D0519783

ANSON'S

LAW OF CONTRACT

ANSON'S
LAW OF
CONTRACT

28th Edition

J. BEATSON
QC, DCL, LLD, FBA

Rouse Ball Professor of English Law
University of Cambridge

Honorary Bencher of the Inner Temple

OXFORD
UNIVERSITY PRESS

OXFORD

UNIVERSITY PRESS

Great Clarendon Street, Oxford OX2 6DP

Oxford University Press is a department of the University of Oxford.
It furthers the University's objective of excellence in research, scholarship,
and education by publishing worldwide in

Oxford New York

Auckland Bangkok Buenos Aires Cape Town Chennai
Dar es Salaam Delhi Hong Kong Istanbul Karachi Kolkata
Kuala Lumpur Madrid Melbourne Mexico City Mumbai Nairobi
São Paulo Shanghai Taipei Tokyo Toronto

A catalogue record for this book is available from the British Library

Library of Congress Cataloging in Publication Data

ISBN 978-0-19-876576-9

7 9 10 8 6

Typeset by RefineCatch Limited, Bungay, Suffolk
Printed in Great Britain by
Ashford Colour Press Ltd.,
Gosport, Hampshire

PREFACE

It is only four years since the last edition of this book, but the legislature and the courts have been active. The mass of material has made the task of reducing it to an intelligible statement of the basic principles of the law of contract a challenging one.

The Contracts (Rights of Third Parties) Act 1999 has meant that the chapter on privity of contract has been substantially rewritten and renamed 'Third Parties'. The replacement of the Unfair Terms in Consumer Contracts Regulations 1994 by the 1999 Regulations and the decision of the House of Lords in *Director-General of Fair Trading* v. *First National Bank plc* has led to an expansion in the treatment of the Regulations both in Chapter 4 (in the context of exemption clauses) and in Chapter 7 (in the context of unconscionable bargains). The chapter on illegality has been rearranged, with the common law and statutory controls of anti-competitive agreements treated alongside each other, and consideration of the policy against agreements tending to encourage speculative litigation in the light of the Access to Justice Act 1999. There have been a number of significant House of Lords' decisions on remedies (notably *Alfred McAlpine Construction Ltd.* v. *Panatown Ltd.*, *Attorney-General* v. *Blake*, and *Farley* v. *Skinner*) and the treatment of damages for the losses of third parties has been relocated to the chapter on damages. Undue influence has been reconsidered in the light of the decision of the House of Lords in *Royal Bank of Scotland plc* v. *Etridge (No. 2)*. Chapters 2 (the agreement), 5 (capacity), and 21–23 (agency) have been pruned. Although the text of the book is 39 pages longer, this is primarily a reflection of the new and more generous design format: in terms of number of words the book is almost the same size as the 27th edition.

The approach of other European systems is mentioned where it is directly germane to English law, as in the case of the use by the Unfair Terms in Consumer Contracts Regulations of the civilian concept of good faith. There are also brief references to European principles and international conventions where these are thought to put the problems faced by English law into perspective.

I am grateful to friends, colleagues, and students who have answered my questions or made useful suggestions for improvements, to Toby Milsom, and to Sir John Smith, whose perceptive review has led to a number of changes in this edition. David Wills, Lesley Dingle, and Peter Zawada of the Squire Law Library provided invaluable assistance in tracking down material. The team at OUP, especially Jane Kavanagh and Sophie Rogers, have been very supportive. But my biggest debts are to Anthony Sinclair and Ed Powles who provided efficient and dedicated research assistance over the last year, and to Felicity Eves who calmly coped with and deciphered my almost illegible riders to the mounted pages. St John's College and the Cambridge Faculty of Law continue to be splendid institutions in which to work. The law is stated as at 10 December 2001, but it has been possible to include some material since that date.

Higher Bury   J.B.
2 April 2002

OUTLINE CONTENTS

DETAILED CONTENTS

PART II FACTORS TENDING TO DEFEAT CONTRACTUAL LIABILITY

PART IV   PERFORMANCE AND DISCHARGE

PART V   REMEDIES FOR BREACH OF CONTRACT

TABLE OF STATUTES

TABLE OF STATUTORY INSTRUMENTS

TABLE OF EUROPEAN COMMUNITY LEGISLATION

TABLE OF INTERNATIONAL AND OTHER NATIONAL LEGISLATION AND RESTATEMENTS

TABLE OF CASES

(Pages on which the facts of a case are given are printed in bold type)

SOME ABBREVIATIONS USED IN REFERENCE

The Table of Cases contains the English Report references for cases reported in the Nominate Reports

Reports

A. & E.	Adpolphus & Ellis	Q.B.	1834–1840
A.L.J.R.	Australian Law Journal Reports	Australia	1927–date
Aleyn	Aleyn	K.B.	1646–1648
All E.R.	All England Reports	All	1936–date
A.L.R.	Australian Law Reports	Australia	1973–date
Amb.	Ambler	Ch.	1737–1783
Anst.	Anstruther	Exch.	1792–1797
Atk.	Atkyns	Ch.	1736–1754
B. & Ad.	Barnewall & Adolphus	K.B.	1830–1834
B. & Ald.	Barnewall & Alderson	K.B.	1817–1822
B. & C.	Barnewall & Cresswell	K.B.	1822–1830
B. & P.	Bosanquet & Puller	C.P.	1796–1804
B. & S.	Best & Smith	Q.B.	1861–1869
B.C.L.C.	Butterworths Company Law Cases	All	1983–date
Beav.	Beavan	Rolls Court	1838–1866
Bing.	Bingham	C.P.	1822–1834
Bing. N.C.	Bingham, New Cases	C.P.	1834–1840
Build. L.R.	Building Law Reports	All	1976–date
Brown, P.C.	Brown, Parliamentary Cases	H.L.	1701–1800
Bulst.	Bulstrode	K.B.	1609–1626
Burr.	Burrow	K.B.	1756–1772
C. & J.	Crompton & Jervis	Exch.	1830–1832
C. & K.	Carrington & Kirwan	Nisi Prius	1843–1850
C. & M.	Crompton & Meeson	Exch.	1832–1834
C. & P.	Carrington & Payne	Nisi Prius	1823–1841
C.B.	Common Bench	C.P.	1845–1856
C.B.N.S.	Common Bench, New Series	C.P.	1856–1865
C.L.C.	CCH Commercial Law Cases	All	1994–date
C.L.R.	Commonwealth Law Reports	Australia	1903–date
C.L.Y.B.	Current Law Year Book	All	1947–date
C.M. & R.	Crompton, Meeson & Roscoe	Exch.	1834–1836
Cab. & El.	Cababé & Ellis	Q.B.	1882–1885
Camp.	Campbell	Nisi Prius	1807–1816
Carth.	Carthew	K.B.	1687–1700
Cl. & Fin.	Clark & Finnelly	H.L.	1831–1846
Co. Rep.	Coke	K.B.	1572–1616
Colles, P.C.	Colles	H.L.	1697–1713

Com. Cas.	Commercial Cases	All	1895–1941
Con.L.R.	Construction Law Reports	All	1985–date
Cowp.	Cowper	K.B.	1774–1778
Cox	Cox's Equity	Ch.	1783–1796
Cr. & Ph.	Craig & Phillips	Ch.	1840–1841
Cro. Eliz.	Croke, of the reign of Elizabeth	C.P., Q.B.	1582–1603
Cro. Jac.	Croke, of the reign of James	C.P., K.B.	1603–1625
Dalison	Dalison	C.P.	1546–1574
D.L.R.	Dominion Law Reports	Canada	1912–date
De G. & J.	De Gex & Jones	Ch.	1857–1859
De G. & Sm.	De Gex & Smale	Ch.	1846–1852
De G.F. & J.	De Gex, Fisher & Jones	Ch.	1859–1862
De G.J. & S.	De Gex, Jones & Smith	Ch.	1862–1865
De G.M. & G.	De Gex, Macnaghten & Gordon	Ch.	1851–1857
Doug. K.B.	Douglas	K.B.	1778–1781
Dr. & Sm.	Drewry & Smale	V.-C.	1860–1865
Drew.	Drewry	V.-C.	1852–1859
E. & B.	Ellis & Blackburn	Q.B.	1852–1858
E. & E.	Ellis & Ellis	Q.B.	1858–1861
E.B. & E.	Ellis, Blackburn & Ellis	Q.B.	1858
E.M.L.R.	Entertainment & Media Law Reports	All	1993–date
E.C.R.	European Court Reports	E.E.C.	1954–date
East	East's Term Reports	K.B.	1800–1812
Eden	Eden	Ch.	1757–1766
Esp.	Espinasse	Nisi Prius	1856–1857
Est. Gaz.	Estates Gazette	All	1858–date
E.G.L.R.	Estates Gazette Law Reports	All	1975–date
Exch.	Exchequer Reports	Exch.	1862–1865
F.L.R.	Family Law Reports	All	1980–date
F. & F.	Foster & Finlason	Nisi Prius	1856–1867
H. & C.	Hurlstone & Coltman	Exch.	1862–1866
H. & N.	Hurlstone & Norman	Exch.	1856–1862
H. Bl.	Henry Blackstone	C.P., Exch.	1788–1796
H.L.C.	House of Lords Cases	H.L.	1847–1866
Hare	Hare	V.-C.	1841–1853
Hob.	Hobart	K.B.	1603–1625
I.C.R.	Industrial Cases Reports	All	1972–date
I.R.L.R.	Industrial Relations Law Reports	All	1972–date
Ir. Rep.	Irish Reports	Ireland	1838–date
Ir. C.L.	Irish Reports, Common Law	Ir. Q.B.	1866–1878
J. & H.	Johnson & Hemming	V.-C.	1859–1862
J. & W.	Jacob & Walker	Ch.	1819–1821
J.P.	Justice of the Peace and Local Government Review	All	1837–date
John.	Johnson	V.-C.	1858–1860
K. & J.	Kay & Johnson	V.-C.	1854–1858
Keen	Keen	Rolls Court	1836–1838
Keilwey	Keilwey	K.B., C.P.	1496–1531
L.G.R.	Local Government Reports	All	1903–date

L.J.C.P.	Law Journal, Common Pleas	C.P.	
L.J.Ch.	Law Journal, Chancery	Ch.	
L.J.Ex.	Law Journal, Exchequer	Exch.	1832–1949
L.J.Q.B.	Law Journal, Queen's Bench	Q.B.	
L.T.	Law Times Reports	All	1859–1947
Ld. Raym.	Lord Raymond	K.B., C.P.	1694–1732
Lev.	Levinz	K.B., C.P.	1660–1697
Ll. L.R.	Lloyd's List Law Reports	All	1919–1950
Lloyd's Rep.	Lloyd's (List) Law Reports	All	1951–date
M. & G.	Manning & Granger	C.P.	1840–1844
M. & S.	Maule & Selwyn	K.B.	1813–1817
M. & W.	Meeson & Welsby	Exch.	1836–1847
Madd.	Maddock	V.-C.	1815–1821
Mer.	Merivale	Ch.	1815–1817
Mod.	Modern Reports	All	1669–1755
My. & K.	Mylne & Keen	Ch.	1832–1835
N.Z.L.R.	New Zealand Law Reports	N.Z.	1883–date
Nev. & M.	Nevile & Manning	K.B.	1832–1836
Noy	Noy	K.B.	1559–1649
P. & C.R.	Property and Compensation Reports	All	1950–date
Peake	Peake	Nisi Prius	1790–1812
Peere Wms.	Peere Williams	Ch.	1695–1735
Ph.	Phillips	Ch.	1841–1849
Q.B.	Queen's Bench Reports	Q.B.	1841–1852
R.P.C.	Reports of Patent Cases	Pat. Cas.	1884–date
Russ.	Russell	Ch.	1823–1829
S.C.	Session Cases	Scotland	1906–date
Salk.	Salkeld	All	1689–1712
Sid.	Siderfin	All	1657–1670
Sim.	Simons	V.-C.	1826–1849
Sm. & G.	Smale & Giffard	V.-C.	1852–1857
St. Tr.	State Trials	—	1163–1820
Stra.	Strange	All	1716–1749
Swan.	Swanston	Ch.	1818–1819
T.L.R.	Times Law Reports	All	1884–1952
Taunt.	Taunton	C.P.	1807–1819
Term R.	Term Reports	K.B.	1785–1800
Ventr.	Ventris	All	1668–1691
Ves. Jun.	Vesey Junior	Ch.	1789–1817
Ves. Sen.	Vesey Senior	Ch.	1746–1755
W. Bl.	William Blackstone	K.B.	1746–1779
W.R.	Weekly Reporter	All	1853–1906
Wilmot	Wilmot	All	1757–1770
Wils.	Wilson	K.B., C.P.	1742–1774
Y. & C. Ch.	Younge & Collyer (Chancery)	V.-C.	1841–1843
Y. & J.	Younge & Jervis	Exch.	1826–1830
Y.B.	Year Books (with regnal year)		

Law Reports, 1865–date

L.R.C.P.	Common Pleas	
L.R. Ch. App.	Chancer Appeals	
L.R. Eq.	Equity Cases	
L.R. Ex.	Exchequer	
L.R.H.L.	House of Lords, English and Irish Appeals	1865–1875
L.R.P.C.	Privy Council Appeals	
L.R.Q.B.	Queen's Bench	
L.R. Sc. App.	Scottish Appeals	
C.P.D.	Common Pleas Division	
Ex. D.	Exchequer Division	1875–1880
App. Cas.	Appeals Cases	
Ch. D.	Chancery Divison	
P.D.	Probate Division	1875–1890
Q.B.D.	Queen's Bench Division	
A.C.	Appeal Cases	
Ch.	Chancery Division	1891–date
K.B. or Q.B.	King's (Queen's) Bench Division	
P.	Probate Division	1891–1971
Fam.	Family Division	1972–date
W.L.R.	Weekly Law Reports	1953–date

Neutral Citations (to reports available on the internet)

E.W.C.A. Civ.	England & Wales Court of Appeal, Civil	2000–date
U.K.H.L.	United Kingdom, House of Lords	1996–date
U.K.P.C.	United Kingdom, Privy Council	2001–date

Periodicals

Aust. L.J.	Australian Law Journal
C.L.J.	Cambridge Law Journal
Can. Bar Rev.	Canadian Bar Review
Const. L.J.	Construction Law Journal
Conv. (N.S.)	Conveyancer and Property Lawyer (New Series)
Harv. L.R.	Harvard Law Review
J.A.L.T.	Journal of the Association of Law Teachers
J.B.L.	Journal of Business Law
J.C.L.	Journal of Contract Law
L.M.C.L.Q.	Lloyd's Maritime and Commercial Law Quarterly
L.Q.R.	Law Quarterly Review
L.S.	Legal Studies
M.L.R.	Modern Law Review
O.J.L.S.	Oxford Journal of Legal Studies
R.L.R.	Restitution Law Review
S.A.L.J.	South African Law Journal
S.J.	Solicitor's Journal

1

INTRODUCTION

The principles of the English law of contract are almost entirely the creation of the English Courts, and the legislature has, until recently, played a relatively small part in their development. They are also, for the most part, a development of the last 200 years; for contract law is the child of commerce, and has grown with the growth of Britain from a mainly agricultural into a mainly commercial and industrial nation. In Blackstone's *Commentaries on the Laws of England*, which were first published in 1756, it is significant of the comparative unimportance of the subject that he devoted 380 pages to the law of real property, and only 28 to contract. The industrial revolution, however, brought about a fundamental change in the structure of the British economy. Land was no longer the primary source of wealth. Mills, mines, and factories sprang up and raw materials were converted by process of manufacture into products for sale in the markets of the world. The capital required for these enterprises was beyond the capacity of most private individuals and it was raised by public subscriptions for shares in joint stock companies or by loans from banks and other financial institutions. The growth of international trade further led to the creation of international commodity, shipping, insurance, and money markets, many of which were centred on London. All of these commercial developments depended and still do depend for their successful operation upon contract.

This introductory chapter considers briefly: first, the nature and function of contract; secondly, the history of contractual obligations in English law; thirdly, the content of the contract law as set out in this book which is concerned with the 'general principles' of contract rather than the detailed rules applicable to different types of contracts; fourthly, the location of contract as part of the law of obligations and its relation to other parts of the law of obligations, tort and restitution, and to property law.

I. THE NATURE AND FUNCTION OF CONTRACT

(a) PROMISE OR AGREEMENT

The law of contract may be provisionally described as that branch of the law which determines the circumstances in which a promise shall be legally binding on the person making it. Section 1 of the American Law Institute's *Restatement Second of the Law of Contracts* gives the following definition:

A contract is a promise or set of promises for the breach of which the law gives a remedy, or the performance of which the law in some way recognises as a duty.

This definition is broadly acceptable, provided that it is realized that, in law, a promise may be constituted by an assurance that a thing *has been* or *is* (for example, that the engine of a car has been recently overhauled or is now in good mechanical condition) as well as that a thing *will be*, and provided that it is also appreciated that most, but not all, contracts take the form of an agreement, that is to say, each party agrees to accept the promise or promises of the other in return for the promise or promises made by itself.[1]

(b) FUNCTIONS OF CONTRACT

The above definition is, however, very much a lawyer's definition and gives little indication of the nature of contract, and still less of its function. Most readers of this book will have some general notion of what a contract is. Indeed, they will enter into a contract very frequently, in some cases almost every day, for example, a contract of carriage (travel by bus or train), or a contract for the sale of goods (the purchase of groceries), or for the supply of services (a haircut), or one involving both sale and the supply of services (having a meal at a restaurant). But the law which will be found in the following pages of this book is law which is derived, for the most part, not from such simple consumer transactions, but from commercial transactions between businesspeople and companies. Commercial transactions involve the exchange of land, goods, or services for money. This exchange is not immediate, as in a supermarket, but is to take place in the future. Contract has an important function of securing that the expectations created by a promise of future performance are fulfilled, or that compensation will be paid for its breach.

Take the example of the construction of an office building. The developer must first purchase the site, and this will often be done with money borrowed from a bank, the developer promising to repay the loan with interest at some future date. It must then engage an architect to design the building, a quantity surveyor to draw up bills of quantities, and a solicitor to do the legal work connected with the development. The building work will be put out to tender and the successful tenderer will be awarded the contract as main contractor. In its turn, the main contractor will often subcontract parts of the work to other contractors. It may be that the developer will put the office space on the market while the building is still under construction and would-be occupants will agree to take a tenancy once it is completed. All of these relationships will depend on the promise of the participating parties that they will carry out their obligations in the future, whether these consist in the payment of money, or otherwise, and that they will be legally bound to their promised performance. No doubt, as a normal rule, each participant will duly fulfil its promise without the need for any intervention, or threatened intervention, by the law.[2] But, in the last

---

[1] Agreement is unnecessary for the enforcement of a promise in a deed (*post*, p. 73) and is not an altogether appropriate description of a unilateral contract, on which see *post*, pp. 29, 35, 52.

[2] Macaulay (1963) 28 American Sociological Review 55.

resort, the recipient of the promise ('the promisee') will rely upon the law to reinforce by appropriate sanctions the promise of performance given. By entering into a contract, the promisee is able to have recourse to those sanctions.

Another important function of contract is a constitutive one: to facilitate forward planning of the transaction and to make provision for future contingencies.[3] The more complex the transaction the greater will be the need for such planning and the more detailed the provisions that are likely to be made. First, and most obviously, contract will normally establish the value of the exchange, that is, how much is to be paid for the land, goods, or services to be provided. In the above example, the developer will need to measure the likely cost of the development against anticipated revenue. While this may to a considerable extent be a matter of estimate, the developer will seek, so far as is practicable, to establish by contract the value of the items that go to make up that cost, for instance, the interest to be paid for the loan and the price to be paid to the main contractor.

Secondly, contract will establish what are the respective responsibilities of the parties and the standard of performance to be expected of them. The building contract will incorporate the specifications for the work, sorting out what is to be done, the nature and quality of the materials to be used, and the date for completion of the work. It will provide for stage payments to be made by the developer. The respective responsibilities of the developer, architect, contractor, and sub-contractors will also be established by contract.

Thirdly, contract enables the economic risks involved in the transaction to be allocated in advance between the parties. The building contract may provide, for example, for an increase in the price in the event of an increase in the cost of labour or materials to the contractor, and who is to bear the risk of strikes, bad weather, or fire. The party affected by the risk may then be able to cover it by insurance.

Finally, contract may provide for what is to happen if things go wrong. Suppose that the contractor fails to remedy defects when required to do so by the architect. Or suppose that the developer fails to pay for work which is certified to have been done. The contract can provide for payment in advance,[4] and can determine whether the party not in default is entitled to terminate the contract and on what terms.[5] The contract may also provide for payment by the contractor of a specified sum by way of 'liquidated damages'[6] in the event of delay in completion beyond the date fixed.

Contract is, in effect, the instrument by which the separate and conflicting interests of the participants can be reconciled and brought to a common goal.[7] The importance accorded by English law to the planning function is shown by its preference for rules that provide certainty, particularly in commercial contracts where speed and certainty have been said to be of paramount importance.[8]

[3] *Ibid.*
[4] See *post*, pp. 631, 646.
[5] See *post*, p. 134.
[6] See *post*, p. 624.
[7] See Gurvitch, *Sociology of Law* (1947).
[8] See *post*, pp. 31, 61, 139, 143, 626.

(c) FREEDOM OF CONTRACT

The significance of the role played by contract in any economic system can scarcely be denied. The issue is the extent to which the law does, or should, assume that parties enjoy freedom of economic decision when entering into contracts. The concept of freedom of contract has two meanings. The first is the freedom of a party to choose to enter into a contract on whatever terms it may consider advantageous to its interests, or to choose not to. Contractual obligation is thereby attributed to the will of the parties. This was one of the cornerstones of nineteenth-century *laissez-faire* economics.[9] Adam Smith in his *Wealth of Nations*, published in 1776, offered the first systematic account of economic affairs, championing the cause of freedom of trade against the economic protectionism current at that time, and freedom of contract was taken up as an ideal into classical economic theory.

When, therefore, in 1861, Sir Henry Maine wrote his *Ancient Law*, he postulated that the movement of progressive societies had hitherto been a *movement* from status (with its entrenched protection of privilege by legal and social restrictions) to contract. He considered this movement to be not only desirable, but inevitable. 'Imperative law', he said,[10] 'has abandoned the largest part of the field which it once occupied, and has left men to settle rules of conduct for themselves with a liberty never allowed to them till recently.'

But freedom of contract also referred to the idea that as a general rule there should be no liability without consent embodied in a valid contract. This second and negative aspect of freedom of contract was influential in narrowing the scope of those parts of the law of obligations which deal with liability imposed by law: tort and restitution.[11]

Today the position is seen in a different light. Freedom of contract is generally regarded as a reasonable social ideal only to the extent that equality of bargaining power between contracting parties can be assumed, and no injury is done to the economic interests of the community at large. In the more complicated social and industrial conditions of modern society it has ceased to have much idealistic attraction except, perhaps, to the proponents of a completely free market economy, who have advanced it in recent years in a modern and sophisticated way, some using the tools of micro-economic analysis.[12] But whatever its status may be as an ideal, the concept of freedom of contract has suffered severe inroads as the result of developments in modern social life and policy.

(i) Statutory restrictions

In the first place, statute law today interferes at numerous points with inroads into the freedom of the parties to make what contract they like. The relations between

---

[9] See Friedmann, *Law in a Changing Society* (1959), ch. 4; Gilmore, *The Death of Contract* (1977); Atiyah, *The Rise and Fall of Freedom of Contract* (1979); Cornish and Clark, *Law and Society in England, 1750–1950* (1989), pp. 201–3, 226.

[10] (1930), ch. ix, p. 322.

[11] *Post*, p.17.

[12] Posner, *Law and Economics*, 4th edn. (1992), ch. 4; Cooter and Ulen, *Law and Economics*, 2nd edn. (1996), ch. 6. Fried, in *Contract as Promise* (1981), provides a non-economic approach.

employers and employees, for example, have been regulated by statutes designed to ensure that employees are properly protected against redundancy and unfair dismissal, and that they know their terms of service. The public has been protected against economic pressure by such measures as the Rent Acts,[13] the Unfair Contract Terms Act 1977,[14] the Unfair Terms in Consumer Contracts Regulations 1999,[15] the Consumer Credit Act 1974,[16] and other similar enactments. These legislative provisions will override any contrary terms which the parties may make for themselves. Freedom of contract is also affected by statutorily imposed 'implied terms' which set the 'default' rule, although in certain circumstances this can be varied by the parties.[17] Further, both national[18] and European Community[19] legislation has been enacted to promote competition in industry and to safeguard the interests of consumers, and the Financial Services and Markets Act 2000 contains provisions to safeguard the interests of investors.

There are also wide-ranging statutory restrictions on discrimination on the grounds of sex, race, and disability in the provision of goods, facilities, and services, and in the selection of employees and in the terms upon which they employed.[20] These are a significant departure from the general freedom at common law to refuse to contract.[21] Although these primarily give rise to compensation orders, they can exceptionally lead to specific relief.[22] The prohibition on discrimination in the provision of goods, facilities, and services applies where the provision is made to the public or a section of the public.[23]

(ii) Standard form contracts: contracts of adhesion

Most contracts entered into by ordinary people are not in fact the result of individual negotiation. An employee's contract of employment, for example, will often be determined by a collective agreement made between trade unions and employers. Standard form contracts are also frequently used, even between businesses. These will lay down the terms on which the supplier is prepared to do business, or embody or incorporate by reference the terms of a trade association. The freedom of the parties to negotiate is limited by such standard form contracts. Although a party, often a consumer, is free to decide not to deal with a particular retailer and to negotiate prices, delivery dates and so on, in many areas similar terms will be offered by other

[13] In particular the Rent Act 1977 (as amended by the Housing Act 1988), and the Landlord and Tenant Acts 1985, 1987 and 1988.

[14] *Post*, p. 185.

[15] S.I. 1999 No. 2083, *post*, pp. 200, 300.

[16] *Post*, p. 300.

[17] e.g. Sale of Goods Act 1979, ss. 12–15, *post*, p. 153; Defective Premises Act 1972, s. 1(1); Law of Property (Miscellaneous Provisions) Act 1994, Part I.

[18] Fair Trading Act 1973; Restrictive Trade Practices Act 1976; Competition Act 1998, *post*, pp. 378–9.

[19] *Post*, pp. 378–9.

[20] Race Relations Act 1976, ss. 4(1)(c), 17, 20–1; Sex Discrimination Act 1975, s. 6(1)(c); Disability Discrimination Act 1995, ss. 4, 5, 12, 19.

[21] *Timothy* v. *Simpson* (1834) 6 C & P 499. Cf. *Constantine* v. *Imperial Hotels Ltd.* [1944] A.C. 693.

[22] Race Relations Act 1976, s. 56; Sex Discrimination Act 1975, s. 65(1)(c); Disability Discrimination Act 1995, s. 8(2)(c).

[23] *Gill* v. *El Vino* [1983] Q.B. 425; *Quinn* v. *Williams Furniture Ltd.* [1981] I.C.R. 328.

retailers so that the individual has either to accept the terms laid down *in toto*, or go without. Since, however, it is not feasible to go without many such goods or services, the individual is effectively compelled to adhere to those terms. In certain types of standard form contracts, however, for example those for the charter of ships, the standard form is often extensively modified or supplemented by other terms appropriate to the particular charterparty.

(iii) 'Compulsory' transactions

In the case of utilities such as water or electricity, which are in effect necessities of modern life, but the supplier is a monopoly or near monopoly, there may be a legal compulsion to supply, at least domestic consumers. Under the legislation regulating such utilities, including gas and telephones where it may now be possible to choose an alternative supplier, there is a duty to supply those who wish to be supplied,[24] there are prohibitions on undue preference and undue discrimination,[25] and a statutory regulator is given power to control prices and other terms of supply. This may be the modern equivalent of the common law duty on common innkeepers and common carriers to serve all comers on a reasonable basis,[26] probably because of their monopoly or near monopoly position. These common law doctrines have not, however, been developed and the field has been left to the anti-discrimination legislation, and that for the control of monopolies and restrictive trade practices, and for regulating utilities. Where there is a statutory obligation to supply and no or little power to negotiate about the incidents of the relationship, the Courts may regard its compulsory nature as incompatible with its being contractual.[27]

(iv) Implied terms and the standard of 'reasonableness'

Finally, the negative aspect of freedom of contract, that there should be no liability without consent embodied in a valid contract, sits uneasily with the practice of implication of terms into the contract, and the use of the standard of 'reasonableness' as a way of dealing with gaps in the contractual language.[28] Terms are implied not only under statute, but also at common law. Although the basis of such implication is said to be 'necessity'[29] or in the case of custom 'presumed consent',[30] in many cases this is rather artificial, and in truth in many standard transactions the implied terms are the legal incidents of the transaction,[31] from which the parties are, subject to statute, often free to deviate. Freedom of contract is also difficult to reconcile with the adoption of the 'objective theory' which provides, in essence, that a person (A), whose conduct is

[24] Gas Act 1986, s. 10; Electricity Act 1989, s. 16.
[25] Telecommunications Act 1984, ss. 3, 8(1)(d); Gas Act 1986, s. 14(3); Electricity Act 1989, ss. 3(2) and 18(4); Water Industry Act 1991, ss. 2(3)(a)(ii), 2(5).
[26] *Clarke* v. *West Ham Corp.* [1909] 2 K.B. 858, at pp. 879–82. Note that almost all carriers contract out of their common law liability.
[27] *Norweb plc* v. *Dixon* [1995] 1 W.L.R. 637; *Read* v. *Croydon Corp.* [1938] 4 All E.R. 631.
[28] e.g. *Tillmanns & Co.* v. *S.S. Knutsford Ltd.* [1908] A.C. 406; *Abu Dhabi National Tanker Co.* v. *Product Star Shipping Co. Ltd. (No. 2)* [1993] 1 Lloyd's Rep. 397, at p. 404.
[29] *Liverpool City Council* v. *Irwin* [1977] A.C. 239, at p. 254. See *post*, pp. 149–50.
[30] *Produce Brokers Co. Ltd.* v. *Olympia Oil & Cake Co. Ltd.* [1916] 1 A.C. 314, at p. 324. See *post*, p. 151.
[31] *Mears* v. *Safecar Securities Ltd.* [1983] Q.B. 54, at p. 78.

such that the other party reasonably believes that A has assented to the terms of a contract, will be bound no matter what A's real intention is.[32] This rule can lead to the imposition of non-consensual obligations, since what creates the obligation is not consent in fact but acting as if consent is being given.

(v) Summary

In many areas of contract, freedom of contract in the classical sense is manifestly lacking. But English law and English judges still to a great extent proceed on the assumption that the parties are free to choose whether or not they will enter into a contract and on what terms. The formulation of the test for implied terms has been noted, and, as recently as 1980, in the House of Lords, Lord Diplock observed:[33] 'A basic principle of the common law of contract ... is that the parties are free to determine for themselves what primary obligations they will accept'. It may be objected that the general principles of contract law therefore present an inadequate, if not distorted, picture of modern economic life. This may be so, but it is nevertheless the fact that the law does still rest on the assumption of freedom of choice, and where a relationship is entered into in which there is no choice, a Court may hold that it is not contractual.[34]

(d) SANCTITY OF CONTRACTS

Closely associated with the concept of freedom of contract is yet another principle, that of the sanctity of contracts.[35] Businesspeople in particular are concerned to ensure that the parties to a contract keep to their bargain and that as few avenues as possible should be afforded for escape from contractual obligations. In general, English law is reluctant to admit excuses for non-performance. But the Draconian requirements of commercial convenience have to be reconciled with the moral qualifications introduced by the need to discourage the grosser forms of unfair dealing. Thus the common law, and even more so equity, the influence of which has been more apparent in recent times, have admitted defences based on fraud, misrepresentation, mistake, duress (including economic duress), and undue influence, and endeavoured to curb the economic exploitation (in particular) of employees by the doctrine of restraint of trade. Although there is no general principle of 'inequality of bargaining power',[36] Courts take account of this in interpreting the contract and applying these doctrines. Additionally, statutory protection overrides unfair terms in certain types of contracts, for instance those made between consumers and businesses, and employees and employers. It should not be imagined, however, that contractual obligations can be repudiated by one party merely because that party was in the weaker bargaining position. In the 'rough and tumble' of commercial relationships, various types of

---

[32] *Post*, p. 31.

[33] *Photo Production Ltd.* v. *Securicor Transport Ltd.* [1980] A.C. 827, at p. 848.

[34] *Ante*, p. 6.

[35] See Hughes Parry, *The Sanctity of Contracts in English Law* (1959), and *post*, p. 17.

[36] *National Westminster Bank plc* v. *Morgan* [1985] A.C. 686, *post*, p. 298.

pressure are frequently brought to bear and terms may be imposed which are, objectively, harsh; but the contract will still bind.

Further, the law will not permit a person of full age and understanding who failed to read the contract or to appreciate its full import and effect to escape from the contract. It will not re-write a contract for the parties or imply additional provisions merely because it would be reasonable so to do. And it will, in general, give effect to a written contract in accordance with its recorded terms, and not admit evidence to show that one party intended them to be construed in a different way from that which they actually express.

In certain situations, however, the law will pronounce that the parties are relieved from performance of their obligations by reason of a change of circumstances occurring after the contract was made. But this principle—that of 'frustration of the contract'[37]—is very limited in scope, and will not apply, for example, merely because a subsequent event changes the financial equilibrium of the transaction and forces a party who expected to make a profit from the transaction into a position of loss. The event must be of such a serious and fundamental character that to enforce the contract in the changed circumstances would be to enforce a different contract from the one which the parties made.

(e) THE INTERESTS PROTECTED BY CONTRACT

The entering into of a contract creates an interest in each party that the contract will be performed.[38] The obligation may be strict, for example a seller's undertaking that it has good title to the goods sold, or it may be qualified, for example to use reasonable care, as is the case in many aspects of contracts for services by professionals such as lawyers or surveyors. If one party fails, in whole or in part, to perform the obligations undertaken in the contract, the other party, whose economic, physical, and, in some cases, psychological interests will be affected, will be entitled to redress. But what form will that redress take?

Where the breach of contract consists of a failure to pay money, whether for goods bought and delivered or for services rendered, the redress for breach will often take the form of (direct) specific enforcement of the contract by an action (in debt) for the sum due.[39] Where the breach consists of the failure to render a non-monetary performance, for example, a seller's failure to deliver goods to a buyer, in some cases the injured party will also be entitled to (direct) specific performance of the other party's obligation. Normally, however, the redress will not take the form of specific performance of the contract, but will consist of monetary compensation.[40] How is that compensation to be assessed?

---

[37] See *post*, Chapter 14.
[38] See Fuller and Perdue (1936–37) 46 Yale L.J. 52, 573; Atiyah (1978) 94 L.Q.R. 193; Taylor (1982) 45 M.L.R. 139; Burrows (1983) 99 L.Q.R. 217; Friedmann (1995) 111 L.Q.R. 628; Coote [1997] C.L.J. 537.
[39] *Post*, p. 630. Cf. p. 590.
[40] *Post*, p. 596.

(i) Reliance on the promise

On one view, the injured party would be entitled to compensation for the loss incurred in reliance on the promise, for example, in the case of a seller of goods, the expense incurred in obtaining the materials and manufacturing the goods, less what can be obtained on a substitute sale. And the law does indeed recognize such 'reliance loss' as an appropriate head of damages.[41]

(ii) Expectation of performance

But the basic object of damages in contract is to put the injured party in the same position as it would have been had the contract been duly performed. The injured party is entitled to protection of its interest in the performance of the contract. Suppose, for example,[42] a port authority by contract promises a car ferry operator that it will allow it to use the port facilities for car ferry operations during the coming year, but in breach of that contract repudiates the contract almost immediately after it is made. The reliance loss sustained by the ferry operator may be no more than (say) the trifling expense of having prepared draft timetables of ship movements for the contract period. But it will nevertheless be entitled to be compensated in damages for loss of its expectation of performance, that is to say, the profit which it would have made on the car ferry operations during the year in question. Compensation assessed on this basis is, in effect, a substitute for the performance of the other party's obligation, whether by the payment of a debt that has accrued due[43] or by the rendering of other forms of performance.[44] This protection of performance interests (also called 'expectation' interests) is not peculiar to the English law of contract. It is a consequence of contract in all developed legal systems. Even if the contract is wholly executory, that is to say, nothing has been done by either party under it at the time of its breach, damages for lost performance ('expectations') will be recoverable.[45]

(iii) Restitution

The restitution interest in contract is of a less obvious nature. It usually arises where a contract is discharged as the result of a breach leaving one party in receipt of a benefit which it would be unjust to retain at the expense of the other, so that party will be compelled by the law to restore that benefit (or its value) to the other.[46] There are also many situations where, without any contract, a similar duty is imposed. These independent restitutionary claims fall outside the scope of contract law and thus of this book.[47]

---

[41] *Post*, p. 599.

[42] See *Thoresen Car Ferries Ltd.* v. *Weymouth Portland B.C.* [1972] 2 Lloyd's Rep. 614.

[43] *Post*, p. 630.

[44] *Post*, p. 632.

[45] But see the criticisms of Atiyah (1978) 94 L.Q.R. 193, and in *The Rise and Fall of Freedom of Contract* (1979).

[46] *Post*, p. 642.

[47] But see *post*, pp. 40, 63, 87, 215, 225, 229.

II. THE HISTORY OF CONTRACTUAL OBLIGATIONS IN ENGLISH LAW

The modern law of contract contains much which can properly be explained (if at all) only in the light of its history. Hence, even in a book which aims only at stating the principles of the modern law, it is desirable to give some account of how that law came to take the form which has just been indicated in outline. We shall see that it has not been by any process of analysis and elucidation of the essential nature of a contract that the law has been moulded. Indeed, the very idea of enforcing promises or agreements as such, which seems most natural to us, may not be an early one in the history of any legal system. We shall find the key to the story by examining the conditions which the Courts have attached at different stages to the actions which they were willing to admit for the enforcement of the kind of rights which we now regard as contractual. The story can here be given only in the barest outline,[48] and it should be understood that there are some points in it which remain obscure or controversial.

(a) THE EARLY ACTIONS

(i) 'Wager of law'

Actions in what we call contract and tort were at first within the jurisdiction of local and manorial courts. The action would commonly end in a general denial of liability, upon which the defendant would 'wage his law', that is undertake to come at the next court day and swear to this denial in the presence of neighbours (their number specified by the Court) who would then swear to their belief in this oath. If on the day all the oaths were made correctly, the defendant won. The efficacy of this depended partly on the fear of damnation for perjury, and partly upon standing among the neighbours (the city of London, for example, which lived by the credit of its citizens, set particular store by this mode of proof). This social sanction would be lost as lawsuits were diverted from the local setting into royal courts in Westminster.

(ii) Trespass

In the field of tort, for which the very rough medieval equivalent is 'trespass', a case would come to a royal court only if there was some royal interest, normally a 'breach of the king's peace'. That allegation had two other effects. It precluded the defendant from answering by wager of law and required the case to go to a jury. And as between the main royal courts, it gave jurisdiction to the King's Bench concurrently with the Common Pleas. The allegation itself became increasingly fictionalized in the early

---

[48] For fuller treatment, see Atiyah, *The Rise and Fall of Freedom of Contract* (1979); Baker, *Introduction to English Legal History*, 3rd edn. (1990), pp. 360–426; Baker and Milsom, *Sources of English Legal History* (1986), pp. 209–96, 358–505, hereafter 'Baker and Milsom'; Cornish and Clark, *Law and Society in England, 1750–1950* (1989), pp. 197–226; Milsom, *Historical Foundations of the Common Law*, 2nd edn. (1981), pp. 243–360; Simpson, *A History of the Common Law of Contract* (1975); Stoljar, *A History of Contract at Common Law* (1975).

fourteenth century; and around the middle of the century the Chancery began to make writs of trespass returnable into royal courts with no mention of the king's peace. This was the effective beginning of 'actions on the case'; and logically plaintiffs should not have been able to sue in the King's Bench, and defendants should have been permitted to wage their law. But on both points logic was overruled. All actions of trespass and case could go to either of the royal courts, and all went to jury trial; and this was a cause of developments to which we shall come, by which remedies in contract came to be sought by actions in tort.

In the field of contract, jurisdiction as between local and royal courts came to depend upon the amount at stake. From a beginning in the thirteenth century, originally concerned only with the recovery of debts, a general jurisdictional barrier developed at 40 shillings, then a sum so large that very few transactions of ordinary people would reach it. But the amount was never altered, so that a period of rapid inflation in the sixteenth century brought transactions of falling real value to Westminster, and therefore to the modes of proof in use there. In particular, since there had been no equivalent of the king's peace to affect proof as well as jurisdiction, wager of law was often available; but those who swore to the defendant would be not neighbours but persons hired in Westminster. In the old contract actions, therefore, the focus of attention for lawyers and litigants was not some substantive law of contract but modes of proof.

(iii) Covenant

The word 'covenant' (*conventio*, agreement) is the nearest medieval equivalent to our 'contract'. But even in local courts an action for money due under a contract would be called not covenant but debt (or detinue if the action was for a specific chattel lent or bought, for example), so that actions called covenant mainly concern breaches of agreement for services like building or for sales or leases of land. The primary claim was for performance, and in royal courts the action was begun by a *praecipe* writ ordering the defendant to keep the agreement; but judgments ceased to order specific performance and damages were awarded instead. Some think that the plaintiff would have to have done his part of the bargain, but we are not informed about the early requirements; and in the royal courts the question was suppressed by a new requirement about proof. Early in the fourteenth century it became settled that the plaintiff was not entitled to an answer unless he could produce a document under the defendant's seal (in illiterate times the equivalent of a signature) setting out the terms of the agreement. Soon after this the action of covenant fell out of use, not because of this requirement but because the kind of sealed document to which we are about to turn proved more effective. But covenant retained a negative importance: parties might contract for the building of a house for example, not thinking of royal courts or sealing wax, and find the natural remedy barred.

(iv) Debt

Any claim for a fixed sum of money or a fixed quantity of fungible goods would in the royal court be made by the *praecipe* writ of debt. At first even a claim for specific goods would be made by the same writ, so that one who borrowed money and a book was seen to owe the book in the same way that the money was owed; but the separation of detinue need not be discussed here. In royal as in local courts, the defendant could normally answer by wager of law; and one lending a large sum or selling goods for a large price might take precautions, and this led to a separation between two principal uses to which the single writ of debt might be put.

(a) Debt on an obligation. The simplest precaution for, say, a lender was to require the borrower to execute a document under seal, a bond. This was evidence not of a promise to pay but of indebtedness itself, and it was conclusive. The defendant could not deny that the debt was owed, though he could deny that the deed was his (*non est factum*). But that was a risky issue to take: it went to a jury, who would compare seals etc.; and if they found against the defendant he would go to prison. At law the defendant could not even say that payment had been made; and though he eventually got equitable protection from the Chancery in this situation, that was only after a long struggle between the competing goods of general certainty and individual justice.

But bonds were put to wider uses than ensuring that a lender or a seller would get the money that was due. One hiring a builder to build a house, for example, would take from him a bond by which the builder would acknowledge that he owed the customer an essentially penal sum, which bond would be void if conditions (written sometimes on the back of the bond, sometimes in a separate indenture) were satisfied; and those conditions specified the site, dimensions, materials, completion date, etc. of the house. If the customer sued it would be on the bond for the penalty, and the builder could of course plead that he had satisfied the conditions. Conversely, the builder would take a bond from the customer, commonly for double the agreed price, to be void if the agreed price was duly paid. Such conditional bonds became the principal vehicle for large transactions; and they continued to be so until the Chancery began to relieve against penalties and until *assumpsit* provided a simpler mechanism.

(b) Debt on a covenant. A sealed document was never required in debt as it was in covenant. The lender could always sue for the repayment of the money lent, the seller for the price, and the builder or other provider of services for the agreed payment. But normally this was only possible when the plaintiff had done his part of the bargain, when the defendant had had his *quid pro quo*. And the medieval word 'contract' did not have its modern meaning: it meant precisely the obligation 'contracted' by a debtor who had received his *quid pro quo*. But much of the reality is hidden by the defendant's usual denial by wager of law—not a denial of any specific facts but just that he owed. And the availability of wager had a further consequence. Only the debtor himself could swear that he did not owe: even if the debt had been publicly incurred it might have been privately paid. So the executor of a dead debtor could not wage law, and it was held by a perverse logic that the executor could not be sued. But that applied only to debt on a contract: the executor could be sued if the plaintiff had a bond which would any way exclude wager.

The combined effect of these actions may be described in terms of an agreement to build a house. Well-advised parties would set it up by conditional bonds, so that the party alleged to be in breach would be sued in debt for the penalty and could plead that the conditions had been satisfied. If the agreement was informally made, the builder who had built could sue in debt for the price (normally answerable by wager of law). But the customer could not bring covenant if the builder did not build, because he had no document under seal; and probably he could not even bring debt to recover any money he had paid. This inequity played its part in the rise of *assumpsit*; but it is important not to suppose that from the beginning lawyers saw that *assumpsit* was to become a general contractual remedy.

(b) ASSUMPSIT

(i) Misfeasance

Among the tort actions which came to royal courts when the need to allege a breach of the king's peace was dropped were some in which there was a contractual background to the wrong. In 1348 a ferry-man was sued: he had undertaken to ferry a horse across the Humber, but so mismanaged it that the horse was drowned.[49] Its owner sued in tort, and the defendant (knowing there was no sealed document) argued that the proper action would be covenant. The action was held to be rightly brought in tort: the plaintiff complained of the killing of his horse, not the failure to transport it; and such claims for 'misfeasance' regularly succeeded.

(ii) Nonfeasance

There was more difficulty if the defendant had made an undertaking but done nothing in the matter at all: this was clearly 'covenant' rather than 'trespass'. Many attempts to get 'trespass' remedies were made, mostly in situations in which performance of the *praecipe* order in covenant would be impossible (e.g. the date by which the house was to be built has passed) or would be no sufficient remedy (e.g. timbers have rotted because the roof was not mended as promised). These would have been arguments for not suing in covenant even if the builder or roof-mender had made their promises under seal; and this may have been among the reasons why customers set up their agreements by conditional bonds in which the penalty would cover any consequential damage as well as the value of the performance. And one must remember that all these early attempts to use *assumpsit* for a nonfeasance were by plaintiffs who had omitted the proper formalities. Perhaps they were caught out by the only transaction of a lifetime large enough to come to a royal court. But their hard cases seemed to a judge in 1425 to threaten bad law: 'if this action' (against one who had not built a mill as promised) 'should be maintained . . . then a man would have an action of trespass for every broken covenant in the world'.[50]

  He was to be proved a prophet: but his logic was hard to overcome and we cannot be sure how and when it happened. A stage seems to be marked by a case of 1442 in

---

[49] *Bukton v. Tounesende, The Humber Ferry Case* (1348), translated in Baker and Milsom (*supra*, n. 48), p. 358.

[50] *Watkins' (or Wykes') Case* (1425) translated in Baker and Milsom (*supra*, n. 48), p. 380, *per* Martin J., at p. 383.

which the defendant agreed to sell and convey land to the plaintiff from whom she took money. But she actually conveyed to a third party; and the plaintiff sued in tort for a deceit.[51] The agreement was made in London about land outside. If the land had been inside the city, the action would have been brought in city courts under the custom of London by which (a) actions in covenant did not require a document under seal, (b) the normal remedy in covenant was an order for performance, and (c) one who had put it out of his power to perform would be sued in deceit and imprisoned until he made fine with the city and repaid the money to his plaintiff. In London therefore the plaintiff's action would not have been a dodge to get round the absence of a sealed document but the natural remedy, essentially in rescission. In Westminster the logic got the plaintiff a remedy: but the Court could not order imprisonment (and therefore repayment of the money) but only damages.

This looked like enforcement rather than rescission, and the king's courts were left with a distinction without a real difference: the disappointed buyer who had paid for the land could get damages if his seller had conveyed to a third party, but not otherwise. Many approaches were tried; and around 1500 it begins to appear that nonfeasance was becoming remediable, at first only when the plaintiff had actually paid or there was some other detrimental reliance (and at any period one who has suffered no damage would normally prefer to hire somebody else rather than sue). Mutual promises do not become actionable until later in the century, by equally obscure stages; and the underlying illogicality is increasingly masked by elaborate and unreal allegations of deceit.

(iii) Assumpsit for money

From the use of *assumpsit* in lieu of covenant (where the absence of a sealed document might leave a plaintiff entirely without remedy) we turn to its use in lieu of debt (where the plaintiff always had a remedy, but might be faced by wager of law). But again one must not think that the end was aimed at from the beginning. The beginning is early in the sixteenth century in cases involving not money but fungible goods: a brewer contracts to buy malt or barley, and when it is not delivered has either to buy at a much higher price or to let his brewery go off stream.[52] The substantial claim goes not to the goods themselves but to the damage flowing from reliance upon the promise to deliver them; and this may be reflected in the language of deceit. When money is involved the reliance claim seems first to have appeared in situations involving third parties. Seller sells to Buyer in reliance upon the promise of a third party to pay if Buyer does not. It is Buyer who got the *quid pro quo* and contracted the debt; and any liability of the third party must be on the basis of reliance.[53]

One must not assume that the first use of the same logic as between two parties was intended as a conscious circumvention of debt. Debtor owes Creditor, and when pressed promises to pay the amount at a specified future date. Relying upon this promise, Creditor makes other bargains with third parties. When Debtor does not pay

---

[51] *Shepton v. Dogge (Nos 1 and 2)* (1442), translated in Baker and Milsom (*supra*, n. 48), pp. 390–5.
[52] For example, see the cases in Baker and Milsom (*supra*, n. 48), pp. 406 and 411.
[53] Such cases are cited in argument in Baker and Milsom (*supra*, n. 48), pp. 414–15.

Creditor, Creditor cannot pay the third parties; and, particularly if he is a merchant, this failure so damages his own credit that he is ruined. This consequential damage is the gist of this action, not the original debt, which is not in principle even claimed. But jurors would include the amount of the debt in their assessment of damages; and such actions soon came to be used to recover debts but exclude wager of law.

Since debt was in the exclusive jurisdiction of the Common Pleas, it was the King's Bench that led in this development and an unseemly difference of practice arose. On the general issue of *Non assumpsit* the Common Pleas would direct the jury that if they were to find for the plaintiff they must find both that the defendant was *indebitatus* and that he made an express promise to pay the debt, the King's Bench that they need find only the indebtedness (because every debtor could be presumed to promise to pay: every contract executory imports in itself an *assumpsit*). But since the issue would be tried at *nisi prius*, the judge actually directing the jury might not come from the Court in which the action had been begun. It seems clear that in *Slade's Case* the judges at *nisi prius* made a conscious effort to have the matter resolved. The jury was induced to bring in a special verdict that the debt was owed but that there was no subsequent promise to pay it. This was reported to the King's Bench, in which the action had been started; and instead of giving judgment that Court referred it to the Court of Exchequer Chamber, not really a Court but an informal conference of all the judges. That body was unable to agree; the King's Bench gave judgment for the plaintiff in accordance with their own practice; and this result was unwillingly accepted by the Common Pleas.[54]

Various consequences followed. Since the *indebitatus assumpsit* action was formally for reliance damage and not the debt, it now had to be made clear that the debt itself was recoverable as well as any damage, that the actions were alternative, and that the one barred the other. And since formally the reliance damage flowed entirely from the promise to pay the debt, there was no logical need to specify how the debt had arisen; and so a defendant in the *indebitatus* action might not know the actual case he was to answer. The Courts therefore required minimum particulars to be given; and a series of 'common counts' developed stating that the debt was for goods sold and delivered, for work and materials, and so on. More importantly *Slade's Case* marked the effective end of wager of law; and it was necessary to make explicit the important consequence that executors could now be sued for simple contract debts. Nor was the ending of wager unmixedly beneficial: it turned out that jury trial could be manipulated by fraudulent plaintiffs; and in 1677 the Statute of Frauds provided that in certain situations action could be brought only if there was some written evidence signed by the defendant.

With the important exception of agreements supported by sealed documents, in which covenant or debt still could and had to be brought, all contract litigation after *Slade's Case* was brought in *assumpsit*; and it was from this that the modern law of contract developed. It is indeed a law of contract rather than a law about particular contracts as in Rome. But its beginnings in tort, which remained obvious in the

---

[54] 1602 4 Co. Rep. 91a.

persistent language of deceit until the nineteenth century, inhibited the development of a satisfactory theoretical structure. Instead we have the 'doctrine' of consideration. There has been much speculation about its 'origin', on the basis that it must have developed from some earlier phenomenon. Consideration as detriment to the plaintiff looks much like the damage he suffered when the case was put in terms of deceit or reliance, and this provides some explanation of the uselessness of past consideration and of the rule that consideration must move from the plaintiff. Consideration as benefit to the defendant looks much like the *quid pro quo* of debt; and it must be remembered that after *Slade's Case* the debt and therefore the *quid pro quo* was the only issue in *indebitatus*. Other origins have been suggested, such as the canonist idea of *causa* which indeed played some part in the Chancery. But the reality seems to be that sixteenth century pleadings used the word to mean the reason for which the promise was given, and judges then and later decided which of these were a sufficient basis for legal action. If so, consideration is not so much a 'doctrine' as a considerable body of the substantive rules of contract.

(c) SUBSEQUENT DEVELOPMENTS

There has been much later development, too detailed and perhaps too little explored by historians, to consider in this summary. Lord Mansfield in the eighteenth century and Lord Denning in the twentieth sought to rationalize consideration, but the substantive changes needed were too obtrusive. The English promissory estoppel, for example, is a pale shadow of the American, perhaps because the lesser weight given in the USA to deeds left more obvious injustice when gratuitous promises were relied on. And the American reliance basis for remedy, essentially as alternative to consideration, is a reminder of the mongrel nature of the common law of contract.

The law started with covenant (or contract) as something essentially different from trespass (or tort). That difference was the continuing obstacle in the rise of *assumpsit*; and its overcoming introduced continuing confusion. It was nineteenth century judges and writers, including Anson, who sought to restore contract law as a thing in itself: rules mostly about the formation of binding agreements, with ancillary rules about the damages recoverable for breach.[55] The impulse may have been partly juristic, partly due to commercial demands for certainty and for more sophisticated rules to deal adequately with the expansion of trade and commerce that resulted from the industrial revolution. Consideration (or a deed) is then represented as something like offer and acceptance: one of the requirements for formation. But it sprang from a law about tort, about damage suffered by the plaintiff at the end of the story rather than about the beginning of a binding relationship between the parties. Like many mongrels the result may not be elegant; but it is strong.

(i) The nineteenth century

We have noted that the concepts of freedom of contract and sanctity of contract were

---

[55] See Simpson (1975) 91 L.Q.R. 247.

at their strongest during the nineteenth century. In 1875 Sir George Jessel M.R. stated:[56]

if there is one thing more than another which public policy requires, it is that men of full age and competent understanding shall have the utmost liberty in contracting, and that their contracts, when entered into freely and voluntarily, shall be held sacred and shall be enforced by Courts of Justice.

This was said to have led to the reduction of supervision over the contractual terms to a bare minimum[57] and the deprivation of the tools available for such control of much of their effectiveness. The doctrine of consideration acquired a predominantly formal meaning, although it was on occasion used to invalidate unfair agreements.[58] A substantial part of the law of contract was attributed to the parties' agreement, and the role of equity, with its discretionary remedies, and its ability to avoid common law rules, was less central.

At the same time, non-contractual liability was kept within narrow boundaries. In restitution (then known as quasi-contract), Bowen L.J.'s famous statement that '[l]iabilities are not to be forced upon people behind their backs'[59] was profoundly influential. Indeed, Lord Sumner and Sir William Holdsworth argued that all such claims were founded upon an implied contract.[60] If there could not be a contract, there could not be an implied contract; there was no independent non-contractual claim. Tort liability was restricted by what was later called the 'privity of contract' fallacy, that duties which originated in a contract were confined to the parties.[61] It was also mainly concerned with the protection of proprietary interests and with providing a remedy for certain categories of physical injury. Although a number of economic torts were developed, notably deceit, injurious falsehood, inducement of breach of contract, and conspiracy, they required wilful misconduct. There was no liability for pure economic loss which was inflicted negligently.

(ii) The twentieth century

In the modern period there is evidence of the reshaping of contract law accompanied by an expansion of non-contractual obligations in tort, in particular for negligent misrepresentation causing purely economic loss, and in restitution. There has been a dilution of formal requirements and increased regard is given to considerations of substantive fairness. The erosion of the doctrine of consideration in the context of contract re-negotiation, and its replacement by rules of equitable estoppel[62] and economic duress is perhaps the most prominent example, but there are others,

---

[56] *Printing & Numerical Registering Co.* v. *Sampson* (1875) L.R. 19 Eq. 462, at p. 465.

[57] Atiyah, *The Rise and Fall of Freedom of Contract* (1979). But cf. Simpson (1979) 46 U. Chi. L.Rev. 533; Barton (1987) 103 L.Q.R. 118.

[58] *Stilk* v. *Myrick* (1809) 2 Camp. 317; 6 Esp. 129, *post*, pp. 104–5.

[59] *Falcke* v. *Scottish Imperial Insurance Co.* (1886) 34 Ch. 234, at p. 248.

[60] *Sinclair* v. *Brougham* [1914] A.C. 398, at p. 452 (overruled by *Westdeutsche Landesbank Girozentrale* v. *Islington London Borough Council* [1996] A.C. 669); Holdsworth (1939) 55 L.Q.R. 37. Cf. Lord Wright (1938) 6 C.L.J. 305, at pp. 312 ff.

[61] *Winterbottom* v. *Wright* (1842) 10 M. & W. 109.

[62] *Post*, p. 112.

including an approach to discharge of contract, whether by breach or frustration, that gives greater emphasis to the consequences of an event than to the, often fictional, intentions of the parties.[63] The evolution of new doctrines and approaches has been gradual, and there have been exceptions and inconsistencies. For instance, when, in 1976, economic duress was first recognized as a factor vitiating contract, its theoretical basis was said to be 'coercion of the will', i.e. absence of consent. But this was rejected in less than a decade, whereas in the case of frustration, first recognized in 1863, it took almost a hundred years for the Courts to turn away from regarding implied contract as the basis of that doctrine.

(iii) Legislation

The last hundred years have also seen a rapid growth in the importance of statute law. There were great codifying Acts of the nineteenth century for particular types of contract, such as the Bills of Exchange Act 1882 and the Sale of Goods Act 1893. We have noted the considerable, and increasing, amount of regulatory legislation, which is designed to protect certain classes of the community or to implement government policy. There are also a number of reforming statutes such as the Law Reform (Frustrated Contracts) Act 1943, the Misrepresentation Act 1967, the Civil Liability (Contribution) Act 1978, the Minors Contracts Act 1987, and the Contracts (Rights of Third Parties) Act 1999 which have been passed to remedy defects or to make good particular deficiencies in the common law.

(iv) Codification

In 1872, the Indian Contract Act was enacted, which codified (with some variations) the general English law of contract for use in the Indian sub-continent. But English law remained, and still remains, predominantly judge-made law. In 1965, the Law Commission of England and Wales and the Scottish Law Commission announced their intention to codify the English and Scots law of contract.[64] The code as originally envisaged was to be a uniform body of law applying throughout England and Scotland, and it was to embody amendments to the existing law of both countries. Subsequently, however, the Scottish Law Commission withdrew from this enterprise. In 1973, therefore, the Law Commission decided to suspend its work on a contract code.[65] Since then it has examined particular areas of the law of contract, and has either recommended reform, as in the case of minors' contracts, implied terms as to quality in the sale of goods, formalities and covenants of title in the sale of land,[66] contributory negligence as a defence in contract, and contracts for the benefit of third parties,[67] or has concluded that no legislation is necessary, as in the case of the parol

---

[63] *Post*, pp. 544–5, 578–9.

[64] Diamond (1968) 31 M.L.R. 361.

[65] An early draft has since been published: see McGregor, *The Contract Code* (1993).

[66] Law Com No. 79 (1977); Law Com No. 134 (1984); Law Com No. 160 (1987); Law Com No. 164 (1987); Law Com No. 199 (1991), implemented respectively by the Civil Liability (Contribution) Act 1978, Minors Contracts Act 1987, the Sale and Supply of Goods Act 1994, and the Law of Property (Miscellaneous Provisions) Acts 1989 and 1994.

[67] Law Com No. 219 (1993), on which see *post*, p. 617 and Law Com No. 242 (1996) implemented by the Contracts (Rights of Third Parties) Act 1999, on which see *post*, p. 429.

evidence rule.[68] It is currently working on illegal contracts. It seems, however, unlikely that the project of codification will be revived.

III. EUROPEAN AND INTERNATIONAL INFLUENCES

The English law of contract is beginning to be exposed to the influence of the European Community and the predominantly civilian systems of its Members because of the perceived importance of its harmonization in the development of a single market in the Community. To date the most significant initiatives affecting contract law have been the Directives on Unfair Terms in Consumer Contracts[69] and those which seek to ensure that there is no discrimination in tendering procedures for major contracts for public works, supplies, and services.[70]

There is also a movement to develop common principles of European contract law.[71] Those who favour this argue that there are many benefits to be derived from a formulation of principles of contract law within Europe. These include the facilitation of cross-border trade, the strengthening of the single European market, the provision of an infrastructure for European community laws governing contract and of guidelines for national courts and legislatures, and the construction of a bridge between common law and civil law systems.

Furthermore, the provisions of the European Convention for the Protection of Human Rights, in particular the right to a fair trial under Article 6 and to the protection of property under Article 1 of the First Protocol to the Convention also have an impact on English contract law as a result of the Human Rights Act 1998.[72]

There are, moreover, wider international initiatives, such as the Unidroit Principles for International Commercial Contracts, the United Nations (Vienna) Convention on Contracts for the International Sale of Goods (the 'CISG'), and growing numbers of international standard form contracts. Renewed consideration is being given to the ratification by the United Kingdom of the CISG which has not yet been ratified because of a perception by some that English contract law is more sophisticated, and fear that uncertainty would result from the broadly formulated provisions of the Convention.[73]

While this book is concerned with English law, the approach of other European systems is mentioned where, as in the case of the use by the Unfair Terms in

---

[68] Law Com No. 154 (1986), *post*, p. 133.

[69] Council Directive 93/13/EEC (O.J. L 95, 21 April 1993, p. 29), implemented by the Unfair Terms in Consumer Contracts Regulations 1994 (S.I. No. 3159), now the 1999 Regulations (S.I. 1999 No. 2083), *post*, pp. 200, 300. See also the Package Travel, Package Holidays and Package Tours Regulations 1992 (S.I. 1992 No. 3288), *post*, pp. 193, 203, 249 and the Timeshare Act 1992.

[70] The main implementing regulations are S.I. 1991 Nos. 2679–2680 and S.I. 1992 No. 3279.

[71] See Lando and Beale, *The Principles of European Contract Law Parts 1 & II* (2000); Kötz, *European Contract Law* (trs. Weir) (1997).

[72] *Wilson* v. *First County Trust Ltd. (No. 2)* [2001] 3 W.L.R. 42; *Shanshal* v. *Al Kishtaini* [2001] 2 All E.R. (Comm) 601.

[73] Hobhouse (1990) 106 L.Q.R. 530. Cf. Steyn, in Birks ed., *The Frontiers of Liability* (vol II) p. 11.

Consumer Contracts Regulationas of the civilian concept of good faith, these are now directly germane to English law. There are also brief references to European principles and international conventions where these might be of use in giving a comparative perspective to problems faced by English law.

IV. THE CONTENT OF CONTRACT LAW

(a) A LAW OF CONTRACT OR OF CONTRACTS

The increasingly complex social and commercial relationships of the twentieth century have produced a situation where it is no longer safe to assume that there is a law of contract rather than of contracts. Particular principles and rules of law are applicable, sometimes as the result of statutory definition, say, to contracts of sale of goods, insurance, the carriage of goods by sea, contracts of employment, consumer contracts, which are peculiar to those contracts. In the past, a number of commercial contexts, such as shipping, insurance, and construction, have been particularly influential in the development of contract law. Some have suggested that they have been disproportionately influential. Whatever the influence of particular contexts, however, apart from statutory intervention the ideology of the common law of contract remains that of a single body of general principles of contract law which apply, with or without modification, across the range of such contracts. It is those general principles of contract law that this book seeks to expound.

The contract law contained in this book follows, for the most part, the subject-matter established by Sir William Anson in the seventh edition of his *Principles of the English Law of Contract and of Agency in its Relation to Contract.* It deals with the Formation of Contract, the Limits of the Contractual Obligation, Performance and Discharge, Remedies for Breach of Contract, and Agency. It also deals with those factors which tend to vitiate a contract, such as incapacity, misrepresentation, duress and undue influence, mistake, and illegality. A word must be said about these.

(b) EFFECT OF VITIATING FACTORS

Not all the factors that vitiate a contract are uniform in effect. Some of them may render a contract void or illegal, others voidable, while others still may make the contract unenforceable at the suit of one or other of the parties. These terms (void, illegal, voidable, and unenforceable) therefore denote different degrees of ineffectiveness, and they are in constant use in the law of contract. They are, however, not infrequently used with insufficient precision,[74] and even the same term may have a different meaning in different situations.

---

[74] See Turpin (1955) 72 S.A.L.J. 58; Honoré (1958) 75 S.A.L.J. 32.

(i) Void contracts

In the case of a void contract, for example, the basic position is that such a contract is simply one which the law holds to be no contract at all, a nullity from the beginning. The parties would be in the same position as they would have been had the contract never been made. No property would pass under such a contract; so, for example, a third party who purchased goods which had been the subject of a void contract would acquire no title to the goods and have to deliver them up to the true owner.[75] Conversely, money paid in pursuance of a void contract could be recovered from the person to whom it had been paid.[76] This indeed is the meaning of 'void' where a contract is said to be void for mistake. Where a contract is rendered 'null and void' by the Gaming Act 1845,[77] not only do no rights of action arise out of the contract, but any money or other property transferred cannot be recovered. In other cases, however, a void contract may not be so completely without legal effect. A contract for the sale of an interest in land 'can only be made in writing'[78] so that one that is not in writing is not merely unenforceable but void,[79] but, if it is executed, it appears that property will nevertheless pass.[80]

(ii) Illegal contracts

Again, an illegal contract is commonly said to be 'void', but the effects of illegality may vary considerably according to the degree of moral turpitude involved, the culpability of the parties, and whether or not the contract itself is rendered illegal.[81] In this case, the invalidity is imposed *ab extra* by the law, and it is not at the discretion of the contracting parties.

(iii) Voidable contracts

A voidable contract, however, is a contract which one of the parties has the option to rescind or affirm. If the choice is to affirm the contract, or if the right to rescind is not exercised within a reasonable time so that the position of the parties has, in the meantime, become altered, the option to rescind may be lost and the party who had it will be bound by the contract; otherwise that party is entitled to repudiate its liability. Nevertheless, the contract is not a nullity from the beginning. Until it is rescinded, it is valid and binding. A third party, therefore, who purchases goods which have been the subject of a voidable contract acquires a good title to the goods and cannot be compelled to surrender them to their former owner.[82]

---

[75] *Cundy* v. *Lindsay* (1878) 3 App. Cas. 459; *post*, p. 327.

[76] *Couturier* v. *Hastie* (1856) 5 H.L.C. 673; *post*, p. 314; *Westdeutsche Landesbank Girozentrale* v. *Islington London Borough Council* [1996] A.C. 669, *post*, p. 215.

[77] s. 18, *post*, p. 388.

[78] Law of Property (Miscellaneous Provisions) Act 1989, s. 2(1), *post*, p. 81.

[79] Harpum, *Megarry & Wade's Law of Real Property*, 6th edn. (2000) p. 652. See also *United Bank of Kuwait plc* v. *Sahib* [1997] Ch. 107, at p. 122 *per* Chadwick J. and in the Court of Appeal at p. 136 *per* Peter Gibson L.J.

[80] *Tootal Clothing Ltd.* v. *Guinea Properties Ltd.* (1991) 64 P. & C.R. 452, at p. 455, *post*, p. 88.

[81] *Aratra Potato Co. Ltd.* v. *Taylor Johnson Garrett* [1995] 4 All E.R. 695, at pp. 708–10; *Mohamed* v. *Alaga* [1999] 3 All E.R. 699. See further *post*, Chapter 9.

[82] Sale of Goods Act 1979, s. 23.

(iv) Unenforceable contracts

An unenforceable contract is one which is good in substance, though, by reason of some technical defect, one or both of the parties cannot be sued on it. The difference between what is voidable and what is unenforceable is mainly a difference between substance and procedure. A contract may be good, but incapable of enforcement because it is not evidenced by writing as required by statute.[83] But, in some cases, the defect is curable: the subsequent execution of a written memorandum may satisfy the requirements of the law and render the contract enforceable, but it is never at any time in the power of either party to avoid the transaction. The contract itself is unimpeachable, only it cannot be directly enforced in Court.

V. CONTRACT AS PART OF THE LAW OF OBLIGATIONS

The law of obligations has traditionally been divided into contractual obligations, which are voluntarily undertaken and owed to a specific person or persons, and obligations in tort which are based on the wrongful infliction of harm to certain protected interests, primarily imposed by the law, and typically owed to a wider class of persons.[84] Recently it has been accepted that there is a third category, restitutionary obligations, primarily based on the unjust enrichment of the defendant at the claimant's expense,[85] such as where the claimant has mistakenly paid the defendant money or discharged the defendant's debt. Contractual liability, reflecting the constitutive function of contract,[86] is generally for failing to make things better (by not rendering the expected performance), liability in tort is generally for action (as opposed to omission) making things worse, and liability in restitution is generally for unjustly taking or retaining the benefit of the claimant's money or work. It accordingly follows that it is a defence to a claim in restitution that the defendant has changed its position, for example by incurring expenditure in reliance on a payment received from the claimant, so as to make it inequitable to order that the money be repaid.[87]

Although this tripartite division is a useful starting point, as the summary of the history of contract above indicates, it is a rationalization of a less tidy common law. The recent expansion of all these types of obligation also increases the occasions in which the different categories will overlap and it has been argued that the division made between duties which are voluntarily assumed and duties which are imposed by

---

[83] *Post*, p. 78 (contract of guarantee).

[84] Winfield, *Province of the Law of Tort* (1931), p. 380; Cane, *The Anatomy of Tort Law* (1997).

[85] *Lipkin Gorman* v. *Karpnale Ltd.* [1991] 2 A.C. 548; *Kleinwort Benson Ltd.* v. *Glasgow City Council* [1999] 1 A.C. 153. See Burrows, *The Law of Restitution* (1993).

[86] *Ante*, p. 3.

[87] *Lipkin Gorman* v. *Karpnale Ltd.* (*supra*, n. 85) at pp. 579–80.

law is an oversimplification.[88] Moreover, care must be taken not to reverse the contractual allocation of risks by non-contractual actions.[89]

(a) CONCURRENCE OF CLAIMS IN CONTRACT AND TORT

Although the Court may decline to find a duty in tort where the parties are in a contractual relationship,[90] or may hold that a term of a contract has excluded or limited what would otherwise be a tortious duty, pre-contractual events, such as misrepresentation, may give rise to an action in tort.[91] Additionally, it is clear that in many cases, exemplified by negligent failure by professionals, such as solicitors and surveyors, to carry out their undertakings to their clients, a defendant may be liable to the same claimant in both contract and in tort.[92] Indeed the fact that tort liability may be grounded in an 'assumption of responsibility', means that a negligent breach of contract may often give rise to claims in both contract and tort.[93] Where this is so, 'the claimant can advance his claim, as he wishes, either in contract or in tort, and no doubt he will advance the claim on the basis that is most advantageous to him'.[94] The practical differences between contract and tort include, for example, the measure of recovery,[95] the period of limitation, the relevance of the claimant's contributory fault (it is generally irrelevant in contract but relevant in tort),[96] and assignability, since only a contractual claim can generally be assigned.

(b) CONTRACT AND RESTITUTION

Historically, the effect of the implied term theory was that contract was thought in effect to have swallowed up restitution. While it is now clear that restitution is independent of contract, the two overlap in the case of money paid and services rendered under ineffective contracts and contracts discharged by breach or by frustration.[97] It may also be difficult to distinguish restitution from contract where one person has 'freely accepted' or 'acquiesced' in services rendered by the other.[98] Where there is a contract and it makes provision for repayment or recompense, there will be no claim in restitution.[99] Where, however, it does not, a claim may lie, and, for example, in the case of a contract discharged for breach, the innocent party's

---

[88] Atiyah (1978) 94 L.Q.R. 193, at p. 223. Cf. Burrows (1983) 99 L.Q.R. 217.

[89] e.g. *Marc Rich & Co. A.G.* v. *Bishop Rock Marine Co. Ltd.* [1996] A.C. 211, and see *post*, p. 468.

[90] *Tai Hing Cotton Mill* v. *Liu Chong Hing Bank* [1986] A.C. 80, at p. 107; *Greater Nottingham Co-operative Society* v. *Cementation Piling and Foundations Ltd.* [1989] Q.B. 1.

[91] *Hedley Byrne & Co. Ltd.* v. *Heller & Partners Ltd.* [1964] A.C. 465, *post*, p. 247.

[92] *Midland Bank Trust Co. Ltd.* v. *Hett, Stubbs and Kemp* [1979] Ch. 384; *Henderson* v. *Merrett Syndicates* [1995] 2 A.C. 145. Cf. *Williams* v. *National Life Health Foods* [1998] 1 W.L.R. 830.

[93] *White* v. *Jones* [1995] 2 A.C. 207, *post*, p. 434, on which see Weir (1995) 111 L.Q.R. 357.

[94] *Coupland* v. *Arabian Gulf Petroleum Co.* [1983] 3 All E.R. 226, *per* Robert Goff L.J., at p. 228.

[95] *Post*, pp. 245, 249, and 603 (remoteness).

[96] *Post*, p. 617.

[97] *Post*, pp. 215, 225, 557, 642–52.

[98] See Beatson, *The Use and Abuse of Unjust Enrichment* (1991), ch. 2.

[99] *Pan Ocean Shipping Co. Ltd.* v. *Creditcorp Ltd.* [1994] 1 W.L.R. 161.

restitutionary claim may be greater than the contractual claim for damages.[100] We shall also see that a restitutionary remedy may be available in respect of work done by one party during pre-contractual negotiations which do not ripen into a contract.[101]

VI. CONTRACT AND PROPERTY

The law of obligations must be distinguished from the law of property which governs the acquisition of the rights persons have in things, which may be land or moveables, and may be a tangible physical object or an intangible, such as a debt, shares in a company or a patent.[102] Whereas a person's property right in a thing is generally valid against the whole world, the rights under the law of obligations, including contract, are personal and valid only against a specific person or persons. Property rights may be *protected* by the law of tort, as where the use and enjoyment of land is protected by the torts of trespass and nuisance. Property rights may be *transferred* by contract, as where A sells goods to B, and the property passes under section 18 of the Sale of Goods Act 1979, but they may also be transferred in other ways, for example by delivery with the requisite intention, as where a gift is made. As we have seen, property can pass under voidable and unenforceable contracts as well as valid ones, but not normally under void contracts.[103] Where property has so passed (whether under the contract or by delivery), B may in turn resell the goods and pass the property in them to C, even though B may not have paid A, or may have committed some other breach of contract, but an unpaid seller in possession of goods has the power to dispose of them in certain cases.[104] Where property has not passed to B, B is only able to confer a contractual right to the goods upon C. The position of a person who only has a contractual right to a thing is less secure than that of a person who has a property right since contractual rights may generally only be enforced against the other party to the contract (in our example, B) whereas property rights are generally enforceable against all persons. C would therefore only be able to enforce a contractual right against B, and not against A, or anyone who acquires the goods from A. There is, however, a tendency to reduce the discrepancy between the two and in certain circumstances contractual rights will be protected against third parties.[105]

---

[100] *Post*, p. 642.
[101] *Post*, pp. 40, 63.
[102] Lawson and Rudden, *The Law of Property*, 2nd edn. (1982), ch. II.
[103] *Ante*, p. 21.
[104] See Sale of Goods Act 1979, ss. 39(1)(c), 48(3)–(4).
[105] e.g. *Lumley* v. *Gye* (1853) 3 E. and B. 216, *post* p. 457.

PART I

FORMATION
OF CONTRACT

2

THE AGREEMENT

A contract consists of an actionable promise or promises. Every such promise involves at least two parties, a promisor and a promisee, and an outward expression of common intention, and of expectation as to the declaration or assurance contained in the promise.

It has been previously pointed out[1] that this outward expression of a common intention and of expectation normally takes the form of an agreement. In most cases, therefore, it will be necessary to ascertain at the outset whether or not an agreement has been concluded.

I. ESTABLISHING AN AGREEMENT

The fact that an agreement has been reached will frequently be self-evident, since, although as a general rule English law has no requirements of writing or other form,[2] the agreement will be set out in a document signed or initialled by both parties. But, in certain circumstances, it may be more difficult to discover whether the parties have agreed. The alleged agreement may, in whole or in part, have been concluded by word of mouth or by conduct. Difficulties of proof will then arise and the resultant questions of fact will have to be determined by the trial judge from the evidence given by the parties and their witnesses. We are not, however, here concerned with difficulties of proof, but rather with those problems that occur even where there is no dispute as to what the parties said or did. Such problems are not infrequent in practice, especially when the fact of agreement has to be elicited from correspondence, or from an exchange of other types of communication such as telex messages, facsimile, or e-mail.

(a) OFFER AND ACCEPTANCE

To determine whether an agreement has actually been concluded, it is normally necessary to inquire whether in the negotiations which have taken place between the parties there has been a definite offer by one party, and an equally definite acceptance of that offer by the other. For most contracts are reducible by analysis to the acceptance of an

---

[1] See *ante*, p. 2.
[2] On such requirements, see *post*, Chapter 3.

offer. If, for instance, A and B have agreed that A shall purchase from B a property for £100,000, we can trace the process to a moment at which B must have said to A, in effect, 'Will you give me £100,000 for my property?', and A has replied, 'I will'; or at which A has said to B, 'Will you let me have the property for £100,000?' and B has said, 'I will'. There are, however, cases to which this analysis does not readily apply. These include a contract alleged to have come into existence during and as a result of performance,[3] the signature of a prepared document, the acceptance by two parties of terms suggested by a third, negotiations through a single intermediary,[4] and multiparty agreements.[5] Where, however, a contract is alleged to have been made by an exchange of correspondence between the parties in which the successive communications other than the first are in reply to one another, the Court should look at the correspondence to see whether there is an offer by one party and an acceptance by the other party.[6] It would be a mistake to think that all contracts can thus be analysed into the form of offer and acceptance or that, in determining whether an exchange does give rise to an enforceable contract, the sole issue is whether the communications match and are identical. Another issue may be whether a statutory 'cooling off' period has passed.[7] The analysis is, however, a working method which, more often than not, enables us, in a doubtful case, to ascertain whether a contract has in truth been concluded, and as such may usefully be retained.

(i) Offer and acceptance in unilateral and bilateral contracts

The process of 'offer and acceptance' may take place in any one of three ways:

(1) In the offer of an act for a promise: as when a person offers goods or services which when accepted bind the acceptor to reward the offeror for them.

Illustration: A plc knowingly allows B to do work for it or to send it goods under such circumstances that no reasonable person would suppose that B meant to do the work or supply the goods for nothing. A plc will be liable to pay for the work or the goods. The doing of the work or the supply of the goods is the offer; the permission to do it, or the acquiescence in its being done, constitutes the acceptance.[8] Mere failure to disown responsibility to pay is not, however, enough.

---

[3] *New Zealand Shipping Co. Ltd.* v. *A. M. Satterthwaite & Co. Ltd.* [1975] A.C. 154, at p. 167; *G. Percy Trentham Ltd.* v. *Archital Luxfer Ltd.* [1993] 1 Lloyd's Rep. 25, at p. 27.

[4] *Pagnan SpA* v. *Feed Products Ltd.* [1987] 2 Lloyd's Rep. 601, at p. 616.

[5] *Clarke* v. *Earl of Dunraven (The 'Satanita')* [1897] A.C. 59, *post*, p. 30.

[6] *Gibson* v. *Manchester City Council* [1979] 1 W.L.R. 294, *per* Lord Diplock at p. 297. Cf. *Port Sudan Cotton Co.* v. *Govindaswamy Chettiar & Sons* [1977] 2 Lloyd's Rep. 5.

[7] e.g. Consumer Credit Act 1974, ss. 67–8; Consumer Protection (Cancellation of Contracts Concluded away from Business Premises) Regulations 1987 (S.I. 1987 No. 2117), as amended by S.I. 1988 No. 958; Timeshare Act 1992; Package Travel, Package Holidays and Package Tours Regulations 1992 (S.I. 1992 No. 1942).

[8] *St John Tugboat Co. Ltd.* v. *Irving Refinery Co. Ltd.* [1964] S.C.R. 614, at pp. 621–2; *Steven* v. *Bromley & Son* [1919] 2 K.B. 722. In such cases where there is an impediment to the creation of a contract such as incompleteness (*post*, p. 66) or informality (*post*, p. 69) there may be a restitutionary claim for a *quantum meruit*, *post*, pp. 63, 67–8.

(2) In the offer of a promise for an act:[9] as when a person offers a reward for the doing of a certain thing, which being done that person is bound to make good the promise to the doer.

Illustration: C, who has lost her dog, offers by advertisement a reward of £25 to anyone who will bring the dog safely home; a promise is offered in return for an act; and when D, knowing of the reward, brings the dog safely home, the act is done and C is bound to pay the reward.

(3) In the offer of a promise for a promise: in which case, when the offer is accepted by the giving of the promise, the contract consists of an outstanding obligation on both sides.

Illustration: E offers to pay F a certain sum of money if F will promise to dig E's garden for him within a certain time. When F makes the promise asked for, he accepts the promise offered, and both parties are bound, the one to do the work, the other to allow the first to do it and to pay for it.

It will be observed that cases (1) and (2) differ from (3) in an important respect. In (1) and (2), it is performance on one side which makes obligatory the promise of the other; the outstanding obligation is all on one side. In consequence, such a contract is sometimes termed 'unilateral'[10] as only one person is bound. In (3), however, each party is obliged to some act or forbearance which, at the time of entering into the contract, is future; there is an outstanding obligation on each side. This is frequently known as a 'bilateral' contract, and each party is both a promisor and a promisee. It is reasonable to presume in cases of doubt that a bilateral, rather than a unilateral contract has been concluded. Thus if G says to H: 'If you will let me have that table you are making, when it is finished, I will give you £25 for it', and H replies 'All right', there is a bilateral contract and H is bound to deliver the table.[11]

(ii) Promises in deeds

In one exceptional situation, however, it is clear that a contract can come into existence without any need for an 'offer and acceptance'. This is the case of a promise in a deed. For example, if a wealthy person, by a document executed as a deed, promises to pay a college £100,000 in order to establish a scholarship, the promise is binding without any need for an acceptance or even knowledge by the object of the promise[12] and even though it is, in fact, merely a gift.[13]

(iii) Inferences from conduct

The description which has been given of the possible forms of offer and acceptance shows that conduct may take the place of written or spoken words either in the offer

---

[9] Or forbearance. See also *post*, p. 100.

[10] *G.N. Ry.* v. *Witham* (1873) L.R. 9 C.P. 16, at p. 19; *New Zealand Shipping Co. Ltd.* v. *A. M. Satterthwaite & Co. Ltd.* [1975] A.C. 154, at pp. 167–8, 171, 177.

[11] *Restatement of the Law of Contracts* (2d), § 31.

[12] Although he cannot be compelled to accept the benefit: *Townson* v. *Tickel* (1819) 3 B. & Ald. 31.

[13] See *post*, p. 76. On deeds, see generally *post*, Chapter 3.

or in the acceptance. An agreement may also be inferred from conduct alone; the intention of the parties is a matter of inference from their conduct, and the inference is more or less easily drawn according to the circumstances of the case.[14] In day-to-day contracts such inferences are frequent. For example, a person who boards a bus or who hires a taxi thereby undertakes to pay the fare to his destination even though he makes no express promise to do so.[15] Again, a person who puts a coin in an automatic machine thereby enters into a contract with the supplier although no words have been exchanged on either side.

Sometimes the inference from conduct is not so clear, because the contract has assumed a less simple form. If more than two parties are involved, it may not be particularly helpful to look for a definite offer and acceptance. In *Clarke* v. *Earl of Dunraven (The Satanita)*:[16]

The owner of a yacht, the *Satanita*, entered it in a yacht club regatta. The rules of the regatta bound competitors to make good any damage caused by fouling. While coming up into position for the start of a race, the *Satanita* fouled and sank the *Valkyrie*, which had also been entered by its owner under the same rules.

Although the immediate relationship of each owner was not with the other, but with the secretary of the yacht club, it was held that a contract existed between them, and that the owner of the *Valkyrie* could recover damages. Lord Herschell said:[17]

The effect of their entering for the race, and undertaking to be bound by these rules to the knowledge of each other, is sufficient, where those rules indicate a liability on the part of the one to the other, to create a contractual obligation to discharge that liability.

Similar principles mean that in the case of a company or other corporate entity there will, for certain purposes, be a contract both between the entity and its members and between each of the members themselves.[18]

(iv) Inferences from inactivity

Save in the most exceptional circumstances an offer cannot be inferred from inactivity. It has been stated that, where neither party to an arbitration has taken any steps in the proceedings for a very long time, an offer to abandon the arbitration can be inferred.[19] It should be noted that in this context a contract to arbitrate disputes between the parties exists and the question is whether *that* contract can be modified. However, even in this context inactivity on its own, without some overt act, is almost

---

[14] Cited with approval in *Wright & Co. Ltd.* v. *Maunder* [1962] N.Z.L.R. 355, at p. 358.

[15] See *Wilkie* v. *London Passenger Transport Board* [1947] 1 All E.R. 258. See also *Steven* v. *Bromley & Son* [1919] 2 K.B. 722; *Sullivan* v. *Constable* (1932) 48 T.L.R. 369.

[16] [1897] A.C. 59.

[17] *Ibid.*, at p. 63.

[18] *Rayfield* v. *Hands* [1960] Ch. 1 (company); *J. H. Rayner (Mincing Lane) Ltd.* v. *Department of Trade and Industry* [1989] Ch. 72, at p. 190; [1990] 2 A.C. 413, at p. 515 (international organization whose members were states).

[19] *Andre et Compagnie S.A.* v. *Marine Transocean Ltd.* [1981] 2 Lloyd's Rep. 29, at p. 31; *Paal Wilson & Co. A/S* v. *Partenreederei Hannah Blumenthal* [1981] 2 Lloyd's Rep. 438, at p. 439; [1983] 1 A.C. 854, at pp. 865, 885, 914, 916, 924.

always likely to be insufficient.[20] In the case of 'inertia selling' statute has intervened, and the despatch of goods without any prior request may constitute a gift rather than an offer.[21]

(b) THE TEST OF INTENTION

In common with most European legal systems,[22] the test of a person's intention is not a subjective, but an objective one; that is to say, the intention which the law will attribute to a person is always that which that person's conduct bears when reasonably construed by a person in the position of the offeree, and not necessarily that which was present in the offeror's own mind. Thus a person may be held to have made an offer although not appreciating that one was being made[23] as where a rent of £65,000 was mistakenly proposed by a landlord instead of £126,000.[24] Again, words or conduct may suffice although the maker is mistaken if, when reasonably construed, they amount to an offer,[25] provided that the offeree neither knew nor could reasonably have known of the misunderstanding at the time the offer was accepted. The better view is that the offeror need not be aware of the offeree's state of mind.[26] Although the approach is objective, it is not purely objective in the sense that the intentions of the parties are entirely irrelevant so that a contract may be formed which is in accordance with the intention of neither party.[27] It has been stated that 'the judicial task is not to discover the actual intentions of each party; it is to decide what each was reasonably entitled to conclude from the attitude of the other'.[28]

---

[20] *Allied Marine Transport Ltd.* v. *Vale do Rio Doce Navegacao S.A.* [1983] 2 Lloyd's Rep. 411, at p. 417; [1985] 1 W.L.R. 925, at p. 937 (C.A.); *Yamashita-Shinnihon SS Co. Ltd.* v. *l'Office Cherifien des Phosphates* [1994] A.C. 486. The Arbitration Act 1996, s. 41(6) confers on arbitrators a power to dismiss a claim for want of prosecution.

[21] Unsolicited Goods and Services Acts 1971 and 1975, ss. 1 and 6. The receiver must serve notice on the sender indicating the place where the goods can be collected within 30 days. On acceptance by silence, see *post*, p. 46.

[22] The exception is French law: see Lando & Beale, *Principles of European Contract Law* (2000) pp. 145–6.

[23] *Upton-on-Severn R.D.C.* v. *Powell* [1942] 1 All E.R. 220. But there the liability (to pay for the provision of fire fighting services) is probably (see *William Lacey (Hounslow) Ltd.* v. *Davis* [1957] 1 W.L.R. 932, at p. 938) best regarded as restitutionary rather than contractual because neither party believed it was entering into a contract: the fire brigade rendering the services (the 'offeree') believed it was under a duty to provide the service without charge. Cf. *Henkel* v. *Pape* (1870) L.R. 6 Ex. 7.

[24] *Centrovincial Estates plc* v. *Merchant Investors Assurance Co. Ltd.* [1983] Com. L.R. 158.

[25] *Moran* v. *University College Salford (No. 2)*, The Times, 23 November 1993 (mistaken unconditional offer of university place); *O.T. Africa Line Ltd* v. *Vickers plc* [1996] 1 Lloyd's Rep. 700 (payment of £150,000 mistakenly offered instead of $150,000). See also *post*, pp. 323–326.

[26] *Paal Wilson & Co. A/S* v. *Partenreederei Hannah Blumenthal* [1983] 1 A.C. 854, at p. 924 (Lord Brightman); see also *ibid.*, at p. 914 (Lord Brandon) and cf. *ibid.*, at p. 916 (Lord Diplock); *Edmonds* v. *Lawson* [2000] Q.B. 501. See generally Spencer [1973] C.L.J. 104, 106–13; Cartwright, *Unequal Bargaining* (1991), pp. 5–24.

[27] Cf. *Upton-on-Severn R.D.C.* v. *Powell* [1942] 1 All E.R. 220, *ante*, n. 23; *Solle* v. *Butcher* [1950] 1 K.B. 671, at p. 691; *Furness Withy (Australia) Pty. Ltd.* v. *Metal Distributors (U.K.) Ltd.* [1990] 1 Lloyd's Rep. 236, at p. 243; Williston, *Law of Contracts*, 3rd edn. (1957), § 95. On the merits and demerits of this 'detached objectivity', see Howarth (1984) 100 L.Q.R. 265; Vorster (1987) 104 L.Q.R. 274.

[28] *Gloag on Contract*, 2nd edn. (1929), p. 7; approved by Lord Reid in *McCutcheon* v. *David Macbrayne Ltd.* [1964] 1 W.L.R. 125, at p. 128.

II. THE OFFER

An offer is an intimation, by words or conduct, of a willingness to enter into a legally binding contract, and which in its terms expressly or impliedly indicates that it is to become binding on the offeror as soon as it has been accepted by an act, forbearance, or return promise on the part of the person to whom it is addressed. A statement of fact made merely to supply information cannot be treated as an offer, and accepted, so as to create a valid contract. In *Harvey* v. *Facey*:[29]

A telegraphed to B 'Will you sell us Bumper Hall Pen? Telegraph lowest cash price, answer paid'. B replied by telegram, 'Lowest price for Bumper Hall Pen £900'. A telegraphed, 'We agree to buy Bumper Hall Pen for £900 asked by you'. Bumper Hall Pen was a plot of land, and A claimed that this exchange of telegrams constituted a valid offer and acceptance.

The Judicial Committee of the Privy Council pointed out that the first telegram of A asked two questions, (1) as to the willingness of B to sell, and (2) as to the lowest price; and that the word 'telegraph' was addressed to the second question only. They held that no contract had been made, that B in stating the lowest price for the property was not making an offer but supplying information, that the third telegram set out above was an offer by A—not the less so because he called it an acceptance and that this offer had never been accepted by B.

(a) OFFERS AND INVITATIONS TO TREAT

It is sometimes difficult to distinguish statements of intention which cannot, and are not intended to, result in any binding obligation from offers which admit of acceptance, and so become binding promises. A person advertises goods for sale in a newspaper, or announces that they will be sold by tender or by auction; a shopkeeper displays goods in a shop window at a certain price; or a bus company advertises that it will carry passengers from A to Z and will reach Z and other intermediate stops at certain times. In such cases it may be asked whether the statement or act made is an offer capable of acceptance or merely an invitation to make offers, and do business; one that contemplates that further negotiations will take place. A statement or act of this nature, if it is not intended to be binding, is known as an 'invitation to treat'.

As the classification of any particular act or statement as being either an offer or an invitation to treat depends on intention to be bound rather than upon any *a priori* principle of law, it is not easy to reconcile all the cases or their reasoning. Where the intention is unclear the Court will take account of the surrounding circumstances and consequences of holding an act or statement to be an offer as well as what is in fact said.

(i) Advertisements

Generally speaking advertisements in newspapers or periodicals that the advertiser

---

[29] [1893] A.C. 552. See also *Schuldenfrei* v. *Hilton (I.T.)* [1999] S.T.C. 821, at pp. 831, 833.

has goods for sale are not offers.[30] Neither are catalogues or price lists.[31] Again, a display of goods marked at a certain price by a shopkeeper in a shop window[32] does not bind the shopkeeper to sell at that price or to sell at all. The display is merely an invitation to treat; it is for the customer to offer to buy the goods, and, subject to anti-discrimination legislation,[33] the shopkeeper may choose either to accept or to refuse the offer. One reason given for this conclusion is that otherwise the advertiser, catalogue publisher, and shopkeeper would be obliged to sell to every person who accepted such an 'offer', even where supplies had run out. In the case of displays on shelves in a self-service shop, which are also generally invitations to treat, it is said that if the display were an offer, once an article was selected and placed in the receptacle, the customer would have no right to change his mind.[34] Another reason given is that if a display was an offer a shopkeeper might be forced to contract with his worst enemy: a 'shop is a place for bargains, not for compulsory sales'[35] but this is less convincing in the light of modern regulation of trading practices, for example the prohibition of sex and racial discrimination[36] and the statutory protection of consumers.[37] Where the display clearly states that the goods will be sold to a person who pays the required price it is, however, likely to be held to be an offer. For example, a notice stating 'We will beat any TV HiFi and Video price by £20 on the spot' was held to be 'a continuing offer' and the shop manager was criminally liable for a misleading indication as to the price at which goods may be available.[38]

(ii) Transactions by machine

Different considerations apply where the transaction is effected through a machine[39]

---

[30] *Partridge* v. *Crittenden* [1968] 1 W.L.R. 1204 (advertisement of 'Bramblefinch cocks and hens' for sale). The position is the same in Germany but not in France: Lando & Beale, *Principles of European Contract Law* (2000) p.162. Cf. advertisements of a *unilateral* contract, which are offers: *Carlill* v. *Carbolic Smoke Ball Co. Ltd.* [1893] 2 Q.B. 49, *post*, p. 36; *Bowerman* v. *A.B.T.A.* [1995] 145 N.L.J.R. 1815; the 'reward' cases, *post*, p. 48.

[31] *Grainger & Son* v. *Gough* [1896] A.C. 325 (bookseller's catalogue with prices); *Seacarriers A/S* v. *Aoteraroa International Ltd.* [1985] 2 Lloyd's Rep. 419 (quotation of freight rates).

[32] *Timothy* v. *Simpson* (1834) 6 C. & P. 499 (*infra*, n. 36); *Fisher* v. *Bell* [1961] 1 Q.B. 394 (on which, see now, Restriction of Offensive Weapons Act 1961, s. 1); *Esso Petroleum Ltd.* v. *Commissioners of Customs and Excise* [1976] 1 W.L.R. 1 (indication of price at which petrol to be sold at attended service station not an offer).

[33] *Infra*, n. 36.

[34] *Pharmaceutical Society of Great Britain* v. *Boots Cash Chemists (Southern) Ltd.* [1952] 2 Q.B. 795 aff'd. [1953] 1 Q.B. 401. See Unger (1953) 16 M.L.R. 369 for criticism and note (i) the context, whether the display constituted an unlawful 'sale' of drugs unsupervised by a registered pharmacist under the Pharmacy and Poisons Act 1933, s. 18(1), and (ii) in the USA it has been held that there is no acceptance until the goods are presented at the checkout: *Lasky* v. *Economic Stores* 5 N.E. 2d 305 (1946).

[35] Winfield (1939) 55 L.Q.R. 499, 518. See *Said* v. *Butt* [1920] 3 K.B. 497 (theatre manager refused entry to critic who had got someone else to buy a ticket for him to a first night performance).

[36] Sex Discrimination Act 1975; Race Relations Act 1976, *ante*, p. 5. See also *Quinn* v. *Williams Furniture* [1981] I.C.R. 328; *Gill* v. *El Vino* [1983] Q.B. 425. Cf. *Timothy* v. *Simpson* (1834) 6 C. & P. 499 (a person who went into a shop asked to pay 7/6d although item was marked at 5/11d and shop assistant said 'don't let him have it, he's only a Jew. Turn him out').

[37] *Post*, n. 38.

[38] *Warwickshire C.C.* v. *Johnson* [1993] 1 All E.R. 299, at p. 302; See also Consumer Protection Act 1987 s. 20(1); *Jenkins* v. *Lombard North Central plc* [1984] 1 W.L.R. 307.

[39] *Thornton* v. *Shoe Lane Parking Ltd.* [1971] 2 Q.B. 163, at p. 169 (machine controlling entry to car park).

as where the display is on a vending machine or where, as in many self-service petrol stations, the product purchased cannot easily be retrieved from the buyer's property. In such cases the display is likely to be an offer. In *Re Charge Card Services*[40] an open offer to sell at pump prices was held to have been accepted by a motorist putting petrol in the tank.

(iii) Auctions

In the case of auctions a difficult distinction has been made between an advertisement that an auction sale shall be 'without reserve', which has been said to be an offer,[41] and an advertisement that an auction will take place on a certain day, which has been held to be an invitation to treat.[42]

(iv) Carriage of persons

There is a similar diversity in the cases on the status of acts or statements about the carriage of persons. A statement in a railway timetable that a certain train will run at a certain time has been said to be an offer capable of acceptance by a passenger who goes to the station to buy a ticket,[43] although regulations[44] in effect provide that no contractual liability is to arise.

(v) Tenders

An announcement inviting tenders is not normally an offer; unless accompanied by words indicating that the highest or the lowest tender will be accepted,[45] it is a mere attempt to ascertain whether an acceptable offer can be obtained.[46] In a case where there is no offer to contract with the highest or lowest bidder, if the invitation to tender prescribes a clear, orderly, and familiar procedure, it may be an offer to consider all conforming tenders. Thus, where, a local authority's staff failed to clear a letterbox and the authority did not consider a tender submitted before the deadline, it was held liable for breach of contract.[47] In the case of tenders for major contracts for public works, supplies, and services the freedom to decide which tender to accept has been limited by European Community law.[48]

---

[40] [1989] Ch. 417, at p. 512. See also *Chapelton* v. *Barry U.D.C.* [1940] 1 K.B. 532 (display of deck chairs for hire an offer). On non-self service petrol sales, see *supra*, n. 32.

[41] *Warlow* v. *Harrison* (1858) 1 E. & E. 309, discussed *post*, p. 54.

[42] *Harris* v. *Nickerson* (1873) L.R. 8 Q.B. 286.

[43] *Denton* v. *Great Northern Railway Co.* (1856) 5 E. & B. 860, *per* Lord Campbell C.J. and Wightman J. (Crompton J. dissenting). See also *Wilkie* v. *L.P.T.B.* [1947] 1 All E.R. 258 (contract formed when passenger boarded bus, i.e. running the bus constituted the offer).

[44] Made by the Railways Board and the independent railways contractors under the Transport Act 1962 and the Railways Act 1993. In the context of bus services, see Public Passenger Vehicles Act 1981 and regulations made under it.

[45] *Harvela Investments Ltd.* v. *Royal Trust of Canada (C.I.) Ltd.* [1986] A.C. 207.

[46] *Spencer* v. *Harding* (1870) L.R. 5 C.P. 561. Contrast *G.N. Ry.* v. *Witham* (1873) L.R. 9 C.P. 16; *Percival Ltd.* v. *L.C.C. Asylums etc. Committee* (1918) 87 L.J.K.B. 677.

[47] *Blackpool and Fylde Aero Club Ltd.* v. *Blackpool B.C.* [1990] 1 W.L.R. 25. See *post*, p. 591 on the remedy for breach of this obligation.

[48] See *post*, p. 214.

(b) GENERAL OFFERS

An offer need not be made to an ascertained person,[49] but no contract can arise until it has been accepted by an ascertained person.

This proposition is best understood by an illustration:

An insurance company offers a reward to any person who finds and returns a valuable diamond brooch insured by them. X who knows of the offer, finds and returns the brooch. She is entitled to claim the reward.[50]

An offer, by way of advertisement, of a reward for the rendering of certain services, addressed to the public at large, *prima facie* creates a power of acceptance in every person to whom it is made or becomes known. But a contractual obligation to pay the reward only comes into existence when an individual person performs the stipulated services, and not before.[51] A general offer may be susceptible of acceptance either by only one person or by a number of persons.

In some cases, such as the offer of a reward for information or the return of a lost possession, the offer is exhausted when once accepted. The offeror clearly does not intend to pay many times over for the same thing. So, where a reward is offered for information and the information asked for reaches the offeror from several sources, it has been held that the person who gave the earliest information is entitled to the reward.[52]

In other cases the nature of the act asked for by the offeror and the circumstances in which the offer is made mean that it remains open for acceptance by any number of persons, such acceptance being signified by performance of its terms. In *Carlill* v. *Carbolic Smoke Ball Co.*:[53]

The defendant offered by advertisement to pay £100 to any one 'who contracts the increasing epidemic influenza colds, or any disease caused by taking cold, after having used the ball three times daily for two weeks, according to the printed directions'. It was added that £1,000 was deposited with the Alliance Bank 'showing our sincerity in the matter'. Mrs Carlill used the Smoke Ball as required by the directions; she afterwards suffered from influenza and sued the company for the promised reward.

The defendant was held liable. It was urged that a notification of acceptance should have been made to it but the Court held that this was one of the class of cases in which, as in the case of a reward offered for information or for the recovery of lost property, there need be no acceptance of the offer other than performance of the condition. The further argument that the alleged offer was merely an advertisement or puff which no reasonable person would take to be serious was rejected because the statement that £1,000 had been deposited to meet demands was regarded as evidence

---

[49] A proposal not addressed to one or more specific persons is presumptively merely an invitation to treat under CISG Art. 14(2) but presumptively an offer under Art. 1336(1) of the Italian Civil Code.

[50] For the position where X does not know of the offer, see *post*, pp. 48–9.

[51] *New Zealand Shipping Co. Ltd.* v. *A. M. Satterthwaite & Co. Ltd.* [1975] A.C. 154, at p. 168. See also *Williams* v. *Carwardine* (1833) 4 B. & Ad. 621, *post*, p. 49.

[52] *Lancaster* v. *Walsh* (1838) 4 M. & W. 16.

[53] [1893] 1 Q.B. 256. See also *Bowerman* v. *A.B.T.A.* [1995] 145 N.L.J.R. 1815.

of the sincerity of the offer. The advertisement was an offer which was capable of being accepted by a number of persons, and which had been accepted by Mrs Carlill when she performed the stipulated conditions.

(c) COMMUNICATION OF THE OFFER

In general an offer is effective when, and not until, it is communicated to the offeree. It follows that there can in general be no acceptance in ignorance of an offer, and, despite one somewhat unsatisfactory contrary decision,[54] this is undoubtedly correct in principle.

(i) Cross-offers

The necessity for the communication of the offer, and for its consequent acceptance, appears to be the reason why two identical cross-offers do not ordinarily make a contract. Two manifestations of a willingness to make the same bargain do not constitute a contract unless one is made with reference to the other.[55] In *Tinn* v. *Hoffman & Co.*:[56]

On 28 November 1871, H wrote to T offering to sell him 800 tons of iron at 69s. per ton, together with a further quantity at the same price. On the same day, T wrote to H offering to buy 800 tons at 69s., together with a further quantity at a lower price. The letters crossed in the post. T contended that there was, at all events, a good contract for 800 tons at 69s. per ton.

A majority of the Court of Exchequer Chamber expressed the opinion that H would not be bound as a result of the simultaneous offers, each being made in ignorance of the other.

(ii) Offer by rendering services must be communicated

Although conduct, such as the rendering of services can constitute an offer, where that offer is not communicated to the party to whom it is intended to be made there is no opportunity of rejection and no presumption of acceptance. Thus, if A does work for B without the request or knowledge of B, A can only sue in contract for the value of the work where there is evidence of a recognition or acceptance of the work by B. This is clearly illustrated by *Taylor* v. *Laird*:[57]

T was engaged to command L's ship and to conduct certain explorers on an expedition up the River Niger. He threw up his command in the course of the expedition, but helped to work the vessel home, though without the knowledge of the defendant. He then claimed to be remunerated for the services thus rendered.

[54] *Gibbons* v. *Proctor* (1891) 64 L.T. 594, 55 J.P. 616. For criticism and contrary authority, see *post*, pp. 48–9.

[55] If one is made with reference to the other, there is no reason why a contract should not be held to exist, even though it is expressed to be an 'offer' and not an acceptance: but see *Gibson* v. *Manchester City Council* [1979] 1 W.L.R. 294.

[56] (1873) 29 L.T. 271, at pp. 275, 277, 278, 279; *Restatement* (2d), § 23.

[57] (1856) 25 L.J. Ex. 329. See also *Forman & Co. Pty. Ltd.* v. *Ship Liddesdale* [1900] A.C. 190.

It was held that he could not recover. L never had the option of accepting or refusing the services while they were being rendered; and he repudiated them when he became aware of them. T's offer, being uncommunicated, did not admit of acceptance and could not give him any contractual rights against L. Pollock C.B. said:[58]

Suppose I clean your property without your knowledge, have I a claim on you for payment? How can you help it? One cleans another's shoes; what can the other do but put them on? Is that evidence of a contract to pay for the cleaning?

In certain circumstances, for instance where the services rendered are necessary services,[59] or where they are freely accepted,[60] restitutionary liability may arise but such liability is not contractual.

III. THE ACCEPTANCE

If a contract is to be made, the offeree must accept the offer. Acceptance of an offer is the expression, by words or conduct,[61] of assent to the terms of the offer in the manner prescribed or indicated by the offeror.

(a) OFFER AND ACCEPTANCE MUST CORRESPOND

The intention of the offeree to accept must be expressed without leaving room for doubt as to the fact of acceptance, or as to the coincidence of the terms of the acceptance with those of the offer. These requirements may be summed up in the general rule, sometimes called the 'mirror image' rule, that the acceptance must be absolute, and must correspond with the terms of the offer.

In determining whether or not an acceptance is conclusive, an alleged acceptance must be distinguished from (i) a rejection and counter-offer; (ii) an acceptance with some variation or addition of terms; or (iii) an acceptance which is equivocal, or which is qualified by reference to the subsequent arrangement of terms.

(i) Counter-offer and rejection

A counter-offer amounts to a rejection of the offer, and so operates to bring it to an end. In *Hyde* v. *Wrench*,[62] for example:

W offered to sell a farm to H for £1,000. H said that he would give £950. W refused, and H then said he would give £1,000, and, when W declined to adhere to his original offer, H tried to obtain specific performance of the alleged contract.

---

[58] At p. 332.

[59] *Jenkins* v. *Tucker* (1788) 1 Hy. Bl. 90 (burial of the dead); *Re Rhodes* (1890) 44 Ch. D. 94 (restitution in respect of the maintenance of a mentally incapable person recognized in principle but no recovery on facts because there was no intention to charge for the services).

[60] See also *Way* v. *Latilla* [1937] 3 All E.R. 759, at pp. 764–5. See *post*, pp. 40, 63.

[61] *Ante*, p. 29.

[62] (1840) 3 Beav. 334.

The Court held that an offer to buy at £950 in response to an offer to sell for £1,000 was a refusal followed by a counter-offer, and that no contract had come into existence. But making express what would otherwise be implied[63] or inquiring whether the offeror will modify his terms does not necessarily amount to a counter-offer. So in *Stevenson, Jacques & Co.* v. *McLean*,[64] the offeree could still accept an offer of a certain quantity of iron 'at 40s. nett *cash* per ton', even though he had telegraphed to the offeror requesting information as to possible terms of credit. It was held that this was not a counter-offer, but was 'a mere inquiry, which should have been answered and not treated as a rejection of the offer'.[65]

(ii) Change of terms

A purported acceptance of an offer may introduce terms at variance with or not comprised in the offer. Although, exceptionally in such a situation the response may be regarded as an acceptance with an offer to enter a further contract,[66] generally, in such cases no contract is made, for the offeree in effect rejects the offer and makes a counter-offer.[67]

In the case of *Jones* v. *Daniel*:[68]

A offered £1,450 for a property belonging to B. In accepting the offer B enclosed with the letter of acceptance a contract for the signature of A. This document contained various terms as to payment of deposit, date of completion, and requirement of title which had never been suggested in the offer.

The Court held that there was no contract; B had not accepted A's offer but made a counter-offer of his own, which was never accepted by A.

(iii) 'Battle of the forms'

In modern commercial practice, a particular problem has arisen which is that of the 'battle of the forms'. A firm may, for example, offer to buy goods from another on a form which contains or refers to its standard conditions of trade. The seller 'accepts' the offer by a confirmation on a form which contains or refers to its (the seller's) standard conditions of trade. These may differ materially from those of the buyer. It may then deliver the goods. Two questions typically arise; is there a contract and, if there is, do the buyer's or the seller's conditions prevail?

One possible solution to this problem is by what might be called the 'first shot' approach. Under this the seller-offeree, by purporting to accept the buyer-offeror's offer, is said to have waived its own conditions of trade, so that the contract is

---

[63] *Lark* v. *Outhwaite* [1991] 2 Lloyd's Rep. 132, at p. 139.

[64] (1880) 5 Q.B.D. 346. See also *Brown & Gracie Ltd.* v. *F. W. Green & Co. (Pty.) Ltd.* [1960] 1 Lloyd's Rep. 289, at p. 297; *Gibson* v. *Manchester City Council* [1979] 1 W.L.R. 294, at p. 302.

[65] At p. 350.

[66] *Monvia Motorship Corp.* v. *Keppel Shipyard (Private) Ltd.* [1983] 1 Lloyd's Rep. 356 (P.C.).

[67] The position is similar in many European systems; see Lando & Beale, *Principles of European Contract Law* (2000), p.179.

[68] [1894] 2 Ch. 332. See also *Brogden* v. *Metropolitan Ry. Co.* (1877) 2 App. Cas. 666, *post*, pp. 40–1. Cf. *Global Tankers Inc.* v. *Amercoat Europa N.V.* [1975] 1 Lloyd's Rep. 666, at p. 671.

concluded subject to the buyer's conditions.[69] In *Butler Machine Tool Co. Ltd.* v. *Ex-cell-o Corporation (England) Ltd.*,[70] however, a majority of the Court of Appeal applied the 'mirror image' rule and stated that the seller's confirmation amounts to a counter-offer. This is capable of acceptance by the buyer. The buyer may indicate that it accepts the counter-offer made to it by some act or performance; e.g. the receipt and acceptance of the goods or by, for instance, the return of an 'acknowledgement' form containing the seller's conditions. This can be called the 'last shot' approach. In our example such an acceptance would conclude a contract subject to the seller's conditions, since it was the seller who fired the 'last shot' in the battle of the forms.

The difficulty is, however, that the operation of the 'last shot' approach depends upon chance and can be arbitrary. Furthermore, unless and until the counter-offer is accepted, there is no contract, even though both buyer and seller may firmly believe that a contract has been made.[71] Where they have acted on that basis and the transaction is executed, it may be possible to treat a matter not finalized in negotiations as inessential[72] but this is not always so. The position, especially in relation to executory transactions, is not satisfactory. The 'first shot' approach, however, can also be arbitrary.

It is suggested that, in these circumstances, the following solution, which reflects business practice[73] and international conventions and which only represents a minor departure from the 'mirror image' rule should be adopted. If an offeror receives a reply to an offer which purports to be an acceptance but which contains additional or different terms which do not materially alter the terms of the offer, and does not promptly object to the offeree about the discrepancy, the terms of the contract consist of the terms of the offer subject to the modifications contained in the acceptance.[74] In effect this simply puts the burden on the offeror to object to such additional or different terms;[75] the requirement that they do not materially alter the terms of the offer substantially preserves the requirement of objective agreement. Under the Convention on the International Sale of Goods most non-trivial variations are likely to be regarded as 'material'.[76] Article 19(3) provides that alterations relating, among other

---

[69] See also *Chas. Davis (Metal Brokers) Ltd.* v. *Gilyott & Scott Ltd* [1975] 2 Lloyd's Rep. 422, *per* Donaldson J. at p. 425.

[70] [1979] 1 W.L.R. 401, at pp. 406, 407. See also *British Road Services* v. *Arthur Crutchley Ltd.* [1968] 1 All E.R. 811; *A. Davies & Co. (Shopfitters)* v. *William Old* (1969) 67 L.G.R. 395.

[71] [1979] 1 W.L.R. 401, at p. 406.

[72] *G. Percy Trentham Ltd.* v. *Archital Luxfer Ltd.* [1993] 1 Lloyd's Rep. 25 (facts compared to 'battle of the forms').

[73] Beale & Dugdale (1975) 2 B.J.L.S. 45, 49–51.

[74] See the Uniform Laws on International Sales Act 1967, Sched. 2, Art. 7(2); CISG Art. 19; von Mehren (1990) 38 Am. J. Comp. Law. 265. See also Lord Denning M.R. in *Butler Machine Tool Co. Ltd.* v. *Ex-cell-o Corporation (England) Ltd.* [1979] 1 W.L.R. 401 (but cf. the House of Lords' disapproval of his approach to formation in *Gibson* v. *Manchester City Council* [1979] 1 W.L.R. 294, at pp. 297, 302 (H.L.)). Cf. the broader approach of the United States' Uniform Commercial Code § 2–207 which applies even where a variation is material but which has been said (Farnsworth, *Contracts*, 2nd edn. (1990), p. 172) to raise as many questions as it answers.

[75] See *post*, p. 46 on acceptance by silence.

[76] See Nicholas (1988) 105 L.Q.R. 201, at p. 217; Scot. Law Com. No. 144 (1993), § 4.19. Cf. Schlectreim, *Commentary on the CISG* (1998), pp. 140–141.

things, to the price, quantity, and quality of the goods, place and time of delivery, extent of one party's liability to the other, or to the settlement of disputes are material alterations.

In cases where there is no contract even though services have been rendered or goods delivered, the rendering of services or delivery of goods may give rise to a restitutionary obligation to pay a reasonable sum.[77] But in such cases, while restitution may protect the performer by the award of the reasonable value of the performance rendered, a recipient, who may have had certain requirements as to the time of performance or its quality may be unprotected. This is because, in the absence of a contract, the party rendering the services or delivering the goods will not be liable in damages for delay or for defective performance.[78]

(iv) Equivocal or qualified acceptance

The acceptance must assent unequivocally and without qualification to the terms of the offer. For example, the reply 'Your order is receiving our attention' is probably too indefinite to amount to an acceptance.[79] The acceptance may also be qualified by reference to the preparation of a more formal contract or by reference to terms which have still to be negotiated. In such a case the agreement is incomplete[80] and there is no binding contract.

(b) COMMUNICATION OF THE ACCEPTANCE

(i) Mental assent insufficient

Acceptance means, in general, communicated acceptance, which must be something more than a mere mental assent. A tacit formation of intention is insufficient.

In an old case in the Year Books[81] it was argued that where the produce of a field was offered to a man at a certain price if he was pleased with it on inspection, the contract was made and the property passed when he had seen and approved of the subject of the sale. But Brian C.J. said:

It seems to me the plea is not good without showing that he had certified the other of his pleasure; for it is trite learning that the thought of man is not triable, for the devil himself knows not the thought of man; but if you had agreed that if the bargain pleased then you should have signified it to such an one, then I grant you need not have done more, for it is matter of fact.

Lord Blackburn approved this decision in *Brogden* v. *Metropolitan Railway Co.*:[82]

---

[77] *Peter Lind & Co. v. Mersey Docks & Harbour Board* [1972] 2 Lloyd's Rep. 234. For the conditions of such liability see *post*, pp. 63, 68.

[78] McKendrick (1988) 8 O.J.L.S. 197, 212–13; Ball (1983) 99 L.Q.R. 572. A contract will also have implied terms as to quality, description, and title: see *post*, p. 153 (Sale of Goods Act 1979 and the Supply of Goods and Services Act 1982).

[79] *Rees* v. *Warwick* (1818) 2 B. & Ald. 113; *Restatement* (2d), § 57.

[80] See *post*, p. 66.

[81] *Anon.* (1477) Y.B. Pasch. 17 Edw. IV, f. 1, pl. 2.

[82] (1877) 2 App. Cas. 666.

B altered a draft coal supply agreement sent to him by M and returned it signed and marked 'approved'. M's agent put it in a drawer. The parties appear to have ordered and supplied coal upon the terms stated but, a dispute having arisen, B contended that he was not bound by the agreement.

It was held that there was a contract between the parties. This had not, however, come into existence at the time M's agent acquiesced in the offer by putting the letter in his drawer but later, when coal was ordered and accepted by M.

(ii) Notification of offeror

Even if there is some overt act or speech to give evidence of the intention to accept, English law stipulates, in addition, that acceptance is not complete *unless and until it is communicated to the offeror*. In the words of Lindley L.J.: 'Unquestionably, as a general proposition, when an offer is made, it is necessary in order to make a binding contract, not only that it should be accepted, but that acceptance should be notified'.[83] Thus, if an offer is made by telephone, and in the middle of the reply the line goes dead, so that the offeror does not hear the words of acceptance, there is no contract.[84] Again, if a person shouts to another across a river or courtyard, but the offeror does not hear the reply because it is drowned by an aircraft flying overhead, there is no contract at that moment and the offeree must repeat the acceptance in order that it might be effective.

(iii) Communication other than by offeree

The justification for the rule requiring communication is that the offeror is entitled to know whether a binding contract has been concluded by acceptance. In principle, therefore, there would seem to be no reason (other than one of certainty) why a contract should not come into existence if the offeror is made aware or is informed that the offer has been accepted even though the acceptance is not communicated to the offeror by the offeree.[85] *Powell* v. *Lee*,[86] however, appears to hold that it is necessary that the acceptance be communicated by the offeree or by his duly authorized agent.

The managers of a school resolved to appoint the plaintiff to the headmastership of a school. One of the managers, acting in his individual capacity, informed the plaintiff of what had occurred. He received no other communication and subsequently the resolution was rescinded.

It was held that there was no concluded contract. It was said: 'the mere fact that the

---

[83] *Carlill* v. *Carbolic Smoke Ball Co.* [1893] 1 Q.B. 256, at p. 262. See also *Robophone Facilities Ltd.* v. *Blank* [1966] 1 W.L.R. 1428; *Allied Marine Transport Ltd.* v. *Vale do Rio Doce Navegacao* [1985] 1 W.L.R. 925, at p. 937; CISG Art. 23. Cf. *post*, p. 49 (no need for communication where offer stipulates a prescribed mode of acceptance).

[84] *Entores* v. *Miles Far East Corporation* [1955] 2 Q.B. 327 *per* Denning L.J. at p. 332; Winfield (1939) 55 L.Q.R. 499, 514; *Restatement* (2d), § 65. But cf. *post*, p. 43 for the different rule which applies to acceptance by post, telegram, or telemessage.

[85] *Levita's Case* (1867) L.R. 3 Ch. App. 36. See also *Dickinson* v. *Dodds* (1876) 2 Ch.D. 463, *post*, p. 57 (third party notification of revocation of offer effective).

[86] (1908) 99 L.T. 284.

[whole body of] managers did not authorize such a communication, which is the usual course to be adopted, implied that they meant to reserve the power to reconsider the decision at which they had arrived'.[87] In the absence of facts giving rise to such an implication, however, communication by a third party should, it is submitted, suffice.

The general rule that acceptance must be communicated before it can take effect is subject to a number of exceptions, to which we now turn.

(iv) Waiver of communication

The general rule that an acceptance of an offer made ought to be notified to the offeror is for the benefit of the offeror, who may expressly or impliedly waive the requirement of notification and agree that an uncommunicated acceptance will suffice. Thus acceptance may in certain circumstances be held to have been made even though it has not yet come to the notice of the offeror. In such a case two things are necessary. There must be an express or implied intimation from the offeror that a particular mode of acceptance will suffice. And there must be some overt act or conduct on the part of the offeree which is evidence of an intention to accept, and which conforms to the mode of acceptance indicated by the offeror.

In *Carlill* v. *Carbolic Smoke Ball Co.*,[88] previously discussed, it will be remembered that the manufacturers of the smoke balls advertised inviting performance of a condition, and it was sufficient for the purposes of binding them that Mrs Carlill had performed the condition without communicating to them the acceptance of the offer. Bowen L.J. stated:[89]

The person who makes the offer may dispense with notice to himself if he thinks it desirable to do so, and I suppose there can be no doubt that where a person in an offer made by him to another person, expressly or impliedly intimates a particular method of acceptance as sufficient to make the bargain binding, it is only necessary for the other person to whom such offer is made to follow the indicated mode of acceptance; and if the person making the offer, expressly or impliedly intimates in his offer that it will be sufficient to act on the proposal without communicating acceptance of it to himself, performance of the condition is a sufficient acceptance without notification.

(v) Promise for an act

In the case of general offers and other offers which indicate performance as a mode of acceptance so as to create a unilateral contract it may well be impossible for the offeree to express acceptance otherwise than by performance of the contract. An offer of reward for the supply of information, or for the return of a lost dog, does not contemplate an intimation of acceptance from every person who, on becoming aware of the offer, decides to ascertain the information or to search for the dog;[90] the offeree

---

[87] (1908) 99 L.T. 284, *per* Channell J. at p. 286.

[88] [1893] 1 Q.B. 256, *ante*, p. 35.

[89] *Ibid.*, at p. 269. Lindley L.J. (*ibid.*, at p. 262) said such cases were either an exception to the rule or ones in which acceptance need not precede the performance. See also *Manchester Diocesan Council for Education* v. *Commercial & General Investments Ltd.* [1970] 1 W.L.R. 241, at p. 245.

[90] *Carlill* v. *Carbolic Smoke Ball Co.* (*supra*, n. 88), at p. 270.

may already have the information or have found the dog, and can do no more than send it on to the offeror.

The position differs in the case of an offer capable of acceptance by performance. The nature and terms of the offer need to be considered more carefully to ascertain whether they entitle the offeree to dispense with notice of acceptance. If A tells B by letter that he will receive and pay for certain goods if B will send them to him, such an offer may be accepted by sending the goods.[91]

(vi) Acceptance by post, telegram, or telemessage

A distinction is drawn between acceptance by instantaneous methods such as telex, telephone, and probably fax, e-mail and electronic data interchange, and acceptance by non-instantaneous methods such as post, telegram, or telemessage. Instantaneous methods, where the acceptor will generally know that his communication has not arrived at once and can try again, are subject to the general requirement that acceptance must be communicated to the offeror.[92] Where, however, it is reasonable for the offeree to notify acceptance by post, telegram,[93] or telemessage, the acceptance is completed when the letter is posted,[94] the telegram handed in,[95] or possibly when the telemessage is dictated.[96] The offeror is bound from that time although the acceptance has not been delivered and may never be delivered.

The postal acceptance rule was laid down in *Adams* v. *Lindsell*:[97]

On 2 September 1817, L wrote offering to sell to A a certain quantity of wool, and added 'receiving your answer in course of post'. If the letter containing this offer had been properly directed, an answer might have been received by the 7th; but it was misdirected and did not reach A until the 5th so that their acceptance, posted the same day, was not received by L until the 9th. On the 8th, however, that is before the acceptance had arrived, L sold the wool to another. A sued for breach of contract.

It was argued on behalf of L that there was no contract between the parties until the letter of acceptance was actually received. The Court replied:[98]

---

[91] *Harvey* v. *Johnston* (1848) 6 C.B. 295, at p. 304; *Newcomb* v. *De Roos* (1859) 2 E. & E. 271. Cf. *Kennedy* v. *Thomassen* [1929] 1 Ch. 426; *Restatement* (2d), § 56. But cf. *Rust* v. *Abbey Life Assurance Co. Ltd.* [1978] 1 Lloyd's Rep. 386, at p. 392 (offer to invest in property bond accepted by allocation of units; no need to send policy to offeror).

[92] *Entores* v. *Miles Far East Corporation* [1955] 2 Q.B. 327; *Brinkibon Ltd.* v. *Stahag Stahl und Stahlwaren-handelsgesellschaft m.b.H* [1983] 2 A.C. 34 (telex).

[93] *Henthorn* v. *Fraser* [1892] 2 Ch. 27, at p. 33.

[94] *Dunlop* v. *Higgins* (1848) 1 H.L.C. 381; *Re Imperial Land Co. of Marseilles (Harris' Case)* (1872) L.R. 7 Ch. App. 587; *Household Fire and Carriage Accident Insurance Co. Ltd.* v. *Grant* (1879) 4 Ex. D. 216; *Henthorn* v. *Fraser* (*supra*, n. 93); *Port Sudan Cotton Co.* v. *Govindaswamy Chettiar & Sons* [1977] 2 Lloyd's Rep. 5.

[95] *Stevenson, Jacques & Co.* v. *McLean* (1880) 5 Q.B.D. 346; *Bruner* v. *Moore* [1904] 1 Ch. 305, at p. 316.

[96] There is no authority on this but if, see *infra*, the rationale of the postal acceptance rule is to protect an offeree who but for the rule may not know until it is too late that his acceptance has not reached the offeror, telemessages should be classified with letters and telegrams rather than with instantaneous means of communication; *Chitty on Contracts*, 28th edn. (1999), § 2–031. Cf. Winfield (1939) 55 L.Q.R. 499, 515.

[97] (1818) 1 B. & Ald. 681.

[98] *Ibid.*, at p. 683. The *ratio decidendi* of the case is complicated by the assertion that the delay was caused by the defendants' negligence in misdirecting their offer. It would seem that the effect of such delay is to extend the permissible period within which the offer may be accepted (see *post*, p. 58) unless the offeree knows or has reason to know of the delay: *Restatement* (2d), § 51.

If that were so, no contract could ever be completed by post. For if [L] were not bound by their offer when accepted by [A] until the answer was received, then [A] ought not to be bound till they had received the notification that [L] had received their answer and assented to it. And so it might go on *ad infinitum*.

The logic of this passage is questionable, but it was undoubtedly necessary for the Court to establish some definite rule as to the time of a postal acceptance.

One of the more obvious consequences of the postal acceptance rule is that the offeror must bear the risk of the letter of acceptance being delayed or lost. In *Household Fire and Carriage Accident Insurance Co. Ltd.* v. *Grant*[99] the Court of Appeal held that the defendant, to whom a letter of allotment had been posted, but which had not reached him, was nevertheless liable as a shareholder. Where, however, the delay or loss is due to the fault of the offeree, as in the case of an acceptance which is improperly addressed or insufficiently stamped, it would seem that it only takes effect if and when it is received by the offeror, provided that this occurs within the time within which a regular acceptance would have been received.[100]

Where the postal acceptance rule does not apply, however, as we have seen,[101] the offeree bears the risk of the acceptance going astray, save where a particular mode of acceptance has been prescribed, in which case communication is not always necessary.[102]

(vii) Place of contracting

Whether the postal acceptance rule applies also determines *where* a contract is made. If the means of communication is by letter, telegram, or telemessage, the contract is complete when the letter is posted or the telegram is handed in[103] and possibly when the telemessage is dictated,[104] and it is there that the contract is made. In other cases the general rule that the contract is made when and where the acceptance is received applies.[105] On the other hand, if the means of communication is by letter or telegram, a different rule prevails.

(viii) Rationale of postal rule

Various attempts have been made to justify the postal acceptance rule analytically.[106] One line of reasoning attempts to eliminate any difficulties as to consensus by treating the post office as the agent of the offeror not only for delivering the offer, but for

---

[99] (1879) 4 Ex. D. 216.

[100] *Getreide-Import-Gesellschaft* v. *Contimar S.A. Compania Commercial y Maritima* [1953] 1 W.L.R. 793; *Restatement* (2d), §§ 67–8.

[101] *Ante*, pp. 40–1.

[102] *Manchester Diocesan Council for Education* v. *Commercial & General Investments Ltd.* [1970] 1 W.L.R. 241, at p. 245 and *ante*, p. 42.

[103] *Cowan* v. *O'Connor* (1888) 20 Q.B.D. 640.

[104] See *supra*, n. 96.

[105] *Brinkibon Ltd.* v. *Stahag Stahl und Stahlwarenhandelsgesellschaft m.b.H* [1983] 2 A.C. 34 approving *Entores* v. *Miles Far East Corporation* [1955] 2 Q.B. 327 where an offer by telex from Holland to London was held to constitute a contract made in England.

[106] Winfield (1939) 55 L.Q.R. 499; Nussbaum (1936) 36 Col. L. Rev. 920.

receiving the notification of its acceptance;[107] yet the post office is clearly not an agent to whom acceptance is or could be communicated. Another is based on the fact that posting the acceptance puts it irretrievably out of the offeree's control. The same can, however, be said of communication by telex which is not completed until receipt[108] so this does not explain why posting exceptionally constitutes an acceptance without notification.

The better explanation would seem to be that the rule is based, not on logic, but on commercial convenience.[109] If hardship is caused, as it obviously may be, by the delay or loss of a letter of acceptance, some rule is necessary, and the rule at which the Courts have arrived is probably as satisfactory as any other would be.[110]

First, it is always open to the offeror to secure protection by requiring actual notification of the acceptance.[111] The nature of the offer or the circumstances in which it was made may indicate that notification is required and Courts may be willing to displace what has been termed an 'artificial concept of communication'.[112] Secondly, the rule is a pragmatic way of limiting the power to revoke an offer before acceptance,[113] even where the offeror has promised not to.[114] It also prevents the offeree from being able to nullify the acceptance while it is in transit and thus from speculating by watching the market and deciding whether to send an overtaking rejection.[115] Further, in the event of delay or loss of the letter of acceptance, it is the offeror who is more likely to be the first to enquire why no reply has been received to the offer, rather than the offeree to enquire whether the acceptance has been received.

The rule has, however, been criticized.[116] The number of different modes of communication now available[117] have been said to give rise to an increasing number of problems of demarcation and it is argued that the law would be much more coherent if there were only one rule for all means of communication. It has also been said that the law should not, as the postal acceptance rule does, favour the offeree because,

---

[107] *Household Fire and Carriage Accident Insurance Co. Ltd. v. Grant* (1879) 4 Ex. D. 216, at p. 221; *Hebb's Case* (1867) L.R. 4 Eq. 9, at p. 12.

[108] *Entores* v. *Miles Far East Corporation* [1955] 2 Q.B. 327.

[109] *Re Imperial Land Co. of Marseilles (Harris' Case)* (1872) L.R. 7 Ch. App. 587, at p. 594; *Brinkibon Ltd.* v. *Stahag Stahl und Stahlwarenhandelsgesellschaft m.b.H* [1983] 2 A.C. 34, at pp. 41, 48.

[110] Winfield (1939) 55 L.Q.R. 499, at p. 506. Three principal systems seem to be in operation in other countries: (i) *information*: when the offeror is actually informed of the acceptance; (ii) *expedition*: when the offeree despatches the letter of acceptance; and (iii) *reception*: when the acceptance is received at its destination, whether the offeror is actually informed or not. See Evans (1966) 15 I.C.L.Q. 553. Under CISG Arts. 18(2), 24 and 21(2) the acceptance becomes effective at the moment the indication of assent is delivered at the address of the offeror; if the letter is lost, there is no contract, but if it is delayed, there is normally a contract, unless the offeror has promptly informed the offeree that he considers his offer as having lapsed.

[111] *Holwell Securities Ltd.* v. *Hughes* [1974] 1 W.L.R. 155.

[112] *Ibid.*, at pp. 157, 158, 161; *New Hart Builders Ltd.* v. *Brindley* [1975] Ch. 342 (rule displaced where contracts required 'notice to . . .' or 'to notify').

[113] *Re Imperial Land Co. of Marseilles (Harris' Case)* (1872) L.R. 7 Ch. App. 587, at p. 594.

[114] *Post*, p. 53. Nussbaum (1936) 36 Col. L. Rev. 920, 922–7. The Scottish Law Commission, which rejects the rule (Scot. Law Com. No. 144 (1993), §§ 4.4–4.7), does not consider this.

[115] *Post*, p. 50. See also Farnsworth, *Contracts*, 2nd edn. (1990), p. 183.

[116] e.g. by Gardner (1992) 12 O.J.L.S. 170; Scot. Law Com. No. 144 (1993), §§ 4.4–4.7.

[117] Apart from telex, fax, e-mail and the various types of electronic document interchange, there are also couriers, private messenger delivery, and document exchange services.

while the offeror is in ignorance as to the actions of the offeree, the offeree has full knowledge of what the position is. The offeree knows that the acceptance has been posted and knows or ought to know that mail is not infrequently delayed.[118] Nevertheless, the ability of the offeror to control the method of acceptance, the offeror's ability to revoke even a 'firm' offer before acceptance[119] and the desirability of preventing speculation by the offeree are, it is suggested, good reasons for the rule. It is significant that the Scottish Law Commission's proposal to abolish it was made together with a proposal to prohibit the offeror from revoking a 'firm' offer.[120]

The rule may in any event not be as anomalous as it appears when compared only with the rules governing instantaneous modes of communication. We have seen that, in the case of a prescribed mode of acceptance, a contract results as soon as the offeree does the stipulated act, whether it has come to the notice of the offeror or not.[121] In a previous edition of this work, it was argued that the principles governing postal acceptance were merely examples of a wider principle that where the offeror either expressly or impliedly indicates the mode of acceptance and this, as a means of communication, proves to be nugatory or insufficient, he does so at his own risk.[122] Suppose that A sends an offer to B by messenger across a lake with a request that B, if she accepts, will at a certain hour communicate her acceptance by firing a gun or lighting a fire. Why, it was asked, should B suffer if a storm renders the gun inaudible or a fog obscures the light of the fire? Although, as we have seen,[123] this 'risk' approach does not apply where instantaneous communication is concerned, it is suggested that it has validity in cases where there is bound to be a substantial interval between the time when the acceptance is sent and the time when it is received.[124]

(ix) Acceptance by silence

In principle, it is difficult to see how the silence or inaction of an offeree who fails to reply to an offer can ever operate as an acceptance, for there will have been no communication of the acceptance to the offeror. But if the offeror has waived[125] communication by indicating that acceptance by silence will suffice, it is clear that the offeror cannot confront the offeree with the alternative of either refusing the offer or being subjected to a contractual obligation by reason of the failure to reply. Although a form or time of acceptance may be prescribed, an offeror cannot prescribe the form or time of refusal so as to impose a contract on the other party if the other party does

---

[118] Scot. Law Com. Memorandum No. 36 [1977], § 48, quoted in Scot. Law Com. No. 144 (1993), § 4.5.

[119] *Ante*, p. 43, *post*, p. 53.

[120] Art. 16(2), *post*, p. 54). Prevention of speculation by the offeree, who unlike the offeror has *full* knowledge, does not appear to have been considered by the Scottish Law Commission: Scot. Law Com. No. 144 (1993), §§ 4.4–4.7. See also §§ 3.10–3.14.

[121] *Manchester Diocesan Council for Education* v. *Commercial & General Investments Ltd.* [1970] 1 W.L.R. 241, at p. 245 and *ante*, p. 42.

[122] Anson, 20th edn., p. 36.

[123] *Entores* v. *Miles Far East Corporation* [1955] 2 Q.B. 327; *Brinkibon Ltd.* v. *Stahag Stahl und Stahlwaren-handelsgesellschaft m.b.H* [1983] 2 A.C. 34, *ante*, p. 41.

[124] *Brinkibon Ltd.* v. *Stahag Stahl und Stahlwarenhandelsgesellschaft m.b.H* [1983] 2 A.C. 34, at p. 48.

[125] On infering an offer from inactivity, see *ante*, p. 30.

not refuse in some particular way or within some particular time.[126] In *Felthouse* v. *Bindley*, for example:[127]

F offered by letter to buy his nephew's horse for £30. 15*s*., adding, 'If I hear no more about him I shall consider the horse mine at £30. 15*s*.'. No answer was returned to this letter, but the nephew told B, an auctioneer, to keep the horse out of a sale of his farm stock, as he intended to reserve it for his uncle F. B sold the horse by mistake, and F sued him for conversion of his property.

The Court held that as the nephew had never signified to F his acceptance of the offer before the auction sale took place, there was no bargain to pass the property in the horse to F, and therefore he had no right to complain of the sale. Willes J. said:[128] 'It is clear that the uncle had no right to impose upon the nephew a sale of his horse for £30 15*s*. unless he chose to comply with the condition of writing to repudiate the offer'.

In more modern times this same principle may be illustrated by the practice of sending out unsolicited goods. A publisher may, for example, without previous order, send a book to a prospective customer with a letter saying, in effect, 'If you do not return the book by a certain day, I shall presume that you have bought it'. It is clear that he cannot by these means impose a contract on the unwilling recipient. But persons with no knowledge of the law may well be misled into thinking that they are bound to pay for the book, and the subsequent letters which they receive may frequently be designed to foster this misapprehension. As a result, in 1971, the legislature enacted the Unsolicited Goods and Services Act whereby the recipients of unsolicited goods may, in certain circumstances, treat them as if they were an unconditional gift to themselves, and suppliers may be guilty of a criminal offence if they demand or threaten legal proceedings for payment.

On the other hand, circumstances can arise where acceptance could more legitimately be presumed from silence. Previous dealings between the parties may have been conducted on the basis, for example, that orders for goods have been fulfilled by the seller without any notification of acceptance other than the despatch of the goods, and the offeror has thereby been led to believe that the practice will continue.[129] It is even arguable by analogy with the cases we have noted on waiver by the offeror of the need for communication of acceptance, that, if the offeror stipulates that acceptance may be constituted by silence or inaction, an unequivocal manifestation of an intention to accept on the part of the offeree (or, possibly, detrimental reliance on the offer by the offeree),[130] should bind the offeror. This, however, would run counter to the decision in *Felthouse* v. *Bindley*, where, it will be noted, the nephew made known his intention to accept his uncle's offer but that, like other authorities that support the general rule, was a case where an offeror sought to impose on the offeree a term as to acceptance by

---

[126] Pollock, *Principles of Contract*, 13th edn. (1950), p. 22.

[127] (1862) 11 C.B.N.S. 869, aff'd (1863) 7 L.T. 835. See also *Allied Marine Transport Ltd.* v. *Vale do Rio Doce Navegacao S.A.* [1985] 1 W.L.R. 925, at p. 937 (C.A.). See further Miller (1972) 35 M.L.R. 489.

[128] At p. 875.

[129] *Restatement* (2d), § 72.

[130] Cf. *Fairline Shipping Cpn.* v. *Adamson* [1975] Q.B. 180; *Schuldenfrei v. Hilton (I.T)* [1999] S.T.C. 821, at pp. 831, 833. See also, *post*, p. 112 (equitable estoppel).

silence. No doubt, in many cases, silence is ambiguous[131] and therefore cannot constitute an acceptance. But if, as in *Felthouse* v. *Bindley* itself, the necessary intention to accept could be proved, there seems to be no convincing reason why a contract should not come into existence, particularly where the offeree has relied on the terms of the offer and it is the offeror who now denies that there is a contract. Recent *dicta* support this. Thus, it has been stated:[132]

[W]here the offeree himself indicates that an offer is to be taken as accepted if he does not indicate to the contrary by an ascertainable time, he is undertaking to speak if he does not want an agreement to be concluded. I see no reason in principle why that should not be an exceptional circumstance such that the offer can be accepted by silence.

In any event, acceptance may be inferred where the offeree takes the benefit of an offered performance which he has had a reasonable opportunity to reject.[133] If the offeror sends an unsolicited pot of jam to the offeree in circumstances which show that payment is expected, the offeror should be able to recover its price if the offeree accepts the benefit of this performance by consuming the jam.[134]

(c) ACCEPTOR MUST HAVE KNOWLEGE OF OFFER

If A offers a promise for an act and B does the act in ignorance of the offer, can B claim performance of the offer on becoming aware of its existence? As illustrated by the case of cross-offers,[135] the answer is not really in doubt: if B has not heard of the offer before doing the act, it cannot be accepted.[136] In *Gibbons* v. *Proctor*,[137] however, a Divisional Court held that a police officer was entitled to claim a reward, offered by handbills, for information given to a superintendent of police, although it seems the officer did not know of the handbills before giving the information. The decision, as reported, is an unsatisfactory one, for the facts of the case are by no means clear. Accordingly, it cannot be considered as of compelling authority, and a New York case, *Fitch* v. *Snedaker*,[138] is usually cited to the contrary. It was there laid down that a reward cannot be claimed by one who did not know that it had been offered. The latter decision is undoubtedly correct in principle. A person who does an act for which a reward has been offered in ignorance of the offer cannot say either that there

---

[131] *Ante*, pp. 29–30.
[132] *Re Selectmove Ltd.* [1995] 1 W.L.R. 474, *per* Peter Gibson L.J. at p. 478. See also *Vitol S.A.* v. *Norelf Ltd.* [1996] A.C. 800, at p. 812.
[133] *St John Tugboat Co. Ltd.* v. *Irving Refinery Co. Ltd.* (1964) 46 D.L.R. (2d) 1 (Canada); *Way & Waller Ltd.* v. *Ryde* [1944] 1 All E.R. 9. See also *Rust* v. *Abbey Life Insurance Co. Ltd.* [1979] 2 Lloyd's Rep. 334. Cf. *Yona International Ltd.* v. *La Reunion Francaise S.A.* [1996] 2 Lloyd's Rep. 84, at p. 110.
[134] *Weatherby* v. *Banham* (1832) 5 C. & P. 228.
[135] See *Tinn* v. *Hoffman & Co.* (1873) 29 L.T. 271, *ante*, p. 36.
[136] *Taylor* v. *Allon* [1966] 1 Q.B. 304, at p. 311; *Tracomin S.A.* v. *Anton C. Nielsen* [1984] 2 Lloyd's Rep. 195, at p. 203.
[137] (1891) 64 L.T. 594, 55 J.P. 616. Cf. *Neville* v. *Kelly* (1862) 12 C.B.N.S. 740. See Hudson (1968) 84 L.Q.R. 503.
[138] (1868) 38 N.Y. 248. See also *Bloom* v. *American Swiss Watch Co.* 1915 A.D. 100 (South Africa); *R.* v. *Clarke* (1927) 40 C.L.R. 227 (Australia); *Restatement* (2d), § 51 and Comment a.

was a consensus of wills with the offeror, or that the act was done in return for or in reliance on the promise offered. On no view of contract could that person set up a right of action. If, however, the acceptor knows of the offer, but is inspired to performance by a motive other than that of claiming the reward, such a motive is immaterial. So in *Williams v. Carwardine*[139] where the plaintiff, with knowledge of the reward, supplied information leading to the conviction of an assailant for murder, but only did this 'to ease her conscience, and in hopes of forgiveness hereafter', she was held entitled to claim the £20 offered. Her acceptance could be referred to the offer.

(d) PRESCRIBED MODE OF ACCEPTANCE

If the terms or the circumstances of the offer do no more than suggest a mode of acceptance, it seems that the offeree would not be bound to this mode so long as the mode used was one which did not cause delay, and which brought the acceptance to the knowledge of the offeror. A departure from the usual or suggested method of communication would probably throw upon the offeree the risk that the acceptance would be delayed, but, subject to this, an offer delivered by hand could be accepted by post, or an offer made by post could be accepted by telegram or telex. Is, however, an offeror who expressly prescribes the method of communication free to treat any departure from this method as a nullity? In the American case, *Eliason v. Henshaw*:[140]

E offered to buy flour from H, requesting that an answer should be sent to him at Harper's Ferry by the wagon which brought the offer. H sent a letter of acceptance by mail to Georgetown, thinking that this would reach E more speedily. He was wrong, and the letter arrived after the time that the reply might have been expected.

The Supreme Court of the United States held that E was entitled to refuse to purchase:[141]

It is an undeniable principle of the law of contracts, that an offer of a bargain by one person to another, imposes no obligation upon the former, until it is accepted by the latter, according to the terms in which the offer was made. Any qualification of, or departure from, those terms, invalidates the offer, unless the same be agreed to by the person who made it.

The same rule probably applies in English law: an offeror, who by the terms of the offer insists upon its acceptance in a particular manner, is entitled to say that he is not bound unless acceptance is effected or communicated in that precise way.[142] Nevertheless, if the stipulation as to the mode of acceptance is inserted at the instance of and for the protection or benefit of the offeror, the offeror may by conduct or otherwise waive strict compliance with it, provided that the offeree is not adversely affected.[143]

---

[139] (1833) 4 B. & Ad. 621; the fact of her knowledge is disclosed by the report in (1833) 5 C. & P. 566; *Lark v. Outhwaite* [1991] 2 Lloyd's Rep. 132, at p. 140. Cf. *R. v. Clarke* (*supra*, n. 138).

[140] (1819) 4 Wheaton 225.

[141] *Ibid., per* Washington J. at p. 228.

[142] *Manchester Diocesan Council for Education* v. *Commercial & General Investments Ltd.* [1970] 1 W.L.R. 241, at p. 246.

[143] *Ibid.*; *Carlyle Finance Ltd.* v. *Pallas Industrial Finance Ltd.* [1999] All E.R. (Comm.) 659.

It will be noted, however, that, in *Eliason* v. *Henshaw*, the letter was sent both to a different place and by a method which proved to be less expeditious than that chosen by the offeror. There would seem to be no supportable reason why a different mode of acceptance, which is not less advantageous to the offeror, should not be held to conclude a contract,[144] unless the offeror has stipulated that acceptance shall be made in that way only and in no other manner.

(e) REVOCATION OF THE ACCEPTANCE

One final problem remains: the question of the revocation of an acceptance. Since the general rule is that acceptance is not complete until it has been communicated to the offeror, it follows that an acceptance can be revoked at any time before this occurs, provided, of course, that the revocation itself is communicated before the acceptance arrives. But what is the position in relation to postal acceptances? Since the acceptance is complete as soon as the letter of acceptance is posted, a telephone call or telegram revoking the acceptance would be inoperative, though it reached the offeror before the letter. This, it is argued, is both the logical and fair conclusion; otherwise the offeree could blow both hot and cold, having the benefit of certainty in the postal acceptance, and the opportunity to revoke it if the offer turned out suddenly to be disadvantageous. On the other hand, it is contended that such a revocation can in no way prejudice the offeror, who could not know of the acceptance until it arrived, by which time he would already be aware of the revocation. There is no direct English authority on this point,[145] but the better view is that the offeree cannot so revoke. If, for example, shares are offered on a fluctuating market, it would clearly be most unfair if the offeree could bind the offeror by a postal acceptance when the shares advanced in price, but send off a revocation if the market fell. There is no reason why an offeree who chooses to accept by post should have an opportunity of changing his mind which would not have been available if the contract had been made *inter praesentes*.

This solution should not, however, be operated to the detriment of the offeror. If the offeror acts on the purported revocation, e.g. by selling the shares which are the subject-matter of the offer, the offeree would not be permitted once again to change his mind and rely on the postal acceptance rule in order to claim damages for breach of contract.

---

[144] *Tinn* v. *Hoffman & Co.* (1873) 29 L.T. 271, at pp. 274, 278; *Manchester Diocesan Council for Education* v. *Commercial & General Investments Ltd.* (*supra*, n. 142), at p. 246; *Restatement* (2d), §§ 29, 68; Winfield (1939) 55 L.Q.R. 499, 516.

[145] In *Household Fire and Carriage Accident Insurance Co. Ltd.* v. *Grant* (1879) 4 Ex. D. 216, Bramwell L.J. at p. 255, was of the opinion that the revocation would be effective. See also *Dick* v. *U.S.* 82 Fed. Supp. 326 (1949); Ellison Kahn (1955) 72 S.A.L.J. 246, 257; Hudson (1966) 82 L.Q.R. 169.

[146] In *Dunmore (Countess of)* v. *Alexander* (1830) 9 S. 190 (Scotland), Lord Craigie (dissenting) held that an offeree could not revoke her acceptance, but the majority of the Court treated the case as one of the revocation of an offer. See also *Wenkheim* v. *Arndt* (1873) 1 J.R. 73 (N.Z.); *Kinch* v. *Bullard* [1999] 1 W.L.R. 423.

IV. TERMINATION OF THE OFFER

Once the acceptance has been communicated to the offeror it cannot be recalled or undone. But until an offer is accepted, it creates no legal rights, and it may be terminated at any time. Termination of the offer may come about in a number of ways: it may be revoked before acceptance, or the offeree may reject the offer. Also an offer may lapse for want of acceptance or be determined by the death of the offeror or offeree.

(a) REVOCATION OF THE OFFER

The law relating to the revocation of an offer may be summed up in two rules; (1) an offer may be revoked at any time before acceptance, and (2) an offer is made irrevocable by acceptance.

(i) Revocable before acceptance

The first of these rules may be illustrated by the case of *Offord* v. *Davies*:[147]

D made a written offer to O that, if he would discount bills for another firm, they (D) would guarantee the payment of such bills to the extent of £600 during a period of twelve calendar months. Some bills were discounted by O, and duly paid, but before the twelve months had expired D, the guarantors, revoked their offer and notified O that they would guarantee no more bills. O continued to discount bills, some of which were not paid, and then sued D on the guarantee.

It was held that the revocation was a good defence to the action. The alleged guarantee was an offer, for a period of 12 months, of promises for acts, of guarantees for discounts. Each discount turned the offer into a promise, *pro tanto*, but the entire offer could at any time be revoked except as regards discounts made before notice of revocation.

(ii) Irrevocable after acceptance

The rule that an offer is made irrevocable by acceptance is illustrated by *Great Northern Railway Co.* v. *Witham*,[148] which, like that in *Offord* v. *Davies*, involved a continuing relationship:

The G.N.R. company advertised for tenders for the supply of such iron articles as it might require between 1 November 1871, and 31 October 1872. W sent in a tender to supply the articles required on certain terms and in such quantities as the company 'might order from time to time', and his tender was accepted by the company. Orders were given and executed for some time on the terms of the tender but finally W was given an order which he refused to execute. The company sued him for breach of contract in that he had failed to perform this order.

---

[147] (1862) 12 C.B.N.S. 748; *Scammell* v. *Dicker* [2001] 1 W.L.R. 631.
[148] (1873) L.R. 9 C.P. 16. Contrast *Percival Ltd.* v. *L.C.C. Asylums etc. Committee* (1918) 87 L.J.K.B. 677.

It is important to note the exact relationship of the parties. The company by advertisement invited all dealers in iron to make tenders, that is, to state the terms of the
offers which they were prepared to make. W's tender stated the terms of an offer
which might be accepted at any time, or any number of times, in the ensuing 12
months. The acceptance of the tender did not in itself make a contract; it was merely
an intimation by the company that it regarded W's tender as a standing offer, which
on its part it would be willing to accept as and when it required the articles to be
supplied. Each fresh order constituted an acceptance of this standing offer. If W
wished to revoke his offer he could have done so, but only as to the future; in the
meantime he was bound to perform any order already made. The Court therefore
held that he was liable for breach of contract.

(iii) Unilateral contracts

Some difficulty is experienced in the case of 'unilateral' contracts, previously referred
to,[149] where an act is done in return for a promise. If one person promises a certain
sum to another on performance by that other of a stipulated act, at what point in
time is the acceptance of the offer complete? The traditional answer to this question
is that the acceptance is complete only when the act has been completely performed.[150]
It therefore follows that up to this time the offeror is at liberty to revoke the offer.
If, for example, a firm of breakfast food manufacturers were to offer to pay £100
to any person who consumed one hundredweight of their breakfast food within the
next three months, they would be able to revoke their offer after two months had
elapsed—to the detriment of those who had almost completed their part of the
bargain, and with profit to themselves. Or to use a judicial example,[151] if one man
offers another £100 if he will go to York, he can revoke when the other is half-way
there.

In order to avoid such an inequitable result,[152] Sir Frederick Pollock argued that
a distinction should be drawn between the acceptance of the offer and the performance of the stipulated act: the acceptance is complete once the offeree has
unequivocally commenced performance (so that the offeror cannot effectively
revoke the offer after this time), but the offeror is not bound to pay the £100 until
the act has been completely performed.[153] This view has some judicial support. In
Errington v. *Errington*,[154] where a father promised his son and daughter-in-law that
a house in which they were living should belong to them as soon as they had paid
off the instalments of a mortgage on the premises, and they commenced to pay

---

[149] See *ante*, pp. 29, 36.

[150] See *ante*, pp. 42–3.

[151] *Rogers* v. *Snow* (1573) Dalison 94; *G.N. Ry.* v. *Witham* (1873) L.R. 9 C.P. 16, at p. 19.

[152] It has been contended that there is no injustice, since the offeree is not bound to go to York and may
give up at any time. The offeror, it is argued, ought to have a similar right to give up his side of the transaction:
Wormser (1916) 26 Yale L.J. 136. This reasoning is not attractive.

[153] Pollock, *Principles of Contract*, 13th edn. (1950), p. 19; see also *Offord* v. *Davies* (1862) 12 C.B.N.S. 748,
at p. 753; Law Revision Committee, Sixth Interim Report (Cmd. 5449 1937), § 39; *Restatement* (2d), § 45;
CISG, Art. 16(2)(b).

[154] [1952] 1 K.B. 290.

them to his knowledge, Denning L.J. considered that this promise could not be revoked:[155]

The father's promise was a unilateral contractual promise of the house in return for their act of paying the instalments. It could not be revoked by him once the couple entered on performance of the act, but it would cease to bind him if they left it incomplete and unperformed.

On this view, the offeror is unable to revoke his offer; but his duty to perform his obligation is conditional upon performance of the stipulated act by the offeree.

Another view was put forward in *Morrison Steamship Co. Ltd.* v. *The Crown.*[156] In that case, Viscount Cave L.C. doubted whether a conditional offer was converted into a contract by commencement of performance. The offeree could not therefore insist on completing performance and claiming the promised sum.[157] But he suggested that 'when work is done and expense incurred on the faith of a conditional promise, the promisor comes under an obligation not to revoke his promise, and if he does so he may be sued for damages or on a *quantum meruit*'.

It may well be, of course, that the nature of the offer itself, or the circumstances under which it was made, indicate that it was never intended to be irrevocable by the offeror.[158] But otherwise it is submitted that English law will not deny the offeree a remedy if the offer is revoked before the performance requested has been completed.

(iv) 'Firm' offers

It will be noted that in *Offord* v. *Davies*, discussed above, the mere fact that the defendants promised to guarantee payment for 12 months did not preclude them from revoking before that period had elapsed.[159] It is a rule of English law that a promise to keep an offer open needs consideration to make it binding and would thus only become so if the offeror gets some benefit, or the offeree incurs some detriment, in respect of the promise to keep the offer open. The offeree in such a case is said to 'purchase an option'; that is, the offeror, in consideration usually of a money payment, sometimes nominal,[160] makes a separate contract not to revoke the offer during a stated period. The position is similar where the offeree expressly or impliedly promises to do or refrain from doing something in exchange for the offeror's promise not to revoke the offer. For example, the offeree may promise not to negotiate with anyone else for a fixed period.[161] Again, a builder tendering for a construction contract may have invited quotations for a fixed period (i.e. firm offers) from electricity or carpentry sub-contractors and expressly or impliedly promised to use the figures

[155] At p. 295. See also *Harvela Investments Ltd.* v. *Royal Trust of Canada (C.I.) Ltd.* [1986] A.C. 207 (submitting bid in response to invitation to tender).
[156] (1924) 20 Ll. L.R. 283, at p. 287. See also *Daulia Ltd.* v. *Four Millbank Nominees Ltd.* [1978] Ch. 231, at p. 239.
[157] Cf. *White and Carter (Councils) Ltd.* v. *McGregor* [1962] A.C. 413; *post*, pp. 566, 632.
[158] *Luxor (Eastbourne) Ltd.* v. *Cooper* [1941] A.C. 108.
[159] See also *Dickinson* v. *Dodds* (1876) 2 Ch. D. 463, *post*, p. 57; *Routledge* v. *Grant* (1828) 4 Bing. 653.
[160] *Mountford* v. *Scott* [1975] Ch. 258. See further, *post*, p. 97.
[161] *Pitt* v. *P.H.H. Asset Management Ltd.* [1994] 1 W.L.R. 327, at p. 332, *post*, p. 60 although this is probably better explained as a unilateral contract.

contained in those offers in its tender. In these cases the offeror by its promise precludes itself from exercising its right to revoke the offer; but where it receives no consideration for keeping the offer open, it says in effect, 'You may accept within such and such a time, but this limitation is entirely for my benefit, and I make no binding promise not to revoke my offer in the meantime'. The Law Revision Committee recommended that 'an agreement to keep an offer open for a definite period of time or until the occurrence of some specified event shall not be unenforceable by reason of the absence of consideration'.[162] Despite this criticism, subject to two exceptions,[163] it seems to be good law.

A firm offer may, moreover, also become irrevocable where the transaction can be characterized as a unilateral contract and the offeree has relied on the offer by embarking on performance of the specified act.[164] We shall see that in its present state of development English law does not recognize a general principle based on the protection of reliance.[165] Unless a unilateral contract can be found or the action in reliance has been requested by the offeror and amounts to consideration, an offeree who relies on a firm offer will not be protected by the law of contract. Similarly there is unlikely to be a remedy in tort for revoking an offer that has been relied on[166] but, where the offeree's action in reliance consists in the rendering of services or the delivery of goods, unless the offeree can be said to have taken the risk that the offer might be withdrawn, as may well be the case in the context of tendering, the offeror may be obliged by the law of restitution to pay a reasonable sum in respect of the services or goods.[167]

(v) Auction sales 'without reserve'

Where goods are put up for sale by auction upon an advertised condition that the sale shall be 'without reserve' the auctioneer thereby indicates to prospective buyers that the bid of the highest *bona fide* bidder will be accepted, and that the goods will not at any stage be withdrawn, for example, on the ground that the reserve price has not yet been reached. An auctioneer who does so withdraw the goods is said to be liable for breach of contract with such a bidder. In *Warlow* v. *Harrison*:[168]

An auctioneer advertised a brown mare for sale by auction 'without reserve'. The owner's name was not disclosed. The plaintiff bid 60 guineas; the owner bid 61 guineas, and the

---

[162] Sixth Interim Report (Cmd. 5449 1937), § 38. The Vienna Convention on Contracts for the International Sale of Goods, Art. 16(2), provides that an offer indicating that it is irrevocable or one that has been relied on by the offeree cannot be revoked.

[163] Offers in a deed (*Beesly* v. *Hallwood Estates Ltd.* [1961] Ch. 105; *Restatement* (2d), § 25 comment c) and an application for shares (Companies Act 1985, s. 82(1)).

[164] *Ante*, p. 53.

[165] See *post*, p. 118 ff. (the limits of equitable estoppel) and *post*, p. 122 for criticisms.

[166] *Holman Construction Ltd.* v. *Delta Timber Co. Ltd.* [1972] N.Z.L.R. 1081 (negligent pre-contractual statement).

[167] *Ante*, pp. 39–40; *post*, p. 63.

[168] (1858–59) 1 E. & E. 295, 309; *Johnston* v. *Boyes* [1899] 2 Ch. 73. Contrast *Fenwick* v. *Macdonald, Fraser & Co. Ltd.* (1904) 6 F. 850 (Scotland). By the Sale of Goods Act 1979, s. 58(4) the seller is now precluded without notification from the bidding himself or employing anyone to bid for him, and any sale contravening this rule may be treated as fraudulent by the buyer.

auctioneer knocked down the mare to him. The plaintiff claimed damages from the auctioneer as being the highest *bona fide* bidder.

A majority of the Court of Exchequer Chamber considered that the auctioneer was liable on a contract that the auction sale was to be 'without reserve'.[169] The judgments have, however, been criticized as inconsistent with established principles.

First, it is clear that a bid at an auction is only an offer which can be retracted at any time before the fall of the hammer.[170] This rule is now to be found in section 57(2) of the Sale of Goods Act 1979. No contract for the sale of the goods in the auction, therefore, comes into existence until a bid is accepted by the auctioneer.

Secondly, an advertisement that an auction of certain articles will take place on a certain day does not bind the auctioneer to sell the goods, nor does it make the auctioneer liable upon a contract to indemnify persons who have incurred expense in order to attend the sale.[171] Such an advertisement is an invitation to treat.

So, where goods are advertised for sale without reserve, until the auctioneer accepts by the fall of the hammer, no contract of sale is concluded with the buyer. If, therefore, the auctioneer withdraws the goods prematurely, refusing to knock them down to the highest bidder, there can be no possible action on any *contract of sale* because none has yet come into existence. The Court in *Warlow* v. *Harrison* stated that the plaintiff was not suing upon the contract of sale (which would at that time have been required by the Statute of Frauds to be evidenced in writing),[172] but upon a different, collateral, contract with the auctioneer. When the auctioneer put up the mare for sale 'without reserve' he contracted that this would be so, that this contract was made with the highest *bona fide* bidder, and it was broken upon a bid being made by or on behalf of the owner.[173]

Several objections have been taken to this analysis.[174] If an advertisement that an auction sale will be held is merely an invitation to treat, how can it be said that a stipulation contained in it that the sale will be 'without reserve' amounts to an offer? Secondly, if a bid may be retracted, or outbid, at any time before it is accepted, how can it be said that it is certain who is the highest bidder? Thirdly, what is the consideration for the promise, since the promisee is not bound to purchase, but may withdraw the bid at any time? While there is a certain artificiality in treating the bidder as having provided consideration by bidding, i.e. by exposure to the risk that the bid would be accepted by the auctioneer, this unilateral contract analysis[175] accords with the modern approach to similar situations and has been recently followed.[176]

[169] The minority held that the auctioneer would be liable for breach of warranty of authority: see *post*, p. 691. In fact, a new trial was ordered but never took place.
[170] *Payne* v. *Cave* (1789) 3 Term R. 148.
[171] *Harris* v. *Nickerson* (1873) L.R. 8 Q.B. 286.
[172] See *post*, p. 74.
[173] (1858) 1 E. & E. 309, at p. 317.
[174] See Slade (1952) 68 L.Q.R. 238; Gower (1952) 68 L.Q.R. 456; Slade (1953) 69 L.Q.R. 21; Cox (1982) 132 New L.J. 719.
[175] *Ante*, pp. 35, 54.
[176] *Barry* v. *Davies* [2001] 1 W.L.R. 1962. See, on tenders, *Harvela Investments Ltd.* v. *Royal Trust of Canada (C.I.) Ltd.* [1986] A.C. 207; *Blackpool and Fylde Aero Club Ltd.* v. *Blackpool B.C.* [1990] 1 W.L.R. 25.

(vi) Revocation must be communicated

It remains to state that revocation, as distinguished from lapse, if it is to be operative, must be communicated. In the case of acceptance we have seen that, in certain circumstances, it is not necessary that the acceptance should have actually come to the notice of the offeror; the posting of a letter, the doing of an act, may constitute an acceptance and make a contract. A revocation of an offer cannot, however, be communicated in the same way, by the posting of a letter of revocation, or by the sale to A of an article offered to B to purchase but must be brought to the notice of the offeree. The law on this subject was settled by *Byrne & Co.* v. *Leon Van Tienhoven & Co.*:[177]

VT, writing from Cardiff on 1 October, made an offer to B in New York asking for a reply by cable. B received the letter on the 11th, and at once accepted in the manner requested. In the meantime, however, VT had, on 8 October, posted a letter revoking the offer. This letter did not reach B until the 20th.

Lindley J. held, first, that a revocation was inoperative until communicated, and secondly, that the revocation of an offer was not communicated by the mere posting of a letter; therefore B's acceptance on 11 October could not be affected by the fact that VT's letter of revocation was already on its way. He pointed out the inconvenience which would result from any other conclusion:[178]

If [VT's] contention were to prevail no person who had received an offer by post and had accepted it would know his position until he had waited such a time as to be quite sure that a letter withdrawing the offer had not been posted before his acceptance of it. It appears to me that both legal principles, and practical convenience require that a person who has accepted an offer not known to him to have been revoked, shall be in a position safely to act upon the footing that the offer and acceptance constitute a contract binding on both parties.

It has been stated that a revocation must be 'brought to the mind' of the offeree[179] but it is submitted that where it arrives at its address it will be effective when it would, in the ordinary course of business, have come to the offeree's attention.[180] Where the offeree refrains from opening a letter or neglects to pay attention to the telex or fax machine[181] it should, therefore, be effective on arrival. The requirement that a revocation be communicated means that, in law, an offeror may be bound by an agreement which it does not believe itself to have made; but, again, if one of the two parties must

---

[177] (1880) 5 C.P.D. 344. See also *Thomson* v. *James* (1855) 18 D. 1 (Scotland); *Stevenson* v. *McLean* (1880) 5 Q.B.D. 346; *Henthorn* v. *Fraser* [1892] 2 Ch. 27. But in *Shuey* v. *United States* 92 U.S. 73 (1875), where a reward was offered in a newspaper, it was held that this offer could be 'withdrawn through the same channel by which it was made', even though the revocation did not come to the notice of the offeree.

[178] At p. 348.

[179] *Henthorn* v. *Fraser* [1892] 2 Ch. 27, *per* Lord Herschell at p. 32. See also *ibid.*, *per* Kay L.J. at p. 37 ('actual knowledge', 'actually received').

[180] *Tenax S.S. Co. Ltd.* v. *The Brimnes (Owners)* [1975] 1 Q.B. 929, at pp. 945, 966, 969 (revocation by telex). See also CISG, Arts. 16(1) and 24 (revocation effective if it 'reaches' the offeree's place of business or mailing address before he has dispatched an acceptance).

[181] *Ibid.* But not where it arrives after or near the close of a working day and is not seen on that day; *ibid.*, at p. 970; *Brinkibon Ltd.* v. *Stahag Stahl und Stahlwarenhandelsgesellschaft m.b.H.* [1983] 2 A.C. 34, at p. 42; *ante*, p. 45.

suffer, there would seem no good reason why it should be the offeree rather than the offeror.

The case of *Dickinson* v. *Dodds*[182] establishes that an offeree who knows that an offer has been withdrawn cannot accept it even if the communication has not come from the offeror:

On 10 June 1874, Dodds made a written offer to Dickinson to sell certain premises for £800, and stating that this offer would remain open until 9 a.m. on 12 June. On the 11th, however, he sold the property to a third person without notice to Dickinson. Dickinson had in fact been informed of the sale, though not by anyone acting under the authority of Dodds. Nevertheless before 9 a.m. on the 12th he purported to accept Dodds' offer. He then brought an action for specific performance of the contract.

The Court of Appeal held that there was no contract. James L.J., after stating that a promise to keep the offer open could not be binding, and that at any moment before a completed acceptance of the offer one party was as free as the other, went on to say:[183]

[I]n this case, *beyond all question, the plaintiff knew* that Dodds was no longer minded to sell the property to him as plainly and clearly as if Dodds had told him in so many words, 'I withdraw the offer'.

Is it then the case that information of the offeror's intention to revoke, from whatever source it reaches the offeree, is good notice of revocation? The inconvenience might be grave. Suppose a company receives an offer of a consignment of goods from a distant correspondent, with liberty to reserve an answer for some days. In the meantime an unauthorized person tells the offeree-company that the offeror has sold or promised the goods to another. What is the offeree to do? The informant may be right, and then, if the offeree accepts, the acceptance may be worthless. Or the informant may be a gossip or mischief-maker and if, because of what the offeree has been told, it refrains from accepting it may lose a bargain. The answer would appear to be that it is open to an offeror, who has revoked an offer without direct communication to the offeree, to show that the offeree knew, from a trustworthy source, that the offer had been withdrawn.[184] The Court would have to decide every such case on the facts presented, but the onus would be upon the offeror to establish that the information ought reasonably to have been believed.

(b) REJECTION OF THE OFFER

An offer will be held to have terminated once it has been rejected by the offeree. The rejection need not be express, provided that the offeror is justified in inferring that the offeree does not intend to accept the offer.[185] It would seem, therefore, that a rejection

---

[182] (1876) 2 Ch. D. 463.

[183] At p. 472; see also Mellish L.J. at p. 474.

[184] *Cartwright* v. *Hoogstoel* (1911) 105 L.T. 628; *Restatement* (2d), § 42.

[185] *Restatement* (2d), § 37. The position is similar in many European systems, see, e.g. Germany, BGB § 146; Lando & Beale, *Principles of European Contract Law* (2000), p. 168.

would not operate so as to destroy the power of acceptance until it comes to the notice of the offeror:

Suppose that A makes an offer to B by letter. Immediately on receiving the letter B writes a letter rejecting the offer. Before the rejection arrives, B changes her mind and telephones her acceptance.

There would be a contract between A and B.[186] It should not be supposed, however, that an uncommunicated rejection would always be without effect. It would, in certain circumstances, preclude the operation of the rule that a letter of acceptance is complete when posted:

Suppose that C Ltd. makes an offer to D Ltd. Immediately on receiving the offer D writes a letter rejecting the offer. Before the rejection arrives, D changes its mind and posts a letter accepting the offer.

Although there is no English authority on this point, it would not seem possible for D to claim that the normal rule as to postal acceptance applied. The letter of acceptance would only create an obligation if received by the offeror before the rejection.[187]

(c) LAPSE OF THE OFFER

An offer may be considered to have lapsed owing to the passing of time.

(i) Offer for a fixed time

The parties may expressly fix a time within which an offer is to remain open. Where the offeror prescribes a specific time limit for acceptance, the offer is conditional upon acceptance within that time.[188] For example, 'This offer to be left open until Friday, 9 a.m. 12 June', allows the offeree to accept the offer, if unrevoked, at any time up to the hour named, after which the offer would lapse.[189] Similarly, an offer to supply goods of a certain sort at a certain price for a year from the present date,[190] or an offer to guarantee the payment of any bills of exchange discounted for a third party for a year from the present date,[191] are offers which may be revoked at any time, except as regards orders already given or bills already discounted, and which will, in any event, lapse at the end of a year from the date of offer.

(ii) No fixed time

In most cases, however, the offeror will not specify any particular time, and it is left to the Court, in the event of litigation, to say what is a reasonable time within which an offer may be accepted. We have already seen that an offer is accepted when acceptance

---

[186] Winfield (1939) 55 L.Q.R. 499, 513; *Restatement* (2d), § 39.

[187] *Restatement* (2d), § 39.

[188] The offeror could nevertheless waive this condition, and treat the late acceptance as valid, provided he did not thereby adversely affect the offeree.

[189] *Dickinson* v. *Dodds* (1876) 2 Ch. D. 463, *ante*, p. 57.

[190] *G.N. Ry.* v. *Witham* (1873) L.R. 9 C.P. 16.

[191] *Offord* v. *Davies* (1862) 12 C.B.N.S. 748.

is made in a manner prescribed or indicated by the offeror.[192] If the circumstances of the offer, for example, if it is made by telegram, suggest that a reply is required urgently, the offer will be considered to have lapsed if the offeree does not quickly decide whether to accept, or chooses a means of communication which will delay the notification of the acceptance.[193] In other cases, the effluxion of a reasonable time will terminate the offer. An instance of this is provided by *Ramsgate Victoria Hotel Co.* v. *Montefiore*:[194]

The defendant, M, offered by letter dated 8 June to purchase shares in the plaintiff company. No answer was received by him until 23 November, when he was informed that shares were allotted to him. He refused to accept them.

It was held that M's offer had lapsed by reason of the delay of the company in notifying its acceptance, and that he was not bound to accept the shares.

(iii) Express or implied condition

The terms of the offer may expressly indicate that its continuance is conditional upon the existence of circumstances other than time; and a condition of this nature may also be implied. For example, where the contract requires for its performance the existence of a particular thing, and before acceptance the thing is destroyed or substantially damaged, the offer is terminated unless the offeror has assumed the risk of such mischance.[195] Thus, in *Financings Ltd.* v. *Stimson*:[196]

S signed an 'agreement' whereby he undertook to buy a motor-car on hire-purchase terms from F company. The agreement contained a clause which stated that it was to become binding only upon acceptance by signature on F's behalf. Before F signed, the motor-car was stolen by thieves. It was subsequently recovered in a damaged condition.

It was clear that the 'agreement' was in fact only an offer since it contemplated acceptance by F. The Court of Appeal held that this offer was only capable of acceptance if the car remained in substantially the same condition as it was when the offer was made. Since this was not the case, the offer had lapsed and there was no binding contract.

(d) EFFECT OF DEATH

In principle, an offeree cannot accept after being informed of the death of the offeror.[197] An acceptance communicated to the offeror's personal representatives will not bind them, unless the offer is one which could not have been revoked by the

---

[192] *Ante*, p. 49.
[193] *Quenerduaine* v. *Cole* (1883) 32 W.R. 185.
[194] (1866) L.R. 1 Ex. 109. See also *Manchester Diocesan Council for Education* v. *Commercial & General Investments Ltd.* [1970] 1 W.L.R. 241, at pp. 247–9; *Chemco Leasing S.p.A.* v. *Rediffusion Ltd.* [1987] 1 F.T.L.R. 201.
[195] *Restatement* (2d), § 266.
[196] [1962] 1 W.L.R. 1184.
[197] *Coulthart* v. *Clementson* (1870) 5 Q.B.D. 42.

offeror during his lifetime.[198] Where the offeree accepts in ignorance of the offeror's death the position is less clear. One view is that the offer is terminated automatically and that knowledge is irrelevant.[199] The alternative, and it is submitted better, view[200] is that an offeree who does not know of the offeror's death should be entitled to accept the offer, unless the offer on its true construction indicates the contrary,[201] e.g. where the offer is personal to the offeror.

It would seem that an offer is in any event determined by the death of the offeree;[202] his personal representatives could not accept the offer on behalf of the offeree's estate.

V. UNCERTAIN AND INCOMPLETE AGREEMENTS

Although the parties may have reached agreement in the sense that the requirements of offer and acceptance have been complied with, there may be no contract because the terms of the agreement are uncertain or because the agreement is qualified by reference to the need for a future agreement between them. For 'unless all the material terms of the contract are agreed there is no binding obligation. An agreement to agree in future is not a contract; nor is there a contract if a material term is neither settled nor implied by law and the document contains no machinery for ascertaining it'.[203]

The terms of a contract must provide a basis for determining the existence of a breach and for giving an appropriate remedy.[204] Nevertheless, as we shall see, although there are differences of approach in the cases, the law is generally anxious to uphold the contract wherever possible lest it should be criticized as the destroyer of bargains.[205] In addition, where uncertainty or incompleteness prevent an agreement from constituting a contract the factual situation may give rise to liability in tort, for instance for misrepresentation,[206] or in restitution in respect of benefits received or work done.[207]

---

[198] *Errington* v. *Errington* [1952] 1 K.B. 290, at p. 295. Even in this case, death may terminate the offer where it is dependent on the personality of the offeror.

[199] *Dickinson* v. *Dodds* (1876) 2 Ch. D. 463, at p. 475; *Restatement* (2d), § 48.

[200] *Bradbury* v. *Morgan* (1862) 1 H. & C. 249, often said to support this, was in fact (like *Lloyd's* v. *Harper* (1880) 16 Ch. D. 290) a case where a contract had been concluded before death.

[201] *Harris* v. *Fawcett* (1873) L.R. 8 Ch. App. 866, at p. 869; *Coulthart* v. *Clementson* (1870) 5 Q.B.D. 42, at p. 46.

[202] *Re Cheshire Banking Co. (Duff's Executor's Case)* (1886) 32 Ch. D. 301; *Reynolds* v. *Atherton* (1921) 125 L.T. 690, at p. 695, but see (1922) 127 L.T. 189, 191 (H.L.); *Somerville* v. *National Coal Board* 1963 S.L.T. 334 (Scotland).

[203] *Foley* v. *Classique Coaches Ltd.* [1934] 2 K.B. 1, *per* Maugham L.J. at p. 13.

[204] *Restatement* (2d), § 33(2). See also Lando & Beale, *Principles of European Contract Law* (2000), p. 146, Art. 2:103.

[205] *Hillas* v. *Arcos* (1932) 147 L.T. 503, *per* Lord Tomlin at p. 512.

[206] *Post*, pp. 64 and 247.

[207] *Post*, p. 63.

(a) CERTAINTY OF TERMS

The law requires the parties to make their own contract; it will not construct a contract for them out of terms which are indefinite or unsettled. A vague or uncertain promise does not accordingly give rise to an enforceable contract. Thus:

C agreed to sell land to D, that the price was to be paid by instalments and that on each payment 'a proportionate part' of the land was to be conveyed. It was held that, since the part to be conveyed on each occasion could not be identified, the agreement as a whole was uncertain and unenforceable.[208]

Similarly when a motor-van was to be bought on the understanding that part of the price should be paid on 'hire-purchase' terms,[209] and when woollen goods were to be bought 'subject to war clause',[210] there was no contract in either case, for 'hire-purchase' terms, and 'war clauses' may take many forms, and it is for the parties, and not for the Court, to define them.

On the other hand, in many transactions, particularly those for future performance over a period, the parties may neither be able nor desire to specify all matters. A transaction which at first sight seems to leave some essential term of the bargain undetermined may, by implication, if not expressly, provide some method of determination other than a future agreement between the parties. In that event, since it is a maxim of the law that that is certain which can be made certain, there will be a good contract.[211] In every case the function of the Court is to put a fair construction on what the parties have said and done, though the task is often a difficult one. As Lord Wright stated:[212]

Business men often record the most important agreements in crude and summary fashion; modes of expression sufficient and clear to them in the course of their business may appear to those unfamiliar with the business far from complete or precise. It is accordingly the duty of the Court to construe such documents fairly and broadly, without being too astute or subtle in finding defects; but, on the contrary, the Court should seek to apply the old maxim of English law, *verba ita sunt intelligenda ut res magis valeat quam pereat.*

The line between discovering the agreement of the parties and imposing an agreement on the basis of what the Court considers the parties ought to have intended can be fine. The Court must be satisfied that the parties have in fact concluded a contract, and not merely expressed willingness to contract in the future. It may have regard to what has been said and done, the context in which it was said or done, the relative

---

[208] *Bushwell Properties Ltd.* v. *Vortex Properties Ltd.* [1976] 1 W.L.R. 591; *Montreal Gas Co.* v. *Vasey* [1900] A.C. 595; *Jacques* v. *Lloyd D. George & Partners* [1968] 1 W.L.R. 625. See also *Stabilad Ltd.* v. *Stephens & Carter Ltd. (No 2)* [1999] 2 All E.R. (Comm.) 651 (performance left to discretion of promisor).

[209] *G. Scammell & Nephews Ltd.* v. *Ouston* [1941] A.C. 251.

[210] *Bishop & Baxter* v. *Anglo-Eastern Trading Co. and Industrial Ltd.* [1944] K.B. 12; *British Electrical and Associated Industries (Cardiff) Ltd.* v. *Patley Pressings Ltd.* [1953] 1 W.L.R. 280.

[211] *Id certum est quod certum reddi potest.* See Fridman (1960) 76 L.Q.R. 521; Samek (1970) 47 Can. Bar Rev. 203.

[212] *Hillas & Co.* v. *Arcos Ltd.* (1932) 147 L.T. 503, at p. 514.

importance of the unsettled matter, and whether the parties have provided machinery for settling it.

If the contract contains an indefinite, but subsidiary provision, the Courts have felt at liberty to strike it out as being without significance, and to give effect to the rest of the contract without the meaningless term.[213]

(i) Previous transactions; trade custom

In *Hillas & Co. v. Arcos Ltd.*[214] the terms were ascertained from previous transactions between the same parties and the custom of the particular trade:

In 1930 P agreed to sell D a quantity of Russian softwood timber 'of fair specification'. The contract contained a clause giving to P an option to purchase further timber in 1931, but the option gave no particulars as to the kind or size or quality of the timber, nor of the manner of shipment. When P sought to exercise the option, D pleaded that the clause was too indeterminate and uncertain to indicate an unequivocal intention to be bound, and that it was merely an agreement to negotiate a future agreement.

The House of Lords held that, in the light of the previous dealings between the parties, there was a sufficient intention to be bound: the terms left uncertain in the option could be ascertained by reference to those contained in the original contract and from the normal practice of the timber trade.[215]

(ii) The standard of reasonableness

Alternatively, where the intention to buy and to sell is clear, incidents of the transaction may be determined by the standard of reasonableness, or by rules of law. Thus, in *Hillas v. Arcos* the phrase 'of fair specification' was held to mean timber distributed over kinds, qualities, and sizes in fair proportions having regard to the season's output, a matter which, if the parties fail to agree, could be ascertained by the Court determining what is reasonable.[216] Similar principles apply to standards provided in the agreement such as 'market value'[217] 'open market value',[218] and that hire shall be 'equitably decreased'.[219] In the case of price, in transactions for the sale of goods or the supply of services the matter is now governed by statute. By section 8 of the Sale of Goods Act 1979:[220]

(1) The price in a contract of sale may be fixed by the contract, or may be left to be fixed in a manner agreed by the contract, or may be determined by the course of dealing between the parties.

---

[213] *Nicolene Ltd. v. Simmonds* [1953] 1 Q.B. 543. See also *Adamastos Shipping Co. Ltd. v. Anglo-Saxon Petroleum Co. Ltd.* [1959] A.C. 133; *Whitlock v. Brew* (1968) 118 C.L.R. 445 (Australia).
[214] (1932) 147 L.T. 503.
[215] On the terms implied by trade custom and law see further, *post*, p. 151.
[216] (1932) 147 L.T. 503, at pp. 512, 513, 516. See also *Mamidoil-Jetoil Greek Petroleum Co. S.A. v. Okta Crude Oil Refinery AD* [2001] 2 Lloyd's Rep. 76, at p. 91 (reasonable fees for services).
[217] *Brown v. Gould* [1972] Ch. 53.
[218] *Gillatt v. Sky Television Ltd* [2000] 2 B.C.L.C. 103.
[219] *Didymi Cpn. v. Atlantic Lines and Navigation Co. Ltd.* [1988] 2 Lloyd's Rep. 108.
[220] See also Supply of Goods and Services Act 1982, s. 15(1). Cf. CISG Art. 55 ('current trade price').

(2) Where the price is not determined as mentioned in subsection (1) above the buyer
must pay *a reasonable price.*

In such cases, the Court will allow an action to recover a reasonable sum for what
the goods or services are worth.[221]

Section 8(2) of the Sale of Goods Act provides for silence as to the price, and will
not apply where an agreement states that the parties will subsequently agree the price
to be paid.[222]

(iii) Executed transactions

The Court will also have regard to what has been done by the parties. Where a
transaction has been wholly or partially performed it will be:

difficult to submit that the contract is void for vagueness or uncertainty. Specifically, the fact
that the transaction is executed makes it easier to imply a term resolving any uncertainty, or,
alternatively, it may make it possible to treat a matter not finalised in negotiations as
inessential.[223]

In the case of executed transactions, the basis of liability is not, however, always
contractual. In some cases the objective test of intention[224] may mean that a contract
comes into existence as a result of the performance and liability can be characterized
as consensual.[225] In others, however, as noted in the context of 'the battle of the
forms',[226] no contractual analysis is possible and, where it is held that there is liability,
it is imposed by the Court in the form of a restitutionary obligation upon the defendant to pay a reasonable sum for the work done or the goods received.[227] Where the
liability is restitutionary, however, the interests of the recipient of the goods or services may not adequately be protected.[228] Moreover, in determining whether to give a
restitutionary remedy, considerations of 'risk' and 'fault' in relation to the reason the
transaction fails to come to fruition as a contract are taken into account so that a
person who is held to have taken the risk of the transaction failing or to have been

[221] *British Bank for Foreign Trade Ltd.* v. *Novinex* [1949] 1 K.B. 623; *Powell* v. *Braun* [1954] 1 W.L.R. 401
(executed transactions); *Hondly* v. *M'Laine* (1834) 10 Bing. 482 (executory transaction).

[222] *May & Butcher* v. *R.* [1934] 2 K.B. 17n; *King's Motors (Oxford) Ltd.* v. *Lax* [1970] 1 W.L.R. 426; *Smith* v.
Morgan [1971] 1 W.L.R. 803.

[223] *G. Percy Trentham Ltd.* v. *Archital Luxfer Ltd.* [1993] 1 Lloyd's Rep. 25, *per* Steyn L.J. at p. 27. See also
F. & G. Sykes (Wessex) Ltd. v. *Fine Fare Ltd.* [1967] 1 Lloyd's Rep. 53, at pp. 57–8; *Foley* v. *Classique Coaches Ltd.*
[1934] 2 K.B. 1.

[224] *Ante,* p. 31.

[225] *Foley* v. *Classique Coaches Ltd.* [1934] 2 K.B. 1; *Way* v. *Latilla* [1937] 3 All E.R. 759. But cf. *ibid.,* at pp.
764–5.

[226] *Ante,* p. 38.

[227] *British Steel Cpn.* v. *Cleveland Bridge and Engineering Co. Ltd.* [1984] 1 All E.R. 504, at p. 511 in the
context of goods delivered under a letter of intent, *post,* p. 67. Birks, *An Introduction to the Law of Restitution*
(1985), pp. 271–2, explains *Way* v. *Latilla* [1937] 3 All E.R. 759 in this way and see *ibid.,* at pp. 764–5. Cf.
Dietrich [2001] L.S. 153.

[228] *Ante,* p. 40.

responsible for this will not be entitled to recompense for the work done or the services rendered.[229]

(iv) Machinery for ascertainment

A contract will not fail for uncertainty even though a material term is to be agreed in future if the contract itself provides machinery for ascertaining it. So, for example, if the contract provides that the parties are to agree a price or quantities for delivery, but also contains an arbitration clause which covers a failure to agree the price or the quantities, the Courts will imply that, in default of agreement, a reasonable price is to be paid, such price to be determined by arbitration.[230] Moreover, in the case of a lease, if premises are let to a tenant for (say) a term of 10 years at a fixed rent for the first five years, but at a rent 'to be agreed' thereafter, the Court will itself determine by inquiry what is a reasonable rent for the premises should the parties fail to agree.[231] Unless the machinery is held to be an essential part of the agreement, the Court will similarly intervene if, for any reason, its operation is stultified, for example, by the refusal of one of the parties to appoint a valuer or an arbitrator.[232]

(v) Agreements to negotiate and not to negotiate

The position of agreements to negotiate and agreements not to negotiate was considered by the House of Lords in *Walford* v. *Miles*:[233]

On 17 March M agreed that, provided that W's bank confirmed that W had the necessary financial resources to purchase M's photographic processing business for £2 million, they would 'break off any negotiations with any third party and would not consider any other alternative and would not accept a better offer but would deal exclusively with W, with a view to concluding the deal as soon as possible after April 6'. M continued to keep in touch with the other interested party and on 27 March withdrew from the negotiations with W. M later sold the business to the third party. W sued for breach of contract and for misrepresentation.

It was found that M had represented that they were not in negotiation with the other interested party and W were awarded tortious damages for misrepresentation.[234] The contractual claims, however, failed.

    It was held that an agreement to negotiate is like an agreement to agree and is

---

[229] *Jennings & Chapman Ltd.* v. *Woodman, Matthews & Co.* [1952] 2 T.L.R. 409; *William Lacey (Hounslow) Ltd.* v. *Davis* [1957] 1 W.L.R. 932; *Regalian Properties plc* v. *London Dockland Development Cpn.* [1995] 1 W.L.R. 212.

[230] *Foley* v. *Classique Coaches Ltd.* [1934] 2 K.B. 1; *F. & G. Sykes (Wessex) Ltd.* v. *Fine Fare Ltd.* [1967] 1 Lloyd's Rep. 53; *Vosper Thornycroft Ltd.* v. *Ministry of Defence* [1976] 1 Lloyd's Rep. 58; *Queensland Electricity Generating Board* v. *New Hope Collieries Pty Ltd.* [1989] 1 Lloyd's Rep. 205, at p. 210.

[231] *Beer* v. *Bowden* [1981] 1 W.L.R. 522.

[232] *Sudbrook Trading Estate Ltd.* v. *Eggleton* [1983] 1 A.C. 444.

[233] [1992] 2 A.C. 128.

[234] These amounted to £700 and were in respect of the expenses of the negotiation and the preparation of the contract documents: [1992] 2 A.C. 128, at p. 135. On damages for misrepresentation, see *post*, pp. 245, 247.

unenforceable 'simply because it lacks the necessary certainty'.[235] Two reasons have been given for this conclusion. First, in *Walford* v. *Miles* Lord Ackner asked how the Court is to police such an agreement and questioned whether it is possible to tell whether it has been breached:[236] 'How can a court be expected to decide whether, *subjectively*, a proper reason existed for the termination of negotiations?'. The position of parties in negotiations was stated to be adversarial and to entitle them to pursue their own interests so long as they avoided making misrepresentations and, if they so wished, to withdraw from the negotiations at any time and for any reason. It was said not to be possible to cure this uncertainty by asking whether the negotiations have been conducted 'in good faith' because a duty to negotiate in good faith 'is as unworkable in practice as it is inherently inconsistent with the position of a negotiating party'. Secondly, it has been said that 'no court could estimate the damages because no one can tell whether the negotiations would be successful or would fall through: or if successful, what the result would be'.[237]

There are, however, difficulties with this aspect of the decision. First, it is unlikely to give effect to the reasonable expectations of business people which it is an important object of the law of contract to facilitate.[238] It appears to require a higher degree of certainty and less willingness to use the standard of reasonableness to resolve ambiguity than some of the cases considered above. Secondly, it is not the case that it is a fundamental attribute of a negotiation that the parties should have absolute freedom to walk away from it for any reason or no reason at all. The law does in fact permit a party to a negotiation to give up this freedom: an agreement to use 'reasonable' or even 'best' endeavours to agree appears to have the necessary certainty to constitute a contract.[239] In such a case the Court may have to determine the difficult question of whether the agreement has been broken, i.e. whether 'reasonable' or 'best' endeavours have in fact been used.[240] It is submitted that there is no satisfactory distinction between such an agreement and an agreement to negotiate in good faith. The objection that it would not be possible to assess damages is also open to question. As will be seen, in other contexts in which the transaction contains a large amount of chance, it has been possible to assess damages and the Court has not held that there is no contract.[241]

[235] [1992] 2 A.C. 128, at p. 138. See also *Courtney & Fairbairn Ltd.* v. *Tolaini Bros (Hotels) Ltd.* [1975] 1 W.L.R. 297; *Mallozzi* v. *Carapelli S.p.A.* [1976] 1 Lloyd's Rep. 407 (C.A.). Cf. *Hillas* v. *Arcos* (1932) 147 L.T. 503, *per* Lord Wright at p. 515.

[236] [1992] 2 A.C. 128, at p. 138.

[237] *Courtney & Fairbairn Ltd.* v. *Tolaini Bros (Hotels) Ltd.* [1975] 1 W.L.R. 297, *per* Lord Denning M.R. at p. 301.

[238] F.P. (1932) 48 L.Q.R. 141; Davenport (1991) 107 L.Q.R. 366.

[239] *Walford* v. *Miles* [1992] 2 A.C. 128, *per* Lord Ackner at p. 138; *Lambert* v. *H.T.V. Cymru (Wales) Ltd.* [1998] E.M.L.R. 629. In *Queensland Electricity Generating Board* v. *New Hope Collieries Pty Ltd.* [1989] 1 Lloyd's Rep. 205, at pp. 209–10 (P.C.) an obligation to make reasonable endeavours was implied and in Re Debtors (*Nos. 4449 and 4450 of 1998*) [1999] 1 All E.R. (Comm.) 149 at pp. 157–8 an obligation to negotiate in good faith was imposed on Lloyds as it was performing functions in the public interest. Cf. *Scandinavian Trading Co. A.B.* v. *Flota Petrolera* [1981] 2 Lloyd's Rep. 425, at p. 432, aff'd on other grounds [1983] 2 A.C. 694.

[240] Neill (1992) 108 L.Q.R. 405, 409–10; Cohen in Beatson and Friedmann, eds., *Good Faith and Fault in Contract Law* (1995), pp. 37 ff.

[241] *Allied Maples Group* v. *Simmons & Simmons* [1995] 1 W.L.R. 1602, at p.1620 and *post*, p. 591.

It is unfortunate that Lord Wright's *dictum* in *Hillas* v. *Arcos*,[242] which recognized a contract to negotiate, has now been rejected by the House of Lords.

An agreement not to negotiate with any third party, a 'lock out' agreement, has been held not to be enforceable where, as in *Walford* v. *Miles*, it does not specify a time limit for its duration apparently on the ground that it would impose indirectly a duty to negotiate in good faith which, for the reasons given above, could not be a contract.[243] But such an agreement is sufficiently certain if it is limited to a fixed period.[244] The distinction between these cases is difficult to justify. It is submitted that neither indirectly imposes a duty to negotiate in good faith since the obligation is a negative one and that it should have been possible to resolve the uncertainty in the first case by applying the standard of reasonableness.[245]

(b) INCOMPLETE AGREEMENT

The parties may agree on certain points, but nevertheless leave other points unresolved. The question then arises whether or not their agreement is complete. Difficulties of interpretation most frequently arise where a contract has to be made out of a correspondence involving lengthy negotiations. The parties discuss terms, approach, and recede from an agreement; proposals are made and met by the suggestion of fresh terms; finally there is a difference, and one of the parties asserts that a contract has been made, and the other that matters have never gone beyond the discussion of terms. Where such a correspondence appears to result, at any moment of its course, in an agreement, it is necessary to ask whether this agreement amounts to a completed agreement, or whether there are other terms of the intended contract, beyond and besides those expressed in the agreement, which are still in a state of negotiation only, and without the settlement of which the parties have no idea of concluding any contract.[246] Where, however, the correspondence shows that the parties have definitely come to terms, even though certain material points may still be left open, a subsequent revival of negotiations cannot, except with the consent of both parties, affect the contract so made.[247]

These cases turn rather on the meaning to be given to the words of the parties than on rules of law.

---

[242] (1932) 147 L.T. 503, at p. 515. A majority of the New South Wales Court of Appeal has rejected the view that every promise to negotiate in good faith is unenforceable: *Coal Cliff Collieries Pty Ltd.* v. *Sijehama Pty Ltd.* (1991) 24 N.S.W.L.R. 1, at p. 26. In the USA the majority view gives contractual effect to an agreement to negotiate: Farnsworth (1987) 87 Colum. L. Rev. 217, 265–7.

[243] *Walford* v. *Miles* [1992] 2 A.C. 128, at p. 140.

[244] *Pitt* v. *P.H.H. Asset Management Ltd.* [1994] 1 W.L.R. 327.

[245] Neill (1992) 108 L.Q.R. 405, 413. Bingham L.J., dissenting in the Court of Appeal, was of this view: (1990) 62 P. & C.R. 410. The agreement provided a standard in stating that the transaction was to be concluded as soon as possible after 6 April: [1990] 1 E.G.L.R. 212.

[246] *Hussey* v. *Horne Payne* (1879) 4 App. Cas. 311.

[247] *Perry* v. *Suffields Ltd.* [1916] 2 Ch. 187; *Mitsui Babcock Energy Ltd.* v. *John Brown Engineering Ltd.* (1996) 51 Con. L.R. 129, at pp. 167, 175, 179.

(i) Effect of reference to further agreement

The classic statement of the issues involved in cases where the agreement is couched in general terms, but reference is made to a contract in which the intentions of the parties may be more precisely stated, is to be found in the judgment of Parker J. in *Von Hatzfeldt-Wildenburg* v. *Alexander*.[248]

If the documents or letters relied on as constituting a contract contemplate the execution of a further contract between the parties, it is a question of construction whether the execution of the further contract is a condition or term of the bargain or whether it is a mere expression of the desire of the parties as to the manner in which the transaction already agreed to will in fact go through. In the former case there is no enforceable contract either because the condition is unfulfilled or because the law does not recognize a contract to enter into a contract. In the latter case there is a binding contract and the reference to the more formal document may be ignored.

(ii) Letters of intent

Difficulties frequently arise where parties in negotiations reach 'points of agreement' or exchange 'letters of intent' or 'letters of comfort', but nevertheless contemplate that a formal document is later to be drawn up. In such situations the question whether or not a binding contract has been concluded is a matter of interpretation for the Court. While such a letter can have contractual effect where it contains an express promise as to future conduct,[249] the Court may be unwilling to imply such a promise from a statement of present fact because the language is often vague or equivocal or because the surrounding circumstances, including previous negotiations, indicate that all that is assumed is a moral responsibility.[250]

The position may be even further complicated by the fact that the parties often act on their informal agreement pending the execution of a formal contract. Where a formal contract is eventually concluded, the Court may be prepared to imply a term that, although the informal agreement is not legally binding, the formal contract is to have retrospective effect. It will, in consequence, apply to work done and services rendered before it was made.[251] Where no formal contract is concluded, work done or goods delivered under a letter of intent which is not legally binding may give rise to a restitutionary obligation to pay a reasonable sum for the work or the goods.[252]

(iii) Agreement 'subject to contract'

The initial agreement for the sale or lease of land is usually entered into 'subject to

---

[248] [1912] 1 Ch. 284, at p. 288.

[249] *Chemco Leasing S.p.A.* v. *Rediffusion* [1987] 1 F.T.L.R. 201 (C.A.) (comfort letter an offer but lapsed before acceptance). See also Staughton J.'s judgment quoted in *Kleinwort Benson Ltd.* v. *Malaysia Mining Cpn. Bdh.* [1988] 1 W.L.R. 799, at pp. 805–6.

[250] *Kleinwort Benson Ltd.* v. *Malaysia Mining Cpn. Bdh.* [1989] 1 W.L.R. 379, at pp. 388, 391, 393. Cf. *Wilson Smithett & Cape (Sugar) Ltd.* v. *Bangladesh Sugar Industries Ltd.* [1986] 1 Lloyd's Rep. 378 (letter of intent for the supply of sugar specifying amount, price, and shipping details held to be an acceptance).

[251] *Trollope & Colls Ltd.* v. *Atomic Power Construction Ltd.* [1963] 1 W.L.R. 333. See Ball (1983) 99 L.Q.R. 572.

[252] *British Steel Cpn.* v. *Cleveland Bridge & Engineering Co. Ltd.* [1984] 1 All E.R. 504. See *ante*, p. 63.

contract' or 'subject to formal contract'. Such an agreement gives rise to no legal liability.[253] Thus in *Winn* v. *Bull*:[254]

A written agreement was drawn up whereby the defendant agreed to take a lease of a house for a definite period and at a fixed rent, but 'subject to the preparation and approval of a formal contract'.

It was held there was no contract. Jessel M.R. explained:[255]

It comes, therefore, to this, that where you have a proposal or agreement made in writing expressed to be subject to a formal contract being prepared, it means what it says; it is subject to and is dependent upon a formal contract being prepared.

The insertion of the words 'subject to contract' renders the agreement nugatory in fact, and this is so notwithstanding that a deposit may have been paid.[256] As a normal rule, a binding contract for the sale of land will come into existence only when a formal 'exchange of contracts' contained in writing signed by or on behalf of each party[257] has taken place.[258] Up to this time either party is free to renegotiate the price, or even to withdraw entirely from the transaction and to do so because of movements in the value of property. The use of the words 'subject to contract' has also been held to preclude a claim in restitution for expenses incurred in respect of the intended contract; the use of those words was said to mean that the parties had in effect expressly agreed that there should be no legal obligation by either party to the other unless and until a formal contract had been entered into.[259]

On the other hand, an agreement for the sale or lease of land will be binding if the terms of the further formal contract are in existence and known to the parties, and not merely in contemplation. For example:

An offer was made to buy land, and 'if offer accepted, to pay deposit and sign contract on the auction particulars'; this was accepted, 'subject to contract as agreed'. The acceptance clearly embodied the terms of the contract mentioned in the offer, and constituted a complete contract.[260]

---

[253] See Law Com. No. 65, *'Subject to Contract' Agreements* (1975) and Law Com. No. 164, *Formalities for Contracts for Sale etc. of Land* (1987), §§ 1.4, 4.15.

[254] (1877) 7 Ch. D. 29. See also *Galliard Homes Ltd.* v. *J. Jarvis & Sons plc* (1999) 71 Con. L.R. 219, at pp. 235–6, 243.

[255] At p. 32.

[256] *Coope* v. *Ridout* [1921] 1 Ch. 291; *Chillingworth* v. *Esche* [1924] 1 Ch. 97; *Eccles* v. *Bryant and Pollock* [1948] Ch. 93; *Tiverton Estates Ltd.* v. *Wearwell Ltd.* [1975] Ch. 146.

[257] Law of Property (Miscellaneous Provisions) Act 1989, s. 2, on which see *post*, p. 81.

[258] Cf. *Alpenstow Ltd.* v. *Regalian Properties Ltd.* [1985] 1 W.L.R. 721 (an agreement 'subject to contract' drawn up by a lawyer after five months of negotiation containing detailed and mandatory provisions of the approval, amendment, and exchange of contracts was very exceptionally held binding). In *Attorney-General of Hong Kong* v. *Humphreys Estates (Queens Gardens) Ltd.* [1987] 1 A.C. 114, at pp. 127–8, the possibility (said to be unlikely) of the parties being estopped from refusing to proceed was accepted. See also *Akiens* v. *Saloman* (1992) 65 P. & C.R. 364, at p. 370. See further, *post*, p. 123.

[259] *Regalian Properties plc* v. *London Dockland Development Cpn.* [1995] 1 W.L.R. 212, at p. 225. See also *Jennings & Chapman Ltd.* v. *Woodman, Matthews & Co.* [1952] 2 T.L.R. 409; *William Lacey (Hounslow) Ltd.* v. *Davis* [1957] 1 W.L.R. 932.

[260] *Filby* v. *Hounsell* [1896] 2 Ch. 737; *Rossiter* v. *Miller* (1878) 3 App. Cas. 1124.

Further, if the parties use the phrase 'a provisional agreement', they then agree to be bound from the beginning, even though they stipulate that a formal document is to be drawn up later on.[261]

(iv) Contracts subject to condition

There are, moreover, situations which at first sight appear to be cases of incomplete agreement, but really turn out to be cases where there is an immediate binding contract, although some of the parties' rights and obligations may be dependent upon the happening of a particular event.[262] For example, the agreement may contain such a term as 'subject to the purchaser's solicitors approving the title'. Until this approval is given the contract need not be implemented, although neither party is free to withdraw from it unilaterally. Alternatively, the contract may be fully operative at once, but upon the happening of a particular event it is thereby discharged.[263] The insertion of such conditions produces a quite different effect from a reservation like 'subject to contract' which prevents the formation of any contract at all. They are dealt with in Chapter 4, The Terms of the Contract.

VI. INTENTION TO CREATE LEGAL RELATIONS

Although a separate requirement of intention to create legal relations did not exist until the nineteenth century,[264] it is now established that an agreement will not constitute a binding contract unless it is one which can reasonably be regarded as having been made in contemplation of legal consequences. A mere statement of intention made in the course of conversation will not constitute a binding promise, though acted upon by the party to whom it was made,[265] and even negotiated agreements do not necessarily give rise to legal obligations. For example, a collective agreement between employers and trade unions is conclusively presumed not to have been intended by the parties to be legally enforceable unless it is in writing and contains a provision stating that the parties intend it to be a legally enforceable contract.[266]

---

[261] *Branca v. Cobarro* [1947] K.B. 854. See also *Damon Comp. Nav. S.A. v. Hapag-Lloyd International S.A.* [1985] 1 W.L.R. 434, at pp. 443, 452; *Global Container Lines Ltd. v. State Black Sea S.S. Co.* [1999] 1 Lloyd's Rep. 127, at p. 156.

[262] *Smith v. Butler* [1900] 1 Q.B. 694; *Marten v. Whale* [1917] 2 K.B. 480. Cf. *Pym v. Campbell* (1856) 6 E. & B. 370, *post*, p. 137.

[263] *Head v. Tattersall* (1871) L.R. 7 Ex. 7, *post*, p. 138.

[264] Simpson (1975) 91 L.Q.R. 247, 263–5; Hedley (1985) 5 O.J.L.S. 391.

[265] *Weeks v. Tybald* (1605) Noy 11; *Guthing v. Lynn* (1831) 2 B. & Ad. 232. But these cases appear to turn on uncertainty and vagueness rather than lack of intent. On the link between uncertainty and lack of intention to contract, see *ante*, pp. 67–8; *post*, p. 71.

[266] Trade Union and Labour Relations (Consolidation) Act 1992, s. 179, see *N.C.B. v. N.U.M.* [1986] I.C.R. 736. The position at common law was similar: *Ford Motor Co. Ltd. v. A.U.E.F.W.* [1969] 1 W.L.R. 339.

(a) SOCIAL ENGAGEMENTS

Sometimes it is clear from the nature of the agreement that there was no intention to enter into a binding contract. Thus, social engagements do not admit of being regarded as business transactions. This is not always because such engagements are not reducible to a money value, for they often may be. The acceptance of an invitation to dinner or to play in a cricket match,[267] of an offer to share the cost of petrol used on a journey,[268] or to take part in a golf club's competition[269] or between friends relating to musical performances by them[270] form agreements in which the promisee may incur expense in reliance on the promise. The damages resulting from breach might be ascertainable, but the Courts would hold that, if no legal consequences could reasonably have been contemplated by the parties, no action will lie.

In *Balfour* v. *Balfour*, Atkin L.J. stated:[271]

It is necessary to remember that there are agreements between parties which do not result in contracts within the meaning of that term in our law. The ordinary example is where two parties agree to take a walk together, or where there is an offer and an acceptance of hospitality. Nobody would suggest in ordinary circumstances that those agreements result in what we know as a contract.

(b) FAMILY ARRANGEMENTS

Family arrangements are another category of agreement in which there may be no intention to create legal relations. In *Balfour* v. *Balfour*:

A husband was employed in a government post in Ceylon. He returned with his wife to England on leave, but she was unable to go back to Ceylon with him for medical reasons. He consequently promised orally to make her an allowance of £30 a month until she rejoined him. He failed to make this payment, and she sued him.

The Court of Appeal held that, although it was not impossible for a husband and wife to enter into a contract for maintenance, in this case they never intended to make a bargain which could be enforced in law. While that decision has been criticized,[272] agreements between spouses and between parents and children[273] are, as we shall see, presumed not to be enforceable contracts. Thus, it has been said that a parent's promise to pay a child an allowance while at university ordinarily creates only a moral obligation.[274]

---

[267] See Atkin L.J. in *Balfour* v. *Balfour* (*infra*, n. 271) at p. 578.

[268] *Coward* v. *Motor Insurers' Bureau* [1963] 1 Q.B. 259; *Buckpitt* v. *Oates* [1968] 1 All E.R. 1145. But see now Road Traffic Act 1988, ss. 145, 149.

[269] *Lens* v. *Devonshire Club*, The Times, 4 December 1914, *per* Scrutton J., referred to in *Rose and Frank Co.* v. *J. R. Crompton & Bros. Ltd.* [1923] 2 K.B. 261, at p. 288. Cf. *Clarke* v. *Earl of Dunraven* [1897] A.C. 59, *ante*, p. 30 (contract between competitors in yacht club regatta).

[270] *Hadley* v. *Kemp* [1999] E.M.L.R. 589, at p. 623.

[271] [1919] 2 K.B. 571, at p. 578. See also *Vaughan* v. *Vaughan* [1953] 1 Q.B. 762, at p. 765; *Gould* v. *Gould* [1970] 1 Q.B. 275.

[272] *Post*, p. 72.

[273] *Jones* v. *Padavatton* [1969] 1 W.L.R. 328.

[274] *Fleming* v. *Beeves* [1994] 1 N.Z.L.R. 385, at p. 389 (New Zealand).

(c) DETERMINING INTENTION

The test of an intention to effect legal relations is an objective one. It may be that the promisor never anticipated that the promise would give rise to any legal obligation, but if a reasonable person would consider there was an intention so to contract, then the promisor will be bound.[275] It has therefore been contended that the common law does not require any positive intention to create a legal obligation as an element of contract, and that 'a deliberate promise seriously made is enforced irrespective of the promisor's views regarding his legal liability'.[276] This view commands considerable respect, but it is submitted that there are difficulties in the way of its acceptance.

In the first place, the parties to a business transaction may deliberately state that they do not intend to enter into any legal obligation, and the Court will then treat their promises as binding in honour only. Thus in *Appleson v. Littlewood Ltd.*,[277] it was held that a competitor who claimed to have sent in a successful coupon in a football pool, of which one of the conditions was that the conduct of the pools and everything done in connection therewith was not to be 'attended by or give rise to any legal relationship whatsoever', could have no claim which a Court would enforce. Again, an agreement between a person appointed to serve as a curate and the church authorities has been held not to be intended to create a contractual relationship of any kind.[278] Moreover, until recently the Crown and civil servants were held not to be in a contractual relationship because the Civil Service Pay and Conditions Code's statement that 'a civil servant does not have a contract of employment enforceable in the courts' meant that the Crown did not have the requisite intention to contract.[279] The context in which an agreement is made,[280] what was said when it was made,[281] and the vagueness of the language used[282] may be held to be inconsistent with an intent to contract. Where the agreement is made in a commercial context, however, the onus on a party who asserts that an agreement was made without the intent is a heavy one.[283]

Secondly, where the agreement falls into that class of cases where legal contracts are not normally made, exemplified by social or family arrangements, it will be presumed

[275] *Carlill v. Carbolic Smoke Ball Co.* [1893] 1 Q.B. 256, *ante*, p. 35; *British Airways Board v. Taylor* [1976] 1 W.L.R. 13. See *ante*, p. 31.
[276] 1 Williston, *Contracts*, § 21; Hepple [1970] C.L.J. 122; Hedley (1985) 5 O.J.L.S. 391; *Restatement* (2d), § 21B.
[277] [1939] 1 All E.R. 464. See also *Rose and Frank Co. v. Crompton & Bros. Ltd.* [1925] A.C. 445; *Jones v. Vernons' Pools* [1938] 2 All E.R. 626. Cf. *Edwards v. Skyways Ltd.* [1964] 1 W.L.R. 349 ('*ex gratia*' payment); *Home Insurance Co. Ltd. v. Administratia Asigurarilor* [1983] 2 Lloyd's Rep. 674, at p. 677 (agreement to be 'interpreted as an honourable engagement').
[278] *Diocese of Southwark v. Coker* [1998] I.C.R. 140.
[279] *R. v. Civil Service Appeal Board, ex parte Bruce* [1988] I.C.R. 649, [1989] I.C.R. 171; *McLaren v. Home Office* [1990] I.C.R. 84; *R. v. Lord Chancellor's Department, ex parte Nangle* [1991] I.C.R. 743; Trade Union and Labour Relations (Consolidation) Act 1992, ss. 62(7) and 245.
[280] *President of the Methodist Conference v. Parfitt* [1984] Q.B. 368 (Minister not in contractual relationship because of spiritual nature of functions).
[281] *Orion Insurance Co. plc v. Sphere Drake Insurance plc* [1992] 1 Lloyd's Rep. 239.
[282] *Vaughan v. Vaughan* [1953] 1 Q.B. 762, at p. 765; *Kleinwort Benson Ltd. v. Malaysia Mining Cpn. Bdh.* [1988] 1 W.L.R. 799; [1989] 1 W.L.R. 379, *ante*, p. 67.
[283] *Edwards v. Skyways Ltd.* (*supra*, n. 277), at p. 355; *Orion Insurance Co. plc v. Sphere Drake Insurance plc* (*supra*, n. 281), at pp. 263, 292.

that no intent to create an enforceable contract is present, even though there may have been an exchange of mutual promises and a 'consideration' moving from the promisee.[284] On the other hand, this presumption may be rebutted upon proof of the true intention of the parties, which is to be inferred from the language they use and the circumstances in which they use it. Thus in *Parker* v. *Clark*:[285]

The defendants, an elderly couple, agreed with the plaintiffs, who were 20 years younger, that if the latter would sell their cottage and come to live with the defendants, sharing household expenses, the male defendant would leave them a portion of his estate in his will. The plaintiffs sold their cottage and moved in with the defendants. Difficulties developed between the two couples, and the defendants repudiated the agreement by requiring the plaintiffs to find somewhere else to live. The plaintiffs claimed damages for breach of contract.

It was argued that the agreement amounted to no more than a family arrangement of the type considered in *Balfour* v. *Balfour*, but Devlin J. held that the circumstances indicated that the parties intended to effect their legal relations and that the defendants were therefore liable. Indeed *Balfour* v. *Balfour* has been said to be an extreme example of this presumption,[286] which has also been said to be of limited assistance in family cases,[287] and there are several cases in which it has been held that a husband's promise to his wife, from whom he was about to separate, that she could have the matrimonial home, was enforceable as a contract.[288] Again, an informal family arrangement to share the winnings of a football pool entry,[289] was similarly enforceable since the necessary intention was present.

Thirdly, it has been clearly established that the distinction between a warranty, which is a term of a contract, and a 'mere representation' depends upon whether the parties intended the statement to have contractual effect.[290] It would be somewhat curious if contractual intention could be dispensed with in proving the existence of a contract, but not in proving the terms of which it is necessarily composed.

The conclusion is that an intention to effect legal relations is essential to the formation of a contract in English law.

---

[284] *Balfour* v. *Balfour* [1919] 2 K.B. 571, at p. 578; *Buckpitt* v. *Oates* [1968] 1 All E.R. 1145; *Jones* v. *Padavatton* [1969] 1 W.L.R. 328.

[285] [1960] 1 W.L.R. 286. Cf. *Re Goodchild* [1997] 1 W.L.R. 1216.

[286] *Pettitt* v. *Pettitt* [1970] A.C. 777, at pp. 806, 816.

[287] *Fleming* v. *Beeves* [1994] 1 N.Z.L.R. 383, at p. 389 (New Zealand).

[287] *Ferris* v. *Weaven* [1952] 2 All E.R. 233; *Merritt* v. *Merritt* [1970] 1 W.L.R. 1121; *Eves* v. *Eves* [1975] 1 W.L.R. 1338 (cohabitation); *Re Windle* [1975] 1 W.L.R. 1628; *Tanner* v. *Tanner* [1975] 1 W.L.R. 1346 (cohabitation). Cf. *Vaughan* v. *Vaughan* [1953] 1 Q.B. 762; *Spellman* v. *Spellman* [1961] 1 W.L.R. 921; *Morris* v. *Tarrant* [1971] 2 Q.B. 143; *Horrocks* v. *Forray* [1976] 1 W.L.R. 230 (cohabitation). See *post*, p. 85 (requirements of form). Where there is no contract, a constructive trust may arise (*post*, p. 86).

[289] *Simkins* v. *Pays* [1955] 1 W.L.R. 975.

[290] *Heilbut Symons & Co.* v. *Buckleton* [1913] A.C. 30, at p. 51; *Oscar Chess Ltd.* v. *Williams* [1957] 1 W.L.R. 370, at p. 374. See *post*, p. 128.

3

FORM, CONSIDERATION, AND PROMISSORY ESTOPPEL

I. FORMAL REQUIREMENTS

Having dealt with the mechanics of agreement, certainty, and intention, we now turn to other formal and substantive requirements of a legally enforceable contract. English law does not regard a bare promise or agreement as legally enforceable but recognizes only two kinds of contract, the contract made by deed, and the simple contract. A contract made by deed derives its validity neither from the fact of the agreement nor because it is an exchange but solely from the *form* in which it is expressed.

A simple contract as a general rule need not be made in any special form, but requires the presence of consideration which, we shall see, broadly means that something must be given in exchange for a promise. The paradigm of the simple contract is thus a bargain but we shall see that the requirement of consideration can be satisfied by nominal consideration, such as a peppercorn. In such cases it has been argued that consideration is really no more than a requirement of form. In some simple contracts, statute imposes (in addition to the requirement of consideration) the necessity of some kind of form, such as writing, either as a condition of their existence or as a requisite of proving the contract.

In modern law requirements of consideration and writing may be circumvented by the operation of the equitable doctrine of estoppel. Under this, where the parties are in a legal relationship, a party who promises not to insist on his or her strict legal rights will, even though the promise is not supported by consideration, not be allowed to go back on it provided the promisee has relied on the promise and it would be inequitable for the promisor to insist on his or her strict legal rights. In such a case a promise can in effect be enforced even though it is not made by deed, is not in writing, and is not supported by consideration.

This topic will be dealt with under five headings: (1) contracts by deed, (2) contracts for which writing is required, (3) consideration, (4) promissory estoppel, and (5) an appraisal of consideration and promissory estoppel. Before doing so, it is useful briefly to consider one matter. The formal nature of contracts by deed, requirements of writing, and in some cases of consideration has been noted. What then is the role of such requirements of form?

Historically, formal requirements played a large role in the English law of contract because the Statute of Frauds 1677 provided that many important and widely used types of contract, in particular contracts for the sale or disposition of an interest in land and, until 1954, contracts for the sale of goods of over £10 in value, were unenforceable unless supported by a note or memorandum in writing.[1]

The significance of formal requirements has now diminished, save in sales of land and a limited number of other types of contract, notably to protect parties (such as tenants, consumers, borrowers, and employees) who are in the weaker bargaining position. Nevertheless, although it has been stated that the advantages of requirements of formality are purely negative in nature and consist in the avoidance of various evils,[2] it should not be forgotten that formality serves a number of useful functions.[3] First, there is the historically important evidential function.[4] A requirement such as writing facilitates and renders certain the existence of a transaction and its terms as well as identifying the intention of the parties. The particularly significant issues of authenticity and integrity which arise in the case of contracts made by e-mail can, for example, be addressed by a suitable formal requirement for such transactions.[5] Secondly, there is the paternalistic and cautionary function of helping to ensure that a party deliberately considers whether to contract and to prevent people accidentally binding themselves on impulse or because of improper pressure. For instance, classes of contractors considered to be weaker, such as tenants, employees, borrowers, and guarantors may be protected by requiring a written agreement and clear language.[6] In some such cases (consumer credit, timeshare, and package travel) there may also be a statutory 'cooling off' period. This is a paternalistic qualification to the substantive requirement of agreement rather than a formal requirement, but the requirement that notice must be given to the protected person of this right to cancel[7] is a requirement of form. The corollary of the evidential and cautionary functions is that formal requirements allow parties to bind themselves with certainty and to know to what they are binding themselves.[8]

As against these useful functions, if the form is complex, it can be inconvenient, mysterious, and inaccessible to ordinary people. Formal requirements may also affront social and commercial attitudes to promises ('my word is my bond') since requiring, for instance, a deed or writing implies mistrust. The result of either or both of these may be that the required form is not used, whether deliberately or by accident, and thus the requirement can have the effect of reducing rather than promoting the security of transactions.

Formal requirements thus prevent impulsiveness, coercion, inadequate evidence, and manufactured evidence, but they may undermine security of transactions if

---

[1] This requirement was repealed by the Law Reform (Enforcement of Contracts) Act 1954.

[2] Jhering, *Geist des Roemishen Rechts*, 480–2.

[3] Law Com. No. 164, *Formalities for Contracts for Sale etc. of Land* (1987), §§ 1.4, 2.3–2.11.

[4] *Ibid.*, § 2.5. See also Holdsworth, *A History of English Law* 7th edn. (1956), 380, 388–90; Simpson, *A History of the Common Law of Contract* (1975), ch. XIII.

[5] *Post*, p. 78.

[6] *Writing*: Consumer Credit Act 1974, s. 60; Unsolicited Goods and Services Act 1971, s. 3A. *Notice of specified terms*: Landlord and Tenant Act 1962, s. 1; Estate Agents Act 1979, s. 18; Employment Rights Act 1996, ss. 1–2, 4–6; Timeshare Regulations 1997 (S.I. 1997 No. 1081).

[7] See *ante*, p. 28, n 7.

[8] e.g. Consumer Credit Act 1974, s. 64.

either their complexity or social or commercial morality mean they are not observed.

II. CONTRACTS BY DEED

(a) HOW A CONTRACT BY DEED IS MADE

At common law it was often said that a contract by deed was executed by being 'signed, sealed and delivered'. The position is now largely governed by section 1 of the Law of Property (Miscellaneous Provisions) Act 1989.[9] To be a deed an instrument must make it 'clear on its face that it is intended to be a deed by the person making it, or as the case may be, by the parties to it (whether by describing itself as a deed or expressing itself to be executed or signed as a deed or otherwise)'.[10] The 1989 Act does not, however, lay down any prescribed manner of making it clear because to do so 'would invalidate what would otherwise be perfectly acceptable deeds merely for failure to include one vital word'.[11]

(i) Signature and attestation

In the case of deeds executed by an individual the requirement of sealing has been abolished.[12] The instrument must either be signed by the person making it in the presence of an attesting witness or, where it is not signed by that person, perhaps because of some physical incapacity, it must be signed at the direction and in the presence of that person and in the presence of two attesting witnesses.[13] In the case of a company incorporated under the Companies Acts either its common seal must be affixed or the instrument must be signed by two directors or one director and the company secretary and expressed to be executed by the company.[14] The requirement of sealing still applies to corporations sole and corporations incorporated under other statutes or by royal charter.[15] In modern times, seals are often very much of a legal fiction, being merely an adhesive wafer attached to the document or even a printed circle containing the letters 'L.S.' (*locus sigilli*).[16] Even a document bearing no indication of a seal at all will suffice, provided that there is evidence (e.g. attestation) that it was intended to be executed as a deed.[17] Failure to have a signature witnessed and

---

[9] Implementing Law Com. No. 163, *Deeds and Escrows* (1987). Section 1 applies to all deeds, and not just those relating to land, made on or after 31 July 1990; S.I. 1990 No. 1175.

[10] Law of Property (Miscellaneous Provisions) Act 1989, s. 1(2)(a). For the similar rule for companies, see Companies Act 1985, s. 36A(5).

[11] 1988/89 503 H.L. Deb. 599 (The Lord Chancellor, Second Reading Debate).

[12] Law of Property (Miscellaneous Provisions) Act 1989, s. 1(1)(b).

[13] *Ibid.*, s. 1(3)(a). 'Signature' includes making one's mark: *ibid.*, s. 1(4).

[14] Companies Act 1985, s. 36A(4).

[15] Law of Property (Miscellaneous Provisions) Act 1989, s. 1(9)–(10).

[16] *First National Securities Ltd.* v. *Jones* [1978] Ch. 109.

[17] *First National Securities Ltd.* v. *Jones* (*supra*, n. 16); *Commercial Credit Services* v. *Knowles* [1978] 6 Current Law 64. Cf. *T.C.B. Ltd.* v. *Gray* [1986] Ch. 621.

attested or, where this is still required, to have the document sealed, will not be fatal if the signatory has taken the benefit of the deed or is estopped from denying its validity because another has detrimentally relied on it.[18]

(ii) Delivery

The 1989 Act preserves the requirement of 'delivery'[19] which, in this context does not signify handing over to the other party, but means an act done or word said so as to make it clear that the person making the deed regards it as binding. Thus, a deed may be 'delivered' even though it is retained in the custody of the grantor.[20]

(iii) Escrow

A deed may be delivered subject to a condition; it then does not take effect until the condition is performed. For example, on a sale of land the vendor does not normally intend the deed to operate until the purchase price has been paid and (where appropriate) the deed has been executed by the purchaser. In such a case, it is termed an *escrow*, but if the condition is fulfilled within a time which is reasonable in all the circumstances,[21] it becomes operative as from the date of its delivery.[22] At one time an escrow could not be handed to one who was a party to it, or else it took effect at once, on the ground that such handing over in fact outweighed oral conditions. But nowadays the intention of the parties prevails if they clearly mean the deed to be delivered conditionally.[23]

(b) WHEN IT IS ESSENTIAL TO CONTRACT BY DEED

Statute sometimes makes it necessary to use an instrument in the form of a deed if the transaction is to be valid. For example, the conveyance of a legal estate in land must normally be made by deed in accordance with the provisions of the Law of Property Act 1925.[24]

Common law now[25] requires a deed only in the case of a gratuitous promise, or contract in which there is no consideration for the promise made on one side and accepted on the other. Thus, one of the most common uses today of a deed (outside conveyances of land) is that of a gratuitous payment to a charity.

---

[18] *T.C.B. Ltd.* v. *Gray* (*supra*, n. 17); Law Com. No. 163, § 2.15.

[19] s. 1(3)(b). Authority by a party making a deed to an agent to deliver it need not be given by deed: *ibid.*, s. 1(1)(c).

[20] *Xenos* v. *Wickham* (1867) L.R. 2 H.L. 296; *Macedo* v. *Stroud* [1922] A.C. 330; *Vincent* v. *Premo Enterprises Ltd.* [1969] 2 Q.B. 609; *D'Silva* v. *Lister House Development Ltd.* [1971] Ch. 17.

[21] *Beesly* v. *Hallwood Estates Ltd.* [1961] Ch. 105; *Kingston* v. *Ambrian Investment Co. Ltd.* [1975] 1 W.L.R. 161. Cf. *Glessing* v. *Green* [1975] 1 W.L.R. 863.

[22] *Alan Estates Ltd.* v. *W. G. Stores Ltd.* [1982] Ch. 511.

[24] ss. 52, 54, as amended by the Law of Property (Miscellaneous Provisions) Act 1989, s. 1(8), Sched. 1, para. 2.

[25] The rule that the contracts of a corporation aggregate had to be made under the corporate seal was abolished by the Corporate Bodies' Contracts Act 1960. On the execution of deeds by companies, see Law Com No. 253 (1998).

III. CONTRACTS FOR WHICH WRITING IS REQUIRED

(a) STATUTORY REQUIREMENTS OF WRITING

We have now dealt with the contract which is valid by reason of its form alone, and we pass to the simple or *parol* contract which depends for its validity upon the presence of consideration.

Although there is a popular belief that only contracts in writing are enforceable, this belief is completely illusory and forms no part of the English common law. In certain exceptional cases, however, the law requires writing, sometimes as a condition of the validity of the contract itself, but sometimes only as evidence without which it cannot be enforced. It should be borne in mind that consideration is as necessary in these contracts as in those in which no writing is required: 'If contracts be merely written and not specialties, they are parol, and a consideration must be proved'.[26] The following are examples of contracts which must, by statute, be made in writing:

(1) The Bills of Exchange Act 1882[27] requires that a bill of exchange or promissory note and the acceptance of a bill of exchange must be in writing.

(2) Contracts of marine insurance are void unless made in writing in the form of a policy.[28]

(3) A consumer credit agreement, e.g. a hire-purchase or loan agreement, must be in writing and be signed by the hirer or debtor and by or on behalf of the owner or creditor. It must also be made in a certain form and contain certain information including prominent notices advising the hirer or debtor of the protection and remedies, including the right to cancel, available under the Act and the annual percentage rate of charge.[29]

(4) A bill of sale is void unless made in a certain form.[30]

Other contracts are not required by statute to be made in writing, but merely to be evidenced by writing before they can be enforced in legal proceedings. Until 1954 the most frequent examples of such contracts were provided by those specified in the Statute of Frauds 1677.[31] The object of these statutory requirements was 'for prevention of many fraudulent practices which are commonly endeavoured to be upheld by perjury and subornation of perjury'.[32] But almost from its inception, this requirement of writing exhibited a tendency to encourage, rather than to prevent, dishonest dealing. The attempts of the judges consequently to circumvent the Statute of Frauds, and

[26] *Rann* v. *Hughes* (1778) 7 Term R. 350n.
[27] ss. 3(1), 17(2).
[28] Marine Insurance Act 1906, s. 22.
[29] Consumer Credit Act 1974, ss. 60, 64; Consumer Credit (Agreements) Regulations 1983 (S.I. 1983 No. 1553), as amended.
[30] Bills of Sale Act (1878) Amendment Act 1882, s. 9.
[31] *Ante*, p. 73.
[32] Statutes of the Realm, vol. V, p. 840.

the niceties of legal learning which resulted, rendered its operation both arbitrary and artificial. By the Law Reform (Enforcement of Contracts) Act 1954,[33] most of its provisions, together with their re-enacting statutes,[34] were repealed.

Two classes of contract were, however, exempted from this repeal. These are contracts of guarantee, and contracts for the sale or other disposition of land.

(b) ELECTRONIC CONTRACTS

The Electronic Communications Act 2000 empowers the modification of any enactment for the purpose of authorizing or facilitating the use of electronic communications for the making of contracts.[35] Moreover, the E.C. Directive on Electronic Commerce requires member states to ensure that their legal systems allow contracts to be concluded by electronic means and that such contracts are not deprived of legal effectiveness on account of their being made by electronic means.[36] There are exceptions to this, in particular contracts creating or transferring rights in real estate (except for rental rights), and contracts of guarantee granted by persons acting outside their trade or business. The Law Commission has advised the Government that, with the exception of marine insurance, it will not be necessary to amend statutory requirements of form to enable the use of most current forms of electronic communications in commercial transactions. Important issues of authenticity and integrity arise in respect of electronic communications and electronic signatures which have to be addressed.[37]

(c) CONTRACTS OF GUARANTEE

The Statute of Frauds provides:

No action shall be brought . . . whereby to charge the defendant upon any special promise to answer for the debt, default, or miscarriage of another person . . . unless the agreement upon which such action shall be brought or some memorandum or note thereof shall be in writing, and signed by the party to be charged therewith or some other person thereunto by him lawfully authorized.

Such a promise is a contract of guarantee or suretyship and can usually be reduced to this form: 'Deal with X, and if X does not meet his obligations, I will be answerable'.

(i) Guarantee distinguished from contract of indemnity

A guarantee must be distinguished from a contract of indemnity, which is not subject

---

[33] See the Sixth Interim Report of the Law Revision Committee (Cmd. 5449, 1937), and the First Report of the Law Reform Committee (Cmd. 8809, 1953).

[34] Sale of Goods Act 1893, s. 4 (writing required for contracts for the sale of goods of over £10 in value).

[35] s. 8(1).

[36] EC Directive 2000/31, O.J. L178/1 17 July 2000. See also the Law Commission's Advice to Government (December 2001).

[37] See e.g. the Judicial Studies Board's Digital Signature Guidelines (2000) on public or dual key cryptography as a method of authenticating electronic communications.

to any statutory requirement of writing. In a contract of guarantee there must always be three parties in contemplation: a principal debtor (whose liability may be actual or prospective), a creditor, and a promisor (the guarantor) who promises to discharge the debtor's liability *if the debtor should fail to do so*. The guarantor's liability is therefore secondary to that of the principal debtor. In a contract of indemnity, however, the promisor is primarily liable, either alone or jointly with the principal debtor, and undertakes to discharge the liability *in any event* whether or not the principal debtor makes default.[38]

(ii) Guarantor's liability is secondary

In a contract of guarantee there must, in fact, be an expectation that another person will perform the obligation which the promisor has undertaken. If the promisor is primarily liable the promise is not within the Statute, and need not be in writing.[39] The question whether the undertaking is primary or secondary is determined, not merely from the particular words of the promise, but from the general circumstances of the transaction.[40] In the result, the borderline is often very artificial and the subject 'has raised many hair-splitting distinctions of exactly that kind which brings the law into hatred, ridicule and contempt by the public'.[41]

(iii) Nature of liability guaranteed

The liability guaranteed may arise out of tort as well as out of contract.[42] It may also be prospective at the time the promise is made, as, for example, in consideration of a future advance of money; or it may be past, provided some new consideration is given.[43] Yet there must be a principal debtor at some time; if not there is no contract of guarantee, and the promise though not in writing will nevertheless be actionable. This is illustrated by *Lakeman* v. *Mountstephen*:[44]

M. stated that he would construct certain drains provided that L, the Chairman of a local Board of Health or the Board would become responsible for payment. L. responded, 'Go on, [M.], and do the work, and I will see you paid'. The Board repudiated liability on the ground that it had never entered into any agreement with L. When sued, L. pleaded that his statement was a promise to be answerable for the debt of another within the Statute of Frauds and, not being in writing, was unenforceable.

The House of Lords held that M was entitled to succeed. The Board had incurred no liability which could be guaranteed, and there could be no contract of guarantee unless there was a principal debtor. L's words, when properly construed, indicated that he would therefore be liable, not as guarantor, but as sole debtor, by reason of his oral promise to the respondent.

---

[38] *Guild & Co.* v. *Conrad* [1894] 2 Q.B. 885, at p. 896.
[39] *Birkmyr* v. *Darnell* (1704) 1 Salk. 27, at p. 28.
[40] *Keate* v. *Temple* (1797) 1 B. & P. 158.
[41] *Yeoman Credit Ltd.* v. *Latter* [1961] 1 W.L.R. 828, *per* Harman L.J. at p. 892.
[42] *Kirkham* v. *Marter* (1819) 2 B. & Ald. 613.
[43] *Board* v. *Hoey* (1948) 65 T.L.R. 43.
[44] (1874) L.R. 7 H.L. 17.

(iv) A continuing liability

The promise must also not effect a release of the original debtor, whose liability must be a continuing liability. If there is an existing debt for which a third party is liable to the promisee, and if the promisor undertakes to be answerable for it, still there is no guarantee if the terms of the agreement are such as to extinguish the original liability. If A says to B, 'Give C Ltd. a receipt in full for its debt to you, and I will pay the amount', this promise would not fall within the Statute of Frauds; for there is no suretyship, but a substitution of one debtor for another.[45]

(v) Exceptions

In two exceptional situations a contract of guarantee has been held to fall outside the Statute, even though it is a promise to answer for the debt, default, or miscarriage of another.

The first is where the guarantee is merely incidental to a larger contract and not the sole object of the parties to the transaction. So in *Sutton & Co. v. Grey*,[46] where the defendants entered into an oral agreement with a stockbroker to introduce business to him on the terms that they were to receive half the commissions earned and to pay half the losses in the event of a client introduced by them failing to pay, it was held that their promise to answer for the debt of such a client did not fall within the Statute. It was incidental to a wider transaction and did not have to be evidenced in writing.

Secondly, where the main purpose of the guarantor is to acquire or retain property, and the guarantee is given to relieve the property from some charge or incumbrance in favour of a third party, it is not within the Statute. Thus if A buys goods from B which are subject to a lien in favour of C, and in order to discharge the lien A promises C to pay B's debt if B does not do so, this promise need not be evidenced in writing.[47] But the interest to be acquired or retained must be substantial and proprietary. An oral promise by a shareholder in a company to guarantee the company's debts in order to prevent an execution being levied on its assets does not come within this exception. The interest of a shareholder in the company's assets is purely personal, and is not a proprietary interest.[48]

These legal niceties have, however, little to commend them. The administration of justice is not a game, and it is a matter for regret that, if special protection was to be afforded by the law to guarantors, it should not have been embodied in a statute requiring the terms of all contracts of guarantee or indemnity to be set out in a written document,[49] instead of perpetuating subtle distinctions.

---

[45] *Goodman v. Chase* (1818) 1 B. & Ald. 297.

[46] [1894] 1 Q.B. 285.

[47] *Fitzgerald v. Dressler* (1859) 7 C.B.N.S. 374.

[48] *Harburg India Rubber Comb Co. v. Martin* [1902] 1 K.B. 778.

[49] As in the case of certain contracts of guarantee and indemnity given in relation to regulated consumer credit agreements: Consumer Credit Act 1974, s. 105(1).

(d) CONTRACTS FOR THE SALE OR OTHER DISPOSITION OF LAND

The most important class of contracts subject to requirements of form are contracts relating to land. The Law Commission recently considered and rejected the abolition of all formal requirements, primarily because of the need for certainty, but also for protective, paternalistic reasons; time to reflect and, if necessary to seek legal advice 'is especially important in the case of contracts dealing with land because they often involve acceptance of a complexity of rights and duties'.[50] Indeed the Commission's recommendations, substantially enacted by the Law of Property (Miscellaneous Provisions) Act 1989 (the '1989 Act'), are in important respects more rigorous than what had hitherto been required.[51] By section 2(1) of the 1989 Act, contracts for the sale or other disposition of an interest in land:

can only be made in writing and only by incorporating all the terms which the parties have expressly agreed in one document or, where contracts are exchanged, in each.

The section applies to a 'disposition'[52] of an interest in land, and 'interest in land' is defined as 'any estate, interest or charge in or over land or over the proceeds of sale of land'.[53] Thus, the section applies to a lease, a mortgage, a release and a disclaimer. It applies where neither party has any proprietary interest in the relevant property.[54] Contracts for the grant of a lease for a period not exceeding three years,[55] those made in the course of a public auction, and those regulated by the Financial Services and Markets Act 2000 (for instance unit trusts investing in land) are excluded.[56]

An example of the increased rigour is provided by the position of equitable mortgages by deposit of title deeds. These were previously valid without any writing, but have now been held to be subject to section 2 of the 1989 Act and void if they do not comply with it, because the basis of such equitable mortgage is contract.[57] An option granted by the vendor of land is also a 'contract' within section 2[58] but the subsequent exercise of that option is a unilateral act and not within the section: 'It would destroy

---

[50] Law Com. No. 164, *Formalities for the Sale etc. of Land*, §§ 2.7–2.9 (1987). For other advantages of formality, see *ante*, p. 74.

[51] Contracts made before the 1989 Act came into force on 27 September 1989 must comply with Law of Property Act 1925, s. 40(1) which substantially re-enacted the relevant portion of the Statute of Frauds, s. 4. The principles are therefore substantially the same as those for guarantees, on which see *post*, p. 83. For fuller discussion of s. 40(1) and the doctrine of part performance, see the 26th edition of this book, pp. 70–8 and *Chitty on Contracts*, 28th edn. (1999), § 4–005 ff.

[52] It has the same meaning as in the Law of Property Act 1925: Law of Property (Miscellaneous Provisions) Act 1989, s. 2(6).

[53] Law of Property (Miscellaneous Provisions) Act 1989, s. 2(6).

[54] *Singh* v. *Beggs* (1995) 71 P. & C.R. 120.

[55] Contracts to grant leases of under three years need no formality (Law of Property (Miscellaneous Provisions) Act 1989, s. 2(5)) because the grant of such a lease itself needs no formality if it takes effect in possession, but contracts to assign such leases are subject to section 2: see Law Com. No. 164 (1987), § 4.10.

[56] Law of Property (Miscellaneous Provisions) Act 1989, s. 2(5)(b), (c). See Law Com. No. 164, §§ 4.11–4.12.

[57] *United Bank of Kuwait* v. *Sahib* [1997] Ch. 107, rejecting the argument that such deposits are equitable charges rather than agreements to mortgage. But cf. *Target Holdings Ltd.* v. *Priestley* (1999) 79 P. & C.R. 305 (writing not needed for agreement which disposed of a mortgage).

[58] *Spiro* v. *Glencrown Properties Ltd.* [1991] Ch. 537; Law Com. No. 164, § 4.3.

the very purpose of the option if the purchaser had to obtain the vendor's counter-signature to the notice by which it was exercised'.[59] A 'lock-out' agreement, where the owner of property agrees with a prospective purchaser not to consider any other offers for property for a fixed period, is, however, not subject to section 2 because its negative nature—the vendor cannot sell to a third party but is not committed to a sale to the prospective purchaser—means that there is no disposition of an interest in land.[60] Again, contracts which are preliminary to the acquisition of such an interest, or such as deal with a remote and inappreciable interest, would appear to be outside the section.[61]

In one respect the 1989 Act probably requires a greater degree of formality than the Law Commission recommended. It appears that it is no longer possible to have an enforceable contract by written offer and acceptance in correspondence; there must either be a single document incorporating all the terms agreed and signed by the parties or each party must sign a document incorporating the terms in the expectation that the other has also executed or will execute a corresponding document incorporating the same terms.[62]

Separate supplementary or collateral agreements to contracts relating to land are not within section 2. For instance, a contract to grant a lease, whereby the prospective tenant agreed to carry out certain work on the premises in exchange for payment has been held to be outside it.[63] The line between the contract relating to land and the supplementary or collateral one is, however, not always easy to draw, particularly where, as commonly occurs, the contract has been duly signed and is awaiting exchange, but a further term is orally agreed immediately prior to exchange. In *Record v. Bell*, for instance:[64]

The vendor of property had not received a copy of the entries from the Land Registry by the day before the contract, which had been drawn up, was to be exchanged. He agreed with the purchaser, who was concerned about undisclosed entries, to warrant his title if the purchaser exchanged contracts and this oral agreement was confirmed by letters. Contracts were exchanged and the title was as warranted but the purchaser, whose financial position had deteriorated, refused to complete and relied *inter alia* on non-compliance with section 2 of the 1989 Act, since all the terms were not in either the contracts exchanged or the exchange of letters.

---

[59] *Ibid., per* Hoffmann J. at p. 541. See also *Trustees of the Chippenham Golf Club* v. *North Wiltshire D.C.* (1991) 64 P. & C.R. 527, at p. 530.

[60] *Pitt* v. *P.H.H. Asset Management Ltd.* [1994] 1 W.L.R. 327, *ante*, p. 66.

[61] e.g. *Angel* v. *Duke* (1875) L.R. 10 Q.B. 174 (agreement to repair house for prospective tenant); *Bligh* v. *Brent* (1836) 2 Y. & C. 268; *Humble* v. *Mitchell* (1839) 11 A. & E. 205 (agreement to transfer shares in company possessed of land). Cf. *Driver* v. *Broad* [1893] 1 Q.B. 744 (contract to sell debentures of company possessed of land is subject to the statute). These decisions concerned the Statute of Frauds.

[62] *Commission for New Towns* v. *Cooper (Great Britain) Ltd.* [1995] Ch. 259; *Firstpost Homes Ltd.* v. *Johnson* [1995] 1 W.L.R. 1567. N.B. clause 1(1) of the Draft Bill attached to the Report differs from section 2 and see Law Com. No. 164, § 4.15. But cf. *Hooper* v. *Sherman*, 30 November 1994 (C.A.), which did not refer to the Act's difference from the Law Commission's Draft Bill and relied on § 4.15.

[63] *Tootal Clothing Ltd.* v. *Guinea Properties Ltd.* (1991) 64 P. & C.R. 452, *per* Scott L.J. at pp. 455–6, Wilde (1993) 109 L.Q.R. 191; *Record* v. *Bell* [1991] 1 W.L.R. 853.

[64] [1991] 1 W.L.R. 853; Smith (1992) 108 L.Q.R. 217; Harpum [1991] C.L.J. 399. Cf. *McCausland* v. *Duncan Lawrie Ltd.* [1997] 1 W.L.R. 38 (a variation of material term had to comply with section 2).

Although the purchaser seemed to be thinking in terms of amending the main contract rather than a separate contract, the agreement was held to be a collateral contract and outside the section:

[i]t would be unfortunate if common transactions of this nature should nevertheless cause the contracts to be avoided. It may, of course, lead to a greater use of the concept of collateral warranties than has hitherto been necessary.[65]

(e) THE FORM REQUIRED

Until the enactment of the 1989 Act this was substantially the same for both contracts of guarantee and contracts for the disposition of an interest in land. The provisions of the Statute of Frauds 1677, which still govern guarantees, were substantially re-enacted by section 40(1) of the Law of Property Act 1925. Many of the decisions under the Statute of Frauds and section 40(1) concerning contracts for the sale of land are applicable to guarantees. The fundamental change effected by the 1989 Act is that in the case of an agreement subject to section 2, failure to comply with the formalities renders the contract void,[66] whereas a contract subject to but which does not comply with the Statute of Frauds exists but is unenforceable. Before discussing the consequences of this difference, the requirements for the two types of contract will be set out.

(i) Signature

A guarantee does not have to be signed by both parties, but only by the party to be charged or that person's agent.[67] The signature need not be an actual subscription of the party's name, it may be a mark; nor need it be in writing, it may be printed or stamped; nor need it be placed at the end of the document, it may be at the beginning or in the middle.[68] Section 2(3) of the 1989 Act requires all the parties to a contract for the sale or disposition of an interest in land or their agents to sign the document incorporating the terms.[69]

(ii) Parties and subject-matter

In a contract of guarantee, the parties and the subject-matter of the contract must appear in the note or memorandum. Where the parties are not named they must be so described as to be identified with ease and certainty.[70] All the material terms of the guarantee must be accurately set out in the memorandum, but by section 3 of the Mercantile Law Amendment Act 1856, the consideration need not be stated.

---

[65] *Ibid.*, at p. 64. This was anticipated by the Law Commission, Law Com. No. 164, § 5.7. On collateral contracts, see *post*, p. 130.

[66] *Post*, pp. 84–6.

[67] *Ante*, p. 78.

[68] *Leeman* v. *Stocks* [1951] Ch. 941. See also *Walker* v. *Copp Clark Publishing Co. Ltd.* (1962) 33 D.L.R. (2d) 338, at p. 344.

[69] For the position where the contract is made by an agent on behalf of an unnamed or undisclosed principal, see *post*, p. 691.

[70] *Rossiter* v. *Miller* (1878) 3 App. Cas. 1124. Cf. *Potter* v. *Duffield* (1874) L.R. 18 Eq. 4.

In a contract for the disposition of an interest in land the parties must all be identified by their signature and all the express terms must be incorporated in the document. Section 2 does not require the inclusion of implied terms, such as a landlord's covenant of quiet enjoyment,[71] and, if the parties have reached agreement but fail to record all the terms in writing or record one or more of them wrongly, the Court may order the written document to be rectified.[72] Where the written agreement is so rectified, the order does not necessarily have retrospective effect; 'the contract shall come into being ... at such time as may be specified in the order'.[73] Where contracts are exchanged each document must contain the express terms and be signed by the parties.[74]

(iii) Several documents

The note or memorandum of a guarantee may consist of various letters and papers, but they must be connected and complete.[75]

In a contract for the disposition of an interest in land the incorporation of the express terms in the document can occur either by their being set out or by reference to some other document or documents. Formerly, implied reference in the signed document sufficed.[76] Although it is not clear from the wording of section 2(2) of the 1989 Act, which differs from the Law Commission's Draft Bill, whether such reference will suffice, the Commission was content for the established rules as to joinder to apply,[77] and it appears that section 2(2) was intended to allow reference to more than one document.[78] Where the document has not been incorporated, it may, as we have seen, nevertheless be effective if it is a separate supplementary or collateral agreement.

(f) THE EFFECT OF NON-COMPLIANCE

The fundamental change effected by the 1989 Act is that, whereas the form required under the earlier legislation is merely evidentiary and does not go to the *existence* of the contract, the form required by section 2 of the 1989 Act does.

The effect of a failure to comply with the provisions of the Statute of Frauds is simply that the contract is not void, or voidable, but it cannot be enforced against a party who has not signed a note or memorandum because it is incapable of proof.[79] No action can be brought until the omission is made good. Thus, provided the note or

---

[71] *Markham* v. *Paget* [1908] 1 Ch. 697.

[72] On rectification see *post*, p. 339.

[73] Law of Property (Miscellaneous Provisions) Act 1989, s. 2(4). See Law Com. No. 164, § 5.6.

[74] 1989 Act, s. 2(1), *ante*, p. 82.

[75] *Stokes* v. *Whicher* [1920] 1 Ch. 411, at p. 418; *Elias* v. *George Saheley & Co. (Barbados) Ltd.* [1983] 1 A.C. 646. Cf. *Timmins* v. *Moreland Street Property Ltd.* [1958] Ch. 110.

[76] Law of Property Act 1925, s. 40(1); *Timmins* v. *Moreland Street Property Ltd.* [1958] Ch. 110.

[77] Law Com. No. 164, § 4.6.

[78] 503 H.L. Deb. 1988/89 col. 610 (Lord Mackay of Clashfern L.C.).

[79] *Leroux* v. *Brown* (1852) 12 C.B. 801; *Maddison* v. *Alderson* (1883) 8 App. Cas. 467, at p. 474.

memorandum acknowledges the existence of the contract,[80] it may be made at any time before the commencement of the action,[81] and it does not matter that it was never intended to serve as a note or memorandum but was prepared for some entirely different purpose.[82]

As a contract for the disposition of an interest in land 'can only be made in writing and only by incorporating all the [express] terms', as noted above, an agreement not complying with the requirements of section 2 is a nullity.[83] Thus, whereas a guarantee may be enforceable either by having a written agreement signed by the party to be charged or by his agent or by having a note or memorandum of the agreement, which could be oral, similarly signed at a later date,[84] an oral agreement subject to section 2 of the 1989 Act cannot be subsequently validated in this way. The Law Commission stated that a regime, such as those under the Statute of Frauds 1677 and the Law of Property Act 1925, s. 40(1), which 'allows oral contracts to be binding but unenforceable and which may later become enforceable, but sometimes only against one party, is indefensibly confusing'.[85]

At the heart of the Law Commission's recommendations was the view that the equitable doctrine of part performance should 'no longer have a role to play in contracts concerning land'.[86] Under this doctrine, the Courts, in certain cases, allowed an unenforceable oral contract concerning land to be proved by oral evidence, when the party seeking to enforce the contract had done acts in performance of its obligations under it, provided that the performance was referable to some contract,[87] the acts were performed by the person seeking to enforce the contract,[88] and the contract was one which, if properly evidenced, would have been specifically enforceable.[89] This requirement meant the doctrine had no application to contracts of guarantee which equity would not specifically enforce.

Under the new law, although the doctrine of part performance can no longer apply as such, the Commission considered that the parties to an agreement that does not comply with the statutory requirements would not simply be left without a remedy.[90]

---

[80] *Buxton v. Rust* (1872) L.R. 7 Ex. 279 (notwithstanding announcement of intention to repudiate contract). See also *Reuss v. Picksley* (1866) L.R. 1 Ex. 342; *Parker v. Clark* [1960] 1 W.L.R. 286 (written offer containing all material terms suffices though contract concluded by subsequent oral acceptance). Cf. *Thirkell v. Cambi* [1919] 2 K.B. 590 (writing denying agreement or a material term insufficient); *Tiverton Estates Ltd v. Wearwell Ltd.* [1975] Ch. 146 (agreement 'subject to contract' insufficient).

[81] *Re Hoyle* [1893] 1 Ch. 84; *Elpis Maritime Co. Ltd. v. Marti Chartering Co. Inc.* [1992] 1 A.C. 21.

[82] *Jones v. Victoria Dock Co.* (1877) 2 Q.B.D. 314 (entry in company's minute book); *Phillips v. Butler* [1945] Ch. 358 (receipt for deposit).

[83] *United Bank of Kuwait v. Sahib* [1997] Ch. 107, at pp. 122, 136; Law Com. No. 164, § 6.4.

[84] *Elpis Maritime Co. Ltd. v. Marti Chartering Co. Inc.* [1992] 1 A.C. 21, at p. 28.

[85] Law Com. No. 164, § 4.2.

[86] *Ibid.*, § 4.13.

[87] *Rawlinson v. Ames* [1925] Ch. 96; *Steadman v. Steadman* [1976] A.C. 536 (mere payment of a sum of money could amount to a sufficient act of part performance, but differing views were expressed as to whether the acts performed must be referable to some contract *concerning land*: *ibid.*, at pp. 542, 547, 554, 562, 568–70, on which see *Re Gonin* [1979] Ch. 16; *Sutton v. Sutton* [1984] Ch. 184). Cf. *Maddison v. Alderson* (1883) 8 App. Cas. 467.

[88] *Caton v. Caton* (1865) L.R. 1 Ch. App. 137, at p. 148, aff'd. (1867) L.R. 2 H.L. 167.

[89] *Britain v. Rossiter* (1882) 11 Q.B.D. 123; *McManus v. Cooke* (1887) 35 Ch. D. 681, at p. 697.

[90] Law Com. No. 164, §§ 5.1–5.2.

The use of collateral contracts and the remedy of rectification have been mentioned above.[91] It should also be noted that where the void contract has been performed, for example by the execution of a valid lease or the completion of a conveyance, a property right will have been created and the parties may not need to rely on the void contract.[92] But the primary tools the Commission anticipated would be used to enable justice to be achieved between the particular parties are the equitable doctrine of estoppel and restitutionary obligations to repay money or make recompense for work done.

(g) ESTOPPEL AND RESTITUTIONARY REMEDIES

Under the doctrine of proprietary estoppel, which is considered in section V(d) of this chapter, a party to a transaction who either detrimentally relies on the belief (encouraged or acquiesced in by the other party) that he has or will acquire rights in the property of the other or who has conducted dealings in reliance on an underlying assumption as to a present, past, or future state of affairs, or a promise by the other that strict legal rights will not be insisted upon, will be protected by equity. Thus, the Law Commission pointed to a case in which acquiescence in improvements to a property was held to justify the conveyance of the fee simple[93] and another in which non-contractual assurances that a housekeeper could remain in a house were protected by equitable relief.[94] Proprietary estoppel, will, however, generally only be available to protect a purchaser. Moreover, in its present state of development in English law,[95] the doctrine of promissory estoppel only operates to modify an existing legal relationship and does not create new causes of action where, as in the case of an agreement that is void for non-compliance with section 2 of the 1989 Act, none existed before. Since section 2(5) of the 1989 Act only takes the 'creation or operation of resulting, implied or constructive trusts' out of the section it may therefore only cover proprietary estoppel. Even in the case of proprietary estoppel, if granting relief will in substance have the effect of enforcing a void contract, as it sometimes can in cases of estoppel,[96] it is arguable that it subverts the policy underlying section 2.[97] Although the Courts are likely to be unsympathetic to those who seek to rely on the statute in ways considered to be unmeritorious,[98] they will have to overcome considerations such as these either by reference to the intention of the Law Commission or by willingness to find a constructive trust based on a common understanding or arrangement which has been relied upon by the claimant.[99] A constructive

---

[91] *Ante*, p. 83, n. 65; p. 84, n. 72.

[92] *Tootal Clothing Ltd.* v. *Guinea Properties Ltd.* (1991) 64 P. &. C.R. 455.

[93] *Pascoe* v. *Turner* [1979] 1 W.L.R. 431.

[94] *Greasley* v. *Cooke* [1980] 1 W.L.R. 1306.

[95] See *post*, pp. 122–4 for criticism of the present position.

[96] See, e.g. *Crabb* v. *Arun D.C.* [1976] Ch. 179, *post*, p. 120.

[97] *Godden* v. *Merthyr Tydfil Housing Association* (1997) 74 P. & C.R. D1, *per* Simon Brown L.J.; *Yaxley* v. *Gotts* [2000] Ch. 162.

[98] *McCausland* v. *Duncan Lawrie Ltd.* [1997] 1 W.L.R. 38, *per* Morrit L.J. at p. 50.

[99] As in *Yaxley* v. *Gotts* [2000] Ch. 162 (such a trust found in circumstances in which doctrine of part performance might have applied before the 1989 Act).

trust of this sort is closely akin to if not indistinguishable from proprietary estoppel.[100]

The parties to an agreement that does not comply with section 2 may also be entitled to a restitutionary remedy. In principle a purchaser of land who has paid a deposit to the vendor under such an agreement, i.e. a void contract, may recover it,[101] except where the purchaser has received part of the benefit bargained for in the contract, for example by entering into possession.[102] A guarantor who has paid money under an oral guarantee believing that the contract was enforceable may be able to recover it as money paid under a mistake,[103] but as the contract is unenforceable not void, recovery may not otherwise be possible.[104]

Where services are rendered under an agreement concerning land which does not comply with the requirements of section 2 in the belief that there was a valid contract, the party conferring the services may be able to recover their reasonable value.[105] Thus, for example, reasonable recompense should be awarded in respect of alterations to property effected by a lessor or vendor at the request of prospective tenants or purchasers in the belief that there was a valid contract.[106] In principle, recompense should also be awarded in respect of services rendered by the prospective purchaser or lessee, for example improvements to the property and other services rendered at the request of or with the acceptance of the owner of property. As this would be limited to the executed part of the transaction, it would not seem to undermine the policy of section 2, just as recompense in respect of services rendered under contracts unenforceable for non-compliance with the Statute of Frauds and similar provisions has not been held to undermine the policy of those provisions.[107]

It is apparent that both estoppel and restitutionary obligations may provide what in many cases was hitherto provided by the doctrine of part performance: a remedy in a situation in which a party has acted on the void contract. Indeed, there are significant overlaps. Both estoppel and part performance can be seen as manifestations of the equitable principle that a person may not rely on strict legal rights where to do so is unconscionable,[108] and the rendering of bargained-for performance, which is the key to the availability of restitutionary recompense, looks very much like part performance under another name. There is, however, a significant difference since under the doctrine of part performance the executory parts of a contract that has

[100] *Ibid.*, *per* Robert Walker L.J. at p. 176.

[101] See *Rover International Ltd.* v. *Cannon Film Sales Ltd. (No. 3)* [1989] 1 W.L.R. 912, at pp. 925, 938; *Westdeutsche Landesbank Girozentrale* v. *Islington L.B.C.* [1996] A.C. 669.

[102] *Linz* v. *Electric Wire Co. of Palestine* [1948] A.C. 371, at p. 377. On what count as such benefits, see *post*, p. 644. Note that the requirement that the failure of consideration be *total* has been put into question, see *post*, p. 645.

[103] *Kleinwort Benson Ltd.* v. *Lincoln C.C.* [1999] 2 A.C. 349 (mistake of law).

[104] *Monnickendam* v. *Leanse* (1923) 39 T.L.R. 445 (a case on the Statute of Frauds).

[105] *Rover International Ltd.* v. *Cannon Film Sales Ltd. (No. 3)* (*supra*, n. 101), at pp. 926–8. Cf. *Guinness plc* v. *Saunders* [1990] 2 A.C. 663, *per* Lord Templeman at pp. 689, 694.

[106] By analogy with *Brewer Street Investments Ltd.* v. *Barclays Woollen Co. Ltd.* [1954] 1 Q.B. 428, *ante*, p. 40 (anticipated contract which failed to materialize).

[107] *Deglman* v. *Guaranty Trust Co. of Canada* [1954] 3 D.L.R. 785 (Canada); *Pavey & Matthews Pty Ltd.* v. *Paul* (1986–87) 162 C.L.R. 221 (Australia).

[108] *Yaxley* v. *Gotts* [2000] Ch. 162, at pp. 176–7, 180, 181, 188, 193; *Gillett* v. *Holt* [2001] Ch. 210, at p. 225.

been part-performed could be enforced, whereas both estoppel and restitution only seek respectively to give relief for the executed part of the transaction. These equitable and restitutionary remedies and the fact, noted above, that completion of the void contract by the execution of a lease or a conveyance creates a property right so that the parties no longer need to rely on the contract explain the statement in one case that:[109]

[S]ection 2 is of relevance only to executory contracts. It has no relevance to contracts which have been completed. If parties choose to complete an oral land contract or a land contract that does not in some respect or other comply with section 2, they are at liberty to do so. Once they have done so, it becomes irrelevant that the contract they have completed may not have been in accordance with section 2.

It has been suggested[110] that the uncertainties of the Statute of Frauds and section 40(1) of the Law of Property Act 1925 stemmed from the tendency of the judges to prevent technical and unmeritorious circumvention of obligations by relying on non-compliance with the statutory requirements. The early indications are of a similar approach to the 1989 Act with its new uncertainties. The Law Commission's recognition that it would be necessary to rely on estoppel, restitution, and collateral contracts 'to do justice between parties in individual otherwise hard cases'[111] in which the strict application of the statutory requirement would result in injustice, accepted this substantial qualification to its stated aim of increasing certainty.

IV. CONSIDERATION

(a) CONSIDERATION DEFINED

It has already been stated that consideration is a universal requisite of contracts not made by deed. A promise is not accordingly of itself enforceable in English law. Consideration is the doctrine designed to establish which promises should be legally enforceable.[112] What, then, is it? In *Currie* v. *Misa*[113] Lush J. stated:

A valuable consideration, in the sense of the law, may consist in some right, interest, profit, or benefit accruing to the one party, or some forbearance, detriment, loss, or responsibility given, suffered, or undertaken by the other.

This brings out the idea of reciprocity as the distinguishing mark; it is the gratuitous promise that is unenforceable in English law.

We shall, however, see that consideration reflects a variety of policies and serves a

---

[109] *Tootal Clothing Ltd.* v. *Guinea Properties Ltd.* (1991) 64 P. & C.R. 452, *per* Scott L.J. at p. 455; Wilde (1993) 109 L.Q.R. 191.

[110] *Ante*, pp. 77, 80.

[111] Law Com. No. 164, §§ 5.7. See also *ibid.* §§ 5.2, 5.4, 5.8.

[112] See Atiyah, *Essays on Contract* (1986), ch. 8; Treitel (1976) 50 A.L.J. 439.

[113] (1875) L.R. 10 Ex. 153, at p. 162. See also *Thomas* v. *Thomas* (1842) 2 Q.B. 851, at p. 859; *Bolton* v. *Madden* (1873) L.R. 9 Q.B. 55, at p. 56.

number of functions.[114] First, enforceability may depend on the content of the promise or the circumstances in which it was made.[115] Thus, promises to do what one is
already obliged to do, particularly where a contract has been renegotiated or the
promise is not made at the request of the promisee have, as we shall see, caused
difficulties. Secondly, consideration has been said to identify which promises the
parties intend to be legally enforceable. They may so intend either where there is a
substantive bargain, or where they have put the transaction into the form of an
exchange, for instance by providing that the promisee should pay a nominal price to
the promisor. It thus serves an evidential and formal function.[116] Thirdly, consideration is sometimes seen as a requirement which ensures that a promisor has deliberately decided to contract and prevents parties accidentally binding themselves on
impulse.[117]

(i) Benefit or detriment

It will be seen from the definition in *Currie* v. *Misa* that consideration consists either
in some benefit to the promisor or some detriment to the promisee; but there is
considerable controversy as to the relative importance of these two factors. It is
universally conceded that detriment to the promisee is a good consideration, since
detriment is, as Sir Frederick Pollock has succinctly stated, 'the price for which the
promise of the other is bought'.[118] On the other hand, many modern authorities
consider that benefit to the promisor is merely an accident, particularly in view of
the rule that consideration must move from, i.e. be provided by, the promisee.[119] Yet
the element of benefit cannot be entirely disregarded, since there are some cases in
which a promise has been held not to be gratuitous on the ground that it secured
some benefit including 'practical' benefit to the promisor, though without any real
detriment to the promisee. So, for example, there was a contract between a pupil
barrister and the chambers whose offer of pupillage she had accepted. Even though
no detriment was suffered by her, the benefit to the chambers in having a pool of
pupil barristers who would compete for recruitment as members of chambers
sufficed.[120]

(ii) Given in return for the promise

The consideration must necessarily be given in return for the promise, and it is

---

[114] Llewellyn (1941) 41 Col. L. Rev. 777, 778, 863; Simpson (1975) 9 L.Q.R. 247, at p. 263.

[115] *Post*, pp. 281–2 (pre-existing duties and duress).

[116] Fuller (1941) 41 Col. L. Rev. 799; Cohen (1933) 46 Harv. L. Rev. 553, 582–3; *post*, pp. 124–6.

[117] *Pillans* v. *Van Mierop* (1765) 3 Burr. 1663, *per* Wilmot J. at p. 1670.

[118] *Principles of Contract*, 13th edn. (1950), p. 133 (and earlier editions), approved in *Dunlop Tyre Co. Ltd.*
v. *Selfridge Ltd.* [1915] A.C. 847, at p. 855, and by the Sixth Interim Report of the Law Revision Committee,
Statute of Frauds and the Doctrine of Consideration (Cmd. 5449, 1937), p. 12. Cf. Atiyah, *Essays on Contract*
(1986), p. 183 (consideration is a 'reason for the recognition of an obligation').

[119] See *post*, p. 95.

[120] *Edmonds* v. *Lawson* [2000] Q.B. 501. See also *Alliance Bank Ltd.* v. *Broom* (1864) 2 Dr. & Sm. 289, *post*,
p. 100; *De la Bere* v. *Pearson* [1908] 1 K.B. 280, *post*, p. 97 n. 164; *Ward* v. *Byham* [1956] 1 W.L.R. 496, at p. 498,
post, p. 103; *Chappell & Co. Ltd.* v. *Nestlé Co. Ltd.* [1960] A.C. 87, *post*, p. 90; *Williams* v. *Roffey Bros. & Nicholls
(Contractors) Ltd.* [1991] 1 Q.B. 1, at pp. 15–16, *post*, p. 106.

usually, although not invariably,[121] given at the request of the promisor. The promisee must, therefore, prove either an exchange of promises (e.g. a promise to supply goods in return for a promise to pay for them) or some act or forbearance on the part of the promisee in return for the promise made. A benefit conferred or a detriment suffered otherwise than in return for the promise of the other party cannot constitute consideration.[122] In particular, there will be no consideration merely because there is detrimental action by the promisee in *reliance* on the promise, but not in *return* for it. Thus, in *Combe* v. *Combe*,[123] where a husband, upon divorce, promised his wife a permanent allowance of £100 a year, the Court of Appeal refused to hold that a consequent forbearance on the part of the wife to apply for maintenance amounted to consideration. The husband had not requested her to forbear, and her action could not be said to have been in return for his promise to pay.

(iii) Consideration and condition

Consideration must also be distinguished from the fulfilment of a condition. If A says to B, 'I will give you £500 if you break your leg', there is no contract, but simply a gratuitous promise subject to a condition.[124] Where the condition consists of the performance of some act by the promisee, the position may be more doubtful. If C says to D, 'You can have my flat if you move in and look after me', there may still be only a conditional gift, unless performance of the stipulation is regarded by the parties as the price to be paid for the promise.[125] This issue was discussed in *Chappell & Co. Ltd.* v. *Nestlé Co. Ltd.*:[126]

C were the owners of the copyright of a tune called 'Rockin' Shoes' and N were manufacturers of chocolate. N offered to the public gramophone records of this tune in return for 1s./6d. and the wrappers from three bars of their chocolate. Under the statutory provisions then in force[127] any person had an automatic right to use a copyright tune for a record, provided he paid a certain percentage of the 'ordinary retail selling price' of the record to the copyright owner. C contended that N could not rely on the statute, since it contemplated a price consisting of money alone, whereas in this case the consideration for the record included three chocolate wrappers.

The House of Lords, by a bare majority, held that the wrappers formed part of the selling price (consideration) for the record. The object of selling the record was to increase the sales of chocolate and the stipulated evidence of such sales formed part of

----

[121] Goodhart (1951) 67 L.Q.R. 456 effectively demonstrates that a request is not essential to a binding obligation provided that the consideration is referable to the promise. Cf. Smith (1953) 69 L.Q.R. 99. See also *Ball* v. *National and Grindlays Bank Ltd.* [1973] Ch. 127.

[122] *Wigan* v. *English and Scottish Law Life Assurance Association* [1909] 1 Ch. 291; *Lipkin Gorman* v. *Karpnale Ltd.* [1991] 2 A.C. 548, at pp. 561, 575, *post*, p. 98.

[123] [1951] 2 K.B. 215; see *post*, p. 119.

[124] *Shadwell* v. *Shadwell* (1860) 9 C.B.N.S. 159, *per* Byles J. at p. 177.

[125] *Ellis* v. *Chief Adjudication Officer* [1998] 1 F.L.R. 184 (no intent to contract and condition not performed).

[126] [1960] A.C. 87.

[127] Copyright Act 1956, s. 8. The statutory licence to record was abolished by the Copyright, Designs and Patents Act 1988, s. 170 and Sched. 1, para. 21.

the consideration. The acquisition of the wrappers was not simply a condition limiting the class of persons qualified to purchase records.

(iv) Consideration and gift

There may also be difficulty in distinguishing consideration from a gift. In *Esso Petroleum Co. Ltd. v. Customs and Excise Commissioners*,[128] a petrol company offered one coin, depicting a World Cup footballer, to every customer who purchased four gallons of petrol. A majority of the House of Lords held that the coin was an offer of consideration to the customer to enter into a contract of sale of petrol,[129] but the minority considered that the coin was a gift.

(b) NECESSITY FOR CONSIDERATION

Consideration is necessary for the formation of every simple contract; a promise (unless in a deed) made without consideration is not actionable as a contract[130] in English law.

As we have seen, from the very beginning of the action of *assumpsit*, a plaintiff who could not produce a sealed instrument had to show that he had contributed to the bargain by furnishing a valuable consideration of some kind.[131] In 1756, however, Lord Mansfield became Chief Justice of the King's Bench, and the doctrine of consideration was attacked by him in two fundamental respects. In the first place, he asserted that consideration was only one of several modes of supplying evidence of the promisor's intention to be bound; and that if the terms of a contract were reduced to writing by reason of commercial custom, or in obedience to statutory requirement, such evidence dispensed with the need for consideration.[132] In *Rann v. Hughes*, however, Lord Mansfield's proposal was overruled. Skynner C.B. stated:[133]

All contracts are by the law of England divided into agreements by speciality and agreements by parol; nor is there any such third class as some of the counsel have endeavoured to maintain as contracts in writing. If they be merely written and not specialties, they are parol, and a consideration must be proved.

Lord Mansfield's second attack was to hold that the existence of a previous moral obligation was sufficient to support an express, but gratuitous, promise.[134] This looser usage of consideration as equivalent to the civilian requirement of 'causa' was finally rejected in *Eastwood v. Kenyon*:[135]

---

[128] [1976] 1 W.L.R. 1.

[129] Or (Lord Fraser) to pay the money price.

[130] But see Denning (1952) 15 M.L.R. 1, and *post*, p. 113.

[131] *Ante*, pp. 13–16.

[132] *Pillans v. Van Mierop* (1765) 3 Burr. 1663. This is the position in Scotland: Lord Normand (1939) 55 L.Q.R. 358.

[133] (1778) 7 T.R. 350n. It should be noted, however, that the only report of the actual decision of the House of Lords states that the case was decided on the ground of failure to comply with the Statute of Frauds: (1778) 4 Brown P.C. 27.

[134] *Lee v. Muggeridge* (1813) 5 Taunt. 36, at p. 46 *per* Sir James Mansfield C.J. (who was Chief Justice of Common Pleas).

[135] (1840) 11 A. & E. 438.

E had been guardian and agent of Mrs K while she was a minor, and had incurred expenses in the improvement of her property: he did this voluntarily, and, in order to do so, was compelled to borrow money, for which he gave a promissory note. When Mrs K came of age she assented to the transaction, and after her marriage her husband promised to pay the note. He was sued upon this promise.

It was held that the moral obligation to fulfil such a promise was insufficient where the consideration was wholly past. 'Indeed', said Lord Denman,[136] 'the doctrine would annihilate the necessity for any consideration at all, inasmuch as the mere fact of giving a promise creates a moral obligation to perform it'.

From that time onwards, every promise not in a deed has been subject to a general and uniform test of actionability. In each case it became necessary to ask whether the promisor gets any benefit or the promisee sustains any detriment, present or future, in respect of the promise. If not, the promise was gratuitous, and was not binding. The variety of policies that may be reflected in the doctrine of consideration has been noted. In working out this doctrine to its logical results it has, no doubt, happened from time to time that the Courts have been compelled to hold a promise to be invalid which the parties intended to be binding, or that the slightness of the benefit or detriment which has been held to constitute a consideration has tended to bring the requirement into ridicule. The Courts are reluctant to describe a promise made in a commercial context as gratuitous and it has been said that 'a defence of lack of consideration rarely has merit'[137] and that 'businessmen know their own business best even when they appear to grant an indulgence'.[138] The doctrine has therefore been the subject of considerable criticism,[139] but it is advisable to reserve a discussion of this until the general rules governing the application of consideration to contracts have been examined.

(c) EXECUTORY AND EXECUTED CONSIDERATION

As far as the relation of the consideration to the promise in respect of time, is concerned, a consideration may be *executory*, a promise given for a promise; or it may be *executed*, an act or forbearance given for a promise.

An *executory* consideration consists of a promise to do, forbear, or suffer, given in return for a like promise. Thus mutual promises, for example, a promise to do work in return for a promise of payment, are illustrations of executory consideration. The fact that the promise given for a promise may be dependent upon a condition does not affect its validity as consideration. A promises B to do a piece of work for which B

---

[136] At p. 450. See also *Guinness Mahon & Co. Ltd. v. Kensington & Chelsea R.B.C.* [1999] Q.B. 215, *per* Robert Walker L.J. at p. 236 ('potentially very confusing').

[137] *Thorensen Car Ferries Ltd. v. Weymouth Portland B.C.* [1977] 2 Lloyd's Rep. 614, *per* Donaldson J. at p. 619.

[138] *Woodhouse A.C. Israel Cocoa Ltd. S.A. v. Nigerian Produce Marketing Co. Ltd.* [1972] A.C. 741, *per* Lord Hailsham L.C. at pp. 757–8. See also *New Zealand Shipping Co. Ltd. v. Satterthwaite* [1975] A.C. 154, at p. 157, *post*, p. 103.

[139] See the Sixth Interim Report of the Law Revision Committee (Cmd. 5449, 1937).

promises to pay if the workmanship is approved by a third party. The promise of B is consideration for the promise of A.

A contract arises upon a present or *executed* consideration when one of the two parties has, either in the act which constitutes an offer or the act which constitutes an acceptance, done all that party is bound to do under the contract, leaving an outstanding liability on one side only. The case of an act which constitutes an offer may be illustrated by the example of one who offers to do work or provide goods in circumstances that show an obvious expectation that payment be made; the contract arises when the work or goods are accepted by the person to whom they are offered, and that person by accepting them becomes bound to pay a reasonable price. So if a wine merchant sends to a customer a selection of wines, and the customer retains some and returns the rest, the customer will be bound to pay for those retained, since the tender of the wine will be at once the offer and the consideration for the obligation.[140] On the other hand, a contract for which the consideration is the act which constitutes an acceptance is best illustrated by the case of an advertisement of a reward for services, which becomes a binding promise when the service is rendered. In such cases it is not the offeror, but the acceptor, who has performed at the moment when the contract is entered into. If A makes a general offer of reward for information and B supplies the information, A's offer is turned into a binding promise by the act of B, and B simultaneously concludes the contract and furnishes consideration by performance.[141]

(d) PAST CONSIDERATION

Executed consideration must be distinguished from *past* consideration which is a mere sentiment of gratitude or honour prompting a return for benefits received. In the case of executed consideration, both the promise and the act which constitutes the consideration are integral and co-related parts of the same transaction.[142] In the case of past consideration, however, the promise is subsequent to the act and independent of it; they are not in substance part of the same transaction. Thus if A saves B from drowning, and B later promises A a reward, A's action cannot be relied on as consideration for B's promise for it is past in point of time. Past consideration is, in effect, no consideration at all; that is to say it confers no benefit on the promisor, and involves no detriment to the promisee in return for the promise. It is merely an act or forbearance in time past by which a person has benefited without incurring any legal liability. If afterwards, whether from good feeling or interested motives, the person who has benefited makes a promise to the person whose act or forbearance led to the benefit, and that promise is made upon no other consideration than the past benefit, it is gratuitous and cannot be enforced. In *Roscorla* v. *Thomas*[143] this principle was clearly stated:

---

[140] *Hart* v. *Mills* (1846) 15 M. & W. 85; Cf. *Taylor* v. *Laird* (1856) 1 H. & N. 266; *ante*, p. 36.
[141] *Ante*, pp. 35 and 39. See *Carlill* v. *Carbolic Smoke Ball Co.* [1893] 1 Q.B. 256.
[142] *Westminster C.C.* v. *Duke of Westminster* [1991] 4 All E.R. 136, at p. 145.
[143] (1842) 3 Q.B. 234. See also *Re McArdle* [1951] Ch. 669; *Savage* v. *Uwechia* [1961] 1 W.L.R. 455.

The plaintiff purchased a horse from the defendant, who afterwards, in consideration of the previous sale, warranted that the horse was sound and free from vice. It was in fact a vicious horse.

The Court held that the sale itself created no implied warranty that the horse was not vicious. The warranty had therefore to be regarded as independent of the sale and as an express promise based upon a previous transaction. It fell, therefore, 'within the general rule that a consideration past and executed will support no other promise than such as would be implied by law'.

The general rule is, however, subject to certain exceptions.

(i) Previous request of the promisor

A past consideration will, it has been said, support a subsequent promise, if the consideration was given at the request of the promisor. Originally this was an unqualified exception based on the fact that, as was said in 1615 in *Lampleigh* v. *Brathwait*:[144]

the promise though it follows, yet it is not naked, but couples itself with the suit before, and the merits of the party procured by that suit, which is the difference.

In the nineteenth century, however, with the rejection of Lord Mansfield's view that a previous moral obligation might be good consideration,[145] the scope of the exception was restricted. By the end of the nineteenth century it was clear that a past service performed at the request of the promisor will only amount to consideration if it was assumed at the time that the service was ultimately to be paid for.

In *Re Casey's Patents, Stewart* v. *Casey*,[146] the owners of certain patent rights promised their manager a one-third share of the patents in consideration of his services in having worked for them. The Court of Appeal rejected the argument that this consideration was past. It held that the fact of the services by the manager raised an implication that they were to be paid for; the subsequent promise to pay was then an admission of a bargain and fixed the amount of the remuneration on the basis of which the services were originally rendered.

In *Pau On* v. *Lau Yiu Long*[147] the Judicial Committee of the Privy Council stated the conditions in which this exception will apply as follows:

An act done before the giving of a promise to make a payment or to confer some other benefit can sometimes be consideration for the promise. The act must have been done at the promisor's request, the parties must have understood that the act was to be remunerated either by a payment or the conferment of some other benefit, and payment, or the conferment of a benefit, must have been legally enforceable had it been promised in advance.

In that case the defendant had requested the plaintiff to promise not to sell certain shares for a year and later promised to indemnify the plaintiff if the shares fell below a

---

[144] (1615) Hob. 105, at p. 106 (subsequent promise to pay for requested attempt to obtain pardon held enforceable).

[145] *Ante*, p. 91.

[146] [1892] 1 Ch. 104. See also *Kennedy* v. *Broun* (1863) 13 C.B.N.S. 677, at p. 740.

[147] [1980] A.C. 614, at p. 629. See *post*, p. 105 for the facts.

certain price. The defendant contended that the consideration for the indemnity was past but it was held that all three conditions mentioned above were satisfied.

It is arguable, however, that this exception is an apparent rather than a real departure from the general doctrine as to past consideration. When a request is made which is in substance an offer of a promise upon terms to be afterwards ascertained, and an act is done in pursuance of that request, a subsequent promise to pay a fixed sum or to confer some other benefit may be regarded as a part of the same transaction, the effect of the promise being merely to render certain that which was uncertain before.

(ii) An antecedent debt

It has long been decided that the existence of an existing debt is sufficient consideration for a subsequent promise to pay that debt.[148] It should not be supposed, however, that the existence of a debt from A to B will always be consideration for any subsequent promise which A may make. There must be present consideration in the form of a forbearance to sue, or else, if a security is given by the debtor, it must be communicated to the promisee and induce such a forbearance.[149]

(iii) Negotiable instruments

By section 27(1) of the Bills of Exchange Act 1882, valuable consideration for a bill may be constituted by (a) any consideration sufficient to support a simple contract; or (b) an antecedent debt or liability. So if A, whose account at the bank is overdrawn, negotiates to its banker a cheque drawn by a stranger, the banker becomes a holder for value of the cheque, as the antecedent debt of A is consideration for the instrument.[150] This is a genuine exception to the rule.

(e) CONSIDERATION MUST MOVE FROM THE PROMISEE

A party to a contract who wishes to enforce the contract must furnish or have furnished consideration for the promise of the other party. It is not, however, necessary that it should have been intended to benefit the other party. It must move from the promisee but it need not move to the promisor.

This rule must be distinguished from the common law doctrine of *privity of contract*, with which it is often confused. Until the enactment of the Contracts (Rights of Third Parties) Act 1999, it was a general rule of English law that a contract cannot confer any rights on one who is not a party to it, even though the very object of the contract may have been to benefit the non-party or third party.[151] The third party was unable to sue because there is no privity of contract between the third party and the promisor. This inability of one who is not a party to the contract to acquire rights under it followed from the view which English law formerly adopted as to the operation of contract generally and *which persons* can sue and be sued on a contract. It has

---

[148] *Slade's Case* (1602) 4 Co. Rep. 91a, *ante*, p. 15. Note that such promises, if in writing, can have the effect of extending the limitation period, *post*, p. 656.

[149] *Wigan* v. *English and Scottish Law Life Assurance Association* [1909] 1 Ch. 291.

[150] But see *Oliver* v. *Davis* [1949] 2 K.B. 727.

[151] *Post*, Chapter 10.

no particular connection with the doctrine of consideration, which is concerned with the separate policy question of *which promises* should be enforced.[152] Nevertheless, an additional reason for refusing an action would be that the third-party will normally have furnished no consideration.[153] For example, in *Tweddle* v. *Atkinson*[154] a contract between the fathers of a married couple provided that each should make a payment to the husband who should have power to sue for the payments. It was held that the husband could not sue: he was not only not a party to the contract, but also no consideration had moved from him, and so the promise was, as far as he was concerned, a gratuitous one.

It is perhaps because the rules of privity and of consideration sometimes coincide in this way that some see them as opposite sides of the same coin, so that even if a party to the contract has provided consideration, a third party could not sue on it because the person seeking to enforce the contract must have provided the consideration.[155] But the rules do not, in fact, always coincide in this way. If, for example, A and B enter into an agreement under which A promises B that if C will dig A's garden, A will pay £10 to B, B cannot enforce the promise. B is the promisee under the agreement but has provided no consideration. B has suffered no detriment (unless B impliedly undertook to procure that C would dig the garden) and, although A has received a benefit, that benefit was conferred by a third party, C, and not by B. The rule that consideration must move from the promisee is thus distinct from that of privity of contract. It is not enough that consideration should have been given; it must have been given by the promisee.[156] The separation of the two rules has been confirmed by the Contracts (Rights of Third Parties) Act 1999, since where a third party is able to enforce a contract under that Act it is necessary for the promisee to have given consideration and it is not necessary for the third party to have done so.

There are, however, a number of exceptions to this rule. In the case of negotiable instruments, for example, it is not necessary that the person seeking to enforce the instrument should personally have furnished consideration, provided that consideration has at some time during the history of the instrument been given.[157] Trusts constitute another major exception, and other instances where the rule need not be observed will be found in the chapter on third parties below.[158]

---

[152] *Tweddle* v. *Atkinson* (1861) 1 B. & S. 393; *Dunlop Pneumatic Tyre Co Ltd* v. *Selfridge and Co Ltd* [1915] AC 847, at p. 853; Law Revision Committee, Sixth Interim Report, (1937) para. 37 supports the view that the rules are distinct, as does the Law Commission, albeit more equivocally, Law Com No. 242 (1996) Part VI.

[153] *Dunlop Pneumatic Tyre Co. Ltd.* v. *Selfridge & Co. Ltd.* [1915] A.C. 847, at p. 855; *post*, p. 423.

[154] [1861] 1 B. & S. 393; *post*, p. 422.

[155] Furmston (1960) 23 M.L.R. 373; Smith, *The Law of* Contract (2nd edn.) p. 94.

[156] Cf. *Coulls* v. *Bagot's Executor and Trustee Co. Ltd.* [1967] A.L.R. 385 (consideration supplied by one of two joint promisees); *McEvoy* v. *Belfast Banking Co. Ltd.* [1935] A.C. 24, at p. 43 (consideration supplied by one of two joint and several promisees).

[157] Bills of Exchange Act 1882, s. 27(2).

[158] *Post*, Chapter 10.

(f) CONSIDERATION NEED NOT BE ADEQUATE

Consideration need not be adequate to the promise, but it must be of some value in the eye of the law. The Courts will not make bargains for the parties and, if a person gets what has been contracted for, will not inquire whether it was an equivalent to the promise which was given in return. The consideration may be of benefit to the promisor, or to a third party, or may be of no apparent benefit to anybody, but merely a detriment to the promisee; in any case 'the adequacy of the consideration is for the parties to consider at the time of making the agreement, not for the Court when it is sought to be enforced'.[159] The most trifling detriment or benefit will suffice, and the following cases will show that the Courts have been prepared to find a contract where the consideration was virtually non-existent.

We have already seen that in *Chappell & Co. Ltd. v. Nestlé Co. Ltd.*[160] wrappers from chocolate bars were held to be part of the consideration for the sale of a record. In *Bainbridge v. Firmstone:*[161]

At the request of F, B allowed him to weigh two boilers provided he returned them in as good a condition as they were lent. F dismantled the boilers to weigh them and returned them in this state. B sued for breach of the agreement.

F was held liable. 'The consideration', said Patteson J.,[162] 'is that the plaintiff, at the defendant's request, had consented to allow the defendant to weigh the boilers. I suppose the defendant thought he had some benefit; at any rate, there is a detriment to the plaintiff from his parting with the possession for even so short a time'.

In *Haigh v. Brooks,*[163] the consideration of a promise to pay certain bills was the surrender of a document supposed to be a guarantee, which turned out to be of doubtful validity. The worthlessness of the document surrendered was held to be no defence to an action on the promise. The Court was not concerned with the adequacy or inadequacy of the price paid or promised. 'The plaintiffs were induced by the defendant's promise to part with something which they might have kept, and the defendant obtained what he desired by means of that promise'.[164]

The consequence of the rule that the Court is not concerned with the adequacy of consideration is that the requirement can be satisfied by nominal consideration. At common law 'a contracting party can stipulate for what consideration he chooses. A peppercorn does not cease to be good consideration if it is established that the

---

[159] *Bolton v. Madden* (1873) L.R. 9 Q.B. 55, *per* Blackburn J. at p. 57.

[160] [1960] A.C. 87, *ante*, p. 90. Cf. *Lipkin Gorman v. Karpnale Ltd.* [1991] 2 A.C. 548, at p. 561 (gaming chips not consideration, *inter alia*, because they were 'worthless'). See also *ibid.* at pp. 575, 577.

[161] (1838) 8 A. & E. 743.

[162] At p. 744.

[163] (1839) 10 A. & E. 309; aff'd *sub nom. Brooks v. Haigh* (1840) 10 A. & E. 323, where it was said by Maule J. that the delivery of the paper alone would suffice. See also *Veitch v. Sinclair* [1975] 1 N.Z.L.R. 264.

[164] (1839) 10 A. & E. 309, *per* Lord Denman C.J. at p. 320. See also *De la Bere v. Pearson* [1908] 1 K.B. 280 (possible benefit to newspaper in publishing letter held to be consideration for offer to give financial advice) although liability today would probably lie in tort: *Hedley Byrne & Co. Ltd. v. Heller & Partners Ltd.* [1964] A.C. 465.

promisee does not like pepper and will throw away the corn'.[165] Statute, however, may make the adequacy of consideration relevant in a particular context. Thus, property legislation distinguishes a transaction for 'nominal' consideration differently from one for 'valuable' consideration,[166] and the term 'consideration' in the Local Government Act 1972 only includes elements of commercial or monetary value.[167]

In the Roman law of sale, and in certain continental systems, the price had to be a fair and serious one, and if this was not so, the seller could rescind the contract unless the buyer was willing to come up to the fair price. This doctrine of *laesio enormis* forms no part of the English common law. Even where statute has intervened to protect a class of contractor, such as consumers, it does not always require a 'fair' or 'reasonable' or 'market' price.[168] In equity, however, inadequacy of consideration is treated as affording corroborative evidence of fraud or undue influence, such as may enable a promisor to resist a suit for specific performance, or to get the promise cancelled.[169] Mere inadequacy of consideration is not of itself a ground on which specific performance of a contract will be refused unless it is such as to constitute of itself conclusive evidence of fraud[170] or unconscientious conduct.[171] Thus specific performance was ordered of an option to purchase a house for £10,000 even though the consideration for the grant of the option was the nominal sum of £1.[172]

(g) CONSIDERATION MUST BE REAL

Though consideration need not be adequate, it must be real. It must be 'something which is of some value in the eye of the law'. Thus, 'it is no consideration to refrain from a course of action which it was never intended to pursue'.[173] This section examines those cases where the reality of consideration has been questioned or defined.

(i) Motive and consideration

Motive must be distinguished from consideration. In *Thomas* v. *Thomas*:[174]

A deceased husband's executor promised to allow his widow to occupy a house the deceased had owned in return for her promise to keep it in repair and to pay a ground rent of £1

---

[165] *Chappell & Co. Ltd.* v. *Nestlé Co. Ltd.* (*supra*, n. 160), *per* Lord Somervell at p. 114. See also *ante*, p. 90.
[166] Land Charges Act 1925, s. 20(8); Law of Property Act 1925, ss. 84(2) and 205(1)(xxi); *Westminster C.C.* v. *Duke of Westminster* [1991] 4 All E.R. 136, at p. 146. See also Insolvency Act 1986, s. 238 (transactions at undervalue).
[167] *R* v. *Pembrokeshire CC, ex parte Coker* [1999] 4 All E.R. 107.
[168] Unfair Terms in Consumer Contracts Regulations 1999 (S.I. 1999 No. 2083), r. 6(2)(b), on which see *post*, p. 200. Cf. Rent Act 1977, s. 70(1) (fair rent); Agricultural Holdings Act 1986, s. 12(2) (prudent and willing parties).
[169] *Post*, pp. 289, 297.
[170] *Coles* v. *Trecothick* (1804) 9 Ves. Jun. 234, *per* Lord Eldon at p. 246.
[171] *Post*, p. 634.
[172] *Mountford* v. *Scott* [1975] Ch. 258.
[173] *Arrale* v. *Costain Civil Engineering Ltd.* [1976] 1 Lloyd's Rep. 98, at p. 106. But an act may be consideration even if it is not solely induced by the promise: *Brikom Investments Ltd.* v. *Carr* [1979] Q.B. 467, at p. 490.
[174] (1842) 2 Q.B. 851.

per annum. The executor stated that the agreement was entered into 'in consideration of' the expressed desire of the deceased that his wife should have the use of the house during her lifetime.

It was held that the desire to carry out the wishes of the deceased did not amount to consideration: 'Motive is not the same thing with consideration. Consideration means something which is of some value in the eye of the law, moving from the plaintiff'.[175] In one sense, however, motive is relevant in that the consideration must be given in return for the promise; but the motive of the promisor must be to obtain a legally recognizable return for the obligation incurred, and not something which is of no value in the eye of the law. So, the desire of one member of a pop group to avoid the danger of internal dissention that might result if he had a larger income than others in the group did not constitute consideration for his promise to make payments to the others.[176]

It has already been noted that at one time the common law courts appear to have been attracted to the equitable principle that natural love and affection within a family could constitute a 'good' consideration; and that the moral obligations to make a return for past benefit was an equivalent to consideration. But past consideration is no consideration, and what the promisor gets in such a case is the satisfaction of motives of affection or gratitude. The question was settled once and for all in *Eastwood* v. *Kenyon*,[177] and the final blow given to the doctrine that consideration for a promise could consist in a motive or obligation resting on the promisor.

(ii) Impossibility

Impossibility, either physical or legal, which exists at the time of formation of the contract and is obvious upon the face of it, makes the consideration unreal. The impossibility must be obvious, such as is, 'according to the state of knowledge of the day, so absurd that the parties could not be supposed to have so contracted'.[178] Thus a covenant in a charterparty that a ship would sail on a date which was already past at the time the contract was executed was held to be void for unreality in the consideration furnished.[179] Again, the old case of *Harvy* v. *Gibbons*,[180] where a bailiff was promised £40 in consideration of a promise made by him that he would release a debt due to his master, is an example of legal impossibility. The Court held that the bailiff could not sue; that the consideration furnished by him was 'illegal', for a servant could not release a debt due to his master. By 'illegal' it is plain that the Court meant legally impossible.

---

[175] *Ibid., per* Patteson J. at p. 859. The issue arose because the executor had argued that the widow's case was procedurally defective because her declaration referred only to her promise to repair and pay rent and omitted to state part of the consideration, i.e. the desire of her deceased husband. The Court rejected this and found for the widow.

[176] *Hadley* v. *Kemp* [1999] 2 E.M.L.R. 589, *per* Park J. at p. 625.

[177] (1840) 11 A. & E. 438; *ante*, p. 91.

[178] *Clifford (Lord)* v. *Watts* (1870) L.R. 5 C.P. 577, *per* Brett J. at p. 588.

[179] *Hall* v. *Cazenove* (1804) 4 East 477.

[180] (1675) 2 Lev. 161.

(iii) Uncertainty

A promise which purports to be a consideration may be of too vague and unsubstantial a character to be enforced. Thus a promise which in terms leaves performance exclusively in the discretion of the promisor will not be enforceable; the consideration being illusory.[181] Again, in *White v. Bluett*:[182]

In proceedings by his father's executors on a promissory note, a son alleged that the father had promised to discharge him from liability in consideration of his promise to cease complaining, as he had been used to do, that he had not enjoyed as many advantages as his brothers.

It was said that the son's promise was no more than a promise 'not to bore his father', and was too vague to form a consideration for the father's promise to waive his rights on the note although, in another case, a promise to make a child happy was stated to be part of the consideration.[183] Again, it has been held that a promise to co-operate in the recovery from a joint debtor was sufficiently certain to form a consideration for a forbearance.[184] Other instances of uncertainty have already been given in connection with incomplete agreements[185] and it is possible that the recognition of 'practical' benefit as consideration[186] will mean that uncertainty should not be seen as an aspect of consideration.

(iv) Forbearance

There is a clear public interest in encouraging the avoidance of litigation and the resolution of disputes by the parties provided that the settlement or compromise is genuine, and entered into freely without the concealment of essential information, the taking of undue advantage,[187] or the exertion of illegitimate pressure.[188] A forbearance to sue, even for a short time, may be consideration for a promise, although there is no waiver or compromise of the right of action. In *Alliance Bank Ltd.* v. *Broom*:[189]

Messrs Broom were asked to give security for moneys they owed to the bank. They promised to assign the documents of title to certain goods; they failed to do so, and the bank sued for specific performance of the promise.

The Court held that the bank was entitled to this remedy:

Although there was no promise on the part of the plaintiffs to abstain for any certain time

---

[181] *Stabilad Ltd.* v. *Stephens & Carter Ltd. (No. 2)* [1999] 2 All E.R. 651, *per* Peter Gibson L.J. at p. 660.

[182] (1853) 23 L.J. Ex. 36.

[183] *Ward* v. *Byham* [1956] 1 W.L.R. 496; *post*, p. 103. See also *Dunton* v. *Dunton* (1892) 18 V.L.R. 114 (Australia); *Hamer* v. *Sidway* 27 NE 256 (1891) (USA).

[184] *Bank of Nova Scotia* v. *MacLellan* (1977) 78 D.L.R. (3d) 1 (Canada).

[185] See *ante*, p. 66.

[186] *Pitt* v. *P.H.H. Asset Management Ltd.* [1994] 1 W.L.R. 327, at p. 332; *Williams* v. *Roffey Bros. & Nicholls (Contractors) Ltd.* [1991] 1 Q.B. 1, *post*, p. 106.

[187] *Colchester B.C.* v. *Smith* [1992] Ch. 421, at p. 435. Payments made to close a transaction are irrecoverable even if there is no consideration: *Woolwich B.S.* v. *I.R.C.* [1993] A.C. 70, at p. 165; Law Com No. 227, *Restitution: Mistakes of law and ultra vires public authority receipts and payments* (1994), §§ 2.25–2.38.

[188] *Huyton S.A.* v. *Peter Cremer G.m.b.H.* [1999] 1 Lloyd's Rep. 620, at pp. 629–30.

[189] (1864) 2 Dr. & Sm. 289.

from suing for the debt, the effect was that the plaintiffs did, in effect, give, and the defend-ant received, the benefit of some degree of forbearance; not, indeed, for any definite time, but, at all events, some extent of forbearance . . . The circumstances necessarily involve the benefit to the debtor of a certain amount of forbearance, which he would not have derived if he had not made the agreement.[190]

The consideration in such a case clearly consists in the benefit received by the prom-isor in that the promise 'stays the hand of the creditor'.[191]

In order that the forbearance should be a consideration, some liability should be shown to exist, or to be reasonably supposed to exist, by the parties. If the claim is not only invalid, but is known by the party forbearing to be so, there is no consider-ation.[192] It would also seem that the claim must be an honest claim and one which the promisee *bona fide* intends to pursue.[193] Where the claim arises out of an illegal agreement, such as a wagering contract, a forbearance to sue on that claim is not sufficient consideration.[194]

(v) Compromise of a dispute

The same public interest in encouraging the avoidance of litigation and the resolution of disputes applies to a compromise of a dispute, for instance by a promise to pay a proportion of a disputed sum claimed, again provided that it is genuine, and entered into freely without the concealment of essential information, the taking of undue advantage, or the exertion of illegitimate pressure.[195] The difference between forbear-ance and compromise is that in compromise the claim is not admitted and the claimant promises to abandon the claim. It has, however, been argued that if the claim compromised is of an unsubstantial character the consideration fails. The answer is to be found in the judgment of Cockburn C.J. in *Callisher* v. *Bischoffsheim*:[196]

Every day a compromise is effected on the ground that the party making it has a chance of succeeding in it, and if he *bona fide* believes that he has a fair chance of success, he has a reasonable ground for suing, and his forbearance to sue will constitute a good consideration. When such a person forbears to sue he gives up what he believes to be a right of action, and the other party gets an advantage, and, instead of being annoyed with an action, he escapes from the vexations incident to it . . . It would be another matter if a person made a claim which he knew to be unfounded, and, by a compromise, derived an advantage under it: in that case his conduct would be fraudulent.

In that case, the defendant agreed to deliver to the plaintiff certain securities in consideration that the plaintiff would cease to press a claim against the Honduras

---

[190] At p. 292.

[191] Cf. *Cook* v. *Wright* (1861) 1 B. & S. 559, at p. 569.

[192] *Wade* v. *Simeon* (1846) 2 C.B. 548, at p. 564.

[193] *Miles* v. *New Zealand Alford Estate Co.* (1886) 32 Ch. D. 266, at p. 284; *Colchester B.C.* v. *Smith* (*supra*, n. 187), at p. 435. See also *B.C.C.I. S.A.* v. *Ali* [2001] 2 W.L.R. 735 (equitable relief against release procured by concealment of facts).

[194] *Poteliakhoff* v. *Teakle* [1938] 2 K.B. 816; *Hill* v. *Hill (William) (Park Lane) Ltd.* [1949] A.C. 530; *post*, p. 389. But cf. *post*, n. 198.

[195] *Huyton* v. *Cremer* [1999] 1 Lloyd's Rep. 620, at p. 629. On duress, see Ch. 7 *infra*.

[196] (1870) L.R. 5 Q.B. 449, at p. 452.

Government. The claim was worthless, but there was no evidence that the plaintiff knew this.[197] It was held that there was consideration for the agreement. If, however, one of the parties to the compromise has no case, and knows that there is no case, the agreement to compromise will not be held binding.

As in the case of forbearance, the compromise of a claim arising out of an illegal contract is insufficient as consideration, unless the compromise arises out of a dispute of fact as to whether the contract is in fact illegal.[198]

(h) PERFORMANCE OF AN EXISTING DUTY

Where what is done, forborne, suffered, or promised is no more than that to which the promisee is legally bound, and if nothing is got in return for the promise but that to which the promisor is already legally entitled, the consideration seems unreal.[199] This may occur where the promisee is already under an existing duty to do something and then promises to do that thing. If you have to do an act anyway, how can it be to your detriment to reaffirm your obligation? If the act will be done anyway, how does it benefit me to pay you to do it? We shall see that there can be actual or 'practical' detriment and benefit in such situations whatever the theoretical position based on legal entitlement. The law draws a distinction between the performance of a public duty, the performance of an existing duty to a third party, and the performance of an existing duty owed to the promisor. In the first case there will be no consideration for the promise. In the second the law holds that valuable consideration is present. In the third case it has recently been held that only where there is, in the particular circumstances, a 'practical' benefit to the promisee is there consideration.

(i) Performance of a public duty

Where the promisee is already under an existing public duty, an express promise to perform, or performance of, that duty will not amount to consideration.[200] There will be no detriment to the promisee or benefit to the promisor over and above their existing rights and liabilities. In *Collins* v. *Godefroy*:[201]

The plaintiff received a subpoena to appear at a trial as a witness on behalf of the defendant. The defendant promised him a sum of money for his trouble. A person who receives a subpoena is bound to attend and give evidence.

It was held that there was no consideration for the promise, the plaintiff being under a public duty to attend.

Where the undertaking is to do more than that to which the promisee is legally bound, this may be consideration, even though it is an act of the same kind as the

---

[197] See also *Wigan* v. *Edwards* (1973) 1 A.L.R. 497 (Australia) (honest claim sufficient).
[198] *Binder* v. *Alachouzos* [1972] 2 Q.B. 151, *per* Lord Denning M.R. at p. 158.
[199] See Davis (1937) 6 C.L.J. 202; Reynolds and Treitel (1965) 76 Malaya L.R. 1.
[200] *Thorensen Car Ferries Ltd.* v. *Weymouth Portland B.C.* [1977] 2 Lloyd's Rep. 614, at p. 619. Earlier cases tend to suggest that an agreement of this nature is invalid on grounds of public policy: *Wathen* v. *Sandys* (1811) 2 Camp. 640; *Bilke* v. *Havelock* (1813) 3 Camp. 374.
[201] (1831) 1 B. & Ad. 950.

subject of the obligation. In *Glasbrook Brothers Ltd.* v. *Glamorgan County Council*,[202] a police authority sued for the sum of £2,200 promised to it by a colliery company for whose mine the authority had provided a stronger guard during a strike than was in its opinion necessary. It was held that it was entitled to maintain an action on the promise.[203] Again, in *Ward* v. *Byham* it was held that there was consideration for a promise to pay a weekly sum to the mother of an illegitimate child if the mother proved the child was 'well looked after and happy'.[204] Morris and Parker L.JJ. considered the mother had promised more than her statutory duty to maintain the child. Denning L.J.'s view[205] that she was only promising to do what she was bound to do but this sufficed because it was a benefit to the promisee (the child's father) was not shared by them.

More recently *Ward* v. *Byham* has been explained as an instance of the recognition that the mother's promise was a 'practical' benefit to the father which thus amounted to consideration for his promise.[206] It is possible the recognition that such 'practical' benefit can constitute consideration may lead to the reassessment of the general rule but, in the context of pre-existing public duties, it is important to bear in mind that it may be contrary to the public interest to give such recognition to a 'practical' benefit and that this should only be done where 'there is nothing in the transaction which is contrary to the public interest'.[207] For instance, the enforcement of an agreement to make a payment for the performance of a public duty such as the giving of evidence[208] or the renewal of a licence[209] might be thought to be contrary to the public interest in ensuring impartiality in the administration of justice and probity in government and local administration.

(ii) Performance of a duty owed to a third party

It is now established that consideration which consists in the performance of, or the promise to perform, an existing contract with a third party may be a real consideration. In these cases the promisee obtains the benefit of a direct obligation which can be enforced.[210]

As far as performance of such a duty is concerned, in *Shadwell* v. *Shadwell*:[211]

The plaintiff was engaged to be married. His uncle wrote to him stating that he was pleased

---

[202] [1925] A.C. 270.

[203] See also *England* v. *Davidson* (1840) 11 A. & E. 856; *Neville* v. *Kelly* (1862) 12 C.B.N.S. 740 (rewards for police officers) and *Goulden* v. *Wilson Barca* [2000] 1 W.L.R. 167 (payment to expert witness).

[204] [1956] 1 W.L.R. 496. See also *Williams* v. *Williams* [1957] 1 W.L.R. 148 (husband's promise to pay weekly sum to wife who had deserted him, and thus forfeited right to maintenance, if she maintained herself and undertook not to pledge his credit held enforceable).

[205] At p. 498. See also *Williams* v. *Williams* (*supra*, n. 204), at p. 150.

[206] *Williams* v. *Roffey Bros. & Nicholls (Contractors) Ltd.* [1991] 1 Q.B. 1, *per* Glidewell L.J. at p. 13, *post*, p. 106. Cf. Purchas L.J. at p. 20.

[207] *Williams* v. *Williams* [1957] 1 W.L.R. 148, *per* Denning L.J. at p. 150. Note that, although Denning L.J.'s views on the general enforceability of a promise or performance of an existing duty have been disapproved, what he said about the relevance of the public interest has not.

[208] *Collins* v. *Godefroy* (*supra*, n. 201). But see now Supreme Court Act 1981, s. 36(4) (tender of expenses).

[209] *Morgan* v. *Palmer* (1842) 2 B. & C. 729, at p. 739.

[210] *New Zealand Shipping Co. Ltd.* v. *A. M. Satterthwaite & Co. Ltd.* [1975] A.C. 154, at p. 168.

[211] (1860) 9 C.B.N.S. 159.

to hear of the intended marriage and that as he promised to assist the plaintiff at starting, would pay him £150 yearly until the plaintiff's income as a Chancery barrister amounted to six hundred guineas. The plaintiff married. He never earned as much as six hundred guineas. The annuity fell into arrear; the uncle died, and the plaintiff sued his executors.

A majority of the Court thought that there was a benefit to the uncle in that the marriage was 'an object of interest to a near relative', and a detriment to the plaintiff because 'he might have made a most material change in his position and have induced the object of his affections to do the same, and might have incurred pecuniary liabilities resulting in embarrassments' if the promised income had been withheld.

In *Scotson* v. *Pegg*:[212]

S promised to deliver to a third party X, or to his order, a cargo of coal then on board S's ship. X made an order in favour of P. P then made an agreement with S that if S would deliver the coal to him, he would in return unload and discharge the coal at a fixed rate each day from the date when the ship was ready for discharge. When sued for breach, P pleaded that S had promised no more than he was bound under his contract with X to perform so there was no consideration for P's promise to unload in the manner specified.

The Court held that P was liable. Wilde B. said:[213] 'If a person chooses to promise to pay a sum of money in order to induce another to perform that which he has already contracted with a third person to do, I confess I cannot see why such a promise should not be binding'.

There are certain points about these cases which are unsatisfactory. For example, in *Shadwell* v. *Shadwell*, as Byles J., who dissented,[214] pointed out, the uncle derived no personal benefit from the marriage; the engagement was in no way induced by his promise, nor was the plaintiff's subsequent change of position in return for his under-taking. Again, the promise to deliver to P at a fixed rate in *Scotson* v. *Pegg* may have involved duties more onerous than the existing obligation to deliver to X or there may have been some dispute as to P's right to have the coals.[215] Nevertheless, a majority of the Privy Council in *New Zealand Shipping Co. Ltd.* v. *A. M. Satterthwaite & Co. Ltd.* (*The Eurymedon*),[216] took them as establishing that actual performance of an existing duty to a third party can be sufficient consideration, even though that performance is no additional detriment to the promisee. In *The Eurymedon* the unloading by steve-dores of goods from a ship (which the stevedores were bound by a contract with a third party to do) was held to be consideration for a promise to relieve them of the liability for damaging the goods.

(iii) Promise to perform duty owed to a third party

The question then arises whether a distinction should be drawn between cases where

---

[212] (1861) 6 H. & N. 295.

[213] At p. 300.

[214] His view was approved by Salmon L.J. in *Jones* v. *Padavatton* [1969] 1 W.L.R. 328, at p. 333.

[215] At p. 299, *per* Martin B. See *ante*, p. 101.

[216] [1975] A.C. 154. See also *Adams* v. *London Improved Motor Coach Builders Ltd.* [1921] 1 K.B. 495, at pp. 501 and 504 (trade union's undertaking to pay solicitor the costs of services rendered to a member did not preclude the member from also being liable to the solicitor).

the consideration alleged is *executed*, i.e. by performance of an existing duty to a third party, and cases where the consideration is *executory*, consisting of a promise to perform. In principle a promise to perform an existing duty owed to a third party should also constitute consideration because the promisor thereby foregoes the liberty to cancel the contract with the third party by mutual agreement.[217] The Judicial Committee of the Privy Council so held in *Pao On* v. *Lau Yiu Long*:[218]

The plaintiffs agreed with a company (Fu Chip) to sell certain shares in return for an allotment to them of 4.2 million shares in Fu Chip. If all the newly allotted shares had been immediately sold in the market, this would have depressed the value of the shares. Accordingly the plaintiffs undertook in their agreement with Fu Chip not to sell or transfer for one year 60 per cent of the allotted shares. Subsequently the plaintiffs refused to complete the agreement unless the defendants (who were the majority shareholders in Fu Chip) promised to indemnify them against any fall in value of the allotted shares during the one year period. The defendants gave that indemnity. The allotted shares fell greatly in value, and, in answer to a claim on the indemnity, the defendants pleaded that there was no consideration for their promise to indemnify.

It was held that the consideration for the indemnity was the promise of the plaintiffs to perform their pre-existing contractual obligations to Fu Chip. 'Their Lordships', said Lord Scarman,[219] 'do not doubt that a promise to perform, or the performance of, a pre-existing contractual obligation to a third party can be a valid consideration'.

(iv) Performance of a duty owed to the promisor

Where the promisee merely undertakes to fulfil the conditions of an existing contract with the promisor, the perception that it is not detrimental to do what one is obliged to do or beneficial to receive what one is entitled to receive has led to the conclusion that there is no consideration. In this context the need to discourage improper pressure by threatening not to perform one's contract unless the other party offers to pay more has been an important factor, although the pre-existing duty rule was rather a blunt weapon for this since it invalidated non-extortive as well as extortive renegotiations. The regulation of renegotiations was, as we shall see, left to the equitable doctrine of promissory estoppel. Although the development of a concept of economic duress[220] means that the common law now has a more direct and precise method of controlling coercion, normally the performance of a duty owed to the promisor will not be consideration.[221] The general position is illustrated by the old case of *Stilk* v. *Myrick*:[222]

---

217 *De Cicco* v. *Schweizer* 221 N.Y. 431 (1917); Hamson (1938) 54 L.Q.R. 233, at p. 237.
218 [1980] A.C. 614.
219 At p. 632.
220 *Post*, p. 279.
221 *North Ocean Shipping Co. Ltd.* v. *Hyundai Construction Co. Ltd.* [1979] Q.B. 705, at p. 712; *Syros Shipping Co. S.A.* v. *Elaghill Trading Co. Ltd.* [1980] 2 Lloyd's Rep. 390; *Pao On* v. *Lau Yiu Long* [1980] A.C. 614, at p. 633; *Vantage Nav. Cpn.* v. *Suhail & Saud Bahwan Building Materials Llc.* [1989] 1 Lloyd's Rep. 138, at p. 147; *Williams* v. *Roffey Bros. & Nicholls (Contractors) Ltd.* [1991] 1 Q.B. 1, at pp. 16, 19, 20, *post*, p. 106; *Hadley* v. *Kemp* [1999] 2 E.M.L.R. 589, at p. 626.
222 (1809) 2 Camp. 317. But see the report of the same case in 6 Esp. 129, and *Harris* v. *Watson* (1791) Peake 102 (promise invalid by reason of public policy).

In the course of a voyage from London to the Baltic and back two seamen deserted, and the captain, being unable to replace them, promised the rest of the crew that, if they would work the vessel home, the wages of the two deserters should be divided amongst them.

It was held that:

There was no consideration for the ulterior pay promised to the mariners who remained with the ship. Before they sailed from London they had undertaken to do all they could under all emergencies of the voyage ... The desertion of a part of the crew is to be considered an emergency of the voyage as much as their death; and those who remain are bound by the terms of their original contract to exert themselves to the utmost to bring the ship in safety to her destined port.[223]

The decision would have been otherwise if the existing contract had been terminated and a new agreement substituted[224] at a higher rate of pay, or if the promise had been made to compromise a dispute,[225] or if uncontemplated risks had arisen.[226] Then the crew would have provided consideration by entering into the new agreement, or forbearing to exercise what were or were believed to be their legal rights or by undertaking to do more than they were contractually bound to do.

(v) Performance of a duty owed to the promisor and 'practical benefit'

Even where the promise is only to perform the existing contractual obligation, the performance may in fact be detrimental to a performing party whose time or money could have been used to greater advantage elsewhere. It may also be beneficial to the promisee because 'a bird in the hand is worth more than a bird in the bush'[227] and because damages for breach of contract might not compensate fully.[228] In *Williams* v. *Roffey Bros. & Nicholls (Contractors) Ltd.*:[229]

R & N Ltd. contracted to refurbish a block of 27 flats. It sub-contracted the carpentry work to W for an agreed price of £20,000. W completed nine of the flats but got into financial difficulties because the agreed price was too low and because he failed to supervise his workforce adequately. R & N was concerned about delay because the main contract contained a penalty clause. It offered to pay W an additional £10,300 at the rate of £575 for each flat in which the carpentry work was completed. Eight further flats were completed but R & N made only one further payment of £1,500. W ceased work and sued for the additional sum promised. One of the grounds on which R & N resisted this claim was that W had given no consideration for their promise to pay the additional sum since he was promising to do no more than he was already bound to do by his sub-contract.

---

[223] *Per* Lord Ellenborough C.J. at p. 319.

[224] See *post*, p. 516.

[225] *Wigan* v. *Edwards* (1973) 1 A.L.R. 497; see *ante*, p. 102.

[226] *Hartley* v. *Ponsonby* (1857) 7 E. & B. 872.

[227] *Corbin on Contracts* (1963), § 172. See also *Foakes* v. *Beer* (1884) 9 App. Cas. 605, *per* Lord Blackburn at p. 622.

[228] *Post*, pp. 593, 600, 618 (limitations on damages).

[229] [1991] 1 Q.B. 1.

This defence failed. In the Court of Appeal Glidewell L.J. stated:[230]

(i) If A has entered into a contract with B to do work for, or to supply goods or services to, B in return for payment by B; and (ii) at some stage before A has completely performed his obligations under the contract B has reason to doubt whether A will, or will be able to, complete his side of the bargain; and (iii) B thereupon promises A an additional payment in return for A's promise to perform his contractual obligations on time; and (iv) as a result of giving his promise, B obtains in practice a benefit, or obviates a disbenefit; and (v) B's promise is not given as a result of economic duress or fraud on the part of A; then (vi) the benefit to B is capable of being consideration for B's promise, so that the promise will be legally binding.

The Court identified several 'practical' benefits to R & N. These were: W's continued performance, avoiding a penalty for delay under the main contract, avoiding the trouble and expense of engaging others to complete the carpentry, and replacing a haphazard method of payment by a more formalized scheme which produced more orderly performance by W and thus enabled R & N to direct its other traders to do work in the completed flats which otherwise would have been held up until W completed his work.[231] It is clear that it was the development of economic duress as a method of controlling improper pressure that enabled the Court to take a more flexible approach to the requirement of consideration:[232]

Now that there is a properly developed doctrine of the avoidance of contracts on the grounds of economic duress, there is no warrant for the court to fail to recognize the existence of some consideration even though it may be insignificant and even though there may have been no mutual bargain in any realistic use of that phrase.[233]

The recognition of 'practical' benefit as consideration could be a significant step towards the overt recognition that all promises made without duress in a commercial context give rise to enforceable contractual obligations. Several factors, however, make it difficult to assess whether this decision will be the catalyst or whether its impact will be more limited. First, the principle in *Stilk* v. *Myrick*, although refined and limited, was not overruled.[234] It appears from this that, where there is no 'practical' benefit to the promisor, the promise will be 'gratuitous' and unenforceable. Secondly, on the facts of *Williams* v. *Roffey Bros.*, although W did not undertake to do any work additional to that which he had originally undertaken to do, the institution of and adherence to the new work scheme was consideration since he was not obliged to

---

[230] At pp. 15–16. On 'practical benefit', see also *Anangel Atlas Comp. Nav. S.A.* v. *Ishikawajima-Harima Heavy Industries Co. Ltd. (No. 2)* [1990] 2 Lloyd's Rep. 526, at pp. 554–5; *Simon Container Machinery Ltd.* v. *Emba Machinery AB* [1998] 2 Lloyd's Rep. 429, at p. 435.

[231] At pp. 11, 19, 20.

[232] At pp. 13–14, 21. See also *Pao On* v. *Lau Yiu Long* [1980] A.C. 614, at pp. 624–35, *ante*, p. 105.

[233] *Vantage Navigation Cpn.* v. *Suhail and Saud Bahwan Building Materials Llc. (The Alev)* [1989] 1 Lloyd's Rep. 138, *per* Hobhouse J. at p. 147. See also *Huyton S.A.* v. *Peter Cremer G.m.b.H* [1999] 1 Lloyd's Rep. 620, *per* Mance J. at pp. 629–30.

[234] At pp. 16, 19, 20.

perform in that way.[235] Thirdly, as will be seen, in the context of part-payment of a money debt, the Court of Appeal has, since *Williams* v. *Roffey Bros.*, declined to have regard to 'practical' benefit.[236]

The notion of 'practical' benefit has been criticized[237] as imprecise, as including the chance of a benefit, as putting into question the adequacy of contract damages, and as undermining the strength of the obligation to perform a contract by recognizing, as Purchas L.J. did,[238] that a contracting party can rely upon his own breach to establish consideration. We shall, however, see that rigid adherence to the pre-existing duty rule has also been criticized as invalidating many commercially desirable renegotiations and that, before the development of economic duress, it was necessary to have recourse to equitable principles to protect the renegotiated transaction. Now that adequate safeguards exist against improper pressure there would seem to be no very convincing reason why a promise to perform, or performance of, any existing duty, including public duties, should not be sufficient consideration provided that it is not contrary to public policy.[239]

(i) DISCHARGE OF AN EXISTING DUTY

The principle that the performance of an existing duty owed to the promisor is an unreal consideration has been applied not only to the creation of a new obligation, but also to the discharge of the existing duty itself. Thus if A owes B a debt of £200, and B agrees to accept £100 in full satisfaction of the debt, B is not bound by the agreement and may subsequently sue for the whole amount. The payment by a debtor of a smaller sum in satisfaction of a larger is not a good discharge of a debt. Such payment is no more than the promisee is already bound to do, and is no consideration for a promise, express or implied, to forgo the residue of the debt.

(i) The general rule

The rule that the payment of a smaller sum in satisfaction of a larger is not a good discharge of a debt is often known as the rule in *Pinnel's Case*,[240] although it is not part of the *ratio decidendi* of that case.

Pinnel brought an action in debt on a bond against Cole for payment of £8 10s. on 11

---

[235] It seems clear that this consideration can be found in the *performance*; i.e the contract was *unilateral*. It is less clear that there was a new bilateral contract because, although Russell L.J. (at p. 19) considered that 'the terms upon which [W] was to carry out the work were varied', Purchas L.J. (at p. 23) stated that there was 'no obligation added to the contractual duties' and Glidewell L.J. did not address the point.

[236] *Re Selectmove Ltd.* [1995] 1 W.L.R. 474, at p. 481, *post*, p. 109.

[237] Chen Wishart, in Beatson and Friedmann eds., *Good Faith and Fault in Contract Law* (1995), Ch. 5; Coote (1990–91) 3 J.C.L. 23.

[238] [1991] 1 Q.B. 1, at p. 23.

[239] *Williams* v. *Williams* [1957] 1 W.L.R. 148, *per* Denning L.J. at 150 (*ante*, p. 103, n. 204); *Huyton S.A.* v. *Peter Cremer G.m.b.H* [1999] 1 Lloyd's Rep. 620, *per* Mance J. at pp. 629–30.

[240] (1602) 5 Co. Rep. 117a. In *Vanbergen* v. *St. Edmund's Properties Ltd.* [1933] 2 K.B. 223, however, it was stated that the new element must not have been introduced merely to oblige the debtor and without any independent benefit to the creditor.

November 1600. Cole pleaded that, at the instance of Pinnel, he had paid him the sum of £5 2s. 2d. on 1 October, and that Pinnel had accepted this in full satisfaction of the debt.

The Court of Common Pleas stated that the payment of a lesser sum on the day in satisfaction of a greater was no satisfaction of the whole. The rule was considered and reaffirmed by the House of Lords nearly three centuries later in *Foakes* v. *Beer*.[241]

Dr Foakes was indebted to Mrs Beer on a judgment for the sum of £2,090. Mrs Beer agreed that if Foakes paid her £500 in cash and the balance of £1,590 in instalments she would not take 'any proceedings whatever' on the judgment. Foakes paid the money exactly as required, but Mrs Beer then claimed an additional £360 as interest on the judgment debt. When sued, Foakes pleaded that his duty to pay interest had been discharged by the promise not to sue.

Their Lordships differed as to whether, on its true construction, the agreement merely gave Foakes time to pay, or was intended to cover interest as well, but they held that, even on the latter construction, there was no consideration for the promise. Foakes therefore remained bound to pay the additional sum. 'It is', said the Earl of Selborne,[242] 'not really unreasonable or practically inconvenient that the law should require particular solemnities to give to a gratuitous contract the force of a binding obligation'.

(ii) Irrelevance of 'practical benefit'

Lord Blackburn recognized that business people 'do every day recognise and act on the ground that prompt payment of a part of their demand may be more beneficial to them than it would be to insist on their rights',[243] particularly where the credit of the debtor is doubtful, but the House of Lords decided that a practical benefit of that nature is not good consideration. In *Re Selectmove Ltd.*[244] it was said that the principle that 'practical' benefit may amount to consideration recognized in *Williams* v. *Roffey Bros. & Nicholls (Contractors) Ltd.*[245] could not, consistently with the doctrine of precedent, be extended to an obligation to make payment because 'it would in effect leave the principle in *Foakes* v. *Beer* without any application'.

(iii) Any difference in performance suffices

If, however, there is a dispute as to the amount due[246] or the thing done or given by the promisee debtor is different from that which the recipient was entitled to demand,[247] however slight the difference, it will be sufficient consideration for the promise to

---

[241] (1884) 9 App. Cas. 605.

[242] At p. 613.

[243] At p. 622. See also *ibid.*, *per* Lord Fitzgerald at p. 630.

[244] [1995] 1 W.L.R. 474, *per* Peter Gibson L.J. at p. 481. See Peel (1994) 110 L.Q.R. 353. See also *Ferguson* v. *Davis* [1997] 1 All E.R. 315.

[245] *Ante*, p. 106.

[246] *Ante*, p. 101.

[247] Even a negotiable instrument (such as a cheque) for the smaller amount would at one time suffice, provided it was accepted by the creditor in discharge of the obligation (*Goddard* v. *O'Brien* (1882) 9 Q.B.D. 37), but this is no longer the case (*D. & C. Builders Ltd.* v. *Rees* [1966] 2 Q.B. 617).

discharge. Even the performance of the identical obligation will be effective if it is to take place at an earlier date or in a different place.

The Court in *Pinnel's Case* recognized that 'the gift of a horse, hawk or robe, etc. in satisfaction is good' because it 'might be more beneficial to the plaintiff than the money ...., or otherwise the plaintiff would not have accepted it in satisfaction'. Judgment was given for the plaintiff on a technical point of pleading;[248] but the fact that the payment and the acceptance of part of the money had taken place before the due day would otherwise have resulted in judgment for the defendant, for the difference in time would have constituted sufficient consideration for the promise to discharge the debt.

(iv) Appraisal of rule

It has been argued that the rule is supportable on the ground that the law should not favour a person who is excused money which he ought to pay any more than a person who is promised money which has not been earned. On the other hand, it is open to the criticism that it not only runs counter to ordinary commercial practice, but that, taken in conjunction with the rule that the law will not inquire into the adequacy of consideration, it may lead to absurd results. 'According to English Common Law', said Jessel M.R.,[249] 'a creditor may accept anything in satisfaction of his debt except a less amount of money. He might take a horse, or a canary, or a tomtit if he chose, and that was accord and satisfaction; but, by a most extraordinary peculiarity of the English Common Law, he could not take 19s. 6d. in the pound'. There is also now a distinction which is difficult to justify on principle between obligations to render services, where practical benefit is recognized, and obligations to pay money, where it is not. The rule enables a creditor to go back on an agreement solemnly entered into and intended to affect legal relations; and there are no strong policy considerations which would demand the application of the doctrine of consideration to the discharge, as opposed to the formation, of contracts.[250]

The Law Revision Committee, in 1937,[251] recommended the abolition of the rule in *Pinnel's Case* where the promisee had carried out his side of the agreement, but this reform has never been implemented. It would seem that the only way forward is for the House of Lords to reconsider its decision in *Foakes* v. *Beer* in the light of the recognition of 'practical' benefit and other developments, in particular the neutralization of the rule by the equitable principle of promissory estoppel in cases where the debtor's position has been altered in reliance on the promise. Before considering the equitable principle we shall consider two common law exceptions to the rule. The first

---

[248] See generally Simpson, *A History of the Common Law of Contract* (1975), pp. 105–6.

[249] *Couldery* v. *Bartrum* (1881) 19 Ch. D. 394, at p. 399.

[250] Sir Frederick Pollock, *Principles of Contract*, 13th edn. (1950), p. 150 (extension of the doctrine from formation to discharge was illegitimate). See also Kötz, *European Contract Law* (1997), pp. 68–71; CISG Art. 29(1) ('a contract may be modified or terminated by the mere agreement of the parties').

[251] Cmd. 5449. In Canada, provincial statutes have now abolished the rule by providing, as the Ontario Mercantile Law Amendment Act R.S.O. 1990, s. 16 does, that 'Part performance of an obligation either before or after the breach thereof, when expressly accepted by the creditor in satisfaction or rendered in pursuance of an agreement for that purpose, though without any new consideration, shall be held to extinguish the obligation'.

is where a debtor makes a composition with creditors; the second is where part payment of a debt is made by a third party to the contract. It will be seen that these two exceptions are based on reasons of policy rather than on logical evasions of the strict doctrine of consideration.

(v) Compositions with creditors

A composition with creditors (apart from the statutory prohibition of preference by debtors who later become bankrupt)[252] is an exception to the rule, inasmuch as each creditor undertakes to accept a lesser sum than is due in satisfaction of a greater. All are bound, both at common law and by virtue of statute.[253] As far as the common law position is concerned, there is no difficulty as to the consideration between the creditors *inter se*; it is the forbearance on the part of each of them to claim the whole amount of their debt so that no one creditor may gain at the expense of the others. But it is difficult to see how the debtor's promise to pay, or the payment of, a portion of the debt can constitute the consideration upon which the creditor renounces the residue.[254]

The consideration must, then, be something other than the payment of a smaller sum in satisfaction of a larger, and it has been suggested that it consists in the procuring of a promise from each creditor to accept less than the full amount of the individual debt, thereby conferring a benefit on the creditors generally.[255] This solution is satisfactory so far as it goes, for there is no doubt that such a consideration would be sufficient, but it cannot apply to a case in which the debtor does not in fact procure the creditors' promises.[256] In such cases the consideration does not move from the debtor.[257] A more acceptable reason for the existence of this exception would seem to be that a party to such an arrangement cannot claim the original debt because to do so would be to commit a fraud on the other creditors.[258]

(vi) Part payment by third party

The second exception to the general rule, that a creditor who accepts, in full satisfaction, part payment of a debt by a third party cannot later recover the balance from the debtor, is also based on the need to prevent fraud on a third party. In *Hirachand Punamchand* v. *Temple*:[259]

A father wrote to the plaintiffs, his son's creditors, offering to pay part of a debt due on a promissory note in satisfaction of the whole, and enclosing a draft for that amount. The plaintiffs cashed the draft, and then sued the son for the balance.

---

[252] Insolvency Act 1986, ss. 340–2 (*post*, p. 354). See also Deeds of Arrangement Act 1914.

[253] *Ibid.*, s. 260(2). A voluntary arrangement pursuant to the statute is not a contract with the debtor: *Johnson* v. *Davies* [1999] Ch. 117.

[254] *Fitch* v. *Sutton* (1804) 5 East 230, at p. 232.

[255] *Good* v. *Cheesman* (1831) 2 B. & Ad. 328.

[256] Cf. *West Yorkshire Darracq Agency Ltd.* v. *Coleridge* [1911] 2 K.B. 326.

[257] *Ante*, p. 95.

[258] *Wood* v. *Roberts* (1818) 2 Stark. 417. Another reason (*Corbin on Contracts* (1963), § 190) is that, subject to the statutory prohibition on preferences (Insolvency Act 1986, s. 340), the debtor's consideration lies in giving up the opportunity of treating his creditors unequally.

[259] [1911] 2 K.B. 330. See also *Welby* v. *Drake* (1825) 1 C. & P. 557.

The Court of Appeal held that the creditors must be deemed to have accepted the draft in full satisfaction, and that the son's debt was extinguished. It approved a *dictum* of Willes J. in *Cook* v. *Lister*:[260] 'If a stranger pays part of the debt in discharge of the whole, the debt is gone, because it would be a fraud on the stranger to proceed'.

V. PROMISSORY ESTOPPEL

In practice the most significant limit to the rule in *Pinnel's Case* is to be found in equitable principle of estoppel, in this context promissory estoppel which, as noted, neutralizes the effect of the rule in many cases. Here we consider the extent to which promissory estoppel operates in effect as an alternative to consideration in the discharge or modification of existing duties and its potential to operate in this way in the formation of contracts.

Before turning to the requirements for the establishment of a promissory estoppel, it should be noted that it is only one form of estoppel. We saw in Section III of this chapter that equity may, by the principle of estoppel, provide a remedy in respect of an agreement that does not comply with statutory requirements of form. Promissory estoppel is one strand in a broader equitable principle whereby parties to a transaction who have conducted their dealings in reliance on an underlying assumption as to a present, past, or future state of affairs, or a promise or representation by words or conduct by one that strict legal rights will not be insisted upon will not be allowed to go back on that assumption, promise or representation when it would be unfair or unjust to do so.[261] The Court will do what is necessary, but not more, to prevent a person who has relied upon such an assumption, promise, or representation from suffering detriment.[262] Promissory estoppel also has similarities to the common law principle of waiver by which the right to performance in accordance with the contract may be lost by a party who in effect promises (albeit without consideration) not to insist on strict adherence to the contract. Waiver is considered in the chapter on Discharge by Agreement.[263]

(a) EFFECT ON EXISTING DUTY

Promissory estoppel was invoked in *Central London Property Trust Ltd.* v. *High Trees House Ltd.*:[264]

---

[260] (1863) 13 C.B.N.S. 543, at pp. 594, 595. This is not also an exception to the rule that a non-party to a contract (here the debtor) cannot enforce it (*post*, p. 421) because the transaction between the creditor and the person who pays is best seen as an executed (complete) gift to the debtor of the discharge of the debt: see Birks and Beatson (1976) 92 L.Q.R. 188, 193–99.

[261] *Post*, pp. 122–4.

[262] *Crabb* v. *Arun D.C.* [1976] Ch. 179, at p. 198; *Commonwealth* v. *Verwayen* (1990) 170 C.L.R. 394, at p. 413 (Australia).

[263] *Post*, Chapter 13.

[264] [1947] K.B. 130.

In 1937 the plaintiff leased to the defendant a block of flats for a term of 99 years at a rent of £2,500 a year. In 1940, many of the flats were empty, on account of the war, and the plaintiff agreed to reduce the rent to £1,250. By 1945 the flats were again full. A receiver for the debenture holders of the plaintiff brought an action against the defendant claiming the full original rent both for the future and also for the last two quarters of 1945.

Denning J. held that the action should succeed. The parties intended the reduction of rent to be a temporary expedient while the flats could not be fully let. This had ceased to be the case early in 1945; therefore the full rent was payable for the last two quarters of 1945, which was all that was actually claimed in the action. The importance of the judgment, however, lies in Denning J.'s contention that, had the plaintiff sued for the full rent between 1940 and 1945, it would have been *estopped* by its promise from asserting its legal right to demand payment in full.

He relied on the decision of the House of Lords in *Hughes* v. *Metropolitan Railway Co.*:[265]

H served on M a notice to repair, within six months, houses held on lease from him. Failure to comply with this notice would entitle H to forfeit the lease. The parties then negotiated for the purchase by H of M's lease and these continued for almost the entire period of the notice. Shortly before the notice was due to expire, H broke off the negotiations, and, upon expiry, brought an action for possession claiming to have forfeited the lease.

The House of Lords held that, by entering into negotiations, H impliedly promised to suspend the notice previously given and that M had acted upon this promise by doing nothing to repair the premises. H was not to be allowed to take advantage of the forfeiture which occurred, and therefore the six months' period was to run only from the breakdown of the negotiations. Lord Cairns described the principle as follows:[266]

If parties who have entered into definite and distinct terms involving certain legal results— certain penalties or legal forfeiture—afterwards by their own act or with their own consent enter upon a course of negotiation which has the effect of leading one of the parties to suppose that the strict rights arising under the contract will not be enforced, or will be kept in suspense, or held in abeyance, the person who otherwise might have enforced those rights will not be allowed to enforce them where it would be inequitable having regard to the dealings which have thus taken place between the parties.

Denning J. stated that the application of this principle led logically to the conclusion that 'a promise to accept a smaller sum in discharge of a larger sum, if acted upon, is binding notwithstanding the absence of consideration'.[267]

The correctness of Denning J.'s *dictum*[268] has, however, been the subject of considerable controversy.[269] In particular, two criticisms have been levelled against it.

---

[265] (1877) 2 App. Cas. 439. See also *Birmingham and District Land Co.* v. *L. & N.W. Ry.* (1888) 40 Ch. D. 268. Contrast the view of this case advanced by Gordon [1963] C.L.J. 222.

[266] At p. 448.

[267] [1947] K.B. 130, at p. 135.

[268] Being based on hypothetical facts, it is *obiter dictum* and not *ratio decidendi*.

[269] As well as the articles cited *post*, see Cheshire and Fifoot (1947) 63 L.Q.R. 283; (1948) 64 L.Q.R. 28; Wilson (1951) 67 L.Q.R. 330; Lord Denning (1952) 15 M.L.R. 1; Sheridan (1952) 15 M.L.R. 338; Bennion (1953) 16 M.L.R. 441; Wilson [1965] C.L.J. 93; Thompson [1983] C.L.J. 257.

First, it was argued that the concept of 'promissory' estoppel offends against the rule in *Jorden* v. *Money*[270] in which it was held that only a representation of existing or past fact, and not one relating to future conduct, will ground an estoppel. Estoppel would not therefore apply, as in the *High Trees* case, to a promise as to the future. The rule in *Jorden* v. *Money*, however, is not an absolute one, and it is qualified by a number of exceptions.[271] One of these exceptions is that principle expressed in *Hughes* v. *Metropolitan Railway Co.*, which applies where two parties stand together in a contractual or other similar legal relationship, and one of them makes to the other a promise to forbear from enforcing its strict legal rights. To this situation the rule in *Jorden* v. *Money* has no application.

Secondly, it was said that the *dictum* of Denning J. is inconsistent with the decision of the House of Lords in *Foakes* v. *Beer*. But the principle upon which he relied in the *High Trees* case was that of estoppel, which must be specially pleaded. A plea of estoppel was never raised in *Foakes* v. *Beer*.

(b) SCOPE OF THE PRINCIPLE

The principle of promissory estoppel has subsequently been recognized,[272] and with this recognition has come a more precise definition of its scope.

(i) A clear promise

In the first place, the promise must be clear and unequivocal,[273] although it need not be express and may be implied from words or conduct.[274] No estoppel can arise if the language of the promise is indefinite or imprecise and silence and inaction, for example the absence of protest about a breach, will not normally estop a party from relying on the breach.[275] Where, however, the language is clear, no question arises of any particular knowledge by the promisor.[276]

(ii) Inequitable to go back on promise

Secondly, it must be inequitable for the promisor to go back on the promise and insist

---

[270] (1854) 5 H.L.C. 185, and applied in *Citizen's Bank of Louisiana* v. *First National Bank of New Orleans* (1873) L.R. 6 H.L. 352; *Maddison* v. *Alderson* (1883) 8 App. Cas. 467, at p. 473.

[271] See Jackson (1965) 81 L.Q.R. 84, 223.

[272] *Tool Metal Manufacturing Co. Ltd.* v. *Tungsten Electric Co. Ltd.* (1950) 69 R.P.C. 108 and [1955] 1 W.L.R. 761 was the first case. As well as the cases discussed below, see *Bremer Handelsgesellschaft m.b.H.* v. *Vanden Avenne-Izegem* [1977] 1 Lloyd's Rep. 133, at p. 165, aff'd [1978] 2 Lloyd's Rep. 109, at p. 127 (H.L.); *The 'Stolt Loyalty'* [1993] 2 Lloyd's Rep. 281. Cf. *Woodhouse A.C. Israel Cocoa Ltd. S.A.* v. *Nigerian Produce Marketing Co. Ltd.* [1972] A.C. 741, at pp. 758, 762.

[273] *Woodhouse A.C. Israel Cocoa Ltd. S.A.* v. *Nigerian Produce Marketing Co. Ltd.* (*supra*, n. 272), at pp. 757, 758, 761, 762, 767–8, 771; *Scandinavian Trading Tanker Co. A.B.* v. *Flota Petrolera Ecuatoriana* [1983] Q.B. 549 (aff'd. [1983] 2 A.C. 694).

[274] *Hughes* v. *Metropolitan Railway Co.* (*supra*, n. 265). It is unlikely to arise where the negotiations are 'subject to contract': *Attorney-General for Hong Kong* v. *Humphreys Estates (Queen's Garden)* [1987] 1 A.C. 114.

[275] *Société Italo-Belge pour le Commerce et l'Industrie* v. *Palm & Vegetable Oils (Malaysia) Sdn. Bdh.* [1982] 1 All E.R. 19, at p. 25; *Vitol S.A.* v. *Esso Australia Ltd.* [1989] 2 Lloyd's Rep. 451, at p. 460.

[276] *Youell* v. *Bland Welch & Co. Ltd.* [1990] 2 Lloyd's Rep. 423, at pp. 448–50. (Cf. waiver where knowledge of all material facts is required.)

on the strict legal rights under the contract. This is illustrated by *D. & C. Builders Ltd.* v. *Rees*:[277]

R owed £482 to D & C, a small building company, in respect of work done for him. He delayed payment for several months, and then offered D & C £300, stating in effect that if it did not accept this sum it would get nothing. As D & C was in desperate financial straits, it accepted the £300 in full settlement of the debt. It then sued for the balance.

Lord Denning M.R. took the view that it was not inequitable for D & C to go back on its promise; the settlement was not truly voluntary as R had improperly taken advantage of D & C's weak financial situation.[278] R was therefore liable for the balance. Although there has been little other guidance as to when it will not be inequitable for a person to go back on such a promise, pointers as to what conduct will and what conduct will not be acceptable while renegotiating a contract can be found in the developing doctrine of duress.[279]

(iii) Alteration of position

Thirdly, it has been said that the promisee must have 'altered his position' in reliance on the promise made.[280] There is, however, some doubt as to what is meant by this requirement. Normally, where it is sought to prove an estoppel, it must be shown that the person to whom the representation is made has acted detrimentally in reliance on it. If these ideas are regarded as fundamentally similar, then the alteration of position which results from the promise must be such that, if the promise is revoked, the promisee will be in a worse position than if the promise had never been made. It is because the position of the promisee has been prejudiced that it is inequitable for the promisor to go back on the promise. In *Hughes* v. *Metropolitan Railway Co.* this requirement was clearly satisfied, since M had refrained from carrying out repairs in reliance on the promise and had thus lost the time which it would have enjoyed had the negotiations never taken place. On the other hand, in the *High Trees* case, no evidence was adduced to show any alteration of position by the tenant company, in the sense that it arranged, or omitted to arrange, its affairs any differently as a result of the promise.[281] The only thing it did in reliance on the promise was to pay part of the debt which it was contractually bound to pay. If the landlord had gone back on its promise, and claimed the full rent between 1940 and 1945, the tenant would have been in no worse position than if the promise had never been made. The *High Trees* case cannot in consequence be regarded as completely identical to *Hughes* v.

---

[277] [1966] 2 Q.B. 617. See also *P.* v. *P.* [1957] N.Z.L.R. 854.

[278] Cf. Danckwerts and Winn L.JJ. at pp. 626, 632–3, who applied the rule in *Pinnel's Case*.

[279] *Huyton S.A.* v. *Peter Cremer G.m.b.H.* [1999] 1 Lloyd's Rep. 620, *per* Mance J. at p. 629. See also *post*, p. 281.

[280] *Tungsten Electric Co. Ltd.* v. *Tool Metal Manufacturing Co. Ltd.* (1950) 69 R.P.C. 108, at pp. 112, 115–16; *Tool Metal Manufacturing Co. Ltd.* v. *Tungsten Electric Co. Ltd.* [1955] 1 W.L.R. 761, at pp. 764, 784; *Ajayi* v. *R. T. Briscoe (Nigeria) Ltd.* [1964] 1 W.L.R. 1326, at p. 1330; *Re Wyvern Developments Ltd.* [1974] 1 W.L.R. 1097, at p. 1104.

[281] It could be suggested that the tenants had 'altered their position' by relying on the informal promise and failing to secure a formal release under seal or by refraining from seeking alternative finance or declaring themselves bankrupt.

Metropolitan Railway Co. although, at common law, the waiver of an existing obligation does not require such detrimental reliance so long as it has been accepted and
acted upon by the other party.[282]

That a weaker form of reliance will suffice is supported by Lord Cairns's statement
of principle. He said that the person seeking to enforce his rights will not be allowed
to do so 'where it would be inequitable having regard to the dealings which have thus
taken place between the parties'. It is therefore arguable that it is for the Court to
decide, on the totality of the evidence produced to it, whether the dealings between
the parties are such as to render it inequitable for the promisor to go back on the
promise. The promisee may have acted differently as a result of the promise even
though it cannot be proved that any prejudice has been suffered as a result of
the making of the promise. For instance, in *Société Italo-Belge pour le Commerce et
l'Industrie* v. *Palm and Vegetable Oils (Malaysia) Sdn. Bdh.*:[283]

> The buyers of a cargo of palm oil did not protest about the sellers' failure to make a
> 'declaration of ship' in writing as soon as possible after sailing and asked the sellers to pass
> the shipping documents to a sub-buyer, a request that was held to be a representation that
> they were prepared to accept them and a waiver of any defect in them. The sub-buyer
> rejected the documents within 2 days and the buyers purported to do so as well.

It was stated that to establish inequity within Lord Cairns's principle, 'it is not necessary to show detriment; indeed the representee may have benefited from the representation, and yet it may be inequitable, at least without reasonable notice, for the
representor to enforce his legal rights'.[284] Thus, on facts such as those in the *High Trees*
case although the tenant may have benefited from the reduction in rent, it may have
been lulled into a state of false security[285] and have conducted its affairs on the basis
that it would only have to pay rent at the lower rate, and not for instance attempting
to renegotiate the transaction or seeking alternative finance, or by deciding not to
declare itself bankrupt. Such an alteration of position by the promisee would be a
cogent factor to be taken into account in deciding this issue.[286] It does not, however,
follow that in every case where there is such reliance by the promisee that it will be
inequitable for the promisor to enforce the contract and in *Société Italo-Belge pour le
Commerce et l'Industrie* v. *Palm and Vegetable Oils (Malaysia) Sdn. Bdh.*, although the
sellers had actively relied on the buyers' representation by presenting the documents,
the very short time between the representation and the rejection of the documents
meant that, in the absence of evidence that the sellers' position had been prejudiced,

---

[282] *W. J. Alan & Co. Ltd.* v. *El Nasr Export and Import Co. Ltd.* [1972] 2 Q.B. 189, at p. 213, but cf. *ibid.*, at p.
221, for the view that there was detrimental reliance. See *post*, p. 522 and see further Clarke [1974] C.L.J. 260.

[283] [1982] 1 All E.R. 19. See also *Scandinavian Trading Tanker Co. A.B.* v. *Flota Petrola Ecuatoriana* [1983]
Q.B. 549 (aff'd. [1983] 2 A.C. 694); *Goldsworthy* v. *Brickell* [1987] Ch. 378, at p. 411.

[284] At p. 27.

[285] *Amalgamated Investment & Property Co. Ltd.* v. *Texas Commerce International Bank Ltd.* [1982] Q.B. 84,
at p. 108.

[286] *Combe* v. *Combe* [1951] 2 K.B. 215, at pp. 220, 225; *Tool Metal Manufacturing Co. Ltd.* v. *Tungsten
Electric Co. Ltd.* [1955] 1 W.L.R. 761, at p. 799 (where, see *infra*, the promisees continued to produce over
quota); *Brikom Investments Ltd.* v. *Carr* [1979] Q.B. 467, at p. 482; *Youell* v. *Bland Welch & Co. Ltd.* [1990] 2
Lloyd's Rep. 423, at pp. 452–4.

it was not inequitable for the buyers to enforce their legal right to reject the documents.

Despite the absence of a requirement of 'detriment', the requirement that the promise be 'acted upon' means that there is, in this respect, a clear distinction from contracts supported by consideration which are enforceable even if wholly executory.[287]

(iv) Suspensive or extinctive?

Finally, it has been suggested that promissory estoppel only serves to suspend, and not wholly to extinguish the existing obligation; the promisor may, on giving due notice, resume the right which has been waived and revert to the original terms of the contract.[288] Thus in *Tool Metal Manufacturing Co. Ltd.* v. *Tungsten Electric Co. Ltd.*:[289]

In 1938 the appellant granted to the respondent a licence to import, make, use, and sell certain hard metal alloys it had patented. The respondent was to pay royalties, and, if the amount of material made exceeded a named quota, 'compensation'. On the outbreak of war, the appellant agreed to suspend its right to compensation, the parties contemplating that a new agreement would be entered into when the war ended.

In 1945, the appellant claimed to have revoked its suspension and to be entitled to compensation from 1 June 1945. This claim failed on the ground that the revocation was premature as no adequate notice had been given to the respondent.

In 1950, the appellant brought the present action, claiming compensation from 1 January 1947, at which date the respondent was fully aware that the appellant was determined to revert to the original agreement.

The House of Lords held that the appellant had effectively revoked its promise to suspend its legal rights and that it was entitled to the compensation claimed; the equitable principle enunciated in *Hughes* v. *Metropolitan Railway Co.* was applicable to the situation, but the promisor might, on giving adequate notice to the promisee, resume its rights under the original agreement. As Bowen L.J. had said in an earlier case:[290]

If persons who have contractual rights against others induce by their conduct those against whom they have such rights to believe that such rights will either not be enforced or will be kept in suspense or abeyance for some particular time, those persons will not be allowed by a Court of Equity to enforce the rights until such time has elapsed, without at all events placing the parties in the same position as they were before.

The temporary effect of the estoppel raised is, it has been argued, the characteristic of the doctrine and the reason why it should be considered a 'quasi-estoppel' rather than a true example of estoppel in equity or at common law.

---

[287] See *Waltons Stores (Interstate) Ltd.* v. *Maher* (1988) 164 C.L.R. 387, *per* Mason C.J. and Wilson J. at p. 406, *post*, p. 122. Cf. Lord Denning, who has contended extra-judicially that the repudiation of a promise solemnly given, and intended to effect legal relations, is in itself inequitable: (1952) 15 M.L.R. 1, 6–8.

[288] *Birmingham and District Land Co.* v. *L. & N.W. Ry.* (1888) 40 Ch. D. 268, at p. 286; *Ajayi* v. *R. T. Briscoe (Nigeria) Ltd.* [1964] 1 W.L.R. 1326, at p. 1330. See also Wilson (1951) 67 L.Q.R. 330; [1965] C.L.J. 93.

[289] [1955] 1 W.L.R. 761.

[290] *Birmingham and District Land Co.* v. *L. & N.W. Ry.* (1888) 40 Ch. D. 268, at p. 286.

It is, however, submitted that this is not a necessary limitation, and that promissory estoppel can extinguish, as well as suspend the promisee's obligations. For example, it is clear that the promise will become 'final and irrevocable if the promisee cannot resume his position'.[291] Otherwise, the effect of the estoppel will depend on the terms and intent of the promise. No doubt, as a normal rule, where the contract imposes an obligation to make periodic payments of money, such as the 'compensation' in the *Tool Metal* case, rent under a lease,[292] or instalments under a hire-purchase agreement,[293] a promise to waive part of these payments will be construed to mean that the promisor reserves to himself the right, on giving reasonable notice, to demand that future payments be made in full.[294] But it has been assumed, although not decided, that the right to claim the balance of past payments is foregone and is thus extinguished,[295] unless the promise is one which simply allows the promisee to postpone payment but does not extinguish the debt.[296] This assumption seems correct. If the promise is such as unequivocally to indicate the intention of the promisor wholly to abandon all right to payment of the money contractually due, whether periodically or as a lump sum, there is no reason why the estoppel should not be held to have permanent effect.[297]

(c) PROMISSORY ESTOPPEL AND THE FORMATION OF CONTRACTS

It has been seen that the principle of promissory estoppel has been employed to obviate the necessity for consideration in cases where parties are already bound contractually one to the other and one of them promises to waive, modify, or suspend its strict legal rights. The question therefore arises whether the principle might similarly be employed as a supplement or alternative to consideration as a necessary element in the formation of contracts. If it could be so employed, there would be two routes to the legal enforceability of a promise; first the furnishing of consideration by the promisee in the form of the incurring of detriment or the conferral of benefit in return for the promise, and secondly, where the promise was intended to effect legal relations and to be acted upon by the promisee, where the promisee's position had been altered in reliance on the promise.[298] This has occurred in some jurisdictions[299] but not yet in England where it is thought illegitimately to outflank the requirement of consideration and where the main doctrinal vehicle for reconciling promissory estoppel and consideration has been the rule that promissory estoppel does not create

---

[291] *Ajayi* v. *R. T. Briscoe (Nigeria) Ltd.* [1964] 1 W.L.R. 1326, at p. 1330. See also *Nippon Yusen Kaisha* v. *Pacifica Navigacion S.A.* [1980] 2 Lloyd's Rep. 245.

[292] *Central London Property Trust Ltd.* v. *High Trees House Ltd.* [1947] K.B. 130.

[293] *Ajayi* v. *R. T. Briscoe (Nigeria) Ltd.* (*supra*, n. 291).

[294] *Banning* v. *Wright* [1972] 1 W.L.R. 972, at p. 981.

[295] *Central London Property Trust Ltd.* v. *High Trees House Ltd.* (*supra*, n. 292); *Tungsten Electric Co. Ltd.* v. *Tool Metal Manufacturing Co. Ltd.* (1950) 69 R.P.C. 108; *P.* v. *P.* [1957] N.Z.L.R. 854.

[296] *Ledingham* v. *Bermejo Estancia Co. Ltd.* [1947] 1 All E.R. 749.

[297] *Brikom Investments Ltd.* v. *Carr* [1979] Q.B. 467, at pp. 484–5; *Sydenham & Co. Ltd.* v. *Enichem Elastometers Ltd.* [1989] 1 E.G.L.R. 257. See also *Maharaj* v. *Chand* [1986] A.C. 898, at p. 908.

[298] See *ante*, p. 115.

[299] *Post*, p. 123.

new causes of action where none existed before; it is 'a shield and not a sword'.[300] It has been said 'that it would be wrong to extend the doctrine of promissory estoppel, whatever its precise limits at the present day, to the extent of abolishing in a back-handed way the doctrine of consideration'.[301] Thus in *Combe* v. *Combe*:[302]

A husband, upon divorce, promised his wife £100 a year as a permanent allowance. In reliance upon this promise, the wife forbore to apply to the Courts for maintenance. The husband failed to make the payments, and the wife sued him on the promise.

The Court of Appeal held that there was no consideration for the promise as the wife's forbearance had not been requested and was not in return for the promise made to her; nor could the wife rely on promissory estoppel, for as Denning L.J. put it:[303]

Seeing that the principle can never stand alone as giving a cause of action in itself, it can never do away with the necessity of consideration when that is an essential part of the cause of action. The doctrine of consideration is too firmly fixed to be overthrown by a side-wind. Its ill-effects have been largely mitigated of late, but it still remains a cardinal necessity of a formation of a contract, though not of its modification or discharge.

There are similar statements in other cases[304] but the restriction of promissory estoppel to situations in which no new cause of action is created has not been adhered to consistently and is difficult to justify on any principled basis. First, the pre-existing legal relationship need not be a contractual one; promissory estoppel has been applied to a relationship between neighbouring landowners,[305] to one derived from statute,[306] and even an exchange of correspondence.[307] Secondly, there are cases in which, despite *Combe* v. *Combe*, Courts appear to have been willing to use promissory estoppel as a sword enabling a person to establish the constituent elements of a cause of action.[308] Thirdly, promissory estoppel is only one form of estoppel and it is possible to found a

---

[300] *Combe* v. *Combe* [1951] 2 K.B. 215, at p. 224.

[301] *Brikom Investments Ltd.* v. *Carr* [1979] Q.B. 467, *per* Roskill L.J. at p. 486; *Argy Trading Development Cpn. Ltd.* v. *Lapid Developments Ltd.* [1977] 1 W.L.R. 444; *Azov Shipping Co. Ltd.* v. *Baltic Shipping Co. (No. 3)* [1999] 2 Lloyd's Rep. 159, at p. 175; *Thornton Springer* v. *N.E.M. Insurance Co. Ltd.* [2000] 2 All E.R. 489, at p. 516.

[302] [1951] 2 K.B. 215. See also *Morris* v. *Tarrant* [1971] 2 Q.B. 143, at p. 160; *Argy Trading Development Co. Ltd.* v. *Lapid Developments Ltd.* [1977] 1 W.L.R. 444, at p. 457; *Syros Shipping Co. S.A.* v. *Elaghill Trading Co. Ltd.* [1980] 2 Lloyd's Rep. 390, at p. 393; *Hiscox* v. *Outhwaite (No. 3)* [1991] 2 Lloyd's Rep. 524, at p. 535.

[303] At p. 220. See *ante*, p. 90.

[304] *Argy Trading Development Co. Ltd.* v. *Lapid Developments Ltd.* [1977] 1 W.L.R. 444, at p. 457; *Syros Shipping Co. S.A.* v. *Elaghill Trading Co.* [1981] 3 All E.R. 189.

[305] *Crabb* v. *Arun D.C.* [1976] Ch. 179 (*infra*, n. 310).

[306] *Robertson* v. *Minister of Pensions* [1949] 1 K.B. 227 (soldier and military authorities); *Durham Fancy Goods Ltd.* v. *Michael Jackson Fancy Goods Ltd.* [1968] 2 Q.B. 839 (statutory liability on director).

[307] *Pacol Ltd* v. *Trade Lines Ltd.* [1982] 1 Lloyd's Rep. 456, at p. 466 and *K. Lokumal & Sons (London) Ltd.* v. *Lotte Shipping Co. Pte. Ltd.* [1985] 2 Lloyd's Rep. 28 but cf. *Shearson Lehman Hutton Inc.* v. *MacLaine Watson & Co. Ltd.* [1989] 2 Lloyd's Rep. 570, at pp. 596, 604.

[308] *Re Wyvern Developments Ltd.* [1974] 1 W.L.R. 1097, at p. 1104 (although there may have been consideration in this case, Atiyah (1974) 38 M.L.R. 65, 67, the detriment to the promisee was not requested); *Durham Fancy Goods Ltd.* v. *Michael Jackson Fancy Goods Ltd.* [1968] 2 Q.B. 839, at p. 847; *Nippon Yusen Kaisha* v. *Pacifica Navegacion S.A.* [1980] 2 Lloyd's Rep. 245; *Pacol Ltd.* v. *Trade Lines Ltd.* [1982] 1 Lloyd's Rep. 456, at pp. 466–8.

cause of action on other forms, in particular proprietary estoppel and estoppel by convention which are considered below. It has, indeed, been stated that the language used in connection with the 'shield, not a sword' limitation is no more than a matter of semantics.[309]

(d) PROPRIETARY ESTOPPEL

Proprietary estoppel arises where a person acts in reasonable reliance and to his or her detriment on the belief that he or she has or will acquire rights in or over the property of another in circumstances in which it is unconscionable for the property owner to deny the rights. Thus, in *Crabb* v. *Arun D.C.*:[310]

The council built a road along the boundary between its property and C's and gave C a point of access to the road. Later C wished to divide his land and sell off one portion. For this purpose C needed a second point of access and, at a site meeting with officers of the council at which he said he would need access at an additional specified point, he was assured that would be acceptable to the council. Later the council fenced off the boundary and erected gates at the two agreed access points. After C sold the front plot without reserving any right of way from the back plot, the council removed the gates at the access point for the back plot and erected a fence, thus leaving the plot landlocked. It then asked C for £3,000 for a right of access. C sought a declaration claiming that he had a right of way over the second point of access.

The Court of Appeal granted the relief sought. There was no consideration for the council's undertaking and the formality requirements for a contract for the transfer of an interest in land had not been satisfied. But the council, at the meeting and by its conduct in putting up the gates, had led C to believe that he had or would be granted a right of access at the specified point and it was inequitable for it to insist on its strict title.

The basis of proprietary estoppel lies in cases of improvements to specific property in the mistaken belief that the improver has or will be given ownership with the owner positively encouraging this detrimental reliance[311] or by standing by and acquiescing in it.[312] Not all cases, however, involve such improvements; in some others services were rendered in the belief that ownership would be given.[313] This form of estoppel is narrower than promissory estoppel in requiring detrimental reliance[314] and the belief

---

[309] *Azov Shipping Co. Ltd.* v. *Baltic Shipping Co.* [1999] 2 Lloyd's Rep. 159, at p. 174.

[310] [1976] Ch. 179, on which see Atiyah (1974) 92 L.Q.R. 174; Millett, *ibid.*, 342.

[311] *Ramsden* v. *Dyson* (1866) 1 H.L. 129, at p. 170; *Dillwyn* v. *Llewellyn* (1862) 4 D., F. & J. 517; *Pascoe* v. *Turner* [1979] 1 W.L.R. 431; *Gillett* v. *Holt* [2001] Ch. 210. See also Allan (1963) 79 L.Q.R. 238; Jackson (1965) 81 L.Q.R. 84, 223; Moriarty (1984) 100 L.Q.R. 376.

[312] *Taylors Fashions Ltd.* v. *Liverpool Victoria Trustee Co. Ltd.* [1982] Q.B. 133, at pp. 151–2. See also *Att.-Gen. of Hong Kong* v. *Humphreys Estates (Queen's Gardens)* [1987] 1 A.C. 114, at p. 124.

[313] *Tanner* v. *Tanner* [1975] 1 W.L.R. 1346 (property management); *Greasley* v. *Cooke* [1980] 1 W.L.R. 1306 (nursing).

[314] Detriment is not a narrow or technical concept and need not consist of quantifiable financial detriment so long as it is something substantial: *Gillett* v. *Holt* [2001] Ch. 210, *per* Robert Walker L.J. at p. 232.

that a legal right over property has or will be given but broader in not requiring an unequivocal representation and in its ability to create new rights.[315] One reason given for allowing the creation of new rights is that the legal owner of the property would otherwise be unjustly enriched by getting the benefit of the improved property for nothing. This does not, however, account for all the cases. For instance, in *Crabb* v. *Arun D.C.* the council would not have been unjustly enriched in this way. Scarman L.J. stated that he did not find the distinction between promissory and proprietary estoppel helpful,[316] and that case has been said to have virtually equated the two as mere facets of the same principle, the root of which is unconscientiousness.[317]

(e) ESTOPPEL BY CONVENTION

When the parties have acted in a transaction upon a common assumption (either of fact or law, whether due to mistake or misrepresentation) that a given state of facts is to be accepted between them as true, then as regards that transaction each will be estopped against the other from questioning the truth of the statement of the facts so assumed where it would be unjust and unconscionable to resile from that common assumption.[318] There must be some mutually manifest conduct by the parties, which is based on a common but mistaken assumption[319] which the parties have agreed on, and such agreement may be inferred from conduct or even from silence.[320] In *Amalgamated Investment & Property Co. Ltd.* v. *Texas Commerce International Bank Ltd.*:[321]

A.I.P. negotiated with the T.C.I. bank for a loan to one of its subsidiaries to be secured *inter alia* by a guarantee by A.I.P. T.C.I. decided to make the loan through Portsoken, a subsidiary company it bought for the purpose, but A.I.P.'s guarantee related to *moneys due to you*, i.e. T.C.I. A.I.P got into financial difficulties and was wound up. T.C.I. had sold property belonging to A.I.P. and applied $750,000 of the proceeds in payment of the outstanding balance of the loan made through Portsoken. A.I.P's liquidator sought a declaration that A.I.P. was under no liability for loans made by Portsoken, and that T.C.I. had not been entitled to apply the money in this way.

---

[315] In principle this should include all forms of property but the cases, while contemplating property in goods, only provide authority for land.

[316] [1976] Ch. 179, at p. 193.

[317] *Taylors Fashions Ltd.* v. *Liverpool Victoria Trustee Co. Ltd.* [1982] Q.B. 133, at p 153. See also *Amalgamated Investment & Property Co. Ltd.* v. *Texas Commerce International Bank Ltd.* [1982] Q.B. 84, at pp. 103–4, 122, and *infra*. See also *Sledmore* v. *Dalby* (1996) 72 P. & C.R. 196 (no longer inequitable to allow the expectation created to be defeated by the enforcement of legal rights).

[318] *Amalgamated Investment & Property Co. Ltd.* v. *Texas Commerce International Bank Ltd.* [1982] Q.B. 84, at pp. 126, 130; *Hiscox* v. *Outhwaite* [1992] 1 A.C. 562, *per* Lord Donaldson M.R. at p. 575; *Norwegian American Cruises A/S* v. *Paul Mundy Ltd.* [1988] 2 Lloyd's Rep. 343, at pp. 351–2 (approving *Hamel-Smith* v. *Pycroft & Jetsave Ltd.*, 5 February 1987, *per* Peter Gibson J.). The estoppel applies only 'for the period of time and to the extent required by the equity which the estoppel has raised': *Troop* v. *Gibson* (1986) 277 Est. Gaz. 1134, at p. 1144.

[319] *Lokumal & Sons (London) Ltd.* v. *Lotte Shipping Co. Pte. Ltd.* [1985] 2 Lloyd's Rep. 28, *per* Kerr L.J. at pp. 34–5.

[320] *Republic of India* v. *India Steamship Co. Ltd. (The Indian Grace) (No. 2)* [1997] 2 W.L.R. 538, *per* Staughton L.J. at p. 549.

[321] [1982] Q.B. 84.

The Court of Appeal held that the guarantee, on its true interpretation, applied to loans by Portsoken, but also stated that even if it did not, A.I.P. was estopped from denying the fact by an estoppel by convention: both had assumed that the guarantee would cover loans by Portsoken. Again, although estoppel by convention differs from promissory estoppel since it does not require a representation, the tenor of the judgments is that the different forms of estoppels should not be divided into rigid categories and could be merged together into one general principle shorn of technicalities. Moreover, if the guarantee did not in fact cover loans by Portsoken, in substance T.C.I. was founding a cause of action on the estoppel, although in form it used the estoppel as a defence to the plaintiff's claim for declaratory relief. Brandon L.J. stated that while a person 'cannot in terms found a cause of action on an estoppel, he may, as a result of being able to rely on an estoppel, succeed on a cause of action on which, without being able to rely on that estoppel, he would necessarily have failed'.[322]

(f) A GENERAL PRINCIPLE OF ESTOPPEL PREVENTING UNCONSCIENTIOUSNESS?

The tendency to regard the different forms of estoppel as aspects of a wider doctrine makes it difficult to justify restricting promissory estoppel to situations in which a promisee in the position of a defendant seeks to prevent a promisor from enforcing his strict legal rights, or a promisee in the position of a claimant has an independent cause of action and seeks to prevent a promisor from setting up a defence in breach of the promise which he has given. The High Court of Australia recognized this and has built on and gone further than *Crabb* v. *Arun D.C.* and *Amalgamated Investment & Property Co. Ltd.* v. *Texas Commerce International Bank Ltd.* In *Waltons Stores (Interstate) Ltd.* v. *Maher*:[323]

M was in negotiations with W to whom he hoped to lease premises which were to be demolished and redeveloped to W's specifications. Solicitors had been instructed to prepare formal documents and W's solicitors told M's solicitors that 'we believe approval will be forthcoming. Let you know tomorrow if any amendments not agreed to'. Later M submitted a contract and this was sent to W 'by way of exchange'. W did not respond for 2 months because it was privately reconsidering the whole deal and had instructed its solicitors 'to go slow'. Because it believed exchange would take place shortly and because, if the timetable for occupation specified by W was to be met, there was urgency, M started work. Two months later, when he had demolished the old premises and was well advanced with the new premises, W told him it intended to withdraw. M argued *inter alia* that W was estopped from denying that a concluded contract existed.

The majority of the Court, declining to fragment the unity of estoppel, held that promissory estoppel could found a cause of action and extended to the enforcement of voluntary promises; W was accordingly estopped. They did not believe this would abolish the doctrine of consideration 'in a back-handed way' because the two

[322] [1982] Q.B. 84, at p. 132. See also *per* Lord Denning M.R. at p. 122. Cf. Eveleigh L.J. at p. 126.
[323] (1988) 164 C.L.R. 387. See also *Restatement* (2d), § 90 (USA); *Harris* v. *Harris* [1989] N.Z. Conv. C. 190, 406 (New Zealand). See generally Spence, *Protecting Reliance* (1999).

protected different interests. An estoppel remedy only seeks to effect the minimum equity needed to avoid the detriment from reliance and unconscionable conduct whereas, where a promise is supported by consideration, the expectations of the promisee are protected even if the promise is entirely executory and there has been no reliance on it.[324] For instance, on the facts of *Williams* v. *Roffey Bros. & Nicholls (Contractors) Ltd.*,[325] W's expectation was to earn the total contract price (£20,000 plus the additional £10,300 promised) for the carpentry work in the flats but his reliance loss was the value of his work and the cost of materials in the flats in which he had worked, a lesser sum. Moreover, the unconscionability necessary to found an estoppel does not exist wherever a person goes back on a promise. What is necessary, save in the case of estoppel by convention, is the creation or encouragement by the party who is to be estopped (the 'promisor') of an assumption in the other ('the promisee') that a contract will come into existence or a promise will be performed and reliance on that assumption by the promisee to his detriment to the knowledge of the promisor.

This step still has to be taken in England, in part because of the perceived need to protect the doctrine of consideration. For example, in *Johnson* v. *Gore Wood & Co.*[326] Lord Goff stated that it was not possible for the test for estoppel by convention—acting on a common assumption—to apply to promises as opposed to existing facts because that would amount to the abandonment of the doctrine of consideration. Nevertheless, as well as the cases considered above, it has been said that it would be possible for a party to negotiations set out in a document to raise some form of estoppel to prevent the other party from refusing to proceed with the transactions envisaged by the document.[327] We have also seen that where negotiations have not led to the conclusion of a contract, reliance in the form of the rendering of services or delivery of goods by one party on assumptions created or encouraged by the other may give rise to a restitutionary remedy.[328] There are, moreover, examples of reliance generating a contract through unilateral contracts in which promises are rendered legally enforceable by virtue of the performance of an act by the promisee (i.e. reliance), often where the promisor has not expressly requested the performance of the act[329] and more recently by the recognition that performance of an existing obligation

---

[324] (1988) 164 C.L.R. 387, at p. 406. On the remedial consequences of this difference, see *post*, pp. 596, 599.

[325] [1991] 1 Q.B. 1, *ante*, p. 106.

[326] [2001] 2 W.L.R. 72, at pp. 98–99, citing Spencer Bower & Turner, *The Law Relating to Estoppel by Representation* (3rd edn., 1977), pp. 167–8. See also Colman J. in *Azov Shipping Co. Ltd.* v. *Baltic Shipping Co.* [1999] 2 Lloyd's Rep. 159, at p. 175 and *Thornton Springer* v. *N.E.M. Insurance Co. Ltd.* [2000] 2 All E.R. 489, at p. 516.

[327] *Att.-Gen. of Hong Kong* v. *Humphreys Estates (Queen's Gardens)* [1987] 1 A.C. 114, at pp. 127–8. See also *Akiens* v. *Salomon* (1992) 65 P. & C.R. 364, *per* Evans L.J., dissenting. But cf. *First National Bank plc* v. *Thompson* [1996] Ch. 231, *per* Millett L.J. at 236 (the 'attempt to demonstrate that all estoppels . . . are now subsumed in the single and all embracing estoppel by representation . . . has never won general acceptance').

[328] *Ante*, pp. 40, 63 and *Brewer St. Investments Ltd.* v. *Barclays Woollen Co. Ltd.* [1954] 1 Q.B. 428.

[329] *Warlow* v. *Harrison* (1858) 1 E. & E. 309, *ante*, p. 56; *Carlill* v. *Carbolic Smoke Ball Co.* [1893] 1 Q.B. 256, *ante*, p. 35; *Collen* v. *Wright* (1857) 8 E. & B. 647; *Spiro* v. *Lintern* [1973] 1 W.L.R. 1002; *New Zealand Shipping Co. Ltd.* v. *Satterthwaite & Co. Ltd.* [1975] A.C. 154, at pp. 167–8.

may be a 'practical' benefit.[330] The doctrinal foundations thus exist for it to be held that promissory estoppel is capable itself of creating a cause of action, notwithstanding that the promisee has provided no consideration.[331] It may be that it has not been *necessary* to do so in the cases that have come before the Courts because either a restitutionary remedy could be found or a bargain exchange could be implied. It is, however, arguable that, until this step is taken, it will not be possible to take up the suggestion made by Lord Hailsham L.C. in 1972 and reduce the sequence of cases based on promissory estoppel to a coherent body of doctrine.[332]

It has, moreover, been argued that it is better to deal with such promises by estoppel than by expanding the concept of consideration, for instance by including 'practical' benefit.[333] This, it is said, would maintain a desirable distinction between non-bargain promises where only reliance is protected and bargains, where expectations are also protected. This does not, however, adequately reflect the fact that in several of the promissory estoppel cases the Court has concluded that the minimum equity needed to avoid unconscientiousness will not be satisfied by anything short of enforcing the promise. Thus, for instance, the effect of the estoppel in the *High Trees* case would have been to prevent the landlord recovering the full rent between 1940 and 1945 and in *Crabb* v. *Arun D.C.* it was to grant C the right of way the council had undertaken to give him. In *Waltons Stores (Interstate) Ltd.* v. *Maher* the effect of the High Court of Australia's ruling that W was estopped from denying that a concluded contract existed appears to have been that M was entitled to damages in lieu of specific performance.[334] In these cases it appears that equitable relief went beyond the protection of reliance.[335]

VI. APPRAISAL OF CONSIDERATION AND PROMISSORY ESTOPPEL

Attempts have been made to justify the doctrine of consideration on the ground that it is essential both to the form and the substance of a contract. Consideration, it has been argued, is a formal necessity which serves to distinguish those promises by which

---

[330] *Ante*, p. 106.

[331] Thompson [1983] C.L.J. 257; Lunner [1992] Conv. 239.

[332] *Woodhouse A.C. Israel Cocoa Ltd. S.A.* v. *Nigerian Produce Marketing Co. Ltd.* [1972] A.C. 741, at p. 758.

[333] Chen-Wishart, in Beatson and Friedmann eds., *Good Faith and Fault in Contract Law* (1995), p. 141ff, also pointing out (*ibid.*, p. 134) that in *Williams* v. *Roffey Bros. & Nicholls (Contractors) Ltd.* [1991] 1 Q.B. 1, *ante*, p. 106, damages appear only to have been awarded for reliance loss, on which see *post*, p. 599.

[334] The trial judge's decision to this effect was affirmed by the New South Wales Court of Appeal (1986) 5 N.S.W.L.R. 407, and the High Court of Australia (1988) 164 C.L.R. 387. Such damages are assessed on the same basis as damages at common law, see *post*, pp. 630–2.

[335] Atiyah, *Essays on Contract* (1986), pp. 239–40; Yorio and Thel (1991) 101 Yale L.J. 111. See also *Commonwealth of Australia* v. *Verwayen* (1990) 170 C.L.R. 394, at pp. 412–13, 429, 487, 501 (not, however, a contract case).

the promisor intends to be legally bound from those which are not seriously meant: 'buyers intend business where philanthropists may not'.[336] But English law already requires an intent to effect legal relations as a distinct element of a contract. Consideration is cogent evidence of the existence of such an intent, but it is by no means conclusive proof that it is present.[337] The abolition of the doctrine would therefore simply mean that the test of contractual intention would assume a greater significance in the law of contract. Few persons would contend that this constituted an insuperable objection to a change in the law,[338] for civil law systems seem to exist quite happily without the need for consideration.[339]

Similarly, aspects of the doctrine, in particular the pre-existing duty rule, have been justified by the need to discourage improper pressure and coercion, a function now more directly and effectively served by the recent recognition of economic duress ground for avoiding a contract.[340]

It has also been argued that English law has made the empirical choice of enforcing bargains in the sense of exchanges rather than promises: 'consideration, offer and acceptance are an indivisible trinity, facets of one identical notion which is that of bargain'.[341] But this does not explain why it is thought better to enforce bargains.[342] Indeed the opposite appears to be the case. Desire to enforce promises had led the Courts on occasion to find a derisory consideration and to construct a bargain where none in fact was present since there was no real exchange. It has been stated that 'ultimately the question of consideration is a formality as in the use of a seal or the agreement to give a peppercorn'[343] and the recognition that a 'practical' benefit will make a promise enforceable[344] makes it difficult to sustain a purely bargain view of contract. Elsewhere, the absence of consideration may enable one of the parties to 'snap his fingers' at a promise deliberately made, and which the person seeking to enforce it has a legitimate interest to enforce.[345] The perception that this is incompatible with such legitimate interests led to the development of promissory estoppel in the context of the part performance of an existing duty. This development makes it difficult to regard bargain as the fundamental principle of contract. When put together with common law 'waiver',[346] it is arguable that consideration has been effectively confined to the formation of contracts and the error

---

[336] Smith and Thomas, *A Casebook on Contract*, 2nd edn. (1961), p. 126.

[337] *Balfour* v. *Balfour* [1919] 2 K.B. 571; *Coward* v. *Motor Insurers' Bureau* [1963] 1 Q.B. 259, *ante*, p. 70.

[338] Cf. Atiyah, *Consideration in Contracts: A Fundamental Restatement* (1971).

[339] Cf. Chloros (1968) 17 I.C.L.Q. 137; Markesinis [1978] C.L.J. 53.

[340] *Ante*, pp. 105, 107; *post*, p. 279 ff.

[341] Hamson (1938) 54 L.Q.R. 233, at p. 234.

[342] It has been said that non-bargain promises are economically sterile (Posner (1977) 6 J. Leg. Stud. 411) and that they should only be enforced if relied upon and only to the extent of the reliance (Eisenberg (1979) 47 U. of Chicago L.R. 1, 3–7).

[343] *Vantage Navigation Cpn.* v. *Suhail & Saud Bahwan Building Materials Llc. (The Alev)* [1989] 1 Lloyd's Rep. 138, *per* Hobhouse J. at p. 147.

[344] *Ante*, p. 106.

[345] *Ante*, p. 102 (pre-exisiting duty cases) and, albeit in the context of a contract for the benefit of a third party, *Dunlop Pneumatic Tyre Co. Ltd.* v. *Selfridge & Co. Ltd.* [1915] A.C. 847, *per* Lord Dunedin at p. 855.

[346] *Post*, p. 523.

in making it also regulate the discharge of contracts[347] has been substantially corrected.

It has been noted that consideration reflects a variety of policies and serves a number of functions. The doctrine has in the past been the Swiss army knife of the law, performing these functions[348] in an ingenious but imperfect way. Professor Simpson has described the identification and separation of these policies and functions and the development in the last 200 years of new, more targeted doctrines.[349] We now have a doctrine of offer and acceptance, a requirement of intention to create legal relations, a concept of economic duress, and a doctrine of privity of contract. There is considerable force in the conclusion of the Law Revision Committee in 1937,[350] which stated that in many cases consideration was a mere technicality, irreconcilable either with business expediency or common sense. In *Johnson* v. *Gore Wood & Co.*[351] Lord Goff stated that although 'the doctrine of consideration may not be very popular nowadays . . . [it] still exists as part of our law'. It is, however, submitted that its role should be confined to the formation of contracts and that there it should be supplemented by the principle of estoppel. The two protect different interests; estoppel will only come into play where there has been reliance, whereas if there is consideration the expectations of the promisee are protected even if the promise is entirely executory. Although an estoppel can only be raised where there has been reliance, where it is, as in a number of the cases discussed above,[352] relief may go beyond the protection of that reliance. Although an estoppel remedy only seeks to effect the minimum equity to avoid the detriment from reliance and unconscionable conduct, such cases are arguably explained as ones in which the Court concluded that unconscientiousness could only be prevented by enforcing the promise or otherwise protecting the promisee's expectations.

---

[347] Pollock, *Principles of Contract*, 12th edn. (1950), p. 146. See also Kötz, *European Contract Law* (1997), pp. 68–71.

[348] *Ante*, pp. 88–9.

[349] (1975) 91 L.Q.R. 247, 263.

[350] Cmd. 5449.

[351] [2001] 2 W.L.R. 72, at p. 99.

[352] *Ante*, p. 115.

4

THE TERMS OF
THE CONTRACT

In most cases the contract is composed of a number of contractual terms. This chapter considers the nature and import of those terms and the form which they may take. First, the terms of a contract will be distinguished from other representations or assertions not intended to be an integral part of the agreement. Secondly, the different types of terms which have been expressly inserted by the parties themselves are examined, as well as those which will be implied by the law.

The terms of a contract are often contained in some 'standard form' document drawn up by one of the parties or a trade association and frequently contain clauses excluding or limiting liability. The last section of this chapter considers special rules of notice between the contracting parties, the special rules of construction and interpretation with regard to exemption clauses, and legislative control of such clauses.

I. PROOF OF TERMS

(a) TERMS AND REPRESENTATIONS

During the course of negotiations leading to the conclusion of a binding agreement, one or other of the contracting parties may make a statement or give an assurance calculated to produce in the mind of the other party a belief that facts exist which render the proposed bargain advantageous to the interests of the other party. A Court may later have to decide whether this statement or assurance formed part of the contract, or whether it was merely a 'representation' or inducement, in the sense that the party making it did not undertake to make it good. Although, a representation which proves to be false renders the agreement voidable at the suit of the party misled[1] and, since 1964, may if made negligently give rise to damages nevertheless it cannot of itself give rise to an action for breach of contract.[2] Such an action will only lie for breach of a contractual term. The question whether a particular statement is a term of the contract or a representation is frequently one of considerable difficulty and the basis of the distinction between the two has been criticized.[3]

---

[1] *Post*, Chapter 6.
[2] *Behn* v. *Burness* (1863) 3 B. & S. 751, at p. 753.
[3] Williston (1913) 27 Harv. L. Rev. 1; Atiyah, *Essays on Contract* (1986), p. 275.

(i) Intention to promise

The primary test is of *contractual intention*, that is, whether there is evidence of an intention by one or both parties that there should be contractual liability in respect of the accuracy of the statement.[4] The question therefore is: on the totality of evidence, must the person making the statement be taken to have *warranted* its accuracy, i.e. promised to make it good? If the facts of the case are such as to show this intention the Court may construe as a term of the contract a statement or assurance made anterior to the final agreement. In *Bannerman* v. *White*:[5]

B offered hops for sale to W. W asked if any sulphur had been used in the treatment of the year's growth, as brewers were refusing hops contaminated with sulphur. B said 'No'. W said that he would not even ask the price if sulphur had been used. They then discussed the price, and W ultimately purchased by sample B's entire growth. After the hops were delivered he repudiated the contract on the ground that the hops contained sulphur. B sued for their price. It was proved that sulphur had been used on five of B's three hundred acres. B had used it for the purpose of trying a new machine, and had either forgotten the matter or thought it unimportant.

The jury found that the statement made as to the use of sulphur was not wilfully false, and so the question whether W was entitled to reject the hops turned upon whether it should be regarded as a condition of the agreement that the hops might be rejected if sulphur had been used. It was argued that 'the conversation relating to the sulphur was preliminary to entering on the contract and no part thereof', but the jury found it was understood and intended by the parties to be part of the contract of sale. The Court of Common Pleas upheld this finding, and said that B's assurance was the condition upon which the parties contracted and the breach of it discharged W from liability to take the hops.[6]

(ii) Inferring intention to promise

One question is whether the requisite intention must be positively shown or whether it can be inferred from the circumstances in which the statement was made. Although there is authority supporting the latter,[7] in *Heilbut, Symons & Co.* v. *Buckleton*, the House of Lords suggested that intention must be positively shown.[8]

B telephoned H.S.'s agent and said 'I understand you are bringing out a rubber company'. The reply was 'We are'. B asked for a prospectus, and was told there were none available. He then asked 'if it was all right', and the agent replied 'We are bringing it out'. On the faith of this, B bought shares which turned out to be of little value. The company was not accurately

---

[4] *Heilbut, Symons & Co.* v. *Buckleton* [1913] A.C. 30, at p. 51 (*post*, n. 8).

[5] (1861) 10 C.B.N.S. 844. Contrast *Hopkins* v. *Tanqueray* (1854) 15 C.B. 130, which is probably wrongly decided.

[6] [1913] A.C. 30.

[7] *Schawel* v. *Reade* [1913] 2 Ir. R. 64, at pp. 84, 86 (H.L.), *per* Lord Atkinson and Lord Moulton.

[8] [1913] A.C. 30, at pp. 38, 42, 49–50, *per* Lord Haldane L.C., Lord Atkinson and Lord Moulton. See also *Independent Broadcasting Authority* v. *EMI Electronics Ltd.* (1980) 14 B.L.R. 1, at pp. 22–3, 32, 41 (H.L.) (in respect of a statement made *long* after the contract).

described as 'a rubber company', although this assurance had not been given in bad faith. B claimed damages for breach of contract.

The House of Lords held that no breach of contract had been committed. There had been merely a representation and no warranty. There was no intention on the part of either or both of the parties that there should be contractual liability in respect of the accuracy of the statement. *Heilbut, Symons & Co.* v. *Buckleton* has been criticized[9] and Courts are no longer as reluctant to find that a pre-contractual statement amounts to a term of the contract.[10]

The difficulty of ascertaining intention, however, means that the dividing line between the two categories of statement remains one that is not easy to draw in practice. For example, in *Oscar Chess Ltd.* v. *Williams*,[11] a private seller sold a motor-car to a firm of dealers. He told them that the car was a 1948 model, and the car log-book showed that it had been first registered in 1948. In fact it was a 1939 model. The log-book had been altered by some unknown person. The Court of Appeal (Morris L.J. dissenting) held that the seller's statement was not a term of the contract, but merely a representation not giving rise to any action for breach of contract. On the other hand, in *Dick Bentley Productions Ltd.* v. *Harold Smith (Motors) Ltd.*,[12] a statement made by a motor dealer to a private purchaser, based on a reading of the milometer, that it had done only 20,000 miles, whereas in fact it had done 100,000, was held to be a contractual term. The *Oscar Chess* case was distinguished on the ground that the seller 'honestly believed on reasonable grounds that [the statement] was true', whereas the motor dealer in the latter case 'who was in a position to know, or at least to find out the history of the car', 'stated a fact that should be within his own knowledge. He had jumped to a conclusion and stated it as a fact'.[13]

In endeavouring to reach a conclusion on this point, the Courts can be said to take into account a number of factors. First, they may have regard to the time which elapsed between the time of making the statement and the final manifestation of agreement; if the interval is a long one, this points to a representation.[14] Secondly, they may consider the importance of the statement in the minds of the parties; a statement which is important is likely to be classed as a term of the contract.[15] Thirdly, if the statement was followed by the execution of a formal contract in writing, it is more likely to be regarded as a representation where it is not incorporated in the written document.[16] Finally, where the maker of the statement is, *vis-à-vis* the other party, in a better position to ascertain the accuracy of the statement or has the primary

---

[9] Williston (1913) 27 Harv. L. Rev. 1; Greig (1971) 87 L.Q.R. 179, Atiyah, *Essays on Contract* (1986), pp. 277–8.

[10] *J. Evans & Son (Portsmouth) Ltd.* v. *Andrea Merzario Ltd.* [1976] 1 W.L.R. 1078, at p. 1081; *Esso Petroleum Co. Ltd.* v. *Mardon* [1976] Q.B. 801, at p. 817; *Howard Marine and Dredging Co. Ltd.* v. *A. Ogden & Sons (Excavations) Ltd.* [1978] Q.B. 574, at p. 590.

[11] [1957] 1 W.L.R. 370. Cf. *Beale* v. *Taylor* [1967] 1 W.L.R. 1193.

[12] [1965] 1 W.L.R. 623.

[13] At pp. 628, 629.

[14] *Routledge* v. *McKay* [1954] 1 W.L.R. 615; *Howard Marine and Dredging Co. Ltd.* v. *A. Ogden & Sons (Excavations) Ltd.* [1978] Q.B. 574, at p. 591. Cf. *Birch* v. *Paramount Estates Ltd.* (1956) 167 Est. Gaz. 396.

[15] *Bannerman* v. *White* (1861) 10 C.B.N.S. 844. Cf. *Oscar Chess Ltd.* v. *Williams* (*supra*, n. 11).

[16] *Heilbut, Symons & Co.* v. *Buckleton* [1913] A.C. 30, at p. 50. Cf. *Miller* v. *Cannon Hill Estates Ltd.* [1931] 2 K.B. 113, and see *post*, p. 130 (collateral warranty).

responsibility for doing this, the Courts will tend to regard it as a contractual term[17] unless it relates to a process, such as a medical procedure, the results of which are inherently unpredictable.[18]

(iii) The influence of wider considerations

The precise place in which the dividing line between representations and terms is drawn may have also been affected by other factors. One of these was the distorting effect of the rule that, before 1964, precluded a damages remedy for negligent mis-statement. While parties seeking to escape from this much criticized feature of English law would often argue that a statement was a warranty, at times when Courts have been conscious of the need to maintain the integrity of the rule, as in *Heilbut, Symons & Co.* v. *Buckleton*, they have not been receptive to such arguments.[19] Although the purpose of making the distinction is no longer to determine whether the maker of the statement is liable in damages, there are still remedial differences. Damages for breach of contract do not depend on establishing negligence and the measure of damages for breach of contract differs from that for misrepresentation.[20] Secondly, in the past it was generally not possible to adduce extrinsic, e.g. oral, evidence to contradict or vary the terms of a written agreement.[21] This 'parol evidence' rule meant that whatever the intention of the parties and however important the oral statement, it could only exceptionally be held to be a term of the contract and had, therefore, normally to be classified as a representation.[22]

(b) COLLATERAL WARRANTIES

Where a preliminary statement or assurance is not a term of the principal agreement the Courts may be prepared to treat it as a contract or 'warranty', collateral to the principal agreement.[23] In particular, in the past, this device has been used where the principal agreement has been reduced to writing, since the parol evidence rule gener-ally prevented the assurance from constituting a term of that contract. But the Courts will, provided the necessary contractual intention is present, construe the assurance as a collateral contract or warranty, conferring a right to damages.[24] Thus where tenants executed leases upon the oral assurance of the landlord that the drains were in good order,[25] or that the landlord would not enforce a covenant against residing on the

---

[17] *Schawel* v. *Reade* (*supra*, n. 7); *Dick Bentley Productions Ltd.* v. *Harold Smith* (*Motors*) *Ltd.* (*supra*, n. 12). See also *Harlingdon and Leinster Enterprises Ltd.* v. Christopher Hull Fine Art [1991] 1 Q.B. 564, at pp. 577, 585. Cf. *Heilbut, Symons & Co.* v. *Buckleton* (*supra*, n. 8); *Beale* v. *Taylor* (*supra*, n. 11).

[18] *Thake* v. *Maurice* [1986] Q.B. 644 (statement that vasectomy was irreversible not a warranty).

[19] Cf. *Heilbut, Symons & Co.* v. *Buckleton* [1913] A.C. 30, at p. 51 and *Esso Petroleum Co. Ltd.* v. *Mardon* [1976] Q.B. 801, at p. 817.

[20] *Post*, pp. 245, 247.

[21] *Post*, p. 132.

[22] For a modern example, see *Lambert* v. *Lewis* [1982] A.C. 225, at p. 263.

[23] Wedderburn [1959] C.L.J. 58.

[24] *Morgan* v. *Griffith* (1871) L.R. 6 Ex. 70; *Newman* v. *Gatti* (1907) 24 T.L.R. 18, at p. 20; *Miller* v. *Cannon Hill Estates Ltd.* [1931] 2 K.B. 113; *Birch* v. *Paramount Estates Ltd.* (1956) 167 Est. Gaz. 396; *Frisby* v. *B.B.C.* [1967] Ch. 932.

[25] *De Lassalle* v. *Guildford* [1901] 2 K.B. 215.

premises,[26] the tenant was held entitled to enforce the assurance as a collateral warranty. In particular, a statement will be likely to found a warranty where one party refuses to enter into a contract unless the other gives it an assurance on a certain point.[27] In 1913, Lord Moulton said of such collateral warranties that they are 'viewed with suspicion by the law. They must be proved strictly', and that they 'must from their very nature be rare'.[28] Nevertheless, since that time the Courts have showed themselves much more willing to treat pre-contractual statements as collateral warranties, and they are no longer rare. In *Esso Petroleum Co. Ltd.* v. *Mardon*,[29] for example:

Esso found a site on a busy main street which it considered suitable for the erection of a petrol filling station. An experienced employee estimated that the throughput of petrol at the station would reach 200,000 gallons in the third year of operation. But the planning authority refused permission for the forecourt and pumps to be sited on the main street and they had to be sited at the rear of the premises where they were only accessible by side streets. M applied for a tenancy of the filling station. He was interviewed by the experienced employee, who gave him the same estimate of throughput but failed to take account of the fact that the filling station was now 'back to front'. In reliance on the estimate, M took a 3-year lease of the filling station. Despite his best efforts, the site proved incapable of a throughput of more than 60,000 to 70,000 gallons. In an action by Esso for possession of the station and monies due for petrol supplied, M counterclaimed damages for (*inter alia*) breach of a collateral warranty.

The Court of Appeal rejected the argument that the estimate could not amount to a warranty because it was a forecast or statement of opinion. It was held that the statement as to potential throughput amounted to a collateral warranty—not in the sense that Esso guaranteed that the throughput would reach 200,000 gallons—but a warranty that the forecast had been prepared with reasonable care and skill. Since Esso negligently made 'a fatal error' in the forecast given to M, and on which he took the tenancy, they were liable to him in damages.

(c) FLOATING WARRANTIES

This device of a collateral warranty has also been employed where the principal contract is one to which either the person giving, or the person receiving, the assurance is not a party. In *Shanklin Pier Ltd.* v. *Detel Products Ltd.*:[30]

The owners of Shanklin Pier in the Isle of Wight wished to paint the pier and consulted D, a firm of paint manufacturers. D told the owners that its paint was suitable for the purpose,

---

[26] *City and Westminster Properties (1934) Ltd.* v. *Mudd* [1959] Ch. 129. See also *Erskine* v. *Adeane* (1873) 8 Ch. App. 756 (landlord's assurance that the game upon the land would be culled).

[27] *Erskine* v. *Adeane* (*supra*, n. 26); *De Lassalle* v. *Guildford* (*supra*, n. 25); *Couchman* v. *Hill* [1947] K.B. 554.

[28] *Heilbut, Symons & Co.* v. *Buckleton* [1913] A.C. 30, at p. 47.

[29] [1976] Q.B. 801. Cf *Jonathan Wren & Co. Ltd.* v. *Microdec plc* (1999) 65 Con. L.R. 157 (Lord Moulton's approach 'applies strongly' where it is sought to make a third party additionally liable for some performance).

[30] [1951] 2 K.B. 854. See also *Wells (Merstham) Ltd.* v. *Buckland Sand & Silica Co. Ltd.* [1965] 2 Q.B. 170; *Lambert* v. *Lewis* [1982] A.C. 225, at p. 263.

and, relying on this statement, the owners caused to be inserted in their agreement with the contractors who were to paint the pier a term requiring the use of D's paint. The paint proved unsuitable and the owners sued the D for breach of warranty.

McNair J. held that the owners were entitled to damages. He said:[31]

I see no reason why there may not be an enforceable warranty between A and B supported by the consideration that B should cause C to enter into a contract with A or that B should do some other act for the benefit of A.

This principle is particularly applicable to cases of hire-purchase where a dealer first sells the article to a hire-purchase finance company which then lets it on hire to the hirer. If the dealer gives a warranty, which induces the hirer to enter into the contract of hire, this warranty is enforceable against the dealer by the hirer, even though the actual contract of hire purchase is not made between them.[32]

(d) EXTRINSIC EVIDENCE

Where the parties put their agreement in a written document, the question arises whether extrinsic evidence may be led to establish the existence of a term or to explain the words used in the document.[33] It has often been said that 'it is firmly established as a rule of law that parol evidence cannot be admitted to add to, vary or contradict a deed or other written instrument', including a contract.[34] Although the purpose of this rule (which was more favoured in the past than it is now)[35] is to promote certainty[36] and to save time in the conduct of litigation,[37] it has long been the subject of a large number of exceptions which have resulted in uncertainty. Thus, extrinsic evidence is admissible to prove the factual background known to the contracting parties. Apart from the previous negotiations of the parties, the 'background' includes anything reasonably available to the parties which would have affected the way in which the language of the document would have been understood by a reasonable person.[38] Extrinsic evidence is thus admissible to prove the aim of the transaction,[39] to ascertain the true meaning of ambiguity in a written agreement,[40] to prove the

---

[31] At p. 856.

[32] *Andrews* v. *Hopkinson* [1957] 1 Q.B. 229; *Yeoman Credit Ltd.* v. *Ogders* [1962] 1 W.L.R. 215.

[33] See Steyn [1988] C.L.P. 23 and *post*, p. 160 on the construction of terms.

[34] *Jacobs* v. *Batavia and General Plantations Trust* [1924] 1 Ch. 287, at p. 295; *Bank of Australasia* v. *Palmer* [1897] A.C. 540, at p. 454; *Rabin* v. *Gerson Berger Association Ltd.* [1986] 1 W.L.R. 526, at p. 530; *Adams* v. *British Airways plc* [1995] I.R.L.R. 577, at p. 583.

[35] Law Com. No. 154, *The Parol Evidence Rule* (1986), §§ 2.3–2.4.

[36] *Shore* v. *Wilson* (1842) 9 C.L. & F. 355, 565–6; *Inglis* v. *John Buttery & Co.* (1878) 3 App. Cas. 552, at p. 577; *Mercantile Agency Co. Ltd.* v. *Flitwick Chalybeate Co.* (1897) 14 T.L.R. 90.

[37] *Prenn* v. *Simmonds* [1971] 1 W.L.R. 1381, at p. 1384.

[38] *Investors Compensation Scheme Ltd.* v. *W. Bromwich B.S.* [1998] 1 W.L.R. 896, *per* Lord Hoffmann at p. 913.

[39] *Prenn* v. *Simmonds* (*supra*, n. 37) at p. 1382; *International Fina Services A.G.* v. *Katrina Shipping Ltd.* [1995] 2 Lloyd's Rep. 344, at p. 350; *Charter Reinsurance Co.* v. *Fagan* [1996] 2 Lloyd's Rep. 113, at pp. 119, 123. See also *Hayden* v. *Lo & Lo* [1997] 1 W.L.R. 198, at p. 205.

[40] *L. G. Schuler AG* v. *Wickman Machine Tool Sales Ltd.* [1974] A.C. 235, at p. 261.

existence of a collateral agreement,[41] to establish implied terms[42] and, more importantly, if it is shown that the document was not intended to express the entire agreement between the parties.[43] It is also admissible to show that the contract is not operative[44] and to impugn the validity of the contract on the grounds of fraud, illegality, misrepresentation,[45] mistake, or duress.

The width of the exceptions led the Law Commission to conclude that:

although a proposition of law can be stated which can be described as the 'parol evidence' rule it is not a rule of law which, correctly applied, could lead to evidence being unjustly excluded. Rather it is a proposition of law which is no more than a circular statement: when it is proved or admitted that the parties to a contract intended that all the express terms in their agreement should be recorded in a particular document or documents, evidence will be inadmissible (because irrelevant) if it is tendered only for the purpose of adding to, varying, subtracting from or contradicting the express terms of that contract.[46]

The Commission concluded[47] that there is no *rule of law* precluding the admissibility of evidence solely because a document exists which looks like a complete contract and that there was accordingly no need for legislation to abrogate the supposed rule as it had provisionally recommended in its Working Paper.[48] The presumption that a document which looks like a contract is the whole contract is only a presumption,[49] and, save where the document states that it contains the entire contract,[50] is unlikely to preclude the receipt of evidence of other terms not included expressly or by reference in the document. Although the traditional description of a parol evidence *rule* may have a lingering influence,[51] the Commission's approach has been judicially approved[52] and is also attractive from a policy point of view. This is because, although facilitating the parties' intentions is an important function of contract law, regarding

---

[41] *Ante*, p. 130.

[42] *Gillespie Bros. & Co.* v. *Cheney Eggar & Co.* [1896] 2 Q.B. 59 (term implied under the Sale of Goods Act 1979); *Hutton* v. *Warren* (1836) 1 M. and W. 466 (custom).

[43] *Mercantile Bank of Sydney* v. *Taylor* [1893] A.C. 317, at p. 321; *Gillespie Bros. & Co.* v. *Cheney, Eggar & Co.* (*supra*, n. 42), at p. 62; *J. Evans & Son (Portsmouth) Ltd.* v. *Andrea Merzario Ltd.* [1976] 1 W.L.R. 1078, at p. 1083.

[44] *Pym* v. *Campbell* (1856) 6 E. & B. 370.

[45] *Thomas Witter Ltd.* v. *T.B.P. Industries Ltd.* [1996] 2 All E.R. 573, at p. 595.

[46] Law Com. No. 154 (1986), § 2.7. See generally Wedderburn [1959] C.L.J. 58.

[47] § 2.17.

[48] Law. Com. W.P. No. 76 (1976).

[49] *Gillespie Bros. & Co.* v. *Cheney Eggar & Co.* (*supra*, n. 42).

[50] *McGrath* v. *Shaw* (1987) 57 P. & C.R. 452, at pp. 459–60. But even such a clause may not prevent a claim for misrepresentation: *Thomas Witter Ltd.* v. *T.B.P. Industries Ltd.* [1996] 2 All E.R. 573, at pp. 595–7.

[51] e.g. *Perrylease Ltd.* v. *Imecar AG* [1988] 1 W.L.R. 463; *A. G. Securities* v. *Vaughan* [1990] 1 A.C. 417, at pp. 468–9, 475; *Guardian Ocean Cargos Ltd.* v. *Banco de Brasil S.A.* [1991] 2 Lloyd's Rep. 68 (but evidence admitted and approach consistent with Law Commission's). Administration of Justice Act 1982, s. 21, permitting the limited receipt of extrinsic evidence in the interpretation of wills, appears to assume the existence of a 'rule'.

[52] *Wild* v. *Civil Aviation Authority* (C.A., 25 September 1987); *Haryanto (Yani)* v. *E.D. & F. Man (Sugar) Ltd.* [1986] 2 Lloyd's Rep. 44, at p. 46. See also *Rosseel N.V.* v. *Oriental Commercial and Shipping Co. (U.K.) Ltd.* [1991] 2 Lloyd's Rep. 625, at p. 628; *State Rail Authority of New South Wales* v. *Heath Outdoor Pty. Ltd.* (1986) 7 N.S.W.L.R. 170, at p. 192; *Norwest Beef Industries Ltd.* v. *P & O Steam Navigation Co.* (1987) 8 N.S.W.L.R. 568, at p. 570.

the issue as governed by a rule of law can have the effect of excluding much evidence of the intentions of the parties without achieving the certainty which the 'rule' aimed to achieve.

II. EXPRESS TERMS

(a) TYPES OF TERMS

Contracts are normally made up of various terms, differing in character and importance. The parties may regard some of these as vital, others as subsidiary, or collateral to the main purpose of the contract. Where a term is broken, the approach of the Courts has been to discover, from the tenor of the contract, the expressed intention of the parties, or the consequences of the breach, whether it was vital to the contract or not.

(i) Conditions and warranties

On one approach, which is reflected in the Sale of Goods Act 1979,[53] the term is classified at the time the contract is made as either a condition or a warranty. If the parties regarded the term as essential, it is classified as a *condition*: any breach of a condition gives the innocent party the option of being discharged from further performance of the contract. The innocent party can also claim damages for any loss sustained by the fact that the contract has not been performed. If the parties did not regard the term as essential, but as subsidiary or collateral, it is classified as a *warranty*; its failure gives rise to a claim for such damages as have been sustained by the breach of that particular term, but the innocent party is not given the option of being discharged from further performance. The classification of a term as being either a 'condition' or a 'warranty' will therefore determine the legal remedies available to the innocent party in the event of its breach.

Nevertheless, it is right to observe that the word 'condition' is sometimes used, even in legal documents, to mean simply 'a stipulation, a provision', and does not carry the meaning given to it by lawyers as a term of art.[54] Moreover, in the context of non-consumer sales, statute has restricted the right of a buyer to reject goods by reason of certain implied conditions if the breach is so slight that it would be unreasonable to reject them.[55] The word 'warranty' is also employed in a variety of senses, and in many of the earlier cases and also in insurance law[56] it is not infrequently used simply to mean a term of the contract, whether a warranty proper or a condition. Whether or not the words 'condition' or 'warranty' are employed in their technical sense must,

---

[53] See *post*, p. 153.

[54] *L. G. Schuler AG* v. *Wickman Machine Tool Sales Ltd.* [1974] A.C. 235.

[55] Sale of Goods Act 1979, ss. 15A, 30A, *post*, p. 153.

[56] Marine Insurance Act 1906, ss. 33–41; *Bank of Nova Scotia* v. *Hellenic Mutual War Risks Association (Bermuda) Ltd.* [1992] 1 A.C. 233.

therefore, depend upon the intention of the parties to be ascertained from their agreement and from the subject-matter to which it relates.

(ii) Intermediate terms

Another approach, often seen as more modern but in fact with older roots,[57] rejects the proposition that every term of a contract can be classified as either a condition or a warranty. On this approach there is a third category of *intermediate* (or 'innomin-ate'[58]) terms. The legal consequences of the breach of such a term (i.e. whether or not the innocent party is entitled to treat itself as discharged) do not follow automatically from a prior classification of the undertaking but depend upon the nature and consequences of the breach.

(b) CONDITIONS

A condition may be defined as a statement of fact, or a promise, which forms an essential term of the contract.[59] If the statement of fact proves untrue, or the promise is not fulfilled, the breach may be treated as a repudiation which discharges the innocent party from further performance of the contract.

An illustration of a statement of fact forming a condition is the case of *Behn* v. *Burness*,[60] where a ship was stated in the contract of charterparty to be 'now in the port of Amsterdam'. The fact that the ship was not in the port at the date of the contract discharged the charterer from performance. An example of a promise is provided by the case of *Glaholm* v. *Hays*:[61]

A charterparty provided that a vessel was to go from England to Trieste and there load a cargo: 'the vessel to sail from England on or before the 4th day of February next'. The vessel did not sail for some days after the 4th February, and on its arrival at Trieste the charterers refused to load a cargo and treated the contract as repudiated.

It was held that the charterers were entitled to be discharged from the contract. The Court of Common Pleas stated:[62]

Whether a particular clause in a charter-party shall be held to be a condition, upon the non-performance of which by the one party, the other is at liberty to abandon the contract, and consider it at an end; or whether it amounts to an agreement only, the breach whereof is to be recompensed by an action for damages, must depend upon the intention of the parties to be collected, in each particular case, from the terms of the agreement itself, and from the subject-matter to which it relates . . . [W]e think the intention of the parties to this contract

---

[57] e.g. *Freeman* v. *Taylor* (1831) 8 Bing. 124, at p. 138. See also *Boone* v. *Eyre* (1779) 1 H. Bl. 273n; *Davidson* v. *Gwynne* (1810) 12 East. 381; *Clipsham* v. *Vertue* (1843) 5 Q.B. 265; *McAndrew* v. *Chapple* (1866) L.R. 1 C.P. 643, at p. 648.

[58] This terminology was first used by Smith and Thomas, *A Casebook on Contract*, 4th edn. (1961).

[59] See also *post*, Chapter 15.

[60] (1862) 1 B. & S. 877; (1863) 3 B. & S. 751.

[61] (1841) 2 M. & G. 257. See also *Petrotrade Inc.* v. *Stinnes Handel GmbH* [1995] 1 Lloyd's Rep. 142, at p. 149.

[62] At pp. 266, 268.

sufficiently appears to have been, to insure the ship's sailing at the latest by the 4th February, and that the only mode of effecting this is by holding the clause in question to have been a condition precedent; which we consider it to have been.

(i) Promissory and contingent conditions

The idea which underlies the use of the word 'condition' in *Glaholm* v. *Hays* is that the term is so vital to the operation of the contract that its fulfilment by one party is a condition precedent to liability on the part of the other. But a condition also usually means an essential undertaking in the contract which one party *promises* will be made good. If it is not made good, not only will the other party be entitled to treat itself as discharged, but also *to sue for damages for breach*. A condition is therefore normally a 'promissory' condition, that is to say, the breach of it entitles the innocent party to be released from further performance of the contract and to be compensated by damages.

Alternatively, and exceptionally, however, a condition may be a 'contingent' condition. For instance, it may be provided that a contract shall not take effect unless or until the condition is fulfilled or that a particular duty under the contract does not become due unless or until the fulfilment of the condition.[63] The existence or enforceability of the contract or the particular obligation is dependent upon the fulfilment of the condition, but there is no guarantee or promise that it will be fulfilled.

The distinction between promissory conditions and the first type of contingent condition was illustrated by Denning L.J. in *Trans Trust SPRL* v. *Danubian Trading Co. Ltd.*[64] when considering a stipulation in a contract of sale of goods which related to the opening by the buyer of a letter of credit[65] in favour of the seller:

> What is the legal position of such a stipulation? Sometimes it is a condition precedent to the formation of a contract, that is, it is a condition which must be fulfilled before any contract is concluded at all. In those cases the stipulation 'subject to the opening of a credit' is rather like a stipulation 'subject to contract'.[66] If no credit is provided, there is no contract between the parties. In other cases, a contract is concluded and the stipulation for a credit is a condition which is an essential term of the contract. In those cases the provision of the credit is a condition precedent, not to the formation of a contract, but to the obligation of the seller to deliver the goods. If the buyer fails to provide the credit, the seller can treat himself as discharged from further performance of the contract and can sue the buyer for damages for not providing the credit.

This does not, however, take account of the situation in which the stipulation operates to qualify not the contract but the particular obligation but is nevertheless contingent.

---

[63] *Restatement* (2d), § 224 provides that a condition is 'an event, not certain to occur, which must occur, unless occurrence is excused, before performance under a contract comes due'.

[64] [1952] 2 Q.B. 297, at p. 304.

[65] See *post*, p. 445.

[66] See *ante*, p. 67. The parallel is not an exact one, for in the case of an agreement 'subject to contract' there is no obligation at all, whereas in the case of a contingent condition there may be an implied obligation to facilitate, or not to prevent, the fulfilment of the condition: *Dodd* v. *Churton* [1897] 1 Q.B. 562; *MacKay* v. *Dick* (1881) 6 App. Cas. 251: *Thompson* v. *ASDA-MFI plc* [1988] Ch. 241.

The examples below show that the insertion of a contingent condition may produce one of several effects.[67]

First, it may prevent the formation of any immediately binding contract, as in *Pym v. Campbell*[68] where the parties entered into an agreement for the sale and purchase of part of the proceeds of an invention on the express oral understanding that it should not bind them until a third party approved the invention. In such a situation, either party may withdraw from the transaction at any time before the condition is fulfilled.

Secondly, one party may assume an immediate unilateral obligation, say, to sell or to buy land or goods from the other, but subject to a condition. In this case, there is a contract from the start imposing a unilateral obligation from which one party cannot withdraw;[69] but no bilateral contract of sale, binding on both parties, comes into existence until the condition is fulfilled.[70] Many options in leases and hire purchase agreements are of this nature; in such cases the fulfilment of the condition depends on the will of the option holder.

Thirdly, the parties may enter into an immediately binding contract, the operation of which is suspended pending fulfilment of the condition. So, for example, an agreement 'conditional on the seller securing all relevant approvals from the Secretary of State'[71] is a contract from which neither party can resile until it can be definitely ascertained that the condition will not be fulfilled. Alternatively, while the operation of the contract is not suspended, that of a particular obligation under it is. Thus, the obligation of an insurer to pay does not arise until the occurrence of the loss.

In none of these situations, however, does either party render itself liable in damages to the other in the event of non-fulfilment of the condition. Even if, as is often the case, the Court is prepared to imply a term that one of the parties will use all reasonable endeavours to secure fulfilment of the condition, as, for example, where a sale of land is conditional upon planning permission being obtained,[72] or goods are sold subject to an import or export licence,[73] the fact that the condition is contingent, and not promissory, will prevent any liability from arising if that party's reasonable endeavours prove unavailing. Although, however, non-fulfilment of a contingent condition does not give rise to a claim in damages, non-fulfilment may, when the time has elapsed for its performance, give either party the right to treat the contract as at an end.[74]

---

[67] For a more detailed account of these effects, see *United Dominions Trust (Commercial) Ltd. v. Eagle Aircraft Services Ltd.* [1968] 1 W.L.R 74, at p. 82; *Wood Preservation Ltd. v. Prior* [1969] 1 W.L.R. 1077, at p. 1090; *L. G. Schuler AG v. Wickman Machine Tool Sales Ltd.* [1972] 1 W.L.R. 840, at pp. 850–1 (C.A.), [1974] A.C. 235 (H.L.).

[68] (1856) 6 E. & B. 370. See also *Aberfoyle Plantations Ltd. v. Cheng* [1960] A.C. 115; *William Cory & Son Ltd. v. I.R.C.* [1965] A.C. 1088. Cf. *Haslemere Estates Ltd. v. Baker* [1982] 1 W.L.R. 1109.

[69] *Smith v. Butler* [1900] 1 Q.B. 694.

[70] *United Dominions Trust (Commercial) Ltd. v. Eagle Aircraft Services Ltd.* (*supra*, n. 67). Cf. *Eastham v. Leigh, London & Provincial Properties Ltd.* [1971] Ch. 871.

[71] *Total Gas Marketing Ltd. v. Arco British Ltd.* [1998] 2 Lloyd's Rep. 209, at pp. 215, 221.

[72] *Hargreaves Transport Ltd. v. Lynch* [1969] 1 W.L.R. 215.

[73] *Re Anglo-Russian Merchant Traders Ltd. v. John Batt & Co. (London) Ltd.* [1917] 2 K.B. 679; *Coloniale Import-Export v. Loumidis & Sons* [1978] 2 Lloyd's Rep. 560.

[74] *Total Gas Marketing Ltd. v. Arco British Ltd.* (*supra*, n. 71), at pp. 218, 221, 226. But not so as to discharge liabilities which had accrued unconditionally: *Kazakstan Wool Processors (Europe) Ltd. v. Nederlansche Credietrzekering Maatschappij NV* [2000] 1 All E.R. (Comm.) 708; *post*, p. 578.

(ii) Conditions subsequent

Another sense in which the word 'condition' is used is that of a condition subsequent. Here the parties agree that the contract is to be immediately binding, but if certain facts are ascertained to exist or upon the happening of a certain event, then either the contract is to cease to bind or one party is to have the option to cancel the contract. In *Brown* v. *Knowlsey B.C.*[75] a contract of employment provided that a temporary teacher's appointment was to last only as long as sufficient funds were provided either by the Manpower Services Commission or other sponsors. It was held that the contract was terminated when such funds ceased to be provided.

Such conditions may also take the form of promises or covenants which impose upon one of the parties to the contract an obligation which he is contractually bound to perform. For example, in many leases there is an express provision for forfeiture of the lease in the event of the tenant's failure to repair.[76]

(c) WARRANTIES

Breach of a warranty, does not entitle the innocent party to treat the contract as repudiated, but only to claim damages.

A warranty has been said to be 'an agreement which refers to the subject matter of a contract, but, not being an essential part of the contract either intrinsically or by agreement, is collateral to the main purpose of such a contract'.[77] The nature of a warranty is illustrated by the case of *Bettini* v. *Gye*:[78]

B contracted with G, the director of the Royal Italian Opera in London, for the exclusive use of his services as a singer in operas and concerts for a period of 3 months. B undertook *inter alia* that he would be in London at least 6 days before the commencement of his engagement, for rehearsals, but only arrived 2 days beforehand. G refused to go on with the contract and was sued by B for breach.

The Court held that, having regard to the length of the contract and the nature of the performances to be given, the rehearsal clause was not vital to the agreement. It was not a condition but merely a warranty. Accordingly its breach did not entitle G to treat the contract as at an end.

It is reasonable to assume that, in the particular circumstances of *Bettini* v. *Gye*, any breach of the rehearsal clause could have been compensated for by damages. But in most cases it would be misleading to conclude that damages would be a sufficient remedy for every breach of even a seemingly unimportant term. The consequences of the breach of such a term might be so serious as to go to the root of the contract. Unless, therefore, a term has been specifically designated a 'warranty' by statute,[79] or

---

[75] [1986] I.R.L.R. 102. See also *Head* v. *Tattersall* (1871) L.R. 7 Ex. 7; *Gyllenhammer & Partners* v. *Sour Brodogradevna* [1989] 2 Lloyd's Rep. 403.

[76] *Post*, p. 647.

[77] *Dawsons Ltd.* v. *Bonnin* [1922] 2 A.C. 413, *per* Lord Haldane at p. 422. See also Sale of Goods Act 1979, s. 61(1).

[78] (1876) 1 Q.B.D. 183. Cf. *Poussard* v. *Spiers* (1876) 1 Q.B.D. 410.

[79] Sale of Goods Act 1979, ss. 12(2), (4), (5) and (5A) and 61(1); Supply of Goods (Implied Terms) Act 1973, ss. 8(1)(b), (2) and (3); *post*, p. 153.

the parties have expressly so provided in their agreement, there are few situations[80] where a Court would be likely to hold, at the present day, that the parties intended that any breach of the term should give rise to a right to claim damages only, and so place the term within this category.

(d) EVALUATION OF THE *AB INITIO* CLASSIFICATION OF TERMS

The dominant approach of the Courts in the 70 years following the enactment of the Sale of Goods Act in 1893 was to classify terms *ab initio* as conditions or warranties. The one clear and obvious advantage in this approach is that of certainty.[81] At least in commercial transactions it is important that parties (or their legal advisers) should be able to know, immediately and unequivocally, what their rights are in the event of a breach by the other party, and to make their decision accordingly. If the term broken is a condition, it will be known with certainty that the breach entitles the innocent party to terminate the contract forthwith.

This certainty is particularly important where the contract is one of a 'string' of contracts under which B buys goods from A and then sells them to C who in turn sells them to D. 'Members of the "string" will have many ongoing contracts simultaneously and they must be able to do business with confidence in the legal results of their actions'.[82] Certainty as to whether there is a right to terminate the contract is also important in cases where it would be difficult for the innocent party to quantify the loss suffered and therefore difficult for the Court to assess damages for a breach of the contract.[83]

On the other hand, the advantage of certainty has to be weighed against the need to reach a fair and just decision in individual cases. Since *any* breach of condition gives rise to a right of termination, the innocent party can refuse to perform the contract even though the breach is trivial in nature, and even though little or no loss has been suffered as a result. For example, it is a condition of a c.i.f. contract for the sale of goods that the goods must be shipped within the shipment period specified in the contract. If the goods are shipped one day later—or even earlier[84]—than the specified shipment period, the buyer is entitled to treat the contract as repudiated and to reject the goods, notwithstanding that the breach has caused no loss. A party may seek to rely on such a breach of condition to get out of a contract which has proved unprofitable, perhaps because of changes in the market.[85] It has been said that 'in principle contracts are made to be performed and not to be avoided according to the whims of market fluctuation and where there is a free choice between two possible constructions . . . the Court should tend to prefer that construction which will ensure

---

[80] But see *Anglia Commercial Properties v. North East Essex Building Co.* (1983) 266 Est. Gaz. 1096 (time limit clause in building contract).

[81] *The Mihalis Angelos* [1971] 1 Q.B. 164, at p. 205; *A/S Awilco of Oslo v. Fulvia S.p.A. (The Chikuma)* [1981] 1 W.L.R. 314, at p. 322; *Bunge Corpn. v. Tradax Export S.A.* [1981] 1 W.L.R. 711, at pp. 718, 720, 725.

[82] *Bunge Corp. v. Tradax Export S.A.* [1981] 1 W.L.R. 711, *per* Lord Lowry at p. 720.

[83] *Ibid.*

[84] *Bowes v. Shand* (1877) 2 App. Cas. 455.

[85] *Arcos Ltd. v. Ronaasen & Son Ltd.* [1933] A.C. 470.

performance, and not encourage avoidance of contractual obligations'.[86] Moreover, as noted above, in the context of non-consumer sales, statute has restricted the right of a buyer to reject goods by reason of certain implied conditions if the breach is so slight that it would be unreasonable to reject them.[87]

(e) INTERMEDIATE TERMS

The distinction between 'conditions' and 'warranties', which placed considerable emphasis on *ab initio* classification of the quality of the term broken, that is to say, whether it was of major or minor importance, and on initial certainty, has fallen out of favour. A new emphasis has been given to a more flexible test which bases the right of termination on the gravity of the breach and of its consequences, a test that has its roots in older authorities.[88] In *Hongkong Fir Shipping Co. Ltd.* v. *Kawasaki Kisen Kaisha Ltd.*, Diplock L.J. said:[89]

There are, however, many contractual undertakings of a more complex character which cannot be categorised as being 'conditions' or 'warranties' . . . Of such undertakings all that can be predicated is that some breaches will and others will not give rise to an event which will deprive the party not in default of substantially the whole benefit which it was intended he should obtain from the contract; and the legal consequences of a breach of such under-taking, unless provided for expressly in the contract, depend upon the nature of the event to which the breach gives rise and do not follow automatically from a prior classification of the undertaking, as a 'condition' or a 'warranty'.

In that case,[90] it was argued on behalf of the charterers of a ship that the shipowners' obligation to provide a seaworthy vessel was a condition, any breach of which entitled the charterers to treat themselves as discharged. The Court of Appeal rejected this contention. The undertaking as to seaworthiness was not a condition, but an *inter-mediate* or 'innominate' term. Breach of such a term would not give rise to a right to treat the charterparty as repudiated unless the conduct of the shipowners, and the actual or anticipated consequences of the breach, were so serious as to frustrate the commercial purpose of the venture. The reason was thus explained by Upjohn L.J.:[91]

Why is this apparently basic and underlying condition of seaworthiness not, in fact, treated as a condition? It is for the simple reason that the seaworthiness clause is breached by the slightest failure to be fitted 'in every way' for service. . . . If a nail is missing from one of the timbers of a wooden vessel or if proper medical supplies or two anchors are not on board at the time of sailing, the owners are in breach of the seaworthiness stipulation. It is contrary to

---

[86] *Cehave N.V.* v. *Bremer Handelsgesellschaft mbH* [1976] Q.B. 44, at p. 71 (the rejected goods were later bought by the same buyers at a lower price and used for the same purpose). See also *Reardon Smith Line Ltd.* v. *Hansen-Tangen* [1976] 1 W.L.R. 989, *post*, p. 142.

[87] Sale of Goods Act 1979, ss. 15A, 30A, *post*, p. 153.

[88] *Ante*, p. 135 n. 57.

[89] [1962] 2 Q.B. 26, at p. 70. See also *Hardwick Game Farm* v. *Suffolk Agricultural Poultry Producers' Assn.* [1966] 1 W.L.R. 287, at p. 341 (aff'd [1969] 2 A.C. 31). See further Reynolds (1963) 79 L.Q.R. 534; Lord Devlin [1966] C.L.J. 192.

[90] For the facts of this case, see *post*, p. 579.

[91] [1962] 2 Q.B. 26, at p. 62.

common sense to suppose that in such circumstances the parties contemplated that the charterer should at once be entitled to treat the contract as at an end for such trifling breaches.

Where a failure of performance is not a breach of condition, but of an intermediate term, the right of the innocent party to treat itself as discharged from further performance will depend upon the gravity of the breach and of its consequences. The expressions used to describe the circumstances that justify discharge, are discussed in the chapter on Discharge by Breach.[92] A test frequently applied is whether the failure of performance is such as to deprive the innocent party of substantially the whole benefit which it was intended that it should obtain as the consideration for the performance of its own undertakings.[93] The test is a strict one. Thus, in the *Hongkong Fir* case, which concerned a two-year charterparty, the ship was off hire because of unseaworthiness for all but eight and a half weeks in the first seven months of the charter, but the charterer was held not to be entitled to treat the contract as discharged. Accordingly, in many cases, the innocent party may have to 'wait and see' whether the consequences of the breach turn out to have so serious an effect.

(f) DISTINGUISHING INTERMEDIATE TERMS AND CONDITIONS

Whether a term will be classified as a condition depends in part on the Court 'making what is in effect a value judgement about the commercial significance of the term in question'.[94] A term is most likely to be classified as 'intermediate' if, as in the *Hongkong Fir* case, it is capable of being broken either in a manner that is trivial and capable of remedy by an award of damages or in a way that is so fundamental as to undermine the whole contract. However, the Courts have recognized that the greater flexibility involves more uncertainty and have indicated that in suitable cases they will not be reluctant to hold that an obligation has the force of a condition.[95] In the modern law, it is probably safe to say that any term of a contract will be classified as an intermediate term, and not as a condition, unless the Court concludes that it falls within one of the following situations:

(i) Categorization as condition by statute

The Sale of Goods Act 1979[96] and the Supply of Goods (Implied Terms) Act 1973[97] expressly define certain implied obligations in contracts of sale of goods or hire-purchase as being 'conditions' or 'warranties'. There can be no doubt that such classification is binding. But in *Cehave N.V. v. Bremer Handelsgesellschaft mbH*[98] the

---

[92] See *post*, p. 565.
[93] *Hongkong Fir Shipping Co. Ltd. v. Kawasaki Kisen Kaisha Ltd.* [1962] 2 Q.B. 26, at p. 66; see also *post*, p. 578. Cf. CISG Art. 25.
[94] *State Trading Cpn. of India Ltd. v. M. Golodetz Ltd.* [1989] 2 Lloyd's Rep. 277, *per* Kerr L.J. at p. 283.
[95] *Bunge Corp. v. Tradax Export S.A.* [1981] 1 W.L.R. 711; *Cie Commerciale Sucres et Denrées v. Czarnikow Ltd.* [1990] 1 W.L.R. 1337; *Petrotrade Inc. v. Stinnes Handel GmbH* [1995] 1 Lloyd's Rep. 142, at p. 149.
[96] See *post*, pp. 153–9.
[97] See *post*, p. 159.
[98] [1976] Q.B. 44. See also *Tradax International S.A. v. Goldschmidt* [1977] 2 Lloyd's Rep. 604.

Court of Appeal rejected the argument that the Sale of Goods Act created a statutory dichotomy which divided *all* terms in contracts of sale of goods into conditions and warranties and held that an express term 'shipment to be made in good condition' was an intermediate term the breach of which had to be so serious as to go to the root of the contract in order to entitle the buyer to reject the goods.

(ii) Categorization as condition by judicial decision

A particular term may have been categorized as a condition by previous judicial decision. Examples are mainly to be found in certain familiar terms in commercial contracts. Thus stipulations in a voyage charterparty as to the time at which the chartered vessel is expected ready to load[99] or in a time charterparty as to the date by which hire is to be paid,[100] and stipulations in a c.i.f. contract for the sale of goods as to the time within which the goods must be shipped[101] or a letter of credit opened,[102] have been held to be conditions, any delay in which entitles the other party to treat itself as discharged. It has, however, been stated[103] that a number of previous decisions on such terms are 'excessively technical' and are open to re-examination by the House of Lords.

(iii) Designation in contract

The parties may have expressly provided in their contract either that a particular term is to be a condition (in the technical sense)[104] or that the consequences of its non-performance by one party are to be that the other party is to have the right to treat himself as discharged. A stipulation as to the time of performance where time is expressly stated to be 'of the essence of the contract' is an example of this situation.[105] Again, stating that a party 'guarantees' to obtain approval within a specified period indicates that the term is a condition.[106]

(iv) Implication from nature of contract, subject-matter, or circumstances

Finally, if the nature of the contract or the subject-matter or the circumstances of the case lead to the conclusion that the parties must, by necessary implication, have intended that the innocent party would be discharged from further performance of its obligations in the event that a particular term was not fully and precisely complied with, that term will be held to be a condition.[107] This is more likely to be the case in single-performance contracts and contracts requiring the performance of particular acts at specified times and in sequence. It is less likely to be the case where the contract

---

[99] *The Mihalis Angelos* [1971] 1 Q.B. 164. See also *Behn* v. *Burness* (1863) 3 B. & S. 751 (*ante*, p. 135).

[100] *Mardorf Peach & Co. Ltd.* v. *Attica Sea Carriers Cpn. of Liberia* [1977] A.C. 850.

[101] *Bowes* v. *Shand* (1877) 2 App. Cas. 455.

[102] *Ian Stach Ltd.* v. *Baker Bosley Ltd.* [1958] 2 Q.B. 130.

[103] *Reardon Smith Line Ltd.* v. *Yngvar Hansen-Tangen* [1976] 1 W.L.R. 989, *per* Lord Wilberforce at p. 998.

[104] Cf. *L. G. Schuler AG* v. *Wickman Machine Tool Sales Ltd.* [1974] A.C. 235.

[105] *United Scientific Holdings Ltd.* v. *Burnley B.C.* [1978] A.C. 904, at pp. 923, 937, 944.

[106] *B.S. & N. Ltd.* v. *Micado Shipping Ltd (Malta)* [2001] 1 Lloyd's Rep. 341, at pp. 349–350.

[107] *United Scientific Holdings Ltd.* v. *Burnley B.C.*, (*supra*, n. 105), at pp. 937, 941, 944, 950, 958; *Bremer Handelsgesellschaft mbH* v. *Vanden Avenne-Izegem P.V.B.A.* [1978] 2 Lloyd's Rep. 109, at p. 133; *Bunge Cpn.* v. *Tradax Export S.A.* [1981] 1 W.L.R. 711, at pp. 716, 717, 720, 729.

is for performance over a long term[108] when substantial performance may have been rendered by the contract-breaker before breach and where the term is of a broad and loose nature.

(v) Adherence to terms fundamental to transaction

A term is also likely to be held to be a condition where adherence to it is fundamental to the transaction in the sense that it cannot proceed without it and where the term is not one which admitted to different types of breach. So, for example, a stipulation in a conditional sale agreement that the seller was at the date of the agreement the owner of the item sold has been held to be a condition.[109]

(vi) Illustrations

In *Bremer Handelsgesellschaft mbH* v. *Vanden Avenne-Izegem P.V.B.A.*[110] a term in a contract for the sale of United States soya bean meal, which required the sellers to advise the buyers 'without delay' of impossibility of shipment by reason of a prohibition of export, was held by the House of Lords to be an intermediate term, since it did not establish any definite time limit within which the advice was to be given. But further provisions in the same contract, which took effect upon a number of events impeding performance and which established a time-table of fixed periods within which the occurrence was to be notified, an extension of time claimed, and the buyer was to have the option of cancelling the contract, were held to be conditions. Punctual compliance with these stipulations was required as part of a 'complete regulatory code'. Again in *Bunge Corporation* v. *Tradax Export S.A.*,[111] a case which also concerned a contract for the sale of soya bean meal:

The sellers were required, by 30 June 1975, to load the goods on board ship at a single United States Gulf port to be nominated by them. The contract further provided that the buyers should give to the sellers 'at least 15 consecutive days' notice of probable readiness of vessel(s) and of the approximate quantity required to be loaded'. The buyers did not give that notice until 17 June, by which time less than 15 days of the loading period remained. The sellers declared the buyers in default and claimed damages for repudiation of the contract on the ground that the term as to notice was a condition.

The House of Lords held that the term, though not expressly stated in the contract to be a condition, was one by implication, so that its breach entitled the sellers to treat themselves as discharged. Their Lordships pointed out that, in general, time was of the essence in mercantile contracts,[112] and in particular in this case where the sellers needed the information to know which loading port they should nominate, so as to

---

[108]   *L. G. Schuler AG* v. *Wickman Machine Tool Sales Ltd.* [1974] A.C. 235; *Decro-Wall S.A.* v. *Practitioners in Marketing Ltd.* [1971] 1 W.L.R. 361.

[109]   *Barber* v. *NWS Bank plc*, The Times, 27 November 1995. Such a condition would otherwise be *implied* by the Sale of Goods Act 1979, s. 12, *post*, p. 153.

[110]   [1978] 2 Lloyd's Rep. 109.

[111]   [1981] 1 W.L.R. 711.

[112]   At pp. 716, 719, 725. See also *Toepfer* v. *Lenersan-Poortman N.V.* [1980] 1 Lloyd's Rep. 143; *Bunge GmbH* v. *Landbouwbelang G.A.* [1980] 1 Lloyd's Rep. 458. But this is not always the case; see *Torvald Klaveness A/S* v. *Arni Maritime Cpn.* [1994] 1 W.L.R. 1465, at pp. 1475–6 (redelivery date of chartered ship).

ensure that the goods would be available for loading on the ship's arrival at that port before the end of the loading period.[113]

(g) LOSS OF THE RIGHT OF DISCHARGE

Certain qualifications must be made to the rule that a breach of condition discharges the innocent party from further performance.

(i) Waiver and affirmation

Where one party has been guilty of a breach of condition, the other party need not necessarily treat itself as discharged. Compliance with the condition can, if the innocent party so wishes, be waived[114] and the contract can be enforced as if it had been omitted. Alternatively, the innocent party can elect to affirm the contract, that is to say, with knowledge of the breach to treat the contract as still binding and to rest content with damages, which are available as a remedy in any event.

These principles have been given statutory force in relation to contracts of sale of goods by section 11(1) of the Sale of Goods Act 1979:

Where a contract of sale is subject to a condition to be fulfilled by the seller, the buyer may waive the condition, or may elect to treat the breach of the condition as a breach of warranty and not as a ground for treating the contract as repudiated.

But they are of general application in the law of contract.

(ii) 'Acceptance' and substantial benefit

Affirmation is voluntary; but an innocent party may, in certain circumstances, be compulsorily required to treat the breach as a breach of warranty and thus restricted to a remedy for damages. For example, an innocent party who has taken a substantial benefit under the contract may sometimes be precluded from opting to be discharged by reason of a breach of condition, and have to sue for damages only.[115] The Sale of Goods Act 1979 also provides that a buyer cannot treat the contract as repudiated for breach of condition where the goods which are the subject-matter of the sale have been 'accepted'. By section 11(4) of the Act:[116]

where a contract of sale is not severable and the buyer has accepted the goods or part of them, the breach of a condition to be fulfilled by the seller can only be treated as a breach of warranty, and not as a ground for rejecting the goods and treating the contract as repudiated, unless there is an express or implied term of the contract to that effect.

Two points, however, require explanation. In the first place, the word 'accept' in the

---

[113] [1981] 1 W.L.R. 711, at p. 729; *Petrotrade Inc. v. Stinnes Handel GmbH* [1995] 1 Lloyd's Rep. 142, at p. 149. Cf. *Universal Bulk Carriers Ltd. v. Andre et Cie SA* [2000] 1 Lloyd's Rep. 459 (provision that laydays to be narrowed not a condition); on appeal to the Court of Appeal: [2001] E.W.C.A. Civ. 588.

[114] Provided that it is exclusively for its own benefit and not for the benefit of both parties.

[115] *Graves v. Legg* (1854) 9 Exch. 709, at p. 717; *Pust v. Dowie* (1865) 5 B. & S. 33; *Behn v. Burness* (1862) 1 B. & S. 877; (1863) 3 B. & S. 751.

[116] The terms 'condition' and 'warranty' are used in the Act in the senses given above; see Sale of Goods Act 1979, ss. 11(3), 61(1).

phrase 'and the buyer has accepted the goods' bears a technical meaning. The buyer is deemed to have accepted the goods when he intimates to the seller that he has accepted them, or when the goods have been delivered and the buyer does any act in relation to them which is inconsistent with the ownership of the seller, or when after the lapse of a reasonable time the buyer retains the goods without intimating to the seller that the goods have been rejected.[117] There is no mention of any requirement that the buyer should *know* of the breach of condition before losing the right to reject, although, in the case of an intimation of acceptance or an act inconsistent with the seller's ownership, 'acceptance' will not be deemed to have taken place unless and until the buyer has had a reasonable opportunity of examining the goods for the purpose of ascertaining whether they are in conformity with the contract[118] and the availability of a reasonable opportunity of examining goods is a material factor in determining whether a 'reasonable' time has elapsed.[119] Where the buyer has the right to reject goods by reason of a defect that affects all or some of them but accepts some of the goods the right to reject the rest is not lost by that partial acceptance.[120]

Secondly, acceptance does not necessarily have this effect if the contract is severable, for example, if delivery of the goods is to be made by instalments which are to be separately paid for. In such a case the Act provides that 'where the seller makes defective deliveries in respect of one or more instalments, or the buyer neglects or refuses to take delivery of or pay for one or more instalments, it is a question in each case depending on the terms of the contract and the circumstances of the case, whether the breach of contract is a repudiation of the whole contract, or whether it is a severable breach giving rise to a claim for compensation but not to a right to treat the whole contract as repudiated'.[121]

The right of the innocent party to treat itself as discharged may thus be lost either voluntarily or as the result of the operation of a rule of law.

.

III. IMPLIED TERMS

The law may imply into a contract terms which the parties have not themselves inserted. In some cases, in particular contracts for the sale and supply of goods and services, contracts of employment, and contracts between landlord and tenant, terms are implied by statute.

In the absence of statutory provision the cases in which the Courts will imply a term into a contract are strictly limited: it is not their task to make contracts for the parties concerned, but only to interpret the contracts already made.[122] Nevertheless, in

---

[117] Sale of Goods Act 1979, s. 35, as amended by the Sale and Supply of Goods Act 1994.

[118] Sale of Goods Act 1979, s. 35(2).

[119] *Ibid.*, ss. 35(5) and 34. Cf. *Bernstein* v. *Pamson Motors (Golders Green) Ltd.* [1987] 2 All E.R. 220; *Shine* v. *General Guarantee Cpn.* [1988] 1 All E.R. 911.

[120] Sale of Goods Act 1979, s. 35A(1).

[121] Sale of Goods Act 1979, s. 31(2).

[122] *Phillips Electronique Grand Publique S.A.* v. *B.S.B. Ltd.* [1995] E.M.L.R. 472, *per* Sir Thomas Bingham M.R. at p. 481.

certain circumstances the Courts are prepared to imply terms into even a written contract. A distinction has developed between two broad categories of case. First, where it is sought to insert into a particular, sometimes detailed, contract a term that the parties have not expressed. In such cases a strict test is applied. The Courts do not imply terms where it would be reasonable to do so but only where it is necessary to give business efficacy to the contract. Here the implication of a term is normally said to depend upon an intention imputed to the parties from their *actual* circumstances; i.e. the express terms of the agreement and the surrounding circumstances.[123] Secondly, there are cases in which the Court is considering a common relationship, for example sale, carriage, landlord and tenant, employment, and that between a regulated dominant supplier (for example a telephone or electricity supplier) and its customer where the parties may have left a lot unsaid. In such cases, when the Court implies a term, it is sometimes laying down a general rule that in all contracts of a defined type some provision is to be implied as an incident of the particular type of contractual relationship unless the parties have expressly excluded it, and it is somewhat artificial to attribute such terms to the unexpressed or implied intention of the parties.[124] A similar process takes place where a term is implied by a trade custom.[125]

(a) BUSINESS EFFICACY AND NECESSITY

Where the parties to a contract, either through forgetfulness or through bad drafting, fail to incorporate into the contract terms which, had they adverted to the situation, they would certainly have inserted to complete the contract, the Courts may, in order to give 'business efficacy' to the transaction, imply such terms as are necessary to effect that result.

In *The Moorcock*, a shipowner and the owner of a jetty contracted to allow a steamship to be discharged and loaded at the jetty. The ship was grounded and damaged at low tide. The Court of Appeal held that the parties must have intended to contract on the basis that the ground was safe for the vessel at low tide, and therefore a term would be implied that the berth was reasonably safe for the purpose of loading and unloading. For a breach of this implied term the defendants were liable.

Bowen L.J. said:[126]

Now, an implied warranty, or, as it is called, a covenant in law, as distinguished from an express contract or express warranty, really is in all cases founded on the presumed intention of the parties, and upon reason. The implication which the law draws from what must obviously have been the intention of the parties, the law draws with the object of giving

---

[123] *Luxor (Eastbourne) Ltd.* v. *Cooper* [1941] A.C. 108, at p. 137; *Shell U.K. Ltd.* v. *Lostock Garages Ltd.* [1976] 1 W.L.R. 1187, at p. 1196; *Anglo-Japanese Bank (International)* v. *Credit du Nord S.A.* [1989] 1 W.L.R. 255, at p. 263. See also *Codelfa Construction Pty. Ltd.* v. *State Rail Authority of New South Wales* (1981–82) 149 C.L.R. 337, *per* Mason J. at p. 353 (account should be taken of the presumed intention of the parties in deciding whether a term is to be implied: High Court of Australia).

[124] *Liverpool City Council* v. *Irwin* [1977] A.C. 239, at pp. 253–4 and 257–8; *Shell U.K. Ltd.* v. *Lostock Garages Ltd.* (*supra*, n. 123), at p. 1196; *Mears* v. *Safecar Security Ltd.* [1983] Q.B. 54, at p. 78; *Scally* v. *Southern Health and Social Services Board* [1992] 1 A.C. 294, at pp. 306–7.

[125] *Post*, p. 151.

[126] (1889) 14 P.D. 64, at p. 68.

efficacy to the transaction and preventing such a failure of consideration as cannot have been within the contemplation of either side . . .

But this principle has subsequently become unpopular, and it has been said to be the last resort of counsel in distress.[127] For instance, in *Easton* v. *Hitchcock*[128] the Court refused to imply a term into a contract for the hire of a private detective that ex-employees of the detective agency would not divulge confidential information, although it was clearly necessary to the running of a detective agency that secrecy should be maintained.

(i) Obvious terms

The principle in *The Moorcock* is applied where, without the implied term, the contract will not be workable. But the Court is also prepared to imply a term if it was so obviously a stipulation in the agreement that it goes without saying that the parties must have intended it to form part of their contract. This test, which often overlaps with the business efficacy test,[129] is applied by asking whether, if an officious bystander were to suggest some express provision for a matter in the agreement, the parties would testily suppress him with a common 'Oh, of course!'.[130] Such an implication will only be made if the Court is satisfied that both parties would, as reasonable persons, have agreed to the term had it been suggested to them, so that the differing commercial motives of the parties will often preclude this type of implication.[131]

Clearly, however, the Court will be reluctant to make such an implication where the parties have entered into a carefully drafted written contract containing detailed terms agreed between them[132] or in a novel or particularly risky contract.[133] It must be possible to formulate the term with a sufficient degree of precision, and without over-complication and artificiality,[134] and the term to be implied must not be inconsistent

---

[127] *Shirlaw* v. *Southern Foundries (1926) Ltd.* [1939] 2 K.B. 206, *per* MacKinnon L.J. at p. 227.

[128] [1912] 1 K.B. 535. See also *Yorkshire Water Services Ltd.* v. *Sun Alliance & London Insurance plc* [1997] 2 Lloyd's Rep. 21.

[129] e.g. *Ali S. S. Corp.* v. *Shipyard Trogir* [1999] 1 W.L.R. 314, *per* Potter L.J. at p.326; *Codelfa Construction Pty. Ltd.* v. *State Railway Authority of New South Wales* (1982) 149 C.L.R. 337, at p. 347 (High Court of Australia).

[130] *Shirlaw* v. *Southern Foundries (1926) Ltd.* [1939] 2 K.B. 206, *per* MacKinnon L.J. at p. 227. See also *McClelland* v. *Northern Ireland General Health Service Board* [1957] 1 W.L.R. 594; *Weg Motors Ltd.* v. *Hales* [1961] Ch. 176, at p. 192; *Bronester* v. *Priddle* [1961] 1 W.L.R. 1294, at p. 1304; *Liverpool City Council* v. *Irwin* [1977] A.C. 239, at p. 254; *Alpha Trading Ltd.* v. *Dunnshaw-Patten Ltd.* [1981] 1 Lloyd's Rep. 122, at p. 128; *Equitable Life Assurance Society* v. *Hyman* [2000] 3 W.L.R. 529 (implication to give effect to reasonable expectations). See further Phang [1998] J.B.L. 1.

[131] *Luxor (Eastbourne) Ltd.* v. *Cooper* [1941] A.C. 108; *Attica Sea Carriers Cpn.* v. *Ferrostaal Poseidon Bulk Reederei GmbH* [1976] 1 Lloyd's Rep. 250; *Liverpool City Council* v. *Irwin* (*supra*, n. 130), at p. 266; *Hughes* v. *Greenwich L.B.C.* [1994] 1 A.C. 170, at p. 179. Cf. *Paragon Finance plc* v. *Nash* [2002] 2 W.L.R. 685 (implied term that power to set interest rates was not to be set arbitrarily). See also *post*, p. 680.

[132] *Shell U.K. Ltd.* v. *Lostock Garages Ltd.* [1976] 1 W.L.R. 1187, at p. 1200. See also *Yorkshire Water Services Ltd.* v. *Sun Alliance & London Insurance plc* [1997] 2 Lloyd's Rep. 21.

[133] *Phillips Electronique Grand Publique S.A.* v. *B.S.B. Ltd.* [1995] E.M.L.R. 472, *per* Sir Thomas Bingham M.R. at pp. 482–3.

[134] *Ibid.*, at p. 497; *Luxor (Eastbourne) Ltd.* v. *Cooper* (*supra*, n. 131), *per* Viscount Simon L.C. at p. 117; *Ashmore* v. *Corporation of Lloyds (No. 2)* [1992] 2 Lloyd's Rep. 620, at pp. 626–9. But note that the term implied may involve a flexible criterion such as to take 'reasonable' care.

with the express terms of the contract.[135] For example, where a party taking out insurance is contractually required to provide a correctly completed direct debit mandate to the insurance company, the company will be under an implied duty to implement the direct debit mandate.[136]

(ii) Must be necessary

In any event, the term to be implied must in all the circumstances be reasonable.[137] But this does not mean that a term will be implied merely because it would be reasonable to do so,[138] or because it would improve the contract[139] or make its performance more convenient.[140] It must be necessary to imply such a term: 'The touchstone is always *necessity* and not merely *reasonableness*'.[141] For example, where parties to a contract are subject to the rules of a regulatory body there is no need to imply those rules into the contract.[142]

(b) STANDARDIZED TERMS IN COMMON RELATIONSHIPS

In certain types of contract, however, terms have become standardized, and they will be implied in all contracts of that type in the absence of any contrary intention. For example, if a builder undertakes to build a house for a purchaser, it is an implied term of the contract that the work will be done in a good and workmanlike manner, that the builder will supply good and proper materials, and that the house will be reasonably fit for human habitation when built or completed.[143] Again, if a travel agent undertakes to arrange for services, such as accommodation and excursions, to be provided by others, it is an implied term of the contract that it would use reasonable care and skill in selecting the service-providers, but if the travel agent itself undertakes to supply the services, it is an implied term of the contract that the services themselves will be carried out with reasonable care and skill, even where the agent has arranged

[135] *Duke of Westminster* v. *Guild* [1985] Q.B. 688, at p. 700; *Johnstone* v. *Bloomsbury H.A.* [1992] 1 Q.B. 333, *per* Browne-Wilkinson V.-C. and Leggatt L.J. at pp. 347 and 350, the former stating that powers created by an express term may be qualified by an implied duty to exercise those powers reasonably: *Imperial Tobacco Pension Trust* v. *Imperial Tobacco* [1991] I.R.L.R. 66 (employer's power to refuse consent to increases in pensions).

[136] *Weldon* v. *GRE Linked Life Assurance* [2000] 2 All E.R. Comm. 914, at pp. 919–921.

[137] *Young & Marten* v. *McManus Childs Ltd.* [1969] 1 A.C. 454, at p. 465; *Liverpool City Council* v. *Irwin* (*supra*, n. 130), at p. 262; *Wong Mee Wan* v. *Kwan Kin Travel Services Ltd.* [1996] 1 W.L.R. 38, at pp. 46–7, relying, *inter alia*, analogically on the Package Travel, Package Holidays and Package Tours Regulations 1992 (S.I. 1992 No. 3288), esp. reg. 15.

[138] *Reigate* v. *Union Manufacturing Co. (Ramsbottom) Ltd.* [1918] 1 K.B. 592, at p. 598; *Liverpool City Council* v. *Irwin* (*supra*, n. 130).

[139] *Trollope & Colls Ltd.* v. *N.W. Metropolitan Regional Hospital Board* [1973] 1 W.L.R. 601, at p. 609.

[140] *Russell* v. *Duke of Norfolk* [1949] 1 All E.R. 109.

[141] *Liverpool City Council* v. *Irwin* (*supra*, n. 130), *per* Lord Edmund-Davies at p. 266. See also *Baker* v. *Black Sea & Baltic General Insurance Co.* [1998] 1 W.L.R. 974, *per* Lord Lloyd at p. 980; *Equitable Life Assurance Society* v. *Hyman* [2000] 3 W.L.R. 529, at p. 539; Bryan & Ellinghaus (2000) 22 Syd. L. Rev. 636, 644 ('objective necessity').

[142] *Clarion Ltd.* v. *National Provident Institution* [2000] 1 W.L.R. 1899, at p. 1896.

[143] *Miller* v. *Cannon Hill Estates Ltd.* [1931] 2 K.B. 113; *Lynch* v. *Thorne* [1956] 1 W.L.R. 303; *Hancock* v. *Brazier (Anerley) Ltd.* [1966] 1 W.L.R. 1317.

for its obligation to be performed by others.[144] Some of these standardized terms have subsequently been codified by statute.[145] Others, as will be seen, continue to emerge by a process of common law development.

In these cases concerning a common relationship, for example sale, carriage, landlord and tenant, or employment, the parties may have left a lot unsaid and the process of implication is different. It involves the Court determining, in the light of general considerations of policy, the standard incidents of the particular type of relationship rather than constructing a hypothetical bargain. Although it has sometimes been said that the criterion for this form of implication is also 'necessity'[146] rather than 'reasonableness',[147] it does appear that a broader approach is taken. The Courts will consider how the proposed implied term will sit with existing law, will affect the parties to the relationship, and wider issues of fairness.[148] While the parties can exclude or modify the standard incidents of the relationship by express words, unless they do so they will form part of the obligation as a legal incident of the particular kind of contractual relationship.[149] Such standardized terms, implied by law, have been said to 'operate as default rules'.[150] In these cases it has been said[151] that the problem of implication is to be solved by asking:

[H]as the law already defined the obligation or the extent of it? If so, let it be followed. If not, look to see what would be reasonable in the general run of such cases . . . and then say what the obligation shall be.

In such cases the contract may be partly but not wholly stated in writing and 'in order to complete it, in particular to give it a bilateral character, it is necessary to take account of the parties and the circumstances', that is the nature of the contract and the relationship established by it.[152] In *Liverpool City Council* v. *Irwin*:[153]

---

[144] *Wong Mee Wan* v. *Kwan Kin Travel Services Ltd.* [1996] 1 W.L.R. 38, at pp. 42 and 46–7. In the second situation the contractor may be liable despite the absence of personal negligence.

[145] e.g. Defective Premises Act 1972, s. 1(1); Sale of Goods Act 1979, ss. 12–15 (*post*, p. 153); Supply of Goods and Services Act 1982, s. 13.

[146] *Liverpool City Council* v. *Irwin* (*supra*, n. 130), *per* Lord Wilberforce at p. 254 and *Scally* v. *Southern Health and Social Services Board* (*supra*, n. 124), *per* Lord Bridge at p. 307; *Ashmore* v. *Corporation of Lloyd's (No. 2)* [1992] 2 Lloyd's Rep. 620, at p 627; *Ali* v. *Christian Salvesen Food Services Ltd.* [1997] I.C.R. 25.

[147] *Liverpool City Council* v. *Irwin* (*supra*, n. 130), *per* Lord Cross at p. 258 and *Shell U.K. Ltd.* v. *Lostock Garages Ltd.* (*supra*, n. 132), *per* Lord Denning M.R. at p. 1196. See also *Lister* v. *Romford Ice & Cold Storage Co. Ltd.* [1957] A.C. 555, *per* Viscount Simonds and Lord Tucker at pp. 576, 594.

[148] Peden (2001) 117 L.Q.R. 459, 467.

[149] *Mears* v. *Safecar Security Ltd.* [1983] Q.B. 54, at p. 78.

[150] *Malik* v. *Bank of Credit & Commerce International S.A.* [1998] A.C. 20, *per* Lord Steyn at p. 45. See also Rakoff, in Beatson and Friedmann, eds., *Good Faith and Fault in Contract Law* (1995), p. 191; Riley (2000) 20 O.J.L.S. 367.

[151] *Shell U.K. Ltd.* v. *Lostock Garages Ltd.* (*supra*, n. 132), *per* Lord Denning M.R. at p. 1196. See also *Liverpool City Council* v. *Irwin* (*supra*, n. 130), *per* Lord Cross at pp. 257–8; *Scally* v. *Southern Health and Social Services Board* [1992] 1 A.C. 294, at p. 307. Cf. *Reid* v. *Rush & Tomkins Group plc* [1990] 1 W.L.R. 212 (no such term implied because extent of obligation raised issues of social policy which could only be resolved by the legislature); *Johnson* v. *Unisys Ltd.* [2000] 2 W.L.R. 1076 (term not implied where statute provided limited remedy for conduct complained of).

[152] *Liverpool City Council* v. *Irwin* (*supra*, n. 130), at p. 254; *Lister* v. *Romford Ice & Cold Storage Ltd.* [1957] A.C. 555, at p. 579.

[153] [1977] A.C. 239.

Tenants in a council tower block withheld rent as a protest at conditions in the building. They alleged that the council was in breach of its duty to repair and maintain the lifts, staircases, and rubbish chutes in the common parts of the building which it controlled. There was no formal lease; merely a document entitled 'conditions of tenancy' and the conditions set out only related to the tenants' obligations. They contained nothing about the landlord's obligations.

It was held that the tenants were to have an implied easement over the common parts for access to their premises and to the rubbish chutes and that the landlord was also under an implied obligation to take *reasonable care* to maintain the common parts in a *reasonable state of repair* because the contract had not placed the obligation to maintain on the tenants individually or collectively, and the landlord retained control of this essential means of access. Again, in recent years an implied obligation of mutual trust and confidence has been recognized in contracts of employment by which both employer and employee are obliged not to conduct themselves in a manner calculated and likely to destroy or seriously damage the relationship of confidence and trust between them.[154] It has also been suggested that an apparently unrestricted contractual power to terminate a telephone service on a month's notice should be interpreted as subject to an implied term that the power to terminate should not be exercised without demonstrable reason or cause.[155]

The distinction between terms implied as the incidents of a defined relationship and those implied to give business efficacy to a particular transaction was also applied in *Scally* v. *Southern Health and Social Services Board*:[156]

A contract of employment contained a term giving certain employees the right to acquire a valuable additional pension benefit if they took certain action within a certain time. The term derived from a collective bargain negotiated by the employees' representatives and trade unions. The plaintiffs, employees who had not been informed of this right, claimed damages for, *inter alia*, breach of contract.

It was held that a term obliging the employer to take reasonable steps to inform its employees of this right should be implied into the contract because this term of the contract was not the result of individual negotiation but of a collective bargain, and the employees could not thus be expected to be aware of the term unless it was drawn to their attention. The implied obligation to inform employees did accordingly not apply to all contracts of employment. If this is an indication that the categories of defined relationships may be sub-divided into smaller and more numerous categories with terms that have a less general application, the distinction between implication of terms in cases concerning a common relationship and implication in those

---

[154] *Malik* v. *Bank of Credit & Commerce International* [1998] A.C. 20.

[155] *Timeload Ltd.* v. *British Telecommunications plc* (1995) 3 E.M.L.R. 459, *per* Sir Thomas Bingham M.R. at p. 467. Some analogical assistance appears to have been derived from section 3 of the Unfair Contract Terms Act 1977, *post*, pp. 272, 278.

[156] [1992] 1 A.C. 294. Cf. *Ali* v. *Christian Salvesen Food Services Ltd.* (*supra*, n. 146); *University of Nottingham* v. *Eyett (No. 1)* [1999] 2 All E.R. 437.

concerning a particular contract may be a fragile one.[157] It has, however, been argued that it can be maintained by having recourse to trade usage in identifying what are the defined types of contractual relationship.[158]

(c) TERMS IMPLIED BY CUSTOM

Another situation in which the Court lays down a general rule that some provision is to be implied in all contracts of a defined type unless the parties have expressly excluded it is where a term is implied by the custom of a locality or by the usage of a particular trade. Such a custom must be strictly proved. It must be notorious, as certain as the written contract, and reasonable.[159] Furthermore, the custom must not offend against the intention of any legislative enactment.

In *Hutton* v. *Warren*,[160] a term was implied by the custom of the country into an agricultural tenancy giving the outgoing tenant the right to a reasonable allowance for seeds and labour expended on the land even though the lease contained no express term to this effect. *Harley & Co.* v. *Nagata*[161] is an example of a term implied by the usage of a particular trade. It was held that, in the case of a time charterparty, a custom that the commission of the broker who negotiated the charterparty should be paid out of the hire that was earned, and should not be payable at all unless hire was in fact earned, should be imported into the brokerage contract. Again in *Mount* v. *Oldham Corporation*[162] an obligation to give a term's notice of an intention to withdraw a child from a private school or to pay a term's fees in lieu of notice was implied by custom.

Certain usages of the mercantile community at large have been codified, for example, those relating to negotiable instruments in the Bills of Exchange Act 1882.

(i) A certain and uniform course of conduct

A course of conduct which is said to form a custom must be both identifiable and uniform. It is these qualities that give the course of conduct the required certainty. The requirement of uniformity does not require total consistency of conduct. Thus, it has been stated that the continued adherence of 85 per cent of the Lancashire weaving mills to a custom was sufficient to maintain it,[163] although a higher degree of uniformity may be required for the creation of a new custom.[164] Once a custom has been

---

[157] See Phang [1993] J.B.L. 242; [1994] J.B.L. 255 and note *Ashmore* v. *Corporation of Lloyd's (No. 2)* [1992] 2 Lloyd's Rep. 620, at p. 631 (no common relationship in many thousands of contracts between Lloyd's underwriters and the Corporation entered into on the same terms).

[158] Peden (2001) 117 L.Q.R. 459, 463.

[159] *Nelson* v. *Dahl* (1879) 12 Ch. D. 568, at p. 575.

[160] (1836) 1 M. & W. 466.

[161] (1917) 23 Com. Cas. 121.

[162] [1973] Q.B. 309. See also *Lord Eldon* v. *Hedley Brothers* [1935] 2 K.B. 1.

[163] *Sagar* v. *H. Ridehalgh & Son Ltd.* [1931] 1 Ch. 310.

[164] *Con-Stan Industries of Australia Pty. Ltd.* v. *Norwich Insurance (Australia) Ltd.* (1985–86) 160 C.L.R. 226 (High Court of Australia), although instances of inconsistency were 'minute': [1981] 2 N.S.W.L.R. 879, at pp. 889–90.

proved in a sufficient number of cases, the Court will take judicial notice of it without the need for further evidence.[165]

(ii) Notoriety

To be notorious a custom need not be known to all the world, nor even to both parties to the contract.[166] It must, however, be well known in the market to which it applies and readily ascertainable by any person entering into a contract of which it will form a part.[167]

(iii) Recognized as having binding effect

The fact that a course of conduct is uniform, certain, and notorious is not, in itself, enough to give rise to a binding custom. It must also be shown that the course of conduct was intended to have a legally binding effect and that compliance with it was the result of a belief in a legal obligation to do so. A custom must therefore be distinguished from a course of conduct that is frequently, or even habitually, followed in a particular commercial community as a matter of grace or commercial convenience.[168] The clearest way of establishing this is to show that the custom has been 'enforced' but this is not necessary and it is sufficient for it to be established that the custom has been acted upon.[169] Where the conduct is required by the rules of a trade or professional association, that will be good evidence that compliance is the result of belief in an obligation to do so.[170]

(iv) Reasonableness

Reasonableness is a question of law and, to qualify, a custom must be 'fair and proper and such as reasonable, honest, and fair-minded men would adopt'.[171] Although evidence of the unreasonableness of a course of conduct may be used to show that it was not generally accepted or known and does not therefore amount to a custom,[172] where a custom has been sufficiently proved, the Courts' tendency to support freedom of bargaining in commercial markets means that it is unlikely to be held to be unreasonable.[173] Where the contracting parties are in a fiduciary relationship, as in the

---

[165] *Universo Insurance Co. of Milan* v. *Merchant's Marine Insurance Co. Ltd.* [1897] 2 Q.B. 93 (judicial notice taken of a broker's liability for unpaid premium in the marine insurance market). See also *J.A. Chapman & Co. Ltd.* v. *Kadirga Denizcilik Ve Ticaret* [1998] Lloyd's Rep. I.R. 377.

[166] *Grissell* v. *Bristowe* (1868) L.R. 3 C.P. 112, at p. 128, rev'd on the facts of the case, (1868) L.R. 4 C.P. 36; *Buckle* v. *Knoop* (1867) L.R. 2 Exch. 125, at p. 129, aff'd *ibid.*, at p. 333.

[167] *Strathlorne S.S. Co. Ltd.* v. *Hugh Baird & Sons Ltd.*, 1916 S.C. (H.L.) 134, *per* Lord Buckmaster L.C. at p. 136.

[168] *General Reinsurance Cpn.* v. *Forsakringsaktiebolaget Fennia Patria* [1983] Q.B. 856, *per* Slade L.J. at p. 874.

[169] *Cunningham* v. *Fonblanque* (1833) 6 C. & P. 44, at p. 49; *Hall* v. *Benson* (1836) 7 C. & P. 711; *Johnson* v. *Clarke* [1908] 1 Ch. 303, at p. 309. Cf. *Sea Steamship Co. Ltd.* v. *Price, Walker & Co. Ltd.* (1903) 8 Com. Cas. 292, at p. 295.

[170] *Cunliffe-Owen* v. *Teaher & Greenwood* [1967] 1 W.L.R. 1421 (Stock Exchange rules); *Shearson Lehman Hutton Inc.* v. *MacLaine Watson & Co. Ltd.* [1989] 2 Lloyd's Rep. 570 (London Metal Exchange).

[171] *Produce Brokers Co. Ltd.* v. *Olympia Oil and Cake Co. Ltd.* [1916] 2 K.B. 296, at p. 298.

[172] *Bottomley* v. *Forbes* (1838) 5 Bing. (N.C.) 121, at p. 128.

[173] *Moult* v. *Halliday* [1898] 1 Q.B. 125, at p. 130.

case of an agent or a broker, a stricter approach is taken. The variation, by a trade custom, of a fiduciary duty such as the rule that fiduciaries must not place themselves in a position where their own interest conflicts with that of their customer, is less likely to be held to be reasonable,[174] although in some cases it may be so held.[175]

(v) Exclusion of customary terms

A custom or usage which would otherwise become an implied term of the contract may be expressly or impliedly excluded by the parties. Thus, in *Les Affréteurs Réunis Société Anonyme* v. *Leopold Walford (London) Ltd.*[176] the custom that in a time charter the broker's commission was only payable if the hire was earned was excluded by an express provision that 'a commission of 3 per cent on the estimated gross amount of hire is due (to the broker) *on signing this charter*', in other words, whether any hire was earned or not.

(d) SALE OF GOODS

Contracts for the sale of goods are of such everyday occurrence, and are commonly made with so little consideration of the exact legal results which the parties would desire to produce by it, that if their rights and obligations were to be determined only by what they say or do when they make the contract their reasonable expectations would often be defeated. Consequently certain conditions and warranties are *implied* in a contract of sale,[177] originally by common law, but since 1893 pursuant to sections 12–15 of the Sale of Goods Act 1893, now re-enacted (with amendments) in the Sale of Goods Act 1979.[178] In principle the statutorily implied terms may be negatived or varied by express agreement, by the course of dealing between the parties, or by a binding usage.[179] This freedom of the parties is, however, made subject to the Unfair Contract Terms Act 1977 and the Unfair Terms in Consumer Contracts Regulations 1999 which contain significant restrictions. In the context of consumer sales the statutorily implied terms are compulsory and in other sales they can only be excluded if the Court is satisfied that the term doing so is reasonable.[180] In the case of non-consumer sales a buyer may not reject goods by reason of a breach of a condition implied by sections 13–15 of the Sale of Goods Act if the breach is so slight that it would be unreasonable to reject them.[181]

---

[174] *Robinson* v. *Mollett* (1875) L.R. 7 H.L. 802; *Anglo-African Merchants Ltd.* v. *Bayley* [1970] 1 Q.B. 311; *North and South Co.* v. *Berkeley* [1971] 1 W.L.R. 470.

[175] *Jones* v. *Canavan* [1972] 2 N.S.W.L.R. 236; *Kelly* v. *Cooper* [1993] A.C. 205, at p. 214 (although this implication may have been on the ground of business efficacy).

[176] [1919] A.C. 801, *post*, p. 440.

[177] See *Benjamin's Sale of Goods*, 5th edn. (1997). On the loss of the right to reject goods for breaches of these provisions, see *ante*, p. 144. On a proposed E.C. Directive on this topic, see Com (95) 520, 18 June 1996; H.L. Select C'ttee on the E.C., 10th Report 1996/97, H.L. 57.

[178] Amended by the Sale and Supply of Goods Act 1994, substantially implementing the Report of the Law Commission, *Sale and Supply of Goods* (Law Com. No. 160, 1987).

[179] Sale of Goods Act 1979, s. 55.

[180] Unfair Contract Terms Act 1977, s. 6, *post*, p. 191.

[181] Sale of Goods Act 1979, s 15A.

(i) Title

By section 12 of the Sale of Goods Act 1979 the following terms are implied:

(1) a condition on the part of the seller that in the case of a sale he has a right to sell the goods, and in the case of an agreement to sell he will have such a right at the time when the property is to pass:

(2) a warranty that

(a) the goods are free, and will remain free until the time when the property is to pass, from any charge or encumbrance not disclosed or known to the buyer before the contract is made, and

(b) the buyer will enjoy quiet possession of the goods except so far as it may be disturbed by the owner or other person entitled to the benefit of any charge or encumbrance so disclosed or known.

Different and more limited warranties are implied in a contract of sale where 'there appears from the contract or is to be inferred from the circumstances of the contract an intention that the seller should transfer only such title as he or a third person may have'.[182] The seller can, by an express term of the contract, indicate an intention to pass only a limited title and such an intention may also be inferred. Where the goods are sold by an auctioneer[183] the intention of the parties to the contract may be that the buyer should have such title only to the goods, and such right only to take possession of them, as the seller has in fact acquired.[184] But where the seller purports to sell only such title as he or a third person may have, the warranties of freedom from encumbrances and quiet possession are not thereby wholly excluded. The seller must disclose to the buyer, before the contract is made, any known encumbrances, and further warrants that neither he nor anyone claiming under him (or the third person) will disturb the buyer's quiet possession of the goods.[185]

The exclusion or restriction of liability for breach of the terms implied by section 12 is absolutely prohibited[186] and they are accordingly a compulsory part of a contract for the sale of goods.

(ii) Sale by description

By section 13 of the Act:

(1) In a contract for the sale of goods by description, there is an implied condition that the goods will correspond with the description.

(2) If the sale is by sample as well as by description it is not sufficient that the bulk of the goods corresponds with the sample if the goods do not also correspond with the description.

---

[182] Sale of Goods Act 1979, s. 12(3).

[183] *Niblett* v. *Confectioners' Materials Co. Ltd.* [1921] 3 K.B. 387, at p. 401; *Rowland* v. *Divall* [1923] 2 K.B. 500, at p. 505.

[184] *Bagueley* v. *Hawley* (1867) L.R. 2 C.P. 625, at p. 629.

[185] Sale of Goods Act 1979, s. 12(4), (5).

[186] Unfair Contract Terms Act 1977, s. 6(1). An express term concerning title will be a condition: *Barber* v. *NWS Bank plc*, The Times, 27 November 1995 (C.A.).

(3) A sale of goods is not prevented from being a sale by description by reason only that, being exposed for sale or hire, they are selected by the buyer.

A sale of goods by description is a sale in which the buyer contracts in reliance on a description, express or implied,[187] even though the buyer has seen the goods[188] and may have selected the goods, e.g. in a self-service shop. Thus, it was held that a person who agreed to buy a second-hand reaping machine described as 'new the previous year and only used to cut 50 acres' was entitled to reject the machine on delivery when he found that it was, in fact, a very old machine.[189] Not all descriptive words are, however, conditions; the words must identify the subject-matter of the contract. So, for instance, words identifying the yard in which a ship that is being sold is to be built are not within section 13.[190]

(iii) Satisfactory quality

Ordinarily there is no implied condition or warranty of the quality of goods sold or of their fitness for any particular purpose: *caveat emptor*. But, where goods are sold in the course of a business,[191] the Act, as amended by the Sale and Supply of Goods Act 1994, contains important qualifications of this principle. By section 14:

(2)   Where the seller sells goods in the course of a business, there is an implied condition[192] that the goods supplied under the contract are of satisfactory[193] quality.

(2C) There is no such condition as regards any matter making the quality of the goods unsatisfactory which is specifically drawn to the buyer's attention before the contract is made; or where the buyer examines the goods before the contract is made, as regards defects which that examination ought to reveal.

Prior to the 1994 amendment the requirement was that the goods be of 'merchantable' quality, a criterion that was criticized[194] as too open-ended, inappropriate for consumer transactions, and as not expressly requiring reasonable durability.[195] The Law Commission had recommended that the criterion be 'acceptable quality'[196] but this was not accepted, *inter alia*, because of concern that a buyer might decide reluctantly that the goods were of 'acceptable' quality even if, by objective standards

---

[187] *Wallis, Son & Wells* v. *Pratt & Haynes* [1911] A.C. 394.

[188] *Grant* v. *Australian Knitting Mills Ltd.* [1936] A.C. 85, at p. 100; *Nicholson & Venn* v. *Smith Marriott* (1947) 177 L.T. 189.

[189] *Varley* v. *Whipp* [1900] 1 Q.B. 513.

[190] *Reardon Smith Line Ltd.* v. *Hansen Tangen* [1976] 1 W.L.R. 989. See also *Ashington Piggeries* v. *Christopher Hill Ltd.* [1972] A.C. 441, at pp. 503–4.

[191] This is to be given a broad meaning. There is no restriction that the goods be of a type that the seller deals in (cf. Unfair Contract Terms Act 1977, s. 12, *post*, p. 185): *Stevenson* v. *Rogers* [1999] Q.B. 1028 (fisherman selling boat).

[192] Sale of Goods Act 1979, s. 14(6).

[193] Defined *infra*.

[194] *Cehave N.V.* v. *Bremer Handelsgesellschaft mbH* [1976] Q.B. 44, *per* Ormrod L.J. at p. 80; Law Com. No. 162, *Sale and Supply of Goods* (1987), § 2.9 ff.

[195] But see *Mash & Murrell* v. *Joseph I. Emmanuel* [1962] 1 W.L.R. 16; *Lambert* v. *Lewis* [1982] A.C. 225, at p. 276.

[196] Law Com. No. 162 (*supra*, n. 194), §§ 3.22, 3.27.

the quality was not 'satisfactory'.[197] The new criterion, is 'satisfactory quality' and is defined in section 14 of the Sale of Goods Act 1979:[198]

(2A) Goods are of satisfactory quality if they meet the standard that a reasonable person would regard as satisfactory, taking account of any description of the goods, the price (if relevant) and all other relevant circumstances.

(2B) The quality of goods includes their state and condition and the following (amongst others) are in appropriate cases aspects of the quality of goods; fitness for all the purposes for which goods of the kind in question are commonly supplied, appearance and finish, freedom from minor defects, safety, and durability.

The indications are that recourse to decisions on the old law should only be had in exceptional cases[199] but, in the absence of guidance as to what 'satisfactory quality' means, they provide useful indications of what is likely to be required. Thus, in *Rogers v. Parish (Scarborough) Ltd.*[200] it was said that:

Starting with the purpose for which ['goods of the kind in question'][201] are commonly bought, one would include in respect of any passenger vehicle not merely the buyer's purpose in driving the car from one place to another but of doing so with the appropriate degree of comfort, ease of handling and reliability and, one might add, of pride in the vehicle's outward and interior appearance. What is the appropriate degree and what relative weight is to be attached to one characteristic of the car rather than another will depend on the market at which the car is aimed.[202]

In that case, a new car had been delivered with substantial defects to its engine, gearbox, and bodywork and attempts to rectify these defects over a six-month period had failed. It was held that the car was not of 'merchantable quality' and the buyer was entitled to reject it, even though the defects did not render it unroadworthy. Again, apart from the factors listed in subsection 2(B), the Court is likely to consider the consequences of the defect and the ease or otherwise with which it could be remedied and whether this would produce a result 'as good as new'.[203]

Second-hand goods sold as such and goods sold as 'seconds' or imperfect must still measure up to a reasonable standard, even though not to the standard of a new or perfect article.[204] The price of the goods may frequently be of relevance: a buyer who, for example, buys a cheap carpet cannot expect it to achieve the same quality of resilience or wear as a more expensive one.[205]

---

[197] 237 H.C. Deb (1993/94), col. 633. See further 139 H.C. Deb. (1987/88) W.A. 705; 165 H.C. Deb. (1989/90), col. 1225.

[198] Inserted by the Sale and Supply of Goods Act 1994, s. 1(1).

[199] *Rogers* v. *Parish (Scarborough) Ltd.* [1987] Q.B. 933, *per* Mustill L.J. at pp. 942–3.

[200] [1987] Q.B. 933.

[201] The bracketed words reflect the 1994 amendments. Before those, s. 14(6) referred to 'goods of that kind'.

[202] *Rogers* v. *Parish (Scarborough) Ltd.* (*supra*, n. 199), at p. 944.

[203] *Bernstein* v. *Pamson Motors (Golders Green) Ltd.* [1987] 2 All E.R. 220.

[204] *Bartlett* v. *Sydney Marcus Ltd.* [1965] 1 W.L.R. 1013; *Business Appliance Specialists Ltd.* v. *Nationwide Credit Cpn. Ltd.* [1988] R.T.R. 332; *Shine* v. *General Guarantee Cpn.* [1988] 1 All E.R. 911.

[205] Cf. *B. S. Brown & Son Ltd.* v. *Craiks Ltd.* [1970] 1 W.L.R. 752.

The condition as to satisfactory quality extends to 'the goods supplied under the contract' including packaging, containers and extraneous items mixed with the goods sold. Thus, in *Wilson* v. *Rickett, Cockrell & Co. Ltd.*[206] it was held that a ton of 'Coalite' which contained, unknown to either party, a detonator did not meet the statutory standard. The argument that there was nothing wrong with the 'Coalite' itself was rejected and the defendant was held liable for damage from an explosion caused when a bucketful of the fuel containing the detonator was put on a fire.

The condition is, however, excluded if the defects are pointed out to the buyer before the contract is made, or if, before the contract is made, the buyer examines the goods, then as regards defects which the examination which has been made ought to have revealed.[207]

(iv) Fitness for purpose

Section 14(3) of the 1979 Act deals with the fitness for purpose of the goods sold:

(3) Where the seller sells goods in the course of a business and the buyer, expressly or by implication, makes known—

(a) to the seller, or

(b) where the purchase price or part of it is payable by instalments and the goods were previously sold by a credit-broker to the seller, to that credit-broker,

any particular purpose for which the goods are being bought, there is an implied [condition][208] that the goods supplied under the contract are reasonably fit for that purpose, whether or not that is a purpose for which such goods are commonly supplied, except where the circumstances show that the buyer does not rely, or that it is unreasonable for him to rely, on the skill or judgment of the seller or credit-broker.

The application of this sub-section is illustrated by two cases concerning the purchase of food. In *Wallis* v. *Russell*[209] the plaintiff bought from a fishmonger 'two nice fresh crabs for tea' and in *Chaproniere* v. *Mason*[210] the plaintiff bought a bath bun from the defendant's baker's shop. The crabs were not fresh and the plaintiff suffered food poisoning after eating the crabs; the bath bun contained a stone and the plaintiff broke a tooth when he bit it. In the first case the plaintiff expressly made it known through her agent[211] that she required the crabs for eating and relied on the fishmonger to select fresh crabs. In the second case, in buying the bun from a baker, the plaintiff clearly made it known by implication that he required it for the purpose of

[206] [1954] 1 Q.B. 598.
[207] Sale of Goods Act 1979, s. 14(2C); *R & B Customs Brokers Co. Ltd.* v. *United Dominions Trust Ltd.* [1988] 1 W.L.R. 321. Cf. *Thornett and Fehr* v. *Beer & Son* [1919] 1 K.B. 486 (on the previous and different wording of the proviso to s. 14(2) of the 1893 Act).
[208] Sale of Goods Act 1979, s. 14(6).
[209] [1902] 2 Ir. Rep. 585.
[210] (1905) 21 T.L.R. 633. See also *Priest* v. *Last* [1903] 2 K.B. 148 (hot-water bottle bursts); *Frost* v. *Aylesbury Dairy Co. Ltd.* [1905] 1 K.B. 608 (typhoid germs in milk); *St Albans City & D.C.* v. *International Computers Ltd.* [1996] 4 All E.R. 481, at p. 494 (computer disk with defective program).
[211] The purchase was made by the plaintiff's granddaughter on her behalf. On agency, see *post*, p. 663.

eating and relied on the baker's skill and judgement. Both defendants were liable in damages for breach of this implied condition.

The reliance will usually arise by implication in a purchase by a private individual of goods from a shop, for such a person 'goes to the shop in the confidence that the tradesman has selected his stock with skill and judgement';[212] and where two business people who are equally knowledgeable are dealing with one another, it may still be that the buyer reasonably relies on the seller's skill or judgement.[213] It is possible, however, that the reliance will be only partial. If, for example, the buyer procures the seller to manufacture goods in accordance with the buyer's formula or specifications, there will be no implied condition that the formula or specifications will produce goods which are reasonably fit for the purpose made known to the seller by the buyer, yet the buyer may rely on the skill or judgement of the seller to ensure that the materials to be compounded in the formula are not toxic or harmful[214] or there may be an area of expertise outside the specifications in respect of which the skill or judgement of the seller is relied on.[215]

(v) Sections 14(2) and 14(3) compared

The two sub-sections of section 14, to some extent, overlap, for both the definition of 'satisfactory quality' and section 14(3) refer to fitness for a purpose for which goods are commonly bought or supplied. A buyer who requires the goods for some special or unusual purpose, however, can recover, if at all, only under section 14(3). The special or unusual purpose must be made known to the seller and the buyer must show reliance on the seller's skill and judgement. Under section 14(2) it is not necessary to show such reliance. Where the goods are unfit for a special or unusual purpose, but nevertheless fit for all purposes for which such goods are commonly supplied, they will still be of 'satisfactory quality' and there will be no breach by the seller of section 14(2). Where, however, they are only fit for some of the purposes for which such goods are commonly supplied they will not be of 'satisfactory quality'.[216] As amended in 1994, the sub-section thus places the risk of unfitness for any of the common purposes on the seller. It is said that the seller who knows that its goods are not fit for one or more of the purposes for which goods of that kind are commonly supplied can protect itself by ensuring that the description of the goods excludes any common purpose for which they are unfit or by otherwise indicating that the goods are not fit for all their common purposes.[217] The amendment has therefore given the characterization of a purpose as 'common' or 'unusual' a new importance.

---

[212] *Grant* v. *Australian Knitting Mills Ltd.* [1936] A.C. 85, *per* Lord Wright at p. 99.

[213] *Henry Kendall & Sons* v. *William Lillico & Sons Ltd.* [1969] 2 A.C. 31. Cf. *Slater & Slater* v. *Finney Ltd.* [1997] A.C. 473 (no reliance because of unusual feature in buyer's machinery).

[214] *Ashington Piggeries Ltd.* v. *Christopher Hill Ltd.* [1972] A.C. 441.

[215] *Cammell Laird & Co. Ltd.* v. *Manganese Bronze & Brass Co. Ltd.* [1934] A.C. 402.

[216] Sale of Goods Act 1979, s. 14(2B), *ante*, p. 156.

[217] See Law Com. No. 162, *Sale and Supply of Goods* (1987), § 3.36. Prior to the amendment it was not necessary for the goods to be fit for *all* of their common purposes: *Sumner, Permain & Co. Ltd.* v. *Webb & Co. Ltd.* [1922] 1 K.B. 55; *Aswan Engineering Establishment Co.* v. *Lupine Ltd.* [1987] 1 W.L.R. 1, and see *Henry Kendall & Sons* v. *William Lillico & Sons Ltd.* [1969] 2 A.C. 31, at p. 77.

(e) SALE BY SAMPLE

In a sale by sample there are two implied conditions. First, that the bulk will correspond with the sample in quality. Secondly, that the goods will be free from any defect
making their quality unsatisfactory, which would not be apparent on reasonable
examination of the sample.[218] The meaning of this last condition was considered in
Godley v. *Perry*.[219]

A 6-year-old boy bought from a retailer in his shop a toy catapult made of brittle poly-
styrene which fractured while he was using it, blinding him in one eye. He sued the retailer
for damages under section 14(2) and (3) of the Sale of Goods Act. The retailer joined the
wholesaler from whom he had bought the catapult by sample as a third party and the
wholesaler likewise joined the importer who had supplied him.

The retailer was held liable but it was argued that the wholesaler and importer were
not liable for breach of the condition as to satisfactory quality in a contract of sale by
sample because a reasonable examination of the catapult would have revealed its
fragility. Edmund Davies J. said:[220]

Counsel . . . suggested that by holding the toy down with one's foot and then pulling on the
elastic its safety could be tested and . . . its inherent fragility would thereby inevitably be
discovered. True, the potential customer might have done any of these. He might also, I
suppose, have tried biting the catapult, or hitting it with a hammer, or applying a lighted
match to ensure its non-inflammability, experiments which, with all respect, are but slightly
more bizarre than those suggested by counsel.

The phrase 'reasonable examination' was to be construed by the common-sense
standards of everyday life: 'Not extreme ingenuity, but reasonableness, is the statutory
yardstick.' The wholesaler and importer were held liable.

(f) OTHER STATUTORY TERMS

Certain terms are implied by sections 8–11 of the Supply of Goods (Implied Terms)
Act 1973[221] into all contracts of hire-purchase. These implied terms resemble very
closely those implied in contracts of sale of goods, and relate similarly to title, quality,
and fitness for purpose, and correspondence with description or sample. Statutory
terms are also implied by the Supply of Goods and Services Act 1982 into contracts
for work and materials, contracts of hire, and contracts for the supply of services. For
example, in a contract for the supply of services, there are implied terms that the
supplier will carry out the service with reasonable care and skill and (if no time for
completion is fixed) that he will carry out the service within a reasonable time. Finally,
the covenants for title which are implied on a disposition of property are set out in
Part I of the Law of Property (Miscellaneous Provisions) Act 1994.

---

[218] Sale of Goods Act 1979, s. 15.
[219] [1960] 1 W.L.R. 9.
[220] At p. 15.
[221] As amended by the Consumer Credit Act 1974, Sched. 4 and the Sale and Supply of Goods Act 1994, s.
7, Sched. 2, para. 4.

IV. CONSTRUCTION OF TERMS

This section deals shortly with certain general principles which govern the construction of terms which have been reduced to writing,[222] premising that the construction of a contract is always a matter of law for the Court to determine.

(a) INTENTION MUST NORMALLY BE ASCERTAINED FROM DOCUMENT ITSELF

The professed object of the Court in construing a written contract is to discover the mutual intention of the parties,[223] the written declaration of whose minds it is. Subject to the exceptions discussed above[224] this intention must be ascertained from the document itself. Accordingly, the parties cannot themselves give direct evidence to show that their real intentions were at variance with the provisions of the document[225] and the task of the Court is to construe the contractual term without any preconception as to what the parties intended.[226]

Evidence of prior negotiations cannot therefore be received in aid of the construction of a written document; but the Court must place itself in thought in the same factual matrix as that in which the parties were. Thus evidence may be admitted of the factual background existing at or before the date of the contract including evidence of the genesis and, objectively, of the 'aim' of the transaction.[227] In *Investors Compensation Scheme Ltd. v. West Bromwich Building Society*[228] Lord Hoffmann stated that, apart from previous negotiations and declarations of subjective intent, the factual background includes absolutely everything reasonably available to the parties which would have affected the way in which the language of the document would have been understood by a reasonable person. In a later case he qualified this by stating that it only included that which the reasonable person would have regarded as relevant.[229] But it has also been formulated more narrowly to include only facts which both parties would have had in mind when making the contract.[230]

The subsequent conduct of the parties may not be used as an aid to interpretation

---

[222] See generally Staughton [1999] C.L.J. 303.

[223] *Pioneer S.S. Ltd. v. B.T.P. Tioxide* [1982] A.C. 724, at p. 736; *International Fina Services A.G. v. Katrina Shipping Ltd.* [1995] 2 Lloyd's Rep. 344, at p. 350.

[224] *Ante*, p. 132. See also *post*, p. 165.

[225] *Prenn v. Simmonds* [1971] 1 W.L.R. 1381, at p. 1385; *Hyundai Merchant Marine Co. Ltd. v. Gesuri Chartering Co. Ltd.* [1991] 1 Lloyd's Rep. 100, at p. 102. See also *British Movietonews Ltd. v. London & District Cinemas Ltd.* [1952] A.C. 166; *Zoan v. Rouamba* [2000] 1 W.L.R. 1509, at p. 1523.

[226] *Pagnan SpA v. Tradax Ocean Transportation S.A.* [1987] 1 All E.R. 81, at p. 88, aff'd [1987] 3 All E.R. 565.

[227] *Prenn v. Simmonds* [1971] 1 W.L.R. 1381; *Reardon Smith Line Ltd. v. Yngvar Hansen-Tangen* [1976] 1 W.L.R. 989; *Codelfa Construction Pty. Ltd. v. State Railway Authority of N.S.W.* (1982) 149 C.L.R. 337, at pp. 345–53 (High Court of Australia).

[228] [1998] 1 W.L.R. 898, at p. 912.

[229] *B.C.C.I S.A. v. Ali* [2001] 2 W.L.R. 735, at p. 749.

[230] *Bank of Scotland v. Dunedin Property Investments Co. Ltd.* (1998) SC 657; *Scottish Power plc v. Bristol (Exploration) Ltd.*, The Times, 2 December 1997; Staughton [1999] C.L.J. 303, 307–8.

of a written contract because it is equally referable to what the parties intended to say as to the meaning of what they in fact said[231] and because 'otherwise one might have the result that a contract meant one thing on the day it was signed, but by reason of subsequent events meant something different a month or a year later'.[232] Subsequent conduct may, however, be used to show that a contract exists,[233] and it may also amount to a variation of its terms or give rise to an estoppel or a waiver.[234]

(b) RULES APPLIED TO WRITTEN AGREEMENTS

There are certain other rules of a general nature which are applied by the Courts in the case of written agreements:

(1) Words are to be understood in their plain and literal meaning. This does not necessarily mean the dictionary sense of the word, but that in which it is generally understood,[235] subject always, however, to admissible evidence being adduced to show that the word is to be understood in some other technical or special sense. The rule may also be departed from where it would involve an absurdity[236] or inconsistency with the rest of the instrument.[237] A Court is unlikely to conclude that the parties intended a construction that leads to an unreasonable result,[238] particularly in the case of a poorly drafted contract.[239] But although 'in the process of interpreting the meaning of the language of a commercial document the Court ought generally to favour a commercially sensible construction',[240] 'to force upon the words a meaning which they cannot fairly bear is to substitute for the bargain actually made one which the court believes could be better made'.[241]

(2) Words susceptible of two meanings receive that which will make the instrument valid rather than void or ineffective.[242] Where a guarantee was expressed to be given to the plaintiffs 'in consideration of your *being* in advance' to J.S., it was argued that this showed a past consideration; but the Court held that the words might mean a prospective advance, and be equivalent to 'in consideration of your *becoming* in advance', or '*on condition* of your being in

---

[231] *Schuler AG v. Wickman Machine Tool Sales Ltd.* [1974] A.C. 235, at pp. 261, 263.

[232] *Whitworth Street Estates (Manchester) Ltd. v. James Miller & Partners Ltd.* [1970] A.C. 583, at p. 603.

[233] *Ibid.; Wilson v. Maynard Shipbuilding Consultants AG Ltd.* [1978] Q.B. 665.

[234] *Ante*, p. 112; *post*, p. 523.

[235] *Robertson v. French* (1803) 4 East 130, at p. 135.

[236] *Abbott v. Middleton* (1858) 7 H.L.C. 68, at p. 69. See also *Investors Compensation Scheme Ltd. v. West Bromwich B.S.* [1998] 1 W.L.R. 898 (H.L.).

[237] *Watson v. Haggitt* [1928] A.C. 127.

[238] *Schuler AG v. Wickman Machine Tool Sales Ltd.* [1974] A.C. 235, *per* Lord Reid at p. 251.

[239] *Mitsui Construction Co. Ltd. v. A. G. of Hong Kong* (1986) 33 B.L.R. 14, *per* Lord Bridge.

[240] *Lord Napier and Ettrick v. R. F. Kershaw Ltd. (No. 2)* [1999] 1 W.L.R. 756, *per* Lord Steyn at p. 763. See also *Antaios Cia Naviera SA v. Salen Rederierna* [1985] A.C. 191, *per* Lord Diplock at p. 201.

[241] *Charter Reinsurance Co. Ltd. v. Fagan* [1997] A.C. 313, *per* Lord Mustill at p. 388, limiting Lord Reid's statement in *Schuler AG v. Wickman Machine Tool Sales Ltd.* (*ante*, n. 238).

[242] *Verba ita sunt intelligenda ut res magis valeat quam pereat*: Bac. Max. 3.

advance'.[243] So strong is this rule in favour of supporting the document that, in suitable cases, the Court is prepared to restrict the written words to those applicable in the agreement, supply obvious omissions, and to transpose or even reject words and phrases if the intention of the parties is clear.

(3) 'An agreement ought to receive that construction which its language will admit, which will best effectuate the intention of the parties, to be collected *from the whole of the agreement*, and greater regard is to be had to the clear intent of the parties than to any particular words which they may have used in the expression of their intent.'[244] The proper mode of construction is to take the instrument as a whole, to ascertain the meaning of words and phrases from their general context, and to try and give effect to every part of it.[245] However, if the words of a particular clause are clear and unambiguous, they cannot be modified by reference to the other clauses in the agreement.

Subsidiary to these main rules there are various others, all tending to the same end, the effecting of the intention of the parties as ascertained from the written document:

(4) Where there is an express mention in the instrument of a certain thing, this will exclude any other thing of a similar nature: *expressio unius est exclusio alterius.*[246] So where a conveyance was made of an iron foundry and two houses, together with the fixtures in the houses, the fixtures in the foundry were held not to pass even though they otherwise would have done so.[247]

(5) The meaning of general words may be narrowed and restrained by specific and particular descriptions of the subject-matter to which they are to apply. Thus in construing a charterparty where liability to deliver cargo was excluded if through 'war, disturbance, or any other cause' it was not possible to do so, it was held that the words 'any other cause' were restricted to events of the same kind as war and disturbance, and so excluded ice.[248] But this rule (the so-called *ejusdem generis* rule) is again only a canon of construction for the purpose of ascertaining what may be presumed to have been the meaning and intention of the parties to the contract. It is not a rule of law and is therefore subordinate to the parties' real intention and does not control it. It will have no application if the parties can be shown to have intended a different interpretation to be given to the language which they have used.

(6) The words of written documents are construed more forcibly against the party putting forward the document.[249] The rule is based on the principle that a

---

[243] *Haigh* v. *Brooks* (1839) 10 A. & E. 309; *Steele* v. *Hoe* (1849) 14 Q.B. 431.

[244] *Ford* v. *Beech* (1848) 11 Q.B. 852, *per* Parke B. at p. 866.

[245] *Ex antecedentibus et consequentibus fit optima interpretatio*: 2 Co. Inst. 317; *Barton* v. *Fitzgerald* (1812) 15 East 529, at p. 541.

[246] Co. Litt. 210a.

[247] *Hare* v. *Horton* (1833) 5 B. & Ad. 715.

[248] *Tillmanns* v. *S. S. Knutsford* [1908] 2 K.B. 385, aff'd [1908] A.C. 406; *Thorman* v. *Dowgate Steamship Co. Ltd.* [1910] 1 K.B. 410.

[249] *Verba chartarum fortius accipiuntur contra proferentem*: Bac. Max. 3; Unfair Terms in Consumer Contracts Regulations 1999 (S.I. 1999 No. 2083), reg. 7. See *post*, p. 169.

party putting forward the wording of a proposed agreement may be assumed to have looked after its own interests, is responsible for ambiguities in its own expression, and has no right to induce another to make a contract on the supposition that the words mean one thing, and then to argue for a construction by which they would mean another thing, more to its advantage.[250]

V. EXEMPTION CLAUSES

(a) STANDARD FORMS OF CONTRACT

One of the most important developments has been the appearance of the standard form of contract,[251] or 'contract of adhesion'.[252] The idea of an agreement freely negotiated between the parties has given way to the necessity for a uniform set of printed conditions which can be used time and time again, and for a large number of persons, and at less cost than an individually negotiated contract. Each time an individual travels by air, bus or train, buys a motor car, takes clothes to the dry-cleaner, buys household goods, or even, in some cases, takes the lease of a house or flat, a standard form contract, devised by the supplier, will be provided which the individual must either accept *in toto*, or, theoretically, go without. In fact, there is little alternative but to accept; the individual does not negotiate, but merely adheres. In some respects, therefore, it would be more correct to regard the relationship which arises not as one of contract at all, but as one of status. The contracting party has the status of a consumer.

The use of standard terms and conditions is not, however, confined to contracts made with consumers. Many contracts between business people—indeed, perhaps the majority of such contracts—are today entered into on the basis of a standard form of document, such as an order form, confirmation of order, catalogue or price list, put forward by one party,[253] or that person's standard form of agreement, or which incorporate by reference the standard terms and conditions of trade associations.

Until recently, the ordinary principles of the law of contract applied to such contracts. But these principles may not be capable of providing a just solution for a transaction in which freedom of contract exists on one side only. In particular, the party delivering the document may allocate the risks of non-performance or defective performance to the other party. While such allocation of risks should in principle lead to lower costs, it is only justifiable if at least some of the cost saving is passed on and if the other party is aware of the contractual allocation of risks. In fact the party

---

[250] *Tan Wing Chuen v. Bank of Credit and Commerce Hong Kong Ltd.* [1996] 2 B.C.L.C. 69, *per* Lord Mustill at p. 77.
[251] See Sales (1953) 16 M.L.R. 318; Gower (1954) 17 M.L.R. 155; Turpin (1956) 73 S.A.L.J. 144; Coote, *Exception Clauses* (1964); Yates, *Exclusion Clauses in Contracts*, 2nd edn. (1982).
[252] Saleilles, *De la Déclaration de la Volonté* (1901).
[253] For the 'battle of the forms', see *ante*, p. 38.

delivering the document may seek unfair exemption from certain common law liabilities, and thus seek to deprive the other party of the compensation which that person might reasonably expect to receive for any loss or injury or damage arising out of the transaction. Moreover, standard form contracts with consumers are often contained in some printed ticket, or notice, or receipt, which is brought to the attention of the consumer at the time the agreement is made and which a prudent consumer would read from beginning to end. In fact, however, the consumer normally has neither the time nor the energy to do this, and, even if this was done, it would be of little assistance for the consumer could not vary the terms in any way. It is not until some dispute arises that the consumer realizes how few are the rights in the contract.

Acting within the limitations imposed on them by the contractual framework of these transactions, the Courts nevertheless endeavoured to alleviate the position of the recipient of the document by requiring certain standards of notice in respect of onerous terms, and by construing the document wherever possible in that person's favour. It has been said that 'the judicial creativity, bordering on judicial legislation' which marked the development of these rules was a 'desperate remedy invoked because it was considered necessary to remedy a widespread injustice'.[254] These rules are still important in determining the efficacy of clauses which purport to exempt one party from common law liability. But the measure of protection which they offered against unfair exemption clauses is somewhat slender, and the power of the Courts to control such clauses has been greatly increased since the enactment of the Unfair Contract Terms Act 1977 and the Unfair Terms in Consumer Regulations 1999.[255]

(b) NOTICE OF PRINTED TERMS

A person who *signs* a document which contains contractual terms is normally bound by them even though that person has not read them and is ignorant of their precise legal effect.[256] But if the document is not signed, being merely delivered to the other party, then the question arises whether adequate notice was given of the terms of the contract.

(i) The notice must be contemporaneous with the contract

In order that a term should become binding as part of the contract it must be brought to the notice of the contracting party before or at the time that the contract is made. If it is not communicated until afterwards, it will be of no effect unless there is evidence that the parties have entered into a new contract on a different basis.[257]

An illustration of the necessity for contemporaneity is provided by *Olley* v. *Marlborough Court Ltd.*:[258]

---

[254] *B.C.C.I. S.A.* v. *Ali* [2001] 2 W.L.R. 735, *per* Lord Hoffmann at p. 756.

[255] See *post*, pp. 185, 200.

[256] *Parker* v. *South Eastern Ry.* (1877) 2 C.P.D. 416, at p. 421; *L'Estrange* v. *F. Graucob Ltd.* [1934] 2 K.B. 394; *Levison* v. *Patent Steam Carpet Cleaning Co. Ltd.* [1978] Q.B. 69.

[257] *Levison* v. *Patent Steam Carpet Cleaning Co. Ltd.* (supra, n. 256).

[258] [1949] 1 K.B. 532. See also *Hollingworth* v. *Southern Ferries Ltd.* [1977] 2 Lloyd's Rep. 70 (sailing tickets delivered after booking made).

O and her husband registered at the defendant's hotel, paid for a week's board and lodging in advance, and then went up to their room. There a notice was exhibited stating: 'The proprietors will not hold themselves responsible for articles lost or stolen, unless handed to the manageress for safe custody'. Owing to the negligence of the hotel staff, a thief gained access to the room and stole some of their property.

The Court of Appeal held that the notice formed no part of the contract since O could not have seen it until after the contract was made; the defendant was accordingly liable for the loss. Also, a customer who parked a car in a garage and received at the entrance a ticket from an automatic machine, was held not to be bound by the conditions printed on the ticket; the machine caused the ticket to be issued when the car was driven to the entrance to the garage, and the customer could not be affected by conditions brought to his notice after this time.[259]

(ii) Course of dealing

An exception clause will not necessarily be incorporated into a contract by virtue of a *previous* course of dealing between the same parties on similar terms.[260] But such a clause may be incorporated where each party has led the other reasonably to believe that it intended that their rights and liabilities should be ascertained by reference to the terms of a document which had been consistently used by them in previous transactions.[261] Where the clause is a usual one in the trade, and the parties are of equal bargaining power, less will be required in terms of the consistency of the previous course of dealing for it to be included in the contract.[262] In such cases the process of incorporation has been said to be based on a common understanding and appears to be very similar to that of implication on the basis of trade custom. It is, however, clear that one party cannot unilaterally, *after* the conclusion of the contract, impose upon the other onerous conditions without consent: any variation of a concluded contract can only take place by mutual consent of both parties.

(iii) The meaning of notice

In what circumstances will a party receiving a ticket, receipt, or common form document at the time the contract is made be bound by the conditions contained in it? In order that a contract should come into existence, normally the terms of the contract should be communicated, that is to say the offeree should be made subjectively aware of their nature and extent. But a more objective idea of *consensus* applies to such standard form contracts.

---

[259] *Thornton* v. *Shoe Lane Parking Ltd.* [1971] 2 Q.B. 163 (only Lord Denning M.R. found that the contract was concluded at that moment. Megaw L.J. and Sir Gordon Willmer reserved their opinions on this point).

[260] *Hollier* v. *Rambler Motors (A.M.C.) Ltd.* [1972] 2 Q.B. 71 (plaintiff had signed a form containing exemption clauses on three or four occasions over a five-year period). See also *McCutcheon* v. *David Macbrayne Ltd.* [1964] 1 W.L.R. 125.

[261] *Henry Kendall & Sons* v. *William Lillico & Sons Ltd.* [1969] 2 A.C. 31 (parties had contracted three or four times a month over a three-year period). See also *Spurling (J.) Ltd.* v. *Bradshaw* [1956] 1 W.L.R. 461, at p. 467; *Gillespie Bros. & Co. Ltd.* v. *Roy Bowles Transport Ltd.* [1973] Q.B. 400; *Circle Freight Int. Ltd.* v. *Medeast Gulf Exports Ltd.* [1988] 2 Lloyd's Rep. 427.

[262] *British Crane Hire Cpn. Ltd.* v. *Ipswich Plant Hire Ltd.* [1975] Q.B. 303 (usual term incorporated on the basis of two transactions months before).

Take the example of a railway or cloakroom ticket, which the person receiving it puts into his pocket unread; three general rules have been laid down to determine whether the traveller or depositor will be bound by the terms contained in the ticket:[263]

(1) A person receiving the ticket who did not see or know that there was any writing on the ticket will not be bound by the conditions.

(2) A person who knows there was writing, and knows or believes that the writing contained conditions, is bound by the conditions.

(3) A person who knows that there was writing on the ticket, but does not know or believe that the writing contained conditions, will nevertheless be bound where the delivery of the ticket in such a manner that the writing on it could be seen is reasonable notice that the writing contained conditions.

It is the third of these rules which is at once the most frequently to be applied and the most difficult in its application. It is sometimes known as the requirement of 'reasonable sufficiency of notice'.

(iv) Reasonable sufficiency of notice

A person may be bound by an exemption clause in a standard form document, even though subjectively ignorant of its content, if the party seeking to rely on the clause has done what was reasonably sufficient in the circumstances to bring it to the other party's notice. The principles were discussed in *Parker* v. *South Eastern Railway Co.*:[264]

P deposited a bag in the defendant's station cloakroom. He received a paper ticket which said on its face 'See back' and on the back were a number of printed conditions, including a condition limiting liability for any package to £10. P admitted that he knew there was writing on the ticket, but stated that he had not read it, and did not know or believe that the writing contained conditions. The bag was lost, and P claimed £24 10*s.*, for its value.

The jury was directed to consider whether P had read or was aware of the special condition upon which the bag was deposited. It answered this question in the negative and accordingly judgment was entered for P. On appeal by the defendant, the Court of Appeal held that the jury had been misdirected. The real question was whether the defendant had done what was reasonably sufficient to give P notice of the condition. A new trial was ordered.

(v) Question of fact

The question whether all that is reasonably necessary to give notice has been done is a question of fact,[265] in answering which the tribunal must look at all the circumstances and the situation of the parties.[266] *Thompson* v. *L.M. & S. Railway Co.*[267] represents a

---

[263] *Parker* v. *South Eastern Ry.* (1877) 2 C.P.D. 416, at pp. 421, 423; approved in *Richardson, Spence & Co.* v. *Rowntree* [1894] A.C. 217; *Burnett* v. *Westminster Bank* [1966] 1 Q.B. 742.

[264] (1877) 2 C.P.D. 416; *Hood* v. *Anchor Line (Henderson Bros.) Ltd.* [1918] A.C. 837.

[265] *Parker* v. *South-Eastern Ry.* (1877) 2 C.P.D. 416; *Richardson, Spence & Co.* v. *Rowntree* [1894] A.C. 217.

[266] *Hood* v. *Anchor Line (Henderson Bros.) Ltd.* [1918] A.C. 837, *per* Lord Haldane at p. 844.

[267] [1931] 1 K.B. 41.

very liberal approach to what constitutes reasonable notice. There a passenger travelling on an excursion ticket was injured by the alleged negligence of the defendant railway company. It was held that a clause exempting the company from liability,[268] printed in its timetable, was sufficiently, although circuitously, incorporated into the contract since the ticket referred to the timetables and excursion bills (the latter also referred to the timetables). But in *Richardson, Spence & Co. v. Rowntree*,[269] a term limiting the liability of a steamship company to $100 in a steamship ticket was held not to be incorporated. The ticket had been handed to the plaintiff folded up, and the conditions were obliterated in part by a stamp in red ink. The jury found that, although the plaintiff knew there was writing on the ticket, she did not know the writing contained conditions, and that reasonably sufficient notice had not been given. The House of Lords refused to upset this finding. If the notice is otherwise sufficient, the fact that a particular plaintiff is under some non-legal disability, for example, unable to speak English, or blind,[270] or, as in *Thompson v. L.M. & S. Railway Co.*, illiterate,[271] will be treated as irrelevant.

If there is no reference on the face of a ticket to the fact that there are conditions printed on the back, the Courts have consistently held that such a notification is defective.[272] Strictly, of course, the issue is one of fact in each particular case, but this requirement may now fairly be said to be one of law.

(vi) Unusual terms

Although a term must be construed in its context, it is not enough to look at a set of printed conditions as a whole. If the particular condition relied upon by the party seeking exemption is one which is unusual in that class of contract, special measures may be required fairly to bring it to the notice of the other party. It has even been said that some clauses 'would need to be printed in red ink on the face of the document with a red hand pointing to it before the notice could be held to be sufficient'.[273] In *Interfoto Picture Library Ltd. v. Stiletto Visual Programmes Ltd.*:[274]

Interfoto hired 47 transparencies to Stiletto. The transparencies were despatched to Stiletto in a bag containing a delivery note containing conditions printed in small but visible

---

[268] The Unfair Contract Terms Act 1977, s. 2(1) now prevents the exclusion or restriction of liability for death or personal injury resulting from negligence, *post*, pp. 190–1.

[269] [1894] A.C. 217. See also *Union Steamships v. Barnes* (1956) 5 D.L.R. (2d) 535 (Canada).

[270] Cf. *Geier v. Kujawa, Weston and Warne Bros. (Transport) Ltd.* [1970] 1 Lloyd's Rep. 364, at p. 368 (where the plaintiff's ignorance of English was known). The term there, excluding the liability of a driver of a motor vehicle to a passenger, would now be invalid under the Road Traffic Act 1988, s. 149.

[271] However, the ticket had been bought on the plaintiff's behalf by her niece and it was found that the niece's father had ascertained, before the ticket was taken, that there were conditions for excursion tickets.

[272] *Henderson v. Stevenson* (1875) L.R. 2 H.L. Sc. App. 470; *White v. Blackmore* [1972] 2 Q.B. 651, at p. 664. See also *Poseidon Freight Forwarding Co. Ltd. v. Davies Turner Southern Ltd.* [1996] 2 Lloyd's Rep. 388 (reference to terms on back of faxed document but terms not communicated).

[273] *Spurling (J.) Ltd. v. Bradshaw* [1956] 1 W.L.R. 461, *per* Denning L.J. at p. 466; *Thornton v. Shoe Lane Parking Ltd.* [1971] 2 Q.B. 163; *Shearson Lehman Hutton Inc. v. MacLaine Watson & Co. Ltd.* [1989] 2 Lloyd's Rep. 570, at p. 612. Cf. *Ocean Chemical Transport Inc. v. Exnor Craggs Ltd.* [2000] 1 Lloyd's Rep. 446, at p. 454 (red hand approach doubted for commercial contract).

[274] [1989] Q.B. 433.

lettering on the face of the document, including condition 2, which stated that 'a holding fee of £5 plus VAT per day will be charged for each transparency which is retained . . . longer than . . . 14 days'. The daily rate per transparency was many times greater than was usual but nothing whatever was done by Interfoto to draw Stiletto's attention particularly to condition 2. Stiletto returned the transparencies 4 weeks later and Interfoto claimed £3,783.50.

The Court of Appeal held that the contract was made when, after the receipt of the transparencies, Stiletto accepted them by telephone. Although, to the extent the conditions were common form or usual terms, they were incorporated into the contract, it was held that condition 2 had not been so incorporated.[275] Bingham L.J. stated:[276]

[Stiletto] are not to be relieved of . . . liability because they did not read the condition, although doubtless they did not; but in my judgment they are to be relieved because [Interfoto] did not do what was necessary to draw this unreasonable and extortionate clause fairly to their attention.

(vii) Exhibited notices

Printed notices containing conditions, for example, the notices exhibited at the counter of a left-luggage office at a railway station, have been held to become part of the contract where the ticket or receipt refers to the notice[277] and probably even where it does not, provided the notice is sufficiently prominent and can be plainly seen before or at the time of making the contract.[278] But there is also authority for the view that the terms of the notice must be 'brought home' to the party affected and accepted by that party as part of the contract.[279]

(viii) The notice must be in a contractual document

If the document is one which the person receiving it would scarcely expect to contain conditions, for example, if it consisted of the sort of ticket which a reasonable person would suppose to be merely a voucher or receipt, it cannot be said that the notice given was reasonably sufficient in the circumstances. It would be 'quite reasonable that the party receiving it should assume that the writing contained in it no condition, and should put it in his pocket unread'.[280]

In *Chapelton* v. *Barry U.D.C.*:[281]

C wished to hire a deck chair on the beach. He took two from a pile belonging to the defendant, paying 2*d.* for each and receiving two tickets from an attendant. He set the chairs up firmly, sat on one—and went through the canvas. C sued the defendant for personal

---

[275] Interfoto could only recover a holding fee assessed on the basis of a *quantum meruit*, here £3.50 per transparency *per* week beyond the 14-day period: [1989] Q.B. 433, at pp. 439, 445.

[276] [1989] Q.B. 433, at p. 445. See also *The Northern Progress* [1996] 2 Lloyd's Rep. 321; *A.E.G. (U.K.) Ltd.* v. *Logic Resources Ltd.* [1996] C.L.C. 265, *per* Hirst L.J. at p. 273, but cf. Hobhouse L.J. *ibid.*, at p. 277.

[277] *Watkins* v. *Rymill* (1883) 10 Q.B.D. 178.

[278] *Olley* v. *Marlborough Court Ltd.* [1949] 1 K.B. 532, at p. 549; *Ashdown* v. *Samuel Williams & Sons Ltd.* [1957] 1 Q.B. 409.

[279] *Harling* v. *Eddy* [1951] 2 K.B. 739, at p. 748; *McCutcheon* v. *David Macbrayne Ltd.* [1964] 1 W.L.R. 125; *Smith* v. *Taylor* [1966] 2 Lloyd's Rep. 231; *Mendelssohn* v. *Normand Ltd.* [1970] 1 Q.B. 177, at p. 182.

[280] *Parker* v. *South-Eastern Ry. Co.* (1877) 2 C.P.D. 416, *per* Mellish L.J. at p. 422.

[281] [1940] 1 K.B. 532.

injuries sustained, and the defendant pleaded an exemption clause printed on the back of the ticket: 'The council will not be liable for any accident or damage arising from the hire of the chair'. C had glanced at the ticket but had not realized that it contained conditions.

The Court held that the defendants were not protected. A cheque-book cover[282] and a parking ticket issued by an automatic machine[283] have similarly been held to be non-contractual documents.

(c) CONSTRUCTION OF EXEMPTION CLAUSES

Assuming that reasonably sufficient notice of a standard form contract has been given to the person who receives the printed document, the next issue is the way in which the terms of the document are to be construed. The disparity between the bargaining power of consumers and large enterprises (both private and public) means that terms have often been imposed upon consumers which are unfair in their application and which exempt the enterprise putting forward the document, either wholly or in part, from its just liability under the contract. This was one of the reasons why, at common law, the Courts evolved certain canons of construction which normally work in favour of the party seeking to establish liability and against the party seeking to claim the benefit of the exemption. These canons of construction do not, however, render exemption clauses generally ineffective. If the clause is appropriately drafted so as to exclude or limit the liability in question, then the Courts must (subject to the powers conferred on them by the Unfair Contract Terms Act 1977 and the Unfair Terms in Consumer Contracts Regulations 1999)[284] give effect to it.

   As between businesses, exemption clauses can, however, perform a useful function. They may, for example, anticipate future contingencies which hinder or prevent performance, establish procedures for the making of claims and provide for the allocation of risks as between the parties to the contract. In a business transaction, the effect of an exemption clause may simply be to determine which of the parties is to insure against a particular risk. Exemption clauses in business transactions are not necessarily unfair or inequitable. But even in business transactions the Courts must be satisfied that the clause, on its wording, does have the effect contended for by the person relying on it, that is, the party seeking to exclude or restrict its liability.

(i) Strict interpretation

'If a person is under a legal liability and wishes to get rid of it, he can only do so by using clear words.'[285] The words of the exemption clause must exactly cover the liability which it is sought to exclude. So an exemption clause in a contract excluding liability for 'latent defects' will not exclude the condition as to fitness for purpose implied by the Sale of Goods Act;[286] exclusion of *implied* conditions and warranties

282 *Burnett* v. *Westminster Bank* [1966] 1 Q.B. 742.
283 *Thornton* v. *Shoe Lane Parking Ltd.* [1971] 2 Q.B. 163.
284 See *post*, pp. 200 and 300.
285 *Alison (J. Gordon) Ltd.* v. *Wallsend Shipway and Engineering Co. Ltd.* (1927) 43 T.L.R. 323, *per* Scrutton L.J. at p. 324.
286 *Henry Kendall & Sons* v. *William Lillico & Sons Ltd.* [1969] 2 A.C. 31.

will not exclude a term which is actually expressed;[287] and a clause excluding liability for breach of *warranty* will not exclude liability for breach of condition.[288] In the leading case of *Wallis, Son & Wells* v. *Pratt & Haynes*:[289]

W bought seed described as 'common English sainfoin' subject to an exemption clause that 'the sellers give no *warranty* express or implied, as to growth, description, or any other matters'. The seed turned out to be giant sainfoin, indistinguishable in seed, but inferior in quality and of less value. W was forced to compensate those to whom it had subsequently sold the seed, and sued to recover the money lost. P & H pleaded the exemption clause.

It was held by the House of Lords that, even though W had accepted the goods and could therefore only sue for breach of warranty *ex post facto*,[290] there was nevertheless originally a breach of the *condition* implied by section 13 of the Sale of Goods Act,[291] and this had not been successfully excluded.

Since the enactment of the Unfair Contract Terms Act 1977, which proscribes certain exemption clauses and subjects many others to a requirement of 'reasonable-ness', there are indications of a slightly less strict approach to construction. Thus, although 'the reports are full of cases in which what would appear to be very strained constructions have been placed upon exclusion clauses',[292] mainly in consumer contracts and standard form contracts, it has been said that:

in commercial contracts negotiated between businessmen capable of looking after their own interests and of deciding how risks . . . can be most economically borne . . . it is wrong to place a strained construction upon words in an exclusion clause which are clear and fairly susceptible of one meaning.[293]

(ii) The '*contra proferentem*' rule

The principle whereby the words of written documents are construed more forcibly against the party putting forward the document has been considered.[294] In the case of exemption clauses this is the party seeking to impose the exemption. This rule of construction is only applied where there is doubt or ambiguity in the phrases used, and provides that such doubt or ambiguity must be resolved against the party proffer-ing the written document and in favour of the other party. In *Lee (John) & Son (Grantham) Ltd.* v. *Railway Executive*:[295]

The lease of a railway warehouse contained a clause exempting the lessors from liability for 'loss damage costs and expenses however caused . . . (whether by act or neglect of the

---

[287] *Andrews Bros. Ltd.* v. *Singer & Co. Ltd.* [1934] 1 K.B. 17.

[288] *Baldry* v. *Marshall* [1925] 1 K.B. 260.

[289] [1911] A.C. 394.

[290] See *ante*, p. 144.

[291] See *ante*, p. 154.

[292] *Photo Production Ltd.* v. *Securicor Transport Ltd.* [1980] A.C. 826, *per* Lord Diplock at p. 851.

[293] *Ibid.* See also *ibid.*, at p. 843, *post*, p. 176.

[294] *Ante*, p. 162.

[295] [1949] 2 All E.R. 581. See also *Adams* v. *Richardson & Starling Ltd.* [1969] 1 W.L.R. 1645, at p. 1653 (construction of so-called 'guarantee'); *Tor Line A.B.* v. *Alltrans Group of Canada Ltd.* [1984] 1 W.L.R. 48, at p. 56 (H.L.).

company or their servants or agents or not) which but for the tenancy hereby created . . .
would not have arisen'. Goods in the warehouse were damaged by fire owing to the alleged
negligence of the lessors in allowing a spark to escape from their railway engines. The lessors
claimed that the clause exempted them from liability.

The Court of Appeal held that, applying the *contra proferentem* rule, the operation of
the clause was confined by the words 'but for the tenancy hereby created' to liabilities
which arose only by reason of the relationship of landlord and tenant created by the
lease. The clause was capable of a wider meaning, but it had to be construed against
the grantor, and the defendants were not protected.

(iii) Exclusion of liability for negligence

The ability of contracting parties to exclude themselves from liability for negligence
has been substantially restricted by legislation.[296] Apart from statutory restrictions,
although it is possible to exclude liability in negligence, the Courts have traditionally
approached clauses which are said to exclude such liability on the assumption that it is
'inherently improbable' that the innocent party would have agreed to the exclusion of
the contract-breaker's negligence.[297] To have this effect the contractual term in question must exclude liability for negligence clearly and unambiguously. Where it does,
and a contracting party is so protected from the consequences of its negligence, it is
not permissible for the other party to disregard the contract and to allege a wider
liability in tort.[298] In *Rutter* v. *Palmer*,[299] for example:

R left his car at P's garage to be sold. The contract provided that 'customers' cars are driven
by your [P's] servants at customers' sole risk'. The car was taken for a trial run by one of P's
drivers, there was a collision and the car was damaged.

It was held that the clause effectively placed the risk of negligence on R and so his
claim failed. Similarly, such phrases as: 'will not be liable for any damage however
caused',[300] 'will not in any circumstances be responsible',[301] 'arising from any cause
whatsoever'[302] will ordinarily be construed to cover liability for negligence.

On the other hand, there may be some ground of liability (other than negligence)
to which the party seeking exemption is subject in respect of the loss or damage

---

[296] Unfair Contract Terms Act 1977, s. 2, *post*, p. 190; Unfair Terms in Consumer Contracts Regulations
1999 (S.I. 1999 No. 2083), Sched. 2, para. 1(a).

[297] *Gillespie* v. *Bowles (Roy) Transport Ltd.* [1973] Q.B. 400, *per* Buckley L.J. at p. 419; *Caledonia Ltd.* v.
Orbit Valve Co. Europe [1994] 1 W.L.R. 1515, *per* Steyn L.J. at p. 1523; *Smith* v. *South Wales Switchgear Co. Ltd.*
[1978] 1 W.L.R. 165, *per* Viscount Dilhorne at p. 168 (indemnity clause).

[298] *Tai Hing Cotton Mill Ltd.* v. *Liu Chong Hing Bank Ltd.* [1986] A.C. 80, *per* Lord Scarman at p. 107.

[299] [1922] 2 K.B. 87. See also *Levison* v. *Patent Steam Carpet Cleaning Co. Ltd.* [1978] Q.B. 69 ('at the
owner's risk'); *Scottish Special Housing Assoc.* v. *Wimpey Construction UK Ltd.* [1986] 1 All E.R. 956 ('at the
sole risk of the Employer'); *Thompson* v. *T. Lohan (Plant Hire) Ltd.* [1987] 1 W.L.R. 649 ('the hirer . . . alone
shall be responsible for all claims . . . ').

[300] *Joseph Travers & Sons Ltd.* v. *Cooper* [1915] 1 K.B. 73; *Ashby* v. *Tolhurst* [1937] 2 K.B. 242; *White* v.
Blackmore [1972] 2 Q.B. 651. Cf. *Bishop* v. *Bonham* [1988] 1 W.L.R. 742.

[301] *Harris Ltd.* v. *Continental Express Ltd.* [1961] 1 Lloyd's Rep. 251; *Carter (J.) (Fine Worsteds) Ltd.* v.
Hanson Haulage (Leeds) Ltd. [1965] 2 Q.B. 495.

[302] *A. E. Farr Ltd.* v. *Admiralty* [1953] 1 W.L.R. 965; *Lamport & Holt Lines Ltd.* v. *Coubro & Scrutton (M. &
I.) Ltd.* [1982] 2 Lloyd's Rep. 42.

suffered, e.g. a strict liability for breach of contract.[303] If the alternative ground is not
so fanciful or remote that he cannot be supposed to have desired protection against
it,[304] the exemption clause will be construed as extending to that ground alone, even if
the words used are *prima facie* wide enough to cover negligence.[305] In *Canada Steamship Lines Ltd.* v. *The King*,[306] for example, a lease of a freight shed provided that the
lessee should 'not have any claim against the lessor for damage to goods' in the shed.
Owing to the negligence of the lessor's employees, a fire broke out and the lessee's
goods in the shed were destroyed. The Judicial Committee of the Privy Council
held that a strict liability was imposed upon the lessor by the Civil Code of Lower
Canada and the exemption clause should be confined to that head of liability. The
lessor was accordingly liable for the negligent destruction of the goods. English
Courts, including the House of Lords,[307] have since applied this decision and it has
been said that:[308]

Commercial contracts are drafted by parties with access to legal advice and in the context of
established legal principles as reflected in the decisions of the courts … The parties to
commercial contracts must be taken to know what those principles are and to have drafted
their contract taking them into account; when the suggested result could have been easily
obtained by an appropriate use of language but the parties instead only used general language, the result of the general principle is that the parties will not be taken to have intended
to include the consequences of a party's negligence.

It was at one time supposed that, where the head of damage in respect of which
liability is sought to be imposed by an exemption clause is one which rests on negligence and nothing else, the clause *must* be construed as extending to that head of
damage, because if it were not so construed 'it would lack subject matter'.[309]

But this rule no longer applies. The scope of an exemption clause depends in each
case on its precise wording. All that can be said is that, if the only liability of the party
pleading the exemption is a liability for negligence, the clause will more readily operate to exempt him;[310] but it will not inevitably do so. In *Hollier* v. *Rambler Motors
(A.M.C.) Ltd.*:[311]

H arranged by telephone to have his car repaired by R.M. and subsequently sent the car to
R.M.'s premises for this purpose. On at least two previous occasions when R.M. had carried

---

[303] *White* v. *John Warwick & Co. Ltd.* [1953] 1 W.L.R. 1285.
[304] *Canada Steamship Lines Ltd.* v. *The King* [1952] A.C. 292; *Smith* v. *South Wales Switchgear Co. Ltd.*
(*supra*, n. 297), at p. 178; *Lamport & Holt Lines Ltd.* v. *Coubro & Scrutton (M. & I.) Ltd.* (*supra*, n. 302).
[305] *Alderslade* v. *Hendon Laundry Ltd.* [1945] K.B. 189, at p. 192; *Canada Steamship Lines Ltd.* v. *The King*
(*supra*, n. 304), at p. 208; *Sonat Offshore S.A.* v. *Amerada Hess Development Ltd.* [1988] 1 Lloyd's Rep. 145, at p.
157; *Shell Chemicals U.K. Ltd.* v. *P. & O. Roadtanks Ltd.* [1995] 1 Lloyd's Rep. 297, at p. 301. Cf. *Ailsa Craig
Fishing Co. Ltd.* v. *Malvern Fishing Co. Ltd.* [1983] 1 W.L.R. 964, at p. 970.
[306] [1952] A.C. 292.
[307] *Smith* v. *South Wales Switchgear Co. Ltd.* [1978] 1 W.L.R. 165.
[308] *Caledonia Ltd.* v. *Orbit Valve Co. Europe* [1994] 1 W.L.R. 221, *per* Hobhouse J. at pp. 228, 232, approved
by the Court of Appeal [1994] 1 W.L.R. 1515, at p. 1521. See also *Shell Chemicals U.K. Ltd.* v. *P. & O. Roadtanks
Ltd.* [1995] 1 Lloyd's Rep. 297, at p. 301.
[309] *Aldersdale* v. *Hendon Laundry Ltd.* [1945] K.B. 189, at p. 192.
[310] *Rutter* v. *Palmer* [1922] 2 K.B. 87, *per* Scrutton L.J. at p. 92.
[311] [1972] 2 Q.B. 71.

out repairs for him he had signed a form on which appeared the printed words: 'The company is not responsible for damage caused by fire to customer's cars on the premises'. While on the premises, the car was damaged by a fire caused by R.M.'s negligence.

The Court of Appeal held that there was no sufficient previous course of dealing to incorporate the exemption clause into the oral contract;[312] but, in any event, the language of the clause did not unequivocally cover negligence. Although the only ground of liability on the part of R.M. would have been liability in negligence, the clause was not so plain as to indicate that R.M. was exempting itself in respect of damage caused by fire due to its own negligence. H therefore succeeded in an action against R.M. for breach of the contract of bailment.

(iv) Exclusion and limitation clauses

It has been held that a less rigorous approach governs clauses that merely limit the compensation payable but do not totally exclude liability. In *Ailsa Craig Fishing Co. Ltd.* v. *Malvern Fishing Co. Ltd. and Securicor (Scotland) Ltd*,[313] a case from Scotland:

S undertook to provide continuous security cover in respect of A.C.F.'s fishing vessel in Aberdeen harbour, but by reason of negligence and breach of contract the vessel fouled the boat berthed next to her and sank. The loss of the vessel cost A.C.F. £55,000. S's standard conditions of contract provided *inter alia* that its liability 'whether under express or implied terms of the contract, or at common law or in any other way' for any loss or damage was limited to £1,000.

The House of Lords held that, although the *contra proferentem* rule applied to limitation clauses, such clauses were not to be construed by the specially exacting standards applicable to clauses totally excluding liability and indemnity clauses. A number of reasons were given for this distinction. First, it was said that there was a higher degree of improbability that a contracting party would agree to a total exclusion of liability than to a limitation of liability, particularly where, as in that case, '. . . the potential losses that might be caused by the negligence of the proferens or its servants are so great in proportion to the sums that can reasonably be charged for the services contracted for'.[314] It was also said that limitation clauses 'must be related to other contractual terms, in particular to the risks to which the defending party may be exposed, the remuneration which he receives, and possibly also the opportunity of the other party to insure'.[315]

It is, however, somewhat difficult to see why such a clear distinction should be drawn between these two types of exemption clauses. In particular, it is not clear why only limitation clauses are 'related to other contractual terms' and to 'the opportunity of the other party to insure'. There may also be practical difficulties. Take the example of first, a clause *excluding* all liability, but not until three months after the delivery of

---

[312] See *ante*, p. 165.
[313] [1983] 1 W.L.R. 964 (H.L.).
[314] *Ibid.*, *per* Lord Fraser at p. 970. This statement was approved by the House of Lords in *George Mitchell (Chesterhall) Ltd.* v. *Finney Lock Seeds Ltd.* [1983] 2 A.C. 803, at pp. 810, 813, 817.
[315] *Ailsa Craig Fishing Co. Ltd* v. *Malvern Fishing Co. Ltd.* (*supra*, n. 305), *per* Lord Wilberforce at p. 966.

goods,[316] and then a clause *limiting* liability to £100, but from the start.[317] Which is to be construed more generously? It is submitted that '[t]here is no difference in principle between words which save [contracting parties] from having to pay at all and words which save them from paying as much as they would otherwise have had to pay'.[318] It has been suggested that the two types of clause should be characterized by reference to the substance of their provisions rather that the particular wording used, and that the more extreme the consequences are, in terms of excluding or modifying the liability which would otherwise arise, the more stringent the Court's approach should be in requiring that the exclusion or liability be clearly and unambiguously expressed.[319]

(d) 'FUNDAMENTAL' TERMS AND 'FUNDAMENTAL BREACH' OF CONTRACT

The rules of construction referred to are of limited utility because the skill of the person drafting an exemption clause can prevail over any reluctance of the Courts to uphold an abuse of contractual freedom. Very gradually, however, there developed a principle which seemed to offer some escape from even the most carefully drafted exemption clauses. This was the principle of the 'breach of a fundamental term' or of 'fundamental breach'.[320]

There were, it was said, in every contract certain *terms* which were fundamental, the breach of which amounted to a complete non-performance of the contract. A fundamental term was conceived to be something more basic than a warranty or even a condition. It formed the 'core' of the contract, and therefore could not be affected by any exemption clause.[321] For example, 'If a man offers to buy peas of another, and he sends him beans, he does not perform his contract; but that is not a warranty; there is no warranty that he should sell him peas; the contract is to sell peas, and if he sends him anything else in their stead, it is a non-performance of it' against which no exemption clause could prevail.[322]

Closely connected with this principle was yet another; that no party to a contract

---

[316] *Atlantic Shipping & Trading Co. Ltd.* v. *Louis Dreyfus & Co.* [1922] 2 A.C. 250. See also 'cesser' clauses in charterparties excluding the charterer's liability for breach once a cargo is shipped and replacing it with an alternative remedy by way of lien on the cargo: *Overseas Transport Co.* v. *MineralImportExport* [1972] 1 Lloyd's Rep. 201.

[317] See the combined operation of the package, unit, and weight limitations of Article IV, r. 5, of the Hague/Visby Rules and the one year time bar under Article III, r. 6: Carriage of Goods by Sea Act 1971.

[318] *Atlantic Shipping & Trading Co. Ltd.* v. *Louis Dreyfus & Co.* (*supra*, n. 316), *per* Lord Sumner at p. 260. See also *Darlington Futures Ltd.* v. *Delco Australia Pty. Ltd.* (1986) 161 C.L.R. 500, at p. 510 (High Court of Australia), disapproving the statements in *Ailsa Craig Fishing Co. Ltd.* v. *Malvern Fishing Co. Ltd* (*supra*, n. 305).

[319] *B. H. P. Petroleum Ltd.* v. *British Steel plc* [2000] 2 Lloyd's Rep. 277, at p. 285.

[320] See Guest (1961) 77 L.Q.R. 98; Reynolds (1963) 79 L.Q.R. 534; Lord Devlin [1966] C.L.J. 192; Jenkins [1969] C.L.J. 251; Legh-Jones and Pickering (1970) 86 L.Q.R. 513; Baker (1970) 33 M.L.R. 441; Weir [1970] C.L.J. 180; Coote [1970] C.L.J. 221; Dawson (1975) 91 L.Q.R. 380; Coote (1977) 40 M.L.R. 31.

[321] *Smeaton Hanscomb & Co. Ltd.* v. *Sassoon I. Setty, Son & Co.* [1953] 1 W.L.R. 1468, at p. 1470.

[322] *Chanter* v. *Hopkins* (1838) 4 M. & W. 399, at p. 404. See also *Bowes* v. *Shand* (1877) 2 App. Cas. 455, at p. 480.

could exempt himself from responsibility for a fundamental *breach*. Its limits were never precisely defined, but it was said that a party could only claim the protection of an exemption clause 'when he is carrying out his contract, not when he is deviating from it or is guilty of a breach which goes to the root of it'.[323] So, for example, if those having charge of a railway cloakroom allowed an unauthorized person to have access to and remove luggage of a depositor without production of the cloakroom ticket, this was a 'fundamental breach' and the railway was not protected by an exemption clause excluding liability for loss or misdelivery.[324]

The two principles were in some cases used interchangeably;[325] and they appeared to establish that, however extensive an exemption clause might be, it could not exclude liability in respect of the breach of a fundamental term or of a fundamental breach. Expressed in this way, the principle constituted a substantive rule of law which operated irrespective of the intention of the parties and limited their freedom of contract.

The 'rule of law' approach was, however, rejected. In *U.G.S. Finance Ltd.* v. *National Mortgage Bank of Greece.*[326] Pearson L.J. stated:

I think there is a rule of construction that normally an exception or exclusion clause or similar provision in a contract should be construed as not applying to a situation created by a fundamental breach of contract. This is not an independent rule of law imposed by the court on the parties willy-nilly in disregard of their contractual intention. On the contrary it is a rule of construction based on the intention of the contracting parties.

This opinion was subsequently unanimously endorsed by the House of Lords in *Suisse Atlantique Société d'Armement Maritime S.A.* v. *N.V. Rotterdamsche Kolen Centrale.*[327] In that case:

S.A. chartered to the respondent the m.v. *Silvretta* for a period of 2 years. It was agreed that, in the event of delays in loading or unloading the vessel, R.K.C. would pay to S.A. $1,000 a day by way of demurrage.[328] Lengthy delays occurred for which S.A. alleged R.K.C. was responsible, but it nevertheless allowed R.K.C. to continue to have the use of the ship for the remainder of the term. On conclusion of the contract, S.A. sued R.K.C. for damages, claiming a sum in excess of that stipulated for as demurrage. R.K.C. relied on the demurrage clause as limiting its liability.

It was argued that the breaches would have entitled S.A. to treat the contract as repudiated; that these breaches amounted to a fundamental breach of contract; and that in consequence R.K.C. could not rely upon the clause which limited their liability to $1,000 a day. The House of Lords rejected this argument. They held that the demurrage clause was not an exemption clause but an 'agreed damages' provision.[329]

---

[323] *Spurling (J.) Ltd.* v. *Bradshaw* [1956] 1 W.L.R. 461, *per* Denning L.J. at p. 465.

[324] *Alexander* v. *Railway Executive* [1951] 2 K.B. 882.

[325] Cf. Lord Upjohn in the *Suisse Atlantique* case [1967] 1 A.C. 361 at p. 421.

[326] [1964] 1 Lloyd's Rep. 446, at p. 450.

[327] [1967] 1 A.C. 361; noted by Treitel (1966) 29 M.L.R. 546.

[328] Demurrage is a sum agreed by the charterer to be paid to the owner as liquidated damages for delay beyond a stipulated or reasonable time for loading or unloading.

[329] See *post*, p. 624.

Nevertheless, even if it had been considered an exemption clause, their Lordships considered that as a matter of construction it covered the breaches which had occurred. Assuming that these breaches amounted to a fundamental breach of contract, in the sense that S.A. would have been entitled to treat itself as discharged from further performance, there was no rule of law which would prevent the application of an exemption clause to such a breach.

Certain statements in the *Suisse Atlantique* case were nevertheless open to the interpretation that in some situations a substantive doctrine of 'fundamental breach' still existed[330] and the heresy that a 'fundamental breach' of contract deprived the party in breach of the benefit of an exemption clause was not finally laid to rest by the House of Lords until *Photo Production Ltd.* v. *Securicor Transport Ltd.*:[331]

S agreed to provide a visiting patrol service to P.P's factory at a charge of £8.15*s.* a week, approximately 26*d.* per visit. The contract contained an exemption clause, the most relevant part of which stated: 'Under no circumstances shall the company [S] be responsible for any injurious act or default by any employee ... unless such act or default could have been foreseen and avoided by the exercise of due diligence on the part of the company ... '. An employee of S, while on patrol, deliberately lit a fire in the factory. The fire spread, and a large part of the premises were burned down.

The Court of Appeal held that, since S had been engaged to safeguard the factory, the deliberate act of their employee in starting a fire was not covered by the exemption clause. The House of Lords reversed this decision. On the true construction of the clause in the context of the contract, in particular the limited nature of the contractual task, the modesty of the charge, and the ability of the factory owners to insure against fire more economically, the House concluded that the risk assumed by S was a modest one.[332] Accordingly, S had effectively modified its obligation under the contract to the exercise of due diligence in its capacity as an employer, and there was no evidence of any lack of due diligence on its part to foresee or prevent the fire. S was therefore absolved from liability. Their Lordships once again affirmed their opinion that the question whether or not an exemption clause protected a party to a contract in the event of breach, or in the event of what would (but for the presence of the exemption clause) have been a breach, depended upon the construction of the contract. Even if the breach was so serious as to entitle the injured party to treat the contract as repudiated,[333] or to render further performance impossible, the other party was not prevented from relying on the clause.

The need for a substantive principle of fundamental breach has largely been obviated by the enactment of the Unfair Contract Terms Act 1977,[334] although certain

---

[330] [1967] 1 A.C. 361, at pp. 398, 427, 432. See *Harbutt's 'Plasticine' Ltd.* v. *Wayne Tank and Pump Co. Ltd.* [1970] 1 Q.B. 447 (exemption clause did not apply where further performance impossible or innocent party accepted breach as terminating contract). See also *Wathes (Western) Ltd.* v. *Austins (Menswear) Ltd.* [1976] 1 Lloyd's Rep. 14; *Kenyon, Son & Craven Ltd.* v. *Baxter Hoare & Co. Ltd.* [1971] 1 W.L.R. 519.

[331] [1980] A.C. 827. See also *George Mitchell (Chesterhall) Ltd.* v. *Finney Lock Seeds Ltd.* [1983] 2 A.C. 803; *Kenya Railways* v. *Antares Co. Pte. Ltd.* [1987] 1 Lloyd's Rep. 424; Unfair Contract Terms Act 1977, s. 9.

[332] [1980] A.C. 827, at pp. 846, 851, 852.

[333] See *post*, p. 578.

[334] See *post*, p. 185.

types of contract are excepted, either wholly or partly from the operation of that Act.[335] In the *Photo Production* case, Lord Diplock stated[336] that, if the expression 'fundamental breach' was to be retained, it should be confined to the ordinary case of a breach of which the consequences are such as to entitle the innocent party to elect to put an end to all primary obligations of both parties remaining unperformed.[337] Similarly it may be supposed that, if the expression 'fundamental term' is to be retained, it should be employed simply as an alternative method of describing a promissory condition.[338] There does not now exist in English law any special rule or rules applicable to cases of 'fundamental breach' where exemption clauses are concerned. No doubt, in deciding whether an exemption clause is, on its true construction, applicable to a particular breach, the Court may reach the conclusion that the parties never intended the clause to apply to the breach in question because its nature or seriousness is such as not to fall within the contemplated ambit of the clause. The parties are less likely to be taken to have agreed that one of them shall be excused in the case of a total non-performance or a performance which is wholly at variance with the object of the contract as ascertained from its other terms and the circumstances surrounding it. But there is no separate category of 'fundamental breaches' against which exemption clauses cannot prevail, and, if sufficiently clear, they will do so against the most serious and deliberate breach. So, for example, the one year time bar in the Hague-Visby Rules applies to fundamental and deliberate breaches.[339] Moreover, in Australia it has been held that an exemption clause which stated it applied 'whether or not loss . . . is caused by . . . fundamental breach of contract' prevailed against a fundamental breach,[340] but it is not clear that such a general clause would have this effect in England.[341]

(e) ILLUSTRATIONS OF CONSTRUCTION

It is now appropriate to consider how the Courts have approached the construction of exemption clauses, particularly with reference to certain familiar types of contract such as sale of goods, hire-purchase, carriage of goods, and bailment.[342]

(i) Sale of goods

We have already seen that, in a contract of sale of goods, sections 12–15 of the Sale of Goods Act 1979 imply certain conditions as to title, correspondence with description

---

[335] See *post*, p. 185.

[336] [1980] A.C. 827, at p. 849.

[337] See *post*, p. 580.

[338] See *Suisse Atlantique Société d'Armement Maritime S.A. v. N.V. Rotterdamsche Kolen Centrale* [1967] 1 A.C. 361, at pp. 398, 427, 432–5.

[339] *Kenya Railways* v. *Antares Co. Pte. Ltd.* [1987] 1 Lloyd's Rep. 424, at pp. 429–430, *post*, p. 182; *Comp. Portorafti Comm. S.A. v. Ultramar Panama Inc.* [1990] 1 Lloyd's Rep. 310.

[340] *Glebe Island Terminals Pty. Ltd. v. Continental Seagram Pty. Ltd* [1994] 1 Lloyd's Rep. 213 (New South Wales Court of Appeal) cf. Handley J.A. dissenting, at p. 230.

[341] *Tor Line A.B.* v. *Alltrans Group of Canada Ltd.* [1984] 1 W.L.R. 48, at p. 54; *Wibau Maschinenfabrik Hartman S.A.* v. *Mackinnon Mackenzie & Co.* [1989] 2 Lloyd's Rep. 494, at p. 505.

[342] See also Howarth (1985) 36 N.I.L.Q. 101.

and sample, fitness for purpose, and satisfactory quality.[343] By virtue of section 6 of the Unfair Contract Terms Act 1977,[344] the power of a seller to exclude these implied conditions has been abrogated, either absolutely or subject to certain qualifications, except where the contract is one for the international sale of goods. But at common law, for example, the Courts have refused to apply an exemption clause covering 'defects in quality' to situations where there was a gross disparity between the goods described in the contract of sale and those delivered, or where the goods were so defective that they were completely unfit for the purpose for which they were required.[345] For example, where copra cake contained so great an admixture of castor beans as to render it dangerous to cattle, a clause disclaiming responsibility for 'defects' was held inapplicable, because what was delivered was not truly copra cake at all.[346] As Lord Wilberforce pointed out in the *Suisse Atlantique* case:[347] 'Since the contracting parties could hardly have been supposed to contemplate such a mis-performance, or to have provided against it without destroying the whole contractual substratum, there is no difficulty here in holding exemption clauses to be inapplicable'. But this is a matter of construction only and, as we have seen,[348] this will be affected by the contractual context. So, 'if an anxious hostess is late in the preparation of a meal, she can perfectly well say: "Send me peas or if you haven't got peas, send beans; but for heaven's sake send something". That would be a contract for peas, beans or anything else *ejusdem generis* and it is a perfectly sensible contract to make'.[349]

(ii) Hire-purchase

The exclusion of terms implied in hire-purchase contracts is governed by similar principles at common law to those in sales, and is now also subject to section 6 of the Unfair Contract Terms Act 1977.[350] A case of this nature arose in *Karsales (Harrow) Ltd.* v. *Wallis*:[351]

W was shown a second-hand Buick motor-car in excellent condition, and wished to buy it on hire-purchase. His agreement with the finance company contained an exemption clause excluding liability for breach of conditions or warranties of any description. After the contract had been concluded, the car was towed at night to W's premises in a deplorable state. Many detachable parts had been removed; new parts replaced by old; the engine was now so defective that the car would not go. W refused to accept it, and was sued by K, the assignee of the finance company.

---

[343] *Ante*, pp. 153–8.

[344] See *post*, p. 191.

[345] e.g. *Munro & Co. Ltd.* v. *Meyer* [1930] 2 K.B. 312; *Champanhac & Co. Ltd.* v. *Waller & Co. Ltd.* [1948] 2 All E.R. 724. Cf. *Smeaton Hanscomb & Co. Ltd.* v. *Sassoon I. Setty, Son & Co.* [1953] 1 W.L.R. 1481; *George Mitchell (Chesterhall) Ltd.* v. *Finney Lock Seeds Ltd.* [1983] 2 A.C. 807.

[346] *Pinnock Brothers* v. *Lewis and Peat Ltd.* [1923] 1 K.B. 690.

[347] [1967] 1 A.C. 361, at p. 433.

[348] *Ante*, p. 132.

[349] Lord Devlin [1966] C.L.J. 192, at p. 212. On this example, see *ante*, p. 174, n. 322.

[350] See *post*, p. 191.

[351] [1956] 1 W.L.R. 936. See also *Yeoman Credit Ltd.* v. *Apps* [1962] 2 Q.B. 508; *Charterhouse Credit Co. Ltd.* v. *Tolly* [1963] 2 Q.B. 638; *Farnworth Finance Facilities* v. *Attryde* [1970] 1 W.L.R. 1053.

The Court of Appeal held that the exemption clause was ineffective because what was contracted for had not been delivered: 'a car that would not go was not a car at all'.[352] On the other hand, a similar clause has been held to cover the delivery of a car which, though unroadworthy and unsafe when hired and in a 'lamentable condition', did still function as a car. These defects were covered by the clause.[353]

(iii) Carriage of goods

A carrier who deviates without justification from the recognized or agreed route, steps outside the 'four corners' of the contract and cannot claim the benefit of a clause designed to protect only when the carrier is acting in pursuance of its provisions.[354] Most of the cases concern the carriage of goods by sea but the same principles apply to carriage by land.[355]

If a ship contracted to carry goods from A to B deviates from her ordinary route, the contract voyage comes to an end, and the shipowner cannot thereafter rely upon an exemption clause in the contract even though the loss or damage to the goods is not attributable to the deviation.[356]

Contracts made between businesses for the carriage of goods by ship fall, as respects loss of or damage to the cargo, outside the Unfair Contract Terms Act 1977,[357] so that the 'deviation cases' continue to be of considerable importance in this context. Such cases are based on the assumption that the parties did not intend the clause to apply to a journey not contemplated by the contract. However, the contract may confer upon the carrier a liberty to deviate, and such a provision will be upheld if clearly expressed.[358] Such a clause will, however, be so construed as not to defeat the main purpose or object of the contract voyage[359] unless possibly the occurrence of the events stipulated in the exemption clause will *always* result in the defeat of the main object since, in that case, 'there will be no scope for holding that that object requires the conclusion that the exemption clause is not applicable to that event'.[360]

Where a carrier has undertaken to stow cargo below deck but carries it on deck, it is a question of construction whether an exemption clause applies to such unauthorized deck carriage. While it has been held that a clause limiting liability to a specified sum

---

[352] *Per* Birkett L.J. at p. 942. See also Parker L.J. at p. 943.

[353] *Handley* v. *Marston* (1962) 106 S.J. 327. See also *Astley Industrial Trust Ltd.* v. *Grimley* [1963] 1 W.L.R. 584.

[354] e.g. *Cunard S.S. Co. Ltd.* v. *Buerger* [1927] A.C. 1; *Stag Line Ltd.* v. *Foscolo, Mango & Co. Ltd.* [1932] A.C. 328. See *Suisse Atlantique Société d'Armement Maritime S.A.* v. *N.V. Rotterdamsche Kolen Centrale* [1967] 1 A.C. 361, at pp. 390, 399, 411, 422, 433.

[355] *London & North Western Ry.* v. *Neilson* [1922] 2 A.C. 263 (disclaimed liability for loss of goods 'in transit' did not cover deviation).

[356] *Thorley (J.) Ltd.* v. *Orchis Steamship Co. Ltd.* [1907] 1 K.B. 660.

[357] Sched. 1, para. 2(c); see *post*, p. 186.

[358] *G. H. Renton & Co. Ltd.* v. *Palmyra Trading Corporation of Panama* [1957] A.C. 149; *Mayfair Photographic Supplies (London) Ltd.* v. *Baxter Hoare & Co. Ltd.* [1972] 1 Lloyd's Rep. 410.

[359] *Leduc* v. *Ward* (1888) 20 Q.B.D. 475; *Glynn* v. *Margetson & Co.* [1893] A.C. 351.

[360] *Nissho Iwai Australia Ltd.* v. *Malaysian International Shipping Cpn. Bhd.* (1988–89) 167 C.L.R. 219, at p. 227 (High Court of Australia).

per package of cargo did not so apply,[361] it has also been held that a clause requiring all claims to be brought within one year does apply.[362]

By the same token it is the duty of a carrier to carry the goods expeditiously to their destination, and delay may lie outside the scope of an exemption clause where the parties cannot be taken to have intended the clause to extend to the period of the delay,[363] or to a risk consequent upon the delay which is wholly at variance with the contract of carriage.[364]

Misdelivery of the goods by the carrier may be covered by an appropriately drafted exemption clause.[365] But where the main object and intent of the contract is that delivery should be made to a certain person or persons, the Court may be prepared to limit the operation of the clause to the extent that it is inconsistent with that main object and intent. In *Sze Hai Tong Bank Ltd.* v. *Rambler Cycle Co. Ltd.*:[366]

R despatched goods by sea from England to Singapore. The bill of lading required the goods to be delivered 'unto order or assigns' and stated that 'the responsibility of the carrier shall be deemed to cease absolutely after the goods are discharged from the ship'. After the goods were discharged from the ship, the carrier's agents did not deliver them 'unto order or assigns', but released the goods to the consignees without production of the bill of lading, with the result that R was never paid for the goods.

The Judicial Committee of the Privy Council held that, although the exemption, on the face of it, could hardly have been more comprehensive, 'it must at least be modified so as not to permit the shipping company deliberately to disregard its obligations as to delivery'.[367] To hold otherwise would defeat the main object and intent of the contract. The carrier was therefore liable.

(iv) Bailment

Principles of a similar nature have also been applied to contracts of bailment. As Lord Hodson pointed out in the *Suisse Atlantique* case:[368]

Under a contract of carriage or bailment if the carrier or bailee uses a place other than that agreed on for storing the goods, or otherwise exposes the goods to risks quite different from those contemplated by the contract, he cannot rely on clauses in the contract designed to

---

[361] *Wibau Maschinenfabrik Hartman S.A.* v. *Mackinnon Mackenzie & Co.* [1989] 2 Lloyd's Rep. 494, at p. 505 (see Hague-Visby Rules, Art. III, para. 5, contained in the Schedule to the Carriage of Goods by Sea Act 1971). See also *J. Evans & Sons (Portsmouth) Ltd.* v. *Andrea Merzario* [1976] 1 W.L.R. 1078.

[362] *Kenya Railways* v. *Antares Co. Pte. Ltd.* [1987] 1 Lloyd's Rep. 424 (Hague-Visby Rules, Art. III, para. 6).

[363] *The Cap Palos* [1921] P. 458 (towage).

[364] *Thomas National Transport (Melbourne) Pty. Ltd.* v. *May & Baker (Australia) Ltd.* [1966] 2 Lloyd's Rep. 347; *Bontex Knitting Works Ltd.* v. *St. John's Garage* [1943] 2 All E.R. 690; aff'd [1944] 1 All E.R. 381n. But see *Suisse Atlantique* case, at p. 435; cf. *Colverd (A. F.) & Co. Ltd.* v. *Anglo-Overseas Transport Co. Ltd.* [1961] 2 Lloyd's Rep. 352.

[365] *Chartered Bank* v. *British India Steam Navigation Co.* [1909] A.C. 369; *Pringle of Scotland* v. *Continental Express* [1962] 2 Lloyd's Rep. 80.

[366] [1959] A.C. 576. See also *Motis Exports Ltd.* v. *Dampskibsselskabet AF 1912 Akt.* [2000] 1 Lloyd's Rep. 211, at pp. 216–217.

[367] At p. 587.

[368] [1967] 1 A.C. 361, at p. 412.

protect him against liability within the four corners of the contract, and has only such protection as is afforded by the common law.

It is first, however, necessary to determine what are the 'four corners' of the contract. If, for instance, a railway company contracts to keep an item in a station cloakroom but keeps it elsewhere in the station and it is stolen or damaged, it will not be able to rely on a clause exempting it, for instance, from liability in respect of loss or damage. But if, on its true construction, the contract is not to keep the item necessarily in the cloakroom, but to keep it at the station, reliance can be placed on the clause.[369] Again, it has been held that warehousemen who stored groundnuts in a warehouse otherwise suitable but not ratproof could rely on a term of the contract excluding liability in the absence of 'wilful neglect or default' when sued in respect of damage to and contamination of the nuts by rats.[370] Although the warehousemen's storage had been negligent, the place where the nuts were stored was one permitted by the contract and the risk to which they were exposed was not one which was wholly uncontemplated by the contract. Since no wilful neglect or default had been proved, the warehousemen were not liable.

The Courts are extremely unlikely to allow a bailee who has converted the goods to shelter under the provisions of an exemption clause, which simply disclaimed liability for loss or damage to the goods bailed, unless the clause specifically authorized the bailee to do the act in question, e.g. to sell the goods in the event that they were not claimed.[371] A simple disclaimer of liability cannot have been intended by the parties to permit the bailee 'to give the goods away to some passerby, or to burn them or throw them into the sea'.[372] Similarly, if a bailee, without authority, sub-contracts its obligations to a third party, it will not be protected by an exemption clause, for example for non-delivery, which is intended to apply only while the goods are in its possession and control.[373]

On the other hand, an exemption clause, if appropriately drafted, has been held, at common law, to cover an honest, but negligent, re-delivery of the goods to the wrong person.[374]

Contracts of bailment, where the bailor is a consumer or if the goods are bailed on the bailee's written standard terms of business, are subject to section 3 of the Unfair Contract Terms Act 1977.[375] If the goods are lost or damaged by negligence, any exemption clause will also be subject to section 2(2) of the Act.[376] In either case, the clause will be of no effect unless it satisfies the requirement of reasonableness.

---

[369] *Gibaud* v. *Great Eastern Railway* [1921] 2 K.B. 426.

[370] *Kenyon, Son & Craven Ltd.* v. *Baxter Hoare & Co. Ltd.* [1971] 1 W.L.R. 519.

[371] *Alexander* v. *Railway Executive* [1951] 2 K.B. 882, at p. 889; *Garnham, Harris & Elton Ltd.* v. *Ellis (Transport) Ltd.* [1967] 1 W.L.R. 940, at p. 946.

[372] *Sze Hai Tong Bank Ltd.* v. *Rambler Cycle Co. Ltd.* [1959] A.C. 576, at p. 587.

[373] *Garnham, Harris & Elton Ltd.* v. *Alfred W. Ellis (Transport) Ltd.* [1967] 1 W.L.R. 940. See also *Davies* v. *Collins* [1945] 1 All E.R. 247; *The Berkshire* [1974] 1 Lloyd's Rep. 185.

[374] *Hollins* v. *J. Davy Ltd.* [1963] 1 Q.B. 844.

[375] See *post*, p. 192.

[376] See *post*, p. 190.

(v) Deliberate breaches

The view that, whereas a negligent breach could be covered by an exemption clause, a wilful or deliberate breach necessarily fell outside its scope,[377] was firmly rejected by the House of Lords in the *Suisse Atlantique* case. Lord Wilberforce said:[378]

> Some deliberate breaches ... may be, on construction, within an exceptions clause (for example, a deliberate delay for one day in loading). This is not to say that 'deliberateness' may not be a relevant factor: depending on what the party in breach 'deliberately' intended to do, it may be possible to say that the parties never contemplated that such a breach would be excused or limited; ... but to create a special rule for deliberate acts is unnecessary and may lead astray.

(vi) Burden of proof

The party seeking to rely on an exemption clause must show that the loss or damage to the other party is within the scope of the clause. But the other party must first plead and prove that the loss or damage which has been sustained was caused by some breach of contract or duty on the part of the defendant. A bailor may well be assisted in this task by a particular rule of law, e.g. that it is for a bailee who is sued in respect of the loss of the goods bailed to it to prove that the loss occurred without its negligence.[379] The burden of proof, however, rests on the party seeking to establish liability.[380]

(f) EXEMPTION CLAUSES AND THIRD PARTIES

A contracting party (A) may seek exemption from liability to the other party to the contract (B) not only for itself but also for persons who are not parties to the contract, for example, its employees or sub-contractors who participate in the performance of the contract.[381] This is because A's employees and sub-contractors, while not in a contractual relationship with B, may nevertheless be under duties to B imposed by the law of tort or the law of bailment. If the employees or independent contractors are not able to rely on the exemption clause as a defence to an action by B, they in turn may have a right to be indemnified by A. Even where there is no right to be indemnified, A may, particularly in the case of employees, nevertheless agree to meet the damages

---

[377] e.g. *Sze Hai Tong Bank Ltd.* v. *Rambler Cycle Co. Ltd.* [1959] A.C. 576.

[378] [1967] A.C. 361, at p. 435. See also *ibid.*, at pp. 394, 414, 415, 429; *Photo Production Ltd.* v. *Securicor Transport Ltd.* [1980] A.C. 827 (*ante*, p. 176); *Comp. Portorafti Comm. S.A.* v. *Ultramar Panama Inc.* [1990] 1 Lloyd's Rep. 310, *ante*, p. 177, n. 339; *China Shipbuilding Corp.* v. *Nippon Yusen Kabukishi Kaisha* [2000] 1 Lloyd's Rep. 367, at p. 376.

[379] *Houghland* v. *R. R. Low (Luxury Coaches) Ltd.* [1962] 1 Q.B. 694; *Port Swettenham Authority* v. *T. W. Wu & Co.* [1979] A.C. 580.

[380] With the demise of the principle of 'fundamental breach', it can no longer be said that the defendant (e.g., a bailee) carries the burden of disproving fundamental breach. Cf. *Woolmer* v. *Delmer Price Ltd.* [1955] 1 Q.B. 291; *Levison* v. *Patent Steam Carpet Cleaning Co. Ltd.* [1978] Q.B. 69. Contra *Hunt & Winterbotham (West of England) Ltd.* v. *B.R.S. Parcels Ltd.* [1962] 1 Q.B. 617; *Glebe Island Terminals Pty. Ltd.* v. *Continental Seagram Pty. Ltd.* [1994] 1 Lloyd's Rep. 213, at p. 238 (N.S.W. C.A.).

[381] See Law Com. No. 242, *Privity of Contract: Contracts for the Benefit of Third Parties* (1996), §§ 2.19–2.35.

awarded to B.[382] In both cases the risk is ultimately borne by A, thus defeating the purpose of the exemption clause. Whether or not it is A who ends up paying, permitting B to succeed against the employees or independent contractors will in many cases upset the allocation of risks and consequent pattern of insurance in the transaction, since A and its employees and independent contractors will have expected B to insure against the relevant loss and not done so themselves.[383] Nevertheless such attempts to rely on exemption clauses encountered great difficulties at common law because of the doctrines of consideration and 'privity of contract'. Under the Contracts (Rights against Third Parties) Act 1999, however, a person who is not a party to a contract may enforce a term of the contract, including an exclusion or limitation clause,[384] if the contract expressly so provides or if the term purports to confer a benefit on the third party. This is dealt with in the chapter on Third Parties.[385]

(g) OTHER COMMON LAW LIMITATIONS

The operation of exemption clauses may be further limited by the application of certain other rules of the common law of a heterogeneous nature.

(i) Express undertakings

A collateral oral warranty may be enforced even though it runs counter to the terms (including exemption clauses) of the principal agreement.[386] There is a still more general principle, i.e. that where an express undertaking is given which is inconsistent with the printed clauses of a standard form document, the latter must be rejected in so far as they are repugnant to the express undertaking. In *J. Evans & Son (Portsmouth) Ltd. v. Andrea Merzario Ltd.*:[387]

E, an importer of machines, arranged the carriage of the machines to England under contract with A.M., a forwarding agent. A.M. orally assured E that machines shipped in containers would be carried under deck. Nevertheless, eight containers carrying E's machines were subsequently loaded on deck. One container fell overboard and was a total loss. A.M. denied liability, relying on an exemption clause in the contract of carriage.

It was held that A.M.'s oral assurance overrode the exemption clause, and that it was liable for breach of the warranty given. Similarly, in *Mendelssohn v. Normand Ltd.*[388] M parked in N's garage on the terms that N would 'accept no responsibility for any loss or damage sustained by the vehicle its accessories or contents however caused'. M left the car unlocked because one of N's employee's stated that the car must be left

---

[382] *Adler* v. *Dickson* [1955] 1 Q.B. 158.

[383] For example where there is a limitation clause, the non-party performer would be expected to insure up to the limit and the contracting party (B) beyond that: see *post*, p. 461, n. 309.

[384] See sections 1(1) and 1(6).

[385] *Post*, p. 421.

[386] *Ante*, p. 128. On the overriding of an exemption clause see *Webster* v. *Higgin* [1948] 2 All E.R. 127.

[387] [1976] 1 W.L.R. 1078. See also *Couchman* v. *Hill* [1947] K.B. 544; *Gallagher* v. *British Road Services Ltd.* [1970] 2 Lloyd's Rep. 440.

[388] [1970] 1 Q.B. 177.

unlocked and that the employee would lock it for him. It was held that the loss by theft of valuables in the car was not covered by the exemption clause.

(ii) Misrepresentation or fraud

A party who misrepresents (albeit innocently) the contents or effect of a clause inserted by it into a contract cannot rely on the clause in the face of the misrepresentation.[389] So in *Curtis* v. *Chemical Cleaning & Dyeing Co.*:[390]

C took a dress to the defendant company for cleaning. She signed a receipt containing a clause exempting the defendant from all liability for damage to articles cleaned after the defendant's servant told her that it would not accept liability for certain specified risks, including damage to the beads and sequins on the dress. When it was returned, the dress was badly stained.

It was held that, as C had been induced to believe that the clause only referred to the beads and sequins, the defendant was not entitled to rely on it in respect of damage by staining. Denning L.J., dealing with the question of exemption clauses generally, said:[391]

Any behaviour, by words or conduct, is sufficient to be a misrepresentation if it is such as to mislead the other party about the existence or extent of the exemption. If it conveys a false impression, that is enough.

It should also be noted that an exemption clause can never exclude liability for personal fraud.[392]

(iii) Reasonableness

The theory of freedom of contract presupposed that any party to a contract is free to choose whether or not to enter into it, and regarded a party who chose to enter into a contract which is onerous as only having itself to blame.[393] But it is now seen that the bargaining powers of the parties may be so unequal that one can virtually dictate terms to the other. Even in 1877 in *Parker* v. *South Eastern Railway Co.*[394] Bramwell L.J. asked what the position would be if some unreasonable condition were inserted, as, for instance, to forfeit £1,000 if goods in a station cloakroom were not removed within 48 hours. He thought that 'there is an implied understanding that there is no condition unreasonable to the knowledge of the party tendering the document and not insisting on its being read—no condition not relevant to the matter in hand'. Lord Denning M.R. has on numerous occasions[395] maintained that an exemption clause will not be given effect if it is unreasonable, or if it would be unreasonable to apply it

---

[389] *Jacques* v. *Lloyd D. George & Partners Ltd.* [1968] 1 W.L.R. 625.

[390] [1951] 1 K.B. 805.

[391] At p. 808.

[392] *Pearson (S.) & Son Ltd.* v. *Dublin Cpn.* [1907] A.C. 351; *Armitage* v. *Nurse* [1998] Ch. 241.

[393] See *ante*, p. 4.

[394] (1877) 2 C.P.D. 416, at p. 428.

[395] e.g. *Gillespie Bros. & Co. Ltd.* v. *Roy Bowles Transport Ltd.* [1973] Q.B. 400, at p. 416; *Levison* v. *Patent Steam Carpet Cleaning Co. Ltd.* [1978] Q.B. 69, at p. 161; *Photo Production Ltd.* v. *Securicor Transport Ltd.* [1978] 1 W.L.R. 856, at. p. 865 (rev'd [1980] A.C. 827).

in the circumstances of the case, for 'there is the vigilance of the common law which, while allowing freedom of contract, watches over to see that it is not abused'.[396]

This doctrine of 'abuse of freedom of contract' has not been accepted as part of the common law and it is clear that the Courts have no general power at common law to strike down a contractual term merely because it is unreasonable or unfair.[397] Such a power has, however, been conferred by statute, notably by section 3 of the Misrepresentation Act 1967,[398] by the Unfair Contract Terms Act 1977, and by the Unfair Terms in Consumer Contracts Regulations 1999.

VI. STATUTORY CONTROL OF EXEMPTION CLAUSES

(a) UNFAIR CONTRACT TERMS ACT 1977

The purpose of the Unfair Contract Terms Act 1977[399] is to limit, and in some cases to take away entirely, the right to rely on exempting clauses in certain situations.

(i) Scope of the Act

The title of the Act is somewhat misleading. In the first place, it is not confined to contract terms. The Act also extends to non-contractual notices containing provisions exempting from liability in tort,[400] although this book is concerned solely with contract terms. Secondly, the Act does not confer upon the Courts a general power to strike down any term of a contract on the ground that the term is unfair or oppressive; it applies, for the most part,[401] only to terms that 'exclude or restrict liability', i.e. exemption clauses. The Act also does not, in general, purport to affect the basis of liability,[402] so that the first enquiry must normally be whether or not the person seeking to rely on the term is in fact under any liability (or obligation), for example, in negligence or for breach of contract. Also logically prior to the application of the Act is the question whether the relevant term has become a term of the contract,[403] and, if so, whether on its true construction in the light of the rules discussed above it applies to the liability which it is sought to exclude or restrict.[404] The tests of incorporation and construction, considered earlier in this chapter, must be applied

---

[396] *John Lee & Son (Grantham) Ltd.* v. *Railway Executive* [1949] 2 All E.R. 581, at p. 584.

[397] *Suisse Atlantique Société d'Armement Maritime S.A.* v. *N.V. Rotterdamsche Kolen Centrale* [1967] 1 A.C. 361, at p. 406; *Photo Production Ltd.* v. *Securicor Transport Ltd.* [1980] A.C. 827, at p. 848.

[398] See *post*, p. 260.

[399] See Coote (1978) 41 M.L.R. 312; Sealy [1978] C.L.J. 15; Palmer and Yates [1981] C.L.J. 108; Adams and Brownsword (1988) 104 L.Q.R. 94. The Act derives substantially from recommendations made by the Law Commission: Law Com. No. 69 (1975); Scot. Law Com. No. 39 (1975).

[400] s. 2. See Markesinis and Deakin, *Tort Law*, 4th edn. (1999), pp. 701–6.

[401] But see 1977 Act, ss. 3(2)(b), 4. Cf. the Unfair Terms in Consumer Contracts Regulations 1999 (S.I. 1999 No. 2083), *post*, p. 200.

[402] But see 1977 Act, ss. 3(2)(b), 4.

[403] *Ibid.*, s. 11(2). See *ante*, p. 164.

[404] See *ante*, p. 169.

before considering the Act. It has been said that the existence of the statutory controls makes these strict tests unnecessary.[405] But, whatever the test, it is important that the application of the test of reasonableness should not be considered until it has been decided that, applying the tests of incorporation and construction, the exemption or limitation clause in question forms part of the contract and covers the events that have occurred. If it is either not incorporated or does not cover those events, then, however reasonable the clause, it will not apply.

(ii) Pattern of control

Many of the provisions of the 1977 Act overlap, so that, when applying it to a particular situation, it is often necessary to consider whether more than one section is relevant.[406] The pattern of control is also somewhat complicated. There are three broad divisions of control: first, control over contract terms that exclude or restrict liability for 'negligence'[407] (which includes a failure to exercise reasonable care and skill in the performance of a contract);[408] secondly, control over contract terms that exclude or restrict liability for breach of certain terms implied by statute or by common law in contracts of sale of goods, hire-purchase, and in other contracts for the supply of goods;[409] thirdly, a more general control in consumer contracts and standard form contracts over terms that exclude or restrict liability for breach of contract, or which purport to entitle one of the parties to render a contractual performance substantially different from that expected or to render no performance at all.[410]

  If the contract term is subject to the control of the Act, the control may assume one of two forms: the restriction or exclusion of liability may be rendered absolutely ineffective,[411] or it may be effective only in so far as the term satisfies the requirement of reasonableness.[412]

(iii) Excepted contracts

Certain very important contracts are wholly or partially excepted from the operation of the Act. These include contracts of insurance,[413] commercial charterparties,[414] and contracts for the carriage of goods by sea,[415] international supply contracts,[416] contracts of employment (except in favour of an employee),[417] and any contract so far as

---

[405] *Photo Production* v. *Securicor Transport* [1980] A.C. 827, *per* Lord Wilberforce at p. 843; *A.E.G. (U.K.) Ltd.* v. *Logic Resources Ltd.* [1996] C.L.C. 265, *per* Hobhouse L.J. at p. 277.

[406] e.g. 1977 Act, ss. 2, 3 and 7.

[407] Defined in *ibid.*, s. 1(1).

[408] *Ibid.*, ss 2, 4, 5; see *post*, p. 190.

[409] *Ibid.*, ss. 6, 7; see *post*, p. 191.

[410] *Ibid.*, s. 3; see *post*, p. 193.

[411] *Ibid.*, ss. 2(1), 5, 6(1), (2), 7(2).

[412] *Ibid.*, ss. 2(2), 3, 4, 6(3), 7(3), (4).

[413] 1977 Act, Sched. 1, para. 1(a).

[414] *Ibid.*, Sched. 1, para. 2.

[415] *Ibid.*, Sched. 1, para. 3.

[416] *Ibid.*, s. 26.

[417] *Ibid.*, Sched. 1, para. 4.

Unfair Contract Terms Act 1977: Pattern of Control

Types of Contract	Type of Liability	Business	Non-Business
Any Contract*	Negligent personal injuries	Unexcludable UCTA, s. 2(1)	Common Law
	Negligent loss or damage	Reasonableness UCTA, ss. 2(2) and 11	
Consumer Contract*	Any term	Reasonableness UCTA, ss. 3(2) and 11	
	Sale of Goods Act, ss. 13, 14, 15 undertakings as to title, description, quality and fitness for purpose	Unexcludable UCTA, ss. 3(2) and 7(2)	
Standard Form Contract*	Any term	Reasonableness UCTA, s. 3(2)	
Sale of Goods	Sale of Goods Act s. 12 undertakings as to title	Unexcludable UCTA, ss. 6(1) and 7(4)	
	Sale of Goods Act, ss. 13–15, undertakings as to description, quality or fitness for purpose	Reasonableness UCTA, ss. 6(3), 7(3) Schedule 2	

* Save types of contract excluded by Schedule 1, on which see *ante*, p. 186.

it relates to[418] the creation or transfer of an interest in land,[419] any intellectual property,[420] or the creation or transfer of securities.[421] In many of these, however, there are specific legislative controls on exemption clauses,[422] and, in the case of consumer contracts, most will also be subject to the Unfair Terms in Consumer Contracts Regulations 1999.[423]

---

[418] See *Micklefield* v. *S. A. C. Technology Ltd.* [1990] 1 W.L.R. 1002 (share option); *Unchained Growth III plc* v. *Granby Village (Manchester) Management Co. Ltd.* [2000] 1 W.L.R. 739 (maintenance charge in lease integral to and thus 'relates to' interest in land).

[419] Sched. 1, para. 1(b).

[420] Sched. 1, para. 1(c); Trade Marks Act 1994, s. 106(1) and Sched. 4, para. 1; *Salvage Association* v. *CAP Financial Services Ltd.* [1995] F.S.R. 654.

[421] Sched. 1, para. 1(d).

[422] *Post*, p. 203.

[423] S.I. 1999 No. 2083, *post*, p. 200.

(iv) Varieties of exemption clauses

Subject to certain exceptions,[424] the 1977 Act only applies to contract terms 'excluding or restricting' specific types of liability; but these are extended to include terms:[425]

(1) making the liability or its enforcement subject to restrictive or onerous conditions;

(2) excluding or restricting any right or remedy in respect of liability, or subjecting a person to any prejudice in consequence of his pursuing any such right or remedy;

(3) excluding or restricting rules of evidence or procedure.

Certain sections[426] also prevent excluding or restricting liability by reference to terms which exclude the relevant obligation or duty. The intention is clearly to embrace terms which, though they do not specifically exclude or restrict *liability*, have a similar effect and thus to prevent the evasion of the policy of the Act. For example, terms which require one party to make a claim within a certain time limit,[427] which take away the right to reject defective goods or to withhold payment (because of a counter-claim),[428] which state that an architect's certificate shall be 'conclusive evidence' that building work has been properly carried out, or which declare that the other party does not 'give any warranty or undertaking, express or implied, in respect of the goods supplied' or accept any responsibility with respect to the accuracy of a property valuation it supplies[429]—all of these are subject to control.

The difficulty, however, is to distinguish such terms from provisions which prevent a contractual duty from arising or circumscribe its extent, or which merely allocate the responsibilities under the contract between the parties.[430] For example, a seller's warning that goods should not be used after a specified time and a statement that the seller of a painting had no expertise in paintings of that type have been held to preclude the implication of obligations of fitness for purpose and correspondence with description under the Sale of Goods Act and not to exclude or restrict them.[431] It has been stated that the test is one of substance[432] but also that one has to ask whether 'but for' the clause there would be liability;[433] a formal test. It is submitted that,

---

[424] 1977 Act, ss. 3(2)(b), 4.

[425] *Ibid.*, s. 13.

[426] *Ibid.*, ss. 2, 5, 6, 7.

[427] *Green (R. W.) Ltd.* v. *Cade Bros.* [1978] 1 Lloyd's Rep. 602.

[428] *Stewart Gill* v. *Horatio Myer & Co.* [1992] 1 Q.B. 600; *Skipskredittforeningen* v. *Emperor Navigation* [1998] 1 Lloyd's Rep. 66; *Schenkers Ltd.* v. *Overland Shoes Ltd.* [1998] 1 Lloyd's Rep. 498 (set-off).

[429] *Smith* v. *Eric S. Bush* and *Harris* v. *Wyre Forest D.C.* [1990] A.C. 831, *post*, p. 449.

[430] *Thompson* v. *T. Lohan (Plant Hire) Ltd.* [1987] 1 W.L.R. 649.

[431] *Wormell* v. *R.H.M. Agriculture (East) Ltd.* [1987] 1 W.L.R. 1091 (1977 Act, s. 14(3)); *Harlington & Leinster Enterprises Ltd.* v. *Christopher Hull Fine Art Ltd.* [1990] 1 All E.R. 737 (1977 Act, s. 13). See *ante*, p. 154, on these implied terms.

[432] *Phillips Products Ltd.* v. *Hyland (Note)* [1987] 1 W.L.R. 659, at p. 666; *Johnstone* v. *Bloomsbury Health Authority* [1992] Q.B. 333, at p. 346.

[433] *Smith* v. *Eric S. Bush* (*supra*, n. 429), at p. 857 (*per* Lord Griffiths). N.B. the notice there was a non-contractual disclaimer.

although it has the attraction of certainty, the latter test is too broad and that the Courts should determine whether a term in a contract 'excludes or restricts' liability by asking whether it deprives a contracting party of the contractual performance which the parties reasonably expected.[434]

(v) 'Business liability'

The 1977 Act is concerned, for the most part,[435] with terms that exclude or restrict 'business liability', that is, 'liability for breach of obligations or duties arising—(a) from things done or to be done by a person in the course of a business (whether his own business or another's), or (b) from the occupation of premises used for business purposes of the occupier'.[436] The word 'business' has, however, been described as 'an etymological chameleon',[437] and it will not always be easy to determine whether or not there is a business liability, for example, in the case of a university or college, since it does not appear necessary for a business that an activity be carried on with a view to profit.[438]

(vi) 'Deals as consumer'

In certain provisions of the 1977 Act, a distinction is drawn between cases where the party to a contract against whom the exemption clause is raised deals as consumer in relation to the other party, and cases where that person deals otherwise than as consumer. As a general rule, greater protection is afforded by the Act to a person who deals as consumer than to one who does not. In order that a party should have dealt as consumer, two conditions must have been satisfied.[439] First, the party must not have made the contract in the course of a business or held himself or herself out as doing so. Secondly, the other party must have made the contract in the course of a business. A partnership or company may deal as consumer.[440] In *R. & B. Customs Brokers Co. Ltd.* v. *United Dominions Trust Ltd.*[441] it was held that a firm of customs brokers had dealt as consumer when it purchased a four-wheel-drive vehicle for the use of one of its directors, on the ground that, to be in the course of a business, the transaction must either form an integral part of the buyer's business or, if incidental to it, be of a type that is regularly carried on by the buyer. The firm had purchased two or three cars in the past but this did not suffice to constitute a pattern of regular purchases. In

---

[434] Macdonald [1992] L.S. 277. See also Law Com. No. 69 (1975), § 146.

[435] Except 1977 Act, s. 6 (exclusion of implied terms in contracts of sale of goods and hire-purchase): see *post*, p. 191. But certain terms will only be implied if the seller or owner sells or hires the goods in the course of a business: see *ante*, p. 155.

[436] *Ibid.*, s. 1(3). Cf. the Unfair Terms in Consumer Contracts Regulations 1999 (S.I. 1999 No. 2083), reg. 3, seller or supplier need only be acting for purposes *relating to* its business.

[437] *Town Investments Ltd.* v. *Department of the Environment* [1978] A.C. 359 *per* Lord Diplock at p. 383.

[438] See the partial definition in 1977 Act, s. 14.

[439] *Ibid.*, s. 12(1)(a), (b).

[440] Under the Unfair Terms in Consumer Contracts Regulations 1999 reg. 3(1) (*supra*, n. 436) a 'consumer' means a 'natural person'.

[441] [1988] 1 W.L.R. 321. See also *Rasbora Ltd.* v. *J.C.L. Marine Ltd.* [1977] 1 Lloyd's Rep. 645 (where a sale of a boat to a company formed for the purpose of buying the boat to be used by an individual was held to be a consumer sale).

addition, if the contract is one for the supply of goods—a contract of sale or hire-purchase,[442] or some other contract under which possession or ownership of goods passes (such as hire)[443]—a third condition must be satisfied; the goods supplied must be of a type ordinarily supplied for private use or consumption, i.e. not a steam-roller.[444] But on a sale by auction or by competitive tender the buyer is not in any circumstances to be regarded as dealing as consumer.[445] It has, however, been held that 'artificial though this meaning is', an employee deals as a consumer *vis à vis* his employers provided the employee neither made the contract nor held himself out as so doing in the course of a business and the employers did make the contract in the course of their business.[446]

The burden of proving that a party did not deal as consumer rests upon the party relying on the exemption clause.[447]

(vii) Liability for negligence

Restrictions are placed by section 2 of the 1977 Act on the power of a party to a contract to secure exemption from business liability for negligence.[448] It is prohibited to exclude or restrict liability for death or personal injury resulting from negligence by reference to any contract term.[449] In the case of other loss or damage, a party to a contract cannot exclude or restrict liability for negligence except in so far as the term satisfies the requirement of reasonableness.[450] Where, in a contract between A and B, a term purports to transfer from A to B responsibility for injury or damage caused to B by A's employees, that term has been held to fall within section 2.[451] But a term requiring B to indemnify A against injury or damage caused to third parties by A's negligence has been held not to on the ground that it was not an 'exclusion or restriction' of A's liability to the third party victim but an arrangement by A and B as to the responsibility for compensating the victim.[452]

Section 5 of the Act further prohibits absolutely the exclusion or restriction of the negligence liability of a manufacturer or distributor of goods by means of a written 'guarantee', such as is often provided, for example, by manufacturers of electrical

---

[442] 1977 Act, s. 6.

[443] *Ibid.*, s. 7.

[444] *Ibid.*, s. 12(1)(c).

[445] *Ibid.*, s. 12(2).

[446] *Brigden* v. *American Express Bank Ltd.* [2000] I.R.L.R. 94.

[447] *Ibid.*, s. 12(3).

[448] 'Negligence' includes a common law duty to take reasonable care or use reasonable skill and also breach of the duty of care under the Occupiers' Liability Acts 1957 and 1984.

[449] *Ibid.*, s. 2(1), (3); *Johnstone* v. *Bloomsbury H.A.* [1992] Q.B. 333, at pp. 343, 346. Terms exempting a party from liability for non-negligently caused death or personal injury may be controlled by 1977 Act, s. 6 (sale of goods); the Consumer Protection Act 1987, ss. 5 and 7 (product liability) or the Defective Premises Act 1972, s. 1.

[450] 1977 Act, s. 2(2), (3).

[451] *Phillips Products Ltd.* v. *Hyland (Note)* [1987] 1 W.L.R. 659; *Flamar Interocean Ltd.* v. *Denmore Ltd.* [1990] 1 Lloyd's Rep. 434 ('deemed servant' clauses).

[452] *Thompson* v. *T. Lohan (Plant Hire) Ltd.* [1987] 1 W.L.R. 649; *Hancock Shipping Co. Ltd.* v. *Deacon & Trysail (Private) Ltd.* [1991] 2 Lloyd's Rep. 550. See also *Neptune Orient Lines Ltd.* v. *J.C.V. (U.K.) Ltd.* [1983] 2 Lloyd's Rep. 438, at p. 442 (promise not to sue third party).

equipment—compact disc players, razors, hair dryers and the like. But the goods must be of a type supplied for private use or consumption, and the loss or damage must have arisen from the goods proving defective while in consumer use, i.e. when a person is using them, or has them in his or her possession for use, otherwise than exclusively for the purposes of a business.

(viii) Indemnity clauses

By section 4 of the 1977 Act, a person who deals as consumer cannot, by any contract term, be compelled to indemnify another in respect of the latter's business liability for negligence or breach of contract, except in so far as the term satisfies the requirement of reasonableness. Thus, for example, if a car hire firm hires a car to a consumer subject to a term that the hirer will indemnify the firm against third party claims arising out of the hirer's use of the car, then that indemnity is subject to the test of reasonableness. But indemnities given by persons who do not deal as consumer are not affected by section 4, and, as seen in the context of section 2,[453] the Act does not control provisions in contracts which require one party (who does not deal as consumer) to indemnify the other against the latter's liability in negligence to third parties.

(ix) Sale of goods and hire-purchase

Section 6 of the 1977 Act restricts the ability of sellers of goods to exempt themselves from liability for breach of the stipulations implied in contracts of sale by sections 12–15 of the Sale of Goods Act 1979. In the first place, it prohibits absolutely the exclusion or restriction of liability for breach of the provisions of section 12 of the 1979 Act (stipulations as to title).[454] Secondly, it prohibits absolutely the exclusion or restriction of liability for breach of the provisions of sections 13 to 15 of the 1979 Act as amended (conditions as to satisfactory quality, fitness for purpose, and correspondence with description or sample) where the buyer *deals as consumer*.[455] If the buyer does not deal as consumer, liability for breaches of sections 13 to 15 can be excluded or restricted, but only in so far as the term satisfies the requirement of reasonableness.[456]

Section 6 of the 1977 Act further contains similar provisions which prohibit, either absolutely or subject to the test of reasonableness, terms excluding or restricting liability for breach of the stipulations implied by the Supply of Goods (Implied Terms) Act 1973 in contracts of hire-purchase.[457]

(x) Supply contracts

Section 7 of the 1977 Act is concerned with contract terms excluding or restricting

---

[453] *Ante.*

[454] 1977 Act, s. 6(1).

[455] *Ibid.*, s. 6(2). This provision is fortified by *criminal* sanctions imposed by the Consumer Transactions (Restrictions on Statements) Orders (S.I. 1976 No. 1813 and S.I. 1978 No. 127). See *Hughes* v. *Hall & Hall* [1981] R.T.R. 430.

[456] 1977 Act, s. 6(3).

[457] See *ante*, p. 159.

business liability for breach of an implied obligation in a contract 'where the possession or ownership of goods passes under or in pursuance of the contract' (other than
a contract of sale of goods or hire-purchase, or on the redemption of trading stamps).
Examples of such contracts are contracts of hire, and—most important of all—
contracts for work and materials, such as building and engineering contracts. At
common law, the obligations to be implied in such contracts were often indeterminate
or imprecise, and varied according to the nature of the contract and the circumstances
in which it was made. However, the Supply of Goods and Services Act 1982[458] now
implies into such contracts terms similar to those implied in contracts of sale of goods
in respect of the goods' correspondence with description or sample, or their quality or
fitness for purpose. The 1977 Act absolutely prohibits the exclusion or restriction of
liability for breach of these implied terms as against a person *dealing as consumer*.[459]
As against a person dealing otherwise than as consumer, such liability can be excluded
or restricted, but only in so far as the exempting term satisfies the requirement
of reasonableness.[460] Terms excluding or restricting liability for breach of implied
terms as to title to or quiet possession of the goods are also subject to the test of
reasonableness.[461]

(xi) Business liability to consumers and under standard terms of business

A more wide-ranging and general control is effected by section 3 of the 1977 Act,
which deals with contractual liability. This section may apply, in addition to sections 6
and 7 mentioned above, to contracts of sale and hire-purchase and supply contracts.
But it may also apply to any contract, unless it is of a type expressly excepted by the
Act. Thus, it may apply, for example, to a contract with a holiday tour operator, a
contract for the dry-cleaning of clothes or the repair of a watch, and a contract for the
garaging of a car or for the storage of furniture. The section, however, only applies as
between contracting parties where one of them deals (1) as consumer,[462] or (2) on the
other's written standard terms of business, and the liability which it is sought to
exclude or restrict is a business liability. Thus, the many contracts, not only with
consumers but also between businesses, made by reference to standard terms and
conditions printed in order forms, confirmations of order, or in catalogues or price
lists are subject to section 3.

Where a standard form of agreement is used but it has been altered to fit the
circumstances of the individual transaction, the question whether section 3 applies
has been said to be one of fact and degree.[463] Clearly differences as to price and date of
delivery will not prevent the section applying to the rest of the terms. The test has

---

[458] 1977 Act, ss. 3, 4, 5, 8, 9, 10.

[459] *Ibid.*, s. 7(2).

[460] *Ibid.*, s. 7(3). See *Stewart Gill Ltd.* v. *Horatio Myer & Co. Ltd.* [1992] Q.B. 600.

[461] 1977 Act, s. 7(4). Cf. *ibid.*, s. 7(3A); Supply of Goods and Services Act 1982, ss. 2, 7.

[462] *Ante*, p. 189.

[463] *Chester Grosvenor Hotel Co. Ltd.* v. *Alfred McAlpine Management Ltd.* (1991) 56 Build. L.R. 115, at pp.
131–3; *St Albans City & D.C.* v. *International Computers Ltd.* [1996] 4 All E.R. 481, at p. 491. Cf. *Flamar
Interocean Ltd.* v. *Denmore* [1990] 1 Lloyd's Rep. 434, at p. 438; *Shearson Lehman Hutton Inc.* v. *MacLaine,
Watson & Co. Ltd.* [1989] 2 Lloyd's Rep. 570, at p. 611; *Salvage Association* v. *CAP Financial Services Ltd.*
[1995] F.S.R. 654.

been said to be one of habitual use,[464] and it is submitted that terms may overall be 'standard' even though, for example, a single provision in a standard form has been altered. Where the contract uses model forms drafted by a third party, such as a professional or trade organization, it has been suggested that unless the model form is invariably or at least usually used by a party, it cannot be that party's 'standard' terms of business.[465]

The control imposed by the section is as follows:[466]

As against that party,[467] the other cannot by reference to any contract term—

    (a) when himself in breach of contract, exclude or restrict any liability of his in respect of the breach; or

    (b) claim to be entitled—

        (i)   to render a contractual performance substantially different from that which was reasonably expected of him, or

        (ii) in respect of the whole or any part of his contractual obligation, to render no performance at all,

    except in so far as . . . the contract term satisfies the requirement of reasonableness.

The wording of the first limb (a) of this provision, relating to the exclusion or restriction of liability in respect of breach of contract, is relatively easy to interpret. But the second limb (b) is more difficult to construe. It would appear to be the intention of (b) that it should apply in cases where there is *no breach of contract at all*, but one party claims to rely on a term of the contract which purports to entitle it either to render a contractual performance substantially different from that which was reasonably expected at the time of the contract or in respect of the whole or part of the contractual obligation to render no performance at all.[468]

It has been held that the second limb (b) did not apply to a term permitting an employer to dismiss an employee during the first two years of employment without going through the contractual disciplinary procedure.[469] Although expressed in negative terms, it merely set out the employee's entitlement and the limit of his rights. Examples of the application of the second limb (b) are likely to include the following. First, where a holiday tour operator agrees to provide a holiday for a consumer at a certain hotel at a certain resort, but nevertheless reserves the right, in certain circumstances, to accommodate the consumer at another hotel, or to switch the holiday to a different resort, or to cancel the holiday in whole or in part.[470] Again, it has been

---

[464] *Chester Grosvenor Hotel Co. Ltd.* v. *Alfred McAlpine Management Ltd.* (*supra*, n. 463).

[465] *British Fermentation Products Ltd.* v. *Compare Reavell Ltd.* (1999) 66 Con. L.R. 1.

[466] 1977 Act, s. 3(2).

[467] i.e. the consumer or the person dealing on the other's written standard terms of business.

[468] *Shearson Lehman Bros. Inc.* v. *Maclaine, Watson & Co. Ltd.* (*supra*, n. 463), at p. 612.

[469] *Brigden* v. *American Express Bank Ltd.* [2000] I.R.L.R. 94. See also *Paragon Finance plc* v. *Nash* [2002] 1 W.L.R. 686.

[470] *Anglo Continental Holidays Ltd.* v. *Typaldos Lines (London) Ltd.* [1967] 2 Lloyd's Rep. 61. Package holidays are now subject to the Package Travel, Package Holidays and Package Tours Regulations 1992 (S.I. 1992 No. 3288) which (reg. 12) require the organization to permit the consumer to withdraw from the contract without penalty if it 'is constrained' to alter significantly an essential term.

suggested that a clause which gives a telephone company power to disconnect a telephone service without demonstrable reason or cause purports to permit partial or different performance from that which the customer expected.[471] Moreover, in a commercial agreement, a *force majeure* clause may excuse a trader from delivering goods to be supplied under the contract, or to suspend or cancel the contract without any further liability on its part upon the happening of events beyond the trader's control, such as strikes, war, civil commotion, inability to obtain supplies, etc. In the cases of the holiday tour operator and the telephone company, it might be held that such provisions do not satisfy the requirement of reasonableness. But it seems unlikely that a *force majeure* clause in a commercial agreement would be held to be unreasonable[472] in the absence of special circumstances.[473]

(xii) The 'reasonableness' test

Except in those instances where the 1977 Act prohibits absolutely the exclusion or restriction of liability,[474] the contract terms controlled by the Act are subject to the test of reasonableness.[475] The question to be decided by the Court in all cases where the 'reasonableness' test is applied in relation to a contract term is whether the term is a fair and reasonable one to have been included 'having regard to the circumstances which were, or ought reasonably to have been, known to or in the contemplation of the parties when the contract was made'.[476] It is therefore clear that the crucial time is the time of the making of the contract, and not the time at which liability arises.[477] The reasonableness of a contract term is therefore not affected by the nature or seriousness of the loss or damage sustained, except to the extent that it was or ought to have been in contemplation at the time the contract was made. It is also clear that circumstances solely known to one party, i.e. the person relying on the exemption clause, such as the experimental nature of the product supplied or the market difficulties involved in procuring it, are to be treated as irrelevant if they were not known, and could not reasonably have been known, to the other party at the time the contract was made.

In order to assist the Court in determining whether a term satisfies the requirement of reasonableness, the Act sets out certain 'guidelines' of circumstances to be taken into account:[478]

---

[471] *Timeload Ltd. v. British Telecommunications plc* (1995) 3 E.M.L.R. 459, *per* Sir Thomas Bingham M.R. at p. 468. But cf. *Paragon Finance plc v. Nash* [2002] 1 W.L.R. 686, paras. 71–77.

[472] *Shearson Lehman Hutton Inc. v. MacLaine, Watson & Co. Ltd.* (*supra*, n. 463), at. p. 612. See also *Brigden v. American Express Bank Ltd* [2000] I.R.L.R. 94, at p. 96.

[473] e.g. in an exclusive dealing agreement (see *post*, p. 379) where the supplier is entitled to suspend in the event of *force majeure* but the purchaser is not entitled, during the suspension, to purchase supplies from elsewhere.

[474] 1977 Act, ss. 2(1), 5, 6(1), (2), 7(2).

[475] *Ibid.*, ss. 2(2), 3(2), 4, 6(3), 7(3), (4).

[476] *Ibid.*, s. 11(1).

[477] *Stewart Gill v. Horatio Myer & Co.* [1992] 1 Q.B. 600, at pp. 607, 608. The reasonableness of a non-contractual notice is determined having regard to the circumstances when the liability arose or would have arisen: 1977 Act, s. 11(3); *Smith v. Eric S. Bush* [1990] A.C. 831, at pp. 848, 857.

[478] 1977 Act, s. 11(2), Sched. 2. For the guidelines under the Unfair Terms in Consumer Contracts Regulations 1999 (S.I. 1999 No. 2083), see *post*, p. 200.

(1) the strength of the bargaining positions of the parties relative to each other, taking into account (among other things) alternative means by which the customer's requirements could have been met;

(2) whether the customer received an inducement to agree to the term, or in accepting it had an opportunity of entering into a similar contract with other persons, but without having to accept a similar term;

(3) whether the customer knew or ought reasonably to have known of the existence and extent of the term (having regard, among other things, to any custom of the trade and any previous course of dealing between the parties);

(4) where the term excludes or restricts any relevant liability if some condition is not complied with, whether it was reasonable at the time of the contract to expect that compliance with that condition would be practicable;

(5) whether the goods were manufactured, processed, or adapted to the special order of the customer.

It will be seen that these guidelines could open up quite extensive enquiries, for instance, as to the market position at the time the contract was made. The Court should not, however, be too ready to focus on remote possibilities or to conclude that a clause fails the test by reference to relatively uncommon or unlikely situations.[479] Strictly the guidelines are applicable to the test of reasonableness only in respect of the exclusion or restriction of liability for breach of the implied obligations as to description and quality in contracts of sale of goods and hire-purchase,[480] and supply contracts.[481] But 'the considerations there set out are normally regarded as being of general application to the question of reasonableness'.[482] However, even where the guidelines are directly applicable, they are not exhaustive; the Court is required to have regard 'in particular' to those matters, but it can also take account of any other relevant circumstances.

If a contract term seeks to restrict liability to a specified sum of money (as, for example, in the case of a term which states that a seller's total liability for loss or damage arising from defects in the goods shall be limited to £20,000) and the question arises whether the term satisfies the requirement of reasonableness, the 1977 Act requires that regard is also to be had in particular to (1) the resources which he would expect to be available to him for the purpose of meeting the liability should it arise, and (2) how far it was open to him to cover himself by insurance.[483]

The burden of proving that a contract term satisfies the requirement of reasonableness rests upon the person who claims that it is reasonable.[484]

The control of exemption and limitation clauses by a test of reasonableness means

---

[479] *Skipskredittforeningen* v. *Emperor Navigation* [1998] 1 Lloyd's Rep. 66, at pp. 75–76.

[480] 1977 Act, s. 6(3).

[481] *Ibid.*, s. 7(3), (4).

[482] *Stewart Gill* v. *Horatio Myer & Co.* [1992] 1 Q.B. 600, *per* Stuart-Smith L.J. at p. 608. See also *Flamar Interocean Ltd.* v. *Denmore* [1990] 1 Lloyd's Rep. 434, at p. 438; *Smith* v. *Eric S. Bush* [1990] A.C. 831, *per* Lord Griffiths at p. 858.

[483] 1977 Act, s. 11(4).

[484] *Ibid.*, s. 11(5). See *A.E.G. (U.K.) Ltd.* v. *Logic Resources Ltd.* [1996] C.L.C. 265.

that decisions are likely to be made on a case by case basis and to turn on the type of
contract and the precise nature of the relationship between the parties rather than the
application of rules. The consequence is a body of law that is more flexible but less
certain. Decisions of judges at first instance as to whether a clause is reasonable can be
seen as broadly similar to exercises of structured discretion.[485] It has been stated that
Courts must entertain a wide 'range of considerations, put them into the scales on
one side or the other, and decide at the end of the day on which side the balance
comes down'.[486] In such circumstances there will be room for a legitimate difference
of judicial opinion as to the correct answer, and for this reason the decision of the
judge at first instance will be treated 'with the utmost respect' and appellate courts
will 'refrain from interference with it unless satisfied that it proceeded upon some
erroneous principle or was plainly and obviously wrong'.[487] An example of such an
error was where the trial judge considered the reasonableness of the part of the
exemption clause that was in issue, requiring a purchaser to return defective goods
at its own expense, separately from the rest of the clause, which in effect excluded all
other warranties and conditions including those implied by the Sale of Goods
Act.[488]

(xiii) Factors taken into account

It has been said that 'it is impossible to draw up an exhaustive list of factors to be
taken into account' in assessing the reasonableness of an exemption or limitation
clause.[489] The decided cases, however, give guidance as to the most significant
factors.[490]

The statutory guidelines concerning contracts of sale, which have a wider importance, and the statutory requirements that regard is to be had to the capacity of the
party seeking exclusion to meet the liability and its insurability are set out above.[491]
Thus, the Court will consider the relative bargaining strength of the parties.[492] A
clause that has been imposed by one side is less likely to be reasonable than one that
was the product of negotiations between representative bodies, or had evolved over

---

[485] In the sense that there is significant scope for setting the reasons and standards (and assessing the
relative importance of conflicting reasons and standards) according to which the decision is to be made
within a broad but not unlimited statutory framework: see Galligan, *Discretionary Powers* (1986), p.21.

[486] *George Mitchell (Chesterhall) Ltd.* v. *Finney Lock Seeds Ltd.* [1983] 2 A.C. 803, at p. 816.

[487] *Ibid., per* Lord Bridge at p. 810. See also *Phillips Products Ltd.* v. *Hyland* [1987] 1 W.L.R. 659, at p. 669.

[488] *A.E.G. (U.K.) Ltd.* v. *Logic Resources Ltd.* [1996] C.L.C. 265.

[489] *Smith* v. *Eric S. Bush* [1990] 1 A.C. 831, at p. 858.

[490] As well as decisions on the 1977 Act, guidance is gained from those on the Misrepresentation Act 1967,
s. 3 (*post*, p. 260, and *Howard Marine and Dredging Co. Ltd.* v. *A. Ogden & Sons (Excavations) Ltd.* [1978] Q.B.
574), the Sale of Goods Act 1893, s. 55 (as amended by the Supply of Goods (Implied Terms) Act 1974 but
now replaced by the Unfair Contract Terms Act 1977, ss. 6–7), but see *Rasbora Ltd.* v. *J.C.L. Marine Ltd.* [1977]
1 Lloyd's Rep. 645; *George Mitchell (Chesterhall) Ltd.* v. *Finney Lock Seeds Ltd.* [1983] 2 A.C. 803.

[491] *Ante*, p. 195.

[492] *Howard Marine and Dredging Co. Ltd.* v. *A. Ogden & Sons (Excavations) Ltd.* [1978] Q.B. 574, *per* Lord
Denning M.R. at p. 594; *George Mitchell (Chesterhall) Ltd.* v. *Finney Lock Seeds Ltd.* [1983] Q.B. 284, at p. 302;
Smith v. *Eric S. Bush* [1990] 1 A.C. 831, at p. 858; *Singer Co. (U.K.) Ltd.* v. *Hartlepool Port Authority* [1988] 2
Lloyd's Rep. 164, at p. 169; Guideline (a) in Sched. 2 to the 1977 Act; Sched. 2(a) to the Unfair Terms in
Consumer Contracts Regulations 1994 (S.I. 1994 No. 3159).

time as a result of trade practice.[493] Again, the Court will have regard not only to whether the customer was obliged to use the services of the supplier, but also to the question of how far it would have been practicable and convenient to go elsewhere.[494] Where a party seeking to rely on a clause has given the other party the opportunity to pay more for the contractual performance without the clause, the clause is more likely to be held to be reasonable. For instance, in a number of standard forms governing contracts for the carriage of goods, the liability of the carrier is limited unless the owner of the goods declares their value and pays an increased charge.[495] The size of the limit compared with other limits in widely used standard terms may also be relevant.[496]

(xiv) Insurance

While the availability of insurance is a factor, it is by no means a decisive factor.[497] The statutory requirement that regard is to be had to how far it was open to the party seeking exclusion to cover itself by insurance[498] was inserted to protect the small business, and possibly also professional persons who might not have the resources to meet unlimited liability should it arise, and who might not be able to obtain insurance cover against such liability. In their case, it might well be reasonable to impose a financial limit to liability. The provision may, however, be held to operate against larger companies with considerable assets, or to render a 'financial limit' clause unreasonable where insurance cover can in fact be obtained. Thus, it has been held that a limitation of liability of £100,000 by a multinational company with insurance cover of £50 million was unreasonable.[499] It is to be noted that the statute makes no reference to the *cost* of such cover, but it has been stated that 'the cost of insurance must be a relevant factor when considering which of two parties should be required to bear the risk of a loss'.[500]

(xv) Negligence

Negligence on the part of the party seeking to rely on the clause is also an important factor. The Court will take into account whether there has been such negligence, and, if so, whether it was reasonably practicable for the other party to have done anything

---

[493] *Howard Marine and Dredging Co. Ltd.* v. *A. Ogden & Sons (Excavations) Ltd.* [1978] Q.B. 574, *per* Lord Denning M.R. at p. 594; *George Mitchell (Chesterhall) Ltd.* v. *Finney Lock Seeds Ltd.* [1983] Q.B. 284, at pp. 302, 307, 314; [1983] 2 A.C. 803, at p. 817; *Schenkers Ltd.* v. *Overland Shoes* [1998] 1 Lloyd's Rep. 498, at p. 507. Trade practice without negotiation is not a weighty factor.

[494] *Overseas Medical Supplies Ltd.* v. *Orient Transport Services Ltd* [1999] 2 Lloyd's Rep. 272, at p. 277.

[495] *Gillespie* v. *Roy Bowles Transport Ltd.* [1973] Q.B. 400, at p. 446. See, for example, clause 29(A) and (D) of the British International Freight Association's Standard Trading Conditions, 1989 edn. See also Guideline (b) in Sched. 2 to the 1977 Act; *Singer Co. (U.K.) Ltd.* v. *Hartlepool Port Authority* [1988] 2 Lloyd's Rep. 164, at p. 170.

[496] *Overseas Medical Supplies Ltd.* v. *Orient Transport Services Ltd* [1999] 2 Lloyd's Rep. 272, at p. 277.

[497] *Ibid.*

[498] 1977 Act, s. 11(4).

[499] *St Albans City & D.C.* v. *International Computers Ltd.* [1995] F.S.R. 686, aff'd [1996] 4 All E.R. 481, at p. 491. See also *Salvage Association* v. *CAP Financial Services Ltd.* [1995] F.S.R. 654.

[500] *Smith* v. *Eric S. Bush* (*supra*, n. 489), *per* Lord Griffiths at p. 858. See also *ibid.*, at pp. 851–4; *George Mitchell (Chesterhall) Ltd.* v. *Finney Lock Seeds Ltd.* [1983] 2 A.C. 803, at p. 817.

to avoid the loss.[501] Excluding or limiting liability for negligence may be reasonable provided it is reasonably practicable for the other party to obtain the service from an alternative source, if the task is very difficult with a high risk of failure, or where it would be impossible to obtain adequate insurance cover against a potential liability that would be ruinous without insurance.[502]

(xvi) Clarity

The clarity of the clause has been described as an 'overriding' factor; businesses must take the consequences of the uncertainty which their 'small print' has created; 'uncertainty' involves unfairness to the other side.[503] A clause is also less likely to be reasonable if the innocent party has not had an opportunity of discovering the defect or damage. Thus a term in a bulk sale of seed potatoes requiring claims to be made within three days of delivery was held not to protect the seller when the potatoes were infected by virus, a defect not discoverable by inspection.[504]

(xvii) Ratio of damage to price

Finally, there is the magnitude of the damage in relation to the contract price. There have been statements that where the price is small but the damages very large, as in the case considered in the next paragraph, this favours a finding of reasonableness.[505]

(xviii) An illustration

The operation of many of the above factors is illustrated by *George Mitchell (Chesterhall) Ltd.* v. *Finney Lock Seeds Ltd.*,[506] a case concerning the reasonableness test in section 55 of the Sale of Goods Act 1893 (now repealed),[507] which required the Court to consider the reasonableness of *reliance* upon the term and not, as is required by the 1977 Act, whether it is reasonable to include it in the contract. In that case:

G.M., a firm of farmers, purchased from F, a seed merchant, a quantity of Dutch winter white cabbage seeds, described as 'Finney's Late Dutch Special' for £201. F negligently supplied seeds of a very inferior variety of autumn cabbage, and as a result the crop failed. G.M.'s loss was £61,513 but F relied on exemption clauses contained in its standard conditions of sale which limited its liability to replacement of the seeds or a refund of the price paid, and excluded any express or implied condition, statutory or otherwise.

---

[501] *George Mitchell (Chesterhall) Ltd.* v. *Finney Lock Seeds Ltd.* [1983] Q.B. 284, at pp. 307, 313; 2 A.C. 803, at p. 817. See also *Walker* v. *Boyle* [1982] 1 W.L.R. 495, at p. 507; *Smith* v. *Eric S. Bush* [1990] 1 A.C. 831, at p. 858 (non-contractual notice); *Britvic Soft Drinks Ltd.* v. *Messer U.K. Ltd.* [2002] 1 Lloyd's Rep. 20, at p. 59.

[502] *Smith* v. *Eric S. Bush* [1990] 1 A.C. 831, at pp. 858–9. See *ante*, p. 197 (s. 11(4)).

[503] *George Mitchell (Chesterhall) Ltd.* v. *Finney Lock Seeds Ltd.* [1983] Q.B. 284, *per* Kerr L.J. at p. 314; *Monarch Airlines Ltd.* v. *London Luton Airport* [1998] 1 Lloyd's Rep. 403, at p. 414. See, similarly, Unfair Terms in Consumer Contracts Regulations 1999 (S.I. 1999 No. 2083), regs. 6 and 7(1), *post*, p. 301. Note the overlap with the rules of construction, *ante*, pp. 169–71.

[504] *R. W. Green* v. *Cade Bros. Farms* [1978] 1 Lloyd's Rep. 602; *R. & B. Customs Brokers Co. Ltd.* v. *United Dominions Trust Ltd.* [1988] 1 W.L.R. 321.

[505] *George Mitchell (Chesterhall) Ltd.* v. *Finney Lock Seeds Ltd.* [1983] Q.B. 284; [1983] 2 A.C. 803 (Lord Denning M.R. and Lord Bridge, cf. Kerr L.J.). See also *Smith* v. *Eric S. Bush* [1990] 1 A.C. 831, at pp. 859–60 (non-contractual notice).

[506] [1983] 2 A.C. 803.

[507] *Ante*, p. 153.

The House of Lords held that F could not rely on the clause. Although similar terms were incorporated universally in the terms of trade between seed merchants and farmers, they were never negotiated; the breach was due to negligence for which F was responsible and seed merchants could insure against crop failure caused by supplying the wrong seeds without materially increasing the price of the seeds. There was also evidence that, in practice, seed merchants always negotiated settlements of claims for damages in excess of the price of seeds if they thought that the claims were 'genuine' and 'justified'. The fact that merchants had not sought to rely on the limitation in the past showed that it would not be reasonable to allow such reliance in this case. Although, under the 1977 Act, reasonableness must be determined at the time of the contract and subsequent reliance is not relevant,[508] it is submitted that it is unlikely to be reasonable to include a term which has never in the past been relied on in a trade and that the absence of such reliance *before* the contract under consideration was made remains relevant under the 1977 Act.

(xix) Powers of the Court

Although the Act uses the words 'except in so far as the term satisfies the requirement of reasonableness', the powers of the Court under the 'reasonableness' provisions of the Act are limited to declaring the term either to be effective or of no effect and are probably more limited than its powers under the Unfair Terms in Consumer Contracts Regulations 1999.[509] It could not re-write the term[510] or, for example, where the term limited liability to a particular sum, render a 'judgement of Solomon' by raising that sum to an amount which it considered reasonable in the circumstances.[511]

On the other hand, if a single term both excludes liability which by the Act cannot be excluded (for example, for death or personal injury resulting from negligence) and liability which can be excluded subject to the test of reasonableness (for example, liability in negligence for other loss or damage), it is arguable that the term could nevertheless be upheld, if reasonable, in respect of the exclusion of the latter liability.[512]

(xx) Effect of the 1977 Act

It is difficult to assess the impact of the 1977 Act on contracting behaviour but, in the area of consumer transactions, the level of complaints about unfair terms and conditions has remained quite high, although a small percentage of total complaints.[513] In 1996 the Office of Fair Trading stated that it was 'very disturbed' to find that unfair terms often conflict with consumer protection legislation that has been in place for

---

[508] *Stewart Gill Ltd.* v. *Horatio Myer & Co. Ltd.* [1992] Q.B. 600.

[509] S.I. 1999 No. 2083, reg. 8. *Post,* pp. 200 and 300.

[510] *Quaere* whether the Court could sever words that made the term unreasonable.

[511] *George Mitchell (Chesterhall) Ltd.* v. *Finney Lock Seeds Ltd.* (*supra,* n. 505), at p. 816; *Stewart Gill Ltd.* v. *Horatio Myer & Co. Ltd.* [1992] Q.B. 600.

[512] This point was left open by Parker J. in *George Mitchell (Chesterhall) Ltd.* v. *Finney Lock Seeds Ltd.* [1981] 1 Lloyd's Rep. 476, at p. 480. But see *R. W. Green Ltd.* v. *Cade Bros. Farms* [1978] 1 Lloyd's Rep. 602, *ante,* p. 198 (three-day time bar invalid, limitation of damages to contract price valid).

[513] According to the Office of Fair Trading, there were some 16,200 complaints in 1989: *Trading Malpractices* (1990).

some time, including the 1977 Act.[514] It would seem that reliance on individual action by parties to contracts is insufficient and that administrative action, either under Part II of the Fair Trading Act 1973 or by the Office of Fair Trading proceeding against traders under Part III of that Act, or under the Unfair Terms in Consumer Contracts Regulations 1999,[515] is necessary.[516]

(b) UNFAIR TERMS IN CONSUMER CONTRACTS REGULATIONS 1999

Unlike the Unfair Contract Terms Act 1977, the Unfair Terms in Consumer Contracts Regulations 1999[517] are not restricted to exemption and limitation clauses, but subject all the terms of a contract between a seller or supplier of goods or services and a consumer which have not been 'individually negotiated'[518] to a requirement of 'fairness'. For this reason, the operation of the Regulations is considered in Chapter 7, which deals with other common law and statutory controls on unfair and unconscionable bargains.[519] As, however, many of the terms controlled by the 1999 Regulations will in fact either be exemption or limitation clauses, it is useful here to indicate the main differences between the two statutory regimes.

(i) Scope

First, the Regulations apply to some contracts, notably insurance,[520] excluded from the 1977 Act. Sales of land, which are excluded from the 1977 Act, are included although the wording of the Regulations is not altogether clear. Although the Regulations only apply to contracts between a seller or a supplier and a consumer, in the context of Community law those words are capable of applying to the creation and transfer of interests in land.[521] But the Regulations do not apply to some matters which are covered by the 1977 Act. For instance, they do not apply to non-contractual notices, and although contracts 'relating to employment' are no longer expressly excluded from their regime,[522] the Commission's view appears to be that an

---

[514] Office of Fair Trading, *Unfair Contract Terms*, Bulletin 2, p. 5.

[515] S.I. 1999 No. 2083, *infra*.

[516] See generally Beale, in Beatson and Friedmann, eds., *Good Faith and Fault in Contract Law* (1995), ch. 9. *Post*, p. 204.

[517] S.I. 1999 No. 2083, replacing S.I. 1994 No. 3159, which implemented EEC Council Directive 93/13, O.J. No. L. 95, 21 April 1993, p. 29. See generally Beale, (*supra*, n. 516); Collins (1994) 14 O.J.L.S. 229; Bright (2000) 20 L.S. 331.

[518] S.I. 1999 No. 2083, reg. 5. They may, accordingly, catch, for instance, clauses by a principal restricting his agent's authority: cf. *Overbrooke Estates Ltd.* v. *Glencombe Properties Ltd.* [1974] 1 W.L.R. 1355, *post*, p. 262.

[519] *Post*, p. 300 ff. Apart from exemption and limitation clauses, according to the Office of Fair Trading, the most common categories of unfair terms are clauses excluding from the contract anything done or said by the salesman ('entire agreement' clauses), clauses hidden before the contract is made (*ante*, p. 164), clauses penalizing consumers, and clauses permitting the supplier to vary its price.

[520] But note the Directive states that terms which clearly and plainly define or circumscribe the insured risk and the insurer's liability will not be assessed for fairness Directive 93/13, Art. 4(1) and Recital 19, since these restrictions are taken into account in calculating the premium paid.

[521] *Unfair Contract Terms* No. 8 (OFT) para. 1.5. See Bright (2000) 20 L.S. 331, 339–341. The position was less clear under the 1994 Regulations (*ante*, n. 517): Bright and Bright (1995) 111 L.Q.R. 655.

[522] Para. (a) of Sched. 1 to the 1994 Regulations. Cf. the more limited exemption in the 1977 Act, *ante*, p. 186.

employment contract is not one that can be made between a seller or supplier and a consumer.[523] Again, under the Regulations only a natural person can be a 'consumer',[524] whereas, under section 12 of the 1977 Act, a company may qualify.[525] But the Regulations have a broader definition of 'seller' and 'supplier' since they only require a 'seller' or 'supplier' to be 'acting for purposes relating to his business'[526] and not, as under the 1977 Act, 'in the course of a business' and with some regularity.[527]

Secondly, the broader scope of the Regulations is accompanied by protection which is, in some respects, less certain than that in the 1977 Act. For example, there are no absolute bans, only factors[528] and an 'indicative and non-exhaustive list of the terms which may be regarded as unfair'.[529] A number of the terms in this list would be of no effect under the 1977 Act[530] or under the common law.[531]

(ii) The test of 'fairness'

A term will be 'unfair' where, 'contrary to the requirement of good faith', it 'causes a significant imbalance in the parties' rights and obligations arising under the contract, to the detriment of the consumer'.[532] It is, as yet, not clear to what extent the three elements of this test differ from the 'reasonableness' test of the 1977 Act. Some of the factors to be taken into account in the determination of 'reasonableness' under the 1977 Act are also to be taken into account in determining 'good faith' and 'fairness', under the Directive although not expressly referred to in the 1999 Regulations.[533] Either test is likely in most cases to lead to a very similar result. There is, as yet, only one significant judicial decision[534] but many of the cases the Director-General of Fair Trading has considered administratively, as part of the duty to prevent the continued use of unfair terms,[535] have involved 'reasonableness' and the plainness and intelligibility of the language and do not show a sharp difference from the approach taken in the cases on the 1977 Act. For example, following complaints suppliers have agreed to withdraw or amend certain types of clause. Thus clauses excluding liability for a

---

[523] See Tonreiro and Karston in *Rechtsangeichung und nationale privatrechte*, p. 12, on which see Bright (2000) 20 L.S. 331, 341. Cf. *ante*, p. 186 for the different position under the 1977 Act.

[524] *Ibid.*, reg. 3(1).

[525] *Ante*, p. 189.

[526] *Ibid.*, reg. 3(1).

[527] *Ante*, p. 189.

[528] *Ibid.*, reg. 6(1). See further, *post*, pp. 201–2).

[529] *Ibid.*, reg. 5(5) and Sched. 2.

[530] For instance, excluding or limiting liability for death or personal injury (*ante*, p. 190), or for breach of implied undertakings as to fitness for use and quality in sales to consumers (*ante*, p. 191, but note that the EC Directive on the Sale of Consumer Goods and Guarantees, would introduce a similar ban.

[531] For instance requiring a consumer in breach to pay a disproportionately high sum in compensation, *post*, p. 625.

[532] *Ibid.*, reg. 5(1), *post*, p. 300.

[533] See the factors listed in Recital 16 to Directive 93/13 which may be referred to in interpreting the Regulations. Cf. Schedule 2 to the 1994 Regulations. The factors listed there are strikingly similar to those in Schedule 2 to the 1977 Act. Cf. also reg. 4(2) and section 11 of the 1977 Act.

[534] *Director-General of Fair Trading* v. *First National Bank plc.* [2001] 3 W.L.R. 1297, *post*, p. 303. This case concerned the 1994 Regulations.

[535] S.I. 1999 No. 2083, reg. 10. Reg. 12 also empowers regulatory bodies and the Consumers Association to apply for injunctive relief against any person or body using or recommending the use of unfair terms.

failure to supply have either been withdrawn or limited to situations in which the failure is beyond the supplier's reasonable control. Clauses excluding delay have either been withdrawn or limited to delay for a reasonable period. Similarly, suppliers have agreed either to withdraw clauses preventing a consumer from withholding any part of the contractual payment where the goods or services are defective or to amend them to prohibit such withholding in the case of a minor defect beyond a proportionate amount of the contractual sum. Finally, suppliers have agreed to withdraw clauses excluding liability for damage if concerned with death or personal injury or to limit them to damage which has not been caused negligently.[536]

But the two tests are not the same. For instance, regulation 6(2) provides that the assessment of fairness of a term shall not relate to the adequacy of the price or the definition of the main subject-matter provided the relevant term is in 'plain intelligible language'. But, as we have seen, under section 3(2)(b) of the 1977 Act, exemption clauses shrinking the contractual obligation are subject to control and the reasonableness test if they permit a contractor to perform in a way that is 'substantially different from that which was reasonably expected'. Conceivably, under the Regulations, a term permitting such performance would escape control by the 'fairness' test if it was in 'plain intelligible language'. The House of Lords has, however, held that regulation 6(2) should be given a restrictive interpretation. Since, in a sense all terms of the contract are in some way related to the price or remuneration, unless regulation 6(2) is interpreted restrictively, it 'will enable the main purpose of the scheme to be frustrated by endless formalistic arguments as to whether a provision is a definitional or an exclusionary provision'.[537] It was held that a provision concerning the rate of interest to be paid on a breach of contract, i.e. the consequences of default, neither defined the main subject of the contract nor realistically concerned the adequacy of the price.[538] To construe such a provision as falling within regulation 6(2) would leave 'a gaping hole in the system' and mean that 'almost any provision containing any part of the bargain would be capable of falling within the reach of regulation [6(2)].'[539] Again, the assessment of the fairness of a term is, as under the 1977 Act, to be made in the light of the circumstances at the time the contract was concluded.[540] But, unlike the 1977 Act, the Regulations expressly require regard to be had to 'all the other terms of the contract'.[541] The determination of fairness will thus take account of the entire contractual package and a term which, in isolation, might appear to be unfair, might not be when looked at in the light of the contract as a whole. We have noted that the Regulations probably permit a broader approach to severance since they provide that 'the contract shall continue to bind the parties if it is capable of continuing in existence without the unfair term'.[542]

---

[536] See Office of Fair Trading Bulletins on *Unfair Contract Terms*.

[537] See *Director-General of Fair Trading* v. *First National Bank plc.* [2001] 3 W.L.R. 1297, para 34, (*post*, p. 303).

[538] *Ibid.*, at paras. 12, 43, 64.

[539] [2000] Q.B. 672, at p. 686 (C.A.).

[540] S.I. 1999 No. 2083, reg. 6(1). Note that, unlike s. 11(1) of the 1977 Act, *ante*, p. 194, there is no express reference to circumstances which 'ought to have been' known to or in the contemplation of the parties at the time of contracting.

[541] S.I. 1999 No. 2083, reg. 6(1).

[542] *Ibid.*, reg. 8(2).

More fundamentally, the broad test of 'good faith', with its conceptual roots in civilian systems of law, which has not been a general requirement in the English law of contract, is, as we shall see,[543] likely to lead to a wider inquiry than that under the 1977 Act. For instance, the Preamble to the Directive upon which the Regulations are based states that the requirement of 'good faith' is satisfied where the seller or supplier 'deals fairly and equitably with the other party *whose legitimate interests he also takes into account*'.[544] This question is considered in Chapter 7, dealing with unfair bargains.[545]

(c) OTHER LEGISLATIVE INTERVENTION

The exclusion or restriction of liability for misrepresentation is controlled by section 3 of the Misrepresentation Act 1967.[546] This is dealt with in Chapter 6. Legislative intervention has also occurred in a number of other important, but limited, spheres, as in the case of consumer credit,[547] consumer safety,[548] defective premises,[549] package holidays,[550] carriage by land,[551] sea,[552] or air,[553] insurance,[554] and employment.[555]

More generally, under the Fair Trading Act 1973,[556] a Director General of Fair Trading has been appointed and a Consumer Protection Advisory Committee has been set up. The Director, or the Secretary of State for Trade and Industry or any other Minister, may refer to the Advisory Committee the question whether a consumer trade practice specified in the reference adversely affects the economic interests of consumers in the United Kingdom. The Advisory Committee will consider this reference and formulate a Report, which may then be followed by legislative action (i.e. a statutory instrument) by the Secretary of State.[557] The Act refers specifically to the situation where it appears to the Director that 'a consumer trade practice has the effect, or is likely to have the effect, of causing the terms or conditions, on or subject to which consumers enter into relevant consumer transactions, to be so adverse to them

[543] *Post*, p. 300.
[544] Recital 16 of the Preamble to EEC Council Directive 93/13 (emphasis added). On the use of the preamble to a Directive in interpreting the implementing regulations, see Case C-106/89, *Marleasing S.A. v. La Commercial* [1992] 1 C.M.L.R. 305.
[545] *Post*, p. 300.
[546] As amended by the Unfair Contract Terms Act 1977, s. 8; see *post*, p. 260.
[547] Consumer Credit Act 1974, s. 173(1).
[548] Consumer Protection Act 1987, Part I.
[549] Defective Premises Act 1972, s. 6(3).
[550] Package Travel, Package Holidays and Package Tours Regulations (S.I. 1992 No. 3288), esp. reg. 15.
[551] Carriage of Goods by Road Act 1965; Carriage of Passengers by Road Act 1974; Carriage by Air and Road Act 1979; Public Passengers Vehicles Act 1981; International Transport Conventions Act 1983.
[552] Carriage of Goods by Sea Act 1924, Art. III, r. 8; Carriage of Goods by Sea Act 1971; Merchant Shipping Act 1995.
[553] Carriage by Air Act 1961; Carriage by Air and Road Act 1979.
[554] Industrial Assurance Acts 1923 and 1968; Road Traffic Act 1988, s. 148; Transport Act 1980, s. 61.
[555] Employment Rights Act 1996; the latest consolidation of legislation concerning individual employment.
[556] Parts I to III.
[557] See S.I. 1976 No. 1812, S.I. 1976 No. 1813, S.I. 1978 No. 127, S.I. 1977 No. 1918.

as to be inequitable'.[558] In addition to these general powers, the Act enables[559] the Director to take action against particular persons, firms, or companies who persist in a course of conduct which is detrimental to the interests of consumers in the United Kingdom or which is to be regarded as unfair to consumers. If the Director is unable to obtain a satisfactory written assurance that the conduct complained of will cease, he may institute proceedings before the Restrictive Practices Court, which can make an order (breach of which will be punishable as a contempt of Court) against the person, firm, or company concerned. We have noted that public action such as is possible under this Act and other legislation may be more effective in controlling the use of undesirable exemptions and limitation clauses.

[558] Fair Trading Act 1973, s. 17(2)(c).
[559] *Ibid.*, Part III.

PART II

FACTORS TENDING TO DEFEAT CONTRACTUAL LIABILITY

5

INCAPACITY

I. CAUSES OF CONTRACTUAL INCAPACITY

The law limits the capacity of certain persons to bind themselves by a promise, or to enforce a promise made to them. These persons are:

(1) The Crown and public authorities;

(2) minors;

(3) corporations;

(4) mentally disordered and drunken persons.

The consequences of contractual incapacity are not identical. In some cases the contract is void, in others voidable, while in others it is unenforceable at the suit of one or both parties.

The underlying policy of rules limiting contractual capacity is to protect those under the incapacity. In the case of public authorities the policy seeks to protect the public finances and taxpayers, and, in the case of companies, investors and creditors. We shall see that this protective policy can inflict hardship upon those who deal with an incapacitated person in good faith and in ignorance of the lack of capacity. More-over, until recently, the non-recognition of independent restitutionary obligations[1] meant that an incapacitated party to whom money had been paid or property trans-ferred might be unjustly enriched at the expense of the other. The practical import-ance of the limitations on contractual capacity has been reduced. In the case of minors this is the result of the reduction in the age of majority from 21 to 18. In the case of local authorities and companies there has been substantial statutory modifica-tion of the *ultra vires* doctrine so as to make many contracts enforceable,[2] thus enhancing security of transactions between local authorities and companies and those who deal with them. Moreover, the development of the law of restitution means that, even where the contract is void or unenforceable, money paid and property transferred will, in general, be recoverable, unless this would amount to indirect enforcement of the contract.[3]

---

[1] See now *Lipkin Gorman* v. *Karpnale Ltd.* [1991] 2 A.C. 548, *ante*, p. 22.

[2] *Post*, pp. 212, 231.

[3] *Westdeutsche Landesbank Girozentrale* v. *Islington L.B.C.* [1994] 4 All E.R. 890, aff'd [1996] 2 A.C. 669 *post*, pp. 215, 225, 232, 235.

II. THE CROWN AND PUBLIC AUTHORITIES

(a) THE CROWN

(i) Application of public law

Since the passing of the Crown Proceedings Act 1947, actions by or against the Crown or a government department in contract are, for the most part, governed by the same rules of procedure as actions between subjects[4] and the same remedies are available, save that no injunction or order of specific performance can be made against the Crown in 'civil proceedings'.[5] Crown contracts are subject to the procurement procedures and remedies required by European Community law, which are considered later in this chapter.[6]

Although contracts made with government departments or Crown officers are not subject to the *ultra vires* doctrine,[7] rules which arise from the fact that such bodies have statutory and prerogative powers and duties of a public law nature affect contracts made by them. In both Crown contracts and the contracts of public authorities, it is therefore necessary to consider these public law rules as well as the common law and statutory position.

(ii) Parliamentary funds

In *Churchward* v. *The Queen*[8] the Admiralty undertook to pay C £18,000 a year for the carriage of cross-channel mails from Dover to Calais and Ostend. Appropriation of funds for this contract was expressly forbidden by Parliament. C sued for the promised sum but failed on the ground that the contract provided for payment to be 'out of moneys provided by Parliament' and no such moneys were provided. Shee J. went further, stating that 'the providing of funds by Parliament is a condition precedent to [the covenant] attaching'. On the basis of this *dicta* it has been said that 'all obligations to pay money undertaken by the Crown are subject to the implied condition that the funds necessary to satisfy the obligation shall be appropriated by Parliament',[9] but the better view is that the Crown is under no antecedent incapacity in this respect. Parliamentary approval, or the lack of it, in no way affects the validity of a Crown contract, and the provision of funds is simply a condition to be fulfilled before actual

---

[4] See generally Turpin, *Government Contracts* (1989); Arrowsmith, *The Law of Public and Utilities Procurement* (1996).

[5] Crown Proceedings Act 1947, s. 21. Although injunctive relief may be given in proceedings for judicial review: (*M.* v. *Home Office* [1994] 1 A.C. 377), judicial review is not generally available for disputes concerning contracts: *Mercury Energy Ltd.* v. *Electricity Cpn. of New Zealand Ltd.* [1994] 1 W.L.R. 521. cf. *Williams Construction Ltd.* v. *Blackman* [1995] 1 W.L.R. 102.

[6] *Post*, pp. 214–15.

[7] But the powers of certain Ministers have been defined by statute (e.g. Supply Powers Act 1975; Ministers of the Crown Act 1975) which may limit the capacity of the Crown (*Cugden Rutile (No. 2) Ltd.* v. *Chalk* [1975] A.C. 520) or the authority of its agents (*post*, p. 211).

[8] (1865) L.R. 1 Q.B. 173, at p. 210.

[9] *New South Wales* v. *The Commonwealth (No. 1)* (1932) 46 C.L.R. 155, at p. 176; *Att.-Gen.* v. *Great Southern and Western Ry. of Ireland* [1925] A.C. 754, at p.773.

payment by the Crown, a condition that is satisfied where there is a fund in existence out of which payment can lawfully be made.[10]

(iii) Fettering future executive action

It is an important principle of public law that public bodies, including the Crown, should preserve the discretionary powers granted to them by statute or the prerogative, and not divest themselves of those powers.[11] This principle may conflict, however, with the principle of sanctity of contracts. In *Rederiaktiebolaget Amphitrite* v. *The King* Rowlatt J. stated that 'It is not competent for the Government to fetter its future executive action, which must necessarily be determined by the needs of the community when the question arises. It cannot by contract hamper its freedom of action in matters which concern the welfare of the State'.[12] In that case:

During the First World War the British legation in Stockholm promised the Swedish owners of the ship *Amphitrite* that, if the ship sailed to England with an approved cargo, she would not be detained. The ship was nevertheless detained and her owners brought a petition of right against the Crown claiming breach of contract.

Rowlatt J. held that the guarantee was not a contract for the breach of which damages could be sued for in a court of law; it was merely an expression of intention to act in a particular way in a certain event, because the Crown could not fetter its future executive action by contract.

Rowlatt J.'s statement has been powerfully criticized on the ground that it is expressed too generally.[13] Three issues must be separated; the validity of the contract *ab initio*; secondly, whether, assuming the contract is valid, the Crown is thereafter under a duty to exercise its powers in a manner consistent with it; and thirdly, whether, assuming there is no valid contract, the Crown is nevertheless precluded from exercising its discretion in a particular way by an estoppel or the application of the emerging public law principle of legitimate expectation.[14]

As far as the first issue is concerned, Rowlatt J. acknowledged that the Crown can bind itself by a commercial contract.[15] *The Amphitrite* was not such a case, but the distinction between 'commercial' and 'non-commercial' contracts has been criticized as unworkable in practice because commercial contracts tend to conflict with 'governmental' obligations,[16] and it is difficult to see how, for instance, procurement contracts involving large capital expenditure are to be classified.

---

[10] *New South Wales* v. *Bardolph* (1934) 52 C.L.R. 455.

[11] See *post*, pp. 212–13, and see generally Wade and Forsyth, *Administrative Law*, 8th edn. (2000), p. 333 ff.

[12] [1921] 3 K.B. 500, at p. 503.

[13] *Robertson* v. *Minister of Pensions* [1949] 1 K.B. 227; *per* Denning J. at p. 231; *Ansett Transport Industries (Operations) Pty. Ltd.* v. *Commonwealth* (1977) 139 C.L.R. 54, at pp. 74, 113–14; *A* v. *Hayden (No. 2)* (1984) 56 A.L.R. 82, at p. 86 (Australia). But see *Commissioners of Crown Lands* v. *Page* [1960] 2 Q.B. 274, *per* Lord Evershed M.R. at p. 287.

[14] *Post*, p. 210.

[15] [1921] 3 K.B. 500, at p. 503. See also *Robertson* v. *Minister of Pensions* [1949] 1 K.B. 22; *per* Denning J. at p.231. Estoppels may arise in respect of such contracts: *Att.-Gen. of Hong Kong* v. *Humphreys Estate (Queen's Gardens)* [1987] A.C. 114, at pp. 127–8.

[16] Mitchell, *The Contracts of Public Authorities* (1954), p. 62. See also *Ansett Transport Industries (Operations) Pty. Ltd.* v. *Commonwealth* (1977) 139 C.L.R. 54, at p. 113.

Where a Crown contract has been validly entered into, the Crown's freedom to exercise its discretionary powers (whether statutory or prerogative) will not, as a matter of construction, be impliedly excluded by the contract. Even in the case of commercial contracts, the Crown must be free to exercise the discretionary powers conferred upon it for the public good. 'No one can imagine, for example, that when the Crown makes a contract which could not be fulfilled in time of war, it is pledging itself not to declare war for so long as the contract lasts.'[17] Thus, it has been held that an *implied* covenant for quiet enjoyment in a Crown lease did not prevent the Crown from requisitioning the premises.[18] The Crown must be at liberty to detain ships, to requisition property, or to perform other essential acts in time of war, and, although the position of an *express* undertaking is less clear,[19] it is submitted that 'no contract would be enforced in any case where some essential governmental activity would be thereby rendered impossible or seriously impeded'.[20] Furthermore, in such cases, a party is unlikely to be able to invoke the principle of estoppel; it is generally recognized that 'estoppel cannot be allowed to hinder the formation of government policy'.[21] A negligent misstatement by the Crown may, however, give rise to liability in tort.[22]

In practice the rule stated in *The Amphitrite* does not often have to be applied since many contracts falling within its scope contain cancellation clauses which usually make provision for compensation.[23]

(iv) Liability of Crown to employees

The general rule is that persons in Crown employment hold office during the pleasure of the Crown, and at common law Crown servants can be dismissed at any time by the Crown and no action lies for wrongful dismissal.[24] In the older cases the reason given for this rule was that the relationship between the Crown and its servants is not one of contract at all, but of status.[25] But this may in fact reflect the absence of an intention to contract on the part of the Crown and more recently it has been said that 'there is nothing unconstitutional about civil servants being employed by the Crown pursuant

---

[17] *Commissioners of Crown Lands* v. *Page* (*supra*, n. 13), *per* Devlin L.J. at p. 292.

[18] *Ibid.*

[19] Devlin L.J. *ibid.*, at p. 292 thought nothing turned on this but Evershed M.R. and Ormrod L.J. reserved their position. Devlin L.J.'s view is inferentially supported in *Ansett Transport Industries (Operations) Pty. Ltd.* v. *Commonwealth* (*supra*, n. 16).

[20] Mitchell, *The Contracts of Public Authorities* (1954), p.7. Cf. Holdsworth (1929) 45 L.Q.R. 166.

[21] *Laker Airways Ltd.* v. *Department of Trade* [1977] Q.B. 643, at pp. 680–2, 707, 709, 728; *Hughes* v. *D.H.S.S.* [1985] A.C. 776.

[22] *Ministry of Housing and Local Government* v. *Sharp* [1970] 2 Q.B. 223. Cf. *Yuen Kun Yeu* v. *Att.-Gen. of Hong Kong* [1988] A.C. 175.

[23] See generally Turpin, (*supra*, n. 4), at pp. 243–6.

[24] *Shenton* v. *Smith* [1895] A.C. 229; *Dunn* v. *The Queen* [1896] 1 Q.B. 116; *Terrell* v. *Colonial Secretary* [1953] 2 Q.B. 482; *Riordan* v. *War Office* [1959] 1 W.L.R. 1046; *Att.-Gen. for Guyana* v. *Nobrega* [1969] 3 All E.R. 1064; *Thomas* v. *Att.-Gen. of Trinidad and Tobago* [1982] A.C. 113. Cf. *Reilly* v. *R.* [1934] A.C. 176, at p. 179 but note *Terrell* v. *Secretary of State for the Colonies* [1953] 2 Q.B. 482, at pp. 498–9.

[25] *Shenton* v. *Smith* (*supra*, n. 24); *Rodwell* v. *Thomas* [1944] K.B. 596; *Inland Revenue Commissioners* v. *Hambrook* [1956] 2 Q.B. 641.

to contracts of service'.[26] The modern and better view is that there can be a valid contract of employment, although this is always determinable at the pleasure of the Crown.[27] But there are conflicting decisions as to whether the use of language of obligation or even of the word 'contract' suffices to indicate an intention by the Crown to enter into a contractual relationship.[28]

Whether or not the relation is contractual, the power of the Crown to dismiss at pleasure without payment of compensation is now limited by statute. The remedies available for unfair dismissal now contained in the Employment Rights Act 1996 extend to Crown employees, including members of the military services.[29]

Although dismissal in breach of the terms of the appointment will not, according to the bulk of the authorities, give rise to a cause of action at common law, it may be susceptible to the public law remedy of judicial review where it is *ultra vires*, an abuse of discretion, or where the principles of procedural fairness have not been observed.[30]

(v) Liability of employees to Crown

Where an intention to contract is established, it is submitted that the Crown can sue its employees for breach of contract.[31] Equitable and restitutionary remedies may also be available against the employees in certain circumstances, such as breach of confidence, or where the employee has profited from a breach of duty.[32]

(vi) Crown agents

If a servant or agent of the Crown enters into an unauthorized contract, the Crown will not be bound unless it has held the agent out to have authority.[33] 'The right to act for the Crown in any particular matter must be established by statute or otherwise'.[34] It is only if the act is within the agent's ostensible authority that the Crown may be estopped from going back on a representation which the agent has made.[35] Furthermore, an agent of the Crown who contracts on behalf of the Crown cannot be sued, either on the contract or for breach of warranty of authority.[36]

---

[26] *R.* v. *Civil Service Board, ex. parte Bruce* [1988] I.C.R. 649, *per* May L.J. at p. 660, aff'd [1989] I.C.R. 171.

[27] *Kodeeswaran* v. *Att.-Gen. of Ceylon* [1970] A.C. 1111, at p. 1123.

[28] Cf. *McClaren* v. *Home Office* [1990] I.C.R. 84 (no contract) and *R.* v. *Lord Chancellor's Department, ex parte Nangle* [1991] I.C.R. 743 (contract).

[29] Employment Rights Act 1996, s. 192. See also Trade Union and Labour Relations (Consolidation) Act 1992, ss. 152, 273 (dismissal on grounds of trade union membership, activities, or non-membership).

[30] *R.* v. *Secretary of State for the Home Department, ex parte Benwell* [1985] Q.B. 554; *Council of Civil Service Unions* v. *Minister for the Civil Service* [1985] 1 A.C. 374. See also Walsh [1989] P.L. 131; Fredman and Morris (1991) 107 L.Q.R. 298; [1991] P.L. 485. On estoppel, see *ante*, pp. 112, 118; *post*, p. 213.

[31] But see *Fisher* v. *Steward* (1920) 36 T.L.R. 395. The terms are deemed to constitute a contract for the purposes of the economic torts: Trade Union and Labour Relations (Consolidation) Act 1992, s. 245.

[32] *Att.-Gen.* v. *Blake* [2001] 1 A.C. 268.

[33] *Att.-Gen. for Ceylon* v. *Silva* [1953] A.C. 461; *Robertson* v. *Minister of Pensions* [1949] 1 K.B. 227; *per* Denning J. at p. 231.

[34] *Ibid.*, at p. 479.

[35] *Robertson* v. *Minister of Pensions* [1949] K.B. 227. But contrast *ibid.*, at p. 232, and see *Re L. (an infant)* [1971] 3 All. ER. 743; *Laker Airways Ltd.* v. *Department of Trade* [1977] Q.B. 643. See also, *post*, p. 213.

[36] *Dunn* v. *Macdonald* [1897] 1 Q.B. 555 criticized by Wade and Forsyth, *Administrative Law*, 8th edn. (2000), pp. 813–14. Cf. the position of other agents, *post*, pp. 687, 691.

(b) PUBLIC AUTHORITIES

(i) Doctrine of ultra vires

Public authorities whose powers are the product of and defined by statute are subject to the doctrine of *ultra vires*, which is a necessary consequence of the statutory nature of the powers of such authorities. So, at common law the contracts of local authorities will be void unless they relate to functions which the authority is authorized, expressly or impliedly, to perform, or unless the acts are calculated to facilitate, or are incidental to, the discharge of those functions.[37]

The purpose of the *ultra vires* rule is to protect the public funds entrusted to such bodies, in the case of local authorities, by local taxpayers. But it has proved a trap for the unwary and can inflict grave hardship on persons who deal *bona fide* with an authority in ignorance of its lack of capacity. So banks which participated in housing or recreational schemes by local authorities either as a joint venturer or a guarantor, and other banks which entered into interest rate swaps with local authorities, could not sue on their contracts when they were held to be *ultra vires*.[38] The result was uncertainty and concern that private sector companies would be reluctant to enter into transactions with local authorities.

(ii) Statutory modification of ultra vires doctrine

The Local Government (Contracts) Act 1997 governs contracts by local authorities for the purposes of or in connection with the discharge of any of their functions which are intended to operate for a period of at least five years. Section 2 provides that where a local authority has issued a certificate stating that it has power to enter into the contract and containing information about the statutory provisions conferring the power and the purpose of the contract, the contract has effect 'as if the local authority had had power to enter into it (and exercised that power properly in entering into it)'. The purpose of the legislation is to render contracts enforceable, and it will still be possible to challenge the power of an authority to enter a contract in judicial review proceedings or an audit of the authority's activities.[39]

(iii) Incompatibility with statutory purpose

Those dealing with public authorities may also encounter the rule considered above that a public authority is not competent to fetter a statutory discretion if this would disable it from fulfilling the primary purpose for which it was created. 'If a person or public body is entrusted by the legislature with certain powers and duties expressly or impliedly for public purposes, those persons or bodies cannot divest themselves of these powers and duties. They cannot enter into any contract or take any action

---

[37] See, e.g. *Hazell* v. *Hammersmith & Fulham L.B.C.* [1992] 2 A.C. 1; *Credit Suisse* v. *Allerdale B.C. and Waltham Forest L.B.C.* [1997] Q.B. 306 and 362. But see Local Government Act 1972, s. 137, and cf. *ibid.*, s.161. See also *ibid.*, s. 135.

[38] *Hazell* v. *Hammersmith & Fulham L.B.C.* (*supra*, n. 37) and *Credit Suisse* v. *Allerdale B.C. and Waltham Forest L.B.C.* (*supra*, n. 37).

[39] Local Government (Contracts) Act 1997, s. 5.

incompatible with the due exercise of their powers or the discharge of their duties'.[40] Thus in *York Corporation* v. *Henry Leetham & Sons*:[41]

Y entered into a covenant with H.L. to allow them to use two rivers which Y maintained and managed under statutory authority in return for an annual payment of £800 in place of the tolls Y was authorized to charge by the statute.

It was held that this covenant was not one which Y was competent to make because it thereby disabled itself from exercising its statutory powers to increase tolls as necessary in order to perform its statutory duty.

On the other hand, in *Birkdale District Electric Supply Co.* v. *Southport Corporation*:[42]

B, the statutory undertaker for the supply of electricity in Birkdale, was sued by S on an agreement by which B had bound itself not to charge higher prices for electricity than those charged in the borough of Southport. It repudiated this agreement on the ground that it was incompatible with the due discharge of its statutory duties.

The House of Lords held that the agreement was nevertheless binding upon B. It was not wholly incompatible with the fulfilment of the purposes of the statute which empowered B to act as an electricity undertaking. The distinction between this case and the *York Corporation* case is by no means clear but it would seem that a public authority is only incompetent to contract where the contract in question is clearly proved to be incompatible with the full observance of the terms and the full attainment of the purposes for which the statutory powers have been granted. But it possesses contractual capacity where the agreements are mere contracts restricting the undertakers' freedom of action in respect of the business management of their undertaking.[43]

(iv) Estoppel and legitimate expectation

A public authority cannot be estopped by its previous conduct so as to hinder its obligation to carry out its statutory powers or duties. But it has been held that a defect in procedure can be cured, so, if an officer, acting within the scope of his ostensible authority, purports to waive an irregularity, on which another person acts, the public authority may be bound by it.[44]

A public authority may also be under a public law duty to act consistently with an arrangement which does not give rise to a contract or an estoppel. This is because a person who, as a result of the words or conduct of a public authority, has a legitimate

---

[40] *Birkdale District Electric Supply Co.* v. *Southport Cpn.* [1926] A.C. 355, *per* Lord Birkenhead at p. 364. But see *Lever (Finance) Ltd.* v. *Westminster Cpn.* [1971] 1 Q.B. 222 (estoppel).

[41] [1924] 1 Ch. 557. See also *Ayr Harbour Trustees* v. *Oswald* (1883) 8 App. Cas. 623; *Cory (William) & Son Ltd.* v. *London Cpn.* [1951] 2 K.B. 476; *Dowty Boulton Paul Ltd.* v. *Wolverhampton Cpn.* [1976] Ch. 13.

[42] [1926] A.C. 355.

[43] *Ibid., per* Lord Sumner at pp. 369, 370.

[44] *Lever (Finance) Ltd.* v. *Westminster Corp.* [1971] 1 Q.B. 222; *Western Fish Products Ltd.* v. *Penwith D.C.* [1981] 2 All E.R. 204.

expectation that a benefit will be granted or continue to be enjoyed, may be able to argue that later inconsistent action is an abuse of power and reviewable on the ground of unfairness.[45] Inconsistency is, however, not necessarily unfair, and the Courts will not let an arrangement that has given rise to a legitimate expectation hinder the formation of policy. For example, an authority that has received and resolved to receive a tender from its own workforce might choose to abandon the project or seek fresh tenders.[46]

(v) Pre-contractual procedures and refusal to contract

Although the general rule, based upon the principle of freedom of contract, is that a person can choose with whom to contract and with whom not to contract,[47] in the case of public authorities this freedom is limited. Both legislation and the regulations implementing European Community Directives on public sector contracts, and the general principles governing the exercise of discretionary powers may invalidate refusals to contract at all or only on particular terms. Such refusals may be based on a policy that amounts to an improper fetter on an authority's discretion or be 'unfair' in the light of an individual's legitimate expectations. For instance, a decision not to contract with a company in part motivated by the wish to induce it to cease trading with South Africa during the apartheid era was held to be *ultra vires*.[48]

(vi) Statutory and E.C. controls

Under the Local Government Act 1988, local authorities are required to exercise their contracting functions (including invitations to tender) without reference to 'non-commercial matters'.[49] Under the Local Government Act 1999 local authorities are required to 'make arrangements to secure continuous improvement in the way in which [their] functions are exercised, having regard to a combination of economy, efficiency and effectiveness'.[50] The Act and any regulations made under it give government extensive powers to require local and other authorities to achieve 'best value' by a programme of contracting out.[51] The Secretary of State is also empowered to provide that a specified matter cease to be a 'non-commercial matter' for the purposes of section 17 of the Local Government Act 1988.

Public authorities (broadly defined so as to include all bodies 'governed by public law') must, furthermore, not discriminate against nationals or products of other

---

[45] *Council for Civil Service Unions* v. *Minister for the Civil Service* [1985] A.C. 374, at p. 408.

[46] *R.* v. *Walsall M.B.C., ex parte Yapp* [1994] I.C.R. 528. See also *Hughes* v. *D.H.S.S.* [1985] A.C. 776.

[47] But there may be a requirement to conform to specified tendering requirements; *Blackpool and Fylde Aero Club* v. *Blackpool B.C.* [1990] 1 W.L.R. 1195, *ante*, p. 34. See also *R.* v. *Lord Chancellor, ex parte Hibbert & Saunders* [1993] C.O.D. 326.

[48] *R.* v. *Lewisham L.B.C., ex parte Shell U.K. Ltd.* [1988] 1 All E.R. 938. See also *Mercury Ltd.* v. *Electricity Corp.* [1994] 1 W.L.R. 521 (reviewability of termination of contract).

[49] s. 17. See *R.* v. *Islington L.B.C., ex parte Building Employers Confederation* [1989] I.R.L.R. 383; *R.* v. *Enfield L.B.C., ex parte T.F. Unwin (Roydon) Ltd.* (1989) 46 Build.L.R. 1. See also Local Government Act 1972, s. 135; Environmental Protection Act 1990, s. 51.

[50] Section 3(1).

[51] *Ibid.*, section 18.

European Community states in awarding major contracts.[52] To this end publicity in the form of Community-wide advertising and standard tendering procedures are required, non-discriminatory specifications and standards must be used, and authorities are required either to accept the lowest price or the 'most economically advantageous' tender. Where a contract has been awarded in breach of these requirements, the only remedy open to a disappointed tenderer is to bring proceedings for damages within three months.[53] Once concluded, the contract between the public authority and the successful tenderer cannot be set aside on the application of a third party.[54]

(vii) Recovery of payments made under void contracts

Payments made under an *ultra vires* contract with a public authority, whether made to or by the incapacitated party, are recoverable in a restitutionary action,[55] although where, as in the interest swaps cases, payments have been made both ways, restitution is only available to a party on the basis that credit is given for what has been received.[56]

III. MINORS

By section 1 of the Family Law Reform Act 1969 the age of majority was lowered from 21 to 18. All persons under that age are known technically as minors (or infants). On attaining their majority they legally become adults. The rights and liabilities of minors under contracts entered into by them during minority rest upon common law rules as altered by the Minors Contracts Act 1987.[57] The desire to protect minors on the one hand and the wish to safeguard the interests of traders on the other has led to a complicated body of law.

(a) COMMON LAW: INTRODUCTION

At common law, the only class of contract to which minority did not afford some sort of defence was a contract for 'necessaries' in the sense to be explained later. In all other cases, common law treated a minor's contracts as being voidable at the option of the

---

[52] 93/36, 93/37, 93/38 E.E.C. O.J. L199/1, 54, 84, implemented by the Public Works Contracts Regulations 1991 (S.I. 1991 No. 2060); Public Supply Contracts Regulations 1991 (S.I. 1991 No. 2679); Utility Supply and Works Contracts Regulations 1992 (S.I. 1992 No. 3279); Public Services Contracts Regulations 1993 (S.I. 1993 No. 3228); Utility Contracts Regulations 1996 (S.I. 1996 No. 2911), amended by Public Contracts (Works Services and Supply) (Amendment) Regulations 2000 (S.I. 2000 No. 2009). See generally Arrowsmith, *The Law of Public and Utilities Procurement* (1996).

[53] S.I. 1993 No. 3228, reg. 32(4)(b). See *Matra Communications S.A.S.* v. *Home Office* [1999] 1 W.L.R. 1646; *R.* v. *Tower Hamlets L.B.C., ex parte Luck* (1999) 15 Const. L.J. 235.

[54] See, e.g. S.I. 1991 No. 2679, reg. 26(2), (5)(b); S.I. 1992 No. 3279, reg. 30(1), (5)(b)(ii); S.I. 1993 No 3228 reg. 32(b).

[55] *Westdeutsche Landesbank Girozentrale* v. *Islington L.B.C.* [1994] 4 All E.R. 890, aff'd [1996] 2 A.C. 669; *Woolwich B.S.* v. *I.R.C.* [1993] A.C. 70; *Guinness Mahon & Co. Ltd.* v. *Kensington & Chelsea L.B.C.* [1999] Q.B. 215.

[56] *Ibid.*

[57] Implementing the recommendations in Law Com. No. 134, *Minors' Contracts* (1984).

minor, either before or after becoming an adult. But these voidable contracts were divided into two classes.

First, contracts in which the minor acquired an interest of a permanent or continuous nature were binding until the minor *disclaimed* them, either during minority or within a reasonable time after becoming an adult. An example of such contract is one by which a minor acquired an interest in land. These will be referred to as 'positive voidable contracts'.

Secondly, the common law rule for contracts which were not thus continuous in their operation, was that they were not binding on a minor unless ratified within a reasonable time after majority. So, for example, a promise by a minor to perform an isolated act, such as to pay for goods supplied other than necessaries, or for work and labour done, required an express ratification after majority before the minor would be bound. These will be referred to as 'negative voidable contracts'.[58]

Since, at common law, both these classes of contracts were only voidable at the option of the minor and not wholly void, there was no objection to the minor enforcing them, though the other party could not enforce them. But a minor's position differed from that of parties of full contractual capacity in that he or she might recover damages for breach but not obtain specific performance of the contract.[59] Specific performance is granted at the discretion of the Court, which will not grant it where it would not be prepared to enforce the contract at the suit of either party.[60] Since the contract could not be enforced against the minor, equity would not allow the minor to obtain specific performance against the other party.

(b) CONTRACTS FOR NECESSARIES AND OTHER BENEFICIAL CONTRACTS

It has already been stated that, at common law, the only class of contract which was not voidable at the option of a minor was a contract for 'necessaries'.[61] The meaning of the term 'necessaries', however, requires further explanation. We first consider contracts for necessary goods, and then contracts of employment or training, and then other agreements beneficial to the minor.

Part of the common law on this matter has been given statutory form by section 3 of the Sale of Goods Act 1979. This provides:

(1) Capacity to buy and sell is regulated by the general law concerning capacity to contract and to transfer and acquire property.

(2) Where necessaries are sold and delivered to a minor or to a person who by reason of

---

[58] It is, perhaps, strictly misleading to refer to these contracts as 'voidable' for the essence of a voidable contract is that it is binding unless repudiated whereas these contracts were not binding unless affirmed. However, the terminology is a convenient one, and it would be inadvisable to reject it merely on purist grounds.

[59] *Flight* v. *Bolland* (1828) 4 Russ 298.

[60] Cf. *post*, 639.

[61] But such a contract may be held invalid if the minor was not capable of understanding the nature of the transaction: see *R.* v. *Oldham Metropolitan Borough Council* [1993] 1 F.L.R. 645, *per* Scott L.J. at pp. 661–2.

mental incapacity or drunkenness is incompetent to contract, he must pay a reasonable price for them.

(3) In subsection (2) above 'necessaries' mean goods suitable to the condition in life of the minor or other person concerned and to his actual requirements at the time of the sale and delivery.

(i) What are necessaries?

We must first consider what the word 'necessaries' includes. It has always been held that a minor may be liable for the supply, not merely of the necessaries of life, but of things suitable to his or her station in life and particular circumstances at the time. Minors are liable for *necessaries*, and not merely for *necessities*.[62] Certain things may be obviously outside the range of possible necessaries. So in *Ryder* v. *Wombwell*:[63]

W, a minor with an income of £500 a year, bought from R a pair of crystal, ruby, and diamond solitaires and an antique goblet in silver gilt.

It was held that neither of these articles could be a necessary, even though W was the son of a deceased baronet and 'moved in the highest society'. Other things may be of a useful character but the quality or quantity supplied may take them out of the character of necessaries. In *Nash* v. *Inman*:[64]

A tailor supplied a Cambridge undergraduate with clothing which included 11 fancy waist-coats at 2 guineas each. It was proved that, although he was a minor, he had already a sufficient supply of clothing according to his position in life.

The Court of Appeal held that the tailor had failed to prove that the clothing was suitable to the undergraduate's actual requirements at the time of the sale and delivery.

Necessaries also vary according to the minor's station in life or peculiar circumstances at the time of the contract.[65] The Court must take into consideration the character of the goods supplied, the actual circumstances of the minor, and the extent to which the minor was already supplied with them. It is necessary to emphasize the words 'actual circumstances', because a false impression conveyed to the person dealing with the minor as to the station and circumstances of the minor will not affect the minor's liability. A shop which supplies expensive goods to a minor thinking that the minor's circumstances are better than they really are, or which supplies goods of a useful class not knowing that the minor is already sufficiently supplied, does so at its peril.[66]

The Sale of Goods Act 1979, section 3, also requires that the goods should be necessary to the minor 'at the time of the sale *and* delivery'. This might seem to indicate that the seller would have to prove them to be necessary at both of these

[62] The Law Commission did not consider that the narrowing of the category in this way was, on balance, desirable: Law Com. No. 134, *Minors' Contracts* (1984), §§ 5.4–5.6.

[63] *Ryder* v. *Wombwell* (1868) L.R. 3 Ex. 90, aff'd (1869) L.R. 4 Ex. 32.

[64] [1908] 2 K.B. 1.

[65] *Peters* v. *Fleming* (1840) 6 M. & W. 42.

[66] The burden of proof is on the supplier: *Nash* v. *Inman* (*supra*, n. 64), at p. 5.

times. But, it is probable that this is simply a reference to the action for goods sold and delivered, which is the normal action for a seller who wishes to recover the purchase price.[67] The seller would have to prove them to be necessary at the time of their delivery alone.

(ii) Loans for necessaries

A loan of money to a minor to pay for necessaries was not recoverable at common law, for 'it may be borrowed for necessaries, but laid out and spent at a tavern'.[68] But in equity it was held that if a minor borrowed money to pay a debt for necessaries, and the debt was actually paid therewith, the lender stood in the place of the person paid and was entitled to recover the money lent.[69] This rule is a branch of the equitable doctrine of subrogation. It is not possible, however, to sue a minor on a negotiable instrument given for the price of necessaries, even though it may have been negotiated to a third party.[70] Also, an account stated with a minor is still void although the items in the account may consist of necessaries.[71]

(iii) Contracts of employment and training

A minor may enter into a contract of employment so as to earn a living or into a contract for the purpose of obtaining instruction or education so as to qualify for a suitable trade or profession whereby he or she may profit himself afterwards.[72] Provided that they are beneficial to the minor, these contracts are binding. In *Clements* v. *London and North Western Railway Company*,[73] a minor entered into a contract of employment with a railway company, promising to accept the terms of an insurance against accidents in lieu of his rights of action under the Employers' Liability Act 1880. It was held that the contract was, taken as a whole, for his benefit and that he was bound by his promise.

On the other hand, a contract of this class which is more onerous than beneficial to the minor will impose no liability. So in *De Francesco* v. *Barnum*:[74]

B, aged 14 years, agreed to become De F's apprentice in 'the art of choreography' for 7 years. De F was to teach her stage dancing, and during the period of apprenticeship B was not to take any professional engagement without the consent of De F, nor was she to marry. She was to receive certain payments for any performances she might give, but there was no provision for any other remuneration and De F did not undertake to find her any engagements. The effect of the deed was to place B entirely at the disposal of De F.

Fry L.J. held that the contract was not beneficial to B and was unenforceable. It should, however, be noted that even though a minor's contract of service contains

---

[67] *Post*, p. 222. See also Winfield (1942) 58 L.Q.R. 82, at p. 90.
[68] *Earle* v. *Peale* (1711) 1 Salk. 386 (except where necessaries are purchased at minor's request).
[69] *Marlow* v. *Pitfeild* (1719) 1 Peere Wms. 558.
[70] *Re Soltykoff, ex parte Margrett* [1891] 1 Q.B. 413. Cf. Bills of Exchange Act 1882, s. 22.
[71] *Williams* v. *Moor* (1843) 11 M. & W. 256.
[72] Co. Litt. 172a.
[73] [1894] 2 Q.B. 482, at p. 491.
[74] (1890) 45 Ch. D. 430. See also *Leng (Sir W. C.) & Co.* v. *Andrews* [1909] 1 Ch. 763.

some terms which are not for the benefit of the minor, the minor cannot necessarily repudiate it, still less select which terms will or will not be followed. 'The Court must look at the whole contract, having regard to the circumstances of the case, and determine . . . whether the contract is or is not beneficial'.[75]

(iv) Other beneficial contracts

The class of contracts under consideration is not, however, limited to contracts of employment and training. It includes numerous contracts for 'necessaries' other than goods, for example, for medical attendance,[76] for the preparation of a marriage settlement by a solicitor,[77] or the hire of a car to fetch a minor's luggage from the railway station.[78] Provided that these are reasonable and beneficial to the minor, the other party can enforce them. Yet the class does not include ordinary trading contracts, as, for instance, the hire-purchase of a motor lorry by a haulage contractor who is a minor.[79] Such contracts may be necessary to the minor's business, and so of benefit to the minor, but they are not binding. Thus, in *Cowern* v. *Nield*,[80] a contract to sell a consignment of hay by a hay and straw dealer who was a minor was held not to be a contract for 'necessaries' because it was a trading contract.

The class is thus a limited one although the limits are not easy to state. In *Doyle* v. *White City Stadium Ltd.*,[81] for instance:

A professional boxer, who was a minor, in consideration of his receiving a licence from the British Boxing Board of Control, agreed to be bound by the rules of the Board in all his professional engagements. A purse of £3,000 was withheld from him by the Board, in accordance with its rules, on the ground that he had been disqualified in a contest for hitting below the belt.

It was held that the agreement was binding on him despite his being a minor. The ground of this decision was that the licence was practically essential in order to enable him to become proficient in his profession, and when the conditions attached to the issue of the licence were incorporated in a particular beneficial contract of employment—in this case, an engagement to box for a heavyweight championship—both contracts became binding on the minor, as they were both for his benefit. Also in *Chaplin* v. *Leslie Frewin (Publishers) Ltd.*:[82]

C, a minor who was the son of Charlie Chaplin, had been eking out a Bohemian existence in London. In return for an advance of royalties, he assigned to LF publishers the exclusive right to publish an autobiography of himself (entitled *I Couldn't Smoke the Grass on my*

---

[75] *Ibid.*, at p. 439. See also *Slade* v. *Metrodent Ltd.* [1953] 2 Q.B. 112.
[76] *Dale* v. *Copping* (1610) 1 Bulst. 39. See also *Gillick* v. *W. Norfolk and Wisbech Area Health Authority* [1986] 1 A.C. 112, at pp. 166–7, 183, 195.
[77] *Helps* v. *Clayton* (1864) 17 C.B.N.S. 553.
[78] *Fawcett* v. *Smethurst* (1914) 84 L.J.K.B. 473.
[79] *Mercantile Union Guarantee Corporation* v. *Ball* [1937] 2 K.B. 498.
[80] [1912] 2 K.B. 419.
[81] [1935] 1 K.B. 110.
[82] [1966] Ch. 71 (Lord Denning M.R. dissenting).

Father's Lawn) which was to be written by 'ghost' writers. The completed work, so he alleged, showed him to be 'a depraved creature', and he sought to repudiate the assignment.

The Court of Appeal held that he could not do so. The contract was binding on him since it was one which enabled him to make a start as an author and thus to earn money to keep himself and his wife.[83] It was a beneficial contract, because, as Danckwerts L.J. put it,[84] 'The mud may cling but the profits will be secured'.

The judgments in these two cases do not set out to define the contracts which are binding when beneficial to a minor, but they perhaps indicate a tendency to enlarge the class; for the contracts which the minors had made were arguably merely incidental to the carrying on of a trade or profession and therefore of a kind which had not hitherto been believed to be binding, even when beneficial.

(c) NEGATIVE VOIDABLE CONTRACTS

As explained above, a negative voidable contract is one which is made during minority and which will not bind the minor at common law unless ratified by the minor within a reasonable time after attaining majority. Generally, such contracts were one-offs and not continuous in nature. Until recently this common law rule was displaced by statute which made it impossible for a person of full age to be sued on a contract entered into during minority, even though he or she had ratified such a contract and even though there was some new consideration for the ratification.[85] However, this did not stop the minor enforcing the contract against the other party. The repeal of that statute means that the common law rule as it existed prior to the legislation has again become the law.

This class of contracts is large; it includes all contracts other than contracts for necessaries and contracts falling within the 'positive voidable' category.

(d) POSITIVE VOIDABLE CONTRACTS

A minor who acquires an interest in permanent property to which obligations attach, or enters into a contract involving continuous rights and duties, benefits and liabilities, and takes some benefit under the contract, will be bound, unless he or she expressly disclaims the contract during the minority or within a reasonable time of coming of age.

Examples of such contracts are the acquisition of an interest in land (such as a lease or tenancy), and of shares in a company. Up to the time that the minor disclaims such a contract he or she will be bound to carry out the obligations under it, provided that

---

[83] The Court also held that, even if the contract had been voidable by the minor, it could not have been rescinded because it had been executed by the transfer of the copyright.

[84] At p. 95.

[85] See Infants Relief Act 1874, s. 2 (now repealed) discussed in A.G. Guest, *Anson's Law of Contract*, 26th edn. (1984), pp. 184–92.

these accrue before repudiation.[86] A minor cannot renounce the liabilities until he or she renounces the interest. So a lessee who is a minor is liable for rent until the lease is disclaimed,[87] and if a shareholder, is under a similar liability in respect of calls on the shares until they are expressly repudiated.[88]

(i) Partnership

The position of a member of a partnership who is a minor differs from that of a shareholder. It is true that partnership is a continuous relationship between the partners, but by becoming a partner a minor does not acquire an interest in a subject of a permanent nature to which obligations are attached. During the minority of a partner, the minor is not liable for debts incurred by the partnership; but equally is not entitled to any share of the partnership assets until the firm's debts have been paid.[89] A minor who continues to act as a partner after majority will be liable, equally with the other partners, for the debts subsequently incurred. A minor may also be liable for such debts if, though ceasing to act as a partner, he or she gives no adequate notice of this withdrawal to persons dealing with the firm.[90] The minor's liability in this case, however, merely illustrates a general rule of the law of partnership applicable to any retired partner, and does not depend on any principle peculiar to the law of minors.

(ii) Time of disclaimer

In order that a minor's disclaimer of a permanent interest may take effect, the contract must be repudiated during minority or within a reasonable time of the minor's coming of age. What is a reasonable time will depend upon the circumstances of each particular case. In *Edwards* v. *Carter*[91] the House of Lords held that a minor who entered into a marriage settlement and covenanted to bring into the settlement any property which might come to him under his father's will could not repudiate it nearly five years after coming of age and one year after his father died leaving him property by will.

(iii) Effect of disclaimer

The effect of a valid disclaimer of a contract that binds until repudiated is to release the minor from future obligations under it. A minor who has paid to the other party in the mistaken belief that the contract is enforceable may be able to recover the payment.[92] But in the absence of such a mistake the minor will not be able to recover

---

[86] There is some doubt as to whether a minor is bound to pay unpaid calls which accrued due before the repudiation, but the better opinion is that he is so bound. See *Cork & Bandon Ry.* v. *Cazenove* (1847) 10 Q.B. 935. Cf. *N.W. Ry.* v. *M'Michael* (*infra*, n. 88), at p.125, and *Newry and Enniskillen Ry.* v. *Coombe* (1849) 3 Exch. 565.

[87] *Blake* v. *Concannon* (1870) 4 Ir. Rep. C.L. 320. By the Law of Property Act 1925, ss. 1(6), 19 a minor can no longer hold a legal estate in land; but can have an equitable interest, and so be bound in the same way: *Davies* v. *Benyon-Harris* (1931) 47 T.L.R. 424.

[88] *Steinberg* v. *Scala (Leeds) Ltd.* [1923] 2 Ch. 452, at p. 463; *North Western Railway Co.* v. *M'Michael* (1850) 5 Exch. 114, aff'd *sub nom. L. & N. W. Ry* v. *M'Michael* (1850) 5 Exch. 855.

[89] *Lovell and Christmas* v. *Beauchamp* [1894] A.C. 607.

[90] *Goode* v. *Harrison* (1821) 5 B. & Ald. 147.

[91] [1893] A.C. 360. See also *Carnell* v. *Harrison* [1916] 1 Ch. 328.

[92] *Kleinwort Benson Ltd.* v. *Lincoln C.C.* [1999] 2 A.C. 349.

anything unless there has been a total failure of the consideration for which the money has been paid. Where, for example shares have been allotted to the minor, money paid for them will be irrecoverable whether or not a dividend has been paid or any other real advantage received.[93] The minor will have received something which had a marketable value and which was the very consideration for which he or she had bargained.

(e) THE NATURE OF THE LIABILITY OF MINORS

Where there is an enforceable obligation against a minor, for example, for necessaries, it remains to characterize that obligation. Two theories have been put forward.

(i) Liability in restitution

The first is that the liability arises in restitution rather than contract. The obligation is imposed by the law because the minor has actually received the benefit of performance, and not as consensually a result of entering a valid contract. This was the view taken by Fletcher Moulton L.J. in *Nash* v. *Inman*:[94]

An infant, like a lunatic, is incapable of making a contract of purchase in the strict sense of the words; but if a man satisfies the needs of the infant or lunatic by supplying to him necessaries, the law will imply an obligation to repay him for the services so rendered, and will enforce that obligation against the estate of the infant or lunatic. The consequence is that the basis of the action is hardly contract. Its real foundation is an obligation which the law imposes on the infant to make a fair payment in respect of needs satisfied.

(ii) Liability in contract

The second theory is that the liability is contractual. The minor can, it is said, enter into a valid contract for necessaries just like any other person. 'The plaintiff', said Buckley L.J. in the same case:[95]

when he sues the defendant for goods supplied during infancy, is suing him in contract on the footing that the contract was such as the infant, notwithstanding infancy, could make. The defendant, although he was an infant, had a limited capacity to contract. In order to maintain his action the plaintiff must prove that the contract sued on is within that limited capacity.

The problem is not academic since, unless the liability is contractual in nature, the minor will not be liable where the contract is executory. In the case of necessary goods, section 3 of the Sale of Goods Act 1979 indicates that the obligation is restitutionary. It deals only with 'necessaries sold and delivered', and says nothing of necessaries sold to a minor and not delivered, that is to say, of a contract of sale which is still

---

[93] *Steinberg* v. *Scala (Leeds) Ltd.* [1923] 2 Ch. 452. See also *Holmes* v. *Blogg* (1818) 8 Taunt. 508.

[94] [1908] 2 K.B. 1, at p. 8; *Re Rhodes* (1890) 44 Ch. D. 94, at p. 105; *Re J.* [1909] 1 Ch. 574, at p. 577; *Elkington* v. *Amery* [1936] 2 All E.R. 86, at p. 88.

[95] At p. 12. See also *Gillick* v. *West Norfolk Area Health Authority* [1986] A.C. 112, at p. 169 (child could enter into a 'contract').

executory.[96] There does not seem to be a single case since the seventeenth century[97] in which a minor has been held liable for the non-acceptance of necessaries or on a contract for necessaries bargained and sold but not delivered. Since necessity is in part determined at the time of delivery, it is in fact difficult to know whether an executory contract is or is not one for necessaries.[98] Moreover, even if the goods are delivered, the plaintiff will not necessarily recover the contractual price but only 'a reasonable price for them'. This does not suggest a consensual contract.[99]

Contracts of employment, apprenticeship and the like, provided that they are beneficial to the minor, have, however, always been regarded as merely one variety of contracts for 'necessaries',[100] and there seems to be no authority for regarding the nature of the liability which they create as resting on a different basis from that of contracts for the supply of necessary goods. Nevertheless in *Roberts* v. *Gray*:[101]

G, a minor, entered into a contract by which he agreed to join R, a famous billiard player, in a world tour as 'professional billiardists'. R incurred certain necessary expenses as a result of preparations for the tour, but, before the tour began, G repudiated the contract.

The Court of Appeal held that to play in company with a noted billiard player such as R was instruction of the most valuable kind for a minor who wished to make billiard playing his occupation, and they upheld an award of £1,500 damages for the breach. They rejected the view that a contract for necessaries in this wider sense was not binding on a minor while it was still executory. 'I am unable to appreciate', said Hamilton L.J.,[102] 'why a contract which is in itself binding, because it is a contract for necessaries not qualified by unreasonable terms, can cease to be binding merely because it is still executory'. This decision and that in *Doyle* v. *White City Stadium Ltd.*,[103] considered above, imply that when the minor is liable the nature of the liability does not differ from that of a contracting party of full capacity; that it is, in fact, a true contractual liability and not restitutionary.

In principle, there is much to be said for the contractual explanation. The law governing minors' contracts is based on the principle of 'qualified unenforceability';[104] the minor has a limited capacity to contract, and within that limited capacity, there is no reason to deny the contractual nature of liability. Moreover, the other party is liable for non-delivery and other non-performance,[105] and it has been argued that section 3 of the Sale of Goods Act 1979 does not exclude the possibility of liability

---

[96] In 1979 Act, s. 3. Cf. the wording of the Infants Relief Act 1874 (now repealed), s. 1 of which might have suggested the contrary: 'contracts . . . for goods supplied *or to be supplied* (other than contracts for necessaries)'. See generally Winfield (1942) 58 L.Q.R. 82.

[97] *Ive* v. *Chester* (1619) Cro. Jac. 560; *Delavel* v. *Clare* (1652) Latch. 156.

[98] *Benjamin's Sale of Goods*, 5th edn. (1997), § 2–031.

[99] *Pontypridd Union* v. *Drew* [1927] 1 K.B. 214, *per* Scrutton L.J. at p. 220. See also Birks, *An Introduction to Restitution* (1985), p. 436.

[100] *Walter* v. *Everard* [1891] 2 Q.B. 369.

[101] [1913] 1 K.B. 520. See also *Hamilton* v. *Bennett* (1930) 94 J.P.N.136.

[102] *Ibid.*, at p. 530.

[103] [1935] 1 K.B. 110; *ante*, p. 219.

[104] Law Com. No. 134 (1984), § 1.12.

[105] *Farnham* v. *Atkins* (1670) 1 Sid. 446; *Bruce* v. *Warwick* (1815) 6 Taunt. 118. See also *Cowern* v. *Nield* [1912] 2 K.B. 419, *ante*, p. 219.

being contractual. This is because a contract for necessaries only binds a minor where it is not, on balance, onerous to the minor. Thus a minor 'will not, in any case, be bound by a contract for necessaries for which more than a reasonable price is charged', a position unaffected by the Sale of Goods Act, the provisions of which 'are consistent with the view that [a minor] may be liable on an executory contract for necessaries provided that the terms are not onerous'.[106] But in the present state of the authorities it is difficult to state the nature of the minor's liability with assurance.

(iii) Liability for positive and negative voidable covenants

If the contract is a positive voidable contract not disclaimed in time or a negative voidable contract which has been ratified, it is clear that it may be enforced as a contract. The real issue, however, concerns the non-contractual liability of the minor. That is, the tortious or restitutionary liability of the minor in the case where a positive voidable contract has been disclaimed or a negative voidable contract has not been ratified. On what basis may the minor be liable? We address this below.

(f) LIABILITY OF MINORS IN TORT

A minor is generally liable for torts committed, but a breach of contract may not be treated as a tort so as to make the minor liable. The tort must be more than a misfeasance in the performance of a contract, and must be separate from and independent of it. Thus tort liability may arise whether the obligation of the minor under an alleged contract is an enforceable one, say for necessaries, or an unenforceable one.

For instance, in *Jennings* v. *Rundall*[107] where a minor hired a mare to ride and injured her by over-riding, it was held that he could not be made liable by framing an action really arising out of contract as an action in tort. And in *Fawcett* v. *Smethurst*,[108] it was said that a minor who hired a car to take his luggage from the station would be under no liability in tort if he used the car to drive several miles further than the station, and there met with an accident. Minors who obtain a loan by falsely representing their age cannot be made to repay the amount of the loan in the form of damages for deceit,[109] nor can minors who buy goods on credit be forced to pay for them by charging them with conversion.[110] 'One cannot make an infant liable for the breach of a contract by changing the form of action to one ex delicto.'[111]

But this is not to say that every tort of a minor which originates in a contract is not

---

[106] Goff and Jones, *The Law of Restitution*, 5th edn. (1998), p. 639. But note the difficulty of ascertaining this at that stage, *ante*, p. 223.

[107] (1799) 8 Term R. 335.

[108] (1914) 84 L.J. K.B. 473, although in that case the minor was, in fact, not guilty of any tort.

[109] *Johnson* v. *Pye* (1665) 1 Sid. 258; *Stikeman* v. *Dawson* (1847) De G. & Sm. 90; *Leslie (R.) Ltd.* v. *Sheill* [1914] 3 K.B. 607.

[110] *Manby* v. *Scott* (1659) 1 Sid. 109, at p. 129.

[111] *Burnard* v. *Haggis* (1863) 32 L.J.C.P. 189, *per* Byles J. at p. 191, cited by Lord Sumner in *Leslie (R.) Ltd.* v. *Sheill* [1914] 3 K.B. 607, at p. 611.

actionable. If the wrongful action is of a kind not contemplated by the contract,[112] the minor may be exposed to tortious liability. So in *Burnard* v. *Haggis*:[113]

A minor hired a mare for riding. He was given strict instructions 'not to jump or lark with her'. He lent her to a friend who jumped and killed her.

It was held that the minor was liable, for, as Willis J. said:[114]

It appears to me that the act of riding the mare into the place where she received her death-wound was as much a trespass, notwithstanding the hiring for another purpose, as if, without any hiring at all, the defendant had gone into a field and taken the mare out and hunted her and killed her. It was a bare trespass, not within the object and purpose of the hiring.

In a more modern case,[115] a minor was successfully sued for the non-return of a microphone and amplifier which he had hired and improperly parted with to a friend. The Court of Appeal held that 'the circumstances in which the goods passed from his possession and ultimately disappeared were outside the purview of the contract of bailment altogether',[116] and the minor was liable. In considering the extent of the contract, it seems that the terms of the agreement, the presence or absence of an express prohibition, and the nature of the subject-matter of the contract must all be considered to be relevant, although not necessarily determining, factors.

(g) LIABILITY OF MINORS IN RESTITUTION

(i) Common law

Where, overall, a contract for necessaries is not beneficial to the minor and is not therefore binding, the minor will nevertheless be liable to pay a reasonable price for any necessaries supplied.[117] But a claimant who seeks restitution of money paid or benefits in kind conferred on the minor under a contract cannot simply rely on the normal grounds for independent restitutionary recovery, in particular mistake, failure of consideration, and acceptance. This is because the Court will take care not to grant restitution where this would amount to indirectly enforcing the void contract, as it would be if, for example, the minor is ordered to repay a loan. There is authority to the effect that a minor can only be made liable in restitution if it can be shown that a wrong quite independent of the contract has been committed,[118] and that otherwise minority affords a good defence.[119] Thus in *Cowen* v. *Nield*[120] a hay and straw dealer

---

[112] *Burnard* v. *Haggis* (1863) 14 C.B.N.S. 45, *per* Willis J. at p. 53; *Fawcett* v. *Smethurst* (1914) 84 L.J.K.B. 473, *per* Atkin J. at p. 474; *Leslie (R.) Ltd.* v. *Sheill* [1914] 3 K.B. 607, *per* Kennedy L.J. at p. 620; *Ballett* v. *Mingay* [1943] K.B. 281, *per* Lord Greene M.R. at p. 283.
[113] (1863) 14 C.B.N.S. 45.
[114] At p. 53.
[115] *Ballett* v. *Mingay* [1943] K.B. 281.
[116] *Ibid.* at p. 283.
[117] *Ante*, p. 216.
[118] *Cowern* v. *Nield* [1912] 2 K.B. 419.
[119] *Leslie (R.) Ltd.* v. *Sheill* [1914] 3 K.B. 607, *post*, p. 226; *Thavorn* v. *Bank of Credit & Commerce International SA* [1985] 1 Lloyd's Rep. 259.
[120] [1912] 2 K.B. 419.

who was a minor was held entitled to retain money paid to him as the price of a consignment of hay which he had failed to deliver in accordance with his contract. But these decisions reflect the now discredited 'implied contract' theory of liability in such cases, and should be rejected now that it has been accepted that the basis of restitutionary liability is the unjust enrichment of the defendant, here the minor.[121] There is force in the argument that a restitutionary claim against a minor should be allowed so long as its effect would not be to enforce the contract indirectly.[122]

(ii) Equitable relief against a fraudulent minor

Minors who fraudulently represent themselves to be of full age and thereby induce other persons to enter into contracts, are nevertheless not liable under the contracts despite the fraud. Equity, however, will, in certain circumstances, intervene in order to prevent minors from taking advantage of their own deceit. 'Minors', said Lord Chancellor Hardwicke,[123] 'are not allowed to take advantage of infancy to support a fraud'. This equitable intervention is distinct and separate from the contract. The principle was succinctly stated by Lord Sumner in *Leslie (R.) Ltd.* v. *Sheill*:[124]

When an infant obtained an advantage by falsely stating himself to be of full age, equity required him to restore his ill-gotten gains, or to release the party deceived from obligations or acts in law induced by the fraud, but scrupulously stopped short of enforcing against him a contractual obligation, entered into while he was an infant, even by means of a fraud.

The exact extent of such equitable relief is the subject of some dispute. It is clear that a minor who obtains property, whether consisting of goods or money or any other security, by means of a false representation of full age, can be compelled to restore that property to the person deceived, provided that it is identifiable and still in the minor's possession. It is equally clear that it is impossible to make the minor repay a loan of money which has been borrowed by such a fraud and subsequently spent. In the words of Lord Sumner in *Leslie (R.) Ltd.* v. *Sheill*:[125] 'Restitution stops where repayment begins'. In that case:

L were a firm of registered moneylenders, and they sued S, to whom they had made two loans of £200 each, to recover £475, being the amount of the loans with interest. At the time of obtaining the loans, S was a minor, but he had falsely represented to L that he was of full age.

The Court of Appeal held that no action could be maintained for the recovery of the money. The loan was rendered void by the Infants Relief Act 1874 then in force and the minor could not be forced to repay:[126]

The money was paid over in order to be used as S's own and he has so used it and, I suppose, spent it. There is no question of tracing it, no possibility of restoring the very thing got by

---

[121] *Lipkin Gorman* v. *Karpnale Ltd.* [1991] 2 A.C. 548.

[122] Goff and Jones, *The Law of Restitution*, 5th edn. (1998), pp. 644–66.

[123] *Earl of Buckinghamshire* v. *Drury* (1760) 2 Eden 60, at p. 71.

[124] [1914] 3 K.B. 607, at p. 618; Atiyah (1959) 22 M.L.R. 273.

[125] *Ibid.*

[126] *Ibid., per* Lord Sumner at p. 619.

the fraud, nothing but compulsion through a personal judgment to pay an equivalent sum out of his present or future resources, in a word nothing but a judgment in debt to repay the loan. I think this would be nothing but enforcing a void contract.

Once the identity of the property has been lost because it has been dissipated, it is no longer possible to invoke the aid of the equitable doctrine of restitution.

So much is clear; the difficulty arises when the minor has parted with the property obtained by the fraud, but stands possessed of other money or property which represents it. Suppose, for example, that a minor obtains certain goods by the misrepresentation, and then sells the goods and stands possessed of the proceeds of sale. Is it possible to claim that the money represents the goods and so ought to be restored to the person deceived? In *Stocks* v. *Wilson*:[127]

W, a minor, by falsely representing himself to be of full age, induced S to sell and deliver to him certain goods for which he promised to pay £300. The goods were not necessaries. He subsequently sold some of the goods for £30, and granted a bill of sale over the remainder as security for the sum of £100 lent to him by a third party. These goods were later sold by him to the grantee of the bill of sale. S claimed, by way of equitable relief, the value of the goods.

Lush J. held that S was not entitled to recover the value of the goods from W as this would be to enforce a void contract. Equity, however, had the power to prevent a minor from retaining the benefit of what had been obtained by reason of his fraud, and since W had obtained the sum of £130 by parting with the goods, he was liable to account to S for this sum. This decision was criticized, but not overruled, by the Court of Appeal in *Leslie (R.) Ltd.* v. *Sheill* on the ground that Lush J. had proceeded on the false assumption that a minor who had obtained money by a false representation of full age could be compelled to refund it. This may, perhaps, be reconciled with *Stocks* v. *Wilson* on the assumption that it is possible for the party defrauded to 'trace' the value of the goods into the proceeds of their sale.[128] If this is so, then the defrauded party's right is similar to that of a beneficiary in respect of a trust fund in the hands of a trustee.[129] It is possible to trace so long as there is an identifiable fund in existence against which the defrauded party can enforce its claim *in rem*; but, once the fund has been dissipated, it is no longer possible to obtain a judgment *in personam* against the infant for the amount.

Equity will also relieve the party deceived of obligations imposed upon that party by the minor's fraud. Thus it has ordered the setting aside of a lease[130] and the giving up of promissory notes[131] obtained by false representation of age. The Court

---

[127] [1913] 2 K.B. 235.

[128] *Leslie (R.) Ltd.* v. *Sheill* [1914] 3 K.B. 607, at p. 618. See also *Thavorn* v. *Bank of Credit & Commerce International S.A.* [1985] 1 Lloyd's Rep. 259, at p. 264; Atiyah (1959) 22 M.L.R. 273. *Stocks* v. *Wilson* may fairly be criticized, since it appears that judgment was given *in personam* against the minor and without any proper inquiry as to whether the money had been spent.

[129] The representation of full age might be considered to raise an 'equity' in the defrauded party similar to that possessed by a beneficiary of a fiduciary relationship.

[130] *Lemprière* v. *Lange* (1879) 12 Ch. D. 675.

[131] *Clarke* v. *Copley* (1789) 2 Cox 173.

scrupulously refrained from enforcing the contracts, and merely restored the status quo affected by the minor's fraud. For example, a claim by the lessor for damages for use and occupation of the premises was dismissed as being inconsistent with this relief.

Where, by a false misrepresentation of age by the minor, a person is thereby induced to lend money, after the minor comes of age the lender is entitled to prove in any bankruptcy proceedings against the minor.[132] The reason seems to be that the lender has a claim, not against the minor personally, but against the minor's assets in competition with the other creditors.[133]

(iii) Minors' Contracts Act 1987

Apart from rights to restitution that may arise at common law and in equity, there is a statutory scheme allowing for restitution. Section 3 of the Minors' Contracts Act 1987[134] provides:

(1) Where—

    (a) a person ('the plaintiff') has after the commencement of this Act entered into a contract with another ('the defendant'), and

    (b) the contract is unenforceable against the defendant (or he repudiates it) because he was a minor when the contract was made,

the court may, if it is just and equitable to do so, require the defendant to transfer to the plaintiff any property acquired by the defendant under the contract, or any property representing it.

The provision leaves the issue of restitution to the discretion of the Court. There is no requirement of fault or fraud. It is also only concerned with property acquired under the contract (or property acquired in exchange for property acquired under the contract) and not property gained in any other way. It appears that money is included within this notion of property. The Law Commission's policy was to extend the equitable remedy available against a fraudulent minor to a case where the minor, though not guilty of fraud, had failed to pay for goods obtained on credit.[135] That equitable relief extended, as in *Stocks* v. *Wilson*[136] and as recognized by the Law Commission, to money which was the proceeds of the property sold to the minor and resold by him or her. But if property delivered to a minor has been consumed or lost, there will be no remedy under the 1987 Act. The Law Commission considered that to order the minor to pay to the seller a sum equivalent to the purchase price or the value of the property 'would amount to the enforcement of the contract' against the minor.[137]

---

[132] *Re King, ex parte Unity Joint-Stock Mutual Banking Association* (1858) 3 De G. & J. 63; *Re Jones, ex parte Jones* (1881) 18 Ch. D. 109, at p. 125.

[133] *Leslie (R.) Ltd.* v. *Sheill* [1914] 3 K.B. 607, at p. 616.

[134] See Law Com. No. 134, *Minors' Contracts* (1984).

[135] *Ibid.,* § 4.21.

[136] [1913] 2 K.B. 235, *ante,* p. 227.

[137] See Law Com. No. 134 (1984), § 4.23.

(h) RESTITUTION IN FAVOUR OF MINORS

In order to recover money paid to the other party under a contract which does not bind the minor, a ground for restitution must be established, i.e. that the money was paid by mistake, under compulsion, or that there has been a failure of consideration. Where the ground of recovery is failure of consideration, in the present state of the authorities, it would appear that what is required is a *total* failure of consideration, so that, as noted above,[138] receipt by the minor of any part of the other party's performance will be fatal. But, as will be seen,[139] the indications are that the requirement of totality is being reconsidered, and it is submitted that the authority of the cases requiring it in this context has been fatally undermined. Provided the minor can return what has been received or give recompense for it in a way that does not amount to indirect enforcement of the contract, the minor should, in principle, be able to recover money paid.

(i) THIRD PARTIES

An interesting question arises as to the effect the invalidity of a minor's contract has on third parties. So far, we know that although a minor may enforce a contract the other party to the contract can only enforce it if it is a valid contract for necessaries or if it is a positive voidable contract that has not been disclaimed or a negative voidable contract that has been ratified. If the contract is not enforceable what is the position of, say a guarantor of the minor's obligations. Section 2 of the Minors' Contracts Act 1987 provides:

Where—

(a) a guarantee is given in respect of an obligation of a party to a contract made after the commencement of this Act, and

(b) the obligation is unenforceable against him (or he repudiates the contract) because he was a minor when the contract was made,

the guarantee shall not for that reason alone be unenforceable against the guarantor.[140]

---

[138] *Ante*, p. 222. On the recovery of property, see *Pearce* v. *Brain* [1929] 2 K.B. 310 but cf. *Chaplin* v. *Leslie Frewin (Publishers) Ltd.* [1966] Ch. 71.

[139] *Post*, pp. 644–5.

[140] Cf. the position under the Infants Relief Act 1874, s. 1 (now repealed) which rendered loans to infants void rather than unenforceable: see *Coutts & Co.* v. *Browne-Lecky* [1947] K.B. 104. See also Law Com. No. 134 (1984), § 4.15.

IV. CORPORATIONS AND UNINCORPORATED ASSOCIATIONS

(a) CORPORATIONS

(i) Doctrine of ultra vires

At common law any act done by a corporation incorporated by statute[141] outside its statutory powers is *ultra vires* and void. Since the corporation has no existence independent of the statute which creates the corporation or authorizes its creation, it follows that its capacity is limited to the exercise of such powers as are actually conferred by, or may reasonably be deduced from, the language of the statute. Thus at common law a company is bound by the objects listed in its memorandum of association, for it is incorporated for the purposes set out in the memorandum. The company can make no contracts inconsistent with, those objects,[142] and, if it does so, a contract so made is, at common law, void and unenforceable as being *ultra vires*.

In *Ashbury Railway Carriage and Iron Co.* v. *Riche*:[143]

A company was incorporated with the object (set out in the memorandum of association) to make, and sell, or to lend on hire, railway wagons and carriages and other rolling stock. The company contracted to assign to another company a concession which it had bought for the construction of a railway in Belgium.

The House of Lords held that the contract, being related to the actual construction of a railway, as opposed to railway stock, was *ultra vires* the objects in the memorandum and void. Even if the shareholders subsequently ratified the contract, it could not thereby be rendered binding on the company.

The explanation given in this case for the existence of the *ultra vires* rule was not only that it was a necessary consequence of statutory incorporation but also that the rule was required to protect investors in, and creditors of, the company.[144] 'It ensured that an investor in a gold mining company did not find himself holding shares in a fried fish shop, and it gave those who allowed credit to a limited company some assurance that its assets would not be dissipated in unauthorized enterprises'.[145] Nevertheless, the application of the rule not infrequently led to injustice. Persons who entered into an *ultra vires* contract with a company could not enforce it. If they supplied goods to the company or performed services under the contract, they could not obtain payment.[146] If they lent money to the company, and the borrowing was

---

[141] A corporation created by charter by virtue of the Royal Prerogative is not so limited. If it exceeds its powers, the effect is not to avoid the contract, but to give cause for forfeiture of the charter: see Gower (1952) 68 L.Q.R. 214; *Jenkin* v. *Pharmaceutical Society* [1921] 1 Ch. 392, at p. 398.

[142] Matters which are reasonably incidental to that which is authorized by the memorandum are not *ultra vires* unless expressly prohibited: *Att.-Gen.* v. *Great Eastern Ry.* (1880) 5 App. Cas. 473, at p. 478.

[143] (1875) L.R. 7 H.L. 653.

[144] *Ibid.*, *per* Lord Cairns at pp. 667–8.

[145] Gower, *The Principles of Modern Company Law*, 3rd edn. (1969), p. 87.

[146] *Re Jon Beauforte (London) Ltd.* [1953] Ch. 131.

ultra vires, the non-recognition of restitution as a claim based on unjust enrichment independent of contract meant that, in general, they could not recover their money.[147] In theory, before entering into the contract with the company, such persons would first scrutinize the memorandum to ascertain the extent of the company's powers. In practice, however, they did not do so, but were nevertheless deemed to have 'constructive notice' of the contents of the memorandum despite the fact that they had no actual knowledge of them. As a result, the doctrine of *ultra vires* proved to be a trap for the unwary and from time to time inflicted grave hardship on persons who dealt *bona fide* with the company in ignorance of its lack of capacity.[148]

(ii) Lack of capacity distinguished from abuse of power

An *ultra vires* contract which is 'beyond the capacity of the company and therefore wholly void'[149] should be distinguished from a contract made by the exercise of a power which the company undoubtedly has but for a *purpose* which is unauthorized. Transactions of the latter sort involve an abuse of power rather than a lack of capacity and will be enforceable against the company unless the other party had notice of the abuse of power.[150]

(iii) Statutory modification of ultra vires doctrine

The *ultra vires* doctrine was criticized by two committees on the reform of company law,[151] and in 1972, although it was not abolished, statutory protection[152] was given to those dealing with a company[153] in good faith in respect of transactions decided upon by the directors which were within the capacity of the company, although in fact unauthorized. In 1989 the second and third requirements were removed in provisions introduced by the Companies Act 1989, amending the Companies Act 1985.

Section 35(1) of the Companies Act 1985 as amended provides that the 'validity of an act done by a company shall not be called into question on the ground of lack of capacity by reason of anything in the company's memorandum'. The effect of this section is that a transaction entered into by a company cannot be held invalid merely because it appears outside the objects listed in the company's memorandum. There is also provision for the company to ratify an *ultra vires* act,[154] although given the width of section 35(1) this will rarely if ever be needed for the protection of a third party who has dealt with the company. Moreover, although a shareholder may apply for an

---

[147] e.g. *Sinclair* v. *Brougham* [1914] A.C. 398. But see now *Westdeutsche Landesbank Girozentrale* v. *Islington L.B.C.* [1996] 2 A.C. 669, *ante*, p. 215, *post*, 232.

[148] e.g. *Re Jon Beauforte (London) Ltd.* (*supra*, n. 146).

[149] This depends solely upon the true construction of the memorandum of association: *Rolled Steel Products (Holdings) Ltd.* v. *B.S.C.* [1986] 1 Ch. 246, at p. 306.

[150] *Ibid.*, at pp. 306–7. On 'notice', see Companies Act 1985, ss. 35A(1) and 35B.

[151] Cohen Committee (Cmnd. 6659), § 12; Jenkins Committee (Cmnd. 1749), §§ 35–42.

[152] European Communities Act 1972, s. 9, implementing Art. 9 of the first Directive 68/151/EEC on Company Law, 1968 O.J. L65/7.

[153] The company itself could not enforce an *ultra vires* contract: *Bell Houses Ltd.* v. *City Wall Properties Ltd.* [1966] 1 Q.B. 207 (reversed on other grounds, [1966] 2 Q.B. 656). See Furmston (1961) 24 M.L.R. 715.

[154] Companies Act 1985, s. 35(3).

injunction to prevent an act outside the objects of a company, it is not possible for the shareholder to obtain such an injunction in respect of an act to be done by the company in fulfilment of a legal obligation arising from a previous act of the company.[155] A shareholder cannot therefore seek to subvert the effect of section 35(1) by seeking to prevent the company proceeding with a transaction within section 35(1) into which it has already entered and is obliged to carry out.

With respect to 'constructive notice', which was discussed above, by section 35B, a party to a transaction with a company is not bound to enquire as to whether it is permitted by the company's memorandum or as to any limitation on the powers of the board of directors to bind the company or authorize others to do so. In effect therefore the doctrine of constructive notice is now a dead letter.

(iv) Powers of directors

At common law similar limitations existed in respect of contracts which, though within the powers of the company, were entered into by the directors of the company and other officers without authority or in breach of its internal constitution.[156] The Companies Act 1985, as amended by the 1989 Act, preserves the duty of directors to observe any limitations on their powers flowing from the company's memorandum.[157] But section 35A(1) protects those dealing with a company in good faith by providing that the power of the board of directors to bind the company, or authorize others to do so, shall be deemed to be free of any limitation under the company's constitution.[158]

(v) Form of contracts

Since the passing of the Corporate Bodies' Contracts Act 1960 a corporation can, in general, contract in the same manner as any natural person of full age and capacity and is not only bound by contracts made under its corporate seal.[159]

(vi) Restitution of benefits conferred under an ultra vires contract

Payments made to or by a company under an *ultra vires* contract are recoverable in a restitutionary action,[160] and a party which has done work under such a contract will be entitled to reasonable remuneration.[161] But, the provisions of section 35 of the Companies Act 1985 mean that restitutionary obligations will be of less significance in the context of companies.

---

[155] Companies Act 1985, s. 35(2). See also *ibid.*, s. 35A(4).

[156] See *Royal British Bank* v. *Turquand* (1856) 6 E. & B. 327; Campbell (1959) 75 L.Q.R. 469; (1960) 76 L.Q.R. 115.

[157] s. 35(3).

[158] See *ibid.*, s.35A(2) for the meaning of 'deals with' and 'good faith'. Cf. *ibid.*, s. 322A in respect of contracts involving directors of the company.

[159] On the execution of deeds by companies, see Companies Act 1985, s. 36A and Law Com. C.P. No. 143 (1995).

[160] *Westdeutsche Landesbank Girozentrale* v. *Islington L.B.C.* [1994] 4 All E.R. 890, aff'd [1996] 2 A.C. 669; *Rover International Ltd.* v. *Cannon Film Sales (No. 3)* [1989] 1 W.L.R. 912.

[161] *Rover International Ltd.* v. *Cannon Film Sales (No. 3)* (*supra*, n. 160).

(b) UNINCORPORATED ASSOCIATIONS

(i) Contractual capacity

An unincorporated association has no legal personality. It cannot therefore contract, or sue or be sued in its name, unless such a course is authorized by statute or by rules of Court. But a contract which purports to have been entered into by or with an unincorporated association is not necessarily invalid. The person or persons who actually made the contract, for example, the secretary or committee of a club, may be held to have contracted personally and be personally liable on the contract.[162] Further, under the rules of agency, they may be held to have contracted on behalf of the members of the association, and, in certain circumstances, a representative action[163] may be brought by or against one or more of the members, including the trustees of the funds of the association,[164] as representing the others, so as to avoid the necessity of joining numerous persons as parties to the action.

(ii) Partnerships

A partnership can normally sue and be sued in the firm's name,[165] and contracts entered into by one of the partners will, as a general rule, bind the firm since each partner has authority to act for the others in the ordinary course of the partnership business.[166]

(iii) Trade unions

A trade union stands juridically in a somewhat anomalous position. Section 10 of the Trade Union and Labour Relations (Consolidation) Act 1992 provides that a trade union is not nor is it to be treated as a body corporate. Nevertheless, that sub-section goes on to provide that it is to be capable of making contracts,[167] that it is to be capable of suing or being sued in its own name,[168] and that any judgment, order, or award made in any proceedings of any description brought against a trade union is to be enforceable against any property held in trust for it to the like extent and in the like manner as if the union were a body corporate.[169] The same capacity and liability attaches to an employers' association which is an unincorporated association.[170]

At common law, a member of a trade union who is improperly expelled from the union in breach of union rules or in defiance of the rules of natural justice can bring an action for breach of contract against the union and recover damages.[171]

---

[162] *Bradley Egg Farm Ltd.* v. *Clifford* [1943] 2 All E.R. 378. See also *Artistic Upholstery Ltd.* v. *Art Forma (Furniture) Ltd.* [1999] 4 All E.R. 277.

[163] C.P.R. r.19.6(1).

[164] *Ideal Films Ltd.* v. *Richards* [1927] 1 KB. 374. But see *Prudential Assurance Co. Ltd.* v. *Newman Industries Ltd. (No. 2)* [1981] Ch. 257, [1982] Ch. 204; *News Group Newspapers Ltd.* v. *S.O.G.A.T.* (1986) 15 I.R.L.R. 227.

[165] R.S.C. Ord. 81 r.1, now in C.P.R. Sched. 1.

[166] See *post*, p. 669.

[167] 1992 Act, s. 10(1)(a).

[168] *Ibid.*, s. 10(1)(b).

[169] *Ibid.*, s. 12.

[170] *Ibid.*, s. 127.

[171] *Bonsor* v. *Musician's Union* [1956] A.C. 104.

Under the 1992 Act, a member of a union has the right not to be unjustifiably disciplined.[172]

V. MENTALLY DISORDERED AND DRUNKEN PERSONS

Under Part VII of the Mental Health Act 1983 the Court of Protection is given wide discretionary powers where, after considering medical evidence, it is satisfied that a person is incapable, by reason of mental disorder, of managing and administering his or her property and affairs. A person as to whom the judge is so satisfied is referred to as a 'patient' for the purposes of this part of the Act, and it is possible that such a person is absolutely incapable of entering into a valid contract.[173] Otherwise, however, a mentally disordered person has full contractual capacity, although such a person may be entitled to avoid a contract which has been made; and this is also the law in the case of drunken persons.

The contract of a mentally disordered or drunken person is not binding if it can be shown that at the time of making the contract he or she was incapable of understanding the general nature of what was being done, and that the other party was aware of this incapacity. This principle was established by Lord Esher M.R. in *Imperial Loan Co.* v. *Stone*:[174]

When a person enters into a contract, and afterwards alleges that he was so insane at the time that he did not know what he was doing, and proves the allegation, the contract is as binding upon him in every respect, whether it is executory or executed, as if he had been sane when he made it, unless he can prove further that the person with whom he contracted knew him to be so insane as not to be capable of understanding what he was about.

Authority for the view that, even if the condition of the mentally disordered or drunken person was not known to the other party, the contract may be set aside if it was unconscionable[175] was disapproved by the Judicial Committee of the Privy Council in *Hart* v. *O'Connor*.[176]

A contract made in such circumstances is voidable at the option of the incapacitated person, who can elect either to avoid the contract or to affirm it, in which case it is binding. Thus in *Matthews* v. *Baxter*:[177]

---

[172] 1992 Act, s. 64 (which includes expulsion). See also *ibid.*, ss. 65–7 and s. 174.

[173] The law on this point is uncertain; see *Re Walker* [1905] 1 Ch. 160; *Re Marshall* [1920] 1 Ch. 284. Contrast *Baldwyn* v. *Smith* [1900] 1 Ch. 588; *In the Estate of Walker* (1912) 28 T.L.R. 466. All of these decisions relate to the Lunacy and Mental Treatment Acts 1890 to 1930 (now repealed). See Fridman (1963) 79 L.Q.R. 502; (1964) 80 L.Q.R. 84. Cf. s. 96(1)(h) of the 1983 Act.

[174] [1892] 1 Q.B. 599, at p. 601; *York Glass Co. Ltd.* v. *Jubb* (1925) 134 L.T. 36; *Hart* v. *O'Connor* [1985] A.C. 1000. See also Law Com. No. 231, *Mental Incapacity* (1995), §§ 3.5–3.6, 3.16–3.19.

[175] *Molton* v. *Camroux* (1848) 2 Exch. 487, at p. 503 (aff'd (1849) 4 Exch. 17); *Archer* v. *Cutler* [1980] 1 N.Z.L.R. 386 (New Zealand): mental disorder. *Cooke* v. *Clayworth* (1811) 18 Ves. 12; *Wiltshire* v. *Marshall* (1866) 14 L.T. (N.S.) 396; *Blomley* v. *Ryan* (1956) 99 C.L.R. 362 (Australia): drunkenness. See *post*, p. 313–14.

[176] [1985] A.C. 1000.

[177] (1873) L.R. 8 Ex. 132.

B, while drunk, agreed at an auction sale to purchase from M certain houses and land. Afterwards, when sober, B affirmed the contract, and then repented of his bargain. When sued on the contract, he pleaded that he was drunk at the time he made it, and to M's knowledge.

The Court held that although B had once an option in the matter and might have avoided the contract, he was now bound by his affirmation of it. 'I think', said Martin B.[178] 'that a drunken man when he recovers his senses, might insist on the fulfilment of his bargain, and therefore that he can ratify it, so as to bind himself to a performance of it'. It will be seen from this case that the contract of a mentally disordered or drunken person is voidable at the option of the incapacitated person and not completely void. Therefore if property is transferred as the result of such a contract and subsequently passes to a *bona fide* purchaser for value, it seems that the innocent purchaser would acquire a good title.

Section 3 of the Sale of Goods Act 1979, which has already been quoted in respect of minors' contracts for necessaries, provides that 'where necessaries are sold and delivered to a person who by reason of mental incapacity or drunkenness is incompetent to contract, he must pay a reasonable price for them'. There is little doubt that this liability arises in restitution[179] and that an executory contract for necessaries would therefore be unenforceable.

---

[178] At p. 134.
[179] *Re Rhodes* (1890) 44 Ch. D. 94; *Re F.* [1990] 2 A.C. 1. See also Winfield (1942) 58 L.Q.R. 82, at p. 87.

6

MISREPRESENTATION AND NON-DISCLOSURE

I. INTRODUCTION

This chapter is concerned with relief for misrepresentation and for the exceptional cases in which there may be relief for non-disclosure. Although, as we shall see, there is some overlap between these two vitiating factors in cases in which there has been partial disclosure, the rationale for the intervention of the law where a false or misleading statement is made is fundamentally different from that for imposing a duty upon a party to disclose to the other party information about the subject-matter of the proposed contract.

The general rule of the common law is that a person contemplating entering a contract with another is under no duty to disclose information to that other. '[T]he failure to disclose a material fact which might affect the mind of a prudent contractor does not give the right to avoid the contract.'[1] The parties must look out for their own interests and ensure they acquire the information necessary to avoid a bad bargain. Thus, a person who visits an antiques shop and sees a rare George II table being sold as a nineteenth century piece need say nothing to the seller before buying it. Neither does the oil prospector who discovers that there is probably oil under a given piece of land have to inform the land owner. There are, however, both common law and statutory exceptions to the general rule, in particular contracts *uberrimae fidei*, contracts of the 'utmost good faith', the prime example of which are insurance contracts, in which there is a duty to disclose and where failure to do so makes the contract voidable.

The effect of a misleading statement made during the negotiations leading to a contract, a misrepresentation, is however, subject to certain limitations, to render the agreement voidable at the suit of the party misled. A person who has been induced to enter into a contract by reason of a misrepresentation can refuse to carry out the undertaking, resist any claim for specific performance, and, if necessary, have the contract set aside by means of the equitable remedy of *rescission*. Where the representation has been incorporated as a term of the contract, the party misled will be able to claim *damages* for breach of contract. The circumstances in which it will be so incorporated are dealt with in Chapter 4. This chapter deals with misrepresentations which have not been incorporated as a term. In such cases the party misled will

---

[1] *Bell v. Lever Bros. Ltd.* [1932] A.C. 161, *per* Lord Atkin at p. 227.

sometimes be entitled to claim tortious *damages* in respect of any loss which may have been sustained by reason of the misrepresentation. If the representation is fraudulent, damages for deceit can be recovered. If it was made without reasonable care being taken to ascertain its truth, the party misled will likewise be entitled to damages by virtue of statute and at common law. Where the party making the representation believed, and had reasonable ground to believe, that the facts represented were true, although the contract is still voidable at the suit of the party misled, damages in addition to rescission cannot be claimed but it may be possible to claim damages in lieu of rescission. A pre-contractual misrepresentation therefore may give rise to contractual, tortious, statutory, and equitable remedies.

II. MISREPRESENTATION

(a) PUFFS, REPRESENTATIONS, AND TERMS

A misleading statement made during the negotiations leading to a contract may fall into one of three categories. First, it may be a mere 'puff', a commendatory expression which by virtue of its vagueness or extravagance would not be expected to and does not ground any form of liability. Secondly, the preliminary statement may be intended by neither party to have contractual effect, but nevertheless may seriously affect the inclination of one party to enter into the contract. It is then known as a 'representation'. If it proves false, the party misled will not be entitled to claim damages for breach of contract, for no contractual stipulation has been broken; but will be entitled to claim the relief accorded by the law in the case of misrepresentation. Thirdly, the preliminary statement may be a term of the contract, or constitute a warranty collateral to the contract, if the party making the statement undertakes or guarantees that it is true.[2] There is an overlap between the second and third categories because a statement that is a misrepresentation may become a term of the contract. In such cases there will be a choice of remedy since the party misled will be entitled to claim damages for breach of contract and to relief for misrepresentation.

(b) REQUIREMENTS OF LIABILITY

An operative misrepresentation consists in a false statement of existing or past fact (or possibly of law) made by one party (the 'misrepresentor') before or at the time of making the contract, which is addressed to the other party (the 'misrepresentee') and which induces the other party to enter into the contract.

(i) There must be a false representation

Mere silence does not constitute a misrepresentation.[3] There must be some positive

---

[2] See *ante*, pp. 127–34.
[3] *Keates* v. *Lord Cadogan* (1851) 10 C.B. 591.

statement, or some conduct from which a statement can be implied, in order to amount to an operative misrepresentation. With regard to conduct, 'a nod or a wink, or a shake of the head or a smile may suffice',[4] as may a photograph.[5] It has been held that the participation by the Spice Girls in the making of a commercial to be shown in the future constituted a representation by conduct that none of the group had an existing declared intention to leave the group before it was shown.[6] And the use of a cheque guarantee card, credit card, or cheque implies that such use is authorized by the bank or credit card company.[7]

In assessing whether a complex pre-contractual document contains a misrepresentation, it has been suggested that it is preferable to look at the matter broadly and to assess whether overall the statements in the document are substantially correct rather than to focus 'more and more microscopically so as to concentrate on each sentence, phrase or word'.[8]

(ii) Partial non-disclosure and active concealment

A partial non-disclosure may constitute a misrepresentation. Suppression of material facts can render that which is stated false, as where a seller of land told a purchaser that all the farms on the land were fully let, but omitted to inform him that the tenants had given notice to quit.[9] But this is only so if the facts are known to the person making the statement or possibly if he or she has the means of knowledge.[10] Further, if a person makes a representation which is true at the time when it is made, but which the representor knows has subsequently become false, the representor is bound to disclose the change in circumstances to the other party.[11]

There is also some authority for the view that if a person does some positive act in order deliberately to conceal defects in the goods, as where the seller of a ship takes the vessel from the slipway into the water in order to conceal its rotten hull,[12] such active concealment will constitute a misrepresentation.

(iii) Representations of opinion normally insufficient

A mere expression of opinion, which turns out to be unfounded, will not invalidate a contract. There is a wide difference between the seller of property saying that it

---

[4] *Walters v. Morgan* (1861) 3 De G.F. & J. 718, *per* Lord Campbell at p. 725. See also *R. v. Charles* [1977] A.C. 177; *R. v. Lambie* [1982] A.C. 449.

[5] *Atlantic Estates plc v. Ezekiel* [1991] 2 E.G.L.R. 202.

[6] *Spice Girls Ltd. v. Aprilia World Service B.V.* [2000] E.M.L.R. 478.

[7] *R. v. Gilmartin* [1983] Q.B. 953.

[8] *Avon Insurance plc. v. Swire Fraser Ltd.* [2000] 1 All E.R. (Comm.) 573, *per* Rix J. at p. 632.

[9] *Dimmock v. Hallett* (1866) L.R. 2 Ch. App. 21; *Southwestern General Property Ltd. v. Martin* [1982] 263 E.G. 1090.

[10] *Sindell v. Cambridgeshire C.C.* [1994] 1 W.L.R. 1016.

[11] *Davies v. London & Provincial Marine Insurance Co.* (1878) 8 Ch. D. 469, at p. 475; *With v. O'Flanagan* [1936] Ch. 575; *Dietz v. Lennig Chemicals Ltd.* [1969] 1 A.C. 170. See also Misrepresentation Act 1967, s. 2(1). Cf. *Turner v. Green* [1895] Ch. 205; *Wales v. Wadham* [1977] 1 W.L.R. 199; *English v. Dedham Vale Properties Ltd.* [1978] 1 W.L.R. 93.

[12] *Schneider v. Heath* (1813) 3 Camp. 505; *Cottee v. Douglas Seaton (Used Cars) Ltd.* [1972] 1 W.L.R. 1408, at p. 1417. See also *Tradex Export S.A. v. Dorada Comp. Nav. S.A.* [1982] 2 Lloyd's Rep. 140, at pp. 157–8.

is worth so much, and a statement that the seller gave so much for it. The first is an opinion which the buyer may or may not choose to adopt; the second is an assertion of fact which, if false to the knowledge of the seller, is also a fraudulent misrepresentation.[13] Thus in *Bisset* v. *Wilkinson*:[14]

W agreed to purchase from B certain lands at Avondale, in the Southern Island of New Zealand, for the purpose of sheep-farming, and in reliance on B's statement that he estimated the lands would carry two thousand sheep. B had not, and no other person had at any time, carried out sheep-farming on the lands in question. When B claimed the balance of the purchase price, W counter-claimed rescission of the contract on the ground of misrepresentation.

The Judicial Committee of the Privy Council held that the statement was merely of an opinion which B honestly held and accordingly the claim for rescission failed. Again, in *Economides* v. *Commercial Union Assurance Co. plc*[15] a statement that the cost of replacing the contents of a flat was £16,000 made by a 21-year-old student with no special knowledge was a statement of opinion. It should not be imagined, however, that a statement of opinion can never constitute a representation of fact. In one sense it always does so, for it asserts that the opinion is actually held. Also the opinion will usually be based upon facts; so the person making the representation impliedly states that facts are known which justify that opinion. This is especially the case where the situation is such that the representor must know the facts much better than the other party. If it is shown that the representor had no reasonable grounds for that opinion, or failed to investigate the facts which gave rise to it, there may well be an actionable misrepresentation.[16]

(iv) Mere commendatory 'puffs' insufficient

Commendatory expressions, such as advertisements to the effect that a certain brand of beer 'refreshes the parts that other beers cannot reach', or that a perfume will irresistibly attract members of the opposite sex, are not dealt with as serious representations of fact. A similar latitude is allowed to a person who wants to gain a purchaser, though it must be admitted that the borderline of permissible assertion is not always easily discernible. At a sale by auction, land was stated to be 'fertile and improvable'; it was in fact partly abandoned and useless. This was held to be 'a mere flourishing description by an auctioneer'.[17] But where in a sale of a hotel the property was said to be let to 'a most desirable tenant', whereas the rent could only be obtained under pressure and was currently much in arrears, such a statement was held to entitle the purchaser to rescind the contract.[18]

---

[13] *Lindsay Petroleum Co.* v. *Hurd* (1874) L.R. 5 P.C. 221, at p. 243.

[14] [1927] A.C. 177. See also *Anderson* v. *Pacific Fire and Marine Insurance Co.* (1872) L.R. 7 C.P. 65.

[15] [1998] Q.B. 587. See also Marine Insurance Act 1906, s. 20(3), (4).

[16] *Smith* v. *Land and House Property Corporation* (1884) 28 Ch. D. 7; *Brown* v. *Raphael* [1958] Ch. 636; *Sirius International Insurance Corp.* v. *Oriental Insurance Corp.* [1999] 1 All E.R. (Comm.) 699.

[17] *Dimmock* v. *Hallett* (1866) L.R. 2 Ch. App. 21. See also *Lambert* v. *Lewis* [1982] A.C. 225, at pp. 262–3.

[18] *Smith* v. *Land and House Property Corporation* (1884) 28 Ch. D. 7.

(v) Expression of intention or prediction normally insufficient

There is normally no liability in respect of a promise or a prediction about the future. Neither can be regarded as true or false at the time when it is made, except in so far as a person may misrepresent the state of the maker's own mind or power to bring an event to pass.[19] Thus there is a distinction between a promise which the promisor intends to perform and one which the promisor intends to break or knows cannot be performed. In the first case the representation is truly one of an intention that something shall take place in future. In the second case there is a misrepresention of the representor's existing intention: not only is a promise made which is ultimately broken, but when it is made, the maker of the statement's ability to perform or state of mind is represented to be something other than it really is. Such a misrepresentation is one of fact. Bowen L.J. said:[20]

The state of a man's mind is as much a fact as the state of his digestion. It is true that it is very difficult to prove what the state of a man's mind at a particular time is, but, if it can be ascertained, it is as much a fact as anything else. A misrepresentation as to the state of a man's mind is, therefore, a misstatement of fact.

Thus it has been held that, if a person buys goods having at the time no means to pay or having formed an intention not to pay for them, that person makes a fraudulent misrepresentation.[21] There may also be a misrepresentation of fact behind a negligent misprediction. Thus it has been held that a forecast of sales potential by a person with special knowledge and skill contains a representation of fact that the maker of the statement had exercised reasonable care in making it.[22] Again, a prediction by a bank manager that the granting of a loan facility would be a formality once supported by insurance from the Export Credit Guarantee Department has been held to contain a statement of fact as to the existing policy of the bank.[23]

(vi) Representation of law

In the present state of the authorities, a misrepresentation of law does not render the contract voidable as against the person making it.[24] But it has been held that in the context of claims for the recovery of money paid under a mistake, a distinction should not be made between mistakes of law and mistakes of fact.[25] In principle, similar reasoning should apply to cases of misrepresentation. It has, moreover, been very difficult to distinguish between a representation of law and one of fact. Many

---

[19] *R. v. Sunair Holidays Ltd.* [1973] 1 W.L.R. 1105, at p. 1109; *British Airways Board* v. *Taylor* [1976] 1 W.L.R. 13, at pp. 17, 21, 23, 27. See also *R.* v. *Gilmartin (supra* n. 7).

[20] *Edgington* v. *Fitzmaurice* (1885) 29 Ch. D. 459, at p. 483. See also *Goff* v. *Gauthier* (1991) 62 P. & C.R. 388.

[21] *Re Shackleton* (1875) L.R. 10 Ch. App. 446; *Ray* v. *Sempers* [1974] A.C. 370. On cheques, and credit and cash cards, see *ante*, p. 238, n. 4.

[22] *Esso Petroleum Co.* v. *Mardon* [1976] Q.B. 801, on which see *ante*, p. 131.

[23] *Box* v. *Midland Bank Ltd.* [1979] 2 Lloyd's Rep. 391, at p. 399; [1981] 1 Lloyd's Rep. 434.

[24] *Beattie* v. *Lord Ebury* (1872) L.R. 7 Ch. App 777; *Solle* v. *Butcher* [1950] 1 K.B. 671, *post*, p. 312.

[25] *Kleinwort Benson Ltd.* v. *Lincoln C.C.* [1999] 2 A.C. 349.

statements of fact contain implicit propositions of law and vice versa. If a dwelling-house is represented to be a 'new' dwelling-house for the purposes of the Rent Acts, is this a representation of fact or of law?[26] A misrepresentation that planning permission exists for the business use of premises has been treated as a representation of fact.[27] Misrepresentations as to private rights (as distinct from the general law)[28] or as to the content or effect of documents[29] have also been held to entitle the party misled to rescind the contract. A misrepresentation of foreign law has also been treated as a representation of fact.[30] And there is no good reason why a *wilful* misrepresentation of law should not be treated in the same way as a statement of opinion which is not actually held.[31]

(vii) The representation must be addressed to the party misled

The representation must have been addressed by the representor to the party misled. In *Peek* v. *Gurney*:[32]

The promoters of a company were sued by P who had purchased shares on the faith of false statements contained in a prospectus issued by them. P was not a person to whom shares had been allotted on the first formation of the company; he had merely purchased shares from such allottees.

The House of Lords held that the prospectus was only addressed to the first applicants for shares; that it could not be supposed to extend to others than these; and that on the allotment 'the prospectus had done its work; it was exhausted'.

A statement made directly to the party misled is clearly addressed to that party; but will also be held to have been so addressed where the person is one to whom the representor intended the statement to be passed on.[33] If this fact is established, it is immaterial that the party misled is merely one of a class of persons, even of the public at large.[34]

(viii) The representation must induce the contract

The representation must form a real inducement to the party to whom it is addressed, and whether or not a person who has entered into a contract was induced to do so by a particular representation is in each case a question of fact.

The burden of proving that the representation induced the contract rests upon the

---

[26] *Solle* v. *Butcher* [1950] 1 K.B. 671 at p. 695.

[27] *Laurence* v. *Lexcourt Holdings Ltd.* [1978] 1 W.L.R. 1128.

[28] *Cooper* v. *Phibbs* (1867) L.R. 2 H.L. 149, *post*, p. 345.

[29] *Hirshfeld* v. *L.B. & S.C. Ry* (1876) 2 Q.B.D. 1; *Wauton* v. *Coppard* [1899] 1 Ch. 92; *Re Roberts* [1905] 1 Ch. 704; *Horry* v. *Tate & Lyle Refineries Ltd.* [1982] 2 Lloyd's Rep. 416.

[30] *Andre & Cie S.A.* v. *Ets. Michel Blanc & Fils* [1979] 2 Lloyd's Rep. 427.

[31] *West London Commercial Bank* v. *Kitson* (1884) 13 Q.B.D. 360, at p. 362.

[32] (1873) L.R. 6 H.L. 377, applied in *Al Nakib Investments Ltd* v. *Longcroft* [1990] 1 W.L.R. 1390.

[33] *Commercial Banking Co. of Sydney Ltd.* v. *R.H. Brown & Co.* [1972] 2 Lloyd's Rep. 360 (Australia); *Smith* v. *Eric S. Bush* [1990] 1 A.C. 831. Cf. *Gross* v. *Lewis Hillman Ltd.* [1970] Ch. 445.

[34] *Andrews* v. *Mockford* [1896] 1 Q.B. 372 (prospectus part of wider scheme of fraud).

party misled.[35] But such inducement may be inferred. Thus it was said by Lord Blackburn:[36]

I think that if it is proved that the defendants with a view to induce the plaintiff to enter into a contract made a statement to the plaintiff of such a nature as would be likely to induce a person to enter into a contract, and if it is proved that the plaintiff did enter into the contract, it is a fair inference of fact that he was induced to do so by the statement.

It will not be inferred that a representation induced the contract where it would not have induced a reasonable person to contract but, in such a case, a representee who proves that he or she was in fact so induced will be entitled to relief.[37]

On the other hand a person who was not actually influenced by a false representation cannot be said to have been induced to enter a contract by it. The representation may have been immaterial, in the sense that the representee's judgment was never affected[38] or the representee did not become aware, until after the conclusion of the contract, that a representation had been made.[39] In *Horsfall* v. *Thomas*,[40] for example:

T bought a cannon which had been manufactured for him by H. The cannon had a defect which made it worthless, which H had endeavoured to conceal by inserting a metal plug into the weak spot in the gun. T never inspected the gun and upon using it the gun burst.

It was held that, the attempted concealment having had no operation upon T's mind or conduct, he could not successfully set up a plea of fraud. 'If the plug, which it was said was put in to conceal the defect, had never been there, his position would have been the same; for, as he did not examine the gun or form any opinion as to whether it was sound, its condition did not affect him.'[41]

(ix) Opportunities for inspection

The mere fact that the party misled has had the opportunity of investigating and ascertaining whether the representation is true or false will not necessarily deprive that person of the right to claim to have been deceived by it;[42] but if the representee does investigate, and consequently relies not so much upon the misrepresentation as upon the accuracy of those investigations, the action will fail, as it can no longer be said that the representation was the reason for entering the

---

[35] *Arkwright* v. *Newbold* (1880) 17 Ch. D. 301, at p. 324. See also *Downs* v. *Chappell* [1997] 1 W.L.R. 426, at p. 435; *South Australia Asset Management Cpn.* v. *York Montague Ltd.* [1997] A.C. 191, at pp. 212–15; *Bristol & West B.S.* v. *Mothew* [1998] Ch. 1.

[36] *Smith* v. *Chadwick* (1884) 9 App. Cas. 187, at p. 196. See also *Barton* v. *County Natwest Ltd.* [1999] Lloyd's Rep. (Bank) 408.

[37] *Museprime Properties Ltd.* v. *Adhill Properties Ltd.* (1991) 61 P. & C.R. 111, at p. 124; *Goff* v. *Gauthier* (1991) 62 P. & C.R. 388.

[38] *Smith* v. *Chadwick* (*supra*, n. 36); *JEB Fasteners* v. *Marks, Bloom & Co.* [1983] 1 All E.R. 583.

[39] *Re Northumberland and Durham District Banking Co.* (1858) 28 L.J. Ch. 50.

[40] (1862) 1 H. & C. 90. Cf. *Smith* v. *Hughes* (1871) L.R. 6 Q.B. 597, at p. 605.

[41] At p. 99, *per* Bramwell B.

[42] *Central Ry. Co. of Venezuela* v. *Kisch* (1867) L.R. 2 H.L. 99, at p. 120; *Redgrave* v. *Hurd* (1881) 20 Ch. D. 1; *Laurence* v. *Lexcourt Holdings Ltd.* [1978] 1 W.L.R. 1128; *Alliance & Leicester B.S.* v. *Edgestop* [1993] 1 W.L.R. 1462.

contract.[43] The representation need not, however, be the sole or decisive inducement, provided that it did, in fact, materially affect the other party's intention to enter into the agreement.[44] Thus a person who bought shares in a company on the faith of fraudulent statements contained in a prospectus, but also in the erroneous belief that he would be entitled to the benefit of a charge on the company's assets, was able to rescind on the ground that he had been materially misled by the statements.[45]

(c) CATEGORIES OF MISREPRESENTATION

Once it has been established that there is an operative misrepresentation, the next step is to inquire into the state of mind of the person making the misrepresentation. In the modern law misrepresentations which merely induce the formation of a contract may either be fraudulent, negligent, or innocent. The following sections consider the requirements of each of these categories and the different remedies available. It should, however, be noted that, prior to 1963, the significant difference was between fraudulent misrepresentations for which the contract could be set aside (i.e. 'rescinded') and for which damages were available, and non-fraudulent misrepresentations (known as 'innocent misrepresentations') for which only rescission was available.[46]

The explanation for this lay in the distinction between common law and equity. Whereas in equity a contract could be rescinded for non-fraudulent misrepresentation, damages, a legal remedy, was not available in the Court of Chancery. But while the common law courts awarded damages for fraud and the breach of a contractual term, they gave no remedy whatsoever for a non-fraudulent misrepresentation which merely induced the formation of a contract.[47] The Judicature Act 1873,[48] which enabled equitable remedies to be granted in any division of the High Court, in no way affected the substantive rule that damages in addition to rescission cannot be awarded for innocent misrepresentation, and did little to change this situation. The important developments were the decision of the House of Lords in 1963 in *Hedley Byrne & Co. Ltd.* v. *Heller & Partners Ltd.*,[49] and the enactment of the Misrepresentation Act 1967.

(d) FRAUDULENT MISREPRESENTATION

At common law a *fraudulent* misrepresentation not only renders the contract voidable at the suit of the party misled, but also gives rise to an action for damages in respect of the deceit.[50] If, therefore, the misrepresentation was made fraudulently, the injured

---

[43] *Attwood* v. *Small* (1838) 6 Cl. & Fin. 232, at p. 395.

[44] *Barton* v. *Armstrong* [1976] A.C. 104, at p. 119.

[45] *Edgington* v. *Fitzmaurice* (1885) 29 Ch. D. 459.

[46] *Heilbut Symons & Co.* v. *Buckleton* [1913] A.C. 30, at p. 48; *Gilchester Properties Ltd.* v. *Gomm* [1948] 1 All E.R. 493.

[47] *Kennedy* v. *Panama, New Zealand, and Australian Royal Mail Co. Ltd.* (1987) L.R. 2 Q.B. 580, at p. 587.

[48] 1873 Act, ss. 24(1), (2), and 25(11). See now the Supreme Court Act 1981, s. 49.

[49] [1964] A.C. 465, *post* p. 247.

[50] There are also statutory remedies in respect of certain fraudulent statements: Financial Services and Markets Act 2000, s. 382 (restitution order) and Banking Act 1987, s. 35 (criminal liability).

party will be entitled to recover damages in respect of any loss which may have been suffered by reason of the fraud.

(i) The meaning of fraud at common law

The meaning of fraud was laid down by the House of Lords in *Derry* v. *Peek*:[51]

A company obtained a statutory right to run trams by animal power or, if the consent of the Board of Trade was obtained, by steam or mechanical power. The directors believed that the Board would give this consent as a matter of course, as they had already submitted plans to the Board without any objection being made. They therefore issued a prospectus saying that the company had the right to run trams by steam or mechanical power. Peek took up shares in the company on the faith of the representation. The Board of Trade ultimately refused its consent, and the company was wound up.

Peek sued in tort for deceit, and to succeed in such an action fraud had to be proved. Lord Herschell stated:[52]

First, in order to sustain an action of deceit, there must be proof of fraud, and nothing short of that will suffice. Secondly, fraud is proved when it is shewn that a false representation has been made, (1) knowingly, or (2) without belief in its truth, or (3) recklessly, careless whether it be true or false. Although I have treated the second and third as distinct cases, I think the third is but an instance of the second, for one who makes a statement under such circumstances can have no real belief in the truth of what he states.

Lord Herschell went on to point out that making a false statement through want of care falls far short of fraud; so too does a false representation honestly believed, though on insufficient grounds. But he also pointed out that when a false statement has been made, the question whether there were reasonable grounds for believing it, and what were the means of knowledge in the possession of the person making it, are weighty matters for consideration, for the ground upon which an alleged belief is founded is an important test of its reality. In the present case, there were obviously present reasons which had led the directors to make the untrue statement, and they 'honestly believed what they stated to be a true and fair representation of the facts'.[53] The respondent's action therefore failed.

Derry v. *Peek* thus establishes that a negligent misrepresentation will not amount to deceit, however gross the negligence may be.[54] Nothing short of fraud will suffice. On the other hand, it also shows that it is not necessary to constitute fraud, that there should be a clear knowledge that the statement made was false. What is essential is the absence of any belief in its truth. Further, it has been held that the motive of the person making the representation is irrelevant. It is no justification to show that

---

[51] (1990) 14 App. Cas. 337.

[52] At p. 374.

[53] *Ibid.*, at p. 376.

[54] *Angus* v. *Clifford* [1891] 2 Ch. 449, at. 464; *Thomas Witter Ltd.* v. *T.B.P. Industries Ltd.* [1996] 2 All E.R. 573, at pp. 587–8.

the representation was made without criminal dishonesty, bad motive, or that there was no intention to cheat or cause loss to another by the deception.[55]

With regard to the statement itself, it is not necessary to prove any specific representation to have been false. It is fraud intentionally to give a false impression and induce a person to act upon it, even though each fact stated taken by itself may be literally true.[56] So it is possible by stating a thing partially to make a statement which, in the sense that it must be known it will be understood, is really false.[57] A half-truth may be fraudulent because further relevant facts are suppressed. Also a statement which is believed to be true when made and which is subsequently discovered to be false, will be considered to be fraudulent if the mistake is not communicated to the other person before that person acts on it.[58]

(ii) Remedies

The remedies for fraudulent misrepresentation are several. The injured party may either affirm the contract and bring an action for damages for deceit or may elect to rescind the contract, i.e. have it set aside, and sue for damages for any loss suffered.[59] If the injured party is sued for specific performance or damages, the fraud may be set up as a defence and a counterclaim for damages for any loss suffered may be brought. If the contract has not yet been executed, the injured party may repudiate it and recover any money paid in an action for money had and received,[60] but it has been held that an account of profits made by the fraudster does not lie.[61]

Measure of damages. Although fraud is discussed here in a contractual context, the measure of damages recoverable is essentially that applicable to the tort of deceit. A wider liability is imposed upon an intentional wrongdoer than a negligent or innocent one in order to deter fraud, because 'moral considerations militate in favour of requiring the fraudster to bear the risk of misfortunes directly caused by his fraud',[62] and also because damages for fraud are frequently a restitutionary remedy.[63] Accordingly, all actual losses directly flowing from the fraud are recoverable even if they could not reasonably have been foreseen[64] and, as contributory negligence is not a

---

[55] *Bradford Building Soc.* v. *Borders* [1941] 2 All E.R. 205, at p. 211; *Brown Jenkinson & Co. Ltd.* v. *Percy Dalton (London) Ltd.* [1957] 2 Q.B. 621; *Standard Chartered Bank* v. *Pakistan National Shipping Corp. (No. 2)* [2000] 1 Lloyd's Rep. 218.

[56] *Jewson & Sons Ltd.* v. *Arcos Ltd.* (1933) 39 Com. Cas. 59.

[57] *Peek* v. *Gurney* (1873) L.R. 6 H.L. 377, at pp. 400, 403; *R.* v. *Kylsant* [1932] 1 K.B. 442.

[58] *Davies* v. *London and Provincial Marine Insurance Co.* (1878) 8 Ch. D. 469, at p. 475. See also *ante*, p. 238.

[59] On rescission, see *post*, p. 253.

[60] *Vaughan* v. *Matthews* (1849) 13 Q.B. 187, at p. 190; *Kettlewell* v. *Refuge Assurance Co.* [1908] 1 K.B. 545, [1909] A.C. 243.

[61] *Halifax B.S.* v. *Thomas* [1996] Ch. 217. But in so far as doubts were cast on the availability of restitutionary damages for fraud, *sed quaere*. See *South Australia Asset Management Cpn.* v. *York Montague Ltd.* [1997] A.C. 191, at p. 215; *Attorney-General* v. *Blake* [2001] 1 A.C. 268.

[62] *Smith New Court Securities Ltd.* v. *Citibank N.A.* [1997] A.C. 254, *per* Lord Steyn at p. 280.

[63] *South Australia Asset Management Cpn.* v. *York Montague Ltd.* [1997] A.C. 191, *per* Lord Hoffmann at p. 215.

[64] *Doyle* v. *Olby (Ironmongers) Ltd.* (*infra*, n. 71); *East* v. *Maurer* (*infra*, n. 73); *Smith New Court Securities Ltd.* v. *Citibank N.A.* (*supra*, n. 62) at pp. 267, 279.

defence to fraud, damages will not be reduced on this ground.[65] The defrauded party is, however, required to mitigate the loss once aware of the fraud[66] but where it is claimed that there has been a failure to mitigate the burden lies on the wrongdoer to show both that the defrauded party has failed to act reasonably and that the failure had in fact resulted in an increased loss.[67]

Damages in tort are assessed in accordance with what we may call the 'out of pocket' rule, that is to say, the amount by which the injured party is worse off by entering into the contract than if he had not contracted at all.[68] Unless the representation has become a term of the contract, there is no entitlement, as there would be on breach of the contract, to recover 'the loss of the bargain', that is to say, an amount which serves to put the injured party into the position in which that party would have been had the representation been true. This can be illustrated by an example loosely based on the facts in *Smith New Court Securities Ltd.* v. *Citibank N.A.* in which the House of Lords stated the applicable principles.[69]

Suppose a person has been fraudulently induced to buy shares for £24 million. They are in fact worth £12 million at the date of the contract. If the representation had been true they would have been worth £26 million. The injured party will be entitled to recover the amount by which it is out of pocket (£12 million), but not for the loss of the bargain (£14 million). The injured party must give credit for any benefits received as a result of the transaction, including, as a general rule, the market value of the property acquired. Account will not generally be taken of a fall in the market value after the date of the contract unless, as in the case of *Smith New Court Securities Ltd.*, the fraudulent misrepresentation continued to operate after that date or the party misled is unable to sell the property because of the fraud.[70] On the other hand, the party misled can undoubtedly recover in respect of consequential damage, such as injury to the person or property, or, say, the expense involved in moving into a house which that party has been fraudulently induced to buy,[71] or even for distress caused by the fraud.[72] The party misled may also recover in respect of opportunities foregone as a result of entering the contract. Thus, in *East* v. *Maurer*,[73] the purchasers of a hair salon bought in reliance on a fraudulent representation that the seller had no intention of regularly working at another salon he owned in the same town recovered, *inter alia*, the profit they would have made if the false representation had not been made, i.e. the profit they might have been expected to make in another hairdressing

---

[65] *Alliance & Leicester B.S.* v. *Edgestop Ltd.* [1993] 1 W.L.R. 1462; *Standard Chartered Bank* v. *Pakistan National S.S. Corp (No. 4)* [2001] Q.B. 167. The position is different under the Misrepresentation Act 1967, s. 2(1), see *post*, p. 248.

[66] *Smith New Court Securities Ltd.* v. *Citibank N.A.* (*supra*, n. 62) at p. 266.

[67] *Standard Chartered Bank* v. *Pakistan National S.S. Corp.* [2001] 1 All E.R. (Comm.) 822.

[68] *Peek* v. *Derry* (1887) 37 Ch. D. 541, at p. 594; *Clef Aquitaine SARL* v. *Laporte Ltd.* [2001] Q.B. 488 (though transaction not loss-making, a more profitable one would have been entered into but for defendant's deceit).

[69] [1997] A.C. 254, *per* Lord Browne Wilkinson at p. 267.

[70] *Ibid.*

[71] *Doyle* v. *Olby (Ironmongers) Ltd.* [1969] 2 Q.B. 158.

[72] *Shelley* v. *Paddock* [1979] Q.B. 120; *Archer* v. *Brown* [1985] Q.B. 401.

[73] [1991] 1 W.L.R. 461. See also *Smith New Court Securities Ltd.* v. *Citibank N.A.* (*supra*, n. 62) at p. 282.

business bought for a similar sum. As Sedley L.J. noted in a later case, 'it does not follow that the proper mode of ascertaining damage in certain cases of tort may not mimic reasoning more familiar in contract.'[74]

(e) NEGLIGENT MISREPRESENTATION

(i) Common law

A person who has been induced to enter into a contract as the result of a negligent misrepresentation made to him or her by the other party to the contract is entitled to rescind as in the case of fraud.[75] But before the passing of the Misrepresentation Act 1967, in the absence of a fiduciary relationship,[76] there was no definitive authority for the proposition that there was also an entitlement to claim damages. In 1963, in the case of *Hedley Byrne & Co. Ltd.* v. *Heller & Partners Ltd.*[77] the House of Lords extended liability in damages in tort to negligent misstatement and held that a duty of care could exist where there was an assumption of responsibility such as to create a 'special relationship' between the person making the statement and the person to whom it was made. The principle is not restricted to statements that induce a contract[78] and the effect of this decision on such statements and the law relating to misrepresentation was not directly considered,[79] nor were the tests advanced by their Lordships for determining the existence of this special relationship uniform in their terminology.[80] Nevertheless, it is clear that the existence of a contract between the parties does not exclude a parallel or concurrent duty of care in tort.[81] Moreover, it has been held that a negligent misrepresentation made by one party to the other preparatory to entering into a contract can give rise to an action for damages in tort for negligent misstatement if the person making it has or professes to have special knowledge or skill in respect of the facts stated[82] or if the representation, in the context in which it is made, is to be regarded as neither casual nor unconsidered, but to be relied on.[83] The burden of proving negligence rests on the party alleging it, i.e. on the representee.

Measure of damages. Again, the tort measure applies, but for a negligent misstatement only losses that are foreseeable can be recovered. Recent cases have considered the

---

[74] *Clef Aquitaine SARL* v. *Laporte Ltd.* [2001] Q.B. 488, at p. 513.

[75] On rescission, see *post*, p. 253.

[76] On the liability and more rigorous duties of a fiduciary, see *Nocton* v. *Lord Ashburton* [1914] A.C. 932, at p. 954 and *post*, p. 267.

[77] [1964] A.C. 465.

[78] *Box* v. *Midland Bank Ltd.* [1979] 2 Lloyd's Rep. 391; *Williams* v. *Natural Life Health Foods Ltd.* [1998] 1 W.L.R. 830, at pp. 834–5.

[79] But see Lord Pearce, *ibid.*, at p. 539.

[80] [1964] A.C. 465, at pp. 486, 503, 514, 528, 529.

[81] *Henderson* v. *Merrett Syndicates Ltd.* [1995] 2A.C. 145, *per* Lord Goff at pp. 186–91.

[82] *Esso Petroleum Co. Ltd.* v. *Mardon* [1976] Q.B. 801; *Cornish* v. *Midland Bank plc* [1985] 3 All E.R. 512; *Gran Gelato Ltd.* v. *Richcliff (Group) Ltd.* [1992] Ch. 560. Contrast *Oleificio Zucchi S.p.A.* v. *Northern Sales Ltd.* [1965] 2 Lloyd's Rep. 496, at p. 519; *Argy Training Development Co. Ltd.* v. *Lapid Developments Ltd.* [1977] 1 W.L.R. 444.

[83] *Howard Marine and Dredging Co. Ltd.* v. *A. Ogden & Sons (Excavations) Ltd.* [1978] Q.B. 574, at pp. 592, 600.

position where the duty is not to advise but is only to take care that information is correct, for example the valuation of a property by a surveyor or information given by a solicitor to a client. In such cases the damages are not based on an assessment of what the injured party's position would have been had accurate information been given, which might, where that party would not have entered into the transaction at all, have included a fall after the date of the contract in the market value of the property purchased. It has been held[84] that because the duty of a valuer is to take care to ensure that information regarding value is correct, a valuer is only liable for the foreseeable loss of the information being wrong, so that the damages are the difference between the valuation given and the true value of the property at the time of the breach. This has been criticized as inappropriately capping the tort measure by reference to the contractual bargain[85] and as redefining 'duty' in a way that prevents inquiry into the other legal issues; namely causation, remoteness, and measure of damages.[86]

(ii) Misrepresentation Act 1967

The uncertainties concerning the way in which the principle laid down in the case of *Hedley Byrne & Co. Ltd.* v. *Heller & Partners Ltd.* operated in respect of pre-contractual statements were largely removed by section 2(1) of the Misrepresentation Act 1967,[87] which establishes a statutory right to damages:

Where a person has entered into a contract after a misrepresentation has been made to him by another party thereto and as a result thereof he has suffered loss, then, if the person making the misrepresentation would be liable to damages in respect thereof had the misrepresentation been made fraudulently, that person shall be so liable, notwithstanding that the misrepresentation was not made fraudulently, unless he proves that he had reasonable ground to believe and did believe up to the time the contract was made that the facts represented were true.

The use of the words 'reasonable ground to believe' might suggest that the duty imposed upon the representor is equivalent to the duty of care in negligence, the extent of which may vary according to the circumstances in which the representation is made. But in *Howard Marine and Dredging Co. Ltd.* v. *A. Ogden & Sons (Excavations) Ltd.*:[88]

O entered into a charterparty by which it chartered from H.M. two barges. In the course of negotiations leading to the contract, H.M.'s manager represented to O that the barges had a payload of 1,600 tonnes. He based this figure on his recollection of a statement in Lloyd's Register that the deadweight capacity of the barges was 1,800 tonnes. That statement was in fact erroneous and the German shipping documents (which the manager had seen) relating

---

[84] *South Australia Asset Management Cpn.* v. *York Montague Ltd.* [1997] A.C. 191. See also *Bristol & West B.S.* v. *Mothew* [1998] Ch. 1; *Swindle* v. *Harrison* [1997] 4 All E.R. 705 (breach of fiduciary duty). Cf. *Aneco Reinsurance Underwriting Ltd.* v. *Johnson & Higgins Ltd.* [2002] 2 Lloyd's Rep. 157, paras 36–9 (duty to advise).

[85] Stapleton (1997) 113 L.Q.R. 1. See also McLaughlan *ibid.* at p. 421; [1997] J.C.L. 114, cf. Dugdale [1995] J.B.L. 533.

[86] *Kenny & Good Pty Ltd.* v. *M.G.I.C.A. (1992) Ltd.* (1999) 163 A.L.R. 611, *per* Gummow J. at pp. 634–5.

[87] Implementing the Tenth Report of the Law Reform Committee (Cmd. 1782, 1962), § 17. The precedent for s. 2(1) was in s. 43 of the Companies Act 1948. See now Financial Services and Markets Act 2000, s. 90; *post*, p. 270.

[88] [1978] Q.B. 574.

to the barges gave the true deadweight capacity at 1,055 tonnes. O refused to pay the agreed hire charges and H.M. withdrew the barges and sued for the balance due. O counterclaimed £600,000 on the grounds of misrepresentation, being the loss which it alleged it had sustained because of the low carrying capacity of the barges.

The Court of Appeal was divided as to whether the circumstances were such as to impose a duty of care in negligence at common law.[89] But a majority of the Court held[90] that H.M. was liable under section 2(1), since the sub-section goes further than the common law, does not require a special relationship or special skill and does not depend upon the representor being under a duty of care the extent of which may vary according to the circumstances in which the representation is made. The statute imposes an absolute obligation not to state facts which the representor cannot prove it had reasonable ground to believe were true. The burden thus lies on the representor and not, as at common law, on the representee and it may be a heavy one to discharge, particularly since reasonable ground for belief in the truth of the statement must be shown to exist up to the time the contract is made.

It should, however, be noted that the sub-section is narrower than the common law because it only applies where a person has (a) entered into a contract after a misrepresentation has been made to that person and (b) the misrepresentation is made by another party to the contract, and not by a third party. Thus if A enters into a contract with B as a result of a misrepresentation made to B by C, no action will lie under the sub-section unless C is B's agent; nor will C be liable to A under this provision, though C might be liable under a collateral warranty,[91] or in tort for negligent misstatement if a special relationship of care or reliance is shown to exist.

Liability in damages has also been imposed in respect of negligent statements in the listing of particulars of securities,[92] and misleading information in literature concerning package holidays.[93] It is also a criminal offence for an estate agent or property developer to make false or misleading statements concerning the description of property.[94]

Measure of damages. The effect of section 2(1) of the 1967 Act is to confer upon the representee a right to damages for misrepresentation in circumstances in which there would have been such a right had the misrepresentation been fraudulent. It is now clear[95] that the measure of damages is the tortious measure, i.e. reliance losses so as to put the representee in the position he would have been in had he never entered into the contract.[96] But the equation with fraud has given rise to certain problems.[97] Most

[89] Lord Denning M.R. and Shaw L.J. Bridge L.J. expressed no concluded view on this issue.

[90] Bridge and Shaw L.JJ. (Lord Denning M.R. dissenting).

[91] *Ante,* p. 130.

[92] Financial Services and Markets Act 2000, s. 90. Those responsible must show they had reasonable grounds for believing the statement was true and not misleading: *ibid.,* Sched. 10, para. 2.

[93] Package Travel, Package Holidays and Package Tours Regulations 1992 (S.I. 1992 No. 3288) implementing Council Directive 90/314/EC.

[94] Property Misdescription Act 1991, s. 1.   [95] Cf. *Watts* v. *Spence* [1976] Ch. 165, at p. 178.

[96] See generally Atiyah and Treitel (1967) 30 M.L.R. 369, 372–5. Cf. the different formulation in Financial Services and Markets Act 2000, ss. 90, 150, 166.

[97] *Sharneyford Supplies Ltd.* v. *Edge* [1987] Ch. 305; *Naughton* v. *O'Callaghan* [1990] 3 All E.R. 191, at p. 196; *Royscott Trust Ltd.* v. *Rogerson* [1991] 2 Q.B. 297. See also *André et Cie S.A.* v. *Ets. Michel Blanc et Fils* [1977] 2 Lloyd's Rep. 166, at p. 181. On the effect of a fall in market value, see *ante,* pp. 246, 248.

importantly, it appears that under the sub-section it is the fraud measure rather than that for negligent misstatement at common law which applies. This allows the recovery of all damages directly flowing from the misrepresentation even if not foreseeable. In *Royscott Trust Ltd.* v. *Rogerson*:[98]

A finance company was induced to advance a greater sum than it would otherwise have done by a car dealer's misrepresentation that a 20 per cent deposit had been paid by a prospective hire-purchaser of a car. The hire-purchaser later ceased to pay the instalments due and dishonestly sold the car. It was held that whether or not the sale by the hire-purchaser was foreseeable, the loss to the finance company of the unpaid instalments was recoverable under section 2(1) of the 1967 Act from the car dealer.

The argument that as a matter of policy it was undesirable to adopt the fraud measure for what is basically negligence liability since fools should not be treated as if they were rogues,[99] was rejected by the Court of Appeal as incompatible with the literal words of the statute. There may, nevertheless, be reluctance to apply the fraud measure, for example taking the view that, at the margin, 'a misrepresentation should not be too easily found'.[100] The point is, however, not beyond argument. First it was not necessary in *Royscott*'s case to choose between the tort and the fraud measures. This was because the act of disposing of the car by the hire-purchaser was held to be foreseeable so the unpaid instalments would have been recoverable in any event. Secondly, not all the consequences of fraud follow in the case of liability under section 2(1) of the 1967 Act. It has been held that damages under section 2(1) may be reduced for contributory negligence where the loss was partly the fault of the representee.[101] As has been seen,[102] common law damages for fraudulent misrepresentation may not be reduced for contributory negligence. Again, the extended limitation period for fraud may not apply to liability under section 2(1).[103] There are, moreover, indications that the House of Lords would be reluctant to find that what Lord Steyn described as 'the rather loose wording' of the statute 'compels the court to treat a person who was morally innocent as if he was guilty of fraud when it comes to the measure of damages'.[104]

[98] [1991] 2 Q.B. 297. See also *William Sindall plc* v. *Cambridgeshire C.C.* [1994] 1 W.L.R. 1016, at p. 1037; *South Australia Asset Management Cpn.* v. *York Montague Ltd.* [1997] A.C. 191, at p. 216.

[99] Fairest [1967] C.L.J. 239, at p. 244; Hooley (1991) 107 L.Q.R. 547, at pp. 549–51. Cf. Atiyah and Treitel (1967) 30 M.L.R. 369, at p. 373; Cartwright, *Unequal Bargaining* (1991), pp. 131–2.

[100] *Avon Insurance plc.* v. *Swire Fraser Ltd.* [2000] 1 All E.R. (Comm.) 573, at p. 633.

[101] *Gran Gelato Ltd.* v. *Richcliff (Group) Ltd.* [1992] Ch. 560, at p. 574. But note that Nicholls V-C. stated, at p. 573, that 'in short liability under the Misrepresentation Act 1967 is essentially founded on negligence' and see Cane (1992) 108 L.Q.R. 539, at p. 544.

[102] *Ante*, pp. 245–6.

[103] *Garden Neptune Shipping Ltd.* v. *Occidental Worldwide Investment Cpn.* [1990] 1 Lloyd's Rep. 330, at p. 335.

[104] *Smith New Court Securities Ltd.* v. *Citibank N.A.* [1997] A.C. 254, at p. 283. See also *ibid., per* Lord Browne Wilkinson at p. 267.

(f) INNOCENT MISREPRESENTATION

(i) Meaning of 'innocent' misrepresentation

It has been noted that historically all non-fraudulent misrepresentations were known as 'innocent misrepresentations'. Now that liability in damages for negligent misrepresentation has been created first in 1963 by the common law and then by section 2(1) of the Misrepresentation Act 1967, the term 'innocent misrepresentation' must be understood to mean a misrepresentation in which *no element of fraud or negligence is presented*. A person who has been induced to enter into a contract as the result of an innocent misrepresentation made to him by the other party to the contract is entitled to the remedy of rescission or to damages in lieu of rescission; but, in contrast with cases of fraudulent or negligent misrepresentation, cannot obtain damages in addition to rescission, only an indemnity.

(ii) Refusal of specific performance

Where there has been an innocent misrepresentation, the party misled may plead the misrepresentation as a defence to an action against him for specific performance of the contract. Specific performance is a discretionary remedy and it will be refused where it would be inequitable for one party to insist on performance of the contract by the other. Thus it will be refused where the party against whom it is sought would not have entered into the contract but for the misrepresentation.[105]

(iii) Rescission

The ability to resist specific performance may not, however, suffice to protect the party misled who does not wish to perform, since, if the contract is not set aside, it may leave that person exposed to an action for damages. The party misled may therefore also obtain rescission of the contract, either as a defence to an action brought by the misrepresenter or by bringing proceedings. Thus in *Redgrave* v. *Hurd*:[106]

R induced H to enter into a contract for the purchase of his house and, together with the house, his practice as a solicitor. He misstated the value of his practice and H refused to complete the purchase of the house. When sued for specific performance, H counterclaimed for rescission of the contract and for the return of the deposit which he had paid.

The Court of Appeal held that specific performance should be refused and the contract rescinded; H accordingly recovered his deposit. The requirements and limits of rescission are considered below.[107]

(iv) Indemnity

When a contract is rescinded, each party is entitled to be relieved of the obligations under the contract and to recover any benefit which has been conferred upon the other party. The object of rescission is to restore the *status quo ante*, and with this end

---

[105] *Lamare* v. *Dixon* (1873) L.R. 6 H.L. 414.
[106] (1881) 20 Ch. D. 1.
[107] *Post*, p. 253.

in view the party misled can claim an indemnity against any obligations which may be incurred, or which have been incurred, as a result of the contract.

The exact principle upon which an indemnity is to be assessed is not, however, entirely clear. In *Newbigging* v. *Adam*:[108]

N entered into a partnership with A and provided £10,000 of new capital. He was induced to enter into the partnership agreement by a material innocent misrepresentation as to the capacity of certain machinery. The business failed, and N sued for rescission of the agreement, for recovery of his capital, and for an indemnity against all claims which might be made against him by virtue of his having become a partner.

The Court of Appeal agreed that N was entitled to the relief for which he asked, that the right to an indemnity must be less extensive than the right to damages, and that the principle underlying the award of an indemnity is to restore the party misled to his old position. But they differed in their conclusion as to how the *status quo ante* should in general be achieved. Fry L.J. was inclined to hold that the party misled 'is entitled to an indemnity in respect of all obligations entered into under the contract when those obligations are within the necessary or reasonable expectation of both of the contracting parties at the time they made the contract'.[109] But an award made on this basis would differ in no way from damages, and it is submitted that a narrower and more satisfactory test was propounded by Bowen L.J. when he said the party misled 'is not to be replaced in exactly the same position in all respects, otherwise he would be entitled to recover damages, but he is to be replaced in his position so far as regards the rights and obligations which have been *created by the contract* into which he has been induced to enter'.[110]

The distinction between damages and an indemnity as it works out in practice may be illustrated by the case of *Whittington* v. *Seale-Hayne*,[111] where the Court adopted the narrower principle suggested by Bowen L.J.:

Poultry farmers had been induced to take a lease by the defendant's innocent oral misrepresentation that the premises were sanitary. This was not the case, and in consequence of the contamination of the water supply, their manager fell ill and the poultry died. They claimed rescission of the lease, and an indemnity to cover the value of the stock, loss of profit on sales, loss of breeding season, medical expenses of the manager, rates, rent, and money spent on outbuildings, etc. They had also been compelled by the local council to renew the drains, and this item, too, was included.

It was held that the poultry farmers were entitled to have the lease rescinded, and to recover what they had spent on rent, rates, and the renewal of the drains, since these were expenses incurred under the covenants in the lease or arising necessarily out of the occupation of the property, and thus 'obligations created by the contract'. Their claim for payment in respect of the other items of loss was not allowed, since these

---

[108] (1886) 34 Ch. D. 582, aff'd *sub nom. Adam* v. *Newbigging* (1888) 13 App. Cas. 308.
[109] At p. 596. Cotton L.J. at p. 589, agreed.
[110] At p. 593.
[111] (1900) 82 L.T. 49.

were damages, there being no obligation to carry on a poultry farm on the leased premises.

(g) RESCISSION

Rescission is, in principle, available for all classes of operative misrepresentation.[112] When a person has been induced to enter into a contract by a misrepresentation of any description, the effect on the contract is not to make it void, but to give the party misled an option, either to avoid it, or, alternatively, to affirm it.

A party who is misled and elects to avoid the contract may take steps to have it set aside by the Courts or may resist an action for specific performance, or for damages, brought by the representor, and rescind by way of counterclaim.[113] Rescission, however, is not merely a judicial remedy. The party misled can therefore rescind without seeking the assistance of a Court, and any property transferred under the contract will revest in the party who has so rescinded the contract.

(i) Mode of rescission

As a normal rule, rescission must be communicated to the other party.[114] But where a seller of goods has a right to avoid the contract for fraud, it suffices if the seller at once, on discovering the fraud, takes all possible steps to regain the goods. In *Car and Universal Finance Co. Ltd. v. Caldwell*:[115]

C was fraudulently induced to sell a motor car to a purchaser in return for a bad cheque. When the cheque was dishonoured, C immediately informed the police and the Automobile Association, but the purchaser had deliberately absconded and could not be found. The purchaser subsequently sold the car. It came into the hands of the plaintiff who bought it in good faith.

The Court of Appeal held that C had effectively rescinded the contract even though he had not communicated his rescission to the purchaser. The title to the car had revested in the defendant on rescission and so the plaintiff had no claim to the vehicle.

(ii) Limits to right to rescind

Certain limitations have been placed by the law on the right to rescind. In a number of situations, the party misled may be precluded from rescinding the contract. It is important to note, however, that the loss of the remedy of rescission will not prevent a claim for damages for fraud or negligent misstatement or under section 2(1) of the Misrepresentation Act 1967. The right to damages, where this exists, still survives.

There are five limitations on the right to rescind.

(a) Affirmation. If after becoming aware of the misrepresentation the representee

---

[112] On the similar principles governing rescission for undue influence, see *post*, p. 293.

[113] The setting up of the misrepresentation by way of defence has in some instances been treated as equivalent to rescission: *Clough* v. *London & N.W. Ry.* (1871) L.R. 7 Ex. 26. Cf. *Berg* v. *Sadler & Moore* [1937] 2 K.B. 158.

[114] *Scarfe* v. *Jardine* (1882) 7 App. Cas. 345, at pp. 360, 361.

[115] [1961] 1 Q.B. 525. Cf. *Newtons of Wembley Ltd.* v. *Williams* [1965] 1 Q.B. 560.

affirms the contract either by express words or by an act which shows an intention to affirm it, rescission cannot be obtained. So, for example, if persons who have purchased shares on the faith of a misrepresentation subsequently become aware of its falsity, but neglect to remove their name from the register of shareholders,[116] or accept dividends paid to them,[117] they will not be permitted to avoid the contract. In *Long* v. *Lloyd*:[118]

Long was induced to purchase a lorry by Lloyd's representation that it was 'in excellent condition'. On the first journey after the sale, the dynamo broke and Long noticed several other serious defects. Lloyd was informed of these and offered to pay half the cost of some of the repairs. On the next long journey, the lorry broke down completely and Long realized that it was in a deplorable condition. He claimed to rescind the contract.

The Court of Appeal held that, although the first journey did not amount to an affirmation of the contract as it had been undertaken merely to test the truth of Lloyd's representation, the second journey did constitute such an affirmation since Long then had knowledge that the representation was untrue.

It has been held that the right to rescind will not be lost by affirmation unless the representee has knowledge of the facts and that these give rise to the right to rescind.[119] Where there is no such knowledge, however, the conduct of the representee may, if relied on by the representor, give rise to an estoppel precluding rescission.[120]

The position thus differs from that concerning the right to reject for breach of condition in contracts for the sale of goods which may be lost by 'acceptance' without such knowledge.[121] In *Long* v. *Lloyd*, where there may not have been such knowledge, the Court may have considered that rescission for misrepresentation should be barred where the right to reject for breach of condition has been lost.[122]

(b) Lapse of time. Lapse of time may in certain circumstances bar the right to rescind. It may be treated as evidence of affirmation where the party misled fails to exercise the right to rescind for a considerable time after discovering the representation to be untrue.[123] But, since knowledge is required for affirmation, mere lapse of time does not normally have this effect.[124] Exceptionally, however, the passage of time may operate so as to preclude rescission even though the representee has no knowledge of the untruth of the representation. Thus, in the case of an executed contract of sale of goods, it has been held that rescission for innocent misrepresentation may be barred

---

[116] *Re Scottish Petroleum Co.* (1883) 23 Ch. D. 413, at p. 434.

[117] *Scholey* v. *Central Ry Co. of Venezuela* (1867) L.R. 9 Eq. 266.

[118] [1958] 1 W.L.R. 753.

[119] *Peyman* v. *Lanjani* [1985] Ch. 457, at pp. 486–7.

[120] *Ibid.*, at p. 488; *Motor Oil Hellas (Corinth) Refineries S.A.* v. *Shipping Corp. Of India* [1990] 1 Lloyd's Rep. 391, at pp. 398–9, *per* Lord Goff.

[121] Sale of Goods Act 1979, s. 35 as amended by the Sale and Supply of Goods Act 1994, *ante*, p. 144.

[122] See *Leaf* v. *International Galleries* [1950] 2 K.B. 86, at p. 91; Atiyah (1959) 22 M.L.R. 76; Davies (1959) 75 L.Q.R. 32.

[123] *Clough* v. *L. & N.W. Ry* (1871) L.R. 7 Ex. 26, at p. 35. Cf. *Allen* v. *Robles* [1969] 1 W.L.R. 1193.

[124] *Armstrong* v. *Jackson* [1917] 2 K.B. 822, at p. 830.

where the lapse of time amounts to an acceptance of the goods.[125] In *Leaf* v. *International Galleries*:[126]

L bought from I.G. a picture of Salisbury Cathedral which I.G. innocently represented to him at the time of the purchase to have been painted by Constable. Five years later, when he tried to sell it, he discovered this was not the case. He endeavoured to return the picture and recover the price. I.G. refused, whereupon he brought an action claiming rescission of the contract of sale.

The Court of Appeal held that the right to rescind had been lost.

(c) Right of third parties. Since the contract is voidable and not void, being valid until rescinded, if third parties *bona fide* without notice and for value acquire rights in the subject-matter of the contract, those rights are valid against the party misled, provided that the contract has not before that time been rescinded.[127] The standard illustration of this principle is provided by a shareholder who wishes to rescind a contract to take up shares in a company; this must be done before winding-up, for once winding-up commences, the rights of the creditors become fixed, since they stand in the position of *bona fide* purchasers for value.[128] Also where goods are obtained by means of a fraud, a person who, before rescission, acquires the goods in good faith and for value from the fraudulent purchaser cannot be displaced by the party defrauded.[129]

(d) Ability to restore. It has been said that when a party 'exercises his option to rescind the contract, he must be in a state to rescind; that is, he must be in such a situation to be able to put the parties into their original state before the contract'.[130] Each must give back what has been transferred. But the purpose of this limitation is to prevent the unjust enrichment of the party seeking to rescind[131] and it should not be too strictly construed. Thus the mere fact that the subject-matter of the contract may have deteriorated before the truth is discovered is not sufficient to prevent a *restitutio in integrum* and so to destroy the right to rescind a contract.[132] In *Adam* v. *Newbigging*[133] rescission was granted of a partnership agreement even though the partnership business was then 'worse than worthless'.

The Courts have refrained from defining the scope of this equitable remedy by any rigid rules;[134] as a condition of rescission there must be *restitutio in integrum*, but at

---

[125] See *post*, p. 258.

[126] [1950] 2 K.B. 86.

[127] *Babcock* v. *Lawson* (1880) 5 Q.B.D. 284.

[128] *Oakes* v. *Turquand* (1867) L.R. 2 H.L. 325.

[129] Sale of Goods Act 1979, s. 23; *Phillips* v. *Brooks Ltd.* [1919] 2 K.B. 243. Cf. *Car and Universal Finance Co. Ltd.* v. *Caldwell* (*ante*, p. 253)—goods acquired after rescission.

[130] *Clarke* v. *Dickson* (1858) E.B. & E. 148, *per* Crompton J. at p. 154; 'You cannot both eat your cake and return your cake', Kinglake Serjt. *arguendo*.

[131] *McKenzie* v. *Royal Bank of Canada* [1934] A.C. 468; *Bouygues Offshore* v. *United Transport Contractors* [1996] 2 Lloyd's Rep. 153, at p. 159.

[132] *Armstrong* v. *Jackson* [1917] 2 K.B. 822, at p. 829; *Lagunas Nitrate Co.* v. *Lagunas Syndicate* [1899] 2 Ch. 392; *Alati* v. *Kruger* (1955) 94 C.L.R. 216 (Australia).

[133] (1888) 13 App. Cas. 308, *ante*, p. 252.

[134] *Hulton* v. *Hulton* [1917] 1 K.B. 813, *per* Swinfen Eady L.J., at p. 821.

the same time the Court has full power to make all just allowances. It was said by Lord Blackburn in *Erlanger* v. *New Sombrero Phosphate Co.*[135] that the practice had always been for a Court of Equity to give relief by way of rescission whenever by the exercise of its powers it can do what is practically just by directing accounts, ordering equitable compensation,[136] and making allowances, though it cannot restore the parties precisely to the state they were in before the contract.

How this goal of doing 'what is practically just' may be reached depends on the circumstances of the case. For instance, the Court may think that justice requires the making of some allowance for the deterioration, or the improvement, as the case may be, of the subject-matter of the contract. Again, it may require compensation for losses incurred by the representor[137] or recompense for services rendered to the representee.[138] The Court will be more drastic in exercising its discretionary powers in a case of fraud than in a case where no fraud is present; it will be 'less ready to pull a transaction to pieces where the defendant is innocent, whereas in the case of fraud the Court will exercise its jurisdiction to the full in order, if possible, to prevent the defendant from enjoying the benefit of his fraud at the expense of the innocent plaintiff'.[139] But, even in a case of fraud, rescission will not be ordered where it is not possible to achieve a broadly just result by orders for monetary adjustment to reflect benefits and detriments which have accrued under the contract since to do so would unjustly enrich the defrauded party.[140]

(iii) No power to award partial rescission

Nothwithstanding the flexibility of equity, it was held in *T.S.B. Bank plc* v. *Camfield*[141] that because, save as is otherwise provided by statute, the right to rescind is that of the representee and not of the Court, there is no power to order partial rescission. In that case, as a result of an innocent misrepresentation, a woman charged her interest in a house to a bank to secure the debts of her husband's business believing that the maximum liability under the charge was £15,000 when it was in fact unlimited. Despite her willingness to charge the property for £15,000, the charge was set aside in its entirety. This result has not been followed in Australia[142] and is open to question.[143] It is in marked contrast to the approach of equity in analogous situations. Thus, mortgagees' claims have been upheld only to the extent of the other party's

---

[135] (1878) 3 App. Cas. 1218, at p. 1278.

[136] See *Mahony* v. *Purnell* [1996] 3 All E.R. 61 (undue influence).

[137] *Spence* v. *Crawford* [1939] 3 All E.R. 271, *per* Lord Thankerton at 283 (loss to representor from sale by bank of shares held as security conceded to be recoverable). See also *Cheese* v. *Thomas* [1994] 1 W.L.R. 129 (undue influence).

[138] *Atlantic Lines & Navigation Co. Inc* v. *Hallam Ltd.* [1983] 1 Lloyd's Rep. 188, *per* Mustill J. at p. 202 (services of chartered ship); *O'Sullivan* v. *Management Agency and Music Ltd.* [1985] 1 Q.B. 428.

[139] *Spence* v. *Crawford* [1939] 3 All E.R. 271, *per* Lord Wright at p. 288.

[140] *Society of Lloyd's* v. *Wilkinson (No. 2)* (1997) 6 Re. L.R. 214, at p. 222, *ibid.*, at pp. 289, 296.

[141] [1995] 1 W.L.R. 430. See also *de Molestina* v. *Ponton* [2002] 1 Lloyd's Rep. 271, at pp. 286–8.

[142] *Vadasz* v. *Pioneer Concrete (S.A.) Pty. Ltd.* (1995) 184 C.L.R. 102.

[143] The matter was left open by the Privy Council in *Scales Trading Ltd.* v. *Far Eastern Shipping Co. Ltd.* [2001] 1 All E.R. (Comm.) 319 at p. 326 although the New Zealand Court of Appeal had expressed a strong preference for the flexible approach in *Vadasz's* case (*supra* n. 142).

understanding of the amount of the mortgage.[144] Again, in rescission for undue influence, the Court is concerned to achieve 'practical justice' for both parties. It has been noted that the party seeking rescission may be required to pay the other reasonable remuneration for beneficial services rendered,[145] and, where the market value of property transferred has fallen, to bear a proportionate part of the loss.[146] Where the objectionable parts of a transaction can be severed without rewriting it, setting aside is, moreover, not invariably an 'all or nothing process'.[147] The inflexible approach in *T.S.B. Bank plc.* v. *Camfield*[148] is also in marked contrast to the statutory power in the Court to award damages in lieu of rescission, to which we now turn.[149]

(iv) Damages in lieu of rescission

Except in cases of fraud,[150] the Court has a discretion to refuse to allow rescission and to award damages in lieu of this remedy. This power is conferred by section 2(2) of the Misrepresentation Act 1967, which states:

Where a person has entered into a contract after a misrepresentation has been made to him otherwise than fraudulently, and he would be entitled, by reason of the misrepresentation, to rescind the contract, then, if it is claimed in any proceedings arising out of the contract, that the contract ought to be or has been rescinded, the court or arbitrator may declare the contract subsisting and award damages in lieu of rescission, if of opinion that it would be equitable to do so, having regard to the nature of the misrepresentation and the loss that would be caused by it if the contract were upheld, as well as to the loss that rescission would cause to the other party.

The reason for this provision is that rescission in some situations may be too drastic a remedy; for example, a car might be returned to the seller because of a trifling misrepresentation about the mileage done since the engine was last overhauled.[151] Section 2(2) allows the Court to take into account the relative importance or unimportance of the facts which have been misrepresented. It also allows the Court to take into account the relationship of the loss caused to the representee by the misrepresentation and the loss which would be caused to the representor if the contract is

[144] *Bristol & West B.S.* v. *Hemming* [1985] 1 W.L.R. 778 and *Skipton B.S.* v. *Clayton* (1993) 66 P. & C.R. 233. See Ferguson (1995) 111 L.Q.R. 555.

[145] *O'Sullivan* v. *Management Agency and Music Ltd.* [1985] 1 Q.B. 428.

[146] *Cheese* v. *Thomas* [1994] 1 W.L.R. 129. See also Jones and Goodhart, *Specific Performance*, 2nd edn. (1996), p. 293 (purchaser's action for specific performance with compensation).

[147] *Barclays Bank plc.* v. *Caplan* [1998] 1 F.L.R. 532, at p. 546.

[148] [1995] 1 W.L.R. 430.

[149] Misrepresentation Act 1967, s. 2(2), *post*, p. 259. In *T.S.B. Bank plc* v. *Canfield* the bank conceded that it could not invoke section 2(2) directly and since an award of damages against the husband would have been an empty remedy no court could have formed the view that it would be equitable to exercise its power under section 2(2).

[150] It is uncertain whether fraud will embrace cases of constructive fraud in equity, e.g. the breach of a fiduciary duty: see *post*, p. 267.

[151] See the Tenth Report of the Law Reform Committee (Cmnd. 1782, 1962), § 11.

rescinded. Where the former is significantly less than the latter it is likely that damages in lieu of rescission will be awarded.[152]

(a) Unavailable where rescission barred. Is there power to award damages of this nature where the right to rescind, though once in existence, has become barred, e.g. by reason of affirmation, lapse of time, the intervention of third party rights, or an inability to make *restitutio in integrum*? The sub-section and its legislative history are ambiguous,[153] but no such power was proposed by the Law Reform Committee.[154] Statements in the cases indicate a divergence of view but it is submitted that the better view is that, while a power to award damages although rescission is barred might be desirable, no such power was created by the sub-section.[155] Although it has been suggested that the time for determining entitlement to rescind is the time of the Court's order,[156] the better view is that the relevant time is the commencement of proceedings, or the time the representee purports to rescind the contract. The reasons that preclude rescission are often practical and have no relevance to the question whether damages should be awarded and the Law Reform Committee's report, which relied on the analogy of damages in lieu of specific relief,[157] supports the earlier time. The Court's discretion, however, appears unimpaired where the misrepresentation has subsequently been incorporated as a term of the contract. As we shall see, a misrepresentation retains its character as such even though it is incorporated as a contractual term,[158] so that the representee continues to enjoy a right to rescind. The Court in this case could still refuse to allow rescission for misrepresentation and award damages in lieu.[159]

(b) Measure of damages. The measure of damages to be awarded under this sub-section is the loss caused by the misrepresentation as a result of the refusal to allow rescission of the contract not the loss caused by entering into the contract.[160] This, in a contract for the sale of land, for example, would be the difference in value between what the representee was misled into thinking was being bought and the value of what was received.

---

[152] *William Sindall plc* v. *Cambridgeshire C.C.* [1994] 1 W.L.R. 1016, at p. 1038 (loss to representee £18,000 to divert a sewer; loss to representor some £6 million in return of purchase price and interest for land the value of which had substantially fallen).

[153] Atiyah and Treitel (1967) 30 M.L.R. 369, at pp. 375–9.

[154] Tenth Report (Cmd. 1782, 1962), § 27.

[155] *Atlantic Lines and Navigation Co. Inc.* v. *Hallam Ltd.* [1983] 1 Lloyd's Rep. 188; *Government of Zanzibar* v. *British Aerospace (Lancaster House) Ltd.* [2000] 1 W.L.R. 2333. Cf. *Thomas Witter Ltd.* v. *T.B.P. Industries Ltd.* [1996] 2 All E.R. 573 relying (at p. 590) on a statement of the Solicitor-General on the third reading of the Bill (741 H.C. Deb., col. 1387, 20 February 1967) but contrast the Lord Chancellor and Viscount Colville of Culross (274 H.L. Deb., col. 929, 17 May 1966; 277 H.L. Deb., col. 53, 18 October 1966). See further Beale (1995) 111 L.Q.R. 385.

[156] *Atlantic Lines & Navigation Co. Inc.* v. *Hallam Ltd.* [1983] 1 Lloyd's Rep. 188.

[157] Tenth Report (Cmd. 1782, 1962), § 11. See also *William Sindall plc* v. *Cambridgeshire C.C. (supra,* n. 152) at p. 1037.

[158] Misrepresentation Act 1967, s. 1(a); *post*, p. 260.

[159] The right of the representee to repudiate for breach of condition, if the misrepresentation has become a condition, would not, it seems, be affected.

[160] *William Sindall plc* v. *Cambridgeshire C.C.* [1994] 1 W.L.R. 1016.

It has been stated that the damages under the sub-section should never exceed what the claimant would have got had the representation been a term. As section 2(2) was enacted because it was thought it might be a hardship to the representor to be deprived of the whole of the benefit of the bargain on account of a minor mis-representation, 'it could not possibly have been intended the damages in lieu be assessed on a principle which would invariably have the same effect'.[161] Moreover, account is not taken of losses due to a general fall in market values after the contract is made. It will be remembered, moreover, that, where a misrepresentation is made without reasonable ground for belief in its truth, damages can be claimed under section 2(1) of the 1967 Act,[162] and that the measure of these damages is that applic-able in tort, i.e. an amount which puts the party misled in the position in which that party would have been had he never entered into the contract.[163] In certain transac-tions there may be no difference between the damages recoverable under section 2(1) and section 2(2); but since consequential damage can be recovered under section 2(1)[164] and account may be taken of losses due to a general fall in the market after the contract,[165] damages under that sub-section will in many cases be more extensive than those recoverable under section 2(2). It is not possible to recover damages twice over under both section 2(1) and section 2(2), for the Act provides that any award under section 2(2) shall be taken into account in assessing the liability of the representor under section 2(1).[166]

Where the misrepresentation is innocent, but the Court refuses rescission, the representee is, of course, not entitled to an indemnity in addition to damages under section 2(2). An indemnity is part of the remedy of rescission and is awarded so that the restoration of the *status quo ante* may be achieved. Since, however, the representee would have been entitled to an indemnity had rescission been granted, the Court should, in assessing the damages under section 2(2), take account of any sum recover-able as an indemnity[167] in computing the loss which has been suffered as a result of the refusal of rescission.

(v) Limitations removed by the 1967 Act

(a) Executed contracts. Before the passing of the Misrepresentation Act 1967, in the case of innocent misrepresentation, there could be no rescission of a contract after it had been executed by the transfer of property under it.[168] The extent of this rule was somewhat uncertain and it was the subject of much criticism,[169] for in many cases the falsity of a misrepresentation cannot be discovered until, for example, a lease of a

---

[161] *Ibid., per* Hoffmann L.J. at p. 1038.

[162] See *ante*, p. 248.

[163] See *ante*, p. 249.

[164] *Davis & Co. (Wines) Ltd.* v. *Alfa-Minerva (E.M.I.) Ltd.* [1974] 2 Lloyd's Rep. 27.

[165] *Ante*, pp. 246, 248.

[166] 1967 Act, s. 2(3).

[167] *Ante*, p. 251.

[168] *Seddon* v. *N.E. Salt Co. Ltd.* [1905] 1 Ch. 326; *Angel* v. *Jay* [1911] 1 K.B. 666.

[169] See e.g. *Lever Bros. Ltd.* v. *Bell* [1931] 1 K.B. 557, at p. 588, aff'd [1932] A.C. 161; *Leaf* v. *International Galleries* [1950] 2 K.B. 86, at pp. 90, 91, 95; Tenth Report of the Law Reform Committee (Cmd. 1782, 1962), §§ 6–10.

house has been executed and the tenant has moved into occupation of the premises. Section 1(b) of the Act therefore provides that a contract is to be capable of rescission notwithstanding that it has been performed. This does not affect the other bars to rescission, and the circumstances in which a Court will exercise its discretion under section 2(2) of the 1967 Act are more likely to be present when a contract has been executed than when it is still executory.

(b) Incorporation as term. If a misrepresentation is subsequently incorporated as a term of the contract, it was previously believed that the right to rescind was lost: the situation was treated simply as involving the breach of a contractual term, for 'the representation becomes merged in the higher contractual right'.[170] This rule was criticized because the representee would be worse off if the misrepresentation were incorporated in the contract as a mere warranty. The representee would then have no right to rescind the contract but only to claim damages. Section 1(a) of the 1967 Act now provides that rescission is still open notwithstanding that the misrepresentation has become a term of the contract. The present rule is: 'once a misrepresentation, always a misrepresentation'. It is doubtful, however, whether the representee can both rescind the contract and claim damages for breach of a contractual term, since, by rescinding it, the contract is effectively set aside for all purposes, including the right to claim damages for the breach of it.

(h) EXCLUSION OF LIABILITY

(i) Common law

At common law, a party to a contract was entitled, by means of an appropriately drafted exemption clause, to limit or exclude his liability for misrepresentation, except in cases of personal fraud.[171]

(ii) Statute

The Misrepresentation Act 1967, the Unfair Contract Terms Act 1977 (in respect of liability under *Hedley Byrne & Co. Ltd. v. Heller & Partners Ltd.*[172]) and the Unfair Terms in Consumer Contracts Regulations 1999[173] restrict the freedom to exclude liability for misrepresentation. Section 3 of the 1967 Act provides:

If any contract contains a term which would exclude or restrict:

   (a) any liability to which a party to a contract may be subject by reason of any misrepresentation made by him before the contract was made; or

---

[170] *Pennsylvania Shipping Co. v. Compagnie Nationale de Navigation* [1936] 2 All E.R. 1167, at p. 1171.

[171] *Pearson (S.) & Son Ltd. v. Dublin Corporation* [1907] A.C. 351; *Toomey* v. *Eagle Star Insurance Co. Ltd. (No. 2)* [1995] 2 Lloyd's Rep. 88, at pp. 91–2. Cf. *HIH Casualty and General Insurance Ltd. v. Chase Manhattan Bank* [2001] 1 Lloyd's Rep. 30, at pp. 43–45 (in principle possible at common law to exclude liability for fraudulent misrepresentation by a contracting party).

[172] [1964] A.C. 465; *ante*, pp. 247, 248.

[173] S.I. 1999 No. 2083 implementing the Directive on Unfair Terms in Consumer Contracts 93/13/EEC, as to which see *ante*, p. 200, *post*, p. 300.

(b) any remedy available to another party to the contract by reason of such a misrepresentation,

that term shall be of no effect except in so far as it satisfies the requirement of reasonableness as stated in section 11(1) of the Unfair Contract Terms Act 1977; and it is for those claiming that the term satisfies that requirement to show that it does.[174]

The exemption clause is therefore *prima facie* invalid, but the Court is empowered to give effect to it if it was a fair and reasonable term to be included in the contract having regard to all the circumstances which were, or ought reasonably to have been, known to or in the contemplation of the parties when the contract was made.[175] A clause purporting to exclude liability for fraudulent misrepresentation will generally not be held to be reasonable.[176] The approach in the case of exclusion of liability for negligent misrepresentation can be illustrated by *Walker* v. *Boyle*.[177] A seller in response to preliminary enquiries represented to the purchaser that she was not aware of any disputes regarding the boundaries of the property to be sold, although she should have been aware of such a dispute. It was held that condition 17 of the National Conditions of Sale which stated that 'no error, misstatement or omission in any preliminary answer concerning the property ... shall annul the sale' did not satisfy the test of reasonableness required by the 1977 Act even though it was a long-standing common-form clause.[178] This was a case where the purchaser was a private individual; but, even as between businesses, a term excluding or restricting liability for misrepresentation may be held unreasonable.[179]

The question arises whether it is possible to avoid the application of section 3 of the 1967 Act by means of a contract term, for example, that statements made are 'not to be construed as assertions of fact', or that they are 'statements of opinion or belief only'. In *Cremdean Properties Ltd.* v. *Nash*,[180] the defendants, by whom it was alleged a misrepresentation had been made, relied on the following clause:

These particulars are prepared for the convenience of an intending purchaser or tenant and although they are believed to be correct their accuracy is not guaranteed and any error, omission or misdescription shall not annul the sale or the grounds on which compensation may be claimed and neither do they constitute any part of an offer of a contract. Any intending purchaser or tenant must satisfy himself by inspection or otherwise as to the correctness of each of the statements contained in these particulars.

The Court of Appeal rejected the defendants' argument that the effect of this clause was to bring about a situation as if no representation at all had been made. The Court

---

[174] Substituted by the Unfair Contract Terms Act 1977, s. 8(1).

[175] *Ibid.*, s. 11(1); see *ante*, p. 194.

[176] *Thomas Witter Ltd.* v. *TBP Industries* [1996] 2 All E.R. 573, at p. 598; *South West Water Services Ltd.* v. *International Computers Ltd.* [1999] B.L.R. 420.

[177] [1982] 1 W.L.R. 495. Cf. *McCullagh* v. *Lane Fox & Partners* (1996) 49 Con. L.R. 124 (estate agent's disclaimer about size of plot reasonable).

[178] It was not the product of negotiation between the representatives of those affected, on which see *ante*, p. 196.

[179] *Howard Marine and Dredging Co. Ltd.* v. *Ogden & Sons (Excavations) Ltd.* [1978] Q.B. 574, *ante*, p. 248.

[180] (1977) 244 E.G. 547.

further doubted whether, even if the defendants' argument were correct, it would be possible thus to defeat the application of section 3 of the 1967 Act. It would therefore seem that, if a representation has in fact been made, a contract term which purports to deny one or more of the conditions to be fulfilled before a representation is effective[181] will be subject to section 3, and to the test of reasonableness provided for in that section. It should, however, be noted that in this case, the Court of Appeal left open the question of the effect of the final part of this clause on the issue as to whether the plaintiffs in fact relied upon the representation, although in *Walker* v. *Boyle* it was held that a similar admonition did not negative a representation of fact which the seller knew was likely to be relied on.[182]

In *Overbrook Estates Ltd.* v. *Glencombe Properties Ltd.*,[183] on the other hand:

An auctioneer sold property belonging to O to G, and in the course of so doing made a misrepresentation as to local authority plans with respect to the property. G refused to proceed with the sale because of the misrepresentation and O brought an action for specific performance of the contract. O relied upon a term in the conditions of sale which stated that the auctioneer had no authority to make any representation in relation to the property.

Brightman J. held that section 3 of the 1967 Act did not operate to qualify the right of a principal publicly to limit the authority of an agent and was therefore inapplicable. Where, despite a term limiting an agent's actual or ostensible authority, the principal expressly authorizes the agent to make the representation in question, section 3 should apply.[184] The cases permitting the limitation of an agent's authority concern auctioneers and estate agents, and it is not clear whether an employer could rely on a term limiting an employee's actual or ostensible authority to avoid the operation of section 3.[185]

The Unfair Terms in Consumer Contracts Regulations 1999, which apply to all unfair terms and not only to exclusion or limitation clauses, will also affect clauses excluding or restricting a consumer's remedies for misrepresentation.[186] A term limiting the seller or supplier's obligation to respect commitments undertaken by his agents is one of those included in the indicative and illustrative list of terms which may be regarded as unfair[187] and it therefore appears that clauses such as that in *Overbrook Estates Ltd.* v. *Glencombe Properties Ltd.* will only be effective if they satisfy the tests of good faith and absence of a significant imbalance in the parties' rights to the detriment of the consumer.

[181] See *ante*, pp. 237–43.
[182] [1982] 1 W.L.R. 495, at p. 501. See also *Goff* v. *Gauthier* (1991) 62 P. & C.R. 388, at p. 401.
[183] [1974] 1 W.L.R. 1355. This decision was accepted as correct by Bridge L.J. in *Cremdean Properties Ltd.* v. *Nash* (*supra*, n. 180). At p. 549. See also *Collins* v. *Howell-Jones* (1980) 259 E.G. 331.
[184] *Museprime Properties Ltd.* v. *Adhill Properties Ltd.* (1991) 61 P. & C.R. 111. Cf. *Collins* v. *Howell-Jones* (1980) 259 E.G. 331, *per* Waller L.J., at 332; but note Murdoch (1981) 97 L.Q.R. 518, at p. 524.
[185] Cf. *Mendelssohn* v. *Normand Ltd.* [1970] 1 Q.B. 177, *ante*, pp. 182–3.
[186] See generally, *ante*, p. 200 ff.
[187] S.I. 1999 No. 2083, Sched. 2, para (n).

III. DUTIES OF DISCLOSURE

(a) NO GENERAL DUTY TO DISCLOSE

We have noted that silence does not normally amount to a misrepresentation and that at common law there is in general no duty of disclosure of material facts before the contract is made.[188] The examples were given of the person who visits an antiques shop and sees a rare George II table being sold as a nineteenth century piece and the oil prospector who discovers that there is probably oil under a given piece of land. Neither have to inform the other party. Nor does a bank have to inform its customer that a more attractive rate of interest is available in a different account.[189] This reflects a major difference between English law and civil law systems since in most civil law systems a party who deliberately does not disclose a relevant fact to the other party may be liable for fraud.[190] The justification for the common law rule is said to be the need to give people an incentive to invest in the acquisition of skill and knowledge and consequently to allow 'good deals' to the more intelligent or the hard-working.[191] Even in civil law systems there is no duty to disclose information 'which is the product of one's own efforts in evaluating market conditions or ascertaining the attributes of property which enhance its value'.[192] This economic argument does not obviously apply to information which has been acquired by pure chance or without any investment. Nor can it be conclusive where the information is acquired by a method regarded by the law as illegitimate—for example where it is 'insider' information about the position of a company. There may also be situations where it may be economically efficient to impose a duty of disclosure. In the case of house sales, the present rule means that it is the intending purchaser who commissions the survey and where several people are interested in a property each will have to invest in the search for information, whereas if sellers were obliged to disclose key elements concerning the state of their houses to all potential buyers, the cost of surveying would in many cases be incurred only once.[193] Less compellingly, the rule has also been justified by the great difficulty in imposing any sensible limits on a duty of disclosure,[194] because the information which had to be disclosed may be unreliable or doubtful or inconclusive, and because disclosure may expose the informer to criticism or litigation.[195]

---

[188] *Ante*, p. 236. See *Bell* v. *Lever Bros. Ltd.* [1932] A.C. 161, *per* Lord Atkin at p. 227; *Clarion Ltd.* v. *National Provident Institution* [2000] 1 W.L.R. 1888 at p. 1905.

[189] *Suriya & Douglas* v. *Midland Bank* [1999] 1 All E.R. (Comm.) 612.

[190] Lando and Beale, *Principles of European Contract Law* (2000), p. 256.

[191] See generally Duggan, Bryan, and Hanks, *Contractual Non-Disclosure* (1994); Kronman (1978) 7 J.L.S. 1; Nicholas in Harris and Tallon eds., *Contract Law Today* (1989); Fried, *Contract as Promise* (1981), p. 77 ff; Trebilcock, *The Limits of Freedom of Contract* (1993), p. 106 ff.

[192] Kötz, *European Contract Law* (1997) p. 201.

[193] Fabre-Magnan, in *Good Faith and Fault in Contract Law* (eds. Beatson and Friedmann), pp. 117–18.

[194] *Laidlaw* v. *Organ* 15 US (2 Wheat) 178 (1817).

[195] *Banque Financiere de la Cite SA* v. *Westgate Insurance Co. Ltd.* [1991] 2 A.C. 249, where a narrower range of policy issues relevant to the imposition of a duty of disclosure were addressed in the leading speech by Lord Templeman who concluded that 'A professional should wear a halo but need not wear a hairshirt'.

As well as the exceptions to the general rule, discussed below, there may be situations in which English law affords protection which in a civil law system might be afforded by a duty to disclose by the use of implied terms, such as the implied term that goods should be of satisfactory quality.[196] Moreover, as we shall see, where A knows that B has misunderstood the *terms* of an offer made by A, no contract will be formed if A does not inform B of its true nature.[197]

(b) CONTRACTS 'UBERRIMAE FIDEI'

There are some contracts in which more is required than abstinence from misrepresentation. They are known as contracts *uberrimae fidei*—of the utmost good faith—and they may be avoided unless there has been a full disclosure of all material facts. Also, in certain situations, a duty of disclosure is imposed by statute.

Two reasons account for most situations where, at common law or in equity, or by statute, contracts have been held to be subject to a duty of disclosure. The first is that, in certain classes of contract, one of the parties is presumed to have means of knowledge which are not accessible to the other, either at all or only by incurring disproportionately high costs. The party who is presumed to have the information is therefore bound to disclose everything which may be supposed likely to affect the judgment of the other party. Contracts of insurance of every kind are of this nature.[198] The second reason is that, in certain situations, the relationship between the contracting parties is not a pure arm's length commercial relationship but one of trust and confidence or one of dependence which imposes upon the party in whom confidence is reposed a duty to make disclosure. The clearest examples of such situations arise where there is a fiduciary relationship. The Misrepresentation Act 1967 does not apply in its terms to cases of non-disclosure as opposed to a 'misrepresentation made'. The remedies for non-disclosure are therefore not affected by the provisions of the Act.[199]

(c) CONTRACTS OF INSURANCE

Before a contract of insurance is made, the intending assured is under an obligation to disclose to the insurer all material information affecting the risk.[200] This duty to disclose is mutual and the insurer must also disclose all material information although disclosure by the insurer will in practice be rare because the material circumstances are normally known only to the intending assured.[201] While the foundation of this obligation was in the past regarded as an implied term in the contract

---

[196] Zimmermann and Whittaker, *Good Faith in European Contract Law* (2000) pp. 194–5, *ante* p. 145 ff.

[197] *Hartog* v. *Colin & Shields* [1939] 3 All E.R. 566, *post*, p. 325.

[198] *Carter* v. *Boehm* (1766) 3 Burr. 1905, *per* Lord Mansfield at p. 1909.

[199] *Banque Keyser Ullman S.A.* v. *Skandia (U.K.) Insurance Co. Ltd.* [1990] 1 Q.B. 665, at p. 789, aff'd. on other grounds [1991] 2 A.C. 249. Cf. Hudson (1969) 85 L.Q.R. 524.

[200] *Carter* v. *Boehm* (1766) 3 Burr. 1905. See generally Hasson (1969) 35 M.L.R. 625; Clarke, *Policies and Perceptions of Insurance* (1996) pp. 80–108; Bennett [1999] L.M.C.L.Q. 165.

[201] *Banque Keyser Ullman S.A.* v. *Skandia (U.K.) Insurance Co. Ltd* [1990] 1 Q.B. 665, at p. 770; [1991] 2 A.C. 249, at pp. 268 and 281.

itself,[202] the weight of modern authority is that the obligation, like the duty not to misrepresent, arises before the contract is made and is therefore non-contractual[203] and probably based on equity's jurisdiction to prevent impropriety which in this context works on a principle of good faith.[204] The difference may lie in different perceptions of the nature of an implied term: 'it is often said that a term is implied in a contract when in truth a positive rule of law is applied because of the category in which a particular contract falls'.[205]

If there has been non-disclosure by one party, the other party is entitled to avoid the contract[206] if it has been induced to enter into the policy on the relevant terms,[207] but is not entitled to damages. Although the principle of good faith also applies during the performance of an insurance contract, at that stage its content is different. It is a duty of honesty and does not require the assured to reveal all facts which the insurer might have an interest in knowing.[208]

(i) Marine insurance

So far as regards marine insurance, the common law rules are now codified in the Marine Insurance Act 1906. Section 18 of the Act provides that:

(1) The assured must disclose to the insurer, before the contract is concluded, every material circumstance which is known to the assured, and the assured is deemed to know every circumstance which, in the ordinary course of business, ought to be known by him. If the assured fails to make such disclosure, the insurer may avoid the contract.

(2) Every circumstance is material which would influence the judgment of a prudent insurer in fixing the premium, or determining whether he will take the risk.

So if the assured insures goods upon a voyage for an amount largely in excess of their value,[209] or fails to inform the insurer that they will be carried on deck, where it is unusual for such goods to be carried,[210] the contract may be avoided even though the non-disclosure was made without any fraudulent intention.

It will be observed that under the Act the assured is, for the purpose of

---

[202] *Blackburn, Low & Co.* v. *Vigors* (1886) 17 Q.B.D. 553, at pp. 578, 583; (1886) 12 App. Cas. 531, at p. 539. Cf. *ibid.*, at pp. 536 and 542; *Bank of Nova Scotia* v. *Hellenic Mutual War Risks Association (Bermuda) Ltd.* [1988] 1 Lloyd's Rep. 514, *per* Hobhouse J. at p. 547.

[203] *Joel* v. *Law Union and Crown Insurance Co.* [1908] 2 K.B. 863, at p. 886; *March Cabaret Club & Casino Ltd.* v. *London Assurance* [1975] 1 Lloyd's Rep. 169, at p. 175; *Banque Keyser Ullman S.A.* v. *Skandia (U.K.) Insurance Co. Ltd.* [1990] 1 Q.B. 665, at pp. 777–8, aff'd on other grounds [1991] 2 A.C. 249; *HIH Casualty & General Insurance Ltd.* v. *Chase Manhattan Bank* [2001] 1 Lloyd's Rep. 30, at p. 41.

[204] *Merchants' and Manufacturers' Insurance Co.* v. *Hunt* [1941] 1 K.B. 295, at pp. 313 and 318; *Manifest S.S. Co. Ltd.* v. *Uni-Polaris S.S. Co. Ltd.* [2001] 2 W.L.R. 170, at pp. 184–6.

[205] *Banque Keyser Ullman S.A.* v. *Skandia (U.K.) Insurance Co. Ltd.* [1990] 1 Q.B. 665, *per* Steyn J. at p. 702. See generally *ante*, p. 148.

[206] *Morrison* v. *Universal Marine* (1872) L.R. 8 Exch. 197. See also *Black King Shipping Corp.* v. *Massie* [1985] 1 Lloyd's Rep. 437, at pp. 514–16.

[207] *Pan Atlantic Insurance Co. Ltd.* v. *Pine Top Insurance Co. Ltd.* [1995] 1 A.C. 501; *St. Paul Fire & Marine Insurance Co. Ltd.* v. *McConnell Dowell Constructors Ltd.* [1996] 1 All E.R. 96.

[208] *Manifest S.S. Co. Ltd.* v. *Uni-Polaris Co. Ltd.* [2001] 2 W.L.R. 170, at pp. 186, 189, 204, 207.

[209] *Ionides* v. *Pender* (1984) L.R. 9 Q.B. 531.

[210] *Hood* v. *West End Motor Car Packing Co. Ltd.* [1917] 2 K.B. 38.

communication, 'deemed to know' every circumstance which, in the ordinary course of business ought to be known by it.

(ii) Non-marine insurance

Although section 18 of the 1906 Act is one of a group of sections which apply to all classes of insurance because they codified the common law,[211] in non-marine insurance the duty of disclosure extends only to material facts which are actually known to the assured.[212] But the test of what is material and the degree of good faith which is required is otherwise the same in all classes of insurance:[213] was the fact one that would have an effect on the mind of the prudent insurer in estimating the risk even if it did not have a decisive effect on the acceptance of the risk or the amount of the premium?[214] Thus the fact that the assured has been so unlucky as to have had several previous fires,[215] or several previous burglaries[216] is material to a fire or theft policy, as is also the fact that the risk has been declined by another company.[217] It has even been held that, in a proposal for fire insurance, the non-disclosure of a conviction for robbery[218] or of the refusal of another insurance company to insure the proposer's motor vehicle[219] may amount to the non-disclosure of a material fact entitling the insurer to repudiate the policy.

(iii) Practice of insurers

In practice, however, insurance companies frequently insert a 'basis of the contract' clause in the proposal form by which the proposer is made to warrant the accuracy of the information supplied by him to the company, with a proviso that the company may avoid the agreement and forfeit the premium if any part of the information proves untrue. The assured is thus compelled to assume responsibility for the truth of even non-material facts,[220] and of facts which he did not know, or did not appreciate, were false. Thus where an applicant for life insurance declared that she had not had any 'operation' when, in fact, she had given birth to a child by Caesarian section, the insurance company was held to be entitled to avoid the policy on the ground that there was a breach of a condition precedent to the company's liability.[221] Such provisions may work injustice to the assured by conferring on insurers a discretion to repudiate the policy on technical grounds alone. Lord Greene M.R. described them as

---

[211] *P.C.W. Syndicates* v. *P.C.W. Reinsurers* [1996] 1 W.L.R. 1136, *per* Staughton L.J. at 1140. See also *Economides* v. *Commercial Union Assurance Co. plc* [1998] Q.B. 587, at p. 598.

[212] *Joel* v. *Law Union and Crown Insurance Co.* [1908] 2 K.B. 863, at p. 884; *Economides* v. *Commercial Union Assurance Co. plc* (*supra*, n. 211).

[213] *Lambert* v. *Co-operative Insurance Society Ltd.* [1975] 2 Lloyd's Rep. 485.

[214] *Pan Atlantic Insurance Co. Ltd.* v. *Pine Top Insurance Co. Ltd.* [1995] 1 A.C. 501. Cf. the 'risk presented is different from true risk' test: [1995] 1 A.C. 501, at pp. 515 and 559 (Lord Templeman and Lord Lloyd dissenting) and [1993] 1 Lloyd's Rep. 496, *per* Steyn L.J. at pp. 505–6.

[215] *Marene Knitting Mills Pty. Ltd.* v. *Greater Pacific General Insurance Ltd.* [1976] 2 Lloyd's Rep. 630.

[216] *Rozanes* v. *Bowen* (1928) 32 Ll. L.R. 98.

[217] *London Assurance Co.* v. *Mansel* (1879) 11 Ch. D. 363.

[218] *Woolcott* v. *Sun Alliance and London Insurance Ltd.* [1978] 1 W.L.R. 493.

[219] *Locker and Woolf Ltd.* v. *West Australian Insurance Co. Ltd.* [1936] 1 K.B. 408.

[220] *Thomson* v. *Weems* (1884) 9 App. Cas. 671, at p. 689; *Dawsons Ltd.* v. *Bonnin* [1922] 2 A.C. 413.

[221] *Kumar* v. *Life Insurance Cpn. of India* [1974] 1 Lloyd's Rep. 147.

'particularly vicious' and 'mere traps' which should be construed strictly[222] and the insurance industry's statements of practice provide, *inter alia*, that insurers should not repudiate liability on grounds of non-disclosure of a fact which the assured could not reasonably be expected to disclose. The Law Commission's recommendation that such clauses should be ineffective[223] has not been implemented, but in consumer contracts they will now be subject to the fairness tests in the Unfair Terms in Consumer Contracts Regulations 1999,[224] which few are likely to satisfy.

(d) CONTRACTS BETWEEN THOSE IN A FIDUCIARY OR 'SPECIAL' RELATIONSHIP

Those in a fiduciary relationship with another are under a duty to make full disclosure of all material facts which might be considered likely to affect a transaction with those to whom the duty is owed. This is a component of wider and rigorous equitable obligations. While not all fiduciaries owe the same duties in all circumstances,[225] they are broadly obliged to act in good faith, not to place themselves in a position where their duty and their interest may conflict, or to act for their own benefit or the benefit of a third person without the informed consent of those to whom the duty is owed.[226] Breach of these duties is sometimes, rather misleadingly, called 'equitable' or 'constructive' fraud.

(i) Who is a fiduciary?

By contrast to a contractual relationship where, subject to the terms of the contract, the parties may legitimately act for their own interests, albeit sometimes in co-operation with the other party, the key feature of fiduciary relationships is a duty to act in the interests of another.[227] Fiduciary relationships can be divided into two categories, those that are status-based and those that are fact-based.[228] Examples of the former include principal and agent, solicitor and client, guardian and ward, and trustee and beneficiary.

The second category arises where, in the absence of an inherently fiduciary status, the factual situation of the particular relationship between the parties gives rise to a fiduciary relationship.[229] The relationship of the parties may be contractual but a contractual relationship gives rise to particular fiduciary obligations only where specific contractual obligations have been undertaken which place one party in the position in which equity imposes its rigorous duties on that party in addition to the contractual obligations.[230] While fiduciary duties should not be superimposed on

---

[222] *Zurich General Accident and Liability Insurance Co. Ltd.* v. *Morrison* [1942] 2 K.B. 53, at p. 58. See also *Joel* v. *Law Union and Crown Insurance Co.* (*supra*, n. 212), at p. 885.

[223] Law Com. No. 104, *Non-Disclosure and Breach of Warranty* (1980), 7.1–7.11.

[224] S.I. 1999 No. 2083, *ante*, p. 200, *post*, p. 300.

[225] *Henderson* v. *Merrett Syndicates Ltd.* [1995] 2 A.C. 145, *per* Lord Browne Wilkinson at p. 206.

[226] See generally Finn, *Fiduciary Obligations* (1977). Fiduciaries are also under a duty to use care and skill: *Nocton* v. *Lord Ashburton* [1914] A.C. 932, at p. 954.

[227] *Bristol and West B.S.* v. *Mothew* [1998] 1 Ch. 1, at p. 18.   [228] Flannigan (1989) 9 O.J.L.S. 285.

[229] *Reading* v. *Attorney-General* [1951] A.C. 507; *Hospital Products Ltd.* v *United States Surgical Corp.* (1984–85) 156 C.L.R. 41(High Court of Australia).

[230] *Nottingham University* v. *Fishel* [2000] I.C.R. 1462, at p. 1491.

common law contractual duties simply to improve the nature or extent of the remedy available,[231] they may arise where one party is in a position of influence over another, is in receipt of information imparted in confidence by the other, or has undertaken to act in the interests of another or placed himself or herself in a position where he or she is obliged so to act.[232] In such cases the fiduciary obligation is, however, circumscribed by the contractual terms: equity cannot alter the terms of a contract validly undertaken.[233] Examples of such fact-based fiduciary relationships may be seen in certain joint ventures[234] and employment relationships.[235]

(ii) Disclosure

The duty to disclose all material facts which might be considered likely to affect a transaction can be illustrated by examples. Thus a broker who is employed to buy shares for a client, cannot sell his own shares unless a full and accurate disclosure of this fact is made to the client and the client's consent is obtained.[236] Again, the promoters of a company, who stand in a fiduciary relationship with the company, are required to make a full disclosure of their interest either to an independent board of directors or to the intended shareholders.[237] In some situations, all that equity requires is disclosure of material facts. In others, however, where the fiduciary relationship gives rise to a presumption of undue influence[238] disclosure in itself may be insufficient, and it must be shown that the transaction is the result of the act of a free and independent mind. Breach of the duty to make full disclosure will entitle the innocent party to rescind the contract or transaction, to be restored to the pre-contractual position, and to recover any profit made by the other party as a result of the breach.

(iii) Employment

The relationship between an employer and employee is not inherently 'fiduciary' but it may be the foundation for a fiduciary relationship as a result of the terms of the particular contract or where, for example, the employee is in receipt of confidential information. An employee is not, however, under a duty to disclose his own misconduct. In *Bell* v. *Lever Brothers Ltd.*[239] the respondent, Lever Brothers, had entered into an agreement with two of its employees whereby it promised to pay, and did in

---

[231] *Norberg* v. *Wynrib* (1992) 92 D.L.R. (4th) 449, at p. 481.

[232] Millett (1998) 114 L.Q.R. 214.

[233] *Nottingham University* v. *Fishel*, supra, n. 230., at p. 1491; *Hospital Products Ltd.* v *United States Surgical Corp.* (1984–85) 156 C.L.R. 41, at p. 97. See also *Kelly v Cooper* [1993] A.C. 205.

[234] *Lac Minerals Ltd.* v. *International Corona Resources Ltd.* [1989] 2 S.C.R. 574 (Supreme Court of Canada).

[235] *Nottingham University* v. *Fishel*, supra, n. 230.

[236] *Armstrong* v. *Jackson* [1917] 2 K.B. 822. See also *Regier* v. *Campbell-Stuart* [1939] Ch. 766; *English* v. *Dedham Vale Properties Ltd.* [1978] 1 W.L.R. 93, and *post*, p. 675. For an example of contractual modification of fiduciary duty cf. *Kelly* v. *Cooper* [1993] A.C. 205.

[237] *Erlanger* v. *New Sombrero Phosphate Co.* (1878) 3 App. Cas. 1218; *Lagunas Nitrate Co.* v. *Lagunas Syndicate* [1899] 2 Ch. 392; *Gluckstein* v. *Barnes* [1900] A.C. 240. See now Financial Services and Markets Act 2000, s. 90, *post*, p. 270.

[238] See *post*, p. 287.

[239] [1932] A.C. 161, *post*, p. 311.

fact pay, considerable sums to them in compensation for the premature termination of their contracts of employment. This contract, however, was strictly unnecessary, for during their employment the two men had been guilty of certain breaches of duty which would have entitled Lever Brothers to dismiss them immediately. When Lever Brothers discovered this fact, it claimed to avoid the contract and recover the money paid on the ground, *inter alia*, that the employees were bound to disclose to them these breaches of duty. No member of the House of Lords was prepared to accept this contention,[240] and Lord Atkin said[241] that he was aware of no authority which placed contracts of service within the limited category of contracts *uberrimae fidei*. Nevertheless, it has subsequently been held that in certain circumstances an employee may be under a duty to report to the employer misconduct on the part of fellow employees.[242]

(iv) Special relationships

We have seen that, under the principle enunciated in *Hedley Byrne & Co. Ltd* v. *Heller & Partners Ltd.*,[243] a special relationship, giving rise to a duty of care, may arise between parties negotiating a contract. That duty may be more extensive than merely to refrain from making negligent misstatements, and may impose upon the party in whom confidence is reposed an obligation to disclose to the other party information relevant to the contract[244] or to provide an adequate explanation of the contract into which the other party is about to enter.[245] *Prima facie* the breach of such a duty would give rise to an action in damages in tort only, and not to a claim that the contract be rescinded. But it could be argued that, at least in some situations, the presence of such a duty made the contract one requiring *uberrima fides*, so that its breach would entitle the party to whom the duty was owed to avoid the contract.

(e) CONTRACTS PRELIMINARY TO FAMILY SETTLEMENTS

An example of a situation of confidence recognized by equity is that of contracts for family settlements and arrangements. These require not only an absence of misrepresentation by the parties entering into them, but also a full disclosure of all material facts within their knowledge. Thus in *Gordon* v. *Gordon*,[246] a family arrangement entered into without a secret marriage being disclosed by one side to the other was set aside under this principle. And parties who are divorcing and make an agreement about the division of the property which is to be embodied in a Court order are

---

[240] Although it was accepted by the Court of Appeal: [1931] 1 K.B. 337.

[241] At p. 227.

[242] *Swain* v. *West (Butchers) Ltd.* [1936] 1 All E.R. 224; *Sybron Cpn.* v. *Rochem Ltd.* [1984] Ch. 112. See also *P.C.W. Syndicates* v. *P.C.W. Reinsurers* [1996] 1 W.L.R. 1136.

[243] [1964] A.C. 465, *ante*, p. 247.

[244] *Al-Kandari* v. *J. R. Brown & Co.* [1988] Q.B. 665, at p. 674; *Banque Keyser Ullman S.A.* v. *Skandia (U.K.) Insurance Co. Ltd.* [1990] 1 Q.B. 665, at pp. 790–805; aff'd. on other grounds [1991] 2 A.C. 249. Cf. *Dillingham Construction Pty. Ltd.* v. *Downs* [1972] 2 N.S.W.R. 49 (Australia). See also *Horry* v. *Tate & Lyle Refineries Ltd.* [1982] 2 Lloyd's Rep. 416.

[245] *Rust* v. *Abbey Life Assurance Co. Ltd.* [1982] 2 Lloyd's Rep. 386, at p. 391; aff'd. [1979] 2 Lloyd's Rep. 334.

[246] (1821) 3 Swan. 400.

under a statutory obligation to make a full and frank disclosure *to the Court which made the order*. But, although the duty was owed to the Court and not to the other party it has been held that a party affected by such non-disclosure could rely on it as a ground for setting the agreement aside.[247]

(f) CONTRACTS FOR THE ALLOTMENT OF SHARES

Promoters and directors of a company have information at their disposal which is not available to the general public. When they invite the public to subscribe for shares they:[248]

are bound to state everything with strict and scrupulous accuracy, and not only to abstain from stating as fact that which is not so, but to omit no one fact within their knowledge, the existence of which might in any degree affect the nature, or extent, or quality of the privileges and advantages which the prospectus holds out as inducements to take shares.

'[T]he duty of disclosure is not the same in a prospectus inviting share subscriptions as in the case of a proposal for marine insurance',[249] nor is there any fiduciary relationship between those issuing the prospectus and the public. In an honest prospectus, except under statute, the non-disclosure even of facts which some intending shareholders might regard as material in influencing their judgment, will be no ground for rescission, unless the omission makes what is stated actually misleading.

Further protection to persons applying for shares is, however, afforded by the Financial Services and Markets Act 2000.[250] This imposes a general duty of disclosure in listing particulars of all information investors and their advisers would reasonably require and reasonably expect.[251] The statute also gives a right to compensation from those responsible to persons who have sustained loss by subscribing for shares on the faith of an untrue statement in the listing particulars unless those responsible can show that up to the time of the allotment they had reasonable ground to believe and did believe the statement to be true.[252]

(g) OTHER INVESTMENT BUSINESS

The Financial Services and Markets Act 2000 also establishes a regulatory regime over those conducting investment business in order to protect the purchasers of the products of the financial services industry, namely insurance policies, investments, and advice. Detailed treatment of this area would be out of place in the present textbook,[253] but a brief summary may be given. Protection is achieved by a licensing

---

[247] *Jenkins* v. *Livesey* [1985] A.C. 424, at p. 439. But cf. *Wales* v. *Wadham* [1971] 1 W.L.R. 199 (no disclosure required at common law).

[248] *New Brunswick and Canada Railway Co.* v. *Muggeridge* (1860) 1 Drew. & Sm. 363, at p. 381, approved in *Central Ry. Co. of Venezuela* v. *Kisch* (1867) L.R. 2 H.L. 99, at p. 113.

[249] *Aaron's Reefs Ltd.* v. *Twiss* [1896] A.C. 273, at p. 287.

[250] There has been statutory protection for over 100 years; see the Directors Liability Act 1890.

[251] Financial Services and Markets Act 2000, ss. 80, 82. On unlisted securities, see s. 87, Sched. 9.

[252] *Ibid.*, s. 90, Sched. 10.

[253] See generally Lomnicka and Powell, *Encyclopaedia of Financial Services Law* (1987).

system and by close control of the way those licensed conduct their businesses, including statutory 'cooling-off' periods after an agreement has been made. Many financial services practitioners, will be in a fiduciary relationship with their clients.[254] The Financial Services and Markets Act 2000 replaced specific requirements in the Financial Services Act 1986[255] with a general rulemaking power[256] and a duty to act in a way that is compatible with the regulatory objectives.[257] These objectives are maintaining confidence in the market, promoting awareness of the benefits and risks of different kinds of investments, protecting consumers by, *inter alia*, advice and accurate information and reducing financial crime.[258] Practitioners continue to be obliged to subordinate their interests to those of their clients, and to make proper provision for disclosure of interests and facts material to transactions entered into or advice given, and the basis, method and frequency of payment by the customer and in certain cases termination provisions.[259] Private investors are given a right to civil damages for contravention of regulatory rules.[260]

(h) SURETYSHIP

Contracts of suretyship or guarantee are not *uberrimae fidei* and therefore non-disclosure, to avoid such a contract, must amount to a misrepresentation. The creditor may be bound to disclose unusual circumstances which the surety would expect not to exist, for the omission to mention such a circumstance can amount to an implied misrepresentation that the circumstance does not exist.[261] Such contracts do not, however, require the same fullness of disclosure as is necessary in a contract *uberrimae fidei*.

Nevertheless it is not always easy in practice to draw the line between contracts of guarantee in the strict sense of contracts to answer for the debt, default, or miscarriage of another and contracts of insurance taking the form of contracts to indemnify against some risk stated in the contract.[262] It was pointed out by Romer L.J., in *Seaton v. Heath*,[263] that many contracts may with equal propriety be called contracts of insurance or contracts of guarantee, and that whether a contract requires *uberrima fides* or not depends not upon what it is called, but upon its substantial character and how it came to be effected. Generally, in a contract of insurance the person desiring to be insured has means of knowledge of the risk which the insurer does not possess, and he puts the risk before the insurer as a business transaction. In a contract of guarantee, on the other hand, the creditor does not as a rule go to the surety, explain the risk, and ask the surety to undertake it. The surety is often a friend or relation of the debtor and

---

[254] *Ante*, p. 267.
[255] Schedule 8.
[256] ss. 138–140.
[257] s. 2(1)(a).
[258] ss. 3–6.
[259] See F.S.A. *Conduct of Business Sourcebook*, sections 5–7.
[260] Financial Services and Markets Act 2000, s. 150.
[261] *Lee* v. *Jones* (1864) 17 C.B.N.S. 482, at pp. 503, 504.
[262] *Trade Indemnity Co. Ltd.* v. *Workington Harbour and Dock Board* [1937] A.C. 1.
[263] [1899] 1 Q.B. 782, at p. 792.

knows the risk to be undertaken, or the circumstances indicate that as between the creditor and the surety it is contemplated that the surety will ascertain what the risk is. Only in the exceptional cases when a contract of guarantee has the characteristics which occur normally in a contract of insurance is the former a contract *uberrimae fidei.*

Accordingly, it is settled that there is no duty of full disclosure where a surety guarantees to a bank the account of one of the bank's customers.[264] On the other hand, when an employer takes a bond from a surety for the 'fidelity', i.e. honesty, of an employee, he must disclose to the surety any previous acts of dishonesty of the employee within his knowledge,[265] and even any subsequent acts of dishonesty which would entitle the surety to withdraw the guarantee.[266] Similarly, where the creditor is put on inquiry that the surety may be subjected to undue influence or misrepresentation by the principal debtor, as is the case where the surety is a wife or cohabitee, the creditor must take reasonable steps to satisfy itself that the surety entered into the obligation freely and in knowledge of the true facts.[267]

(i) PARTNERSHIP

There seems to be no rule requiring full disclosure in the formation of a contract of partnership, but since, when the partnership has been formed, the parties stand to one another in the confidential relation of principal and agent, each partner is bound to disclose to the others all material facts, and to exercise the utmost good faith in all that relates to their common business. The duties of partners are, however, for the most part regulated by the provisions of the Partnership Act 1890.[268]

(j) CONTRACTS FOR THE SALE OF LAND

Contracts for the sale of land have been said in some respects to be contracts *uberrimae fidei*; but no special relationship of confidence exists between the parties.[269] *Caveat emptor* is just as much the general rule in contracts for the sale of land as it is in contracts of sale of goods.

(i) Misdescription

Nevertheless, a seller must be able to convey precisely that which he has contracted to sell. If the land or the nature of the seller's right or interest in the land, has been *misdescribed*, so that the purchaser is unable to obtain that which he contracted to purchase, the purchaser will be entitled to refuse to complete the sale and to the return of the deposit. A seller, for example, who has contracted to sell absolute freehold

---

[264] *National Provincial Bank v. Glanusk* [1913] 3 K.B. 335; *Cooper v. National Provincial Bank* [1946] K.B. 1.

[265] *London General Omnibus Co. Ltd. v. Holloway* [1912] 2 K.B. 72.

[266] *Phillips v. Foxall* (1872) L.R. 7 Q.B. 666.

[267] *Barclays Bank plc v. O'Brien* [1994] 1 A.C. 180, *post*, p. 287. See also *Royal Bank of Scotland v. Etridge (No. 2)* [2001] 3 W.L.R. 1021, *post*, p. 285.

[268] Partnership Act 1890, ss. 28–30.

[269] See generally Harpum (1992) 108 L.Q.R. 280, 320–33.

property cannot enforce the contract if his title is possessory only and not absolute[270] or if the land is subject to restrictive covenants of which the purchaser was not made aware.[271] Further, a seller cannot, by a condition of the contract, compel the purchaser to accept a title which the seller knew to be a bad title, but did not disclose,[272] unless the defect is patent.[273] This means that it is virtually impossible to exclude liability for failure to disclose latent defects in the title. The consequence is that in effect a 'duty of disclosure' is imposed on the seller.[274]

(ii) Remedies

If the defect is a serious one, equivalent, in fact, to a substantial misdescription, it can legitimately be claimed that the purchaser has not got what was contracted for. The purchaser is then entitled to resist specific performance and, if necessary, to rescind the contract while it is still executory;[275] and will not be prevented from doing so by a stipulation which provides that errors, misstatements, or omissions shall not annul the sale but are to be a matter of compensation only.[276] Alternatively, the purchaser can affirm the contract and claim specific performance with an abatement of the purchase price.[277]

If, however, the defect is slight, and the purchaser gets substantially what was contracted for, he can be compelled to complete the sale subject to compensation to be made by the seller.[278]

The right of the purchaser to rescind the contract or to resist specific performance on the ground of substantial misdescription is available, not only where the misdescription is a term of the contract of sale, but also where it arises from a misrepresentation made in the course of negotiations leading to the contract. But if the misdescription is the result of a misrepresentation, even though this is sub-sequently embodied as a contractual term,[279] the right to rescind can be exercised after

---

[270] *Re Brine and Davies' Contract* [1935] Ch. 388.

[271] *Flight* v. *Booth* (1834) 1 Bing. N.C. 370; *Charles Hunt Ltd.* v. *Palmer* [1931] Ch. 287.

[272] *Re Banister* (1879) 12 Ch. D. 131, at pp. 146, 147; *Nottingham Patent Brick Co.* v. *Butler* (1887) 16 Q.B.D. 778, at p. 786; *Farugi* v. *English Real Estates Ltd.* [1979] 1 W.L.R. 963; *Walker* v. *Boyle* [1982] 1 W.L.R. 495.

[273] *Bowles* v. *Round* (1800) 5 Ves. 508; *Yandle & Sons* v. *Sutton* [1922] 2 Ch. 199, at p. 204. Where the contract is to sell free from incumbrances it is irrelevant that the defect is patent: Harpum (1992) 108 L.Q.R. 280, 284.

[274] *Reeve* v. *Berridge* (1888) 20 Q.B.D. 523, *per* Fry L.J. at p. 528; *Carlish* v. *Salt* [1906] 1 Ch. 335; *Peyman* v. *Lanjani* [1985] Ch. 457. Cf. *William Sindall plc* v. *Cambridgeshire C.C.* [1994] 1 W.L.R. 1016 (National Conditions of Sale only required vendor to disclose incumbrances of which it had knowledge or means of knowledge).

[275] *Re Russ and Brown's Contract* [1934] Ch. 34. If the contract is executed by conveyance, the purchaser must rely on the covenants as to title contained in the conveyance, for the contract is merged in the conveyance: Law of Property (Miscellaneous Provisions) Act 1994, ss. 2–5.

[276] *Flight* v. *Booth* (1834) 1 Bing. N.C. 370, at p. 337; *Re Arnold* (1880) 14 Ch. D. 270; *Walker* v. *Boyle* [1982] 1 W.L.R. 495.

[277] Cf. *Gilchester Properties Ltd.* v. *Gomm* [1948] 1 All E.R. 433, but note damages in lieu of rescission may be awarded: Misrepresentation Act 1967, s. 2(2), *ante*, p. 257.

[278] *McQueen* v. *Farquhar* (1805) 11 Ves. 467. But the purchaser may be deprived of his right to compensation by a term of the contract.

[279] *Charles Hunt Ltd.* v. *Palmer* [1931] Ch. 287; *Laurence* v. *Lexcourt Holdings Ltd.* [1978] 1 W.L.R. 1128.

conveyance.[280] A claim for damages may also lie under section 2(1) of the Misrepresentation Act 1967.[281]

(k) THE FUTURE

Although there is no serious move away from the general rule of non-disclosure, there are concerns about its scope. In other words, should a more liberal approach be taken to the exceptions? Are they too narrow? Take the case of the couple who are divorcing and make an agreement about the division of the property. If the negotiations prior to the agreement proceeded on the basis of the husband's belief, based on the wife's conscientious and religious objections to divorce, that the wife would never remarry, is the agreement vitiated in any way by the failure of the wife to disclose that she had earlier become engaged to be married? On pure common law analysis, on such facts, after considering whether any of the common law and equitable exceptions applied, it has been held that none did and there was no duty to disclose.[282] Although, as we have seen, the common law position has been affected by statute where the property settlement is embodied in a Court order, it was said that this *contractual* aspect of the decision is not open to criticism in any way.[283] But is it right in principle that there should be no duty to disclose in such a case? The economic arguments do not appear applicable, let alone compelling, and it was certainly very difficult and probably impossible for the husband to acquire the information from another source. One commentator who supports the general rule has described the decision as 'quite unreasonable'.[284] The position might have been different if a broader view had been taken of the concept of 'fiduciary' relationship or if it had been possible to look at the statutory as well as the common law exceptions to the rule. But, as Nicholas comments, the statutory provisions have been regarded as isolated irruptions into the body of the common law and have not been seen as expressing a policy from which a principle could be synthesized.[285]

We have mentioned section 18 of the Marine Insurance Act 1906 and the requirements of the Financial Services and Markets Act 2000 and the rules made under it. Other examples are to be found in the Consumer Credit Act 1974,[286] in the labelling

---

[280] See *ante*, p. 259 (subject to the Misrepresentation Act 1967, s. 2(2), *ante*, p. 257).

[281] *Watts* v. *Spence* [1976] Ch. 165; *Walker* v. *Boyle* (*supra*, n. 276).

[282] *Wales* v. *Wadham* [1977] 1 W.L.R. 199.

[283] *Jenkins* v. *Livesey* [1985] AC 424, at p. 439, *ante*, pp. 269–70.

[284] Atiyah, *An Introduction to the Law of Contract*, 5th edn. (1995), p. 252. The decision, but not the reasoning, may, however, be justified on the merits since the husband had not made a full disclosure of his assets.

[285] In Harris and Tallon eds., *Contract Law Today* (1989), p. 178. Cf. the different approach in France, Ghestin, in Harris and Tallon eds., pp. 153–5. See also Legrand (1986) 6 O.J.L.S. 322.

[286] s. 55 empowers regulations to be made requiring pre-contractual disclosure of specified information but none have been made, perhaps because the requirement that credit agreements subject to the Act contain specified information (*ibid.*, s. 60 and S.I. 1983 No. 1533, amended by S.I. 1984 No. 1600, S.I. 1985 No. 666, S.I. 1988 No. 2047) when coupled with the right of consumers to cancel the agreement within a specified period (s. 67 and S.I. 1987 No. 2117, amended by S.I. 1988 No. 958) achieves the same end.

and advertising provisions in the Medicines Act 1968,[287] the Hallmarking Act 1973,[288] and in the Energy Act 1976,[289] and the Package Travel, Package Holiday and Package Tours Regulations 1992.[290]

The financial services and consumer credit statutes reflect a legislative decision that consumers buying on credit and the purchasers of the products of the financial services industry require protection. Although there are many differences between the financial services and the consumer credit regimes, they have similar disclosure and 'cooling-off' provisions. Both regimes also exercise close control over the content of advertisements. The fact that the legislative schemes are so detailed means that it is not unreasonable to see them as self-contained codes and that no common law duty should be superimposed on them.[291] However, that part of the regimes which relates to disclosure might arguably be of wider significance. In both contexts the relationship is one of inequality; in financial services (and probably in consumer credit) there is also imbalance of information in the sense that the professional has information that the client cannot acquire from any other source—or cannot do so without incurring considerable expense. We have noted that this imbalance is also at the root of the duty of disclosure in contracts *uberrimae fidei* and the other non-statutory exceptions.

It is submitted that it is arguable that the fact that the legislature has imposed a duty of disclosure in the specified cases can be seen, alongside the cases in which a duty exists at common law, as an indication of the underlying rationale and principle of such a duty. If so, such legislative duties could therefore assist a Court which is considering the scope of the exceptions or the extension of the duty to a new fact situation.[292] We have seen that the Marine Insurance Act 1906 is used in this way for all types of insurance; it is either 'directly applicable, or else indirectly because the Act codified the common law applicable to all classes of insurance'.[293]

---

[287] e.g. ss. 85(2), 95(4)(a) and 96.

[288] s. 11 (disclosure of information explaining hallmarks).

[289] s. 15 and see S.I. 1983 No. 1486, r. 14.

[290] S.I. 1992 No. 3288, rr. 7–8.

[291] *Aldrich* v. *Norwich Union Life Assurance Co. Ltd.* [1999] 2 All E.R. (Comm.) 707 (Financial Services Act 1986, s. 47); *Payne* v. *Barnet L.B.C.* (1998) 30 H.L.R. 295 (Housing and Planning Act 1986, s.125 (4A)).

[292] See *Timeload Ltd.* v. *British Telecommunications plc* (1995) 3 E.M.L.R. 459; *Malik* v. *Bank of Credit & Commerce International S.A.* [1998] 1 A.C. 20 *per* Lord Steyn at p. 52–53; Beatson (2001) 117 L.Q.R. 247; *post,* p. 350. Cf. the different approach in *Banque Financiere de la Cite SA* v. *Westgate Insurance Co. Ltd.* [1991] 2 A.C. 249, 273–4.

[293] *P.C.W. Syndicates* v. *P.C.W. Reinsurers* [1996] 1 W.L.R. 1136, *per* Staughton L.J. at 1140. See also *Economides* v. *Commercial Union Assurance Co. plc* [1998] Q.B. 587, at p. 598.

7

DURESS, UNDUE INFLUENCE, AND UNCONSCIONABLE BARGAINS

I. INTRODUCTION

This chapter considers three vitiating factors based on the improper conduct of one party, the vulnerability of the other, or a combination of the two. Because of their narrow scope these were, in the past, considered to be relatively unimportant in the law of contract, but they are of more significance in the modern law.

Duress and undue influence occur where one party to a contract has coerced the other or exercised such domination that the other's independence of decision was substantially undermined. Although in some respects undue influence is the equitable equivalent of common law duress, in equity, owing to the development of constructive fraud, relief was granted in cases of pressure or coercion where the common law provided no remedy.[1] Moreover, in some cases the primary concern of equity is to protect certain relationships and it does so by a presumption of undue influence. Since the Judicature Act 1873, it has been the duty of the Courts to apply the common law and equitable rules concurrently, and in the event of any conflict or variance between them, the equitable rules are to prevail. The common law and equitable rules have, therefore, now to be treated in the light of their combined effect.[2] Duress, like fraud and misrepresentation, is primarily concerned with the process by which the contract was made (procedural unfairness or impropriety) rather than whether the terms of the contract are in fact harsh or unconscionable (substantive unfairness or impropriety). While undue influence is also said to be primarily concerned with procedural unfairness, especially in cases of overt acts of improper pressure or coercion, because it also has a role in protecting the excessively vulnerable, the position is more complicated and it has significant substantive aspects.

In the limited category of cases in which the doctrine of unconscionable bargains operates, it is necessary to show not only that the process by which the contract was made was unfair but that there is contractual imbalance, i.e. the doctrine extends to the actual substance of the contract and the fairness of its terms. The role of unconscionability was restricted in the nineteenth century by the assumption that parties

---

[1] *Royal Bank of Scotland plc. v. Etridge (No. 2)* [2001] 3 W.L.R. 1021, at paras. 6–8, 103.
[2] *United Scientific Holdings Ltd. v. Burnley B.C.* [1978] A.C. 904.

enjoy freedom of economic decision when entering into contracts which enables them to choose to enter into a contract on whatever terms they may consider advantageous to their interests, or to choose not to,[3] and more recently by the view that the task of limiting such freedom so as to relieve inequality of bargaining power is essentially a legislative task for Parliament.[4] In the case of consumer contracts there has been significant statutory intervention to protect consumers against unfair terms.[5] Employment and landlord and tenant relationships are also regulated by statute so as to protect employees and tenants from unfairness.[6] As in the case of statutory duties of disclosure,[7] it is arguable that to the extent that the statutory regimes can be seen as expressing a policy from which a principle can be derived they may be of some analogical assistance in developing the common law.[8]

II. DURESS

(a) NATURE OF DURESS

A contract which has been induced by unlawful or illegitimate forms of pressure or intimidation is voidable[9] on the ground of duress.[10] A restitutionary claim lies for the recovery of money paid under duress, and in many cases the duress will also be tortious and give rise to an action for damages, for example for assault, wrongful interference with property and, in the case of economic duress, intimidation.[11]

(i) Unlawful pressure distinguished from illegitimate pressure

Unlawful pressure occurs where the coercive party threatens to do something that is a breach of a common law or statutory duty. The act may be a crime, a tort, or, subject to the qualifications set out below, a breach of contract. Where an unlawful act is threatened, provided it induces the contract, in principle the contract may be set aside by the other party. No distinction is drawn, as it was until recently, between the effect of different categories of duress. In the words of Lord Devlin, '[a]ll that matters to the

---

[3] *Ante*, p. 4.

[4] *National Westminster Bank plc* v. *Morgan* [1985] A.C. 686, *per* Lord Scarman at p. 708.

[5] *Post*, p. 300.

[6] *Ante*, p. 200.

[7] *Ante*, p. 264.

[8] *Timeload Ltd.* v. *British Telecommunications plc.* (1995) 3 E.M.L.R. 459; *Malik* v. *B.C.C.I. S.A.* [1998] A.C. 20, at pp. 52–3. See generally Beatson (2001) 117 L.Q.R. 247.

[9] Coke 2 Inst. 483; *Whelpdale's Case* (1605) 5 Co. Rep. 119a; *North Ocean Shipping Co. Ltd.* v. *Hyundai Construction Co. Ltd.* [1979] Q.B. 705; *Pao On* v. *Lau Yiu Long* [1980] A.C. 614; *Universe Tankships Inc. of Monrovia* v. *International Transport Workers Federation* [1983] 1 A.C. 366. Cf. *Barton* v. *Armstrong* [1976] A.C. 104, at p. 120. Cf. Lanham (1966) 29 M.L.R. 615, who contends that duress renders the contract void.

[10] Beatson, *The Use and Abuse of Unjust Enrichment* (1991) ch. 5; Cartwright, *Unequal Bargaining* (1991), ch. 7; Dawson (1947) 45 Mich. L. Rev. 253; Hale (1943) 43 Col. L. Rev. 603; Halson (1991) 107 L.Q.R. 649; Smith [1997] C.L.J. 343.

[11] *Universe Tankships Inc. of Monrovia* v. *International Transport Workers Federation* (*supra*, n. 9) at pp. 385, 400; *Rookes* v. *Barnard* [1964] A.C. 1129.

plaintiff is that, metaphorically speaking, a club has been used. It does not matter to the plaintiff what the club is made of—whether it is a physical club or an economic club or an otherwise illegal club'.[12]

The position is different where what is threatened is not an unlawful act. Ordinarily it is not duress to threaten to do that which one has a legal right to do, for instance to refuse to enter into a contract or to terminate a contract lawfully. But exceptionally such a threat may constitute duress when coupled with a demand. Although such pressure is not unlawful, it is 'illegitimate'.

(ii) Juridical basis of duress

It was originally stated that a contract could only be set aside for duress if the will of the victim was coerced so as to vitiate consent.[13] But the fallacy of this approach was exposed in *Universe Tankships Inc. of Monrovia* v. *International Transport Workers Federation*.[14] A person subjected to duress is fully aware of the nature and terms of the contract which is thus entered. The victim still intends to contract, though the contract is made unwillingly. 'The classic case of duress is . . . not the lack of will to submit but the victim's intentional submission arising from the realisation that there is no other practical choice open to him'.[15] The rationale of duress is thus not lack of knowledge or consent but illegitimate pressure which means that the victim's apparent consent is treated in law as revocable, unless approbated expressly or by implication after the pressure has ceased to operate on the victim's mind.[16]

(b) UNLAWFUL PRESSURE

(i) Types of duress

(a) Duress of the person. Until 1976, despite some authority to the contrary,[17] the received view was that the only form of duress that could vitiate a contract was actual or threatened violence to the person,[18] for example threats to kill the party to the contract or perhaps a close relative.[19] How serious the action threatened must be in order to render the contract voidable will depend upon the ability of the person threatened to resist the pressure improperly brought to bear.[20] But once it is

---

[12] *Rookes* v. *Barnard* [1964] A.C. 1129, at p. 1209.

[13] *Occidental Worldwide Investment Cpn* v. *Skibs A/S Avanti* [1976] 1 Lloyd's Rep. 293, at p. 336; *North Ocean Shipping Co. Ltd.* v. *Hyundai Construction Co. Ltd.* [1979] Q.B. 705, at pp. 717, 719; *Pao On* v. *Lau Yiu Long* [1980] A.C. 614, at p. 635. See also *Barton* v. *Armstrong* (*infra*, n. 19) at p. 121; *Alec Lobb (Garages) Ltd.* v. *Total Oil Great Britain Ltd.* [1983] 1 W.L.R. 87, at p. 93.

[14] [1983] 1 A.C. 366. See also *Lynch* v. *D.P.P. of Northern Ireland* [1975] A.C. 653, at pp. 670, 675, 680, 690–1, 695, 703, 709; Atiyah (1982) 98 L.Q.R. 197, (1983) 99 L.Q.R. 353; Beatson (1976) 92 L.Q.R. 496, *The Use and Abuse of Unjust Enrichment* (1991), pp. 113–17.

[15] [1983] 1 AC 366, *per* Lord Scarman at p. 400. See also Lord Diplock at p. 384.

[16] See *post*, p. 294.

[17] *Tamvaco* v. *Simpson* (1866) L.R. 1 C.P. 363; *Government of Spain* v. *North of England S.S. Co. Ltd.* (1938) 54 T.L.R 852, 61 Ll.L. Rep. 44.

[18] Co. 2 Inst. 483; Co. Litt. 253b; 1 Roll. Abr. 687, pl. 5, 6; *Skeate* v. *Beale* (1841) 11 A. & E. 983.

[19] *Barton* v. *Armstrong* [1976] A.C. 104.

[20] *Scott* v. *Sebright* (1886) 12 P.D. 21, at p. 24.

established that the threats contributed to the decision of the person threatened to enter into the contract, that person is entitled to relief, even though the contract might well have been entered into all the same if no threats had been made.[21]

At common law, a threat of *lawful* imprisonment, e.g. a criminal prosecution, would not ordinarily amount to duress, but in equity a threat by one party to prosecute the other for a criminal offence could constitute a ground on which the contract would be set aside,[22] and today the equitable rule prevails.[23]

(b) Duress of goods. A contract entered into as the result of actual or threatened violence to or the illegal seizure of goods or other property can be set aside on the ground of duress.[24] Older authority to the contrary can possibly be explained as the voluntary compromise of a claim,[25] or as involving facts in which the degree of coercion applied was in fact insufficient to constitute duress.[26] It was in any event inconsistent with authority granting the recovery of money paid under protest for the release of goods from unlawful detention.[27]

(c) Economic duress. It is also now established that, in certain circumstances, a contract can be set aside for economic duress.[28] So it has been held that an unlawful threat by a trade union to continue the 'boycotting' of a ship[29] and a threat to break an existing contract[30] can be a sufficient ground to render voidable a contract, supported by consideration, entered into as a result of its pressure. In particular, one party may threaten to break an existing contract unless the contract is re-negotiated in its favour, and the other party may accede to this demand in order to avoid the adverse financial consequences which would ensue from the threatened breach.[31] In *Atlas Express Ltd.* v. *Kafco (Importers and Distributors) Ltd.*:[32]

K had agreed to supply basketware to a chain of retail shops and made a contract for its delivery with A, a carrier. A had erroneously estimated that each load would contain over

[21] *Barton* v. *Armstrong* [1976] A.C. 104.

[22] *Williams* v. *Bayley* (1886) L.R. 1 H.L. 200.

[23] *Mutual Finance Co. Ltd.* v. *John Wetton & Sons Ltd.* [1937] 2 K.B. 389.

[24] *Vantage Navigation Cpn.* v. *Suhail & Saud Bahwan Building Materials Llc. (The Alev)* [1989] 1 Lloyd's Rep. 138. See also *Lloyds Bank Ltd.* v. *Bundy* [1975] Q.B. 326, at p. 337; *Occidental Worldwide Investment Cpn.* v. *Skibs A/S Avanti* [1976] 1 Lloyd's Rep. 293, at pp. 335–6; *North Ocean Shipping Co. Ltd.* v. *Hyundai Construction Co. Ltd.* [1979] Q.B. 705, at p. 715; *Pao On* v. *Lau Yiu Long* [1980] A.C. 614, at p. 635.

[25] *Occidental Worldwide Investment Cpn.* v. *Skibs A/S Avanti* (*supra*, n. 24); Beatson, *The Use and Abuse of Unjust Enrichment* (1991), pp. 105–6. On compromises, see *ante*, p. 101.

[26] *Skeate* v. *Beale* (1840) 11 A. & E. 983, at p. 990.

[27] *Astley* v. *Reynolds* (1731) 2 Str. 915; *Maskell* v. *Horner* [1915] 3 K.B. 106.

[28] *Occidental Worldwide Investment Cpn.* v. *Skibs A/S Avanti* (*supra*, n. 24), at p.336; *North Ocean Shipping Co. Ltd.* v. *Hyundai Construction Co. Ltd.* (*supra*, n. 24); *Pao On* v. *Lau Yiu Long* (*supra*, n. 13), at p.635; *Universe Tankships Inc. of Monrovia* v. *International Transport Workers Federation* [1983] 1 A.C. 366, at pp. 383, 391, 397, 400; *Alec Lobb (Garages) Ltd.* v. *Total Oil Great Britain Ltd.* [1983] 1 W.L.R. 87, at p. 93.

[29] *Universe Tankships Inc. of Monrovia* v. *International Transport Workers Federation* (*supra*, n. 28).

[30] *North Ocean Shipping Co. Ltd.* v. *Hyundai Construction Co. Ltd.* (*supra*, n. 24); *Pao On* v. *Lau Yiu Long* (*supra*, n. 13). See also *Occidental Worldwide Investment Cpn.* v. *Skibs A/S Avanti* (*supra*, n. 24) (threat to put company into liquidaton).

[31] On the distinction between a 'threat' and a 'warning' which will not suffice, see *post*, p. 281.

[32] [1989] Q.B. 833.

400 cartons and, on this basis, had agreed a price of £1.10 per carton. The first load was for a smaller number of cartons, and A, believing that carrying such a load at the agreed rate was not financially viable, said that it would not perform unless K agreed to pay a minimum of £440 a load. Because K's commercial survival depended on the contract with the retail chain and it could not find an alternative carrier, it agreed to A's demand but then refused to pay.

It was held that the new terms were agreed under economic duress. In that case there was a direct threat to repudiate the contract, but the threat may be indirect. Thus, in *B & S Contracts and Design Ltd.* v. *Victor Green Publications Ltd.* an indication by a party to a contract that it was prepared to allow its workers to strike unless the other party agreed to make a payment in addition to the contract price was held to be a veiled threat and to constitute duress because the other party had no other practical choice open to it but to agree to pay.[33] Good faith in the sense that the contractual difficulty is not the fault of the party seeking to renegotiate does not preclude a finding of economic duress.[34]

(ii) Causation

Not every threat to break a contract unless its terms are renegotiated will amount to duress. It is also necessary for the threat to induce the renegotiation, and in this context a number of factors will be taken into account. These include the availability of an adequate alternative remedy, whether there has been a compromise or a submission to a claim made in good faith, and whether the victim has protested or taken independent advice. Thus, in *Pao On* v. *Lau Yiu Long*,[35] where one party was coerced into accepting the renegotiation of a business transaction by a threat by the other party to break an existing contract, but did so with legal advice and without protest, and after a considered appraisal of the risk involved, it was held by the Privy Council that the renegotiated agreement would not be set aside on the ground of economic duress. In cases of duress of the person the Court may be willing to infer, in the absence of evidence to the contrary, that the duress induced the contract.[36] But in cases of economic duress, it is for the party seeking to have the contract set aside to establish that the duress was a significant cause of the contract.[37]

(iii) Alternative remedies

A person threatened with duress of goods or a breach of contract can stand up to the threat and, if the other party breaches the contract, sue for damages. In the context of duress of goods the presence of an alternative remedy, such as an action in tort for wrongful interference with goods, is not necessarily a bar to relief; the threatened party might have had 'such an immediate want of his goods that [such an action]

---

[33] [1984] I.C.R. 419, at pp. 426, 428.

[34] *Huyton S.A.* v. *Peter Cremer G.m.b.H. & Co.* [1999] 1 Lloyd's Rep. 620, at p. 627.

[35] [1980] A.C. 614, *ante*, pp. 103–4. See also *Alec Lobb (Garages) Ltd.* v. *Total Oil Great Britain Ltd.* (*supra*, n. 28).

[36] *Barton* v. *Armstrong* [1976] A.C. 104, at p. 120.

[37] *Huyton S.A.* v. *Peter Cremer G.m.b.H. & Co.* [1999] 1 Lloyds Rep. 620, at pp. 636, 638–9. Cf. *Crescendo Management Pty. Ltd.* v. *Westpae Banking Corp.* (1998) 19 N.S.W.L.R. 40, *per* McHugh J.A. at p. 46.

would not do'[38] and in any event there is no *right* to recover the goods themselves as opposed to damages in an action in tort.[39]

In the case of duress by threatened breach of contract, although damages and, where available, specific relief may be adequate, there will be situations in which such remedies do not adequately protect the victim, for example where it is imperative that there be no interruption in performance or where, as in *Atlas Express Ltd.* v. *Kafco (Importers and Distributors) Ltd.*, it is not possible to obtain the contractual services from another source. The existence and adequacy of an alternative remedy is taken into account in such cases. There is some support for treating this as purely evidential and not conclusive, i.e. one of the factors (with protest and independent advice) which the Court takes into account in determining whether the victim was in fact coerced by the threat.[40] But it is submitted that, since the basis of the doctrine of duress is the absence of a practical alternative on the part of the victim to submission to the threat, the better view is that the existence of an adequate alternative remedy goes to the essence of and precludes a finding of duress.[41]

(c) DURESS DISTINGUISHED FROM LEGITIMATE RENEGOTIATION

We noted in Chapter 3 of this book that it may well be reasonable for a party to seek to renegotiate a contract and that one of the functions of promissory estoppel is to protect reasonable renegotiations. Where the party seeking to renegotiate honestly believes that in the circumstances it is entitled not to perform, we have seen that the result will generally be a binding compromise.[42] But where it does not, the development of duress makes it important that parties who genuinely face difficulties if they complete performance on the contract terms and wish to renegotiate know what is and what is not permissible conduct.

(i) Was there a threat?

In *Williams* v. *Roffey Bros. & Nicholls (Contractors) Ltd.*[43] R & N, noticing their carpentry sub-contractor's difficulties, offered an additional payment which, as we have seen, was held binding. But surely the renegotiation would not automatically have been vitiated by duress if it was the sub-contractor who had taken the initiative. It should not necessarily be seen as a threat to point out that without renegotiation it

---

[38] *Astley* v. *Reynolds* (1731) 2 Str. 915, at p. 916; *Maskell* v. *Horner* [1915] 3 K.B. 106, at p. 122. See also *Kanhaya Lal* v. *National Bank of India* (1913) 29 T.L.R. 314. Cf. *Vantage Navigation Cpn.* v. *Suhail & Saud Bahwan Building Materials Llc. (The Alev)* (*supra*, n. 24) at pp. 146–7.

[39] By the Torts (Interference with Goods) Act 1977, ss. 3(2)(a), 3(3)(b) an order for delivery of the goods may be made at the discretion of the court.

[40] *Pao On* v. *Lau Yiu Long* (*supra*, n. 24), *per* Lord Scarman at pp. 635, 640; *Huyton S.A.* v. *Peter Cremer G.m.b.H. & Co.* [1999] 1 Lloyd's Rep. 620, at p. 638.

[41] *Vantage Navigation Cpn.* v. *Suhail & Saud Bahwan Building Materials Llc. (The Alev)* (*supra*, n. 24); *Hennessy* v. *Craigmyle & Co. Ltd.* [1986] I.C.R. 461.

[42] *Ante*, p. 101.

[43] [1991] 1 Q.B. 1, *ante*, p. 106.

will not be possible to continue performance,[44] provided that this is so in fact. This is particularly so where, as in the *High Trees* case,[45] changes of circumstances have affected the risks originally undertaken.[46] It must be recalled that, save for specifically enforceable contracts, it is open for a party to a contract to be in deliberate breach of contract in order to cut its losses commercially.[47] We have seen that the *bona fides* of the person making a demand are relevant in determining whether there is a compromise or whether the doctrine of promissory estoppel applies.[48] They should also be relevant in determining whether there is duress.[49] Thus, in *B & S Contracts and Design Ltd.* v. *Victor Green Publications Ltd.*, considered above,[50] it seems that the fact that the contractor had not made reasonable efforts to avoid a strike by its workers before demanding an additional payment from the other party to the contract was a factor in the conclusion that the demand was a veiled threat.

(ii) Is it commercially reasonable to renegotiate?

One way to determine what is permissible is by a test, similar to that in paragraph 176(2) of the *Restatement of Contracts 2d*, which would ask whether it was commercially reasonable to seek to renegotiate and whether, as in the case of promissory estoppel, the renegotiated terms are 'fair and equitable'.[51] But it is difficult to see how the Courts could do this without becoming more involved in an examination of the fairness of both the original contract and the renegotiation than they have hitherto been.[52] It is, however, equally difficult to see any way of distinguishing permissible and impermissible conduct during renegotiations that does not ultimately involve some monitoring of the substantive fairness of the contract, although this should be kept to the absolute minimum by emphasizing that duress is primarily a doctrine of *procedural* impropriety focusing on conduct.

(d) THREATS OF LAWFUL ACTION

(i) Ordinarily not duress

It is not ordinarily duress to threaten to do that which one has a right to do, for

---

[44] See, on the difference between a 'threat' and a 'warning' in the context of economic torts, *Conway* v. *Wade* [1909] A.C. 506, at p. 510; *Rookes* v. *Barnard* [1964] A.C. 1129, at p. 1166; *Camilla Tanker Ltd.* v. *International Transport Workers Federation* [1976] I.C.R. 274, at pp. 284, 296. See also *Hodges* v. *Webb* [1920] 2 Ch. 70; Beatson, *The Use and Abuse of Unjust Enrichment* (1991), pp. 118–20; Smith [1997] C.L.J. 343, 346–50.

[45] [1947] K.B. 130, *ante*, pp. 112–13.

[46] See *Watkins & Sons Inc.* v. *Carrig* 21 A. 2d. 591 (1941) (hard rock unexpectedly struck during excavations) but cf. *North Ocean Shipping Co. Ltd.* v. *Hyundai Construction Co. Ltd.* (*supra*, n. 28) at p. 714; *Williams* v. *Roffey Bros. & Nicholls (Contractors) Ltd.* (*supra*, n. 43) at p. 20.

[47] *Williams* v. *Roffey Bros. & Nicholls (Contractors) Ltd.* (*supra*, n. 43) *per* Purchas L.J. at p. 23.

[48] *D. & C. Builders* v. *Rees* [1966] 2 Q.B. 617, *ante*, p. 115.

[49] *CTN Cash and Carry Ltd.* v. *Gallagher Ltd.* [1994] 4 All E.R. 714 (lawful act duress, see *post*, p. 283).

[50] [1984] I.C.R. 419, *ante*, p. 280.

[51] *D. & C. Builders* v. *Rees* (*supra*, n. 48), *ante*, p. 115.

[52] Beatson, *The Use and Abuse of Unjust Enrichment* (1991), pp. 126–9, 135; Goff and Jones, *The Law of Restitution*, 5th edn. (1998), p. 329.

instance to refuse to enter into a contract or to terminate a contract lawfully.[53] In the cut-and-thrust of business relationships various types of pressure may be brought to bear in differing situations. Where there are shortages in goods or services the person who wishes to acquire them has little choice. Thus a private person or undertaking is generally permitted to refuse to deal with another at all or except on specified terms,[54] and the poor person who has to agree to pay a high rent to get a roof over his head is nevertheless bound. 'No bargain will be upset which is the result of the ordinary interplay of [market] forces'[55] and a contracting party will not be permitted to escape from its contractual obligations merely because it was coerced into making a contract by fear of the financial consequences of refusing to do so.[56] In *CTN Cash & Carry Ltd.* v. *Gallagher Ltd.* it was held that a wholesale buyer of cigarettes who, following an honest but mistaken demand by the seller, paid a sum not due because the seller had threatened, as it was entitled to do, to withdraw credit facilities from the buyer, could not recover it on the ground of duress.[57] It was said that this enables people to know where they stand, avoids the reopening of settled accounts, and provides certainty as to what is acceptable conduct in the bargaining process.[58] Although this approach leaves many forms of socially objectionable conduct unchecked, as a general rule the determination of when socially objectionable conduct which is not in itself unlawful should be penalized is for the legislature rather than the judiciary.[59]

(ii) Exceptional cases: 'illegitimate' pressure as duress

Exceptionally a threat of lawful action may constitute duress and render a contract voidable. It has been said that the threat, if not wrongful, must be immoral or unconscionable.[60] We have seen that a threat by one party to prosecute the other for a criminal offence could constitute a ground on which the contract would be set aside.[61] Similarly, in the context of salvage, a refusal to rescue a vessel in distress or those on board save on extortionate terms has led to the resulting contract being set aside.[62] Again, it is inconceivable that the Courts would give effect to an agreement obtained by threats amounting to blackmail, although in one sense the blackmailer may only be threatening to do some act which he is lawfully entitled to do, e.g. to tell

[53] *Leyland Daf Ltd.* v. *Automotive Products plc* [1994] 1 B.C.L.R. 244, at pp. 249–50, 257; *Smith* v. *Charlick Ltd.* (1923) 34 C.L.R. 38, at pp. 56, 64–5 (High Court of Australia).
[54] For the position of a public body see *R.* v. *Lewisham L.B.C., ex parte Shell U.K. Ltd.* [1988] 1 All E.R. 938 and the statutory controls discussed *ante*, pp. 212, 214.
[55] *Lloyds Bank Ltd.* v. *Bundy* [1975] Q.B. 326, at p. 336.
[56] *Hardie and Lane Ltd.* v. *Chilton* [1928] 2 K.B. 306: *Eric Gnapp Ltd.* v. *Petroleum Board* [1949] 1 All E.R. 980.
[57] [1994] 4 All E.R. 714. See also *Leyland Daf Ltd.* v. *Automotive Products plc* [1994] 1 B.C.L.R. 244.
[58] *Ibid.*, at p. 719.
[59] *CTN Cash and Carry Ltd.* v. *Gallagher Ltd.* (*supra*, n. 49), *per* Steyn L.J. at pp. 718–19, and see Birks, *An Introduction to the Law of Restitution* (1985), p. 177.
[60] *Alf Vaughan* v. *Royscot Trust Ltd.* [1999] 1 All E.R. (Comm.) 856.
[61] *Mutual Finance Co. Ltd.* v. *John Wetton & Sons Ltd.* [1937] 2 K.B. 389, *ante*, p. 279.
[62] *The Port Caledonia* [1903] P. 184 ('£1,000 or no rope'). See also *The Rialto* [1891] P. 175 (agreement to pay £6,000 when proper sum was £3,000).

a wife of her husband's adultery, or to appoint a receiver.[63] Lord Scarman has stated that:[64]

[d]uress can, of course, exist even if the threat is one of lawful action: whether it does so depends upon the nature of the demand. Blackmail is often a demand supported by a threat to do what is lawful, e.g. to report criminal conduct to the police.

In the typical case of blackmail, the blackmailer has no economic interest in the outcome apart from getting what has been demanded, and it is for this reason that the threat is regarded as illegitimate. Where the person making the threat has some economic or other interest in the outcome apart from getting what has been demanded, the question will be whether the demand is 'unwarranted' in the sense of being unrelated to any 'legitimate' interest of the party making the demand. It is submitted that, as in the criminal law, a demand will not be unwarranted where the person making it believes that there are reasonable grounds for making it and the use of the menaces is a proper means of reinforcing the demand.[65] Since in the typical case of coercion by the threat of a lawful act concerning an existing or future contractual relationship, the threatener will have a direct economic interest, the demand will, in the majority of cases, be 'legitimate'.[66] The tort of conspiracy to injure, which also does not involve unlawful means, provides a useful guide. In that context the pursuit of more profit, of a larger share of the market, price stability, and of higher wages have all been held to be legitimate purposes.[67] For these reasons, while in principle a threat to do what is lawful can constitute duress, this form of pressure is unlikely to have much practical impact save where the relationship between the parties is one accorded special protection by the law.[68]

III. UNDUE INFLUENCE

We have already seen that the term 'fraud' was used in a sense wider and less precise in the Court of Chancery than in the common law courts.[69] This followed naturally from the remedies which they respectively administered. The common law gave damages for a wrong, and was compelled to define with care the wrong which furnished a cause

---

[63] *Westpac Banking Corp.* v. *Cockerill* (1998) 152 A.L.R. 267.

[64] *Universe Tankships Inc. of Monrovia* v. *International Transport Workers Federation* [1983] 1 A.C. 366, at p. 401. See also Lord Diplock, *ibid.*, at p. 385. See further *Thorne* v. *Motor Trade Association* [1937] AC. 797, at p. 822; *Dimskal Shipping Co. S.A.* v. *International Transport Workers Federation (The Evia Luck)* [1992] 2 A.C. 152. Cf. *Royal Boskalis Westminster N.V.* v. *Mountain* [1997] 2 All E.R. 929, at p. 981.

[65] Theft Act 1968, s. 2(1); Criminal Law Revision Committee, Eighth Report (Cmnd. 2977); *R.* v. *Hervey* (1980) 72 Cr. App. R. 139.

[66] For a possible example of an unwarranted demand see *Norreys* v. *Zeffert* [1939] 2 All E.R. 186.

[67] *Mogul Steamship Co.* v. *McGregor* [1892] A.C. 25; *Thorne* v. *Motor Trade Association* [1937] A.C. 797; *Crofter Hand Woven Harris Tweed Co. Ltd.* v. *Veitch* [1942] A.C. 435.

[68] See *post*, pp. 287 (presumed undue influence) and 296 (unconscionability) for consideration of such relationships.

[69] *Ante*, p. 267.

of action. Equity refused specific performance of a contract or set aside the transaction, with or without compensation, where one party had acted unfairly by the other. Fraud in equity was often used in the sense of unconscientious dealing although, in the words of Lord Haldane, a great equity lawyer, this was unfortunate.[70] One such form of dealing is commonly described as 'undue influence'. The nature and operation of undue influence has recently been considered by the House of Lords in eight appeals heard together and reported as *Royal Bank of Scotland plc. v. Etridge (No. 2)*.[71] The principles are set out in the speech of Lord Nicholls with whom, although there are some differences of expression and approach, the other members of the Appellate Committee agreed.[72]

(a) NATURE OF UNDUE INFLUENCE

The term 'undue influence' has sometimes been used by the Courts to describe the equitable doctrine of coercion referred to above,[73] but it also includes, and it would perhaps be more helpful to confine it to, forms of pressure much less direct or substantial than those already discussed. It may also arise where the parties are in a relation of confidence or dependence which puts one of them in a position to exercise over the other an influence which may be perfectly natural and proper in itself, but is capable of being unfairly used.[74] Courts, including the House of Lords in *Etridge's* case, have been careful not to define precisely the sort of influence which will be regarded as 'undue'.[75] Nevertheless, it is accepted that equity identified broadly two forms of unacceptable conduct, which Lord Nicholls described as follows:[76]

The first comprises overt acts of improper pressure or coercion such as unlawful threats. . . . The second form arises out of a relationship between two persons where one has acquired over another a measure of influence or ascendancy, of which the ascendant person then takes unfair advantage. . . . In cases of this latter nature the influence one person has over another provides scope for misuse without any specific overt acts of persuasion. The relationship between two individuals may be such that, without more, one of them is disposed to agree a course of action proposed by the other. Typically, this occurs when one person places trust in another to look after his affairs and interests, and the latter betrays this trust by preferring his own interests. He abuses the influence he has acquired.

The first type of case, the direct analogue of common law duress, has been called 'actual' undue influence. The second type of case, where the parties are in a

---

[70] *Nocton v. Lord Ashburton* [1914] A.C. 932, at p. 953.

[71] [2001] 3 W.L.R. 1021.

[72] *Ibid.*, at para. 3. See also paras. 91, 100, 192.

[73] *Mutual Finance Co. Ltd. v. John Wetton & Sons Ltd.* [1937] 2 K.B. 389; *Royal Bank of Scotland plc v. Etridge (No. 2)* [2001] 3 W.L.R. 1021, at paras. 7–8.

[74] Winder (1939) 3 M.L.R. 97. See also Cartwright, *Unequal Bargaining* (1991), ch. X. Cf. Birks and Chin in Beatson and Friedmann (eds.), *Good Faith and Fault in Contract Law* (1995), ch. 3 (undue influence is about impaired consent, not exploitation).

[75] *National Westminster Bank plc v. Morgan* [1985] A.C. 686, at p. 709.

[76] *Royal Bank of Scotland plc v. Etridge (No. 2)* [2001] 3 W.L.R. 1021, at paras. 8–9. See also paras. 103–5 (Lord Hobhouse) and 151–8 (Lord Scott). But Lord Clyde, at para. 92 questioned the wisdom of attempting to make classifications of cases of undue influence.

relationship in which duties of care and confidence are imposed on one party towards the other, has been called 'presumed' undue influence.

It is often said that, in the first type of case, evidence of express influence must be adduced by the party seeking to impeach the transaction, whereas, in the second, undue influence is presumed by the law in the absence of evidence to the contrary.[77] While this is undoubtedly true, it can be somewhat misleading, as once it is established that one person is in a position to exercise undue influence over the other, it is presumed that such influence has been exercised until the contrary is proved,[78] although, as seen below, the nature of the presumption differs in different categories of case.

(b) ACTUAL UNDUE INFLUENCE

Where one party exercised such domination over the mind and will of the other that the latter's independence of decision was substantially undermined, and this domination brought about the transaction, the victim will be entitled to relief on the ground of undue influence.

There is no need for any special relationship (of the type mentioned below) to exist between the parties, although, of course, it may do so. The mere fact that domination was exercised is sufficient; no abuse of confidence need be proved. In *Smith* v. *Kay*,[79] for example, a young man, only just of age, incurred liabilities to the appellant by the contrivance of an older man who had acquired a strong influence over him, and who professed to assist him in a career of extravagance and dissipation. It was held that influence of this nature, though in no way 'fiduciary', entitled the young man to the protection of the Court. Similarly, in *Morley* v. *Loughnan*[80] executors sued to recover £140,000 paid by the deceased to a member of the 'Exclusive Brethren' in whose house he had lived for some years, and under whose religious influence he had been. Wright J., in giving judgment for the plaintiffs, said that it was unnecessary to decide whether or not any special relationship existed between the deceased and the defendant, for he 'took possession, so to speak, of the whole life of the deceased, and the gifts were not the result of the deceased's own free will, but the effect of that influence and domination'.[81]

Many older cases on this point have unfortunately concerned spiritual 'advisers' who have used their expert knowledge of the next world to obtain material advantages in this. In more recent times the cases have often concerned men who have put pressure on their wives or partners to secure business debts by mortgaging the family home.[82] While heavy family pressure will not in itself suffice to constitute domination, in one case wounding and insulting language and demeaning comparisons between

---

[77] *Allcard* v. *Skinner* (1887) 36 Ch. D. 145, *per* Lindley L.J. at p. 181.

[78] *Ibid.*, at p. 183. See also *Goldsworthy* v. *Brickell* [1987] 1 Ch. 378, at p. 401.

[79] (1859) 7 H.L.C. 750. See also *Royal Bank of Scotland plc.* v. *Etridge (No. 2)* [2001] 3 W.L.R. 1021, at para. 103.

[80] [1893] 1 Ch. 736.

[81] At p. 756.

[82] e.g. *C.I.B.C. Mortgages Ltd.* v. *Pitt* [1994] 1 A.C. 200.

what a husband characterized as his wife's disloyalty and his relations' loyalty amounted to moral blackmail and coecion.[83]

Actual undue influence itself suffices for relief. It is not necessary that the transaction induced by it be not readily explicable or be manifestly disadvantageous to the victim,[84] although it has been said that in the nature of things questions of undue influence will not usually arise where the transaction is innocuous.[85] In this, as will be seen, actual undue influence differs from presumed undue influence.[86]

(c) PRESUMED UNDUE INFLUENCE

Even if it cannot be proved that the claimant's mind was a 'mere channel through which the will of the defendant operated',[87] relief may be given if there existed between the parties some special relationship of confidence which the defendant has abused:

Wherever two persons stand in such a relation that, while it continues, confidence is necessarily reposed by one, and the influence which naturally grows out of that confidence is possessed by the other, and this confidence is abused, or the influence is exerted to obtain an advantage at the expense of the confiding party, the person so availing himself of his position will not be permitted to retain the advantage, although the transaction could not have been impeached if no such confidential relation had existed.[88]

Prior to *Etridge's* case Slade L.J.[89] had divided presumed undue influence into two classes, an approach approved by the House of Lords in *Barclays Bank plc* v. *O'Brien*.[90] The first (class 2A) was where the duties of care and confidence arose as a matter of law by virtue of the relationship between the parties. The second (class 2B) was said to occur where the duties arose in the special circumstances of the parties' association with each other, i.e. because on the facts of the particular case the claimant placed trust and confidence in the other party and the transaction between the parties was one calling for an explanation.

In *Etridge's* case, however, their Lordships considered that it was only in class 2A cases that there is a true presumption of undue influence, arising from the law's 'sternly protective attitude towards certain types of relationship'. In such cases the claimant 'need not prove he actually reposed trust and confidence in the other party. It is sufficient for him to prove the existence of the relationship'.[91] In class 2B cases, however, although described by generations of equity lawyers as cases in which a presumption of undue influence arises, there is no true presumption but only a shift

---

[83] *Bank of Scotland* v. *Bennett* [1997] 1 F.L.R. 801, at pp. 822–7; [2001] 3 W.L.R. 1021, at paras. 312–15.

[84] *C.I.B.C. Mortgages Ltd.* v. *Pitt* (*supra*, n. 82).

[85] *Royal Bank of Scotland plc.* v. *Etridge (No. 2)* [2001] 3 W.L.R. 1021, at para. 12.

[86] *Ibid.*, at para. 26.

[87] *Tufton* v. *Sperni* [1952] 2 T.L.R. 516, at p. 530.

[88] *Tate* v. *Williamson* (1866) L.R. 2 Ch. App. 55, *per* Lord Chelmsford at p. 61.

[89] *B.C.C.I.* v. *Aboody* [1990] 1 Q.B. 923, at p. 953.

[90] *Barclays Bank plc* v. *O'Brien* [1994] 1 A.C. 180, at pp. 189–190.

[91] [2001] 3 W.L.R. 1021, *per* Lord Nicholls at para. 18. See also *ibid.*, at paras. 107, 161.

in the evidential onus on a question of fact. The burden of proving undue influence rests on the claimant, but will normally be discharged by proof that he or she placed trust and confidence in the other party and that the transaction between the parties is one which calls for explanation. Proof of those two facts is *prima facie* evidence that the defendant abused the influence he or she acquired in the relationship, and it is then for the defendant to counter the inference which should otherwise be drawn. Accordingly, a claimant who succeeds does so because he or she has established a case of undue influence.[92] Analytically, the general burden of proof remains on the claimant, but this can be discharged by establishing a sufficient *prima facie* case.[93] Despite this difference, since there is a shift in the evidential onus and since the requirement that the transaction must be one calling for an explanation is relevant in both categories of case, the two different types of presumption are considered in this section. In both there are two components required for the establishment of a situation in which undue influence will be presumed. The first is the nature of the relationship, and the second is the nature of the transaction, which must be one calling for an explanation; i.e. not be readily explicable by the relationship of the parties, but also, less satisfactorily, described as one that is 'manifestly disadvantageous' to the victim.

(i) The nature of the relationship

A true presumption that one party acquires influence over another who is vulnerable is made as a matter of law in respect of certain relationships. In other situations, proof that on the particular facts trust and confidence has been reposed by one party in the other and that the transaction is one which calls for explanation, will lead to a shift in the evidential onus.

(a) True presumption raised as a matter of law. It is not every fiduciary relationship that as a matter of law raises a presumption of undue influence.[94] It must be one of a limited class which the Courts regard as suggesting undue influence. While it has been stated that the relations which fall into this category cannot be listed exhaustively,[95] they include those between parent (or person *in loco parentis*) and child,[96] solicitor and client,[97] doctor and patient,[98] trustee and beneficiary,[99] spiritual adviser and any person to whom that person stands in that relationship,[100] and, in certain circumstances, fiancé and fiancée.[101] But the relationship of husband and wife is not one to which this presumption applies as a matter of law.[102]

---

[92] *Ibid.*, at paras. 13–14.
[93] *Ante*, p. 286.
[94] *Re Coombe* [1911] 1 Ch. 723, at p. 728 (principal and agent will not suffice).
[95] *Royal Bank of Scotland plc.* v. *Etridge (No. 2)* [2001] 3 W.L.R. 1021, at para. 10.
[96] *Bainbrigge* v. *Browne* (1881) 18 Ch. D. 188.
[97] *Wright* v. *Carter* [1980] 1 Ch. 27.
[98] *Mitchell* v. *Homfray* (1881) 8 Q.B.D. 587.
[99] *Beningfield* v. *Baxter* (1886) 12 App. Cas. 167.
[100] *Huguenin* v. *Baseley* (1807) 14 Ves. Jun. 273; *Allcard* v. *Skinner* (1887) 36 Ch. D. 145.
[101] *Re Lloyds Bank Ltd.* [1931] 1 Ch. 289. Cf. *Zamet* v. *Hyman* [1961] 1 W.L.R. 1442.
[102] *Barclays Bank plc* v. *O'Brien* [1994] 1 A.C. 180; *Royal Bank of Scotland plc.* v. *Etridge (No. 2)* [2001] 3 W.L.R. 1021. Cf. *Backhouse* v. *Backhouse* [1978] 1 W.L.R. 243, at p. 251.

In *Etridge's* case Lord Nicholls stated that the test is whether one party has reposed sufficient trust and confidence in the other rather than whether the relationship belongs to a particular type, that the principle is not confined to cases of abuse of trust and confidence but includes cases where a vulnerable person has been exploited, and that there is no single touchstone for determining whether the principle is applicable.[103] It is submitted that this provides insufficient certainty and that it is preferable for the law to mark out certain relationships where, 'as a matter of policy, the law requires the dominant party to justify the righteousness of the transaction'.[104]

It is important to note that the presumption is that one party has acquired influence over the other, it is not a presumption that the influence has been abused. If all that has happened is that a client has left a small bequest to his family solicitor, no inference of abuse or unfair dealing will arise.[105]

(b) Shift in the evidential onus as a result of the facts of the particular case. Where, as in the case of husband and wife, the presumption does not apply as a matter of law, one of the parties may nevertheless be able to demonstrate that on the facts of the particular case he or she placed trust and confidence in the other. In such a case, the degree of trust may be such that (provided, see below, the transaction is one that calls for an explanation) the court can infer that, in the absence of a satisfactory explanation, the transaction can only have been procured by undue influence. In such cases there is a rebuttable evidential presumption of undue influence. In the case of wives, it has been stated that 'this special tenderness of treatment' is attributable to the fact that in many cases a wife is able to demonstrate that she placed trust and confidence in her husband in relation to her financial affairs and because 'the sexual and emotional ties between the parties provide a ready weapon for undue influence: a wife's true wishes can easily be overborne because of her fear of destroying or damaging the wider relationship between her and her husband if she opposes his wishes'.[106] Similar principles apply to all other cases where there is an emotional relationship between unmarried cohabitees.[107]

The list of situations in which such a relationship exists on the facts of the particular case is not a closed one. The principle applies to every case where influence is acquired and abused, where confidence is reposed and betrayed.[108] All the circumstances have to be considered to determine whether such a relationship does exist,[109] and it is not necessary to show that it is one of domination. It suffices that the party in

---

[103]   *Royal Bank of Scotland plc.* v. *Etridge (No. 2)* [2001] 3 W.L.R. 1021, at paras. 10–11. See also Lord Clyde, at para. 92.

[104]   *Ibid., per* Lord Scott at para. 158. See also Lord Hobhouse at para. 104.

[105]   *Ibid., per* Lord Hobhouse at para. 104.

[106]   *Barclays Bank plc* v. *O'Brien (supra*, n. 102) *per* Lord Browne-Wilkinson at pp. 190–1, 196. For a sociological analysis of the law and practice relating to surety wives and partners, see Fehlberg, *Sexually Transmitted Debt* (1997).

[107]   *Ibid.,* at p. 198. See also [2001] 3 W.L.R. 1021, at para. 47.

[108]   *Smith* v. *Kay* (1859) 7 H.L.C. 750, *per* Lord Kingsdown at p. 779.

[109]   *Lloyds Bank Ltd.* v. *Bundy* [1975] Q.B. 326, at p. 342.

whom trust and confidence is reposed is in a position to exert influence over the party who reposes it. Thus in *Tate* v. *Williamson*:[110]

An undergraduate, T, aged 23 years, was being pressed to pay his college debts, which amounted to some £1,000. Being estranged from his father, he asked his great-uncle to advise him how he should find the means to pay. The great-uncle was unable to advise in person owing to ill health, but he deputed the defendant, his nephew, to do so. Conversations took place between T and the defendant in which T expressed the desire to sell part of his estate, upon which the defendant offered to buy it for £7,000. Before the sale was completed, the defendant obtained a report from a surveyor on the property, and this valued it at £20,000. The defendant did not disclose this fact to T, but proceeded with the purchase. Excessive drinking led to T's death one year later. It was held that the purchase must be set aside. The defendant, having been asked to give advice, stood in a confidential relationship to T, and this prevented him from becoming a purchaser of the property without the fullest communication of all material information which he had obtained as to its value.

Similarly, in *Tufton* v. *Sperni*,[111] the situation was such that a confidential relationship arose:

T and S were fellow members of a committee formed to establish a Moslem cultural centre in London, it being understood that T would provide the funds for the centre. S induced T to buy his (S's) own house for the purpose at a price which grossly exceeded its market value.

The Court of Appeal set the contract aside. The situation was not one which was comprehended by the established categories, nor was there any domination of T by S; yet, as Evershed M.R. pointed out:[112]

If a number of persons join together for the purpose of furthering some charitable or altruistic objective, it would seem not unreasonable to conclude that in regard to all matters related to that objective, each 'necessarily reposes confidence' in the others and each possesses accordingly that 'influence which naturally grows out of confidence'.

(ii) A transaction which is not readily explicable by the relationship and calls for an explanation

In *Goldsworthy* v. *Brickell*, drawing on Lindley L.J.'s classic nineteenth century formulation in *Allcard v Skinner*,[113] Nourse L.J. stated:

---

[110] (1866) L.R. 2 Ch. App. 55. See also *Cheese* v. *Thomas* [1994] 1 W.L.R. 129 (great nephew and aged great-uncle); *Grosvenor* v. *Sherratt* (1860) 28 Beav. 659 (executor and young woman); *Re Craig* [1971] Ch. 95 (secretary-companion and man of 84 years); *Goldsworthy* v. *Brickell* (*infra*, n. 112) (85-year-old farmer and farm manager); *Lloyds Bank Ltd.* v. *Bundy* (*supra*, n. 109) (banker and customer) but cf. *National Westminster Bank plc* v. *Morgan* [1985] 1 A.C. 686; *Horry* v. *Tate & Lyle Refineries Ltd.* [1982] 2 Lloyd's Rep. 416 (injured employee and employer's insurers); *O'Sullivan* v. *Management Agency and Music Ltd.* [1985] Q.B. 428 (unknown pop musician and internationally recognized manager). Perhaps the high watermark is *Credit Lyonnais Bank Nederland N.V.* v. *Burch* [1997] 1 All E.R. 144 (employer and employee) which is perhaps better regarded, see Chen-Wishart [1997] C.L.J. 60, as a case of unconscionability, on which see *post*, p. 296.

[111] [1952] 2 T.L.R. 516. See also *Roche* v. *Sherrington* [1982] 1 W.L.R. 599.

[112] At p. 523. See also *Goldsworthy* v. *Brickell* [1987] 1 Ch. 378.

[113] (1887) 36 Ch. D. 145, *per* Lindley L.J. at p. 185.

the presumption is not perfected and remains inoperative until the party who has ceded the trust and confidence makes a gift so large, or enters a transaction so improvident, as not to be reasonably accounted for on the ground of friendship, relationship, charity or other ordinary motives on which men act. Although influence might have been presumed beforehand, it is only then that it is presumed to have been undue.[114]

The reason for this requirement is to prevent the presumption applying to obviously innocuous transactions between those in a relationship of trust and confidence, such as a moderate gift as a Christmas present by a child to a parent, an agreement by a client to pay the reasonable fees to a solicitor, or a moderate bequest to one's doctor.[115] But in *National Westminster Bank plc* v. *Morgan*[116] Lord Scarman stated that the transaction must be 'manifestly disadvantageous'. This formulation has been widely criticized because its primary focus appears to be financial, i.e. the adequacy of the consideration given in exchange for the money paid or property transferred.

'Manifest disadvantage' can generally be shown where a person agrees to guarantee the debts of another and is, of course, an inherent feature of gifts, which have been the subject of many cases of undue influence.[117] It would also exist where a charge over a matrimonial home secured not only money borrowed under the proposed transaction but also any other transaction entered into by the debtor. But in the case of a guarantee of the debts of a business it may be more difficult to determine whether the transaction is 'manifestly disadvantageous'. In the sense that the guarantor undertakes a serious financial obligation with no personal financial return it is disadvantageous. But where the guarantor has an interest in the business, as in the case of a shareholder or a wife where the business is the source of the family income, it may not be.[118] Moreover, the formulation does not readily allow non-financial factors to be taken into account. Where the requisite relationship of trust and confidence exists between two persons, the fact that an offer by one to buy land or a valuable oil painting from the other is for the full or even an enhanced market price should not necessarily prevent the transaction being presumed to be vitiated by undue influence. The person subjected to the influence should not be presumed to wish to sell a family home or business, or an item of particular sentimental value, even for the full market price. A relationship and the influence resulting from it may be abused 'even though the transaction is, on the face of it, one which, in commercial terms, provides reasonably equal benefits for both parties'.[119] In *Etridge's* case it was accepted that the label 'manifest disadvantage' can give rise to misunderstanding and should be discarded. Lord Nicholls stated that the better approach was to adhere more directly to the classic test which asks whether the transaction can be 'reasonably accounted for on the

[114] [1987] Ch. 378, at p. 401. This requirement does not apply to cases of 'actual' undue influence, *ante*, p. 286.

[115] *Royal Bank of Scotland plc.* v. *Etridge (No. 2)* [2001] 3 W.L.R. 1021, paras. 24, 104, 156.

[116] [1985] A.C. 686.

[117] e.g. *Allcard* v. *Skinner* (1887) 36 Ch. D. 145, *post*, p. 294.

[118] *Royal Bank of Scotland plc.* v. *Etridge (No. 2)* [2001] 3 W.L.R. 1021, paras. 28–29.

[119] *National Westminster Bank plc.* v. *Morgan* [1983] 3 All E.R. 85, *per* Slade L.J., at p. 92. Although the House of Lords disagreed ([1985] A.C. 686 at p. 704), see *Barclays Bank plc.* v. *Coleman* [2001] Q.B. 20, *per* Nourse L.J. at p. 31.

ground of friendship, relationship, charity or other ordinary motives' as well as whether it is 'improvident'.[120]

(iii) Rebutting the presumption

Where undue influence is shown to exist, the presumption of its exercise can only be rebutted by proof that the party reposing the confidence has been 'placed in such a position as will enable him to form an entirely free and unfettered judgment, independent altogether of any sort of control'.[121] The most obvious way of establishing this is to show that the party reposing the confidence received independent legal advice and took it. In some (possibly extreme) cases, very cogent evidence has been required to be adduced by the defendant to prove that the significance of the advice was brought home to the other party. In *Powell* v. *Powell*:[122]

A settlement was executed by a young woman, under the influence of her stepmother, by which she shared her property with the children of the stepmother's second marriage. She received some independent advice from a solicitor, but he was acting for some of the other parties to the settlement as well as for the plaintiff. It appeared that, although he had expressed disapproval of the transaction, he had not carried his disapproval to the point of withdrawing his services.

It was held that the settlement should be rescinded. And in *Huguenin* v. *Baseley*, where a woman made over her property to a clergyman in whom she reposed confidence, Lord Eldon said:[123]

The question is, not, whether she knew what she was doing, had done, or proposed to do, but how the intention was produced: whether all that care and providence was placed round her, as against those, who advised her, which, from their situation and relation with respect to her, they were bound to exert on her behalf.

But this is not the only way of rebutting the presumption. The essential thing is to show that the transaction was 'the result of the free exercise of independent will'.[124] If this is established, the transaction will be upheld despite the absence of independent advice.[125] On the other hand, such advice will not necessarily rebut the presumption. There must be a full appreciation of the facts. In *Tate* v. *Williamson*, for example, the young man, T, was referred to independent solicitors, but such fair dealing in other respects was, said Lord Chelmsford, 'of no consequence, when once it is established that there was a concealment of a material fact, which the defendant was bound to disclose'.[126]

---

[120] [2001] 3 W.L.R. 1021, paras. 28–29. See also *ibid.*, paras. 104, 156.

[121] *Archer* v. *Hudson* (1844) 7 Beav. 551, *per* Lord Langdale M.R. at p. 560. See also *Zamet* v. *Hyman* [1961] 1 Ch. 1442, at p. 1446; *Re Craig* [1971] Ch. 95, at p. 105; *Goldsworthy* v. *Brickell* [1987] 1 Ch. 378, at pp. 408–9.

[122] [1900] 1 Ch. 243. See also *post*, p. 296.

[123] (1807) 14 Ves. Jun. 273, at p. 300. See also *Credit Lyonnais Bank Nederland N.V.* v. *Burch* [1997] 1 All E.R. 144, *per* Millett L.J. at pp. 155–6.

[124] *Inche Noriah* v. *Shaik Allie Bin Omar* [1929] AC. 127, at p. 135.

[125] *Re Brocklehurst* [1978] Ch. 14.

[126] (1866) L.R. 2 Ch. App. 55, at p. 65.

(d) RESCISSION

The right to rescind contracts and to revoke gifts made under undue influence is similar to the right of rescinding contracts induced by fraud and misrepresentation. The conditions for and bars to rescission considered in Chapter 6 above in principle apply here.

(i) The need for restitution

If the transaction is to be set aside, the parties must be restored to their original positions.[127] Each must give back what has been received, although here too the flexibility of equity means that the impossibility of restoring the parties precisely to their original position will not bar the remedy.[128] The Court will grant relief whenever, by directing accounts and making allowances, it can do what is practically just. Moreover, since it is restitution that has to be made, not damages paid,[129] when reversing a transaction under which both parties had made a financial contribution to the acquisition of an asset from which they were both to benefit but the value of which has fallen, if the conduct of the party presumed to have exercised influence was not morally reprehensible, the Court may order the loss in the value of the asset to be borne by the parties in proportion to their contributions to the purchase price.[130]

Another example of equity's flexibility where complete restitution is impossible is provided by *O'Sullivan* v. *Management Agency and Music Ltd.*[131] In that case a management agreement between an inexperienced pop musician and an internationally known firm of managers presumed to have been entered as a result of undue influence was set aside although the parties could not be restored to their original position, *inter alia*, because the musician had since achieved considerable fame. The managers were ordered to account for the profit they had made from the agreement, but were also held to be entitled to reasonable remuneration for their skill and work in promoting the musician and making a significant contribution to his success. Where taking an account of profits will not do justice, the defendant may be ordered to pay equitable compensation to the claimant.[132]

(ii) Severance

A finding of undue influence normally vitiates effective consent, so that it will rarely be possible to sever the objectional parts of the transaction leaving the parts uncontaminated by undue influence enforceable. But, where a person's consent can be regarded as having been freely given in relation to part of the transaction and it is possible to sever that part without rewriting the contract, this will be possible.[133]

---

[127] *Dunbar Bank plc* v. *Nadeem* [1998] 3 All E.R. 877 (party setting aside transaction required to restore beneficial interest in lease).

[128] *Cheese* v. *Thomas* [1994] 1 W.L.R. 129. See *ante*, p. 255.

[129] *Ibid., per* Nicholls V.-C. at p. 135.

[130] *Ibid.* See Chen-Wishart (1994) 110 L.Q.R. 173.

[131] [1985] 1 Q.B. 428.

[132] *Mahoney* v. *Purnell* [1996] 3 All E.R. 61. See Heydon (1997) 113 L.Q.R. 8.

[133] *Barclays Bank plc* v. *Caplan* [1998] 1 F.L.R. 532. Cf. *Allied Irish Bank plc* v. *Byrne* [1995] 2 F.L.R. 325 and the position concerning rescission for misrepresentation, *ante*, p. 253.

(iii) Affirmation of transaction

The right to rescind may be lost by affirmation, and so soon as the undue influence is withdrawn, the action or inaction of the party influenced becomes liable to the construction that he or she intended to affirm the transaction. Thus in *Mitchell v. Homfray*[134] a jury found as a fact that a patient who had made a gift to her physician determined to abide by her gift after the confidential relationship of physician and patient ceased, and the Court of Appeal held that the gift could not be impeached. Also in *Allcard* v. *Skinner*:[135]

A was introduced by her spiritual adviser and confessor to S who was the lady superior of a Protestant community called 'The Sisters of the Poor'. A subsequently became a professed member of the community and bound herself to observe rules of poverty, chastity, and obedience. The rule of poverty bound her to relinquish all earthly possessions, and the rule of obedience not to seek the advice of anyone outside the community without permission. In 1872 she came into possession of certain stocks, which she transferred to S as superior of the community; she also made a will in S's favour. In 1879, she left the sisterhood. She immediately revoked the will, but took no steps to retrieve the property which she had conveyed to S until some 6 years had elapsed.

It was held that, by her inactivity after she had been freed from the spiritual influence of S, she had acquiesced in the gift, and her claim was barred by this acquiescence.[136]

An affirmation will not be valid unless there is an entire cessation of the undue influence which had brought about the contract or gift. The necessity for such a complete relief of the will of the injured party from the dominant influence was stated in *Moxon* v. *Payne*:[137]

Frauds or impositions of the type practised in this case cannot be condoned; the right to property acquired by such means cannot be confirmed in this Court unless there be full knowledge of all the facts, full knowledge of the equitable rights arising out of those facts, and an absolute release from the undue influence by means of which the frauds were practised.

The same principle is applied where someone parts with a valuable interest under pressure of poverty and without proper advice. Acquiescence is not presumed from delay alone; on the contrary, 'it has always been presumed, that the same distress, which pressed him to enter into the contract, prevented him from coming to set it aside'.[138]

(iv) Third parties

As transactions affected by undue influence are voidable, not void, third parties who

---

[134] (1881) 8 Q.B.D. 587.

[135] (1887) 36 Ch. D. 145.

[136] See also *Nicholl* v. *Ryder* [2000] E.M.L.R. 632 (acquiescence based on solicitor's knowledge which was imputed to defendant).

[137] (1873) L.R. 8 Ch. App. 881, *per* James L.J. at p. 885. See also *Re Pauling's Settlement Trusts* [1964] Ch. 303; *Goldsworthy* v. *Brickell* [1987] 1 Ch. 378, at pp. 410, 417 (*quaere* whether knowledge of the right to rescission is needed, *post*, pp. 295, 527).

[138] *Fry* v. *Lane* (1888) 40 Ch. D. 312, *per* Kay J. at p. 324.

acquire some interest in the subject-matter of the contract in good faith and for value cannot be displaced by the person seeking rescission.[139]

(a) Third parties with notice and volunteers. A transaction into which a person has been induced to enter by the exercise of duress or undue influence may be set aside, not only as against the person exercising compulsion or influence, but also as against a party having notice of the fact that the compulsion or influence was used.[140] Money or property transferred can be recovered from such a person, and from a person who, even though ignorant of the undue influence, has furnished no consideration: 'Let the hand receiving it be ever so chaste, yet, if it comes through a polluted channel, the obligation of restitution will follow it'.[141]

(b) Actual and constructive notice. In this context notice includes imputed or constructive as well as actual notice. This can be illustrated from the cases in which a wife has guaranteed a loan made by a bank to her husband, although it is not confined to such cases.[142] Where the bank knows of facts which put it on inquiry that the wife may have the right, as against the husband, to avoid the transaction, it will be held to have constructive notice of her right unless it has taken reasonable steps to ensure that her agreement had been properly obtained.[143] A bank will be put on inquiry where the transaction is on its face not to the financial advantage of the wife, as where she guarantees the husband's business debts,[144] but not where there was nothing to indicate to the bank that the transaction was anything other than a normal advance of funds to the husband and wife for their joint benefit.[145] In the case of a family company where the wife who is a guarantor has an interest in the business, the lender will be put on notice where the security given is out of all proportion to the interest in the company.[146]

(c) Proof of notice. The burden of proving that the lender has actual or constructive notice of the duress or undue influence has been held to lie on the guarantor but is *prima facie* discharged where it is shown that it knows the relationship between the guarantor and debtor is non-commercial.[147] If the guarantor (in our scenario the

---

[139] *Bainbrigge* v. *Browne* (1881) 18 Ch. D. 188.

[140] *Lancashire Loans Ltd.* v. *Black* [1934] 1 K.B. 380; *Kesarmel s/o Letchman Das* v. *Valliappa Chettiar (N.K.V.) s/o Nagappa Chettiar* [1954] 1 W.L.R. 380. Cf. Bills of Exchange Act 1882, s. 30(2); *Talbot* v. *Von Boris* [1911] 1 K.B. 854.

[141] *Bridgeman* v. *Green* (1757) Wilmot 58, *per* Wilmot J. at p. 65.

[142] Guarantors in other relationships include employees (*Credit Lyonnais Bank Nederland N.V.* v. *Burch* [1997] 1 All E.R. 144) and friends (*Banco Exterior Internacionale S.A.* v. *Thomas* [1997] 1 W.L.R. 221).

[143] *Barclays Bank plc* v. *O'Brien* [1994] 1 A.C. 180, at p. 195 ff. See also *Allied Irish Bank plc* v. *Byrne* [1995] 2 F.L.R. 325 (no such steps taken).

[144] *Ibid.*, *Royal Bank of Scotland plc* v. *Etridge (No. 2)* [2001] 3 W.L.R. 1021, paras. 44, 46, 109–13, 163–5.

[145] *C.I.B.C. Mortgages Ltd.* v. *Pitt* [1994] 1 A.C. 200, at p. 211 (advance to enable parties to purchase shares). The facts of *National Westminster Bank plc* v. *Morgan* [1985] A.C. 686 (refinancing of existing debt) may be another example.

[146] *Bank of Scotland* v. *Bennett* [1997] 1 F.L.R. 801; *Credit Lyonnais Bank Nederland N.V.* v. *Burch* [1997] 1 All E.R. 144. Cf. *Brittania Building Society* v. *Pugh* [1997] 2 F.L.R. 7.

[147] *Royal Bank of Scotland plc.* v. *Etridge (No. 2)* [2001] 3 W.L.R. 1021, para. 87. See also *Barclays Bank plc* v. *Boulter* [1999] 1 W.L.R. 1919, *per* Lord Hoffmann at p. 1925.

wife) shows that the lender knew she was a wife living with her husband and that the transaction was, on its face, not to her advantage the burden is then upon the lender to show that it took reasonable steps to satisfy itself that her consent was properly obtained. Normally it will be able to do so by warning the person entering the transaction, in our example the wife, at a meeting not attended by the principal debtor, of the amount of the existing indebtedness and of the proposed new loan, of the potential liability and of the risks involved, and advising her to take independent legal advice.[148] The lender will not, however, have to take these steps where it has a reasonable belief that legal advice has been given to the guarantor by a lawyer acting for her who has knowledge of the amount of the existing indebtedness and of the proposed new loan. If so, the lender is entitled to assume that the legal adviser has carried out its professional duty to advise the guarantor.[149] Provided the legal adviser is acting for the wife, this will be so even where the adviser is also the debtor's lawyer, where the legal adviser has agreed to act as the lender's agent on completion, or where the lender instructed the legal adviser to explain the transaction to the guarantor and to confirm that she appeared to understand it.[150] Unless the legal adviser is acting for the lender, the lender is not fixed with constructive notice of what the legal adviser learns in the course of advising the guarantor since such knowledge is not acquired in the adviser's capacity as the lender's lawyer.[151] Where the lender is put on inquiry, it has no duty to ask about the guarantor's motives.

IV. UNCONSCIONABLE BARGAINS

(a) UNCONSCIENTIOUS DEALING

There is another class of cases in which equity also throws the burden of justifying the righteousness of a bargain on the party who claims the benefit of it.[152] Lord Selborne describes these cases in *Earl of Aylesford* v. *Morris*[153] as cases:

which, according to the language of Lord Hardwicke,[154] raise, 'from the circumstances or conditions of the parties contracting—weakness on one side, usury on the other, or extortion, or advantage taken of that weakness'—a presumption of fraud. Fraud does not here mean deceit or circumvention, it means an unconscientious use of the power arising out of these circumstances and conditions; and when the relative position of the parties is such as *prima facie* to raise this presumption, the transaction cannot stand unless the person claiming the

[148] *Barclays Bank plc* v. *O'Brien* (*supra*, n. 143) at p. 196. See also *Credit Lyonnais Bank Nederland N.V.* v. *Burch* (*supra*, n. 146).

[149] *Royal Bank of Scotland plc* v. *Etridge* (*No. 2*) [2001] 3 W.L.R. 1021, paras. 56, 114, 171.

[150] *Ibid.*, at paras. 69–74, 115, 173–4. See also *Banco Exterior Internacional* v. *Thomas* [1997] 1 W.L.R. 221; *National Westminster Bank plc* v. *Beaton* (1997) 30 H.L.R. 99.

[151] *Ibid.*, at paras. 77, 115, 180. See also *Halifax Mortgage Services Ltd.* v. *Stepsky* [1996] Ch. 207.

[152] Waddams (1976) 39 M.L.R. 369; Bamforth [1995] L.M.C.L.Q. 538.

[153] (1873) L.R. 8 Ch. App. 484, at p. 490. See also *Hart* v. *O'Connor* [1985] A.C. 1000, at p. 1024.

[154] *Earl of Chesterfield* v. *Janssen* (1751) 2 Ves. Sen. 125, at p. 157.

benefit of it is able to repel the presumption by contrary evidence, proving it to have been in point of fact fair, just, and reasonable.

Thus although equity will not normally intervene to protect a contracting party against the consequences of his or her own folly, some protection is offered to poor and ignorant persons who are overreached in the absence of independent advice. This ground of relief differs from undue influence in that it is concerned with 'the nature and circumstances of the bargain' whereas undue influence is concerned 'with the prior relationship between the parties and with whether that was the motivation or reason for which the bargain was entered into'.[155]

A particular case of the application of this principle was the protection given by equity to 'expectant heirs', that is, to those persons who have expectations (in the popular sense) of succeeding to property on the death of another.[156] But this is but one illustration, and the principle also applies generally to what have been called 'catching bargains', that is to say, whenever the parties 'meet under such circum-stances as, in the particular transaction, to give the stronger party dominion over the weaker'.[157]

In ordinary cases each party to a bargain must take care of his own interest, and it will not be presumed that undue advantage or contrivance has been resorted to on either side; but in the case of the 'expectant heir', or of persons under pressure without adequate protection, and in the case of dealings with uneducated ignorant persons, the burden of shewing the fairness of the transaction is thrown on the person who seeks to obtain the benefit of the contract.[158]

Thus in *Fry* v. *Lane*[159] it was held that when a purchase had been made from a poor and ignorant man at a considerable undervalue, the vendor having had no independ-ent advice, equity would set aside the transaction. At common law, the nearest ana-logue is to be found in the cases on salvage, mentioned above,[160] in which extortionate bargains made to rescue ships in distress have been set aside.

The cases suggest that three elements are necessary if the Court is to intervene.[161] First, one party must be at a serious disadvantage to the other through, for example poverty, ignorance or lack of advice. Secondly, this weakness must be exploited by the other party in some morally culpable manner; and thirdly, the resulting transaction must be, not merely harsh or improvident, but overreaching and oppressive. The last requirement means that, in the case of a sale by the disadvantaged party, the sale must

---

[155] *Irvani* v. *Irvani* [2000] 1 Lloyd's Rep. 412, at p. 424.

[156] By the Law of Property Act 1925, s. 174, a bargain with an expectant heir, made in good faith, and without unfair dealing, is not to be set aside merely on the ground of undervalue. But the jurisdiction of the Court to set aside or modify unconscionable bargains is not affected in other respects.

[157] *Earl of Aylesford* v. *Morris* (1873) L.R. 8 Ch. App. 484, *per* Lord Selborne L.C. at p. 491.

[158] *O'Rorke* v. *Bolingbroke* (1877) 2 App. Cas 814, *per* Lord Hatherley at p. 823.

[159] (1888) 40 Ch. D. 312. See also *Cresswell* v. *Potter* [1978] 1 W.L.R. 255n; *Boustany* v. *Pigott* (1993) 69 P. & C.R. 298.

[160] *Ante*, p. 283.

[161] *Alec Lobb (Garages) Ltd.* v. *Total Oil (Great Britain) Ltd* [1983] 1 W.L.R. 87, *per* Peter Millett Q.C. at pp. 94–5. This aspect of his judgment was not varied by the Court of Appeal: see [1985] 1 W.L.R. 173, at pp. 182–3.

not merely be at an undervalue, but at a *substantial* undervalue which 'shocks the conscience of the Court'.[162] And the second requirement means that a gross disparity in the price does not suffice, however serious the disadvantage of the weaker party. In *Hart v. O'Connor*[163] it was held by the Judicial Committee of the Privy Council that a contract made with a person who, although apparently of full capacity was mentally disordered, could not be set aside as unconscionable unless the other party was aware of the mental disorder at the time the contract was made. So, for relief to be granted, both procedural and substantive unconscionability must be shown.

Although there have been expressions of support for a wider role for this doctrine,[164] particularly by giving a broad meaning to the concept of 'serious disadvantage',[165] there has been no fundamental change. The fact that procedural unconscionability must be present means that there will often be an overlap with the doctrines of duress and undue influence, and some cases which would perhaps have been best regarded as cases of unconscionability have been treated as cases of duress or undue influence.[166] This is in contrast to the position in other common law jurisdictions, particularly Australia and the USA, where a general doctrine of unconscionability has been developed.[167]

(b) INEQUALITY OF BARGAINING POWER?

The intervention of equity in all these cases of coercion, undue influence, and unconscionable bargains, and also in certain other cases such as penalties[168] and forfeiture, has been stated by Lord Denning M.R.[169] to be grounded upon the same general principle: that of 'inequality of bargaining power'. In *Lloyds Bank Ltd. v. Bundy*:[170]

B, an elderly farmer, and his only son, had been customers of the bank for many years. The son founded a company which banked at the same bank. In 1966, B guaranteed the company's overdraft for £1,500 and charged his farm to the bank to secure that sum. Subsequently the overdraft was increased and the bank sought further security. In May 1969, B, having taken legal advice, signed a further guarantee in favour of the bank for £5,000 and a further charge for £6,000. In December 1969, the bank manager visited B and indicated to

---

    [162] *Ibid.*

    [163] [1985] A.C. 1000.

    [164] See, e.g. *A. Schroeder Music Publishing Ltd.* v. *Macaulay* [1974] 1 W.L.R. 1308, *per* Lord Diplock at p. 1315, *post*, p. 382; *Alec Lobb (Garages) Ltd.* v. *Total Oil (Great Britain) Ltd.* [1985] 1 W.L.R. 173. See also the cases on penalties and forfeiture, *post*, pp. 624–9. For criticism, see Trebilcock (1976) 26 U. of Tor. L.J. 359.

    [165] *Cresswell* v. *Potter* [1978] 1 W.L.R. 255n; *Backhouse* v. *Backhouse* [1978] 1 W.L.R. 243; *Watkin* v. *Watson-Smith*, The Times, 3 July 1986.

    [166] *Credit Lyonnais Bank Nederland N.V.* v. *Burch* [1997] 1 All E.R. 144 (undue influence, but see Chen-Wishart [1997] C.L.J. 60); *CTN Cash and Carry Ltd.* v. *Gallagher Ltd.* [1994] 4 All E.R. 714, *per* Sir Donald Nicholls V.-C., at p. 720 (and see Carter and Tolhurst [1996] 9 J.C.L. 220).

    [167] *Commercial Bank of Australia Ltd.* v. *Amadio* (1983) 151 C.L.R. 447; *Louth* v. *Diprose* (1992) 175 C.L.R. 621 (Australia); Uniform Commercial Code §2–302 (USA); *Paris* v. *Machnik* (1972) 32 D.L.R. (3d) 723 (Canada).

    [168] See *post*, pp. 624, 647.

    [169] *Lloyds Bank Ltd.* v. *Bundy* [1975] Q.B. 326, at p. 339.

    [170] [1975] Q.B. 326.

him that continuance of the company's overdraft facility was dependent upon B executing in favour of the bank a further guarantee for £11,000 and a further charge for £3,500. The bank manager did not advise B to seek independent advice, and B signed the required guarantee and charge without such advice.

The Court of Appeal held that this last guarantee and charge should be set aside for undue influence, since a special relationship of confidence existed between B and the bank in the particular circumstances of the case. But Lord Denning M.R. also considered that the guarantee and charge were voidable on the larger ground of inequality of bargaining power:[171]

There are cases in our books in which the courts will set aside a contract, or a transfer of property, where the parties have not met on equal terms—when the one is so strong in bargaining power and the other so weak that, as a matter of common fairness, it is not right that the strong should be allowed to push the weak to the wall.

His Lordship nevertheless pointed out that no bargain should be upset which was the result of the ordinary interplay of economic forces, but only 'where there has been inequality of bargaining power such as to merit the intervention of the court'. Such a general principle has not, however, yet been accepted in English law which has generally regarded it as involving undue uncertainty. Moreover, in *National Westminster Bank plc* v. *Morgan*[172] the need for it was questioned. First, it was said that the development of the doctrine of undue influence was a preferable technique. Secondly, it was said that the task of restricting freedom of contract was essentially a legislative rather than a judicial task, and one that Parliament has undertaken in legislation protecting, for example, consumers, employees, tenants, and investors.[173] We now turn to two examples of such statutory intervention. As we have noted, there are examples of statutory regimes which express a policy from which a principle can be derived being used analogically in developing the common law.[174] This has not, however, yet occurred in the context of undue influence and unconscionable bargains. But in *Timeload Ltd.* v. *British Telecommunications plc*[175] Sir Thomas Bingham M.R. said, in relation to section 3 of the Unfair Contract Terms Act 1977, that it was arguable that 'the common law could, if the letter of the statute does not apply, treat the clear intention of the legislature expressed in the statute as a platform for invalidating or restricting the operation of an oppressive clause'.

---

[171] At p. 336. See also *Clifford Davis Management Ltd.* v. *W.E.A. Records Ltd.* [1975] 1 W.L.R. 61; *Arrale* v. *Costain Civil Engineering Ltd.* [1976] 1 Lloyd's Rep. 98; *Cresswell* v. *Potter* [1978] 1 W.L.R. 255n.; *Backhouse* v. *Backhouse* [1978] 1 W.L.R. 243, at p. 252; *A. Schroeder Music Publishing Ltd.* v. *Macaulay* [1974] 1 W.L.R. 1308. Cf. *Alec Lobb (Garages) Ltd.* v. *Total Oil Great Britain Ltd.* [1985] 1 W.L.R. 173.

[172] [1985] A.C. 686, at p. 708. See also *Pao On* v. *Lau Yiu Long* [1980] A.C. 614, at p. 634; *Horry* v. *Tate & Lyle Refineries Ltd.* [1982] 2 Lloyd's Rep. 416, at p. 423.

[173] *Ante*, pp. 4–5.

[174] *Ante*, pp. 274–5. Beatson (2001) 117 L.Q.R. 247.

[175] (1995) 3 E.M.L.R. 459, at p. 468.

(c) CREDIT AGREEMENTS

Certain types of contract which may give rise to the kind of oppressive dealing which equity discourages have been dealt with by statute in the Consumer Credit Act 1974.[176] These are credit agreements: for example, a moneylending contract or a contract of hire-purchase. The Act enables a Court, if it finds a credit transaction to be extortionate, to reopen the agreement so as to do justice between the parties.[177] A credit agreement may be held to be extortionate if it requires the debtor to make payments which are grossly exorbitant having regard, not only to objective factors such as prevailing interest rates and the degree of risk accepted by the creditor, but also to subjective factors such as the debtor's age, experience, business capacity, and state of health, and the degree to which, at the time of entering into the transaction, the debtor was under financial pressure. In one case an interest rate of 48 per cent was held not to be extortionate since little security was offered for the loan.[178] Although there is no specific requirement that the subjective factors should have been known to the lender, some cases have required that the lender 'take advantage' of the borrower.[179] A credit agreement may also be reopened on the ground that it is extortionate because it 'grossly contravenes ordinary principles of fair dealing'.[180]

(d) UNFAIR TERMS IN CONSUMER CONTRACTS

By E.E.C. Council Directive 93/13,[181] a term in a contract between a seller or supplier of goods or services and a consumer which has not been 'individually negotiated'[182] is subjected to a requirement of 'fairness' containing three elements; absence of 'good faith', 'significant imbalance', and 'detriment to the consumer'. The Directive was originally implemented in 1994 but the 1994 Regulations[183] were revoked and replaced by the Unfair Terms in Consumer Contracts Regulations 1999[184] which follow the language of the Directive more closely. While it is ultimately for the Courts to decide whether any term is unfair, the Regulations are also enforced administratively by the Director-General of Fair Trading who is under a duty to prevent the use of unfair terms. The Office of Fair Trading publishes guidance as to what the Director-General considers fair and unfair.[185]

(i) The scope of the Regulations

The scope of the Regulations and their relationship to the Unfair Contract Terms Act

---

[176] Repealing the Moneylenders Act 1900, s. 1, and the Moneylenders Act 1927, s. 10.

[177] Consumer Credit Act 1974, ss. 137–40.

[178] *A. Ketley Ltd.* v. *Scott* [1982] I.C.R. 241.

[179] *Davies* v. *Directloans Ltd.* [1986] 1 W.L.R. 823; *Coldunell Ltd.* v. *Gallon* [1986] Q.B. 1184.

[180] Consumer Credit Act 1974, s. 138(1).

[181] O.J. L. 95, 21 April 1993, p. 29.

[182] S.I. 1999 No. 2083, reg. 2(1).

[183] S.I. 1994 No. 3159.

[184] S.I. 1999 No. 2083. See generally *ante*, p. 200; Beale in Beatson and Friedmann (eds.), *Good Faith and Fault in Contract Law* (1995), ch. 9; Collins (1994) 14 O.J.L.S. 229; Dean (1993) 56 M.L.R. 581; Macdonald [1994] J.B.L. 441.

[185] See, e.g. *Unfair Contract Terms Guidance* (OFT311) (February 2001).

1977 has been considered in Chapter 4 above.[186] It was noted that in general the Regulations have a broader scope and permit a broader approach than the 1977 Act. In particular, the Regulations apply to all terms, not just to exemption and limitation clauses. It was, however, also noted that the broader scope of the Regulations is accompanied by a narrower definition of 'consumer' and by protection which is, in some respects, less certain than that in the 1977 Act. For example, there are no absolute bans, only factors and an 'indicative and non-exhaustive list of the terms which may be regarded as unfair'.[187]

(ii) The test of unfairness

Regulation 5(1) provides that a contractual term which has not been individually negotiated will be 'unfair' where:

contrary to the requirement of good faith, it causes a significant imbalance in the parties' rights and obligations under the contract to the detriment of the consumer.

Some guidance is provided by regulation 6(1) and by the 'indicative and non-exhaustive list' of terms in Schedule 2. Regulation 6(1) provides:

. . . the unfairness of a contractual term shall be assessed, taking into account the nature of the goods or services for which the contract was concluded and by referring, at the time of the conclusion of the contract, to all circumstances attending the conclusion of the contract and to all the other terms of the contract or of another contract on which it is dependent.

A term which, in isolation, might appear to be unfair, might thus not be when looked at in the light of the contract as a whole. Thus while a term may create an imbalance between the parties' rights and obligations, it might be one that is justified as fair (or reasonable) say in a high risk or speculative contract or where a seller is dependent on a third party who may (because of market strength) supply only on very restrictive terms.

Schedule 2 contains 17 categories of term, which 'may' be unfair. These include terms authorizing or enabling the seller or supplier to dissolve the contract on a discretionary basis where the same facility is not given to the consumer,[188] to terminate a contract of indeterminate duration without reasonable notice except where there are serious grounds for doing so,[189] to alter the terms of the contract unilaterally without a valid reason which is specified in the contract,[190] to determine whether goods or services supplied are in conformity with the contract,[191] and terms requiring a consumer in breach of contract to pay 'a disproportionately high sum in compensation'[192] or to fulfil all his obligations where the supplier does not perform his.[193]

---

[186] *Ante*, pp. 185, 200.
[187] 1999 Regulations, Sched. 2.
[188] *Ibid.*, para. 1(f).
[189] *Ibid.*, para. 1(g).
[190] *Ibid.*, para. 1(j).
[191] *Ibid.*, para. 1(m). See also para. 1(k).
[192] *Ibid.*, para. 1(e). This will normally be void as a penalty at common law: *post*, p. 624.
[193] *Ibid.*, para. 1(c).

The Office of Fair Trading's guidance emphasizes that it is unlikely to find clauses leaving undue discretion to suppliers and permitting action such as cancellation or variation in the absence of clear and specific reasons to be fair, and is likely to find clauses reflecting the ordinary law, for example permitting cancellation if the consumer is in serious breach, to be fair.[194] Its starting point in assessing the fairness of a term is normally to ask what would be the position of a consumer if it did not appear in the contract. It has stated that 'the principle of freedom of contract can no longer be said to justify using standard terms to take away protection consumers would otherwise enjoy. The regulations recognize that contractual small print is in no real sense freely agreed with consumers. Where a term changes the normal position seen by the law as striking a fair balance it is regarded with suspicion.'[195] It considers that 'transparency is also fundamental to fairness' and that terms may be unfair 'if the language used could mislead an ordinary person even though it might be clear to a lawyer, or if consumers are not given an adequate chance to read them before becoming bound by them'.

(a) Exclusion of main subject-matter and price. Regulation 6(2) contains an important exclusion from the assessment of the fairness of a term. It provides that terms concerning the definition of the main subject matter of the contract or the adequacy of the price or remuneration are to be left out of account provided they are in plain intelligible language. In this respect the Regulations are probably narrower than the 1977 Act because, as we have noted,[196] under section 3(2)(b) of the 1977 Act, exemption clauses shrinking the contractual obligation are subject to the reasonableness test if they permit a contractor to perform in a way that is 'substantially different from that which was reasonably expected'. Under the Regulations, it is possible that a term permitting such performance would escape the control of the 'fairness' test if it is in 'plain intelligible language'.

While it has been stated that the test is not whether a term can be called a 'core term',[197] regulation 6(2) seeks to make a distinction between terms containing the substance of the bargain and other terms. The Office of Fair Trading considers that the purpose of the exemption 'is to allow freedom of contract to prevail in relation to terms that are genuinely central to the bargain between consumer and supplier' and that it sees the exemption as 'conditional upon such terms being expressed and presented in such a way as to ensure that they are, or at least are capable of being, at the forefront of the consumer's mind in deciding whether to enter the contract'.[198] The distinction between terms expressing the substance of the contract and other terms has been recognized by the House of Lords which has held that the regulation should be given a restrictive interpretation. Thus, a provision concerning the rate of interest to be paid on a breach of contract was held neither to define the main subject

---

[194] *Unfair Contract Terms Guidance* (OFT311) (February 2001) paras. 6.14, 7.4, 10.3.
[195] *Ibid.,* p. 2.
[196] *Ante,* p. 193.
[197] *Director-General of Fair Trading* v. *First National Bank plc* [2000] Q.B. 672, at p. 686. Cf. [2001] 3 W.L.R. 1297, *per* Lord Bingham at para. 12.
[198] *Unfair Contract Terms Guidance* (OFT311) (February 2001) para. 19.13.

of the contract nor realistically to concern the adequacy of the price.[199] To construe such a provision as falling within regulation 6(2) would mean that 'almost any provision containing any part of the bargain would be capable of falling within the reach of [the] regulation'[200] and leave 'a gaping hole in the system' of protection.[201]

(b) Significant imbalance. The basic question whether a term causes a significant imbalance in the parties' rights and obligations is primarily concerned with the substantive fairness of the contract.[202] For instance, a term which gives a significant advantage to the seller or supplier without a countervailing benefit to the consumer (such as a price reduction) might fail to satisfy this part of the test of an unfair term.[203] Despite this, it is submitted that for the reasons given below the test as a whole will in practice be primarily concerned with procedural fairness, unfair surprise, and the absence of real choice.

The meaning of 'significant imbalance' was considered by the House of Lords in *Director General of Fair Trading* v. *First National Bank plc.* The case concerned the fairness of a term in a bank's loan agreement that, should the borrower default on his repayments, interest would continue to be payable at the contractual rate until any judgment was satisfied. Delegated legislation provides that no statutory interest is payable on a county court judgment given in proceedings to recover money under an agreement regulated by the Consumer Credit Act 1974. It was argued that in these circumstances it was unfair to allow the recovery of contractual interest because that would expose the borrower to further liability after all the instalments the Court ordered him to pay had been paid in full. Lord Bingham stated that:

the requirement of significant imbalance is met if a term is so weighted in favour of the supplier as to tilt the parties' rights and obligations under the contract significantly in his favour. This may be by the granting to the supplier of a beneficial option or discretion or power, or by the imposing on the consumer of a disadvantageous burden or risk or duty.[204]

The House of Lords upheld the term. It held that the essential bargain in a bank loan is to make available funds which will be repaid with interest until full repayment. There was nothing unbalanced or detrimental to the consumer in requiring interest to be paid after judgment; indeed the absence of such a term would unbalance the contract to the detriment of the lender.[205] Their Lordships considered that any unfairness in exposing the borrower to further liability after judgment is due to the fact that the judgment does not cover the whole of the indebtedness, not from any inherent unfairness in the contractual term.

(c) Good faith. The significant imbalance must be contrary to the requirement of good faith. In *Director General of Fair Trading* v. *First National Bank plc* Lord Bingham

---

[199] *Director-General of Fair Trading v. First National Bank plc.* [2001] 3 W.L.R. 1297 at paras. 12, 34, 43, 64.
[200] *Ibid.* [2000] Q.B. 672, at p. 686 (C.A.).
[201] [2001] 3 W.L.R. 1297, para. 34.
[202] [2001] 3 W.L.R. 1297, *per* Lord Steyn at para. 37.
[203] *Ibid.*, [2000] Q.B. 672, at p. 687.
[204] [2001] 3 W.L.R. 1297 at para. 17.
[205] *Ibid.*, paras. 22–4, 38, 55–7.

stated that good faith looked to good standards of commercial morality and practice. The House of Lords held that the requirement of 'good faith' sought to promote fair and open dealing, and to prevent unfair surprise and the absence of real choice. Lord Bingham stated that 'openness requires that the terms should be expressed fully, clearly and legibly, containing no concealed pitfalls or traps',[206] and the Court of Appeal stated that 'terms must be reasonably transparent and must not operate to defeat the reasonable expectations of the consumer' who 'should be put in a position where he can make an informed choice'.[207] While that case was concerned with the 1994 Regulations, the position should be the same under the 1999 Regulations.

Guidance is also provided by Recital 16 of the Preamble to the Directive.[208] This states that in making an assessment of 'good faith', account should be taken of the strength of bargaining positions of the parties, whether the consumer had an inducement to agree to the term, and whether the goods were sold or supplied to the consumer's special order. These factors, which were contained in the 1994 Regulations but are not in the 1999 Regulations, look much like some of the guidelines to the reasonableness test in the 1977 Act.[209]

Recital 16 also states that the requirement of 'good faith' is satisfied where the seller or supplier 'deals fairly and equitably with the other party *whose legitimate interests he also takes into account*'. The implication is that where the other party's legitimate interests are not taken into account, the requirement will not be satisfied. This is in contrast to the common law position since, as Lord Ackner's speech in *Walford* v. *Miles*[210] shows, parties to a contractual negotiation are generally considered to be in an adversarial relationship in which they are entitled to pursue their own interests so long as they avoid making misrepresentations.

(d) Procedural or substantive fairness. How should English law proceed to put flesh on the bare bones of the elements of 'good faith' and 'significant imbalance', which have been said to overlap substantially?[211] There are a number of possibilities. First, although good faith is not a concept wholly unfamiliar to English lawyers, its conceptual roots lie in the civil law systems, making it appropriate to use one of the civil law systems. However, their concepts of good faith differ radically. They range from French law's substantive use of the concept to avoid unreasonable and onerous conditions, to the more procedural notions of unfair surprise and absence of real choice which characterize Dutch and German law.[212] Alternatively, the statutory concept of 'reasonableness' in the 1977 Act might be deployed, perhaps reinforced by support

---

[206] *Ibid.*

[207] [2000] Q.B. 672, at p. 687.

[208] *Marleasing S.A. v. La Commercial* (Case C-106/89) [1992] 1 C.M.L.R. 305 permits reference to be made to the Directive and probably also to the preamble in interpreting the Regulations.

[209] *Ante*, p. 194.

[210] [1992] 2 A.C. 128, at p. 138, *ante*, p. 65.

[211] *Director-General of Fair Trading* v. *First National Bank plc.* [2000] Q.B. 672, at p. 686; [2001] 3 W.L.R. 1297, *per* Lord Steyn at para. 37.

[212] Beale, (*supra*, n. 184), pp. 243–5 cites *inter alia*, on French law, Ghestin, *Le Contrat: Formation*, 2nd edn. (1988) para. 608–2; on Dutch law, Storme, *La bonne foi dans la formation des contrats en droit neerlandais* (1992); decision of the Hoge Raad H.R. 15–11–1957; Article 6.233 of the New Netherlands Civil Code; on German law B.G.B. para. 242; Micklitz (1989) 41 Rev. int. droit comparé 101, 109.

from the equitable concepts of unconscionability and undue influence considered earlier in this chapter and the rules on penalty and forfeiture clauses considered in Chapter 17 below.[213] This gains some support from the similarity of the guidelines in Recital 16 of the preamble to the Directive to those in the 1977 Act.[214] Finally, an autonomous European Community concept of 'good faith' could be developed.[215] This last appears to have been the favoured approach in *Director General of Fair Trading* v. *First National Bank plc*. It was stated that one of the objectives of the Directive was partially to harmonize the law among all member states of the European Union and that the language used in expressing the test is clear and not reasonably capable of differing interpretations.[216]

What then is this autonomous European Community concept of 'good faith'? There is clearly a substantive component in the test and the controlling concept of 'significant imbalance' is primarily a substantive one. The fact that some clauses may cause such a serious imbalance that they should always be treated as being contrary to good faith,[217] also has a substantive flavour. Moreover, Lord Steyn has stated that 'any purely procedural or even predominantly procedural interpretation of the requirement of good faith must be rejected'.[218] Lord Bingham's statement that fair dealing requires that a supplier should not, 'unconsciously' take advantage of the consumer's necessity, indigence, lack of experience, unfamiliarity with the subject matter of the contract, or weak bargaining position,[219] also suggests a substantive concept.

It is, however, submitted that most commentators were correct in considering the test as a whole to be primarily concerned with procedural fairness.[220] The requirement in Regulation 6(2) that terms concerning the price and defining the main subject-matter of the contract are left out of account (provided they are in plain intelligible language) makes it difficult to regard the test as primarily substantive, because those, particularly 'price' are central to substantial fairness.[221] Moreover, the absence of any absolutely prohibited terms and the fact that 'the indicative and non-exhaustive list of the terms which may be regarded as unfair' are couched in an open-textured way also suggest that the Regulations are not primarily concerned with substantive fairness but with the prevention of unfair surprise and the absence of real choice. So the Courts are likely to be primarily concerned with the requirements of openness which, as

---

[213] See MacNeil (1995) 40 Jur. Rev. 146, 148, citing *Fiddelaar* v. *Commission* (Case 44/59) [1960] E.C.R. 535, at p. 547; Weatherill, *E.C. Consumer Law & Policy* (1997) p. 82. Cf. *Chitty on Contracts*, 28th edn. (1999) para. 15–049.

[214] *Ante*, p. 304.

[215] Unfair Contract Terms Act 1977, s. 11 and Sched. 2.

[216] *Director-General of Fair Trading* v. *First National Bank plc* [2001] 3 W.L.R. 1297, para. 17. See also *ibid.*, paras. 32, 45.

[217] Beale, (*supra*, n. 184), at p. 245. Some of the terms contained in the indicative list of terms which might be regarded as unfair may fall into this category, e.g. excluding or limiting liability for death or personal injury, making the seller or supplier's duty to perform a matter for its discretion, or giving it the right to determine whether the goods or services are in conformity with the contract or the exclusive right to interpret any term: see Schedule 2 to the 1999 Regulations.

[218] [2001] 3 W.L.R. 1297, para. 36.

[219] *Ibid.*, para. 17. Cf. the requirements for common law unconscionability, *ante*, p. 296.

[220] *Supra*, n. 184. Cf. Smith (1994) 47 C.L.P. 5, 8.

[221] Collins (1994) 14 O.J.L.S. 229, 249.

stated by Lord Bingham, are that the terms should be expressed fully, clearly, and legibly, should contain no concealed pitfalls or traps, and accord appropriate prominence to terms which might operate disadvantageously to the customer.[222]

To this extent, despite taking a different approach to that taken by the common law, the result achieved is, as Bingham L.J. acknowledged in *Interfoto Picture Library Ltd.* v. *Stiletto Visual Programmes Ltd.*[223] and as the similarity of three of the guidelines in the Regulations to those in the 1977 Act suggests, not likely to be very different to that under the 1977 Act in relation to terms excluding or limiting liability.[224] But it is clear from the above discussion that in certain respects the Regulations permit a broader approach than the 1977 Act. Notwithstanding this, the experience of administrative enforcement by the Office of Fair Trading suggests that there will not be a sharp difference from that previously taken in English law under the 1977 Act. In part this is because of the similarity of the problems, but in part it is because of an understandable tendency to retreat to familiar ground when confronted by unfamiliar concepts on which there is little guidance. In the long term, however, it is submitted that English contract lawyers will be forced to become comparative lawyers so that they can properly and sensitively transpose the concept of good faith into English law in this context when putting flesh on the concept of 'significant imbalance'. Whether this spills over into other contractual contexts as some commentators have suggested,[225] is, of course another matter, but the experience of the impact of European law in other contexts, notably public law,[226] suggests that it might.

(iii) Plain, intelligible language

Regulation 7 requires a seller or supplier to ensure that any written term of a contract is expressed in plain, intelligible language and, as at common law, where it is not it is construed *contra proferentem*, so that the interpretation most favourable to the consumer shall prevail. We have noted that the immunity of a term defining the main subject matter of the contract or concerning the price given by regulation 6(2) will be lost if it is not in plain, intelligible language. The Office of Fair Trading does not consider that plain vocabulary alone meets the requirement and also regards an illegible term or one hidden away in small print as potentially unfair.[227]

(iv) Effect of term being held to be unfair

An unfair term is not binding on the consumer but 'the contract shall continue to bind the parties if it is capable of continuing in existence without the unfair term'.[228]

---

[222] *Director-General of Fair Trading* v. *First National Bank plc.* [2001] 3 W.L.R. 1297, para 17.

[223] [1989] Q.B. 433. See also *Balfour Beatty Civil Engineering* v. *Docklands Light Railway* [1996] C.L.C. 1435, at p. 1442.

[224] Dean (1994) 56 M.L.R. 581, 585.

[225] Clarke (1996) 81 Svensk Jurist Tidning 145.

[226] *M.* v. *Home Office* [1994] A.C. 377 (spilling over from *Brasserie du Pecheur* v. *Germany* (Case C-43/93) and *R.* v. *Secretary of State for Transport, ex parte Factortame Ltd.* (Case C-48/93) [1996] E.C.R. I-1029) and *Woolwich Building Society* v. *Inland Revenue Commissioners* [1993] A.C. 70 (spilling over *inter alia* from *Amministrazione della Finanze dello Stato* v. *San Giorgio* (Case 199/82) [1983] E.C.R. 3595).

[227] *Unfair Contract Terms Guidance* (OFT311) (February 2001) para. 19.12.

[228] 1999 Regulations, reg. 8(2).

This is a broader approach to severance than under the Unfair Contract Terms Act 1977 and probably enables the remainder of the contract to continue to bind the parties in all cases save where the unfair term is a 'core term' which has failed the requirement of plainness and intelligibility.

(v) Prevention of unfair terms

The Regulations give the Director-General of Fair Trading and a number of other bodies (currently local authorities, utility regulators, and the Consumers Association) power to apply for an injunction to prevent the use of, or the recommending the use of, an unfair term in contracts concluded with consumers.[229] Normally, however, cases are resolved by the Director-General accepting informal undertakings to amend the offending terms in lieu of Court proceedings. The Director-General applies the same test of fairness as a Court but looks forward rather than backwards and considers the circumstances that are generally likely to obtain, not those attending the conclusion of a particular contract.[230] The Director-General and the qualifying bodies have wide powers to obtain documents and information[231] and the Director-General is under a duty to consider any complaint that a contract term is unfair unless the complaint is frivolous or vexatious or one of the other qualifying bodies has stated that it will consider it.[232]

---

[229] *Ibid.*, reg 12.
[230] *Unfair Contract Terms*, OFT Bulletin No 4 (December 1997) p. 21.
[231] 1999 Regulations, reg. 12.
[232] *Ibid.*, reg. 10(1).

8

MISTAKE

I. INTRODUCTION

This chapter is concerned with the circumstances in which a contract will be held to be defective if one, or both, of the parties enter into it under some misapprehension or misunderstanding but would not have done so had they known the true position. Mistake is one of the most difficult topics in the English law of contract. The principles have never been precisely settled, the decided cases are open to a number of varying interpretations and the position is further complicated by two factors.

First, there has been a distinct change in the attitude of the judges towards the question of mistake during the last hundred years. In the past, in reliance on the *consensus* theory of contract and influenced by the eighteenth century French jurist Pothier, the Courts were more readily disposed to hold that, where there was no 'true, full and free' consent, there was no valid contract.[1] At the present time, however, the Courts are very reluctant to intervene in this manner and the role of mistake is narrower than in many European legal systems.[2]

The reasons for this change are first that, at common law, if a contract is entered into under a legally operative mistake, it is void *ab initio*; it has no legal effect whatever. Consequently, if the subject-matter of the contract consists of goods, no property in the goods will pass under the contract. A third party who takes the goods in good faith and for value will acquire no title to them, and will have to deliver them up to the true owner.[3] Secondly, there is a feeling that, once the parties are ostensibly in agreement in the same terms and upon the same subject-matter, they ought to be held to their bargain; they must rely on the terms of the contract for protection from the effect of facts unknown to them.[4] This has led to increased reliance on objectivity where matters are judged by the external standard of the reasonable person.[5] Limiting the circumstances in which a third party in good faith cannot safely rely on what is objectively the apparent position promotes the certainty and finality of transactions

---

[1] Pothier, *Traité des Obligations*, P. I, c. 1, s. 1, Art. III, para. 1, was cited in *Smith* v. *Wheatcroft* (1878) 9 Ch. D. 223, at p. 230; *Gordon* v. *Street* [1899] 2 Q.B. 641, at p. 647; *Phillips* v. *Brooks* [1919] 2 K.B. 243, at p. 248; *Lake* v. *Simmons* [1927] A.C. 487, at p. 501; *Sowler* v. *Potter* [1940] 1 K.B. 271, at p. 274. Cf. *Lewis* v. *Averay* [1972] 1 Q.B. 198, *per* Lord Denning at p. 206.

[2] Lando and Beale, *Principles of European Contract Law* (2000) p. 235.

[3] *Cundy* v. *Lindsay* (1878) 3 App.Cas. 459; *post*, p. 327.

[4] *Bell* v. *Lever Brothers Ltd.* [1932] A.C. 161, *per* Lord Atkin at p. 224.

[5] *Smith* v. *Hughes* (1871) L.R. 6 Q.B. 597, *ante*, p. 31, *post*, p. 324.

which has been the hallmark of the English law of contract. Thirdly, there is a fear that parties to a contract will plead mistake to get out of a bad bargain or to reallocate the risks and consequently undermine the sanctity of contract.[6] This is coupled with a perception, also used to justify the absence of a general duty of disclosure, that a person who has acquired an expertise in the subject-matter of the contract, for instance antique Chinese porcelain, could not be deprived of the benefit of a bargain made with an uninformed counter-party without imperilling the market system.[7] Where there is no contractual bargain to set aside or avoid, the common law recognizes a broader role for mistake. Thus any payment caused by a mistake is *prima facie* recoverable.[8]

Nevertheless, cases will undoubtedly arise in which it would be unjust to hold the parties strictly to their agreement. Such cases will occur quite independently of any express warranty, or misrepresentation, or fraud, and relief must be sought, if at all, on the ground of mistake. To meet this difficulty the Courts have, side by side with their general refusal to apply the doctrine of common law mistake, developed the use of certain equitable remedies which are, in some ways, more satisfactory as they are discretionary and, further, do not render the contract void *ab initio*. Thus as in the position of a contract vitiated by fraud, misrepresentation, or duress, the position of third parties who take goods in good faith is protected.

The separate development of common law and equitable doctrine before the Judicature Act 1873 is the second complicating factor in this topic. In principle, the state of the law with a narrow doctrine of common law mistake with potentially harsh effects on third parties supplemented by the broader and flexible doctrine of mistake in equity in which third parties are protected is 'entirely sensible and satisfactory'.[9] But it is not easy to state the precise relationship of the equitable remedies with the common law doctrine of mistake and there appear to be differences, not easy to justify, between the operation at law and in equity of the policies against the use of mistake to get out of a bad bargain or to reallocate the risks of the contract. There are some indications of a more integrated approach, but there has, as yet 'been little merging of the streams of common law and equity'.[10] Accordingly, the present state of the law requires us first to discuss the effect of mistake, at common law, and then in equity, remembering that the principles here laid down should in no way be regarded as definitive, but rather as an attempt to extract a *rationale* from cases decided on a more empirical basis.

Before doing so we should note that it has been argued[11] that there is a close

---

[6] e.g. *Riverlate Properties Ltd.* v. *Paul* [1975] Ch. 133, at pp. 140–1; *Associated Japanese Bank (International) Ltd.* v. *Crédit du Nord* [1989] 1 W.L.R. 255, at p. 264.

[7] *Smith* v. *Hughes* (1871) L.R. 6 Q.B. 597, at pp. 604, 606. See generally Kronman (1978) 7 J.L.S. 1. On disclosure, see *ante*, pp. 236, 263.

[8] *Kleinwort Benson Ltd.* v. *Lincoln C.C.* [1999] 2 A.C. 349.

[9] *Associated Japanese Bank (International) Ltd.* v. *Crédit du Nord S.A.*, (*supra*, n. 6) at pp. 267–8. See *post*, p. 313.

[10] *Clarion Ltd.* v. *National Provident Institution* [2000] 1 W.L.R. 1888, at pp. 1905–6.

[11] *Associated Japanese Bank (International) Ltd.* v. *Crédit du Nord S.A.* [1989] 1 W.L.R. 255, at p. 268 (mistake can be regarded as a type of 'pre-contractual frustration'); *William Sindall plc* v. *Cambridgeshire C.C.* [1994] 1 W.L.R. 1016, at pp. 1035, 1039. See generally McKendrick, *Contract Law* (4th edn) pp. 289, 318; Smith (1994) 110 L.Q.R. 400, at p. 403. Cf. Treitel, *The Law of Contract* (10th edn) p. 862.

310 FACTORS DEFEATING CONTRACTUAL LIABILITY

relationship between mistake, which is concerned with misapprehensions or mis-understandings at the time of the formation of an apparent contract, and the doctrine of frustration, which concerns uncontemplated events occurring after that time. Both mistake and frustration are concerned with the allocation of risk in which the construction of the contract is central, and the Courts are conscious that both may be pleaded to get out of a bad bargain or to reallocate the risks.[12] Moreover, the two situations may appear factually similar, as where it is an accident whether the uncontemplated event occurred before or after the making of the contract.[13] But it is important to remember that they are 'different juristic concepts'.[14] Mistake relates to the formation of a contract and, where operative, renders it void or voidable *ab initio*, whereas frustration relates to its discharge and only discharges it from the time of the frustrating event. Where a contract is voidable for mistake we have noted that the power to set it aside is discretionary, but frustration discharges a contract automatically, and its effects are regulated by statute. Frustration is considered in Chapter 14.

II. MISTAKES WHICH INVALIDATE A CONTRACT

This section is concerned with that form of mistake which invalidates a contract by negativing or nullifying consent.[15] Three topics, superficially connected with the subject, should be eliminated at the outset.

First, there are cases in which there is not even the outward semblance of agreement, because offer and acceptance never coincided in their respective terms.[16] Such cases, where the mistake has brought about a failure to agree, are analytically different from cases in which there has been a genuine agreement but the existence of a material mistake raises a question about the voluntariness of the consent of one or both of the parties. Any tendency to treat them together stems from Pothier's civil law analysis[17] which, though influential in the past, is no part of English law.[18]

Secondly, there are cases where the parties are genuinely agreed, although the terms employed in making their agreement do not convey their true meaning. In such cases the Courts may be willing to correct their error; but this is a question which concerns the rectification, and not the formation, of a contract.[19]

Nor, lastly, are we concerned with cases in which one party finds the obligation of a contract more onerous than expected, or is disappointed in the performance received from the other party. If the terms of a contract do not express what one party

---

[12] *Amalgamated Investment & Property Co. Ltd.* v. *Walker & Sons Ltd.* [1977] 1 W.L.R. 164, at p. 172. See also *supra* n. 6.

[13] *Ibid.* Compare also the facts of *Griffith* v. *Brymer* (1903) 19 T.L.R. 434 (*post*, p. 320, n. 77) and *Krell* v. *Henry* [1903] 2 K.B. 740 (*post* p. 534).

[14] *Joseph Constantine Steamship Line Ltd.* v. *Imperial Smelting Corporation Ltd.* [1942] A.C. 154, at p. 186.

[15] *Bell* v. *Lever Brothers Ltd.* (*supra*, n. 4), at p. 217.

[16] *Ante*, p. 37.

[17] See generally Ibbetson, *A Historical Introduction to the Law of Obligations*, (1999) p. 225 ff.

[18] *Lewis* v. *Averay* [1972] 1 Q.B. 198, at p. 206.

[19] *Post*, p. 339.

intended them to express, that party's failure to find words appropriate to the intended meaning does not invalidate the contract.

The cases of operative mistake with which we have to deal fall into two main classes:

(1) cases in which the parties, though genuinely agreed, have both contracted in the mistaken belief that some fact which lies at the root of the contract is true. This type of mistake is generally known as *mutual* mistake, as it is shared by both parties;

(2) cases where, although to all outward appearances the parties are agreed, there is in fact no genuine agreement between them, and the law therefore does not regard a contract as having come into existence. This type of mistake is sometimes known as *unilateral* mistake,[20] as the mistake is on one side only.

Until recently, for a mistake to be operative at common law, and to invalidate a contract, it had to be one of fact and not of law.[21] But this distinction was based on the position in the law of restitution and it has recently been rejected in that context. Money paid under a mistake is *prima facie* recoverable whether the mistake is of fact or of law.[22] Although the policy favouring finality of transactions is stronger where there is an apparent contract, it is submitted this policy does not require the maintenance of the distinction where there is an apparent contract.

(a) MISTAKES GOING TO THE ROOT OF THE CONTRACT

In this type of mistake—mutual mistake—the parties, though genuinely *ad idem*, contract on the basis of an assumption which subsequently proves to be false.

(i) *Bell* v. *Lever Brothers Ltd.*

The leading case is that of *Bell* v. *Lever Brothers Ltd.*[23] The facts of the case are fairly simple, but the judgments are difficult to interpret.

L, entered into two agreements with B and S. The first was a service contract by which B and S were appointed to the Board of the Niger Company, a subsidiary of L, for a period of five years at salaries of £8,000 and £6,000 p.a. respectively. The second was a compensation contract by which L, in consideration of their retiring within the service period, promised to pay B £30,000 and S £20,000.

While they were acting under their appointments, both B and S had secretly entered on their own account into speculative transactions in cocoa, a course of conduct which would have given L the right to dismiss them summarily and without compensation. L had entered into the compensation contract, and paid the sums therein promised in ignorance of this fact. They now sought rescission of this contract and recovery of the money on the ground that it had been paid under a mistake of fact.

---

[20] e.g. by Lord Atkin in *Bell* v. *Lever Brothers Ltd.* [1932] A.C. 161, at p. 217.

[21] *British Homophone Ltd.* v. *Kunz* (1932) 152 L.T. 589.

[22] *Kleinwort Benson Ltd.* v. *Lincoln C.C.* [1999] 2 A.C. 349.

[23] [1932] A.C. 161.

The jury found that B and S had been guilty of no fraud and that, at the time they entered into the compensation contract, they did not have in mind their breaches of duty. The case must therefore be considered as one of *mutual* mistake, that is, one where the parties had both contracted under the same mistaken assumption. L would nevertheless never have entered into the contract had they known the true state of affairs, and they therefore alleged that the contract was a nullity from the beginning. The Court of Appeal[24] upheld this contention; but the House of Lords, by a bare majority, held that the contract was valid and binding.

There has been considerable discussion as to what this case in fact decides. Lord Blanesburgh, while stating that he was in accord with the other majority opinions, based his own decision mainly on a point of pleading.[25] The other two majority members, Lord Atkin and Lord Thankerton, in the course of their speeches, formulated a number of propositions which, although directed to the same end, tend not to be easily reconcilable one with the other. The speeches therefore provide support for a variety of conflicting interpretations of the doctrine of mutual mistake.

First, it is said that the case establishes that there is no doctrine of mistake, rendering the contract void *ab initio*, in English law.[26] In *Solle* v. *Butcher*, for example, Denning L.J. said:[27]

The correct interpretation of [*Bell* v. *Lever Brothers Ltd.*], to my mind, is that, once a contract has been made, that is to say, once the parties, whatever their inmost states of mind, have to all outward appearances agreed with sufficient certainty in the same terms on the same subject matter, then the contract is good unless and until it is set aside for failure of some condition on which the existence of the contract depends, or for fraud, or on some equitable ground. Neither party can rely upon his own mistake to say that it was a nullity from the beginning, no matter that it was a mistake which to his mind was fundamental, and no matter that the other party knew that he was under a mistake. A fortiori, if the other party did not know of the mistake but shared it.

Some support for this contention can be found in the speech of Lord Atkin,[28] but both he and other members of the House of Lords assume throughout that certain types of mistake will avoid a contract, although they differ as to the circumstances in which it will do so and it has been stated that Denning L.J.'s view does not do justice to the speeches of the majority.[29] Nevertheless, it is clear that the effect of the decision in *Bell* v. *Lever Brothers* is to confine the doctrine of mutual mistake within the most narrow limits; it is only in the most extreme cases that the Court will intervene.

---

[24] [1931] 1 K.B. 557.

[25] He also pointed out (pp. 180–1, 183, 197) that the payments made to Bell and Snelling were, at any rate in part, voluntary payments because their agreement was with the Niger Company not Lever Brothers, and so could not be recovered as money paid under a mistake: see *Morgan* v. *Ashcroft* [1938] 1 K.B. 49, at pp. 66, 71, 77.

[26] Slade (1954) 70 L.Q.R. 385; Shatwell (1955) 33 Can. Bar Rev. 164; Smith (1994) 110 L.Q.R. 400.

[27] [1950] 1 K.B. 671, at p. 691, *post*, p. 342. Bucknill and Jenkins L.JJ. did not mention *Bell* v. *Lever Brothers Ltd.*

[28] *Bell* v. *Lever Brothers Ltd.* [1932] A.C. 161, at p. 224.

[29] *Associated Japanese Bank (International) Ltd.* v. *Crédit du Nord S.A.* [1989] 1 W.L.R. 255, at p. 267. But cf. Smith (1994) 110 L.Q.R. 400, at pp. 412–13.

Secondly, it is said that the case establishes that a contract is void at law only if some term can be implied in both offer and acceptance which prevents the contract from coming into operation.[30] Lord Atkin expressly states that this is a proposition to which few would demur,[31] but cogently goes on to point out that it does not take us very far in the inquiry how to ascertain whether the contract does contain such a term.

An example is provided by *Associated Japanese Bank (International) Ltd.* v. *Crédit du Nord S.A.*[32]

A fraudulent party purported to sell to A.J.B. and lease-back from it certain machines which in fact did not exist. C.N. guaranteed the fraudulent party's obligations under the sale and lease-back. When the fraudulent party was adjudged bankrupt, A.J.B. sued on the guarantee.

It was held that as the guarantee provided that substitution of the subject of the contract, i.e. the machines, could only be made with the guarantor's consent, it was subject to an express condition precedent that the lease related to existing machines. Alternatively, it was stated that the contextual background and the fact that both parties were informed that the machines existed meant that such a condition could be implied.[33]

Thirdly, it is suggested that the application of the doctrine of mutual mistake depends upon the true construction of the contract made between the parties.[34] As a general rule, one or other of them will be considered to have assumed the risk of the ordinary uncertainties which exist when an agreement is concluded. Normally, because of the principle *caveat emptor*, the buyer is held to have taken the risk that property sold might prove defective or might be in some way different from that which the parties believed it to be. Alternatively, this risk will have been assumed by the seller if there was an express or implied warranty as to quality or description in the contract. A mutual misunderstanding will not therefore normally nullify the contract.

It is only where the terms of the contract, construed in the light of the nature of the contract and of the circumstances believed to exist at the time it was made,[35] show that it was never intended to apply to the situation which in reality existed at that time, and the risk of the relevant mistake has not been allocated to one of the parties, that the contract will be held void.[36] In *Bell* v. *Lever Brothers Ltd.*, for example, since B and S were under no duty to disclose their breaches of the service agreement to their employers, the risk that such breaches might have taken place was one which was assumed by L when they entered into the contract to pay compensation. In the view of

---

[30] This, as in the case of frustration, may be a fiction: see *post*, p. 542.

[31] [1932] A.C. 161, at p. 225. See also *Whittaker* v. *Campbell* [1984] Q.B. 318, at p. 327; Goldberg and Thomson [1978] J.B.L. 150.

[32] [1989] 1 W.L.R. 255, at p. 263.

[33] *Ibid*. See also *Financings Ltd*. v. *Stimson* [1962] 1 W.L.R. 1184.

[34] Atiyah (1957) 73 L.Q.R. 340; Atiyah & Bennion (1961) 24 M.L.R. 421; McTurnan (1963) 41 Can. Bar Rev. 1.

[35] Extrinsic evidence is admissible to assist in the construction of the contract: *Pritchard* v. *Merchants' and Tradesmen's Life Assurance Society* (1858) 3 C.B. (N.S.) 622.

[36] *Associated Japanese Bank (International) Ltd*. v. *Crédit du Nord S.A.* [1989] 1 W.L.R. 255, at p. 268; *William Sindall Plc.* v. *Cambridgeshire C.C.* [1994] 1 W.L.R. 1016, at pp. 1035, 1039; *Amalgamated Investment & Property Co. Ltd*. v. *John Walker & Sons Ltd*. [1977] 1 W.L.R. 164, and *post*, p. 319 and cf. *Gamerco S.A.* v. *I.C.M./Fair Warning (Agency) Ltd*. [1995] 1 W.L.R. 1226.

the majority of the House of Lords, the terms of this contract were still applicable notwithstanding the fact that L would have been entitled, had they known the true position, to treat the contract of service as at an end: an agreement to terminate a broken contract was not radically different from an agreement to terminate an unbroken contract since the party paying for the release got exactly what he bargained for.[37]

No systematic test can be laid down to determine whether the obligations envisaged by the parties extend to cover the situation which has unexpectedly emerged; but a number of factual situations have been considered by the Courts, and these may be conveniently marshalled into four categories:

(1) mistake as to the existence of the subject-matter of the contract;

(2) mistake as to title;

(3) mistake as to the quality or the substance of the thing contracted for;

(4) a false and fundamental assumption going to the root of the contract.

(ii) Mistake as to the existence of the subject-matter of the contract

If the subject-matter of the contract is a *res extincta*, that is it has, at the time of the contract, and unknown to the parties, ceased to exist, or if it has never been in existence, then the contract may be void for mutual mistake.

In a contract for the sale of goods, for example, where the terms of the contract indicate that the parties intended it to take effect only if the goods were in existence, the non-existence of the goods will produce a situation not contemplated by the contract and to which it cannot apply.[38] It is also enacted in section 6 of the Sale of Goods Act 1979[39] that, where there is a contract for the sale of specific goods, and the goods without the knowledge of the seller have perished at the time when the contract is made, the contract is void. As well as physical destruction, 'perishing' includes cases in which the goods are so damaged that they become for business purposes something other than the description under which they were sold.[40]

The leading case is that of *Couturier* v. *Hastie*:[41]

A contract was made for the sale of a cargo of corn, which the parties believed was being shipped from Salonica to England. The corn had, in fact, before the date of sale, deteriorated and had been unloaded at Tunis and sold. The buyer contended that, since the cargo of corn was not in existence, he was not bound to pay the price. But the seller argued that, on the true construction of the contract, 'this was not a mere contract for the sale of an ascertained cargo, but that the purchaser bought the adventure, and took upon himself all risks from the shipment of the cargo'.

---

[37] *Bell* v. *Lever Brothers Ltd.* [1932] A.C. 161, at pp. 223–4. See *post*, p. 319.

[38] *Ibid., per* Lord Atkin at p. 217.

[39] See *Barrow, Lane, and Ballard Ltd.* v. *Phillip Phillips & Co.* [1929] 1 K.B. 574 (subject-matter of sale stolen prior to it). But contrast s. 55(1) of the Act which, it has been argued, enables contractual variation of this rule: Atiyah (1957) 73 L.Q.R. 340, at pp. 348–9; *The Sale of Goods*, 10th edn. (2000), p. 96.

[40] *Asfar & Co.* v. *Blundell* [1896] 1 Q.B. 123; *Oilfields Asphalts* v. *Grovedale Coolstores (1994) Ltd.* [1998] 3 N.Z.L.R. 479 (account taken of contemplated use or purpose for goods).

[41] (1856) 5 H.L.C. 673. See also Atiyah (1957) 73 L.Q.R. 340.

The House of Lords held that the purchaser was not liable to pay for the corn. The contract contemplated a sale of existing goods. Neither Coleridge J., who delivered the judgment of seven judges in the Exchequer Chambers,[42] nor Lord Chancellor Cranworth in the House of Lords, actually mentioned the word 'mistake', for they considered the case purely as one of the construction of the contract; but they intimated that the contract would be void, inasmuch as 'it plainly imports that there was something which was to be sold at the time of the contract, and something to be purchased', whereas the object of the sale had ceased to exist.[43]

Similarly, in *Strickland v. Turner*,[44] S bought and paid for an annuity on the life of a man who was, unknown to both parties, already dead. He was able to recover the purchase money as the annuity had ceased to exist at the time of sale.

In these cases it is not difficult to see that the non-existence of the subject-matter of the contract gave rise to a total failure of consideration. If a cargo does not exist, it cannot be delivered; if an annuity is purchased on the life of a dead person, the purchaser gets nothing for his money. It does not matter whether the contract is valid or void. In neither case can the seller claim to recover, or retain, the purchase money. The consideration for the contract has totally failed. It is only when the buyer brings an action for *damages* for non-delivery that the crucial question of the validity of the contract will arise. So in *McRae* v. *Commonwealth Disposals Commission*:[45]

The Commonwealth Disposals Commission invited tenders for the purchase of a wrecked vessel described as 'an oil tanker on Jourmaund Reef approximately 100 miles north of Samarai' in New Guinea. M's tender was accepted, and he thereupon fitted out a salvage expedition at considerable expense. In fact there was no oil tanker in the locality indicated, nor was there even such a reef as Jourmaund Reef. M claimed damages against the Commission for the loss sustained by him in the expedition.

The Commission, whose conduct was described by the High Court of Australia as 'reckless and irresponsible', resisted the claim to damages on the ground that the contract was void *ab initio*. It relied on *Couturier* v. *Hastie* for the proposition that mutual mistake as to the existence of the subject-matter of a contract nullifies consent and avoids the contract. The Court did not, however, accept this argument, considering that the question of the validity of the contract had never arisen in that case; it was merely concerned with the failure of the consideration. If it had arisen, the decision would have depended upon whether the contract was subject to an implied condition precedent that the cargo existed at the time of the contract. No such condition could, in any event, be implied in the case before the Court, for the Commission had clearly contracted that there was a tanker in the position specified, and they must be held liable for breach.

It has been argued that the reasoning of the High Court of Australia in *McRae's* case negatives the existence of any doctrine of mutual mistake; indeed, it is said that a

---

[42] (1853) 9 Exch. 102, reversing the Court of Exchequer at (1852) 8 Exch. 40.

[43] (1856) 5 H.L.C. 673, at p. 681. Ibbetson states (*A Historical Introduction to the Law of Obligation* (1999) p. 228) that the 'reanalysis' of this decision was 'pivotal' to the rooting of mistake in English law.

[44] (1852) 7 Exch. 208. See also *Hitchcock* v. *Giddings* (1817) 4 Price 135.

[45] (1951) 84 C.L.R. 377 (noted (1952) 15 M.L.R. 229).

contract concerning subject-matter which is non-existent is always valid and binding, unless a term can be implied to the contrary.[46] It is submitted, however, that this is not the case. The merit of the decision in *McRae* v. *Commonwealth Disposals Commission* is that it shows that, save where section 6 of the Sale of Goods Act applies,[47] invalidity is not an invariable consequence of such a contract. The question is one of the construction of the agreement.

When properly construed, the contract may indicate that the seller assumed responsibility for the non-existence of the subject-matter. This was so in *McRae's* case, where the seller was held to have guaranteed the existence of the tanker.[48] Alternatively the contract may indicate that the buyer took the risk that the subject-matter might not exist and undertook to pay in any event. This was the point at issue in *Couturier* v. *Hastie*, where the House of Lords was called upon to decide whether or not the buyer had purchased merely the expectation that the cargo would arrive, and the securities (i.e. the shipping documents) against the contingency of its loss. There is therefore no absolute rule that a contract for the sale of a *res extincta* is necessarily void in English law. But if the true construction of the contract is that the parties entered into it on the footing that the subject-matter was in existence, and that neither of them should bear the responsibility if this was not so, then the contract is void for mutual mistake.

This would seem to be the most satisfactory approach to the question of mistake as to the existence of the subject-matter of the contract.

(iii) Mistake as to title

Where a person agrees to purchase property which, unknown to itself and the seller, is already owned by the buyer i.e. a *res sua*, the contract may be void.

In *Bell* v. *Lever Brothers*, Lord Atkin said:[49]

Corresponding to mistake as to the existence of the subject-matter is mistake as to title in cases where, unknown to the parties, the buyer is already the owner of that which the seller purports to sell to him. The parties intended to effectuate a transfer of ownership: such a transfer is impossible: the stipulation is *naturali ratione inutilis*.

So if A agrees to take from B a lease of land of which, contrary to the belief of both parties at the time of the contract, A is already tenant for life, the contract is void at common law.[50] But this principle must not be applied too widely. Normally a seller is taken to warrant title to the property sold; even though the parties both contract under a mistaken belief as to the title of the seller, there is a valid contract, and the seller may be made liable in damages. It is only where the buyer happens to purchase

---

[46] Slade (1954) 70 L.Q.R. 385. See also Smith (1994) 110 L.Q.R. 400, at p. 402.

[47] It did not apply in *McRae's* case because the goods had not perished, but never been in existence. But cf. *ante*, p. 314, n. 39.

[48] At p. 407. See also *Barr* v. *Gibson* (1838) 3 M. & W. 390; *Tommey* v. *Finextra* (1962) 106 S.J. 1012.

[49] [1932] A.C. 161, at p. 218.

[50] *Cooper* v. *Phibbs* (1867) L.R. 2 H.L. 149—a case in equity where the contract was rescinded for mistake; but see the view of Lord Atkin at p. 218 and Lord Thankerton at p. 236 of *Bell* v. *Lever Brothers Ltd.* on its validity at common law. Cf. Matthews (1989) 105 L.Q.R. 599.

his own property, and where no warranty can be implied, that the contract is a nullity from the beginning. For both parties must necessarily have accepted in their minds as an essential and integral element of the subject-matter of the transaction that the seller was, and that the buyer was not, entitled to the property.[51]

(iv) Mistake as to the quality or the substance of the thing contracted for

This has proved to be one of the most contentious categories in the law of mutual mistake. In *Bell* v. *Lever Brothers*, Lord Atkin said:

Mistake as to quality . . . will not affect assent unless it is the mistake of both parties, and is as to the existence of some quality which makes the thing without the quality *essentially different* from the thing as it was believed to be.

In reliance on this statement, it has been suggested that while a mistake as to *quality* (or attributes) will not avoid the contract, a mistake as to *substance* (or essence) will.[52]

Some support may be gained from *Kennedy* v. *Panama, New Zealand, and Australian Royal Mail Co. Ltd.*:[53]

K was induced to take shares in a further issue of capital by the defendant company by a statement in the prospectus that the new capital was required to carry out a contract recently entered into with the New Zealand government for the carriage of mails. The contract, which the company believed to be valid, had been made with an unauthorized agent of the New Zealand government and the government refused to ratify it. The shares fell greatly in value and K claimed to return the shares and recover back the purchase price.

The Court of Queen's Bench refused to allow K to do so. It held that the shares which had been received were not, because of the difference in value, different in substance from those which the company had contracted to deliver. Blackburn J., delivering the judgment of the Court, referred to the Digest of Civil Law[54] which distinguished substance and quality. He considered that the principle of English law was the same as that of Roman law,[55] and that, at common law, if the mistake was as to quality, there was no remedy in the absence of fraud, or of a definite warranty. Although there was no remedy at common law, on the facts of the case, equitable relief by way of rescission would have been available on the ground of misrepresentation.

That a mistake as to quality will not generally avoid the contract can scarcely be doubted. We may give some examples, both actual and hypothetical:

A agrees to buy from B a certain parcel of oats which both believe to be old oats. They are in fact new oats, and unsuitable for the purpose for which A wants them. There is a valid contract despite the mistake.[56]

C buys from D a picture which both believe to have been painted by Constable. Several

---

[51] [1932] A.C. 161, *per* Lord Thankerton at pp. 235, 236.

[52] Tylor (1948) 11 M.L.R. 257.

[53] (1867) L.R. 2 Q.B. 580 (a common law case), expressly approved in *Bell* v. *Lever Brothers Ltd.*, *passim*. Cf. *Emmerson's Case* (1866) L.R. 1 Ch. App. 433 (company in liquidation).

[54] At p. 588. Digest, 18.1.9, 10, 11.

[55] Cf. Lawson (1936) 52 L.Q.R. 79.

[56] *Smith* v. *Hughes* (1871) L.R. 6 Q.B. 597; *post*, p. 324.

years later, when C tries to sell the picture, he finds that it was not painted by Constable at all. The mistake, though 'fundamental', does not avoid the contract.[57]

E agrees to buy from F '100 bales of Calcutta kapok, Sree brand'. The sale is by sample, but both parties believe that this particular brand of kapok is pure kapok, consisting of tree cotton, whereas it in fact contains an admixture of bush cotton and is a commercially inferior product. The contract is valid.[58]

G buys from H a car which both believe to be a 1948 model. It is actually a 1939 model, and worth very much less. There is no mistake at common law.[59]

In the case of a mistake as to substance, however, this type of mistake does not in fact necessarily avoid the contract. In *Solle* v. *Butcher*:[60]

B made structural alterations to a flat and let it to S for seven years at a rent of £250 per year, both parties mistaken in believing that it was a 'new' dwelling-house and not subject to a controlled rent of £140.

The Court of Appeal held that, although there was a mistake as to the identity of the flat, and this was, in the social context, a mistake on a matter of considerable importance, nevertheless the lease was not void at common law. The mistake would afford grounds for relief in equity, but the lease was not a nullity from the beginning. Similarly in another case, where the parties contracted to buy and sell 'horsebeans', in the belief that they were the same as 'feveroles', an entirely different sort of bean, the contract was not avoided.[61]

It is evident then that there is no clear rule which states that a mistake as to the substance of the thing contracted for will avoid the contract although there are possibly circumstances in which it will do so. Where the mistake is as to 'an essential and integral element in the subject-matter of the bargain'[62] so that it renders the subject-matter 'essentially and radically different from the subject matter which the parties believed to exist'[63] the contract will be void. Accordingly, the following contracts of sale have been held to be void: of a quantity of Georgian table linen erroneously described in the particulars of sale as 'the authentic property of Charles I' and as bearing the arms of that unhappy monarch;[64] of a breeding cow which was mistakenly believed to be a sterile cow and sold by the pound for beef;[65] and of a plot of land, zoned as building land, for which, however, due to the absence of sewage facilities, it was impossible to obtain a building permit.[66]

The distinction between substance and quality is at best an arbitrary one, for there

---

[57] *Leaf* v. *International Galleries* [1950] 2 K.B. 86; *ante*, p. 255; *Harlingdon & Leinster Enterprises Ltd.* v. *Christopher Hull Fine Art Ltd.* [1991] 1 Q.B. 564, at p. 576.

[58] *Harrison & Jones Ltd.* v. *Bunten and Lancaster Ltd.* [1953] 1 Q.B. 646.

[59] *Oscar Chess Ltd.* v. *Williams* [1957] 1 W.L.R. 370, *ante*, p. 129.

[60] [1959] 1 K.B. 671, followed in *Grist* v. *Bailey* [1967] Ch. 532.

[61] *Frederick E. Rose (London) Ltd.* v. *William H. Pim Junior & Co. Ltd.* [1953] 2 Q.B. 450; *post*, p. 340.

[62] *Bell* v. *Lever Brothers Ltd.* [1932] A.C. 161, *per* Lord Thankerton, at p. 236.

[63] *Associated Japanese Bank (International) Ltd.* v. *Crédit du Nord S.A.* [1989] 1 W.L.R. 255, at p. 263.

[64] *Nicholson and Venn* v. *Smith Marriott* (1947) 177 L.T. 189.

[65] *Sherwood* v. *Walker* 33 N.W. 919 (1887), (Michigan).

[66] *Alessio* v. *Jovica* (1974) 42 D.L.R. (3d) 242 (Canada). Cf. *Amalgamated Investment & Property Co. Ltd.* v. *John Walker & Sons Ltd.* [1977] 1 W.L.R. 164.

is no metaphysical 'substance' independent of qualities.[67] Moreover, 'the principle enunciated in *Bell* v. *Lever Brothers Ltd.* is markedly narrower in scope than the civilian doctrine' and 'it is therefore no longer useful to invoke the civilian distinction'.[68] It is better to enquire what exactly the parties intended in their contract, i.e. whether the risk has been assigned to one of the parties or whether to enforce the contract would compel one or other of them to assume a risk which it was never intended should be undertaken.[69] The contract is then void because on its true construction it does not apply.

(v) A false and fundamental assumption

Where the parties contract under a false and fundamental assumption, going to the root of the contract, and which both of them must be taken to have had in mind at the time they entered into it as the basis of their agreement, the contract may be void.

This category is not separate and distinct from those categories of mistake already mentioned, but rather a more compendious statement of the type of error required. It received the approval of both Lord Atkin[70] and Lord Thankerton[71] in *Bell* v. *Lever Brothers Ltd.*, although some doubts were expressed as to its value owing to the necessary vagueness of its formulation. One thing, however, is certain. It is not sufficient for one party to establish that the mistake was as to the effect or commercial consequences of the contract,[72] or that, had the true facts been known, that party would never have entered into the bargain. Indeed, there may be assumptions which may be regarded by one, or both, of the parties as, in one sense, 'fundamental' – for example, that a picture is the work of an old master, or that a flat is free from rent control. Yet the contract will still bind. As Lord Thankerton points out:[73]

The phrase 'underlying assumption by the parties', as applied to the subject-matter of a contract . . . can only properly relate to something which both must have necessarily accepted in their minds as an essential and integral element of the subject-matter.

In *Bell* v. *Lever Brothers Ltd.* itself, this requirement was not fulfilled. On its true construction, the agreement to pay compensation applied notwithstanding the fact that the contract of service had been broken:

The contract released is the identical contract in both cases, and the party paying for release gets exactly what he bargains for. It seems immaterial that he could have got the same result in another way, or that if he had known the true facts he would not have entered into the bargain.[74]

The discovery of the new facts must, it was said, destroy the identity of the contract.

---

[67] Glanville Williams (1945) 61 L.Q.R. 293. Cf. Tylor (1948) 11 M.L.R. 257.

[68] *Associated Japanese Bank (International) Ltd.* v. *Crédit du Nord S.A.* [1989] 1 W.L.R. 255, *per* Steyn J., at p. 268.

[69] *Ante*, pp. 313–14.

[70] [1932] A.C. 161, at p. 225.

[71] *Ibid.*, at p. 236.

[72] *Clarion Ltd.* v. *National Providential Institution* [2000] 1 W.L.R. 1888, at p. 1899.

[73] *Ibid.*, at p. 235.

[74] *Ibid.*, *per* Lord Atkin at p. 223. Cf. *Horcal* v. *Gartland* [1983] I.R.L.R. 459.

It is not surprising that the strictness of this test has resulted in a dearth of cases on the subject of fundamental mistake. In *Scott* v. *Couslon*,[75] however, a contract for the assignment of a policy of life insurance was made upon the basis of an erroneous belief, shared by both parties, that the assured was still alive. It was held that the vendor was entitled to the return of the policy and also the moneys payable under it. Similarly the following have been held to be void: a separation deed entered into by a husband and wife on the erroneous assumption that their marriage was valid;[76] a contract for the hire of rooms to watch a coronation procession made in ignorance that the procession had already been cancelled;[77] and an agreement as to the amount due under two contracts of sale entered into in the erroneous belief that the results in the two certificates of analysis had been transposed.[78]

The operation of this principle can also be illustrated by *Sheikh Brothers Ltd.* v. *Ochsner*,[79] a case from Kenya, decided by the Judicial Committee of the Privy Council under section 20 of the Indian Contract Act 1872. Inspired by Pothier's civilian analysis,[80] section 20 provides: 'Where both the parties to an agreement are under a mistake as to a matter of fact essential to the agreement, the agreement is void'.

The appellants granted the respondent a licence to cut and manufacture all sisal grown on a particular estate. As well as paying for the licence, the respondent undertook to deliver to the appellants 50 tons of sisal each month. The estate was, in fact, not capable of producing such a quantity of sisal as would meet this requirement.

The Judicial Committee held, following the statements in *Bell* v. *Lever Brothers Ltd.*, that the contract was void. In this case, however, there was nothing in the contract to indicate that one or other of the parties took the risk that the estate would not produce so much sisal. The decision would have been otherwise if, on a true construction of the contract, the appellants had guaranteed the yield of the estate or the respondent had agreed to pay in any event.[81]

(vi) Effect of negligence

A party wishing to rely on an operative mutual mistake must have had reasonable grounds for entertaining the belief on which the mistake was made. Such a party who does not and is at fault, is not allowed to rely on the mistake. In *McRae* v. *Commonwealth Disposals Commission*, it was said:[82]

At least it must be true to say that a party cannot rely on a mutual mistake where the mistake consists of a belief which is, on the one hand entertained by him without any reasonable ground, and, on the other hand, deliberately induced by him in the mind of the other party.

---

[75] [1903] 2 Ch. 249.

[76] *Galloway* v. *Galloway* (1914) 30 T.L.R. 531.

[77] *Griffith* v. *Brymer* (1903) 19 T.L.R. 434.

[78] *Grains & Fourrages S.A.* v. *Huyton* [1997] 1 Lloyd's Rep. 628.

[79] [1957] A.C. 136. See also *Clifford* v. *Watts* (1870) L.R. 5 C.P. 577; *Associated Japanese Bank (International) Ltd.* v. *Crédit du Nord S.A.* [1989] 1 W.L.R. 255, at p. 269, *ante*, p. 313 (guarantee of machine lease agreement said to be void because machines did not exist).

[80] Ibbetson, *A Historical Introduction to the Law of Obligations* (1999) p. 227.

[81] *Bute (Marquis of)* v. *Thompson* (1844) 13 M. & W. 487; *Jeffries* v. *Fairs* (1876) 4 Ch. D. 448.

[82] (1950) 84 C.L.R. 377, *per* Dixon and Fullagar JJ. at p. 408; see *ante*, p. 315.

In *Associated Japanese (International) Bank Ltd.* v. *Crédit du Nord S.A.* this qualification of the positive rules regarding mistake was said to preclude a person who makes a contract with a minimal knowledge of the facts to which the mistake relates but is content that it is a good speculative risk, from relying on a mutual mistake which consists of a belief entertained without any reasonable grounds for such belief.[83] The qualification was said to rest on policy and good sense rather than principles such as estoppel or negligence.

(b) ABSENCE OF A GENUINE AGREEMENT

It follows from the essential nature of a contract that if there is no genuine agreement between the parties, or, as is commonly said, if the parties are not *ad idem*, there is no contract. This is only another way of saying that offer and acceptance must correspond exactly, or no contract will ensue. Therefore, if the offeree thinks that the offeror is some person other than he really is, or that the thing offered is something different, or that the terms proposed by the offeror are other than those actually proposed, and if she accepts on that mistaken assumption, it is clear that there is no genuine agreement, for the offer which she has accepted is not the offer made by the other party.

But the offeree may nevertheless be held to have accepted the real offer, and not that which exists merely in her mind, if an agreement can reasonably be inferred from objective facts. For it is a rule of our law that the intention of the parties must be inferred from their words and conduct as interpreted by a reasonable person:

If, whatever a man's real intention may be, he so conducts himself that a reasonable man would believe that he was assenting to the terms proposed by the other party, and that other party upon that belief enters into the contract with him, the man thus conducting himself would be equally bound as if he had intended to agree to the other party's terms.[84]

It is evident that in the vast majority of cases the operation of this objective test will exclude the plea that the parties were not in agreement. It will be remembered that in Chapter 2, The Agreement[85] and Chapter 4, The Terms of the Contract,[86] it was stated that, as a general rule, the intention of the parties must be construed objectively. So it is clear that the cases in which mistake affects a contract must be considered to be the rare exceptions to this general rule. Parties are bound by agreements to which they have expressed a clear assent. If they exhibit all the outward signs of agreement the law will hold that they have agreed.

Nevertheless it may happen that the law regards a contract as void though at first sight it appears perfectly valid. This may occur in one of four situations:

---

[83] [1989] 1 W.L.R. 255, at p. 268. See also the requirement of absence of fault in equity: *Solle* v. *Butcher* [1950] 1 K.B. 671, at p. 693; *post*, p. 344.

[84] *Smith* v. *Hughes* (1871) L.R. 6 Q.B. 597, *per* Blackburn J. at p. 607. See also *Centrovincial Estates plc* v. *Merchant Investors Assurance Co. Ltd.* [1983] Com. L.R. 158; *O.T. Africa Line Ltd.* v. *Vickers plc* [1996] 1 Lloyd's Rep. 700.

[85] *Ante*, p. 31.

[86] *Ante*, p. 160.

(1) where, despite outward appearances, there is no real coincidence between the terms of the offer and those of the acceptance;

(2) where there is a mistake as to the promise known to the other party;

(3) where there is a mistake as to the identity of the person with whom the contract is made;

(4) where there is a mistake in relation to a written document.

(i) Offer and acceptance not coincident

It may happen that, owing to a mistake on the part of one party, an offer may be innocently accepted in a different sense from that in which it was intended by the offeror, and the terms in which the contract is expressed may suffer from such latent ambiguity that it is impossible to say that the conduct of the parties points to one solution rather than another. In such a case one party may say that she did not attach the same meaning to the terms as the other party, and it will be impossible to say that her conduct would have induced a reasonable person to make one deduction rather than the other. The contract will be void because the terms of the offer and the acceptance did not coincide.[87]

If, for example, two things have the same name, and A makes an offer to B referring to one of them, which offer B accepts thinking that A is referring to the other, then provided there is nothing in the terms of the contract to identify one or other as its subject-matter, evidence may be given to show that the mind of each party was in fact (and subjectively) directed to a different object: that A offered one thing and B accepted another. So in *Raffles* v. *Wichelhaus*:[88]

W agreed to buy from R 125 bales of cotton 'to arrive [in Liverpool] *ex Peerless* from Bombay'. There were two ships called *Peerless*, and both sailed from Bombay, but W meant a *Peerless* which sailed in October, and R a *Peerless* which sailed in December.

It was held that there was no contract. There was nothing in the agreement which would point to one or other of the vessels as being the one identified in the contract; the offer and acceptance did not coincide.

Similarly, if A makes to B an offer which is ambiguous in its terms, or is rendered ambiguous by the circumstances surrounding it, and B accepts the offer in a different sense from that in which it is meant, then unless an objective construction requires otherwise, B may effectively maintain that there is no binding contract. In *Scriven Bros. & Co.* v. *Hindley & Co.*:[89]

S instructed an auctioneer to sell certain bales of hemp and tow. These bore the same shipping mark and were described in the auction catalogue as so many bales in different lots with no indication of the difference in their contents. H examined samples of the hemp before the sale intending to bid for the hemp alone. At the auction, the tow was put up for

---

[87] Cited with approval in *Alampi* v. *Swartz* (1963) 38 D.L.R. (2d) 300 (Canada).

[88] (1864) 2 H. & C. 906. See Simpson, *Leading Cases on the Common Law* (1995), ch. 6.

[89] [1913] 3 K.B. 564. See also *Thornton* v. *Kempster* (1814) 5 Taunt. 786; *Henkel* v. *Pape* (1870) L.R. 6 Ex. 7; *Falck* v. *Williams* [1900] A.C. 176; *Lloyds Bank plc* v. *Waterhouse* (1991) 10 Tr. L.R. 161, at pp. 185, 191.

sale, and H's buyer, believing it to be hemp, made a bid which was a reasonable one if it had been intended for hemp, but an excessive one for tow. This bid was accepted by the auction-eer, who did not realize the buyer's mistake, but merely thought the bid an extravagant one for tow. S sought to enforce the contract by suing for the price.

It was clear that offer and acceptance did not coincide. S intended to sell tow; H's buyer, misled by the auction catalogue, intended to buy hemp. The Court held that there was nothing in H's conduct which would estop them from pleading that the parties were not in agreement as to the subject-matter of the sale. Accordingly, no contract had come into existence, and H was not liable.

It has been said that these are not truly cases of mistake, but rather cases where there is merely no concurrence between the terms of the offer and those of the acceptance. This is true, but it is convenient to deal with them here as proof of a mistake must be adduced before a flaw can be found in the ostensible agreement.

(ii) Mistake as to the promise known to the other party

In entering into contracts people must use their own judgment or, if they cannot rely upon their judgment, must take care that the terms of the contract secure to them what they want. *Caveat emptor* is a general rule of the law of contracts. One party is not bound to disclose to the other all material circumstances which might affect the bargain and which are known to that party alone. Even if it is known that the other party is contracting under a misapprehension, the general rule is that there is no duty to disillusion the mistaken party.[90] The position is different if the contract contains statutory implied terms;[91] or is *uberrimae fidei*;[92] or there has been some active fraudulent concealment.[93] Save in these cases mere silence will not constitute a mis-representation, and each party must protect itself from the consequences of its own mistake.

Nevertheless the law will not recognize that a contract has come into existence when one party makes or accepts an offer which that party knows that the other understands in a fundamentally different sense from that in which the offer was made or accepted. So we find that a mistake by one party as to the *promise*, i.e. the terms of the contract, if known to the other party, will avoid the contract. Only a mistake as to the promise is sufficient; any other mistake, for example, as to the quality or the substance of the thing contracted for, will not affect consent in this way.[94] Moreover, although, in the current state of the authorities, the mistake must be known to the other party, and, if it is not, the party mistaken will be prevented from denying the apparent agreement; *dicta* suggest that a mistake by one party of which the other ought reasonably to have known will suffice. This is the case, at least, where there was

---

[90] *Bell* v. *Lever Brothers Ltd.* [1932] A.C. 161; *ante*, p. 311. See also *G.S. Fashions Ltd.* v. *B. & Q. plc* [1995] 1 W.L.R. 1088.

[91] *Ante*, p. 153, 159.

[92] *Ante*, p. 264.

[93] *Ante*, p. 243.

[94] *Bell* v. *Lever Brothers Ltd.* (*supra*, n. 90), at p. 218.

something in the conduct of the other party making it inequitable for that party to insist on the apparent bargain, including wilfully shutting her eyes to the obvious.[95]

We can best illustrate these propositions by an imaginary sale:

A sells X a piece of china.

(1) X thinks that it is Dresden china. A thinks it is not. Each takes a chance. X may get a better thing than A intended to sell, or a worse thing than X intended to buy; in neither case is the validity of the contract affected.

(2) X thinks that it is Dresden china. A knows that X thinks so, and knows that it is not. The contract holds. A must do nothing to deceive X, but she is not bound to prevent X from deceiving himself as to the quality of the thing sold. X's error is one of motive alone, and although it is known to A, it is insufficient.

(3) X thinks that it is Dresden china and thinks that A intends to contract to sell it as Dresden china; and A knows that it is not Dresden china, but does not know that X thinks that A is contracting to sell it as Dresden china. A reasonably believes that X is assenting to a sale of china in general terms. The contract holds. The misapprehension by X of the extent of A's promise, *if unknown to A*, has no effect, unless, as in *Scriven Brothers & Co. v. Hindley & Co.*,[96] A has caused or contributed to X's misapprehension.

(4) X thinks it is Dresden china, and thinks that A intends to contract to sell it as Dresden china. A knows that X *thinks A is contracting to sell it as Dresden china*, but does not mean to, and in fact does not, offer more than china in general terms. There is no contract to sell the particular piece of china. X's error was not one of judgment as to the quality of the china, as in (2), but was an error as to the nature of A's promise, and A, knowing that her promise was misunderstood, nevertheless allowed the mistake to continue. The apparent agreement is not a contract if A knows that X has accepted her offer in terms different from those in which it was in fact made. Moreover, A's knowledge in principle should deprive her of the right to deny the agreement as understood and intended by X, i.e. for Dresden china.

These propositions can be illustrated by two cases. The first is *Smith v. Hughes:*[97]

S sued H for the price of oats sold and delivered, and for damages for not accepting the oats. S had offered to sell to H, by sample, a parcel of oats at 35s. a quarter. According to H, S described the oats as 'good *old* oats', but S denied that the word 'old' had been used. This offer was rejected by H's counter-offer of 34s. a quarter, which in turn was accepted by S's delivery of the oats. When they were delivered, they were found to be new oats, and unsuitable for S's purpose.

The trial judge directed the jury to consider:

(1) whether the word 'old' had been used by S or H in making the contract. If so, they were to give a verdict for H;

---

[95] *Centrovincial Estates plc* v. *Merchant Investors Assurance Co. Ltd.* [1983] Com. L.R. 158; *Taylor* v. *Johnson* (1983) 151 C.L.R. 422 at p. 432; *O.T. Africa Line Ltd.* v. *Vickers plc* [1996] 1 Lloyd's Rep. 700. See also *Mannai Investment Co. Ltd.* v. *Eagle Star Life Assurance Co. Ltd.* [1997] A.C. 749; *Clinton* v. *Windsor Life Ass. Co. Ltd* [1998] 2 C.L. 120. Cf. the test for rectification in cases of unilateral mistake, *post*, p. 340.

[96] [1913] 3 K.B. 564; see *ante*, p. 322.

[97] (1871) L.R. 6 Q.B. 597.

(2) if the word 'old' had not been used, whether they were of the opinion that S believed H to believe, or to be under the impression, that he was contracting for the purchase of old oats. If so, they were to give a verdict for H.

The jury found for H without stating on which ground they had based their verdict. On a motion for a new trial, the majority of the Court of Queen's Bench were of the opinion that the second of these two directions would not sufficiently bring to the minds of the jury the distinction between agreeing to take the oats under the belief that they were old, and agreeing to take the oats under the belief that S *contracted* that they were old.[98] Hannen J. said:[99]

If, therefore, in the present case, [S] knew that [H], in dealing with him for oats, did so on the assumption that [S] was contracting to sell him old oats, he was aware that [H] apprehended the contract in a different sense to that in which he meant it, and he is thereby deprived of the right to insist that [H] shall be bound by that which was only the apparent, and not the real bargain.

But this was not necessarily so. H might merely have been mistaken as to the age of the oats, and not as to the plaintiff's promise. If such were the case, the contract would be valid, and a verdict should have been given for S:[100]

In order to relieve [H], it was necessary that the jury should find not merely that [S] believed [H] to believe that he was buying old oats, but that he believed [H] to believe that he, [S], was contracting to sell old oats.

Accordingly, a new trial was ordered.

The second case, in which the same rule was applied in slightly different circumstances, is *Hartog* v. *Colin & Shields:*[101]

C & S offered to sell to H 3,000 Argentine hare skins, but by a mistake they offered them at so much per *pound* instead of so much per *piece*. H accepted the offer. It was shown that it was the usual practice of the trade to charge on a per piece basis and that the written and oral negotiations leading up to the sale had proceeded throughout on a price per piece. As a pound contained on average three pieces the price under the agreement was roughly one-third of what it would have been on a per piece basis. H sought to enforce the sale in the terms of the offer, and sued for non-delivery.

Singleton J. held that H must have known and did in fact know that, when he accepted C & S's offer, they were under a mistake, and that this mistake amounted to a stipulation of the contract.[102] The *apparent* agreement (i.e. so much per pound) was

---

[98] (1871) L.R. 6 Q.B. 597, *per* Blackburn J. at p. 608.

[99] At p. 610.

[100] *Ibid., per* Hannen J. at p. 611.

[101] [1939] 3 All E.R. 566, followed in *McMaster University* v. *Wilcher Construction Ltd.* (1971) 22 D.L.R. (3d) 9 (Canada) aff'd (1973) 69 DLR 3d 410.

[102] *Sed quaere* whether it is sufficient that a reasonable person would have known of the other's mistake (see *McMaster University* v. *Wilcher Construction Ltd.* (*supra,* n. 101), at p. 32; *Centrovincial Estates plc* v. *Merchant Investors Assurance Co. Ltd.* [1983] Com. L.R. 158, at p. 159; *O.T. Africa Line Ltd.* v. *Vickers plc* [1996] 1 Lloyd's Rep. 700) or whether, as the analogy with rectification suggests (*post,* p. 341), actual knowledge, as in *Hartog* v. *Colin & Shields,* is necessary.

therefore void. It was not decided whether C & S could enforce the *intended* contract (i.e. so much per piece) but both principle and the analogy of rectification in cases of unilateral mistake[103] suggest that they should have been able to.

(iii) Mistake as to the identity of the person with whom the contract is made

Mistakes of this sort can only occur where A contracts with B, believing B to be C: that is, where a party has in contemplation a definite and identifiable person with whom he intends to contract. Further, the identity of the other party must be material: at the time when the contract is made, one party must regard the identity of the other party as a matter of vital importance.[104] One who, for example, accepts a bid at a public auction cannot normally allege that he is concerned with the identity of the person who makes the bid.[105] In the case of a contract wholly in writing, the identity of the parties is established by the names in the written contract.[106]

Mistake as to identity has posed particular difficulties for the Courts because often the issue of its effect on an apparent agreement arises not as between the parties to the agreement but in determining which of two innocent people defrauded by a third party who has vanished is to bear the loss. This has resulted in a complicated body of cases with divergent reasoning by judges in the same case, and fine and not always convincing distinctions, some of which may reflect an unarticulated judicial policy as to the incidence of loss between the innocent parties.

(*a*) *An offer can only be accepted by the person to whom it is addressed.* We may start with the proposition that a person cannot constitute himself a contracting party with one whom he knows or ought to know has no intention of contracting with him. An offer can be accepted only by the person to whom it is addressed. In *Boulton* v. *Jones*:[107]

B had taken over the business of one Brocklehurst, with whom J had been used to deal. J had a running account with Brocklehurst and was entitled to a set-off in respect of sums owed to him by Brocklehurst. J sent an order for goods to Brocklehurst, which B supplied without informing J that the business had changed hands. When J learned that the goods had not come from Brocklehurst, he refused to pay for them, and was sued by B for the price.

It was held that he was not liable to pay for the goods. Pollock C.B. said:[108]

It is a rule of law that if a person intends to contract with A, B cannot give himself any right under it. Here the order in writing was given to Brocklehurst. Possibly Brocklehurst might have adopted the act of [B] in supplying goods and maintained an action for their price. But

---

[103] *Post*, p. 340. See also *Commission for the New Towns* v. *Cooper (Great Britain) Ltd.* [1995] Ch. 259 (false and misleading statements made to divert mistaken party's attention).

[104] *Ingram* v. *Little* [1961] 1 Q.B. 31, at p. 57; *Lewis* v. *Averay* [1972] 1 Q.B. 198, at p. 209.

[105] *Dennant* v. *Skinner* [1948] 2 K.B. 164.

[106] *Hector* v. *Lyons* (1988) 58 P. & C.R. 156; *Shogun Finance Ltd.* v. *Hudson* [2002] 2 W.L.R. 867.

[107] (1857) 2 H. & N. 564. From the report of this case in (1857) 6 W.R. 107 it appears that Boulton knew of the existence of the set-off.

[108] At p. 565.

since [B] had chosen to sue, the only course [J] could take was to plead that there was no contract with him.

Nevertheless it must be remembered that offer and acceptance must here, as elsewhere, be understood in an objective sense. The test is not merely 'Did the offeror intend to contract with the person to whom the offer was made?' but also 'How would a reasonable person in the position of the offeree have interpreted the offer?' So if A makes an offer to B in mistake for C, and B, reasonably believing the offer is intended for him, accepts, then A is bound even though he can prove that he had made a mistake. An extreme application of this principle can be seen in *Upton-on-Severn R.D.C. v. Powell*:[109]

The defendant sent for the Upton fire brigade in mistake for the Pershore fire brigade, in whose area he was, and the call was accepted in good faith by the Upton brigade.

It was held that the defendant was contractually bound to pay for their services despite his mistake and despite the fact that neither party thought they were entering a contract; the defendant thought he was calling the brigade the services of which he was entitled to without charge, and the fire brigade thought they were answering a call within their area for which there would be no charge.[110]

But no contract will be formed if a person accepting an offer believes on reasonable grounds that he is accepting an offer from someone other than the person by whom it has in fact been made, and this fact is known to the offeror. In *Cundy v. Lindsay*:[111]

L received an order for goods from one Blenkarn, who gave as his address '37 Wood Street, Cheapside'. He imitated the signature of a respectable firm named Blenkiron & Co., who were known by reputation to L and who carried on business at 123 Wood Street. L was thus fraudulently induced to send the goods to Blenkarn's address, which goods he afterwards sold to C. L sued C for the return of the goods.

If the contract between L and Blenkarn was merely voidable for fraud, C would be entitled to retain the goods as they had taken them in good faith and for value. If the contract was void for mistake, Blenkarn could pass no title to the goods to C because as between him and L there was no contract. The House of Lords held that L were entitled to succeed. Lord Cairns said:[112]

Of him [Blenkarn] they knew nothing, and of him they never thought. With him they never intended to deal. Their minds never, even for an instant of time rested upon him, and as between him and them there was no *consensus* of mind which could lead to any agreement or any contract whatever. As between him and them there was merely the one side to a contract, where, in order to produce a contract, two sides would be required.

When his offer was accepted, Blenkarn knew that L thought they were entering into a contract with Blenkiron & Co. The contract was therefore void *ab initio*. Again, in *Shogun Finance Ltd. v. Hudson*[113] a finance company agreed to sell a car on hire purchase terms to a fraudster who then sold it to the defendant. As proof of identity the fraudster had produced a genuine but unlawfully obtained driving licence in the name of a Mr Patel, and the company had checked Mr Patel's credit rating. It was held that the hire purchase agreement, if it was made with anyone, was made between the company and Mr Patel.[114] Accordingly the defendant did not obtain title to the car and the finance company was entitled to it.

(b) The general rule: need for identifiable third person. If A's mistake does not go to the *identity* of the other party, if A does intend to make a contract with that particular person, then the fact that he would not have made it if he had not been labouring under some mistake regarding the personality of the other party will not prevent the formation of a contract. It is sometimes stated that mistake as to *attributes*, for example, as to the solvency or social position of that person or whether that person holds a driving licence,[115] is insufficient. There is, in fact, no more intrinsic validity in the distinction between *identity* and *attributes* than that, considered above, between *substance* and *qualities*. 'A man's very name is one of his attributes. It is also the key to his identity.'[116] The law does, however, conveniently distinguish between cases where there are two individuals in the picture (i.e. A contracts with B in mistake for C) and cases where there is only one (i.e. A contracts with B in the belief that B is not B). Glanville Williams stated cogently:[117]

The conclusion is that a so-called 'error of identity' consists in misapprehending (the attributes of) two or more persons. An 'error of attributes' consists in misapprehending (the attributes of) a single person.

In *King's Norton Metal Co. Ltd. v. Edridge, Merrett & Co, Ltd.*:[118]

K.N., a metal manufacturer, received a letter purporting to come from 'Hallam & Co.' in Sheffield asking for quotations for metal wire. On the letterhead was a picture of a large factory and a list of overseas depots. K.N. replied, and Hallam & Co. ordered the wire. In fact, the firm of 'Hallam & Co.' consisted solely of a fraudulent person named Wallis. The letters had been written, and the writing paper prepared, by him. Wallis subsequently sold the wire so obtained to the defendant. K.N. sued the defendant, contending that the contract with Hallam & Co. was void, and that the wire was therefore still its property.

---

[113] [2002] 2 W.L.R. 867.

[114] Dyson and Brooke L.JJ. applied *Hector* v. *Lyons* (*supra* n. 106), Dyson L.J. also considered the agreement was void because the company intended to contract only with Mr Patel. Sedley L.J. dissented, considering the agreement to be voidable because the garage's manager who had faxed the fraudster's licence and a draft agreement to the finance company was, for this limited purpose, the company's agent so that the 'face to face' rule (*infra* p. 330) applied.

[115] *Whittaker* v. *Campbell* [1984] Q.B. 318, at p. 329.

[116] *Lewis* v. *Averay* [1972] 1 Q.B. 198, at p. 206.

[117] (1945) 23 Can. Bar Rev. 278. Cf. Wilson (1954) 17 M.L.R. 515, and the reply by Unger (1955) 18 M.L.R. 259.

[118] (1897) 14 T.L.R. 98. Cf. *Newborne* v. *Sensolid (Great Britain) Ltd.* [1954] 1 Q.B. 45.

The Court of Appeal held that K.N. had intended to contract with the writer of the letter. Although it would not have done so if it had known what sort of a person the writer was, and that he was using an *alias*, a contract had been made which was not void on the ground of mistake, but only voidable for fraud. Consequently the property in the goods delivered had passed under it to Wallis, and an innocent purchaser from him acquired a good title to them. A.L. Smith L.J. put the question as follows:[119]

With whom, upon this evidence, which was all one way, did [K.N.] contract to sell the goods? Clearly with the writer of the letters. If it could have been shown that there was a separate entity called Hallam & Co. and another entity called Wallis then the case might have come within the decision in *Cundy* v. *Lindsay*.

Therefore, in order to establish mistake as to identity, the party contracting must prove not merely that she did not intend to contract with the person with whom the apparent contract was concluded, but also that there was a third identifiable person with whom there was an intention to contract.[120]

(c) The exception: no third party in existence. The general position must be distinguished from that where A contracts with B in the belief that B is not B, and B knows of this error.[121]

Suppose that B, knowing that A will refuse to contract with him, disguises himself so as to conceal his identity, and effects a purchase of goods from A.

It might be thought that this situation is no different from that where A contracts with B in mistake for C, and B realizes the mistake. There is in fact a considerable difference. In the latter situation the contract is void because B cannot accept an offer which he knows is not intended for himself but for C. In the former, there is no third person to whom the offer is really addressed: it is addressed to B, even though A mistakenly believes that he is not B. B is not, therefore, prevented from accepting an offer addressed to himself, and the contract will be valid and binding.

   In certain circumstances, however, the offer made by A may expressly or impliedly contain a stipulation that excludes B. These are the terms upon which A is prepared to contract, and, as we have seen,[122] it is not possible for an offeree to accept an offer which he knows is made to him in different terms from those in which he purports to accept it. B cannot, therefore, accept such an offer. For example, the offer may be made to a limited class of persons, such as the members of a club or college, of whom B is not one. B may know, by reason of a previous refusal, that he is a person with whom A is unwilling to contract: a drama critic who is refused a ticket for a theatre

---

[119] At p. 99.
[120] See also *Citibank N.F.* v. *Brown Shipley & Co. Ltd.* [1991] 2 All E.R. 690, at p. 702 (mistake as to identity of messenger insufficient). See generally Goodhart (1941) 57 L.Q.R. 228; Unger (1955) 18 M.L.R. 259. Cf. Wilson (1954) 17 M.L.R. 515.
[121] This section relies heavily on the convincing argument of Professor Goodhart in (1941) 57 L.Q.R. 228, at pp. 241 ff.
[122] *Ante*, p. 322.

performance cannot conclude a contract by going to the box office in disguise, or by employing a friend to buy a ticket for him.[123]

The difficulty is to know in what circumstances such a term is to be *implied* into the offer. In *King's Norton Metal Co. Ltd. v. Edridge, Merrett & Co. Ltd.*,[124] the mistaken plaintiff was unable to satisfy the Court that such an implication should be made. This decision does not appear to have been cited in the case of *Sowler v. Potter*[125] in which it was held that the identity of the tenant was a vital element in a tenancy contract and that therefore *any* mistake with regard to her identity rendered the contract void *ab initio*. But this does not constitute a sound positive test of mistake in English law. The proper approach in such a case as *Sowler v. Potter* would be to inquire whether a stipulation could be implied into the offer that the offer excluded the particular person as a tenant, and whether this stipulation was known to the offeree. The answer is clear: no such stipulation could possibly be implied, and the contract should not have been held to be void. The decision in *Sowler v. Potter* has incurred almost unanimous disapproval, and must now be taken to have been overruled.[126]

(d) Transactions concluded in the parties' presence. Where the parties are not at a distance from one another but deal face to face, there is a presumption that each intended to deal with the other and not with someone else. In *Phillips v. Brooks Ltd.*:[127]

A man, North, called at P's shop and selected some pearls and a ring. He wrote out a cheque for £3,000, saying 'I am Sir George Bullough' (a person of credit whose name was known to P) and giving Sir George Bullough's address. P, finding on reference to a directory that Sir George lived at that address, allowed North to take away the ring which North then pledged to the defendants for £350. The defendants had no notice of the fraud. P sued for the return of the ring, alleging that he had never parted with the property in it.

Horridge J. held that, although the plaintiff believed the person to whom he was handing the ring was Sir George Bullough, he in fact contracted to sell and deliver it to the person who came into his shop. His intention was 'to sell to the person present and identified by sight and hearing'.[128] The contract, therefore, was not void on the ground of mistake, but only voidable on the ground of fraud, and the defendants had acquired a good title to the ring.

It does not, however, follow from this decision that there can be no operative mistake as to identity where the parties are in each other's presence. The proper inference that each intended to contract with the other is not inevitable. In *Lake v. Simmons*:[129]

---

[123] *Said v. Butt* [1920] 3 K.B. 497 (this case was primarily concerned with the question of an undisclosed principal and not with mistake).

[124] *Ante*, p. 328.

[125] [1940] 1 K.B. 271.

[126] *Solle v. Butcher* [1950] 1 K.B. 671, at p. 691; *Gallie v. Lee* [1969] 2 Ch. 17, at pp. 33, 41, 45 aff'd [1971] A.C. 1004; *Lewis v. Averay* [1972] 1 Q.B. 198, at p. 206; *Shogun Finance Ltd. v. Hudson* [2002] 2 W.L.R. 867, *per* Dyson L.J. at para. 34 (approving the suggestion as to the proper approach in this and previous editions of this book). Cf. *Gordon v. Street* [1899] 2 Q.B. 641.

[127] [1919] 2 K.B. 243, criticized by Goodhart (1941) 57 L.Q.R. 228, at p. 241.

[128] *Edmunds v. Merchant Despatch Co.* (1883) Mass. 283, *per* Morton C.J. at p. 286.

[129] [1927] A.C. 487.

L, a jeweller, was insured with a company against loss by theft, with the exception of jewellery 'entrusted to a customer'. A woman named Esme Ellison, posing as the wife of a wealthy customer, one Van der Borgh, made a few purchases from L to inspire confidence, and then was allowed to take away two pearl necklets of considerable value 'on approval' for her supposed husband. She made away with the necklets, and the question arose whether the loss was covered by the insurance policy, or came within the exception clause.

The House of Lords held that the loss was covered by the insurance. Viscount Haldane considered that the answer to the question turned on whether there was a contract between L and Esme Ellison, and said:[130]

[L] thought that he was dealing with a different person, the wife of Van der Borgh, and it was on that footing alone that he parted with the goods. He never intended to contract with the woman in question.

The contract was therefore void. It could, of course, be argued that L intended to contract with the woman in the shop, merely investing her with attributes of Mrs Van der Borgh,[131] but Viscount Haldane thought otherwise. He distinguished *Phillips* v. *Brooks Ltd.* by pointing out that, in that case 'the jeweller was prepared to sell to North individually as a casual customer who had entered the shop. All that remained to be subsequently arranged was the payment of the price'.[132] The mention of Sir George Bullough induced therefore, not the making of the contract, but only the delivery of the goods. This would seem to suggest that if North had introduced himself as Sir George Bullough on entering the shop, it might well have been that the proper conclusion to be drawn would have been that the plaintiff had intended to contract with Sir George Bullough and no one else, and this fact being known to North, the contract would not have been voidable but void.

Two more recent cases, the facts of which closely resemble those in *Phillips* v. *Brooks Ltd.*, illustrate the difficulty of deciding whether a contract is void for mistake as to identity, or merely voidable for fraud. In *Ingram* v. *Little*:[133]

Miss Elsie and Miss Hilda Ingram advertised their car for sale. A rogue who called himself Hutchinson visited them and offered to buy the car. When he made as if to pay them by cheque, they refused to accept it and insisted on payment in cash. He then gave his initials and an address, describing himself as a respectable business man living in Caterham. One of the Ingrams then went to the local post office and ascertained from the telephone directory that there was such a person living at that address. They then allowed the rogue to take away the car in return for a worthless cheque and the rogue sold the car to the defendants who took it in good faith.

The Court of Appeal held that the contract between the Ingrams and 'Hutchinson' was void for mistake as to identity and that the vehicle was still their property. The

---

130 At p. 500. See also *Hardman* v. *Booth* (1863) 1 H. & C. 803. Cf. *Citibank NA* v. *Brown Shipley & Co. Ltd.* [1991] 2 All E.R. 690, at p. 700.

131 She did not exist. Van der Borgh was a widower. Esme Ellison was his mistress.

132 At p. 501 (no trace of this as a material distinction can be found in the judgment in *Phillips* v. *Brooks Ltd.*). See also *Ingram* v. *Little* (*infra*, n. 133), at pp. 51, 60; *Lewis* v. *Averay* [1972] 1 Q.B. 198, at pp. 206, 208.

133 [1961] 1 Q.B. 31 (Devlin L.J. dissenting). Cf. *Fawcett* v. *Star Car Sales Ltd.* [1960] N.Z.L.R. 406.

circumstances (particularly the investigation of the telephone directory) indicated that it was with Hutchinson that the plaintiffs intended to deal and not with the rogue who was physically present before them. On the other hand, in *Lewis* v. *Averay*:[134]

L, a post-graduate chemistry student, advertised his car for sale. A rogue, posing as the well-known television actor Richard Greene, called on L and offered to buy the car. L accepted the offer, and the rogue wrote out a cheque, signing it 'R.A. Green'. The rogue wished to take away the car at once, but L was not willing for him to have it until the cheque had been cleared. At L's request the rogue produced 'proof' that he was Richard Greene in the form of a special pass of admission to Pinewood studios bearing the name 'Richard A. Green' and an address, a photograph of the rogue and an official stamp. L was satisfied on seeing this pass and allowed the rogue to have the car. The cheque was worthless and the rogue sold the car to A, a music student, who bought it in good faith.

The Court of Appeal held that A intended to contract with the person actually present before him. The contract was therefore merely voidable for fraud, and A in consequence acquired the property in the car as against L.

(e) Critique. It is by no means easy to draw any convincing distinction between these various cases, and it is doubtful whether the statements of principle contained in them can be reconciled. While it can be argued that *Ingram* v. *Little*, if rightly decided, depends on 'the very special and unusual facts of the case'[135] for its decision, as we have seen from *Shogun Finance Ltd.* v. *Hudson*[136] (albeit in the context of a transaction held not to have been concluded in the parties' presence), the same unsatisfactory outcome can occur in other scenarios. There is considerable merit in the suggestion made by Lord Denning M.R. in *Lewis* v. *Averay* that such fine distinctions as exist, for example, between mistake as to identity and mistake as to attributes and the precise time of any statement as to identity, are a reproach to the law. But, as Sedley L.J. has observed, the decision of the House of Lords in *Cundy* v. *Lindsay*, which was not referred to in *Lewis* v. *Averay*, stands in the way of a better test for the allocation of loss than now exists, but any decision of the Court of Appeal 'which ignored or marginalised it would create a conflict which would assist neither the standing of the law nor the ability of people to know where they stood'.[137] It would be preferable if effect were given to a recommendation made by the Law Reform Committee[138] that, where goods are sold under a mistake as to the buyer's identity, the contract should, so far as third parties are concerned, be considered voidable and not void. It is after all the seller who has accepted the identity and given credit to the fraudulent buyer on the basis of what may be fairly perfunctory inquiries.

(iv) Mistake in relation to a written document

We now deal with a class of mistake which is peculiar to the law of written contracts. This is due to the existence of the common law defence of *non est factum* which

---

[134] [1972] 1 Q.B. 198.
[135] *Ibid., per* Phillimore L.J. at p. 208.
[136] [2002] 2 W.L.R. 867, *ante* p. 328.
[137] *Ibid.*, at para 13.
[138] Twelfth Report of the Law Reform Committee (Cmd. 2958, 1966), 15.

permits one who has signed a written document, which is essentially different from that which he intended to sign, to plead that, notwithstanding his signature, 'it is not his deed' in contemplation of law.[139] The term properly applies to a deed but is equally applicable to other written contracts.

The effect of a successful plea of *non est factum* is that the transaction contained in the document is not merely voidable against the person who procured its execution, but is entirely void into whosesoever hands the document may come.

It must be emphasized that the defence of *non est factum* is a narrow one. Those too lazy or too busy to read through a document before signing it cannot rely upon it. Neither can those who sign a document containing objectionable terms or terms the legal effect of which they are unaware. As Donovan L.J. explained in *Muskham Finance Ltd.* v. *Howard*:[140]

Much confusion and uncertainty would result in the field of contract and elsewhere if a man were permitted to try to disown his signature simply by asserting that he did not understand that which he signed.

In *Blay* v. *Pollard & Morris*,[141] the defendant signed a document which he knew to relate to the dissolution of a partnership of which he was a member. Unknown to him, the document contained a term which had not been mentioned in a previous oral agreement, and which made him liable to indemnify his fellow partner in respect of certain partnership liabilities. It was held that he was bound by his signature.

The narrowness of *non est factum* is also explained by the fact that it can be invoked against third parties:

Where a fraudster has tricked, first, the signer of the document, in order to induce the signature, and then some third party, who is induced to rely on the signed document, which of the two victims is the law to prefer. The authorities indicate that the answer is, almost invariably, the latter. The signer of the document has, by signing, enabled the fraud to be carried out, enabled the false document to go into circulation.[142]

(a) Essentially different transaction. In order for the defence to succeed, the person executing the document must show[143] that the transaction which the document purports to effect is essentially different in substance or in kind from the transaction intended. At one time it was thought that the plea of *non est factum* would not succeed if the mistake was as to the contents of a document, as opposed to its essential nature or character.[144] This distinction between contents and character is not an intelligible one,[145] for a document takes its character from its contents and in *Saunders* v. *Anglia*

---

[139] *Scriptum predictum non est factum suum*. See *Thoroughgood's Case* (1582) 2 Co. Rep. 9a; Holdsworth, *H.E.L.* viii, p. 50; Simpson, *A History of the Common Law of Contract* (1975), 98.

[140] [1963] 1 Q.B. 904, at p. 914.

[141] [1930] 1 K.B. 628.

[142] *Norwich and Peterborough B.S.* v. *Steed (No. 2)* [1993] Ch. 116 *per* Scott L.J., at p. 125.

[143] The burden of proof lies on the person wishing to establish the defence of *non est factum*: [1971] A.C. at pp. 1016, 1019, 1027, 1038; *Crédit Lyonnais* v. *P.T. Barnard & Associates Ltd.* [1976] 1 W.L.R. 557; *Norwich and Peterborough B.S.* v. *Steed (No. 2)* [1993] Ch. 116.

[144] *Howatson* v. *Webb* [1907] 1 Ch. 537, aff'd., [1908] 1 Ch. 1.

[145] See Glanville Williams (1945) 61 L.Q.R. 179, at p. 194; *Gallie* v. *Lee* [1969] 2 Ch. 17, at pp. 31, 41, 43, *sub. nom. Saunders* v. *Anglia Building Society* [1971] A.C. 1004, at pp. 1017, 1022, 1025, 1039.

Building Society,[146] it was rejected by the House of Lords in favour of a more flexible test: that there must be a 'radical' or 'essential' or 'fundamental' or 'serious' or 'very substantial' difference between the document signed and that which the person signing intended to sign. If, for example, a person signs a guarantee for £10,000 believing it to be a guarantee of a lesser sum, it will depend on the amount of the lesser sum and the surrounding circumstances of the case whether or not the difference between the two transactions is sufficient to satisfy this test. The question is one of degree.

In *Saunders* v. *Anglia Building Society*,[147] the House of Lords held that the test had not been satisfied:

The appellant, an elderly widow, gave the title deeds of her house to her nephew, intending to make a gift to him of the house in order that he could borrow money on the security of the property. It was a condition of the gift that he was to permit her to reside there for the rest of her life. She was subsequently requested by a friend of her nephew, whom she knew to be assisting him to obtain a loan, to sign a document. The friend told her that it was 'to do with the gift by deed to Wally (her nephew) for the house'. As she had broken her spectacles, she signed the document without reading it. The document was in fact a deed conveying the house on sale to the friend. The friend did not pay the appellant or her nephew, but subsequently mortgaged the house to the respondents.

The plea of *non est factum* failed. At first sight there might seem to be an essential difference between a gift of the house to the nephew and a sale of the house to his friend. But, as Russell L.J. pointed out in the Court of Appeal,[148] the appellant intended to transfer the house so that the transferee could raise money on it, and she knew that her nephew and his friend were engaged jointly on this project. The 'object of the exercise' might well have been achieved by means of a sale if the friend had been honest and paid the nephew. Although their Lordships were by no means unsympathetic to the appellant's situation,[149] they held that the document which she had executed was not of a fundamentally different nature from the document which she believed she was signing. The building society could therefore enforce the mortgage.

We must now examine two cases in which the plea of *non est factum* was successful. The first is that of *Foster* v. *Mackinnon*:[150]

Mackinnon, 'a gentleman far advanced in years', was fraudulently induced to indorse a bill of exchange for £3,000 on the assurance that it was a guarantee of a similar nature to one which he had previously signed. Later the bill was indorsed for value to Foster, who took it in good faith.

It was held that the defence of *non est factum* was available to Mackinnon, as he never intended to make such a contract, and had been guilty of no negligence.

---

[146] [1971] A.C. 1004, at pp. 1017, 1019, 1021, 1026, 1039.
[147] *Ibid.*
[148] *Gallie* v. *Lee* [1969] 2 Ch. 17, at pp. 40–1.
[149] The building society, in fact, undertook not to evict the appellant during her lifetime.
[150] (1869) L.R. 4 C.P. 704.

The second is *Lewis* v. *Clay*.[151]

Lord William Nevill came to the defendant and asked him to witness some deeds for him. He produced a roll of papers covered by blotting paper, in which there were cut four openings, and explained that it was 'a private matter'. Believing that he was witnessing Lord Nevill's signature, the defendant signed in the spaces indicated. It turned out that the papers were promissory notes to the value of £11,000 made out in favour of Lewis who took them in good faith and for value.

The jury found that the defendant had signed in misplaced confidence, but without negligence; and Lord Russell C.J. held that he was not liable because 'his mind never went with the transaction', but was 'fraudulently directed into another channel by the statement that he was merely witnessing a deed or other document'.

(b) Effect of negligence of party signing. In *Saunders* v. *Anglia Building Society*[152] it was held that, even if the document signed is essentially different from that which the person signing it intended to sign, as against a third party he will not be entitled to disown his signature unless he proves that he exercised reasonable care. What is reasonable care will depend on the circumstances of the case and the nature of the document being signed. If one of two innocent parties is to suffer for the fraud of a third, the sufferer should be the one whose negligence has contributed to the loss suffered.

As a normal rule, therefore, if a person of full understanding and capacity forbears, or carelessly omits, to read what he signs, the defence of *non est factum* will not be available.[153] However, as Lord Wilberforce pointed out in *Saunders'* case:[154]

There still remains a residue of difficult cases. There are still illiterate or senile persons who cannot read, or apprehend, a legal document; there are still persons who may be tricked into putting their signature on a piece of paper which has legal consequences different from anything they intended . . . Accepting all that has been said by learned judges as to the necessity of confining the plea within narrow limits, to eliminate it altogether would, in my opinion, deprive the courts of what may be, doubtless on sufficiently rare occasions, an instrument of justice.

There is support for the view that, where no third party is involved, negligence is irrelevant.[155] But it has also been suggested that in two party cases remedies for fraud, misrepresentation, or unilateral mistake should be used rather than *non est factum*.[156]

(c) Documents signed in blank. Where a person signs a document in blank, leaving it to another to fill in the terms of the contract in accordance with an oral agreement

---

151 (1898) 67 L.J.Q.B. 224.

152 [1971] A.C. 1004, at pp. 1019, 1023, 1027, 1037–8. *Carlisle and Cumberland Banking Co.* v. *Bragg* [1911] 1 K.B. 489, criticized by Anson (1912) 28 L.Q.R. 190; Guest (1963) 79 L.Q.R. 346, was overruled.

153 Cf. Stone (1972) 88 L.Q.R. 190; Spencer [1973] C.L.J. 104.

154 [1971] A.C. 1004, at p. 1025. See also *Petelin* v. *Cullen* (1975) 132 C.L.R. 355 (Australia); *Lloyds Bank plc* v. *Waterhouse* [1993] 2 F.L.R. 97.

155 *Petelin* v. *Cullen* (1975) 132 C.L.R. 355, at p. 360; *Bradley West Solicitors Nominee Co. Ltd.* v. *Keenan* [1994] 2 N.Z.L.R. 111, at p. 118.

156 *Lloyds Bank plc* v. *Waterhouse* [1993] 2 F.L.R. 97, at pp. 117, 122–3.

reached between them, it would seem that he could in theory rely on the defence of *non est factum* if the terms inserted render the transaction essentially different in substance or in kind from the transaction intended. However, unless there are exceptional circumstances present, a person who signs a document in blank accepts responsibility for it; and he takes the risk if, through fraud or error, the document is filled in in some different way.[157] He cannot therefore avoid his liability as against an innocent third party.

III. MISTAKE IN EQUITY

The effect of a mistake at common law, if it operates at all, is to render the contract void *ab initio*; but, as we have already seen in the case of innocent misrepresentation, equity may be prepared to grant relief where the common law refuses to intervene. One reason for a less restrictive approach is that equity acts *in personam* so that innocent third parties who have given value are protected. In the case of mistake three equitable remedies are relevant:

(1) specific performance, which may be refused where there has been a mistake;

(2) rectification of a written contract;

(3) rescission of the contract.

In no case, however, does equitable relief take the form of a decree that the contract is a nullity from the beginning; at the most, the contract is voidable, and not void.

The equitable remedies in respect of contracts are only one aspect of a much wider equitable jurisdiction to relieve from the consequences of mistake, a jurisdiction which extends to gifts and is less concerned with the nature of the mistake.[158] This, coupled with the fact that the jurisdiction has developed primarily by reference to the remedy sought, has meant that attention has not always been paid to the allocation of risks in the contract or the need to prevent a party pleading mistake to get out of a contract that has turned out to be a bad bargain.

Before turning to the equitable remedies something must be said about their relationship with the doctrine of mistake at common law.

(a) EQUITABLE AND COMMON LAW MISTAKE

(i) Before the Judicature Act

Before the Judicature Act 1873, common law and equity were administered in separate jurisdictions. If a plaintiff applied to the Court of Chancery for equitable relief on the

---

[157] *United Dominions Trust Ltd. v. Western* [1976] Q.B. 513. Cf. *Mercantile Credit Co. Ltd. v. Hamblin* [1965] 2 Q.B. 242. See Allcock (1982) 45 M.L.R. 18.

[158] Mistake of law was not a bar: see e.g. *Gibbon v. Mitchell* [1990] 1 W.L.R. 1304, at p. 1309.

ground of contractual mistake,[159] the Court had its own remedies and followed its own principles in granting or refusing relief.[160] It did not first have to inquire whether or not the contract was void at common law and it is therefore misleading to suggest, as does Denning L.J. in *Solle* v. *Butcher*,[161] first, that the intervention of equity *presupposed* that the contract was good at law, or secondly (and somewhat inconsistently) that if the contract was void at law, equity would automatically have had to follow the law. The truth is that the Court of Chancery did not trouble itself about the position at law, unless, of course, there had been actual judgment. Even where a contract might have been void at common law,[162] the Court of Chancery decided the case on equitable principles alone.

(ii) Relationship since 1875

Since 1875 the rules of common law and equity have been applied in all divisions of the High Court of Justice, and the particular rule to be applied in the case of contractual mistake has depended upon the nature of the relief demanded. In *Cundy* v. *Lindsay*,[163] for example, the case was decided according to common law principles because the plaintiff pleaded that the contract was void. In *Paget* v. *Marshall*,[164] on the other hand, the plaintiff's claim to have the contract rescinded or rectified meant that the case was to be determined according to equitable rules. Until *Solle* v. *Butcher* there had been no real consideration of their relationship one with the other.

In that case, however, Denning L.J. put forward the opinion that equity has somehow superseded the common law where contractual mistake is concerned.[165] For instance, he considered that *Smith* v. *Hughes*[166] and *Cundy* v. *Lindsay*[167] would nowadays be cases where the contract would be voidable and not void. The authority for this view would presumably be that provision in the Judicature Act 1873,[168] which lays down that where there is any conflict or variance between the rules of equity and common law with reference to the same matter, the rules of equity are to prevail. It is doubtful, however, whether this is a proper case for the application of this provision. The better view[169] is that the Court must first consider, if so pleaded, the question of common law mistake. If the contract is pronounced void, as it would be on the facts of *Cundy* v. *Lindsay*, no question of equitable relief will arise. If, on the other hand, the contract is not void, the Court may then proceed to consider the possibility of any

[159] See Grunfeld (1952) 15 M.L.R. 297.

[160] See, e.g., *Wood* v. *Scarth* (1855) 2 K. & J. 33 (equity); (1858) 1 F. & F. 293 (law).

[161] [1950] 1 K.B. 671, at pp. 692, 694.

[162] See, e.g. *Cooper* v. *Phibbs* (1867) L.R. 2 H.L. 149, *ante*, p. 316, n. 50 (mistake as to title) and *Webster* v. *Cecil* (1861) 30 Beav. 62, *post*, p. 324 and *Garrard* v. *Frankel* (1862) 30 Beav. 445, and *ante*, pp. 323, 325 (snapping up).

[163] *Ante*, p. 327.

[164] (1884) 28 Ch. D. 255.

[165] [1950] 1 K.B. 671, at pp. 692–3, *ante*, p. 312, *post*, p. 342. See also *Magee* v. *Pennine Insurance Co. Ltd.* [1969] 2 Q.B. 507, at p. 514. Elsewhere he seems to conceive of the role of equity as merely supplementary.

[166] *Ante*, p. 324.

[167] *Ante*, p. 327.

[168] s. 25(11), now the Supreme Court Act 1981, s. 49.

[169] *Grist* v. *Bailey* [1967] Ch. 532; *Associated Japanese Bank (International) Ltd.* v. *Crédit du Nord S.A.* [1989] 1 W.L.R. 255, at p. 270; *William Sindall plc* v. *Cambridgeshire C.C.* [1994] 1 W.L.R. 1016, at p. 1039.

further relief in equity which may have been asked for by the parties. The mere fact that the contract is good at common law does not preclude rescission in equity on similar grounds[170] or other equitable relief.

(b) REFUSAL OF SPECIFIC PERFORMANCE

In the case of breaches of contracts for the sale or transfer of property, the common law remedy is damages but equity would compel the transfer of the property involved by means of an order for specific performance. If, however, one of the parties contracted under a mistake which would render it inequitable for the other to enforce the contract, this would afford a good defence to an action for specific performance of the contract. In *Webster* v. *Cecil*:[171]

C offered to sell W several plots of land. Immediately after he had despatched the offer he discovered that, by a mistake in adding up the prices of the plots, he had offered his land for sale at £1,250 instead of the £2,250 which he had intended. He informed W of the mistake without delay, but not before W had accepted the offer. W must have been taken to have known of the mistake as C had previously refused an offer of £2,000. W now sought specific performance of the contract.

This was refused. W was left to such action at law as might be available.[172]

Specific performance is a discretionary remedy[173] and the Court will not order it where it would cause undue hardship in the circumstances of the case. Mistake of a type which is insufficient to render the contract void at law may thus be a ground for resisting specific performance, as it would be harsh to enforce performance of a contract against one who has entered into it under a mistake. In *Malins* v. *Freeman*[174] where a purchaser bid for and bought one lot of land at an auction in the belief that he was buying a wholly different lot, the Court refused to order specific performance of the contract. The defendant's mistake was due to his own carelessness and to no fault of the plaintiff, but the Court was prepared to exercise its discretion in his favour, leaving the plaintiff to claim damages at law. On the other hand, in *Tamplin* v. *James*,[175] the defendant bid for and bought an inn and outbuildings in the mistaken belief that the lot also included two pieces of garden attached thereto. There was little excuse for this misapprehension as the plans of the property to be sold were exhibited at the sale. The Court made an order for specific performance of the agreement.

---

[170] *Munro (Robert A.) & Co. Ltd.* v. *Meyer* [1930] 2 K.B. 312, at pp. 333–5; *Frederick E. Rose (London) Ltd.* v. *William H. Pim Jnr. & Co. Ltd.* [1953] 2 Q.B. 450, at p. 460; *Oscar Chess Ltd.* v. *Williams* [1957] 1 W.L.R. 370, at p. 373.

[171] (1861) 30 Beav. 62. See also *Wood* v. *Scarth* (1855) 2 K. & J. 33.

[172] In fact there would be no action for the contract would be void: see *Hartog* v. *Colin and Shields* [1939] 3 All E.R. 566; *ante*, p. 325.

[173] See *post*, p. 634ff.

[174] (1837) 2 Keen 25. See also *Baskcomb* v. *Beckwith* (1869) L.R. 8 Eq. 100; *Denny* v. *Hancock* (1870) L.R. 6 Ch. App. 1; *Burrow* v. *Scammell* (1881) 19 Ch. D. 175, at p. 182.

[175] (1880) 15 Ch.D. 215.

(c) RECTIFICATION OF WRITTEN CONTRACTS

(i) Mutual mistake

Where a contract has been reduced to writing, or a deed executed, and the writing or deed, owing to mutual mistake, fails to express the concurrent intentions of the parties at the time of its execution, the Court will rectify the document in accordance with their true intent.

In *Craddock Brothers* v. *Hunt*,[176] for example:

A vendor agreed orally to sell to a purchaser a certain piece of property. By a mistake, the written contract embodying this agreement included an adjoining yard which the parties had excluded from the sale and the subsequent conveyance actually conveyed this land to the purchaser.

The Court ordered that the conveyance should be rectified to bring it into line with the parties' oral agreement.

Before the remedy of rectification is made available the following conditions must be satisfied.

(a) Full and final agreement. The document which it is sought to rectify must fail to express the common intentions and common outward accord of the parties. Such accord cannot be shown where there is confusion as to what has been agreed[177] or where a matter is omitted from a document as a result of forgetfulness; an absence of intention does not suffice.[178] The accord does not, however, as some cases suggested, have to amount to a complete concluded contract.[179] It is now clearly established that there is jurisdiction to rectify where the parties have made a mistake in their attempt to embody in the document their concurrent intentions existing at the time it was put into writing or executed.[180] A concluded contract need not be shown.

(b) Clear evidence of mistake. The party seeking to have a document rectified must adduce convincing evidence that its terms do not accurately record the common intention of the parties at the time.[181] Unless the court is sure of the mistake and of the existence of a prior agreement, '[c]ertainty and ready enforceability would be hindered by constant attempts to cloud the issue by reference to pre-contractual negotiations'.[182] Parol evidence is, however, admissible even where the contract is one which is required to be in writing.[183]

---

[176] [1923] 2 Ch. 136. See also *U.S.A.* v. *Motor Trucks Ltd.* [1924] A.C. 196, at p. 200.

[177] *Cambro Contractors Ltd.* v. *John Kennelly Sales Ltd.*, The Times, 14 April 1994 (C.A.).

[178] *Olympia Sanna Shipping Co. S.A.* v. *Shinwa Kaiun Kaisha* [1985] 2 Lloyd's Rep. 364, at p. 370; *Kemp* v. *Neptune Concrete* (1989) 57 P & C.R. 369, at pp. 377, 379–80.

[179] *Mackenzie* v. *Coulson* (1869) L.R. 8 Eq. 368, at p. 375; *Faraday* v. *Tamworth Union* (1916) 86 L.J. Ch. 436, at p. 438; *Higgins (W.) Ltd.* v. *Northampton Cpn.* [1927] 1 Ch. 128, at p. 136; *U.S.A.* v. *Motor Trucks Ltd.* [1924] A.C. 196, at p. 200.

[180] *Shipley U.D.C.* v. *Bradford Cpn.* [1936] Ch. 375; *Crane* v. *Hegemann-Harris Co., Inc.* [1939] 1 All E.R. 662, aff'd [1939] 4 All E.R. 68; *Joscelyne* v. *Nissen* [1970] 2 Q.B. 86. See also Bromley (1971) 87 L.Q.R. 532.

[181] *Joscelyne* v. *Nissen* (*supra*, n. 180), at p. 98; *Luk Leamington Ltd.* v. *Whitnash plc* [2002] 1 Lloyd's Rep. 6.

[182] *Ets George et Paul Levy* v. *Adderley Nav. Co. Panama S.A.* [1980] 2 Lloyd's Rep. 67, at p. 73. See also *Thomas Bates & Son* v. *Wyndhams Ltd.* [1981] 1 W.L.R. 505. Cf. *Atlantic Marine Transport Corp.* v. *Coscol Petroleum Corp.* [1991] 1 Lloyd's Rep. 246, at p. 250.

[183] *Craddock Bros.* v. *Hunt* [1923] 2 Ch 136; *U.S.A.* v. *Motor Trucks Ltd.* [1924] A.C. 196.

(c) Continuing intention. Thirdly, the intention of the parties as expressed in the prior accord must have continued unchanged up to the time of the execution of the written instrument.[184]

(d) Literal disparity. Rescission is not an appropriate remedy where the mistake relates to the transaction itself rather than to the document which purports to record it. Accordingly, there must be a literal disparity between the terms of the agreement and the document. Proof of an inner misapprehension is insufficient. In *Frederick E. Rose (London) Ltd.* v. *William H. Pim Jnr. & Co. Ltd.*:[185]

Rose received from its Middle East associates an order for up to five hundred tons of 'Moroccan horsebeans described here as feveroles'. Rose did not know what feveroles were, and asked Pim. Pim replied that they were simply horsebeans, and so Rose orally contracted to buy from Pim a quantity of horsebeans to meet this order. A subsequent written agreement embodied the same terms. In fact, however, feveroles were quite another type of bean, and Rose claimed to have the written agreement rectified to read 'feveroles', intending to claim damages on the agreement if so rectified.

The Court of Appeal refused rectification. Both the oral and the written contracts were for horsebeans. There was no literal disparity between them. The only mistake was in the minds of the parties at the time. As Denning L.J. put it:[186]

Rectification is concerned with contracts and documents, not with intentions. In order to get rectification it is necessary to show that the parties were in complete agreement on the terms of their contract, but by an error wrote them down wrongly; and in this regard, in order to ascertain the terms of their contract, you do not look into the inner minds of the parties—into their intentions—any more than you do in the formation of any other contract.

It has, however, been held that, where the parties have expressly agreed what is the meaning of particular words used in a written contract, the contract can be rectified to make it clear that the words bear the meaning agreed.[187]

(ii) Unilateral mistake

The remedy of rectification was originally granted only in cases of mutual mistake, to correct the erroneous expression of the common intentions of *both* parties. But it has been extended to cases of unilateral mistake, where, due to a mistake of one party alone, the document fails to reflect that party's intentions at the time of its execution.[188] If, however, the mistake is unilateral, the knowledge or conduct of the party

[184] *Fowler* v. *Fowler* (1859) 4 De G. & J. 250.

[185] [1953] 2 Q.B. 450. See also *Agip S.p.A.* v. *Nav. Alta Italia S.p.A.* [1984] 1 Lloyd's Rep. 353, at p. 359; *Ets George et Paul Levy* v. *Adderley Nav. Co. Panama S.A.* [1980] 1 Lloyd's Rep. 67, at p. 72.

[186] At p. 461.

[187] *London Weekend Television Ltd.* v. *Paris & Griffith* (1969) 113 S.J. 222; *Joscelyne* v. *Nissen* [1970] 2 Q.B. 86, at p. 98; *Re Butlin's Settlement* [1976] Ch. 251; *Partenreederei M.S. Karen Oltmann* v. *Scarsdale Shipping Co. Ltd.* [1976] 2 Lloyd's Rep. 708.

[188] *Roberts & Co. Ltd.* v. *Leicestershire C.C.* [1961] Ch. 555; *Riverlate Properties Ltd.* v. *Paul* [1975] Ch. 133, at p. 140; *Thomas Bates & Son Ltd.* v. *Wyndham's (Lingerie) Ltd.* [1981] 1 W.L.R. 505.

who was not mistaken must be such as to make it inequitable for that party to object to rectification.

The Court will not order rectification unless three conditions are satisfied.[189] First, the other party must have actual knowledge of the mistaken party's intentions and of the mistake.[190] In this context the knowledge of an agent will not suffice[191] but a party who has wilfully shut its eyes to the obvious or wilfully and recklessly failed to make such inquiries as an honest and reasonable person would have made will be taken to have actual knowledge.[192] Secondly, the party not under a mistake must have failed to draw the mistaken party's attention to the mistake. Thirdly, the mistake must be such that the party not under a mistake would derive a benefit,[193] or the mistaken party would suffer a detriment,[194] if the inaccuracy in the document were to remain uncorrected. Previously there was some authority for the view that the conduct of the party who was not mistaken had to amount to fraud,[195] or at least involve a degree of sharp practice on his part;[196] but this is no longer required.[197] Nevertheless, it is clear that if a party executes a document in ignorance that the other party is under a mistake, the remedy of rectification will be denied.[198]

(b) RESCISSION

We have already seen that a party to a contract may obtain the right to rescind the contract where he has been induced to enter into it by a material misrepresentation,[199] or by fraud, whether actual or constructive,[200] or by non-disclosure of a material fact where the transaction is one which is *uberrimae fidei*.[201]

(i) Mutual mistake

Rescission is also available in certain circumstances where both parties have contracted under a *mutual* mistake. Thus in *Laurence* v. *Lexcourt Holdings Ltd.*,[202] tenants of office premises obtained an order that the lease of the premises to them should be rescinded on the ground that, at the time of the letting, both parties to the lease had assumed that there was planning permission for the whole of the premises to be used as offices, whereas the permission related to part only of the premises.

---

[189] *Thomas Bates and Son Ltd.* v. *Wyndham's (Lingerie) Ltd.* (*supra*, n. 188), at pp. 515–16, 520–1.

[190] *Riverlate Properties Ltd.* v. *Paul* [1975] Ch. 133, at p. 140.

[191] *Kemp* v. *Neptune Concrete* (1989) 57 P. & C.R. 369.

[192] *Commission for the New Towns* v. *Cooper (G.B.) Ltd.* [1995] Ch. 259.

[193] *Thomas Bates and Son Ltd.* v *Wyndham's (Lingerie) Ltd.* (*supra* n. 188), at p. 516.

[194] *Ibid.*, at p. 521.

[195] *May* v. *Platt* [1900] 1 Ch. 616, at p. 623.

[196] *Riverlate Properties Ltd.* v. *Paul* (*supra*, n. 190), at p. 140.

[197] *Thomas Bates and Son Ltd.* v. *Wyndham's (Lingerie) Ltd.* (*supra*, n. 188).

[198] *Riverlate Properties Ltd.* v. *Paul* (*supra*, n. 188); *Agip s.p.A* v. *Nav. Alta Italia s.p.A.* [1984] 1 Lloyd's Rep. 353, at p. 362.

[199] *Ante*, p. 251.

[200] *Ante*, pp. 245, 267.

[201] *Ante*, p. 264.

[202] [1978] 1 W.L.R. 1128, following *Solle* v. *Butcher* [1950] 1 K.B. 671, *post*, p. 342 but cf. *William Sindall plc* v. *Cambridgeshire C.C.* [1994] 1 W.L.R. 1016, at p. 1035.

Earlier authority for the proposition that a contract may be rescinded for mutual mistake is provided by *Huddersfield Banking Co., Ltd.* v. *Henry Lister & Son, Ltd.*:[203]

A company went into liquidation. In the company's factory were 33 looms. If these were attached to the realty, they would be fixtures and belong to the plaintiff bank as mortgagees; if not, they would pass to the Official Receiver and be sold for the benefit of the company's creditors. Representatives of the bank and the Receiver inspected the factory and found that they were not attached. In reliance upon this assumption, the bank concurred in a consent order for their sale. It later appeared that the looms had been wrongfully loosened. The bank successfully sought to have the consent order set aside.

Kay L.J. said:[204]

It seems to me that, both on principle and on authority, when once the Court finds that an agreement has been come to between parties who were under a common mistake of a material fact, the Court may set it aside, and the Court has ample jurisdiction to set aside the order founded upon that agreement.

Similarly in *Allcard* v. *Walker*,[205] an order consenting to the variation of a post-nuptial marriage settlement was rescinded, the parties having erroneously assumed the settlement to be valid.

In *Solle* v. *Butcher*,[206] noted above, these and other cases were used by Denning L.J. as the basis of a new and general doctrine of mistake in equity. Despite criticism[207] it has been followed,[208] has stood for over 50 years, and is now regarded as good law and 'on occasion the passport to a just result'.[209]

In *Solle* v. *Butcher* the parties contracted under a mutual mistake of fact that a flat leased to S was a 'new' dwelling-house for the purpose of the Rent Restriction Acts and so could be let at a rent of £250 per year instead of the £140 which might lawfully be demanded. To an action by S to recover the rent overpaid, B pleaded that the lease should be rescinded on the ground of mistake. The Court ordered the rescission of the lease but on the terms (*inter alia*) that S should be permitted to elect whether to accept the rescission or to claim a new lease at the full agreed rent of £250 per year. The judgment of Denning L.J. contains a statement of the circumstances in which the Court will intervene:[210]

Let me next consider mistakes which render a contract voidable, that is, liable to be set aside on some equitable ground. Whilst presupposing that a contract was good at law, or at any

---

[203] [1895] 2 Ch. 273. See also *Wilding* v. *Sanderson* [1897] 2 Ch. 534.

[204] At p. 284. See also Vaughan Williams J. at p. 276. Cf. Lindley L.J. at p. 281.

[205] [1896] 2 Ch. D. 369.

[206] [1950] 1 K.B. 671, *ante*, p. 318.

[207] Goodhart (1950) 66 L.Q.R. 169; Slade (1954) 70 L.Q.R. 385, at p. 407; Atiyah and Bennion (1961) 24 M.L.R. 421 at pp. 440–1; Cartwright (1987) 103 L.Q.R. 594.

[208] *Grist* v. *Bailey* [1967] Ch. 532; *Laurence* v. *Lexcourt Holdings Ltd.* [1978] 1 W.L.R. 1128; *West Sussex Properties Ltd.* v. *Chichester D.C.* [2000] N.P.C. 74.

[209] *West Sussex Properties Ltd.* v. *Chichester D.C.* [2000] N.P.C. 74, *per* Sir Christopher Staughton, at para. 42.

[210] At p. 692.

rate not void, the court of equity would often relieve a party from the consequence of his own mistake, so long as it could do so without injustice to third parties. The court, it was said, had power to set aside the contract whenever it was of opinion that it was unconscientious for the other party to avail himself of the legal advantage which he had obtained: *Torrance* v. *Bolton per* James L.J.[211]

The court had, of course, to define what is considered to be unconscientious, but in this respect equity has shown a progressive development. It is now clear that a contract will be set aside if the mistake of the one party has been induced by a material misrepresentation of the other, even though it was not fraudulent or fundamental; or if one party, knowing that the other is mistaken about the terms of an offer, or the identity of the person by whom it is made, lets him remain under his delusion and concludes a contract on the mistaken terms instead of pointing out the mistake . . .

A contract is also liable in equity to be set aside if the parties were under a common misapprehension either as to facts or as to their relative and respective rights, provided that the misapprehension was fundamental, and that the party seeking to set it aside was not himself at fault.

In cases of mutual mistake Denning L.J. stated that three requirements must be satisfied before the Court will grant relief.

(a) Fundamental mistake. If the mistake is mutual, then in some sense it must be 'fundamental' or 'material' before the Court will intervene. It has been said that 'equity can have regard to a wider and perhaps unlimited category of "fundamental" mistake'.[212] Despite this requirement of 'fundamentality', the fact that the contract in *Solle* v. *Butcher* was rescinded shows that the category of operative mutual mistake is broader in equity than at common law. Rescission has also been ordered where there is a mistake as to the value of the subject matter of the contract.[213] The difference is also shown by *Magee* v. *Pennine Insurance Co. Ltd.*,[214] where the contrast with the common law position as laid down in *Bell* v. *Lever Brothers Ltd.* is highlighted by the similarity of the fact situation. Both concerned a contract made under a mistake as to the status of an earlier contract. In *Magee*'s case the later contract was a compromise of a claim made under the earlier contract, an insurance policy, which in fact was voidable for misrepresentation. The contract of compromise was set aside, Winn L.J. dissenting on the ground that the case was indistinguishable from *Bell* v. *Lever Brothers Ltd.*[215]

(b) Inequitable to rely on contract. The circumstances of the case must be such that it would be inequitable for the party seeking to uphold the contract to rely on his

---

[211] (1872) L.R. 8 Ch. App. 118, at p. 124, *post*, p. 346.

[212] *William Sindall plc.* v. *Cambridgeshire C.C.* [1994] 1 W.L.R. 1016, *per* Evans L.J. at p. 1042. See also *Associated Japanese Bank (International) Ltd.* v. *Crédit du Nord S.A.* [1989] 1 W.L.R. 255, at p. 270.

[213] *Grist* v. *Bailey* [1967] Ch. 532, at p. 541, *post*, p. 344. See also *West Sussex Properties Ltd.* v. *Chichester D.C.* [2000] N.P.C. 74.

[214] [1969] 2 Q.B. 507.

[215] There is doubt as to the ground of the decision. Lord Denning M.R. held the compromise was valid at law but voidable in equity. Fenton Atkinson L.J. agreed with Lord Denning but also (at p. 517) appeared to apply the proposition, based on *Bell* v. *Lever Brothers Ltd.*, that a contract is void when consensus is reached on a particular assumption which is not true.

strict rights at common law. Here, however, and, as we shall see, unlike the case of unilateral mistake, the inequity does not appear to flow from the defendant's conduct.

(c) No fault. Thirdly, the party seeking to set the contract aside must not himself have been at fault.[216] For there to be 'fault' there must be some degree of blameworthiness beyond the mere fact that the mistake has been made but there has been little guidance as to how much. *Solle* v. *Butcher* is consistent with a concept of relative fault since although B, the lessor, was seeking to have the lease rescinded, it was S, the lessee, but also B's agent for letting, who formed the opinion that the flat was not rent-controlled and advised B accordingly.[217] As between the two parties it seems that B was less responsible for the mistake.[218] *Grist* v. *Bailey*,[219] however, suggests that there must be some personal fault to preclude the rescission of the contract.

B contracted to sell to G a freehold house for £850, 'subject to the existing tenancy thereof'. The value of the house with vacant possession was £2,250. Both parties believed the house was occupied by a protected tenant but this was not the case. The person in possession had only a doubtful claim to be a protected tenant and subsequently left the house without making a claim.

It was held that B was not at fault since, although a vendor should generally know who her tenants are, this was a case of a long-standing and informal tenancy. Rescission was ordered on the condition that B entered into a new contract at the proper vacant possession price.[220] Again in, *Laurence* v. *Lexcourt Holdings Ltd.*[221] the defendant's omission to make the searches and inquiries of the local authority which were usually done in a lease of land did not constitute fault.

The combination of a concept of inequity which does not depend on a party's conduct at the time of contracting and a narrow approach to fault means that the scope of equitable relief is potentially very wide and difficult to operate in a principled way. The approach of the Courts to rescission, in cases such as *Grist* v. *Bailey* and *Laurence* v. *Lexcourt Holdings Ltd.*, is also open to the criticism that insufficient attention was paid to the question of contractual allocation of risk.[222] It is arguable that, as in the case of common law, an express or implied allocation of a particular risk should generally preclude the rescission of the contract for mistake.

(d) Setting aside on terms. Rescission is a discretionary remedy, and, in the exercise of its discretion, the Court has power in equity to attach to the rescission such terms as justice may require in order to effect a *restitutio in integrum*. This was done in *Cooper*

---

[216] See *Grist* v. *Bailey* [1967] Ch. 532, at p. 542.

[217] [1950] 1 K.B. 671, at pp. 684, 694. See also *Laurence* v. *Lexcourt Holdings Ltd.* [1978] 1 W.L.R. 1128, at pp. 1137–8.

[218] Denning L.J. considered (at p. 695) that the lease was induced by an innocent misrepresentation by the plaintiff, but did not decide the case on this ground.

[219] [1967] Ch. 532.

[220] At p. 543.

[221] [1978] 1 W.L.R. 1128, *ante*, p. 341.

[222] *William Sindall plc.* v. *Cambridgeshire C.C.* [1994] 1 W.L.R. 1016, *per* Hoffmann L.J. at p. 1035. See also *Associated Japanese Bank (International) Ltd.* v. *Crédit du Nord S.A.* [1989] 1 W.L.R. 255.

v. *Phibbs*,[223] a case in which the House of Lords set aside a contract on the ground of a mistake shared by both parties:

C agreed with P to take a lease of a salmon fishery which both parties believed to be P's property. It was later discovered that the fishery belonged to C as tenant in tail. C filed a petition asking for cancellation of the agreement and for such further relief as 'the nature of the case might admit of, and as to the Court might seem fit'.

Lord Westbury said:[224]

If parties contract under a mutual mistake and misapprehension as to their relative and respective rights, the result is, that that agreement is liable to be set aside as having proceeded upon a common mistake.

But in granting rescission of the contract, the House of Lords ordered that P should have a lien on the fishery for the money which they had spent on improving the property in the belief that it was theirs. Without this lien C would have been unjustly enriched by P's mistaken expenditure.[225]

In *Cooper* v. *Phibbs* the terms had the effect of unwinding the contract and restoring the *status quo ante* but this is not always the effect of such terms. Thus, in *Solle* v. *Butcher*, B was permitted to rescind but S was given the option of accepting this or claiming a new lease at the higher rent. The effect of this option, if taken up, would be to give effect to the expectation of the parties at the time of the original lease: there was no subversion of the bargain they thought they had made. On the other hand, in *Grist* v. *Bailey*, the terms, which as we have noted, gave the purchaser the option of a new contract at the vacant possession price, may have operated to reverse the risks of the original contract. Where payments have been made under an agreement later rescinded on the ground of mistake, the person who made the payments may be entitled to restitution of the payments, subject to any defence of change of position. While the Court has power to impose terms to exclude the recovery of any such payments, it is unlikely to be willing to do so where the payee cannot establish that it has changed its position as a result of the payment so as to make it inequitable for repayment to be ordered.[226]

(ii) Unilateral mistake

Where the mistake is *unilateral*, that is to say, where only the party seeking to have the contract set aside was under a mistake, although it has not been stated that the mistake must be 'fundamental', the cases in which relief has been given have involved mistakes as to the subject matter of the contract or its terms. A mistake as to the effect

---

[223] (1867) L.R. 2 H.L. 149. See also *Bingham* v. *Bingham* (1748) 1 Ves. Sen. 126; *Beauchamp (Earl)* v. *Winn* (1873) L.R. 6 H.L. 223.

[224] At p. 170 he dismissed any misrepresentation as immaterial.

[225] Cf. *Magee* v. *Pennine Insurance Co. Ltd.* [1969] 2 Q.B. 507, *ante*, p. 343, where no terms were imposed on the rescission of the compromise agreement even though this left the insurance company with three years' premiums in respect of a policy for which they were not at risk. *Quaere* whether the premiums would have been recoverable as money paid for a consideration which had totally failed, *post.*, p. 643. Cf. Fletcher [1969] C.L.J. 181, at 182.

[226] *West Sussex Properties Ltd.* v. *Chichester D.C.* [2000] N.P.C. 74, *per* Morritt L.J. at paras. 34–5.

or the commercial consequences of the contract will not suffice.[227] Apart from this the knowledge and conduct of the party who is not mistaken is important although there is some doubt as to precisely what is required. On one view, there must be fraud or misrepresentation on the part of the other party before rescission is available.[228] On another, somewhat wider, view, which, as we have seen, formed the basis of the decision in *Solle* v. *Butcher*,[229] it is sufficient if the other party is guilty of some conduct which would render it inequitable to insist that the contract be performed. In *Torrance* v. *Bolton*:[230]

Property was put up for sale by auction, having been advertised as an 'absolute freehold reversion'. But the conditions of sale, which were read out by the auctioneer, disclosed that it was encumbered by three mortgages. T, who was deaf, did not hear this announcement, and bid on the assumption that he was buying something more substantial than a mere equity of redemption. The property was knocked down to him.

The agreement was set aside. The misleading advertisement cast upon the seller the duty of showing that T had not been misled, and it was clear from T's conduct that he did not know what he was buying. Although, in view of the advertisement, the case can be seen as one of misrepresentation,[231] James L.J. stated that rescission was available in any case 'in which the Court is of the opinion that it is unconscientious for a person to avail himself of the legal advantage which he has obtained'.[232]

The importance of the requirement of unconscionability is shown by *Riverlate Properties Ltd.* v. *Paul*.[233] The Court of Appeal held that there was no power to grant equitable relief on the grounds of mere unilateral mistake unless the party against whom relief is sought was aware, at the time of the transaction, that the other party was contracting under a mistake. Russell L.J. stated:[234]

If a man may be said to be fortunate in obtaining a property at a bargain price, or on terms that make it a good bargain, because the other party unknown to him has made a miscalculation or other mistake, some high-minded men might consider it appropriate that he should agree to a fresh bargain to cure the miscalculation or mistake, abandoning his good fortune. But if equity were to enforce the views of those high-minded men, we have no doubt that it would run counter to the attitudes of much the greater part of ordinary mankind (not least the world of commerce), and would be venturing on the field of moral philosophy.

In the light of this decision, older cases which seem to decide that in cases of unilateral mistake in written contracts equity might give the defendant the option of accepting rectification or having the contract rescinded should perhaps be explained on the

---

[227] *Clarion Ltd.* v. *National Provident Institution* [2000] 1 W.L.R. 1888, at pp. 1898–9.

[228] *May* v. *Platt* [1900] 1 Ch. 616, *per* Farwell J. at p. 623; *London Borough of Redbridge* v. *Robinson Rentals* (1969) 211 E.G. 1125; *Riverlate Properties Ltd.* v. *Paul* [1975] Ch. 133.

[229] [1950] 1 K.B. 671, *ante*, pp. 342–3.

[230] (1872) L.R. Ch. App. 118.

[231] *Clarion Ltd.* v. *National Provident Institution* [2000] 1 W.L.R. 1888, at p. 1900.

[232] At p. 124.

[233] [1975] Ch. 133. See also *Taylor* v. *Johnson* (1983) 151 C.L.R. 422 (High Court of Australia).

[234] At p. 141. See also *William Sindall plc* v. *Cambridgeshire C.C.* [1994] 1 W.L.R. 1016, at p. 1035.

ground that on their facts there was knowledge of the mistake of the other party.[235]
Even where there is such knowledge, the appropriate remedy, in the opinion of the
Court of Appeal, is rectification alone.

[235] *Garrard* v. *Frankel* (1862) 30 Beav. 445 (defendant taken to know of mistake); *Paget* v. *Marshall* (1884)
28 Ch. D. 255 (Bacon V.-C. inclined to the opinion that defendant probably knew of the mistake but hesitated
to find him guilty of fraud). See also *Harris* v. *Pepperell* (1867) L.R. 5 Eq. 1; *Bloomer* v. *Spittle* (1872) L.R. 13
Eq. 427 (mutual mistake).

9

ILLEGALITY

I. INTRODUCTION

Public policy imposes certain limitations upon the freedom of persons to contract. An ostensibly valid contract may be tainted by illegality.[1] The source of the illegality may arise by statute or by virtue of the principles of common law. In some instances the law prohibits the agreement itself, and the contract is then by its very nature illegal but in the majority of cases the illegality lies in the object which one or both parties have in mind or in the method of performance. As a general rule, although all the other requirements for the formation of an agreement are complied with, an agreement that is illegal in one of these ways will not be enforceable.

The subject of illegality is one of great complexity and the effects of illegality are by no means uniform. This is because the seriousness of the illegality varies. Illegal objects may range from those tainted with gross moral turpitude, e.g. murder, to those where the harm to be avoided is relatively small, e.g. breach of licensing requirements or cases in which a person commits an unlawful act in order to escape danger to his or her life.[2] It is not surprising, therefore, that there are differences in the attitude of the judges to those who have an illegal object in view or are parties to an illegal transaction. Attempts have been made to distinguish between 'illegal' contracts and those which are 'nugatory' or 'void'. In the former case, it is said that the law will refuse to aid in any way a person whose cause of action is founded upon such a contract; in the latter case, the law simply says that the contract is not to have legal effect. While some contracts can be classified in this way, it is both impracticable and impossible to apply this classification over the whole field of the subject. Moreover, confusion is created by the fact that the judges have on many occasions treated the terms as interchangeable. It seems better to use the single word 'illegality' to cover the multitude of instances where the law, for some reason of public policy or as a result of a statutory prohibition, denies to one or both of the parties the rights under the contract to which he or she would otherwise be entitled.

---

[1] This chapter is concerned with initial illegality and illegality in performance and not with supervening illegality which is dealt with in Chapter 14, Discharge by Frustration.

[2] *Howard* v. *Shirlstar Container Transport Ltd* [1990] 2 All E.R. 366.

II. STATUTORY ILLEGALITY

This section deals with general principles. The statutory control of anti-competitive agreements and gaming and wagering contracts are dealt with in sections IV and V below.

(a) THE EFFECT OF STATUTORY PROHIBITION

(i) Express prohibition: contract illegal

The nature and effects of statutory illegality may vary considerably. A statute may declare that a certain type of contract is expressly prohibited. There is then no doubt of the intention of the legislature that such a contract should not be enforced. 'What is done in contravention of the provisions of an Act of Parliament cannot be made the subject-matter of an action.'[3] Thus, in *Re Mahmoud and Ispahani*:[4]

A wartime statutory order prohibited the purchase or sale of linseed oil without a licence from the Food Controller. M held a licence to sell to other licensed dealers. I falsely assured him that he had a licence and M agreed to sell a quantity of linseed oil to I. I later refused to accept the oil on the ground that he had no licence. M brought an action for damages for non-acceptance.

The Court of Appeal rejected M's claim even though he was ignorant, at the time the contract was made, of the facts which brought it within the statutory prohibition. 'The Order', said Bankes L.J.,[5] 'is a clear and unequivocal declaration by the Legislature in the public interest that this particular kind of contract shall not be entered into'.

(ii) Implied prohibition: contract illegal

The position is the same where the contract is impliedly prohibited by statute. The statute is to be construed in the ordinary way. The Courts must determine whether the statutory words, construed in context including the purpose of the statute, prohibit and penalize only the prescribed conduct or whether they additionally prohibit the contract.[6] If, for example, the purpose of the statute is to protect the public from injury or fraud the inference is likely to be that contracts made in contravention of its provisions are prohibited.[7] Again,

if a contract has as its whole object the doing of the very act which the statute prohibits, it

---

[3] *Langton* v. *Hughes* (1813) 1 M. & S. 593, *per* Lord Ellenborough C.J. at 596.
[4] [1921] 2 K.B. 716. See also *Chai Sau Yin* v. *Liew Kwee Sam* [1962] A.C. 304; *Wilson, Smithett & Cope Ltd.* v. *Terruzzi* [1976] Q.B. 683; *Hughes* v. *Kingston upon Hull C.C.* [1999] 2 All E.R. 49.
[5] At p. 374.
[6] *St John Shipping Corporation* v. *Joseph Rank Ltd.* [1957] 1 Q.B. 267, at pp. 283, 287. See generally Buckley (1975) 38 M.L.R. 535.
[7] *Anderson* v. *Daniel* [1924] 1 K.B. 138.

can be argued that you can hardly make sense of a statute which forbids an act and yet permits to be made a contract to do it.[8]

But, in the absence of a clear implication, the following pages show that courts are cautious in construing a statute in this way in part because 'so much of commercial life is governed by regulations of some sort or another; which may easily be broken without wicked intent'.[9] Thus, the fact that the purpose of a statute is to limit the scope of companies' commercial activities does not mean that every contract entered into in a prohibited sphere should be invalidated.[10] The absence of a criminal sanction and the presence of a wide array of regulatory remedies indicate that such contracts are not prohibited.[11]

(iii) Contract unenforceable by one party

Frequently, a statute will in express terms or on its true construction render a contract unenforceable only by the party whose duty it is to observe the statutory requirement. In such a case, if that party contravenes the provisions of the statute, the contract will be unenforceable by him or her but may be enforced by the other party.[12]

(iv) Illegal performance

Statutory illegality may also arise in connection with the performance of a contract which is not in itself illegal. The method of performance adopted by one of the parties may violate some statutory prohibition, for example, the vendor of goods may deliver them to a purchaser without the required statutory invoice.[13] In such a situation the party in default will not be able to enforce any claim based on its own illegal performance. But since such a contract is lawful in its inception, notwithstanding that it has been performed in an unlawful manner, there is no reason why the other party, if *innocent*, should not be able to sue. The innocent party does not have to rely on the illegal performance in order to establish a cause of action. Thus in *Marles v. Philip Trant & Sons Ltd.*:[14]

P.T., a firm of seed merchants, bought a quantity of wheat described as 'spring wheat' from a third party. It sold this wheat to various farmers, including M, but the wheat was found not to be spring wheat and the crops failed. M claimed damages from P.T. for breach of warranty. P.T., as it was entitled to do, brought in the third party to the action, claiming from him an indemnity in respect of M's claim, and damages. The third party, however, raised the defence that P.T. had not, at the time of the sale, delivered to M certain particulars in writing

---

[8] *St John Shipping Corporation* v. *Joseph Rank Ltd.* [1957] 1 Q.B. 267, at p. 288; *Mohamed* v. *Alaga & Co.* [2000] 1 W.L.R. 1815, at p.1824.

[9] *Ibid.* See also *Shaw* v. *Groom* [1970] 2 Q.B. 504, at p. 522.

[10] *Fuji Finance Inc.* v. *Aetna Life Insurance Co. Ltd.* [1997] Ch. 173, at pp. 193–4.

[11] *Ibid.*

[12] *Cope* v. *Rowlands* (1836) 2 M. & W. 149; *Victorian Daylesford Syndicate Ltd.* v. *Dott* [1905] 2 Ch. 624; Consumer Credit Act 1974, s. 40; Sex Discrimination Act 1975, s. 77; Race Relations Act 1976, s. 72; Financial Services and Markets Act 2000, ss. 26, 27. See *Deutsche Ruckversicherung A.G.* v. *Walbrook Insurance Co. Ltd.* [1996] 1 All E.R. 791 on the similarly worded Financial Services Act 1986, s. 132.

[13] *Anderson Ltd.* v. *Daniel* [1924] 1 K.B. 138.

[14] [1954] 1 Q.B. 29. See also *Archbolds (Freightage) Ltd.* v. *Spanglett Ltd.* [1961] 1 Q.B. 374 (*post*, p. 399).

as required by section 1(1) of the Seeds Act 1920. He contended that he was not bound to indemnify P.T., as he could not be made liable on a contract which was illegal.

A majority of the Court of Appeal held that the contract between P.T. and M was not illegal from the beginning, but was only rendered illegal later by the method of performance which did not comply with the statutory requirements. M could recover damages for breach of warranty from P.T., since the warranty was given on the lawful stage of the agreement. The third party's contention that he was not liable to compensate P.T. in respect of its liability under this head therefore failed.[15]

On the other hand, if the other party participates in, or assents to the illegal performance, it will likewise be unable to sue. In *Ashmore, Benson, Pease & Co. Ltd.* v. *A. V. Dawson Ltd.*:[16]

The defendant, a road haulage company, contracted with A.B.P. to carry two 25-ton tube banks to a port. A.B.P.'s transport manager and his assistant watched the tube banks being loaded onto two lorries whose lawful maximum load was 20 tons. A.B.P. sued the defendant in respect of damage to one of the tubes when the lorry carrying it toppled over.

The Court of Appeal found that A.B.P.'s manager must have realized that the lorries were overloaded, and that he had participated in the defendants' illegal performance of the contract by sanctioning the loading of the two vehicles with a load in excess of the statutory maximum. A.B.P.'s claim therefore failed.

(v) Statute only imposes a penalty

Although the fact that a statutory offence has been committed in the course of performance of a contract may render the contract unenforceable, it will not necessarily have this effect. For the law to prescribe that the commission of any unlawful act in the course of performing a contract should inevitably deprive the wrongdoer of all contractual remedies might well inflict on the wrongdoer a loss far in excess of the statutory penalty. This would be unreasonable. For example, a road haulier might be unable to claim freight simply on the ground that the driver of the vehicle had exceeded the speed limit or the permitted driving hours or on the ground that the vehicle did not have the appropriate licence.[17] It is therefore necessary, in all cases of statutory illegality to have regard to the statutory language and to its scope and purpose. Was the statute intended to interfere with the contract under consideration, to render it unenforceable at the suit of a party who performs it illegally, or merely to impose a penalty on the offender?[18] Where the purpose of the statute is simply to impose a penalty, even the 'guilty' party can sue. Thus in *St. John Shipping Corporation* v. *Joseph Rank Ltd.*:[19]

[15] Singleton and Denning L.J. Hodson L.J. dissenting, stated the defendants 'cannot rely upon the breach of warranty by a third party to prove their damages when those damages are to be measured by reference to a contract illegally performed by them'.

[16] [1973] 1 W.L.R. 828.

[17] See the facts of *Archbolds (Freightage) Ltd.* v. *Spanglett Ltd.* [1961] 1 Q.B. 374, at pp. 385, 390, *post*, p. 399.

[18] *Hughes* v. *Asset Managers plc* [1995] 3 All E.R. 669, at pp. 673–4; *Nelson* v. *Nelson* (1995) 132 A.L.R. 133 (High Court of Australia) *post*, p. 411.

[19] [1957] 1 Q.B. 267. See also *Cope* v. *Rowlands* (1836) 2 M. & W. 149.

St. J, shipowners, contracted to carry a load of grain but overloaded the ship contrary to the Merchant Shipping (Safety and Loadline Conventions) Act 1932. The master was prosecuted and fined for this offence. J.R., the consignee of part of the cargo, withheld a proportion of the freight due, i.e. a sum equivalent to the freight on the excess cargo carried.

Devlin J. held that J.R. was not entitled to do so. The Act did not render unlawful the contract of carriage, but merely imposed a penalty in respect of its infringement. Similarly, a landlord who fails to provide a tenant with a proper rent-book is exposed to a criminal penalty, but is not precluded from recovering the rent.[20]

(vi) Void contracts

A statute may also declare a contract to be void, that is a nullity. Statutory provisions of this nature are numerous and are often (but by no means invariably)[21] connected with a failure to register the agreement[22] or to comply with certain requirements of form.[23] A party to such a contract cannot enforce it, but may be able to recover money or property transferred under it,[24] provided that this is not precluded by the express words of the statute[25] or by judicial interpretation.[26]

(vii) Contract not void or unenforceable

Finally, where a contract is not directly contrary to the provisions of a statute by reason of any express or implied prohibition or even where the statute expressly states that a breach of its prohibition does not render any contract void or unenforceable,[27] the Court may still refuse to enforce the contract because this could lead to the Court assisting in something illegal or because the contract is associated with or furthers an illegal purpose.[28] This, however, is a question of illegality at common law, which is considered in Part III of this chapter.[29]

III. ILLEGALITY AT COMMON LAW

There are a number of situations where the policy of the common law means that a contract cannot be enforced even though it is not expressly or impliedly prohibited by

---

[20] *Shaw* v. *Groom* [1970] 2 Q.B. 504.
[21] See, e.g. Marine Insurance Act 1906, s. 4(1); Sex Discrimination Act 1975, s. 77; Race Relations Act 1976, s. 72 (a *term* of contract that is unlawfully discriminatory is 'void', but is only unenforceable against the victim of the discrimination).
[22] Bills of Sale Act 1878, s. 10; Companies Act 1985, s. 395.
[23] Bills of Sale Act (1878) Amendment Act 1882, s. 9; Marine Insurance Act 1906, s. 22; see *ante*, p. 77.
[24] *North Central Wagon Finance Co. Ltd.* v. *Brailsford* [1962] 1 W.L.R. 1288.
[25] e.g. Gaming Act 1845, s. 18; *post*, p. 388.
[26] e.g. Life Assurance Act 1774, s. 1; *Harse* v. *Pearl Life Assurance Co.* [1904] 1 K.B. 558; see *post*, pp. 402–3.
[27] See, e.g. Trade Descriptions Act 1968, s. 35.
[28] See *Chase Manhattan Equities Ltd.* v. *Goodman* [1991] B.C.L.C. 897, at pp. 931–4, and *post*, p. 396; *Nelson* v. *Nelson* (1995) 132 A.L.R. 133, at pp. 143, 178 (High Court of Australia).
[29] *Post*.

statute. The origins of the concept of the policy of the law, or public policy, are ancient and obscure. By the begining of the nineteenth century the lack of definition and consequent uncertainty of the concept led to judicial statements against the extension of public policy which was described as 'a very unruly horse'.[30] The view was also expressed that it was not the function of the Courts to create new law, but to interpret and elucidate existing principles,[31] and that there was a public interest in upholding freedom of contract. The effect of the nineteenth century emphasis on freedom of contract was reluctance to interfere with a contract on the ground of public policy.[32] It is in reconciling this freedom of contract with other public interests that the difficulty arises.

By the second half of the twentieth century, however, the positive function of the Courts in matters of public policy was increasingly recognized. As Lord Denning M.R. has said: 'With a good man in the saddle, the unruly horse can be kept in control. It can jump over obstacles'.[33] Moreover, some flexibility is clearly desirable in matters of public policy which cannot remain immutable.[34] Certain aspects of public policy are more susceptible to change than others, though the policy of the law has, on some subjects, been worked into a set of tolerably definite rules. The principles applicable to agreements in restraint of trade, for example, have on a number of occasions been modified or extended to accord with prevailing economic conditions,[35] and this process still continues.[36] So too the principles applicable to transactions between cohabiting couples have been modified to accord with prevailing social conditions,[37] as have those concerning the financing of litigation.[38] For the rest, the application of canons of public policy to particular instances necessarily varies with the progressive development of public opinion and morality, but like any other branch of the common law is governed by the judicial use of precedents.[39]

Contracts which the Courts will not enforce because they are contrary to public policy may be arranged under certain heads.

(a) AGREEMENTS TO COMMIT A CRIME OR CIVIL WRONG, OR TO PERPETRATE A FRAUD

(i) Agreements to commit a crime

The Courts will not enforce an agreement which has as its object the deliberate

[30] *Richardson* v. *Mellish* (1824) 2 Bing. 229, *per* Burrough J. at p. 252.
[31] *Re Mirams* [1891] 1 Q.B. 594, at p. 595; *Mogul Steamship Co.* v. *McGregor, Gow & Co.* [1892] A.C. 25, at p. 45.
[32] *Ante*, p. 4, and see especially *Printing and Numerical Registering Co.* v. *Sampson* (1875) L.R. 19 Eq. 462, *per* Jessel M.R. at p. 465.
[33] *Enderby Town F.C. Ltd.* v. *The Football Association Ltd.* [1971] Ch. 591, at p. 606.
[34] *Nagle* v. *Feilden* [1966] 2 Q.B. 633, *per* Danckwerts L.J. at p. 650.
[35] See *post*, p. 367.
[36] See *post*, pp. 367, 381.
[37] *Post*, p. 362.
[38] *Thai Trading Co.* v. *Taylor* [1998] Q.B. 781.
[39] *Legal Essays and Addresses*, iii. 76, 78.

commission of a criminal offence (whether by statute or at common law),[40] although the fact that an offence is committed in the course of an otherwise legal agreement will not necessarily render the contract unlawful.[41]

(ii) Agreement to commit a civil wrong or fraud

The Courts will not enforce an agreement to commit a tort. An agreement to commit an assault has therefore been held to be void, as in *Allen* v. *Rescous*,[42] where one of the parties undertook to beat up someone. So too, has an agreement involving the publication of a libel,[43] or deceit,[44] or the perpetration of a fraud.[45] In *Mallalieu* v. *Hodgson*[46] a secret agreement by which a debtor agreed to pay M part of his debt in full, when the debtor had agreed to pay all his other creditors was held to be a fraud on the other creditors, each of whom had promised to forgo a portion of his debt in consideration that the others would forgo a similar proportion of their debts. The agreement to prefer one creditor was unenforceable.[47] Similarly, an agreement by the promoters of a company to defraud prospective shareholders,[48] or to rig the market for shares,[49] has been held to be fraudulent and unenforceable.

(iii) Agreements to defraud the revenue

One of the most common types of illegal agreement is one to defraud the revenue, whether that of the central or local government. In *Alexander* v. *Rayson*:[50]

A let a flat in Piccadilly to R at a rent of £1,200 a year. The transaction was effected by two documents: (1) a lease of the flat at a rent of £450 p.a., covering certain services to be rendered by the lessor A, and (2) an agreement to render services (which were substantially the same) in consideration of an extra £750 p.a. A dispute having arisen, R declined to pay an instalment due under the agreement. When sued by A, R pleaded that the object of the two documents was that only the lease was to be disclosed to the local authority in order to deceive them as to the true rateable value of the premises.

The Court of Appeal held that, if the documents were to be used for this fraudulent purpose, A was not entitled to the assistance of the law in enforcing either the lease or the agreement.

---

[40] See, e.g. *Levy* v. *Yates* (1838) 8 A. & E. 129; *Bigos* v. *Bousted* [1951] 1 All E.R. 92 (*post*, p. 405); *Tinsley* v. *Milligan* [1994] 1 A.C. 340.

[41] See *ante*, p. 351.

[42] (1677) 2 Lev. 174.

[43] *Clay* v. *Yates* (1856) 1 H. & N. 73.

[44] *Brown Jenkinson & Co. Ltd.* v. *Percy Dalton (London) Ltd.* [1957] 2 Q.B. 621.

[45] *Willis* v. *Baldwin* (1780) 2 Doug. K.B. 450.

[46] (1851) 16 Q.B. 689.

[47] *Ibid., per* Erle J. at p. 711 ('altogether void'). See also Insolvency Act 1986, ss. 339–40.

[48] *Begbie* v. *Phosphate Sewage Co. Ltd.* (1876) 1 Q.B.D. 679.

[49] *Scott* v. *Brown, Doering, McNab & Co.* [1892] 2 Q.B. 724.

[50] [1936] 1 K.B. 169; see also *Miller* v. *Karlinski* (1945) 62 T.L.R. 85; *Napier* v. *National Business Agency Ltd.* [1951] 2 All E.R. 264; *Corby* v. *Morrison* [1980] I.R.L.R. 218; *Tinsley* v. *Milligan* [1994] 1 A.C. 340, *post*, p. 410 (social security authorities).

(iv) Contracts of indemnity

A contract of indemnity which would enable persons to commit crimes or torts with
impunity is enforceable. Although it has been held that a motorist may recover under
a policy of insurance against third party risks even if the motorist's own gross or
criminal negligence caused the loss,[51] an assured cannot claim indemnity against the
consequences of an intentional wrongful act.[52] In *Geismar* v. *Sun Alliance and London
Insurance Ltd.*,[53] for example:

G had brought into the United Kingdom certain jewellery which he failed to declare to
the customs and on which he failed to pay customs duty. He claimed indemnity
from the defendant insurers for the loss through theft at his home of the uncustomed
jewellery.

It was held that G could not enforce the contract of indemnity. And shipowners, who
had been promised an indemnity by a shipper of cargo if they would issue false bills of
lading, were unable to enforce the promise as it was one to indemnify them against the
consequences of the tort of deceit.[54]

(b) AGREEMENTS WHICH INJURE THE STATE IN ITS RELATIONS WITH OTHER STATES

(i) Contracts with an alien enemy

Contracts with alien enemies are illegal in time of war and it is unlawful to enter into
or to perform such a contract even one made before war broke out.[55] Further, a
contract which expressly provides for the suspension of all rights and obligations
arising under it during a war may yet be held to be void on grounds of public policy as
tending, merely by its continued existence, to promote the economic interests of the
enemy state or to prejudice those of the United Kingdom.[56]

(ii) Contracts hostile to a friendly state

An agreement which contemplates action hostile to a friendly foreign government
cannot be enforced.[57] It is also contrary to public policy to allow the enforcement in
English Courts of agreements to be performed in a foreign state in breach of the laws

---

[51] *Tinline* v. *White Cross Insurance Co. Ltd.* [1921] 3 K.B. 327. See also *Hardy* v. *Motor Insurers' Bureau*
[1964] 2 Q.B. 745; *Cooke* v. *Routledge* [1998] N.I.L.R. 174.

[52] *Gray* v. *Barr* [1971] 2 Q.B. 554; *R.* v. *Chief National Insurance Commissioner* [1981] Q.B. 758 (but see
now the Forfeiture Act 1982, s. 4) (intentional manslaughter); *Lancashire C.C.* v. *Municipal Mutual Insurance
Ltd.*, [1997] Q.B. 743 (exemplary damages). See also *W. H. Smith & Son* v. *Clinton* (1908) 25 T.L.R. 34
(intentional libel).

[53] [1978] Q.B. 383.

[54] *Brown Jenkinson & Co. Ltd.* v. *Percy Dalton (London) Ltd.* [1957] 2 Q.B. 621. See also *Haseldine* v. *Hosken*
[1933] 1 K.B. 822.

[55] *Potts* v. *Bell* (1800) 8 Term. R. 548; *Kuenigl* v. *Donnersmarck* [1955] 1 Q.B. 515; Trading with the Enemy
Act 1939. For the contractual incapacity of an alien enemy, see *Porter* v. *Freudenberg* [1915] 1 K.B. 857.

[56] *Ertel Bieber & Co.* v. *Rio Tinto Co.* [1918] A.C. 260.

[57] *De Wütz* v. *Hendricks* (1824) 2 Bing. 314, at p. 316.

of that state. 'This country', it has been said,[58] 'should not assist or sanction the breach of the laws of other independent states'. Thus the Court of Appeal has refused to entertain an action arising out of certain transactions which had for their object the importation of whisky contrary to the prohibition laws of the United States of America.[59]

This does not, however, mean that the Court must necessarily refuse to enforce a contract merely because its performance will involve a foreign defendant in a breach of its own law.[60] A foreign law that is repugnant to English conceptions of liberty or freedom of action will not be enforced here. Examples of such laws include those involving persecution of such a character that its breach would be regarded as meritorious[61] or imposing a contractual incapacity which is foreign to the ideas of English law.[62] Although the same principle has been said to apply to the penal, political, or revenue laws of other countries,[63] this formulation is too wide; the Court is not prepared to disregard them altogether.[64] And if two people knowingly contract to *break* such a law, they cannot expect the Court to enforce their agreement. In *Regazzoni* v. *K. C. Sethia (1944) Ltd.*:[65]

S agreed to sell and deliver to R at Genoa in Italy a quantity of jute bags to be shipped from India. At that time the government of India was in dispute with the South African government over the treatment of Indian nationals in South Africa and had prohibited the direct export of jute to South Africa, and also imposed penalties on any indirect shipments. Both S and R knew that the jute bags were to be shipped to South Africa in violation of the Indian prohibition. The bags were not delivered and R brought an action for non-delivery.

The House of Lords held that, since the contract required the export of goods from India in breach of the law of that country, it could not be enforced in this country, even though the law might be classed as a political law. R accordingly failed.

---

[58] *Ralli Brothers* v. *Compania Naviera Sota y Aznar* [1920] 2 K.B. 287, *per* Scrutton L.J. at p. 304. See also *Libyan Arab Foreign Bank* v. *Bankers Trust Co.* [1989] 1 Q.B. 728, *per* Staughton J., at p. 743–6; *Soleimany* v. *Soleimany* [1999] Q.B. 785.

[59] *Foster* v. *Driscoll* [1929] 1 K.B. 470.

[60] *Kleinwort Sons & Co.* v. *Ungarische Baumwolle Aktiengesellschaft* [1939] 2 K.B. 678; *British Nylon Spinners Ltd.* v. *I.C.I. Ltd.* [1953] Ch. 37; *Toprak Mahsulleri Ofisi* v. *Finagrain Compagnie Commerciale Agricole et Financiére* [1979] 2 Lloyd's Rep. 98.

[61] *Regazzoni* v. *K. C. Sethia (1944) Ltd.* (infra, n. 65), at p. 325. See also *Lemenda* v. *African Middle East Petroleum Ltd.* [1988] Q.B. 448, at p. 461. Cf. *Westacre Investments Ltd.* v. *Jugoimport SPDR Ltd.* [1999] Q.B. 740, at p. 801; aff'd [2000] Q.B. 288.

[62] *In re Selot's Trusts* [1902] 1 Ch. 488.

[63] *Holman* v. *Johnson* [1775] 1 Cowp. 341, at p. 343; *Government of India Ministry of Finance* v. *Taylor* [1955] A.C. 491; *Brokaw* v. *Seatrain U.K. Ltd.* [1971] 2 Q.B. 476; *Att.-Gen. of New Zealand* v. *Ortiz* [1982] Q.B. 349. Cf. [1984] A.C. 1 at p. 46.

[64] *Re Emery's Investment Trusts* [1959] Ch. 410; *Empresa Exportadora De Azucar* v. *Industria Azucarera Nacional S.A.* [1983] 2 Lloyd's Rep. 171. Cf. *Re Helbert Wagg & Co. Ltd.'s Claim* [1956] Ch. 323, at p. 352.

[65] [1958] A.C. 301. Cf. *Pye* v. *B. G. Transport Service* [1966] 2 Lloyd's Rep. 300; *Fielding & Platt Ltd.* v. *Najjar* [1969] 1 W.L.R. 357.

(c) AGREEMENTS WHICH TEND TO INJURE GOOD GOVERNMENT

(i) Sale of offices

The public has an interest in the proper performance of their duty by public servants, and is entitled to be served by the fittest persons procurable. Contracts which have for their object the sale of public offices are illegal.

(ii) Assignment of public salaries

An agreement to assign the salary of a public officer is also illegal based on a somewhat different principle. The rule has been explained on the ground that 'it is fit that the public servants should retain the means of a decent subsistence, without being exposed to the temptations of poverty'.[66]

(iii) Other contracts injurious to the public service

The law will not uphold a contract whereby one of the parties agrees to use influence or position for the purpose of securing a title, contract, or some other benefit from the government for the other;[67] or an agreement whereby a member of Parliament in consideration of receiving a salary from a political association agreed to vote on every subject in accordance with the directions of the association;[68] or an agreement whereby a donation to a charity is made in consideration of a promise to secure the donor a knighthood.[69] The public has a right to demand that public officials shall not be induced merely by considerations of personal gain to act in a manner other than that which the public interest demands, and that no-one shall enter or refrain[70] from entering the public service for the same reason.

But agreements that may influence the proceedings before a public official are not necessarily against the public interest. Thus, it has been held not to be against public policy for a party to a commercial transaction involving the disposition of an interest in land to enter into a covenant to support and not to oppose a planning application by the other party.[71]

(d) AGREEMENTS WHICH TEND TO PERVERT THE COURSE OF JUSTICE

(i) Agreements not to disclose wrongdoing

The Courts will normally refuse to enforce an undertaking not to disclose misconduct which is of such a nature that it ought in the public interest to be disclosed to others who have a proper interest to receive it.[72] Nevertheless, a promise not to disclose the

---

[66] *Wells* v. *Foster* (1841) 8 M. & W. 149, at p. 151. See also *Roberts* v. *Roberts* [1986] 1 W.L.R. 437 (statutory prohibition of assignment of soldiers' pay and benefits). Cf. *Re Mirams* [1891] 1 Q.B. 594.

[67] *Montefiore* v. *Menday Motor Components Co.* [1918] 2 K.B. 241.

[68] *Osborne* v. *Amalgamated Society of Railway Servants* [1910] A.C. 87.

[69] *Parkinson* v. *College of Ambulance Ltd.* [1925] 2 K.B. 1.

[70] *Re Beard* [1908] 1 Ch. 383 (armed forces).

[71] *Fulham Football Club Ltd.* v. *Cabra Estates plc* [1994] 1 B.C.L.C. 363, *per* Neill L.J. at pp. 390–1.

[72] *Initial Services Ltd.* v. *Putterill* [1968] 1 Q.B. 396; *Lion Laboratories Ltd.* v. *Evans* [1985] 1 Q.B. 526. See also *Att.-Gen.* v. *Guardian Newspapers Ltd.* [1990] 1 A.C. 109 at pp. 268–9.

fact that a crime has been committed may still be lawful. In *Howard* v. *Odhams Press Ltd.* Greene L.J. stated 'It may well be permissible for a person against whom frauds have been and are intended to be committed to give a promise of secrecy in order to obtain information relating to them which will enable him, by taking steps himself, to prevent the commission of future frauds'.[73] But such a promise is void if its effect is not merely to enable the protection of the party to whom the information is given, but to preclude that party from disclosing information as to frauds committed or contemplated against others to whom such information would be of use in preventing the commission of such frauds.

(ii) Compromise of criminal offences

Before 1967, although the compromise of a prosecution for a misdemeanour which was of a private character, e.g. assault or libel, was permissible,[74] an agreement not to prosecute a felony or a misdemeanour of a public nature was not enforceable,[75] and the compounding of a felony was itself a criminal offence.[76] The Criminal Law Act 1967 abolished the distinction between felonies and misdemeanours and further provided that the compounding of an offence (other than treason) was no longer to be criminal by English law. Section 5 of the Act, however, established a new crime of concealing an arrestable offence[77] which is committed if a person accepts as the price of not disclosing such an offence any consideration other than the making good of loss or injury occasioned by the offence, or the making of any reasonable compensation for that loss or injury. The effect of this provision in the law of contract is enigmatic. It can be argued that, subject to the rules of duress,[78] an agreement to compromise a prosecution is now legal and enforceable, provided that it is not one which is rendered criminal by the Act of 1967. The better view, however, is that the abolition of the offence of compounding did not in itself affect the rules of public policy administered by the Courts, for these were not dependent upon the fact that the agreement itself constituted a crime. Further, an agreement to compromise a criminal offence may, in certain circumstances, expose one (or possibly both) of the parties to a charge of attempting or conspiring to pervert the course of justice,[79] and the agreement will in consequence be illegal in that event.

---

[73] [1938] 1 K.B. 1, at p. 42.

[74] *Baker* v. *Townsend* (1817) 7 Taunt. 422; *Fisher & Co.* v. *Apollinaris Co.* (1875) L.R. 10 Ch. App. 297. See also *Keir* v. *Leeman* (1844) 6 Q.B. 308, at p. 321, aff'd (1846) 9 Q.B. 371.

[75] *Windhill Local Board of Health* v. *Vint* (1890) 45 Ch. D. 351 (obstruction of highway); *Clubb* v. *Hutson* (1865) 18 C.B.N.S. 414 (obtaining by false pretences).

[76] It was also probably an offence to compound a misdemeanour of a public nature.

[77] An offence the sentence for which is fixed by law or for which a person may be sentenced to imprisonment for five years, and attempts to commit such an offence.

[78] See *ante*, p. 277.

[79] *R.* v. *Grimes* [1968] 3 All E.R. 179; *R.* v. *Panayiotou* [1973] 1 W.L.R. 1032.

(e) AGREEMENTS WHICH TEND TO ABUSE THE LEGAL PROCESS

(i) The policy against speculative litigation

Agreements encouraging speculative litigation are contrary to public policy and unlawful. It is not thought right that a person should buy an interest in another's quarrel, or should incite another to litigation by offers of assistance for which there is an expectation of payment. Someone who does this might be tempted, for personal gain, to inflame the damages, to suppress evidence, or even to suborn witnesses.[80] This head of public policy, which rests on the perceived need to protect the integrity of public justice,[81] has, however, not been static. In the last century, as much litigation became supported by some association or other, e.g. by trade unions or insurance companies, its operation was progressively redefined and narrowed in scope. It was also significantly altered by the Courts and Legal Services Act 1990 as amended by the Access to Justice Act 1999. The legislation constitutes recognition by Parliament that where legal aid is not available certain agreements which would have been illegal at common law confer a benefit to the public by increasing access to justice.

(ii) Maintenance and champerty

Maintenance and champerty are the names given to agreements which may contravene the policy against the encouragement of speculative litigation. Maintenance occurs where a person supports litigation in which he has no legitimate concern without just cause or excuse.[82] Champerty occurs where it is agreed that the person who maintains another's litigation is to receive a share of the proceeds of the litigation. Champerty has been said to be an aggravated form of maintenance.[83] The Courts, until recently, looked with particular disfavour upon champertous agreements between solicitors and their clients under which the solicitor is to receive a share of the proceeds of the client's litigation.[84]

Agreements which 'savour of champerty' will also be struck down. It is not unlawful to agree to supply information which will enable property to be recovered, in consideration of receiving a part of the property when recovered;[85] but if the person giving such information is to recover the property or actively to assist in the recovery by procuring evidence or other means, the arrangement is contrary to the policy of the law and void.[86] The question to what extent the purchase of a right of action already accrued is obnoxious to the rules against champerty is considered later in connection with the subject of assignment of choses in action.[87]

---

[80] *Re Trepca Mines Ltd.* [1963] Ch. 199, *per* Lord Denning M.R. at p. 219.

[81] *Giles* v. *Thompson* [1993] 3 All E.R. 321, *per* Steyn L.J. at p. 328; [1994] 1 A.C. 142, *per* Lord Mustill at 164.

[82] *Hill* v. *Archbold* [1968] 1 Q.B. 686, at p. 694.

[83] *Giles* v. *Thompson* [1993] 3 All E.R. 321, *per* Steyn L.J. at p. 328.

[84] *Wild* v. *Simpson* [1919] 2 K.B. 544; *Re Trepca Mines Ltd.* [1963] Ch. 199. See also Solicitors Act 1974, s. 59; *Wallersteiner* v. *Moir (No. 2)* [1975] Q.B. 373 (contingency fees); *Aratra Potato Co. Ltd.* v. *Taylor Joynson Garrett (a firm)* [1995] 4 All E.R. 695 (acceptance of a lower fee for lost cases).

[85] *Rees* v. *De Bernardy* [1896] 2 Ch. 437.

[86] *Stanley* v. *Jones* (1831) 7 Bing. 369. See also Theft Act 1968, s. 23.

[87] See *post*, p. 482.

Maintenance and champerty were both torts and crimes at common law. Criminal liability was abolished by the Criminal Law Act 1967.[88] But section 14(2) of the Act expressly provides that this abolition is not to affect cases in which a contract is to be treated as contrary to public policy or otherwise illegal.

(iii) Just cause or excuse

The concept of what is a just cause or excuse has widened considerably as the operation of this head of public policy has narrowed.[89] As a general rule it is, for example, considered legitimate for litigation to be supported by trade unions or insurance companies. Again, it has been held not to be maintenance where an employer supported an action for libel brought by an employee to protect his reputation attacked by reason of acts done by him in the course of his employment,[90] and where a national anglers' society provided funds for an action by a riparian owner against a company alleged to be polluting a particular river.[91] A genuine commercial interest may also suffice.[92] But the legitimacy of the interest of the person supporting the action must be distinct from the benefit which that person seeks to derive from the agreement to support it.[93]

Where a person with a legitimate interest in maintaining an action, agrees to do so but does not agree to pay the costs of action if the action of the person supported does not succeed, the better view is that an agreement by a person with a legitimate interest in maintaining the action will not be illegal solely on the ground that it makes no provision for the maintainer to pay the costs if the action does not succeed.[94]

(iv) Conditional fee agreements

Section 58 of the Courts and Legal Services Act 1990 permits certain speculative actions undertaken on a 'no win, no fee' basis, and validates certain agreements between lawyers and their clients for a percentage uplift in the fees in the event of success. The maximum increase under the regulations is 100 per cent.[95] Such conditional fee agreements must be in writing and must comply with the relevant regula-

[88] ss. 13, 14.

[89] See the historical survey in *Giles* v. *Thompson* [1993] 3 All E.R. 321, *per* Steyn L.J., at pp. 328–33, approved (*ibid.*) [1994] 1 A.C. 142, at 164.

[90] *Hill* v. *Archbold* (*supra*, n. 82). See also *Bourne* v. *Colodense Ltd.* [1985] I.C.R. 291 (support by trade union). Cf. *Neville* v. *London Express Newspaper Ltd.* [1919] A.C. 368 (support by newspaper).

[91] *Martell* v. *Consett Iron Co. Ltd.* [1955] Ch. 363.

[92] *British Cash and Parcel Conveyors Ltd.* v. *Lamson Stores Service Co. Ltd.* [1908] 1 K.B. 1006; *Bourne* v. *Colodense Ltd.* (*supra*, n. 90); *Trendtex Trading Cpn.* v. *Crédit Suisse* [1980] 1 Q.B. 629, at 668; [1982] A.C. 679; *Giles* v. *Thompson* [1994] 1 A.C. 142 at p. 164; *Camdex International Ltd.* v. *Bank of Zambia* [1996] 3 All E.R. 431; *Norglen Ltd.* v. *Reeds Rains Prudential Ltd.* [1999] 2 A.C. 1.

[93] *Giles* v. *Thompson* [1994] 1 A.C. 142 at p. 163.

[94] *Hayward* v. *Giffard* (1838) 4 M. & W. 194, at p. 196; *Shah* v. *Karanjia* [1993] 4 All E.R. 792; *Murphy* v. *Young & Co's Brewery plc* [1997] 1 Lloyd's Rep. 236; *Tharros Shipping Co. Ltd. and Den Norske Bank plc* v. *Bias Shipping Ltd.* [1997] 1 Lloyd's Rep. 246, at p. 250. Cf. *Hill* v. *Archbold* (*supra*, n. 82) at p. 694–5; *McFarlane* v. *E.E. Caledonia (No. 2)* [1995] 1 W.L.R. 366.

[95] Conditional Fees Agreements Order 1995 (S.I. 1995 No. 1674), reg. 3. But the Law Society's conditions provide for the fee to be limited to 75% of the damages recovered.

tions.[96] Conditional fee agreements by clients who do not have legal aid are permitted in proceedings for personal injuries, by or on behalf of insolvent companies, and before the European Commission of Human Rights and the European Court of Human Rights.[97] The Access to Justice Act 1999, which restricts the availability of legal aid in a radical way, also extends the availability of alternative methods of funding litigation by authorizing conditional fee agreements in all money and damages claims except family cases[98] and, by section 27, makes it clear that an agreement between a solicitor to charge a client only if the client succeeds in litigation is valid.

There have been different views about the effect of the legislation on further common law development of this head of public policy. In *Thai Trading Co. (a firm)* v. *Taylor* the Court of Appeal had to consider the enforceability at common law of an agreement by a solicitor only to charge his client if she succeeded in litigation, facts which would now fall within section 27 of the 1999 Act. It took the view that the progressive narrowing by the Courts of this head of public policy during the last half-century meant that, if Parliament wished to freeze further common law development, it had to do so more directly. The agreement was held not to be contrary to public policy.[99] Millett L.J. stated that the policy which had invalidated such agreements in the past was formed in an age when litigation was regarded as an evil and to be discouraged. 'It rings oddly in our ears today when access to justice is regarded as a fundamental human right which ought to be readily available to all.' He considered that current attitudes are exemplified by the passage into law of the Courts and Legal Services Act 1990 which showed that 'the fear that lawyers may be tempted by having a financial incentive in the outcome of litigation to act improperly is exaggerated, and there is a countervailing public policy in making justice readily accessible to persons of modest means'. But in a subsequent case[100] the Court of Appeal was of the view that the carefully crafted legislative scheme shows and defines the extent to which Parliament has decided to make such agreements enforceable. May L.J stated that where Parliament has by successive enactments 'modified the law by which any arrangement to receive a contingency fee was impermissible, there is no present room for the court, by an application of what is perceived to be public policy, to go beyond that which Parliament has provided'.[101]

(f) AGREEMENTS WHICH ARE CONTRARY TO GOOD MORALS

Although it has sometimes been said that contracts *contra bonos mores* are void, the only aspect of immorality with which Courts of law have actually dealt is sexual

---

[96] Conditional Fees Agreements Regulations 1995 (S.I. 1995 No. 1675).

[97] Conditional Fees Agreements Order 1995 (S.I. 1995 No. 1674), reg. 2.

[98] See Access to Justice Act 1999, ss. 27–8, amending the Courts and Legal Services Act 1990. See also Bawden [1997] N.L.J. 1559; Hoon, *ibid.* 1611; Tunkel, *ibid.* 1784; Harrison, *ibid.* 1786.

[99] [1998] Q.B. 781. Cf. the contrary decisions in *British Waterways Board* v. *Norman* (1993) 26 H.L.R. 232 and *Aratra Potato Co. Ltd.* v. *Taylor Johnson Garrett (a firm)* [1995] 4 All E.R. 695.

[100] *Awwad* v. *Geraghty & Co.* [2001] Q.B. 570.

[101] *Ibid.*, at p. 600. See also p. 593. *Thai Trading* may be also open to question on other grounds: see *Thomas Hughes* v. *Kingston upon Hull C.C.* [1999] Q.B. 1193; *Mohamed* v. *Alaga & Co* [2000] 1 W.L.R. 1815, but note that s. 27 of the Access to Justice Act 1999 enshrines it legislatively.

immorality.[102] Formerly the Courts generally refused to enforce any contract which directly or indirectly promotes sexual immorality. Thus a promise by a man to pay a woman money if she would become his mistress has been held to be illegal and unenforceable.[103] And a landlord who let premises to a woman who was, to the knowledge of the landlord's agent, the kept mistress of a man who was in the habit of visiting her there, and who was expected to pay the rent, was not permitted to recover the rent reserved in the lease.[104] The Courts today are unlikely to adopt the same attitude to agreements involving extra-marital cohabitation.[105]

As an Australian judge has said: 'The social judgments of today upon matters of "immorality" are as different from those of the last century as is the bikini from a bustle'.[106] The law has come to terms with the fact that a man and woman may set up home together and produce children in a stable relationship without being married and has afforded to the woman rights in the 'matrimonial home' equivalent to those of a wife.[107] Such rights (which may be contractual in nature) have not been denied on the ground of immorality. And the Court of Appeal has held that an agreement to advertise telephone sex lines is not unenforceable on the grounds of immorality.[108]

On the other hand, it seems unlikely that an agreement which involves prostitution would be enforced. An action cannot be maintained to recover the rent of premises knowingly let for the purposes of prostitution,[109] or upon a contract of employment which requires the employee to procure prostitutes for customers of the employer.[110] Also in *Pearce* v. *Brooks*:[111]

P, a firm of coach-builders, agreed with B, a prostitute to hire to her an ornamental brougham of an intriguing design, with the knowledge that it was to be used by her in the furtherance of her trade. She failed to pay the hire, and P brought an action to recover the money.

It was held that P could not recover.

---

[102] *Coral Leisure Group Ltd.* v. *Barnett* [1981] I.C.R. 503, at p. 506.

[103] *Walker* v. *Perkins* (1764) 1 W. Bl. 517; *Benyon* v. *Nettlefold* (1850) 3 Mac. & G. 94. But a promise made in consideration of past illicit cohabitation merely lacks consideration, and is not illegal: *Beaumont* v. *Reeve* (1846) 8 Q.B. 483.

[104] *Upfill* v. *Wright* [1911] 1 K.B. 506.

[105] See Dwyer (1977) 93 L.Q.R. 386.

[106] *Andrews* v. *Parker* [1973] Qd. R. 93, *per* Stable J. at p. 104.

[107] *Eves* v. *Eves* [1975] 1 W.L.R. 1338; *Tanner* v. *Tanner* [1975] 1 W.L.R. 1346; *Paul* v. *Constance* [1977] 1 W.L.R. 527. See also Part IV of the Family Law Act 1996, especially s. 62 (defining cohabitants); *Davis* v. *Johnson* [1979] A.C. 264; *Tinsley* v. *Milligan* [1994] 1 A.C. 340, *post*, p. 410 (where what made the agreement illegal was that its purpose was to defraud the social security, rather than that it concerned lesbian cohabitees). See also *Barclays Bank plc* v. *O'Brien* [1994] 1 A.C. 180, at p. 198.

[108] *Armhouse Lee Ltd.* v. *Chappell*, The Times, 7 August 1996.

[109] *Girardy* v. *Richardson* (1793) 1 Esp. 13.

[110] Cf. *Coral Leisure Group Ltd.* v. *Barnett* [1981] I.C.R. 503.

[111] (1866) L.R. 1 Ex. 213. See also *Armhouse Lee Ltd.* v. *Chappell*, The Times, 7 August 1996 (agreements to promote sex dating probably illegal).

(g) AGREEMENTS WHICH AFFECT THE FREEDOM OR SECURITY OF MARRIAGE OR THE DUE DISCHARGE OF PARENTAL DUTY

(i) Restraint of marriage

Agreements which restrain the freedom to marry are contrary to policy as injurious to the moral welfare of the citizen. Thus a promise under seal not to marry any person besides the promised, and on breach to pay the promised £2,000 was held void, as there was no promise of marriage on either side and the agreement was purely restrictive.[112]

(ii) Marriage brokage

Promises made upon the consideration of procuring a marriage between two persons, are held illegal 'not for the sake of the particular instance or the person, but of the public, and that marriages may be on a proper foundation'.[113] It has been held that an agreement to introduce a person to others of the opposite sex with a view to marriage is invalid, although there is a choice given of a number of persons, and not an effort to bring about marriage with a particular person.[114] It is submitted that decisions such as these require reconsideration in the light of modern conditions. If they remain good law the transactions between the many marriage bureaux and dating agencies and their clients may be unenforceable.

(iii) Promises by person already married

At common law, a promise to marry after a spouse's death, made by a married person to someone who knew the promisor was married, was not enforceable.[115] Such a contract, it was said, was 'not only inconsistent with that affection which ought to subsist between married persons, but is calculated to act as a direct inducement to immorality'.[116] Actions for breach of promise of marriage have now, however, been abolished.[117]

(iv) Agreements for separation

Agreements providing for the separation of husband and wife are valid if made in prospect of an immediate separation; but it is otherwise if they contemplate a possible separation in the future, because they then give inducements to the parties not to perform their matrimonial duties, in the fulfilment of which society has an interest.[118]

---

112 *Lowe* v. *Peers* (1768) 4 Burr. 2225.

113 *Cole* v. *Gibson* (1750) 1 Ves. Sen. 503, *per* Lord Eldon at p. 506.

114 *Hermann* v. *Charlesworth* [1905] 2 K.B. 123. *Sed quaere*, and note (*post*, p. 405) the liberal approach to the restitution of money paid under such an agreement after substantial performance, and compare the general approach, *post*, p. 403.

115 But if she did not know, she could bring an action for breach: *Shaw* v. *Shaw* [1954] 2 Q.B. 429. See now the Inheritance (Provision for Family and Dependants) Act 1975; *post*, p. 621 n. 198.

116 *Wilson* v. *Carnley* [1908] 1 K.B. 729, *per* Farwell L.J. at p. 740. Cf. *Fender* v. *St. John-Mildmay* [1938] A.C. 1.

117 Law Reform (Miscellaneous Provisions) Act 1970, s. 1. But see s. 2 and *Mossop* v. *Mossop* [1988] 2 F.L.R. 173 (regarding disputes about property).

118 *Cartwright* v. *Cartwright* (1853) 3 De G.M. & G. 982.

(v) Parental duty

For the same reason a parent cannot by contract transfer to another his or her rights and duties in respect of a child, because the law imposes such duties in respect of the minor and for its benefit.[119] In a proper case, however, an adoption order can be obtained from the Court under the Adoption Act 1976. Statute expressly provides that a surrogacy agreement, i.e. an agreement by a woman to carry and bear a child at the behest of another with a view to that other person subsequently assuming the parental role, is unenforceable.[120]

(h) AGREEMENTS WHICH OUST THE JURISDICTION OF THE COURTS

At common law an agreement which purports to oust the jurisdiction of the Courts is contrary to public policy and void.[121] It is the policy of the common law that citizens have the right to have their legal position determined by the ordinary tribunals. In the case of arbitration, the common law position has been substantially modified by statute, particularly in the case of arbitrations involving foreign nationals and companies.

(i) Arbitration clauses

There is no objection to contracts which contain a clause that any dispute or difference between the parties is to be referred to and settled by arbitration. Such a clause is valid and binding. An arbitration clause which requires as a condition precedent to the accrual of any cause of action that the arbitrator shall have made an award is not contrary to public policy. Such a clause is common in arbitration agreements and is known as a 'Scott v. Avery' clause.[122] It does not oust the jurisdiction of the Court but merely provides that the cause of action shall not be complete until the arbitration award is made. A similar provision known as an 'Atlantic Shipping' clause is also frequently inserted, and this provides that no claim shall arise unless it is put forward in writing and an arbitrator appointed within a limited period.[123] Its validity rests upon the same foundation.

   Provision is made in the Arbitration Act 1996 for an appeal to the Court on points of law arising out of an arbitrator's award.[124] There are, however, a number of limits on this right. For example, unless all the parties agree to the appeal then leave of the

---

[119] *Humphreys* v. *Polak* [1901] 2 K.B. 385. See also Children Act 1989, s. 2.

[120] Human Fertilisation and Embryology Act 1990, s. 36. See also *Re P. (Minors) (Wardship: Surrogacy)* [1987] 2 F.L.R. 421.

[121] *Czarnikow* v. *Roth Schmidt* [1922] 2 K.B. 478. But cf. *Jones* v. *Sherwood Computer Services plc.* [1992] 1 W.L.R. 277; Kendall (1993) 109 L.Q.R. 385 (question remitted to expert); *West of England Shipowners Mutual Insurance Association* v. *Crystal Ltd.* [1996] 1 Lloyd's Rep. 370 (a chosen tribunal may be the final arbiter on questions of fact).

[122] *Scott* v. *Avery* (1855) 5 H.L.C. 811. Cf. Arbitration Act 1996, s. 9(4)–(5).

[123] *Atlantic Shipping and Trading Co.* v. *Dreyfus (L.) & Co.* [1922] 2 A.C. 250. But see Arbitration Act 1996, s. 12.

[124] *Ibid.*, s. 69(1). See also ss. 70 and 71.

Court is required.[125] Moreover, the parties may agree to exclude the jurisdiction of the Court. In the case of a domestic arbitration agreement[126] such an exclusion will be upheld if entered into during arbitration proceedings.[127] In the case of non-domestic arbitration agreements, the freedom of the parties to include such a clause is not restricted in any way.[128]

(ii) Foreign jurisdiction clauses

The Courts will normally uphold a clause in a contract whereby any dispute between the parties is to be referred to the exclusive jurisdiction of a foreign Court. But such a clause is not absolutely binding, and may be overridden if England is the more convenient forum.[129]

(iii) Maintenance agreements

Another example of an agreement which ousts the jurisdiction of the Courts is one in which a wife contracts not to apply to the Courts for maintenance in return for a promise by the husband that he will make her a definite allowance.[130] The right of the Court to award maintenance cannot be ousted, although the financial arrangements are not thereby rendered void or unenforceable.[131]

(i) AGREEMENTS IN RESTRAINT OF TRADE

The common law does not favour agreements that prohibit or restrain a person in the exercise of a lawful trade, employment, or profession. It protects the right of individuals to work and prevents them from disabling themselves from earning a living by an unreasonable restriction by the doctrine of restraint of trade. Since a principal aim of this doctrine is to prevent agreements which unreasonably restrict competition, it is considered in the next section, together with statutory control of anti-competitive agreements.

---

125 *Ibid.*, s. 69(2)–(3).

126 Defined in *ibid.*, s. 85, and broadly, not involving foreign nationals, residents, and companies.

127 *Ibid.*, ss. 69 and 87(1).

128 *Ibid.*, s. 69(1).

129 *The Fehmarn* [1958] 1 W.L.R. 159; *The Eleftheria* [1970] P. 54; *The Adolf Warski* [1976] 1 Lloyd's Rep. 107. But see the Civil Jurisdiction and Judgments Act 1982, Sched. 1, art. 17.

130 *Hyman* v. *Hyman* [1929] A.C. 601. See Cretney, in Rose ed., *Consensus ad idem* (1996), pp. 269–74.

131 Matrimonial Causes Act 1973, s. 34. Cf. *Sutton* v. *Sutton* [1984] Ch. 184. A financial agreement which is then embodied in a consent order will bar further application to the Court: *De Lasala* v. *De Lasala* [1980] A.C. 546, at p. 560.

IV. COMMON LAW AND STATUTORY CONTROL OF ANTI-COMPETITIVE AGREEMENTS

(a) INTRODUCTION

There are statutory and common law controls over anti-competitive agreements. The statutory controls are contained in Articles 81 and 82 of the European Community Treaty and the very similar provisions introduced by the Competition Act 1998.

At common law the control is exercised by the doctrine of restraint of trade. This reflects the fact that the 'public have an interest in every person's carrying on his trade freely: so has the individual. All interference with individual liberty of action in trading, and all restraints of trade of themselves, if there is nothing more, are contrary to public policy, and therefore void'.[132] As formulated, this is a *prima facie* rule. Not all restraints of trade are contrary to public policy. For example, the public interest does not necessarily suffer if a person who sells the goodwill of a business undertakes an obligation not to enter into immediate competition with the buyer. An agreement *prima facie* in restraint of trade is enforceable if it is established that the restrictions in it are reasonable in the interests of the parties and of the public.

(b) RESTRAINT OF TRADE DEFINED

An agreement in restraint of trade has been defined as 'one in which a party (the covenantor) agrees with any other party (the covenantee) to restrict his liberty in the future to carry on trade with other persons not parties to the contract in such a manner as he chooses'.[133] This definition is adequate provided it is not applied too literally. In one sense, all commercial contracts restrain trade; for when one person binds another by contract, say to sell a rare Sheraton writing table or a particular cargo of oil, the seller's future liberty to deal lawfully in that subject-matter with persons not parties to the contract is restricted. Yet ordinary commercial contracts are clearly not tainted with invalidity. The issue is how to determine which agreements are 'in restraint of trade'.

Two categories of agreement have long been recognized as 'in restraint of trade'. First, agreements between employers and employees, whereby the employees covenant not to set up business on their own account on leaving the employers' service or to enter into employment with a rival firm. Secondly, agreements between the buyer and seller of a business together with its goodwill, whereby the seller covenants not to carry on a business which will compete with that of the buyer.

Apart from these types of agreement, there is no definitive way of determining

---

[132] *Nordenfelt* v. *Maxim Nordenfelt Guns and Ammunition Co. Ltd.* [1894] A.C. 535, *per* Lord Macnaghten at p. 565.

[133] *Petrofina (Great Britain) Ltd.* v. *Martin* [1966] Ch. 146, *per* Diplock L.J. at p. 180, adopted by Lord Hodson in *Esso Petroleum Co. Ltd.* v. *Harper's Garage (Stourport) Ltd.* [1968] A.C. 269, at p. 317. See also *ibid.*, p. 307 (Lord Morris).

whether or not an agreement is in restraint of trade. As noted above, asking whether a person has agreed to give up some freedom which he or she otherwise had could bring in all commercial contracts. The difficulty is not met by asking whether the agreement only regulates normal commercial relations because this too begs the question. Lord Wilberforce has said:[134]

[I]t would be mistaken, even it were possible, to try to crystallise the rules of this, or any, aspect of public policy into neat propositions. The doctrine of restraint of trade is one to be applied to factual situations with a broad and flexible rule of reason.

The factual situations which invite the application of the doctrine will change with prevailing economic and social conditions, and it is important to bear in mind that those referred to later in this chapter are not exhaustive: 'the classification must remain fluid and the categories can never be closed'.[135] But today, when economic theory indicates that a competitive economy produces more beneficial results—from the point of view of the public—than a non-competitive economy, it is tempting to define a contract in restraint of trade as being one which is designed to restrict competition,[136] although it must be admitted that there is no judicial authority for this formulation and it has been authoritatively stated that the reason for the Courts' intervention in cases of restraint of trade is simply to protect the weaker party against oppression.[137]

The law concerning restraint of trade has also changed from time to time, both in form and in spirit, in response to changes in conditions of trade. In modern law the operation of the common law doctrine, particularly concerning agreements for exclusive dealing and market-sharing, has been significantly affected by both national and European Community legislation which seeks to control anti-competitive practices, which are of wider application than the common law doctrine and which are primarily administered by regulatory authorities.[138]

(c) THE MODERN LAW

The foundation of the modern law on the subject is contained in the speech of Lord Macnaghten in *Nordenfelt* v. *Maxim Nordenfelt Guns and Ammunition Co. Ltd.*:[139]

N was a maker and inventor of guns and ammunition. He sold his business to the M.N. company for £287,500 and entered into a covenant (later to be repeated in a contract of service) that he would not for 25 years 'engage . . . either directly or indirectly in the trade or business of a manufacturer of guns, gun mountings or carriages, gunpowder explosives or ammunition, or in any business competing or liable to compete in any way with that for the time being carried on by the company', but expressly reserved the right to deal in explosives

---

[134] *Esso Petroleum Co. Ltd.* v. *Harper's Garage (Stourport) Ltd.* (*supra*, n. 133), at p. 331.

[135] *Ibid.*, at p. 337.

[136] Guest (1968) 2 J.A.L.T. 3. Contrast *Texaco Ltd.* v. *Mulberry Filling Station Ltd.* [1972] 1 W.L.R. 814, at p. 827; Heydon (1969) 85 L.Q.R. 229.

[137] *A. Schroeder Music Publishing Co. Ltd.* v. *Macaulay* [1974] 1 W.L.R. 1308, *per* Lord Diplock at pp. 1315–16.

[138] *Post*, pp. 378–9, 383.

[139] [1894] A.C. 535.

other than gunpowder, in torpedoes or submarine boats, and in metal castings or forgings. After some years N entered into a business with a rival company dealing with guns and ammunition, and M.N. sought an injunction to restrain him from so doing.

The House of Lords was of the opinion that the covenant not to compete with the company 'in *any* business competing or liable to compete in any way with that for the time being carried on by the company' was unreasonable, as it attempted to protect not only the business as it was when sold, but any future activities of the company. It was therefore void; but this clause was distinct and severable from the rest of the agreement. As for the remainder of the restraint, in so far as it protected the business actually sold, it was reasonable between the parties, because N not only received a large sum of money, but also by his reservation retained scope for the exercise of his inventive and manufacturing skill. Moreover, the wide area over which the business extended necessitated a restraint co-extensive with that area for the protection of the respondents. Finally it could not be said to be contrary to the public interest since it transferred to an English company the making of guns and ammunition for foreign lands. The restraint was therefore valid.

As a result of this decision and later cases in which it has been elucidated, certain propositions of law can be stated:

(1) All restraints of trade, in the absence of special justifying circumstances, are contrary to public policy and do not give rise to legally binding obligations, and in that sense are void.[140] But in this context being void does not mean that the agreement will be disregarded for all purposes, and it has been said that a contract in restraint of trade should more properly be spoken of as one 'which the law will not enforce'.[141] It is not unlawful for the parties to agree to implement it, and if the parties do so the Courts will not later allow them to recover sums paid under the agreement or property transferred on the basis that the agreement is of no effect whatsoever.[142] But, as we shall see, in certain situations it is the effect of an agreement on third parties which renders the agreement in unreasonable restraint of trade, and, in such cases, the third parties may be able to challenge the agreement.[143]

(2) It is a question of law for the decision of the Court whether the special circumstances adduced do or do not justify the restraint; and if a restraint is not justified, the Court will, if necessary, take the point, since it relates to a matter of public policy, and the Court does not enforce agreements which are contrary to public policy.[144]

---

[140] *Mason* v. *Provident Clothing & Supply Co. Ltd.* [1913] A.C. 724.

[141] *Joseph Evans & Co. Ltd.* v. *Heathcote* [1918] 1 K.B. 418, *per* Bankes L.J. at p. 431.

[142] *Boddington* v. *Lawton* [1994] I.C.R. 478, *per* Nicholls V.-C. at pp. 491–3. See also *Joseph Evans & Co. Ltd.* v. *Heathcote* [1918] 1 K.B. 418; *Esso Petroleum Co. Ltd.* v. *Harper's Garage (Stourport) Ltd.* [1968] A.C. 269, at p. 297; *Schroeder Music Publishing Co. Ltd.* v. *Macaulay* [1974] 1 All E.R. 174, at p. 181, aff'd [1974] 1 W.L.R. 1308.

[143] *Post*, p. 384.

[144] *Wyatt* v. *Kreglinger and Fernau* [1933] 1 K.B. 793, at p. 806; *North Western Salt Co. Ltd.* v. *Electrolytic Alkali Co. Ltd.* [1914] A.C. 461, at p. 470.

(3) A restraint can only be justified if it is reasonable (a) in the interests of the contracting parties, and (b) in the interests of the public.

(4) The onus of showing that the restraint is reasonable between the parties rests upon the person alleging that it is so, that is to say, upon the covenantee.[145] The onus of showing that, notwithstanding that a covenant is reasonable between the parties, it is nevertheless injurious to the public interest and therefore void, rests upon the party alleging it to be so, that is to say, usually upon the covenantor.[146] But once the agreement is before the Court it is open to scrutiny in all its surrounding circumstances as a question of law.[147]

(5) Covenants in restraint of trade are construed (a) with reference to the object sought to be obtained, that is the protection of one of the parties against competition in trade, and (b) in their context and in the light of the factual matrix when the agreement was made.[148]

Reasonableness as a test for the validity of a restraint, however, requires further consideration.

(d) REASONABLENESS IN THE INTERESTS OF THE PARTIES

The application of this test will depend on the answers to two questions: what is it that the covenantee is entitled to protect, and how far can such protection extend? A covenant cannot be considered reasonable unless it is designed to protect the legitimate interests of the covenantee. The issue of whether a covenant in restraint of trade is reasonable ultimately falls to be decided by reference to the legitimate interests that are sought to be protected and not by a classification of the relationship between the parties.[149] But the nature of the interests recognized as legitimate by the law will vary according to the subject-matter and nature of the contract.

(i) Subject-matter and nature of agreement

The different approaches of the courts can be illustrated by comparing restraints on the seller of a business and those on former employees. The buyer of a business with its goodwill is entitled to prevent the seller from competing with the business sold. The buyer has acquired a business which, from the nature of the case, has been immune from competition by the person who has sold it, and the goodwill of that business is an interest which the buyer is legitimately entitled to protect. In *Herbert Morris Ltd.* v. *Saxelby* Lord Shaw stated:[150]

When a business is sold the vendor, who, it may be, has inherited it or built it up, seeks to

---

[145] *Mason* v. *Provident Clothing & Supply Co. Ltd.* [1913] A.C. 724, at p. 733; *Herbert Morris Ltd.* v. *Saxelby* [1916] 1 A.C. 688, at p. 700; *Attwood* v. *Lamont* [1920] 3 K.B. 571, at p. 587.

[146] *Herbert Morris Ltd.* v. *Saxelby* (*supra*, n. 145), at pp. 700, 708; *Att.-Gen. of Commonwealth of Australia* v. *Adelaide Steamship Co. Ltd.* [1913] A.C. 781, at p. 795.

[147] *Esso Petroleum Co. Ltd.* v. *Harper's Garage (Stourport) Ltd.* [1968] A.C. 269, at p. 319.

[148] *Clarke* v. *Newland* [1991] 1 All E.R. 397, at p. 402.

[149] *Bridge* v. *Deacons* [1984] 1 A.C. 705, at p. 714.

[150] [1916] 1 A.C. 688, at pp. 713–14.

realize this piece of property, and obtains a purchase upon a condition without which the whole transaction would be valueless. He sells, he himself agreeing not to compete; and the law upholds such a bargain, and declines to permit a vendor to derogate from his own grant. Public interest cannot be invoked to render such a bargain nugatory: to do so would be to use public interest for the destruction of property.

The law will not, however, permit a covenant which merely restricts competition, and does not protect the interest of the buyer in the business actually sold.[151]

A different set of considerations comes into play in the case of restraints upon former employees. An employer cannot prevent competition by a former employee, or restrict the use by the employee of personal skill and knowledge acquired in the course of the employment. The employer is entitled only to protect its trade secrets, and to prevent the use by the employee of influence acquired over its clients or customers.[152]

Where the question of restraint of trade is raised outside these two categories of agreements, the law[153] adopts a much more lenient attitude, and recognizes as a legitimate interest the right of the covenantee to secure its competitive position in the market, or to maintain the effectiveness and stability of its organization.[154] What interests can be protected will therefore depend upon the nature of the contract.

(ii) Extent of protection

Where the covenantee has a legitimate interest which it is entitled to protect, the restriction must not be longer in point of time, or wider in area, or otherwise be more extensive in scope than is necessary to protect that interest.[155] Again, however, the answer to this question in any individual case must necessarily depend upon the interest to be protected, the nature of the contract and the relative positions of the contracting parties.

(iii) Restraint must be reasonable for both parties

The restraint must be reasonable not only in the interests of the covenantee, but of both parties. At first sight it might appear that any restraint, since it protects the covenantee alone, must be opposed to the interests of the covenantor, but if the transaction is regarded as a whole this is clearly not so. If the vendor of a business could not covenant not to compete with the person to whom it is being sold, the business would command a lower price; if employees could not bind themselves not to convey trade secrets to their employers' rivals, they might not so readily obtain proper training or employment.[156]

---

[151] See *post*, p. 375.

[152] *Faccenda Chicken Ltd.* v. *Fowler* [1987] Ch. 117, at p. 137.

[153] See *post*, p. 379–80.

[154] *Eastham* v. *Newcastle United Football Club Ltd.* [1964] Ch. 413; *Esso Petroleum Co. Ltd.* v. *Harper's Garage (Stourport) Ltd.* [1968] A.C. 269. See also *McEllistrim* v. *Ballymacelligott Co-operative Agriculture and Dairy Society Ltd.* [1919] A.C. 548, at pp. 563–4.

[155] See *post*, pp. 373–4, 379–80.

[156] *Herbert Morris Ltd.* v. *Saxelby* [1916] 1 A.C. 688, *per* Lord Parker at p. 707. See also Lord Shaw, quoted *ante*, p. 369.

(iv) Consideration

The quantum of the consideration which the covenantor has received in exchange for the restraint is relevant to the determination of the reasonableness of the contract.[157]

(v) Time

The reasonableness of the restraint is normally determined at the time the covenant was entered into. But in *Shell U.K. Ltd.* v. *Lostock Garage Ltd.*,[158] Lord Denning M.R. held that a covenant which, though at its inception was reasonable, could become unenforceable if it was found afterwards to operate unreasonably or unfairly in circumstances that were not envisaged beforehand. This approach did not, however, receive the support of the other members of the Court of Appeal in the case.[159]

(e) REASONABLENESS IN THE INTERESTS OF THE PUBLIC

Cases in which a restraint has been held void as not being reasonable in the interests of the public are not common. Indeed, in 1913, the Judicial Committee of the Privy Council observed that 'their Lordships are not aware of any case in which a restraint, though reasonable in the interests of the parties, has been held unenforceable because it involved some injury to the public',[160] and it was further said that 'if once the Court is satisfied that the restraint is reasonable as between the parties this onus [of proving injury to the public] will be no light one'.[161] More recently, however, in relation to certain types of agreement such as cartels[162] and other forms of restrictive trading agreements,[163] there has been a distinct shift of emphasis in favour of recognizing the importance of the interests of the public.[164] Such agreements are, as a general rule, freely entered into between traders who are perfectly capable of deciding for themselves what is reasonable in their own interests. So the real point at issue is whether the maintenance of the restraint is detrimental to the interests of the public.

Even where cases are decided on the basis of reasonableness between the parties, it is *ultimately* on the ground of public policy that the Court will decline to enforce an unreasonable restraint. As Lord Pearce has said: 'There is not, as some cases seem to suggest, a separation between what is reasonable on grounds of public policy and what is reasonable as between the parties. There is one broad question: is it in the

---

[157] *Nordenfelt* v. *Maxim Nordenfelt Guns and Ammunition Co. Ltd.* [1894] A.C. 535, at p. 565; *Esso Petroleum Co. Ltd.* v. *Harper's Garage (Stourport) Ltd.* [1968] A.C. 269, at pp. 300, 318, 323; *Allied Dunbar (Frank Weisenger) Ltd.* v. *Weisinger* [1988] I.R.L.R. 60.

[158] [1976] 1 W.L.R. 1187.

[159] Ormrod and Bridge L.JJ.

[160] *Att.-Gen. of Commonwealth of Australia* v. *Adelaide Steamship Co.* [1913] A.C. 781, at p. 795.

[161] *Ibid.*, at p. 797.

[162] See *post*, p. 376.

[163] See *post*, p. 379.

[164] *Esso Petroleum Co. Ltd.* v. *Harper's Garage (Stourport) Ltd.* [1968] A.C. 269, at pp. 300–1, 318–19, 321, 324, 330, 340–1. See also *Dickson* v. *Pharmaceutical Society of Great Britain* [1970] A.C. 403, at p. 441. But cf. the more cautious approach adopted by Ungoed-Thomas J. in *Texaco Ltd.* v. *Mulberry Filling Station Ltd.* [1972] 1 W.L.R. 814, at pp. 826–9; *post*, p. 382. See also *Alec Lobb (Garages) Ltd.* v. *Total Oil (Great Britain) Ltd.* [1985] 1 W.L.R. 173 at p. 191.

interests of the community that this restraint should, as between the parties, be held to be reasonable and enforceable?'[165]

(f) COVENANTS BETWEEN EMPLOYER AND EMPLOYEE

The general approach to such covenants has been noted above. Covenants imposing restraints upon an employee which operate only during the currency of the contract of employment cannot normally be challenged on the ground that they are unreasonable. During this period an employer has the exclusive right to the services of the employee and the doctrine of restraint of trade will have no application unless the employee is too unilaterally fettered or the contract has as its object the sterilizing rather than the absorption of a person's capacity for work.[166]

But if covenants are imposed which restrain the employee's freedom to work *after* the termination of the employment, those covenants must be reasonable in the interests of the parties and of the public. Whether a clause is or is not in restraint of trade will be judged by the effect the clause has in practice,[167] and this is determined by the circumstances that existed at the time of formation.[168]

(i) Interest of employer

An employer is generally entitled to protect its trade secrets or other confidential information, and to prevent the misuse by the employee of acquaintance with the employer's clients or customers.[169] An employer also has an interest in a stable workforce, and will be able to impose restrictions on the solicitation of employees.[170] But an employer cannot inhibit the use of the employee's own skill and experience, even if this is acquired during the course of the employment.[171]

Yet the dividing line between confidential information and personal skill and knowledge may not be easy to draw. In *Sir W. C. Leng & Co. Ltd. v. Andrews:*[172]

---

[165] *Esso Petroleum Co. Ltd. v. Harper's Garage (Stourport) Ltd. (supra,* n. 164), at p. 324.

[166] *Young v. Timmins* (1831) 1 Cr. & J. 331; *Esso Petroleum Co. Ltd. v. Harper's Garage (Stourport) Ltd.* (*supra,* n. 164), at pp. 294, 328, 329; *A. Schroeder Music Publishing Co. Ltd. v. Macaulay* [1974] 1 W.L.R. 1308; *Clifford Davis Management Ltd. v. W.E.A. Records Ltd.* [1975] 1 W.L.R. 61.

[167] See e.g. *Stenhouse Australia Ltd. v. Phillips* [1974] A.C. 391; *Sadler v. Imperial Life Assurance Co. of Canada Ltd.* [1988] I.R.L.R. 388. Cf. *Watson v. Prager* [1991] 1 W.L.R. 726 at p. 749.

[168] *Briggs v. Oates* [1991] 1 All E.R. 407 at p. 417; *Watson v. Prager* [1991] 1 W.L.R. 726 at p. 738. But where the contract has been discharged because of the *employer's* breach, the employee is released from the covenants: *General Billposting Co. Ltd. v. Atkinson* [1909] A.C. 118; *Rock Refrigeration Ltd. v. Jones* [1997] 1 All E.R. 1, Phillips L.J. *dubitante,* and see *post,* pp. 576, 580.

[169] *Faccenda Chicken Ltd. v. Fowler* [1987] Ch. 117 at p. 137; *Systems Reliability Holdings plc v. Smith* [1990] I.R.L.R. 377; *Dawnay, Day & Co. Ltd. v. de Braconier D'Alphen* [1998] I.C.R. 1068. But it has been stated *obiter* (*Faccenda Chicken Ltd. v. Fowler, ibid.,* at p. 136) that confidential information falling short of a trade secret or its equivalent cannot, to the extent that it is inevitably carried away in the employee's head as part of the employee's skill and knowledge, be protected after the employment has ended. *Sed quaere.* Cf. *Roger Bullivant Ltd. v. Ellis* [1987] I.C.R. 464, at p. 473; *Systems Reliability Holdings plc v. Smith* (*supra*) at p. 384.

[170] *Dawnay, Day & Co. Ltd. v. de Braconier D'Alphen* (*supra,* n. 169). See also Sales (1988) 104 L.Q.R. 600.

[171] *Herbert Morris Ltd. v. Saxelby* [1916] 1 A.C. 688, *per* Lord Parker at p. 710. See also *Faccenda Chicken Ltd. v. Fowler* (*supra,* n. 169) at p. 137; *Office Angels Ltd. v. Rainer-Thomas and O'Connor* [1991] I.R.L.R. 214.

[172] [1909] 1 Ch. 763.

A Sheffield newspaper took from one of its junior reporters a covenant that he would not, after leaving his employment, be connected with any other newspaper within 20 miles of that city. The newspaper claimed that this was necessary to protect its 'organization' and 'sources of information'.

It was held that these interests did not merit protection. Today, however, business 'know-how' is regarded as a thing of value, a saleable commodity. Although it is not precisely of the same nature as a trade secret, it is nevertheless not simply part of the employee's stock of experience. If 'know-how' involves an element of confidentiality it can be protected,[173] and in principle the Courts should recognize 'know-how' as an interest capable of protection in its own right where it can be separated from what the employee can legitimately claim to be his own skill and experience, albeit acquired during the course of the employment.[174] The difficulties of recognizing what is and what is not confidential, or who may or may not have been a customer of the employer have led to the suggestion that an anti-competition covenant which is reasonable as to space and time may be the 'most satisfactory form of restraint'.[175]

(ii) Scope of restraint

A covenant will not be adjudged reasonable between the parties unless it does no more than protect the legitimate interests of the employer. The employer is not entitled to restrain the employee from carrying on a business different from that in which the trade secrets exist or the customer connection has been built up and in which the employee was employed. Thus a covenant 'not to carry on any business whatsoever' is void.[176] And a baker cannot restrain an employee employed to sell bread from opening a restaurant, even though he himself keeps a restaurant or contemplates doing so in the future.[177] However, a covenant which appears unduly wide as to scope or area may, on its proper construction, be limited and thus held valid. So, a covenant by a milkman not to sell or solicit orders for 'milk or dairy produce' from any of the employer's customers was held not to include any dairy produce but only that with which the milkman had been concerned in his employment and thus was not too wide.[178] Finally, it has been held that if an employer expressly states the interest to be protected then the employer may not justify the restraint by reference to some other interest.[179]

---

[173] *Printers and Finishers Ltd. v. Holloway* [1965] 1 W.L.R. 1, at p. 5; *Commercial Plastics Ltd. v. Vincent* [1965] 1 Q.B. 623, at p. 642. See also *Lansing Linde Ltd. v. Kerr* [1991] 1 W.L.R. 251, at pp. 260, 270 (trade secrets can include highly confidential information of a non-technical nature, e.g. names of customers and goods they buy); *Johnson & Bloy (Holdings) Ltd. v. Wolstenholme Rink plc* [1989] 1 F.S.R. 135; *Universal Thermosensors Ltd. v. Hibben* [1992] 1 W.L.R. 840.

[174] Cf. *Faccenda Chicken Ltd. v. Fowler,* (*supra* n. 169) at p. 136. See also *Lock International plc v. Beswick* [1989] 1 W.L.R. 1268, at pp. 1273–5.

[175] *Turner v. Commonwealth & British Minerals Ltd.* [2000] I.R.L.R. 114, at p. 117.

[176] *Baker v. Hedgecock* (1888) 39 Ch. D. 520.

[177] *Bromley v. Smith* [1909] 2 K.B. 235, at p. 241.

[178] *Home Counties Dairies Ltd. v. Skilton* [1970] 1 W.L.R. 526. See also *Plowman & Son Ltd. v. Ash* [1964] 1 W.L.R. 568; *Littlewoods Organisation Ltd. v. Harris* [1977] 1 W.L.R. 1472; *Edwards v. Worboys* [1984] 1 A.C. 724 *per* Dillon L.J. at pp. 727–8.

[179] *Office Angels Ltd. v. Rainer-Thomas and O'Connor* [1991] I.R.L.R. 214, at p. 219.

(iii) Area of restraint

The restraint must not be more extensive in area than the employer's interests require. Thus in *Mason* v. *Provident Clothing & Supply Co.*,[180] where a canvasser in the company's Islington branch covenanted not to work in any similar business for three years within 25 miles of London, the restraint was held to be unreasonable as it extended further than was legitimately warranted. But in *Foster & Sons Ltd.* v. *Suggett*[181] a covenant by a works manager not to engage in glass-making anywhere in the United Kingdom was considered reasonable for the protection of his employer's business, as he had been instructed in secret methods of making glass and the employer's trade extended throughout the country. Again, a covenant which is unlimited in area, i.e. is literally world-wide, may be construed by reference to the business of the employer to which it relates, and so be limited to the area in which that business is in fact carried on.[182] But it has been said that Courts should not strive to find implicit limitations within covenants which on their face are too wide and thus to make them enforceable since employers would otherwise have no reason to impose restraints in appropriately limited terms.[183]

(iv) Length of restraint

A restraint may be struck down on the ground that it is too extensive in time. The protection of trade secrets does not justify keeping someone out of trade indefinitely,[184] and an employee's connections with the customers of a former employer must necessarily weaken with the passage of time. So, in *M. & S. Drapers* v. *Reynolds*,[185] where a collector-salesman of a drapery firm covenanted not to canvass his employer's customers for a term of five years from the determination of his employment, this period was held to be too long in view of the humble position which he occupied.[186]

(v) Nature of employment

The nature of the employment is also material. It is clear, for example, that a greater measure of protection will be allowed to the employer against the subsequent activities of a senior employee, such as a managing director,[187] than in the case of a temporary or subordinate employee, such as a travelling sales representative.[188] Each case must be considered in the light of its own circumstances.

---

[180] [1913] A.C. 724. See also *Office Angels Ltd.* v. *Rainer-Thomas and O'Connor* [1991] I.R.L.R. 214 at p. 221.

[181] (1918) 35 T.L.R. 87.

[182] *Littlewoods Organisation Ltd.* v. *Harris* [1977] 1 W.L.R. 1472; *Scully (U.K.) Ltd.* v. *Lee* [1998] I.R.L.R. 259.

[183] *J. A. Mont (U.K.) Ltd.* v. *Mills* [1993] I.R.L.R. 173, *per* Simon Brown L.J at p. 176. See also *post*, p. 413 (severance).

[184] *Kerchiss* v. *Colora Printing Inks Ltd.* [1960] R.P.C. 235.

[185] [1957] 1 W.L.R. 9. See also *Home Counties Dairies Ltd.* v. *Skilton* [1970] 1 W.L.R. 526 (milk roundsman: one year).

[186] [1921] 2 A.C. 158. See also *Bridge* v. *Deacons* [1984] 1 A.C. 705. See further *Edwards* v. *Worboys* [1984] 1 A.C. 724. Cf. *Oswald Hickson Collier & Co.* v. *Carter-Ruck* [1984] 1 A.C. 720.

[187] *Nordenfelt* v. *Maxim Nordenfelt Guns and Ammunition Co. Ltd.* [1894] A.C. 535.

[188] *M. & S. Drapers Ltd.* v. *Reynolds* [1957] 1 W.L.R. 9.

(vi) Public interest

Covenants in a contract of employment which are reasonable between the parties will seldom be invalidated on the ground that they are contrary to the public interest. In *Wyatt* v. *Kreglinger and Fernau*,[189] however, the public interest was considered:

W had worked for K's firm as a wool broker. On his retirement, they wrote him a letter offering him a pension of £200 a year on condition that he did not engage in the wool trade. There was some doubt whether this offer was ever specifically accepted by W, but K paid him the pension for 9 years, after which time they ceased to do so, claiming that there was no proper contract, or if there was a contract, it was unenforceable as being in unreasonable restraint of trade.

The Court of Appeal upheld K's plea. They differed as to whether there was a proper contract, but held unanimously that the restraint was invalid as being contrary to the public interest, as well as being unreasonable between the parties. The reason given was that such covenants deprived the country of the services of able-bodied persons who might still be of benefit to it in their own trade.

   This judgment has been justly criticized, since the person seeking to evade his obligations was the very person who had imposed the unreasonable stipulation and there were several million unemployed at the time.[190] But it is possible to conceive of situations where it would be injurious to the public interest, say, in the case of a distinguished engineer or economist, that a person should be tied by an agreement which, though reasonable from the point of view of the protection of the employer's proprietary interest, is yet detrimental to the community at large. Indeed, in one case, a condition of a pension scheme that a former salesman of a company should not engage in any activity which competed with the company was said to be invalid on the ground that it would deprive the public of his skilled services in promoting the export trade.[191]

(g) SALE OF THE GOODWILL OF A BUSINESS

It has been noted that considerably more latitude is allowed to covenants which accompany the sale of the goodwill of a business than in the case of contracts between employer and employee,[192] but the rules relating to the area and length of the restraint are, in principle, the same.

   Covenants in gross, however, which do not protect the business actually sold, and whose object is merely to restrain competition, will not be upheld. In the *Nordenfelt* case[193] we saw that a covenant 'not to engage in any business liable to compete with that for the time being carried on by the company' was considered unreasonable.

---

[189] [1933] 1 K.B. 793.

[190] But see *Howard F. Hudson Pty. Ltd.* v. *Ronayne* (1972) 126 C.L.R. 449 (Australia).

[191] *Bull* v. *Pitney-Bowes Ltd.* [1967] 1 W.L.R. 273. See also *J. A. Mont (U.K.) Ltd.* v. *Mills* [1993] I.R.L.R. 173.

[192] *Ante*, p. 368.

[193] [1894] A.C. 535; *ante*, p. 367. See also *Vancouver Malt & Saké Brewing Co. Ltd.* v. *Vancouver Breweries Ltd* [1934] A.C. 181.

There seems to be no reported case in which a covenant reasonable as between the parties has been struck down as contrary to the public interest.

(h) CARTEL AGREEMENTS

Business organizations frequently enter into cartels, that is to say, agreements to regulate the production and marketing of the commodities manufactured by them, and to maintain prices and standards in relation to those commodities. Similarly, employers may enter into agreements attempting to regulate labour and to impose mutual restrictions upon the re-employment of former employees. The rules of professional organizations also restrict professionals such as lawyers or doctors as to how they may work, for instance, by restricting advertising or controlling the charges for services. Cartel agreements are, like all other agreements in restraint of trade, *prima facie* void at common law and must be justified as being reasonable in the interests of the parties and of the public.

(i) Reasonableness between the parties

In this type of agreement, which is generally freely negotiated, the parties can be regarded 'as the best judges of what is reasonable between themselves'.[194] They are entered into for the purpose of avoiding undue competition and carrying on trade without excessive fluctuations or uncertainty. As a result, it is difficult for a Court to say that they are unreasonable between the parties, and in fact the Courts have only done so if an agreement contains no provision, or virtually no provision, for voluntary withdrawal.[195]

(ii) Public interest

The position adopted by the common law has been to regard many cartels at least as being not injurious to the public,[196] and in some cases even as positively beneficial.[197] Indeed, the Courts virtually excluded the possibility that a cartel should be held contrary to the public interest by requiring it to be one which was calculated to produce 'a pernicious monopoly, that is to say, a monopoly calculated to enhance prices to an unreasonable extent'.[198] The effect was that in this context the common law did not promote competition.

Even if the Courts had, in fact, adopted a different economic attitude, the doctrine of restraint of trade could not have been employed to any real effect in the suppression of cartels, since, save in exceptional circumstances, a cartel agreement would only have come before the Courts if one of the parties failed to perform it and was sued for the breach.

---

[194] *North Western Salt Co.* v. *Electrolytic Alkali Co. Ltd.* [1914] A.C. 461, at p. 471; *English Hop Growers* v. *Dering* [1928] 2 K.B. 174, at p. 180.

[195] *McEllistrim* v. *Ballymacelligott Co-operative Agriculture and Dairy Society Ltd.* [1919] A.C. 548; *Evans (J.) & Co.* v. *Heathcote* [1918] 1 K.B. 418; *Bellshill and Mossend Co-operative Society* v. *Dalziel Co-operative Society* [1960] A.C. 832.

[196] *Att.-Gen. of Commonwealth of Australia* v. *Adelaide Steamship Co.* [1913] A.C. 781.

[197] *North Western Salt Co. Ltd.* v. *Electrolytic Alkali Co. Ltd.* [1914] A.C. 461.

[198] *Att.-Gen. of Commonwealth of Australia* v. *Adelaide Steamship Co.* (*supra*, n. 196), at p. 796.

(iii) Agreements between employers and professional rules

The exception concerns agreements between employers which attempt to regulate labour and to impose mutual restrictions upon the re-employment of former employees. These may be struck down as being employer-employee covenants in disguise or as being contrary to the public interest.[199] So, in *Eastham* v. *Newcastle United Football Club Ltd.*,[200] a professional football player, who could be debarred by rules in an agreement between his club and the Football Association from playing for any other club, was held entitled to a declaration that the rules were invalid. Wilberforce J. accepted that some restriction was required for the proper and stable organization of the game of football in England, but concluded the rules were more restrictive on the player's liberty of employment than was necessary to protect this interest. He therefore granted a declaration that the system was invalid, not only against the defendant club, but also in respect of the rules of the Football Association. Although these rules constituted an agreement between employers only, they were calculated to affect the employees' freedom of employment and so could be challenged by the player on the same grounds as if they had been contained in an agreement between him and his employer. Similarly, in *Greig* v. *Insole*[201] Slade J. held void as being in unreasonable restraint of trade resolutions of the International Cricket Conference and the Test and County Cricket Board disqualifying from playing in test and county matches any player who took part in a match arranged by a private promoter (Mr Kerry Packer) during a certain period.

The common law doctrine of restraint of trade also extends to cover the rules of professional bodies. Thus the Court of Appeal refused to strike out a claim that a rule of the Jockey Club preventing a woman from holding a trainer's licence was invalid,[202] and a rule of the Pharmaceutical Society restricting the types of goods in which their members might deal has been held invalid.[203] The doctrine may even apply to the rules of professional bodies the members of which do not technically engage in 'trade',[204] though possibly not to those rules which are related solely to the maintenance of professional honour or standards.[205] But the basis upon which a person who is not a member of the relevant professional body, and thus a party to the restrictive

---

[199] *Mineral Water Bottle Exchange and Trade Protection Socy.* v. *Booth* (1887) 36 Ch. D. 465; *Kores Manufacturing Co. Ltd.* v. *Kolok Manufacturing Co. Ltd.* [1959] Ch. 108; *Esso Petroleum Co. Ltd.* v. *Harper's Garage (Stourport) Ltd.* [1968] A.C. 269, at pp. 300, 319. But see Trade Union and Labour Relations Act 1992, s. 128 (purposes of employers' associations, defined in s. 122, not, by reason only that its purpose is in restraint of trade, unlawful or unenforceable).

[200] [1964] Ch. 413 at p. 432. See also *Buckley* v. *Tutty* (1971) 46 A.L.J.R. 23; *Hall* v. *Victorian Football League* [1982] V.R. 64 (Australia).

[201] [1978] 1 W.L.R. 302.

[202] *Nagle* v. *Feilden* [1966] 2 Q.B. 633. See also *Greig* v. *Insole* [1978] 1 W.L.R. 302; *Adamson* v. *N.S.W. Rugby League Ltd.* (1991) 103 A.L.R. 319.

[203] *Pharmaceutical Society of Great Britain* v. *Dickson* [1970] A.C. 403.

[204] *Ibid.*, at pp. 420, 427, 430, 436, 441.

[205] *Ibid.*, at pp. 421, 436.

agreement, can challenge it, has been put into question[206] and in practice the field has largely been left to modern legislation promoting competition or proscribing certain forms of discrimination.

(iv) Legislative control of cartels

In 1956 legislation[207] was enacted rendering restrictive trading agreements affecting the supply, acquisition, or process of manufacture of goods, or the prices to be charged for them void, unless they are shown positively to be in the public interest. Since the accession of the United Kingdom to the European Communities a separate regime of European Community competition law has also been directly applicable in English law, and the Competition Act 1998 replaced the United Kingdom legislation with prohibitions closely based on those in the European Community Treaty.[208]

The provisions of the European Community Treaty that relate to competition are designed not merely to promote competition within the Community, but to ensure that the objective of establishing a common market is not defeated by the existence of agreements which endanger, either directly or indirectly, freedom to trade between Member States. There is a very considerable body of law within the Community on competition, and detailed treatment of that or the similar provisions introduced by the Competition Act 1998 would be out of place in this book.[209]

It suffices to say that agreements directly or indirectly to fix prices, including target prices,[210] and market-sharing and segmentation agreements are covered by Article 81 (ex Article 85(1)) and section 2 of the Competition Act, even where the arrangements between the parties are an informal and non-binding 'gentlemen's agreement'.[211] The concept of 'concerted practices' includes the knowing substitution of practical co-operation for the risks of competition, and although this will not be inferred from parallel behaviour, it will where, in the light of the economic structure of the market, such behaviour cannot be otherwise explained.[212]

In principle, these provisions cover services[213] including the rules of professional bodies. However, certain professional services, such as those of lawyers, doctors, sur-

---

[206] Privity of contract precludes an action in contract at common law (see *post*, Chapter 10), and in *R. v. Disciplinary Committee of the Jockey Club, ex parte Aga Khan* [1993] 1 W.L.R. 909 it was said by Hoffmann L.J. at p. 933 that gaps in private law remedies should not be filled by subjecting them to public law and the judicial review procedure. Where there is unlawful discrimination or the restriction seeks to prevent those subject to the rules from dealing with a non-party, there may be a remedy: *Cutsforth v. Mansfield Inns Ltd.* [1986] 1 W.L.R. 558.

[207] Restrictive Trade Practices Act 1956, re-enacted in 1976, amended in 1977 and 1980, and repealed by the Competition Act 1998.

[208] European Communities Act 1972, s. 2; *De Geus v. Bosch* (Case 13/16) [1962] E.C.R. 45; *Belgische Radio en Televisie v. S.V.S.A.B.A.M.* (Case 127/73) [1974] 1 E.C.R. 51.

[209] See Whish, *Competition Law*, 4th edn. (2001); Albors Llorens, *EC Competition Law and Policy* (2002).

[210] *Cementhandelaren v. Commission* (Case 8/72) [1972] E.C.R. 977.

[211] *A.C.F. Chemiefarma N.V. v. Commission* (Cases 41, 44 and 45/69) [1970] E.C.R. 661.

[212] *I.C.I. v. Commission* (Case 48/69) [1972] E.C.R. 557. Cf. *Ahlström Osakeyhtio v. Commission* (Joined Cases C-89, 104, 114, 116, 117, 125–129/85) [1993] E.C.R. I-1307 (burden on Commission).

[213] See, for example, *Italy v. Commission* (Case 41/83) [1985] E.C.R. 873 (telecommunications); *Verband der Sachversicherer v. Commission* (Case 45/85) [1987] E.C.R. 405 (insurance); *C.B. and Europay v. Commission* (Cases T-39 and T-40/92) [1994] E.C.R. II-49 (banking). See also Council Regulation 2408/92 O.J. 1992, L 240, p. 8 (air transport).

veyors, accountants, and architects will, if designated by the Secretary of State, be excluded from the prohibition in section 2 of the 1998 Act.[214]

Infringement of the prohibitions not only renders a prohibited agreement automatically void and unenforceable,[215] but may expose the parties to the risk of heavy fines[216] or to an order that the infringement be discontinued.[217] By Article 81(3) (ex Article 85(3)) and sections 4 and 6–9 of the 1998 Act, however, provision is made for the individual and 'block' exemption (considered below)[218] of agreements or concerted practices, which

(a) improve production or distribution, or promote technical or economic progress,

(b) allow consumers a fair share of such benefits,

(c) contain only indispensable restrictions, and

(d) do not afford the parties the possibility of eliminating competition in respect of a substantial part of the products in question.

Article 82 (ex Article 86) of the Treaty and section 18 of the 1998 Act also prohibit the abuse by one or more undertakings of a dominant position. The provisions give a number of illustrations of such abuse, for example, 'limiting production, markets or technical development to the prejudice of consumers'. These provisions enable control to be exercised by European and national regulatory authorities and Courts over 'abusive' practices, and over mergers by dominant firms when these substantially reduce competition.[219]

(i) EXCLUSIVE DEALING AGREEMENTS

An agreement by which a firm undertakes to buy all that it requires of a certain commodity from a single seller and from no other source, or to sell its whole output of a certain commodity to a single buyer and to no other generally falls within both the restraint of trade doctrine and the prohibition in Article 81 (ex Article 85) of the European Community Treaty and section 2 of the Competition Act 1998.

(i) 'Solus' ties

In *Esso Petroleum Co. Ltd.* v. *Harper's Garage (Stourport) Ltd.*,[220] the House of Lords held that a 'solus' agreement relating to the purchase of petrol was an agreement in restraint of trade:

---

[214] Competition Act 1998, Schedule 4; S.I. 1999 No. 2546.

[215] Article 81(2) (ex Art. 85(2)). See *Delimitis* v. *Henninger Bräu A.G.* (Case C-234/89) [1991] E.C.R. I-935. Whether severance is possible is governed by English law: *Société de Vente de Ciments et Béton* v. *Kerpen & Kerpen* (Case 319/82) [1983] E.C.R. 4173.

[216] Regulation 17, art. 15(2)(a).

[217] *Ibid.*, art. 3. On the consequences, see *Courage Ltd.* v. *Crehan* (Case C-453/99) [2001] 3 W.L.R. 1646.

[218] *Post*, pp. 383–4.

[219] *Europemballage & Continental Can Co. Inc.* v. *E.C. Commission* (Case 6/72) [1973] 1 E.C.R. 215; *United Brands Co.* v. *E.C. Commission* (Case 27/76) [1978] 1 E.C.R. 207. Cf. *Garden Cottage Foods Ltd.* v. *Milk Marketing Board* [1983] 3 W.L.R. 143.

[220] [1968] A.C. 269. See also *Petrofina (Great Britain) Ltd.* v. *Martin* [1966] Ch. 146.

H.G., owned two garages. In relation to the first garage, it entered into a 'solus' agreement whereby it undertook to purchase from Esso for 4 years and 5 months all its requirements of petrol to be sold at that garage, and to buy from no other source. The agreement contained a 'continuity' clause under which, if H.G. sold the garage, it was bound to procure the buyer to enter into a similar agreement with Esso. The agreement also contained a 'keep open' clause under which H.G. was to keep open the garage at all reasonable times for the sale of petrol. In return H.G. received a certain rebate per gallon off the scheduled wholesale price of the petrol supplied.

In relation to the second garage, in return for a loan of £7,000, H.G. entered into a mortgage of the garage premises in favour of Esso. H.G. covenanted to repay the loan with interest during 21 years, and not to redeem the mortgage before this time. They also covenanted that, during the continuance of the mortgage, they would observe obligations similar in nature to those contained in the agreement relating to the first garage.

H.G. commenced to sell another brand of petrol and, when sued, pleaded that both transactions were in unreasonable restraint of trade.

The House of Lords held that the agreement for four years and five months on the first garage was (despite its onerous covenants) reasonable in the interests of the parties, since it was reasonably required to protect Esso's legitimate interest in securing the continuity of their selling outlets, their system of distribution, and the stability of their sales; it was also not contrary to the public interest. But the agreement for 21 years on the second garage was longer than was necessary to protect Esso's interests and was therefore unenforceable.

(ii) Restrictive covenants on land

The fact that the agreement is contained in a mortgage of land does not prevent the application of the doctrine of restraint of trade. This incursion of restraint of trade into the sphere of land raises some difficult questions as to the extent of the doctrine in this sphere. In the *Esso Petroleum* case a majority of their Lordships considered that it had no application to covenants contained in leases or conveyances on purchase.[221] So a person who purchases a petrol station, or takes a lease of one from an oil company, where the conveyance or lease contains a petrol 'solus' agreement, could not on this view challenge the 'solus' agreement as being in restraint of trade. The reason for this is given by Lord Reid:[222]

Restraint of trade appears to me to imply that a man contracts to give up some freedom which otherwise he would have had. A person buying or leasing land had no previous right to be there at all, let alone to trade there, and when he takes possession of that land, subject to a negative restrictive covenant he gives up no right or freedom which he previously had.

This reasoning does not appear entirely convincing, for the economic effect of a 'solus' agreement contained in a lease or conveyance is no different from one which is contained in a mortgage or is in gross. Undoubtedly, what their Lordships had in mind was the disastrous inconvenience which would occur if familiar restrictive covenants in the form say, not to use leased premises for the purpose of trade, or not to

---

[221] *Ibid.*, at pp. 298, 309, 316–17, 325.
[222] *Ibid.*, at p. 298.

use them for the purpose of carrying on any offensive trade, e.g. a fried fish shop, could be challenged under the restraint of trade doctrine. It is submitted, however, that a more satisfactory criterion would be to inquire whether or not the covenant was imposed in order to restrict the covenantor from competing with the covenantee, or to restrict competition by third parties by removing the covenantor's freedom to trade with them. Most restrictive covenants on lease or on sale are imposed to preserve the amenities of the particular or neighbouring property; they would therefore not be subject to the doctrine. But if the covenant was imposed by a covenantee who owned a fried fish shop, and wished to be secure against competition, or if the covenantee wished to secure the covenantor's custom to the exclusion of any competitors (as in a 'solus' agreement), then the doctrine of restraint of trade could, and should, apply. This would accord with the opinion, previously expressed,[223] that in the modern law the answer to the problem of defining a contract in restraint of trade is to be found in terms of its anti-competitive effect. Nevertheless a number of cases have subsequently endorsed the view that a person's freedom to trade is not restricted when that person takes possession of land under a lease or conveyance which contains restrictions on the use to which the land may be put.[224]

(iii) Lease and lease-back

If the key to the application of the doctrine is contracting to give up some freedom which otherwise a person would have had, a further problem arises. Suppose that P, the proprietor of a filling station, leases it to an oil company for a period of (say) 50 years in return for the payment of a capital sum. Immediately afterwards the company leases the filling station back to P for a term of 50 years less one day by an underlease which contains a 'solus' tie, and P repays the capital sum and interest in the form of rent. Does the fact that the 'solus' tie is now contained in the lease-back place it outside the doctrine of restraint of trade because immediately before it P had no right to trade on the land? Or will the lease and lease-back be treated as a single transaction whereby the filling station proprietor gives up his existing freedom to trade?

It was held in *Alec Lobb (Garages) Ltd.* v. *Total Oil Great Britain Ltd*,[225] that in such a case the lease and lease-back were to be treated as one transaction by which P gave up its existing freedom to trade, and that the doctrine of restraint of trade could not be circumvented by the transparent device of the lease-back to P.

An oil company paid £35,000 and a nominal rent for a 51-year lease of a petrol station forecourt from a family company in financial difficulties. On the same day the oil company sub-leased the forecourt to the company's shareholders for 21 years at a rent of £2,500 per annum and subject to a 'solus' tie in its favour.

---

[223] See *ante*, p. 367.

[224] *Cleveland Petroleum Co. Ltd.* v. *Dartstone Ltd.* [1969] 1 W.L.R. 116; *Robinson* v. *Golden Chips (Whole-sale) Ltd.* [1971] N.Z.L.R. 257; *Quadramain Pty. Ltd.* v. *Sevastopol Investments Pty. Ltd.* (1976) 133 C.L.R. 390 (Australia); *Re Ravenseft Properties Ltd.'s Application* [1978] Q.B. 52; *Irish Shell Ltd.* v. *Elm Motors Ltd.* [1982] I.L.R.M. 519 (Ireland).

[225] [1985] 1 W.L.R. 173. See also *Amoco Australia Pty. Ltd.* v. *Rocca Bros. Motor Engineering Cp. Pty. Ltd.* [1975] A.C. 561 (P.C.)

Notwithstanding the absence of evidence of economic necessity which the decision in the *Esso Petroleum* case stated would be required to uphold a tie of this length (21 years), the Court of Appeal held that the tie was reasonable. This was because of the £35,000 consideration, received by the family company plaintiff,[226] because there was provision for the tie to be ended after seven and 14 years, and because the public interest did not require the tie to be set aside since the land could only be used as a garage and it made no difference to the public who supplied the petrol.[227]

(iv) Other forms of exclusive dealing agreements

A further problem raised in the speeches in the *Esso Petroleum* case is whether other forms of exclusive dealing agreement are subject to the doctrine of restraint of trade. In *A. Schroeder Music Publishing Co. Ltd.* v. *Macaulay:*[228]

M, a young and unknown song-writer, entered an 'exclusive services' agreement with the S music publishing company, under which he undertook to assign the full copyright in present and future works produced by him to S for a period of 5 years, or for 10 years if his royalties exceeded £5,000. S was under no obligation to publish any of the works, could terminate the agreement by one month's notice, and could assign its benefit. In fact M was a great success.

The House of Lords held that the agreement was subject to the doctrine and was unreasonable. It took account of the extent of the inequality of bargaining power between the parties, and the contrast between the total commitment on the part of the song-writer and the lack of obligation on the part of S. But there is more difficulty with 'sole agency' agreements (under which a person is given the sole right to supply a manufacturer's goods within a certain area)[229] and tied public houses.[230] The view was expressed by some of their Lordships in the *Esso Petroleum* case that these were exempt because they had gained general commercial acceptance.

(v) 'Reasonableness in the interests of the public'

In the *Esso Petroleum* case considerable emphasis was placed on the public interest test in the application of the restraint of trade doctrine to exclusive dealing agreements.[231] But what does this mean in this context? In *Texaco Ltd.* v. *Mulberry Filling Station Ltd.*, a case which also concerned the validity of a petrol 'solus' agreement, the parties adduced evidence of a general economic nature in an attempt to show the relative advantages and disadvantages to the public of the abolition or retention of the 'solus' tie system. Ungoed-Thomas J., however, considered that much of this evidence was irrelevant. The public interest test was, in his view, only the expression of a rule of public policy reflecting the desire of the law to secure to every individual the liberty to

---

[226] [1985] 1 W.L.R. 173 at pp. 179, 185, 189–90.

[227] *Ibid., per* Dunn and Waller L.JJ. at pp. 186, 191 (to uphold the tie may encourage the rescue of businesses in financial hardship).

[228] [1974] 1 W.L.R. 1308.

[229] *Esso Petroleum Co. Ltd.* v. *Harper's Garage (Stourport) Ltd.* [1968] A.C. 269, at pp. 296, 310–11, 320, 328, 336.

[230] *Ibid.*, at pp. 298, 325, 333–4, 341.

[231] [1972] 1 W.L.R. 814.

trade; it was not concerned with ultimate economic advantage to the public in general:

> If it refers to interests of the public at large, it might not only involve balancing a mass of conflicting economic, social and other interests which a court of law might be ill-adapted to achieve; but, more important, interests of the public at large would lack sufficiently specific formulation to be capable of judicial as contrasted with unregulated personal decision and application—a decision varying, as Lord Eldon put it, like the length of the Chancellor's foot.[232]

Although, at first sight, this might appear to be a somewhat narrow approach, it is nevertheless true to say that the Courts of common law are unlikely to be willing to assume the task of weighing, without any specific guidance, conflicting economic judgments and predictions. Where, as in *A. Schroeder Music Publishing Co. Ltd.* v. *Macaulay*, the Courts do strike down a restriction, their conclusions may be open to question on economic grounds. So it has been argued, on the basis of an analysis of the risky music publishing business, where there are many failures for every success such as M's, that the effect of the decision would be to make it more difficult for unknown composers to be taken up by publishers.[233] The task of weighing conflicting economic judgments and predictions is, indeed, better entrusted to government, regulatory agencies, such as the Director General of Fair Trading or the Competition Commission, or to specialized tribunals such as the Restrictive Practices Court and the Competition Commission Appeal Tribunal.

Where, however, as in *A. Schroeder Music Publishing Co. Ltd.* v. *Macaulay*, there is great inequality of bargaining power, the primary concern of the Court is the reasonableness of the restriction as between the parties and not the broader economic issues that are involved in determining whether it is 'reasonable in the interests of the public'. The deep concern of the common law with the personal liberty of the citizen led to the legal principle favouring the right of an individual to work and not to be disabled from supporting himself or herself by an unreasonable restriction.

(vi) Legislative control

The prohibition in Article 81 (ex Article 85) and section 2 of the Competition Act 1998, considered above, will often apply to exclusive dealing agreements. For example, in *Consten and Grundig* v. *Commission of the European Communities*:[234]

G, a German manufacturer of radios, television and similar equipment, appointed C, a French company, the sole distributor of its products within France. C undertook (*inter alia*) not to export any of G's products outside France, and, in turn, G imposed on all its other distributors outside France an obligation not to export its products outside their respective territories. It further assigned to C the trademark 'GINT' which would enable C to sue any third party, importing G's products into France, for infringement of this trade mark. The

---

[232] *Ibid.*, at p. 827. Sometimes there will be such evidence. In the *Esso Petroleum* case account was taken of a Report into the Distribution of Retail Petrol (H.C. No. 264 of 1965).

[233] Trebilcock (1976) 26 U. of Tor. L.J. 359.

[234] (Cases 56/64, 58/64) [1966] E.C.R. 299. For the remedies of a third party affected by such an agreement, see *Cutsforth* v. *Mansfield Inns Ltd.* [1986] 1 W.L.R. 558.

object of this arrangement was to confer upon C absolute territorial protection within France from competing G products imported from outside.

The European Court of Justice held that C could not rely upon the agreement with G, nor upon the trade mark or on French national law, to prevent the importation of G's products into France. The agreement prevented other distributors in a national market, i.e. France, from obtaining supplies of G products from elsewhere in the Community. It accordingly fell within Article 85(1).

Certain categories of exclusive dealing agreements have been accorded a block exemption, provided they contain the required provisions and do not contain those proscribed.[235] Where an agreement does not fall within a block exemption, it remains open to the parties to apply for individual exemption provided the requirements of Article 81(3) (ex Article 85(3)) and the 1998 Act are fulfilled.[236]

(j) TRADE UNIONS

Trade unions are, to a large extent, protected from the doctrine of restraint of trade by section 11 of the Trade Union and Labour Relations (Consolidation) Act 1992, which provides that the purposes of any trade union are not, by reason only that they are in restraint of trade, unlawful so as to make any agreement or trust void or voidable and its rules are not similarly unlawful or unenforceable. In *Faramus* v. *Film Artistes' Association*[237] F was expelled from the union because of a rule barring any person who had been convicted of a criminal offence. His challenge to the rule on the ground that it was in unreasonable restraint of trade failed because the agreement constituted by the rules of the union was one which related or was directed to its purposes. It could not therefore be challenged on the ground that it was an unreasonable restraint of trade.

(k) MONOPOLIES

In 1948, Parliament enacted the Monopolies and Restrictive Practices (Inquiry and Control) Act,[238] which set up an advisory body, now named the Competition Commission.[239] The Commission is empowered to investigate and report on monopoly situations,[240] mergers of enterprises,[241] and anti-competitive practices. It is independent of government, but it has itself no power to initiate an investigation or to implement its own recommendations. References to the Commission can be initiated only

---

[235] The major EC ones are: Regulation 1983/83 Exclusive Distribution; Regulation 1984/83 Exclusive Purchasing; Regulation 2349/84 Patent Licensing; Regulation 123/85 Motor Vehicle Distribution; Regulation 418/85 Research and Development; Regulation 4087/88 Franchising; Regulation 556/89 Know-how Licensing. See also Competition Act 1998, s. 6.

[236] *Ante*, p. 379.

[237] [1964] A.C. 925 (decided on the similar wording of the Trade Union Act 1871, s. 3).

[238] This has now been repealed.

[239] Competition Act 1998, s. 45.

[240] The definition of a 'monopoly situation' is a complicated one, but, in general, it exists if one-quarter of goods or services of one description are supplied by or to a single company or group of companies.

[241] Only large mergers are controlled.

by the Secretary of State or by the Director General of Fair Trading and any orders made in consequence of its reports are made by the Secretary of State.

V. GAMING AND WAGERING CONTRACTS

Gaming and wagering contracts have frequently been the subject of statutory intervention and the intricacy of this legislation calls for special analysis.

(a) GAMING AND WAGERING DEFINED

The definition of a gaming contract depends, for the most part, on certain statutory definitions of 'gaming';[242] but the classic definition of a wagering contract is derived from the judgment of Hawkins J. in *Carlill* v. *Carbolic Smoke Ball Co.*[243] There must be two parties, or two sides, professing to hold opposite views, mutual chances of gain and loss, and neither party must have any interest in the contract other than the sum or stake he or she will win or lose. 'It is essential to a wagering contract that each party may under it either win or lose, whether he will win or lose being dependent on an uncertain fact or event.' Thus persons who contribute to a sweepstake, buy a lottery ticket, take part in a bingo session, or enter coupons for a football pool do not make wagering contracts.[244] The organizers can neither win nor lose; they merely pay out a proportion of the money staked to those who are successful, less their own expenses.[245]

Hawkins J. stated that the issue must concern a future uncertain event. But an event may be uncertain, not only because it is a future event, but because it is not yet ascertained, at any rate to the knowledge of the parties. Thus a wager may be made upon the height of the Eiffel Tower, or upon the result of an election which is over, if the parties do not know in whose favour it has gone. The uncertainty then resides in the minds of the parties, and the subject of the wager may be said to be the accuracy of each person's judgment rather than the determination of a particular event.

For a contract to be a wager the determination of the uncertain event must be the sole condition of the contract. The knowledge, skill, or luck of each party is backed against that of the other, and in a true wager this is the whole transaction. The Court will look at the substance of the contract, and not merely to the words in which it is expressed. Thus an agreement to buy a horse on terms that the price was to be £200 if

[242] e.g. Gaming Act 1968, s. 52(1).

[243] [1892] 2 Q.B. 484, at p. 490, aff'd [1893] 1 Q.B. 256; *Weddle, Beck & Co.* v. *Hackett* [1929] 1 K.B. 321, at p. 329.

[244] *Ellesmere* v. *Wallace* [1929] 2 Ch. 1; *Tote Investors Ltd.* v. *Smoker* [1968] 1 Q.B. 509; *Peck* v. *Lateu* (1973) 117 Sol. J. 185; *One Life Ltd.* v. *Roy* [1996] 2 B.C.L.C. 608. But see the Betting, Gaming and Lotteries Act 1962 (as amended), and the Lotteries and Amusements Act 1976 as amended, *inter alia*, by the National Lottery Act 1993.

[245] See also *Kloekner & Co. A.G.* v. *Gatoil Overseas Inc.* [1990] 1 Lloyd's Rep. 177 at p. 192 (agent's contract).

it trotted at 18 miles per hour within one month, but a shilling if it did not, was held to be in reality a wager.[246]

Wagers must, however, be distinguished from certain other transactions in which there may be chances of gain and loss to the parties depending upon the determination of an uncertain event, but in which these chances are merely incidental to some other object which the parties have in view.

(i) Insurance contracts and gaming

Contracts of insurance bear a certain superficial resemblance to wagering contracts, but they are really transactions of a different character because the person taking out the insurance has an interest in the contract other than that which created by the sums paid or to be paid. If A Ltd. insures its cargo with B, an underwriter, that is to say, if A agrees with B that in consideration of its paying a premium of £500, B will pay A £50,000 if the cargo is lost by certain specified perils, A cannot, except by straining the use of words, be said to bet against the safety of its own cargo.[247] A's object is to preserve itself from a financial loss if its property perishes, and not that it should gain and B lose if an uncertain event turns out in a particular way. Similarly, if P insures her life by a policy involving the payment of premiums during her whole life, she cannot, without absurdity, be said to back herself for a short life. What she does do is to buy a certain future provision for her dependants at a price which will be fixed according to the number of years she lives. No doubt, if she has a long life, the transaction will prove financially unprofitable, but almost any commercial transaction may involve chances of profit and loss.

A genuine insurance transaction, therefore, is not a wagering contract, though a transaction purporting to be one of insurance may sometimes turn out to be nothing but a wager. This abuse has been dealt with by the legislature, which makes the existence or non-existence of an 'insurable interest' the distinction between a genuine insurance transaction and a wager.[248] The Marine Insurance Act 1906[249] provides that a contract of marine insurance is to be deemed to be a gaming or wagering contract if the insured has no 'interest', actual or prospective, in the adventure, or if the policy contains words which make proof of interest unnecessary. Also, the Life Assurance Act 1774[250] deals with insurance generally (marine insurance excepted), and forbids insurances on the life of any person or other event wherein the person for whose benefit the policy is made has no interest.[251] This Act[252] further requires that the persons to benefit should be named in or identifiable from the policy, and provides

---

[246] *Brogden* v. *Marriott* (1836) 3 Bing. N.C. 88.

[247] *Wilson* v. *Jones* (1867) L.R. 2 Ex. 139, at p. 150.

[248] See *Anthony John Sharp* v. *Sphere Drake Insurance plc (The Moonacre)* [1992] 2 Lloyd's Rep. 501 at pp. 509–10 (insurable interest); *Newbury International Ltd.* v. *Reliance International Insurance Co.* [1994] 1 Lloyd's Rep. 83, at pp. 85, 91–3 (no insurable interest). See generally Clarke, *Policies and Perceptions of Insurance* (1997), p. 20 ff.

[249] s. 4. See also Marine Insurance (Gambling Policies) Act 1909.

[250] s.1.

[251] *Macaura* v. *Northern Insurance Co. Ltd.* [1925] A.C. 619.

[252] As amended by the Insurance Companies Amendment Act 1973.

that the insured should not recover a sum greater than its interest at the time of insurance.

(ii) Stock Exchange transactions and gaming

The law does not frown upon speculation in stocks and shares as such, but if a transaction is no more than 'an agreement to pay differences', that is to say, if the parties do not intend a real transaction by the purchase and delivery of actual stocks and shares, but only that one shall receive from the other the difference between the contract price of a particular security and its market price on the settling day, they are doing no more than betting on the price of the security at a future date. If a transaction is found as a fact to be essentially an agreement to pay differences, a term to the effect that either party has the option to require completion of the purchase will not be enough to alter its character. Such a term has been said to be inserted only 'to cloak the fact that it was a gambling transaction, and to enable [the parties] to sue one another for gambling debts',[253] and is unenforceable at common law. But a licensed dealer in securities may not plead the Gaming Act,[254] and, where one of the parties to a contract for differences enters into it by way of an investment business, it will be enforceable despite being a wager.[255]

The mere taking or not taking delivery of shares (or the mere existence of a right to call for delivery) is, however, not determinative of whether the contract is or is not a wagering contract. So if a buyer never intended to take delivery of shares but did intend to and did enter into a further sales contract, then the original contract will not be held to be a wager as it is a genuine sale contract and not merely an agreement for the payment of differences.[256]

(iii) Commodity futures and gaming

Similar considerations apply to dealings in commodity futures. If A contracts to sell goods to B, delivery to be made in three months' time, and the price to be the market price at the date of delivery, it may be said that A stands to lose or gain upon a future event, which is uncertain, that is to say, according as the market rises or falls. But this element of chance is merely an incident in the larger transaction of a contract of sale of goods on certain terms; it does not convert that transaction into a wagering contract.[257] If, however, both parties use this means in order to gamble on future price

---

[253] *Universal Stock Exchange Ltd.* v. *Strachan* [1896] A.C. 166, at p. 173. Cf. *Universal Stock Exchange Ltd.* v. *Stevens* (1892) 66 L.T. 612. But sums deposited for the purpose of gambling may be recovered provided the other party to the transaction has not appropriated the money in order to place or pay for a gaming transaction: *Re Futures Index Ltd.* [1985] F.L.R. 147. See also *Strachan* v. *Universal Stock Exchange Ltd. (No. 2)* [1895] 2 Q.B. 697.

[254] Licensed Dealers (Conduct of Business) Rules 1983 (SI 1983 No 585), r. 18(2).

[255] Financial Services and Markets Act 2000, s. 412. See *City Index Ltd.* v. *Leslie* [1992] 1 Q.B. 98 (share price indices).

[256] *Thacker* v. *Hardy* (1878) 4 Q.B.D. 685; *Morgan Grenfell & Co. Ltd.* v. *Welwyn Hatfield D.C.* [1995] 1 All E.R. 1.

[257] *Garnac Grain Co. Inc.* v. *H. M. Faure & Fairclough Ltd.* [1966] 1 Q.B. 650 at p. 674. See also *City Index Ltd.* v. *Leslie* [1992] 1 Q.B. 98 (share price indices and commodity prices); *Morgan Grenfell & Co. Ltd.* v. *Welwyn Hatfield D.C.* [1995] 1 All E.R. 1, at pp. 12–14 (interest rate swaps).

differences and for no other purpose, it being in effect agreed between them that neither party should be entitled to call for performance, then the contract will be held to be a wager[258] and will not be enforced unless validated by statute.[259]

(b) WAGERS AT COMMON LAW

At common law all wagers were enforceable,[260] and, until the latter part of the eighteenth century, were only discouraged by some trifling difficulties of pleading.[261]

But as the Courts found that frivolous or indecent matters were brought before them for decision, rules came to be established that a wager was not enforceable if it could only be proved by evidence which was indecent or was calculated to injure or pain a third person. Moreover, they developed a principle of public policy that any wager which tempted a person to offend against the law was illegal. Strange and even ludicrous reasoning was used by the Courts in their effort to discourage the litigation of wagers. A bet upon the duration of the life of Napoleon was stated to tend to weaken the patriotism of English people.[262] But it is evident that the substantial motive pressing upon the judges was 'the inconvenience of countenancing idle wagers in courts of justice', the feeling that 'it would be a good rule to postpone the trial of every action upon idle wagers till the Court had nothing else to attend to'.[263]

(c) GAMING ACT 1845

Although a number of statutes were passed during the seventeenth and eighteenth centuries[264] which sought to regulate certain aspects of gaming, it was not until 1845 that Parliament took any decisive step to exclude litigation by the parties to a gaming or wagering contract from coming before the Courts.

(i) All wagering contracts 'null and void'

Section 18 of the Gaming Act 1845 provides:

All contracts or agreements, whether by parole or in writing, by way of gaming or wagering, shall be null and void; and no suit shall be brought or maintained in any Court of Law or Equity for recovering any sum of money or valuable thing alleged to be won upon any wager, or which shall have been deposited in the hands of any person to abide the event on which any wager shall have been made.

The section, it will be observed, has three branches. The first makes all gaming and wagering contracts null and void. Thus if A makes a bet with B on the result of the Derby, or on the height of the Eiffel Tower, and wins, A cannot sue B for the amount.

---

[258] *R. Pagnan & Fratelli* v. *N. G. J. Schouten N.V.* [1973] 1 Lloyd's Rep. 319, at pp. 356–7; *Wilson, Smithett & Cope Ltd.* v. *Terruzzi* [1976] Q.B. 683, at p. 710.

[259] *Ante*, p. 387, nn. 254 and 255.

[260] *March* v. *Pigot* (1771) 5 Burr. 2802.

[261] *Jackson* v. *Colegrave* (1694) Carthew 338.

[262] *Gilbert* v. *Sykes* (1812) 16 East. 150, *per* Lord Ellenborough C.J. at p. 159.

[263] *Ibid.*, *per* Bayley J. at p. 162.

[264] Gaming Acts 1664, 1710 and 1835.

If A loses and pays, he cannot recover his money.[265] The second branch prevents any action being brought to recover any money or valuable thing alleged to be won on any wager. At first sight, it might seem that it merely restated in procedural terms a declaration of substantive law already contained in the first branch, but this is not the case.

(ii) Supplementary promises and covenants

The second branch of section 18 precludes the enforcement of a collateral and later promise to pay a sum of money in compensation for the non-payment of the bet. In *Hill v. William Hill (Park Lane) Ltd*:[266]

A racehorse owner, who had failed to pay betting debts to his bookmaker, was ordered to do so by the committee of Tattersalls, which acts as a sort of court of honour for bets on horse-racing. The sanction for non-compliance was to be reported to the Jockey Club which would post him as a defaulter and warn him off the turf. Hill did not comply with the Committee's order but later agreed to do so in consideration of the bookmaker not reporting him to the Jockey Club. No payments were made and the bookmaker sued to recover the money promised to them, pointing out that they were not suing on the void contract of wager but the later agreement which, they argued, was not an agreement 'by way of gaining or wagering'.

The House of Lords, by a majority of four to three, refused to accept the contention that the second agreement was caught neither by the first (substantive) branch of section 18, nor by the second (procedural) branch. They held that the action was brought to recover a sum of money 'alleged to be won upon any wager', and so was caught by the wider language of the second or procedural part. Lord Normand said:[267]

The purpose of this part of s.18 is not to strike a second and an unnecessary blow at contracts and agreements already stricken with nullity, but to strike at any suit for recovering money or valuables won by wagering. The language is appropriate for that purpose and it is a purpose which is a logical sequel and reinforcement of the first branch of the section. The legislature cannot have been unmindful that a provision making gaming and wagering contracts and agreements null and void might be rendered nugatory by additional promises or covenants given or entered into for security or in satisfaction of money lost by gaming or wagering. The preamble to the Act of 1845 shows that such supplementary promises and covenants were familiar to Parliament.

This decision does not necessarily strike down all arrangements between a bookmaker and a defaulting client,[268] but it clearly prevents the recovery, whether directly or indirectly, and even from a third party who would otherwise be liable to pay,[269] of a sum of money or valuable thing alleged to have been won upon the wager. The legislation cannot be circumvented by using chips instead of money. The use of chips

---

[265] *Bridger v. Savage* (1884) 15 Q.B.D. 363, at p. 367. See also *Re Futures Index Ltd.* [1985] F.L.R. 147. Cf. *Universal Stock Exchange Ltd.* v. *Strachan* [1896] A.C. 166 (deposit recoverable).
[266] [1949] A.C. 530.
[267] At p. 565.
[268] *Re Browne* [1960] 1 W.L.R. 692.
[269] *Coral* v. *Kleyman* [1951] 1 All E.R. 518; *A. R. Dennis & Co. Ltd.* v. *Campbell* [1978] Q.B. 365.

acts as a 'convenient mechanism for facilitating gambling with money' and does not affect the invalidity of the gaming contract whether or not the supply of chips is made under a separate contract.[270]

(iii) Restitution: No recovery of money paid to winner

Although *prima facie* money paid under a void contract can be recovered back in a restitutionary action,[271] 'a gaming loss, whenever paid, is a completed voluntary gift from the loser to the winner', and is irrecoverable.[272] It has also been held that a mistaken overpayment to a punter by a bookmaker cannot be recovered, *inter alia* because this would be to recognize 'wagering transactions as producing legal obligations and therefore doing the very thing which the Gaming Act, 1845, does not permit to be done'.[273] But where stolen money has been used for gambling (whether the transaction is illegal or only void under the 1845 Act), the person from whom the money was stolen may recover it as paid without consideration,[274] subject to the restitutionary defence of change of position which protects a payee whose position has so changed that it would be inequitable in the circumstances to require repayment.[275]

(iv) Money deposited with a stakeholder

The third branch of section 18 concerns the situation where the parties deposit money with a stakeholder to await the event of a wager. In such a case the winner cannot sue to recover any winnings. But the construction which has been put upon this part of section 18 is that it does not preclude either party from recovering his or her own deposit from the stakeholder until it has been paid over to the winner.[276]

(v) Agreement for prizes for games and sports

Section 18, however, contains a proviso enabling prizes for the winner of any genuine and 'lawful game, sport pastime or exercise' to be recovered. Moreover, as we have noted, statute exempts certain dealings from section 18, for example contracts for differences entered into by way of investment business.[277]

---

[270] *Lipkin Gorman* v. *Karpnale Ltd.* [1991] 2 A.C. 548 at p. 575. Cf. Lord Templeman *ibid.*, at p. 562 (only one contract) and Lord Goff *ibid.*, at pp. 576–7 (two contracts).

[271] See *ante*, Chapter 5 and *Re London County Commercial Reinsurance Office Ltd.* [1922] 2 Ch. 67 (marine insurance policies void under the Marine Insurance Act 1906, s. 4).

[272] *Lipkin Gorman* v. *Karpnale Ltd.* [1991] 2 A.C. 548 *per* Lord Templeman at p. 562. See also *ibid.*, pp. 561, 575, 577.

[273] *Morgan* v. *Ashcroft* [1938] 1 K.B. 49, at pp. 61, 69.

[274] *Clarke* v. *Shee* (1774) 1 Cowp. 197; *Lipkin Gorman* v. *Karpnale Ltd.* (*supra*, n. 270) at pp. 562, 564, 575, 577.

[275] *Lipkin Gorman* v. *Karpnale Ltd.* (*supra*, n. 270) at pp. 562, 579–80.

[276] *Diggle* v. *Higgs* (1877) 2 Ex. D. 422; *Burge* v. *Ashley & Smith Ltd.* [1900] 1 Q.B. 744 (on the effect of the 1892 Act, *infra*). The stakeholder will even be liable if he disregards the demand: *Hampden* v. *Walsh* (1876) 1 Q.B.D. 189.

[277] *Ante*, p. 387.

(d) SECURITIES

(i) Gaming securities

Section 1 of the Gaming Act 1710 enacted that if a security, e.g. a cheque, is given to the winner by the loser in payment of a sum lost under a gaming contract, the security is 'utterly void, frustrate, and of none effect'. The winner can no more sue on the security than for the amount that has been won.[278]

Cases of hardship, however, resulted where the security consisted of a negotiable instrument (for instance a cheque) which is subsequently transferred to a third party, who might take it for valuable consideration and in ignorance of its origin. Such a person, when seeking to enforce the cheque, would discover, too late, that he had paid value for an instrument which was by statute wholly void as against the party losing at play. Section 1 of the Gaming Act 1835 therefore enacted that securities which would have been void under the 1710 Act should henceforth be deemed to have been made, drawn, accepted, given, or executed *for an illegal consideration*. The effect of this is that the holder of a cheque given as security for a gaming debt may nevertheless enforce it, despite its origin, but only if the holder can affirmatively prove that, subsequent to the illegality, value has in good faith been given for the cheque.[279]

(ii) Non-gaming securities

The 1710 Act only deals with securities given in relation to playing at or betting on *games* (which includes horse-racing).[280] But since the 1845 Act, securities given in respect of non-gaming wagers such as a wager on the result of a contested election are affected by the fact that the transaction in respect of which they were given is said by the statutes to be null and void. Here the defect is not that they are deemed to have been given for an illegal consideration, but that they have been given for no consideration at all. In such a case, the rules which govern the transfer and enforcement of negotiable instruments (such as cheques) provide that, if consideration has at some time during the history of the instrument been given, it is enforceable by the holder of the instrument.[281] Moreover it is for the original drawer of the cheque to *disprove* the giving of such consideration, for the holder is presumed to be a holder in due course unless the contrary is proved. An example illustrates the distinction between gaming and non-gaming securities, and the burden of proof in either case.

Suppose that A makes a bet with B on the result of the Cheltenham Gold Cup, and loses. A gives B a cheque for £100. B indorses the cheque in favour of C Ltd., a trader, in return for a television set.

Since the wager was one on a 'game', namely, horse-racing, the cheque is deemed to have been given for illegal consideration. It is for C to prove that consideration has at some time been given, either by itself or by some other holder, without notice of the

---

[278] *Richardson* v. *Moncreiffe* (1926) 43 T.L.R. 32.
[279] Bills of Exchange Act 1882, s. 30(2), but cf. ss. 29(3), 81. See also *Tatam* v. *Haslar* (1889) 23 Q.B.D. 345; *Woolf* v. *Hamilton* [1898] 2 Q.B. 337; *Ladup Ltd.* v. *Shaikh* [1983] Q.B. 225; and *post*, pp. 490–1.
[280] *Applegarth* v. *Colley* (1842) 10 M. & W. 723.
[281] See *post*, pp. 96, 491.

circumstances which gave rise to the illegality. But had the same bet been made, for instance, on the height of the Eiffel Tower, then this would have been a non-gaming wager. The burden of proof would have been upon A to show that value had not been given. Knowledge of the circumstances of the wager would this time be immaterial.[282]

(iii) Securities for money lent for gaming

The 1710 and 1835 Acts also apply to securities given for the repayment of money knowingly lent for gaming, or betting on the players, or given for the repayment of money lent at the time of play to those gaming or betting. Thus if A lends B a sum of money in order to enable B to bet on a game, and B gives A a cheque as security for the amount of the loan, the cheque is deemed to have been given for an illegal consideration. The same rule applies where A lends no actual money, but provides B with 'chips' which represent money, and receives a cheque as security.[283]

In the case of cheques given in connection with loans for gaming Part II of the Gaming Act 1968[284] establishes a system for the licensing or registration of premises for gaming. If the holder of the licence accepts a cheque and gives in exchange for it cash or tokens to enable a person to take part in gaming, the cheque is enforceable provided certain conditions are fulfilled.[285] It must not be a post-dated cheque, and must be exchanged for cash or tokens to the amount or value for which it is drawn.[286] The holder of the licence must also cause the cheque to be delivered to a bank for payment or collection not more than two banking days after accepting it.

(e) PRINCIPAL AND AGENT

Since the Gaming Act 1845 merely declared that gaming and wagering contracts were void and unenforceable, no taint of illegality attached to a transaction whereby one person employed another to make loans for making or paying bets. The ordinary rules which govern the relation of principal and agent applied in such a case.

Section 1 of the Gaming Act 1892 altered the law in this respect:

Any promise, express or implied, to pay any person any sum of money paid by him under or in respect of any contract or agreement rendered null and void by the Gaming Act 1845, or to pay any sum of money by way of commission, fee, reward, or otherwise in respect of any such contract, or of any services in relation thereto or in connection therewith shall be null and void, and no action shall be brought or maintained to recover any such sum of money.

Accordingly, no action can be brought to recover a commission or reward promised for making or for paying bets. If one person employs another to make bets, the person

---

[282] *Lilley* v. *Rankin* (1887) 56 L.J.Q.B. 248.

[283] *Stuart* v. *Stephen* (1940) 56 T.L.R. 571. The same analysis appears to apply under the Gaming Acts 1845 and 1968 for security given for chips: see *Lipkin Gorman* v. *Karpnale Ltd.* [1991] 2 A.C. 548 and *Crockfords Club Ltd.* v. *Mehta* [1992] 1 W.L.R. 355.

[284] As amended by the Gaming (Amendment) Act 1986. See also the Acts of 1987 and 1990. A security given for a wager that would be invalid under the Gaming Act 1945, s. 18 may also be saved by Financial Services and Markets Act 2000, s. 412.

[285] Gaming Act 1968, s. 16.

[286] *Ladup Ltd.* v. *Shaikh* [1983] Q.B. 225; *Crockfords Club Ltd.* v. *Mehta* [1992] 1 W.L.R. 355, at pp. 365–6.

making the bet (the agent) can bring no action if the principal fails to pay the money due; the contract is clearly caught by the Act.[287] Also if the agent fails to place the bet, no action can be brought for breach of the contract of agency, or to recover the sums which would have been won had the principal's instructions been faithfully carried out by the agent.[288] Likewise, no action lies if the bet made by the agent was not authorized by the principal.[289] It has been held, however, that an agent who receives the winnings cannot keep them. This is money received on behalf of another; there is thus no promise to pay the principal a sum of money *paid* in respect of a wagering contract but there is an implied promise to pay over monies *received* by the agent; and such an action lies outside the provisions of the 1892 Act.[290]

(f) LOANS

By section 1 of the 1892 Act a loan of money made in discharge of the bets of another is irrecoverable if it has been paid direct to the winner, for the lender has paid it 'under or in respect of' a contract avoided by the Act of 1845.[291] By the same token, a loan of money cannot be recovered if it is a term in the contract that the money lent shall be used for the payment of such a debt.[292] But in *Re O'Shea*,[293] the Court of Appeal held that money lent to pay wagering debts can be recovered provided that it is not paid direct to the winner, but remains *at the free disposition of the borrower* to use as the borrower thinks fit. In such a case, the money is not paid 'under or in respect of' a contract rendered null and void by the Gaming Act 1845; accordingly, it does not fall under the Act of 1892, and may still be recovered.

The Act may also possibly prevent the recovery of money lent for the purpose of wagering. It is submitted that, if a loan of money is made subject to a stipulation that it is to be used to make a bet, or if it is otherwise not at the free disposition of the borrower, any promise to repay the money is void and ineffective as it has been paid 'under or in respect of' a contract made void by the Act of 1845.[294] On the other hand, if it is at the free disposition of the borrower, it probably lies outside the Act of 1892. The question is whether the Acts of 1710 and 1835 make such a loan irrecoverable.

It will be remembered that the Acts of 1710 and 1835 deal only with gaming, and in their terms only apply to *securities* given in relation to gaming. If A lends money to B knowing that it will be used for gaming, and B gives A cheque as security for the loan, there is no doubt that A cannot sue B on the cheque. The cheque was void under the 1710 Act, and must now be taken to have been given for an illegal consideration under

---

[287] *Law* v. *Dearnley* [1950] 1 K.B. 400. Unless the agent made the wagers in the course of an investment business: Financial Services and Markets Act 2000, s. 412 and Sched. 2, paras. 2 and 19.

[288] *Cohen* v. *Kittell* (1889) 22 Q.B.D. 680; *Thomas Cheshire & Co.* v. *Vaughan Bros. & Co.* [1920] 3 K.B. 240.

[289] *A. R. Dennis & Co. Ltd.* v. *Campbell* [1978] Q.B. 365.

[290] *Bridger* v. *Savage* (1884) 15 Q.B.D. 363; *De Mattos* v. *Benjamin* (1894) L.J.Q.B. 248. It is unlikely that this has been affected by the decision in *Hill* v. *William Hill (Park Lane) Ltd.* [1949] A.C. 530; *ante*, p. 389.

[291] *Woolf* v. *Freeman* [1937] 1 All E.R. 178. See also *C. H. T. Ltd.* v. *Ward* [1965] 2 Q.B. 63 (provision of 'chips').

[292] *Macdonald* v. *Green* [1951] 1 K.B. 594.

[293] [1911] 2 K.B. 981.

[294] *Carney* v. *Plummer* [1897] 1 Q.B. 634.

the Act of 1835. In *Carlton Hall Club Ltd.* v. *Laurence*[295] it was held that A cannot disregard the security and recover on the contract of loan, which would strictly not be affected by the enactments referred to.[296]

C.H.C. was the proprietor of a social club. It supplied to members wishing to play billiards and poker for money 'chips' in return for cheques made out by those members. The defendant bought some £28 worth of chips, giving C.H.C. a cheque for that amount. The cheque was dishonoured.

The Divisional Court held that the Acts rendered illegal not only the security but also the consideration. The loan was therefore irrecoverable.[297]

This interpretation is open to reconsideration,[298] and it has been criticized. Its effect, as reported in the Law Journal, would either be to prevent any recovery whatever of money knowingly lent for the purpose of playing upon even a perfectly lawful game[299]—a consequence which does not seem to have been intended by the legislature—or to prevent recovery of such a loan only if a security happened to have been given—a distinction which has no basis of logic or public policy. The decision was assumed to be correct by the Court of Appeal in *Crockfords Club Ltd.* v. *Mehta*,[300] although Lloyd L.J. stated that nothing in the Acts of 1710 and 1835 affected the underlying loan.[301] Nevertheless, the *Crockfords* case also showed that the impact of the *Carlton Hall Club* case has been restricted by section 16 of the Gaming Act 1968 which, as we have noted,[302] makes the giving of a cheque which complies with its conditions enforceable, and thus removes the basis for the argument that the underlying loan is illegal or unenforceable.[303]

By section 16 of the Gaming Act 1968 the holder of a gaming licence is prohibited, under criminal penalty, to make directly or indirectly any loan (in money or tokens)[304] in order to enable a person to take part in the gaming, or in respect of any losses incurred by a person in the gaming. Any such loan will therefore be illegal and irrecoverable, although, as noted above, pursuant to section 16(2), subject to certain

[295] (1929) 98 L.J.K.B. 305. This report is considered superior to that in [1929] 2 K.B. 153: see *C.H.T. Ltd.* v. *Ward* [1965] 2 Q.B. 63, at p. 85; *Crockfords Club Ltd.* v. *Mehta* [1992] 1 W.L.R. 355 at p. 366.

[296] The better view appears to be that there is a loan when a cheque is given at the time of an advance: see *R.* v. *Knightsbridge Crown Court, ex parte Marcrest Properties Ltd.* [1983] 1 W.L.R. 300 at p. 309 and *Crockfords Club Ltd.* v. *Mehta* [1992] 1 W.L.R. 355.

[297] Cf. the different position where the loan is governed by the law of another country and is enforceable under that law, because the Gaming Acts do not have extra-territorial effect on transactions, the proper law of which is that of a foreign legal system: *Société Anonyme des Grands Etablissements du Touquet-Paris-Plage* v. *Baumgart* (1927) 43 T.L.R. 278.

[298] *C.H.T. Ltd.* v. *Ward* [1965] 2 Q.B. 63, at p. 86.

[299] *Supra*, n. 295 at p. 307; cf. that in the Law Reports (*supra*, n. 295) at p. 164. At the time of the decision playing these games of chance in a common gaming house was unlawful (*C.H.T. Ltd.* v. *Ward* [1965] 2 Q.B. 63, at p. 85 so explains it) but this had not been raised by the defendant: see 45 T.L.R. 195.

[300] [1992] 1 W.L.R. 355, at pp. 366, 369.

[301] *Ibid.*, at p. 365.

[302] See *ante*, p. 392.

[303] [1992] 1 W.L.R. 355, at pp. 366, 369. The position would be similar where the Financial Services and Markets Act 2000 s. 412 applies.

[304] See *R.* v. *Knightsbridge Crown Court, ex parte Marcrest Properties Ltd.* (*supra*, n. 296); *Crockfords Club Ltd.* v. *Mehta* (*supra*, n. 296).

conditions the acceptance of a cheque in exchange for cash or tokens to enable a person to take part in the gaming does not infringe this enactment and is a lawful grant of credit.[305]

(g) ILLEGAL GAMING

Certain games, such as hazard and roulette, were previously unlawful by statute, as were games of chance if played in a place habitually kept for gaming.[306] But the law has now been altered and consolidated in the Gaming Act 1968.[307] Gaming of certain kinds is now lawful provided that the very stringent conditions laid down by the Act are complied with. But this transition to legality has not of itself, except in so far as the 1968 Act provides to the contrary, altered the law relating to gaming and wagering as laid down in the Gaming Acts discussed above.[308] Gaming which transgresses the provisions of the 1968 Act is unlawful and illegal.

VI. THE EFFECT OF ILLEGALITY

(a) THE FUNDAMENTAL PRINCIPLE OF POLICY

It has already been pointed out that the single word 'illegal' may embrace varying degrees of impropriety,[309] and it should not be supposed that the effect of illegality is always identical.

In some cases, the law adopts a very severe attitude and refuses to assist a person implicated in the illegality in any way whatsoever. In others, public policy does not require that such a person should be so completely denied a remedy. Money paid or property transferred may be recoverable;[310] collateral transactions may not be tainted;[311] and the Court may be prepared to sever the illegal part of the contract from that which is legal, and enforce the legal part alone.[312] In this section, however, unless otherwise stated, we shall be dealing with those situations where the law rigorously discourages the claims of those who found their cause of action upon an illegal transaction. Even in these situations, there is some variation in the rules to be applied.[313] Moreover, in some instances, the Courts will refuse their aid only to a party who intends to break the law; in others, the contract is unlawful *per se.* Thus, although

---

[305] *R. v. Knightsbridge Crown Court, ex parte Marcrest Properties Ltd.* [1983] 1 W.L.R. 300 at p. 310.

[306] Unlawful Games Act 1541; Gaming Act 1845, s. 1.

[307] The Act has been amended by the Gaming (Amendment) Acts of 1973, 1980, 1982, 1986, 1987, and 1990.

[308] *Ladup Ltd.* v. *Shaikh* [1983] Q.B. 225.

[309] See *ante*, p. 348.

[310] See *post*, pp. 402, 405.

[311] See *post*, p. 412.

[312] See *post*, p. 413.

[313] See *post*, pp. 402, 405.

general rules can be set out, each case must be examined in order to discover the precise effect of the illegality.

The fundamental principle upon which the Courts will act when they have to deal with an illegal contract was long ago explained by Lord Mansfield:[314]

The objection, that a contract is immoral or illegal as between plaintiff and defendant, sounds at all times very ill in the mouth of the defendant. It is not for his sake, however, that the objection is ever allowed; but is founded in general principles of policy, which the defendant has the advantage of, contrary to the real justice, as between him and the plaintiff, by accident, if I may so say. The principle of public policy is this: *ex dolo malo non oritur actio.* No court will lend its aid to a man who founds his cause of action upon an immoral or an illegal act. If, from the plaintiff's own stating or otherwise, the cause of action appears to arise *ex turpi causa,* or the transgression of a positive law of this country, there the court says he has no right to be assisted. It is upon that ground the court goes; not for the sake of the defendant, but because they will not lend their aid to such a plaintiff. So if the plaintiff and defendant were to change sides, and the defendant was to bring his action against the plaintiff, the latter would then have the advantage of it; for where both are *equally* at fault, *potior est conditio defendentis.*

It has recently been said that:

the principle is not a principle of justice: it is a principle of policy, whose application is indiscriminate and so can lead to unfair consequences as between the parties to litigation. Moreover the principle allows no room for the exercise of any discretion by the court in favour of one party or the other.[315]

The consequence is that, subject to exceptions, discussed below, no person who is aware of the illegal nature of a contract can enforce it, or recover money or property transferred under it.

Since the justification for the rule that an illegal contract cannot be enforced by a guilty party is not to protect the defendant but because the Courts will not lend their aid to such a claimant it does not matter that the defendant shares the guilt. But, questions of illegality involve varying degrees of impropriety, of participation and responsibility, of injustice because of unjust enrichment, and of relationship between the illegality and the claim.[316] This, as well as the harshness of the consequences of the application of the *ex turpi causa* maxim, led to the adoption in some decisions of an approach, originating in cases concerned with the effect of illegality on a claim in tort,[317] whereby the Courts would help such a claimant unless to do so 'would be an

---

[314] *Holman* v. *Johnson* (1775) 1 Cowp. 341, at p. 343. See also Glanville Williams (1942) 8 C.L.J. 51; Grodecki (1955) 71 L.Q.R. 254.

[315] *Tinsley* v. *Milligan* [1994] 1 A.C. 340, *per* Lord Goff, at p. 355. But cf. Case C-453/99 *Courage Ltd.* v. *Crehan* [2001] 3 W.L.R. 1646 (where E.C. competition law renders agreement illegal a national rule barring relief to an innocent party is precluded by Article 81).

[316] Tan (1988) 104 L.Q.R. 523, at p. 526. See also *ante,* p. 348, *post,* pp. 397, 402–3; Buckley (1994) 110 L.Q.R. 3; Rose (1996) J.C.L. 271.

[317] *Thackwell* v. *Barclays Bank plc* [1986] 1 All E.R. 676; *Saunders* v. *Edwards* [1987] 1 W.L.R. 1116. On the test in tort, see further *Kirkham* v. *Chief Constable of Greater Manchester* [1990] 2 Q.B. 283; *Pitts* v. *Hunt* [1991] 1 Q.B. 24 and *post,* p. 408.

affront to public conscience'.[318] Although the 'public conscience' test seeks to address the underlying policy issues and would lead to a more unified approach to the effect of illegality in the law of obligations, and a greater harmony between common law and equitable rules, it has been rejected by the House of Lords. In *Tinsley* v. *Milligan* their Lordships stated that it was 'inconsistent with numerous authorities' and with Lord Mansfield's principle, it was 'imponderable', and that its adoption would replace a system of rules by a discretionary balancing operation.[319] Lord Goff considered that to introduce a system of discretionary relief[320] is a matter for the legislature after a full inquiry rather than for a Court.

(b) THE INTENTION OF THE PARTIES AND ENFORCEABILITY OF THE CONTRACT

It must, however, be emphasized at the outset that most contracts are not legal or illegal in the same way that eggs are good or bad. The effect of illegality will in most cases turn on the intention of the parties, i.e. whether one or both of them entered into the contract intending to do an act forbidden by the law. Their rights and remedies will depend upon whether they knew of or participated in the illegal intention.

(i) Guilty parties

A party who enters into a contract for an illegal purpose or intending to perform it in an illegal manner, or a contract which to the knowledge of that party involves or has as its object the commission of an illegal act, cannot bring any action upon the contract or enforce it in any way.[321] And if both parties share the unlawful intention, as in *Pearce* v. *Brooks*,[322] where both knew that the brougham was to be used for the purpose of prostitution, no action can be maintained by either party.

(ii) Innocent parties

A party who is innocent of any illegal intention is not without remedy. A number of situations must be distinguished.

(a) Lawful act intended to further illegal purpose. If the contract is one to do

---

[318] *Euro Diam Ltd.* v. *Bathurst* [1990] Q.B. 1, at p. 35. See also *Howard* v. *Shirlstar Container Transport Ltd.* [1990] 1 W.L.R. 1292, although *Tinsley* v. *Milligan* (*supra*, n. 315) at p. 360 has now explained this case as an example of the principle stated in *St John Shipping Corp.* v. *Rank* [1957] 1 Q.B. 267, *ante*, pp. 351–2.

[319] [1994] 1 A.C. 340, respectively at pp. 358 and 361 (*per* Lord Goff), p. 369 (*per* Lord Browne-Wilkinson), and pp. 358 and 363–4 (*per* Lord Goff). This decision is open to criticism on other grounds; *post*, p. 396.

[320] See the New Zealand Illegal Contracts Act 1970 and N.Z. Law Commission Report No. 25 *Contract Statutes Review* (1993) pp. 21, 173 ('in practice' this statute 'has worked reasonably well').

[321] *Alexander* v. *Rayson* [1936] 1 K.B. 169, at p. 182. Cf. *Edler* v. *Auerbach* [1950] 1 K.B. 359. On the attribution of knowledge to a company, see *Meridian Global Funds Management Asia Ltd.* v. *Securities Commission* [1995] 2 A.C. 500. See further *Selangor United Rubber Estates Ltd.* v. *Cradock (No. 3)* [1968] 1 W.L.R. 1555, at p. 1655.

[322] (1866) L.R. 1 Ex. 213; *ante*, p. 362. See also *Alexander* v. *Rayson* (*supra*, n. 321), *ante*, p. 354; *Corby* v. *Morrison* [1980] I.R.L.R. 218.

something which is lawful in itself, but which one of the parties intends to use for the furtherance of some illegal purpose or to perform in an illegal manner, the agreement can be the subject-matter of an action *at the suit of the innocent party*. Provided that there was no knowledge of the illegal intention of the other party, the innocent party is entitled to recover what may be due under the contract, or to obtain damages in full.[323] An innocent party who becomes aware of the illegality before the transaction is completed or while it is still executory, may refuse to perform the contract. Thus in *Cowan* v. *Milbourn*:[324]

M, agreed to let a set of rooms to C for certain days; then he discovered that it was proposed to use the rooms for the delivery of lectures which were unlawful because blasphemous within the meaning of a statute. M refused to carry out the agreement.

It was held that he was entitled to do so. But should the illegal purpose be discovered before it is carried into effect, an innocent party who allows it to proceed none the less cannot recover. In *Cowan* v. *Milbourn*, M could not have recovered the rent of his rooms if, having let them in ignorance of C's intentions, he had allowed the rooms to be used after he had learned of the illegal purpose which his tenant contemplated.

(b) Commission of illegal act. The same principle applies where the contract is not unlawful '*per se*'[325] and one party is unaware that it involves or has as its object the commission of an illegal act. The contract itself is still valid, and an innocent party who was ignorant of the facts which constitute the illegality can enforce it. In *Bloxsome* v. *Williams*:[326]

B contracted with W on a Sunday for the purchase of a horse, W warranting that the horse was not more than 7 years old and sound. Unknown to B, W was a horse-dealer and the Sunday Observance Act 1677 imposed a penalty on a horse-dealer for exercising his trade on a Sunday. The horse was 17 years old and unsound, and B sued for damages for breach of warranty.

The Court of King's Bench held that the illegality was no defence to the action for breach of contract as B was ignorant of the fact that W was a horse-dealer. It is also possible for an innocent party who has executed part of such a contract before discovering the illegality to recover reasonable remuneration for the work already done in a restitutionary action. So in *Clay* v. *Yates*[327] a printer was able to recover the value of work done towards the publication of a treatise which, after the major part of it had been printed, he found to contain defamatory material.

[323] *Mason* v. *Clarke* [1955] A.C. 778, at pp. 793, 805. See also *Fielding & Platt Ltd.* v. *Najjar* [1969] 1 W.L.R. 357; *Newland* v. *Simons and Willer (Hairdressers) Ltd.* [1981] I.C.R. 521.

[324] (1867) L.R. 2 Ex. 230. The definition of blasphemy in this case must be revised in the light of *Bowman* v. *Secular Society Ltd.* [1917] A.C. 406.

[325] See *post*, p. 400.

[326] (1824) 3 B. & C. 232 (the defendant in this case could not have sued: *Fennell* v. *Ridler* (1826) 5 B. & C. 406). See also *Shaw* v. *Shaw* [1954] 2 Q.B. 429; *Bank für Gemeinwirtschaft* v. *City of London Garages Ltd.* [1971] 1 W.L.R. 149 and the cases cited *ante*, pp. 350–1. Cf. *Phoenix General Insurance Co. of Greece S.A.* v. *Halvanon Insurance Co. Ltd.* [1988] 1 Q.B. 216 (effect reversed by the Financial Services Act 1986, s. 132).

[327] (1856) 1 H. & N. 73. Cf. *Taylor* v. *Bhail* [1996] C.L.C. 377, at p. 383 (no such remuneration for guilty party) and *Aratra Potato Co.* v. *Taylor Johnson Garrett* [1995] 4 All E.R. 695, at pp. 709–10 (no *quantum meruit* for work done under champertous agreement).

(c) Legal formation but illegal performance. Different considerations, however, apply where there is no illegal intention at the time the contract is entered into, but one party subsequently performs the contract in an illegal manner. Normally that party will be precluded from enforcing any claim which requires reliance on its own illegal performance.[328] But this is not necessarily the case. As we have seen, if a statutory offence is committed in the course of performing a contract, the intention of the statute may simply be to impose a penalty, and not to prevent the party in default from asserting civil remedies.[329] There may also be other situations where public policy does not require that the commission of an unlawful or immoral act in the course of performance should deprive the 'guilty' party of recourse to the Courts.[330] In any event, the normal contractual remedies are available to the innocent party. In *Archbold's (Freightage) Ltd.* v. *Spanglett Ltd.*:[331]

S agreed with A to carry a consignment of whisky from Leeds to London docks in one of its vans. Unknown to A, the vehicle to be used for this purpose did not possess an 'A' licence entitling it to carry the goods of other persons for reward. Owing to the driver's negligence, the whisky was stolen *en route* and A claimed damages for its loss. S contended that it was not liable as the contract was illegal.

The Court of Appeal refused to accept this contention. The contract was not one prohibited by statute; and it was not rendered illegal merely by the fact that one of the parties (i.e. S) had performed it in an unlawful manner. Thus, even though S might not have been able to enforce the contract, A was ignorant of the illegality and was entitled to damages. In such cases the illegal performance of the contract will not render it unenforceable unless, in addition to knowledge of the facts which make the performance illegal, the party seeking to enforce it actively participates in the illegal method of performance.[332]

(d) Ignorance of law generally no defence. There is, however, an important qualification which must be made to the principles stated above. A party to a contract who has full knowledge of the facts which constitute the illegality, but yet is ignorant of the law will, however, not be held to be innocent, for, in the context of enforcement, *ignorantia juris haud excusat.* In *J. M. Allan (Merchandising) Ltd.* v. *Cloke*[333] the plaintiff sued the defendant for rentals payable in respect of a roulette table hired to the defendant and designed for the playing of 'Roulette Royale', a game which was at that time unlawful by virtue of the Betting and Gaming Act 1960.[334] At the time the parties entered into the hiring agreement, neither knew that the game was illegal, and the plaintiff pleaded that it had no 'wicked intention to break the law'. The Court of

---

[328] *Anderson Ltd.* v. *Daniel* [1924] 1 K.B. 138; *B. & B. Viennese Fashions* v. *Losane* [1952] 1 All E.R. 909.

[329] See *ante*, p. 352.

[330] *Coral Leisure Group Ltd.* v. *Barnett* [1981] I.C.R. 521.

[331] [1961] 1 Q.B. 374.

[332] *Ashmore, Benson, Pease & Co. Ltd.* v. *A. V. Dawson Ltd.* [1973] 1 W.L.R. 828; *ante*, p. 351; *Hall* v. *Woolston Hall Leisure Ltd.* [2001] 1 W.L.R. 225, at pp. 236, 246.

[333] [1963] 2 Q.B. 340. See also *Nash* v. *Stevenson Transport Ltd.* [1936] 2 K.B. 128; *Miller* v. *Karlinski* (1945) 62 T.L.R. 85. Cf. *Shelley* v. *Paddock* [1980] Q.B. 348.

[334] The Act has now been repealed.

Appeal rejected this plea and held that ignorance of the law was no answer to the charge of illegality so as to permit the plaintiff to enforce the agreement.

(e) Ignorance of law a defence where performance legal. In *Cloke*'s case, the parties intended from the beginning that the subject-matter of the contract should be used for an unlawful purpose (the playing of 'Roulette Royale'), and this fact was held to render the contract illegal in its formation. On the other hand, in *Waugh* v. *Morris*:[335]

M chartered a ship belonging to W to take a cargo of hay from Trouville to London, the cargo to be unloaded alongside ship in the river. M subsequently instructed the master to land the hay at a wharf at Deptford Creek, and the master agreed to do so. Unknown to the parties an Order in Council (made before the charterparty was entered into) had forbidden the *landing* of French hay in order to prevent the spread of disease among animals. M, on hearing this, took the cargo from alongside the ship without landing it, and exported it, thus avoiding a breach of the Order in Council. The return of the vessel was delayed, and W sued for damages arising from the delay.

M pleaded as a defence that the charterparty contemplated an illegal act, the landing of French hay contrary to the Order in Council. This defence did not prevail. The charterparty itself merely provided that the hay should be taken and delivered alongside, but not landed; and the Court found as a fact that W never contemplated or believed that M would violate the law. In his judgment, however, Blackburn J. said:[336]

Where a contract is to do a thing which cannot be performed without a violation of the law it is void, whether the parties knew the law or not. But we think, that in order to avoid a contract which can be legally performed, on the ground that there was an intention to perform it in an illegal manner, it is necessary to show that there was the wicked intention to break the law; and if this be so, the knowledge of what the law is becomes of great importance.

It is submitted that Blackburn J. did not intend, by these words, to lay down a general rule that, when a contract is not illegal in its formation, but the illegality resides only in its performance, a party may be excused by ignorance of the law. The principle is more narrow: that if one or both parties contemplate a method of performance which is, unknown to them, illegal, they will not be shut out from their contractual remedies if, on their discovering the illegality, the contract is lawfully performed.[337]

(c) CONTRACTS UNLAWFUL '*PER SE*'

If a contract is expressly or by implication forbidden by statute or by public policy, then it is void and unenforceable, though the parties may have been ignorant of the facts constituting the illegality and did not intend to break the law. Such contracts are unlawful *per se* and the intention of the parties is irrelevant.

[335] (1873) L.R. 8 Q.B. 202.
[336] At p. 208.
[337] See also *Hindley & Co. Ltd.* v. *General Fibre Co. Ltd.* [1940] 2 K.B. 517. Cf. *Reynolds* v. *Kinsey* 1959 (4) S.A. 50 (South Africa).

An example of a contract forbidden by statute has been given in *Re Mahmoud and Ispahani*[338] where the plaintiff, who was ignorant of the fact that the defendant had no licence to purchase linseed oil, was unable to recover damages for non-acceptance in face of a statutory prohibition. An example of a contract forbidden by public policy is one which necessarily involves trading with an alien enemy in time of war. No rights of action will arise, even though one party at the time of the agreement is ignorant of the fact that war has broken out or that the other party has the status of an enemy.[339] The agreement itself is prohibited and cannot be enforced in any way.

It is clear that considerable difficulty may be experienced in deciding whether a particular statute or head of public policy renders the contract unlawful *per se* or merely prevents a guilty party from suing on it. The modern tendency is to hold that a contracting party who has not participated in the unlawful intention should not be denied relief. The state of mind of the parties is the crucial factor. Unless it is clear that the legislature intended, or public policy demands, that the contract be prohibited altogether, the innocent party can sue on the agreement.

Moreover, even if the contract is one which is unlawful *per se*, the innocent party is not necessarily without remedy. If the innocent party has been induced to enter into the contract by a misrepresentation or assurance by the other party, then damages can be recovered for breach of a collateral warranty if such has been given,[340] or for fraud if there is fraud,[341] provided that the conduct of the innocent party is not itself sufficiently culpable to bar that remedy.[342] So in *Strongman (1945) Ltd.* v. *Sincock*[343] a builder recovered damages for the breach of a collateral assurance by his client that he would obtain the necessary licences to enable the work to be carried out, even though a contract to build without a licence was absolutely prohibited by statute. And in *Shelley* v. *Paddock*[344] a woman who was fraudulently induced to agree to buy a house in Spain in ignorance of the fact that the purchase was in breach of the Exchange Control Act 1947 was held entitled to recover damages for the fraud.

(d) BENEFIT FROM ILLEGAL CONTRACTS

It is sometimes said to be a rule of law that no person can take any benefit from a contract, either directly or through a personal representative, when that benefit results

---

[338] [1921] 2 K.B. 716, *ante*, p. 349; *Chai Sau Yin* v. *Liew Kwee Sam* [1962] A.C. 304; *Harse* v. *Pearl Life Assurance Co.* [1904] 1 K.B. 558.

[339] *Sovfracht (v/o)* v. *Van Udens Scheepvaart en Argentuur Maatschappij (N.V. Gebr.)* [1943] A.C. 203.

[340] *Strongman (1945) Ltd.* v. *Sincock* [1955] 2 Q.B. 525, at pp. 536, 539; *Gregory* v. *Ford* [1951] 1 All E.R. 121.

[341] *Burrows* v. *Rhodes* [1899] 1 Q.B. 816; *Road Transport & General Insurance Co.* v. *Adams* [1955] C.L.Y. 2455; *Shelley* v. *Paddock* [1980] Q.B. 348. Rescission on the ground of fraud may also be available, see *Hughes* v. *Clewley (The Siben) (No. 2)* [1996] 1 Lloyd's Rep. 35 (not available in that case), *ante*, pp. 253, 257.

[342] *Askey* v. *Golden Wine Co. Ltd.* [1948] 2 All E.R. 35.

[343] [1955] 2 Q.B. 525.

[344] [1980] Q.B. 348. See also *Hughes* v. *Clewley (The Siben) (No. 2)* [1996] 1 Lloyd's Rep. 35, at p. 63 and *Saunders* v. *Edwards* [1987] 1 W.L.R. 1116, the result, but not the reasoning of which was said to be 'unassailable' by Lord Goff in *Tinsley* v. *Milligan* [1994] 1 A.C. 340, at p. 360.

from the performance by *that person* of an illegal act.[345] In *Beresford* v. *Royal Insurance Co. Ltd.*:[346]

R insured his life with the defendant company for £50,000. A few minutes before the policy was due to lapse, he committed suicide. The policy contained a term avoiding it in the event of suicide within a year of its commencement, but the suicide occurred after the policy had run for some years.

The House of Lords held that the insurance company had agreed to pay in this event, but that the claim was contrary to public policy as the deceased's personal representatives could not obtain any benefit from the assured's illegal act. The case would certainly not be decided the same way at the present day, for suicide is no longer a crime,[347] and the rule itself is probably too widely stated. It is submitted that it will only apply where the statute or head of public policy is such as to require that the offender be deprived of the fruits of the illegal act.[348] Thus, although it has been held that no recovery would be allowed under a policy of insurance when the insured goods had been deliberately imported without payment of customs duty,[349] the same considerations would not apply in the case of unintentional importation or the innocent possession of uncustomed goods.[350] Similarly, in principle no remuneration in the form of a restitutionary *quantum meruit* will be given for work done pursuant to an illegal contract where that would amount to indirect enforcement of the contract.[351]

(e) RECOVERY OF MONEY PAID OR PROPERTY TRANSFERRED

(i) Generally not recoverable

It is scarcely surprising that the Courts will refuse to enforce an illegal agreement at the suit of a person who is implicated in the illegality. But it is also a rule of English law that money paid or property transferred by such a person cannot be recovered. In the colourful words of Wilmot C.J.:

All writers upon our law agree in this, no polluted hand shall touch the pure fountains of

---

[345] *Cleaver* v. *Mutual Reserve Fund Life Association* [1892] 1 Q.B. 147; *Re the Estate of Crippen* [1911] P. 108, at p. 112; *Archbolds (Freightage) Ltd.* v. *Spanglett Ltd.* [1961] 1 Q.B. 374, at p. 388; *Re Giles* [1971] Ch. 544; *Davitt* v. *Titcumb* [1990] 1 Ch. 110. But see the Forfeiture Act 1982; *Re K.* [1985] Ch. 85; *Re S.* [1996] 1 W.L.R. 235.

[346] [1938] A.C. 586. See also *Prince of Wales etc. Association* v. *Palmer* (1858) 25 Beav. 605. Cf. *White* v. *British Empire etc. Assurance Co.* (1868) L.R. 7 Eq. 394.

[347] Suicide Act 1961.

[348] *Marles* v. *Philip Trant & Sons Ltd.* [1954] 1 Q.B. 29, at p. 39; *St. John Shipping Cpn.* v. *Joseph Rank Ltd.* [1957] 1 Q.B. 267, at p. 292; *R.* v. *Chief National Insurance Commissioner* [1981] Q.B. 758, at p. 765; *Gardner* v. *Moore* [1984] 1 A.C. 548; *Thorne* v. *Silverleaf* [1994] 1 B.C.L.C. 637.

[349] *Geismar* v. *Sun Alliance and London Insurance Ltd.* [1978] Q.B. 383; *ante*, p. 355.

[350] *Ibid.*, at p. 395.

[351] *Aratra Potato Co.* v. *Taylor Johnson Garrett* [1995] 4 All E.R. 695, at pp. 709–10 (champertous agreement). But, in the case of statutory illegality, *quaere* whether the test is whether the statute bars restitution as well as enforcement of the executory contract; see by analogy *Scott* v. *Pattison* [1923] 2 K.B. 723; *Pavey & Matthews Pty. Ltd.* v. *Paul* (1986–87) 162 C.L.R. 221 (unenforceable contracts).

justice. Whoever is a party to an unlawful contract, if he hath once paid the money stipulated to be paid in pursuance thereof, he shall not have the help of a court to fetch it back
again.[352]

This principle is expressed in the maxim *in pari delicto potior est conditio defendentis*
and it may be illustrated by the case of *Parkinson* v. *College of Ambulance Ltd.*:[353]

The secretary of a charitable organization promised P that he would secure for him a
knighthood if P made a sufficient donation to the organization's funds. In consideration of
this promise, P paid over £3,000 and promised more when he should receive the honour.
The knighthood never materialized, and P sued for the return of his money.

Although, there was 'a total failure of consideration', which, but for the illegality,
would have grounded a restitutionary claim for the return of the money, it was held
that the action must fail as it was founded upon a transaction which was illegal at
common law.

But there are exceptional cases in which a person will be relieved of the consequences of an illegal contract which that person has entered—cases to which the
maxim just quoted does not apply. They fall into three classes: (i) where the illegal
purpose has not yet been carried into effect before it is sought to recover the money
paid or goods delivered or other property transferred in furtherance of it; (ii) where
the party seeking recovery is not *in pari delicto* with the party resisting recovery; (iii)
where the claimant does not have to rely on the illegal contract to make out the claim,
but can establish a claim based on a legal or equitable property right. Each of these
exceptions will be considered in turn.

(ii) Illegal purpose not yet carried into effect

The first exception relates to cases where money has been paid, or goods delivered, or
other property transferred for an unlawful purpose which has not yet been carried
into effect because the claimant withdrew in time.[354] The law is not quite satisfactorily
settled on this point, and the authorities are difficult to reconcile, but its present
condition would seem to demand that two conditions be satisfied. First, the party
seeking to recover must withdraw from the transaction before the illegal purpose is
executed in whole or in part. Secondly, the withdrawal must be voluntary and not be
merely frustration by circumstances over which the party seeking to recover money
paid or property transferred has no control.

It is, however, highly unlikely that the Courts would allow any opportunity for a
withdrawal or change of mind in the most serious cases of moral reprehensibility, as
for example, where money is paid to another to commit murder.[355]

(a) Repudiation of illegal purpose. While the illegality is still completely executory, the
parties are allowed an opportunity for repentance or change of mind, a *locus poeniten-*

[352] *Collins* v. *Blantern* (1767) 2 Wilson 341, at p. 350.
[353] [1925] 2 K.B. 1. See also *Shaw* v. *Shaw* [1965] 1 W.L.R. 937. For a criticism of the maxim, see Grodecki (1955) 71 L.Q.R. 254.
[354] See Beatson (1975) 91 L.Q.R. 313; Merkin (1981) 97 L.Q.R. 920.
[355] *Kearley* v. *Thomson* (1890) 24 Q.B.D. 742, at p. 747; *Tappenden* v. *Randall* (1801) 2 B. & P. 467.

tiae. But some doubt exists as to when this privilege ceases. In *Taylor* v. *Bowers*[356] it was said by Mellish L.J. that:

If money is paid or goods delivered for an illegal purpose, the person who had so paid the money or delivered the goods may recover them back *before the illegal purpose is carried out*; but if he waits till the illegal purpose is carried out, or if he seeks to enforce the illegal transaction, in neither case can he maintain an action.

The facts of the case to which these words applied were as follows:

T, a debtor, had made a fictitious assignment of his goods to one A in order to defraud his creditors. Two meetings of creditors were then called, but no composition was reached as only one creditor turned up. A had in the meantime, without T's consent, parted with the goods under a bill of sale to the defendant, who was one of the creditors and knew of the fraudulent assignment. T sued the defendant for the recovery of the goods.

It was held that he was entitled to succeed. It could be contended that, in this case, the illegal purpose was still entirely executory, for no creditor had actually been defrauded.[357] But it is difficult to see the fictitious assignment as anything but a part-performance of the illegal purpose, since at the two creditors' meetings the creditors would clearly have been less likely to have pressed their claims in view of the assignment. If this is so, then the facts in *Taylor* v. *Bowers* support the principle stated by Mellish L.J., that recovery is possible at any time before the illegal purpose is carried out, i.e. completed.[358]

Subsequent cases, however, do not endorse this formulation. In *Kearley* v. *Thomson*,[359] for instance:

The defendants, a firm of solicitors acting for a petitioning creditor of one Clarke, a bankrupt, agreed with K, a friend of Clarke, that in consideration of the payment of their costs they would not appear at the public examination of Clarke, nor oppose the order for his discharge. They carried out the first part of the agreement, but before any application was made for Clarke's discharge, K changed his mind and sought to recover the money which he had paid.

K's action failed. It was held that the agreement was illegal as tending to pervert the course of justice, and that recovery was precluded as the illegal purpose had already been partly executed. The principle as formulated by Mellish L.J. in *Taylor* v. *Bowers*, and even the case itself, might, said the Court, require reconsideration.[360] In any event, the case before the Court was distinguishable as there had been 'a partial carrying into effect of an illegal purpose in a substantial manner'.[361] Although the matter is not free

---

[356] (1876) 1 Q.B.D. 291, at p. 300.

[357] *Tinsley* v. *Milligan* [1994] 1 A.C. 340, at p. 374 ; *Tribe* v. *Tribe* [1996] Ch. 107, at pp. 121–2, 124, 132–3. See also *Perpetual Executor & Trustees Assoc.* v. *Wright* (1917) 23 C.L.R. 185, at p. 193 (High Court of Australia).

[358] See also *Singh* v. *Ali* [1960] A.C. 160, at p. 167.

[359] (1890) 24 Q.B.D. 742.

[360] See Millett L.J.'s doubts in *Tribe* v. *Tribe* [1996] Ch. 107, at p. 125. But the decision was cited without disapproval in *Tinsley* v. *Milligan* [1994] 1 A.C. 340, at p. 374.

[361] *Ibid.*, *per* Fry L.J. at p. 747. See also *Apthorp* v. *Neville & Co.* (1907) 23 T.L.R. 575; *Re National Benefit Assurance Co. Ltd.* [1931] 1 Ch. 46; *Parker (Harry) Ltd.* v. *Mason* [1940] 2 K.B. 590.

from doubt,[362] the position now seems to be that money paid or goods delivered in pursuance of an illegal purpose cannot be recovered where that purpose has been executed in whole or in part.[363]

(b) Withdrawal must be genuine. What the law allows in these cases is a *locus poenitentiae,* and therefore, whilst it will help one who repudiates, it will not help a person who has abandoned the illegal purpose only because that purpose has been frustrated by the failure of the other contracting party to fulfil his side of the illegal contract, or in some other way. So, in *Bigos* v. *Bousted*:[364]

In breach of the provisions of the Exchange Control Act 1947, A entered into an agreement with B whereby B agreed to make available £150 worth of Italian currency to enable A's wife and daughter to travel in Italy. As security, A deposited with B a share certificate. The promised money was never forthcoming, and A sued B to recover the certificate.

It was pleaded on A's behalf that he was entitled to a *locus poenitentiae* as the illegal contract had not been performed, but this contention was rejected by Pritchard J. He held that there was no true withdrawal on A's part; the contract had merely been frustrated by B's failure to supply the money.

But although the *withdrawal* must be genuine, it is not necessary that there be genuine repentance. Thus in *Tribe* v. *Tribe*:[365]

A father transferred shares to his son on trust so that they would not be the subject of claims made against him by creditors but the illegal purpose of defrauding the creditors was not carried out because the claims settled. The son refused to transfer the shares back to his father.

The Court of Appeal held that the father was entitled to the benefit of the *locus poenitentiae* doctrine. Millett L.J. stated that 'genuine repentance is not required . . . voluntary withdrawal from an illegal transaction when it has ceased to be needed is sufficient'.[366]

(c) Marriage brokage contracts. Marriage brokage contracts, are an exception to the general rule. In *Hermann* v. *Charlesworth*,[367] a woman who had paid £52 to the proprietor of a newspaper, *The Matrimonial Post and Fashionable Marriage Advertiser*, with a view to obtaining by advertisement an offer of marriage, successfully recovered the money after advertisements had appeared, and several prospective suitors had been introduced, but before any marriage had been arranged.

(iii) Parties not *'in pari delicto'*

Where the parties are not *in pari delicto* the less guilty party may be able to recover

---

[362] Cf. Lord Browne-Wilkinson's formulations (whether illegal purpose 'put into operation' and whether it was 'carried through') in *Tinsley* v. *Milligan* (*supra*, n. 360) at p. 374.

[363] *Tribe* v. *Tribe* [1996] Ch. 107, at pp. 122, 124, 133. Cf. at 134. For an alternative formulation, see Beatson (1975) 91 L.Q.R. 313, at pp. 314–16.

[364] [1951] 1 All E.R. 92. But see *Shelley* v. *Paddock* [1980] Q.B. 348.

[365] [1996] Ch. 107.

[366] *Ibid.*, at p. 135.

[367] [1905] 2 K.B. 123. Cf. *ante*, p. 363 doubting that such contracts should be unenforceable.

money paid, or property transferred, under the contract. This possibility may arise in two basic situations. The first is where the contract is rendered illegal by statute in order to protect a class of persons of whom the claimant is one. The second is where the nature of the restitutionary cause of action shows that the claimant was ignorant or innocent of the illegality.

(a) Class protecting statutes. First, the case of a contract made illegal by statute in the interests of a particular class of persons of whom the claimant is one. As Lord Mansfield explained in *Browning* v. *Morris*:[368]

... [W]here contracts or transactions are prohibited by positive statutes, for the sake of protecting one set of men from another set of men; the one, from their situation and condition, being liable to be oppressed or imposed upon by the other; there, the parties are not *in pari delicto*; and in furtherance of these statutes, the person injured, after the transaction is finished and completed, may bring his action and defeat the contract.

The Rent Acts have furnished an illustration of this type of case. The Rent Act 1977 provides that, where under any agreement a premium is paid which could not lawfully be required or received, the premium is to be recoverable by the person by whom it is paid.[369] But even in the absence of any such express statutory provision, it has been held that a tenant or assignee of a lease, though a willing party to the evasion of the Rent Acts, may recover an illegal premium paid, since the Acts were passed for the protection of such persons.[370]

The intention of the statute is one of prime importance. In *Green* v. *Portsmouth Stadium Ltd.*:[371]

G, a bookmaker, alleged that, over a long period of time, he had been overcharged by the defendants for admission to a greyhound track run by them. The Betting and Lotteries Act 1934, section 13(1), allowed a charge to be made to bookmakers not exceeding five times the highest fee for the public at large, but G had been compelled to pay considerably more. He claimed the excess from the defendants in an action for money had and received.

The Court of Appeal held that the action must fail. The Act was designed to regulate racecourses; it was not a bookmakers' charter. The statute was not passed 'to protect one set of men from another set of men', at any rate, not so as to give bookmakers the right to bring civil proceedings for the recovery of their money.

(b) Fraud. Where a person has been induced to enter into the contract by fraud, recovery will be allowed. In *Hughes* v. *Liverpool Victoria Legal Friendly Society*:[372]

H took up five insurance policies with the defendants on the lives of persons in which she

---

[368] (1778) 2 Cowp. 790, at p. 792.

[369] Rent Act 1977, s. 125. See *Farrell* v. *Alexander* [1977] A.C. 59.

[370] *Gray* v. *Southouse* [1949] 2 All E.R. 1019; *Kiriri Cotton Co. Ltd.* v. *Dewani* [1960] A.C. 192. See also *Ailion* v. *Spiekermann* [1976] Ch. 158.

[371] [1953] 2 Q.B. 190.

[372] [1916] 2 K.B. 482. Cf. *Harse* v. *Pearl Life Assurance Co.* [1904] 1 K.B. 558 where no fraud present. See also *Reynell* v. *Sprye* (1852) 1 De G. M. & G. 660. See also, *ante*, p. 401 (*damages* for fraud).

had no insurable interest. She was induced to do so by a fraudulent misrepresentation on the part of the defendants' agent that the policies were valid and would be paid. They were in fact illegal and void.

It was held that she was entitled to recover the premiums which she had paid.

(c) Oppression and duress. The position is the same where a person has been induced to enter into the contract by improper pressure. In *Atkinson* v. *Denby*:[373]

A, a debtor, offered his creditors a composition of 5s. in the pound. The defendant, an influential creditor, refused to assent to the composition unless A would make him an additional payment of £50 in fraud of the other creditors. This was done and the composition arrangement was carried out. A then sued to recover the £50 on the ground that it was a payment made by him under oppression.

It was held that he could recover. The Court of Exchequer Chamber, affirming the judgment of the Court of Exchequer, observed:[374]

It is said that both parties are *in pari delicto*. It is true that both are *in delicto*, because the Act is a fraud upon the other creditors, but it is not *par delictum*, because one has the power to dictate, the other no alternative but to submit.

(d) Mistake. Where money is mistakenly paid under an invalid or ineffective contract, the payer may recover it subject to defences in the law of restitution such as change of position. This has long been the case for mistakes of fact, even where the contract is illegal. In *Oom* v. *Bruce*[375] insurance premiums paid by the agent of a Russian in ignorance of the outbreak of war between the United Kingdom and Russia (a matter making the contract illegal) were held to be recoverable. Until recently, as a general rule, money paid under a mistake of law was irrecoverable. The rule had been subject to much criticism, and, in 1960, in the context of an illegal contract, Lord Denning had suggested that money paid under a mistake of law should be recoverable whenever the payee is primarily responsible for the mistake.[376] By 1994, when the Law Commission recommended its abolition,[377] the rule was clearly 'on the turn',[378] and, in 1998 the House of Lords, in *Kleinwort Benson Ltd.* v *Lincoln C.C.*,[379] held that it was not part of English law. In that case KB sought to recover payments made to the defendant under interest rate swaps contracts believed to be binding but subsequently held *ultra vires*. In principle, the position should be the same in the case of money paid under an illegal contract.

(e) Fiduciary duty. There is some authority for the view that a person who is under a fiduciary duty to the claimant may not be allowed to retain property, or to refuse to

---

[373] (1861) 6 H. & N. 778, aff'd (1862) 7 H. & N. 934. On duress, see *ante*, p. 277.

[374] (1862) 7 H. & N. 934, at p. 936.

[375] (1810) 12 East 225.

[376] *Kiriri Cotton Co. Ltd.* v. *Dewani* [1960] A.C. 192, at p. 204.

[377] Law Com. No. 227, *Mistakes of Law and Ultra Vires Public Authority Receipts and Payments*, (1994), §§ 3.7–3.12.

[378] *Friends Provident Life Office* v. *Hillier Parker* [1997] Q.B. 85, *per* Auld L.J. at p. 97.

[379] [1999] 2 A.C. 349.

account for monies received, on the ground that the property or the monies have come into his hands as the proceeds of an illegal transaction. In *Re Thomas*,[380] where a client sought to recover from his solicitor money paid in pursuance of a champertous agreement between them, it was held that he was entitled to do so. 'Is every rascally solicitor', said Lindley L.J.,[381] 'to invoke his own rascality as a ground of immunity from the jurisdiction of the Court?' It may also be that an agent who receives money from a third party under an illegal contract is bound to account to the principal for the proceeds.[382] But this exception is by no means clearly established, and it is probable that recovery will be denied where the agency is itself illegal.[383]

(f) Critique. It will be seen from this discussion that until recently only a limited number of situations in which one of the parties will be held not to be *in pari delicto* with the other were recognized. The removal of the bar on recovery of money paid under a mistake of law is an important liberalizing development. But there is also a case for going further, and applying a test similar to that in the *St. John Shipping Corp.* case in the context of enforcement of the contract,[384] i.e. weighing up the comparative merits of the parties in the light of the statutory purposes and policies, and allowing the recovery of money or property when to so so would not undermine them.[385]

(iv) Claimant not relying on the illegal contract

It is settled law that the ownership of property can pass under an illegal contract if the parties so intend, as in the case of goods sold to a buyer under an illegal contract of sale.[386]

Where, however, only a limited interest is transferred, as under a contract of bailment or a lease, or a trust, it is equally well established that the owner of the property who is not forced to found the claim on the illegal contract,[387] but simply relies on his or her title to the property, can recover it from the bailee or lessee.

This principle is extremely difficult to apply since it is frequently hard to determine whether a claimant is relying upon title, or upon the contractual provisions of the illegal agreement. For example, it seems probable that a landlord can recover premises let to a tenant under an illegal agreement once the term of years has expired; but it is a matter of doubt whether the landlord could recover them in the meantime under a

---

[380] [1894] 1 Q.B. 742. But cf. *Kearley* v. *Thomson* (1890) 24 Q.B.D. 742; *Palaniappa Chettiar* v. *Arunasalam Chettiar* [1962] A.C. 294.

[381] At p. 749.

[382] *Tenant* v. *Elliott* (1797) 1 B. & P. 3; *Farmer* v. *Russell* (1798) 1 B. & P. 296; *Bone* v. *Eckless* (1869) 5 H. & N. 925. See also *Bridger* v. *Savage* (1884) 15 Q.B.D. 363.

[383] *Parker (Harry) Ltd.* v. *Mason* [1940] 2 K.B. 590.

[384] [1957] 1 Q.B. 267, *ante*, pp. 351–2.

[385] See *Nelson* v. *Nelson* (1995) 132 A.L.R. 133, *post*, p. 411.

[386] *Scarfe* v. *Morgan* (1838) 4 M. & W. 270, at p. 281; *Elder* v. *Kelly* [1919] 2 K.B. 179; *Singh* v. *Ali* [1960] A.C. 167; *Kingsley* v. *Sterling Industrial Securities Ltd.* [1967] 2 Q.B. 747, at pp. 782, 783; *Belvoir Finance Co. Ltd.* v. *Stapleton* [1971] 1 Q.B. 210; *Tinsley* v. *Milligan* [1994] 1 A.C. 340, *per* Lord Browne-Wilkinson at p. 374; *Aratra Potato Co.* v. *Taylor Johnson Garrett* [1995] 4 All E.R. 695, at p. 710. Cf. *Amar Singh* v. *Kulubya* [1964] A.C. 142 (transfer prohibited). See also Higgins (1962) 25 M.L.R. 149.

[387] *Amar Singh* v. *Kulubya* (*supra*, n. 386); *Tinsley* v. *Milligan* (*supra*, n. 386).

covenant which provided for forfeiture for non-payment of rent.[388] Would the land-lord be relying on his independent right of ownership, or (more probably) upon the contractual provisions of the illegal lease?

(a) Claims based on legal title. In the case of chattels, it has been held that the termination of the bailment puts the bailor in the more favoured position. In *Bow-makers Ltd.* v. *Barnet Instruments Ltd.*:[389]

The defendant entered into a contract whereby it agreed to hire-purchase from Bowmakers certain machine tools. Such an agreement was rendered illegal by a government order which prohibited the disposition of machine tools without a licence from the Ministry of Supply. The defendant failed to make the agreed payments for hire. It further sold some of the tools and refused to deliver up to Bowmakers others still in its possession. Bowmakers sued for damages for conversion.

It was contended on behalf of the defendant that since the contract of hire-purchase was illegal, Bowmakers could have no remedy on it. It pointed to the case of *Taylor* v. *Chester*[390] where a man failed to recover half of a £50 bank note deposited by him to secure the payment of money for a night's debauch in a brothel. To this the plaintiff replied that it was not relying on the contract, but upon its paramount right of ownership, the bailment having come to an end. The case of *Taylor* v. *Chester* was distinguishable because the pledge had not been redeemed, whereas in *Bowmakers'* case all possessory rights of the defendant had been extinguished. This latter argument was adopted by the Court of Appeal. Du Parcq L.J. said:[391]

In our opinion, a man's right to possess his own chattels will as a general rule be enforced against one who, without any claim of right, is detaining them, or has converted them to his own use, even though it may appear either from the pleadings, or in the course of the trial, that the chattels in question came into the defendant's possession by reason of an illegal contract between himself and the plaintiff, provided that the plaintiff does not seek, and is not forced, either to found his claim on the illegal contract or to plead its illegality in order to support his claim.

This case has been criticized[392] on the ground that, although the possessory rights of the defendants in the tools *sold* had come to an end,[393] this was not so in the case of the tools *retained*. In so far as the Court allowed the claim to these latter in pursuance of the terms of the agreement, it was in effect permitting the enforcement of the provisions of an illegal agreement. Nevertheless, the principle has been accepted,[394] even if its application is a matter of dispute.

---

[388] *Jaijbhay* v. *Cassim* 1939 A.D. 537 (South Africa); *Gas Light & Coke Co.* v. *Turner* (1839) 5 Bing. N.C. 666, *per* Tindal C.J. at p. 677; *Alexander* v. *Rayson* [1936] 1 K.B. 169, *per curiam* at p. 186.

[389] [1945] K.B. 65. See also *Tinsley* v. *Milligan* [1994] 1 A.C. 340.

[390] (1869) L.R. 4 Q.B. 309.

[391] [1945] K.B. 65, at p. 71.

[392] Hamson (1949) 10 C.L.J. 249; Paton, *Bailment in the Common Law* (1952), p. 34; *Miles* v. *Watson* [1953] N.Z.L.R. 958. For wider criticism, see *Nelson* v. *Nelson* (1995) 132 A.L.R. 133, at pp. 176, 189–90, *post*, p. 411. The case is stoutly defended by Coote (1972) 35 M.L.R. 38.

[393] An act inconsistent with the bailment, such as pledging or selling the goods bailed, automatically determines the bailment and the immediate right to possession re-vests in the bailor.

[394] *Belvoir Finance Co. Ltd.* v. *Stapleton* [1971] 1 Q.B. 210. Cf. *Lewis & Hall* v. *McBurney* [1970] C.L.Y. 372.

It seems probable that, if the property were of such a kind that it would be absurd to encourage litigation concerning its ownership, such as housebreaking instruments, obscene books, or controlled drugs, the Court would not countenance recovery in any event.[395] But it is difficult to see how a principle that entitles parties to recover their property can properly make a distinction of this sort.[396]

(b) Claims based on equitable interests. In *Tinsley* v. *Milligan*[397] the principle in the *Bowmakers* case was applied to a claim based upon an equitable interest.

T and M purchased a house with funds generated by a joint business venture on the understanding that they had equal interests in it, but registered it in T's name so that M was able to make fraudulent claims for benefit from the Department of Social Security. Later, after the parties had quarrelled, T asserted her legal title and M, who had confessed her wrongdoing and made amends to the Department, counterclaimed for a declaration that T held the house on trust for the parties in equal shares.

It is a rule of equity that (save in the case of certain dealings between spouses and parents and children) where two parties have provided the purchase money to buy property which is conveyed into the name of one alone, that party is presumed to hold the property on a resulting trust for both parties in shares proportionate to their contributions to the price. Such a resulting trust arose in the case of the purchase of the house by T and M, and a majority of the House of Lords[398] held that the counter-claim by M did not therefore rely on the illegality but on her equitable interest. Lord Goff and Lord Keith dissented on the ground that, as M did not have 'clean hands' she could not assert an equitable interest, and the rule in the *Bowmakers* case is not applicable where equitable relief is sought.[399] But the majority thought that if the law is that a party is entitled to enforce a proprietary right acquired under an illegal transaction, the same rule ought to apply to any property right so acquired, whether such right is legal or equitable.

The limited scope and procedural nature of the decision in *Tinsley* v. *Milligan* can be illustrated by comparing the facts of that case with those in *Tribe* v. *Tribe*, considered above, where a father voluntarily transferred shares to his son, and the presumption of resulting trust did not apply. In such cases there is a presumption of advancement, i.e. equity presumes an intention to make a gift so that the person who has transferred property or allowed it to be registered in the name of another will have no equitable interest to assert unless the presumption is rebutted. Lord Browne-Wilkinson considered this would be difficult for the transferor to do without pleading or leading evidence that would reveal the illegal aspect of the transaction, so that the transferor's claim would fail.[400] In *Tribe* v. *Tribe* the Court of Appeal was troubled by

---

[395] *Bowmakers Ltd.* v. *Barnet Instruments Ltd.* (*supra*, n. 389), at p. 72; *Taylor* v. *Chester* (*supra*, n. 390); *Webb* v. *Chief Constable of Merseyside Police* [2000] 1 All E.R. 22.

[396] *Tinsley* v. *Milligan* [1994] 1 A.C. 340, *per* Lord Goff at p. 362. See also *R.* v. *Lomas* (1913) 9 Cr. App. Rep. 220, as explained in *R.* v. *Bullock* [1955] 1 W.L.R. 1.

[397] [1994] 1 A.C. 340. See Buckley (1994) 110 L.Q.R. 3; Enonchong (1995) 111 L.Q.R. 134.

[398] Lord Browne-Wilkinson, Lord Jauncey, and Lord Lowry.

[399] *Ibid.*, at p. 362.

[400] [1994] 1 A.C. 340, at p. 372.

this consequence of the decision of the House of Lords[401] but was able to avoid it because the father fell within the *locus poenitentiae* principle,[402] which M did not in *Tinsley* v. *Milligan* because the illegal purpose had been carried into effect. So, if T had been M's wife or child, so that the presumption of advancement applied, M's claim would have failed.

(c) Critique of the proprietary based approach. The rule established in the *Bowmakers* case and extended to equitable interests in *Tinsley* v. *Milligan* is a manifestation of judicial concern, where there is no question of enforcing the *executory* provisions of an illegal contract or transaction, that people should not be unnecessarily precluded by illegality from enforcing rights already acquired under the completed provisions of such a contract or transaction.[403] But it is submitted that it is open to a number of objections. First, it avoids confronting the issue of illegality, the underlying policy issues, and the merits of the parties, and relies instead on the mechanical application of highly technical and procedural concepts. Secondly, to the extent that the parties can, in their illegal contract, determine who owns the property that is its subject-matter, parties who know that the contract is illegal and nevertheless enter into it may be able to insulate themselves from the consequences of the *in pari delicto* rule. Furthermore, where the illegality consists, as it often does in modern conditions, in the contravention of a statute, the property-based approach takes no account of the statutory purposes.

In *Nelson* v. *Nelson*,[404] where a mother provided the purchase money for a house that was transferred into the names of her two children to enable her unlawfully to obtain a subsidized advance from a governmental body on another property, the High Court of Australia disapproved of both the proprietary based approach of the majority in *Tinsley* v. *Milligan* and the unremitting application by the minority of the rule laid down in *Holman* v. *Johnson*.[405] It applied a similar test to that in the *St. John Shipping Corp.* case in the context of enforcement of the contract,[406] and asked whether the policy of the statute precluded the claim made. McHugh J. stated:[407]

[T]he sanction imposed should be proportionate to the seriousness of the illegality involved ... The statute must always be the reference point for determining the seriousness of the illegality; otherwise the courts would embark on an assessment of moral turpitude independently of and potentially in conflict with the assessment made by the legislature.

Secondly, the imposition of the civil sanction must further the purpose of the statute and

---

[401] [1996] Ch. 107, at pp. 118, 134. See also *Nelson* v. *Nelson* (1995) 123 A.L.R. 132, at pp. 148, 165–6 and Davies in Oakley ed., *Trends in Contemporary Trust Law* (1996), ch. 2.

[402] *Ante*, pp. 403–4.

[403] *Tinsley* v. *Milligan* [1994] 1 A.C. 340, *per* Lord Jauncey at p. 366. See also *Nelson* v. *Nelson* (1995) 132 A.L.R. 133, *per* Toohey J. at p. 176 (High Court of Australia).

[404] (1995) 132 A.L.R. 133.

[405] (1775) 1 Cowp. 341, *ante*, p. 396.

[406] [1957] 1 Q.B. 267, *ante*, p. 351.

[407] (1995) 132 A.L.R. 133, at p. 192. See also (*ibid.*) pp. 146, 149, 167 and McCamus (1987) 25 Osgoode H.L.J. 787.

must not impose a further sanction for the unlawful conduct if parliament has indicated that the sanctions imposed by the statute are sufficient to deal with conduct that breaches or evades the operation of the statute and its policies.

The Court concluded that the policy of the statute did not preclude the claim made, and awarded the mother the relief sought on the condition that she made appropriate recompense to the body that had given her the subsidy.

(f) COLLATERAL TRANSACTIONS

(i) Securities

A transaction which is collateral to an illegal agreement may also be affected by taint of illegality.[408] Any security given to secure payment under, or performance of, an illegal contract is itself illegal, even though not given in pursuance of the contract. Thus in *Fisher* v. *Bridges*[409] a deed executed to secure the payment of the price for land conveyed to the defendant for an illegal purpose was held to be illegal and unenforceable. Jervis C.J., said that the deed:[410]

springs from, and is a creature of, the illegal agreement; and, as the law would not enforce the original illegal contract, so neither will it allow the parties to enforce a security for the purchase money, which by the original bargain was tainted with illegality.

(ii) Bills of exchange

Similarly, if a bill of exchange is made and given to secure payment of money due or about to become due upon an illegal agreement, the rule that a subsequent holder is presumed to be a holder in due course does not apply; the holder can only recover by proving that consideration has been given either by himself or some immediate holder, and without notice of the illegality.[411] Money knowingly lent for the purpose of financing an illegal agreement is also, in principle, irrecoverable.[412]

(iii) No tainting

Not all collateral transactions are necessarily tainted. As noted above, an innocent party may have an action for breach of a collateral warranty.[413] And securities given in respect of an agreement which is not strictly illegal, but merely nugatory and void, can be enforced if supported by independent consideration.[414]

---

[408] *Heald* v. *O'Connor* [1971] 1 W.L.R. 497 (guarantee).
[409] (1854) 3 E. & B. 642.
[410] At p. 649.
[411] Bills of Exchange Act 1882, s. 30(2); see *ante*, p. 391, *post*, p. 490.
[412] *Cannan* v. *Bryce* (1819) 3 B. & Ald. 179; *Spector* v. *Ageda* [1973] Ch. 30.
[413] See *ante*, p. 401.
[414] See *ante*, p. 391.

VII. SEVERANCE

(a) INTRODUCTION

The same contract may contain both legal and illegal terms. In such a case it has long been established that an illegal term, or an illegal part of a term, can in certain circumstances be 'severed', leaving the remainder of the contract in force.[415] In *Pickering* v. *Ilfracombe Railway Co.* Willes J. stated:[416]

The general rule is that, where you cannot sever the illegal from the legal part of a covenant, the contract is altogether void; but, where you can sever them, whether the illegality be created by statute or by the common law, you may reject the bad part and retain the good.

This *dictum* does not indicate the circumstances in which it is, or it is not, possible to sever the illegal from the legal parts of the contract; nor does it indicate that differing criteria have been adopted from time to time by the Courts. For example, in recent years the Courts have moved away from the nineteenth century requirement that an illegal promise could only be severed if it was supported by separate consideration.[417] Emphasis has now shifted to the nature of the illegality involved and whether it accords with public policy that severance should be allowed. Nevertheless, the Courts have to bear in mind that it is not their task to force on the parties an entirely different contract.[418] Before severance is permitted, certain conditions must be satisfied in order to ensure that the elimination of the offending clause still leaves substantially the same agreement.

(b) PUBLIC POLICY

Where there are legal and illegal terms in a contract which are capable of severance, the jurisdiction to enforce the legal terms will only be exercised if the severance is in accordance with public policy.

(i) Illegal conditions

If a stipulation involves a serious element of moral turpitude—if, for example, it is one which has as its object the deliberate commission of a criminal offence—it will so infect the rest of the contract that the Courts will refuse to give any effect to the agreement,[419] at least at the suit of one who knew of or participated in the illegality. Thus in *Napier* v. *National Business Agency Ltd.*:[420]

---

[415] *Henry Pigot's Case* (1614) 11 Co. Rep. 27b. See Marsh (1948) 64 L.Q.R. 230, 347, and (1953) 69 L.Q.R. 111.

[416] (1868) L.R. 3 C.P. 235, at p. 250.

[417] *Waites* v. *Jones* (1835) 1 Bing. N.C. 646, at p. 662; *Walrond* v. *Walrond* (1858) 28 L.J. Ch. 97; *Lound* v. *Grimwade* (1888) 39 Ch. D. 605; *Kearney* v. *Whitehaven Colliery Co.* [1893] 1 Q.B. 700; *Kuenigl* v. *Donnersmark* [1955] 1 Q.B. 515, at p. 537; *post*, p. 414.

[418] *Putsman* v. *Taylor* [1927] 1 K.B. 637, at p. 639.

[419] *Bennett* v. *Bennett* [1952] 1 K.B. 249, at p. 254.

[420] [1951] 2 All E.R. 264. See also *Kenyon* v. *Darwen Manufacturing Co. Ltd.* [1936] 2 K.B. 193; *Miller* v. *Karlinski* (1945) 62 T.L.R. 85 and *Hyland* v. *J. H. Barker (North West) Ltd.* [1985] I.C.R. 861.

The defendant agreed to employ N at a salary of £13 a week as salary, and a further £6 per week for 'expenses'. In fact, N's expenses were nowhere near that sum, and this further provision was merely a device to defraud the income tax authorities. N brought an action to recover his salary, abandoning his claim to the expense allowance.

The Court of Appeal held that the provision as to expenses was contrary to public policy. Its inclusion vitiated the whole agreement and no severance could be allowed. Similarly relief will be refused if severance would be inconsistent with the policy of the Courts or of Parliament to discourage contracts containing an illegal element of the type sought to be severed. Thus, in *Kuenigl v. Donnersmark*,[421] McNair J. refused to sever certain clauses in an agreement which involved dealings with an alien enemy.

On the other hand, if a provision in a contract is illegal by virtue of a statute passed for the protection of a class of persons,[422] there is no ground of public policy to prevent the Court from severing the illegal provision and giving effect to the remainder of the contract in an action brought by a member of the protected class.[423]

(ii) Unenforceable provisions

Public policy does not prevent the severance of provisions that are merely void or unenforceable,[424] and, in particular, of covenants in unreasonable restraint of trade or clauses which oust the jurisdiction of the Courts. Such stipulations are not illegal in the strict sense, and will not taint the entire agreement in which they are contained. Provided that certain requirements are satisfied, they may be severed from the rest of the agreement. As Denning L.J. pointed out in *Bennett v. Bennett*:[425]

The presence of a void covenant of this kind does not render the deed totally ineffective. . . . The party who is entitled to the benefit of the void covenant, or rather who would have been entitled to the benefit of it if it had been valid, can sue upon the other covenants of the deed which are in his favour; and he can even sue upon the void covenant, if he can sever the good from the bad, even to the extent of getting full liquidated damages for a breach of the good part. So also the other party, that is, the party who gave the void covenant and is not bound by its restraints, can himself sue upon the covenants in his favour, save only when the void covenant forms the whole, or substantially the whole, consideration for the deed.

There is no clear delimitation of the types of illegal stipulation which can be severed in this way, but whether or not a particular stipulation can be severed will depend upon considerations of public policy.

(iii) Extent of severance

Public policy may also affect the extent of the severance to be allowed. As we have already seen, the law dislikes employer-employee covenants in restraint of trade and will be jealous to see that freedom of contract is not abused. The question, therefore, arises whether an employer should be permitted to bluff (whether intentionally or

[421] [1955] 1 Q.B. 515.
[422] See *ante*, p. 406.
[423] *Ailion v. Spiekermann* [1976] 1 Ch. 158.
[424] *Bennett v. Bennett* [1952] 1 K.B. 249, at p. 254.
[425] [1952] 1 K.B. 249, at p. 260; *post*, p. 416.

not) the employee into accepting a covenant which is unreasonably wide, and, then, when the bluff is called, to make use of the principle of severance to carve out of that void covenant the maximum of what might validly have been required. In *Mason* v. *Provident Clothing and Supply Co. Ltd.*,[426] Lord Moulton expressed the view that, in such cases, the excess which it is sought to delete must be 'merely trivial'. More recently, however, in *T. Lucas & Co. Ltd.* v. *Mitchell*,[427] the Court of Appeal held that an unreasonable restraint, if it can be regarded as intended by the parties to be separate and separable from a valid restraint,[428] is capable of being severed notwithstanding that it is contained in an agreement between employer and employee. It may be that, in modern times, an employee needs less protection than formerly. But as Lord Moulton pointed out:[429] 'It must be remembered that the real sanction at the back of these covenants is the terror and expense of litigation, in which the servant is at a great disadvantage, in view of the longer purse of his master'.

(c) REQUIREMENTS

Assuming that severance of the contract is in accord with public policy, certain requirements must still be satisfied. It must, however, be stated that the formulation of these requirements has been the subject of much speculation and contradiction. At present, the situation would appear to be as follows.

(i) The 'blue pencil' rule

In the first place, the illegal portion of the contract must be capable at least of being verbally separated from the remainder of the agreement. This is generally known as the 'blue pencil' rule, that is, 'severance can be effected when the part severed can be removed by running a blue pencil through it'[430] without affecting the meaning of the part remaining. The rule in practice can be seen in *Goldsoll* v. *Goldman*:[431]

The defendant sold his jeweller's business in New Bond Street, London to Goldsoll, who was also a jeweller, and covenanted that he would not for the period of 2 years 'either solely or jointly . . . carry on the business of a vendor of or dealer in real or imitation jewellery in the county of London, England, Scotland, Ireland, Wales, or any part of the United Kingdom . . . or in France, the United States of America, Russia, or Spain, or within 25 miles of Potsdamerstrasse, Berlin, or St. Stefans Kirche, Vienna'. The defendant joined a rival firm of jewellers in New Bond Street, and Goldsoll sought an injunction to restrain breach of the covenant.

---

[426] [1913] A.C. 724, at p. 745. See also *Attwood* v. *Lamont* [1920] 3 K.B. 571, at p. 593. Cf. *Nevanas & Co.* v. *Walker* [1914] 1 Ch. 413; *Putsman* v. *Taylor* [1927] 1 K.B. 637.

[427] [1974] Ch. 129. See also *Scorer* v. *Seymour Jones* [1966] 1 W.L.R. 1419.

[428] See *post*, p. 417.

[429] [1913] A.C. 724, at p. 745. A similar concern also affects the construction of such clauses: *J. A. Mont (U.K.) Ltd.* v. *Mills* [1993] I.R.L.R. 173, *ante*, p. 374.

[430] *Attwood* v. *Lamont* [1920] 3 K.B. 571, *per* Lord Sterndale M.R. at p. 578. See also *Business Seating (Renovations) Ltd.* v. *Broad* [1989] I.C.R. 729 at p. 734 and *Ginsberg* v. *Parker* [1988] I.R.L.R. 483.

[431] [1915] 1 Ch. 292. See also *Putsman* v. *Taylor* [1927] 1 K.B. 637; *Ronbar Enterprises Ltd.* v. *Green* [1954] 1 W.L.R. 815.

The Court of Appeal held that, as Goldsoll's business was chiefly confined to imitation jewellery, the covenant was unreasonably wide, and that it was also too wide in area. But it was possible to excise the words 'real or' and also the references to foreign countries, and so to limit the covenant to dealing in imitation jewellery within the United Kingdom. In this form the covenant was unexceptionable and could be enforced. The reason for this somewhat technical rule is that the Court is not prepared to rewrite the agreement for the parties.

(ii) Illegal promise must not form main consideration

Secondly, the illegal promise must not form the whole or the main consideration for the contract. It must go only to a part, and a subsidiary part, of the consideration provided.[432] Otherwise one party would be compelled to perform a promise, the consideration for which would be far less than was ever contemplated when the promise was made. In *Bennett* v. *Bennett*:[433]

A wife entered into a deed with her husband by which she covenanted not to apply to the Court for maintenance for herself or for her children, to maintain the younger herself, and to indemnify her husband against any legal expenses arising out of the deed. The husband undertook to pay his wife and son an annuity, and to convey to her certain property. The husband failed to make the promised payments and was sued by his wife.

It was held that the covenant by the wife not to apply to the Court for maintenance was contrary to public policy and void. Since it formed the main consideration for the contract, it could not be severed from the rest of the agreement. The wife was therefore unable to enforce her claim to the annuity since it was founded upon a consideration which was void. On the other hand, in *Goodinson* v. *Goodinson*:[434]

A husband promised to pay his wife a weekly sum if she would indemnify him against any debts incurred by her, not pledge his credit for necessaries, and forbear to bring any matrimonial proceedings against him.

He fell into arrears with the payments and was sued by her. It was held that there was ample consideration to support the agreement apart from the covenant not to sue, and so the husband was liable.

(iii) Illegal promise must not alter agreement

Thirdly, the Court will not permit severance where the offending provisions are 'inextricably interwoven with the other promises in the agreement'[435] so that severance would 'alter entirely the scope and intention of the agreement'.[436] This is a

---

[432] See *Carney* v. *Herbert* [1985] 1 A.C. 301 (illegal ancilliary provision for the exclusive benefit of the plaintiff).

[433] [1952] 1 K.B. 249. This decision was effectively reversed by the Matrimonial Causes Act 1965, s. 23(1), now the Matrimonial Causes Act 1973, s. 34; *ante*, p. 365. See also *Triggs* v. *Staines U.D.C.* [1969] 1 Ch. 10.

[434] [1954] 2 Q.B. 118.

[435] *Kuenigl* v. *Donnersmark* [1955] 1 Q.B. 515, at p. 538.

[436] *Attwood* v. *Lamont* [1920] 3 K.B. 571, *per* Lord Sterndale M.R. at p. 580. See also *Routh* v. *Jones* [1947] 1 All E.R. 179, 758; *Marshall* v. *N. M. Financial Management Ltd.* [1995] 1 W.L.R. 1461; *Crehan* v. *Courage (No. 1)* [1999] Eur. L. Rep. 834.

sensible rule, for the mechanical deletion of an offending clause could affect the whole nature of the contract. Nevertheless, it is extraordinarily difficult to apply, and our understanding of its application is by no means increased by a study of its leading illustration. In *Attwood* v. *Lamont*:[437]

A was the proprietor of a general outfitter's business. L had been employed as a tailor and cutter in one of A's departments. He was not concerned with any of the other departments. In his contract of service he had bound himself, after the termination of his employment, not to be concerned in the trade or business of a tailor, dressmaker, general draper, milliner, hatter, haberdasher, gentlemen's, ladies', or children's outfitter within 10 miles of his employer's place of business at Kidderminster.

The Court of Appeal held that this covenant was too wide. It attempted to protect against competition all departments of the employer's business, and not merely tailoring. The Divisional Court had found that the covenant was severable by striking out the other trades except that of tailor. The Court of Appeal reversed this finding. Both Lord Sterndale M.R. and Younger L.J. considered that severance was only permissible in a case where the covenant to be severed was 'not really a single covenant, but was in effect a combination of several distinct covenants',[438] and the latter said:[439]

Now, here, I think, there is in truth but one covenant for the protection of the respondent's entire business, and not several covenants for the protection of his several businesses. The respondent is, on the evidence, not carrying on several businesses but one business, and, in my opinion, this covenant must stand or fall in its unaltered form.

It may be presumed that their Lordships intended simply to say that the deletion of the offending trades altered the *nature*, and not merely the *extent*, of the original covenant.[440] But the distinction drawn between 'single' and 'several' covenants is somewhat unprofitable, and cannot easily be applied to covenants such as that in *Goldsoll* v. *Goldman*.[441] It seems better to say that the question of altering the scope and intention of the agreement is one which depends upon the true construction of the covenant and agreement rather than upon this difficult and elusive distinction.

(d) EFFECT OF SEVERANCE

The effect of severance is not uniform in all cases.

(i) True severance

If the illegal and legal undertakings are distinct and separate, each being supported by its own consideration, the Court will strike out the offending conditions, together with the consideration, leaving the rest unimpaired.

---

[437] [1920] 3 K.B. 571. Cf. *Putsman* v. *Taylor* [1927] 1 K.B. 637; *T. Lucas & Co. Ltd.* v. *Mitchell* [1974] Ch. 129 (reversing the decision of Pennycuick J. [1972] 1 W.L.R. 938).

[438] They differed, however, as to how this test should be applied.

[439] At p. 593.

[440] See Lord Sterndale M.R. at p. 578.

[441] See *ante*, p. 415.

Suppose that Government regulations prohibit building on a single property in excess of £1,000 without a licence. A builder undertakes to execute a number of unlicensed works on a single property on a 'cost plus' basis, i.e. the individual items being executed and paid for as required.[442]

Any work ordered or executed within the £1,000 limit will be legal and must be paid for. Work ordered in excess of this limit will be illegal, but it can be severed from the rest of the agreement. Neither a promise to do such work, nor a promise to pay for it, will be enforceable. The illegal part is truly and completely severed.

(ii) One-sided severance

On the other hand, the Court may strike out one or more of the promises on one side, while leaving the consideration on the other side unaffected. *Goldsoll* v. *Goldman*[443] and *Goodinson* v. *Goodinson*,[444] are examples of 'one-sided' severance.[445] The Court excised the offending provisions, but did not interfere with the consideration given for them. The severance was on one side only.

(iii) Restitutio in integrum

If severance would substantially alter the nature of the contract, and neither party is willing to accept the contract in its severed form, there is authority for the view that the Court may order *restitutio in integrum* of benefits obtained under the contract.[446] In *South Western Mineral Water Co. Ltd.* v. *Ashmore*:[447]

A wished to purchase from S.W.M.W. a controlling interest in a company. It was agreed that he should pay £6,000 and be given an option to purchase the assets of the company for £36,500 to be secured by a debenture over the assets. A was let into possession of the company's premises and took delivery of all the assets. It was subsequently realized that the proposed debenture was illegal as it infringed a provision of the Companies Act 1948.

Cross J. held that the stipulation for an illegal debenture did not render the whole agreement void. The agreement could be enforced by S.W.M.W. if they waived the security or by A if he tendered immediate payment. But as neither party was willing to accept an agreement in these terms, S.W.M.W. was to return the £6,000 and A was to give up possession of the premises and restore the assets received.

---

[442] *Frank W. Clifford Ltd.* v. *Garth* [1956] 1 W.L.R. 570.
[443] See *ante*, p. 415.
[444] See *ante*, p. 416.
[445] A term suggested by Somervell L.J. in *Bennett* v. *Bennett* [1952] 1 K.B. 249, at p. 260.
[446] Provided that recovery is not precluded by the maxim *in pari delicto potior est conditio defendentis* (see *ante*, pp. 402–3) if the contract as a whole is tainted.
[447] [1967] 1 W.L.R. 1110.

PART III

LIMITS OF THE CONTRACTUAL OBLIGATION

10

THIRD PARTIES

I. INTRODUCTION

This chapter deals with the scope of a valid contract when formed, and the question, to whom does the obligation extend? This question must be considered under two separate headings: (1) the acquisition of rights by a third party, and (2) the imposition of liabilities upon a third party. At common law the general rule is that no one but the parties to a contract can be entitled under it, or bound by it. This principle is known as that of *privity of contract.*

Both aspects of this principle have long been subject to common law and statutory exceptions. But the first aspect, which prevented parties to a contract from enabling a third party to acquire rights under it, was subject to widespread criticism by judges, law reform bodies, and scholars.[1] Despite these criticisms it has been reaffirmed on several occasions by the House of Lords in the last 50 years. But the limitation on the power of contracting parties has been removed by legislation implementing a Law Commission report.[2] The Contracts (Rights of Third Parties) Act 1999 enables a third party to enforce a contract where the parties so intend.

While the 1999 Act creates a potentially 'general and wide-ranging exception'[3] to the first aspect of the privity principle, it does not abolish it and leaves it intact for cases not covered by the Act. It also preserves the statutory and common law exceptions to the rule.[4] A third party who is able to invoke one of these may be in a better position than one who relies on the 1999 Act.[5] The statutory and common law exceptions to the rule will also continue to be of importance because of the tendency of commercial contracts drafted since its enactment to exclude the Act. Moreover, the Act does not enable a contract term to be directly enforced against a third party and thus does not change the second aspect of the rule under which a burden cannot be imposed on a third party.[6] Accordingly, it remains necessary to consider the common law principle and the exceptions to and circumventions of it.

---

[1] *Post*, p. 427.

[2] Law Commission No. 242, *Privity of Contract: Contracts for the Benefit of Third Parties* (1996), hereafter 'Law Com. No. 242'.

[3] Law Com. No. 242, §§ 5.16, 13.2.

[4] s. 7(1), *post* p. 430.

[5] ss. 2 and 3, *post* pp. 443–5.

[6] H.L. Debs. 11 January 1999, col. 21 (Lord Irvine L.C.). But see *post*, pp. 435, 463.

II. THE ACQUISITION OF CONTRACTUAL RIGHTS
BY THIRD PARTIES

(a) THE DEVELOPMENT OF THE COMMON LAW RULE

If A and B make a contract in which B promises to do something or to refrain from doing something for the benefit of T.P., all three may be willing that T.P. should have all the rights of an actual contracting party.[7] Thus B may promise to pay a sum of money[8] to, or perform a service for,[9] T.P. Alternatively, B may promise not to sue T.P., either at all[10] or in circumstances covered by an exclusion or limitation clause in the contract between A and B.[11] Many systems of law give effect to the intentions of those concerned but the rule of the English common law, now modified by the Contracts (Rights of Third Parties) Act 1999, is that a person who is not a party to a contract can neither sue on nor rely on defences based on that contract.

(i) A relative latecomer

This rule was not clearly established until the middle of the nineteenth century. There are earlier decisions permitting the third party, often a relative of the promisee[12] but not always,[13] to enforce the promise. The development of the rule of privity of contract was linked with that of the doctrine of consideration and the early cases used both strands of reasoning. In *Price* v. *Easton*:[14]

W.P. owed Price £13. W.P. promised to work for E, and in return E undertook to discharge the debt to Price. The work was done by W.P., but E did not pay the money to Price. Price sued E.

It was held that Price could not recover because he was not a party to the contract. However, the reasoning of the judges differed. Lord Denman C.J. said that the plaintiff did not 'shew any consideration for the promise moving from him to the defendant',[15] while Littledale J. said, 'No privity is shewn between the plaintiff and the defendant';[16] and Patteson J. that there was 'no promise to the plaintiff alleged'.[17]

In *Tweddle* v. *Atkinson*,[18] it was also held that no action could be brought by a non-party:

[7] Dowrick (1956) 19 Mod. L.R. 374.

[8] *Beswick* v. *Beswick* [1968] A.C. 58, *post*, p. 423.

[9] *Jackson* v. *Horizon Holidays Ltd.* [1975] 1 W.L.R. 1548, *post*, p. 622 (provision of holiday accommodation).

[10] *Snelling* v. *John Snelling Ltd.* [1973] Q.B. 87, *post*, p. 426.

[11] *Scruttons* v. *Midlands Silicones Ltd.* [1962] A.C. 446, *post*, p. 461.

[12] *Bourne* v. *Mason* (1699) 1 Ventr. 6; *Dutton* v. *Poole* (1672) 2 Lev. 210.

[13] *Marchington* v. *Vernon* (1787) 1 Bos. & P. 101n (doubted in *Phillips* v. *Bateman* (1812) 16 East 356); *Carnegie* v. *Waugh* (1823) 1 L.J.(O.S.) 89.

[14] (1833) 4 B. & Ad. 433.

[15] At p. 434.

[16] At p. 434.

[17] At p. 435.

[18] (1861) 1 B. & S. 393; *ante*, p. 96. Lord Denning M.R. in *Beswick* v. *Beswick* [1966] Ch. 538, at p. 553 said that the action failed because H's father had not done his part under the contract.

H and W married. After the marriage, X and Y, their respective fathers, made a contract by which they undertook that each should pay a sum of money to H, and that H should have power to sue for such sums. After the death of X and Y, H sued the executors of Y for the money promised to him.

Wightman J. said:[19]

Some of the old decisions appear to support the proposition that a stranger to the consideration of a contract may maintain an action upon it, . . . But there is no modern case in which the proposition has been supported. On the contrary, it is now established *that no stranger to the consideration can take advantage of a contract, although made for his benefit.*

The modern rule is based on Lord Haldane's formulation in *Dunlop Pneumatic Tyre Co. Ltd.* v. *Selfridge & Co. Ltd.*:[20]

. . . [I]n the law of England certain principles are fundamental. One is that only a person who is a party to a contract can sue on it. Our law knows nothing of a *jus quaesitum tertio* arising by way of contract. Such a right may be conferred by way of property, as for example, under a trust, but it cannot be conferred on a stranger to a contract as a right to enforce the contract *in personam.*

The House of Lords has reaffirmed the rule in several cases, notably in 1968 in *Beswick* v. *Beswick*:[21]

B, a coal merchant, agreed to transfer the business to his nephew in return for a promise by the nephew to employ him as 'consultant' during his lifetime, and, after his death, to pay an annuity of £5 a week to his widow. On B's death, the nephew failed to pay the money to the widow. She brought an action against him in her personal capacity as the beneficiary of the contract, and also in her capacity as administratrix of her deceased husband's estate.

The House of Lords held that she was not entitled to enforce the obligation in her personal capacity, but she was able to sue as administratrix of the estate, i.e. as her deceased husband's personal representative.

(ii) Relationship with doctrine of consideration

Price v. *Easton* and *Tweddle* v. *Atkinson* might seem to rest solely on the rule that consideration must move from the promisee and it has been argued that the privity rule is really no more than an application of the doctrine of consideration.[22] However, in *Dunlop Pneumatic Tyre Co. Ltd.* v. *Selfridge & Co. Ltd.* Lord Haldane[23] clearly distinguished the two and the balance of authority supports the existence of two

---

[19] At pp. 397–8, emphasis added.

[20] [1915] A.C. 847, at p. 853.

[21] [1968] A.C. 58, at pp. 72, 78, 83, 92, 95, 105. See also *Scruttons Ltd.* v. *Midland Silicones Ltd.* [1962] A.C. 446; *The Eurymedon* [1975] A.C. 154; *Woodar Investment Development Ltd.* v. *Wimpey Construction (U.K.) Ltd.* [1980] 1 W.L.R. 277, at pp. 284, 291, 297, 300; *J. H. Rayner (Mincing Lane) Ltd.* v. *D.T.I.* [1990] 2 A.C. 418, at pp. 479, 506; *White* v. *Jones* [1995] 2 A.C. 207, at pp. 262–3, 266.

[22] Furmston (1960) 23 M.L.R. 373; Smith, *The Law of Contract*, 3rd edn. (1998), p. 90.

[23] [1915] A.C. 847, at p. 853.

distinct rules of consideration and privity.[24] The two rules reflect two logically separate issues of policy.[25] The first, primarily associated with the privity doctrine, relates to who can enforce a contract. The second, primarily associated with consideration, concerns the types of promises that can be enforced.

(b) REMEDIES OF THE PROMISEE

Notwithstanding the fact that the third party cannot personally enforce the contract, the contract is nevertheless binding between the parties to it. The remedies that may be available to the promisee if the promisor fails to perform the promise are only relevant where the promisee is able and willing to enforce the contract for the benefit of the third party. The widow in *Beswick* v. *Beswick* would not have been able to obtain her annuity had Peter Beswick appointed his nephew the executor of his estate instead of his widow. At present, there appears to be no procedure by which an unwilling or unco-operative promisee can be compelled to institute proceedings for specific performance on behalf of the third party.[26] The existence of a right of action in the promisee does not, in consequence, necessarily ensure that the third party will obtain the performance promised in the contract. But even where the promisee seeks a remedy there are certain difficulties.

(i) Damages

The general rule is that damages are for loss suffered by the claimant. Therefore, where the breach of contract consists of failure to perform in favour of the third party, unless, as may be the case in a commercial transaction, the promisee suffers loss by reason of the breach, the damages will generally be only nominal. The general rule and the exceptions to it, whereby substantial damages may be awarded in respect of loss suffered by the third party, are considered in Chapter 17 on Damages.[27]

(ii) Specific performance

The promisee may be able to obtain an order for specific performance against the promisor to compel him to carry out the promise in favour of the third party. Thus in

---

[24] *Vandepitte* v. *Preferred Accident Insurance Corp. of New York* [1933] A.C. 70, 79; *Scruttons Ltd.* v. *Midland Silicones Ltd.* [1962] A.C. 446; *Kepong Prospecting Ltd.* v. *Schmidt* [1968] A.C. 810, at p. 826. See also Atiyah, *Essays on Contract* (1986), p. 220; *K. H. Enterprise* v. *Pioneer Container* [1994] 2 A.C. 324, at p. 355; *White* v. *Jones* [1995] 2 A.C. 207, at pp. 262–3; *Coulls* v. *Bagot's Executor and Trustee Co. Ltd.* (1967) 119 C.L.R. 460, at pp. 478, 486, 493; *Trident General Insurance Co. Ltd.* v. *McNiece Bros Pty. Ltd.* (1988) 165 C.L.R. 107, at p. 164 (High Court of Australia); *London Drugs Ltd.* v. *Kuehene & Nagel International Ltd.* [1992] 3 S.C.R. 299, at p. 417 (Supreme Court of Canada).

[25] Law Revision Committee, Sixth Interim Report 1937 (Cmnd. 5449), § 37; Law Com. C.P. No. 121, *Privity of Contract: Contracts for the Benefit of Third Parties* (1991), § 2.9 and see (albeit more equivocally) Law Com. No. 242, Part VI.

[26] But see the suggestion that the third party be joined as a party to the action made by Lord Denning in *Beswick* v. *Beswick* [1966] Ch. 538, at p. 554, and (in a different context) *Snelling* v. *John Snelling Ltd.* [1973] Q.B. 87 (*post*, p. 426). Contrast *Gurtner* v. *Circuit* [1968] 2 Q.B. 587, at pp. 599, 606; *White* v. *Jones* [1995] 2 A.C. 207, at p. 267.

[27] *Post*, p. 589.

Beswick v. *Beswick*[28] the House of Lords held that the widow, in her capacity as personal representative of Peter Beswick (the promisee), could obtain specific performance of the promise in favour of herself as third party. As Lord Pearce explained: 'The estate (though not the widow personally) can enforce it'.[29]

Specific performance is, as will be seen, a discretionary equitable remedy which is not available as a matter of course. As a general rule, an order for specific performance will not be made against a defendant in any case where damages are an adequate and appropriate remedy,[30] where, had the positions been reversed, the claimant's undertaking could not have been specifically enforced, so 'mutuality' was lacking,[31] or where the contract has been discharged and is no longer in existence.[32] Not all contractual undertakings, particularly those to perform services or to build, are sufficiently precisely defined to be enforced specifically.[33]

In *Beswick* v. *Beswick* an award of damages was considered inadequate and specific performance appropriate for a number of reasons. First, damages would not have taken account of the loss to the third party and would have been purely nominal.[34] Secondly, the defaulting promisor had received the full benefit of the contract by the completed transfer of the business.[35] Thirdly, had the business not been transferred, the defaulting promisor could have obtained specific performance of the promise.[36] Fourthly, specific performance was more appropriate for a promise to make a series of regular payments than a succession of actions for damages which would have had to have been brought as each payment fell due. It does not therefore follow that specific performance will necessarily be ordered in all cases where performance is to be made to a third party.

(iii) Action for the agreed sum

The contracting party to whom the promise is made has normally no claim whatsoever to the money or other performance properly due to the third party.[37]

(iv) Recovery of money paid

Where a contract is made for the benefit of a third party and the promisee has paid money to the promisor in consideration of a promise which the promisor has totally failed to perform, the promisee will be entitled to recover the money as paid on a consideration which has totally failed. This remedy, which might be less advantageous than damages or specific performance, would not be available in the present state of

---

28 [1968] A.C. 58, *ante*, p. 423.

29 *Ibid.*, at p. 89.

30 See *post*, pp. 633.

31 See *post*, p. 635.

32 *Woodar Investment Development Ltd.* v. *Wimpey Construction U.K. Ltd.* [1980] 1 W.L.R. 277, at p. 300.

33 *Forster* v. *Silvermere Gold and Equestrian Centre* (1981) 125 Sol. J. 397, *post*, p. 636.

34 *Ante*, p. 424. This factor alone would not necessarily be conclusive; see *ante*, p. 338 *post*, p. 634 (inadequacy of consideration).

35 [1968] A.C. 58, at pp. 83, 89, 97.

36 *Ibid.*, at p. 89 (Lord Pearce).

37 *Re Stapleton-Bretherton* [1941] Ch. 482; *Re Schebsman* [1944] Ch. 83; *Coulls* v. *Bagot's Executor and Trustee Co. Ltd.* (1967) 119 C.L.R. 460, at p. 502; *Beswick* v. *Beswick* [1968] A.C. 58, at pp. 94, 96. Cf. *Re Sinclair's Life Policy* [1938] Ch. 799.

the law if the promisor had partly performed the promise, as then would not be a total failure of consideration.[38]

(v) Promise not to sue

Where the promisor, either expressly or by necessary implication, promises not to sue a third party, the third party, as a stranger to the contract, cannot rely directly on the terms of the contract as a defence to any action brought by the promisor.[39] But the promisee may obtain a declaration that the promise is binding on the promisor, and thus effectively prevent the promisor from suing the third party. In *Snelling* v. *John Snelling Ltd.*:[40]

Three brothers were shareholders and directors of a family company which owed each of them considerable sums of money. Differences arose between them, and, as part of an effort to settle these, they made a contract, agreeing, *inter alia*, that, in the event of any director resigning, he would immediately forfeit all moneys due to him from the company. Subsequently, one brother (Brian) resigned his directorship and brought an action against the company for payment of the money owed to him. His two brothers applied to be, and were, joined as co-defendants to the action, and they counterclaimed for a declaration that the sums due to Brian from the company had been forfeited.

The question arose whether the company, which was not a party to the agreement, could rely on it. In principle, it could not do so, and so Brian would be entitled to judgment on his claim. The two brothers would, however, also be entitled to a declaration that the provisions of the agreement were binding on Brian. In the view of Ormrod J. the resulting situation was absurd, and he held that the proper order to make was to dismiss Brian's claim. The reality of the situation was that Brian's claim had failed since his two brothers had succeeded in their counterclaim, and the order of the Court should reflect that fact. It would therefore seem that, where all parties are before the Court, the Court may stay[41] or dismiss a claim brought by a contracting party against a third party whom the other contracting party has promised not to sue.

It has been said that for the court to exercise its power to stay or dismiss a claim, the promisee must have a sufficient interest,[42] such as a legal or equitable right to protect,[43] and must be able to show a real possibility of prejudice to himself, for example by being exposed to an action by the third party.[44] In *Snelling's* case the promisees were not subject to this kind of 'legal' prejudice since they would not have been exposed to an action by the company. However, they would have been commercially and financially prejudiced by any deterioration in the company's financial position, as would have occurred had Brian's action succeeded.

---

[38] See *post*, p. 642.

[39] See *post*, p. 461 (exemption clauses).

[40] [1973] Q.B. 87.

[41] This power is now in Supreme Court Act 1981, s. 49(2). But contrast *Gore* v. *Van der Lann* [1967] 2 Q.B. 31.

[42] *Gore* v. *Van der Lann* [1967] 2 Q.B. 31.

[43] *European Asian Bank* v. *Punjab & Sind Bank* [1982] 2 Lloyd's Rep. at p. 356, 369.

[44] *The Elbe Maru* [1978] 1 Lloyd's Rep. 206. Cf. *The Chevalier Roze* [1983] 2 Lloyd's Rep. 438, at p. 443; *The Starsin* [2001] 1 Lloyd's Rep. 437, at pp. 461–2.

(c) RATIONALE AND APPRAISAL OF THE COMMON LAW RULE

(i) Justification of rule

The case for the common law rule rests on a number of factors. First, although consideration has been provided for the promise, it has not been provided by the third party. Secondly, it is unjust that a person could sue on a contract but not be sued upon the contract.[45] Thirdly, if third parties could enforce contracts made for their benefit, the rights of the contracting parties to vary or terminate such contracts would be affected. Fourthly, it is undesirable for the promisor to be liable to two actions from both the promisor and the third party, and the privity rule limits the potential liability of a contracting party to a wide range of possible third party claimants.[46] The Law Commission did not regard any of these explanations as convincing justifications of the rule.[47]

Those who favour the common law rule[48] also point out that it is not absolute. The Courts and the legislature have created exceptions to avoid perceived injustice. It must also be remembered that the rule only precludes the third party from proceeding *in contract*. Where it is possible to base a claim on some other cause of action, for instance in tort or based on a property right, proceedings may succeed.[49] Proceedings may also succeed if the Court can discern a collateral contract between the third party and the promisee under the main contract for the benefit of the third party.

(ii) Criticism of rule

The considerable criticism of the principle that a third party cannot acquire rights under a contract has been noted. Its desirability as a matter of policy has been questioned by judges,[50] law reform bodies,[51] and commentators.[52] Its pedigree has also been criticized on the ground that it was doubtful that the nineteenth century cases on which it is based in fact established its existence and that it was only a rule of procedure.[53] It is said that it serves only to defeat the legitimate expectations of the

---

45 *Tweddle* v. *Atkinson* (1861) 1 B. & S. 393, at p. 398; *London Drugs Ltd.* v. *Kuehene & Nagel International Ltd.* [1992] 3 S.C.R. 299, at pp. 418, 440. But see *ante*, p. 29 for the position in the case of unilateral contracts.

46 *Trident General Insurance Co. Ltd.* v. *McNiece Bros Pty. Ltd.* (1988) 165 C.L.R. 107, at pp. 121–2.

47 *Privity of Contract: Contracts for the Benefit of Third Parties*, Law Com. C.P. No. 121 (1991), §. 4.4; Law Com. No. 242, § 3.1.

48 Kincaid (1994) 8 J.C.L. 51; (1999) 12 J.C.L. 47; (2000) 116 L.Q.R. 43; Smith (1997) 17 O.J.L.S. 643.

49 See *post*, pp. 448 (tort), 439, 447 (property).

50 *Scruttons Ltd.* v. *Midland Silicones Ltd.* [1962] A.C. 446, at pp. 467–8; *Beswick* v. *Beswick* [1968] A.C. 58, at p. 72; *Woodar Investment Development Ltd.* v. *Wimpey Construction U.K. Ltd.* [1980] 1 W.L.R. 277, at pp. 291, 297–8, 300 (H.L.); *Forster* v. *Silvermere Gold and Equestrian Centre* (1981) 125 Sol. J. 397 (C.A.); *Swain* v. *The Law Society* [1983] 1 A.C. 598, at p. 611; *Darlington B.C.* v. *Wiltshier Northern Ltd.* [1995] 1 W.L.R. 68, at pp. 73, 76.

51 Law Revision Committee Sixth Interim Report (Cmnd. 5449); Law Com. No. 242, *Privity of Contract: Contracts for the Benefit of Third Parties* (1996).

52 Corbin (1930) 46 L.Q.R. 12; Furmston (1960) 23 M.L.R. 373; Flannigan (1987) 103 L.Q.R. 564; Andrews (1988) 8 L.S. 14; Adams & Brownsword (1990) 10 L.S. 12. Cf. Kincaid [1989] C.L.J. 243, (1994) 8 J.C.L. 51, (2000) 116 L.Q.R. 43; Smith (1997) 17 O.J.L.S. 643.

53 *Drive Yourself Hire Co. (London) Ltd.* v. *Strutt* [1954] 1 Q.B. 250, at p. 273; *Beswick* v. *Beswick* [1968] Ch. 538, at pp. 553–4, 557, *per* Lord Denning M.R., a particularly vigorous critic.

parties and the third party, who often organize their affairs on the faith of the contract; that it undermines the social interest of the community in the security of bargains; and that it is commercially inconvenient.[54] Above all it defeats the intentions of the parties to the contract. In the standard situation the person who has suffered the loss cannot sue, while the person who has suffered no loss can sue but may be able to obtain only nominal damages.[55] Where the object of the contract is to benefit the third party, the effect of this is tantamount to ruling that the object of the contract is unenforceable.

Defenders of the rule point out that it may be possible to circumvent it by a variety of legal devices. These are considered below.[56] In some, particularly those based on statute, the third party rule is simply overridden. In others the third party claimant does not need to rely on the contract but is able to have recourse to other areas of the law and to rely on a property right, a possessory right, or is able to sue in tort. Alternatively, the third party may be able to establish a collateral contract with the promisor.[57] Other exceptions to and circumventions of the rule may be seen in assignment,[58] agency (including the doctrine of the undisclosed principal),[59] transfer on death,[60] and bankruptcy.[61] But the exceptions and circumventions are complicated and not always available, particularly to those who do not have access to sophisticated legal advice. Moreover, their technicality has led to artificiality and uncertainty.

(iii) Reform

The right of a third party to sue on a contract made for its benefit is recognized by the law of Scotland and the legal systems of the United States. It has also been introduced by statute in several Commonwealth jurisdictions[62] while in others the privity doctrine has been modified judicially.[63] In England, the Courts, while criticizing the principle that a third party cannot acquire rights under a contract, indicated that a radical change in the common law, such as abrogation of the principle, should be introduced by legislation.[64] This reluctance stemmed from the nature of the third party rule itself, which some saw as a 'fundamental' rule and which, in Anson's words,

---

[54] For difficulties in construction and insurance contracts, see Law Com. No. 242 (1996), §§ 3.10–3.27.

[55] *Ante*, p. 424.

[56] See *post*, p. 439 ff, 463.

[57] See generally, *ante*, p. 130 and, on exemption clauses and third parties, *post*, p. 464.

[58] See *post*, p. 470.

[59] See *post*, p. 682.

[60] See *post*, p. 493.

[61] See *post*, p. 494.

[62] Western Australia, Queensland and New Zealand. For a summary of this legislation, see Law Com. No. 242 (1996), Appendix B, and for a summary of the position in other legal systems, including Scotland, the United States, France, and Germany, see the Appendix to Law Com. C.P. No. 121 (1991).

[63] *London Drugs Ltd.* v. *Kuehene & Nagel International Ltd.* [1992] 3 S.C.R. 299, (Canada) *post*, p. 468 (exemption clauses); *Trident General Insurance Co. Ltd.* v. *NcNiece Bros. Pty. Ltd.* (1988) 165 C.L.R. 107 (Australia).

[64] *Scruttons Ltd.* v. *Midland Silicones Ltd.* [1962] A.C. 446, at pp. 467–8; *Beswick* v. *Beswick* [1968] A.C. 58, at p. 72; *Woodar Investment Development Ltd.* v. *Wimpey Construction U.K. Ltd.* [1980] 1 W.L.R. 277, at pp. 291, 297–8, 300. But cf. *K. H. Enterprise* v. *Pioneer Container* [1994] 2 A.C. 324, at p. 335; *Darlington B.C.* v. *Wiltshier Northern Ltd.* [1995] 1 W.L.R. 68. Cf. *The Mahkutai* [1996] A.C. 650, at p. 665.

'seems to flow from the very conception we form of contract'.[65] As such, it fixed 'a reference point for the development of subsidiary rules', here the rules of trust, agency and estoppel. Those who took this view considered that it was not possible to abrogate the rule without leaving open major issues of policy, which it was not appropriate for Courts to decide.[66]

As long ago as 1937 the Law Revision Committee recommended that where a contract by its express terms purports to confer a benefit directly on a third party, the third party should be entitled to enforce the provision in its own name.[67] Although widely supported, the recommendation was not implemented because of the outbreak of the Second World War.[68] In 1991 the Law Commission returned to the subject and in 1996 it recommended that the rule should be reformed so as to enable contracting parties to confer a right to enforce the contract on a third party.[69] The Law Commission saw its proposals 'as achieving at a stroke and with certainty and clarity what a progressive House of Lords might well itself have brought about over the course of time', and as not cutting across the underpinning principles of the common law.[70]

While the simple recognition of some form of third party right might be uncontroversial, the determination of its precise extent is not. The most important difficulties concern the test of enforceable benefit, the validity of defences that would have been available had the promisee sued, and whether the contracting parties should have power to vary or cancel the contract. The way that these issues are dealt with by the Contracts (Rights of Third Parties) Act 1999, which substantially implemented the Law Commission's Report,[71] is considered in the next section.

(d) THE CONTRACTS (RIGHTS OF THIRD PARTIES) ACT 1999

(i) Introduction

The Contracts (Rights of Third Parties) Act 1999 enables the parties to a contract to make it enforceable by a third party.[72] It enables a third party both to sue to enforce a positive provision in the contract, such as a promise to pay money or not to sue,[73] and

---

[65] *Principles of the Law of Contract* (1879), p. 195.

[66] See Brennan and Deane JJ.'s minority judgments in *Trident General Insurance Co. Ltd.* v. *NcNiece Bros. Pty. Ltd.* (1988) 165 C.L.R. 107, at pp. 128, 131–2, 134, 140–1, 142–5 and Beatson (1992) 44 C.L.P. 1.

[67] Sixth Interim Report (Cmnd. 5449), para. 48.

[68] See further Beatson (1992) 44 C.L.P. 1, 10–15.

[69] Law Com. No. 242, *Privity of Contract: Contracts for the Benefit of Third Parties* (1996), §§ 3.29, 3.32, including (see now s. 1(6) of the 1999 Act) the right to rely on clauses limiting or excluding the third party's liability to a contracting party. See Adams, Beyleveld and Brownsword (1997) 60 M.L.R. 238.

[70] Law Com. No. 242, §1.10.

[71] For commentary on the Act see Andrews [2001] C.L.J. 353; Bridge (2001) 5 Edin. L. Rev. 85; Burrows [2000] L.M.C.L.Q. 540; Merkin, *Privity of Contract*, ch. 5 (usefully containing the Law Commission consultation paper, report and the Parliamentary debates on the bill in appendices).

[72] Section 6(2)–(4), exempting contracts of employment and the contract contained in a company's articles from the Act (see *post*, p. 430), are not based on recommendations of the Law Commission and s. 8, on arbitration clauses, differs from the Draft Bill attached to the Commission's Report.

[73] See *Fraser River Pile & Dredge Ltd.* v. *Can-Dive Services Ltd.* [2000] 1 Lloyd's Rep. 199 (third party able to enforce subrogation clause under Canadian legislation). On the common law position of such promises, see *ante*, p. 426.

to rely on an exemption or limitation clause in its favour as a defence.[74] The Act thus removes the limit on the autonomy of the parties represented by the first limb of the privity rule. It is fundamental to the scheme of the Act that the parties to the contract control both whether a third party has an enforceable right and, if so, the extent of such right.[75] The third party's rights are thus derived from the parties' intentions as embodied in the contract. But they are distinct from the rights of the parties, which are preserved.[76] The rights of a third party under the Act are generally supplementary to rights the third party has under the common law or other statutes considered later in this chapter.[77] It will be seen that some of the common law and statutory exceptions give third parties more secure rights than those given by the 1999 Act.

(ii) The scope of the Act

The Act applies to contracts made after 11 May 2000. Although it is general, certain types of contract are not affected by it. The common law position for contracts in the articles of association of a company, binding on the company and its members under section 14 of the Companies Act 1985, is preserved by section 6(2) of the 1999 Act. Moreover, section 6(3) prevents third parties from relying on the 1999 Act to enforce terms in contracts of employment and similar contracts purporting to enable them to sue an employee, a worker, or an agency worker.[78]

A second category of contracts is excluded from the 1999 Act because they are subject to an alternative legislative regime recognizing and regulating third party rights which might otherwise be undermined. Bills of exchange, promissory notes, and negotiable instruments are excluded by section 6(1). Contracts of carriage subject either to the Carriage of Goods by Sea Act 1992 or international conventions governing carriage by road, air and rail to which the United Kingdom is party are, subject to one qualification, excluded by section 6(5). The qualification is that a third party may avail itself of an exclusion or limitation of liability in such a contract.[79] Contracts by way of charterparties are not excluded.[80]

In the case of negotiable instruments, only third parties who are 'holders' of the instrument can sue[81] whereas, if the 1999 Act applied, this would have opened up the possibility of others suing. In the case of contracts of carriage, where third parties are given the right to enforce the contract under the Carriage of Goods by Sea Act 1992 they also take some or all of the burdens, whereas under the 1999 Act the third party takes only the benefits.[82] Moreover, under section 2(1) of the 1992 Act, 'all rights of

---

[74] s. 1(6). See *post*, p. 460ff on exemption clauses and third parties.

[75] s. 1(4), see *post*, pp. 435, 463.

[76] s. 4, see *post*, p. 436.

[77] s. 7(1). See Law Com. No. 242, §§ 12.1–12.2; *post* p. 439ff. But note the position of negotiable instruments and certain contracts of carriage, *infra*.

[78] As defined by ss. 54 and 34–35 of the National Minimum Wage Act 1998. See H.L. Debs. 11 January 1999, col. 21 (Lord Irvine L.C.)

[79] s. 6(5).

[80] See the definitions in ss. 6(6) and (7) of the 1999 Act.

[81] See *post*, p. 486.

[82] See Law Com. No. 242, §§ 12.7–12.16. See *post* p. 492.

suit' are transferred to the third party[83] so that, unlike under the 1999 Act, the promisee is left with no rights of enforcement.

(iii) The tests of enforceability

The 1999 Act contains two tests of enforceability. By section 1:

> (1) Subject to the provisions of this Act, a person who is not a party to a contract (a 'third party') may in his own right enforce a term of the contract if—
>
> (a) the contract expressly provides that he may, or
>
> (b) subject to subsection (2), the term purports to confer a benefit on him.
>
> (2) Subsection (1)(b) does not apply if on a proper construction of the contract it appears that the parties did not intend the term to be enforceable by the third party.

Each will be considered in turn.

(a) Express provision. Section 1(1)(a) of the 1999 Act provides a simple and certain test: a third party acquires an enforceable right where the contract contains an express provision to that effect. Section 1(3) provides that the third party must be expressly identified in the contract by name, class or description.[84] Identification in the course of negotiations does not suffice. But the third party need not be in existence when the contract is made.[85] Accordingly, a contracting party's present and future employees and sub-contractors may qualify, as may unborn children. Third parties who qualify under section 1(1)(a) may enforce a contractual term (including an exclusion or limitation clause) even if they are not intended to be the beneficiaries of the term, as where they are trustees.[86]

The Law Revision Committee had recommended that this should be the only way that a third party could acquire an enforceable right.[87] But, while a requirement of express contractual provision is conducive to certainty, it means that the intentions of contracting parties (including those reflected in trade practice or by the principles governing implied terms)[88] will not always be recognized. Nor would it cover the facts of many of the cases where the privity doctrine caused a problem, such as *Beswick* v. *Beswick*.[89] For these reasons, and because requiring express contractual provision would 'operate to the disadvantage of those who do not have the benefit of (good) legal advice',[90] the Law Commission concluded that there should also be a second test of enforceability to cover situations where the parties do not expressly contract to confer a legal right on the third party.

---

[83] See *post*, p. 493.

[84] In the similarly worded New Zealand legislation, the words 'or nominee' may not sufficiently identify the third party (*Karangahape Road International Village Ltd.* v. *Holloway* [1989] 1 N.Z.L.R. 83) and may be insufficient to indicate an intention to create an enforceable right in the nominee (*Field* v. *Filton* [1988] 1 N.Z.L.R. 482). But cf. *Rattrays Wholesale Ltd.* v. *Meredyth Young and A'Court Ltd.* [1997] 2 N.Z.L.R. 363.

[85] Law Com. No. 242, §§ 8.1–8.16.

[86] Law Com. No. 242, § 7.12ff. Such a third party may also have a common law right of enforcement: see *post*, p. 439.

[87] Law Com. No. 242, §§ 8.1–8.16.

[88] Sixth Interim Report (Cmnd. 5449).

[89] [1968] A.C. 58, *ante*, p. 423. See Law Com. No. 242, § 7.11.

[90] Law Com. No. 242, § 7.11.

(b) Term purporting to confer a benefit on the third party. The effect of section 1(1)(b) and section 1(2) is in general terms to provide for what the Law Commission and the Lord Chancellor described as a rebuttable presumption in favour of there being a third party right where a contractual term purports to confer a benefit on a third party identified by name, class, or description.[91] This will be rebutted where, on the proper construction of the contract as a whole, i.e. including the surrounding circumstances,[92] the parties do not intend the third party to have a right to enforce it.

It has been suggested that the presumption in section 1(1)(b) is triggered only where the third party is to receive a benefit directly from the promisor,[93] but this is not clear from the words of the Act or the Law Commission's report.[94] Moreover, although the phrase 'rebuttable presumption' conveys a useful indication of the starting point, it is important to note that the language of presumption is not entirely appropriate to describe the exercise under section 1(2) which is to construe the contract. The construction of a contract is a matter of law in respect of which no burden of proof lies on either side, although the onus is on a person relying on surrounding circumstances as an aid to construction to prove those circumstances.[95]

The approach of the 1999 Act should avoid a problem which has arisen in the United States where only the 'intention to benefit' test has been used. That test has led to difficult distinctions between the 'intended beneficiary' and the 'incidental beneficiary', the third party who benefits *incidentally* by the performance of a contract by others.[96] Where A contracts with B to construct a new road on B's land, C, whose adjoining land would be enhanced in value by the building of the road, while deriving a factual benefit from the performance of the contract made between A and B, is merely an incidental beneficiary of the contract, the primary benefit of which is conferred upon B. Moreover, while the road may be intended for the benefit of all road-users, it is unlikely that the parties intend that road-users should have a right of action in the event of a delay in construction. It is clear that the 1999 Act does not enable either C or other road-users to enforce the terms of the contract between A and B. Again, a standard liability insurance policy indemnifying the assured against liability to third parties is plainly for the benefit of those who may make claims against the assured. But, in general, payment is to be made to the assured and the term so providing purports to confer a benefit on the assured. It is accordingly difficult to say that the term purports to confer a benefit on a person with a claim against the assured.[97]

---

[91] Law Com. No. 242, § 7.17; H.L. Debs., 2 February 1999, col. 1425. The identification requirement in s. 1(3), *ante* p. 431, also applies to s. 1(1)(b).

[92] See *ante*, at p. 160.

[93] Burrows [2000] L.M.C.L.Q. 540, 544.

[94] Cf. the example in Law Com. No. 242, §§ 7.33, 7.51, based on the facts of *Green* v. *Russell* [1959] 2 Q.B. 226, *post*, pp. 433–4.

[95] *Scott* v. *Martin* [1987] 2 All E.R. 813. See Roe (2000) 63 M.L.R. 887. Cf. Burrows [1996] L.M.C.L.Q. 467, 473 (the presumption is 'a strong one').

[96] *Restatement of Contracts* (1932), §§ 133(1) and 147; *Restatement of Contracts* (2d) (1981), § 302. See Prince (1985) 25 Boston College L. Rev. 919, 934–7, 979.

[97] Merkin, *Privity of Contract*, p. 105; Burrows [2000] L.M.C.L.Q. 540, 544–5.

As noted, the ordinary rules of construction will determine whether there is a
contractual intention to confer enforceable rights on a third party. The Law Commission illustrated the application of the test now contained in section 1(1)(b) by reference to a number of hypothetical situations and some of the celebrated cases in which
the first aspect of the privity principle has caused difficulty.[98] A selection is set out
below. First, there are cases or situations in which the Commission considered the
third party would be able to enforce the term on the basis of what is now section
1(1)(b).

(1) In *Beswick* v. *Beswick*[99] the contract gave Mrs Beswick, who was expressly
    named, a presumed right of enforceability because the nephew promised to
    confer the benefit (the annuity payments) on her. As there was no indication in
    the contract that the parties did not intend her to enforce the term, she would
    have been able to enforce it under section 1(1)(b).

(2) B takes out a policy of insurance with A Ltd. to cover her employees against
    medical expenses. The policy provides that payments under it will be made
    directly to ill employees or, at the discretion of A Ltd., to the provider of the
    medical services in discharge of an employee's liability. C, an employee,
    becomes ill and requires hospitalization. Meanwhile B disappears. C seeks to
    sue as a beneficiary of B's contract of insurance with A Ltd. In the absence of
    some contrary indication in the contract triggering section 1(2), C would be
    able to do so. A Ltd. has promised to confer a benefit (direct payment or the
    discharge of C's liability) on C, who is identified by class.[100]

(3) B Ltd., the owner of land, takes out a liability insurance policy with A Ltd., an
    insurance company, whereby A Ltd. agree to indemnify B Ltd. and B's sub-
    sidiary companies, contractors, and sub-contractors. C, one of B Ltd.'s con-
    tractors, incurs liability while carrying out work for B Ltd. C sees to sue as a
    beneficiary of B's contract of insurance with A Ltd. In the absence of some
    contrary indication in the contract triggering section 1(2), C would be able to
    do so. The contract purported to confer a benefit on C, who is identified by
    class.[101]

(4) B Ltd. takes out a personal accident insurance policy with A Ltd. to cover its
    employees against accidents. By the terms of the policy, payments are to be
    made to B Ltd. C, an employee, is injured and B Ltd. is insolvent. The Commis-
    sion considered this a difficult case because it is arguable that, since payment is
    to be made to B Ltd., it is difficult to say that under the contract A purports to
    confer a benefit on C so as to bring section 1(1)(b) into operation. But it
    concluded that, once received by B Ltd., the money is held on trust for C, so
    that the contract does purport to confer a benefit on C and the provision that

---

[98] Law Com. No. 242, §§ 7.28–7.51. For other examples see Burrows [2000] L.M.C.L.Q. 540, 552–3.

[99] [1968] A.C. 58, *ante*, p. 423. See Law Com. No. 242, § 7.46.

[100] Law Com. No. 242, § 7.32.

[101] *Ibid.*, § 7.50, broadly the facts of *Trident General Insurance Co. Ltd.* v. *McNiece Bros Pty. Ltd.*(1988) 165
C.L.R. 107 (High Court of Australia).

the money be paid to B Ltd. would not show that the parties did not intend C to be able to enforce the term because channelling the money in this way is a matter of administrative convenience.[102]

Secondly, there are those cases or situations in which the Commission considered that the third party would not be able to rely on section 1(1)(b). The first is the clear case where the parties expressly provide that the third party is to have no rights, or where the intention to benefit the third party is not known to one of the parties (illustration (5)). It is also likely to be the case where the third party is an incidental beneficiary of the contract (illustration (6)), or where the transaction is part of a chain of contracts which gives the third party a contractual claim against someone else (illustrations (7) and (8)).

(5) On Mr and Mrs C's marriage, their wealthy relative B buys an expensive set of china dishes as a wedding gift from A Ltd., a well-known department store. The china is delivered to B, who sends it to Mr and Mrs C. The glazing is defective and after two weeks of use the pattern is fading badly. Mr and Mrs C could not sue A Ltd. under the 1999 Act since the contract between A Ltd. and B does not purport to confer a benefit on them and they are not identified in the contract.[103] The position would be different if B had made it clear to A Ltd. when purchasing the china that it was a gift and A Ltd. agreed to deliver it to Mr and Mrs C's home. In such circumstances the Commission concluded that A Ltd. would have promised to confer a benefit (china of satisfactory quality) on Mr and Mrs C, who have been identified by name.[104]

(6) In *White* v. *Jones*[105] a firm of solicitors, A, contracted with B to draw up a will benefiting C but, as a result of the solicitors' negligence, the will was never drawn up. Although the intended legatee is expressly designated as a beneficiary, the contract is not one in which the solicitor promises the testator to confer a benefit on the third party, the intended legatee, but one by which the solicitor is to enable the testator to do so. The relevant contractual beneficiary is the testator who intends to confer on the third party the benefit of his assets after death and not the benefit of the solicitor's promise to draft the will. Accordingly, the contract does not fall within section 1(1)(b) of the 1999 Act. The intended legatee, however, has a claim in tort against the solicitors.[106]

(7) C, the owner of property, contracted with B Ltd. for the erection of a factory. The contract entitled C to nominate sub-contractors and B made a contract

---

[102] *Ibid.*, §§ 7.33, 7.51, broadly the facts of *Green* v. *Russell* [1959] 2 Q.B. 226. See Pearce L.J., *ibid.*, at pp. 246–7.

[103] Based on the example in Law Com. No. 242, § 7.42. On the rejection of a special test for consumers, see *ibid.*, § 7.54 and *post*, p. 451.

[104] Based on the example in Law Com. No. 242, § 7.41.

[105] [1995] 2 A.C. 207.

[106] See Law Com. No. 242, §§ 7.19–7.27, 7.48. Because there was a claim in tort (on which see *post*, p. 449), the Commission was content (Law Com. No. 242, § 7.25) to leave these cases outside its proposed third-party right although 'at a theoretical level' it preferred the view that the right of the prospective beneficiaries more properly belongs within the realm of contract than tort: *ibid.*, § 7.27. *Sed quaere.*

with A, a nominated flooring sub-contractor. The floor was defective. The Commission considered that in such a care, even if A's obligations, including the obligation to use reasonable care in laying the floor, purported to benefit C, who was expressly identified, C would not be able to sue A under section 1(1)(b). It considered that the presumption of an enforceable right would be rebutted because A's sub-contract was part of a wider chain of contracts, under which C's rights for breach of A's obligations, were to lie against B Ltd., the head-contractor.[107]

(8) A person who purchases goods from a retailer against whom he has a claim under the contract of sale is, in general, unlikely to be able to rely on section 1(1)(b) to sue the manufacturer of the goods for breach of the manufacturer's contract with the retailer.[108]

(iv) The nature of the rights under the Act

(a) The third party's rights. The third party's rights are derived from the parties' intentions as embodied in the contract and, apart from negotiable instruments and certain contracts of carriage,[109] are supplementary to rights the third party has under the common law or other statutes. But, as will be seen in the discussion of defences and variation and cancellation below, the third party entitled to sue under the 1999 Act does not specifically step into the shoes of the promisee and is not treated as a party to the contract.[110]

By section 1(5), a third party who has a right to enforce a contractual provision under the 1999 Act will be able to claim any remedy for breach of contract given by the Courts that would have been available if he had been a party to the contract. Accordingly, while the third party may claim damages,[111] an award of an agreed sum, specific performance, and an injunction, the Act does not permit him or her to terminate the contract since termination is a self-help remedy, or to claim restitutionary remedies, since those are not remedies for breach of contract.[112]

Section 1(4) contains an important limitation on the third party's rights. A third party has no right to enforce a term 'otherwise than subject to and in accordance with any other relevant terms of the contract'. In this way, although the Act does not change the rule whereby parties to a contract cannot generally impose an obligation upon a third party, if the benefit conferred is qualified or subject to a condition, the third party cannot ignore the qualification or condition.

The distinction between the imposition of a burden and the conferral of a conditional benefit is easy to draw where the condition does not require any performance

---

[107] Law Com. No. 242, § 7.47, the facts of *Junior Books Co. Ltd.* v. *Veitchi Co. Ltd.* [1983] 1 A.C. 520. The owner successfully sued the sub-contractor in tort in respect of the economic loss suffered; see *post*, p. 450. Macmillan (2000) 63 M.L.R. 721, 725 considers the view that the presumption of enforceability was rebutted to involve a certain circularity.

[108] See Law Com. No. 242, § 7.54.

[109] *Ante*, p. 430.

[110] Save for the limited purposes set out in ss. 1(5) and 3(4), see *post*, p. 437.

[111] See *post*, p. 620.

[112] Law Com. No. 242, § 3.33.

by the third party, for example where the contract states that the benefit is conditional on the third party reaching a certain age or where the contract contains a clause exempting or limiting the promisor's liability to the third party. Where, however, the condition requires performance by the third party, for example the grant of a right of way over a path subject to a condition that the third party keeps the path in repair, the distinction may be less easy to draw. In order to avoid the possibility of the third party being overall worse off by being given the right to enforce, the Commission considered that in such a case the third party should be bound by the condition in the limited sense that the promisor can use the condition as the basis of a defence or set-off to a claim by the third party to enforce the contract.[113]

(b) The promisee's rights. The third party's rights are distinct from the rights of the parties, which are preserved by the provision in section 4 that section 1 'does not affect any right of the promisee to enforce any term of the contract'.[114]

(c) Avoidance of double liability. Since, unless otherwise agreed between the contracting parties, both the promisee and the third party have independent and concurrent rights to sue, the Law Commission was concerned to protect the promisor against double liability. This is not a problem where the promisee either recovers nominal damages or is granted specific performance of the obligation to benefit the third party. The Commission considered that it is also not a problem where the third party first recovers damages because then the promisee will be left with no corresponding loss outstanding. In the occasional cases in which the promisee has suffered personal loss which is independent of the third party's loss, the promisee should be entitled to sue for that loss in its own name.[115] That leaves the situation in which the promisee has recovered substantial damages and the third party then brings an action in reliance on section 1. Section 5 of the 1999 Act provides that in any such action by the third party the Court or arbitral tribunal shall reduce any award to the third party to such extent as it thinks appropriate to take account of the sum recovered by the promisee.

(v) Defences

(a) Defences available against the promisee. Section 3(2) of the Act provides that the rights of the third party are subject to the entitlement of the promisor to raise any defence or set-off which arise out of or in connection with the contract and which would have been available against the promisee.[116] Counterclaims are excluded because a counterclaim may exceed the value of the third party's claim and thus impose a burden on the third party.[117] 'Defences' include matters which render the contract void (such as mistake), voidable (such as misrepresentation), or which have led to the contract being discharged (such as serious breach or frustration). But the Law Commission did not consider that personal bars on the promisee, such as

---

[113] Law Com. No. 242, § 10.27.
[114] On damages in such cases, see *post*, p. 620ff.
[115] Andrews [2001] C.L.J. 353, 371.
[116] Law Com. No. 242, § 10.12. Cf. Law Revision Committee, Cmnd. 5449, § 47.
[117] *Ibid.*, § 10.10.

inequitable conduct by the promisee which would bar a claim by him for specific performance or a failure to mitigate his loss, should automatically bar or restrict the third party's remedy.[118]

The Act enables the parties to the contract either to enlarge the defences available to the promisor to include all defences available against the promisee whether or not they arise out of or are connected with the contract,[119] or to preclude the promisor from raising any defence available against the promisee.[120]

Defences based on an exclusion or limitation clause fall within section 3(2) and so can be raised by the promisor. In this context, the promisor may be in a better position *vis à vis* the third party than it would be in an action by the promisee. This will be the case where the exclusion or limitation clause is subject to the Unfair Contract Terms Act 1977.[121] While a clause restricting or excluding liability for death or personal injury that is unenforceable by virtue of section 2(1) of the 1977 Act will not bind the third party, section 7(2) of the 1999 Act provides that section 2(2) of the 1977 Act shall not apply in proceedings brought by a third party under the 1999 Act. Section 2(2) subjects clauses restricting or excluding liability for negligence to a requirement of reasonableness, so the result is that a clause that might be regarded as unreasonable and unenforceable against the promisee will bind the third party.

(b) *Defences available had the third party been a party to the contract.* By section 3(4) the third party's claim is also subject to the defences, set-offs, and counterclaims (not arising from the contract) that would have been available to the promisor had the third party been a party to the contract. Again, the parties may contract out of this. Section 3(5) enables the parties to provide that such defences, set-offs, and counterclaims are not to be available in a claim by the third party.

(vi) Variation and rescission

Perhaps the most difficult question in deciding on the precise extent of a third party right is when the contracting parties should have power to vary or cancel the contract by agreement. A balance has to be struck between preserving the freedom of the contracting parties to implement their intentions at any particular time and allowing the creation of effective third party rights so that a third party can arrange its affairs with some certainty.[122]

(a) *The range of solutions.* The matter has not been satisfactorily solved in certain jurisdictions which recognize third party rights.[123] The Law Revision Committee considered that third party rights should be subject to cancellation of the contract by the contracting parties at any time before the third party had adopted the contract either

---

[118] *Ibid.,* § 10.2.

[119] 1999 Act, s. 3(3).

[120] *Ibid.,* s. 3(5).

[121] On s. 2 of the 1977 Act, see *ante,* p. 190ff.

[122] Law Com. No. 242, § 9.8.

[123] In Scotland, while *Carmichael* v. *Carmichael's Executrix* 1920 S.C. (H.L.) 195 suggests the right becomes irrevocable when brought to the notice of the third party, the position is unclear; McCormick [1970] Jur. Rev. 228, 236; Scot. Law Com. Memorandum No. 38 (1977).

expressly or by conduct. But this notion lacks precision and may lead to Courts presuming that there has been acceptance.[124] In New Zealand, variation is allowed until the third party has materially altered his position in reliance on the contract[125] and there are advantages in utilizing this familiar concept in this context. In certain cases, such as contracts of insurance[126] and possibly other contracts which expressly name a third party, it is even arguable that the third party's rights should not be subject to cancellation unless the contract expressly provides for this. But the 1999 Act does not exclusively base the right of the third party to sue on express provision (the section 1(1)(a) test); it is also based on identification as a beneficiary (the section 1(1)(b) test). To presume irrevocability within a scheme where the right can be based on identification may lead to unfairness.[127]

The Law Commission sought to balance the freedom of the contracting parties to implement their intentions with the need to create effective third party rights by having a statutory scheme as the 'default' arrangement but allowing the parties to vary it by appropriate provisions in the contract. The Commission considered that reliance should be the primary test for the crystallization of the third party's rights but that there should also be an alternative test of acceptance to enable a third party who has successfully communicated its assent to the promisor to be secure in its entitlement without having to show reliance.

(b) Section 2(1) of the Act. Section 2(1) of the Act gives effect to the Law Commission's recommendations. It provides that the contracting parties' right to vary or rescind the contract by agreement should be lost in two situations. First, where the third party has relied on the term and the promisor is aware of such reliance or could reasonably have foreseen that the third party would rely on it.[128] The third party will have to prove that it has relied on the term. Secondly, the right to rescind is lost where the third party has communicated its assent to the term by words or conduct[129] to the promisor.[130] Communication of the acceptance to the promisee will not suffice and by section 2(2)(b) if sent by post the acceptance shall not be regarded as communicated to the promisor until received by him; the Law Commission considered that it would be inappropriate to apply the postal acceptance rule.[131]

(c) Contractual provision. The Commission's recognition of the autonomy of the parties resulted in it recommending that the contracting parties be able expressly to reserve the right to vary or rescind the third party's right irrespective of reliance or acceptance by the third party, or to provide that the third party's right shall crystallize on the occurrence of an event other than reliance or acceptance. These are enacted in section 2(3)(a) and (b) of the 1999 Act.

---

[124] Law Com. C.P. No. 121 (1991), §§ 4.32, 5.31; Law Com. No. 242, § 9.17.

[125] New Zealand Contracts (Privity) Act 1982, s. 5, set out in Appendix B to Law Com. No. 242 (1996). See also *Restatement of Contracts* (2d), § 311.

[126] As in the case of s.11 of the Married Women's Property Act 1882, *post*, p. 444.

[127] Law Com. No. 242, § 12.25.

[128] S. 2(1)(b) and (c). See Law Com. No. 242, §§ 9.26–9.30.

[129] S. 2(2)(a).

[130] S. 2(1)(a). See Law Com. No. 242, § 9.20, 9.26.

[131] Law Com. No. 242, § 9.20. On postal acceptance, see *ante*, p. 43.

(d) Discretion to dispense with third party's consent. Where the third party's rights have crystallized so that the consent of a third party is required for any variation or rescission of the term by agreement, a Court or arbitral tribunal has power to dispense with such consent in three situations. First, where consent cannot be obtained because the third party's whereabouts cannot reasonably be ascertained.[132] Secondly, where the third party is mentally incapable of giving his consent.[133] Thirdly, where it cannot reasonably be ascertained whether or not the third party has in fact relied on the term.[134]

(e) TRUSTS OF CONTRACTUAL RIGHTS

(i) Rights based on equitable property not contract

Equity allows a third party to enforce a contract where it can be construed as creating a completely constituted trust of the contractual right, also known as a trust of the promise. However, as Lord Haldane stated in *Dunlop* v. *Selfridge*,[135] the rights do not arise by way of contract but are based on the third party's equitable proprietary interest in the subject matter of the contract and the right of the equitable owner to enforce the trust in his favour. Property may be tangible or intangible[136] and certain rights under a contract, 'choses in action', constitute an important example of intangible property.[137]

Thus a promisee under a contract, either at the time when the contract is made or thereafter, may constitute a trust of the right to which the promisee is entitled in favour of a third party which is enforceable in equity.[138] The subject of the trust, the contractual right to money or property,[139] is at law vested in the trustee, that is to say, in the promisee under the contract.

As with the enforcement of equitable rights in general, the person having the legal right in the thing demanded, in this case the contracting party who has thus become a trustee, must in general be a party to the action. 'The trustee then can take steps to enforce performance to the beneficiary by the other contracting party as in the case of other equitable rights. The action should be in the name of the trustee. If, however, the trustee refuses to sue, the beneficiary can sue, joining the trustee as defendant'.[140] A trustee who sues on behalf of the third party may recover not merely nominal

---

[132] s. 2(4)(a).

[133] s. 2(4)(b).

[134] s. 2(5).

[135] [1915] A.C. 847; *ante*, p. 423.

[136] Lawson and Rudden, *The Law of Property* (2nd edn), ch. 2.

[137] *Ibid.*, pp. 26–8. *Post*, p. 470.

[138] Williston (1902) 15 Harvard L.R. 767; Corbin (1930) 46 L.Q.R. 12; Glanville Williams (1944) 7 Mod. L.R. 123; Barton (1975) 91 L.Q.R. 236; Rickett (1979) 32 C.L.P. 1; Law Com. No. 242, §§ 2.8–2.9.

[139] Cf. *Southern Water Authority* v. *Carey* [1985] 2 All E.R. 1077, at p. 1083 (no trust of the benefit of an exemption clause).

[140] *Vandepitte* v. *Preferred Accident Insurance Corporation of New York* [1933] A.C. 70, at p. 79.

damages representing the trustee's own meagre interest in the performance of the contract, but the whole loss suffered by the beneficiary.[141]

Although this equitable principle was first enunciated in the eighteenth century by Lord Hardwicke,[142] the important developments occurred in the nineteenth century. Thus in *Lloyd's* v. *Harper*:[143]

H, whose son was about to be elected a member of Lloyd's, wrote to the committee guaranteeing his son's solvency. When the son became insolvent, Lloyd's claimed against the father on behalf of members who had suffered thereby, and also on behalf of some outsiders.

It was held that the creditors were entitled to the benefit of the contract made, since the committee had entered into it as trustee for all those who had suffered by the insolvency of the son.

The principle was applied by the House of Lords in *Les Affréteurs Réunis Société Anonyme* v. *Leopold Walford (London) Ltd.*:[144]

In a charterparty made between the appellant, the owner of a steamship, and a firm of charterers, the appellant promised to pay a commission of 3 per cent on the gross amount of hire to the respondent, the broker who had negotiated the contract of charterparty. It failed to pay, and the respondent sued to obtain its commission.

The respondent was not a party to the contract. Although it would not normally be entitled to any rights under it, it was the practice for a charterer, if necessary, to sue the shipowner for the amount of a broker's commission *as trustee for the broker*. Here the action had been brought by the brokers themselves, but by consent it was treated as brought by the charterers as trustees for them. The House of Lords recognized the practice and gave judgment in the broker's favour.

(ii) Intention to create trust

To establish a trust of the promise it is necessary to establish that the promisee intended to enter the contract as trustee but, in the absence of express words,[145] there is no satisfactory test to determine whether the requisite intention exists. The consequence is uncertainty.[146]

The different judicial approaches to the question at different stages of the doctrine have led to a complicated body of case law which is not possible to reconcile. *Lloyds* v. *Harper* and *Walford*'s case may suggest that it is possible to infer an intention to create a trust solely from the intention to benefit the third party and, as such, the device of a trust could be fictionally employed as a way round the privity rule.[147] However, the approach of the Courts in more recent times has been stricter. It is said that the

---

[141] *Lloyd's* v. *Harper* (1880) 16 Ch. D. 290.

[142] *Tomlinson* v. *Gill* (1756) Amb. 330.

[143] (1880) 16 Ch. D. 290. See also *Fletcher* v. *Fletcher* (1844) 4 Hare 67.

[144] [1919] A.C. 801.

[145] *Fletcher* v. *Fletcher* (1844) 4 Hare 67.

[146] Glanville Williams (1944) 7 Mod. L.R. 123.

[147] Corbin (1930) 46 L.Q.R. 12, at p. 17; Lord Wright (1939) 55 L.Q.R. 189, at p. 208 (a 'cumbrous fiction').

intention to constitute the trust must be affirmatively proved by substantial evidence,[148] in part because the presence of a trust renders the contract immutable where the parties might otherwise wish to be free to vary it.[149] Thus it will be more difficult to establish a trust where the intention to benefit the third party is not irrevocable,[150] where the contract consists of a complex package of benefits and burdens,[151] or where the third party may not need the benefit.[152]

An example of the differences of approach is provided by the contrast between *Re Flavell*[153] and *Re Schebsman*.[154] In *Re Flavell*:

Partnership articles provided that, in the event of the death of one of the partners, an annuity out of the firm's net profits each year was to be paid to his widow or children as he should appoint and, in default of appointment, to his widow.

It was held that the executors of the deceased partner were trustees for the widow under this contract, and that she was entitled to be paid the promised sums. But in *Re Schebsman*:

In 1940 S's employment was terminated, and, in consideration of his retirement, the company agreed to pay him the sum of £5,500 by instalments. If he died before the completion of the payments to him they were to be paid to his widow and daughter. S later became bankrupt, and then died. His trustee in bankruptcy claimed to intercept the sums being paid to his widow, on the ground that S himself could have intercepted them, and so they were available for his creditors.

The Court refused to hold that the contract created a trust in favour of the widow and daughter; they had therefore no enforceable right to the money. But the company was free to perform its obligation if it so wished, and, if it did so, neither S nor his trustee in bankruptcy could intercept the money and put it in his own pocket. Accordingly, the claim failed. Du Parcq L.J. said:[155]

It is true that, by the use possibly of unguarded language, a person may create a trust, as Monsieur Jourdain talked prose, without knowing it, but unless an intention to create a trust is clearly to be collected from the language used and the circumstances of the case, I think that the Court ought not to be astute to discover indications of such an intention. I have little doubt that in the present case both parties (and certainly the debtor) intended to keep alive their common law right to vary consensually the terms of the obligation undertaken by the company, and if circumstances had changed in the debtor's life-time injustice might

---

[148] *Vandepitte* v. *Preferred Accident Insurance Corp of New York* [1933] A.C. 70, at p. 80.

[149] *Re Schebsman* [1944] Ch. 83, at p. 104; *Green* v. *Russell* [1959] 2 Q.B. 226, at p. 241.

[150] *Re Sinclair's Life Policy* [1938] Ch. 799. Note, however, that it is possible to have a revocable trust: *Wilson* v. *Darling Island Stevedoring and Lighterage Co.* (1956) 95 C.L.R. 43, at p. 67 (Fullagar J.).

[151] *Vandepitte* v. *Preferred Accident Insurance Corp of New York* [1933] A.C. 70, at p. 81; *Swain* v. *The Law Society* [1983] 1 A.C. 598, at p. 612; *Southern Water Authority* v. *Carey* [1985] 2 All E.R. 1077, at p. 1083.

[152] *Vandepitte* v. *Preferred Accident Insurance Corp of New York*, *ibid.*, at p. 80 (contracting party liable for infant third party's torts); *Swain* v. *The Law Society* [1983] 1 A.C. 598, at pp. 612, 621 (third party beneficiary accorded direct action against promisor by statute), *post*, p. 444.

[153] (1883) 25 Ch. D. 89.

[154] [1944] Ch. 83.

[155] [1944] Ch. 83, at p. 104.

have been done by holding that a trust had been created and that those terms were accordingly unalterable.

Similar contrasts can be found in the approach of the Courts to contracts of insurance. Thus while in some cases such contracts have been held to create a trust in favour of third parties,[156] in others they have not.[157] In this context too it would appear that English Courts no longer favour the device of a trust of a contractual right. It has been stated in Australian decisions that this may be too cautious and that there is 'considerable scope for the development of trusts' particularly in the context of insurance policies for the benefit of third persons.[158] One recent English case also indicates less hostility.[159] However, the dominant approach is exemplified by the decision of the Judicial Committee of the Privy Council in *Vandepitte* v. *Preferred Accident Insurance Corporation of New York*[160] on appeal from British Columbia:

B insured his car with the respondent. The contract of insurance was stated to cover not only B himself, but all persons driving the car with his consent. B's daughter, while driving it with his consent, knocked down and injured the appellant, V. She was successfully sued in negligence by V, but the judgment was unsatisfied. By the British Columbia Insurance Act, an injured person could, in such circumstances, avail himself of any rights possessed by the driver of the vehicle against the insurance company. V therefore brought an action against the respondent under this Act.

In order to succeed, he had to establish that the daughter had some rights against the company under the policy, and he could only do this by showing that a trust had been created for her benefit. The Judicial Committee were not satisfied that this was B's intention. First, as British Columbia law provided that a father was liable for the torts of his minor children living with the family, B would 'naturally expect' any claim to be against him.[161] Secondly, a trust was not appropriate for a contract, such as insurance which imposes '. . . serious duties and obligations . . . on any person claiming to be insured, which necessarily involve consent and privity of contract'.[162]

The strict and possibly overcautious approach to the requirement of intention means that, despite its continued use,[163] the trust of a contractual right does not now constitute a major qualification to the doctrine of privity of contract.

---

[156] *Royal Exchange Assurance* v. *Hope* [1928] Ch. 179; *Re Webb* [1941] Ch. 225; *Re Foster's Policy* [1966] 1 W.L.R. 222. See also *Williams* v. *Baltic Insurance Association of London Ltd.* [1924] 2 K.B. 282.

[157] *Re Englebach's Estate* [1924] 2 Ch. 348; *Clay's Policy of Assurance* [1937] 2 All E.R. 548; *Re Sinclair's Life Policy* [1938] Ch. 799; *Green* v. *Russell* [1959] 2 Q.B. 226; *Swain* v. *The Law Society* [1983] 1 A.C. 598; *McCamley* v. *Cammell Laird Shipbuilders Ltd.* [1990] 1 W.L.R. 963, at p. 969.

[158] *Trident General Insurance Co. Ltd.* v. *NcNiece Bros. Pty. Ltd.* (1988) 165 C.L.R. 107, at p. 166 (Toohey J.). See also *ibid.*, at pp. 120–1, 146–51, 156; *Wilson* v. *Darling Island Stevedoring and Lighterage Co.* (1956) 95 C.L.R. 43, at p. 67.

[159] *Darlington BC* v. *Wiltshier (Northern) Ltd* [1995] 1 W.L.R. 68, at pp. 75, 81 (a constructive trust). Cf. Law Com. No. 242, § 2.9.

[160] [1933] A.C. 70. Cf. *Williams* v. *Baltic Insurance Association of London Ltd.* [1924] 2 K.B. 282; Road Traffic Act 1988, s. 148(7).

[161] *Ibid.*, at p. 80.

[162] *Ibid.*, at p. 81.

[163] *Burton* v. *FX Music Ltd.* [1999] E.M.L.R. 826, at pp. 840–1 (trust of promise to pay royalties due under a music distribution agreement).

(iii) Differences from the rights under the 1999 Act

It will clearly be more difficult for a third party to establish a trust of a contractual promise for the third party's benefit than to establish a right to enforce the promise under the 1999 Act. But the rights under the 1999 Act will be more limited. First, rights under the statute can, subject to section 2, be altered or extinguished whereas the third party's rights under a trust of a promise are in principle irrevocable.[164] Secondly, the third party's rights under the statute, but not under a trust, are subject to defences applicable between the parties to the contract.[165] Thirdly, since the third party's rights based on a trust of the promise are founded on an equitable proprietary interest, they will be more effective than those under the 1999 Act where the promisee is insolvent.[166]

There are also procedural differences since, as noted above, it is necessary in an action based on a trust of the promise for the trustee to be joined in the action whereas, under the 1999 Act it is a matter for the Court's discretion.[167]

(f) CONTRACTS OF INSURANCE

Contracts of insurance made for the benefit of third parties cannot in principle be enforced by them, unless a trust is created in their favour.[168] The general principle is, however, subject to a number of important statutory exceptions, including the 1999 Act. The potential application of the 1999 Act to insurance contracts has been noted.[169] This section considers other statutory exceptions.

(i) Road traffic

Under the Road Traffic Act 1988, section 148(7), the person issuing a policy of insurance against death or bodily injury to third parties in accordance with the requirements of the Act is made liable to indemnify not only the persons taking out the policy, but 'the person or classes of persons specified in the policy in respect of any liability which the policy purports to cover'. This means that the driver of a motor vehicle is entitled to the benefit of an insurance policy made with an insurance company by the owner of the vehicle and which purports to cover the driver.[170] The Act also permits an injured third party to proceed directly against the insurance company on obtaining judgment against the assured.[171] It provides a better remedy for a third party than the 1999 Act since it precludes the insurer relying on various

---

[164] On revocable trusts, see *ante*, p. 441, n. 150.

[165] 1999 Act, s. 3, see *ante*, p. 436.

[166] Property held on trust by a bankrupt individual or an insolvent company is not available for distribution to creditors: Insolvency Act 1986, ss. 283, 107; Insolvency Rules 1986 S.I. 1986 No. 1925. See e.g., *Re Kayford Ltd.* [1975] 1 W.L.R. 279.

[167] Civil Procedure Rules, r. 19.1(2).

[168] See *ante*, p. 442, nn. 156 and 157.

[169] See *ante*, pp. 432, 433.

[170] *Tattersall* v. *Drysdale* [1935] 2 K.B. 174.

[171] Road Traffic Act 1988, ss. 151–3. See also the Third Parties (Rights against Insurers) Act 1930, *post*, p. 444.

defences which would have been available in a claim by the assured.[172] Victims of road accidents are also protected by two agreements entered into in 1972 between the Secretary of State for the Environment and the Motor Insurers' Bureau. These are designed to compensate those injured by untraced ('hit and run') drivers and by uninsured drivers. Where the victim claims against the Bureau in respect of injuries sustained, as it is the policy of the Bureau not to raise the defence that the victim is not a party to the agreement between it and the Secretary of State,[173] the victim may proceed and even obtain judgment.[174]

(ii) Liability and indemnity insurance

Although, in general, a third party who has a claim against a defendant who has taken out insurance against liability to third parties will not be able to claim against the insurer under the 1999 Act, as seen above in certain circumstances such a claim will be possible. Additionally, under the Third Parties (Rights against Insurers) Act 1930 a third party who has a claim against a defendant who has taken out insurance against liability to third parties will be able to claim against the insurer where the defendant has become, *inter alia*, insolvent either before or after incurring the liability to the third party. The 1930 Act has several limitations, primarily that the third party has to establish its claim in proceedings against the defendant before obtaining any rights against the insurer.[175] The Law Commission[176] has therefore recommended the replacement of the 1930 Act with legislation under which a third party will be entitled to resolve all issues relating to a claim in a single set of proceedings against the insurer and to improved rights to information about the insurance policy. Where the defendant is insolvent the 1930 Act, despite its several limitations, is likely to provide a better remedy than the 1999 Act which does not give the third party priority over the claims of the defendant's liquidator.[177] Moreover, the limitations in sections 2 and 3 of the 1999 Act will not apply to a claim under the 1930 Act.

Third party rights may also be created by administrative rules made by a regulatory body operating in the public law sphere. Thus a contract to provide indemnity insurance for solicitors made between the Law Society and insurers as part of a compulsory insurance scheme can be directly enforced by solicitors.[178]

(iii) Husband and wife

The Married Women's Property Act 1882, section 11, allows a husband to effect an insurance on his life for the benefit of his wife and children. A wife, too, may effect an insurance on her own life for the benefit of her husband and children. Such an

---

[172] *Ibid.*, ss. 148, 152. Cf. 1999 Act, s. 3 *ante*, p. 436.

[173] *Hardy* v. *Motor Insurers' Bureau* [1964] 2 Q.B. 745, at p. 757; *Gurtner* v. *Circuit* [1968] 2 Q.B. 587, at p. 599.

[174] But see the criticism voiced by Lord Dilhorne in *Albert* v. *Motor Insurers' Bureau* [1972] A.C. 301, at p. 320.

[175] *Bradley* v. *Eagle Star Insurance Co. Ltd.* [1989] A.C. 957 (cf. Companies Act 1989, s. 141); *The Fanti and The Padre Island* [1991] 2 A.C. 1; *Cox* v. *Bankside Members Agency Ltd.* [1995] 2 Lloyd's Rep. 437.

[176] Law Com. No. 272 (2001).

[177] *Ante*, p. 430.

[178] *Swain* v. *Law Society* [1983] 1 A.C. 598.

insurance creates a trust in favour of the objects of the policy, and does not form part of the assured's estate. The Law Revision Committee proposed that this be extended to all life, endowment, and education policies which name a beneficiary[179] but the Law Commission considered that this would only be sensible as part of a general review of insurance.[180] Nevertheless, those named as beneficiaries under such policies may have a right to enforce them by virtue of the 1999 Act, albeit subject to the limits set out in it, in particular those in sections 2 and 3, which exclude those sections where the 1882 Act applies.

(iv) Limited interests

Persons with limited interests in property may also be given the right to sue even though they are not parties to the contract of insurance. In contracts of marine insurance, when several persons have an interest in the merchandise conveyed, any such person 'may insure on behalf and for the benefit of other persons interested as well as for his own benefit'.[181] Similarly, in the case of sales of land, if A contracts to sell land to B and property on the land is damaged or destroyed before the completion of the sale, any insurance moneys received by A must be held by A in trust for B.[182] And a tenant can claim under the landlord's fire insurance policy, and vice versa.[183]

(g) COMMERCIAL PRACTICE

Certain exceptions have been introduced into the doctrine of privity of contract as concessions to commercial practice. Some of these are the result of statutory provisions; others arise out of the agreed practices of merchants as recognized by the Courts.

(i) Negotiable instruments and bills of lading

Negotiable instruments and bills of lading provide important illustrations of statutory exceptions, and are additionally excluded from the operation of the 1999 Act.[184] But since these are dealt with in the section devoted to them later in this book,[185] it is not necessary to elaborate their effect here.

(ii) Letters of credit

The irrevocable letter of credit has often been said to be an example of an exception to privity of contract.[186] The purpose of such letters of credit is to finance contracts for

---

[179] Sixth Interim Report 1937, Cmnd. 5449, § 49.
[180] Law Com. No. 242 (1996), § 12.26.
[181] Marine Insurance Act 1906, s. 14(2).
[182] Law of Property Act 1925, s. 47(1).
[183] Fires Prevention (Metropolis) Act 1774, s. 83.
[184] 1999 Act, s. 6(1) and (5), but a third party may invoke s. 1 to avail itself of an exclusion or limitation of liability in contracts of carriage.
[185] See *post*, p. 486.
[186] See *The Uniform Customs and Practice for Documentary Credits* (1993); Jack, *Documentary Letters of Credit* (1993).

the sale of goods between buyers and sellers in different countries, particularly where the delay between despatch from the place of manufacture and arrival at the destination is a considerable one. It enables short-term credit facilities to be made available, guarantees payment to the seller, and safeguards the parties against currency fluctuations.

There are three stages in the transaction. First, a term is inserted in the contract of sale made between the buyer and the seller whereby the buyer undertakes to furnish an irrevocable letter of credit in favour of the seller.[187] Secondly, the buyer approaches its own banker (usually described as the issuing banker) and instructs it to issue an irrevocable letter of credit, giving the banker details of the transaction. This constitutes a contract between the buyer and the banker. Thirdly, the banker advises the seller that an irrevocable letter of credit has been opened in its favour, that is to say, the banker gives an irrevocable undertaking to pay the seller, or to accept bills of exchange drawn on it, provided the seller tenders the required shipping documents in compliance with the terms of the letter of credit.[188] The seller can then ship the goods in the secure knowledge that it will be paid for them. The shipping documents represent the goods themselves,[189] and they are usually retained by the banker as security against its right to be reimbursed by the buyer.

The irrevocable letter of credit does not fit easily into the common law. If the transaction is regarded simply as a contract between the buyer and its banker, the seller is a third party to this contract and technically would be unable to sue should the banker revoke the letter of credit or for some reason fail to make payment.[190] Nevertheless, it has been established that the banker is legally under an absolute obligation to pay, irrespective of any dispute there may be between the buyer and seller.[191] It has therefore been argued that the irrevocable letter of credit forms an 'exception' to the doctrine of privity of contract; but it seems better to regard the promise of payment given by the banker to the seller as an autonomous undertaking, independent of any other contract. Thus the irrevocable letter of credit is not an exception to privity of contract but to the doctrine of consideration. It is either an irrevocable offer by the banker to the seller (which is accepted by the seller tendering the shipping documents) or a unilateral contract between the banker and the seller to pay on tender of the shipping documents.[192]

---

[187] For the effect of a failure to furnish the letter of credit, see *ante*, p. 136, *post*, p. 524.

[188] An irrevocable letter of credit may also be 'confirmed' by a banker operating in the seller's country (known as the correspondent banker) who, by confirming the credit, adds to the promise of the issuing banker its own undertaking to ensure payment.

[189] See *post*, p. 492.

[190] In the Sixth Interim Report of the Law Revision Committee, 1937 (Cmnd. 5449), § 45, it was pointed out that the liquidator of a bank might be compelled to rely on the defence of privity.

[191] *Urquhart, Lindsay & Co. Ltd.* v. *Eastern Bank Ltd.* [1922] 1 K.B. 318, at pp. 321, 322; *Donald H. Scott & Co. Ltd.* v. *Barclays Bank Ltd.* [1923] 2 K.B. 1, at p. 13; *Trans-Trust S.P.R.L.* v. *Danubian Trading Co. Ltd.* [1952] 2 Q.B. 297, at pp. 304–5; *Midland Bank Ltd.* v. *Seymour* [1955] 2 Lloyd's Rep. 147, at p. 166; *Hamzeh Malas & Sons* v. *British Imex Industries Ltd.* [1958] 2 Q.B. 127, at p. 129.

[192] Ellinger (1962) 4 Malaya L.R. 307. The problem in either case is how, and at what time, consideration for the undertaking is furnished by the seller, so as to render it binding. In *Urquhart's* case (*supra*), at p. 321, Rowlatt J. thought that the banker's undertaking took effect once the seller acted on it, e.g. by commencing performance of their contract with the buyer. Cf. *Dexters Ltd.* v. *Schenker & Co.* (1932) 14 Ll. L.R. 586, at p. 588 (when letter of credit received). The latter is correct.

(iii) Package holidays

Where a consumer makes a contract for the provision of a package holiday, the beneficiaries of that contract (for example family members and others who go on the holiday) are given direct contractual rights against the organizer and the retailer even where they are not parties to the contract.[193]

(h) CONTRACTS CONCERNING LAND

(i) Covenants in a lease

The benefit of covenants in a lease which touch and concern the land demised will run upon an assignment of the lease or of the reversion.[194] Also, under the rule in *Tulk* v. *Moxhay*,[195] a vendor of freehold land may attach to the land sold restrictive covenants as to its future use (for example, that no buildings shall be erected on the land). Provided that the covenant was imposed for the benefit of neighbouring land, any subsequent owner of that land may enforce the covenant if he shows that the benefit of the covenant has become annexed to the land,[196] has been assigned to him, or that its benefit has passed to him under a building scheme.[197] Third parties may thus acquire rights under a covenant to which they were not privy.[198] These rules, however, are simply rules applicable to rights over land.

(ii) Law of Property Act 1925, section 56(1)

A more controversial exception is provided by section 56(1) of the Law of Property Act 1925, which states:

A person may take an immediate or other interest in land or other property, or the benefit of any condition, right of entry, covenant or agreement over or respecting land or other property, although he may not be named as a party to the conveyance or other instrument.

The word 'property' is defined in the Act, unless the context otherwise requires, as including 'any thing in action, and any interest in real or personal property'.[199]

The scope of this sub-section has long been problematical.[200] In the view of some it is merely a conveyancing provision and applies only to land; but others, in particular Lord Denning, have interpreted it much more widely.[201] There has also been

---

[193] Package Travel, Package Holidays and Package Tours Regulations 1992 (S.I. 1992 No. 3288), regs. 2 and 15, implementing EEC Council Directive 90/314, 1990 O.J. L 158/59. See also *Jackson* v. *Horizon Holidays Ltd.* [1975] 1 W.L.R. 1468 *post*, p. 622.

[194] *Spencer's Case* (1583) 5 Co. Rep. 16a.

[195] (1848) 2 Ph. 774; see *post*, p. 453.

[196] In *Federated Homes Ltd.* v. *Mill Lodge Properties Ltd.* [1980] 1 W.L.R. 594 Brightman L.J. indicated this could take place automatically without express words.

[197] Harpum, *Megarry & Wade's Law of Real Property*, 6th edn. (2001), pp. 1034–5.

[198] See ss. 78(1) and 79(1) of the Law of Property Act 1925, and also *Smith and Snipes Hall Farm Ltd.* v. *River Douglas Catchment Board* [1949] 2 K.B. 500.

[199] s. 205(1)(xx).

[200] See Elliott (1956) 20 Conv. (N.S.) 43, 114; Andrews (1959) 23 Conv. (N.S.) 179; Furmston (1960) 23 M.L.R. 373, 380–5; Ellinger (1963) 26 M.L.R. 396; Wade [1964] C.L.J. 66.

[201] See *Smith and Snipes Hall Farm Ltd.* v. *River Douglas Catchment Board* [1949] 2 K.B. 500, at p. 517; *Drive Yourself Hire Co. (London) Ltd.* v. *Strutt* [1954] 1 Q.B. 250, at p. 274; *Beswick* v. *Beswick* [1966] Ch. 538.

considerable doubt as to who can properly rely on it. In its terms the sub-section is wide enough to permit any person who might conceive it of 'benefit' to take advantage of a covenant or agreement made by others, but such could scarcely have been the intention of the legislature. Accordingly, the Courts have construed it in a more limited fashion. In *White* v. *Bijou Mansions Ltd.* Simonds J. said that the only person who could rely on section 56 is one who, although not expressly named, the instrument purports to grant something to, or covenant with.[202]

This, which we may call the orthodox meaning, however, does not assist a person who is not a party to a contract but wishes to sue on that contract. The agreement is not 'made with him', nor does it 'grant something to him' since the sub-section does not give to the non-party a right to the performance of a contract if, apart from the sub-section, that person has no such right.[203] The sub-section did not create any fresh rights to sue under a contract, but only assisted the protection of rights shown to exist.

In *Beswick* v. *Beswick*[204] the House of Lords held unanimously that the context of section 56(1) required that a limited interpretation should be given to the word 'property', but there was no agreement as to what that interpretation should be. Lord Guest thought that it meant land,[205] but Lord Upjohn did not accept that the word was limited to an interest in real property.[206] There was similar disagreement about the orthodox meaning of the scope of the sub-section.[207] And Lord Upjohn expressed the view, based on historical grounds, that the words 'conveyance or other instrument' were confined to documents *inter partes* and under seal.[208] These differences of opinion have yet to be resolved,[209] and the enactment of the 1999 Act with its wider scope for third party enforcement may mean that they will not be. It is, however, clear that section 56(1) does not apply to a simple promise by A to B to pay a sum of money to C.

(i) CONTRACTS GIVING RISE TO TORTIOUS DUTIES OF CARE TO THIRD PARTIES

(i) Tortious duty to third party

A contract between A and B may, in addition to creating obligations between the contracting parties, lead to the creation of a tortious duty of care by one of them

---

[202] [1937] Ch. 610, at p. 625. See also *ibid.* (on appeal) [1938] Ch. 351, at p. 365; *Re Ecclesiastical Commissioners for England's Conveyance* [1936] Ch. 430; *Amsprop Trading Ltd.* v. *Harris Distribution Ltd.* [1997] 1 W.L.R. 1025. Contrast *Stromdale and Ball Ltd.* v. *Burden* [1952] Ch. 223.

[203] *Re Miller's Agreement* [1947] Ch. 615. See also *Re Foster* [1938] 3 All E.R. 357; *Re Sinclair's Life Policy* [1938] Ch. 799; *Green* v. *Russell* [1959] 2 Q.B. 226; *Scruttons Ltd.* v. *Midland Silicones Ltd.* [1962] A.C. 446.

[204] [1968] A.C. 58.

[205] At p. 87.

[206] At p. 105, with whom Lord Pearce agreed (at p. 94).

[207] At pp. 74–5, 81, 87, 94, 106.

[208] At p. 107, with whom Lord Pearce agreed (at p. 94). See also Lord Reid at pp. 76–7.

[209] In *Lynus* v. *Prowsa* [1982] 1 W.L.R. 1044, at p. 1049 and *Amsprop Trading Ltd.* v. *Harris Distribution Ltd.* [1997] 1 W.L.R. 1025 the orthodox meaning was considered correct.

towards a third party.[210] For instance, a contract made by an occupier of land may subject him or her to liability in tort to third party visitors,[211] and professionals such as surveyors and solicitors have been held liable in tort to third parties who have suffered loss by reason of their misrepresentation[212] or defective performance of the contract. For instance, in the two cases of *Smith* v. *Eric S. Bush (a firm)* and *Harris* v. *Wyre Forest District Council:*[213]

S and H applied to borrow money on mortgage to enable them to buy a house. In each case the lender contracted with surveyors to value the house and S and H then bought their respective houses in reliance on the valuations, which had in fact been carried out negligently. Although not party to any contract with the surveyors, S and H successfully sued them in tort; the surveyors knew that they would rely on the valuation and had paid the lenders for a valuation.

A third party who is sued by a party to a contract, may also be able to rely on its terms to show that it was under no duty of care, perhaps because the party to the contract had agreed to bear the risk.[214] This is discussed below[215] when the special problems of exemption clauses and third parties are considered.

(ii) Intended legatees

In *Ross* v. *Caunters*[216] and *White* v. *Jones*[217] solicitors, who had contracted with a testator to draw up wills benefiting third parties, were held liable in tort to the third parties where, as a result of their negligence, in the first case the will was executed in such a way as to invalidate the gift, and in the second case it was never drawn up. In these cases the relationship created by the contract gives rise to a duty of care to a third party who is thus able to sue the contracting party in tort, at least where no loss is suffered by the testator's estate.[218] It has been noted[219] that these cases do not fall within section 1(1)(b) of the 1999 Act and it is submitted that they are best analysed as torts.[220] Although the intended legatee is expressly designated as a beneficiary, the contract is not one in which the solicitor promises the testator to confer a benefit on the third party, the intended legatee, but one by which the solicitor is to enable the testator to do so.[221] The relevant contractual beneficiary is the testator who intended

---

[210] Reynolds (1985) 11 N.Z.U.L.R. 215, at pp. 220–6. See also Whittaker (1996) 14 O.J.L.S. 191.

[211] Occupiers Liability Act 1957, s. 3; Defective Premises Act 1972, ss. 1(1)(b) and 4.

[212] *Hedley Byrne & Co. Ltd.* v. *Heller & Partners Ltd.* [1964] A.C. 465, *ante*, at p. 247.

[213] [1990] 1 A.C. 831. See *ante*, at pp. 434 for a fuller statement of the facts.

[214] *Southern Water Authority* v. *Carey* [1985] 2 All E.R. 1077; *Norwich City Council* v. *Harvey* [1989] 1 W.L.R. 828, at p. 837, *post*, at p. 467. See also, *post*, at p. 456 (bailment).

[215] *Post*, p. 467.

[216] [1980] Ch. 287.

[217] [1995] 2 A.C. 207. See Weir (1995) 111 L.Q.R. 357. See further *Hill* v. *Van Erp* (1997) 142 A.L.R. 687 (Australia).

[218] *Carr-Glyn* v. *Frearsons* [1997] 2 All E.R. 614, at pp. 623–4, 628.

[219] *Ante*, p. 434.

[220] *White* v. *Jones* [1995] 2 A.C. 207, *per* Lord Mustill at p. 273; Barker (1994) 14 O.J.L.S. 137. Cf. Markesinis (1987) 103 L.Q.R. 354; Macmillan (2000) 63 M.L.R. 721, 724. For the Law Commission's position see *ante*, p. 434, n. 106.

[221] *White* v. *Jones* [1995] 2 A.C. 207, at pp. 262–3, 273; *Gartside* v. *Sheffield, Young & Ellis* [1983] N.Z.L.R. 37, at pp. 42, 49.

to confer on the third party the benefit of his assets after death and not the benefit of the solicitor's promise to draft the will.

(iii) Liability in tort not based on intention to benefit third party

The exceptions and qualifications to the privity principle considered above are based on an intention by the contracting parties to benefit the third party. Liability in tort is not based on such an intention and there may be liability where there could be no question of a contractual action. Although the contract is a relevant factor in determining whether a duty of care is owed to or by a third party, the criteria for liability in tort reflect wider considerations than the intentions of the contracting parties and include 'proximity', the type of loss suffered (liability in tort for economic loss is very narrow), assumption of responsibility by the defendant, and whether the claimant has reasonably relied on something said or done by the defendant.

The potential width of tort liability can be demonstrated by *Junior Books Co. Ltd.* v. *Veitchi Co. Ltd.*,[222] a decision of the House of Lords on appeal from Scotland, in which the owner of a factory under construction successfully sued a nominated sub-contractor who had negligently laid a floor for the economic loss suffered. The sub-contractor had contracted with the head-contractor who had in turn contracted with the factory owner. Although Scottish law recognizes that third parties may acquire rights under a contract, the factory owner did not seek to argue that it could sue in contract.[223] It was not known to the Court whether allowing the factory owner to sue the sub-contractor in tort circumvented an exemption clause in the contract between the sub-contractor and the head contractor.[224] Courts have, however, been increasingly reluctant to impose liability in tort for pure economic loss, particularly where this would cut across the contractual structure governing dealings between the defendant and others. Personal injury or damage to property is normally necessary and the reasoning in the *Junior Books* case has been substantially undermined.[225] Detailed discussion of this topic will be found in works on the law of tort.[226]

(j) FURTHER DEVELOPMENT OF THE COMMON LAW

The reluctance of English Courts to reform the third party rule has been noted.[227] What is the effect of the enactment of the Contracts (Rights of Third Parties) Act 1999 on further development of the common law?[228]

The Law Commission stated that it intended that legislation based on its recommendations, which it described as 'relatively conservative and moderate' should not

---

[222] [1983] 1 A.C. 520, *ante*, p. 435.

[223] It is not clear whether the requirements for a contractual action by the third party had been satisfied. On these, see McBryde, *The Law of Contract in Scotland* (1987), p. 412ff.

[224] *Ibid.*, at p. 538 (Lord Roskill).

[225] See *D. & F. Estates* v. *Church Commissioners for England* [1989] A.C. 177, 202; *Caparo Industries plc* v. *Dickman* [1990] 2 A.C. 605; *Murphy* v. *Brentwood D.C.* [1991] 1 A.C. 398; *Henderson* v. *Merrett Syndicates Ltd.* [1995] 2 A.C. 145.

[226] Cane, *Tort Law and Economic Interests* (2nd edn.); Markesinis and Deakin, *Tort Law* (3rd edn.) p. 83ff.

[227] *Ante*, p. 428.

[228] See Beatson (2001) 117 L.Q.R. 106.

hamper the judicial development of third party rights where the Courts decide that in a particular sphere the reform did not go far enough.[229] It is submitted that this cannot mean that, in situations in which the 'intention that the third party should enforce the contract' test is not satisfied, Courts should have no regard to the existence of the 1999 Act and its policy and should continue to develop the common law in the same way as they would have done without the 1999 Act. It may indeed be appropriate for the Courts to identify some common law principle other than the intention of the parties upon which to rest third party rights of suit, for instance 'assumption of responsibility',[230] or 'reasonable reliance'. It may also be appropriate for there to be judicial development where, as in the case of the promisee's remedies in contracts for the benefit of third parties, this has expressly been left to the common law.[231]

If, however, the only basis of any right in the third party could be intention but the requirements of the 1999 Act have not been satisfied, to allow the third party to enforce the contract term at common law would outflank the careful (and reasonably broad) way the 1999 Act has been framed. This would be the effect of any attempt to build on the suggestion, based on *dicta* in *Darlington B.C.* v. *Wilshier (Northern) Ltd.*[232] that, despite an unpromising history, the trust of a promise should be deployed as a way of granting a right of action to a third party. The basis of such a trust is an irrevocable intention to benefit the third party. Similarly, a common law exception applicable to exemption clauses such as has been adopted in Canada[233] would not be subject to the limitations in the 1999 Act, for example that the third party be identified in the contract by name, class, or description.[234] In such cases it would be inappropriate to enlarge the statutory provisions by judicial innovation.[235]

The difficulties can be illustrated by considering one of the examples of possible judicial development given by the Commission. The Commission wished to leave the House of Lords free to decide that, although there was no intention in a given contract to benefit a third party who is a consumer, the consumer should be able to enforce the contract because, in the particular circumstances 'a measure of imposed consumer protection is required'. It is, however, submitted that it is bizarre to leave a development of this sort to judicial development when Parliament has laid down that third parties are to have the right to enforce a contract only where the parties to it so intend.[236] Whether it is desirable to go further and to have 'a measure of imposed consumer protection' involves matters of policy which are, it is suggested, more suitable for a legislative than a judicial determination.

---

[229] Law Com. No. 242, § 5.11. See e.g., the exception for exemption clauses developed by the Supreme Court of Canada in *London Drugs Ltd.* v. *Kuehene & Nagel International Ltd.* [1992] 3 S.C.R. 299, *post*, p. 468.

[230] *White* v. *Jones* [1995] 2 A.C. 207.

[231] Law Com. No. 242, §§ 5.12–5.17. See *Alfred McAlpine Construction Ltd.* v. *Panatown Ltd.* [2000] 3 W.L.R. 946, *per* Lord Goff and Lord Millett (both dissenting) at pp. 551–2, 590. Cf. Lord Clyde at p. 535.

[232] [1995] 1 W.L.R. 68, at pp. 75, 81.

[233] *Post*, p. 468.

[234] s. 1(3), *ante*, p. 431.

[235] *Alfred McAlpine Construction Ltd.* v. *Panatown Ltd.* [2000] 3 W.L.R. 946, *per* Lord Clyde at p. 535.

[236] A proposal to confer rights automatically on third parties in respect of consumer sales regardless of the intentions of the parties was rejected: H.L. Debs., 11 January 1999, col. 31 (Lord Irvine L.C.).

III. THE IMPOSITION OF CONTRACTUAL
LIABILITIES UPON THIRD PARTIES

(a) INTRODUCTION

As a general rule, two persons cannot, by any contract into which they may enter, thereby impose contractual liabilities upon a third party.

This principle may be illustrated by reference to building contracts, where a person (the employer) engages a contractor to carry out certain building work. The contractor frequently sub-contracts parts of the work to sub-contractors. A sub-contractor has no cause of action against the employer for work done or materials supplied under the sub-contract, since the employer is not a party to that contract.[237] Even if the employer has nominated the sub-contractor and taken the benefit of the sub-contractor's work, the employer will not be liable to the sub-contractor for the price, as there is no privity of contract between them. Conversely, the employer has no claim in contract[238] against the sub-contractor,[239] since the sub-contractor is not a party to the main contract between the employer and the contractor.

Further, the principle of privity of contract normally prevents a person from being bound by an exemption clause contained in a contract to which it is not a party. This rule and its exceptions and circumventions are considered later in this chapter.[240]

Nevertheless there are certain situations where contractual liabilities may affect third parties. First, a contract concerning property may impose liabilities on third parties who subsequently acquire the property with notice of the contract. The property may be tangible, as where a contract is made concerning land or goods, or it may be intangible, as where the contract concerns intellectual property such as a patent or copyright. A similar principle may apply where information subject to a contractual obligation of confidentiality comes to the knowledge of a third party with notice of the contract,[241] although confidential information does not have all the attributes of a property interest, and it is not generally treated as such.[242] A second situation arises under the law of bailment. Where the owner of goods transfers possession to another (i.e. bails the goods), and the bailee then sub-bails them to another, the owner may be bound by exemption clauses contained in the contract of sub-bailment although not a party to it. Thirdly, the land law doctrine of restrictive covenants has been said to apply to chattels but, although there is some support in the cases, this approach has been much criticized. Fourthly, a person who knowingly interferes with contractual

---

[237] *Hampton* v. *Glamorgan C.C.* [1917] A.C. 13. See also *Schmaling* v. *Tomlinson* (1815) 6 Taunt. 147 (principal and sub-agent).

[238] But a claim may lie in tort: *Junior Books Ltd.* v. *Veitchi Co. Ltd.* [1983] 1 A.C. 520: see *ante*, p. 450.

[239] Unless there is a collateral warranty: see *ante*, p. 130.

[240] *Post*, p. 460.

[241] See Gurry, *Breach of Confidence* (1984), pp. 271–82; Cornish, *Intellectual Property*, 4th. edn. (1999), pp. 305–6.

[242] *Boardman* v. *Phipps* [1967] 2 A.C. 46, at pp. 127–8; Cornish, *op. cit.*, p. 330. Cf. Gurry, *op. cit.*, pp. 46–56.

rights without justification will be liable in tort and may be restrained from doing so by an injunction.

(b) CONTRACTS CONCERNING LAND

A contract for the sale of land creates an equitable proprietary interest in the land which can be enforced against a subsequent purchaser with notice.[243] Certain kinds of covenants concerning land are enforceable against third parties whether or not there is notice. If A leases land to B, there is privity of contract between them. But covenants in a lease which have reference to the subject-matter of the lease will be enforceable, not only between A and B, but against assignees of the lease or of the reversion.[244]

Also, under an equitable principle known as the rule in *Tulk* v. *Moxhay*,[245] the burden of covenants restricting the use to which land may be put can 'run with the land'. In that case:

T, who owned houses in Leicester Square, sold the garden in the centre of the square to E. E covenanted to maintain the land sold as a garden and not to build on it. The land was sold several times before being purchased by the defendant with notice of the covenant. The defendant proposed to build on the land and T sought an injunction to restrain him.

The injunction was granted. The defendant was not permitted to use the land in a manner inconsistent with the covenant entered into by E. The ground for the decision was the defendant's *notice* of the covenant at the time of the purchase.[246] But in subsequent cases the principle in *Tulk* v. *Moxhay* has undergone a considerable change. It must now be shown that the covenant was imposed for the benefit of neighbouring land owned by the person seeking to enforce it and that the benefit of the covenant has passed to that person.[247] The right of a person entitled to the benefit of the covenant to prevent the inconsistent use has taken on a proprietary quality, an 'equitable interest'[248] in the land burdened by the covenant. A subsequent purchaser of that land buys it subject to the equitable interest and with the burden of the interest attached.[249]

Similar principles are also applied to certain other interests in land such as easements and options to purchase.

---

[243] *London & South West Ry.* v. *Gomm* (1882) 20 Ch. D. 562. See Harpum, *Megarry & Wade's Law of Real Property*, 6th edn. (2001), p. 677.

[244] *Spencer's Case* (1583) 5 Co. Rep. 16a; Law of Property Act 1925, ss. 141, 142.

[245] (1848) 2 Ph. 774.

[246] Such covenants must now be registered under the Land Charges Act 1972.

[247] *London C.C.* v. *Allen* [1914] 3 K.B. 642; see *ante*, p. 447.

[248] *Re Nisbet and Potts' Contract* [1905] 1 Ch. 391, at p. 398; [1906] 1 Ch. 386, at pp. 403, 405.

[249] *Rogers* v. *Hosegood* [1900] 2 Ch. 388, at p. 407.

(c) CONTRACTS CONCERNING CHATTELS AND OTHER PERSONAL PROPERTY

English law has always drawn a distinction between the principles applicable to real and personal property.[250] The general rule set out above is subject to statutory exceptions. It does not apply where a contract or an option to transfer a chattel or an intangible interest creates an equitable interest in property or a possessory interest in the transferee, and the Courts may protect this interest against a third party.[251]

It has also been said that:

> Reason and justice seem to prescribe that, at least as a general rule, where a man, by gift or purchase, acquires property from another, with knowledge of a previous contract, lawfully and for valuable consideration made by him with a third person, to use and employ the property for a particular purpose in a specified manner, the acquiror shall not, to the material damage of the third person, in opposition to the contract and inconsistently with it, use and employ the property in a manner not allowable to the giver or seller.[252]

Although the generalization in this *dictum* has been influential, it will be seen that there are formidable difficulties in regarding it as sound in principle.[253] It is also not entirely clear why it applies to some types of contract (time charters) but not to others (resale price maintenance agreements).[254]

(i) Resale price maintenance

Manufacturers may try to prevent price cutting by imposing a condition on the wholesalers with whom they contract that the goods are not to be re-sold at less than a fixed or minimum price. In this way they attempt to bind retailers and others with whom they have no contractual relationship. Restrictions in such agreements between undertakings which operate at a different level of the production or distribution chain are known as 'vertical' restrictions. At common law such restrictions were ineffective against subsequent purchasers who did not take subject to the price maintenance conditions even where notice of the conditions was attached to the goods.[255]

The matter is now governed by section 2 of the Competition Act 1998 which contains a general prohibition on restrictive agreements, subject to limited exceptions. As noted in Chapter 9, the Competition Act seeks to harmonize UK law with EC competition law, and section 2 has broadly the same effect as the prohibition in Article 81 (ex Article 85) of the EC Treaty which applies where a restriction affects trade between members of the EU.[256]

---

[250] See Cohen-Grabelsky (1982) 45 Mod. L.R. 241; Gardner (1982) 98 L.Q.R. 279; Tettenborn [1982] C.L.J. 58.

[251] *Falke* v. *Grey* (1859) 4 Drew 651; *Erskine Macdonald Ltd.* v. *Eyles* [1921] 1 Ch. 631, 641. See also *Swiss Bank Corp.* v. *Lloyd's Bank Ltd.* [1982] A.C. 584, at pp. 598, 613 (contract did not create charge over property).

[252] *De Mattos* v. *Gibson* (1858) 4 De G. & J. 276, *per* Knight Bruce L.J. at p. 282.

[253] Post, p. 457.

[254] *Law Debenture Trust Cpn.* v. *Ural Caspian Oil Cpn. Ltd.* [1993] 1 W.L.R. 138, *per* Hoffmann L.J., at p. 144, rev'd on other grounds [1995] Ch. 152.

[255] *McGruther* v. *Pitcher* [1904] 2 Ch. 306. See also *Taddy* v. *Sterious & Co.* [1904] 1 Ch. 354.

[256] *Ante*, p. 383. For a full discussion, see Whish, *Competition Law*, 4th edn. (2001); Albors-Llorens, *EC Competition Law and Policy* (2002).

An agreement operating between wholesalers providing for the fixing of resale prices falls within the prohibition.[257] Although there are block exemptions in both UK and EC legislation for certain vertical restrictions,[258] they do not apply to vertical agreements that have as their direct or indirect object the fixing of resale prices. Recommended prices and maximum prices are, however, allowed.[259] Vertical restraints imposed by firms in a dominant market position may also fall within the UK and EC controls on the abuse of such a market position.[260]

(ii) Intellectual property

(a) Patents. A patentee has by statute the sole right to make, use, exercise, and vend an invention; and no other person has the right to sell the patented article except under licence from the patentee, and subject to any conditions attached to the licence.[261] But the rights of a patentee to attach resale price maintenance conditions to goods have now been substantially curtailed by section 2 of the Competition Act 1998 and Article 81 (ex Article 85) of the EC Treaty.[262] Certain other restrictive conditions, in agreements for sales by a direct licensee or assignee, for instance 'tie-in' clauses providing that the patented article is only to be used for manufacture with supplies purchased from the patentee, are rendered void by section 44 of the Patent Act 1977 unless the patentee is willing to supply or license the patented article on reasonable terms and without any such condition.[263]

(b) Copyright. The owner of the copyright in literary, dramatic, musical, or artistic works has a statutory right to prevent it being copied, published, broadcast, or infringed in certain other ways by any unauthorized person.[264] A signed agreement to transfer the copyright in a work not yet in existence will vest legal ownership in the transferee as soon as the work is created if there is no other person with a superior equity.[265] It has been held that a publisher who is granted a contractual option in respect of the future work of an author may restrain another publisher who, although not a party to the contract, with knowledge of the circumstances subsequently contracts with the author to publish the work.[266]

---

[257] Case 243/83 *Binon* v. *Agencie et messagerie de la presse* [1985] E.C.R. 2015, at para. 44; Case 27/87 *Louis Erauw-Jacquery* v. *La Hesbignonne* [1988] E.C.R. 1919, at para. 15.

[258] Competition Act 1998 (Land and Vertical Agreements Exclusion) Order 2000, S.I. 2000 No. 310; Regulation 2790/99 O.J. [1999] L. 336/21, Art. 4.

[259] Case 161/84 *Pronuptia de Paris GmbH* v. *Pronuptia de Paris Irmgard Schillgallis* [1986] E.C.R. 353.

[260] Competition Act 1998, s. 18; EC Treaty, Article 82 (ex Article 86). For a summary, see *ante*, p. 379.

[261] *Columbia Graphophone Ltd.* v. *Murray* (1922) 39 R.P.C. 239; *Dunlop Rubber Co. Ltd.* v. *Long Life Battery Depot* [1958] 1 W.L.R. 1033.

[262] See *ante*, p. 383.

[263] The person supplied or licensee may relieve himself of liability by payment of reasonable compensation: s. 44(4).

[264] Copyright, Designs and Patents Act 1988. See generally Cornish, *Intellectual Property*, 4th edn. (1999), Part IV.

[265] Copyright, Designs and Patents Act 1988, s. 91. Cornish, *op. cit.*, p. 465.

[266] *Erskine Macdonald Ltd.* v. *Eyles* [1921] 1 Ch. 631.

(iii) Bailment

Bailment involves the transfer of possession (or an agreement to transfer possession) of goods to a person (the 'bailee') who holds (or agrees to hold) the goods either for or at the direction of the bailor, to whom they will be returned.[267] The hirer of a car is a bailee as is the dry cleaning firm which takes in a customer's clothes for cleaning. In many situations there will be a series of bailments and the question is whether, if the ultimate sub-bailee loses or damages the goods and is sued by the bailor either in tort or for breach of duties arising from the bailment,[268] it can rely on the terms of the contract it made with its immediate bailor as a defence. In *Morris* v. *C. W. Martin & Sons Ltd.*:[269]

Morris sent a mink stole to a furrier to be cleaned. The furrier did not clean furs himself, so, with the Morris's consent, he delivered it for cleaning to the defendant, one of whose servants later stole it. The contract between the furrier and the defendant contained an exemption clause, on which the defendant sought to rely when sued by Morris.

On the facts the exemption clause was held not to apply, but Lord Denning M.R. said that, had it applied, in principle the defendant could have relied on it. Morris would be bound by the conditions if she had expressly or impliedly consented to the furrier making a sub-bailment containing those conditions. Since she had agreed that the furrier should send the stole to the defendant, she impliedly consented to his making a contract for cleaning on the terms current in the trade.[270]

In *K. H. Enterprise* v. *Pioneer Container*[271] this principle was applied to a contract for the carriage of goods by sea:

K.H.E. contracted for the carriage of goods from Taiwan to Hong Kong. The carrier was permitted to sub-contract 'on any terms' and did so to the defendant who took possession of the goods under bills of lading providing that any dispute was exclusively to be determined in Taiwan. The goods were lost and K.H.E. sued in Hong Kong, contending that it was not bound by the exclusive jurisdiction clause because there was no contract between it and the defendants.

The Judicial Committee of the Privy Council stated that a person who voluntarily takes another person's goods into its custody holds them as bailee of that person (the owner) even if it does so without the owner's consent, but can only invoke the terms of the sub-bailment under which it received the goods from an intermediate bailee (the carrier) as qualifying its responsibility if the owner consented to them.[272] It held

---

[267] *Palmer on Bailment*, 2nd edn. (1991); *Chitty on Contracts*, 28th edn. (1999), para. 33–001ff.
[268] For instance, only to deal with the goods in the manner authorized.
[269] [1966] 1 Q.B. 716.
[270] *Ibid.*, at p. 729. See also Salmon L.J. at p. 741. See also *Singer Co. (U.K.) Ltd.* v. *Tees and Hartlepool Port Authority* [1988] 2 Lloyd's Rep. 164; *The Captain Gregos (No. 2)* [1990] 2 Lloyd's Rep. 395, at p. 405.
[271] [1994] 2 A.C. 324.
[272] *Ibid.*, at p. 342 disapproving *Johnson Matthey & Co. Ltd.* v. *Constantine Terminals Ltd.* [1976] 2 Lloyd's Rep. 215. The principles in *'The Pioneer Container'* were applied in *Sonicare International Ltd.* v. *East Anglia Freight Terminal Ltd.* [1997] 2 Lloyd's Rep. 48 and *Spectra International plc* v. *Hayesoak Ltd.* [1997] 1 Lloyd's Rep. 153.

that consent to sub-contract and therefore to sub-bail 'on any terms' was wide enough to constitute express consent to the clause and K.H.E. was bound by it.

(iv) Ships under charter-party

In *Lord Strathcona Steamship Co. Ltd. v. Dominion Coal Co. Ltd.*:[273]

The D Co. had a long-term time charterparty of a ship. The owners sold the ship, which eventually came into the possession of the L.S. Co., who took it with notice of the charter-party and on the understanding that the agreement should be honoured. They did not honour the agreement, and, when sued by the charterers, L.S. Co. pleaded that they were not bound by the charterparty as there was no privity of contract between them.

The Judicial Committee of the Privy Council upheld the decision of the Courts in Nova Scotia granting the charterers an injunction restraining the L.S. Co. from using the ship inconsistently with the charterparty. The Board relied upon the *dictum* of Knight Bruce L.J. in *De Mattos* v. *Gibson* quoted above.[274] The case was said to fall under the rule in *Tulk* v. *Moxhay* relating to the use of land: whether the subject-matter was land or a chattel, the principle is the same: 'the remedy is a remedy in equity by way of injunction against acts inconsistent with the covenant, with notice of which the land was acquired'.[275]

This reasoning has, however, been the subject of considerable criticism,[276] and it has been said that the case was wrongly decided.[277] In the first place, it is argued that reliance should not have been placed on the *dictum* of Knight Bruce L.J. In *De Mattos* v. *Gibson* an interlocutory injunction was granted to restrain the mortgagee of a ship, who had acquired his mortgage with knowledge of an existing voyage charterparty, from interfering with the performance of the charter. Knight Bruce L.J.'s reasoning did not, however, form part of the concurring judgment of Turner L.J. and has been doubted.[278] When the case came before Lord Chelmsford L.C.,[279] a final injunction was refused.[280] Although the Lord Chancellor expressed the opinion that the mort-gagee was bound to abstain from any act which would have the immediate effect of preventing performance of the charter, he appeared to do so on the ground that any right to an injunction was based on an extension of the principle whereby a person who knowingly induces one party to break his contract with another is liable to that other in tort in respect of any loss which may have been suffered by the breach.[281]

Secondly, in so far as the Judicial Committee in the *Strathcona* case drew an analogy with the rule in *Tulk* v. *Moxhay*, this too will not bear examination. We have seen that

[273] [1926] A.C. 108.
[274] *Ante*, p. 454.
[275] [1926] A.C. 108, at p. 119.
[276] *Greenhalgh* v. *Mallard* [1943] 2 All E.R. 234, at p. 239.
[277] *Port Line Ltd.* v. *Ben Line Steamers Ltd.* [1958] 2 Q.B. 146, at p. 168.
[278] *London C.C.* v. *Allen* [1914] 3 K.B. 642, at p. 658; *Barker* v. *Stickney* [1919] 1 K.B. 121, at p. 132.
[279] (1859) 4 De G. & J. 288.
[280] On the ground that the mortgagee had not interfered with performance of the charter until it was evident that the shipowner was wholly unable to perform it (at pp. 299–300).
[281] *Lumley* v. *Gye* (1853) 3 E. & B. 216. See also Wade (1926) 42 L.Q.R. 139; *The Lord Strathcona* [1925] P. 143; *post*, p. 458, n. 285.

the *Tulk* v. *Moxhay* rule is not now dependent upon notice of the restrictive covenant alone, but upon the ownership of neighbouring land for the benefit of which the covenant was imposed: the person seeking to enforce the covenant must have a continuing proprietary interest in its enforcement.[282] But a charterer under a voyage or time charterparty (even if of long duration) only has a personal right that the shipowner should continue to use the ship to perform the services which he has covenanted to perform. The charterer has no proprietary interest in the subject-matter of the contract, the ship.[283]

Although the principle stated by Knight Bruce L.J. in *De Mattos* v. *Gibson* has subsequently been applied in cases of the mortgage of ships subject to a charterparty[284] these are open to the same criticisms. The better view is that any right of the charterer to an injunction to restrain a use of the ship inconsistent with his charterparty arises if, but only if, the conduct of the purchaser is such as to constitute the tort of knowing interference with the charterer's contractual rights.[285]

There may, moreover, be alternative explanations for the decision in the *Strathcona* case. One is that there was an implied contract between the third party and the charterers, or a 'novation' of the original agreement,[286] for the Board pointed out: 'This is not a mere case of notice of the existence of a covenant affecting the use of the property sold, but it is the case of the acceptance of their property expressly *sub conditione*'.[287] Alternatively, there is some ground for saying that the third party was in the position of a 'constructive trustee'[288] with obligations which a Court of Equity would not permit it to violate.[289]

With these reservations in mind, we have now to consider the scope of the decision. This was considered in *Port Line Ltd.* v. *Ben Line Steamers Ltd.*:[290]

The M.V. *Port Stephens* was chartered to Port Line by its owner, Silver Line Ltd., on a gross time charter for 30 months from March 1955. In February 1956, Silver Line sold the vessel to the defendant, it being agreed that the defendant should immediately charter the ship back to Silver Line by demise in order that it might fulfil its contract with Port Line.

---

[282] See *ante*, p. 453.

[283] *Port Line Ltd.* v. *Ben Line Steamers Ltd.* [1958] 2 Q.B. 146, *per* Diplock J. at p. 166. Unless it is a charterparty by demise, when the charter could be said to acquire a 'possessory interest' in the vessel: see *Baumwoll Manufacturer Von Carl Scheibler* v. *Furness* [1893] A.C. 8. See also *Lorentzen* v. *White Shipping Co. Ltd.* (1943) 74 Ll. L.R. 161.

[284] *Messageries Imperiales* v. *Baines* (1863) 7 L.T. 763; *The Celtic King* [1894] P. 175.

[285] *Lumley* v. *Wagner* (1852) 1 De G.M. & G. 604. See also *Torquay Hotel Co. Ltd.* v. *Cousins* [1969] 2 Ch. 106; *Acrow Ltd.* v. *Rex Chainbelt Inc.* [1971] 1 W.L.R. 1676; *Law Debenture Trust Cpn.* v. *Ural Caspian Oil Cpn. Ltd.* [1995] 152. In *Swiss Bank Cpn.* v. *Lloyd's Bank Ltd.* [1979] Ch. 548, at p. 573 (rev'd [1982] A.C. 584), Browne-Wilkinson J. stated that the principle of Knight Bruce L.J. represented 'the counterpart in equity of the tort of knowing interference with contractual rights'. But although they may cover the same ground they are doctrinally distinct and subject to different requirements: see Cohen-Grabelsky (1982) 45 Mod. L.R. 241, at pp. 265–7; Gardner (1982) 98 L.Q.R. 279, at pp. 289–93; Tettenborn [1982] C.L.J. 58, at p. 82.

[286] See *post*, p. 485.

[287] [1926] A.C. 108, at p. 116.

[288] See *ante*, p. 439.

[289] [1926] A.C. 108, at p. 125. See also *Swiss Bank Cpn.* v. *Lloyd's Bank Ltd.* [1979] Ch. 548, at p. 573 (rev'd [1982] A.C. 584).

[290] [1958] 2 Q.B. 146.

Unfortunately, this second charterparty contained the term that 'If the ship be requisitioned this charter shall thereupon cease', although no such clause appeared in the original time charter-party. The defendant was unaware of this disparity. In August 1956 the ship was requisitioned by the Crown, and as a result Port Line lost the use of the vessel. Its claim against Silver Line was settled, but it then brought an action against the defendant to recover the whole or part of the compensation received by the defendant from the Crown in respect of the period of requisition.

Diplock J. stated that the *Strathcona* case was wrongly decided, but held that even if it was correct Port Line could not bring its claim within its principles, as the defendant had no knowledge at the time of its purchase of Port Line's rights under the time charter. The principle in the *Strathcona* case thus only applies where there is actual knowledge by the subsequent purchaser at the time of the purchase of the charterer's rights.[291] Constructive notice is insufficient.[292] Moreover, Diplock J. considered that, even if notice had been shown, (a) the defendant was in no breach of duty to Port Line since it was by no act of its that the vessel during the period of requisition was used inconsistently with the terms of Port Line's charter —it was by act of the Crown by title paramount—and (b) Port Line was not entitled to any remedy against the defendant except an injunction to restrain the defendant from using the vessel in a manner inconsistent with the terms of the charter.[293]

The charterer cannot obtain specific performance of the contract,[294] nor, it seems, damages or monetary compensation.[295] It would also seem that the Court will not be prepared to grant an injunction if the situation is such that, in any case, the vendor was incapable of further performing the charterparty,[296] or if, in the case of the mortgage of a vessel, the charter is such as substantially to impair the security.[297]

(v) Restrictions on the use of other chattels

There is even more doubt as to whether the principle stated by Knight Bruce L.J. in *De Mattos* v. *Gibson*, and the decision in the *Strathcona* case, would apply to contracts under which the owner of a particular chattel, other than a ship, undertakes to use the chattel to perform its obligations to the other contracting party: for example, where the owner of a costly machine[298] agrees to use the machine to manufacture goods for the other party over a certain period. In *De Mattos* v. *Gibson* Lord Chelmsford L.C. stressed that 'a vessel engaged under a charterparty ought to be regarded as a chattel

---

291 [1958] 2 Q.B. 146, at p. 168.

292 The doctrine of constructive notice does not apply to chattels (*Joseph* v. *Lyons* (1884) 15 Q.B.D. 280, at p. 287) nor to the contents of documents in commercial transactions (*Manchester Trust* v. *Furness* [1895] 2 Q.B. 539, at p. 545).

293 *Port Line Ltd.* v. *Ben Line Steamers Ltd.* [1958] 2 Q.B. 146, at p. 167.

294 *De Mattos* v. *Gibson* (1859) 4 De G. & J. 277, at p. 297.

295 Although the form of the order made in the *Strathcona* case would seem to indicate that damages could be awarded, cf. *Port Line Ltd.* v. *Ben Line Steamers Ltd.* (*supra*), at p. 169; *Law Debenture Trust Cpn.* v. *Ural Caspian Oil Cpn. Ltd.* [1993] 1 W.L.R. 138, at pp. 144; rev'd on another ground [1995] Ch. 152.

296 *Lord Strathcona* [1925] P. 143. See also *ante*, p. 457, n. 280.

297 *The Celtic King* [1894] P. 175.

298 *De Mattos* v. *Gibson* (1858) 4 De G. & J. 288, *per* Knight Bruce L.J. at p. 283.

of peculiar value to the charterer',[299] and it has been said that the *Strathcona* decision may be confined to 'the very special case of a ship under charterparty'.[300] Nevertheless, there would seem to be no reason why the immediate purchaser of a chattel should not be restrained by injunction if it commits or threatens to commit the tort of knowing interference with such a contract.[301] The same would probably apply to any covenant by the owner of a chattel to use[302] or not to use[303] the chattel in a particular manner. But the relief granted against the third party purchaser would depend upon the fact of tortious interference, and not upon notice of any 'interest' in the chattel.

Moreover, it is highly unlikely that any covenant affecting the use of a chattel would be held to 'run with the goods', so as to bind all persons who subsequently purchased the chattel with notice of the covenant.[304] There are good reasons why land-owners should be entitled to prevent neighbouring land from being put to a use that would be prejudicial to their property. But no such reasons would justify the imposition of incumbrances on chattels.

(vi) Hire-purchase and hire

There is no authority as to whether a hire-purchase agreement, under which a chattel is bailed to the hirer with an option to purchase the chattel once all the instalments have been fully paid, will be binding on a third party purchaser of the chattel from its owner. But since such an agreement confers upon the hirer a possessory interest in the chattel and has been said to confer a proprietary interest,[305] the better view is that the purchaser is bound, at least if he or she has notice of the agreement but possibly where there is no such notice.[306] The same principle could possibly apply to a simple bailment for hire.

IV. EXEMPTION CLAUSES AND THIRD PARTIES

(a) BENEFIT TO THIRD PARTIES

It has been noted that at common law problems arose where a contracting party (A) sought to exempt persons who are not parties to the contract, for example, its employees or sub-contractors who participate in the performance of the contract

---

[299] (1859) 4 De G. & J. 288, at p. 299.

[300] *Clore* v. *Theatrical Properties Ltd.* [1936] 3 All E.R. 483, *per* Lord Wright M.R. at p. 490.

[301] See Cohen-Grabelsky (1982) 45 Mod. L.R. 241; Gardner (1982) 98 L.Q.R. 279; Tettenborn [1982] C.L.J. 58.

[302] *Sefton* v. *Tophams Ltd.* [1965] Ch. 1140 (land). But see *Clarke* v. *Price* (1819) 2 Wils. Ch. 157; *Haywood* v. *Brunswick Permanent Benefit Building Socy.* (1876) 3 Ch. D. 694.

[303] *British Motor Trade Association* v. *Salvadori* [1949] Ch. 556 (covenant not to re-sell chattel). See also *Esso Petroleum Co. Ltd.* v. *Kingswood Motors (Addlestone) Ltd.* [1974] Q.B. 142 (land); *Law Debenture Trust Cpn.* v. *Ural Caspian Oil Cpn. Ltd.* [1995] Ch. 152 (shares).

[304] *Taddy* v. *Sterious & Co.* [1904] 1 Ch. 354; *McGruther* v. *Pitcher* [1904] 2 Ch. 306; *ante*, p. 453.

[305] *Whiteley Ltd.* v. *Hilt* [1918] 2 K.B. 808, at pp. 817, 818, 822.

[306] Goode, *Hire Purchase Law and Practice*, 2nd edn., p. 35.

from liability to the other party to the contract (B).[307] It has been seen that A's employees and sub-contractors, although not in a contractual relationship with B, may nevertheless be under duties to B imposed by the law of tort or the law of bailment. If the employees or independent contractors are not able to rely on the exemption clause as a defence to an action by B, they in turn may have a right to be indemnified by A. Even where there is no right to be indemnified, A may, particularly in the case of employees, nevertheless agree to meet the damages awarded to B.[308] In both cases the risk is ultimately borne by A, thus defeating the purpose of the exemption clause. Whether or not it is A who ends up paying, permitting B to succeed against the employees or independent contractors will in many cases upset the allocation of risks and consequent pattern of insurance in the transaction, since A and its employees and independent contractors will have expected B to insure against the relevant loss and not done so themselves.[309]

Despite this, prior to the Contracts (Rights of Third Parties) Act 1999 such attempts to rely on exemption clauses encountered great difficulties, primarily because A's employees or sub-contractors were not parties to the contract, but also because they normally furnished no consideration for the promise.[310] The tension between the doctrine of privity of contract and the commercial expectations of those who take part in multiparty transactions produced a very complicated body of law. At times the Courts applied the doctrine[311] and prevented a defendant from relying on an exemption clause. At other times, and particularly more recently, they have been willing to circumvent the doctrine and even to contemplate some form of modification or exception to it with regard to exemption clauses.

But first, the operation of the doctrine of privity in such cases will be considered. In *Scruttons Ltd.* v. *Midland Silicones Ltd.*:[312]

A drum of chemicals was shipped from New York to London and consigned to the respondents upon the terms of a bill of lading which exempted the carriers from liability in excess of $500 (£179) per package. The drum was damaged by the negligence of the appellants, a firm of stevedores employed by the carriers, and the damage amounted to £593. Although the appellants were not a party to the bill of lading, nor expressly mentioned therein, they claimed to be entitled to the benefit of the clause limiting liability.

In the House of Lords, Lord Denning considered that the appellants were protected by

---

[307] See Law Com. No. 242, §§ 2.19–2.35.

[308] *Adler* v. *Dickson* [1955] 1 Q.B. 158.

[309] For example where there is a limitation clause, the non-party performer would be expected to insure up to the limit and the contracting party (B) beyond that: see *Scruttons Ltd.* v. *Midland Silicones Ltd.* [1962] A.C. 446, where the non-party stevedores only agreed to take out insurance in excess of a $500 limitation where that limitation did not apply, *per* Lord Denning at pp. 481–2. See also *The Mahkutai* [1996] A.C. 650; *London Drugs Ltd.* v. *Kuehene & Nagel International Ltd.* [1992] 3 S.C.R. 299, *per* Iacobucci J. at p. 423.

[310] *Ante*, p. 96.

[311] If the true doctrine is as stated by Lord Haldane in *Dunlop Pneumatic Tyre Co. Ltd.* v. *Selfridge & Co. Ltd.* [1915] A.C. 847, at p. 853, *ante*, p. 423, that 'only a person who is a party to a contract can *sue on it*' (emphasis added), it is arguable that a defendant seeking to rely on an exemption clause is not within the doctrine.

[312] [1962] A.C. 446.

an accepted principle of the law of tort, that of voluntary assumption of risk, since the respondents had assented to the limitation of liability. But the majority of their Lordships unequivocally reasserted the doctrine of privity of contract. They held that the appellants could not claim the benefit of an exemption clause in a contract to which they were not a party.[313]

Exemption clauses are unambiguously brought within the 1999 Act[314] so that effect can now be given to the commercial expectations of those who take part in multi-party transactions. The Act thus sweeps 'away the technicalities applying to the enforcement by expressly designated third parties of exclusion clauses'.[315]

Nevertheless, discussion of the complex common law position remains necessary. First, the common law applies to contracts made before 11 May 2000 and disputes concerning such contracts will continue to come before the Courts for some time. Moreover, there may be cases in which the 1999 Act does not apply or in which, if it does, it will be advantageous for a person to rely on the common law, as where the common law enables the third party to establish a right which arises independently of the contract, for instance one based on tort.[316] Where the third party can formulate its claim in tort nothing in the 1999 Act will affect it, although, as will be seen, regard may be had to the terms of the contract in determining whether a tortious duty has arisen and the scope of such duty.[317]

(b) BURDEN ON THIRD PARTIES

A similar problem arises in relation to the burden of an exemption clause. It is a trite principle of law that a person who is not a party to a contract cannot be subjected to the burden of that contract. So, at common law, an exemption clause will, as a general rule, only operate so as to take away the rights of the contracting parties, and not those of third parties who suffer injury or damage. In *Haseldine* v. *C. A. Daw & Son Ltd.*:[318]

The owners of a block of flats employed the defendant engineers to repair a lift in the building. Owing to their negligence, the lift was badly repaired and H, a visitor to the premises, was injured when the lift fell to the bottom of the lift-shaft.

---

[313] Article IV *bis* (2) of the Hague Rules (as amended), contained in the Schedule to the Carriage of Goods by Sea Act 1971, now extends protection to the servants and agents (but not independent contractors) of the carrier in respect of loss or damage to goods covered by a contract of carriage of goods by sea to which the Rules apply.

[314] 1999 Act, s. 1(6), *ante*, p. 430. This includes such clauses in contracts of carriage which are otherwise excluded from the 1999 Act by s. 6(5).

[315] Law Com. No. 242, §§ 2.35, 3.32.

[316] See *ante*, p. 448. Note also that where the right arises under a separate contract, the Unfair Contract Terms Act 1977 may apply, whereas it may not where the right arises under the 1999 Act: 1999 Act, s. 7(2), see *ante*, p. 437.

[317] See *post*, p. 467.

[318] [1941] 2 K.B. 343. By s. 3(1) of the Occupiers Liability Act 1957, a contract made by an occupier of premises may increase its liability to non-parties beyond the common duty of care but may not reduce it below that duty. Cf., at common law, *Fosbroke-Hobbes* v. *Airwork Ltd.* [1937] 1 All E.R. 108, at p. 112.

The defendant was held liable in tort for negligence. Goddard L.J. said:[319]

> It is, however, argued that it is not right that a repairer who, as in the present case, has stipulated with the person who employs him that he shall not be liable for accidents, should none the less be made liable to a third person. The answer to this argument is that the duty to the third party does not arise out of the contract, but independently of it.

It has been noted[320] that this reasoning is of special importance where a person bails goods to another in order that they may be carried or worked on by the bailee. In turn, the bailee may sub-contract the task of carrying the goods or working on them to a sub-bailee. If the contract between the bailee and sub-bailee contains exemption clauses which exonerate the sub-bailee from liability, the bailor will not automatically be bound. The sub-bailee will not be protected against the bailor, who is not a party to the contract, unless the bailor expressly or impliedly consented to the bailee making a sub-bailment containing those conditions.[321]

The 1999 Act does not affect the principle that a third party to a contract cannot be subjected to the burden of an exemption clause in that contract.[322] But, by section 1(4), a third party who wishes to enforce a term conferring a benefit on him or her can only do so subject to and in accordance with any other terms of the contract. Those other terms may impose burdens and conditions upon the enjoyment of any benefit.

(c) COMMON LAW TECHNIQUES FOR AVOIDING THE DOCTRINE IN RELATION TO EXEMPTION CLAUSES

At one time the proposition was advanced that where a contract contained an exemption clause, any employee or agent while performing the contract was entitled to the same immunity from liability as the employer or principal.[323] But this principle of 'vicarious immunity' was rejected by the House of Lords in *Scruttons Ltd.* v. *Midland Silicones*.[324] There are, however, a number of ways in which the doctrine of privity may be avoided at common law. The willingness of the Courts to do so has varied. The application of the doctrine in some cases can be seen as part of the process by which Courts sought to alleviate the position of those affected by onerous terms,[325] for instance clauses seeking to exclude liability for personal injury resulting from negligence, now prohibited by statute.[326] The reluctance to save negligent people from the normal consequences of their fault, however, extended beyond such cases and may

---

[319] At p. 379.

[320] *Ante*, p. 456.

[321] *K. H. Enterprise* v. *Pioneer Container* [1994] 2 A.C. 324, *ante*, p. 456.

[322] H.L. Debs. 11 January 1999, col. 21 (Lord Irvine L.C.).

[323] *Elder Dempster & Co. Ltd.* v. *Peterson, Zochonis & Co. Ltd.* [1924] A.C. 522, *per* Viscount Cave at p. 534. See also p. 548 (Viscount Finlay) and [1923] 1 K.B. 436, at p. 441 (Scrutton L.J.).

[324] [1962] A.C. 446.

[325] *Ante*, pp. 169, 180.

[326] *Cosgrove* v. *Horsfall* (1945) 62 T.L.R. 140; *Adler* v. *Dickson* [1955] 1 Q.B. 158; and *Genys* v. *Matthews* [1966] 1 W.L.R. 758 concerned such clauses. See now the Unfair Contract Terms Act 1977, s. 2, *ante*, p. 190.

have influenced the decision in *Scruttons Ltd.* v. *Midland Silicones Ltd.*[327] Since that decision, the perceived need to support established commercial practice and to avoid redistributing the risks of transactions has led to greater judicial dissatisfaction with the operation of privity in such situations and a greater willingness to avoid the operation of the doctrine.

There are two methods of avoiding the privity doctrine at common law; a contractual route (see (ii)–(iv) below) and what can broadly be termed a tortious route (see (v) below). The contractual route involves the identification of a second contract between the claimant (B) and the person wishing to rely on the exemption clause. The second route is based on the exemption clause showing that the claimant (B), in its contract with A, assumed the risk of damage or loss resulting from the negligence of the defendant so as to qualify or negate the defendant's tortious duty of care to it or, more narrowly, the duty created by virtue of the defendant being a bailee or sub-bailee of goods. In its wider form this was not favoured by the majority in *Scruttons Ltd.* v. *Midland Silicones Ltd.* but has since attracted some support.[328] Before examining these, the position where the contracting party intervenes to protect the defendant is noted.

(i) Promise not to sue

Where the contract containing the exemption clause can be construed as a promise by the claimant not to sue the third party defendant, if the contracting party intervenes in the proceedings to protect the defendant, the Court may stay or dismiss the claimant's claim.[329]

(ii) Agency

The Courts may be able to imply that a party (A) to a contract containing an exemption clause which is intended to benefit third parties such as its employees or subcontractors was either acting as agent for the third parties or as agent for the other party to the contract (B) so as to create a direct contractual relationship between B and the employees or sub-contractors.

This device was first employed during the nineteenth century, when England was (as it is again) covered by a network of small railway companies and a contract made with one might entitle the holder of a ticket to travel on one or more of them. In such circumstances, the passenger was not allowed to say that only the company which was a party to the primary agreement was protected by the exemption clauses contained in it. The Courts were ready to find either that the contracting company was acting as agent for the other companies,[330] or that it was acting as agent for the passenger.[331] The passenger was thus brought into a direct contractual relationship with the other

---

[327] See [1962] A.C. 446, at p. 472 (*per* Viscount Simonds), relying on *Wilson* v. *Darling Island Stevedoring & Lighterage Co. Ltd.* (1956) 95 C.L.R. 43, at p. 78 (*per* Fullagar J.). See also *The Mahkutai* [1996] A.C. 650, *per* Lord Goff at p. 660.

[328] See *Pacific Associates* v. *Baxter* [1990] 1 Q.B. 933, at p. 1011 (Purchas L.J.); *Norwich C.C.* v. *Harvey* [1989] 1 W.L.R. 828; *Marc Rich & Co. AG* v. *Bishop Rock Marine Co. Ltd., The 'Nicholas H'* [1996] A.C. 211, *per* Lord Steyn at pp. 239–40, *post*, p. 468.

[329] See *ante*, p. 426.

[330] *Hall* v. *N.E. Ry.* (1875) L.R. 10 Q.B. 437, at p. 442.

[331] *Ibid.*, at p. 443.

companies. In reliance on the principle of agency many enterprises have framed contractual clauses designed to protect their employees and sub-contractors from liability.

In *Scruttons Ltd.* v. *Midland Silicones Ltd.*,[332] the House of Lords left open the question whether the stevedores could have been protected if the carriers had contracted as agents on their behalf. Lord Reid said:[333]

I can see a possibility of success of the agency argument if (first) the bill of lading makes it clear that the stevedore is intended to be protected by the provisions in it which limit liability, (secondly) the bill of lading makes it clear that the carrier, in addition to contracting for these provisions on his own behalf, is also contracting as agent for the stevedore that these provisions should apply to the stevedore, (thirdly) the carrier has authority to do that, or perhaps later ratification by the stevedore would suffice, and (fourthly) that any difficulties about consideration moving from the stevedore were overcome.

(iii) Contract by performing specified act

These conditions set out in *Scruttons Ltd.* v. *Midland Silicones Ltd.* were held to have been satisfied in *New Zealand Shipping Co. Ltd.* v. *A. M. Satterthwaite & Co. Ltd. (The Eurymedon)*,[334] where the bill of lading contained a clause by which the carrier, as agent of the stevedore, stipulated that both he and the stevedore should be entitled to the limitation of liability contained in the bill. The Judicial Committee of the Privy Council held that the stevedore had furnished consideration by unloading the goods under its contract with the carrier.[335] The contract was, however, only established by somewhat artificially[336] identifying an offer to the stevedore in the contract between the carrier and the shipper,[337] and it will not be possible to do so in all cases. The carrier may not have authority to act as agent of the stevedore and, although in the majority of cases this may be solved by recourse to the principle of ratification,[338] this may not always be possible.[339] Again, the company seeking the benefit of the exemption clause will only be held to have furnished consideration where it is performing the contract containing the exemption clause.[340] More fundamentally, the exclusion clause may not refer to the employee or subcontractor.[341] Although, in cases of the

---

[332] [1962] A.C. 446; *ante*, p. 461.

[333] At p. 474.

[334] [1975] A.C. 154.

[335] See *ante*, p. 104.

[336] See Reynolds (1974) 90 L.Q.R. 301; Coote (1974) 37 M.L.R. 453; Battersby (1978) 28 U. of Tor. L.J. 75.

[337] The plaintiff was in fact the consignee not the shipper. It would be party to the offer made by the shipper to the stevedore either by statute (then the Bills of Lading Act 1855, now the Carriage of Goods by Sea Act 1992, s. 2) or by presenting the bill of lading to the ship and requesting delivery of the goods thereunder: *Brandt* v. *Liverpool Brazil & River Plate Navigation Co. Ltd.* [1924] 1 K.B. 575.

[338] *The Mahkutai* [1996] A.C. 650.

[339] *The Suleyman Stalskiy* [1976] 2 Lloyd's Rep. 609 (Sup. Ct. of British Columbia); *Lummus Co. Ltd.* v. *East African Harbours Cpn.* [1978] 1 Lloyd's Rep. 317, at pp. 322–3 (High Ct. of Kenya).

[340] *Raymond Burke Motors Ltd.* v. *The Mersey Docks and Harbour Co.* [1986] 1 Lloyd's Rep. 155 (goods damaged while they were being stored and not during loading or unloading).

[341] e.g. in *London Drugs Ltd* v. *Kuehene & Nagel International Ltd.* [1992] 3 S.C.R 299 the clause did not refer to warehouseman's employees. Cf. s.1(3) of the Contracts (Rights of Third Parties) Act 1999, *ante*, p. 431.

carriage of goods by sea, it has been said that stevedores and others performing the contract would normally be protected and that Courts should not search for 'fine distinctions' which would diminish this general position,[342] this approach has not been applied in other contexts.[343] It is in such contexts that the 1999 Act is likely to make a real difference. It is, moreover, inevitable, even in carriage of goods by sea, 'so long as the principle continues to be understood to rest upon an enforceable contract as between the cargo owners and the stevedores entered into through the agency of the shipowner, . . . that technical points of contract and agency law will continue to be invoked'.[344]

(iv) Implied contract

Privity questions may also be avoided by the implication of a contract between the claimant and the third party. The circumstances surrounding the transaction may justify the inference of a collateral contract between them. Again, this brings a claimant into a direct contractual relationship with the third party so that the third party is entitled to the benefit of the exemption clause. In *Pyrene Co. Ltd.* v. *Scindia Navigaton Co. Ltd.*:[345]

P sold to I.S.D. in India certain fire-tenders 'f.o.b. London'. The defendant agreed with I.S.D. to carry the tenders to India. The contract of carriage contained a clause limiting the liability of the defendant to £200. Owing to the negligence of the defendant, a tender was damaged while being loaded. But since it had not yet crossed the ship's side, it was still at P's risk. P made good the damage and sued the defendant for the loss, which amounted to more than £900.

Devlin J. held that P was bound by the exemption clause. Although it was not a party to the contract of carriage, it was entitled to the benefits of the contract and had in consequence also to accept its liabilities. In the *Midland Silicones* case, however, it was stated that this decision could be supported 'only upon the facts of the case, which may well have justified the implication of a contract between the parties'.[346] It may therefore be an example of an implied contract, that is to say, all three parties intended P to participate in the contract of affreightment.

Where the third party is brought into a direct contractual relationship with one of the parties to the contract by reason of the device of agency or of an implied contract,

---

[342] *Port Jackson Stevedoring Pty. Ltd.* v. *Salmond and Spraggon (Australia) Pty. Ltd.* [1981] 1 W.L.R. 138, at p. 144 (Lord Wilberforce). See Reynolds (1979) 95 L.Q.R. 183; Coote [1981] C.L.J. 13. See also *The Starsin* [2001] 1 Lloyd's Rep. 437, at pp. 459–60 (shipowners who were third parties to a contract made by charterers).

[343] *Southern Water Authority* v. *Carey* [1985] 2 All E.R. 1077, at p. 1084 (construction); *Kendall* v. *Morgan* The Times, 2 December 1980 (employment).

[344] *The Mahkutai* [1996] A.C. 650, *per* Lord Goff, at p. 664.

[345] [1954] 2 Q.B. 402.

[346] [1962] A.C. 466, *per* Viscount Simonds at p. 471, and see p. 470 where *Elder Dempster & Co. Ltd.* v. *Paterson, Zochonis & Co. Ltd.* [1924] A.C. 522 was similarly explained. See also *Hispanica de Petroleos S.A.* v. *Vencedora Oceanica S.A., The Kapetan Markos N.L. (No. 2)* [1987] 2 Lloyd's Rep. 321, at p. 331; *Comp. Portorafti Comm. S.A.* v. *Ultramar Panama Inc., The Captain Gregos (No. 2)* [1990] 2 Lloyd's Rep. 395, at pp. 401–3.

the exemption clause relied on will be controlled by statute, in particular the Unfair Contract Terms Act 1977,[347] unless the contract between them is one which is not subject to the control of the legislation.[348] It has been noted that the position is different where the third party proceeds under the 1999 Act.[349]

(v) Assumption of risk; negation of duty

Turning to the non-contractual route, the majority in *Scruttons Ltd.* v. *Midland Silicones*[350] rejected Lord Denning's powerful reasoning based on the general defence to actions in tort where a claimant has voluntarily consented to take the risk of a loss or injury. But we have noted that in the case of bailment a similar principle may protect an employee or sub-contractor. Where a bailor bails goods to a bailee who in turn sub-bails them to third party who damages them, the third party may be able to rely on the terms on which the goods were sub-bailed to it as a defence to an action by the bailor, provided the bailor has expressly or impliedly consented to the bailee making the sub-bailment containing the exemption clause.[351] Where this is so the bailor is bound by an exemption clause in a contract to which it is not a party. A defendant who is sued in tort may also rely on an exclusion clause in a contract to which the claimant but not the defendant is a party as restricting or excluding the duty of care that it would otherwise owe to the claimant. Where this is so the defendant is taking the benefit of an exemption clause in a contract to which it is not a party. So, in *Pacific Associates Inc.* v. *Baxter*[352] a consultant engineer successfully defended a claim for negligence by the contractor by relying on a term of the contract between the employer and the contractor which provided that neither the engineer nor any of his staff 'shall be in any way personally liable for the acts or obligations under the Contract . . . '. Purchas L.J. stated that 'the presence of such an exclusion clause, while not directly binding between the parties, cannot be excluded from a general consideration of the contractual structure against which the contractor demonstrates reliance on, and the engineer accepts responsibility for, a duty in tort, if any, arising out of the proximity established between them by the existence of that very contract'. The contractual structure may be relevant even where there is no express provision seeking to exempt the third party. In *Norwich C.C.* v. *Harvey:*[353]

A building was damaged by fire as a result of the negligence of a roofing sub-contractor. The

---

[347] See *ante*, p. 185.

[348] See *ante*, pp. 186–7.

[349] See *ante*, p. 437.

[350] [1962] A.C. 446. See also *Leigh & Sillavan Ltd.* v. *Aliakmon SS. Co. Ltd.* [1986] A.C. 785, *per* Lord Brandon at p. 817 but cf. Robert Goff L.J. [1985] Q.B. 350 at p. 399. Cf. also the cases considered *infra*.

[351] *Ante*, p. 456 (*K. H. Enterprise* v. *Pioneer Container* [1994] 2 A.C. 324). The position would appear to be the same whether or not the original bailment is a contract. Where it is a contract there may well be an implied contract between the bailor and the sub-bailee; *ante*, p. 466, but note that it has been said that the relationship between bailor and sub-bailee cannot aptly be described as depending on agreement: *Dresser U.K. Ltd.* v. *Falcongate Freight Management Ltd.* [1992] 1 Q.B. 502, *per* Bingham L.J. at p. 511.

[352] [1990] 1 Q.B. 933. See also *Southern Water Authority* v. *Carey* [1985] 2 All E.R. 1077.

[353] [1989] 1 W.L.R. 828.

main contract provided that the building owner was to bear the risk of damage by fire and the sub-contractor contracted on the same terms and conditions as in the main contract. The owner of the building brought an action against the sub-contractor.

It was held that, although there was no direct contractual relationship between the owner and the sub-contractor, nevertheless they had both contracted with the main contractor on the basis that the owner had assumed the risk of damage by fire and the sub-contractor owed no duty in respect of the damage which occurred. It is not, however, necessary for the defendant's contract to contain the exemption clause; what is important is whether the recognition of a duty of care by the defendant would outflank the contractual structure governing dealings between the claimant and others.[354]

(vi) A general common law exception for exemption clauses

The commercial inconvenience that results from the application of the doctrine of privity in the context of exemption clauses has led to the recognition by the Supreme Court of Canada of an exception whereby employees and sub-contractors acting in the course of their employment and performing the services provided for in the main contract can rely on an exemption clause in that contract which is intended to protect them.[355]

Prior to the enactment of the 1999 Act there were indications that the artificiality and technical nature of the approach based on *New Zealand Shipping Co. Ltd.* v. *A. M. Satterthwaite (The Eurymedon)*[356] inclined senior judges to regard the development started in that decision as not yet complete. They appeared to be prepared to recognize a fully fledged exception to the doctrine of privity where a contract clearly provides that (for example) independent contractors such as stevedores are to have the benefit of exceptions and limitations contained in that contract.[357] The case for such recognition is that the reasons for and justifications of the privity doctrine do not apply where a third party seeks to rely on a contractual provision as a defence; there is an identity of interest between the contracting party and the third party as far as the performance of the contracting party's contractual obligations is concerned, and it is commercially undesirable to allow a person to circumvent a contractual

---

[354] *Marc Rich & Co. AG* v. *Bishop Rock Marine Co. Ltd., The Nicholas H* [1996] A.C. 211, *per* Lord Steyn at pp. 239–40 (if the cargo owner recovered from the defendant, a classification society, the cost of insuring against such claims would be passed on to shipowners and the contractual structure governing dealings between shipowners and cargo owners and the limitation of shipowners' liability would be destroyed). See also *Henderson* v. *Merrett Syndicates Ltd.* [1995] 2 A.C. 145, at p. 197.

[355] *London Drugs Ltd.* v. *Kuehene & Nagel International Ltd.* [1992] 3 S.C.R. 299. It may be more problematic to establish a clear intention to extend the protection of an exemption clause to an independent contractor than to an employee; *ibid.*, at p. 441.

[356] [1975] A.C. 154, *ante*, p. 465.

[357] *The Mahkutai* [1996] A.C. 650, at p. 665 (but the exclusive jurisdiction clause was held not to be intended to benefit third parties). See also *Dresser U.K. Ltd.* v. *Falcongate Freight Management Ltd.* [1992] 1 Q.B. 502, *per* Bingham L.J. at p. 511 (describing the principle of bailment on terms as 'a pragmatic legal recognition of commercial reality'); Law Com. C.P. No. 121 (1991), §§ 4.8–4.12; Law Com. No. 242 (1996) § 2.19ff.

exclusion clause and thus redistribute the contractual allocation of risk by suing the employee or sub-contractor of the other party to the contract.[358]

Since, however, a fully fledged common law exception such as the Canadian one would not be subject to the limitations in the 1999 Act, for example that the third party be identified by name, class, or description,[359] the courts may consider it inappropriate to enlarge the statutory provisions by judicial innovation.[360]

[358] *London Drugs Ltd.* v. *Kuehene & Nagel International Ltd.* [1992] 3 S.C.R. 299, at pp. 440–7. For these reasons and justifications, see *ante*, p. 461 and *Privity of Contract: Contracts for the Benefit of Third Parties* Law Com. C.P. No. 121 (1991), § 4.3; Law Com. No. 242 (1996) §§ 2.33–2.35.

[359] s. 1(3), *ante*, p. 431.

[360] *Alfred McAlpine Construction Ltd.* v. *Panatown Ltd.* [2000] 3 W.L.R. 946, *per* Lord Clyde at p. 535. Cf. *ante*, p. 451.

11

ASSIGNMENT AND NEGOTIABILITY

The benefit of a contract may, in certain circumstances, be transferred to a third party. This chapter considers assignment, that is to say, the transfer of rights under contracts to a third party without the concurrence of the other party to the contract, and the transfer of liabilities under contracts, and the nature of negotiable instruments.

I. ASSIGNMENT OF CONTRACTUAL RIGHTS

A party to a contract (the assignor) may, as a general rule, assign its rights under the contract to a third party (the assignee) without the consent of the party (the debtor) against whom those rights are held.[1] Rights under contracts are 'choses in action'.

(a) NO ASSIGNMENT AT COMMON LAW

At common law the benefit of a contract could not be assigned so as to enable the assignee to bring an action upon it in its own name.

'"Choses in action" is a known legal expression used to describe all personal rights of property which can only be claimed or enforced by action, and not by taking physical possession.'[2] The contrasted term is 'chose in possession'. The definition of a chose in action thus includes not only contractual rights but many rights which are not contractual, e.g. patent rights, copyrights, and rights of action in tort. We are concerned here, however, only with the assignment of contractual rights.

The existence of a remedy or remedies is an essential condition for the existence of the chose in action but the remedies are not property in themselves capable of assignment separately from the underlying chose in action. For example, the right to rescind a mortgage is not a chose in action, and may not be assigned separately from the property.[3]

The only exceptions allowed by the common law were assignments by or to the

---

[1] For a more detailed study, see Marshall's *Assignment of Choses in Action* (1950).
[2] *Torkington* v. *Magee* [1902] 2 K.B. 427, *per* Channell J. at p. 430; rev'd [1903] 1 K.B. 644.
[3] *Investors Compensation Scheme Ltd.* v. *W. Bromwich B.S.* [1998] 1 W.L.R. 898.

Crown[4] and by holders of negotiable instruments permitted by the law merchant. The reason for the non-recognition of assignments of choses in action seems to have been that the common law judges feared that to permit assignments would both undermine the doctrine of privity of contract and encourage maintenance and unnecessary litigation.[5] But even at common law it was (and still is) possible for the right to sue on a contract to be conferred on a third party by other, albeit cumbrous and unsatisfactory, means.

In the first place, the contracting party could give to the third party a power of attorney and thus enable the third party to sue the debtor as the contracting party's representative.[6]

Secondly, the contracting party could allow the third party to sue the debtor in the contracting party's name, taking from the third party an indemnity against costs; but he could not be compelled to do this.

Thirdly, with the consent and co-operation of the debtor, the contracting party could effect a transfer by means of a substituted agreement, or 'novation', as follows:

If A plc owes M Ltd £100, and M owes X £100, it may be agreed between all three that A shall pay X instead of M, which thus terminates M's legal relationship with either party. In such a case the consideration for A's promise to pay X is the discharge by X of M's debt; for M's discharge of A, the promise of A to pay X; for X's discharge of M, the discharge by M of A's debt to M.

But a mere written authority from the creditor to the debtor (i.e. from M to A) to pay the amount of the debt over to a third party, even though the debtor acknowledged in writing the authority given, did not entitle the third party to sue for the amount unless the third party had furnished consideration by an express promise to release the creditor from the debt.[7]

(b) ASSIGNMENT IN EQUITY

Equity would permit the assignment of a chose in action, including debts and other contractual rights, whether such chose was equitable or legal.

(i) Equitable choses

An *equitable* chose is one which, before 1875, could only be enforced in the Court of Chancery, such as a share in a trust fund, a legacy, or a reversionary interest under a will. Where there was an assignment of an equitable chose, the assignee was allowed to proceed in its own name, and only an assignor who had an interest in the action had to be made a party to it.[8] The reason for this was that since there was no claim that might be asserted by an action at law, the Court of Chancery had exclusive jurisdiction

---

[4] *Master* v. *Miller* (1791) 4 Term Rep. 320, at p. 340.

[5] *Lampert's Case* (1612) 10 Co. Rep. 46b, at 48a; *Fitzroy* v. *Cave* [1905] 2 K.B. 364, at p. 372.

[6] *Re Bowden* [1936] Ch. 71, at p. 74.

[7] *Liversidge* v. *Broadbent* (1859) 4 H. & N. 603. But cf. *Walker* v. *Rostron* (1842) 9 M. & W. 411 and *Shamia* v. *Joory* [1958] 1 Q.B. 448.

[8] *Goodson* v. *Ellisson* (1827) 3 Russ. 583; *Cator* v. *Croydon Canal Co.* (1841) 4 Y. & C. Ex. 593; *Donaldson* v. *Donaldson* (1854) Kay 711.

over the whole transaction; there was therefore no risk that the trustees of the fund (i.e. the debtors) would be exposed to a second action at law by the assignor.

(ii) Legal choses

A *legal* chose in action is one which, before 1875, could be enforced by an action at law, for example, a right under a contract, a debt, or a claim under a policy of insurance. Equity would recognize the assignment of a legal chose in action, but had here to proceed more carefully. If equity itself enforced the claim of the assignee, that would not prevent the assignor from bringing an action at law; and the debtor would have been put to the inconvenience of resorting to equity to restrain the assignor from enforcing the judgment on the ground that the assignee had already recovered in equity. Consequently, the Court of Chancery did not in the ordinary case enforce the assignee's claim. What it did was to infer from the assignment a duty on the assignor to exercise the right for the benefit of the assignee. On receiving a proper indemnity against costs, the assignor's duty was to permit the assignee to use the assignor's name so that the assignee might bring an action at law. If necessary, it would enforce this duty.[9] So whenever a legal chose in action was assigned in equity—and it could not be assigned otherwise—the action in a Court of law was brought in the assignor's name.[10] This was primarily in the interests of the party liable, so that one action should bind both the legal and equitable title to the chose; and partly in the interests of the assignor, who might dispute the assignment if he thought fit.

Since the Judicature Act 1873 an assignment in equity will be recognized by all divisions of the High Courts of Justice, whether it be of a legal or equitable chose in action. But the rules relating to such assignments (including the use of the assignor's name) are based on those in operation before the passing of the Act. These rules are examined in detail below, but it is first necessary to note that section 25(6) of the Judicature Act (now replaced by section 136(1) of the Law of Property Act 1925) has introduced a form of statutory assignment which takes effect *at law*.

(c) ASSIGNMENT UNDER THE LAW OF PROPERTY ACT 1925

By section 136(1) of the Law of Property Act 1925:

Any absolute assignment by writing under the hand of the assignor (not purporting to be by way of charge only) of any debt or other legal thing in action, of which express notice in writing has been given to the debtor, trustee or other person from whom the assignor would have been able to claim such debt or thing in action, is effectual in law (subject to equities having priority over the right of the assignee) to pass and transfer from the date of such notice—

(a) the legal right to such debt or thing in action;

(b) all legal and other remedies for the same; and

---

[9] *Hammond* v. *Messenger* (1838) 9 Sim. 327.

[10] See, however, the statement of practice by Buller J. in *Master* v. *Miller* (1791) 4 Term Rep. 320, at p. 341, which shows that a Court of law did not always insist on the rule.

(c) the power to give a good discharge for the same without the concurrence of the assignor.

The effect of this section, provided the conditions laid down in it are fulfilled, is to give to the assignee a legal title to the debt or right assigned.[11] The assignee is thus enabled to sue in its own name.[12] It is necessary to examine the words of the section in some detail.

(i) 'Assignment'

The section does not touch the rules of assignment in equity so that equitable assignments remain unimpaired,[13] nor does it make assignable contracts which were not assignable in equity before:

This sub-section is merely machinery; it enables an action to be brought by the assignee in his own name in cases where previously he would have sued in the assignor's name, but only where he could so sue.[14]

(ii) 'Absolute' and unconditional

The Act requires the assignment to be 'absolute' and unconditional. This means that it must be an assignment of a sum due or about to become due, not of an amount which is dependent on any question as to the state of accounts between assignor and assignee.

If the assignment is to take effect or to cease upon the happening of a future uncertain event, so that the original debtor is uncertain as to the person in whom the right to receive the money is vested, it is not absolute. Thus in *Durham Brothers* v. *Robertson*:[15]

A building contractor wrote to the plaintiffs in the following terms: '*Re* Building Contract, South Lambert Road. In consideration of money advanced from time to time we hereby charge the sum of £1,080, being the price ... due to us from [the defendant] on the completion of the above buildings as security for advances, and we hereby assign our interest in the above-mentioned sum until the money with added interest be repaid to you'.

It was held that the assignment was not within the section. It did not transfer the whole debt to the plaintiffs unconditionally, but only until the advances were repaid. The defendant could not be sure that he was paying his debt to the right person without knowing the state of accounts between the assignor and assignee. But an assignment which passes the entire interest of the assignor in the debt may still be absolute despite the fact that it contains a proviso for redemption and reassignment on repayment.[16] The assignment is subject to a condition, but it cannot prejudice the

---

[11] *Warner Bros. Records Inc.* v. *Rollgreen Ltd.* [1976] Q.B. 430.

[12] Subject to the right of a debtor who receives notice of a disputed assignment to call upon the persons giving notice to interplead.

[13] *Brandt's Sons & Co.* v. *Dunlop Rubber Co. Ltd.* [1905] A.C. 454, at p. 461.

[14] *Torkington* v. *Magee* [1902] 2 K.B. 427, *per* Channell J. at p. 435; *Marchant* v. *Morton, Down & Co.* [1901] 2 K.B. 829, at p. 832.

[15] [1898] 1 Q.B. 765. See also *Raiffeisen Zentralbank* v. *Five Star Trading LLC* [2001] 2 W.L.R. 1344.

[16] *Tancred* v. *Delagoa Bay and East Africa Ry.* (1889) 23 Q.B.D. 239.

debtor, who will receive notice first of the assignment, and then of the reassignment, if one is made. The debtor will always know to whom the debt is owed. There may, too, be an absolute assignment of a debt arising out of an existing contract, even though it does not become payable until a date later than the assignment.[17] All contracted rights are vested from the moment the contract is made, even if they are not presently enforceable.[18]

(iii) Not by way of charge

The assignment must also not purport to be by way of charge. An assignment by way of charge is one which merely gives a right to payment out of a particular fund, and does not transfer the fund to the assignee. A good illustration is furnished by *Jones* v. *Humphreys*:[19]

A schoolmaster, in consideration of a loan to him of £15, assigned to the plaintiff so much and such part of his income, salary and other emoluments from his employers as should be necessary and requisite for repayment of the sum borrowed (with interest) or of any further or other sums in which he might thereafter become indebted to the plaintiff.

It was held that this was not an absolute assignment, but was a mere security purporting to be by way of a charge. Even the assignment of a definite part of an existing debt, for example part of a sum deposited in a bank account,[20] is not absolute, but merely a charge upon the whole debt;[21] for otherwise it would be in the power of the original creditor 'to split up the single legal cause of action for the debt into as many separate legal causes of action as he might think fit',[22] thus obviously prejudicing the position of the debtor. But any of these assignments, though not absolute, and therefore outside the section, may still be perfectly good as equitable assignments.

(iv) 'Writing'

The assignment must be in writing and signed by the assignor; signature by an agent may be insufficient.[23]

(v) 'Notice'

The Act requires that express notice in writing should be given to the debtor or trustee. This requirement is peremptory, so that in a case where the debtor was unable to read and it was therefore thought useless to give him written notice, though the assignment was read over to him and understood by him, there was held to be no legal

---

[17] *G. & T. Earle Ltd.* v. *Hemsworth R.D.C.* (1928) 44 T.L.R. 758; *Care S.S. Cpn.* v. *Latin American S.S. Cpn.* [1983] Q.B. 1005.

[18] *Marathon Electrical Mfg. Corp.* v. *Mashreqbank PSC* [1997] C.L.C. 1090, approving Oditah, *Legal Aspects of Receivables Financing* (1991) pp. 28–9.

[19] [1902] 1 K.B. 10. See also *Court Line Ltd.* v. *Akt. Gøtaverken* [1984] 1 Lloyd's Rep. 283.

[20] *Deposit Protection Board* v. *Dalia* [1994] 2 A.C. 367.

[21] *Williams* v. *Atlantic Assurance Co.* [1933] 1 K.B. 81.

[22] *Durham Brothers* v. *Robertson* [1898] 1 Q.B. 765, *per* Chitty L.J. at p. 774; *Forster* v. *Baker* [1910] 2 K.B. 636. See Hall [1959] C.L.J. 99.

[23] *Wilson* v. *Wallani* (1880) 5 Ex. D. 155.

assignment.[24] The written notice, however, need not be in any particular form, provided that it sufficiently indicates the fact of the assignment.[25] The notice takes effect when it is received by the debtor.[26]

(vi) Consideration

An assignment under the Act does not require the assignee to have furnished consideration in order to make it valid as between assignor and assignee or to enable the assignee to sue in its own name.[27]

(vii) Rights assignable

The Act refers to 'any debt or other legal thing in action'.[28] This expression is not, as might appear at first sight, confined to legal choses in action, which were enforceable only in a Court of Common Law, but extends to choses in equity as well; i.e. rights which a Court of Equity would have dealt with as being assignable.[29]

A 'legal thing in action' may therefore be defined as any right the assignment of which a Court of law or equity would, before the Judicature Act, have recognized or enforced.

(d) OTHER STATUTORY ASSIGNMENTS

Statute has also created further exceptions to the rule that there can be no assignment at law. For example, by the Policies of Assurance Act 1867[30] and by the Marine Insurance Act 1906,[31] policies of life and marine insurance can be assigned, but the former Act requires notice to be given by the assignee to the insurance company. Stock and shares in a company are transferable under the provisions of the Companies Act 1985[32] and the Stock Transfer Act 1963, and assignments of patents and copyright are regulated by the Patents Act 1977[33] and the Copyright, Designs and Patents Act 1988.[34]

(e) EQUITABLE ASSIGNMENTS

An assignment which does not comply with one or more of the requirements of section 136(1) of the Law of Property Act 1925 may still be a perfectly good and valid

---

[24] *Hockley* v. *Goldstein* (1922) 90 L.K.J.B. 111.
[25] *Denny, Gasquet & Metcalfe* v. *Conklin* [1913] 3 K.B. 177.
[26] *Holt* v. *Heatherfield Trust Ltd.* [1942] 2 K.B. 1.
[27] *Re Westerton* [1919] 2 Ch. 104.
[28] See, e.g. *King* v. *Victoria Insurance Co. Ltd.* [1896] A.C. 250; *Investors Compensation Scheme* v. *West Bromwich B.S.* [1998] 1 W.L.R. 898.
[29] *Re Pain* [1919] 1 C.E. 38; *Torkington* v. *Magee* [1902] 2 K.B. 427, at p. 430, rev'd on other grounds [1903] 1 K.B. 646.
[30] s. 1.
[31] s. 50(2).
[32] s. 182.
[33] ss. 90, Sched. 1, paras. 25–9.
[34] ss. 90, 94.

equitable assignment. 'The statute does not forbid or destroy equitable assignments or impair their efficacy in the slightest degree.'[35] But whereas a statutory assignee acquires a legal title to the chose assigned, an assignee in equity does not do so.[36] Thus a statutory assignee is entitled to bring an action without the necessity of joining the assignor as a party to the action, but an assignee in equity will not always enjoy this right.

(i) Joinder of the assignor

If the chose in action is *equitable*, the assignee is entitled to sue without joining the assignor as a party unless the assignor still has some interest in the suit. This may arise where there is still some question of accounts outstanding between the assignor and the assignee, or where the assignment consists of a charge upon a trust fund. In such a case the parties interested must be made parties to the action so that the Court may make a final adjudication binding them all.

   If the chose in action is *legal*, the assignee cannot recover damages or other relief without joining the assignor as a party to the action, if the assignor is willing as co-claimant, if not, as co-defendant.[37] Moreover the *assignor* of part of a debt cannot recover the balance in excess of the sum assigned without joining the assignee.[38] Attempts have been made to justify these requirements on the ground that they serve to protect the debtor who might otherwise pay the debt to the wrong person,[39] and that they allow an assignor who wishes to dispute the assignment to do so.[40] But the first reason is only relevant where the assignor retains an interest in the chose, and the second would apply even in the case of a statutory assignment, where the assignee is entitled to sue alone. The rule that an assignor of a legal chose must always be joined as a party seems to be a procedural consequence of the fact that the legal title to the chose assigned does not pass to the assignee, but only an equitable right, the legal title remaining vested in the assignor.[41]

(ii) Form

No particular form is necessary for an equitable assignment, and, except where the interest assigned is an equitable interest or trust within section 53(1) of the Law of Property Act 1925,[42] it need not even be in writing. It may be addressed to the debtor or to the assignee. If it is addressed to the debtor:

---

[35] *Brandt's Sons & Co.* v. *Dunlop Rubber Co. Ltd.* [1905] A.C. 454, *per* Lord Macnaghten at p. 461. See also *Raiffeisen Zentralbank* v. *Five Star Trading LLC* [2001] 2 W.L.R. 1344.

[36] *Warner Bros. Records Inc.* v. *Rollgreen Ltd.* [1976] Q.B. 430.

[37] *Durham Brothers* v. *Robertson* [1898] 1 Q.B. 765, at p. 769; *Performing Right Society Ltd.* v. *London Theatre of Varieties Ltd.* [1924] A.C. 1; *Williams* v. *Atlantic Assurance Co.* [1933] 1 K.B. 81; *Weddell* v. *J. A. Pearce & Major* [1988] Ch. 26; *Three Rivers D.C.* v. *Bank of England* [1996] Q.B. 292. Cf. *Brandt's Sons & Co.* v. *Dunlop Rubber Co. Ltd.* (*supra*, n. 35), at p. 464.

[38] *Walter & Sullivan Ltd.* v. *J. Murphy & Sons Ltd.* [1955] 1 Q.B. 584.

[39] *Ibid.*, *per* Parker L.J. at p. 588.

[40] *Durham Brothers* v. *Robertson* (*supra*, n. 36), *per* Chitty L.J. at p. 770.

[41] *Warner Bros. Records Inc.* v. *Rollgreen Ltd.* [1976] Q.B. 430; *Three Rivers D.C.* v. *Bank of England* [1996] Q.B. 292.

[42] *Grey* v. *I.R.C.* [1960] A.C. 1; *Oughtred* v. *I.R.C.* [1960] A.C. 206. Cf. *Vandervell* v. *I.R.C.* [1967] 2 A.C. 291; *Neville* v. *Wilson* [1997] Ch. 144.

It may be couched in the language of command. It may be a courteous request. It may assume the form of mere permission. The language is immaterial if the meaning is plain. All that is necessary is that the debtor should be given to understand that the debt has been made over by the creditor to some third person.[43]

In *Thomas* v. *Harris*,[44] it was addressed to the assignee:

A father handed to his son certain insurance policies on his life with the request that the son should erect a tombstone in his memory, using the policy monies for this purpose. No notice was given to the insurance company.

It was held that, by this informal act, the father had assigned the policies to his son by way of charge for the cost of the tombstone. There was a valid equitable assignment.

(iii) Notice

No notice to the debtor is necessary; the assignment is effective as between assignor and assignee from the moment it is made.[45] Notice is nevertheless *advisable* for several reasons. In the first place, the assignment will not bind the debtor until notice has been received, not necessarily in writing, of the assignment. So, if, before notice, the debtor pays the assignor, that is a good discharge of the debt[46] but if the debtor pays the assignor after notice that is no answer to a claim by the assignee.[47] Accordingly, to constitute notice a communication to the debtor should make it clear that thereafter payment should not be made to the assignor and should generally be by the assignee.[48] Secondly, notice to the debtor or trustee is necessary to establish priority under the rule in *Dearle* v. *Hall*, which we shall deal with later.[49] Thirdly, notice to the debtor will prevent the debtor from setting up new equities which may mature after the receipt of the notice.

(iv) Consideration

The question whether, as between assignor and assignee, consideration is necessary in an equitable assignment is a difficult one.[50] Equity will not assist a volunteer, and it has been said that 'for every equitable assignment . . . there must be consideration. If there be no consideration, there can be no equitable assignment'.[51] This statement is, however, much too wide, and it is by no means true to say that value is required in every case.

---

[43] *Brandt's Sons & Co.* v. *Dunlop Rubber Co. Ltd.* [1905] A.C. 454, *per* Lord Macnaghten at p. 462. But the assignment must either have been made by prior arrangement with, or be communicated to, the assignee: *Re Hamilton* (1921) 124 L.T. 737.

[44] [1947] 1 All E.R. 444.

[45] *Brandt's Sons & Co.* v. *Dunlop Rubber Co. Ltd.* (*supra*, n. 43), at p. 462.

[46] *Stocks* v. *Dobson* (1853) 4 De G.M. & G. 15.

[47] *Deposit Protection Board* v. *Dalia* [1994] 2 A.C. 367, at p. 387 (C.A.), rev'd. on other grounds, *ibid.*

[48] *Herkules Piling Ltd.* v. *Tilbury Construction Ltd.* (1992) 61 B.L.R. 107, at p. 119 (or possibly by the assignor, if acting on the assignee's behalf).

[49] *Post*, p. 481.

[50] For a discussion of this subject see Megarry (1943) 59 L.Q.R. 58; Hollond (1943) 59 L.Q.R. 129; Sheridan (1955) 33 Can. Bar Rev. 284; Hall [1959] C.L.J. 99; Marshall, *The Assignment of Choses in Action* (1950), p. 109.

[51] *Glegg* v. *Bromley* [1912] 3 K.B. 474, *per* Parker J. at p. 491.

Valuable consideration for this purpose may consist in any consideration sufficient to support a simple contract, or an antecedent debt or liability.[52] Thus if A assigns to B the benefit of a contract in satisfaction of a debt owed by A to B, this is good consideration for the assignment. Similarly, if the assignment is by way of security for an existing debt in such circumstances that a forbearance to sue will be implied on the part of the assignee, this is sufficient to give the assignee a right to sue the debtor.[53] If consideration has been furnished by the assignee, no problem will arise; it is where the assignment is voluntary that some doubt exists.

It is well established that a mere *agreement* to assign a chose in action must, like other contracts, have consideration to support it; if it is voluntary, it is unenforceable.[54] An assignment of a future chose in action also requires consideration.[55] A future chose in action is a mere expectancy which may or may not materialize, such as a share of a trust fund, which will be received only if an uncertain event occurs,[56] damages in an action which is still pending,[57] or the right to payments falling due under contracts not yet made.[58] Such an assignment can only operate as a contract to assign when the subject-matter comes into existence, for 'nothing passes even in equity until the property comes into present existence';[59] it is therefore unenforceable unless value has been given.

But just as it is possible to make a gift of a chattel, so also it is possible to make a gift of (i.e. to transfer without consideration) a chose in action, provided that the transfer is effected in whatever manner is necessary for a transfer of that particular chose. Such a transfer, however, must, as it is said, be 'complete and perfect', for if anything remains to be done by the donor in order to give effect to the donor's intention, the gift will fail. Equity will not intervene to perfect an imperfect gift.[60] The question of consideration in equitable assignments turns, therefore, on whether any act remains to be done by the assignor in order to perfect the assignment; the assignor must have made every effort to complete the transaction.[61]

If the subject-matter assigned is an equitable chose in action, the assignment is complete when the assignor has unequivocally, even though informally, expressed an intention that the chose should henceforth belong to the assignee.[62] The assignee is then, as we have seen, in a position to enforce the right to the chose without more ado:

---

[52] *Currie* v. *Misa* (1875) L.R. 10 Ex. 153; *Leask* v. *Scott* (1877) 2 Q.B.D. 376; (1943) 59 L.Q.R. 208.

[53] *Glegg* v. *Bromley* (*supra*, n. 51).

[54] *Re McArdle* [1951] Ch. 669.

[55] *Tailby* v. *Official Receiver* (1888) 13 App. Cas. 523.

[56] *Re Ellenborough* [1903] 1 Ch. 697. See also *Norman* v. *Federal Commissioner of Taxation* (1963) 109 C.L.R. 9 (future interest and dividends).

[57] *Glegg* v. *Bromley* (*supra*, n. 51).

[58] *E. Pfeiffer Weinkellerei-Weineinkauf GmbH & Co.* v. *Arbuthnot Factors Ltd.* [1988] 1 W.L.R. 150; *Annangel Glory Comp. Nav. S.A.* v. *M. Golodetz, Middle East Marketing Cpn. Ltd.* [1988] 1 Lloyd's Rep. 45.

[59] *Ibid.*, per Parker J. at p. 490.

[60] A similar principle is that in *Milroy* v. *Lord* (1862) 4 De G.F. & J. 264, at p. 274.

[61] *Fortescue* v. *Barnett* (1834) 3 My. & K. 36; (1943) 59 L.Q.R. 58, at pp. 61, 129; [1959] C.L.J. 99.

[62] *Voyle* v. *Hughes* (1954) 2 Sm. & G. 18; *Re Wale* [1956] 1 W.L.R. 1346; cf. *Re Lucan (Earl of)* (1890) 45 Ch. D. 470 where an assignment which failed to create a complete and perfect charge on a reversionary interest was held to be unenforceable for want of consideration.

'such an assignment without any valuable consideration is not a mere agreement but is an actual transfer of the equitable right'.[63] But if the subject of the assignment is a legal chose in action, can a merely equitable assignment of it be said to be complete and perfect? That is the question on which the law is still not altogether clear.

One difficulty of so regarding the transaction is that it leaves the legal title to the chose transferred still outstanding in the assignor. In Australia it has now been settled that, even if the assignment is one which is capable of being a statutory assignment, it does not have to be made in the statutory form, and that the assignor has done everything which is necessary to transfer the legal title to the assignee when the assignor has done those things which it and only it could do.[64] Although the matter has not been settled, it is submitted that this would also be the position in England: the law does not require the assignment of a chose in action to be made only in the statutory form[65] since it continues to recognize the validity of equitable assignments. Furthermore, as noted,[66] it is not now necessary for the assignee to ask the Court to compel the assignor to join as co-claimant, for an unwilling assignor can be made a defendant. In the result, an equitable assignee of a legal chose in action is now able to enforce the rights under the contract against the debtor without seeking the aid either of the assignor or of the Court, and there seems no reason why the assignment should not be regarded as complete and perfect without consideration.[67] There may, of course, be other reasons why a particular equitable assignment is not complete and perfect, e.g. because the assignor fails to complete the transfer of shares or stock in the sole recognized form,[68] or because the necessary consent of a third party to the transfer has not been obtained.[69] But the better view is that, as between assignor and assignee, an equitable assignment of an existing chose in action, whether legal or equitable, is not rendered ineffective merely because it is voluntary.

(f) ASSIGNEE TAKES 'SUBJECT TO EQUITIES'

Whether the assignment of a chose in action is legal or equitable, the assignee takes 'subject to equities', that is, subject to all such defences as might have prevailed against the assignor. 'The general rule, both at Law and in Equity, is that no person can acquire title to a chose in action . . . from one who has himself no title to it.'[70] An assignee of contractual rights must therefore take care to ascertain the exact nature and extent of those rights; for no more than the assignor has to give can be taken and

---

[63] *Voyle* v. *Hughes* (*supra*, n. 62), at p. 30; *Letts* v. *I.R.C.* [1957] 1 W.L.R. 201.

[64] *Corin* v. *Patton* (1990) 169 C.L.R. 540 (High Court of Australia). Cf. *Olsson* v. *Dyson* (1969) 120 C.L.R. 365.

[65] Cf. *Milroy* v. *Lord* (*infra*, n. 68).

[66] *Ante*, p. 476.

[67] *Holt* v. *Heatherfield Trust Ltd.* [1942] 2 K.B. 1; *Harding* v. *Harding* (1886) 17 Q.B.D. 442; *Re Patrick* [1891] 1 Ch. 82; *Re Griffin* [1899] 1 Ch. 408; *German* v. *Yates* (1915) 32 T.L.R. 52; *Re Rose* [1952] Ch. 499; *Pulley* v. *Public Trustee* [1956] N.Z.L.R. 771; *Mascall* v. *Mascall* (1984) 50 P. & C.R. 119.

[68] *Milroy* v. *Lord* (1862) 4 De G. F. & J. 264. But such an 'assignment' could nevertheless take effect as a declaration of trust.

[69] *Re Fry* [1946] 312.

[70] *Crouch* v. *Crédit Foncier of England* (1873) L.R. 8 Q.B. 374, at p. 380.

an assignee cannot be exempt from the effect of transactions by which the assignor may have lessened or invalidated the rights assigned.

(i) Claims arising out of contract assigned

The debtor is entitled to raise, by way of defence to an action brought by the assignee, all claims that directly arise out of the contract or transaction which forms the subject-matter of the assignment, whether such claims accrue before or after notice of the assignment is received. So, for example, despite the fact that the assignee is wholly innocent and has given value for the contractual rights assigned, the debtor can rescind the contract on the ground that it was induced to enter into it by the fraud of the assignor[71] or set off a claim for unliquidated damages for breach of the contract by the assignor,[72] or obtain a stay where the assignor's action would have been stayed for failure to pay the Courts of an earlier action.[73]

But a debtor with a claim of a strictly personal nature against the assignor cannot set that claim up against an innocent assignee. The debtor is restricted to claims which arise out of the contract itself and do not exist independently of it. The line between the two may be fine. For instance, while, as we have seen, the debtor can assert a right to rescind a contract because of the fraud of the assignor, a claim for damages for fraud cannot be asserted by the debtor in proceedings by the assignee. Thus in *Stoddart* v. *Union Trust*:[74]

The Union Trust were fraudulently induced by one Price to buy a newspaper called 'Football Chat' for the sum of £1,000, of which £200 was to be paid immediately, and the balance of £800 by instalments. Price assigned this £800 to the plaintiff, Stoddart, who took in good faith without knowledge of the fraud. When sued by Stoddart, the Union Trust pleaded that they had sustained damage exceeding £800 and that therefore no money was owed by them.

The Court of Appeal rejected this contention and held that the Union Trust could not set off their claim for damages against the assignee. Kennedy L.J. said:[75]

The defendants are claiming damages for the fraud which induced them to enter into the contract on the footing that they are liable under it, and at the same time seeking to repudiate their obligation under it. The claim for damages is a personal claim against the wrong-doer; it is something dehors the contract.

The debtor may also not recover money paid to the assignee, even where a subsequent breach of contract has given rise to an obligation on the part of the assignor to repay the money.[76]

---

[71] *Graham* v. *Johnson* (1869) L.R. 8 Eq. 36; *Banco Santander S.A.* v. *Bayfern Ltd* [2000] 1 All E.R. (Comm.) 776 (letter of credit).

[72] *Young* v. *Kitchin* (1878) 3 Ex. D. 127; *Newfoundland Government* v. *Newfoundland Ry.* (1888) 13 App. Cas. 199. See also *Bank of Boston Connecticut* v. *European Grain and Shipping Ltd.* [1989] A.C. 1056 (if debtor's claim against assignor could not be set off against debt, it cannot be set off against assignee).

[73] *Sinclair* v. *British Telecommunications plc* [2000] 2 All E.R. 461, at p. 469.

[74] [1912] 1 K.B. 181.

[75] At p. 194.

[76] *Pan Ocean Shipping Co. Ltd.* v. *Creditcorp Ltd.* [1994] 1 W.L.R. 161; Tolhurst [1999] C.L.J. 546.

(ii) Claims arising out of other transactions

Where a claim arises out of a contract or transaction other than the one which forms the subject-matter of the assignment, the debtor can set off such a claim against the assignee if but only if the claim accrues[77] *before the debtor has notice of the assignment.* An example is where money on deposit with a bank is assigned, but the bank has a claim against the assignor for taking up and paying bills of exchange.[78] The effect of notice is, therefore, in this case to prevent the debtor from setting up against the assignee any fresh equities which may mature. 'After notice of assignment of a chose in action the debtor cannot by payment or otherwise do anything to take away or diminish the rights of the assignee as they stood at the time of the notice'.[79]

(g) PRIORITIES

It may happen that an assignor makes two or more assignments of the same chose in action to different assignees. If the fund is insufficient to meet all the claims, a problem of their respective priorities will arise. The rule is that *equitable titles have priority according to the priority of notice.*[80] The successive assignees of an obligation rank as to their title, not according to the dates at which the creditor assigned the contractual rights to them respectively, but according to the dates at which notice was given to the party to be charged. This rule is generally known as the rule in *Dearle* v. *Hall.*[81] The reason lying behind it seems to be that, by failing to give notice to the debtor, the first assignee has enabled the assignor to make a second, and possibly fraudulent, assignment to the subsequent assignee. Accordingly, even though the first assignee's assignment was first in time, it ought to be postponed to the later assignment.

But the first assignee will only be postponed to a subsequent assignment of which prior notice has been given, if, at the time of the first assignment, the second assignee had no knowledge of the previous assignment.[82] A second assignee who had such knowledge, could scarcely claim to have been misled.

Except where the interest assigned is an equitable interest in land or in personalty, when the notice must be in writing,[83] no special form is required for a notice to gain priority. Provided it is clear and unequivocal, and brought home to the party charged, oral notice is sufficient. Even a notice in a newspaper read by the debtor has been held to suffice.[84] If the interest assigned is an equitable interest in a trust fund, it is advisable to give notice to all the trustees in order to be perfectly safe; otherwise notice given to one trustee alone may determine with his death or resignation.[85]

---

[77] *Business Computers Ltd.* v. *Anglo-African Leasing Ltd.* [1977] 1 W.L.R. 578.

[78] *Re Pinto Leite and Nephews* [1929] 1 Ch. 221.

[79] *Roxburghe* v. *Cox* (1881) 17 Ch. D. 520, *per* James L.J. at p. 526.

[80] *Marchant* v. *Morton, Down & Co.* [1901] 2 K.B. 829.

[81] (1823) 3 Russ. 1.

[82] *Re Holmes* (1885) 29 Ch. D. 786.

[83] Law of Property Act 1925, s. 137(3).

[84] *Lloyd* v. *Banks* (1868) L.R. 3 Ch. App. 488.

[85] *Re Phillips' Trusts* [1903] 1 Ch. 183.

(h) RIGHTS NOT ASSIGNABLE

Some choses in action are not assignable, and not every right which arises under or out of a contract can be assigned.

(i) Assignment prohibited

In the first place, the contract itself may expressly provide that the rights arising under it, or some of them, shall not be assignable. In such a case, a purported assignment of those rights will be invalid as against the debtor,[86] although it may be effective as between assignor and assignee[87] and enable the assignee to sue the assignor for breach of contract.[88] It has also been held that a clause prohibiting assignment does not necessarily prohibit a declaration of trust in favour of a third party.[89]

(ii) Bare right of action

Secondly, it is said that by reason of the rules against champerty and maintenance[90] a mere right to sue for damages (a 'bare right of action') cannot be assigned.[91] However, rights of action arising out of or incidental to rights of property can be assigned with the property transferred. Thus the purchaser of an estate was permitted to sue for damages for breaches of covenant committed by the vendor's tenants before the sale,[92] and the purchaser of land injuriously affected by a railway to claim compensation in respect of damages already sustained.[93] Again, a debt, as opposed to a mere right to sue for damages, is a species of property and is assignable at law.[94] Further, in *Trendtex Trading Corporation* v. *Crédit Suisse*,[95] the House of Lords made it clear that even an assignment of a bare right of action may be upheld if the assignee has a genuine commercial or financial interest in taking the assignment. An assignment to an insurer, who has indemnified the insured under a policy of insurance, of the insured's right of action has been held valid on the ground that the insurer has a legitimate interest in recouping the loss sustained by paying out on the policy.[96] Likewise, an assignee who has financed the transaction giving rise to the right of action assigned will have a legitimate commercial interest in taking the assignment if its sole object is

---

[86] *Helstan Securities Ltd.* v. *Hertfordshire C.C.* [1978] 3 All E.R. 262; *Linden Gardens Trust Ltd.* v. *Lenesta Sludge Disposals Ltd.* [1994] 1 A.C. 85, at p. 103; *Hendry* v. *Chartsearch Ltd.* [1998] C.L.C. 1382; Goode (1979) 42 M.L.R. 553; Allcock [1983] C.L.J. 328.

[87] *Re Turcan* (1888) 40 Ch. D. 5; *Re Westerton* [1919] 2 Ch. 104. Contrast *Spellman* v. *Spellman* [1961] 1 W.L.R. 921, at p. 928, but cf. at p. 925.

[88] *R v. Chester & North Wales Legal Aid Office, ex parte Queensferry Ltd.* [1998] 2 B.C.L.C. 436; *Bawejem Ltd.* v. *M.C. Fabrications Ltd.* [1999] 1 All E.R. (Comm.) 377.

[89] *Don King Productions Inc.* v. *Warren* [2000] Ch. 291, criticized by Tettenborn [1998] L.M.C.L.Q. 353.

[90] See *ante*, p. 359. This principle is unaffected by the abolition of the torts and crimes of champerty and maintenance: see Criminal Law Act 1967, s. 14(2).

[91] *De Hoghton* v. *Money* (1866) L.R. 2 Ch. App. 164; *May* v. *Lane* (1894) 64 L.J.Q.B. 236; *Torkington* v. *McGee* [1902] 2 K.B. 427, at p. 433 (decision reversed [1903] 1 K.B. 644); *Defries* v. *Milne* [1913] 1 Ch. 98. Cf. *Glegg* v. *Bromley* [1912] 3 K.B. 474 (fruits of action).

[92] *Defries* v. *Milne* (*supra*, n. 91); *Ellis* v. *Torrington* [1920] 1 K.B. 399.

[93] *Dawson* v. *G.N. & City Ry.* [1905] 1 K.B. 260.

[94] *Ellis* v. *Torrington* (*supra*, n. 92) at p. 411; *Camdex International Ltd.* v. *Bank of Zambia* [1998] Q.B. 22.

[95] [1982] A.C. 679, at pp. 694, 696, 697, 703.

[96] *Compania Colombiana de Seguros* v. *Pacific Steam Navigation Co.* [1965] 1 Q.B. 101.

to enable the assignee to recoup its loss on the transaction.[97] On the other hand, in the *Trendtex* case, the purchase with a view to profit of a right of action arising out of the breach and repudiation of a letter of credit was held to be invalid in English law as 'savouring of maintenance', since it involved trafficking in litigation.[98] But where the assignee has a genuine commercial or financial interest an assignment by a party unable to fund litigation to recover damages for breach of contract to a person who can, where the object and effect of the assignment is to enable the litigation to be funded, is not contrary to public policy or unlawful[99] unless there is an obvious disproportion between the assignee's true interest and what it bargained to receive under the assignment.[100]

(iii) Personal relationship

Thirdly, where some relation of personal confidence between the parties or their personal qualifications are of the essence of a contract, one party cannot assign the right to the performance of the obligations of the other, since to do so would be to alter the nature of the contract without the other's consent.

So, for example, a cake manufacturer was held not to be able to assign the right to be supplied with 'all the eggs he should require for manufacturing purposes for one year' to a new company on the amalgamation of the business.[101] What the supplier had undertaken to do was to supply all the eggs that the manufacturer, and not all that any other person or company, should require. Moreover, the manufacturer had undertaken not to buy eggs elsewhere and this introduced a personal element which was most material to the contract. This undertaking would not be binding on the assignee, so that the supplier would be deprived of its benefit. For a similar reason, a motor insurance policy cannot be assigned to the purchaser if the car is sold, unless the insurance company consents to the assignment, for that would be to 'thrust a new assured upon a company against its will'.[102] On the other hand, where it appears from the nature of the contract that no special personal considerations are involved, so that it can make no difference to the party on whom an obligation rests whether the performance is rendered for the original contracting party or another, then the right to the performance of an obligation may be assigned.[103] Moreover, as noted, the fact that a contract is non-assignable has been held not to preclude the making of a declaration of trust of the benefit of the contract for a third party.[104]

---

[97] *Trendtex Trading Cpn.* v. *Crédit Suisse* (*supra*, n. 95), at pp. 694, 696, 697, 703 (but not if the object is to sell on to and divide the 'spoils' with a subsequent assignee).

[98] See also *Re Trepca Mines Ltd. (No. 2)* [1963] Ch. 199; *Laurent* v. *Sale & Co.* [1963] 1 W.L.R. 829; *Re Oasis Merchandising Services Ltd.* [1997] 2 W.L.R. 764.

[99] *Norglen Ltd.* v. *Reeds Rains Prudential Ltd* [1999] 2 A.C. 1; *Circuit Systems Ltd.* v. *Zuken-Redac (U.K.) Ltd.* [1997] 1 W.L.R. 721.

[100] *Advanced Technology Structures Ltd.* v. *Cray Valley Products Ltd.* [1993] B.C.L.C. 723.

[101] *Kemp* v. *Baerselman* [1906] 2 K.B. 604.

[102] *Peters* v. *General Accident and Life Assurance Corporation Ltd.* [1937] 4 All E.R. 628, *per* Goddard J. at p. 633.

[103] *Tolhurst* v. *Associated Portland Cement Manufacturers (1900) Ltd.* [1903] A.C. 414; *Shayler* v. *Woolf* [1946] Ch. 320.

[104] *Don King Productions Inc.* v. *Warren, ante* n. 89.

(iv) Contracts of employment

The paradigm example of a personal contract is a contract of employment but, although at common law an employer could not assign its rights under contracts of employment with employees if it transferred the business without consent,[105] the position has been altered by legislation. On transfers of a business by sale, other disposition or by operation of law (e.g. on insolvency), there is a statutory novation by which all rights, powers, duties, and liabilities under a contract of employment operate between the employee and the transferee[106] unless the employee gives notice that he or she objects to being employed by the transferee.

(v) Salaries of public officers, etc

Finally, for reasons of public policy, no assignment may be made of the salary of a public officer paid out of national funds (for example of a civil servant's pay),[107] of maintenance granted to a wife,[108] or of benefits under social security legislation.[109]

II. ASSIGNMENT OF CONTRACTUAL LIABILITIES

(a) LIABILITIES CANNOT BE ASSIGNED

The burden of a contract can never be assigned without the consent of the other party to the contract.[110] A promisor cannot assign its liabilities under a contract without the consent of the promisee; or, conversely, a promisee cannot be compelled, by the promisor or by a third party, to accept any but the promisor as the person liable on the promise.

The rule is based on sense and convenience, for a contracting party ought not to be permitted to shift the burden of a contract onto the shoulders of a third party without the consent of the other party to the contract. It is illustrated by the case of *Robson and Sharpe* v. *Drummond*:[111]

S hired a carriage to D for 5 years, undertaking to paint it every year and to keep it in repair. R was the partner of S, but the contract was made with S alone. After 3 years S retired from business, and D was informed that R was thenceforth answerable for the painting and repair of the carriage and would receive the payments. D refused to deal with R, and returned the carriage.

---

[105] *Nokes* v. *Doncaster Amalgamated Collieries Ltd.* [1940] A.C. 1014, at p. 1026; *Newns* v. *British Airways* (1992) 21 I.R.L.R. 575, at p. 576.

[106] Transfer of Undertakings (Protection of Employment) Regulations 1981 (S.I. 1981 No. 1794), reg. 5(1); Trade Union Reform and Employment Rights Act 1993, s. 33. See *Secretary of State for Employment* v. *Spence* (1986) 15 I.R.L.R. 248, at p. 251; *Litster* v. *Forth Dry Dock & Engineering Co. Ltd.* (1989) 18 I.R.L.R. 161.

[107] See *ante*, p. 357.

[108] *Re Robinson* (1884) 27 Ch. D. 160.

[109] e.g. Social Security Act 1975, s. 87; Supplementary Benefits Act 1976, s. 16.

[110] *Linden Gardens Trust Ltd.* v. *Lenesta Sludge Disposals Ltd.* [1994] 1 A.C. 85, at p. 103.

[111] (1831) 2 B. & Ad. 303.

It was held that he was entitled to do so. Lord Tenterden stated:[112]

[T]he defendant may have been induced to enter into this contract by reason of the personal confidence which he reposed in [S], and therefore have agreed to pay money in advance. The . . . defendant had a right to object to its being performed by any other person, and to say that he contracted with [S] alone, and not with any other person.

Parke J. stated that D 'had a right to have the benefit of the judgment and taste of [S] to the end of the contract'.[113]

(b) VICARIOUS PERFORMANCE

One limitation to this rule is that there may be circumstances which make it permissible for a contracting party to perform its side of the contract by getting someone else to do in a satisfactory fashion the work for which the contract provides. If A undertakes to do work for B which needs no special skill, and it does not appear that A has been selected with reference to any personal qualification, B cannot complain if A sub-contracts the work to an equally competent sub-contractor. Such cases are sometimes loosely referred to as assignments of a contractual liability, but they are really instances of the *vicarious performance* of a contract. The original contracting party remains liable on the contract and, as a rule, is the only person entitled to sue for payment. This is clearly stated by Lord Greene M.R. in *Davies* v. *Collins*:[114]

In many contracts all that is stipulated for is that the work shall be done and the actual hand to do it need not be that of the contracting party himself; the other party will be bound to accept performance carried out by somebody else. The contracting party, of course, is the only party who remains liable. He cannot assign his liability to a sub-contractor, but his liability in those cases is to see that the work is done, and if it is not properly done he is liable. It is quite a mistake to regard that as an assignment of the contract; it is not.

The circumstances in which a contract may be vicariously performed, which are similar to those which determine whether a contractual right is assignable, are discussed in Chapter 12.

(c) NOVATION

Another way by which the burden of a contract may be 'assigned' to a third party is with the co-operation of the party entitled to performance. A liability may be transferred with the consent of the party entitled; but this is in effect the rescission of one contract and the substitution of a new one in which the same acts are to be performed by different parties. This is called a novation and it can only take place by an

---

[112] At p. 307.
[113] At p. 308.
[114] [1945] 1 All E.R. 247, at p. 249. See also *Stewart* v. *Reavell's Garage* [1952] 2 Q.B. 545.

agreement supported by consideration[115] between the parties; novation cannot be compulsory.[116] It is therefore not properly to be regarded as an assignment.

(d) MUTUAL RIGHTS AND OBLIGATIONS

As a general rule, where the benefit of a contract, involving mutual rights and obligations, is the subject of a valid assignment, the assignee does not acquire the assignor's contractual obligations. But the circumstances may be such as to show that the assignee agreed to accept, not merely the rights, but also the obligations of the contract;[117] alternatively the rights assigned may themselves be qualified or conditional, the condition being that certain restrictions be observed or certain obligations assumed.[118] In such situations, an assignee who takes the benefit of the contract must also bear the burden.

III. NEGOTIABLE INSTRUMENTS

Under the most favourable circumstances the assignment of a contract binds the party chargeable to the assignee only when notice is given, and subject always to the rule that a better title than the assignor possesses cannot be given to the assignee.

There is, however, a class of promises in writing, the benefit of which can be transferred in such a way that the promise may be enforced by the transferee of the benefit without previous notice to the debtor, and without the risk of being met by defences which would have been good against the transferor of the promise. This class of contracts is known as 'negotiable instruments',[119] in which the process of transfer is termed 'negotiation'.[120]

For an instrument to be negotiable these features seem to be essential:

In the first place, the title to it passes by delivery, or, if it is made to order (that is to say, either expressed to be so payable, or expressed to be payable to a particular person) then by the indorsement of the payee completed by delivery.

Secondly, the written promise which it contains gives a right of action to the holder of the document for the time being, though the holder and the fact of the holding may be alike unknown to the promisor.

Thirdly, a *bona fide* holder for value is not prejudiced by defects in the title of the assignor; the holder does not hold 'subject to equities'.

[115] *Commissioners of Customs and Excise* v. *Diners Club Ltd.* [1988] 2 All E.R. 1016, at p. 1023, aff'd. [1989] 1 W.L.R. 1196.
[116] Approved in *Re United Railways of the Havana and Regla Warehouses Ltd.* [1960] Ch. 52, at p. 84, rev'd in part on other grounds *sub nom. Tomkinson* v. *First Pennsylvania Banking and Trust Co.* [1961] A.C. 1007. See also *ante*, p. 448.
[117] *Tito* v. *Waddell (No. 2)* [1977] Ch. 106, at pp. 290–307. See also *Rother Iron Works Ltd.* v. *Canterbury Precision Engineers Ltd.* [1974] Q.B. 1.
[118] *Tolhurst* v. *Associated Portland Cement Manufacturers Ltd.* [1903] A.C. 414.
[119] See generally Chalmers and Guest, *Bills of Exchange*, 15th edn. (1998); Barak (1983) 18 Israel L. Rev. 49.
[120] See *post*, pp. 490–1 for the separate legal notion of 'transferability'.

Fourthly, the instrument is of a type recognized by the law as negotiable. The parties cannot confer negotiability upon a contract which is not recognized by the law to possess this quality.

(a) TYPES OF NEGOTIABLE INSTRUMENT

Certain instruments are negotiable by the custom of merchants recognized by the Courts; others are negotiable by statute. The operation of negotiability can best be illustrated by reference to some of these.

(i) Cheques

Although, since the Cheques Act 1992, a large number of cheques are not negotiable,[121] the cheque remains the most familiar type of negotiable instrument. A cheque is an unconditional order, addressed by its drawer to a banker, directing the banker to pay on demand a certain sum to the person named on the face of the cheque or the bearer. If the cheque is made payable to 'Bearer' or to 'A or Bearer', the mere delivery of it by one holder to another suffices as negotiation and the holder for the time being is entitled to present the cheque for payment without any further formality. But if it is made payable to 'A or Order', it must first be indorsed. Until it is indorsed, a simple delivery does not suffice.[122] For the cheque to be negotiated, A must indorse it, and this is done by A signing on the back.

If the indorsement consists in the mere signature of A, the cheque is said to be indorsed 'in blank'. It then becomes a cheque payable to bearer, that is, negotiable by mere delivery, for A has given his order, though it is an order not mentioning any particular person. The cheque is in fact indorsed over to anyone who becomes possessed of it.

If the indorsement takes the form of an order in favour of B, written on the cheque and signed by A, i.e. 'B or Order', it is called a 'special' indorsement. Its effect is to transfer to B the right to demand payment of the cheque. Once again, B must now indorse the cheque, and may do so specially or in blank. Thus the cheque may pass through several hands before it is ultimately presented for payment.

(ii) Bills of exchange

A bill of exchange is an unconditional order in writing, addressed by A to B, requiring B to pay a sum of money to or to the order of a specified person or to bearer. Usually this specified person is a third person, C, but it need not be. A may draw a bill upon B in favour of A. The order may be addressed to B because B is buying goods from A and it may have been arranged that 'payment' for the goods is to be made to C (a bank) or directly to A by means of a bill instead of cash. Since bills of exchange are here considered merely as illustrative of negotiability, we will adopt the most usual, as it is the most convenient, form of illustration.

---

[121] *Post*, pp. 491–2.
[122] The Cheques Act 1957 removes the necessity for the indorsement of cheques paid into the account of the payee, but this does not apply where it is sought to negotiate the instrument.

A directs B to pay a sum of money 'to the Order of C', or to 'Bearer'. A is then called the drawer of the bill, and by drawing it promises to pay the sum specified in it either to C or to any subsequent holder into whose hands it may come if B does not 'accept' the bill or, having accepted it, fails to pay.

B, upon whom the bill has been drawn, is called the drawee; but on assenting to pay the sum specified, B is said to become the 'acceptor'. Such assent (or 'acceptance') must be expressed by writing on the bill and signed by B. The payee of the bill, in our example C, may transfer it to another person before it has been accepted, and in that case it is for the transferee to present it to B for acceptance. Acceptance may be general or qualified. A general acceptance assents without qualification to the order of the drawer; but the person presenting the bill may be willing to take one qualified by conditions as to amount, time, or place,[123] though this releases the drawer or any previous indorser from liability unless they assent to the qualification.

The rules relating to payment, indorsement, and transfer by delivery are similar to those concerning cheques, and given above. If the bill has been accepted, the holder may demand payment from the acceptor. But in the event of default in acceptance or payment, the holder may also demand compensation either from the original drawer, or from any indorser; for an indorser is to all intents and purposes a new drawer, and becomes therefore an additional security for payment to the holder for the time being.

In modern business practice, the primary function of a bill of exchange is to enable a seller or exporter to obtain cash as soon as possible after the despatch of the goods, and yet enable the buyer or importer to defer payment until the goods reach him, or later. Credit can be obtained if the bill is accepted by a bank, upon whom the parties can rely, and bills can be bought and sold on the discount market.[124]

(iii) Promissory notes

A promissory note is an unconditional promise in writing made by one person to another signed by the maker, engaging to pay, on demand or at a fixed or determinable future time, a sum certain in money, to, or to the order of, a specified person or to bearer.[125] A Bank of England note is a promissory note which by statute is made legal tender.[126]

Bills of exchange were negotiable by the law merchant; promissory notes were originally made so by the Promissory Notes Act 1704; both classes of instrument are now governed by the Bills of Exchange Act 1882.[127] A cheque is in fact a species of bill of exchange, but it possesses certain features of its own not common to all bills of exchange.

---

[123]　But by the Bills of Exchange Act 1882, s. 19(2) a condition as to payment at a particular place is not a qualified acceptance 'unless it expressly states that the bill is to be paid there only, and not elsewhere'. Hence the common form 'accepted payable at X Bank' is not a qualified acceptance.

[124]　Gillett Bros., *The Bill on London* (1964) p. 16.

[125]　Bills of Exchange Act 1882, s. 83(1).

[126]　Currency and Bank Notes Act 1954, s. 1.

[127]　As amended.

(iv) Instruments negotiable by custom

Certain other instruments are negotiable by the custom of merchants recognized by the Courts; such are foreign bonds expressed to be transferable by delivery,[128] and scrip certificates which entitle the bearer to become holder of such bonds or shares in a company.[129] The character of negotiability may from time to time be attached to other instruments by the custom of merchants proved to the satisfaction of the Courts; i.e. notorious, certain, reasonable, and general.[130] The categories of negotiable instruments are never closed.

In *Goodwin* v. *Robarts*[131] the Court of Exchequer Chamber rejected the view that a mercantile custom of recent origin was insufficient to attach to an instrument the character of negotiability:

G purchased scrip issued by the agent of a foreign government from a broker, but allowed the broker to remain in possession of it. The broker fraudulently pledged the scrip to R in order to secure a loan. R took the scrip in good faith and, upon the default of the broker, sold it. If the scrip was negotiable, R acquired a good title; if not, R would be liable to G as true owner.

It was held that the scrip was negotiable according to the custom of merchants. Dealing with the argument that this was a new and unrecognized type of negotiable instrument, Cockburn C.J. said:[132]

We are of the opinion that [this argument] cannot prevail. It is founded on the view that the law merchant thus referred to is fixed and stereotyped, and incapable of being expanded and enlarged so as to meet the wants and requirements of trade in the varying circumstances of commerce. It is true that the law merchant is sometimes spoken of as a fixed body of law, forming part of the common law, and as it were coeval with it. But as a matter of legal history, this view is altogether incorrect. The law merchant thus spoken of with reference to bills of exchange and other negotiable securities, though forming part of the general body of the lex mercatoria, is of comparatively recent origin. It is neither more nor less than the usages of merchants and traders in the different departments of trade, ratified by the decisions of Courts of law, which, upon such usages being proved before them, have adopted them as settled law with a view to the interests of trade and the public convenience.

Negotiability emphasizes the interest which merchants have in dynamic security, in speedy transactions, and the protection of the *bona fide* purchaser, as opposed to static security which is designed to safeguard the title of the true owner.[133] The decision in *Goodwin* v. *Robarts* enables the Courts to give effect to that interest.

[128] *London Joint Stock Bank* v. *Simmons* [1892] A.C. 201.
[129] *Goodwin* v. *Robarts* (1875) 1 App. Cas. 476; *Rumball* v. *Metropolitan Bank* (1877) 2 Q.B.D. 194.
[130] See *ante*, p. 151.
[131] (1875) L.R. 10 Ex. 337, aff'd (1875) 1 App. Cas. 476. See also *Bechuanaland Exploration Co. Ltd.* v. *London Trading Bank Ltd.* [1898] 2 Q.B. 658 and *Edelstein* v. *Schuler & Co.* [1902] 2 K.B. 144; Bosanquet and Palmer (1899) 15 L.Q.R. 130, 245.
[132] (1875) L.R. 10 Ex. 337, at p. 346.
[133] Demogue, *Modern French Legal Philosophy*, p. 418.

(b) ASSIGNABILITY AND NEGOTIABILITY

There are a number of differences between assignability and negotiability.

(i) Notice

In the first place, notice to the debtor is never required in the case of a negotiable instrument. The benefit of the promise to pay is transferable by the mere delivery and the right of action vests in the holder for the time being. In the case of an assigned contract, however, notice is necessary to perfect a statutory assignment, and is advisable in equitable assignments so as to prevent the debtor paying the assignor.

(ii) Title

Secondly, a *bona fide* holder for value without notice[134] obtains a good title to a negotiable instrument; whereas in assignment, the assignee takes 'subject to equities'. So, for example, if the instrument has been stolen, or obtained by fraud, a holder who took the instrument in good faith and for value, and without notice of any defect in the title of the person who negotiated it, will still be entitled to demand payment. Thus in *London Joint Stock Bank* v. *Simmons*:[135]

Negotiable bonds belonging to X were pledged to a bank by X's broker without authority, to secure a loan to the broker. The bank had no notice of these facts. On the broker's insolvency, the bank sold the bonds in satisfaction of the debt due, and the broker's clients sued the bank.

The House of Lords held that the bank was entitled to retain and realize the securities, as it had taken the bonds for value and in good faith. 'It is', said Lord Herschell,[136] 'surely of the very essence of a negotiable instrument that you may treat the person in possession of it as having authority to deal with it, be he agent or otherwise, unless you know to the contrary, and are not compelled, in order to secure a good title to yourself, to inquire into the nature of his title, or the extent of his authority'.

(iii) Consideration

Thirdly, the doctrine of consideration does not always apply to negotiable instruments. The rule in ordinary contracts (including some contracts of assignment) is that consideration must move from the promisee.[137] But in the case of bills of exchange, for example, no consideration need necessarily have been given by the holder of the bill. Section 27(2) of the Bills of Exchange Act 1882 provides that, where value has *at any time* been given for a bill, the holder is deemed to be a holder for value as regards the acceptor and all parties to the bill who became parties prior to

---

[134] A 'holder in due course': Bills of Exchange Act 1882, s. 29(1).
[135] [1892] A.C. 201.
[136] At p. 217.
[137] See *ante*, pp. 95–6.

such time.[138] Once value has been given by a party to the bill, the holder can enforce the bill whether he or she personally gave value or not.[139]

(iv) Holder in due course

Finally, in the case of bills of exchange certain presumptions greatly assist the holder to establish a right to sue on the bill. Every holder of a completed bill of exchange is *prima facie* deemed to be 'a holder in due course'—that is, is presumed to have given value for it in good faith, without notice of any defect in title of the person who negotiated it.[140] The holder will therefore have to do no more than prove the signature of the person sued, everything else being presumed in the holder's favour. The burden will be on the person sued to prove that the holder's title is in some way defective or that no consideration has been given.

There is an important exception to this rule. If in an action on the bill it is admitted or proved that the acceptance, issue, or subsequent negotiation of the bill is tainted with fraud or illegality of some kind, then this presumption no longer holds good. The burden of proof is shifted, and it is now the holder of the bill who must prove affirmatively that, subsequent to the alleged fraud or illegality, value has in good faith been given for the bill, though not necessary by itself.[141] A holder who can do so will still win the action whatever the earlier history of the bill may be, unless the holder was a party to the fraud or illegality alleged. A holder who has been a *party* to the fraud or illegality can never succeed, though mere knowledge of it will not invalidate the holder's title, if it is derived, not from a person whose own title is defective, but from one who is a holder in due course.[142]

(c) LIMITATION OF NEGOTIABILITY

We have spoken all the time of a bill of exchange or promissory note as if it must always be a negotiable instrument. But it is to be noted that a particular bill or note is only negotiable if it is in a condition of negotiability. It may, for example, contain words which prevent its transferability or negotiability. If so, it is valid as between the parties thereto, but is not negotiable.[143] For example, if a bill of exchange is drawn payable 'to P only' it is not transferable and only P can sue on it.[144] However, if a crossed cheque merely bears the words 'not negotiable', it still remains transferable, though the person to whom it is transferred takes it subject to any defect in the title of the transferor.[145] But, by the Cheques Act 1992 a crossed cheque with the words 'account payee' or 'a/c payee' with or without the words 'only' is not transferable.

---

[138] See *Scott* v. *Lifford* (1808) 1 Camp. 246; *Diamond* v. *Graham* [1968] 1 W.L.R. 1061.

[139] *Sed quaere* whether this is so as between immediate parties whose relations regarding the bill arise out of their direct dealings: *Churchill & Sim* v. *Goddard* [1937] 1 K.B. 92, at p. 110; *Pollway Ltd.* v. *Abdullah* [1974] 1 W.L.R. 493; *Hasan* v. *Willson* [1977] 1 Lloyd's Rep. 431, at p. 441.

[140] Bills of Exchange Act 1882, s. 30(2).

[141] *Tatam* v. *Haslar* (1889) 23 Q.B.D. 345; *ante*, p. 344.

[142] Bills of Exchange Act 1882, s. 29(3).

[143] *Ibid.*, s. 8(1).

[144] *Hibernian Bank Ltd.* v. *Gysin and Hanson* [1939] 1 K.B. 483.

[145] Bills of Exchange Act 1882, s. 81 (crossed cheques only).

Cheque books issued by banks often contain these words. Crossing a cheque does not of itself hinder the negotiability of the cheque; it simply means that it cannot be presented for payment over the counter, but must be collected through a banker.

It is also possible for a bill to be restrictively indorsed, e.g. 'Pay Q only', in which case Q has the right to receive payment of the bill and to sue any party thereto that the indorser could have sued, but it gives Q no power to transfer its rights as indorsee unless the indorsement expressly authorized Q to do so.[146]

(d) BILLS OF LADING

Bills of lading, which are affected both by the law merchant and by statute, possess some characteristics which call for separate consideration.[147] They are not, in fact, fully negotiable, but certain rights are transferred by indorsement and delivery of the bill.

A bill of lading may be regarded in three aspects: (i) it is a receipt given by the shipowners acknowledging that the goods specified in the bill have been put on board; (ii) it is a document which contains or evidences the terms of the contract for the carriage of the goods agreed upon between the shipper of the goods and the shipowners whose ship is to carry them; and (iii) it is a 'document of title' to the goods, of which it is the symbol. It is by means of this document of title that the goods themselves may be dealt with by the owner of them while they are still upon the high seas.

Three copies of the bill of lading are usually made, each signed either by the master of the ship or by the agents of the shipowner. One copy is kept by the consignor of the goods and one by the master of the ship, and the original is forwarded to the consignee, who (in the normal case) on receipt of it acquires a property in the goods which can only be defeated by the exercise of the right of the vendor of the goods to stop them in transit.[148] But if, before stoppage, the consignee lawfully transfers a bill of lading by indorsement and delivery to a holder in good faith and for value, that holder has a title to the goods which overrides the vendor's right of stoppage in transit. The holder of the bill can claim the goods in spite of the insolvency of the consignee, and the consequent loss of the price of the goods by the vendor.[149]

At common law, the holder's right was a right of property only. The indorsement of a bill of lading gave a right to the goods alone; it did not give the holder any power to sue on the contract expressed in the bill. This proved very inconvenient and the Bills of Lading Act 1855 provided that an indorsee to whom the property in the goods passed by the indorsement acquired 'all rights of suit' and 'the same liabilities in respect of the goods'.[150] The position is now governed by the Carriage of Goods by

---

[146] *Ibid.*, s. 35(1) and (2).

[147] See generally *Scrutton on Charterparties and Bills of Lading*, 20th edn. (1996).

[148] Stoppage in transit is the right of the unpaid seller who has parted with possession of the goods sold to resume possession of them as long as they are in the course of transit, and to retain them until payment or tender of the price. It may be exercised when the buyer is insolvent. See Sale of Goods Act 1979, ss. 44–6.

[149] Sale of Goods Act 1979, s. 47.

[150] s. 1. For criticism, see Law Com. No. 196, *Rights of Suit in Respect of Carriage of Goods by Sea* (1991).

Sea Act 1992 which provides that the lawful holder of a bill of lading is entitled to assert contractual rights irrespective of the passing of property and regardless of whether the holder has itself suffered loss.[151]

A bill of lading differs from the negotiable instruments which have just been dealt with:

In the first place, its indorsement transfers a remedy *in rem*, the right to claim specific goods, whereas a negotiable instrument confers only a remedy *in personam*, the right to be paid a certain sum of money.

Secondly, although the indorsee is relieved from one of the liabilities to which the consignee of the goods is exposed, namely, the vendor's right of stoppage in transit, it does not acquire proprietary rights independent of the consignee's title: a bill of lading stolen, or transferred without the authority of the person really entitled, gives no such rights even to a *bona fide* indorsee.[152] Again the contractual rights transferred are, in effect, 'subject to equities' because, where the holder takes or demands delivery of the goods or otherwise claims under the contract of carriage against the shipowner, it becomes subject to any contractual liabilities as if it had been a party to the contract of carriage.[153]

IV. ASSIGNMENT BY OPERATION OF LAW

So far we have dealt with the voluntary assignment by parties to a contract of the benefit or the liabilities of the contract. But rules of law may also operate to transfer these rights or liabilities from one to another.

(a) THE EFFECT OF DEATH

The general rule is that rights and liabilities under a contract pass, on the death of a party to the contract, to his or her personal representatives.

But performance of such contracts as depend upon the personal service or skill of the deceased cannot be demanded of personal representatives, nor can they insist upon offering such performance, though they can sue for money earned by the deceased and unpaid at the time of the death.[154] Contracts of agency and of personal service expire with the death of either of the parties to them; thus an apprenticeship contract is terminated by the death of the master, and no claim to the services of the apprentice survives to the executor or administrator.[155]

---

[151] s. 2(1). Where loss is suffered by another the holder's rights are exercised for the benefit of the person who sustained the loss: *ibid.*, s. 2(4).

[152] *Gurney* v. *Behrend* (1854) 3 E. & B. 622, at p. 634. See also Carriage of Goods by Sea Act 1992, ss. 2(1) and 5(2) ('lawful' holder).

[153] Carriage of Goods by Sea Act 1992, s. 3.

[154] *Stubbs* v. *Holywell Railway Co.* (1867) L.R. 2 Ex. 311.

[155] *Baxter* v. *Burfield* (1746) 2 Stra. 1266.

(b) BANKRUPTCY

Bankruptcy is regulated by the Insolvency Act 1986. Proceedings commence with the filing of a petition for a bankruptcy order either by a creditor alleging acts of bankruptcy against the debtor or by the debtor alleging inability to pay the debts.[156] Where the grounds of the petition are established the Court may, in an appropriate case, appoint an insolvency practitioner to ascertain whether the debtor is willing to make a proposal for a voluntary arrangement and a meeting of the creditors should be summoned.[157]

If the creditors decide not to accept a composition or scheme of arrangement, the Court makes a bankruptcy order and a trustee is appointed. To the trustee passes 'all property belonging to or vested in the bankrupt at the commencement of the bankruptcy',[158] or property which may be acquired by or has devolved upon the bankrupt since the commencement of the bankruptcy.[159] The object of the laws of bankruptcy is that 'every beneficial interest which the bankrupt has shall be disposed of for the benefit of his creditors'.[160] It suffices to note that:

(1) Where any part of the property of the bankrupt consists of a chose in action, it is deemed to have been assigned to the trustee.[161]

(2) The trustee may disclaim, and so discharge, unprofitable contracts.[162]

(3) The trustee is excluded from suing for personal injuries arising out of breaches of contract, such as injuries to reputation or credit.[163]

(4) Executory contracts personal to the bankrupt do not pass.[164]

The trustee, as statutory assignee of the bankrupt's choses in action, is in one respect in a more favourable position than an ordinary assignee. If a chose in action has been assigned by the bankrupt *before* the bankruptcy took place, the assignment will be void as against the trustee if (i) it is of a future chose in action for which the consideration is not supplied until after the commencement of the bankruptcy[165] or (ii) it is a

---

[156] Insolvency Act 1986, ss. 264–72.

[157] *Ibid.*, ss. 273–4.

[158] *Ibid.*, s. 283(1). 'Property' includes 'things in action': *ibid.*, s. 436. Between the date of the order and the appointment of the trustee the official receiver is under a duty to act as receiver and manager of the estate: *ibid.*, s. 287.

[159] *Ibid.*, s. 307.

[160] *Smith* v. *Coffin* (1795) 2 H. Bl. 444, at p. 461.

[161] Insolvency Act 1986, s. 311(4). Where there is a cross-claim what is assigned is a claim to the net balance: *ibid.*, s. 323; *Stein* v. *Blake* [1996] A.C. 243.

[162] *Ibid.*, s. 315. An administrative receiver of a company becomes liable on any contract of employment 'adopted' by him: *ibid.*, s. 44; *Powdrill* v. *Watson* [1995] 2 All E.R. 65.

[163] *Wilson* v. *United Counties Bank* [1920] A.C. 102 (credit); *Re Kavanagh* [1949] 2 All E.R. 264, aff'd [1950] 1 All E.R. 39n. (reputation). Cf. *Beckham* v. *Drake* (1849) 2 H.L.C. 579 (wrongful dismissal). See *Heath* v. *Tang* [1993] 1 W.L.R. 1421.

[164] *Gibson* v. *Carruthers* (1841) 8 M. & W. 321 (contract to marry); *Lucas* v. *Moncrieff* (1905) 21 T.L.R. 683 (contract to publish book).

[165] *Wilmot* v. *Alton* [1897] 1 Q.B. 17; *Re Collins* [1925] Ch. 556; *Re de Marney* [1943] Ch. 126. Cf. *Re Davis & Co.* (1888) 22 Q.B.D. 193; *Re Trytel* [1952] 2 T.L.R. 32.

general assignment of book debts by a trader and has not been registered under the Bills of Sale Act.[166]

(c) LAND

If a person acquires an interest in land from another, either by purchase or lease, upon terms which bind that person to observe certain covenants respecting the land, the assignment by either party to the contract of his interest will, in certain circumstances, operate as a transfer to the assignee of the rights and obligations arising out of the covenants.[167] This subject is, however, best studied in the special works on the law of land, and is accordingly omitted here.

---

[166] Insolvency Act 1986, s. 344.
[167] See *ante*, pp. 447, 453.

PART IV

PERFORMANCE AND DISCHARGE

12

PERFORMANCE

I. PERFORMANCE MUST BE PRECISE AND EXACT

(a) STANDARDS OF CONTRACTUAL DUTY

The general rule is that performance of a contract must be precise and exact. That is, a party performing an obligation under a contract must perform that obligation exactly within the time frame set by the contract and exactly to the standard required by the contract. Sometimes that standard will be strict. This is so in the case of many common law obligations such as a seller's obligation to load cargo,[1] not to ship dangerous cargo,[2] and to obtain an export licence.[3] It is also so in the case of the statutory implied terms of quality in contracts for the sale and supply of goods.[4] Sometimes, as in the case of contracts for services, it will only require the exercise of reasonable care[5] or due diligence.[6] Whether the alleged performance satisfies this criterion is a question to be answered by construing the contract, so as to see what the parties meant by performance, and then by applying the ascertained *facts* to that construction, to see whether that which has been done corresponds to that which was promised.

(b) DEVIATION FROM CONTRACTUAL TERMS

If there is the slightest deviation from the terms of the contract, the party not in default will be entitled to say that the contract has not been performed, will be entitled to sue for damages for breach, and, in certain cases, to elect to be discharged. Thus in *Re Moore & Co. and Landauer & Co.*:[7]

---

[1] *Kurt A. Becher G.m.b.H. & Co. K.G.* v. *Roplak Enterprises S.A. (The World Navigator)* [1991] 2 Lloyd's Rep. 23.

[2] *The Anathanasia Cominos* [1990] 1 Lloyd's Rep. 277, at p. 282.

[3] *Pagnan SpA.* v. *Tradax Ocean Transportation SA.* [1987] 3 All E.R. 565.

[4] Sale of Goods Act 1979, ss. 12, 14 (as amended), *ante*, pp. 153–8; Supply of Goods and Services Act 1982, ss. 4 and 9. See also Supply of Goods (Implied Terms) Act 1973, s. 10 (hire purchase).

[5] e.g., *Lister* v. *Romford Ice and Cold Storage Co. Ltd.* [1957] A.C. 555 (driving lorry); *Thake* v. *Maurice* [1986] Q.B. 644, at pp. 684–7, cf. pp. 677–8 (medical treatment); *Smith* v. *Eric S. Bush* [1990] 1 A.C. 831 at p. 843 (surveying house); *Henderson* v. *Merrett Syndicates Ltd.* [1995] 2 A.C. 145, at p. 176 (managing agents of Lloyd's underwriters). See also Supply of Goods and Services Act 1982, s. 13. Cf. *Samuels* v. *Davis* [1943] 1 K.B. 526.

[6] Carriage of Goods by Sea Act 1971, s. 3 (seaworthiness); *Union of India* v. *N.V. Reederij Amsterdam* [1962] 2 Lloyd's Rep. 233 (H.L.).

[7] [1921] 2 K.B. 519.

D agreed to buy from P 3,000 tins of canned fruit from Australia to be packed in cases containing 30 tins. When the goods were tendered it was found that a substantial part of the consignment was packed in cases containing 24 tins.

D was entitled to reject the whole consignment. Even if the performance effected is commercially no less valuable than that which was promised, there is a default in performance. So a contract to ship goods direct from Singapore to New York was held not to have been performed by shipping them to the American Pacific Seaboard and thence to New York by train.[8]

Only if the deviation is 'microscopic' will the contract be taken to have been correctly performed, for *de minimis non curat lex*.[9] A party who does not render precise and exact performance of a contract is nevertheless exceptionally treated as having performed to some extent where that party has attempted (tendered) performance but the other party has prevented that performance, and in certain cases where there has been partial performance of an entire obligation.

II. TIME OF PERFORMANCE

(a) STIPULATIONS AS TO TIME AT COMMON LAW

Where a time was fixed for the performance of an undertaking by one of the parties to the contract, the common law as a general rule held this to be 'of the essence of the contract'. This phrase is often used but is capable of causing confusion because the question relates not to the contract as a whole but to the particular term which has been breached.[10] If the condition as to time was not fulfilled, the other party might treat the contract as broken and elect to terminate it.[11] For instance, in a contract for the sale of a flat where time was stated to be of the essence, the vendor was entitled to terminate when the purchaser tendered the price 10 minutes late.[12]

(b) STIPULATIONS AS TO TIME IN EQUITY

Equity did not regard a condition as to time as of the essence. Where it could do so without injustice to the contracting parties it decreed specific performance notwithstanding failure to observe the time fixed by the contract for completion, and as an

---

[8] *Re L. Sutro & Co. and Heilbut Symons & Co.* [1917] 2 K.B. 348.

[9] *Arcos Ltd.* v. *E. A. Ronaasen & Son* [1933] A.C. 470, *per* Lord Atkin at pp. 479, 480.

[10] *British and Commonwealth Holdings plc.* v. *Quadrex Holdings Inc.* [1989] 1 Q.B. 842, *per* Browne-Wilkinson V.-C. at p. 857.

[11] *United Scientific Holdings Ltd.* v. *Burnley B.C.* [1978] A.C. 904, *per* Lord Simon at pp. 940–1. Cf. *ibid.*, *per* Lord Diplock at pp. 927–8. See further, *ante*, pp. 135, 142 (conditions).

[12] *Union Eagle Ltd.* v. *Golden Achievement Ltd.* [1997] A.C. 514. See also *Comp. Commerciale Sucres et Denrees* v. *C. Czarnikow Ltd.* [1990] 1 W.L.R. 1337, at p. 1347. But cf. Sale of Goods Act 1979, s. 10(1), *post*, p. 502.

incident of specific performance relieved the party in default by restraining proceedings at law based on such failure.[13]

(c) LAW OF PROPERTY ACT 1925, S. 41

Since the passing of the Judicature Acts, the rules of common law and equity have been fused,[14] and section 41 of the Law of Property Act 1925[15] enacts:

Stipulations in a contract, as to time or otherwise, which according to rules of equity are not deemed to be or to have become of the essence of the contract, are also construed and have effect at law in accordance with the same rules.

But this relief is not available in three instances:

(1) where the agreement expressly states that time is of the essence of the contract;[16]

(2) where time was not originally of the essence of the contract, but has been made so by one party, upon a breach by the other party,[17] giving notice to the party in breach requiring performance of the contract within a reasonable time;[18]

(3) where from the nature of the contract, its subject-matter, or the circumstances of the transaction, time must be taken to be of the essence of the agreement. The most common examples of this are provided by mercantile contracts, considered *infra*, but, although time is *prima facie* not of the essence in sales of land,[19] or provisions in leases, such as rent review clauses,[20] in certain cases it will be. Thus, in the case of the sale of a public-house as a going concern,[21] or of a leasehold house required for immediate occupation,[22] or of an option to acquire property,[23] or the power under a 'break' clause in a lease to determine the lease prematurely,[24] time may well be of the essence and, if so, no relief is permitted.

---

[13] *United Scientific Holdings Ltd.* v. *Burnley B.C.* [1978] A.C. 904, at p. 942. See also *Stickney* v. *Keeble* [1915] A.C. 386, at p. 415.

[14] *Ibid.* [1978] A.C. 904, at pp. 924–5, 926–7, 940, 956–7, 964.

[15] Re-enacting the Judicature Act 1873, s. 25(7). Cf. *Raineri* v. *Miles* [1981] A.C. 1050 (damages available).

[16] *Steedman* v. *Drinkle* [1916] 1 A.C. 275.

[17] *Behzadi* v. *Shaftesbury Hotels Ltd.* [1992] Ch. 1; *British and Commonwealth Holdings plc.* v. *Quadrex Holdings Inc.* [1989] 1 Q.B. 842, at pp. 857–8.

[18] *Stickney* v. *Keeble* (*supra*, n. 13); *Behzadi* v. *Shaftesbury Hotels Ltd.* (*supra*, n. 17); *Finkielkraut* v. *Monohan* [1949] 2 All E.R. 234. On 'reasonableness', see also *Oakdown Ltd.* v. *Berstein and Co. (a firm)* (1985) 49 P. & C.R. 282.

[19] *Webb* v. *Hughes* (1870) L.R. 10 Eq. 281; *Chancery Lane Developments Ltd.* v. *Wade's Department Stores Ltd.* (1986) 53 P. & C.R. 306, at p. 312.

[20] *United Scientific Holdings Ltd.* v. *Burnley B.C.* (*supra*, n. 13).

[21] *Tadcaster Tower Brewery Co.* v. *Wilson* [1897] 1 Ch. 705.

[22] *Tilley* v. *Thomas* (1867) L.R. 3 Ch. App. 61.

[23] *Hare* v. *Nicoll* [1966] 2 Q.B. 130.

[24] *United Scientific Holdings Ltd.* v. *Burnley B.C.* (*supra*, n. 13) at p. 929; *Coventry City Council* v. *J. Hepworth & Sons Ltd.* (1982) 46 P. & C.R. 170. But cf. *Metrolands Investments Ltd.* v. *J. H. Dewhurst Ltd.* [1986] 3 All E.R. 659.

(d) MERCANTILE CONTRACTS

In mercantile contracts, time will readily be assumed to be of the essence of the contract. For example, if a contract to purchase shares provides for payment by a fixed date, payment must be made on or before that date, and in default the seller can treat the contract as discharged.[25] Similarly, time is of the essence for payment under a time charterparty of a ship if the owner is given the right to withdraw the vessel in default of 'punctual payment' of hire.[26] However, section 10(1) of the Sale of Goods Act 1979 provides that, unless a different intention appears from the terms of the contract, stipulations as to time of *payment* are not of the essence of a contract of sale of goods. The unpaid seller may, however, give notice of his intention to re-sell perishable goods and, if payment is not tendered within a reasonable time thereafter, re-sell and recover damages for and loss.[27] Whether or not any other stipulation as to time is of the essence of a contract of sale of goods depends upon the terms of the contract;[28] but it is very often held to be so.[29]

Where a person is required to perform on or before a particular date, the performance may normally be carried out during the whole of that day.[30] Thus if payment of hire under a time charterparty is due on 14 June, the charterer has (regardless of banking hours) until midnight on 14/15 June to make the payment, and the ship-owner cannot withdraw the ship for non-payment before that time.[31] Where no time is fixed by the contract for performance, it must be performed within a reasonable time.[32]

III. PLACE OF PERFORMANCE

The place of performance depends upon the express or implied intentions of the parties, judged from the nature of the contract and the surrounding circumstances. If no place of performance is specified even by implication, in a contract for the sale of goods it is basically the duty of the buyer to collect the goods rather than the seller to send them,[33] and in contracts to pay money it is basically the debtor's duty to pay the creditor at the creditor's place of business or residence.[34]

---

[25] *Hare* v. *Nicoll* (*supra*, n. 23). See also *Union Eagle Ltd.* v. *Golden Achievement Ltd.* [1997] A.C. 514, *ante*, p. 500.

[26] *Scandinavian Trading Tanker Co. A.B.* v. *Flota Petrolera Ecuatoriana* [1983] 2 A.C. 694.

[27] Sale of Goods Act 1979 s. 48(3).

[28] *Ibid*, s. 10(2). But see *Hartley* v. *Hymans* [1920] 3 K.B. 475, at p. 483.

[29] *Reuter* v. *Sala* (1879) 4 C.P.D. 239, at pp. 246, 249; *Hartley* v. *Hymans* (*supra*, n. 28), at p. 484; *Finagrain S.A. Geneva* v. *P. Kruse Hamburg* [1976] 2 Lloyd's Rep. 508; *United Scientific Holdings Ltd.* v. *Burnley B.C.* [1978] A.C. 904, at pp. 924, 937, 944, 950, 958; *Bunge Cpn.* v. *Tradax Export S.A.* [1981] 1 W.L.R. 711 (*ante*, p. 143); *Comp. Commerciale Sucres et Denrees* v. *C.Czarnikow Ltd.* [1990] 1 W.L.R. 1337, at p. 1347.

[30] Contrast Sale of Goods Act 1979, s. 29(5) (demand or tender of delivery may be treated as ineffectual unless made at a reasonable hour).

[31] *Afovos Shipping Co. S.A.* v. *R. Pagnan & Filii* [1983] 1 W.L.R. 195.

[32] *Postlethwaite* v. *Freeland* (1880) 5 App. Cas. 599; Sale of Goods Act 1979, s. 29(3).

[33] Sale of Goods Act 1979, ss. 29(1), (2). See also CISG, Art. 31.

[34] *Charles Duval & Co. Ltd.* v. *Gans* [1904] 2 K.B. 685; *Fowler* v. *Midland Electricity Corporation for Power Distribution Ltd.* [1917] 1 Ch. 656 (debenture). On payment through the banking system, see *post*, p. 504.

IV. ORDER OF PERFORMANCE

Where the contract makes no express provision, the order of performance depends on whether the obligation of one party to perform is interdependent on or independent of the other's obligation. The obligations may be interdependent in one of two ways. The obligation of one to perform may either be conditional upon performance by the other or concurrent with the obligation of the other. The determination of this is a matter of intention, and thus of the construction of the contract. The distinction between interdependent obligations (i.e. conditions precedent and concurrent obligations), and independent promises is discussed in Chapters 4 and 15.[35] In a contract of sale, unless the contract provides otherwise, payment and delivery are treated as due simultaneously and as concurrent,[36] but in a contract of employment the general rule is that the performance of the work is a condition precedent to the obligation to pay. The order of performance determines whether one party has to extend credit to the other and whether failure to perform is a breach of contract,[37] and, if so, whether the innocent party is entitled to be discharged from its obligations. The position at common law differs from that in many civil law countries where a party may withhold performance until the other party performs, not only in cases of concurrent obligations but also where the other party has to perform first.[38]

V. PAYMENT

(a) INTRODUCTION

One mode of complete performance of an obligation is by payment. No request or demand for payment is normally necessary[39] unless the contract so provides.[40]

There is a common, but mistaken, belief that payment of a debt can only be proved by the production of a written receipt. But payment may be proved by any evidence,[41] and a receipt is only *prima facie* evidence that a debt has been paid.[42]

Payment normally means payment in cash. The parties may, however, agree, expressly or impliedly, that payment may be made in some other manner, and, in the absence of any express stipulation, the method of payment may be determined by

---

[35] *Ante*, p. 136; *post*, p. 576.

[36] Sale of Goods Act 1979, s. 28.

[37] *Post*, Chapter 15.

[38] Lando & Beale, *Principles of European Contract Law* (2000), p. 407.

[39] *Bell & Co. v. Antwerp, London & Brazil Line* [1891] 1 Q.B. 103, *per* Lord Esher M.R. at p. 107; *Carne* v. *Debono* [1988] 1 W.L.R. 1107, at p. 1112.

[40] *Libyan Arab Foreign Bank Co. v. Bankers Trust Co.* [1989] 1 Q.B. 728, at pp. 748–9. On the need for notice by a tenant of want of repair before landlord's obligation to repair is due, see *Calebar Properties Ltd.* v. *Stitcher* [1984] 1 W.L.R. 287, at p. 298; *British Telecommunications plc* v. *Sun Life Assurance Society plc* [1996] Ch. 69.

[41] *Eyles* v. *Ellis* (1827) 4 Bing. 112. See also Cheques Act 1957, s. 3.

[42] *Wilson* v. *Keating* (1859) 27 Beav. 121.

course of dealing between the parties or by trade custom. If the parties are dealing together on a regular basis, it may be agreed that, at periodic intervals, sums due from one party shall be set off against sums due to that party by the other, and such set-off is then equivalent to an actual cash payment.[43]

(b) INTERBANK TRANSFERS

Nowadays payment is frequently made by use of the banking system. The debtor instructs its bank to pay a specified sum to the account of the creditor at another bank. The transfer may be effected by letter, telegram, telex, or electronically from the one bank to the other. Such payment, when made, 'is the equivalent of cash, or as good as cash' for the purposes of a contract that requires payment in cash.[44] But difficulties can arise. If payment has to be made by a certain date, does the receipt of the payment order by the creditor's bank constitute payment? Or is payment only made when the order has been processed and the amount credited to the creditor's account? In *Mardorf Peach & Co. Ltd.* v. *Attica Sea Carriers Corporation of Liberia*,[45] where the evidence was that the system of processing might take up to 24 hours before the account was credited, members of the House of Lords expressed differing opinions. Lord Salmon[46] and Lord Russell[47] were inclined to the view that, since a payment order was as between banks the equivalent of cash, it should suffice for punctual payment that such cash equivalent was tendered in due time to the creditor's bank to be credited to its account.[48] But Lord Fraser[49] was of the opinion that payment would not take place until the creditor's bank acted on the request in the order and credited the amount to the creditor's account. However, in *A/S Awilco of Oslo* v. *Fulvia S.p.A. di Navigazione of Cagliari (The Chikuma)*:[50]

R chartered A's vessel *Chikuma*. Failing punctual payment of hire in cash in American currency monthly in advance, A was entitled to withdraw the vessel from service. Payment of one instalment of hire fell due on 22 January. On 21 January R instructed its Norwegian bank to make the required payment by credit transfer. By a telex message before noon on the 22nd there was a credit transfer to A's bank in Italy of the sum due. The bank credited this on the same day to A's account. By Italian banking law, however, although A would have immediate access to the money, interest would not start to be paid by the bank until 26 January, and if A had withdrawn the sum credited it would probably have incurred liability to the bank to pay interest for those 4 days. A withdrew the vessel for default in punctual payment.

---

[43]   *Larocque* v. *Beauchemin* [1897] A.C. 358, at pp. 365–6.

[44]   *A/S Awilco of Oslo* v. *Fulvia S.p.A. di Navigazione of Cagliari (The Chikuma)* [1981] 1 W.L.R. 314, at p. 320.

[45]   [1977] A.C. 850.

[46]   At p. 880.

[47]   At p. 889.

[48]   In the case of a transfer between branches of the same bank, *Momm* v. *Barclays Bank International Ltd.* [1977] Q.B. 79 held that payment was effected when the staff of the bank received the debtor's instructions and set in motion the bank's internal procedures for crediting the creditor's account.

[49]   At p. 885.

[50]   [1981] 1 W.L.R. 314 (criticized by Mann (1981) 97 L.Q.R. 379).

The House of Lords upheld their right to do so. The payment on 22 January was not equivalent to cash for it could not be used to earn interest, e.g. by immediate transfer to a deposit account. The fact that A could withdraw the money, but subject to payment of interest, did not make the payment equivalent to cash, since the arrangement amounted in substance to an overdraft facility.

(c) PAYMENT BY NEGOTIABLE INSTRUMENT OR DOCUMENTARY CREDIT

A negotiable instrument,[51] such as a bill of exchange, cheque, or promissory note may, by agreement, be given and accepted in payment. But the presumption where a negotiable instrument is taken in lieu of a money payment is that the parties intend it to be a conditional discharge only:[52]

Suppose that A, being owed a sum of money by B, agrees to take a cheque in payment of the sum due.

So far, B has satisfied the debt.[53] But if the cheque is dishonoured when presented for payment, A's right to sue on the debt revives and A's original rights are restored.[54] Exceptionally, however, a negotiable instrument may be given and accepted as absolute payment. In such a case, in the example given above, B's debt would then be wholly discharged. A would have to rely upon the rights conferred by the cheque, and, if the cheque is dishonoured, A must sue on it, and cannot revert to the original claim for the debt.[55] Similar principles apply to payment by documentary credit.[56]

(d) PAYMENT BY CREDIT OR CHARGE CARD

By contrast, payment by a credit or charge card is an unconditional and absolute payment unless the contract provides otherwise. So, the liability of a cardholder who has paid for goods or services in this way is discharged and the cardholder will not be liable to the seller or supplier if the credit or charge card company fails to pay the seller or supplier the amount charged to the card.[57]

---

[51] See *ante*, pp. 486–93.

[52] *Re Romer and Haslam* [1893] 2 Q.B. 286, at pp. 296, 300, 303.

[53] *Sayer* v. *Wagstaff* (1844) 5 Beav. 415, at p. 423; *Hadley & Co. Ltd.* v. *Hadley* [1898] 2 Ch. 680; *Bolt & Nut Co. (Tipton) Ltd.* v. *Rowlands, Nicholls & Co. Ltd.* [1964] 2 Q.B. 10.

[54] *Sayer* v. *Wagstaff* (*supra*, n. 53); *Re Romer and Haslam* (*supra*, n. 52).

[55] *Sard* v. *Rhodes* (1836) 1 M. & W. 153; *Sibree* v. *Tripp* (1846) 15 M. & W. 23; *Re Romer and Haslam* (*supra*, n. 52), at pp. 296, 300.

[56] *W.J. Alan & Co. Ltd.* v. *El Nasr Export and Import Co.* [1972] 2 Q.B. 189, at pp. 209–12; *Re Charge Card Services Ltd.* [1989] Ch. 497, at p. 511. On documentary credits, see further, *ante*, pp. 445–6.

[57] *Re Charge Card Services Ltd.* [1989] Ch 497; *Customs & Excise Commissioners* v. *Diners Club Ltd.* [1989] 1 W.L.R. 1196.

VI. VICARIOUS PERFORMANCE

There may be circumstances which make it permissible for a contracting party to perform his side of the contract by getting someone else to do in a satisfactory fashion the work for which the contract provides.[58] A contract may be vicariously performed where this is expressly permitted by the contract,[59] or, from the terms of the contract, its subject-matter, and surrounding circumstances, it may properly be inferred that it is a matter of indifference whether the performance is that of the contracting party or his nominee. Thus it has been held that a contract to let out railway waggons and keep them in repair could be vicariously performed.[60] The repairs were 'a rough description of work which ordinary workmen conversant with the business would be perfectly able to execute'.[61] If, however, the person employed has been selected with reference to his individual skill, competence, or other personal qualification, that person is not entitled to sub-contract the performance of the contract to another. Thus it has been held that personal care and skill is an ingredient in contracts by a warehouseman for the storage of furniture,[62] by a publishing firm for the publication of a book,[63] and by an architect in the design of a building.[64] Such contracts cannot be vicariously performed without the consent of the promisee. Contracts of service are normally personal to the contracting parties.[65] Furthermore, payment of a debt which is made by a person other than the debtor or the debtor's agent will not be effective to discharge the debt.[66]

Even where the contract may not, in principle, be vicariously performed, if the promisee in fact agrees to it being performed by a non-party and accepts such performance, the contract will be discharged.[67]

VII. ALTERNATIVE MODES OF PERFORMANCE

A contract can provide for alternative modes of performance in one of two ways.[68] First, it may provide for performance in a particular way, for instance a shipper's obligation to load a cargo of wheat, but give that party the option to perform in an

---

[58] See *ante*, p. 485, for the distinction between vicarious performance and assignment.

[59] e.g. *Société Commerciale de Reassurance* v. *E.R.A.S. International Ltd.* [1992] 1 Lloyd's Rep. 570, at p. 596.

[60] *British Waggon Co. Ltd.* v. *Lea & Co.* (1880) 5 Q.B.D. 149.

[61] *Ibid.*, *per* Cockburn C.J. at p. 153.

[62] *Edwards* v. *Newland & Co.* [1950] 2 K.B. 534.

[63] *Griffith* v. *Tower Publishing Co. Ltd.* [1897] 1 Ch. 21.

[64] *Moresk Cleaners Ltd.* v. *Hicks* [1966] 2 Lloyd's Rep. 338.

[65] *Nokes* v. *Doncaster Amalgamated Collieries Ltd.* [1940] A.C. 1014 (rights). But note the Transfer of Undertakings Regulations 1981 (S.I. 1981 No. 1794 as amended by S.I. 1999 No. 2402), reg. 5(1), *ante*, p. 484.

[66] See *Belshaw* v. *Bush* (1851) 11 C.B. 191; *Walter* v. *James* (1871) L.R. 6 Ex. 124; *Owen* v. *Tate* [1976] 1 Q.B. 402. See generally Beatson and Birks (1976) 91 L.Q.R. 188; Beatson, *The Use and Abuse of Unjust Enrichment* (1991), ch. 7; Friedmann (1983) 99 L.Q.R. 534.

[67] *Belshaw* v. *Bush* (*supra*, n. 66); *Hirachand Punamchand* v. *Temple* [1911] 2 K.B. 483, *ante*, p. 111.

[68] See generally Treitel, *Frustration and Force Majeure* (1994), ch. 10.

alternative way, for instance, to change to a cargo of barley. Secondly, it may permit one party to choose[69] between alternative modes of performance without specifying one as the primary mode, for instance, a shipper's obligation to load a full cargo in the months of September or October.

(a) CONTRACT OPTION

In the first situation, once the option is exercised, the contractual obligation is varied; in the example above, the contract ceases to be one to load wheat and becomes one to load barley. The option must be exercised within a reasonable time and this must be communicated to the other party;[70] if it is not exercised it is lost. But, in considering whether to exercise the option, the promisee is not generally bound to consider the interests of the other party.[71] For example, if the primary mode of performance becomes impossible, the option-holder is not obliged to exercise it in order to avoid the contract being frustrated.[72] But an attempt to rely on the exercise of such an option to render a contractual performance substantially different from that which was reasonably expected may be ineffective against a consumer or a party dealing on the other's written standard terms of business.[73]

(b) PERFORMANCE OPTION

In the second situation there is a truly alternative obligation. The promisor is obliged to perform in any of the authorized modes. If, prior to a choice being made, one mode ceases to be available, that simply narrows the scope of contractually authorized performance.[74] So, in the example given above, if access to the loading port is impossible due to strikes or bad weather during September, that does not affect the obligation to ship a full cargo; the shipper remains liable to load a full cargo in October, even if the shipper had planned to do so in September. But once a party chooses the alternative to be performed, that choice binds.[75]

---

[69] If the contract does not specify which party has the option, it will be the one who has to do the first act: *Reed* v. *Kilburn Co-op* (1875) L.R. 10 Q.B.D. 264.

[70] *Reardon Smith Line Ltd.* v. *Ministry of Agriculture, Fisheries & Food* [1963] A.C. 691, at p. 731.

[71] *Ibid.*, at pp. 719–20, 730. See also *Thompson* v. *ADSA-MFI Group Plc.* [1988] 1 Ch. 241, at pp. 251, 266–7 (no general principle that a party cannot take advantage of own acts to avoid obligations under the contract).

[72] On frustration, see further Chapter 14.

[73] Unfair Contract Terms Act 1977, s. 3(2)(b); Unfair Terms in Consumer Contracts Regulations 1999 (S.I. 1999 No. 2083), Sched. 2, para. 1(b), (c), (h), (l). See generally *ante*, pp. 200, 300.

[74] *Reardon Smith Line Ltd.* v. *Ministry of Agriculture, Fisheries & Food* [1963] A.C. 691, at p. 717, 720, 730; *Atlantic Lines & Navigation Co. Ltd.* v. *Didymi Corp. (The Didymi)* [1984] 1 Lloyd's Rep. 583, at p. 587; *Libyan Arab Foreign Bank* v. *Bankers Trust Co.* [1989] Q.B. 728, at p. 766; *Lauritzen A.S.* v. *Wijsmuller B.V. (The Super Servant Two)* [1990] 1 Lloyd's Rep 1, at p. 9.

[75] *Schneider* v. *Foster* (1857) 2 H. & N. 4; *Gath* v. *Lees* (1865) 3 H. & C. 558. But authority (*Brown* v. *Royal Insurance Co.* (1859) 1 E. & E. 853) suggesting the party remains bound even where it is no longer possible to perform the contract in that way is doubtful since it predates the development of the doctrine of frustration, on which see *post*, Chapter 14.

VIII. RIGHT TO CURE BAD OR INCOMPLETE PERFORMANCE

We have seen that English law treats a serious misperformance, such as incomplete delivery or delivery of goods that are not of satisfactory quality, as the standard example of a breach entitling the innocent party to treat the contract as discharged.[76] Unlike the position in some other systems, the innocent party is not required to serve notice requiring the other party to perform in a stated time[77] and there is only a limited right to cure defective performance.[78] If, however, a bad or incomplete performance is tendered before the time of performance has arrived, the promisor is not generally prevented from making another tender of performance within time that does comply. The promisee would have to accept this fresh tender unless the first amounted to a repudiation which the promisee had acted upon and terminated the contract.[79] One situation in which the defective performance will be treated as a repudiation is where the defective performance has destroyed the confidence of the promisee.[80]

IX. TENDER

Tender is attempted performance; and the word is applied to attempted performance of two kinds, dissimilar in their results. It is applied to a performance of a promise to do something, and of a promise to pay something. In each case the performance is prevented by the act of the party for whose benefit it is to take place.

(a) TENDER OF ACTS

Where one party is obliged by the contract to perform a promise to do something, but the other party refuses to accept the performance when tendered, the promisor is discharged from performing that obligation and may sue for damages. In addition, if the promisee commences an action against the promisor for failure to perform the obligation, the promisor is entitled to set up the refusal to accept the tender as a defence.[81] The promisor will not, however, be treated as having performed the obligation. If the refusal to accept the tender amounts to a repudiation of the contract the promisor can elect to terminate the contract and sue for damages.[82] Although such a

---

[76] *Ante*, pp. 135, 140 (conditions and innominate terms). See further *post*, Chapter 15.

[77] Treitel, *Remedies for Breach of Contract* (1988) p. 327 (German Law's 'Nachfrist').

[78] Treitel, *op cit*, pp. 371–4; CISG Art 48; Restatement of Contract 2nd, § 237 (serious breach initially only justifies suspension of performance by innocent party).

[79] *Borrowman, Phillips & Co. v. Free & Hollins* (1878) 4 Q.B.D. 500; *Motor Oil Hellas (Corinth) Refineries S.A. v. Shipping Corporation of India (The Kanchenjunga)* [1990] 1 Lloyd's Rep 391, at p. 399.

[80] On repudiation, see further *post*, Chapter 15.

[81] *Startup* v. *Macdonald* (1843) 6 M. & G. 593.

[82] *Ibid.*

refusal does not always have this effect,[83] if it is absolute and unqualified it entitles the promisor to elect to be discharged. For example, the Sale of Goods Act 1979, section 37, provides that when the seller is ready and willing to deliver the goods and requests the buyer to take delivery, the buyer must do so within a reasonable time or become liable for any loss occasioned to the seller by the buyer's neglect. But this does not affect the rights of the seller where the non-acceptance amounts to a repudiation of the contract.

(b) TENDER OF PAYMENT

Where, however, the performance due consists of the payment of a sum of money, a tender by the debtor, though refused by the creditor, does not discharge the debtor from the obligation to pay the debt. The debtor is bound in the first instance 'to find out the creditor and pay him the debt when due';[84] if the creditor will not take payment when tendered, the debtor must nevertheless continue to be ready and willing to pay the debt. Then, the debtor, if sued, can plead that a tender had been made, but must pay the money into Court.[85] If the debtor proves this plea, the creditor gets nothing but the money originally tendered, i.e. no interest or damages, while the debtor gets judgment for the costs of the action, and so is placed in as good a position as at the time of the tender.

Tender of payment, to be a valid performance to this extent, must observe exactly any special terms which the contract may contain as to time,[86] place, and mode of payment. The nineteenth century authorities further prescribe extremely strict requirements for a valid tender: it must be unconditional and it must be in legal currency.[87] There must be an offer of money produced and accessible to the creditor, not necessarily of the exact sum, but of such a sum as will allow the creditor to take exactly what is due without being called upon to give change.[88] Finally, it was necessary for the cash to be produced to the creditor in person. 'Great importance', it was said,[89] 'was attached to the production of money, as the sight of it might tempt the creditor to yield'. But these requirements may be dispensed with expressly or impliedly by the creditor,[90] and the requirement of payment in cash must be interpreted against the background of modern commercial practice. In commercial transactions, it would appear that any commercially recognized method of transferring funds, the result of which is to give the transferee the immediate use of the funds transferred, will nowadays suffice.[91]

[83] See, e.g. the Sale of Goods Act 1979, s. 31(2), *ante*, p. 145.

[84] *Walton* v. *Mascall* (1844) 13 M. & W. 452, *per* Parke B. at p. 458.

[85] C.P.R. r. 37.3.

[86] In the absence of such terms a tender of goods must be made at a reasonable hour: Sale of Goods Act 1979, s. 29(5).

[87] The Currency and Bank Notes Act 1954; the Coinage Act 1971 and the Currency Act 1983 define legal tender.

[88] *Betterbee* v. *Davis* (1811) 3 Camp. 70.

[89] *Finch* v. *Brook* (1834) 1 Bing. N.C. 253, *per* Vaughan J. at p. 257.

[90] *Farquharson* v. *Pearl Assurance Co. Ltd.* [1937] 3 All E.R. 124.

[91] *Tenax Steamship Co. Ltd.* v. *The Brimnes (Owners)* [1975] 1 Q.B. 929, at p. 963; *Mardorf Peach & Co. Ltd.* v. *Attica Sea Carriers Cpn. of Liberia* [1977] A.C. 850, at pp. 880, 885, 889; see *ante*, p. 504; *Libyan Arab Foreign Bank Co.* v. *Bankers Trust Co.* [1989] 1 Q.B. 728, at pp. 749–50.

(c) EARLY TENDER

A promisee need not, moreover, accept an early tender, but, as we have seen, if a bad tender is made before the time of performance has arrived, it does not generally prevent the promisor making another tender within time that does comply with the contract.[92]

X. PARTIAL PERFORMANCE

(a) ENTIRE AND DIVISIBLE OBLIGATIONS

Since the performance of a contractual obligation must be precise and exact, where one party's performance is made conditional on complete and entire performance by the other party,[93] at common law[94] the general rule is that the other can recover nothing for incomplete performance. It is immaterial how the failure to effect complete performance comes about. It may be due to a deliberate abandonment of the contract, to a negligent act or omission, or to a simple misfortune occurring without any fault. In *Cutter* v. *Powell*,[95] for example:

A seaman was engaged to act as second mate on a voyage from Jamaica to Liverpool. He was to be paid 30 guineas, almost four times the going rate, in a single payment upon completion of the voyage. Nineteen days out from Liverpool, when the voyage was nearly completed, he died. His widow sued to recover a proportion of the agreed sum.

Her action failed. The seaman's obligation was construed as an entire contract or, more accurately, an entire obligation, that is to say, if the voyage was completed he was to receive the stipulated sum, but, if it was not, he was to receive nothing. As Sir George Jessel M.R. said; 'if a shoemaker agrees to make a pair of shoes, he cannot offer you one shoe and ask you to pay half the price'.[96]

   The reason it is inaccurate to refer to 'entire' contracts, is that it is very unlikely that complete performance of each and every obligation in a contract by one party is a condition precedent to the liability of the other. The contract may, for example, be a complex one, composed of a number of undertakings differing in character or importance; or it may be a promise to do a number of successive acts; or to do a single

---

   [92] *Ante*, p. 508.
   [93] See Williams (1941) 57 L.Q.R. 373; Treitel (1967) 30 M.L.R. 139, at p. 141 ff; Law Com. No. 121, *Pecuniary Restitution on Breach of Contract* (1983). Mr Brian Davenport Q.C. dissented and the government rejected the report: 19th Annual Report (1983–84) Law Com. No. 140, § 2.11.
   [94] For statutory exceptions, see Apportionment Act 1870 (rents, annuities, dividends, and other periodic payments in the nature of income *prima facie* considered as accruing from day to day); Law Reform (Frustrated Contracts) Act 1943, *post*, p. 557.
   [95] (1795) 6 Term R. 320; Stoljar (1956) 34 Can. Bar Rev. 288. But the effect of this decision has been alleviated by statute: see the Law Reform (Frustrated Contracts) Act 1943; *post*, p. 557, and what is now the Merchant Shipping Act 1995, s. 38.
   [96] *Re Hall & Barker* (1878) 9 Ch. D. 538, at p. 545.

act which can be partly or defectively performed.[97] Very often a contract may be entire as to one aspect but 'divisible' or 'severable' (in the sense that the right to payment accrues incrementally as the performance is rendered) as to another. For example, in *Cutter v. Powell*, although the seaman's obligation to complete the voyage was entire, his obligation to exercise reasonable care in the performance of his duty was unlikely to be entire, so that, had he completed the voyage, but had performed his duty badly, it seems he would have been able to recover his wages, subject to a claim against him for poor work.[98] Again, in contracts for the carriage of goods by sea, whereas the obligation to deliver the cargo to the stipulated port is entire, so that no freight at all is payable if delivery is made at an intermediate port,[99] the obligations with respect to the quantity or condition of the cargo are not, so that, if half the cargo is delivered, half the freight is payable,[100] and if all the cargo arrives damaged (but still of the same commercial description), freight will be payable subject to a counterclaim against the carrier for damages.[101]

Because the consequences can be draconian, Courts are reluctant to construe an obligation as 'entire'.[102] But where the payment for the performance was to be a lump sum to be paid after completion they have generally done so, so that the promisee cannot recover anything until the work is completely executed.[103] Thus, apart from *Cutter* v. *Powell*, this construction has been put on obligations by a builder to build two houses and stables for a client,[104] and by a plumber to supply and install a combined central heating and hot water system in a private house.[105]

(i) Rationale of rule

The general rule has been justified in a number of ways.[106] First, the recipient of the performance has not contracted to buy part of the performance for a proportionate part of the price and should not be compelled to pay for performance that is different to that agreed, and, in some cases, insisted upon.[107] Where, like the seaman in *Cutter* v.

---

[97] See the discussion in *Baltic Shipping Co.* v. *Dillon* (1992–93) 176 C.L.R. 344, at pp. 350, 384 (High Court of Australia).

[98] Law Com. No. 121, *Pecuniary Restitution on Breach of Contract* (1983), § 2.12, citing Somervell L.J. in *Hoenig* v. *Isaacs* [1952] 2 All E.R. 176, at p. 178.

[99] *St. Enoch S.S. Co. Ltd.* v. *Phosphate Mining Co.* [1916] 2 K.B. 624; *Metcalfe* v. *Brittania Iron Works Co.* (1877) 2 Q.B.D. 423.

[100] *Ritchie* v. *Atkinson* (1808) 10 East 295, at 530. But where there is a stipulation for lump freight or freight to be computed on loading, the carrier will be entitled to full freight: *Aires Tanker Corp.* v. *Total Transport Ltd (The Aires)* [1977] 1 W.L.R. 185; *Colonial Bank* v. *European Grain & Shipping Ltd. (The Dominique)* [1989] A.C. 1056. See further *Scrutton on Charterparties*, 20th edn. (1996) art. 166.

[101] *Dakin* v. *Oxley* (1864) 15 C.B.(N.S.) 646, at p. 667. See further *Scrutton on Charterparties* (*supra*, n. 100).

[102] *Button* v. *Thompson* (1869) L.R. 4 C.P. 330, at p. 342.

[103] *Appleby* v. *Myers* (1867) L.R. 2 C.P. 651 at pp. 660–1, *The Madras* [1898] P. 90, and *Sumpter* v. *Hedges* [1898] 1 Q.B. 190, *post*, p. 514, appear to adopt this as a general rule. For criticism, see *post*.

[104] *Sumpter* v. *Hedges* (*supra*, n. 103).

[105] *Bolton* v. *Mahadeva* [1972] 1 W.L.R. 1009.

[106] See generally, Waddams in Reiter and Swan, eds., *Studies in Contract Law* (1980) p. 163 ff; Law Com. No. 121, *Pecuniary Restitution on Breach of Contract* (1983), §2.24–2.26.

[107] *Wiluszynski* v. *Tower Hamlets L.B.C.* [1989] I.C.R. 493; *Miles* v. *Wakefield M.B.C.* [1987] A.C. 539, *post*, p. 515; *British Telecommunications plc* v. *Ticehurst* [1992] I.C.R. 383.

Powell, the performer is to be paid significantly more than the going rate for the job, it can also be said that he has accepted the risk of incomplete or defective performance. Secondly, the rule holds people to their contracts and gives them a strong incentive to complete.[108] It is particularly important where there is inequality of bargaining power or scope for opportunistic behaviour, as there often is in contracts for small building works on private houses. It is all too common for a builder not to complete one job before moving on to the next, and the rule enables the householder to withhold all payment unless the job is finished.[109] Thirdly, the losses the innocent party suffers may be ones for which the law finds it difficult to compensate.[110]

(ii) Critique of rule

The principle precluding recovery, however, if rigorously applied, could be productive of great injustice. It is hard to contend, for example, that even the most trivial defect of workmanship in the decoration of a flat,[111] or some momentary slip or inefficiency on the part of an employee,[112] should entitle the 'injured' party to refuse all payment save where the injured party has made it absolutely clear that the trivial defect or breach will have this effect.[113] It should not, accordingly, be inferred, as it has been,[114] that such penal consequences follow from the mere postponement of payment of a lump sum by one party until after the other party has completely performed.[115] Such postponement may be prompted by a number of other reasons, including easing the 'cash-flow' of the party who will have to pay, and protecting that party from the risk that the other may become insolvent. Moreover, the application of the principle would often result in the unjust enrichment of the injured party if that party could retain the benefit of the incomplete performance without the necessity of paying for it. A general acceptance of the risk of incomplete performance by the part performer may not extend to a situation where the other party is incontrovertibly benefited, and a restitutionary remedy does not necessarily constitute a redistribution of risks allocated by the contract.[116]

The unpalatable consequences that can follow have led Courts to seek to avoid construing an obligation as entire. Broadly speaking this can properly be done in two

---

[108] *Munro* v. *Butt* (1858) 8 E. & B. 735, at p. 754; Law Com. No. 121, *Pecuniary Restitution on Breach of Contract* (1983), § 2.25.

[109] *Ibid.*, p. 37 (Mr B. J. Davenport Q.C.'s dissent). A builder may protect itself by requiring payments before the completion of performance, which (*post*, pp. 643, 647) will generally be irrecoverable. Note that in contracts for the sale of goods, consumers have wider power of rejection than others: Sale of Goods Act 1979, ss. 15A(1), 30(2A), *infra*, n. 124.

[110] As in the case of non-pecuniary loss (*Vigers* v. *Cook* [1919] 2 K.B. 475; and see *post*, p. 592) or loss to a third party (*ante*, p. 424).

[111] *Hoenig* v. *Isaacs* [1952] 2 All E.R. 176 (contract price £750, defects remedied for £55).

[112] *Ibid.*, at p. 178.

[113] *Miles* v. *Wakefield M.B.C.* [1987] A.C. 539 at pp. 551, 561, 568; *Wiluszynski* v. *Tower Hamlets L.B.C.* [1989] I.C.R. 493 at pp. 500, 503.

[114] *Supra*, n. 103.

[115] Law Com. No. 121, *Pecuniary Restitution on Breach of Contract* (1983), §§ 2.11, 2.27 and 2.67; Williams (1941) 57 L.Q.R. 373, at pp. 389 ff.

[116] Although it *might* do so; see Beatson, *The Use and Abuse of Unjust Enrichment* (1991), ch. 4, and *Wiluszynski* v. *Tower Hamlets L.B.C.* [1989] I.C.R. 493, *post*, p. 515.

situations; where the injured party has *accepted* the partial performance, and, although this is not so clearly established, where the part performer can establish that the services rendered or the work done has *incontrovertibly benefited* the other party so as to give rise to a claim in restitution. The underdevelopment of the law of restitution until recently and the tendency to construe an obligation as 'entire' simply because the contract provides for a lump sum has, however, also led to authority favouring a remedy in a third situation; where the part performer has *substantially performed* the 'entire' obligation.

(b) DOCTRINE OF 'SUBSTANTIAL PERFORMANCE'

Where the contract is *substantially* performed, there is authority that the injured party is not discharged from the obligation to pay, but is protected by a counterclaim or set-off for any loss which may have been sustained by reason of the incomplete or defective performance.[117] A Court will hold a contract to have been substantially performed if the actual performance falls not far short of the required performance, and if the cost of remedying the defects is not too great in amount in comparison with the contract price.[118] In *Dakin (H.) & Co. Ltd.* v. *Lee*:[119]

D were builders who had contracted to execute certain repairs to L's premises for £1,500. They carried out a substantial part of the contract, but failed to perform it exactly in three unimportant respects (which could have been rectified at a cost of £80). The official referee appointed by the parties held that D were consequently not entitled to recover any part of the contract price.

On appeal, it was held that this finding was erroneous. The contract had been substantially, if not precisely, performed. Pickford L.J. stated that the fact that the work was done badly did not mean that it had not been performed at all.[120] D was accordingly entitled to recover the price less a reduction for the breach. In the USA a more flexible approach has been taken whereby the Court may look at the quality of performance so that, even if the cost of compliance is great, there may still be substantial performance if the work that is done is of the same quality as that contracted for. In *Jacob & Youngs Inc.* v. *Kent* the New York Court of Appeals held that a builder who failed to use galvanized piping of 'Reading manufacture' for the plumbing in a building had substantially performed the contract; the pipes in fact used were of the same quality as those specified and the defect could only be remedied by demolishing a substantial

---

[117] *Boone* v. *Eyre* (1779) 1 H. Bl. 273; *Broom* v. *Davis* (1794) 7 East 480n; *Bolton* v. *Mahadeva* (*supra*, n. 105), at p. 1015; *Sim* v. *Rotherham Metropolitan Borough Council* [1987] Ch. 216, at p. 253; *Wiluszynski* v. *Tower Hamlets L.B.C.* [1989] I.C.R. 493, at p. 499; *Williams* v. *Roffey Bros. & Nicholls (Contractors) Ltd.* [1991] 1 Q.B. 1, at pp. 8–10, 17.

[118] Compare *Hoenig* v. *Isaacs* [1952] 2 All E.R. 176 (cost of remedying defects was 7.3 per cent of contract price) and *Bolton* v. *Mahadeva* [1972] 1 W.L.R. 1009 (no substantial performance where cost of remedying defects was 31 per cent of contract price).

[119] [1916] 1 K.B. 566, at p. 579. Note Greer L.J.'s criticism in *Eshelby* v. *Federated European Bank Ltd.* [1932] 1 K.B. 423, at p. 431 and cf. *Vigers* v. *Cook* [1919] 2 K.B. 475; *Bolton* v. *Mahadeva* [1972] 1 W.L.R. 1009.

[120] This suggests that on true analysis the obligation concerning the *quality* of the work may not have been entire. See Williams (1941) 57 L.Q.R. 373, at pp. 386–7, and see *ante*, p. 511.

part of the building.[121] There are indications that this approach may also be taken in English law.[122]

Since the basis of the rules governing entire obligations is that the parties have made *complete* and *precise* performance by one party a condition to entitlement to performance by the other, it is submitted that it is logically difficult to justify applying a principle of substantial performance to such obligations. To do so is to set aside the contractual allocation of risks. But the cases which have construed an obligation as entire simply because the contract provided for a lump sum to be paid after the completion of performance provide some pragmatic justification, since this fact alone may not truly indicate that the risks of any trivial incompleteness in performance are to lie with the part performer. On principle, however, the correct approach is greater caution in the categorization of an obligation as entire, and development of the emerging restitutionary principles to which we now turn.

(c) ACCEPTANCE OF PARTIAL PERFORMANCE BY INNOCENT PARTY

A party who renders incomplete performance of an entire contract may nevertheless claim remuneration where the other party has freely accepted such partial performance or otherwise waived the need for complete performance. So, if the customer of Sir George Jessel's shoemaker had accepted one shoe he would have been obliged to pay for the shoe he accepted.[123] In the case of the sale of goods, section 30(1) of the Sale of Goods Act 1979 provides:

Where the seller delivers to the buyer a quantity of goods less than he contracted to sell, the buyer may reject them, but if the buyer accepts the goods so delivered he must pay for them at the contract rate.[124]

In most cases, such a claim will arise upon a *quantum meruit*, that is to say, for a reasonable sum in respect of the services rendered or the work done by the partial performance. But it will only do so if the party not in default has the option whether to accept or to refuse the partial performance. Thus in *Sumpter* v. *Hedges*:[125]

S agreed to erect two houses and stables on H's land for £565. He failed to complete the contract. H thereupon completed the buildings himself, using the materials left on the site by S. S brought an action to recover the value of the work done before he abandoned the contract, and also claimed in respect of the building materials used.

It was held that S was entitled to recover the value of the materials left which H used, for H had the choice whether or not to use these to complete the building. But S could

---

[121] 129 NE 889 (1921).

[122] In *Ruxley Electronics Ltd.* v. *Forsyth* [1996] 1 A.C. 344, *post*, p. 598 (not involving an entire obligation), *ibid.*, at p. 363, *Jacob & Youngs Inc.* v. *Kent*, was approved in a slightly different context.

[123] *Ante*, p. 510. See also *Baltic Shipping Co.* v. *Dillon* (1992–93) 176 C.L.R. 344, at p. 378.

[124] But a non-consumer may not reject where the shortfall or breach of the conditions implied by ss. 13–15 of the 1979 Act is so slight that it would be unreasonable for him to do so: 1979 Act, ss. 30(2A), and 15A, inserted by the Sale and Supply of Goods Act 1994.

[125] [1898] 1 Q.B. 673. See also *Munro* v. *Butt* (1858) 8 E. & B. 738; *Forman & Co. Proprietary Ltd.* v. *Ship 'Liddesdale'* [1900] A.C. 190.

not recover for the work he had done, for H had no option but to accept the partly-erected building which was on his land. Similarly, an employer who told employees working 'to rule' and not carrying out part of their contractual services not to come to work at all unless they were prepared to work normally, was not held to have 'accepted' the partial performance simply because it did not send them home; '[a] person is not treated by the law as having chosen to accept that which is forced down his throat despite his objections'.[126]

Originally the basis of this liability was said to be that acceptance of partial performance implies a fresh agreement between the parties to pay for the work already done or goods supplied[127] but the implication of such a contract can be fictional, and, in such cases, it is better to regard the obligation to pay as restitutionary arising from the operation of the principle of unjust enrichment.[128]

(d) INCONTROVERTIBLE BENEFIT

The failure of the claim in respect of the partially-erected building in *Sumpter* v. *Hedges* shows that the mere fact that a person appears to have benefited from the part performance of an entire obligation, does not suffice to ground a claim for recompense.[129] But, where it can be shown that the recipient of the part performance has gained a readily realizable financial benefit or has been saved expense which he must have incurred, there is some support for the view that the part performer would be entitled to reasonable remuneration[130] save where the parties have made it clear that the risk of non-completion is to be borne by the part performer even where there is such a benefit.[131]

---

[126] *Wiluszynski* v. *Tower Hamlets L.B.C.* [1989] I.C.R. 493, *per* Nicholls L.J. at p. 504, but see Mead (1990) 106 L.Q.R. 192. In *Miles* v. *Wakefield M.B.C.* [1987] A.C. 539, at pp. 553, 563, two of their Lordships suggested that, if the employer has not made it clear that reduced or inefficient work will not be accepted, the employee will be entitled to a reasonable sum for that reduced work. But, as the contract had not been discharged, there are formidable difficulties with any restitutionary claim: *post*, p. 651. Cf. Lord Bridge's doubts, *ibid.*, at p. 552. Lord Brandon and Lord Oliver reserved their opinions.

[127] *Sumpter* v. *Hedges* (*supra*, n. 103); *Steele* v. *Tardiani* (1946) 72 C.L.R. 386, at pp. 394, 402 (High Court of Australia).

[128] *Baltic Shipping Co.* v. *Dillon* (1992–93) 176 C.L.R. 344 at pp. 374, 385 (High Court of Australia). For the recognition of unjust enrichment in England, see *Lipkin Gorman* v. *Karpnale* [1991] A.C. 548, *ante*, p. 22.

[129] See also *Bolton* v. *Mahadeva* [1972] 1 W.L.R. 1009.

[130] *Hain S.S. Co. Ltd.* v. *Tate & Lyle Ltd.* (1936) 41 Com. Cas 350, *per* Lord Atkin, Lord Wright M.R., and Lord Maugham, at pp. 358, 367–8, 373; *Procter & Gamble Philippine Manufacturing Corp.* v. *Peter Cremer GmbH & Co. (The Manilla)* [1988] 3 All E.R. 843, at p. 855; *Miles* v. *Wakefield M.B.C.* (*supra*, n. 126) at pp. 553, 563. See also *Britton* v. *Turner* 6 N.H. 481; (1834) (New Hampshire). Cf. Beatson (1981) 98 L.Q.R. 389 at pp. 411, 413.

[131] Law Com. No. 121, *Pecuniary Restitution on Breach of Contract* (1983), §§ 2.66–2.69, 2.73, and see *supra*, n. 126.

13

DISCHARGE BY AGREEMENT

I. INTRODUCTION

Contract rests on the agreement of the parties: as it is their agreement which binds them, so by their agreement they may be discharged. And this mode of discharge may occur in one of four ways: by release under seal; by accord and satisfaction; by rescission of a contract which is still executory; or by the operation of some provision contained in the contract itself.

Two sources of difficulty, however, exist which render the topic of discharge by agreement one of considerable artificiality and refinement.

(a) CONSIDERATION APPLIES TO DISCHARGE

The first is that the doctrine of consideration applies to the discharge as well as to the formation of a contract.[1] As a result, a distinction has to be drawn between those situations where the contract is still *executory* on both sides, and those where the contract has been *executed* on one side. In the case of an executory contract, the consideration for the discharge by agreement is found in the relinquishment by each promisee of its right to performance. Where, however, the contract has been wholly executed by one party, leaving the other party still to perform its side of the obligation, as, for example, where A has sold and delivered goods to B, but B has not yet paid for them, any release of B would be purely gratuitous since A would not receive any benefit, nor would B suffer any detriment, by this action. This distinction was emphasized by Parke B. in *Foster* v. *Dawber*, when he said:[2]

It is competent for both parties to an executory contract, by mutual agreement, without any satisfaction, to discharge the obligation of that contract. But an executed contract cannot be discharged except by release under seal, or by performance of the obligation, as by payment, where the obligation is to be performed by payment.

The agreement to discharge must therefore be under seal, or be supported by some other consideration ('accord and satisfaction') on the part of the person seeking to be released.

---

[1] See *ante*, p. 108.
[2] (1851) 6 Exch. 839, at p. 851.

(b) CONTRACTS EVIDENCED BY WRITING

The second source of difficulty is that certain contracts are required by law to be evidenced by writing,[3] and it has been held that any subsequent variation of such a contract must also be proved by writing. But writing is not required for the rescission by agreement of such a contract, nor for the waiver of a term contained in it. The distinction between rescission, variation, and waiver is, as we shall see, a fine one, and there is much artificiality in the lines to be drawn between almost identical cases. The occasions on which this difficulty can arise have declined greatly since writing is a requirement for very few types of contract.[4] But writing is still required for contracts for the sale or other disposition of land and contracts of guarantee, so that it cannot be said that the difficulties have entirely disappeared.

II. FORMS OF DISCHARGE BY AGREEMENT

(a) RELEASE

The right to performance of a contract can be abandoned by release under seal. If a sealed instrument is employed, it is immaterial that the contract has been executed on one side, for the seal dispenses with the need for consideration. A release not under seal requires consideration. The agreement is then discharged by accord and satisfaction. A release is construed in the same way as any other contract. It has been held that a general release could not be interpreted as covering rights which the parties had no idea existed.[5]

An agreement not to sue in perpetuity amounts to a release,[6] but, at common law, an agreement not to sue for a limited period merely gave rise to a cross-action for damages.[7] Equity, however, would restrain the promisor from suing within that time,[8] and today the equitable rule prevails so that the agreement acts as a bar to the original action.[9]

(b) ACCORD AND SATISFACTION

Discharge of a contract in return for a consideration which consists in some satisfaction other than the performance of the original obligation is termed 'accord and satisfaction':

[3] See *ante*, p. 77.

[4] See *ante*, p. 77.

[5] *B.C.C.I. S.A.* v. *Ali* [2001] 2 W.L.R. 734 (Lord Hoffmann dissenting). It did not release rights to stigma damages (*post*, p. 594) which the law did not recognize at the time of the release.

[6] *Hodges* v. *Smith* (1599) Cro. Eliz. 623. See, however, *Cutler* v. *McPhail* [1962] 2 Q.B. 292, at p. 298.

[7] *Ford* v. *Beech* (1848) 11 Q.B. 852.

[8] *Beech* v. *Ford* (1848) 7 Hare 208.

[9] Supreme Court Act 1981, s. 49.

Accord and satisfaction is the purchase of a release from an obligation, whether arising under contract or tort by means of any valuable consideration, not being the actual performance of the obligation itself. The accord is the agreement by which the obligation is discharged. The satisfaction is the consideration which makes the agreement operative.[10]

It is effective to discharge any contract, whether executory or executed, and even if it is under seal.[11]

(i) Executory satisfaction

Formerly, a contractual obligation, or cause of action arising from the breach of a contract, was not discharged so long as the satisfaction remained executory, that is, so long as the agreement to furnish new consideration had not been carried out.[12] As it was said in an old case:[13] 'Accord executed is satisfaction; accord executory is only substituting one cause of action in the room of another, which might go on to any extent'. But the question is now regarded as one of the construction of the agreement; and the promise only, as distinct from the actual performance of it, may be a good satisfaction and discharge the original obligation, if it clearly appears that the parties so intended.[14] The original obligation or claim is then discharged from the date the promise is accepted. If the promisor fails to perform its promise, the promisee's only remedy is to sue for breach of the promise, and it cannot return to the original obligation or claim.[15]

It must be remembered, however, that the rule in *Pinnel's Case*[16] prescribes that the payment of a smaller sum in satisfaction of a larger is not a good discharge of a debt. So if B owes A the sum of £50 for goods sold and delivered, and A agrees to excuse him £45 out of this amount, the debt is not discharged by the payment of £5. But the receipt by A of some satisfaction different in kind, or of a fixed instead of an uncertain sum, or of a lesser sum at an earlier date or in a different place than that required by the contract, is sufficient. Compromises of a disputed claim,[17] compositions with creditors,[18] and payments by a third party,[19] also afford exceptions to this rule.

(ii) Promissory estoppel

Accord without satisfaction is of no effect, and it is still a matter of some doubt whether the principle of promissory estoppel considered above in Chapter 3 could be

---

[10] *British Russian Gazette and Trade Outlook Ltd. v. Associated Newspapers Ltd.* [1933] 2 K.B. 616, *per* Scrutton L.J. at p. 643.

[11] *Steeds v. Steeds* (1889) 22 Q.B.D. 537.

[12] *Peytoe's Case* (1612) 9 Co. Rep. 79b.

[13] *Lynn v. Bruce* (1794) 2 H. Bl. 317, *per* Eyre L.C.J. at p. 319.

[14] *Good v. Cheesman* (1831) 2 B. & Ad. 328; *Morris v. Baron & Co.* [1918] A.C. 1, at p. 35; *British Russian Gazette and Trade Outlook Ltd. v. Associated Newspapers Ltd.* (*supra*, n. 10), at pp. 650, 654–5; *Jameson v. Central Electricity Generating Board* [1998] Q.B. 323, at p. 335.

[15] *British Russian Gazette and Trade Outlook Ltd. v. Associated Newspapers Ltd.* (*supra*, n. 10), at pp. 644, 654; *Green v. Rozen* [1955] 1 W.L.R. 741.

[16] (1602) 5 Co. Rep. 117a; *ante*, p. 108; *Ferguson v. Davis* [1997] 1 All E.R. 315.

[17] See *ante*, p. 101, and see *Kitchen Design & Advance Ltd. v. Lea Valley Water Co.* [1989] 2 Lloyd's Rep. 221.

[18] See *ante*, p. 111.

[19] See *ante*, p. 111.

successfully relied upon to obviate the necessity for consideration where the accord involves the permanent abandonment by one party of his right to performance by the other. It is questionable whether the principle extends this far. The view has been advanced that promissory estoppel serves only to suspend, and not totally to extinguish, existing rights,[20] although it is probable that this is not a necessary limitation on the doctrine.

(iii) Bills of exchange

One important exception does, however, exist. It was a rule of the law merchant, imported into the common law, that no satisfaction was required for the discharge of a bill of exchange or promissory note. The Bills of Exchange Act 1882, section 62, has given statutory force to this rule, but subject to the provision that the discharge must be in writing, or the bill delivered up to the acceptor.

(c) RESCISSION

(i) By agreement

A contract which is executory on both sides may be discharged by agreement between the parties that it shall no longer bind them. This effects a rescission of the contract, and it releases the parties from their obligations under it. Such an agreement is formed of mutual promises, and the consideration for each promise of each party is the abandonment by the other of its rights under the contract.

(ii) Abandonment

The Court can infer from a long period of delay or inactivity that the parties have agreed to abandon their contract. It must be shown that one party conducted itself in such a way that the other party reasonably assumed that it was agreed that the contract was abandoned.[21] Courts have come close to inferring an offer to abandon a contract from mere silence, although some overt act is almost always likely to be required.[22] In the case of arbitration, legislation now gives arbitrators the power to dismiss a claim for want of prosecution irrespective of whether the arbitration contract has been abandoned.[23]

(iii) Substituted contract

Rescission of a contract may also take place by such an alteration in its terms as substitutes a new contract for the old one. The old contract may be expressly discharged in the new one, or discharge may be implied by the introduction of new terms or new parties. This method of discharge is therefore a form of rescission with a new contract superadded.

---

[20] *Ante*, p. 117.

[21] *Paal Wilson & Co. A/S* v. *Partenreederei Hannah Blumenthal* [1983] 1 A.C. 854, at pp. 865, 885, 914, 916, 924.

[22] On arbitration, see *ante*, pp. 30–1. On landlord and tenant, see *Collin* v. *Duke of Westminster* [1985] 1 Q.B. 581.

[23] Now contained in the Arbitration Act 1996, s. 41(3).

An example of the discharge of a contract by the substitution of new terms is
provided by *Morris* v. *Baron & Co.*:[24]

A dispute had arisen out of a contract for the sale of cloth and an action had been begun.
Before the case came on for trial the parties made an oral arrangement of which the chief
terms were that the action and counterclaim were to be withdrawn, an extension of credit
was to be given to the buyer for a sum admittedly due from him under the old contract, and,
as regards the balance of goods contracted for but undelivered, there was to be substituted
for a firm contract of sale an option for the buyer to take them if he pleased.

The House of Lords held that in these circumstances it must be concluded that the
parties had agreed to abrogate the old contract and substitute a new one for it.

Similarly, the introduction of new parties[25] may impliedly rescind an existing contract and substitute a new one for it:

Suppose A has entered into a contract with B and C, and that B and C agree among
themselves that C shall retire from the contract and cease to be liable upon it.

A may of course insist upon the continued liability of C; but if A continues to deal
with B after becoming aware of the retirement of C, A's conduct will probably justify
the inference that a new contract to accept the sole liability of B has been made, and A
cannot then hold C to the original contract. 'If one partner goes out of a firm, and
another comes in, the debts of the old firm may, by the consent of all three parties—
the creditor, the old firm, and the new firm—be transferred to the new firm',[26] and
this consent may be implied by conduct, if not expressed in words or writing.

(iv) Form of discharge by agreement

As regards the form needed for the expression of an agreement which purports to
rescind an existing contract, the old rule of the common law was that a contract under
seal could only be discharged by agreement expressed under seal. But, in equity, an
agreement to rescind which was not under seal afforded an equitable defence to an
action on the deed. Since the Judicature Acts the rule of equity prevails, and a contract
under seal may be rescinded by a parol contract.[27]

A parol or simple contract, whether in writing or not, may be discharged by a
subsequent agreement, either written or oral. Even when the original agreement is one
required by statute to be in or evidenced by writing, as in the case of contracts for the
sale or other disposition of land, or contracts of guarantee,[28] there is no need for a
written discharge since there is no requirement that they shall be dissolved in writing.
In *Morris* v. *Baron & Co.*,[29] for example, the original contract for the sale of cloth was
one which was required by section 4 of the Sale of Goods Act 1893 (now repealed) to

---

[24] [1918] A.C. 1.

[25] See also 'novation', *ante*, pp. 471, 485–6.

[26] *Hart* v. *Alexander* (1837) 2 M. & W. 484, *per* Parke B. at p. 493. In the case of partnership, these rules are
substantially embodied in the Partnership Act 1890, s. 17(3).

[27] *Berry* v. *Berry* [1929] 2 K.B. 316; Supreme Court Act 1981, s. 49.

[28] See *ante*, p. 77.

[29] [1918] A.C. 1.

be evidenced by writing. The substituted contract was itself unenforceable because it did not comply with that section. Nevertheless, it operated as a discharge of the old contract with the result that the buyer, who claimed damages for non-delivery of the goods alternatively under the original and under the substituted agreement, was unable to succeed on either ground.

Rescission of an agreement by substitution of new terms must, however, be distinguished in form and in effect from (i) variation, and (ii) forbearance or waiver.

(d) VARIATION

The parties to a contract may effect a variation of the contract by modifying or altering its terms by mutual agreement, but without intending to rescind it and to substitute a wholly new contract for it.[30] A contract may also give one of the parties the power unilaterally to vary the obligations, for example by a price variation clause, but in the case of consumer contracts, this power has been restricted by legislation.[31]

(i) Form of variation

A contract under seal may be varied, as it may be rescinded, by a parol contract.[32] A simple contract, again, whether in writing or not, may be varied by a subsequent agreement either written or oral. This in no way conflicts with the rule that extrinsic evidence is not admissible to vary or add to the contents of a written document, for that principle merely refers to the ascertainment of the *original* intention of the parties. It has no application to the case of a *subsequent* variation.[33] But a contract required by law to be evidenced by writing must be varied in writing. In *Goss v. Lord Nugent*:[34]

By an agreement in writing G had contracted to sell to N several lots of land and to make good title to them. It was afterwards discovered that a good title could not be made to one of the lots, and N orally agreed not to insist on a good title to that lot. N later, relying on the defective title, refused to pay the purchase money.

The contract being one for the sale of land, it was required to be evidenced in writing. The promise to accept the defect in title would operate to vary that contract. But the Court held that G could not rely on this variation as it was merely oral, and N was therefore entitled to succeed on the ground that a good title had not been made.

Whether there has been a mere variation of terms or a rescission must depend upon the intention of the parties in each particular case and the question is often not

---

[30] *British and Beningtons Ltd.* v. *North Western Cachar Tea Co. Ltd.* [1923] A.C. 48; Stoljar (1957) 35 Can. Bar. Rev. 485; Dugdale and Yates (1976) 39 M.L.R. 680.

[31] *Lombard Tricity Finance Ltd.* v. *Paton* [1989] 1 All E.R. 916; Unfair Terms in Consumer Contracts Regulations 1999 (S.I. 1999 No. 2083), *ante*, p. 200.

[32] *Berry* v. *Berry* [1929] 2 K.B. 316.

[33] *Goss* v. *Lord Nugent* (*infra*, n. 34), at p. 64.

[34] (1833) 5 B. & Ad. 58. See also *Noble* v. *Ward* (1867) L.R. 2 Ex. 135; *United Dominions Trust (Jamaica) Ltd.* v. *Shoucair* [1969] 1 A.C. 340; *New Hart Builders Ltd.* v. *Brindley* [1975] Ch. 342.

an easy one to determine; but the following test has been suggested by Lord Dunedin:[35]

In the first case [variation] there are no such executory clauses in the second arrangement as would enable you to sue upon that alone if the first did not exist; in the second [rescission] you could sue on the second arrangement alone, and the first contract is got rid of either by express words to that effect, or because, the second dealing with the same subject-matter as the first but in a different way, it is impossible that the two should be both performed. When I say you could sue on the second alone, that does not exclude cases where the first is used for mere reference, in the same way as you may fix a price by a price list, but where the contractual force is to be found in the second by itself.

The changes must go to the 'very root' of the original agreement,[36] and 'there should have been made manifest the intention in any event of a complete extinction of the first contract, and not merely the desire of an alteration, however sweeping, in terms which leave it still subsisting'.[37]

(ii) Consideration for variation

A variation involves a definite alteration, *as a matter of contract*, of contractual obligations by the mutual agreement of both parties.[38] It must be supported by consideration. In most cases, consideration for the variation can be found in a mutual abandonment of existing rights or the conferment of new benefits by each party on the other.[39] Alternatively, consideration may be found in the assumption of additional obligations or the incurring of liability to an increased detriment.[40] Although an agreement whereby one party undertakes an additional obligation, but the other party is merely bound to perform its existing obligations, will, as a general rule, not be effective to vary a contract, as no consideration is present,[41] it has been held that the contract may exceptionally be varied where the Court can identify a 'practical' benefit to the party undertaking the additional obligation.[42] And if one party merely agrees not to enforce one of the terms of the contract to be performed by the other, this does not constitute a variation. Such an agreement may, however, be binding as a waiver[43] or in equity.[44]

---

[35] *Morris* v. *Baron & Co.* [1918] A.C. 1, at p. 26.

[36] *British and Beningtons Ltd.* v. *North Western Cachar Tea Co. Ltd.* [1923] A.C. 48, *per* Lord Sumner at p. 68.

[37] *Morris* v. *Baron & Co.* (*supra*, n. 35), *per* Lord Haldane at p. 19.

[38] *Besseler Waechter Glover & Co.* v. *South Derwent Coal Co.* [1938] 1 K.B. 408, *per* Goddard J. at p. 416.

[39] *Re William, Porter & Co. Ltd.* [1937] 2 All E.R. 361; *W. J. Alan & Co. Ltd.* v. *El Nasr Export and Import Co.* [1972] 2 Q.B. 189.

[40] *North Ocean Shipping Co. Ltd.* v. *Hyundai Construction Co. Ltd.* [1979] Q.B. 705.

[41] *Stilk* v. *Myrick* (1809) 2 Camp. 317; *Syros Shipping Co. S.A.* v. *Elaghill Trading Co.* [1980] 2 Lloyd's Rep. 390; see *ante*, pp. 105–6.

[42] *Williams* v. *Roffey Bros. & Nicholls (Contractors) Ltd.* [1991] 1 Q.B. 1; *Anangel Atlas Compania Naviera S.A.* v. *Ishikawajima-Harima Heavy Industries Co. Ltd. (No. 2)* [1990] 2 Lloyd's Rep 526, *ante*, p. 107. Cf. *Re Selectmove Ltd.* [1995] 1 W.L.R. 474, *ante*, p. 108.

[43] See *infra*.

[44] See *ante*, p. 112; *post*, p. 525.

(e) WAIVER

A party who voluntarily agrees to forbear from insisting on the mode of performance or time of performance fixed by the contract, or forbears from so insisting, will be held to have waived the right to require that the contract be performed by the other party in accordance with its terms. But 'waiver' is a term which bears many meanings, has been criticized as a 'slippery word worn smooth with overuse',[45] and, as we shall see, is also used to refer to an election between inconsistent rights. Waiver is relevant where difficulties of form or absence of consideration mean that there is no variation of the contract. Waiver was developed by the common law mainly as a device for evading the formal requirements of the Statute of Frauds, but because, as we have noted, formal requirements are much less important in the modern law, this aspect is now of less importance, although still relevant for certain types of contract, such as contracts for the sale of land and guarantees.[46]

(i) Form of waiver

Where a contract has to be by deed, or in, or evidenced by, writing, an oral agreement to forbear, for example by acceding to a request to extend the time of performance, might be met by the plea that the contract had been discharged by an alteration of the time of performance, that a new contract was thereby created, and that the new contract was unenforceable for non-compliance with the statutory requirements as to form.[47] Alternatively, the party which agreed to extend the time for performance, if sued by the other party, might plead that the other party was never ready and willing to perform within the time originally fixed for performance. A party thus given more time for performance, could not rely on the assent of the other to this, as this constituted a variation of the contract which was nugatory since it was not in writing.[48]

(ii) Variation and waiver distinguished

In order to overcome these difficulties, and so that statutory requirements of formality might not become a cloak for fraud, the Courts showed themselves willing to draw a distinction between variation on the one hand and mere waiver or forbearance on the other. Whereas the former might, in the cases previously mentioned, be required to be in writing, an oral waiver would be efficacious although not in the statutory form. In *Levey & Co.* v. *Goldberg*,[49] for example:

G agreed in writing to buy from L certain cloth over £10 in value, delivery to be made within a specified time. At the request of G, L orally consented to withhold delivery during that period. Subsequently, however, before delivery was made, G sought to terminate the contract claiming that L had repudiated the contract by not being ready and willing to deliver the cloth within the contract time or within a reasonable time, and pleading the Sale of Goods Act, section 4, as a defence to L's subsequent action for non-acceptance of the goods.

---

[45] Roscoe Pound's forward to Ewart, *Waiver Distributed* (1917), vi. See also Carter (1991) 4 J.C.L. 59.
[46] *Ante*, p. 520, and see generally *ante*, Chapter 3.
[47] *Stead* v. *Dawber* (1839) 10 A. & E. 58.
[48] *Plevins* v. *Downing* (1876) 1 C.P.D. 220, at p. 225.
[49] [1922] 1 K.B. 688.

It was held that the forbearance by L at the request of G to deliver within the defined period did not constitute a variation but was a valid and effective waiver although not in writing. G was therefore liable for his failure to accept the cloth. The distinction between variation and waiver has been said to depend upon the intention of the parties;[50] for there to be a variation the parties must intend permanently to alter the contractual obligation; if the party forbearing wishes to preserve the possibility of reverting to the contract, it is at most, a waiver. The distinction is difficult to apply in practice,[51] and, although now much less important in respect of formal requirements, it is still important in commercial transactions.

(iii) Waiver does not require consideration

Waiver is important because it is an extremely common occurrence in commercial transactions. It is, however, open to the technical objection that it ought to have no binding force since it is gratuitous and made without consideration. As it benefits only the promisee, without any corresponding benefit to the promisor, the element of consideration is lacking. It should therefore be without legal effect. But the Courts have not hesitated to hold that the waiver of a contractual stipulation is valid and binding even though there is no consideration. The party granting the indulgence cannot go back on the promise and require strict adherence to the contract.[52] However, in cases of postponement of performance, if no period of postponement is fixed, that party may give reasonable notice to the other party requiring the contract to be performed within a certain time, and the contract must then be performed within that time.[53] Similarly, in cases of the waiver of other types of contractual term, the party granting the indulgence may as a general rule, upon reasonable notice, require the other party to comply with the original contractual stipulation; but cannot treat the forbearance as of no effect. In *Panoutsos v. Raymond Hadley Corporation of New York*:[54]

P contracted to buy from R.H. 4,000 tons of flour which R.H. was to ship to Greece, by means of separate shipments. The contract required payment to be effected by P opening a bankers' confirmed letter of credit in R.H.'s favour. P did open a letter of credit, but it was not 'confirmed'. R.H. made some shipments and received payment for these by this letter of credit. Subsequently, however, R.H. summarily terminated the remainder of the contract on the ground that the letter of credit was not in accordance with the contractual stipulation. P sued for breach.

It was held that R.H., by its acceptance of payment by means of the unconfirmed letter of credit, had impliedly waived this condition in the contract. This, however, did not

---

[50] *Stead v. Dawber* (1839) 10 A. & E. 57; *Tallerman & Co. Pty. Co. Ltd. v. Nathan's Merchandise (Vic.) Pty. Ltd.* (1954) 91 C.L.R. 288, at p. 297 (High Court of Australia). Dugdale and Yates (1976) 39 M.L.R. 680 distinguish pre-breach statements which are likely to be variations from post-breach ones, which are not.

[51] Compare, e.g. *Goss v. Lord Nugent* (1833) 5 B. & Ad. 58 with *Hickman v. Haynes* (1875) L.R. 10 C.P. 598.

[52] *Leather Cloth Co. v. Hieronimus* (1875) L.R. 10 Q.B. 140; *Bruner v. Moore* [1904] 1 Ch. 305; *Besseler Waechter Glover & Co. v. South Derwent Coal Co.* [1938] 1 K.B. 408; *Tankexpress A/S v. Compagnie Financière Belge des Petroles S.A.* [1949] A.C. 76.

[53] *Charles Rickards Ltd. v. Oppenhaim* [1950] 1 K.B. 616.

[54] [1917] 2 K.B. 473.

mean that it was consequently bound to accept that letter of credit until the end of the contract; it might, by giving reasonable notice, insist on the strict contractual terms. But it was not entitled to cancel the contract in a summary manner.

(iv) Risk borne by party requesting forbearance

The party to whom the forbearance is granted is also bound by its terms.[55] Moreover, if that party asks to have the performance of the contract postponed, it does so at its own risk. For if that party subsequently refuses to accept the goods, and the market value of the goods which it should have accepted at the earlier date has altered at the later date, the measure of damages may be increased as against it by the addition of damages consequent on the delay.[56]

(v) Equitable estoppel

In developing waiver mainly as a common law device for evading the formalities required by the Statute of Frauds, little attempt was made to explain why a gratuitous promise should thus be binding. If it is to be justified analytically, it may be more satisfactory to regard waiver as a species of estoppel. It will be remembered that equity, by use of the principle of promissory estoppel,[57] is also prepared to give effect to a promise made in similar circumstances:

If persons who have contractual rights against others induce by their conduct those against whom they have such rights to believe that such rights will either not be enforced or will be kept in suspense or abeyance for some particular time, those persons will not be allowed by a court of equity to enforce the rights until such time has elapsed, without at all events placing the parties in the same position as they were before.[58]

The party who has waived strict performance may be said to be estopped from going back on the promise or representation to do so, at any rate without giving fair and adequate notice to the promisee.[59]

The similarity between waiver and estoppel was expressly noted by Denning L.J. in *Charles Rickards Ltd. v. Oppenhaim*:[60]

O ordered from C.R. a Rolls Royce car chassis, which was delivered to him. He wished to have a body built on the chassis, and C.R. accepted this order. The job was to be completed by 20 March 1948, at the latest. On that day it was still not completed, but O continued to press for delivery. On 29 June, however, he wrote to C.R. stating he would not take delivery after 25 July. C.R. still having failed to deliver the car, O treated the contract as repudiated.

The Court of Appeal held that he was entitled to do so. Although by his conduct he had impliedly waived the original stipulation as to time, he had given reasonable

---

[55] *Hickman v. Haynes* (1875) L.R. 10 C.P. 598; *Levey & Co. v. Goldberg* [1922] 1 K.B. 688.

[56] *Levey & Co. v. Goldberg* (*supra*, n. 55).

[57] See *ante*, p. 112.

[58] *Birmingham and District Land Co. v. L. & N.W. Ry.* (1888) 40 Ch. D. 268, *per* Bowen L.J. at p. 286.

[59] For recent discussion on waiver in the sense of estoppel see *Motor Oil Hellas (Corinth) Refineries SA v. Shipping Corp. of India (The Kanchenjunga)* [1990] 1 Lloyd's Rep 391; *Commonwealth of Australia v. Verwayen* (1990) 170 C.L.R. 394.

[60] [1950] 1 K.B. 616; cf. Stoljar (1957) 35 Can. Bar. Rev. 485.

notice of his intention to reimpose a new time limit. C.R. having failed even then to perform, the contract was clearly discharged by its breach. Denning L.J. said of O's consent to postponement:[61]

Whether it be called waiver or forbearance on his part, or an agreed variation or substituted performance, does not matter. It is a kind of estoppel. By his conduct he evinced an intention to affect their legal relations. He made, in effect, a promise not to insist on his strict legal rights. That promise was intended to be acted on, and was in fact acted on. He cannot afterwards go back on it.

The analogy, however, is not completely exact. It may be that promissory estoppel is more limited than waiver. For an estoppel to become binding, the promisee must alter its position in reliance on the promise. In fact, when waiver is used in the sense of estoppel, the focus of the law is on whether the dealings between the parties and the prejudice to the party who has been told that strict performance is not required are such as to render it inequitable for the other party to go back on its promise or representation.[62] But the requirement of reliance has not been strictly enforced for waiver,[63] although it is true to say that in cases of waiver of a time fixed for performance (but not in the case of waiver of other types of stipulation) it will usually be found to have been satisfied.

Waiver may also be used in the sense of election, that is, where a party is entitled either under the terms of the contract or by the general law, to choose between alternative and inconsistent rights.[64] Here the law focuses on that party's words, conduct, and knowledge to determine whether an election has been made.[65] Once an election is made it can be said that the party has waived the alternative and inconsistent right. For example, waiver may apply to conditions precedent,[66] to the right of one party to treat itself as discharged by reason of a repudiatory breach by the other,[67] or to terminate a contract for breach under an express contractual provision to that effect.[68] If a party elects to affirm the contract and thus waive its right to terminate, it will not be held to have waived (in the sense of an election) its right to damages for the breach unless the requirements of a waiver in the sense of estoppel are established to that effect.[69] Further, a party may, without the assent of the other party, waive compliance with a term of the con-

---

[61] At p. 623.

[62] See *ante*, pp. 114–15.

[63] *W. J. Alan & Co. Ltd.* v. *El Nasr Export and Import Co. Ltd.* [1972] 2 Q.B. 189, at p. 213, but cf. *ibid.*, at p. 221; *Finagrain S.A. Geneva* v. *P. Kruse Hamburg* [1976] 2 Lloyd's Rep. 508. See *ante*, p. 524.

[64] *Motor Oil Hellas (Corinth) Refineries S.A.* v. *Shipping Corp. of India (The Kanchenjunga)* [1990] 1 Lloyd's Rep 391, *per* Lord Goff at p. 398.

[65] See *United Australia Ltd.* v. *Barclays Bank Ltd.* [1941] A.C. 1, *per* Lord Atkin at p. 30.

[66] See *ante*, p. 135.

[67] See *post*, pp. 578–9.

[68] See *infra*.

[69] *Hain S.S. Co. Ltd.* v. *Tate & Lyle Ltd.* (1936) 41 Com. Cas. 350, at p. 363; [1936] 2 All E.R. 597, at p. 608; *Suisse Atlantique Societe d'Armament Maritime S.A.* v. *N.V. Rotterdamsche Kolen Centrale* [1967] 1 A.C. 361, at p. 395; *Motor Oil Hellas (Corinth) Refineries S.A.* v. *Shipping Corp. of India (The Kanchenjunga)* [1990] 1 Lloyd's Rep 391, at p. 400.

tract which is inserted solely for its own benefit.[70] When used in the sense of an election, waiver is always permanent; it cannot be reversed by the service of a notice.[71] This is to be contrasted to what was said above in relation to waiver in the sense of estoppel which can (but not always) be negated by the service of a notice.[72] In addition, when used in the sense of election there is no requirement of reliance and detriment although there is still a focus on words and conduct. Moreover, when used in the sense of estoppel there is no requirement of knowledge whereas with election there is a requirement that the promisee has knowledge of the facts which give rise to the right to elect and arguably in some cases knowledge of the right itself.[73]

(f) PROVISIONS FOR DISCHARGE CONTAINED IN THE CONTRACT ITSELF

A contract may contain within itself the elements of its own discharge, in the form of provisions, express or implied, for its determination or termination in certain circumstances. Apart from the statutory protection given to those dealing on the other party's standard terms[74] and to consumers,[75] and the power of the Court to give equitable relief against forfeiture,[76] there is no requirement that a party act reasonably when deciding to exercise a contractual power to terminate.

The parties may expressly provide that, upon the happening of a certain event, either the contract shall *ipso facto* determine,[77] or that, on the occurrence of that event, one party is to have the option to cancel the contract.[78]

(i) Automatic termination

Where the event is one over which the parties have no control and cannot bring about themselves, then effect will generally be given to a provision that the contract is *ipso facto* to cease to bind.[79] But if the relevant event is a breach of contract the courts are likely to interpret the contract as nevertheless requiring an election by the innocent party before holding that the contract is terminated. This is an application of the

---

[70] *Hawksley* v. *Outram* [1892] 3 Ch. 359. Cf. *Burgess* v. *Cox* [1951] Ch. 383; *Gregory v. Wallace* [1998] I.R.L.R. 387 (terms inserted for benefit of both parties).

[71] *Kammins Ballrooms Co. Ltd.* v. *Zenith Investments (Torquay) Ltd.* [1971] A.C. 850, at p. 883; *China National Foreign Trade Transportation Corporation* v. *Evologia Shipping Co. S.A. of Panama* [1979] 1 W.L.R. 1018, *per* Lord Scarman at p. 1034–5.

[72] *Motor Oil Hellas (Corinth) Refineries S.A.* v. *Shipping Corp. of India (The Kanchenjunga)* [1990] 1 Lloyd's Rep 391, at p. 399. See *ante*, p. 525 on estoppel.

[73] See *Peyman* v. *Lanjani* [1985] Ch 457. See further *post*, pp. 567–8.

[74] Unfair Contract Terms Act 1977, s. 3(2)(b)(ii).

[75] Unfair Terms in Consumer Contracts Regulations 1999 (S.I. 1999 No. 2083), Sched. 2, esp. para 1(f), (g), *ante*, p. 200; Consumer Credit Act 1974, ss. 76, 86, 87, 88, 98.

[76] This is considered *post*, pp. 647–8. See also Law of Property Act 1925, s. 146 (forfeiture of lease).

[77] *Continental Grain Export Corpn.* v. *S.T.M. Grain Ltd.* [1979] 2 Lloyd's Rep. 460.

[78] *Head* v. *Tattersall* (1871) L.R. 7 Ex. 7; *Brown* v. *Knowlsey B.C.* [1986] I.R.L.R. 102, *ante*, p. 138.

[79] *New Zealand Shipping Co.* v. *Société des Ateliers et Chantiers* [1919] A.C. 1, *per* Lord Wrenbury at p. 15; *Gyllenhammar & Partners International Ltd.* v. *Sour Brodogradevna Industrija* [1989] 2 Lloyd's Rep. 403, *per* Hirst J. at p. 413.

principle that a party may not rely on its own breach to bring the contract to an end;[80] i.e. a party may not take advantage of his or her own wrong.[81] The better view is that this is not an independent rule of law,[82] but a principle of construction reflecting the presumed intention of the parties, and which may be rebutted by the express terms of the contract.[83] Moreover, even if the event triggering the automatic termination provision is not a breach of contract, a party will not be able to take advantage of that provision if their wrongful action gave rise to the event upon which the automatic termination provision is based.[84]

(ii) Termination on notice

More often, a provision is inserted making the contract terminable at the option of one or both of the parties upon notice. This right of termination may be exercisable upon a breach of the contract by one party (whether or not the breach would amount to a repudiation of the contract),[85] or upon the occurrence or non-occurrence of a specified event other than breach,[86] or simply at the will of the party upon whom the right is conferred. For example, the contract may be terminable 'by 3 months' notice in writing on either side'. A similar provision may be incorporated by implication, or by the usage of trade. At common law,[87] for instance, a contract of employment may be terminated by reasonable notice by either party, the length of the notice depending upon the nature of the employment and the intervals at which remuneration is to be paid. Moreover, even where the duration of a written contract is on the face of the instrument indefinite and unlimited, such a provision may sometimes be implied from the nature of the contract,[88] particularly where the contract is for a fixed price[89]

---

[80] The principle does not apply if breach is of a duty owed to a person who is not a party to the contract: *Cheall* v. *Association of Professional Executive Clerical and Computer Staff* [1983] 2 A.C. 180, *per* Lord Diplock at p. 189 and *Thompson* v. *ASDA-MFI Group plc.* [1988] 1 Ch. 241, at p. 266.

[81] *Alghussein Establishment* v. *Eton College* [1988] 1 W.L.R. 587; *Cheall* v. *Association of Professional Executive Clerical and Computer Staff* (*supra*, n. 80); *Brown* v. *Knowsley B.C.* [1986] I.R.L.R. 102.

[82] *New Zealand Shipping Co.* v. *Société des Ateliers et Chantiers* (*supra*, n. 79); *Alghussein Establishment* v. *Eton College* (*supra*, n. 80); *Cheall* v. *Association of Professional Executive Clerical and Computer Staff* (*supra*, n. 81).

[83] See, e.g. *Gyllenhammar & Partners International Ltd.* v. *Sour Brodogradevna Industrija* [1989] 2 Lloyd's Rep. 403, *per* Hirst J. at p. 416.

[84] See *Cheall* v. *Association of Professional Executive Clerical and Computer Staff* (*supra*, n. 81), *per* Lord Diplock at p. 189. This principle means that even where such a provision declares that the contract is to be 'void', it is not absolutely so: *New Zealand Shipping Co.* v. *Société des Ateliers et Chantiers* (*supra*, n. 82) *per* Lord Wrenbury at p. 15. See also *post*, p. 550 (self-induced frustration).

[85] But cf. *Laing Management Ltd.* v. *Aegon Insurance Co. (U.K.) Ltd* (1998) 86 Build. L.R. 70 (reliance on contractual right to terminate did not constitute acceptance of repudiatory breach, *sed quaere*).

[86] *Mannai Investment Co. Ltd.* v. *Eagle Star Life Assurance Co. Ltd.* [1997] A. C. 749 ('break' clause in lease). See also *Head* v. *Tattersall* (1871) L.R. 7 Ex. 7 and, *ante*, p. 138 (condition subsequent).

[87] But see now the Employment Rights Act 1996, s. 86 (minimum periods of notice by employer).

[88] *Crediton Gas Co.* v. *Crediton U.D.C.* [1928] 1 Ch. 447; *Winter Garden Theatre (London) Ltd.* v. *Millennium Productions Ltd.* [1948] A.C. 173; *Re Spenborough U.D.C.'s Agreement* [1968] Ch. 139; Cf. *Kirklees Metropolitan B.C.* v. *Yorkshire Woollen District Transport Co.* (1978) 77 L.G.R. 448 (fixed term agreement could not be terminated by notice). See also Carnegie (1969) 85 L.Q.R. 392.

[89] *Staffordshire Area Health Authority* v. *South Staffs. Waterworks Co.* [1978] 1 W.L.R. 1387, on which see *post*, p. 550. Where there are price variation provisions, such an implied term is unlikely: *The Queensland Electricity Generating Board* v. *New Hope Collieries Pty Ltd.* [1989] 1 Lloyd's Rep. 205; *Watford Borough Council* v. *Watford Rural Parish* (1987) 86 L.G.R. 524 at p. 528.

or is a commercial contract.[90] Thus a partnership for no fixed time is terminable by notice.[91]

Any notice given must be clear and unambiguous in its terms, and if it is to be given in a certain form, e.g. in writing, or within a certain time, or if a specified period of notice must be given, these requirements must normally be strictly complied with, otherwise the notice will be of no effect.[92] Notwithstanding this *prima facie* rule, in interpreting a clause in a contract which lays down a procedure for the termination of the contract, the Court will have regard to the commercial purpose served by the clause.[93]

[90] *Martin-Baker Aircraft Co. Ltd.* v. *Canada Flight Equipment Ltd.* [1955] 2 Q.B. 556, at p. 577; *Re Spenborough U.D.C.'s Agreement* [1968] Ch. 139; *Watford Borough Council* v. *Watford Rural Parish* (*supra*, n. 89) at p. 532.

[91] Partnership Act 1890, s. 26.

[92] *Avofos Shipping Co. S.A.* v. *R. Pagnan & Filii* [1983] 1 W.L.R. 195. Cf. *Bremer Handelsgesellschaft mbH* v. *Vanden Avenne-Izegem P.V.B.A.* [1978] 2 Lloyd's Rep. 109; *ante*, p. 143.

[93] *Mannai Investment Co. Ltd.* v. *Eagle Star Life Assurance Co. Ltd.* [1997] A.C. 749 (minor misdescription did not preclude notice from being effective where, construed in its contractual setting, it would unambiguously inform a reasonable recipient how and when it was to operate); *Ellis Tylin Ltd.* v. *Co-operate Retail Services Ltd.* [1999] Build. L.R. 205.

14

DISCHARGE BY
FRUSTRATION

I. INTRODUCTION

Some legal systems accept that changes of circumstances may justify modifying a contract where to maintain the original contract would produce intolerable results incompatible with justice.[1] But many legal systems, including English law, concerned that modification would undermine certainty and alter the risks allocated by the contract, make provision for the discharge of a contract only where, after its formation, a change of circumstances makes contractual performance illegal or impossible. In English law, such a situation is provided for by the doctrine of frustration.[2] Originally, this term was confined to the discharge of maritime contracts by the 'frustration of the adventure', but it has now been extended to cover all cases where an agreement has been terminated by supervening events beyond the control of either party.[3] But the doctrine is not one of supervening impossibility; some kinds of impossibility may in some circumstances not discharge the contract at all, while impossibility does not accurately describe the cases of frustration of a commercial purpose where the fundamentally different situation which has unexpectedly occurred means that performance would be, as a matter of business, radically different from the contractually stipulated performance.[4] In these cases the contract is discharged although performance is not literally impossible.

The defining characteristics of the doctrine of frustration that have emerged from the case law have been summarized by Bingham L.J.[5] in the following terms:

The doctrine of frustration was evolved to mitigate the rigour of the common law's insistence on literal performance of absolute promises . . . The object of the doctrine was to give

---

[1] Lando & Beale, *Principles of European Contract Law* (2000) p. 328.

[2] See generally, Treitel, *Frustration and Force Majeure* (1994).

[3] Initial impossibility and misunderstandings that exist at the time of the formation of the contract, sometimes referred to as 'pre-contractual frustration', are considered *ante*, in Chapter 8. See esp. p. 313, and note that care should be taken not to treat such cases as frustration, cf. *Gamerco S.A.* v. *I.C.M./Fair Warning (Agency) Ltd.* [1995] 1 W.L.R. 1226, *quaere* wrongly so treated, see Carter and Tolhurst (1996) 10 J.C.L. 264, at pp. 265–6. See also *post*, p. 533.

[4] *Joseph Constantine Steamship Line Ltd.* v. *Imperial Smelting Corporation Ltd.* [1942] A.C. 154, *per* Viscount Simon, at p. 164. See also *Jackson* v. *Union Marine Insurance Co. Ltd.* (*post*, p. 533) and *Krell* v. *Henry* (*post*, p. 534).

[5] *J. Lauritzen A.S.* v. *Wijsmuller B.V. (The Super Servant Two)* [1990] 1 Lloyd's Rep. 1 at p. 8. For the facts, see *post*, p. 551.

effect to the demands of justice, to achieve a just and reasonable result, to do what is reasonable and fair, as an expedient to escape from injustice where such would result from enforcement of a contract in its literal terms after a significant change in circumstances . . . Since the effect of frustration is to kill the contract and discharge the parties from further liability under it, the doctrine is not to be lightly invoked, must be kept within narrow limits and ought not to be extended . . . Frustration brings the contract to an end forthwith, without more and automatically . . . The essence of frustration is that it should not be due to the act or election of the party seeking to rely on it . . . A frustrating event must be some outside event or extraneous change of situation . . . A frustrating event must take place without blame or fault on the side of the party seeking to rely on it.

In this chapter we trace the history of the doctrine and examine the scope of its present application. It should, however, be noted that as the doctrine has developed, so too has the use, particularly in standard form contracts, of *force majeure* clauses, which entitle one or both of the parties to be excused (in whole or in part) from performance of the contract. Such clauses may cover non-frustrating events and may provide for more flexible remedies than total discharge. For instance they may entitle a party to suspend performance, to claim an extension of time for performance, or to be compensated for performance which will be more onerous.[6]

II. EMERGENCE OF THE DOCTRINE

Before 1863 it was a general rule of the law of contract that a person was absolutely bound to perform any obligation which had been undertaken, and could not claim to be excused by the mere fact that performance had subsequently become impossible; for 'where there is a positive contract to do a thing, not in itself unlawful, the contractor must perform it or pay damages for not doing it, although in consequence of unforeseen accidents, the performance of his contract has become unexpectedly burdensome or even impossible'.[7] So in *Paradine* v. *Jane* in 1647:[8]

P sued J for rent due upon a lease. J pleaded 'that a certain German Prince, by name Prince Rupert, an alien born, enemy to the king and kingdom, had invaded the realm with an hostile army of men; and with the same force did enter upon the defendant's possession, and him expelled, and held out of possession . . . whereby he could not take the profits'. This plea was in substance a plea that the rent was not due because the lessee had been deprived, by events beyond his control, of the profits from which the rent should have come.

The Court held that this was no excuse:[9]

---

[6] On such clauses, which fall outside the scope of this book, see generally, *Channel Island Ferries Ltd.* v. *Sealink U.K. Ltd.* [1988] 1 Lloyd's Rep 323; Treitel, *Frustration and Force Majeure* (1994), §12–012 ff; McKendrick, *Force Majeure and Frustration of Contract*, 2nd edn. (1994), esp. chs. 1 and 3. For one other advantage, see *post*, p. 552.

[7] *Taylor* v. *Caldwell* (1863) 3 B. & S. 826, *per* Blackburn J. at p. 833.

[8] (1647) Aleyn 26 and Style 47. On the antecedents of this decision, see Ibbetson, ch. 1 in Rose, ed., *Consensus ad Idem* (1996).

[9] *Ibid.*, at p. 27.

When the party by his own contract creates a duty or charge upon himself, he is bound to make it good, if he may, notwithstanding any accident by inevitable necessity, because he might have provided against it by his contract. And therefore if the lessee covenant to repair a house, though it be burnt by lightning, or thrown down by enemies, yet he ought to repair it.

It has always, however, been open to the parties to introduce an express provision into their agreement that the fulfilment of a condition or the occurrence of an event should discharge one or both of them from some or all of their obligations under it;[10] and just as the parties may expressly discharge their obligation to perform a contract, so there are cases in which a contract, though containing no express provision, will be interpreted by the Courts as containing such a provision by implication. An implication of this nature would, it might be thought, readily be made where, without the fault of either party, an event occurs which renders the contract not merely more onerous, but completely impossible of performance.

This was the device[11] used by the Court of Queen's Bench in 1863 in the case of *Taylor* v. *Caldwell*[12] in order to introduce an exception into the existing law:

C agreed with T to hire to him a music-hall and gardens for the purpose of entertainment. Before the day of performance arrived, the music-hall was destroyed by fire. T sued C for damages for breach of the contract which C, through no fault of his own, was unable to perform.

C was held not liable to pay, for 'the contract is not to be construed as a positive contract, but as subject to an implied condition that the parties shall be excused in case, before breach, performance becomes impossible from the perishing of the thing without default of the contractor'.[13] Blackburn J. said:[14]

The principle seems to us to be that, in contracts in which the performance depends on the continued existence of a given person or thing, a condition is implied that the impossibility of performance arising from the perishing of the person or thing shall excuse the performance. In none of these cases is the promise in words other than positive, nor is there any express stipulation that the destruction of the person or thing shall excuse the performance; but that excuse is by law implied, because from the nature of the contract it is apparent that the parties contracted on the basis of the continued existence of the particular person or chattel.

From this time onwards the Courts showed themselves prepared to hold that, unless a contrary intention appears, the continuance of a contract was conditional upon the possibility of its performance.

It was not long, however, before the new doctrine was extended outside the sphere of literal impossibility to situations where there had been a 'frustration of the adventure'. Most of the early frustration cases arose out of delay, attributable to the fault of neither party, in the carrying out of charterparties; and they seem at first to have been

---

[10] See *ante*, p. 138.
[11] See Trakman (1983) 46 M.L.R. 39.
[12] (1863) 3 B. & S. 826.
[13] At p. 833.
[14] At p. 839.

treated as raising a question which was regarded as connected, rather than identical, with that raised by the cases of impossibility.

In *Jackson* v. *Union Marine Insurance Co. Ltd*.:[15]

J's ship had been chartered to proceed in January to Newport to load a cargo of iron rails for San Francisco. On the way to Newport she ran aground and it took over a month to refloat her. She was then taken into Liverpool and underwent lengthy repairs lasting until August. In the meantime the charterers had chartered another ship. The plaintiffs claimed from the defendant insurance company for a total loss, by perils of the sea, of the freight to be earned under the charterparty.

The question whether or not there had been such a loss depended for the answer on the question whether or not the charterers had been justified in throwing up their contract with J instead of waiting until the ship was repaired and then loading her. The jury found that the time necessary to get the ship off, and to repair her so that she might become a cargo-carrying ship, had been so long as to put an end in a commercial sense to the speculation entered into by J and the charterers; and on this finding the Court held that a voyage undertaken after the ship had been repaired would have been an adventure different from that which both parties had contemplated at the time of the contract. It was, they said, an implied term of the contract that the ship should arrive at Newport within a reasonable time, and her inability to arrive put an end to it. 'The adventure', said Bramwell B.,[16] 'was frustrated by perils of the seas, both parties were discharged, and a loading of cargo in August would have been a new adventure, a new agreement'.

The dislocation of business caused by the war with Germany from 1914 to 1918 brought a large number of frustration cases into the Courts, and it soon became clear that they raised the same questions as those raised by cases previously considered under the head of impossibility. 'When this question arises in regard to commercial contracts', said Lord Loreburn,[17] 'the principle is the same, and the language as to 'frustration of the adventure' merely adapts it to the class of cases in hand'. 'The doctrine of frustration is only a special case of the discharge of contract by an impossibility of performance arising after the contract was made.'[18] The modern practice is to use the term 'frustration' to cover cases of both classes.

III. INSTANCES OF FRUSTRATION

Before turning to the theoretical basis of the doctrine of frustration, we consider examples of factual situations in which the Courts have been ready to infer, from the nature of the contract and from the circumstances surrounding it, that it has been

---

[15] (1874) L.R. 10 C.P. 125.

[16] At p. 148.

[17] *F. A. Tamplin Steamship Co. Ltd*. v. *Anglo-Mexican Petroleum Products Ltd*. [1916] 2 A.C. 397, at p. 404.

[18] *Joseph Constantine Steamship Line Ltd*. v. *Imperial Smelting Corporation Ltd*. [1942] A.C. 154, *per* Viscount Maugham at p. 168.

frustrated by the happening of a subsequent event. While the reasoning in some of these examples is based on the 'implied term' theory of frustration, which, as we shall see, is now discredited, they remain useful illustrations of situations in which a contract may be frustrated.

(a) DESTRUCTION OF SUBJECT-MATTER OF CONTRACT

The most simple case is probably that where the performance of the contract is made impossible by the destruction of a specific thing *essential* to that performance, for example, the destruction of the music-hall in *Taylor v. Caldwell*. So if A agrees with B to supply and install certain machinery in B's factory premises, and the premises are destroyed by fire, the contract will be frustrated.[19] But if the machinery only is destroyed, leaving the premises untouched, then it is still possible to obtain other machinery and A must do the work over again: the contract will not be discharged.[20] Where an agreement for the sale of specific goods has been made and, before the risk passes to the buyer, without any fault on the part of the seller or buyer, the goods perish, the agreement is avoided.[21]

(b) NON-OCCURRENCE OF A PARTICULAR EVENT

The principle of frustration has also been held to apply to cases concerning the cancellation of an expected event. In the so-called 'Coronation cases', which arose out of the postponement of the coronation of King Edward VII owing to his sudden illness, it was applied to contracts the performance of which depended on the existence or occurrence of a particular state of things forming the basis on which the contract had been made. In *Krell v. Henry*,[22] for instance:

H agreed to hire a flat from K for 26 and 27 June 1902; the contract contained no reference to the coronation processions, but they were to take place on those days and to pass the flat. The processions were cancelled.

Two-thirds of the rent had not been paid when the processions were abandoned and the Court of Appeal held that K could not recover it. The Court considered that the processions and the relative position of the flat lay at the foundation of the agreement. The contract was therefore discharged.

It should not be imagined, however, that failure before performance of the factor which induced the parties to enter into the agreement will necessarily discharge the contract; for 'it may be that the parties contracted in the expectation that a particular event would happen, each taking his chance, but that the actual happening of the

---

[19] *Appleby* v. *Myers* (1867) L.R. 2 C.P. 651; *post*, p. 556.

[20] *Ibid.*, at p. 660.

[21] Sale of Goods Act 1979, s. 7. See further *post*, pp. 562–3 (effect of frustration and partial perishing of goods).

[22] [1903] 2 K.B. 740. See also *Chandler* v. *Webster* [1904] 1 K.B. 493 (*post*, p. 556). Cf. *Griffith* v. *Brymer* (1903) 19 T.L.R. 434 (*ante*, p. 320).

event was not made the basis of the contract'.[23] In *Herne Bay Steamboat Co. v. Hutton*:[24]

The defendant chartered from the plaintiff the S.S. *Cynthia* for 28 and 29 June 1902, for the express purpose of taking paying passengers to see the Coronation naval review at Spithead and to tour the fleet. The review was cancelled, but the fleet remained.

The Court of Appeal refused to hold the defendant discharged. They did so, partly on the ground that a tour of the fleet was still possible, but mainly because they considered that it was the defendant's own venture and it was at his risk. The Court pointed out that if the existence of a particular state of things is merely the motive or inducement to one party to enter into the contract, as distinct from the basis on which both contract, the principle cannot be applied. And the example was given of the hire of a vehicle to take the hirer and a party to Epsom to view the races on Derby day; the hirer will not be discharged if the races are cancelled, for the hirer's purpose is not the common foundation of the contract to hire the vehicle.

(c) DEATH, OR INCAPACITY FOR PERSONAL SERVICE

Where performance of obligations under a contract for personal services is rendered impossible or radically different by the death or incapacitating illness of the promisor, the contract will be frustrated. In *Stubbs* v. *Holywell Railway Co.*[25] it was held that a contract for personal services was put an end to by the death of the party by whom the services were to be rendered. And in *Robinson* v. *Davison*:[26]

D's wife, an eminent piano player, promised to perform at a concert, but was prevented from doing so by a dangerous illness. An action was brought against D claiming damages for breach of contract.

It was held that the contract was discharged by D's wife's illness, and it was not therefore broken by her failure to perform, nor, on the other hand, could she have insisted on performing when she was unfit to do so as frustration is not brought about by an act of election.[27] These are examples of cases where performance by the relevant party is personal and cannot be carried out by anyone else so that death or illness gives rise to frustration.[28] Similar decisions have been reached in the case of the discharge of a seaman's contract of service by his internment,[29] and of that of a music-hall artist, by his call-up for service in the army.[30] However, absence—even prolonged absence—through illness will not necessarily determine a contract of employment. A number of factors must be considered: the terms of the contract

---

[23] *Larrinaga & Co. Ltd.* v. *Société Franco-Americaine des Phosphates de Medulla, Paris* (1923) 39 T.L.R. 316, *per* Lord Finlay at p. 318.

[24] [1903] 2 K.B. 683.

[25] (1867) L.R. 2 Ex. 311.

[26] (1871) L.R. 6 Ex. 269.

[27] *Post*, p. 555 ff.

[28] If performance is not of a personal character then the contract is not necessarily frustrated by death or incapacity: *Phillips* v. *Alhambra Palace Co. Ltd.* [1901] 1 Q.B. 59.

[29] *Horlock* v. *Beal* [1916] 1 A.C. 486.

[30] *Morgan* v. *Manser* [1948] 1 K.B. 184.

(including any sick pay provisions), the nature and the expected duration of the employment, the period of past employment, and the nature and duration of the illness and the prospects for recovery.[31] In *Marshall* v. *Harland & Wolff Ltd.*[32] the test for frustration of a contract of employment was formulated as follows, 'Was the employee's incapacity . . . of such a nature, or did it appear likely to continue for such a period, that further performance of his obligations in the future would either be impossible or would be a thing radically different from that undertaken by him and accepted by the employer under the agreed terms of his employment?'. The application of the doctrine of frustration to employment contracts can give rise to results that may appear harsh. In *Notcutt* v. *Universal Equipment Co. (London) Ltd.*[33] frustration was held to have occurred when it became apparent to the parties that an employee who had suffered a heart attack would never work again. This had the effect of automatically terminating the contract of employment and thereby releasing the employer from the contractual provisions which required that notice be given before terminating the contract and the statutory obligation to pay the employee during the period of notice.

(d) REQUISITIONING OF SHIPS AND INTERFERENCES WITH CHARTERPARTIES

A number of cases have arisen concerning charterparties, and these provide some of the most important instances of the application of the doctrine.

In war-time, ships are often requisitioned for such time and for such purposes as the Government may require them. If the ship is under charterparty the question will arise whether or not the requisitioning operates so as to frustrate the rights of the shipowners and charterers under the agreement. In *F. A. Tamplin Steamship Co. Ltd.* v. *Anglo-Mexican Petroleum Products Co. Ltd.*:[34]

The steamship *F. A. Tamplin* was chartered by a time charterparty for 5 years from 4 December 1912, to 4 December 1917. In February 1915 the Government requisitioned the ship for use as a troopship and made certain structural alterations to her for this purpose. The charterers were willing to go on paying the agreed freight under the charterparty, but the owners claimed that the contract had been frustrated by the requisition as they wished to obtain a larger amount of compensation from the Crown.

The House of Lords, by a bare majority, held that the contract still continued. The interruption was not of sufficient duration to make it unreasonable for the parties to

---

[31] *Marshall* v. *Harland & Wolff Ltd.* [1972] 1 W.L.R. 899, at pp. 903–5. Note that an employee who is suspended from work on medical grounds is entitled to be paid by the employer for up to 26 weeks: Employment Rights Act 1996, s. 64.

[32] [1972] 1 W.L.R. 899, at p. 905 *per* Donaldson J. But see *Hart* v. *A. R. Marshall & Sons (Bulwell) Ltd.* [1977] 1 W.L.R. 1067 ('key' worker replaced); *Egg Stores (Stamford Hill) Ltd.* v. *Leibovici* [1977] I.C.R. 260, at p. 264. See also *F.C. Shepherd & Co. Ltd.* v. *Jerrom* [1987] 1 Q.B. 301 (imprisonment of employee).

[33] [1986] 1 W.L.R. 641.

[34] [1916] 2 A.C. 397.

go on. There might be many months during which the ship would be available for commercial purposes before the five years expired.

In *Bank Line Ltd.* v. *Capel (A.) & Co.*,[35] on the other hand:

In February 1915, B.L. chartered the steamship *Quito* to C for a period of 12 months from the time the vessel should be delivered. It was provided in the charterparty that (i) if the steamer had not been delivered by 30 April 1915, C, the charterers, were to have the option to cancel the contract or to proceed with it, and (ii) 'Charterers to have option of cancelling this charterparty should steamer be commandeered by Government during this Charter'. The steamer was not delivered by 30 April, and, on 11 May, before delivery, she was commandeered by the Government and not released until September. She was then sold by B.L., and C sued for non-delivery, having never exercised their options to cancel.

The House of Lords held that the contract had been frustrated. The clauses in the charterparty were not intended to place the shipowners indefinitely at the charterers' mercy, to oblige them to deliver however long the delay. They merely gave to the charterers the option to cancel the contract without the necessity of proving frustration:

A contingency may be provided for, but not in such terms as to show that the provision is meant to be all the provision for it. A contingency may be provided for, but in such a way as shows that it is provided for only for the purpose of dealing with one of its effects and not with all.[36]

Lord Haldane, who dissented, was of the opinion that there was no frustration: the requisition was not of such a permanent character as to make the terms of the charterparty wholly inapplicable.

These differences of opinion within the highest tribunal show that cases of frustration raise most difficult questions of fact and principle. In the *Bank Line* case Lord Loreburn stated[37] that 'the main thing to be considered is the probable length of the total deprivation of the use of the chartered ship compared with the unexpired duration of the charterparty'. On this basis, the two decisions can perhaps be reconciled without undue difficulty, since the *Bank Line* charter was of one year's duration only, whereas that in the *Tamplin* case had still nearly three years to run at the time the requisitioning took place. But it is by no means certain that Lord Loreburn's test is the correct one to apply.[38]

Events other than the seizure or requisitioning of the ship may also frustrate a charterparty. It has already been seen that, in *Jackson* v. *Union Marine Insurance Co. Ltd.*,[39] the charterparty was frustrated by the stranding of and damage to the ship. In a number of cases a charterparty has been held to have been frustrated by the inability

---

[35] [1919] A.C. 435.

[36] [1919] A.C. 435, *per* Lord Sumner at p. 456.

[37] [1919] A.C. 435, at p. 454. See also the *Tamplin* case (*supra*, n. 34), at p. 405.

[38] *International Sea Tankers Inc.* v. *Hemisphere Shipping Co. Ltd.* [1982] 1 Lloyd's Rep. 128, at pp. 131, 133, 135. The alternative tests were discussed by Diplock J. in *Port Line Ltd.* v. *Ben Line Steamers Ltd.* [1958] 2 Q.B. 146. See also *post*, pp. 545.

[39] (1874) L.R. 10 C.P. 125, *ante*, p. 533.

of the ship to leave port, due, for example, to the refusal of a foreign government to allow the ship to depart,[40] or to the outbreak of hostilities, as happened in 1980 when some sixty ships were trapped in the Shatt-el-Arab river upon the outbreak of war between Iran and Iraq,[41] or to the arrest of the ship.[42] More difficulty, however, arises where strikes prevent the loading or unloading of the ship. The charterer of a ship usually undertakes in the contract to load and unload the cargo within a specified number of days, and, in default, to pay a certain sum of money to the shipowner by way of 'demurrage'. If strikes occur at the port of loading or discharge, this does not (in the absence of any express provision to the contrary) absolve the charterer from his liability to pay demurrage in respect of the delay.[43] However, a prolonged strike may in exceptional circumstances frustrate a charterparty, that is if the delay is such as to make further performance something radically different from that which was undertaken in the contract.[44] Prolongation of a voyage by interruption of the contemplated route might also bring about frustration, but did not do so, for example, where the blocking of the Suez Canal necessitated a voyage round the Cape, since the alternative route was not fundamentally different, but merely longer and more expensive.[45]

(e) SALE AND CARRIAGE OF GOODS

Similar principles have been applied to contracts for the sale of goods to be carried by sea. In *Nickoll* v. *Ashton Edridge & Co.*,[46] for example, a cargo sold by the defendants to the plaintiffs was to be shipped 'per steamship *Orlando* . . . during the month of January'. Without default on the defendant's part the ship was so damaged by stranding as to be unable to load in January. It was held that in these circumstances the contract must be treated as at an end.

The Anglo-French invasion of Egypt in 1956 and the consequent closure of the Suez Canal led to a number of cases concerning the frustration of c.i.f. contracts[47] for the sale of goods. Among these was the case of *Tsakiroglou & Co. Ltd.* v. *Noblee Thorl G.m.b.H.*:[48]

---

[40] *Embiricos* v. *Reid (Sydney) & Co.* [1914] 3 K.B. 45; *Scottish Navigation Co.* v. *Souter* [1917] 1 K.B. 222; *Lloyd Royal Belge* v. *Stathatos* (1917) 34 T.L.R. 70.

[41] *International Sea Tankers Inc.* v. *Hemisphere Shipping Co. Ltd.* [1983] 1 Lloyd's Rep. 400; *Kodros Shipping Cpn. of Monrovia* v. *Empresa Cubana de Fletes* [1983] 1 A.C. 736; *Finelvet A.G.* v. *Vinava Shipping Co. Ltd.* [1983] 1 W.L.R. 1469.

[42] See *Adelfamar S.A.* v. *Silos E. Mangimi Martini S.p.A. (The Adelfa)* [1988] 2 Lloyd's Rep. 466.

[43] *Budgett & Co.* v. *Binnington & Co.* [1891] 1 Q.B. 35.

[44] *The Penelope* [1982] P. 180; *Pioneer Shipping Ltd.* v. *B.T.P. Tioxide Ltd.* [1982] A.C. 724.

[45] *Ocean Tramp Tankers Cpn.* v. *V/O Sovfracht (The Eugenia)* [1964] 2 Q.B. 226, overruling *Société Franco Tunisienne D'Armement* v. *Sidermar S.p.A.* [1961] 2 Q.B. 278. See also *Palmco Shipping Inc.* v. *Continental Ore Cpn.* [1970] 2 Lloyd's Rep. 21.

[46] [1901] 2 K.B. 126.

[47] 'C.i.f.' stands for cost, insurance, and freight. In a c.i.f. contract the price will be agreed on the basis that it includes insurance of the goods while in transit and the expenses of carriage (freight) to the port of destination.

[48] [1962] A.C. 93, overruling *Carapanayoti & Co. Ltd.* v. *E. T. Green Ltd.* [1959] 1 Q.B. 131.

T agreed to sell to N.T. a quantity of groundnuts to be shipped from the Sudan to Hamburg during November or December 1956. On 2 November, the Suez Canal was closed and remained closed for the next 5 months. The price of the groundnuts c.i.f. Hamburg was clearly calculated on the basis of shipment *via* the canal, but the contract contained no term to this effect. T refused to perform the contract, claiming that it had been frustrated by the closure of the canal.

The House of Lords held there was no frustration, since it would still be possible to ship the nuts to Hamburg around the Cape of Good Hope. Such a journey would not be commercially or fundamentally different from that by the canal, but merely more expensive. Their Lordships also pointed out that the contract was one of sale of goods, the transport of which is normally of no direct concern to the buyer. Nevertheless, they indicated that, if the goods had been perishable or if a definite date had been fixed for delivery, the contract might possibly have then been frustrated by the necessity for the longer Cape route.

(f) BUILDING CONTRACTS

Further instances of the doctrine of frustration are provided by a group of cases concerning building or construction contracts. Events may occur which hold up completion of the works. Such delays inevitably increase the contractor's costs. If the contract is a fixed-price contract, the contractor may lose the profit which it expected to gain, or even be forced into loss. In *Davis Contractors Ltd.* v. *Fareham U.D.C.*:[49]

In July 1946, D entered into a contract with Fareham U.D.C. to build 78 houses for a fixed sum of £94,424. Owing to the unexpected shortage of skilled labour and of certain materials the contract took 22 months to complete instead of the 8 months expected, and cost some £115,000. D contended that the contract had been frustrated and that they were entitled to claim on a *quantum meruit* for the cost actually incurred.

The House of Lords refused to accept this contention. The mere fact that unforeseen circumstances had delayed the performance of the contract, and rendered it more onerous to the appellants, did not discharge the agreement. The ultimate situation was still within the scope of the contract; the thing undertaken was not, when performed, different from that contracted for.

These strict requirements were, however, fulfilled in the case of *Metropolitan Water Board* v. *Dick, Kerr & Co. Ltd.*:[50]

D.K. & Co. contracted with the M.W.B. to construct a reservoir within 6 years. Two years elapsed when the Minister of Munitions, acting under statutory powers, required them to cease work on their contract and to remove and sell their plant. The M.W.B. brought an action claiming that the contract still continued.

The House of Lords held that the interruption created by the prohibition was of such a character and duration as to make the contract, if resumed, in effect a different contract, and that the original contract was therefore discharged.

[49] [1956] A.C. 696.
[50] [1918] A.C. 119.

(g) CHANGE IN THE LAW

The performance of a contract may be made legally impossible either by a change in the law or by a change in the operation of the law by reason of new facts supervening. The law may actually forbid the doing of some act undertaken in the contract;[51] or it may take from the control of the promisor something in respect of which it has contracted to act or not to act in a certain way, as, for example, where a piece of land subject to a restrictive covenant against building is compulsorily acquired and built upon by Act of Parliament.[52] Such cases are explained by policy and 'the elementary proposition that if further performance of a contract becomes impossible by legislation having that effect the contract is discharged'.[53]

For there to be frustration, the change in the law must be such as to strike at the root of the agreement, and not merely to suspend or hinder its operation in part. So it has been held that a 99-year building lease was not frustrated by Government restrictions on building for only a small part of the term,[54] and that the rights of a payee of a cheque drawn on a bank in Holland were not discharged by an enemy invasion and occupation of that country rendering presentation for payment there illegal, but not elsewhere.[55] Lesser interruptions may, however, be covered by provisions in the contract, for instance clauses providing a seller with an excuse for non-performance in the event of 'prohibition of export . . . preventing fulfilment',[56] although, as will be seen, the presence of such a clause may preclude the application of the doctrine of frustration.

The outbreak of war is another event which, by changing the operation of the law, may have the effect of abrogating obligations outstanding under a contract by reason of supervening illegality, if one of the parties resides in this country and the other in enemy or enemy-occupied territory, and the contract is one which involves commercial dealings with the enemy.[57] So strong are the public policy considerations in this situation that the contract will be wholly frustrated, even though the parties themselves provide that their obligations shall be merely postponed.[58]

---

[51] *Denny, Mott & Dickson Ltd.* v. *Fraser (James B.) & Co. Ltd.* [1944] A.C. 265.

[52] *Baily* v. *De Crespigny* (1869) L.R. 4 Q.B. 180. See also *Brown* v. *London Cpn.* (1862) 13 C.B.N.S. 828; *Studholme* v. *South Western Gas Board* [1954] 1 W.L.R. 313.

[53] *Reilly* v. *The King* [1934] A.C. 176, *per* Lord Atkin at p. 180. On the implications for the theoretical basis of the doctrine, see *post*, pp. 541–6.

[54] *Cricklewood Property and Investment Trust Ltd.* v. *Leighton's Investment Trust Ltd.* [1945] A.C. 221; *post*, p. 553. See also, *Libyan Arab Foreign Bank* v. *Bankers Trust Co.* [1989] 1 Q.B. 728, *per* Staughton J., at p. 772.

[55] *Cornelius* v. *Banque Franco-Serbe* [1942] 1 K.B. 29. See also *Arab Bank Ltd.* v. *Barclays Bank* [1954] A.C. 495 (accrued rights not destroyed).

[56] On such clauses, see *Bremer Handelsgesellschaft mbH* v. *Vanden Avenne-Izegem P.V.B.A.* [1978] 2 Lloyd's Rep. 109; *Bremer Handelsgesellschaft mbH* v. *C. Mackprang Jr.* [1979] 1 Lloyd's Rep. 221; *Bremer Handelsgesellschaft mbH* v. *Westzucker GmbH (No. 3)* [1989] 1 Lloyd's Rep. 198, and Treitel, *Frustration and Force Majeure* (1994) §12–025 ff.

[57] *Ertel Bieber & Co.* v. *Rio Tinto Co. Ltd.* [1918] A.C. 260; *Fibrosa Spolka Akcyjna* v. *Fairbairn Lawson Combe Barbour Ltd.* [1943] A.C. 32 (*post*, p. 528); McNair and Watts, *The Legal Effects of War*, 4th edn. (1966), ch. 3.

[58] *Ertel Bieber & Co.* v. *Rio Tinto Co. Ltd.* (*supra*, n. 57).

(h) PERFORMANCE OF ONLY ONE PARTY AFFECTED

The illustrations above show that, save in cases of supervening illegality, a frustrating event often only affects the ability of one of the parties to perform, while the other party, who usually has to pay money, is still capable of performing. So, in the requisitioning cases considered above, the charterers were able to pay the hire, and may have been willing to do so notwithstanding the non-availability of the ship, since the rate paid by the Government for requisitioned ships was higher than that payable under the charter.[59] Nevertheless, if the event is a frustrating one, it excuses both parties even where this may be to the advantage of the party who is unable to perform.

IV. THE THEORETICAL BASIS OF FRUSTRATION

Considerable judicial attention has been paid to the theoretical basis on which the doctrine of discharge of a contract by frustration rests, perhaps because of a perceived need to explain why a finding of frustration does not constitute a reallocation of risks nor permit an escape from a bad bargain.[60]

Successive pronouncements of the House of Lords have set forth a number of learned, but often contradictory, opinions concerning this issue and a number of theories have been put forward at various times. Since there is now general agreement on the appropriate test to be applied, it is necessary to refer only briefly to the four principal tests or 'theories' which have been advanced.[61]

(a) IMPLIED TERM

At one time the preponderance of judicial opinion favoured the view that frustration of a contract depended upon the implication of a term although, as we have noted, this did not explain discharge where the performance of the contract is made *legally* impossible by a change in the law or its operation.[62] Lord Loreburn's speech in *F. A. Tamplin Steamship Co. Ltd.* v. *Anglo-Mexican Petroleum Products Co. Ltd.*[63] contains the classic exposition of the reasons on which the implied term theory of frustration was based:

---

[59] *F. A. Tamplin Steamship Co. Ltd.* v. *Anglo-Mexican Petroleum Products Co. Ltd.* [1916] 2 A.C. 397, at pp. 405, 410, 422; *Bank Line Ltd.* v. *Capel (A.) & Co.* [1919] A.C. 435, *ante*, p. 537.

[60] *Pacific Phosphates Co. Ltd.* v. *Empire Transport* (1920) 4 L.L.R. 189, at p. 190.

[61] In *National Carriers Ltd.* v. *Panalpina (Northern) Ltd.* [1981] A.C. 675, Lord Hailsham L.C. stated, at p. 687, there were at least five theories; in addition to those considered *infra*, he referred to and rejected one based on total failure of consideration.

[62] In the heyday of the implied contract theory legal impossibility was sometimes said to differ from other categories of frustration: *Joseph Constantine S.S. Line Ltd.* v. *Imperial Smelting Corporation Ltd.* [1942] A.C. 154, at p. 163.

[63] [1916] 2 A.C. 397, at pp. 403–4, see *ante*, p. 536 for the facts. For recent support for this theory, see Smith (1994) 110 L.Q.R. 400, at p. 403.

[A] Court can and ought to examine the contract and the circumstances in which it was made, not of course to vary, but only to explain it, in order to see whether or not from the nature of it the parties must have made their bargain on the footing that a particular thing or state of things would continue to exist. And if they must have done so, then a term to that effect will be implied, though it be not expressed in the contract . . . Sometimes it is put that performance has become impossible and that the party concerned did not promise to perform an impossibility. Sometimes it is put that the parties contemplated a certain state of things which fell out otherwise. In most of the cases it is said that there was an implied condition in the contract which operated to release the parties from performing it, and in all of them I think that was at bottom the principle upon which the Court proceeded. It is in my opinion the true principle, for no Court has an absolving power, but it can infer from the nature of the contract and the surrounding circumstances that a condition which was not expressed was a foundation on which the parties contracted . . . Were the altered conditions such that, had they thought of them, they would have taken their chance of them, or such that as sensible men they would have said, 'If that happens, of course, it is all over between us'?

A contract would therefore be frustrated if a term could be implied that, in the events that subsequently happened, the contract would come to an end. The expression 'an implied term' is, however, ambiguous. It may be used in a subjective sense, that is to say, it may mean a term which the Court reads into the contract in order to give effect to what it regards as the parties' real intention at the time of contracting. As was said in a later case[64] 'the law is only doing what the parties really (though subconsciously) meant to do for themselves'. To such an implied term a number of objections may be raised. In particular, it is difficult to see how the parties could be taken, even impliedly, to have provided for something which never occurred to them.[65] Moreover, had it occurred to them, it is unlikely that they would have agreed that the contract was to come to an end. Lord Wright said:[66]

It is not possible, to my mind, to say that if they had thought of it, they would have said: 'Well, if that happens, all is over between us'. On the contrary, they would almost certainly on the one side or the other have sought to introduce reservations or qualifications or compensations.

That this is so is shown by the widespread use of *force majeure* clauses which specify what is to happen on the occurrence of an event which affects one or both parties' performance.

On the other hand, the implied term may be formulated more objectively. It may mean a term which, in the light of the events which have actually arisen, the parties *as*

---

[64] *Hirji Mulji* v. *Cheong Yue S.S. Co. Ltd.* [1926] A.C. 497, at p. 504.

[65] *Davis Contractors Ltd.* v. *Fareham U.D.C.* [1956] A.C. 696, at p. 728. Also see the example given by Lord Sands in *James Scott & Sons Ltd.* v. *Del Sel* 1922 S.C. 592, at p. 597: 'A tiger has escaped from a travelling menagerie. The milkgirl fails to deliver the milk. Possibly the milkman may be exonerated from any breach of contract: but, even so, it would seem hardly reasonable to base that exoneration on the ground that "tiger days excepted" must be held as if written into the milk contract'. See further, *F.C. Shepherd & Co. Ltd.* v. *Jerrom* [1987] 1 Q.B. 301 *per* Mustill L.J at p. 322.

[66] *Denny, Mott & Dickson Ltd.* v. *Fraser (James B.) & Co. Ltd.* [1944] A.C. 265, at p. 275.

reasonable people would have imported into the contract to deal with that possibility.[67] When used in this sense, the implied term is betrayed by a similar artificiality. The 'reasonable person' has no real existence and represents 'no more than the anthropomorphic conception of justice'; an opinion ascribed to such a person is, in fact, that of the Court, which is and must be the spokesman of the fair and reasonable person.[68] An implied term of this sort is no more than a fiction, something added to the contract by the law.

(b) 'JUST AND REASONABLE RESULT'

In truth, the discharge of a contract by frustration occurs, not because of the actual or imputed will of the parties, but by operation of law. The doctrine of frustration is, as Lord Sumner pointed out, 'a device, by which the rules as to absolute contracts are reconciled with a special exception which justice demands'.[69] In declaring a contract to have been frustrated, the Court exercises a positive function: it releases the parties from further performance of the obligations which they would otherwise be bound to perform.

Recognition of these facts led certain of the judges (and notably Lord Wright and Lord Denning) to the conclusion that the basis of the doctrine of frustration was the desire of the Courts to reach a just and reasonable result.[70] 'The truth is', Lord Wright said,[71] 'that the Court or jury as a judge of fact decides the question in accordance with what seems just and reasonable in its eyes'. This view, however, might be taken to suggest that a Court had the power to release the parties from their obligations whenever it was just and reasonable to do so,[72] even, for example, where the only effect of the subsequent event had been to render the contract financially more onerous than the parties had anticipated. But it is clear that the circumstances in which a contract will be held to have been frustrated are far more limited in scope.[73]

(c) FOUNDATION OF THE CONTRACT

Some test was, therefore, required which would recognize that frustration did not depend on the intentions of the parties, but which would not permit contracts to be too easily discharged. The first such test to be formulated was that of the 'disappearance of the foundation of the contract'. The question to be asked was whether the events that had occurred were of a character and extent so sweeping as to cause the

---

67 *Dahl* v. *Nelson, Donkin & Co.* (1881) 6 App. Cas. 38, at p. 59.

68 *Davis Contractors Ltd.* v. *Fareham U.D.C.* [1956] A.C. 696, *per* Lord Radcliffe at p. 728.

69 *Hirji Mulji* v. *Cheong Yue S.S. Co. Ltd.* [1926] A.C. 497, at p. 510.

70 *Joseph Constantine Steamship Line Ltd.* v. *Imperial Shipping Corporation Ltd.* [1942] A.C. 154, at p. 186.

71 *Legal Essays and Addresses* (1939), p. 259. See also *Denny, Mott & Dickson Ltd.* v. *Fraser (James B.) & Co. Ltd.* [1944] A.C. 265, at pp. 274–6.

72 *British Movietonews Ltd.* v. *London and District Cinemas Ltd.* [1951] 1 K.B. 190, at pp. 201–2 (disapproved on appeal: [1952] A.C. 166).

73 See *Notcutt* v. *Universal Equipment Co. (London) Ltd.* [1986] 1 W.L.R. 641, at pp. 646–7, where the Court of Appeal rejected an argument to the effect that, before a court could determine that a contract was frustrated, it must be shown that it would be unjust to hold the parties to the contract.

foundation of the contract to disappear.[74] It was adopted, for example, by Goddard J. in *W. J. Tatem Ltd.* v. *Gamboa*:[75]

During the Spanish Civil War, T chartered to G, acting on behalf of the Republican Government of Spain, a steamship, for 30 days from 1 July 1937. The ship was to be used for the evacuation of refugees from Northern Spain to French ports. The hire was to be at the rate of £250 a day and was payable until the ship was returned to T. On 14 July, the ship was seized by the Nationalists and detained in the port of Bilbao until 11 September. In answer to T's claim for hire, G pleaded that the contract had been frustrated.

Goddard J. was prepared to assume that the circumstances of the contract (including the very high rate of hire) showed that the parties contemplated that seizure and detention of the vessel might occur. He nevertheless held that the contract was frustrated: the foundation of the contract was destroyed by the seizure, as G thereafter no longer had the use of the vessel. The expression 'foundation' of the contract is, however, imprecise, and it leaves open the question what is the foundation of the contract in a particular case. Moreover, the test is difficult to apply to situations other than those in which the subject-matter of the contract ceases to be available. It has, therefore, been rejected by the House of Lords.[76]

(d) RADICAL CHANGE IN THE OBLIGATION

There is now general agreement that the appropriate test to apply to determine whether a contract has been frustrated is that of a 'radical change in the obligation'. In *Davis Contractors Ltd.* v. *Fareham U.D.C.*, Lord Radcliffe said:

Frustration occurs whenever the law recognizes that without default of either party a contractual obligation has become incapable of being performed because the circumstances in which performance is called for would render it a thing radically different from that which was undertaken by the contract. *Non haec in foedera veni*. It was not this that I promised to do.[77]

This test has been adopted by the House of Lords in several cases,[78] and was

---

[74] *F. A. Tamplin Steamship Co. Ltd.* v. *Anglo-Mexican Petroleum Products Co. Ltd.* [1916] 2 A.C. 397, at p. 406.

[75] [1939] 1 K.B. 132.

[76] *National Carriers Ltd.* v. *Panalpina (Northern) Ltd.* [1981] A.C. 675.

[77] [1956] A.C. 696, at p. 729, for the facts, see *ante*, p. 539. The Latin phrase is said to be drawn from *The Aeneid*, Book 4, lines 338–9 (see Sir John Megaw, letter to *The Times*, 20 December 1980). But whether the relationship between Aeneas and Queen Dido was affected by a supervening event (Mercury's intervention) or an initial mistake (as to the nature of the relationship) is not entirely clear. Neither is it clear that Aeneas's 'excuses' for his planned desertion of Queen Dido, were as shabby as many (from Ovid to Sir John Megaw) consider them to be; see Williams, *Tradition and Originality in Roman Poetry* (Oxford, 1968) pp. 378–6 and John Sparrow, Jackson Knight Memorial Lecture, *Dido* v. *Aeneas: the case for the defence* (Abbey Press, 1973).

[78] *Tsakiroglou & Co. Ltd.* v. *Noblee Thorl G.m.b.H.* [1962] A.C. 93, at p. 131; *Pioneer Shipping Ltd.* v. *B.T.P. Tioxide Ltd.* [1982] A.C. 724, at pp. 744, 745, 751; *Paal Wilson & Co. A/S* v. *Partenreederei Hannah Blumenthal* [1983] 1 A.C. 854, 909, 918. See also *William Sindall plc* v. *Cambridgeshire County Council* [1994] 1 W.L.R. 1016 at p. 1039 (C.A.).

reformulated by Lord Simon in *National Carriers Ltd.* v. *Panalpina (Northern) Ltd.*:[79]

Frustration of a contract takes place when there supervenes an event (without default of either party and for which the contract makes no sufficient provision) which so significantly changes the nature (not merely the expense or onerousness) of the outstanding contractual rights and/or obligations from what the parties could reasonably have contemplated at the time of its execution that it would be unjust to hold them to the literal sense of its stipulations in the new circumstances; in such a case the law declares both parties to be discharged from further performance.

This approach has sometimes been called the 'construction' theory, because it requires the Court first to construe the terms of contract in the light of its nature and the relevant surrounding circumstances when it was made. The original obligation undertaken by the parties can thus be determined. The Court must then consider whether there would be a radical change in that obligation if performance were enforced in the circumstances which have subsequently arisen. A mere rise in cost or expense will not suffice. 'It is not hardship or inconvenience or material loss itself which calls the principle of frustration into play. There must be as well such a change in the significance of the obligation that the thing undertaken would, if performed, be a different thing than that contracted for.'[80]

(i) Application of test

The test is clearly meant to be a difficult one to satisfy. It is, moreover, easier to state than to apply. 'The data for decision are, on the one hand, the terms and construction of the contract, read in the light of the then existing circumstances, and on the other hand the events which have occurred.'[81] If the parties have themselves provided for the situation that has arisen the contract governs and there is no frustration. If they have not provided for it then the new situation must be compared with the situation for which they did provide to see how different it is.[82] The comparison is between the rights and obligations of the parties after the event, assuming the contract still binds them, and what their rights and obligations would have been had the event not occurred. We have noted the factors taken into account in contracts of employment.[83] In contracts for the carriage of goods by sea and charterparties, account may be taken of the extent to which the goods carried or to be carried are liable to damage or to deterioration,[84] or are subject to a seasonal market,[85] and the extent to which the

---

[79] [1981] A.C. 675, at p. 700. See also *ibid*, pp. 688, 717. For the facts, see *post*, p. 554.

[80] *Davis Contractors Ltd.* v. *Fareham U.D.C. (supra,* n. 77), *per* Lord Radcliffe at p. 729. See also *Tsakiroglou & Co. Ltd.* v. *Noblee Thorl G.m.b.H.* [1962] A.C. 93.

[81] *Heyman* v. *Darwins* [1942] A.C. 356, at p. 383.

[82] *Ocean Tramp Tankers Corporation* v. *V/O Sovracht (The Eugenia)* [1964] 2 Q.B. 226, *per* Lord Denning M.R. at p. 239.

[83] *Ante*, pp. 535–6.

[84] *Tsakiroglou & Co. Ltd.* v. *Noblee Thorl G.m.b.H.* [1962] A.C. 93, at pp. 115, 118 and 123. See also *Jackson* v. *Union Marine Insurance* (1874) L.R. 10 C.P. 125, at p. 146 (carriage of ice would be frustrated by shorter delay than carriage of iron rails).

[85] *Jackson* v. *Union Marine Insurance* (1874) L.R. 10 C.P. 125, at p. 115. See also *ibid.* at p. 146.

vessel and crew are fit to proceed in the new circumstances. To constitute frustration, the event or events must make performance of the contract a thing 'radically' or 'fundamentally' different in a commercial sense from that undertaken by the contract. These concepts are elusive and the courts recognize that it is often difficult to draw the line[86] and that the question is one of degree.[87] It is, however, clearly more difficult to frustrate a long-term contract than a short-term one.[88]

(ii) Similarity to test for discharge for breach

The terms 'radical' and 'fundamental' are also used to determine whether a contract may be discharged for breach of an 'intermediate' or 'innominate' term.[89] In *Hong Kong Fir Shipping Co. Ltd.* v. *Kawasaki Kisen Kaisha Ltd.*[90] Diplock L.J. stated that *Jackson* v. *Union Marine Insurance Co. Ltd.*[91] was seeking to apply to frustrating events the same standard as if they had arisen by a breach by one of the parties. For the purpose of determining whether a contract may be discharged it is the happening of the event and not whether the event was the result of a breach that is crucial.[92] Despite this, in practice it is more likely than not that there will be differences between cases of frustration and cases of breach because in the context of breach, factors other than the ratio of failure to the performance undertaken are relevant to the question of whether the breach is fundamental.

(iii) Question of law

The application of the 'radical change in the obligation' test is a matter of law; but once it is shown that a judge or arbitrator has correctly applied the test to the facts found by him, an appellate Court should be slow to differ from his conclusion.[93]

V. INCIDENCE OF RISK

The doctrine of frustration is principally concerned with the incidence of risk—who must take the risk of the happening of the supervening event? The Courts have therefore to determine whether the contract, on its true construction, has made provision for that risk. We have noted that increased expense, even if caused by wholly

---

[86] *Ocean Tramp Tankers Corporation* v. *V/O Sovracht (The Eugenia)* [1964] 2 Q.B. 226, at p. 239.
[87] *National Carriers Ltd.* v. *Panalpina (Northern) Ltd.* [1981] A.C. 675, at p. 688; *Pioneer Shipping* v. *B.T.P. Tioxide (The Nema)* [1982] A.C. 724, at p. 744.
[88] *Lord Strathcona Shipping Co. Ltd.* v. *Dominion Coal Co. Ltd.* [1926] A. C. 108, at p. 115; *National Carriers Ltd.* v. *Panalpina (Northern) Ltd.* [1981] A.C. 675, *per* Lord Hailsham L.C., at p. 691. See also *Larrinaga & Co.* v. *Societe Franco-Americaine des Phosphates de Medulla, Paris* (1922) 28 Com. Cas. 1, at p. 5.
[89] *Post*, p. 578 ff. See also, *ante*, p. 140.
[90] [1962] 2 Q.B. 26, on which, see *post*, p. 578.
[91] *Ante*, p. 533.
[92] [1962] 2 Q.B. 26, at pp. 49, 68. See also, in the same context, *The Hermosa* [1980] 1 Lloyd's Rep. 638, at p. 649 (delay by a variety of events, some the consequences of breach and some not).
[93] *Pioneer Shipping Ltd.* v. *B.T.P. Tioxide Ltd.* (*supra*, n. 87), at pp. 738, 752–3.

abnormal fluctuations in prices, does not frustrate.[94] In this connection, the cases show that a number of difficult questions may arise.

(a) EXPRESS PROVISION

Except in certain cases of illegality[95] there is little doubt that it is open to the parties to provide that the contract shall continue, or be merely suspended, and not discharged, upon the occurrence of a particular event, or to allocate the risks attendant upon that event. Where the contract makes provision (that is, full and complete provision, so intended) for a given contingency, this will preclude the Court from holding that the contract is frustrated.[96] But the parties may fail to make complete provision, as happened in the *Bank Line* case,[97] where the option given to one party, i.e. the charterers, to cancel or continue with the charterparty if the ship should be requisitioned, was held not to be intended to apply to requisitioning of so long a duration as to make the charter, as a matter of business, a wholly different thing. And a provision in a building contract, for example, that the contractor is to be allowed an extension of time in the event of 'delays', may be construed as inapplicable to a situation where the delay which occurs is such as to bring about a radical change in the obligation.[98] In this type of case, the contract can still be frustrated.

It is also open to the parties to provide that the contract is to be suspended or discharged by a non-frustrating event.[99] There are, for example, difficulties in determining whether a given delay or prospective delay frustrates a contract.[100] As a matter of interpretation the Court may conclude that the parties preferred the certainty of termination after a specified period of delay, pursuant to a contractual term, to the uncertainty of possible discharge under the doctrine of frustration.[101]

(b) FORESEEN EVENTS

The second question is whether events which were foreseen by the parties at the time of contracting can be relied upon to establish frustration. In many of the cases reference is made to the occurrence of an 'unforeseen' or 'unexpected' or 'uncontemplated' event, and it may be argued that the parties must be taken to have assumed the

---

[94] *Ante*, p. 539: *Davis Contractors Ltd. v. Fareham U.D.C.* [1956] A.C. 696, *per* Lord Reid at p. 724 and *Tsakiroglou & Co. Ltd. v. Noblee Thorl G.m.b.H.* [1962] A.C. 93. But note that in the latter Lord Reid reserved his position on an increase which reached a wholly astronomical figure, and cf. *William Cory v. L.C.C.* [1951] 1 K.B. 8, aff'd [1951] 2 K.B. 476.

[95] See *ante*, p. 540.

[96] *Bank Line Ltd. v. Capel (A.) & Co.* [1919] A.C. 435, at p. 455; *Joseph Constantine Steamship Line Ltd. v. Imperial Smelting Corporation Ltd.* [1942] A.C. 154, at p. 163. See also *Bangladesh Export Import Co. Ltd. v. Sucden Kerry S.A.* [1995] 2 Lloyd's Rep. 1.

[97] [1919] A.C. 435; *ante*, p. 537. See also *Jackson v. Union Marine Insurance Co. Ltd.* (1874) L.R. 10 C.P. 125 (clause excusing one party only from liability in a given contingency).

[98] *Metropolitan Water Board v. Dick, Kerr & Co. Ltd.* [1918] A.C. 119; *ante*, p. 539.

[99] *Ante*, p. 531.

[100] *Post*, pp. 548–9.

[101] *Total Gas Marketing Ltd. v. Arco British Ltd.* [1998] 2 Lloyd's Rep. 209, *per* Lord Steyn at p. 222.

risk of an event which was present in their minds at the time the contract was made. It is, however, a question of construction of the contract whether it was intended to continue to be binding in that event,[102] or whether, in the absence of any express provision, the issue has been left open,[103] so as to allow the incidence of risk to be determined by the law relating to frustration. In *W. J. Tatem Ltd.* v. *Gamboa*,[104] for example, the fact that seizure of the ship was within the contemplation of the parties did not preclude the operation of frustration since the contract made no express provision for the contingency.

(c) PREVENTION OF PERFORMANCE IN MANNER INTENDED BY ONE PARTY

The third question is whether a contract will be frustrated by an event which prevents performance in a manner intended by one party alone. In *Blackburn Bobbin Co. Ltd.* v. *Allen (T. W.) & Sons Ltd.*:[105]

A agreed to sell and deliver to B.B. at Hull a quantity of Finnish birch timber. A found it impossible to fulfil this contract because the outbreak of war cut off its source of supply from Finland. B.B. was unaware that timber from Finland was normally shipped direct from a Finnish port to England, and that timber merchants did not, in practice, hold stocks of it in England.

The Court of Appeal held that there was no frustration. What had happened was merely that an event had occurred which rendered it practically impossible for the defendants to deliver: that event might have been, but was not, provided for in the contract. To free A from liability, it would have to be shown that the continuance of the normal mode of shipping the timber from Finland was a matter which *both* parties contemplated as necessary for the fulfilment of the contracts. Since this was not the case, A bore the risk.

(d) DELAY

Frequently, as we have seen, a subsequent event causes delay[106] in the performance of the contract, bringing financial loss to one of the parties. But the risk of delay is one which has to be accepted in commercial transactions. Lord Sumner said:[107]

---

[102] *Larrinaga & Co.* v. *Société Franco Americaine des Phosphates de Medulla* (1923) 39 T.L.R. 316; *Maritime National Fish Ltd.* v. *Ocean Trawlers Ltd.* [1935] A.C. 524; *Chandler Bros. Ltd.* v. *Boswell* [1936] 3 All E.R. 179; *Paal Wilson & Co. A/S* v. *Partenreederei Hannah Blumenthal* [1983] 1 A.C. 854, at p. 909.

[103] *W. J. Tatem Ltd.* v. *Gamboa* [1939] 1 K.B. 132, at p. 138; *Ocean Tramp Tankers Corporation* v. *V/O Sovfracht (The Eugenia)* [1963] 2 Q.B. 226, at p. 239; *The Nile Co. for the Export of Agricultural Crops* v. *H. & J.M. Bennett (Commodities) Ltd.* [1986] 1 Lloyd's Rep. 555 at p. 582; *Adelfamar S.A.* v. *Silos E. Mangimi Martini SpA (The Adelfa)* [1988] 2 Lloyd's Rep 466 at p. 471.

[104] [1939] 1 K.B. 132; *ante*, p. 544.

[105] [1918] 2 K.B. 467. It was also said in this case that there could never be frustration of a contract for the sale of unascertained goods, but this is probably too wide: see *Re Badische Co. Ltd.* [1921] 2 Ch. 331; *Tsakiroglou & Co. Ltd.* v. *Noblee Thorl G.m.b.H.* [1962] A.C. 93; *ante*, pp. 538–9.

[106] See Stannard (1983) 46 M.L.R. 738.

[107] *Bank Line Ltd.* v. *Capel (A.) & Co.* [1919] A.C. 435, at p. 458.

Delay even of considerable length and of wholly uncertain duration is an incident of maritime adventure, which is clearly within the contemplation of the parties . . . so much so as to be often the subject of express provisions. Delays such as these may very seriously affect the commercial object of the adventure, for the ship's expenses and overhead charges are running on . . . None the less this is not frustration.

The delay must be such as 'to render the adventure absolutely nugatory',[108] 'to make it unreasonable to require the parties to go on',[109] 'to destroy the identity of the work or service when resumed with the work or service when interrupted',[110] 'to put an end in a commercial sense to the undertaking'.[111] It may, however, be difficult for the parties to determine whether, at any particular point of time, the delay is of this nature. On this point, Lord Roskill, in *Pioneer Shipping Ltd.* v. *B.T.P. Tioxide Ltd.*,[112] has provided guidance:

It is often necessary to wait upon events in order to see whether the delay already suffered and the prospects of further delay from that cause will make any ultimate performance of the relevant contractual obligations 'radically different' . . . from that which was undertaken by the contract. But, as has often been said, business men must not be required to await events too long. They are entitled to know where they stand. Whether or not the delay is such as to bring about frustration must be a question to be determined by an informed judgment based upon all the evidence of what has occurred and what is likely thereafter to occur.

While, therefore, it is for the tribunal to whom the issue has been referred to decide as a question of law whether or not the contract has been frustrated, 'that conclusion is almost completely determined by what is ascertained as to mercantile usage and the understanding of mercantile men'[113] about 'the significance of the commercial differences between what was promised and what in the changed circumstances would now fall to be performed'.[114]

Even where the delay is *prima facie* sufficient, where both parties are responsible for it, the rule that reliance cannot be placed on a self-induced frustration will preclude discharge.[115]

---

[108] *Bensaude & Co.* v. *Thames and Mersey Marine Insurance Co.* [1897] 1 Q.B. 29, *per* Lord Esher at p. 31; [1897] A.C. 609, at pp. 611, 612, 614.

[109] *Metropolitan Water Board* v. *Dick, Kerr & Co. Ltd.* [1918] A.C. 199, *per* Lord Atkinson at p. 131; *F. A. Tamplin Steamship Co. Ltd.* v. *Anglo-Mexican Petroleum Products Co. Ltd.* [1916] 2 A.C. 397, *per* Lord Loreburn at p. 405.

[110] *Metropolitan Water Board* v. *Dick, Kerr & Co. Ltd.* (*supra*, n. 109), *per* Lord Dunedin at p. 128; *Bank Line Ltd.* v. *Capel (A.) & Co.* [1919] A.C. 435, *per* Lord Sumner at p. 460.

[111] *Jackson* v. *Union Marine Insurance Co. Ltd.* (1874) L.R. 10 C.P. 125.

[112] [1982] A.C. 724, at p. 752.

[113] *Tsakiroglou & Co. Ltd.* v. *Noblee Thorl G.m.b.H.* (*supra*, n. 105), at p. 124.

[114] *Pioneer Shipping Ltd.* v. *B.T.P. Tioxide Ltd.* (*supra*, n. 87).

[115] *Paal Wilson & Co. A/S* v. *Partenreederei Hannah Blumenthal* [1983] 1 A.C. 854. See *post*, p. 551.

(e) INFLATION

Finally, some mention must be made of the effects of inflation. In *Staffordshire Area Health Authority* v. *South Staffordshire Waterworks Co.*[116] a contract was entered into in 1929 under which the defendants agreed 'at all times hereafter' to supply water to a hospital at a fixed price of seven (old) pence per 1,000 gallons. By 1978 the equivalent cost of supplying the water was some twenty times the contract price. The Court of Appeal held that the contract was, on its true construction, terminable by the defendants upon reasonable notice.[117] But Lord Denning M.R. expressed the opinion[118] that, by reason of 50 years of continuing inflation, a fundamentally different situation had emerged in which the contract had ceased to bind. His reasoning was not, however, accepted by the other members of the Court of Appeal, and the orthodox view is that any depreciation in the purchasing power of sterling,[119] or the devaluation of a foreign currency in which a debt is expressed,[120] is a risk which must be borne by the creditor. If the creditor does not wish to bear this risk, provision may be made in the contract. In certain contexts, for example leases, it is not unusual for the terms of the contract to provide for modification of the price to take account of inflation.

VI. SELF-INDUCED FRUSTRATION

It is well established that a party whose act or election has given rise to the event which is alleged to have frustrated the contract cannot invoke the doctrine of frustration; reliance cannot be placed upon a self-induced frustration.[121] In *Maritime National Fish Ltd.* v. *Ocean Trawlers Ltd.*:[122]

O.T. chartered to M.N.F. a steam trawler fitted with an otter trawl. Both parties knew at the time of the contract that it was illegal to use an otter trawl without a licence from the Canadian Government. Some months later M.N.F. applied for licences for five trawlers which it was operating, including O.T.'s trawler and three trawlers owned directly or

---

[116] [1978] 1 W.L.R. 1387.

[117] On the implication of a term to this effect (less likely where there is a price variation clause), see *ante*, pp. 528–9.

[118] At pp. 1397–8. He did not, however, hold that the contract was terminated automatically (see *post*, p. 555), but only on reasonable notice.

[119] *Wates Ltd.* v. *G.L.C.* (1987) 25 Build. L.R. 1, at p. 35.

[120] *British Bank for Foreign Trade Ltd.* v. *Russian Commercial and Industrial Bank* (1921) 38 T.L.R. 65; *Re Chesterman's Trusts* [1923] 2 Ch. 466.

[121] *J. Lauritzen A.S.* v. *Wijsmuller B.V. (The Super Servant Two)* [1990] 1 Lloyd's Rep. 1 at p. 8. But where the relevant act is caused by a third party for whose action the party claiming frustration is not responsible the result is not considered to be self-induced frustration: *Adelfamar S.A.* v. *Silos E. Mangimi S.p.A. (The Adelfa)* [1988] 2 Lloyd's Rep. 466 at p. 471.

[122] [1935] A.C. 524 (see [1934] 1 D.L.R 621, esp. at p. 623 and [1934] 4 D.L.R. 288, esp. at p. 299 for a full statement of the facts). See also *Bank Line Ltd.* v. *Capel (A.) & Co.* [1919] A.C. 435, at p. 452; *Ocean Tramp Tankers Corporation* v. *V/O Sovfracht (The Eugenia)* [1964] 2 Q.B. 226, at p. 237; *Denmark Productions Ltd.* v. *Boscobel Productions Ltd.* [1969] 1 Q.B. 699, at pp. 725, 736–7; *Paal Wilson & Co. A/S* v. *Partenreederei Hannah Blumenthal* [1983] 1 A.C. 854.

indirectly by M.N.F. It was informed that only three licences would be granted, and was requested to state for which of the three trawlers it desired to have licences. It named two trawlers that it owned directly or indirectly and a third chartered from a person other than O.T., and then claimed that it was no longer bound by the charterparty as its object had been frustrated.

The Judicial Committee of the Privy Council held that the failure of the contract was the result of M.N.F.'s own election, and that since 'reliance cannot be placed upon a self-induced frustration' there was no frustration. Similar conclusions have been reached where, in breach of contract, a charterer of a ship allowed the ship to enter a war-zone, where she was trapped,[123] and where parties to arbitration proceedings were in breach of their mutual contractual obligations to apply to the arbitral tribunal for directions to prevent delay in the conduct of the arbitration.[124]

(a) CHOOSING BETWEEN DIFFERENT CONTRACTS

The position is more complicated where a party enters into a number of contracts and the supervening event means that, while it is possible to perform one or more of the contracts, it is not possible to perform them all. This was the position in *J. Lauritzen A.S.* v. *Wijsmuller B.V. (The Super Servant Two)*:[125]

In July 1980 W contracted with L to carry a drilling rig from Japan to a location off Rotterdam using, at its option, either the *Super Servant One* or the *Super Servant Two*. It also entered into two contracts with third parties containing similar substitution clauses, one before the contract with L and one afterwards. In its internal schedules W planned to use the *Super Servant Two* for L's contract and the *Super Servant One* for the other two contracts, but, prior to the time set for performance, the *Super Servant Two* sank. W informed L that it would not transport the rig with either the *Super Servant One* or the *Super Servant Two*, but the parties agreed, without prejudice to their rights under the contract, that the drilling rig would be transported by another, more expensive, method. In answer to L's claim for the losses suffered, W counterclaimed *inter alia* that the sinking of the *Super Servant Two* frustrated the contract.

The Court of Appeal held that the contract was not frustrated. Even if the sinking of the *Super Servant Two* occurred without any fault on the part of W, it was not the cause of the inability to perform. The real cause was said to be W's election not to use the *Super Servant One*, something which it would have been physically possible for it to do. It was said that that exercise of choice meant that W had accepted the risk of the *Super Servant Two* being unable to perform with the result that its unavailability

---

[123] *Ocean Tramp Tanker Corporation* v. *V/O Sovfracht (The Eugenia) (supra,* n. 122).

[124] *Paal Wilson & Co. A/S* v. *Partenreederei Hannah Blumenthal (supra,* n. 122). The position in arbitration caused difficulties in commercial practice; see *ante,* pp. 30–1 for another, only partially successful, attempt to deal with the problem of stale arbitrations, which has now been addressed by legislation empowering the arbitrator to dismiss a claim in the case of inexcusable and inordinate delay where the delay results in a substantial risk that it would not be possible to have a fair resolution of the issues or of serious prejudice to the respondent: see now Arbitration Act 1996, s. 41 and *L'Office Cherifien Des Phosphates* v. *Yamashita-Shinnihon Steamship Co. Ltd.* [1994] 1 A.C. 486.

[125] [1990] 1 Lloyd's Rep. 1, affirming [1989] 1 Lloyd's Rep. 149.

gave rise to a breach not a frustrating event. Moreover, to allow W to rely on the unavailability of the *Super Servant One* as a frustrating event would allow it to rely on its own act of election whereas frustration in theory occurs automatically.

The reasoning in this case has been criticized[126] for not taking sufficient account of the fact that, in the *Maritime National Fish* case, it was possible for O.T. to perform all contracts made with third parties, and because the rule that frustration is automatic is not an absolute one.[127] W's 'election' was only as to which contract it was not going to perform and it is submitted that the decision is likely to lead to practical difficulties. It would appear to mean, for instance, where a farmer agrees to sell 250 tons of a crop to be grown on specific land which normally yields over 500 tons to A, and 250 tons to B, if there is a poor harvest and the yield is only 250 tons, that neither contract would be frustrated. But this result is difficult to reconcile with cases, apparently not considered in *The Super Servant Two*, in which neither party to a contract for the sale of a specific crop was held to be liable if the crops failed to materialize.[128] It is also difficult to reconcile with cases in which a seller who, following a partial failure of supply, delivered to other customers or delivered the available supply to all customers on a *pro rata* basis, was held entitled to rely on a *force majeure* clause.[129] In the present state of the law, however, a promisor who wishes protection in the case of a partial failure of supply 'must bargain for the inclusion of a suitable *force majeure* clause in the contract'.[130]

(b) NEGLIGENT ACTS

Where the act of the party pleading frustration was inadvertent and merely negligent the position is not altogether clear. Although there have been frequent statements to the effect that the frustrating event must occur without the 'default' of either party, this point has never been expressly decided. It was discussed by the House of Lords in *Joseph Constantine Steamship Line Ltd.* v. *Imperial Smelting Corporation Ltd.*, where Lord Russell, commenting on the kind or degree of fault which might debar a party from relying on a self-induced frustration, said:[131]

The possible varieties are infinite, and can range from the criminality of the scuttler who

---

[126] Treitel, *Frustration and Force Majeure*, §14–017. Treitel's earlier arguments on the issue were considered and rejected by the Court: [1989] 1 Lloyd's Rep. 148, at pp. 152–3, 154, 158; [1990] 1 Lloyd's Rep. 1, at pp. 9, 13–14.

[127] See *post*, p. 555.

[128] e.g. *Howell v. Coupland* (1876) 1 Q.B.D. 258; *H.R. & S. Sainsbury Ltd.* v. *Street* [1972] 1 W.L.R. 834, on which see *post*, p. 563.

[129] *Intertradex S.A.* v. *Lesieur Tourteaux S.A.R.L.* [1978] 2 Lloyd's Rep. 509, at p. 513; *Bremer Handelsgesellschaft m.b.H.* v. *Mackprang Jr. (No. 2)* [1979] 1 Lloyd's Rep. 221; *Bremer Handelgesellschaft m.b.H.* v. *Continental Grain Co.* [1983] 1 Lloyd's Rep. 169, at p. 292; *Bremer Handelsgesellschaft m.b.H.* v. *Vanden Avenne-Izegem P.V.B.A.* [1978] 2 Lloyd's Rep. 109. In *The Super Servant Two* the *force majeure* cases were said to be of no assistance in the context of frustration: [1989] 1 Lloyd's Rep. 148, at 158; [1990] 1 Lloyd's Rep. 1 at p. 9. *Sed quaere*, see Hudson (1968) 31 M.L.R. 535.

[130] *J. Lauritzen A.S.* v. *Wijsmuller B.V. (The Super Servant Two)* [1989] 1 Lloyd's Rep. 148 *per* Hobhouse J. at p. 158, although the distinction from frustration may be put into question since his Lordship also accepted that protection might be afforded by an implied term.

[131] [1942] A.C. 154, at p. 179.

opens the sea-cocks and sinks his ship, to the thoughtlessness of the prima donna who sits in a draught and loses her voice. I wish to guard against the supposition that every destruction of corpus for which a contractor can be said, to some extent or in some sense, to be responsible, necessarily involves that the resultant frustration is self-induced within the meaning of the phrase.

In that case:

J.C. chartered to I.S.C. its steamship *Kingswood* to proceed to Australia and load a cargo there. Before this could be done, a violent explosion occurred in the boiler of the ship which resulted in such a delay as would discharge the contract. The cause of the explosion was never ascertained, but I.S.C. alleged that J.C. had first to establish that it occurred without its fault before it could rely on the doctrine of frustration and so not be liable for breach of contract.

It was not necessary for the House of Lords to decide whether mere negligence would suffice, for it held that the burden of proving that the event which causes the frustration is due to the act or default of a party lies on the party alleging it to be so. Since I.S.C. failed to satisfy the Court on this point, the contract was discharged. It would appear logical, however, for a finding of negligence to prevent a party claiming that the contract was frustrated where that negligent act caused the alleged frustrating event.[132]

VII. LEASES AND CONTRACTS FOR THE SALE OF LAND

There was at one time considerable doubt as to whether the doctrine of frustration applied to leases of land. In 1945, in *Cricklewood Property and Investment Trust Ltd.* v. *Leighton's Investment Trust Ltd.*[133] the House of Lords held unanimously that, since wartime restrictions preventing the performance of a building lease cover only a small part of the 90 years remaining on the lease, it had not been frustrated. But on the question whether a lease could in any circumstances be terminated by frustration the House was evenly divided. Viscount Simon and Lord Wright considered that, on very rare occasions, frustration could occur, giving as illustrations some vast convulsion of nature which might sweep the property into the sea, or the frustration of a building lease by a perpetual statutory prohibition on building for the remainder of the term. Lord Russell and Lord Goddard took the contrary view. A lease was more than a contract: it vested an estate in land in the lessee, and the contractual obligations which it contained were merely incidental to the relationship of landlord and tenant. If all or some of these should become impossible of performance, the lease would remain.[134]

---

[132] See *J. Lauritzen A.S.* v. *Wijsmuller B.V. (The Super Servant Two)* [1990] 1 Lloyd's Rep. 1, at p. 10.
[133] [1945] A.C. 221.
[134] But there may be excuses for non-performance of covenants short of frustration: *ibid.*, *per* Lord Russell, at p. 233–4; *John Lewis Properties plc* v. *Viscount Chelsea* [1993] 2 E.G.L.R. 77, at p. 82.

The estate in the land would still be vested in the tenant. Lord Porter, the fifth member of the House, refused to express an opinion.

In 1981, this question was re-considered by the House of Lords in *National Carriers Ltd.* v. *Panalpina (Northern) Ltd.*:[135]

P let a warehouse to N.C. for 10 years from 1 January 1974. N.C. covenanted that it would not without P's consent use the premises for any purpose other than that of warehousing in connection with its business, or assign, underlet, or part with possession. In May 1979, the local authority temporarily closed the street which provided the only vehicular access to the warehouse. The closure lasted for 20 months and during this period the warehouse could not be used for the purpose contemplated by the lease. In answer to a claim for rent, N.C. counterclaimed that the lease had been frustrated.

Their Lordships unanimously held that there was no frustration. A majority,[136] however, agreed with Viscount Simon and Lord Wright in the *Cricklewood* case that, in principle, the doctrine of frustration was applicable to leases. 'Coastal erosion as well as the "vast convulsion of nature" . . . can . . . cause houses, gardens, even villages and their churches, to fall into the North Sea.'[137] However, the view was expressed[138] that in practice the doctrine would 'hardly ever' apply. In the present case, having regard to the nature and length of the interruption, and in particular to the fact that the lease would still have some three years to run after the interruption came to an end, it could not be said that the lease had been frustrated.

There appears to be no reported English case in which it has been held that a lease has been frustrated.[139] The reason for this may be the relative indestructibility of land. But the absence of cases of frustration is more likely to be due to the fact that the events which are most likely to occur, for example, fire,[140] are normally expressly provided for in the lease, and the incidence of the risk of less common events (such as requisitioning)[141] may be held to have been assumed by the tenant and not by the landlord. It is also very improbable that some personal incapacity which prevents the tenant from using the premises would be sufficient to terminate the lease,[142] at least if the tenant's personal occupation was not the common basis of the venture.[143] But if commercial premises are let (particularly for a short term) for one principal purpose known to the lessor, and one which gives to the premises a large part of its rental

---

[135] [1981] A.C. 675. For criticism see Price (1989) 10 J.L.H. 90, at pp. 101–3.

[136] Lord Russell of Killowen dissenting.

[137] [1981] A.C. 675, per Lord Hailsham L.C., at p. 691. See also *Holbeck Hall Hotel Ltd.* v. *Scarborough B.C.* (1998) 57 Con. L.R. 113, at pp. 152–3 (point not considered by C.A.: [2000] 2 W.L.R. 1396).

[138] At pp. 692, 697, 717.

[139] Cf. *Rom Securities Ltd.* v. *Rogers (Holdings) Ltd.* (1967) 205 E.G. 427 (agreement for a lease). Contrast *Tay Salmon Fisheries Co. Ltd.* v. *Speedie*, 1929 S.C. 593 (Scotland).

[140] Cf. *National Carriers Ltd.* v. *Panalpina (Northern) Ltd.* [1981] A.C. 675, 690.

[141] *Whitehall Court Ltd.* v. *Ettlinger* [1920] 1 K.B. 680; *Matthey* v. *Curling* [1922] 2 A.C. 180; *Swift* v. *Mackean* [1942] 1 K.B. 375. See also (before the *National Carriers* case) *Simper* v. *Coombs* [1948] 1 All E.R. 306; *Redmond* v. *Dainton* [1920] 2 K.B. 256 (destruction of premises).

[142] *London and Northern Estates Co.* v. *Schlesinger* [1916] 1 K.B. 20 (internment of tenant). See also *Youngmin* v. *Heath* [1974] 1 W.L.R. 135 (death).

[143] See *Sumnall* v. *Statt* (1984) 49 P. & C.R. 367, and *ante*, p. 534.

value, the failure of that purpose by legal prohibition or otherwise might be sufficient to bring about the radical change in the obligation required to frustrate the lease.

Similar problems arise in relation to contracts for the sale of land where a change of circumstances occurs after exchange of contracts but before completion. The risk that the premises may be destroyed or damaged, for example, by fire, is one which must be borne by the purchaser, and in respect of which it is usual to insure. It has further been held that such a contract was not frustrated when the land agreed to be sold was made the subject of a compulsory purchase order[144] and where a building intended for development was listed as being of historic or architectural interest.[145] The position is in doubt, but the answer to the question whether a contract of sale of land can be frustrated would again appear to be 'hardly ever' rather than 'never'.[146]

VIII. EFFECTS OF FRUSTRATION

(a) COMMON LAW

(i) Contract generally determined automatically

Generally, the contract is not merely dischargable at the option of one or other of the parties; it is brought to an end forthwith and automatically. In *Hirji Mulji* v. *Cheong Yue Steamship Co. Ltd.*:[147]

In November 1916 C.Y. chartered its ship, the *Singaporean*, agreeing that it should be placed at H.M.'s disposal on 1 March 1917, for 10 months. Shortly before this date the ship was requisitioned by the Government. Believing that she would soon be released, C.Y. asked if H.M. would be willing to take up the charter. H.M. said that they would. The ship was, however, not released until February 1919, and H.M. then refused to accept her.

The shipowners contended that H.M. had so conducted themselves as to oust the doctrine of frustration. But the House of Lords held that frustration, unlike breach, brings the contract to an end automatically, and could not be waived in this manner.[148]

The rule precluding a party relying on a self-induced frustration, considered above, shows that the rule that discharge is automatic is not absolute. We have seen that the party whose act or default has caused the frustrating event is not entitled to treat

---

[144] *Hillingdon Estates Co.* v. *Stonefield Estates Ltd.* [1952] Ch. 627; *E. Johnson & Co. (Barbados) Ltd.* v. *N.S.R. Ltd.* [1997] A.C. 400.

[145] *Amalgamated Investment & Property Co. Ltd.* v. *John Walker & Sons Ltd.* [1977] 1 W.L.R. 164.

[146] See also *Denny, Mott & Dickson Ltd.* v. *Fraser (James B.) & Co. Ltd.* [1944] A.C. 265, at pp. 274–6 (option to purchase land).

[147] [1926] A.C. 497. See also *J. Lauritzen A.S.* v. *Wijsmuller B.V. (The Super Servant Two)* [1990] 1 Lloyd's Rep. 1, at p. 8.

[148] *Ibid.*, *per* Lord Sumner, at p. 509. See also *B.P. Exploration (Libya) Co. Ltd.* v. *Hunt* [1979] 1 W.L.R. 783, at p. 809 (waiver or estoppel could not prevent reliance on frustration).

himself as discharged. But *F.C. Shepherd & Co. Ltd.* v. *Jerrom*,[149] shows that this will not affect the position of the other party, for whom the event is not 'self'-induced. In that case:

An employee was sentenced to a term of detention, and his employer stated that it would not take him back on his release. Once released, he instituted proceedings for unfair dismissal, which the employer defended *inter alia* on the ground that the contract had been frustrated by the imposition of the sentence of imprisonment.

Although it was clear that the employee could not rely on his detention as frustrating the contract of employment, it was held that the employer could.

(ii) Future obligations discharged

The effect of frustration *at common law* is to release both parties from any further performance of the contract. All obligations falling due for performance after the frustrating event occurred are discharged. In *Appleby* v. *Myers*,[150] for example:

A undertook to erect certain machinery upon M's premises, the agreement providing that the work was to be paid for on completion. While the work was in progress, and before it was completed, the premises and the machinery already erected were wholly destroyed by fire.

The contract was frustrated, but since it had been agreed that payment was to be made only on completion, A could recover nothing for the work already done.

(iii) Accrued obligations remain

Legal rights or obligations already accrued and due, before the frustrating event occurred, are left undisturbed. In *Chandler* v. *Webster*:[151]

C agreed to hire from W a room in Pall Mall to watch the Coronation procession. The price for the hire was to be £141, payable immediately. C paid £100 of this sum, but before he paid the balance, the procession was cancelled. He claimed to recover back the money paid.

It was held not only that he could not recover the £100 already paid, but that he was also liable to pay the other £41 as this obligation had fallen due before the frustrating event occurred. In part because of the underdevelopment of restitutionary principles at that time, the Court of Appeal rejected C's argument that he was entitled to recover the £100 in restitution as money paid under a consideration which had totally failed. The effect of the frustration was not to wipe out the contract altogether but only to release the parties from further performance, so it could not be said that the 'consideration' had failed completely.

---

[149] [1987] 1 Q.B. 301. See also *Joseph Constantine Steamship Line Ltd.* v. *Imperial Smelting Corporation Ltd.* [1942] A.C. 154, *per* Lord Porter, at pp. 199–200; *Notcutt* v. *Universal Equipment Co. (London) Ltd.* [1986] 1 W.L.R. 641.

[150] (1867) L.R. 2 C.P. 651. See also *Compania Naviera General S.A.* v. *Kerametal Ltd.* [1983] 1 Lloyd's Rep. 372.

[151] [1904] 1 K.B. 493.

(iv) Development of a restitutionary response

The harshness of the decision in *Chandler* v. *Webster*, which allocated all the risks of the frustrating event on C, excited considerable criticism,[152] and in 1942 it was overruled by the House of Lords in *Fibrosa Spolka Akcyjna* v. *Fairbairn Lawson Combe Barbour Ltd.*:[153]

The respondent contracted with the appellant, a Polish company, to manufacture certain machinery and deliver it to Gdynia. Part of the price was to be paid in advance, and the appellant accordingly paid £1,000. The contract was frustrated by the occupation of Gdynia by hostile German forces in September 1939. The appellant thereupon requested the return of the £1,000. This request was refused on the ground that considerable work had been done, and expense incurred, under the contract.

Under the rule in *Chandler* v. *Webster* this money would have been irrecoverable, as it had already been paid at the time the frustrating event occurred. The House of Lords, however, allowed the appellants to recover. It was pointed out that an action for the recovery of the sum paid was not an action on the contract, which *ex hypothesi* had ceased to exist, but an action in restitution to recover money paid on a consideration which had totally failed.[154] The House held that, in the context of a claim to recover money paid, the term 'consideration' should be understood not in the sense of the consideration which is necessary to the formation of a contract, but rather in the sense of the performance of an obligation already incurred. A party who has paid money but has received no part of the bargained-for performance, is entitled to recover it, for the consideration has totally failed.

(b) LAW REFORM (FRUSTRATED CONTRACTS) ACT 1943

(i) Underlying principle

The law as the *Fibrosa* case left it was still not satisfactory, for the party who had to return the pre-payment might have incurred expenses for the purpose of the performance of the contract, or might be left with goods which were made valueless by the failure of the contract.[155] Moreover, the insistence that the failure of consideration be total[156] meant that if the party seeking recovery of the money had received any part, however small, of the performance of the contract, the *Fibrosa* case did not apply, and the money was irrecoverable. It was to remedy this situation that the Law Reform (Frustrated Contracts) Act 1943 was passed.[157]

It has been stated that the 'fundamental principle underlying the Act ..., is

---

[152] *Cantiare San Roco S.A.* v. *Clyde Shipbuilding & Engineering Co. Ltd.* [1924] A.C. 226, at p. 257.

[153] [1943] A.C. 32.

[154] See *post*, p. 643.

[155] This was probably not a problem in *Fibrosa* since, although the sellers had done a considerable amount of work in manufacturing the machines ([1942] 1 K.B. 12 at p. 14), it was accepted that they could be resold without loss: [1943] A.C. 32, at p. 49.

[156] See *post*, p. 643.

[157] See Williams, *Law Reform (Frustrated Contracts) Act 1943*; Goff and Jones, *The Law of Restitution*, 5th edn. (1999), p. 557 ff; McKendrick, *Force Majeure and Frustration of Contract*, 2nd edn. (1994), ch. 11.

prevention of the unjust enrichment of either party to the contract at the other's expense' and not the apportionment of the loss caused by the frustrating event between the parties.[158] Although it has been argued that the law is defective in not providing for such loss-apportionment,[159] especially since the line between action in reliance on a contract which results in a benefit and action which does not can be very fine,[160] the case for a financial adjustment is stronger where such pre-frustration action has resulted in a realizable benefit in the hands of one of the parties. But in the present state of the law, it is important not to allow an over-wide interpretation of 'enrichment' or 'benefit' to operate as loss-apportionment by subsuming virtually all action taken by a contracting party in reliance on the contract. The Act does not apply if there is a provision to the contrary in the contract.[161]

(ii) Money paid or payable

By section 1(2) of the 1943 Act:

All sums paid or payable to any party in pursuance of the contract before the time when the parties were so discharged (in this Act referred to as 'the time of discharge') shall, in the case of sums so paid, be recoverable from him as money received by him for the use of the party by whom the sums were paid, and, in the case of sums so payable, cease to be payable:

Provided that, if the party to whom the sums were so paid or payable incurred expenses before the time of the discharge in, or for the purpose of, the performance of the contract, the court may, if it considers it just to do so having regard to all the circumstances of the case, allow him to retain or, as the case may be, recover the whole or any part of the sums so paid or payable, not being an amount in excess of the expenses so incurred.

A careful reading of this sub-section reveals that it has two effects.

In the first place, it embodies the rule in the *Fibrosa* case, although it is now no longer necessary to prove a total failure of consideration. So if A agrees to manufacture and deliver to B certain machinery, B promising to pay £10,000 down and the balance on completion, then even if A has delivered part of the machinery to B before the frustrating event occurs, B can recover the £10,000, if paid, and, if not paid, it ceases to be payable.[162]

(iii) Expenses incurred by payee

The Act goes further than the *Fibrosa* case in that it gives to the Court a discretionary power to allow the payee to set off against the sum so paid or payable a sum not exceeding the value of any expenses which the payee has incurred in or for the

---

[158] *B.P. Exploration (Libya) Co. Ltd.* v. *Hunt (No. 2)* [1979] 1 W.L.R. 783, *per* Robert Goff J. at pp. 799–800. Cf. Lawton L.J. *ibid.* [1981] 1 W.L.R. 232.

[159] Williams, *Law Reform (Frustrated Contracts) Act 1943*, p. 35; McKendrick, 'Frustration, Restitution and Loss Apportionment' in Burrows, ed., *Essays on the Law of Restitution* (1991), p. 147; cf. Posner and Rosenfield (1977) 6 J.L.S. 83, at p. 112 ff (part-performer can generally evaluate the risk better and insure more cheaply than the other party); Stewart and Carter [1992] C.L.J. 66, at pp. 86–9, 109–10; Burrows, *The Law of Restitution* (1993), p. 286.

[160] *Post*, pp. 643–4.

[161] 1943 Act, s. 2(3). Cf. *B.P. Exploration (Libya) Ltd.* v. *Hunt* [1983] 2 A.C. 352, at pp. 372, 373.

[162] A's position may be protected by s. 1(3), on which see *infra*.

purpose of performing the contract before the frustration.[163] So if, in the above
example, A has incurred expenses totalling, say, £6,000, then the Court has power to
permit A to recover or retain the whole or part of this sum from the £10,000 due from
B under the contract. But expenses can only be set off against 'the sums so paid or
payable', i.e. those due before frustration, so that if the expenses amounted to, say,
£12,000, it would not be possible to charge the £2,000 in excess of £10,000 against the
unpaid balance due after the frustrating event occurred.

In *Gamerco S.A. v. I.C.M./Fair Warning (Agency) Ltd.*[164] Garland J. considered three
methods by which the Court should exercise its discretion; allowing the payee to
retain all the expenses incurred[165] as a statutory recognition of the defence of change
of position,[166] equal division of the loss caused by the frustrating event,[167] and a broad
discretion to do what the Court considers just, 'having regard to all the circumstances
of the case'.[168] His Lordship favoured the third, concluding that the task of the Court
'is to do justice in a situation which the parties neither contemplated nor provided for,
and to mitigate the possible harshness of allowing all loss to lie where it has fallen'.[169]
In *Gamerco's* case:

$775,000 was payable by the promoters of a pop concert to the defendant group, Guns N'
Roses, at the time the contract was frustrated, $412,500 of which had been paid. Both parties
had incurred expenses before the date of frustration which were wholly wasted: the defendant $50,000, and the promoters $450,000. Neither party was left with any residual benefit or
advantage.

In these circumstances, and having particular regard to the promoters' loss, and his
view that there was no question of any change of position by the defendant as a result
of the promoters' advance payment,[170] his Lordship made no deduction under the
proviso and ordered repayment of the $412,500.

(iv) Obligations other than to pay money

Section 1(3) of the 1943 Act provides for the adjustment of the financial relations of
the parties:

Where any party to the contract has, by reason of anything done by any other party thereto
in, or for the purpose of, the performance of the contract, obtained a valuable benefit (other
than a payment of money to which the last foregoing sub-section applies) before the time of
discharge, there shall be recoverable from him by the said other party such sum (if any) not

---

[163] 'Expenses' include a reasonable sum in respect of overhead expenses: s. 1(4), and the onus of proof lies
on the payee: *Gamerco S.A. v. I.C.M./Fair Warning (Agency) Ltd.* [1995] 1 W.L.R. 1226, at p. 1235. See also
Lobb v. Vasey Housing Auxiliary (War Widows Guild) [1963] V.R. 239 (Victoria, Australia).

[164] [1995] 1 W.L.R. 1226.

[165] This was favoured by the Law Revision Committee (Cmd. 6009, 1939), p. 7.

[166] As suggested in *B.P. Exploration Co. (Libya) Ltd. v. Hunt (No. 2)* [1979] 1 W.L.R. 783 at p. 800. Note that
this decision was substantially approved by the House of Lords: [1983] 2 A.C. 352.

[167] Williams, *Law Reform (Frustrated Contracts) Act 1943*, pp. 35–6.

[168] Treitel, *Frustration and Force Majeure* (1994), §§15–059–15–060.

[169] [1995] 1 W.L.R. 1226, at p. 1237.

[170] *Sed quaere*, see *Lipkin Gorman v. Karpnale Ltd.* [1991] 2 A.C. 548; Carter and Tolhurst (1996) 10 J.C.L.
265.

exceeding the value of the said benefit to the party obtaining it, as the court considers just, having regard to all the circumstances of the case and, in particular—

(a) the amount of any expenses incurred before the time of discharge by the benefited party in, or for the purpose of the performance of the contract, including any sums paid or payable by him to any other party in pursuance of the contract and retained or recoverable by that party under the last foregoing sub-section, and

(b) the effect, in relation to the said benefit, of the circumstances giving rise to frustration of the contract.

The result is that recompense may be awarded in respect of a valuable benefit conferred by either party upon the other party in pursuance of the contract. In *B.P. Exploration Co. (Libya) Ltd.* v. *Hunt (No. 2)*[171] Robert Goff J. pointed out that the sub-section must be applied in two distinct stages. The first is the identification and valuation of the benefit. The second stage is for the Court to assess what sum (not exceeding the value of the benefit) it considers just to award to the party by whom the benefit has been conferred.

With regard to the identification and valuation of the benefit, there are three situations to be considered. The first is where the performance rendered results in the delivery of an item which is unaffected by the frustrating event. If, for example, in the illustration set out above, A has delivered to B some of the machinery, the machinery so delivered could constitute a benefit to B. The value of that benefit will ordinarily be its value to B at the date of frustration. This may be more or less than the expenses incurred by A in manufacturing and delivering that machinery. It was stated by Robert Goff J. that as a matter of construction 'benefit' in the sub-section normally meant the end product of services rather than the services themselves.[172]

The second is where, although the performance results in the delivery of an item or an end-product, in our example the machinery, the event which frustrates the contract (as in *Appleby* v. *Myers*),[173] destroys it or renders it useless and of no value to B without delivery of the remainder. Under paragraph (b) of the sub-section regard is to be had to 'the effect, in relation to the . . . benefit, of the circumstances giving rise to the frustration of the contract'. The interpretation of this provision is problematical. Robert Goff J. stated[174] that 'benefit' in section 1(3)(b) clearly refers to the end-product of the services, rather than the services themselves, and that the sub-section 'makes it plain that the plaintiff [the party conferring the benefit] is to take the risk of depreciation or destruction by the frustrating event'. If this view is correct,[175] then the

---

[171] [1979] 1 W.L.R. 783 (aff'd by the Court of Appeal [1981] 1 W.L.R. 232, and by the House of Lords [1983] 2 A.C. 352), for the facts see *infra*.

[172] *B.P. Exploration Co. (Libya) Ltd.* v. *Hunt (No. 2)* (*supra*, n. 166) at pp. 801–2.

[173] (1867) L.R. 2 C.P. 651; *ante*, p. 556. See also *Parsons Bros. Ltd.* v. *Shea* (1965) 53 D.L.R. (2d) 86 (Canada).

[174] *B.P. Exploration Co. (Libya) Ltd.* v. *Hunt (No. 2)* [1979] 1 W.L.R. 783, at p. 803. Contrast Glanville Williams, *Law Reform (Frustrated Contracts) Act 1943*, pp. 48–51.

[175] Cf. Treitel, *Frustration and Force Majeure* (1994), § 15–054 (s. 1(3) applies where a valuable benefit has been obtained 'before the time of discharge' and sub-paragraphs (a) and (b) are relevant to the assessment of the just sum, not the identification of the benefit); Birks, *An Introduction to the Law of Restitution* (1985), p. 253.

value of the benefit in such a case will be nil, and no award could be made in favour of A under the sub-section.

The third situation is where the performance rendered is a 'pure' service, without any end-product, such as gardening, surveying, or transporting goods.[176] Here, Robert Goff J. stated that the 'benefit' in the sub-section was the services themselves,[177] and it is these that must be valued. In such cases care must be taken not to cross the line between restitution in respect of a benefit conferred, which is permitted by the sub-section, and recompense for action taken by one party in reliance on the contract: 'if in fact the performance of services has conferred no benefit on the person requesting them, it is pure fiction to base restitution on a benefit conferred'.[178]

The second stage is for the Court to assess what sum (not exceeding the value of the benefit) it considers just to award to the party by whom the benefit has been conferred. This has been termed the 'just sum'. The purpose of the award has been said to be to prevent the unjust enrichment of the other party at his expense.[179] In the example given above, if the machinery delivered remained of value to B after the frustrating event, the just sum would probably be assessed as the reasonable value of that machinery,[180] or a rateable part of the contract price.

The principles were applied in *B.P. Exploration Co. (Libya) Ltd.* v. *Hunt (No. 2)*:[181]

B.P. entered into a contract to explore and develop an oil concession in Libya owned by H. B.P. was to make initial payments and a transfer of oil to Hunt, and in return was to get a 50 per cent share in the concession and 'reimbursement oil' calculated by a formula. A significant oil field was discovered and oil was produced and transferred under the contract for four and a half years, but the contract was then frustrated when both parties' interests were expropriated by the Libyan Government, which paid some compensation to H. B.P. claimed under section 1(3) of the 1943 Act.

It was held that, under section 1(3), the 'valuable benefit' had to be not the work exploring and extracting oil but the end-product of that work, the enhancement of the value of H's concession. But the effect of the frustrating event was to make this valueless and unrealizable by H, and sub-paragraph (b) required this to be reflected in the valuation of the benefit. But H had received considerable amounts of oil produced prior to the expropriation, and compensation thereafter, and half the value of this ($85 million) was held to be the benefit obtained from B.P.'s exploration and development, and the upper limit of any award.[182] The 'just sum' was determined by taking account of the cost to B.P. of the work done for H and the oil it initially transferred to

---

[176] See e.g. *Angus* v. *Skully* 44 NE 674 (1900) (USA) and the facts of *Cutter* v. *Powell* (1795) 6 T.R. 320, *ante*, p. 510.

[177] *B.P. Exploration Co. (Libya) Ltd.* v. *Hunt (No. 2)* (*supra*, n. 166) at p. 803.

[178] *Coleman Engineering* v. *North American Airlines* 420 P. 2d 713, *per* Traynor C.J. at p. 729 (1966) (California).

[179] *Ibid.*, at p. 805.

[180] *Ibid.*, at pp. 805–6.

[181] [1979] 1 W.L.R. 783 (aff'd by the Court of Appeal [1981] 1 W.L.R. 232, and by the House of Lords [1983] 2 A.C. 352).

[182] The other half was attributed to Hunt's ownership of the concession prior to the exploration and development under the contract.

H reduced by the amount of the 'reimbursement oil' it had received. This amounted to just under $35 million. Since this was in effect the value of 'reimbursement oil' due to B.P. but not transferred at the date of frustration, the remedy given approximately corresponded to a scaled-down contract price, that percentage of the contract price which the part-performer had 'earned' by performance before the frustrating event.

Neither under sub-section (2) nor under sub-section (3) can any allowance be made for the time-value of money, that is to say, for the fact that money may have been paid, or expenses incurred, long before the date of frustration.[183]

(v) Carriage of goods by sea and voyage charters

The Act does not apply to contracts for the carriage of goods by sea or a charterparty (other than a time charterparty or a charterparty by way of demise).[184] This recognizes a well-established custom, which has become part of the business practice of shipowners and insurers, that freight paid or payable in advance under such contracts is not recoverable even though the completion of the voyage is frustrated.[185]

(vi) Sale of goods and insurance

The Act is also not applicable to contracts of insurance and certain contracts for the sale of goods. By section 2(5)(c) the Act does not apply to:

Any contract to which section seven of the Sale of Goods Act 1979 (which avoids contracts for the sale of specific goods which perish before the risk has passed to the buyer) applies or . . . any other contract for the sale, or for the sale and delivery, of specific goods, where the contract is frustrated by reason of the fact that the goods have perished.

It will be remembered that the general rule in the case of the sale of goods is that they are at the risk of the person whose property they are: *res perit domino*.[186] Where there is a sale of *specific* goods property in the goods normally passes to the buyer at the time the contract is made,[187] and so it follows that they are also at the buyer's risk. To this type of contract the Act has no application.

Suppose that A buys from a shopkeeper, B, a particular wardrobe, arranging for it to be delivered next day. During the night the shop catches fire and the wardrobe is destroyed. The risk has passed to A, who must pay the purchase price.

But the sub-section quoted above also exempts cases where there is an agreement to sell specific goods and the risk has not yet passed to the buyer. If the goods then perish without the fault of either party, the contract is *avoided* by section 7 of the Sale of Goods Act 1979 and the 1943 Act does not apply.

Specific goods are defined by section 61(1) of the Sale of Goods Act 1979 as 'goods identified and agreed on at the time a contract of sale is made'. Goods which are unascertained at this time do not therefore come within this exception, although it

---

[183] *B.P. Exploration Co. (Libya) Ltd* v. *Hunt (No. 2)* [1979] 1 W.L.R. 783, at p. 800.
[184] 1943 Act, s. 2(5).
[185] *Compania Naviera General S.A.* v. *Kerametal Ltd.* [1983] 1 Lloyd's Rep. 372.
[186] Sale of Goods Act 1979, s. 20.
[187] *Ibid.*, s. 18, Rule 1.

must be noted that the doctrine of frustration rarely then applies. If A agrees to sell to B 'six hundred tons of coal', there can normally be no frustration of this contract. Even though A may have had in mind a particular source, this assumption is not common to both parties. The contract can be fulfilled at any time and A must obtain sufficient coal from another source or be liable for breach.[188] On the other hand, if the goods, though unascertained, are to come from a source which is specifically defined, for example, 'six hundred tons of coal from the ship *Rose Marie* now in dock', and subsequently the ship and cargo are destroyed by fire, this contract is clearly capable of frustration, but there is some doubt as to whether or not it falls outside the 1943 Act. In one case,[189] goods of this nature were held not to be specific goods for the purposes of section 52 of the Sale of Goods Act 1979 (specific performance), and it is submitted that, for the purposes of frustration, the goods are likewise not specific goods and so are subject to the provisions of the 1943 Act.[190]

A similar problem may arise in the type of situation exemplified by *Howell* v. *Coupland*:[191]

C agreed to sell to H 200 tons of potatoes to be grown on a particular field. The crop failed, so that C was able to deliver only 80 tons. In answer to H's claim for non-delivery of the other 120 tons, C pleaded that he had duly delivered all that it was possible for him to deliver and that he was excused from delivering the remainder.

It was held that C was not liable. Mellish L.J. said:[192]

This is not like the case of a contract to deliver so many goods of a particular kind, where no specific goods are to be sold. Here there was an agreement to sell and buy 200 tons of a crop to be grown on specific land, so that it is an agreement to sell what will be and may be called specific things; therefore neither party is liable if the performance becomes impossible.

Despite the use by Mellish L.J. of the word 'specific' in this case, it is clear that the potatoes were not 'specific goods' within the meaning of the Sale of Goods Act. Nevertheless this is not a situation to which the provisions of the 1943 Act would appear to apply. It has been held[193] that a contract of sale of this nature is subject to a condition. Depending on the intention of the parties, the condition which will be implied may be one that neither party shall be liable if any part of the promised goods fails to materialize;[194] alternatively, it may, as in *Howell* v. *Coupland*, be a condition that the buyer can require such performance as remains possible, but the seller is excused from delivering the remainder of the goods.[195]

[188] *Blackburn Bobbin Co. Ltd.* v. *Allen (T. W.) & Sons Ltd.* [1918] 2 K.B. 467; *ante*, p. 548. Cf. *Re Badische Co. Ltd.* [1921] 2 Ch. 331; see *ante*, p. 548.

[189] *Re Wait* [1927] 1 Ch. 606.

[190] See also Hudson (1968) 31 M.L.R. 535.

[191] (1876) 1 Q.B.D. 258.

[192] At p. 262.

[193] *H.R. & S. Sainsbury Ltd.* v. *Street* [1972] 1 W.L.R. 834. See also *Re Wait* [1927] 1 Ch. 606, at p. 631.

[194] See the Sale of Goods Act 1979, s. 5(2) (condition precedent). The sale might also be subject to a condition subsequent: *ante*, pp. 138, 528–9.

[195] *H.R. & S. Sainsbury Ltd.* v. *Street* (*supra*, n. 193).

(vii) Arbitration

There are very few reported decisions on the interpretation of the 1943 Act: most disputes simply concern the amount of each party's liability, and are referred to arbitration.[196]

---

[196] *Pioneer Shipping Ltd. v. B.T.P. Tioxide Ltd.* [1982] A.C. 724.

15

DISCHARGE BY BREACH

If one of two parties to a contract breaks an obligation which the contract imposes, a new obligation will in every case arise—an obligation to pay damages to the other party in respect of any loss or damage sustained by the breach. Besides this, there are circumstances under which the breach not only gives rise to a right of action for damages but also gives the innocent party the right to decide not to render further performance under the contract and to be discharged from its obligations.[1] However, not every breach of contract has this effect. In order to do so the breach must be such as to constitute a repudiation by the party in default of its obligations under the contract.

I. DISCHARGE AT OPTION OF THE INJURED PARTY

It is common to speak of the contract as having been 'discharged by the breach'. The phrase, though convenient, is not strictly accurate. A breach does not, of itself, effect a discharge;[2] what it may do is to justify the innocent party, if that party so chooses, in regarding itself as absolved or discharged from further performance of the contract. It does not automatically terminate the innocent party's obligation since that party has the option either to treat the contract as still continuing or to regard itself as discharged by reason of the repudiation of the contract by the other party. An acceptance of a repudiation must be clear and unequivocal.[3] Once the option is exercised to either keep the contract on foot or terminate it, the decision is not revocable.[4] A fresh option may arise, however, if the repudiation continues or there is another separate repudiatory breach.

---

[1] See Treitel (1967) 30 M.L.R. 139.

[2] See *post*, pp. 571, 578.

[3] *Vitol S.A. v. Norelf Ltd.* [1996] A.C. 800, *per* Lord Steyn at 810–11. See also *Heyman v. Darwins Ltd.* [1942] A.C. 356, at p. 361; *Northwest Holt Group Administration Ltd. v. Harrison* [1985] I.C.R. 668; *Bliss v. South East Thames Regional Health Authority* [1987] I.C.R. 700, at pp. 716–17; *State Trading Corporation of India Ltd. v. M. Golodetz Ltd.* [1989] 2 Lloyd's Rep. 277 at p. 286.

[4] *Motor Oil Hellas (Corinth) Refineries S.A. v. Shipping Corporation of India (The Kanchenjunga)* [1990] 1 Lloyd's Rep. 391 *per* Lord Goff at p. 398; *Peyman v. Lanjani* [1985] Ch. 457.

(a) EFFECT OF UNACCEPTED REPUDIATION

In principle, an innocent party who does not 'accept' the repudiation is entitled to continue to insist on performance because the contract remains in full effect. Thus in *White and Carter (Councils) Ltd.* v. *McGregor*:[5]

W. & C., an advertising contractor, agreed with McG., a garage proprietor, to display advertisements for his garage for 3 years. On the same day, McG refused to perform the agreement and requested W. & C. to cancel the contract. W. & C. refused to do so, and elected to treat the contract as still continuing. It made no effort to relet the space, displayed advertisements as agreed, and sued for the full amount due.

It was contended on behalf of McG. that, since he had renounced the agreement before anything had been done under it, W. & C. was not entitled to carry out the agreement and sue for the price: its remedy, if any, lay in damages. A bare majority of the House of Lords rejected this contention and held that W. & C. was entitled to the full contract sum.

The decision has been criticized as encouraging wasteful and unwanted performance. The criticisms are considered in the context of specific remedies.[6] It is in any event clear from the speeches of the majority in this case that the party not in breach will not always thus be entitled to complete the contract and sue for the contract price. In the first place, if the contract cannot be carried out without the co-operation of the party who has refused to perform, and such co-operation is withheld, the innocent party's only remedy is to sue for damages and not for the price.[7] So an employee who is wrongfully dismissed from employment can only claim damages. The employee cannot claim the salary payable after dismissal on the ground that he is ready, able, and willing to serve the employer if only the employer would allow him to do so.[8] Secondly, the rule in *White and Carter (Councils) Ltd.* v. *McGregor* does not apply 'if it can be shown that a person has no legitimate interest, financial or otherwise, in performing the contract rather than claiming damages',[9] in which case a claimant may be compelled to resort to the remedy of damages, provided the damages are an adequate remedy for any loss suffered.

The need for acceptance of a repudiation for the contract to be discharged led to Asquith L.J.'s famous and influential aphorism that 'an unaccepted repudiation is a thing writ in water'.[10] But an unaccepted repudiation is not altogether without effect.

---

[5] [1962] A.C. 413, on the facts of which, see Rodger (1977) 93 L.Q.R. 168.

[6] Chapter 18.

[7] At pp. 430, 432, 439.

[8] *Vine* v. *National Dock Labour Board* [1956] 1 Q.B. 658, at p. 674; *Denmark Productions Ltd.* v. *Boscobel Productions Ltd* [1969] 1 Q.B. 699; *Hill* v. *C. A. Parsons & Co. Ltd.* [1972] Ch. 305, at p. 314; *Gunton* v. *Richmond L.B.C.* [1980] I.C.R. 755. Cf. *Boyo* v. *Lambeth London Borough Council* [1994] I.C.R. 727 at pp. 742–4, 747.

[9] *White and Carter (Councils) Ltd.* v. *McGregor* [1962] A.C. 413, *per* Lord Reid at p. 431; *Attica Sea Carriers Corp.* v. *Ferrostaal Poseidon Bulk Reederei GmbH (The Puerto Buitrago)* [1976] 1 Lloyd's Rep. 250; *Gator Shipping Cpn.* v. *Trans-Asiatic Oil Ltd. S.A.* [1978] 2 Lloyd's Rep. 357, at pp. 372–4; *Stocznia Gdanska S.A.* v. *Latvian S.S. Co.* [1996] 2 Lloyd's Rep. 132; [1998] 1 W.L.R. 574.

[10] *Howard* v. *Pickford Tool Co. Ltd.* [1951] 1 K.B. 417, at p. 421. See also *Fercometal S.A.R.L.* v. *Mediterranean Shipping Co. S.A.* [1989] A.C. 788 at p. 800; *State Trading Corporation of India Ltd.* v. *M. Golodetz Ltd.* [1989] 2 Lloyd's Rep. 277 at p. 285.

An innocent party who remains ready and willing to perform[11] can rely on the unaccepted repudiation as a defence in an action brought by the guilty party.[12] Again, while the suggestion that contracts of employment are an exception to the normal rule and are discharged by a unilateral repudiation without the need for acceptance has been rejected,[13] it has been held that an employee's right to damages following an unlawful dismissal does not continue beyond the time at which the employer could have lawfully brought the contract to an end.[14]

(b) FAILURE OF PERFORMANCE

In cases of a failure of performance by one party which goes to the root of the contract,[15] the contract is likewise not determined by the breach,[16] and it is open to the innocent party to treat the contract as continuing or to accept the defective performance when tendered. An innocent party who adopts this course is sometimes said to have elected to *affirm* the contract, i.e. to have waived the right to be treated as discharged, although the right to claim damages for the breach is still retained.[17] Affirmation may be express or implied. Affirmation will be implied if, to the knowledge of the party in default, the innocent party does some unequivocal[18] act which shows an intention to go on with the contract regardless of the breach or from which it may be inferred that the right to be treated as discharged will not be exercised.[19] And affirmation must be total. A contracting party cannot affirm part of the contract and disaffirm the rest, for that would be to make a new contract.[20]

(c) AFFIRMATION OF CONTRACT

Affirmation is a voluntary act, and requires knowledge. Although old authorities to the contrary can be found, the traditional position was that a party need only have knowledge of the facts which give rise to the right to affirm or terminate.[21] Recent

---

[11] *Fercometal S.A.R.L.* v. *Mediterranean Shipping Co. S.A. (The Simona)* [1989] A.C. 788.

[12] *Peter Turnbull & Co. Pty. Ltd.* v. *Mundus Trading Co. (Australasia) Pty. Ltd.* (1954) 90 C.L.R. 235, at pp. 245, 251; *Foran* v. *Wight* (1989) 168 C.L.R. 385 at p. 438 (Australia). See further Carter, *Breach of Contract*, 2nd edn. (1991) p. 242 ff.

[13] *Gunton* v. *Richmond L.B.C.* [1980] I.C.R. 755.

[14] *Boyo* v. *Lambeth London Borough Council* [1994] I.C.R. 727.

[15] See *post*, p. 578.

[16] *Photo Productions Ltd.* v. *Securicor Transport Ltd.* [1980] A.C. 827 (overruling *Harbutt's 'Plasticine' Ltd.* v. *Wayne Tank and Pump Co. Ltd.* [1970] 1 Q.B. 447).

[17] See *ante*, p. 134.

[18] *China National Foreign Trade Transportation Cpn.* v. *Evlogia Shipping Co. S.A. of Panama* [1979] 1 W.L.R. 1018; *Yukong Line Ltd. of Korea* v. *Rendsburg Investments Corp. of Liberia* [1996] 2 Lloyd's Rep. 604 (very clear evidence required).

[19] *Bentsen* v. *Taylor, Sons & Co.* [1893] 2 Q.B. 274; *Hain SS. Co. Ltd.* v. *Tate & Lyle Ltd.* (1936) 41 Com. Cas. 350, at pp. 355, 363; *Suisse Atlantique Société d'Armement Maritime S.A.* v. *N.V. Rotterdamsche Kolen Centrale* [1967] 1 A.C. 361.

[20] *Suisse Atlantique Société d'Armement Maritime S.A.* v. *N.V. Rotterdamsche Kolen Centrale* (*supra*, n. 19), at p. 398.

[21] *Matthews* v. *Smallwood* [1910] 1 Ch. 777 at p. 786; *Kammins Ballrooms Co. Ltd.* v. *Zenith Investments (Torquay) Ltd.* [1971] A.C. 850, at pp. 877–8, 883.

cases go further and suggest that a party cannot be called upon to make an election or be held to have made an election, unless, in addition to knowledge of the relevant facts, that party has knowledge of the right to elect.[22] Despite this debate, as we have seen,[23] there are circumstances where the innocent party will be deprived of the right to be treated as discharged even though that party has no knowledge of the breach. There may also be cases where an innocent party who has led the party in default to believe that it will not exercise that right will be estopped from exercising it.[24]

(d) EFFECT OF ELECTION TO ACCEPT REPUDIATION

If the innocent party decides to accept the repudiation, this discharges all the future contractual obligations of that party which have not already been performed. At the same time, the primary obligations of the party in default to perform any of that party's contractual promises which remain unperformed are likewise discharged.[25] However, in the case of the party in default, in place of the primary obligations imposed by the contract there arises a secondary obligation to pay damages for the breach. This point was clearly made in *Moschi* v. *Lep Air Services Ltd*.:[26]

R Ltd., was indebted to L Ltd., the respondent, in the sum of £40,000, which it agreed to pay to L Ltd at the rate of not less than £6,000 *per* week. M, the appellant, guaranteed to L Ltd. the performance by R Ltd. of its obligation to make these payments. R Ltd. defaulted from the outset and, after 3 weeks, paid only some £10,000 of the £18,000 then due. L Ltd. elected to treat this default as a repudiation of the contract which it accepted. R Ltd went into liquidation and L Ltd. sued M in respect of both the accrued and future instalments unpaid.

M argued that, since the repudiation had been accepted, the obligation of the company to pay the outstanding instalments due after that time came to an end, and in consequence his obligation as guarantor also came to an end. The House of Lords found little difficulty in disposing of this argument and held that he was liable on the guarantee. In the first place, upon acceptance of the repudiation, although the company's primary obligation to pay the future instalments came to an end, it was replaced, by operation of law, by a secondary obligation to pay damages for the breach. This secondary obligation was just as much an obligation arising from the contract as were the primary obligations it replaced. Secondly, M had undertaken that R Ltd. would perform its contract and so was in breach of his contract of guarantee.

---

[22] *Peyman* v. *Lanjani* [1985] Ch. 457; *Sea Calm Shipping Co. S.A.* v. *Chantiers Navals de L'Esterel* [1986] 2 Lloyd's Rep. 294. See also *Kendall* v. *Hamilton* (1879) 4 App Cas. 504 at p. 542. Cf. *Motor Oil Hellas (Corinth) Refineries S.A.* v. *Shipping Corpn. of India (The Kanchenjunga)* [1990] 1 Lloyd's Rep. 391 at p. 398.

[23] See *ante*, p. 527.

[24] The incidence of estoppel in this situation depends upon interpretation of the difficult case of *Panchaud Frères S.A.* v. *Etablissements General Grain Co.* [1970] 1 Lloyd's Rep. 53 (esp. at pp. 57–8) and cases consequent thereon.

[25] It may, however, be the intention of the parties that certain primary obligations, for example, an arbitration or jurisdiction clause, should continue notwithstanding that their other primary obligations have come to an end: see *Heyman* v. *Darwins Ltd.* [1942] A.C. 356; *Moschi* v. *Lep Air Services Ltd.* [1973] A.C. 331, at p. 350. See also *ante*, pp. 176–7 (exemption clauses).

[26] [1973] A.C. 331. See also *Photo Production Ltd.* v. *Securicor Transport Ltd.* [1980] A.C. 827, at p. 849.

The damages which R Ltd. had not paid constituted the loss flowing from M's breach of contract for which M was liable.

(e) NO OR BAD REASON FOR CLAIMING TO BE DISCHARGED

Where one party refuses to go on with the contract, giving no reason for this refusal or the wrong or an inadequate reason, the action can still be justified if (even if this is unknown to that party) the other party had at the time committed a breach of contract which would have provided a good reason.[27] So, for example, if an employer dismisses an employee without giving any reason at all, the employer can justify the dismissal should it subsequently be discovered that, prior to the dismissal, the employee had been guilty of dishonesty which would have entitled the employer to dismiss the employee.[28] Similarly if a buyer of goods rejects the goods on the erroneous ground that they are defective in quality, that rejection will still be lawful should the goods turn out not to have been in conformity with the contract description—a breach of contract which would have justified rejection. This rule, though well established, could be criticized on the ground that it allows a party to a contract to 'blow hot and cold', first alleging one reason then in fact relying on another. There is some authority[29] for the view that a party will be estopped from relying on a ground which was not specified at the time of the refusal to perform if that party has thereby led the other party to believe that no reliance would be placed on that ground and it would be unfair or unjust now to allow such reliance.

II. FORMS OF DISCHARGE BY BREACH

The right of a party to be treated as discharged from further performance may arise in any one of three ways: the other party to the contract (a) may renounce its liabilities under it, (b) may by its own act make it impossible to fulfil them, (c) may fail to perform what it has promised.[30] In each of these three cases the contracting party has repudiated its contractual obligations. In the first case, the repudiation is by the refusal to perform; in the second, it is by the inability to perform; in the third, it is by a total or substantial failure to perform, and not the less so because that failure may not have been wilful or deliberate.

[27] *Taylor* v. *Oakes Roncoroni & Co.* (1922) 127 L.T. 267, at p. 269; *British & Beningtons Ltd.* v. *N.W. Cachar Tea Co.* [1923] A.C. 48, at p. 71; *The Mihalis Angelos* [1971] 1 Q.B. 164, at pp. 195, 200, 204; *Scandinavian Trading Co. A/B* v. *Zodiac Petroleum S.A.* [1981] 1 Lloyd's Rep. 81; *Sheffield* v. *Conrad* (1987) 22 Con. L.R. 108.

[28] *Ridgway* v. *Hungerford Market Co.* (1835) 3 A. & E. 171, at pp. 177, 178, 180; *Boston Deep Sea Fishing & Ice Co.* v. *Ansell* (1888) 39 Ch. D. 339, at pp. 352, 364; *Cyril Leonard & Co.* v. *Simo Securities Trust* [1972] 1 W.L.R. 80, at pp. 85, 87, 89. But the rule does not apply to cases of unfair dismissal under statute: *W. Devis & Co.* v. *Atkins* [1977] A.C. 931.

[29] *Panchaud Frères S.A.* v. *Etablissements General Grain Co.* [1970] 1 Lloyd's Rep. 53, at pp. 57–8. See also *Heisler* v. *Anglo-Dal Ltd.* [1954] 1 W.L.R. 1273, at p. 1278.

[30] This statement of the law was approved by Lord Porter in *Heyman* v. *Darwins Ltd.* [1942] A.C. 356, at p. 397 and by Devlin J. in *Universal Cargo Carriers Corporation* v. *Citati* [1957] 2 Q.B. 401, at p. 436 (aff'd in part [1957] 1 W.L.R. 979 and reversed in part [1958] 2 Q.B. 254).

Of these forms of breach the first two may take place not only in the course of performance but also while the contract is still wholly executory, i.e. before either party is entitled to demand a performance by the other of the other's promise. In such a case the breach is usually termed an 'anticipatory breach'.[31] The last can only take place at or during the time for performance of the contract.

(a) RENUNCIATION

Renunciation occurs where one of the parties evinces an intention not to go on with the contract. If there is an express and unqualified refusal to perform, this intention will, of course, be clear and obvious. But it can also be evinced by conduct.

(i) By conduct

The test of whether an intention to renounce a contract is evinced by conduct is 'whether the party renouncing has acted in such a way as to lead a reasonable person to the conclusion that he does not intend to fulfil his part of the contract'.[32] Acts or omissions from which renunciation can be inferred may also entitle the injured party to be treated as discharged on one or both of the two other grounds previously mentioned.[33] But if the injured party relies upon renunciation as a ground for discharge, they must be such as to lead to the conclusion that the other party no longer intends to be bound by the contract.

(ii) Intention to renounce

The importance of this intention was emphasized in the case of *Freeth* v. *Burr*,[34] where there was a failure on the part of the buyer to pay for one instalment of several deliveries of iron, under an erroneous impression that he was entitled to withhold payment as a set-off against damages for non-delivery of an earlier instalment. The seller was not discharged. Keating J. said:[35] 'It is not a mere refusal or omission of one of the contracting parties to do something which he ought to do, that will justify the other in repudiating the contract; but there must be an absolute refusal to perform his part of the contract'. Note here that the word 'repudiating' is being used in the sense of an election to terminate the contract.

Also in *Mersey Steel and Iron Co.* v. *Naylor, Benzon & Co.*:[36]

---

[31] See *post*, pp. 571–3; Dawson [1981] C.L.J. 83.

[32] *Universal Cargo Carriers Corporation* v. *Citati* (*supra*, n. 30), *per* Devlin J. at p. 436. See also *Forslind* v. *Becheley Crundall*, 1922 S.C. (H.L.) 173; *The Hermosa* [1982] 1 Lloyd's Rep. 570; *Nottingham Building Society* v. *Eurodynamics plc.* [1995] F.S.R. 605 at pp. 611–12.

[33] *Mersey Steel and Iron Co.* v. *Naylor, Benzon & Co.* (1884) 9 App. Cas. 434, at p. 441 (renunciation) and p. 444 (failure of performance).

[34] (1874) L.R. 9 C.P. 208 applied in *Aktion Maritime Corpn. of Liberia* v. *S. Kasmas & Brothers Ltd.* [1987] 1 Lloyd's Rep. 283 at p. 306. See also *Mitsubishi Heavy Industries Ltd.* v. *Gulf Bank K.S.C.* [1997] 1 Lloyd's Rep. 343 at pp. 350, 354.

[35] At p. 214.

[36] (1884) 9 App. Cas. 434. See also *Sweet & Maxwell Ltd.* v. *Universal News Services Ltd.* [1964] 2 Q.B. 699; *Alfred C. Toepfer International GmbH* v. *Itex Itagram Export S.A.* [1993] 1 Lloyd's Rep. 360 at p. 361.

N.B. bought from M.S. 5,000 tons of steel, to be delivered at the rate of 1,000 tons each month commencing in January 1881, payment to be made within 3 days of the receipt of the shipping documents. M.S. delivered part only of the first instalment in January, but delivered another in February. Shortly before payment for these was due, a petition was presented for the winding up of M.S., whereupon N.B. refused to pay as it had been erroneously advised not to do so unless M.S. obtained the leave of the Court. M.S. informed N.B. that it would treat this refusal as breach, but N.B. continued to express its willingness to take delivery and to make the payments if possible.

The House of Lords held that M.S. was not entitled to treat itself as discharged. The Earl of Selborne L.C. said:[37]

I cannot ascribe to their [N.B.'s] conduct, under these circumstances, the character of a renunciation of the contract, a repudiation of the contract, a refusal to fulfil the contract. It is just the reverse; the purchasers were desirous of fulfilling the contract; they were advised that there was a difficulty in the way, and they expressed anxiety that that difficulty should be as soon as possible removed.

In neither of these two cases did the breach, in the particular circumstances in which it had been committed, indicate, in the view taken by the Court, an intention in the party in default to throw up the contract altogether, so as to set the other party free. Moreover, a Court may be reluctant to find that there has been a renunciation where a party insists on performing the contract in a particular way which, although ultimately held to be a breach of contract, arose from a *bona fide* belief as to the construction of the contract which is also consistent with its continuance.[38] On the other hand, an unequivocal refusal, by words or conduct, to perform the contract will entitle the other party to be discharged from any further performance of its obligations even where the party who has failed to perform acted in good faith.[39] So, for example, if a buyer contracts to buy goods by instalments and agrees to pay cash for them, but then demands credit in respect of all future deliveries of the goods, the seller may refuse to make any further deliveries.[40] Similarly if, in breach of a contract of employment, a gardener insolently refuses to carry out instructions,[41] or a school teacher refuses to supervise school meals when required to do so,[42] the employer is justified in dismissing that person, i.e. terminating the contract of employment.

Renunciation may take place either before performance is due or during performance itself.

(iii) Renunciation before performance is due : 'anticipatory breach'

The parties to a contract which is wholly executory have a right to something more than the performance when the time arrives. They have a right to the maintenance of

---

[37] At p. 441.

[38] *Vaswani* v. *Italian Motors (Sales and Services) Ltd.* [1996] 1 W.L.R. 270. See also *Woodar Investment Development Ltd.* v. *Wimpey Construction U.K. Ltd.* [1980] 1 W.L.R. 277.

[39] *Federal Commerce & Navigation Co. Ltd.* v. *Molena Alpha Inc.* [1979] A.C. 757; *Farrant* v. *The Woodroffe School* [1998] 2 I.C.R. 184.

[40] *Withers* v. *Reynolds* (1831) 2 B. & Ad. 882.

[41] *Pepper* v. *Webb* [1969] 1 W.L.R. 514.

[42] *Gorse* v. *Durham C.C.* [1971] 1 W.L.R. 775.

the contractual relation right up to that time, as well as to a performance of the contract when due.

The renunciation of a contract by one of the parties before the time for performance has come does not, of itself, put an end to the contract, but the 'anticipatory breach' entitles the other to choose to be discharged and to sue at once for damages. A contract is a contract from the time it is made, and not from the time that performance is due. A leading case upon this subject is *Hochster* v. *De la Tour*:[43]

D engaged P on 12 April to enter into his service as a courier and to accompany him upon a tour; the employment was to commence on 1 June. On 11 May D wrote to P to inform him that his services would no longer be required. P at once brought an action, although the time for performance had not yet arrived.

The Court held that he was entitled to do so.

The rule has also been applied to situations where the performance is not absolute as in *Hochster* v. *De la Tour*, but contingent. In that case a time was fixed for performance, and before it arrived D renounced the contract, but in *Frost* v. *Knight*,[44] performance was contingent upon an event which might not happen within the lifetime of the parties:

K, a bachelor, promised to marry F upon his father's death; but during his father's lifetime he renounced the contract.

F was held entitled to sue on the ground explained above. The principle of anticipatory breach was justified by Cockburn C.J. as follows:[45]

The promisee has an inchoate right to the performance of the bargain, which becomes complete when the time for performance has arrived. *In the meantime he has a right to have the contract kept open as a subsisting and effective contract.* Its unimpaired and unimpeached efficacy may be essential to his interests.

It can also be said that the principle is convenient as it enables the innocent party to assert its rights speedily and so to minimize the damage which may be suffered from the breach. Nevertheless, it is important to note that a party who has been guilty of an anticipatory breach by renunciation is accorded no privilege of withdrawing that renunciation once it has been accepted by the other party,[46] even though the guilty party tenders performance within the time originally fixed by the contract and even though the position of the other party has in no way changed as a result of the renunciation.

The promisee, however, has the right to continue to insist on the performance of the promise and to refuse to accept the renunciation. If this is done, the promisee loses the right to rely on the anticipatory breach and the contract remains in existence for the benefit and at the risk of both parties. Should anything occur subsequently to

---

[43] (1853) 2 E. & B. 678.

[44] (1872) L.R. 7 Ex. 111.

[45] At p. 114 (emphasis added). But see Vold (1928) 41 Harv. L.R. 340.

[46] *Xenos* v. *Danube, etc., Ry.* (1863) 13 C.B.N.S. 824; but see *Aegnoussiotis Shipping Cpn. of Monrovia* v. *A/S Kristian Jebsens Rederi of Bergen* [1977] 1 Lloyd's Rep. 268, at p. 276 (new contract).

discharge the contract from other causes, the promisor, whose renunciation has been refused, may take advantage of such discharge. Thus in *Avery* v. *Bowden*:[47]

A chartered his ship to B. It was agreed that the ship would sail to Odessa, and there take a cargo from B's agent, which was to be loaded within a certain number of days. The vessel reached Odessa, and her master demanded a cargo, but B's agent was unable to supply one. Nevertheless, the master of the ship continued to demand a cargo, but before the specified number of days had elapsed the Crimean War broke out between England and Russia and the performance of the contract became legally impossible. A afterwards sued for breach of the charterparty.

His action failed. If B's agent had positively informed the master that no cargo would be provided, and that there was no use in his remaining there any longer, the master might have treated this as an anticipatory breach and sailed away. A would then have had the right to sue at once upon the contract. But the Court found that as the conduct of B's agent was not such as to constitute a renunciation of the contract there was therefore no breach committed by B before the contract was frustrated. Even, however, if there had been a renunciation of the contract, the Court considered that it could not be treated as a cause of action after the master still continued to insist upon having a cargo in fulfilment of the charterparty. Again, it has been held by the House of Lords[48] that where, following an anticipatory breach by charterers which was not accepted by the shipowners, the owners later failed to tender the vessel ready to load on time, the charterers were entitled to cancel the charterparty.

Despite the utility of the principle of 'anticipatory breach', the term itself is somewhat misleading. It suggests that the cause of action lies in the future breach that will occur on the date fixed for performance, which the innocent party is, in some sense, permitted to anticipate. But it is clear from the cases cited that, at any rate where the anticipatory breach consists of a renunciation of the contract, the breach is constituted by the renunciation itself, and, if this is accepted, the innocent party is immediately entitled to recover by way of damages the true value of the contractual rights which have been lost, subject to the innocent party's duty to mitigate.[49]

(iv) Renunciation during performance

If during the performance of a contract one of the parties by words or conduct unconditionally refuses to perform its side of the contract, the other party is forthwith released from any further performance of its obligations, and is entitled at once to sue.

In *Cort* v. *Ambergate etc. Railway Company*:[50]

C contracted with the defendant to supply it with 3,900 tons of railway chairs, at a certain price, to be delivered in certain quantities at specified dates. After 1,787 tons had been delivered, the defendant requested C to deliver no more, as they would not be wanted.

---

[47] (1855) 5 E. & B. 714; (1856) 6 E. & B. 953. See also *Michael* v. *Hart & Co.* [1902] 1 K.B. 482; *Berners* v. *Fleming* [1925] Ch. 264.

[48] *Fercometal S.A.R.L.* v. *Mediterranean Shipping Co. S.A. (The Simona)* [1989] A.C. 788.

[49] *The Mihalis Angelos* [1971] 1 Q.B. 164.

[50] (1851) 17 Q.B. 127.

C brought an action upon the contract, averring that he was always ready and willing to perform his part, but had been prevented from doing so by the action of the defendant.

C obtained a verdict, and when the defendant moved for a new trial on the ground that he should have proved not merely that he was ready and willing to deliver, but an actual delivery, the Court rejected this submission. Since the contract had been renounced, C could maintain an action without manufacturing and tendering the rest of the goods.

(b) IMPOSSIBILITY CREATED BY ONE PARTY

If, by the act or default of, one party further commercial performance of the contract is made impossible,[51] although that party has not, by words or conduct, renounced the intention to fulfil it, the other party will be discharged.

Renunciation is usually easier to establish because the innocent party need only show that the conduct of the promisor was such as to lead a reasonable person to believe that the promisor did not intend to perform the promise, whereas if reliance is placed on impossibility the innocent party must show that the contract was in fact impossible of performance due to the default of the promisor. But it is an independent ground for discharge, as can be seen from *Universal Cargo Carriers Corporation* v. *Citati:*[52]

U.C.C. chartered a ship to C who agreed to nominate a berth and a shipper, and to provide a cargo, all before a certain day. Three days before the due date C had done none of these things. Although C was willing to perform the contract if he could, U.C.C. cancelled it and found another charterer.

Devlin J. held that C had not renounced the contract, but, since he could not have performed before the delay became so long as to frustrate the commercial purpose of the contract, U.C.C. was entitled to treat this inability to perform as discharging its obligations.

Here also the impossibility may be created either before performance is due or in the course of performance.

(i) Impossibility created before performance is due: anticipatory breach

If the act or default of a promisor which makes performance impossible occurs before the time for performance arrives, the effect is the same as though the promisor had renounced the contract at that time. Such impossibility need not be deliberately created: 'Anticipatory breach was not devised as a whip to be used for the chastisement of deliberate contract-breachers, but from which the shiftless, the dilatory, or the unfortunate are to be spared. It is not confined to any particular class of breach,

---

[51] If the impossibility arises through the occurrence of some external event, which radically alters the nature of the obligation (but not otherwise), the contract may be discharged by frustration: see *ante*, pp. 530, 533.

[52] [1957] 2 Q.B. 401 (aff'd in part [1957] 1 W.L.R. 979 and revs'd in part [1958] 2 Q.B. 254). See also *Sanko Steamship Co. Ltd.* v. *Eacom Timber Sales Ltd.* [1987] 1 Lloyd's Rep. 487 at p. 492.

deliberate or blameworthy, or otherwise; it covers all breaches that are bound to happen'.[53]

The aggrieved party may sue at once. In *Lovelock v. Franklyn*:[54]

F promised to assign to L within 7 years from the date of his promise, all his interest in a lease for the sum of £140. Before the end of 7 years he assigned his interest to another person.

It was held that L need not wait until the end of the seven years to bring an action. Lord Denman C.J. stated:[55]

L has a right to say to F: 'You have placed yourself in a situation in which you cannot perform what you have promised; you promised to be ready during the period of seven years; and, during that period, I may at any time tender you the money and call for an assignment, and expect that you should keep yourself ready; but, if I now were to tender you the money, you would not be ready'. That is a breach of the contract.

Similarly, in *Universal Cargo Carriers Corporation v. Citati (supra)*, the ship-owners' cancellation of the contract was not premature. They were permitted to anticipate a breach which was in fact inevitable.

(ii) Impossibility created during performance

The rule is similar where the complete performance of the contract is made impossible by the act or default of one party. This is illustrated by the case of *O'Neil v. Armstrong*:[56]

O'N, a British subject, was engaged by A, the captain of a warship owned by the Japanese Government, to act as a fireman on a voyage from the Tyne to Yokohama. In the course of the voyage the Japanese Government declared war on China. O'N was informed that performance of the contract would bring him under the penalties of the Foreign Enlistment Act 1870. He consequently left the ship, and sued A for the wages agreed upon.

It was held that he was entitled to succeed in his action, for the act of A's principal, the Japanese Government, had made his performance of the contract legally impossible.

It will be seen from this case that discharge by breach may occur, not only where one party disables itself from performing the contract, but also where it prevents completion of the contract by the other party.[57] The Courts may imply a term that the parties co-operate to ensure performance. A duty to co-operate cannot be imposed so as to compel a party to do something which the contract on its true construction relieved that party from doing, and cannot be used to compel a party to do something which that party is in fact unable to do.[58] But the Courts are often ready to imply a

---

[53] *Ibid.*, at p. 438.

[54] (1846) 8 Q.B. 371.

[55] *Ibid.*, at p. 378. See also *Omnium D'Enterprises v. Sutherland* [1919] 1 K.B. 618.

[56] [1895] 2 Q.B. 418.

[57] See also *Ogdens Ltd. v. Nelson* [1905] A.C. 109. Cf. *Bremer Vulkan v. South India Shipping Co.* [1981] A.C. 909 (both parties in breach).

[58] *North Sea Energy Holdings N.V. v. Petroleum Authority of Thailand* [1999] 1 Lloyd's Rep. 483, at p. 492.

term that each party undertakes to do all that is necessary to secure performance of the contract.[59] Thus if a licence is required for the export of goods, and the buyer fails to provide the seller with the information necessary to obtain the licence, no action will lie against the seller for non-delivery.[60] In some situations, where performance has thus been prevented by the promisee, the contract is taken as satisfied and the promisor can sue for the full remuneration or price.[61] But in most cases the promisor will be forced to sue for damages for the breach, since the contract cannot be fulfilled without the co-operation of the party in default.[62]

(c) FAILURE OF PERFORMANCE

Failure of performance, whether total or partial, is the most common ground for the discharge of a party by breach. But it is not every failure of performance by one party which entitles the other to be discharged from its own liabilities under it. In order to determine if this is so, it is necessary to ask a number of questions.

(i) Are the promises independent?

In certain circumstances, the obligations entered into by each party may be independent of each other in the sense that neither party can claim to be released from its promise by the failure of the other to perform its part. Put in another way, each party can enforce the obligations undertaken by the other even though it has not performed its own. For example, in the case of leases, a tenant's covenant to pay rent is independent of a landlord's covenant to repair; the tenant cannot withhold payment on the ground that the landlord has failed to repair the premises.[63] Again, a covenant by a husband in a separation deed to pay his wife maintenance has been said to be independent of any covenant on her part, e.g. not to molest him.[64] And, because of the involvement of third parties in documentary sales, the obligation of a buyer to pay when the shipping documents are tendered has been held to be independent of the seller's obligation to supply goods conforming to the contract.[65] But the tendency of the Courts is against construing a contract in this way unless the parties clearly intend to do so because such a construction means that both parties are inadequately protected from the risk of non-performance by the other.[66] Thus, in a contract for work

---

[59] *Stirling* v. *Maitland* (1864) 5 B. & S. 840, at p. 852; *Southern Foundries (1936) Ltd.* v. *Shirlaw* [1940] A.C. 701; *The Unique Mariner (No. 2)* [1979] 1 Lloyd's Rep. 37. Cf. *Rhodes* v. *Forwood* (1876) 1 App. Cas. 256; *Luxor (Eastbourne) Ltd.* v. *Cooper* [1941] A.C. 108. See Bateson [1960] J.B.L. 187; Burrows (1968) 31 M.L.R. 390.

[60] *Kyprianou* v. *Cyprus Textiles Ltd.* [1958] 2 Lloyd's Rep. 60.

[61] *Mackay* v. *Dick* (1881) 6 App. Cas. 256. See also *Metro Meat Ltd.* v. *Fares Rural Co. Pty. Ltd.* [1985] 2 Lloyd's Rep. 13.

[62] *Colley* v. *Overseas Exporters* [1921] 3 K.B. 302. Contrast *White and Carter (Councils) Ltd.* v. *McGregor* [1962] A.C. 413 (*ante*, p. 566) where no co-operation necessary.

[63] *Taylor* v. *Webb* [1937] 2 K.B. 283.

[64] *Fearon* v. *Earl of Aylesford* (1884) 14 Q.B.D. 792, at p. 800. See also *Winstone* v. *Linn* (1823) 1 B. & C. 460 (contract of apprenticeship). Cf. *Ellen* v. *Topp* (1851) 6 Exch. 424.

[65] *Gill & Duffus S.A.* v. *Berger & Co.* [1984] A.C. 382 (c.i.f. sale). See also *Vagres Comp. Maritima S.A.* v. *Nissho-Iwai America Corp. (The Karin Vatis)* [1988] 2 Lloyd's Rep. 330 (terms of contract rendered obligation to pay freight when cargo loaded independent of charterer's obligations).

[66] See also, *ante*, pp. 510–15.

or services, the obligation to pay would fall due although the work had not been done.

Normally, however, the obligations of each party will be regarded as *interdependent*. For example, an employee who has been wrongfully dismissed is not bound to observe a covenant in restraint of trade.[67] The clearest example of obligations which are dependent on each other arises if the parties agree that the performance of their respective promise shall be simultaneous, or at least that each shall be ready and willing to perform its promise at the same time. Then the obligation to perform each promise is dependent or conditional on this concurrence of readiness and willingness to perform the other; their mutual promises are *concurrent conditions*. Thus section 28 of the Sale of Goods Act 1979 provides that in a contract for the sale of goods:

Unless otherwise agreed, delivery of the goods and payment of the price are concurrent conditions, that is to say, the seller must be ready and willing to give possession of the goods to the buyer in exchange for the price and the buyer must be ready and willing to pay the price in exchange for possession of the goods.

Failure to tender the goods discharges the buyer from its obligation to pay the price; failure to tender the price discharges the seller from its obligation to deliver the goods.

(ii) Is the obligation 'entire' or 'divisible'?

It has already been pointed out in Chapter 12, Performance,[68] that certain obligations are 'entire' in the sense that the liability of one party is dependent upon the complete performance of the obligation by the other. Subject to the doctrine of substantial performance,[69] if A agrees to make a dress for B in return for a promise to pay for the dress on completion, anything less than complete performance by A will release B from her obligation to pay. It is immaterial how the failure to effect complete performance comes about. It may be due to a deliberate abandonment of the contract, to a negligent act or omission, or, as in *Cutter* v. *Powell* noted above,[70] to a simple misfortune occurring without any fault.

Entire obligations are, however, the exception rather than the rule. The obligations in most bilateral contracts are 'divisible' in the sense that the breach of any one or more of them will not necessarily constitute a ground of discharge. The contract may, for example, be a complex one, composed of a number of undertakings differing in character or importance; or it may be a promise to do a number of successive acts; or to do a single act which can be partly or defectively performed. A failure by one party precisely to perform its obligations under the contract will give a right of action in damages to the other; but it will not necessarily discharge the innocent party from the performance of its own obligations under the contract.

---

[67] *General Billposting Co. Ltd.* v. *Atkinson* [1909] A.C. 118. See also *Rock Refrigeration Ltd.* v. *Jones* [1997] 1 All E.R. 1, but cf. the doubts of Phillips L.J. at pp. 18–19 and note that some primary obligations do continue after discharge, *post*, p. 581.

[68] See *ante*, p. 510.

[69] See *ante*, p. 513.

[70] (1795) 6 Term R. 320, *ante*, p. 510.

(iii) Is the term broken a condition?

Assuming that the obligations in the contract are divisible, and not entire, the question then arises whether the particular term which has been broken is a condition of the contract. From an historical point of view, the right of the innocent party to choose to be treated as discharged was said to turn upon the non-performance of a 'condition precedent' in the contract.[71] Performance by one party of that party's promise or 'covenant' was regarded as a condition precedent to the liability of the other. The classification of contractual terms is dealt with in Chapter 4 of this book.[72] It was there noted that, today, a term will only be classified as a condition if it has been so categorized by statute (for instance by the Sale of Goods Act 1979) or by judicial decision, or if the parties have so agreed in their contract, either expressly or by implication.[73] Any breach of a condition will entitle the innocent party to choose to be treated as discharged.[74] It was also noted, however, that there has now emerged a category of 'intermediate terms', the breach of which will not necessarily produce that effect.[75]

(iv) Does the breach go to 'the root of the contract'?

If the term broken is not a condition, but an intermediate term, the right of the innocent party to choose to be treated as discharged from further performance will depend upon the nature and consequences of the breach. Differing terminology has been used by the Courts to describe the test to be applied, the most common being that the breach must go to 'the root of the contract'.[76] It has also been said that the breach must be 'fundamental',[77] that it must 'affect the very substance of the contract'[78] or 'frustrate the commercial purpose of the venture'.[79] The use of these and similar expressions emphasizes that the breach must be far-reaching in its effect in order to justify discharge. A test which is nowadays frequently applied is that stated by Diplock L.J. in *Hongkong Fir Shipping Co. Ltd.* v. *Kawasaki Kisen Kaisha Ltd.*:[80] 'Does the occurrence of the event deprive the party who has further undertakings to

---

[71] *Pordage* v. *Cole* (1669) 1 Wms. Saund. 319; *Kingston* v. *Preston* (1773) 2 Doug. 689, at p. 691. The history of the expression is expounded in *Cehave N.V.* v. *Bremer Handelsgesellschaft* [1976] Q.B. 44, at pp. 57, 72; *United Scientific Holdings Ltd.* v. *Burnley B.C.* [1978] A.C. 904, at p. 927. See also *Hurst* v. *Bryk* [2000] 2 W.L.R. 740, *per* Lord Millett at p. 747; Dawson [1981] C.L.J. 83, at p. 87.

[72] *Ante*, pp. 134–44.

[73] *Ante*, pp. 141–3.

[74] See, e.g. *Union Eagle Ltd.* v. *Golden Achievement Ltd* [1997] A.C. 514.

[75] *Ante*, p. 140.

[76] *Mersey Steel & Iron Co.* v. *Naylor, Benzon & Co.* (1884) 9 App. Cas. 434, at p. 444; *Heyman* v. *Darwins Ltd.* [1942] A.C. 356, at p. 397; *Suisse Atlantique Société d'Armement S.A.* v. *N.V. Kolen Centrale* [1967] 1 A.C. 361, at p. 422; *Cehave N.V.* v. *Bremer Handelsgesellschaft* [1976] Q.B. 44, at pp. 60, 73; *Federal Commerce & Navigation Co. Ltd.* v. *Molena Alpha Inc.* [1979] A.C. 757, at p. 779.

[77] *Suisse Atlantique Société d'Armement S.A.* v. *N.V. Kolen Centrale* (*supra*, n. 76), at pp. 397, 409–10, 421–2, 431.

[78] *Wallis, Son and Wells* v. *Pratt and Haynes* [1910] 2 K.B. 1003, at p. 1012.

[79] *MacAndrew* v. *Chapple* (1866) L.R. 1 C.P. 643, at pp. 647, 648; *Jackson* v. *Union Marine Insurance Co.* (1874) L.R. 10 C.P. 125, at pp. 145, 147, 148; *Trade and Transport Inc.* v. *Iino Kaiun Kaisha Ltd.* [1973] 1 W.L.R. 210, at p. 223.

[80] [1962] 2 Q.B. 26, at p. 66.

perform of substantially the whole benefit which it was the intention of the parties as expressed in the contract that he should obtain as the consideration for performing those undertakings?' In that case:

H chartered to K the m.v. *Hongkong Fir* for a period of 24 months, on terms that she was 'in every way fitted for ordinary cargo service'. The vessel was an old one, and by reason of its age needed to be maintained by an experienced, competent, careful, and adequate engine room staff. This H did not provide. The chief engineer was addicted to drink and inefficient, and the engine room complement inadequate, with the result that there were many serious breakdowns in machinery. In the first 7 months of the charter the ship was only eight and a half weeks at sea, the rest of the time being spent in breakdowns and repair to make the ship seaworthy; but this was eventually achieved. K refused to continue with the charterparty.

It was argued on behalf of K that the term as to seaworthiness was a condition of the contract, and that it was therefore entitled as of right to treat itself as discharged. This argument was not accepted by the Court of Appeal.[81] The Court then went on to hold, on the facts, that the delays which had already occurred, and the delay which was likely to occur, as a result of the vessel's unseaworthiness, and the conduct of H in taking steps to remedy the same, were not, when taken together, such as to deprive K of substantially the whole benefit which it was the intention of the parties K should obtain from further use of the ship under charterparty. K had therefore unjustifiably treated the contract as repudiated.

The same approach has been adopted with respect to contracts to deliver and pay for goods by instalments. If the seller makes defective deliveries in respect of one or more instalments, or the buyer neglects or refuses to take delivery of or pay for one or more instalments, this will not necessarily permit the innocent party to choose to be treated as discharged. The question will arise whether the breach is a repudiation of the whole contract or whether it is a severable breach giving rise to a claim for damages but not to a right to treat the whole contract as repudiated.[82] The breach or breaches may, of course, amount to an express or implied renunciation of the contract.[83] But if they amount only to a failure of performance, they must go to the root of the contract in order to justify discharge. Thus in *Simpson* v. *Crippin*[84] it was agreed that 6,000 to 8,000 tons of coal should be delivered in equal monthly instalments during a period of 12 months, the buyer to send waggons to receive the coal; the buyer sent waggons for only 158 tons in the first month, but the seller was not held entitled to cancel the contract as the breach did not go 'to the whole root and consideration of the agreement'.

On the other hand, in *Honck* v. *Muller*:[85]

H, in October 1879, bought from M 2,000 tons of pig iron to be delivered 'in November, 1879, or equally over November, December and January next at 6*d. per* ton extra'. H failed to

---

[81] See *ante*, p. 140.

[82] Sale of Goods Act 1979, s. 30(2) and (2A).

[83] See *ante*, p. 570.

[84] (1872) L.R. 8 Q.B. 14.

[85] (1881) 7 Q.B.D. 92. See also *Munro & Co. Ltd.* v. *Meyer* [1930] 2 K.B. 312 (nearly half of goods seriously adulterated).

take delivery of any iron in November, but claimed to have delivery of one-third of the iron in December and one-third in January. M refused, and gave notice that he considered the contract discharged.

H brought an action for breach and failed, as a majority of the Court considered that his failure of performance was so substantial as to discharge M from further liability.[86]

In contracts for the sale and delivery of goods by instalments, the most relevant factors have been said to be, 'First, the ratio quantitatively which the breach bears to the contract as a whole, and secondly the degree of probability or improbability that such a breach will be repeated'.[87] The importance of the second factor was clearly emphasized by Bigham J. in *Millar's Karri and Jarrah Co.* v. *Weddel*:[88]

If the breach is of such a kind, or takes place in such circumstances as reasonably to lead to the inference that similar breaches will be committed in relation to subsequent deliveries, the whole contract may there and then be regarded as repudiated and may be rescinded. If, for instance, a buyer fails to pay for one delivery in such circumstances as to lead to the inference that he will not be able to pay for subsequent deliveries; or if a seller delivers goods differing from the requirements of the contract, and does so in such circumstances as to lead to the inference that he cannot, or will not, deliver any other kind of goods in the future, the other contracting party will be under no obligation to wait to see what may happen; he can at once cancel the contract and rid himself of the difficulty.

It follows that, the further parties have proceeded with the due performance of a contract, the less likely it is that one party will be able to claim that it has been discharged by a single breach.[89]

The right of discharge therefore depends on the answer to this question: Does the breach go so far to the root of the contract as to entitle the injured party to say, 'I have lost all that I cared to obtain under this contract; further performance cannot make good the prior default'?[90]

III. CONSEQUENCES OF DISCHARGE

(a) RELEASE FROM FUTURE OBLIGATIONS

An innocent party who is entitled to, and does, choose to be treated as discharged by the other party's breach, is thereby released from further performance of those future obligations which remain still to be performed.[91] After such discharge the innocent

---

[86] *Maple Flock Co. Ltd.* v. *Universal Furniture Products (Wembley) Ltd.* [1934] 1 K.B. 148, *per* Lord Hewart C.J. at p. 157.

[87] *Ibid.*

[88] (1909) 100 L.T. 128, at p. 129.

[89] *Cornwall* v. *Henson* [1900] 2 Ch. 298, at p. 304.

[90] Cited with approval in *Alkok* v. *Grymek* (1966) 56 D.L.R. (2d) 393 (Canada).

[91] See Shea (1979) 42 M.L.R. 623; Beatson (1981) 97 L.Q.R. 389; Rose (1981) 34 C.L.P. 235; Law Commission Report, *Pecuniary Restitution on Breach of Contract* (1983), No. 121.

party is not bound to accept, or pay for, any further performance by the party in breach. The duty of the party in default to perform future unperformed obligations likewise comes to an end, as does that party's right to perform them.

(b) CONTRACT NOT RESCINDED *AB INITIO*

In the terminology employed in many of the cases, these consequences are often described as a 'rescission' of the contract; or it is stated that the contract is 'terminated' or 'put an end to' by the breach. But these expressions are somewhat misleading:

> To say that the contract is rescinded or has come to an end or ceased to exist may in individual cases convey the truth with sufficient accuracy, but the fuller expression that the injured party is thereby absolved from future performance of his obligations under the contract is a more exact description of the position. Strictly speaking, to say that on acceptance of the renunciation of the contract the contract is rescinded is incorrect.[92]

Certainly, this so-called rescission is quite different from rescission *ab initio*, such as may arise, for example, in cases of misrepresentation or mistake.[93] The contract is not set aside as from the beginning.

(c) ACCRUED OBLIGATIONS REMAIN

Although both parties are discharged from further performance of their obligations, rights are not divested which have already been unconditionally acquired. Rights and obligations which arise from the partial execution of the contract and causes of action which have accrued from its breach alike continue unaffected.[94] So, for instance, if a time charterparty of a ship is repudiated by the charterer, the shipowner can recover arrears of hire charges due but unpaid up to the date of the shipowner's acceptance of the repudiation.[95] Again, if building work is to be paid for by instalments, the builder can sue for any instalment due but unpaid at the time of discharge.[96]

It makes no difference in this respect whether the accrued obligation is one in favour of the innocent or the guilty party. An employee who repudiates a contract of employment, can nevertheless sue for wages earned before that time[97] and, following termination of a partnership agreement, it seems that the innocent partner remains

---

[92] *Heyman* v. *Darwins Ltd.* [1942] A.C. 356, *per* Lord Porter at p. 399. This statement was unanimously approved by the House of Lords in *Johnson* v. *Agnew* [1980] A.C. 367. See also *Bank of Boston Connecticut* v. *European Grain and Shipping Ltd.* [1989] A.C. 1056, at pp. 1098–9 and *State Trading Corpn. of India Ltd.* v. *M. Golodetz Ltd.* [1989] 2 Lloyd's Rep. 277, at p. 286.

[93] *Johnson* v. *Agnew* (*supra*, n. 92), at p. 393.

[94] *McDonald* v. *Dennys Lascelles Ltd.* (1933) 48 C.L.R. 457, *per* Dixon J. at p. 476. But, once the contract has been discharged, equitable relief, e.g. an injunction, cannot be granted: *Walker* v. *Standard Chartered Bank plc* [1992] B.C.L.C. 535.

[95] *Leslie Shipping Co.* v. *Welstead* [1921] 3 K.B. 420. See also *Chatterton* v. *Maclean* [1951] 1 All E.R. 561 (hire-purchase).

[96] *Hyundai Heavy Industries Co. Ltd.* v. *Papadopoulos* [1980] 1 W.L.R. 1129 (H.L.).

[97] *Taylor* v. *Laird* (1856) 25 L.J. Ex. 29. Cf. Apportionment Act 1870, s. 2.

liable for the accrued liabilities of the partnership, provided these were incurred when the innocent party was a partner.[98]

Admittedly, if money has been paid by one party to the other under the contract, and the consideration for the payment has wholly failed, the money may be recoverable in restitution by an action for money had and received.[99] But, in principle, accrued liabilities remain enforceable despite the discharge. Moreover, as we have seen,[100] only the primary obligations of the parties as a general rule come to an end. The primary obligations of the party in default are then replaced by a secondary obligation to pay compensation to the injured party for the breach. Note, however, certain primary obligations will survive discharge and continue to be enforceable. The continued enforcement of such obligations simply reflects the presumed intention of the parties. The best examples of obligations that survive are arbitration clauses and dispute resolution mechanisms.[101] In addition, there are clauses that may only come into operation upon discharge such as certain liquidated damages clauses. It has also been held that an obligation to pay a retainer for a specified period[102] and an agent's duty to provide records to its principal survive discharge.[103]

(d) *QUANTUM MERUIT* CLAIMS

With respect to payments not yet due at the time of discharge, for example, for goods supplied or for services performed under the contract, the innocent party can sue for the reasonable value of these on a *quantum meruit* or *quantum valebat*,[104] or include them in his claim for damages for breach. Whether the guilty party has any claim will depend on whether the contract is entire or divisible. If it is entire, in principle no claim is possible.[105] But if it is divisible, the guilty party may be entitled to claim in respect of performance completed, subject to a counterclaim for damages by the innocent party in respect of loss suffered by the breach.

IV. LOSS OF THE RIGHT OF DISCHARGE

The right of discharge may be lost by waiver, affirmation, acceptance, and operation of law. In addition, a party may be estopped from claiming to be entitled to treat a contract as discharged. This has been dealt with earlier in this book.[106]

---

[98] *Hurst* v. *Bryk* [2000] 2 W.L.R. 740. See also Partnership Act 1890, s. 9.

[99] See *post*, p. 642.

[100] See *ante*, p. 581.

[101] *Heyman* v. *Darwins Ltd.* [1942] A.C. 356.

[102] *Duffen* v. *Frabo SpA* [2000] 1 Lloyd's Rep. 180.

[103] *Yasuda Fire & Marine Insurance Co. of Europe Ltd.* v. *Orion Marine Insurance Underwriting Agency Ltd.* [1995] Q.B. 174.

[104] See *post*, p. 649.

[105] See *ante*, pp. 510–11. But see *post*, p. 645.

[106] See *ante*, pp. 521–7 and 112.

16

DISCHARGE BY OPERATION OF LAW

There are rules of law which, operating upon certain sets of circumstances, will bring about the discharge of a contract, and these we will briefly consider.

I. MERGER

(a) ACCEPTANCE OF HIGHER SECURITY

If a higher security is accepted in place of a lower, the security which in the eye of the law is inferior in operative power,[1] in the absence of a contrary intention manifested by the parties, merges and is extinguished in the higher.

Thus, if two parties to a simple contract embody its contents in a deed which they both execute, the simple contract is thereby discharged. This most often happens in the case of contracts for the sale of land, the written agreements being merged and extinguished in the subsequent conveyance under seal.[2]

The rules governing this process may thus be summarized:

(1) The later security must be of higher efficacy than that which it is sought to replace. A negotiable instrument is not a higher security for the purposes of this rule,[3] although the giving of a negotiable instrument may constitute payment of a debt.[4]

(2) The subject-matter of the two securities must be the same, that is, they must secure the same obligation and be made between the same parties.[5]

---

[1] *Price* v. *Moulton* (1851) 10 C.B. 561.

[2] *Knight Sugar Co. Ltd.* v. *Alberta Ry. and Irrigation Co.* [1938] 1 All E.R. 266, at p. 269. Cf. *Tito* v. *Waddell (No. 2)* [1977] Ch. 107, at p. 284 (contrary intention).

[3] *Drake* v. *Mitchell* (1803) 3 East 251.

[4] See *ante*, p. 505.

[5] *Twopenny* v. *Young* (1824) 3 B. & C. 208; *Holmes* v. *Bell* (1841) 3 M. & G. 213; *Hissett* v. *Reading Roofing Co. Ltd.* [1969] 1 W.L.R. 1757.

(b) RIGHTS VESTING IN SAME PERSON

The rights and liabilities under a contract are also extinguished if they become vested by assignment or otherwise in the same person and in the same right, for it is not possible to contract with oneself. So where a tenant for a term of years retains the lease and acquires the reversion, the lease merges in the reversion and is destroyed.[6] Similarly, a bill of exchange is discharged if the acceptor is or becomes the holder of it at or after its maturity in his own right.[7]

II. DISCHARGE BY JUDGMENT OF A COURT

A right of action arising from breach of contract is discharged by the judgment of a Court of Record[8] in the claimant's favour for the same demand. The right is thereby merged in the more solemn form of obligation called a Contract of Record. The result of legal proceedings taken upon a broken contract may be summarized as follows:

(a) EFFECT OF BRINGING ACTION

The bringing of an action has not itself any effect in discharging the right to bring the action. Another action may be brought for the same cause, although proceedings in such an action would, if they were merely vexatious, be struck out or stayed upon application to the summary jurisdiction of the Court.[9]

(b) EFFECT OF JUDGMENT FOR CLAIMANT

But when judgment is given in the claimant's favour, the cause of action is merged into matter of record, and only the judgment can be enforced.[10] Further, 'damages resulting from one and the same cause of action must be assessed and recovered once for all',[11] so that successive judgments cannot be obtained for different breaches of a single undertaking.[12]

(c) EFFECT OF JUDGMENT FOR DEFENDANT

A person may be estopped *per rem judicatam* from re-litigating in subsequent proceedings a cause of action in respect of which judgment was given against that person

---

[6] *Capital and Countries Bank Ltd.* v. *Rhodes* [1903] 1 Ch. 631. By a rule of equity, however, the intentions of the parties may operate to prevent the occurrence of such merger. Under the provisions of the Law of Property Act 1925, s. 185 the equitable rule now prevails in all cases.

[7] Bills of Exchange Act 1882, s. 61.

[8] A county court is a court of record: County Courts Act 1984, s. 1(2).

[9] C.P.R. rr. 3.4(2), and 3.1(2)(f); County Courts Act 1984, s. 35.

[10] *Kendall* v. *Hamilton* (1879) 4 App. Cas. 504.

[11] *Brunsden* v. *Humphrey* (1884) 14 Q.B.D. 141, *per* Bowen L.J. at p. 147; *Furness, Withy & Co. Ltd.* v. *Hall Ltd.* (1909) 25 T.L.R. 233.

[12] *Conquer* v. *Boot* [1928] 2 K.B. 336. But see *Overstone Ltd.* v. *Shipway* [1962] 1 W.L.R. 117 (separate causes of action).

in earlier proceedings, or an issue raised and determined against him or her in such proceedings.[13] But, for such an estoppel to arise, certain conditions must be satisfied:[14] first, there must have been a final judgment on the merits[15] in the earlier proceedings by a Court of competent jurisdiction;[16] secondly, there must be identity of parties in the two sets of proceedings;[17] thirdly, there must be identity of subject-matter in the two proceedings.[18] Cause of action and issue estoppel are based upon the public interest in finality of litigation.[19]

III. ALTERATION OR CANCELLATION OF A WRITTEN INSTRUMENT

(a) RULE AS TO ALTERATION

If a deed or contract in writing is altered by addition or erasure, it is discharged, except as against a party making or assenting to the alteration, for 'no man shall be permitted to take the chance of committing a fraud, without running any risk of losing by the event, when it is detected'.[20]

This principle is subject to the following rules:

(1) The alteration must be made deliberately by the promisee or by one acting with the promisee's consent;[21] and even an alteration by a stranger while the instrument is in the custody of the promisee will have the same effect.[22] Previous editions of this book stated that this responsibility for the acts of officious burglars, could not be supported, but although recently described as 'a harsh and ancient common law doctrine', it is good law.[23]

---

[13] *Palmer* v. *Temple* (1839) 9 A. & E. 508.

[14] *Carl Zeiss Stiftung* v. *Rayner & Keeler Ltd.* (*No. 2*) [1967] 1 A.C. 853, at pp. 909, 910.

[15] *Hines* v. *Birbeck College* (*No. 2*) [1992] Ch. 33.

[16] *Midland Bank Trust Co. Ltd.* v. *Green* [1980] Ch. 590; *Hines* v. *Birbeck College* (*No. 2*) [1992] Ch. 33; *The European Gateway* [1987] Q.B. 206.

[17] *Gleeson* v. *J. Wippell & Co. Ltd.* [1977] 1 W.L.R. 510; *North West Water Ltd.* v. *Binnie & Partners* [1990] 3 All E.R. 547; *House of Spring Gardens Ltd.* v. *Waite* [1991] 1 Q.B. 241, at p. 252; *Talbot* v. *Berkshire C.C.* [1994] Q.B. 290, at pp. 296–7. Cf. *Marginson* v. *Blackburn B.C.* [1939] 2 K.B. 426; *C (a minor)* v. *Hackney London B.C.* [1996] 1 All E.R. 973.

[18] *Haystead* v. *Commissioner of Taxation* [1926] A.C. 155.

[19] *Republic of India* v. *India Steamship Co. Ltd.* [1993] A.C. 410, at p. 415; *ibid.* (*No. 2*) [1998] A.C. 878, at p. 912; *Thrasyvoulou* v. *Secretary of State for the Environment* [1990] 2 A.C. 273, at p. 289. While a foreign judgment does not operate as a merger, under the Civil Jurisdiction and Judgments Act 1982, s. 34, further proceedings are barred unless waived: [1993] A.C. 410, at pp. 423–4.

[20] *Master* v. *Miller* (1791) 4 Term Rep. 320, *per* Lord Kenyon C.J. at p. 329.

[21] *Pattinson* v. *Luckley* (1875) L.R. 10 Ex. 330; *Hongkong & Shanghai Banking Corporation* v. *Lo Lee Shi* [1928] A.C. 181. Cf. *Co-operative Bank* v. *Tipper* [1996] 4 All E.R. 366, at p. 371 (pencilled alteration insufficient).

[22] *Pigot's Case* (1614) 11 Co. Rep. 26b; *Davidson* v. *Cooper* (1844) 13 M. & W. 343.

[23] *Goss* v. *Chilcott* [1996] A.C. 788; *Co-operative Bank* v. *Tipper* (*supra*, n. 21) at p. 369. But the nullifying operation is confined to cases falling strictly within its ambit: *Farrow Mortgage Services Pty. Ltd.* v. *Slade* (1996) 38 N.S.W.L.R. 636, at p. 640.

(2) The alteration must be made without the consent of the other party, else it would operate as a new agreement.

(3) The alteration must be made in a material part. What amounts to a material alteration necessarily depends upon the character of the instrument, and it is possible for the character of an instrument to be affected by an alteration which does not touch the contractual rights set forth in it. In most cases, a material alteration will be one which imposes a greater liability on the promisor.[24]

(b) BILLS OF EXCHANGE

The Bills of Exchange Act 1882, section 64, provides that a bill shall not be avoided as against holder in due course, though it has been materially altered, if the alteration is not apparent, and the holder may enforce payment of it according to its original tenor.

(c) CANCELLATION AND LOSS

Intentional cancellation of a written instrument by the promisee also discharges the obligation, but the loss of the instrument only affects the rights of the parties in so far as it may occasion a difficulty of proof. In the case of bills of exchange and promissory notes, if the holder of the instrument loses it, *he* may require the drawer to give him another bill upon his giving an indemnity against possible claims.[25]

IV. BANKRUPTCY

A contract is not discharged by bankruptcy of one of the parties to it;[26] but it effects a statutory release from debts and liabilities provable under the bankruptcy, when the bankrupt has obtained from the Court an order of discharge. It is sufficient to call attention to this mode of discharge, without entering into a discussion of the nature and effects of bankruptcy, or the provisions of the Insolvency Act 1986.

---

[24] On the different position of alterations to bank notes, see *Suffell v. Bank of England* (1882) 9 Q.B.D. 555.

[25] Bills of Exchange Act 1882, s. 69.

[26] *Re Edwards, ex parte Chalmers* (1873) L.R. 8 Ch. App. 289; see *ante*, p. 494.

PART V

REMEDIES FOR BREACH OF CONTRACT

17

DAMAGES

I. INTRODUCTION

Where a party performing a contract does not do so to the standard required by the contract[1] or within the timeframe set, that party will breach the contract. Chapter 16 endeavours to state the rules which govern the discharge of a contract by breach, and it now remains to consider the various remedies which are available apart from the entitlement of the innocent party in an appropriate case to be treated as discharged from further performance.

These remedies fall under three heads:[2]

(1) Every breach of contract entitles the injured party to damages for the loss he or she has suffered.

(2) In certain circumstances the injured party may obtain the enforcement of the promise by an order for specific performance of the contract, an injunction to restrain its breach or for the payment of the sum due under the contract.

(3) In certain circumstances the parties to a contract that has been broken may be entitled to the return of money paid, recompense for services rendered or goods transferred, or a money award reflecting the gain to the defendant. These are restitutionary remedies. Although some of them are based on a distinct branch of the law of obligations, restitution, and are not based on breach of contract, others are based on contract.

This and the following three chapters consider each of these remedies in turn, and also how the rights of action created by a breach of contract may be barred by lapse of time.

It will be seen that the development of the law has been marked by a broadening approach to the concept of loss and thus in its ability to protect the claimant's interest in the performance by the other party of the contractual obligations. Except in the case of a debt, the repayment of which may be specifically enforced at common law by an award of the agreed sum, the common law remedy for breach of a contractual promise is that of damages. There has been increased sophistication in identifying and calculating economic interests and in recognizing intangible interests of no economic

---

[1] The standard may be strict or may require only the exercise of reasonable care, *ante* p. 499.

[2] See Burrows, *Remedies for Torts and Breach of Contract*, 2nd edn. (1994); Harris, *Remedies in Contract and Tort* (1988); Treitel, *Remedies for Breach of Contract* (1988).

value but for which a contractor has paid, and in reflecting these in awards of damages. If the claimant's interest in the performance of the contractual obligations cannot adequately be protected by an award of damages, there has been greater willingness to order that the contract be specifically performed where this is possible and practicable.

The overlap between the law of contract and the law of restitution has been mentioned. In certain cases, for example professional negligence cases, there will be overlapping claims in contract and in tort. The rules discussed in this section only apply to contractual damages. However, it should be borne in mind that in cases of overlap with the law of tort an alternative, and sometimes preferable, remedy may be available.[3]

II. COMPENSATORY NATURE OF DAMAGES

Damages for breach of contract are designed to compensate for the damage, loss or injury the claimant has suffered through that breach. A claimant who has not, in fact, suffered any loss by reason of the breach, is nevertheless entitled to a verdict, but the damages recoverable will be purely nominal (usually £2).

Whereas physical losses are the most frequent subject of actions in tort, commercial (i.e. financial) losses are the most frequent subject of actions for breach of contract. However, as will be seen, damages for breach of contract are not necessarily limited to compensation of financial loss alone. Damages may also be awarded in contract to compensate for physical damage to the person or property, for the loss of an attribute of property (such as comfort or privacy) even where this has not affected its value, for inconvenience, and, in certain circumstances, for disappointment.

(a) LOSS TO THE CLAIMANT

In *Alfred McAlpine Construction Ltd.* v. *Panatown Ltd.*[4] the House of Lords affirmed the general principle that damages may only be recovered for a loss which the claimant has suffered. This can, however, lead to difficulties in cases in which the loss is non-financial, is aesthetic or subjective,[5] has been suffered by a third party, or where the defendant has profited from the breach without causing loss to the claimant. In powerful dissenting speeches, Lord Goff and Lord Millett considered that these difficulties were the result of an unduly narrow approach to the concept of loss and the failure of English law to recognize that a contracting party's interest lies in the performance of the contract.[6] Their Lordships considered that these could be addressed

---

[3] *Ante*, p. 23. See, for example, *Henderson* v. *Merrett Syndicates Ltd.* [1995] 2 A.C. 145; *Midland Bank Trust Co. Ltd.* v. *Hett Stubbs & Kemp* [1979] Ch. 384 (limitation). But cf. *Parsons (H.) (Livestock) Ltd.* v. *Uttley Ingham & Co. Ltd.* [1978] Q.B. 791 (remoteness).

[4] [2000] 3 W.L.R. 946, at pp. 948, 961, 987, 999, 1005.

[5] *Radford* v. *de Froberville* [1977] 1 W.L.R. 1262, at p. 1267, see *post*, p. 597, 598.

[6] *Alfred McAlpine Construction Ltd.* v. *Panatown Ltd.* [2000] 3 W.L.R. 946, at pp. 973, 1011–12.

by recognizing that damages may be measured by the value of the party's defeated interest in having the contract performed—giving full recognition to the performance interest as the basis of contractual damages.[7] Lord Millett stated that the difficulties could also be addressed by recognizing that the performance of a contract may have an economic value of its own which is capable of sounding in damages[8]—a wider approach to loss. It should, however, be noted that, if this approach is to be developed, it does not follow that substantial damages will be recoverable where the victim was reasonably able to secure an equivalent alternative at no greater cost, or where it would not be reasonable for the victim to be given specific protection of the performance interest, e.g. where curing defective performance would be unreasonably costly.[9] The performance interest is considered below, as are situations in which substantial damages can be claimed in respect of a third party's loss. The exceptional cases in which a claimant can recover a substantial sum based on the defendant's benefit are considered below in Chapter 19, on restitutionary awards.

(b) DIFFICULTY OF ASSESSMENT NO BAR

Difficulty in assessing damages does not disentitle a claimant from having an attempt made to assess them, unless they depend altogether on remote and hypothetical possibilities. This can be seen from the case of *Simpson* v. *London and North Western Railway Company*,[10] where Simpson was deprived of the opportunity of exhibiting his products at an agricultural show. Although the ascertainment of damages was difficult and speculative, it was held that this was no reason for not giving any damages at all. Again, in *Chaplin* v. *Hicks*,[11] a candidate in a beauty competition, who had successfully passed the earlier stages of the competition, was, in breach of contract, not allowed to compete in the later stages with 49 others from whom 12 winners were to be chosen. She was awarded substantial damages for the loss of the chance of being successful (approximately 25 per cent), of which she had been wrongfully deprived. Similar considerations may affect the measure of damages in the cases where an offer to consider all conforming tenders is held to give rise to an enforceable obligation.[12] The value of the chance depends upon the number of contingencies upon which it depends.[13]

What must, however, be shown is a real and measurable (and not merely a speculative) chance.[14] This will be more difficult to show where, by contrast to the position in *Chaplin* v. *Hicks*, the claimant's loss depends upon the actions of an independent third party,[15] for example, where the breach of contract is said to have caused the loss of the

---

[7] *Ibid.*, at pp. 973, 976, 1011, 1013.

[8] *Ibid.*, at p. 1011.

[9] On 'cost of cure' and mitigation, see *post*, pp. 597, 614.

[10] (1876) 1 Q.B.D. 274; *post*, p. 608.

[11] [1911] 2 K.B. 786. Cf. *Sapwell* v. *Bass* [1910] 2 K.B. 486.

[12] *Blackpool and Fylde Aero Club Ltd.* v. *Blackpool B.C.* [1990] 1 W.L.R. 25, *ante*, p. 34, where the measure of damages was not considered.

[13] *Ministry of Defence* v. *Wheeler* [1998] 1 W.L.R. 637.

[14] *Allied Maples Group* v. *Simmons & Simmons* [1995] 1 W.L.R. 1602.

[15] *Ibid.*, at pp. 1609–11, 1623–5.

chance of obtaining a job.[16] The decision as to whether to offer a job depends (subject to statutory prohibition on discrimination on specified grounds) on the unrestricted volition of the prospective employer. In the absence of evidence that the claimant had a real chance of getting the job, and that the chance was lost because of the breach of contract, it is unlikely that a Court will be able to conclude that a real and measurable chance has been lost.

(c) DAMAGES ARE NOT PUNITIVE

Damages for breach of contract are given by way of compensation for loss suffered, and not by way of punishment for wrong inflicted. The measure of damages is therefore not affected by the motive of the breach. 'Vindictive' or 'exemplary' damages have no place in the law of contract.[17] Contractual damages cannot be used to punish, however outrageous the defendant's conduct. In *Addis v. Gramophone Co. Ltd.*:[18]

A was employed by G as manager of their business in Calcutta at a salary together with a commission on trade done. G wrongfully dismissed A without giving him the required 6 months' notice.

The House of Lords held that, although A might recover a sum representing his salary for the period of notice and the commission he would have earned during that period, his employers were not to be penalized in damages for the sharp and oppressive manner in which they had dismissed him.[19]

(d) COMPENSATION FOR INCONVENIENCE OR DISAPPOINTMENT

Contractual damages may be recovered for substantial physical inconvenience or discomfort arising from a breach. For example, where a family were transported by a railway company to the wrong station, with the result that they had to walk several miles home on a drizzling wet night,[20] and where a man, with his wife and child, was forced to live for two years in discomfort with his wife's parents owing to the failure of a solicitor to take any effective steps to obtain possession of a house,[21] damages for the physical inconvenience were recovered.

---

[16] *B.C.C.I. SA v. Ali & others (No. 2)* [1999] 4 All E.R. 83, at pp. 114–16.

[17] They may be recoverable in certain circumstances in tort: see *Rookes v. Barnard* [1964] A.C. 1129, at p. 1221; *Broome v. Cassell & Co. Ltd.* [1972] A.C. 1027; *A.B. v. South West Water Services* [1993] Q.B. 507. For the arguments for and against the imposition of restitutionary damages in cases of 'cynical' breach, see *post*, p. 653.

[18] [1909] A.C. 488, followed on this point but not others (*post*, p. 594) by *Malik v. Bank of Credit & Commerce International S.A.* [1998] 1 A.C. 20, at pp. 50–1. See also *Co-operative Insurance Society Ltd. v. Argyll Stores (Holdings) Ltd.* [1998] 1 A.C. 1, at p. 15. Cf. McBride (1995) 24 Anglo-American L.Rev. 369 for the argument that punitive damages should be awarded for deliberate breaches of contract.

[19] See also *Malik v. Bank of Credit & Commerce International S.A.* [1998] 1 A.C. 20, at p. 51; *Johnson v. Unisys Ltd.* [1999] 1 All E.R. 854, at p. 861, but note that the manner and circumstances of a dismissal may increase the claimant's financial loss: see *post*, p. 593.

[20] *Hobbs v. L. & S.W. Ry.* (1875) L.R. 10 Q.B. 111.

[21] *Bailey v. Bullock* [1950] 2 All E.R. 1167. Noise can amount to physical discomfort: *Farley v. Skinner* [2001] 3 W.L.R. 899, at paras. 30, 60.

Damages are not generally recoverable for 'any distress, frustration, anxiety, displeasure, vexation, tension or aggravation' caused by the breach even where it was in the contemplation of the parties that the breach would expose the parties to distress.[22] The reparation of such non-pecuniary, non-physical harm poses problems of incommensurability and subjectivity, and difficulties of proof. There is 'no standard measure of assessment by reference to which the harm can be converted into monetary form . . . This incommensurability gives rise to real danger of indeterminacy and of inconsistent awards'.[23]

There are, however, two exceptions to the general rule. Damages for non-physical distress or annoyance can be awarded where the claimant's distress is directly consequential on physical loss caused by the breach of contract.[24] They can also be awarded where the purpose of the contract is to provide enjoyment or peace of mind, or to prevent distress.[25] In *Jarvis* v. *Swans Tours Ltd.*:[26]

J, a solicitor, was entitled to two weeks' paid holiday a year and booked with S Tours a 15-day Christmas winter sports holiday at a hotel in Switzerland. He did so on the faith of S's brochure which described the holiday as a 'house-party', and promised a variety of entertainments including excellent skiing, a yodeller evening, a bar, and afternoon tea and cakes. In the first week there were only 13 people at the hotel and in the second week he was entirely alone. The promised entertainments proved to be wholly inferior in quality in comparison with the description in the brochure.

The Court of Appeal held that J was entitled to damages consisting of the amount which he had paid for the holiday and an additional sum of some £60 to compensate him for the disappointment he had suffered. Similarly, damages were awarded for anxiety and distress suffered by a woman whose solicitors failed to take prompt and effective measures against a man who was pestering her,[27] by a woman whose solicitors had failed to obtain proper financial relief in matrimonial proceedings,[28] by a bride when a photographer failed to keep his promise to be present and take

---

[22] *Watts* v. *Morrow* [1991] 1 W.L.R. 1421, *per* Bingham L.J. at p. 1445. See also *Bliss* v. *S.E. Thames R.H.A.* [1987] I.C.R. 700 (contract of employment); *Hayes* v. *James & Charles Dodd* [1990] 2 All E.R. 815 (solicitor's contract to provide professional services); *Branchett* v. *Beaney* [1992] 3 All E.R. 910 (covenant for quiet enjoyment of property).

[23] Law Com. C.P. No. 132, *Aggravated, Exemplary and Restitutionary Damages* (1993) § 2.12.

[24] *Perry* v. *Sydney Phillips & Son* [1982] 1 W.L.R. 1297 (anxiety and distress of living in a house in poor condition which had been bought in reliance on negligence in breach of contract in a surveyor's report); *Calebar Properties* v. *Sticher* [1984] 1 W.L.R. 287 (unpleasantness of living in deteriorating premises until they became uninhabitable because of landlord's delay in repairing). But such damages should be 'modest': *Watts* v. *Morrow* (*supra*, n. 22) at pp. 1443, 1445. Cf. Lord Cooke (*dissente*) in *Johnson* v. *Gore Wood & Co.* [2001] 2 W.L.R. 72 at p. 108 (distress due to poverty and changed way of life akin to that due to physical loss).

[25] *Ruxley Electronics & Constructions Ltd.* v. *Forsyth* [1996] A.C. 344, *per* Lord Lloyd at p. 374 (cf. Lord Mustill, *ibid*, at pp. 360–1, on which see *post*, p. 598); *Farley* v. *Skinner* [2001] 3 W.L.R. 899 at para. 28; *Johnson* v. *Gore Wood & Co.* [2001] 2 W.L.R. 72, *per* Lord Bingham at p. 96. Lord Cooke, *ibid.*, at p. 108 considered that contracts for status such as membership of a trade union or club are also included.

[26] [1973] Q.B. 233. See also *Jackson* v. *Horizon Holidays Ltd.* [1975] 1 W.L.R. 1468.

[27] *Heywood* v. *Wellers* [1976] Q.B. 446; *McLeish* v. *Amoo-Gottfried & Co.* The Times, 13 October 1995 (solicitor's negligence led to wrongful conviction). Cf. *Cook* v. *Swinfen* [1967] 1 W.L.R. 457, at p. 461; *Hayes* v. *James & Charles Dodd* [1990] 2 All E.R. 815.

[28] *Dickinson* v. *James Alexander & Co.* (1990) 20 Fam. L.R. 137 (C.A.).

photographs at her wedding,[29] and by children when a cemetery owner broke its contract to grant exclusive burial rights in a plot adjacent to that in which their parents were buried.[30] Such damages are nevertheless compensatory in nature and are not designed to inflict retribution on the defendant for inflicting the harm.

Originally this exception only applied if 'the sole' object of the contract was to provide enjoyment or peace of mind, or to prevent distress.[31] Accordingly, a contract with an architect to design a house for a couple who contemplated that it would be their 'dream home' did not qualify.[32] This meant that the non-economic purposes of a party to a contract would be protected where they were the only purposes but would not be where there were also economic purposes, and to this extent part of the purposes of the contract were unenforceable.[33] It has, however, recently been held in *Farley* v. *Skinner* that it suffices that the provision of peace of mind, or the prevention of distress is 'an important object' of the contract.[34] In that case F, a prospective purchaser of a house who wanted peace and quiet, employed a surveyor to report and advise, *inter alia*, whether the house might be affected by aircraft noise. The surveyor advised that it was unlikely that the property would suffer greatly and F bought the house.[35] In fact, the house was near a navigation beacon used by aircraft waiting to land at Gatwick Airport and was substantially affected by noise. It was held by the House of Lords that F was entitled to damages for the significant interference with his enjoyment of the property caused by the noise.

(e) LOSS OF REPUTATION

Although damages cannot be recovered in a contractual action for injury to reputation per se,[36] they may be where the loss of reputation caused by the breach of contract causes financial loss. In *Malik* v. *Bank of Credit & Commerce International S.A.*:[37]

M and other relatively senior employees of B.C.C.I., were made redundant following the bank's insolvency. They claimed that they were unable thereafter to obtain employment in the financial services industry because of the stigma attached to former employees of B.C.C.I., and sought substantial compensation for this handicap in the labour market. For the purposes of the proceedings it was assumed that B.C.C.I. had carried on its business in a corrupt and dishonest manner, that this had become widely known, that M and the other employees were innocent of any involvement, were at a handicap in the labour market because of the stigma, and had suffered financial loss as a result.

[29] *Diesen* v. *Sampson* 1971 S.L.T. (Sh. Ct.) 49.

[30] *Reed* v. *Madon* [1989] Ch. 408.

[31] *Watts* v. *Morrow* [1991] 1 W.L.R. 1421, *per* Bingham L.J. at p. 1445.

[32] *Knott* v. *Bolton* (1995) 45 Con. L.R. 127 (overruled by *Farley* v. *Skinner*).

[33] Capper (2000) 116 L.Q.R. 553, approved in *Farley* v. *Skinner* [2001] 3 W.L.R. 899, at paras. 24, 51.

[34] *Farley* v. *Skinner* [2001] 3 W.L.R. 899.

[35] The price F paid for the house coincided with its market value taking into account aircraft noise, so he had no claim for diminution of value.

[36] *Addis* v. *Gramophone Co. Ltd* [1909] A.C. 488, *ante*, p. 592.

[37] [1998] 1 A.C. 20. Statutory provision precludes the implication of a term in respect of the manner of dismissal: *Johnson* v. *Unisys Ltd.* [2001] 2 W.L.R. 1076.

The House of Lords held that contracts of employment contained an implied term of mutual trust and confidence so that the defendant was under an implied obligation not to carry on a dishonest or corrupt business, and that, in principle, financial loss in respect of damage to reputation caused by breach of this term is recoverable in a contractual action. It will, however, often be difficult to prove a handicap on the labour market. The damage must result from a relevant breach of contract, and in the ordinary way any loss of reputation an employee may suffer from being wrongfully dismissed or from having been associated with an unsuccessful or grossly incompetent business will not found a claim.[38]

The effect of this decision is to establish that financial loss resulting from a loss of reputation caused by a breach of contract is governed by general contractual principles. The contrary statements in *Addis* v. *Gramophone Co. Ltd.*[39] were explained in *Malik*'s case on the basis that the earlier case was decided before the development of the implied obligation of mutual trust and confidence so that the loss of reputation there had not been caused by a breach of contract,[40] and other cases will require reconsideration.[41]

Cases previously regarded as exceptional can now be seen as examples of the general rule. So, where a bank refuses to pay a customer's cheque when it has funds of the customer to meet, it will be liable in respect of any loss to the customer's trade reputation or credit-rating caused by the breach.[42] It is, moreover, no longer necessary to distinguish a breach of contract which causes injury to a reputation which a person already possesses from a breach of a specific undertaking to protect or enhance a person's reputation, for which damages were awarded prior to the decision in *Malik*'s case.[43] So, where a contract entitles an actor to be advertised as playing a leading part at a well-known music-hall, the actor may recover damages for the loss of publicity and for any injury that the failure to appear may cause to the actor's existing reputation.[44] In view of the assumed facts in *Malik*'s case, there was no need to deal with a breach of contract that causes non-financial loss, for instance distress and injured feelings resulting from loss of reputation, but the increased willingness to award contractual damages for such losses[45] suggests that this aspect of *Addis*'s case may also be ripe for reconsideration.[46]

[38] *B.C.C.I. SA* v. *Ali & others (No. 2)* [1999] 4 All E.R. 83, *ante* p. 592.

[39] [1909] A.C. 488, for example *per* Lord Loreburn, at p. 491. For the facts, see *ante*, p. 592.

[40] [1998] 1 A.C. 20, *per* Lord Nicholls, at p. 38 and *per* Lord Steyn at p. 51.

[41] e.g. *Groom* v. *Crocker* [1939] 1 K.B. 194 (solicitors who wrongfully admitted negligence on the part of their motorist client, held not to be liable to him for 'loss of credit' as a careful driver).

[42] *Kpohoror* v. *Woolwich Building Society* [1996] 4 All E.R. 119, suggesting that a distinction between trade and personal transactions should no longer be made.

[43] *Clayton & Waller Ltd.* v. *Oliver* [1930] A.C. 209.

[44] *Marbe* v. *George Edwardes (Daley's Theatre) Ltd.* [1928] 1 K.B. 269, at pp. 281, 288.

[45] For the conditions under which such an award will be made see *ante*, pp. 592–4.

[46] *Johnson* v. *Gore Wood & Co.* (*supra* n. 24) *per* Lord Cooke at p. 109. But cf. *ibid.*, *per* Lord Bingham at p. 97 and Lord Goff at p. 101.

III. BASIS OF ASSESSMENT OF DAMAGES

The general principle that damages are compensatory in nature is nevertheless only a starting point, and the question must still be asked—when a contract is broken and action is brought upon it, how are we to arrive at the amount which the claimant, if successful, is entitled to recover in respect of its loss?

(a) THE 'PERFORMANCE' OR 'EXPECTATION' MEASURE

The object of an award of damages for breach of contract is to place the claimant, so far as money can do it, in the same situation, with respect to damages, as if the contract had been performed.[47] Claimants are thus enabled to recover damages in respect of the loss of gains of which they have been deprived by the breach. For example, if machinery is not delivered to a person or delivered late in breach of contract, that person will have a claim for loss of profits for being deprived of its use. Such a claim, however, is not peculiar to an action in contract, since a similar claim would lie if the machinery were damaged or destroyed by a tort. But the law of contract goes further and entitles claimants (in appropriate circumstances) to damages for the loss of the bargained-for performance, that is to say, for the loss of the particular benefit which it was expected would be received by the contract which has been broken: an art dealer contracts to purchase a painting which is worth far more than the agreed price; a record company by contract obtains for a relatively modest sum the sole right to distribute the records of what proves to be a highly successful pop-group; a caterer obtains an extremely lucrative contract to cater for a banquet. In each case, if the contract is broken by the other party, the damages will be assessed by reference to the claimant's 'performance' or 'expectation' loss, consisting of what would have been received had the contract been duly performed.[48]

(i) Scope of the duty undertaken

It is important to consider the precise scope of the duty undertaken. Thus it has been held that a surveyor's contractual duty to value property is a duty to take reasonable care to provide information on which the other party would decide whether to lend money on mortgage. The performance expected is different and narrower than where the duty undertaken is to advise the potential lender as to whether to make the loan.[49] A person giving negligent advice in breach of a contractual duty to advise will, subject to the rules of remoteness considered below, be responsible for all the loss

---

[47] *Robinson* v. *Harman* (1848) 1 Exch. 850, at p. 855.

[48] See Fuller and Perdue (1936–7) 46 Yale L.J. 52, 573; Taylor (1982) 45 M.L.R. 139; Burrows (1983) 99 L.Q.R. 217; Friedmann (1995) 111 L.Q.R. 628; Coote [1997] C.L.J. 537. Cf. Atiyah (1978) 94 L.Q.R. 193.

[49] Cf. *South Australia Asset Management Co.* v. *York Montague Ltd.* [1997] A.C. 191, *per* Lord Hoffmann at p. 214 (valuers not liable for loss attributable to collapse of property market). See also *Platform Home Loans* v. *Oyston Shipways Ltd.* [2000] 2 A.C. 190, at pp. 208–9. Cf. *Aneco Reinsurance Underwriting Ltd.* v. *Johnson & Higgins Ltd.* [2002] 2 Lloyd's Rep. 157, paras 40–1 (duty to advise) and *Kenny & Good Pty. Ltd.* v. *MGICA* (1999) 199 C.L.R. 413 where the *South Australia* case was criticized as redefining the duty in a way which forecloses questions of causation, remoteness, and measure.

which is a consequence of the advice being taken. A person who negligently provides incorrect information is only responsible for the consequences of the information being wrong.

(ii) Assessment by reference to contract terms

Damages must be assessed by reference to the terms of the contract sued upon, and the Court cannot take account of 'the expectations, however reasonable, of one contractor that the other will do something that it has assumed no legal obligation to do'.[50] Thus an employee who is wrongfully dismissed and sues the employer for breach of contract will be unable to recover contractual damages for the loss of 'fringe benefits' from the employment unless the employer has assumed a contractual obligation to provide those benefits.[51] Also, where the defendant has a choice of two methods of performance, damages will be assessed on the basis of the minimum legal obligation, i.e. that the contract would have been performed by the method least onerous to the defendant and least beneficial to the claimant.[52]

(iii) Diminution in value or 'cost of cure'

In many cases the assessment of the claimant's loss of bargain will be the difference in value between the performance received and that promised in the contract; 'diminution in value'.[53] However, in appropriate circumstances, damages may either be assessed on the basis of what it has cost or will cost the claimant to have the contract performed by a third party; the 'cost of cure',[54] or another basis which reflects the loss truly suffered by the claimant. These alternatives may be more appropriate where the claimant's purpose in contracting is non-monetary. For instance, a contract for small building works on a house may be made to make it 'more comfortable, more convenient, and more conformable' to the owner's particular tastes,[55] or to ensure privacy.[56] These factors may not enhance the value of the property to be benefited or may even reduce it, as where the work consists of redecorating, to the owner's execrable taste, a house in good decorative order.[57] In such cases the value of the promise to the promisee differs from the financial effect on the promisee's position which full performance will ensure. Where the value of the performance to the promisee exceeds the financial enhancement of the promisee's position, the value beyond the market price has been called the 'consumer surplus'.[58]

[50] *Lavarack v. Woods of Colchester Ltd.* [1967] 1 Q.B. 278, at p. 294.
[51] *Ibid.*
[52] *Re Thornett & Fehr and Yuills Ltd.* [1921] 1 K.B. 219; *Abraham v. Herbert Reiach Ltd.* [1922] 1 K.B. 477; *Bunge Cpn. v. Tradax Export S.A.* [1981] 1 W.L.R. 711. Cf. *Paula Lee Ltd. v. Robert Zehil & Co Ltd.* [1983] 2 All E.R. 390. See Hudson (1975) 91 L.Q.R. 20.
[53] See *post*, p. 610; Landlord and Tenant Act 1927, s. 18; Sale of Goods Act 1979, ss. 50(3), 51(3), 53(3).
[54] *Jones v. Herxheimer* [1950] 2 K.B. 106; *East Ham Cpn v. Bernard Sunley & Sons Ltd.* [1966] A.C. 406, at p. 434; *Tito v. Waddell (No. 2)* [1977] Ch. 106, at p. 329; *Radford v. de Froberville* [1977] 1 W.L.R. 1262, at pp. 1269–70; *Ruxley Electronics & Constructions Ltd. v. Forsyth* [1996] 1 A.C. 344. Where the 'cost of cure' is less than the reduction in value, the mitigation principle (*post*, p. 614) will restrict the claimant to the former.
[55] *Ruxley Electronics & Constructions Ltd. v. Forsyth* [1996] 1 A.C. 344, *per* Lord Mustill at pp. 360–1.
[56] *Radford v. de Froberville* (*supra*, n. 54) (the erection of a wall).
[57] See *B.P. Exploration Co. (Libya) Ltd. v. Hunt (No. 2)* [1979] 1 W.L.R. 783, *per* Robert Goff J. at p. 803.
[58] Harris, Ogus, Phillips (1979) 95 L.Q.R. 58; Muris (1983) 12 J.L.S. 379.

If work contracted for is not performed or is performed badly, the claimant is entitled to the cost of substitute or remedial work to be carried out by a third party where it is possible to do so,[59] unless, in all the circumstances, this is unreasonable, as where the cost of cure is wholly disproportionate to any resulting benefit[60] and where it would not be reasonable for the claimant to have the work done, whether or not the claimant does so intend.[61] In such cases, unless the claimant's interest in performance is not wholly financial, only the diminution in value should be recovered. Thus in *Ruxley Electronics & Constructions Ltd.* v. *Forsyth*:[62]

F contracted with R for the construction of a swimming pool in his garden with a diving area 7 feet 6 inches deep at a price of £17,797. In breach of contract the diving area was only 6 feet deep but was suitable for diving and there was no adverse effect on the market value of the pool. The estimated cost of rebuilding the pool to the specified depth was £21,560.

The House of Lords held that F was not entitled to the 'cost of cure'.

(iv) Loss of non-monetary 'consumer surplus'

In *Ruxley Electronics & Constructions Ltd.* v. *Forsyth* it was held that as F had lost his personal preference for a deeper pool he was entitled to £2,500 for loss of amenity. This is best regarded as compensation, albeit imprecise, for F's loss of his performance and of non-monetary 'consumer surplus'.[63] The decision has been said to be an example of the Courts taking steps to recognize and remedy a deficiency in the remedial regime for breach of contract where the claimant's loss is non-financial by giving fuller recognition to the performance interest as the basis of contractual damages.[64] In cases where there was never any question of being able to 'cure' the breach,

---

[59] Cf. *Ward* v. *Cannock Chase D.C.* [1985] 3 All E.R. 537 (a tort case where cost of cure was awarded subject to planning permission) and note that where a surveyor in breach of contract fails to identify defects in the property surveyed the *prima facie* measure is the diminution in the value of the property, not the cost of repairing it: *Phillips* v. *Ward* [1956] 1 W.L.R. 491; *Watts* v. *Morrow* [1991] 1 W.L.R. 1421; *Patel* v. *Hooper & Jackson* [1999] 1 W.L.R. 1792, at p. 1801.

[60] *Ruxley Electronics & Constructions Ltd.* v. *Forsyth* [1996] 1 A.C. 344, at pp. 354, 361; *Sealace SS Co. Ltd.* v. *Oceanvoice Ltd.* [1991] 1 Lloyd's Rep. 120; *Channel Island Ferries Ltd.* v. *Cenargo Navigation Ltd.* [1994] 2 Lloyd's Rep. 160, at p. 167 (plaintiff's interest wholly financial). In principle 'benefit' should include non-monetary benefits such as bathroom tiles matching an existing colour scheme.

[61] *Ruxley Electronics & Constructions Ltd.* v. *Forsyth* (*supra*, n. 60), *per* Lord Jauncey and Lord Lloyd at pp. 354, 359, 372–3. See also *Watts* v. *Morrow* [1991] 1 W.L.R. 1421; *Taylor* v. *Hepworths Ltd* [1977] 1 W.L.R. 659 (tort); *De Cesare* v. *Deluxe Motors Pty. Ltd.* (1996) 67 S.A.L.R. 28, at pp. 33–5 (Australia). Cf. *Tito* v. *Waddell (No. 2)* [1977] Ch. 106, at p. 317; *Radford* v. *de Froberville* (*supra*, n. 54), at p. 1248; *Dean* v. *Ainley* [1987] 1 W.L.R. 1729 (Glidewell L.J. and Sir George Waller).

[62] [1996] 1 A.C. 344, on which see Coote [1997] C.L.J. 537; O'Sullivan, ch. 1 in Rose, ed., *Failure of Contracts* (1997). See also *Harbutt's 'Plasticine' Ltd.* v. *Wayne Tank and Pump Co. Ltd.* [1970] 1 Q.B. 447, at p. 473.

[63] *Ibid.*, *per* Lord Bridge and Lord Mustill at pp. 354, 360–1. Cf. *ibid.*, *per* Lord Lloyd, at p. 374, reserving his position but regarding it as compensation for F's disappointment, on which see *ante*, p. 561.

[64] O'Sullivan, 'Reflections on the Role of Restitutionary Damages to Protect Contractual Expectations', adopted in this context by Lord Goff and Lord Millett in *Alfred McAlpine Construction Ltd.* v. *Panatown Ltd.* [2000] 3 W.L.R. 946, at pp. 973, 1012, discussed *ante*, pp. 590–1.

for example where a carrier provided a low grade delivery service rather than the 'enhanced' service that was promised and paid for, it should, in principle, also be possible to put a figure to any non-monetary loss suffered.[65]

The increased willingness to award damages in such cases is a reflection of recognition that 'the principle of pacta sunt servanda would be eroded if the law did not take account of the fact that the consumer often demands specifications which, although not of economic value, have value to him'.[66]

(b) THE RELIANCE MEASURE

An alternative basis for the assessment of damages is that the claimant should recover its 'reliance loss', that is to say, expenses which it has incurred in preparing to perform or in part performance of the contract and which have been rendered futile by the breach. Even expenses incurred prior to, and in anticipation of, the making of the contract are recoverable, provided it was reasonably in the contemplation of the parties that they would be wasted if the contract was broken. Thus in *Anglia Television Ltd.* v. *Reed,*[67] the television company obtained damages in respect of expenses of £2,750 which had been thrown away by reason of the defendant's refusal, in breach of contract, to play the leading part in a television play, even though the expenses had been incurred before the contract was made. A claimant may be compelled to claim damages for wasted expenses rather than for the loss of its bargain by reason of its inability to prove that financial benefit would have accrued to it had the contract been performed.[68]

If, however, the defendant can prove that the claimant would not have benefited financially had the contract been performed, the claimant will not be permitted to escape from a bad bargain by recovering as damages sums spent in reliance on the contract instead of loss of expectancy.[69] In such a case the claimant would only recover nominal damages because the reliance losses are considered to flow from entering into a losing contract and not from the defendant's breach.[70] A claimant who recovers for the loss of bargain cannot, as a general rule, combine a claim for reliance loss with one for loss of expectation so as to recover twice in respect of the same loss.[71] Thus damages for expenses rendered futile by the breach cannot be sought at the same time as damages for loss of profit, since such expenses would have had to be laid out in order to earn the profit claimed.

---

[65] See Beale (1996) 112 L.Q.R. 205, discussing *White Arrow Express Ltd.* v. *Lamey's Distribution Ltd.* (1995) 15 Tr. L.R. 69.

[66] *Ruxley Electronics & Constructions Ltd.* v. *Forsyth* (*supra*, n. 60), *per* Lord Mustill, at p. 360; *Farley* v. *Skinner* [2001] 3 W.L.R. 899, at paras 21, 79.

[67] [1972] 1 Q.B. 60. See also *Lloyd* v. *Stanbury* [1971] 1 W.L.R. 535.

[68] *Anglia Television Ltd.* v. *Reed* (*supra*, n. 67) (inability to prove what profits from TV play would have been); *McRae* v. *Commonwealth Disposals Commission* (1950) 84 C.L.R. 377 (value of ship to be salvaged too speculative; price paid and cost of salvage expedition recovered).

[69] *C. & P. Haulage* v. *Middleton* [1983] 1 W.L.R. 1461; *CCC (London) Films Ltd* v. *Impact Quadrant Films Ltd.* [1985] Q.B. 16.

[70] Cf. *post*, p. 642 (restitutionary remedies can 'save' a claimant from a bad bargain).

[71] See *Cullinane* v. *British 'Rema' Manufacturing Co. Ltd.* [1954] 1 Q.B. 292, *post*, p. 614.

IV. CAUSATION

In order to establish a right to damages the claimant must show that the breach of contract was a cause of the loss which has been sustained in the sense that the breach of contract is the 'effective' cause of the loss, as opposed to an event which merely gives the opportunity for the claimant to sustain the loss.[72] The Courts have treated the determination of whether a breach was the cause of the loss in a broad way, in the end turning to their 'commonsense'[73] in interpreting the facts. Accordingly, there are few rules of law that can be stated.

Where another event has also affected the fact situation, if that other event was *likely*[74] to happen once the breach of contract had occurred it will generally not be held to break the chain of causation. In *Monarch Steamship Co. Ltd.* v. *Karlshamms Oljefabriker (A/B)*[75] a voyage was delayed by the unseaworthiness of the vessel so that it arrived in European waters after the outbreak of the Second World War and was diverted by the Admiralty to Glasgow. It was held that the outbreak of war and the Admiralty's action did not break the chain of causation; the cause of the cargo-owners' loss was the defendant's breach of contract in failing to provide a seaworthy ship. But where that other event was *not likely* to happen once the breach of contract has occurred, the chain of causation may well be held to have been broken. Thus a breach of contract by a solicitor in wrongfully ceasing to act for a client gave rise to the opportunity for the client to sustain loss by acting without alternative legal advice and lodging a defective application, but was not the cause of such loss.[76] Moreover, if the breach of contract consists of an omission, for example failure to provide equipment or advice, causation depends upon the answer to the hypothetical question: would the claimant have taken action to obtain the benefit that has been lost or to avoid the risk that has been incurred?[77]

V. REMOTENESS OF DAMAGES

Where the test of causation is satisfied the law does not, however, compel the defendant to assume liability for all the loss which the claimant may have suffered as a consequence of the breach. Certain losses may nevertheless be too 'remote', and for these the claimant is not entitled to compensation.

---

[72] *Galoo Ltd.* v. *Bright Grahame Murray* [1994] 1 W.L.R. 1360; *Young* v. *Purdy* [1997] P.N.L.R. 130, disapproving of the 'but for' test. But cf. *Weld-Blundell* v. *Stephens* [1920] A.C. 956; *Banco de Portugal* v. *Waterlow & Sons Ltd.* [1932] A.C. 542; *Compania Naviera Maropan S/A* v. *Bowaters Lloyd Pulp & Paper Mills Ltd.* [1955] 2 Q.B. 68; *Quinn* v. *Burch Bros. (Builders) Ltd.* [1966] 2 Q.B. 370.

[73] *Galoo Ltd.* v. *Bright Grahame Murray* [1994] 1 W.L.R. 1360, at 1374–5.

[74] In the sense used in the context of remoteness, *infra*.

[75] [1949] A.C. 196. On the position where the other event is the act of the claimant, see *post*, pp. 616–17.

[76] *Young* v. *Purdy* [1997] P.N.L.R. 130; *Galoo Ltd.* v. *Bright Grahame Murray* [1994] 1 W.L.R. 1360. See also *South Australia Asset Management Co.* v. *York Montague Ltd.* [1997] A.C. 191, *per* Lord Hoffmann at p. 212–13. Cf. *ibid.* [1995] Q.B. 375, *per* Bingham M.R. at pp. 406, 420–1.

[77] *Allied Maples Group Ltd.* v. *Simmons & Simmons (a firm)* [1995] 1 W.L.R. 1602, at pp. 1609–11.

(a) THE BASIC TWO-BRANCHED RULE

The foundation of the law on this subject is contained in the judgment of Alderson B. in the Court of Exchequer in the case of *Hadley* v. *Baxendale*. Drawing on the civilian principle of foreseeability and Articles 1149–1151 of the French Civil Code, he stated that where the parties have made a contract which one of them has broken damages are recoverable: (1) when they are 'such as may fairly and reasonably be considered arising naturally, i.e., according to the usual course of things' from the breach, or (2) when they are 'such as may reasonably be supposed to have been in the contemplation of both parties at the time they made the contract', provided that in both cases, they are the probable result of the breach.[78] The effect of the rule was explained by Alderson B. as follows:[79]

[I]f the special circumstances under which the contract was actually made were communicated by the plaintiffs to the defendants, and thus known to both parties, the damages resulting from the breach of such a contract, which they would reasonably contemplate, would be the amount of injury which would ordinarily follow from a breach of contract under these special circumstances so known and communicated. But, on the other hand, if these special circumstances were wholly unknown to the party breaking the contract, he, at the most, could only be supposed to have had in his contemplation the amount of injury which would arise generally, and in the great multitude of cases not affected by any special circumstances, from such a breach of contract. For, had the special circumstances been known, the parties might have specially provided for the breach of contract by special terms as to the damages in that case; and of this advantage it would be very unjust to deprive them.

From this it will be seen that liability under the second branch of the rule will depend upon the special circumstances made known to the party in default at the time the contract was made. In the case in which these principles were formulated:

H's mill was stopped by the breakage of a crankshaft, and it was necessary to send the crankshaft to the makers as a pattern for a new one. The defendants, who were carriers, undertook to deliver the shaft to the makers, but the only information given to them was 'that the article to be carried was the broken shaft of a mill, and that H was the owner of the mill'.[80] By some neglect on their part the delivery of the shaft was delayed, and in consequence the mill could not be restarted until some time after it could otherwise have been. H lost profits which he would otherwise have made.

The question was whether this loss of profits ought to be taken into account in estimating the damages. Applying the principles quoted above, the Court pointed out that the circumstances communicated to the defendants did not show that a delay in the delivery of the shaft would entail loss of profits of the mill; H might have had another shaft, or there might have been some other defect in the machinery to cause

[78] (1854) 9 Exch. 341, at p. 354. For the meaning of the term 'probable' in this context, see *post* p. 603.
[79] *Ibid.*, at pp. 354, 355.
[80] *Ibid.*, *per* Alderson B. at p. 355. It was stated by Asquith L.J. in *Victoria Laundry (Windsor) Ltd.* v. *Newman Industries Ltd.* [1949] 2 K.B. 528, at p. 537, that the headnote is misleading in that it wrongly ascribes to the defendants knowledge that the mill was stopped for want of the shaft.

the stoppage. Accordingly they could not recover for this loss because the Court stated[81] that:

[I]n the great multitude of cases of millers sending off broken shafts to third persons by a carrier under ordinary circumstances, such consequences would not, in all probability, have occurred; and these special circumstances were here never communicated by [H] to the defendants.

The rule was further considered in *Victoria Laundry (Windsor) Ltd.* v. *Newman Industries Ltd.*:[82]

V, a launderer and dyer, wished to expand its business, and for this purpose entered into a contract with the defendant to purchase from it a new boiler. It was agreed that the boiler was to be delivered on 5 June, but when V sent to collect the boiler on that day it was informed that it had been damaged by a fall and was not ready. The boiler was not, in fact, delivered until November. In consequence of this delay, V lost the profits which it would have earned during this period, and, in particular, certain highly lucrative dyeing contracts which it could have obtained with the Ministry of Supply. V sued *inter alia* to recover these losses.

Streatfield J. held that V was not entitled to include in its measure of damages the loss of any business profits during the period of delay. His decision was reversed. Asquith L.J., delivering the judgment of the Court of Appeal, pointed out that the defendant knew before, and at the time of the contract, that V was a launderer and dyer and required the boiler for immediate use in its business. From the defendant's own technical experience, and from the business relations existing between the parties, the defendant must be presumed to have anticipated that some loss of profits would occur by reason of its delay. But in the absence of special knowledge on its part, the defendant could not reasonably foresee the additional losses suffered by V's inability to accept the highly lucrative dyeing contracts. The case was therefore to be referred to an Official Referee who would decide as to what loss might reasonably be considered to be normal in the circumstances.

Although there are two branches to the rule in *Hadley* v. *Baxendale*, in essence they both form a part of a single general principle.[83] An attempt to elucidate their relationship was made by Asquith L.J. in *Victoria Laundry (Windsor) Ltd.* v. *Newman Industries Ltd.*[84] The general principle which governs both branches of the rule is that the aggrieved party is only entitled to recover such part of the loss actually resulting from the breach as was at the time of the contract reasonably foreseeable as liable to result from the breach. What was at that time reasonably so foreseeable depends on the knowledge then possessed by the parties or, at all events, by the party who later commits the breach. For this purpose, knowledge 'possessed' is of two kinds: one imputed, the other actual. Everyone, as a reasonable person, is taken to know the 'ordinary course of things' and consequently what loss is liable to result from a breach of contract in that ordinary course. This is the subject-matter of the first branch of the

---

[81] (1854) 9 Exch. 341, *per* Alderson B. at p. 356.
[82] [1949] 2 K.B. 528.
[83] *Koufos* v. *C. Czarnikow Ltd.* [1969] 1 A.C. 350, at pp. 385, 415.
[84] [1949] 2 K.B. 528, at p. 539.

rule. But to this knowledge, which a contract-breaker is assumed to possess whether it is actually possessed or not, there may have to be added in a particular case knowledge which the claimant actually possesses, of special circumstances outside the 'ordinary course of things', of such a kind that a breach in those special circumstances would be liable to cause more loss.[85] Such a situation attracts the operation of the second branch of the rule and makes this additional loss recoverable. Under neither branch is it necessary that the contract-breaker should actually have asked what loss is liable to result from a breach. It suffices that, if the issue had been considered, the contract-breaker would as a reasonable person have concluded that the loss in question was liable to result.

The language of the judgment in the *Victoria Laundry* case has been described as 'a justifiable and valuable clarification of the principles which *Hadley* v. *Baxendale* was intending to express' particularly that the phrase used by Alderson B.—'in the contemplation of the parties . . . as the probable result' did not mean an odds on probability.[86] Nevertheless, there has been some criticism of the way in which Asquith L.J. formulated the general principle in terms of 'reasonable foresight' of the loss 'liable to result'. This, it is said, may engender confusion with the rule regarding remoteness of damage in tort,[87] where a defendant will be held responsible for damage which is reasonably foreseeable as liable to happen even if the risk is very small,[88] because it is said that in tort, unlike in contract, there is often no opportunity for the injured party to protect itself against an unusual risk by informing the defendant.[89] In *Koufos* v. *C. Czarnikow Ltd.*[90] Lord Reid and Lord Morris interpreted Alderson B.'s phrase as meaning the contemplation of a result which was 'not unlikely' to happen rather than an odds on probability;[91] and a majority of their Lordships distinguished the tort rule by requiring that the loss must be 'not very unusual and easily foreseeable',[92] or that there must be 'a real danger' or 'a serious possibility'[93] of its occurrence.

(b) PHYSICAL DAMAGE AND ECONOMIC LOSS

The interrelation of the tests for remoteness of damage in contract and tort was further considered by the Court of Appeal in *Parsons (H.) (Livestock) Ltd.* v. *Uttley Ingham & Co. Ltd.*[94]

---

[85] Knowledge of special circumstances may, however, in some situations be such as to lead the parties to believe that the loss will be reduced: see *Biggin & Co. Ltd.* v. *Permanite Ltd.* [1951] 1 K.B. 422, at p. 436; *Koufos* v. *C. Czarnikow Ltd. (supra,* n. 83), at p. 416.

[86] *Koufos* v. *C. Czarnikow Ltd. (supra,* n. 83), at p. 417. See also p. 399, but contrast pp. 389, 390, 410–11, 424–5. In *R & H Hall Ltd.* v. *W.H. Pim (Junior) & Co Ltd.* (1927) 33 Com. Cas. 324, at p. 330 Lord Dunedin stated that 'probable' did not mean more than an even chance.

[87] *Overseas Tankship (U.K.)* v. *Morts Dock and Engineering Co. (The Wagon Mound)* [1961] A.C. 388.

[88] *Koufos* v. *C. Czarnikow Ltd. (supra,* n. 83), at pp. 385–6, 389.

[89] *Ibid.,* at pp. 385–6, 411, 422–3. But as parties to a tort claim may well be in a contractual or similar relationship this is not an adequate reason. See Burrows (*supra,* n. 2), p. 54.

[90] [1969] A.C. 350.

[91] At pp. 388, 406. See also *per* Lord Pearce at pp. 416–17, Lord Upjohn at p. 424.

[92] At p. 383.

[93] At pp. 414–15, 425.

[94] [1978] Q.B. 791.

U.I. agreed to supply and erect on P's pig farm a bulk food storage hopper for the purpose of storing pig nuts for P's top grade pig herd. When the hopper was installed, U.I. failed to ensure that a ventilator at the top of the hopper was open, with the result that the pig nuts stored in it became mouldy. P fed the mouldy nuts to their pigs believing (as would normally be the case) that no harm could result. But the pigs suffered an attack of E. *coli*, an intestinal infection triggered by feeding on the mouldy nuts, and 254 pigs died.

At first instance, Swanwick J. held that the damage caused was not within the reasonable contemplation of the parties as a result of U.I.'s breach of contract. The Court of Appeal reversed that decision. Lord Denning M.R. expressed the opinion[95] that the observations of the House of Lords in *Koufos* v. *C. Czarnikow Ltd.* were limited to cases where a claimant was claiming for loss of profit or, at any rate, for economic loss. In his view, where the claim was for damages for personal injury or damage to property, or for resulting expenses to which the claimant had actually been put, the rule in contract was the same as that in tort, so that a defendant would be liable for any loss or damage which ought reasonably to have been foreseen at the time of the breach as a possible consequence, even if it was only a slight possibility.

A distinction between loss of profit and physical damage might be justified on the ground that a person is unlikely to consider the possibility of physical injury in advance and thus to disclose unusual risks.[96] However, Orr and Scarman L.JJ., who held that the parties could have contemplated 'a serious possibility' that the pigs might become ill as a result of the breach, considered that neither authority[97] nor principle supported a distinction in law between loss of profit and physical damage. Nevertheless, Scarman L.J. stated[98] that although the formulation of the remoteness test is not the same in tort and contract because the relationship of the parties in a contractual situation differs from that in tort, it would be absurd if the amount of damages recoverable were to depend upon whether the claimant's cause of action was in contract or in tort. In his opinion the difference between 'reasonably foreseeable' (the test in tort) and 'reasonably contemplated' (the test in contract) was semantic, not substantial. This suggests that where there is a contractual relation between the parties and concurrent liability in contract and tort there should, in principle, be no difference between the remoteness tests in contract and tort. But even in such situations the difference may not yet have been eliminated.[99]

---

[95] At pp. 803–4.

[96] Burrows (*supra*, n. 2), p. 53. But this may not be the case for all types of contracts, e.g. a contract for medical services or for instruction in a sporting activity.

[97] The authority relied on by Lord Denning, *Ashington Piggeries Ltd.* v. *Christopher Hill Ltd.* [1972] A.C. 441 and *Kendall (Henry) & Sons* v. *William Lillico & Sons Ltd.* [1969] 2 A.C. 31, in fact applied *Koufos* v. *C. Czarnikow Ltd.* (*supra*, n. 83) as, more recently, did *Kemp* v. *Intasun Holidays Ltd.* [1987] 2 F.T.L.R. 234 (asthmatic attack caused by dirty hotel room too remote).

[98] At pp. 806–7. See also *Archer* v. *Brown* [1985] Q.B. 401, at p. 418.

[99] Cf. *Henderson* v. *Merrett Syndicates Ltd.* [1995] 2 A.C. 145, at p. 185 (remoteness less restricted in tort than in contract) and *Banque Lambert Bruxelles S.A.* v. *Eagle Star Insurance Co. Ltd.* [1995] Q.B. 375, at p. 405 (essence of the test the same) *sub nom. South Australia Asset Management Co.* v. *York Montague Ltd.* [1997] A.C. 191, at p. 211 (scope of the duty is the same); *Kenny & Good Pty Ltd.* v. *MGICA* (1999) 199 C.L.R. 413, at p. 434 *per* McHugh J. (High Court of Australia). See generally Cartwright [1996] C.L.J. 488, at pp. 500–4, 514.

(c) TYPE OF DAMAGE

In the context of physical injury it is established that the word 'damage' refers to the type or kind of damage in question; it is not necessary for a claimant to go further and show contemplation of the exact nature of the damage that has arisen, or the amount of damage of the type or kind.[100] Although it has been said that the same principles apply to cases of loss of profit,[101] this is difficult to reconcile with the decision of the Court of Appeal in the *Victoria Laundry* case in which the 'ordinary' loss of profits were recovered but not that from the highly lucrative Ministry of Supply contracts.[102] An attempt to do this was made in *Brown* v. *K.M.R. Services Ltd.* by Stuart-Smith L.J. who stated that although categorization into types is difficult in the case of financial loss, loss of ordinary business profits is different *in type or kind* from loss flowing from a particular contract which gives rise to very high profits, whereas underwriting losses of a far larger magnitude than any contemplated were of the same *type* as those foreseeable.[103]

(d) DAMAGE ARISING IN THE USUAL COURSE OF THINGS

It will now be convenient to examine separately the operation of each branch of the rule, in view of the fact that each covers a different degree of knowledge possessed by the contracting parties. The first branch of the rule in *Hadley* v. *Baxendale* deals with such damage as may fairly and reasonably be considered arising naturally, i.e., according to the usual course of things, from the breach of contract, as the probable result of the breach. It depends, as we have seen, on the knowledge which the parties are presumed to possess and the scope of the contractual duty undertaken.[104]

(i) Normal business position of parties

Damages will not be too remote if they flow from the normal business position of the parties, for the Court will assume that this is known to both of them. In *Monarch Steamship Co. Ltd.* v. *Karlshamns Oljefabriker (A/B)*,[105] the facts of which are summarized *supra*, as a result of the diversion of the delayed vessel to Glasgow the purchasers of the cargo of soya incurred expenses in having them forwarded to the contractual destination in Sweden.

The House of Lords held that the purchasers were entitled to recover this cost. Lord Wright pointed out that the question in all such cases must always be 'what reasonable business men must be taken to have contemplated as the natural or probable result if the contract was broken. As reasonable business men each must be taken to

---

[100] *Koufos* v. *C. Czarnikow Ltd.* (*supra*, n. 83), at pp. 382, 383, 385–6, 417.

[101] *Parsons (H.) (Livestock) Ltd.* v. *Uttley Ingham & Co. Ltd.* [1978] Q.B. 791, at pp. 804, 813, *Wroth* v. *Tyler* [1974] Ch. 30, at pp. 60–2; *Transworld Oil Ltd.* v. *North Bay S.S. Cpn.* [1987] 2 Lloyd's Rep. 173, at p. 175 (relying on cases of physical injury); *Homsy* v. *Murphy* (1997) 73 P. & C.R. 26, at pp. 36, 45.

[102] *Ante*, p. 602. See also *Islamic Republic of Iran S.S. Lines* v. *Ierax S.S. Co. of Panama* [1991] 1 Lloyd's Rep. 81, at pp. 85–6.

[103] [1995] 4 All E.R. 598, at pp. 620–1.

[104] *South Australia Asset Management Co.* v. *York Montague Ltd.* [1997] A.C. 191, at p. 211, *ante*, p. 596.

[105] [1949] A.C. 196 (*ante*, p. 567). Cf. *Diamond* v. *Campbell-Jones* [1961] Ch. 22.

understand the ordinary practices and exigencies of the other's trade or business'.[106] In this case, the possibility of war must have been present in the minds of the parties, and experienced business people would know that one of the risks that would be consequent upon prolongation of the voyage at that time would be the diversion of the vessel by the order of the Admiralty. The cost of transhipment was therefore not too remote a consequence of the unseaworthiness of the ship.

(ii) Market fluctuations

The Sale of Goods Act 1979 contains statutory provisions for the assessment of damages for breach of a contract of sale which are founded on the first branch of the rule in *Hadley* v. *Baxendale*, and these are considered later in this chapter.[107] But the first branch of the rule applies where the seller fails to deliver or is late in delivering what is on the face of it obviously a profit-earning chattel, for instance, a merchant or passenger ship, or some essential part of such a ship.[108] In such cases the party injured will be entitled to recover the loss of profit which might reasonably be expected to arise if the contract were broken.[109]

In contracts for the carriage of goods, if, by default of a carrier, the goods which he has contracted to deliver are lost or delayed in transit, certain loss will ordinarily be assumed to have been suffered by the consignee as the natural and probable result of the breach. In the case of loss, the normal measure of damages is the market value of the goods at the time when they ought to have arrived, less the freight payable on safe delivery.[110] In the case of delay in delivering the goods, it is the difference between the market value of the goods on the day on which they ought to have arrived and their market value on the day on which they did arrive.[111] Thus in *Koufos* v. *C. Czarnikow Ltd.*:[112]

The respondent, a sugar merchant, chartered the ship *Heron II* from the appellant to carry a cargo of sugar from Constanza to Basrah. The ship deviated without authority from the agreed voyage, with the result that the cargo was delayed. Owing to a fall in the market for sugar at Basrah, the respondent obtained £3,800 less for the sugar than the price obtainable when it should have been delivered.

The appellant contended that he was not liable for this sum as he had no special knowledge of the seasonal and other fluctuations of the sugar market. But the House of Lords held that a shipowner must be presumed to know that prices in a commodity market were liable to fluctuate, and judgment was given against him.

---

[106] At p. 224. See also *Bulk Oil* v. *Sun International* [1984] 1 Lloyd's Rep. 531, at p. 544.

[107] *Post*, p. 609.

[108] *Victoria Laundry (Windsor) Ltd.* v. *Newman Industries Ltd.* [1949] 2 K.B. 528, *per* Asquith L.J. at p. 536. See also *Fletcher* v. *Tayleur* (1855) 17 C.B. 21; *Saint Lines* v. *Richardsons Westgarth & Co.* [1940] 2 K.B. 99.

[109] *Cory* v. *Thames Ironworks & S.S. Co.* (1868) L.R. 3 Q.B. 181 (use of hull as coal store); *Fyffes Group Ltd* v. *Reefer Express Lines Pty Ltd.* [1996] 2 Lloyd's Rep. 171, at p. 203 (sub-charter of vessel on three-year time charter).

[110] *Rodocanachi* v. *Milburn* (1886) 18 Q.B.D. 67, at p. 76.

[111] *Wilson* v. *Lancs. & Yorks. Ry.* (1861) 9 C.B.N.S. 632.

[112] [1969] 1 A.C. 350.

(iii) Exceptional loss not covered

On the other hand, the first branch of the rule in *Hadley* v. *Baxendale* does not cover losses which are the consequence of special facts not known to the party in default at the time the agreement was made. In *Hadley* v. *Baxendale* itself, H was unable to recover damages arising from the fact that they had only one shaft, and in *Victoria Laundry* V was unable to recover in respect of the exceptionally lucrative Ministry of Supply contracts because information about those facts had not been conveyed to the defendants. Again in *British Columbia etc. Saw-Mill Co. Ltd.* v. *Nettleship*:[113]

A number of cases of machinery intended for the erection of a sawmill at Vancouver were shipped on the defendant's vessel. The defendant failed to deliver one of the cases, but was unaware of the fact that it contained a material part without which the sawmill could not be erected at all. B.C. Saw-Mill claimed the cost of replacing the lost parts, and the loss incurred by the stoppage of its works during the time that the rest of the machinery remained useless owing to the absence of the lost parts.

It was held that the measure of damages was the cost of replacing the lost machinery at Vancouver only, and the Court said:[114]

The defendant is a carrier, and not a manufacturer of goods supplied for a particular purpose . . . He is not to be made liable for damages beyond what may fairly be presumed to have been contemplated by the parties at the time of entering into the contract. It must be something which could have been foreseen and reasonably expected, and to which he assented expressly or impliedly by entering into the contract.

This principle will exclude the recovery of damages in respect of loss of profit on actual or contemplated forward contracts where the carrier has no actual or imputed knowledge of these at the time of the contract. The loss of profit on such sales is too remote. An illustration is provided by *Horne* v. *Midland Railway Company*:[115]

H being under contract to deliver military shoes in London for the French army at an unusually high price by a particular day, delivered them to the defendant to be carried, with notice of the contract only as to the date of delivery. The shoes were delayed in carriage, and were consequently rejected by the intending purchasers. H sought to recover, in addition to the ordinary loss for delay, the difference between the price at which the shoes were actually sold and the high price at which they would have been sold if they had been punctually delivered.

It was held that this damage was not recoverable unless it could be proved that the company was informed of the exceptional loss which H might suffer from an unpunctual delivery. Again, it has been held that a person who contracts to purchase land intending to resell it to an identified sub-purchaser at a profit will not be able to recover in respect of the loss of the sub-sale where the seller does not know of the

---

[113] (1868) L.R. 3 C.P. 499.

[114] (1868) L.R. 3 C.P. 499, *per* Bovill C.J. at p. 505.

[115] (1873) L.R. 8 C.P. 131. Although this case was one of an exceptionally lucrative contract, the same principle applies to ordinary loss of profit: *Heskell* v. *Continental Express* [1950] 1 All E.R. 1033.

purchaser's intention and purpose and the consequent exposure of the seller to the risk of such damage in the event of breach.[116]

(iv) Immaterial that breach not contemplated

It is, however, immaterial that the breach was of a type not reasonably to be anticipated, for the parties naturally contemplate performance and not breach. Thus in *Banco de Portugal* v. *Waterlow & Sons Ltd.*:[117]

W & Sons agreed to print for the Bank of Portugal a quantity of Portuguese banknotes of a particular type. They negligently delivered to one M, the head of an international band of criminals, some 580,000 of these notes, and these were subsequently put into circulation in Portugal. Upon discovery of the fraud, the Bank issued notices withdrawing from circulation all notes of that type, and undertook to exchange them for other notes. The Bank then brought an action against W & Sons claiming as damages for breach of contract the value of the notes exchanged, and the cost of printing the genuine notes withdrawn.

It was held by a majority of the House of Lords that these losses were recoverable. The damage suffered, although the result of a breach which could scarcely be said to have been in the contemplation of the parties at the time they made the contract, was nevertheless to be considered as flowing from the business positions of the parties and arising naturally from the breach.

(e) DAMAGE REASONABLY SUPPOSED TO BE IN THE CONTEMPLATION OF THE PARTIES

As we have seen, the application of this second branch of the rule depends upon the knowledge which the contract-breaker possesses at the time of the contract, of special circumstances outside the 'ordinary course of things', of such a kind that a breach in those circumstances will cause more loss. The question is whether the damage is such as may reasonably be supposed to have been in the contemplation of both parties, at the time they made the contract, as the probable result of the breach of it. So, in *Simpson* v. *London and North Western Railway Company*:[118]

S, a manufacturer, was in the habit of sending specimens of his goods for exhibition to agricultural shows. After exhibiting in a show at Bedford, he entrusted some of his samples to an agent of the defendant company for carriage to a show-ground at Newcastle. On the consignment note he wrote: 'Must be at Newcastle Monday certain'. Owing to a default on the part of the company, the samples arrived late for the Newcastle show. S therefore claimed damages for his loss of profits at the show.

It was held that the company was liable. The company's agent had knowledge of the special circumstances, that the goods were to be exhibited at the Newcastle show, and so should have contemplated that a delay in delivery might result in this loss.

---

[116] *Seven Seas Properties* v. *Al Essa (No. 2)* [1993] 1 W.L.R. 1083 (purchaser concealed purpose). See also *Seven Seas Properties* v. *Al Essa* [1988] 1 W.L.R. 1272, at p. 1276.

[117] [1932] A.C. 452. See *The Portuguese Bank-note Case* by Sir Cecil Kisch for an exciting account of this case.

[118] (1876) 1 Q.B.D. 274.

It is usually said that 'bare knowledge' of the special circumstances surrounding the contract is sufficient to make the contract-breaker liable.[119] But there is some authority for the view that, in addition, the contract-breaker should either expressly or impliedly have contracted to assume liability for the exceptional loss. On this view, the mere communication to a party of the existence of special circumstances is not enough: there must be something to show that the contract was made *on the terms* that the defendant was to be liable for that loss.[120]

This view cannot be supported. No doubt a casual intimation would not suffice, for the special circumstances must be disclosed in such a manner as to render it a fair inference of fact that both parties contemplated the exceptional loss as a probable result of the breach. Thus in *Kemp* v. *Intasun Holidays Ltd.*:[121]

While booking a holiday Mrs K remarked to the travel agent that her husband was not present because he was suffering, as he sometimes did, from an asthma attack. In breach of contract Mr and Mrs K were accommodated for the first 30 hours of their holiday in a filthy and dusty room in an inferior hotel and Mr K had an asthma attack throughout the period. The trial judge awarded Mr K *inter alia* £800 for the consequences of having suffered an asthma attack due to the state of the alternative accommodation.

It was held by the Court of Appeal that this casual remark did not suffice to give the defendant the necessary degree of knowledge of special circumstances to make the defendant responsible for the consequences of the asthma attack he had suffered. What is necessary to enlarge the area of contemplation is that the special circumstances should be brought home to the party.[122] But it is unnecessary that it should be a term of the contract that the defendant is to be liable for that loss.[123]

VI. ASSESSMENT OF DAMAGES IN CONTRACTS FOR THE SALE OF GOODS

Useful illustrations of the application of the principles so far discussed are provided by the manner of assessment of damages in contracts for the sale of goods. Sections 50 and 51 of the Sale of Goods Act 1979 state that the measure of damages for non-acceptance or non-delivery of the goods is 'the estimated loss directly and naturally resulting, in the ordinary course of events, from the buyer's or seller's breach of

---

[119] *Patrick* v. *Russo-British Grain Export Co. Ltd.* [1972] 2 K.B. 535, *per* Salter J. at p. 540.

[120] *British Columbia etc. Saw-Mill Co. Ltd.* v. *Nettleship* (1868) L.R. 3 C.P. 499, at p. 509; *Horne* v. *Midland Ry.* (1873) L.R. 8 C.P. 131, at p. 141. See also *Victoria Laundry (Windsor) Ltd.* v. *Newman Industries Ltd.* [1949] 2 K.B. 528, at p. 538; *Seven Seas Properties* v. *Al Essa (No. 2)* [1993] 1 W.L.R. 1083, at p. 1088 (a party should not be exposed to risks of liability going beyond the first branch of *Hadley* v. *Baxendale* without the opportunity of making an informed decision whether to accept such risk and whether to negotiate some exclusion from liability).

[121] [1987] 2 F.T.L.R. 234.

[122] See *Heywood* v. *Wellers* [1976] 1 Q.B. 446, at p. 459, *per* Lord Denning M.R. (tort).

[123] *Koufos* v. *C. Czarnikow Ltd.* [1969] 1 A.C. 350, at p. 422.

contract'; and where there is an available market for the goods in question, this is *prima facie* to be ascertained by the difference between the contract price and the market or current price at the time when the goods ought to have been accepted or delivered, as the case may be, or, if no time was fixed, then at the time of the refusal to accept or deliver. The reason for this *prima facie* 'breach-date' rule[124] is that in a case of non-delivery by the seller the buyer may go into the market and buy alternative goods at the current price and, in a case of the buyer's failure to accept goods, the seller may take his goods into the market and obtain the current price for them.[125]

(a) NON-DELIVERY

Suppose that A promises to sell and deliver to B 1,000 tons of coal at £112 per ton on 8 February. A fails to carry out its contract. On 8 February the market price of coal of that quality is £120 per ton. B can recover as damages for non-delivery the difference between the contract price and the market price on that day, i.e. £8 per ton.

Uncontemplated forward or sub-sales must ordinarily be disregarded. If, for instance, in the expectation of receiving the coal, B has contracted to sell a similar quantity to C at £117 per ton, its damages will still be £8 (and not £5) per ton, since it must go into the market in order to fulfil its contract with C.[126] And the same is probably true where the sub-sale is at a price higher than the market price at the date when delivery should be made.[127]

(b) LATE DELIVERY

Where the seller is late in delivering the goods, the damage is the difference between the market value at the time they ought to have been delivered and the market value at the time when they actually were delivered. Difficulties have arisen where the goods have been resold for more than their market value. In *Wertheim* v. *Chicoutimi Pulp Co. Ltd.*:[128]

The seller was late in delivering the goods. The market price of the goods at the time when they ought to have been delivered was 70*s.* per ton, and, at the time they were delivered, 42*s.* 6*d.* per ton. The measure of damages ought therefore to have been 27*s.* 6*d.* per ton, and this

---

[124] ss. 50(3) and 51(3). For examples of its displacement see *Van den Hurk* v. *R. Martens & Co. Ltd.* [1920] 1 K.B. 850 (sale of goods); *Johnson* v. *Agnew* [1980] A.C. 367, at pp. 400–1 (sale of land); *South Australia Asset Management Co.* v. *York Montague Ltd.* [1997] A.C. 191 at p. 221 (negligent overvaluation). See generally Waddams (1981) 97 L.Q.R. 445.

[125] *Barrow* v. *Arnaud* (1846) 8 Q.B. 604, at p. 609 (Tindal C.J.); *Kaines (U.K.) Ltd.* v. *Osterreichische Warrenhandelgesellschaft etc.* [1993] 2 Lloyd's Rep. 1 (in a volatile market this must be done at the first practical opportunity).

[126] *Williams Bros* v. *E. T. Agius Ltd.* [1914] A.C. 510.

[127] *Great Western Ry.* v. *Redmayne* (1866) L.R. 1 C.P. 329. But contrast *Hall Ltd.* v. *Pim Junr. & Co.* (1928) 139 L.T. 50 (H.L.) and *Coastal International Trading Ltd.* v. *Maroil A.G.* [1988] 1 Lloyd's Rep. 92 where it was contemplated that the buyer might re-sell the particular goods purchased.

[128] [1911] A.C. 301 approved in *Williams Bros.* v. *E.T. Agius Ltd.* [1914] A.C. 510, at p. 522. See also the reasoning in *Pagnan & Fratelli* v. *Corsiba Industrial Agropacuaria* [1970] 1 W.L.R. 1306.

was the sum claimed by the buyer. But proof was adduced that he had actually sold the goods for 65s. per ton.

The Judicial Committee of the Privy Council held that the seller could rely on this sale to reduce the damages to 5s. per ton. Lord Atkinson considered that the *prima facie* market value rule was displaced where the sub-sale proves that the value of the goods to the buyer was more than their market value at the time of delivery and that to assess damages by reference to market value would allow the buyer to be 'compensated for a loss he never suffered'.[129] It does not, however, appear that the buyer was obliged to fulfil the sub-contract by delivering the specific goods received and the case has been rightly criticized for taking account of the sub-sale.[130] The buyer would have been free to resell the goods at the time they ought to have been delivered at their then market price (70s. per ton) and to procure other goods for the sub-contract. In a falling market a buyer is likely to do this and, on the facts of *Wertheim*'s case, to sell one lot at 70s. per ton and to fulfil the 65s. per ton sub-sale by buying in at the market price of 42s. 6d. per ton. The late delivery therefore deprived the buyer in that case of the opportunity to sell at the due date, a fact that was unaffected by the sub-sale.

(c) NON-ACCEPTANCE

The case of a buyer who fails to accept the goods is slightly more complicated. Although the normal rule, as set out in section 50(3) of the Sale of Goods Act 1979, is that the measure of damages is the difference between the contract price and the market price on the day fixed for acceptance, in modern trading conditions the retail price is frequently that recommended by the manufacturers, so that there is no difference between the contract and the market price. The question then arises whether a seller who is a dealer can recover its loss of profit on the sale. In *W.L. Thompson Ltd.* v. *Robinson (Gunmakers) Ltd.*:[131]

The defendant contracted to buy a new Vanguard car from T. T was a motor-car dealer and the price of the car was that fixed by the manufacturers, which it was unable to vary in any way. The defendant refused to accept the car, but T managed to persuade its wholesale suppliers to take the car back. T nevertheless claimed from the defendant the loss of its profit on the sale.

The defendant claimed that T was entitled to only nominal damages, there being no difference between the market price of the car and the contract price. Upjohn J. refused to accept this contention. He held that section 50(3) of the Sale of Goods Act 1979 laid down only a *prima facie* rule, and that it was displaced by proof in this case that the supply of Vanguard cars currently exceeded demand. T therefore acted

[129] *Ibid.*, at pp. 307–8.
[130] *Slater* v. *Hoyle & Smith Ltd.* [1920] 2 K.B. 11, *per* Scrutton L.J., at p. 23. See also *Campbell Mostyn (Provisions) Ltd.* v. *Barnett Trading Co.* [1954] 1 Lloyd's Rep. 65. But in *Bence Graphics Ltd.* v. *Fasson U.K. Ltd.* [1998] Q.B. 87, *Slater*'s case was not followed, it was stated that the earlier decision 'should be reconsidered', and Auld L.J. approved of *Wertheim*'s case. For criticism of the *Bence Graphics* case, see *post*, pp. 613–14.
[131] [1955] Ch. 177. Contrast *Lazenby Garages Ltd.* v. *Wright* [1976] 1 W.L.R. 459 (second-hand B.M.W. 'unique').

reasonably in returning the car to its suppliers, but it had sold one less Vanguard car than it would otherwise and so was entitled to claim its loss of profit on the transaction. It had therefore suffered a loss in the volume of its sales.[132] On the other hand, in *Charter* v. *Sullivan*,[133] the Court of Appeal held that a motor-car dealer could recover only nominal damages for non-acceptance of a car when the state of the motor trade was such that he could sell all the cars he could get, and he in fact sold the vehicle in question within 10 days of the failure to accept; here the breach did not result in loss of volume of sales. Jenkins L.J. went so far as to doubt whether it could be said that there was an 'available market' for the operation of the market price rule when goods could only be sold at a fixed retail price. But the Court was agreed that the dealer in this case could not be held to have made 'only one sale instead of two', since he was limited in the number of sales he could make by the fact that demand exceeded supply. The dealer had therefore suffered no loss of profit by the breach. The conclusion seems to be that loss of profit is not recoverable where demand exceeds supply, but can be recovered where supply equals or exceeds demand.[134]

(d) DELAY

A buyer who delays in accepting delivery may be liable to the seller for any loss occasioned by the delay and also for a reasonable charge for the care and custody of the goods.[135] Otherwise the measure of damages is as above.

(e) BREACH OF WARRANTY

Where goods are delivered in breach of warranty, section 53 of the Sale of Goods Act 1979 provides a *prima facie* rule that the buyer is entitled to the difference between the value of the goods at the time of delivery to the buyer and the value which they would have had if they had fulfilled the warranty.

(i) Sub-sales

Again, in principle, uncontemplated sub-sales are treated as irrelevant.[136] However, if it was within the reasonable contemplation of the parties at the time they made the contract that the goods would probably be re-sold to sub-purchasers on the same or

---

[132] On 'lost volume sellers', see Harris (1962) 60 Mich. L.Rev. 577, at pp. 600–1; (1964) 18 Stan. L. Rev. 66; Childres and Burgess (1973) 48 N.Y.U.L. Rev. 833. Cf. economists' scepticism about an *assumption* of lost volume in the case of retail sales, Goetz and Scott (1979) 31 Stan. L. Rev. 323, at p. 355; Goldberg (1984) 57 S. Cal. Rev. 283.

[133] [1957] 2 Q.B. 117.

[134] See also *Re Vic Mill Ltd.* [1913] 1 Ch. 465.

[135] Sales of Goods Act 1979 s. 37. Also under s. 48(3) of the Act, an unpaid seller has the right to sell perishable goods, or any goods after notice, and to recover from the original buyer damages for any loss occasioned by the breach.

[136] *Slater* v. *Hoyle & Smith Ltd.* [1920] 2 K.B. 11, at p. 23 (the seller did not know of the sub-sale, and the goods were described differently in the sub-sale). *Slater*'s case is inconsistent with *Wertheim* v. *Chicoutimi Pulp Co. Ltd.* [1911] A.C. 301, *ante*, pp. 610–11, and it has been put into question by *Bence Graphics Ltd.* v. *Fasson U.K. Ltd.* [1998] Q.B. 87, *post*, but see Treitel (1997) 113 L.Q.R. 188.

substantially similar terms either as they were or after manufacturing them into another product, the Court may have regard to the sub-sale. The buyer will, for example, be able to recover from the seller any damages which it has been forced to pay to those sub-purchasers together with any costs reasonably incurred in defending an action against him by them. Thus in *Hammond & Co.* v. *Bussey*:[137]

H, a shipping agent, contracted with B, a coal merchant, for the supply of a quantity of 'steam-coal' to be used in steamships, B knowing at the time of the contract that H was buying the coal for resale as fit for this purpose. H resold the coal, which was not fit for the purpose of steamships and they reasonably, but unsuccessfully, defended an action brought against them by their sub-purchaser.

It was held that H might recover not only the damages paid by it to its sub-purchaser, but the costs incurred in defending the action, for this damage came within the second branch of the rule in *Hadley* v. *Baxendale*, B having had special knowledge of the probability of the sub-contracts.

Where, however, the buyer has not been faced with claims by the sub-purchasers, it may not be able to recover from the seller for the difference between the value of the goods delivered and the value which they would have had if they had fulfilled the warranty. Thus in *Bence Graphics Ltd.* v. *Fasson U.K. Ltd.*:[138]

B bought vinyl film from the defendant for some £564,300, and used it to manufacture decals which it then sold to companies to be used to identify bulk containers. It was a term of the contract that the decals should have a 'guaranteed minimum five year life' but due to a latent defect the vinyl film degraded prematurely and many of the decals became illegible. There were many complaints but only one claim, for which the defendant had compensated B. B returned some £22,000 worth of defective decals to the defendant, and the defendant conceded that B was entitled to be reimbursed for this. The lack of durability was found by the trial judge to render the vinyl film worthless, and he awarded B £564,300, the difference between the value of the product had it fulfilled the warranty and its actual value. By the date of the trial, there was no possibility of further claims against B by its customers because the limitation period for such claims had expired.

A majority of the Court of Appeal allowed an appeal by the defendant, and held that since the parties contemplated that the vinyl film would be manufactured and sold on, they contemplated that the measure of damages would be the claimant's liability to the ultimate users, thus displacing the *prima facie* measure of damages in section 53 of the Sale of Goods Act 1979. This greater willingness to depart from the statutory *prima facie* rule has been criticized.[139] First, it is said to treat an issue of the valuation of B's loss as one of remoteness (i.e. whether the loss so identified can be recovered); B had undoubtedly lost the benefit of the performance promised. Secondly, had B's customers brought claims against B, the defendant would have undoubtedly been

---

[137] (1887) 20 Q.B.D. 79. *Biggin & Co. Ltd.* v. *Permanite Ltd.* [1951] 2 K.B. 314. Cf. *Coastal International Trading Ltd.* v. *Maroil AG* [1988] 1 Lloyd's Rep. 92 (terms of sub-sale unusual so loss of profit irrecoverable).

[138] [1998] Q.B. 87.

[139] Treitel (1997) 113 L.Q.R. 188 prefers the reasoning in *Slater* v. *Hoyle & Smith Ltd.* [1920] 2 K.B. 11, which the Court of Appeal refused to follow. But cf. *McGregor on Damages*, 16th edn. (1997), paras. 881–2.

liable for the cost of meeting them so that the effect of the decision gave a defendant who delivered worthless goods a windfall gain, the benefit of the forbearance of
a person's customers from claiming against him or her. Although it might be
thought that this second criticism sits uneasily with the rule, considered *infra*, that
in general a claimant may not recover for loss that has been avoided,[140] for a
compensating advantage to reduce the damages it must arise directly out of or as a
consequence of the breach. But in this case it arose out of the forbearance of B's
customers.

(ii) Reliance loss and loss of profit

If, at the time of making the contract, the seller knew or may be presumed to have
known that goods were to be used to produce a profit, and the breach of warranty
precludes or reduces the profit likely to have been made, the buyer may recover
damages for the loss of profit caused by the breach.[141] Such a buyer who brings an
action for breach of warranty in respect of the quality or performance of goods sold
to it cannot recover both the whole capital loss in the value of the goods (reliance loss)
and also the whole of the profit (where admissible) which it would have made by its
use of them (expectation loss) for this would be to allow the recovery of damages
twice over. In *Cullinane* v. *British 'Rema' Manufacturing Co. Ltd*.:[142]

C purchased from the defendants a clay pulverizing plant, warranted to be capable of
pulverizing clay at the rate of six tons per hour. This warranty was not fulfilled, and C
claimed as damages (a) the difference between the purchase price of the plant and its
residual value, and (b) his loss of profits from the date of installation to the date of trial of
the action.

The Court of Appeal held that these claims could not be cumulative but must be
alternative because the profits would only have been made if the capital expenditure
had been incurred. C could claim one or other, but not both.

VII. MITIGATION OF DAMAGE

A person who has suffered loss from a breach of contract must take any reasonable
steps that are available to mitigate the extent of the damage caused by the breach.[143]
The innocent party cannot claim to be compensated by the party in default for loss
which is really due not to the breach but to its own failure to behave reasonably after
the breach[144] but damages will not be reduced where the failure to mitigate the loss is

---

[140] *Post*, p. 616. The position would have been different if the limitation period for claims by B's
customers had not expired, since it would have still been at risk of such a claim.

[141] *Richard Holden Ltd*. v. *Bostock & Co. Ltd*. (1902) 18 T.L.R. 317.

[142] [1954] 1 Q.B. 292. Cf. *T.C. Industrial Plant Pty. Ltd*. v. *Robert's (Queensland) Pty. Ltd*. [1964] A.L.R.
1083 (Australia).

[143] Bridge (1989) 105 L.Q.R. 398; Harris, *Remedies in Contract and Tort* (1988), ch. 6.

[144] *British Westinghouse Electric Co. Ltd*. v. *Underground Electric Rys. Co. of London Ltd*. [1912] A.C. 673, at
p. 689.

due to the claimant's impecuniosity.[145] The underlying policy is the desirability of avoiding waste, in this context a loss which could have been avoided by reasonable action.

(a) ACTING REASONABLY

An employee who is wrongfully dismissed must make reasonable efforts to obtain, and must accept an offer of, suitable alternative employment. A failure to do so may mean that the employee is, in certain circumstances, entitled to nominal damages only.[146] Again, where a seller wrongfully refuses to deliver goods due under a contract for the sale of goods, a buyer who fails to buy substitute goods which are available will be debarred from claiming any part of the damage which is due to the failure to do so.[147] A claimant may even be required to accept a reasonable offer from the defendant which would make good the loss or part of it.[148] But there is no obligation to do anything other than in the 'ordinary course of business'[149] and it is a question of fact in each case whether the claimant has acted as a reasonable person might have been expected to act. For example, there is no compulsion to accept goods of inferior quality[150] or to risk one's commercial reputation[151] or to embark upon complicated litigation[152] or to undergo an operation with the risk of surgical complications[153] in order to mitigate loss. In cases of wrongful dismissal, an employee is not compelled to accept re-employment if it involves lower status, if relations are irretrievably affected by the circumstances of dismissal (as where there has been a public charge of misconduct), or if it is likely to be less permanent than alternatives.[154]

(b) 'DUTY' TO MITIGATE A MISNOMER

It is often said that the law imposes 'a duty' on claimants to mitigate their loss. But this expression is misleading. Claimants are under no such duty, and are free to act as they judge to be in their best interests. However, a claimant who has acted unreasonably cannot hold the defendant liable for loss which has thus been

---

[145] *Clippens Oil Co. Ltd.* v. *Edinburgh & District Water Trustees* [1907] A.C. 291, 303. See generally *Alcoa Minerals of Jamaica Inc.* v. *Broderick* [2000] 3 W.L.R. 23 (P.C.).

[146] *Beckham* v. *Drake* (1847–9) 2 H.L.C. 579; *Shindler* v. *Northern Raincoat Co. Ltd.* [1960] 1 W.L.R. 1038; *Yetton* v. *Eastwoods Froy Ltd.* [1967] 1 W.L.R. 104.

[147] *Kaines (U.K.)* v. *Osterreichische Warenhandelsgesellschaft Austrowaren Gesellschaft m.b.H.* [1993] 2 Lloyd's Rep. 1 (in volatile market buyer must act quickly); *Coastal (Bermuda) Petroleum Ltd.* v. *VTT Vulcab Petroleum (No. 2)* [1994] 2 Lloyd's Rep. 629, at p. 635.

[148] *Brace* v. *Calder* [1895] 2 Q.B. 253; *Payzu Ltd.* v. *Saunders* [1919] 2 K.B. 581; *Sotiros Shipping Inc.* v. *Sameiet Solholt* [1983] 1 Lloyd's Rep. 605. Cf. Bridge (1989) 105 L.Q.R. 398, at p. 411 ff.

[149] *Dunkirk Colliery Co.* v. *Lever* (1878) 9 Ch. D. 20, at p. 25.

[150] *Heaven & Kesterton Ltd.* v. *Et. Francois Albiac & Cie* [1956] 2 Lloyd's Rep. 316. See also *Strutt* v. *Whitnell* [1975] 1 W.L.R. 870.

[151] *Finlay (James) & Co. Ltd.* v. *N.V. Kwik Hoo Tong H.M.* [1929] 1 K.B. 400; *London & South of England Building Society* v. *Stone* [1983] 1 W.L.R. 1242.

[152] *Pilkington* v. *Wood* [1953] Ch. 770.

[153] *Selvanayagam* v. *University of West Indies* [1983] 1 W.L.R. 585.

[154] *Yetton* v. *Eastwoods Froy Ltd.* [1967] 1 W.L.R. 104. Cf. *Brace* v. *Calder* [1895] 2 Q.B. 253.

suffered.[155] Again, the question of reasonableness is a question of fact. For example, it has been held reasonable to incur hire purchase charges to replace a damaged rotor,[156] legal expenses in proceedings with a third party,[157] advertising to safeguard one's commercial reputation,[158] and voluntary expenses to meet the plaintiff's commercial (but legally unenforceable) obligations to the public.[159]

(c) COMPENSATING ADVANTAGES MAY REDUCE DAMAGES

Where a person mitigates loss and obtains a compensating advantage, the advantage will be deducted from the damages provided it arose directly out of or as a consequence of the breach and the act of mitigation and is not merely an 'indirect' or collateral benefit.[160] Thus where turbines which were less efficient than the contract specification and used more coal were replaced by turbines which resulted in an overall saving of coal over the whole period, the damages had to be reduced by the savings achieved.[161] But, where the benefit is independent of the act of mitigation damages will not be reduced. Thus where a used part of a damaged rotor had to be replaced with a new part which would last longer, the plaintiff was entitled to the full cost of the replacement,[162] and benefits from wholly independent transactions, for example sums due under an insurance policy, will not lead to a deduction.[163]

VIII. CLAIMANT'S CONTRIBUTORY FAULT

(a) NO APPORTIONMENT AT COMMON LAW

As a general rule, where the claimant's loss has been caused partly by the defendant's breach of contract and partly by the claimant's own conduct the damages are not reduced[164] unless the claimant's conduct breaks the chain of causation[165] or itself amounts to a breach of contract.[166]

---

[155] *Sotiros Shipping Inc.* v. *Sameiet Solholt* (*supra*, n. 148), at p. 608.

[156] *Bacon* v. *Cooper (Metals) Ltd.* [1982] 1 All E.R. 397.

[157] *The Antaios* [1981] 2 Lloyd's Rep. 284, 299.

[158] *Holden Ltd.* v. *Bostock & Co. Ltd.* (1902) 18 T.L.R. 317.

[159] *Banco de Portugal* v. *Waterlow & Sons Ltd* [1932] A.C. 452, the facts of which are set out *ante*, p. 608.

[160] *British Westinghouse Co.* v. *Underground Electric Rys Co. of London* [1912] A.C. 673. See also *Dimond* v. *Lovell* [2000] 2 W.L.R. 1121. Cf. *Lavarack* v. *Woods of Colchester* [1967] 1 Q.B. 278; *Hussey* v. *Eels* [1990] 2 Q.B. 227; *Famosa S.S. Co. Ltd.* v. *Armada Bulk Carriers Ltd.* [1994] 1 Lloyd's Rep. 633, at p. 637.

[161] *British Westinghouse Co.* v. *Underground Electric Rys. Co. of London* (*supra*, n. 144).

[162] *Bacon* v. *Cooper (Metals) Ltd.* [1982] 1 All E.R. 397.

[163] *Bradburn* v. *G.W. Ry.* (1874) L.R. 10 Ex. 1; *Arab Bank plc* v. *John D. Wood Commercial Ltd.* [2000] 1 W.L.R. 857.

[164] See generally Law Com. No. 219, *Contributory Negligence as a Defence in Contract* (1993).

[165] *Quinn* v. *Burch Bros. (Builders) Ltd.* [1966] 2 Q.B. 370; *Lambert* v. *Lewis* [1982] A.C. 225; *Schering Agrochemicals Ltd.* v. *Reisbel N.V. S.A.* (1992, C.A.), noted by Burrows (1993) 109 L.Q.R. 175; *Beoco Ltd.* v. *Alfa Laval Co. Ltd.* [1995] Q.B. 137; *County Ltd.* v. *Girozentrale Securities* [1996] 3 All E.R. 834.

[166] *Tennant Radiant Heat Ltd.* v. *Warrington Development Corp.* [1988] 1 E.G.L.R. 41; *Harper* v. *Ashton's Circus Pty Ltd.* [1972] 2 N.S.W.L.R. 395.

(b) LAW REFORM (CONTRIBUTORY NEGLIGENCE) ACT 1945

Where the defendant is liable in contract for failure to use reasonable skill and care and this liability co-exists with liability in the tort of negligence, as may be the case where services are rendered to a client by professionals such as lawyers, builders, or carriers, the Law Reform (Contributory Negligence) Act 1945 empowers the Court to reduce the damages for breach of contract by a proportion commensurate with the claimant's blameworthiness.[167] It is not settled whether the 1945 Act applies where the claimant has a right of action in tort which is not co-extensive with the one it has in contract,[168] but the Act does not apply to breaches of a strict contractual duty[169] or of a duty of care imposed by the contract which does not also give rise to liability in tort.[170] While this position is not entirely logical, particularly in respect of breaches of contractual obligations to exercise reasonable care where the defendant's liability exists solely in contract, it has been argued that permitting apportionment in contract cases would allow Courts to vary an agreed allocation of risks. It has also been said that existing contract doctrines, in particular implied terms obliging claimants to take care for their own interests, mitigation, and causation, recognize and give effect to the principle that account should be taken of the fact that it is the claimant who is part author of the loss suffered. Those who take this view, while recognizing that these doctrines operate in an 'all or nothing' manner either allowing full recovery or no recovery, believe that apportionment would unduly undermine the certainty which is important in the English law of contract. The Law Commission accepted that this would be so in the case of a breach of a strict contractual duty but recommended that apportionment should be available in cases where the defendant is in breach of a purely contractual obligation to exercise reasonable care.[171]

IX. THE TAX ELEMENT IN DAMAGES

Since damages are designed to compensate the claimant for the actual loss suffered and no more, any liability to pay tax may have to be taken into account. In *British Transport Commission* v. *Gourley*,[172] where G claimed for loss of earnings arising out of personal injuries caused by negligence, the House of Lords held that damages

---

[167] *Forsikringsaktieselskapet Vesta* v. *Butcher* [1989] A.C. 852. Cf. the different conclusion of the High Court of Australia in *Astley* v. *Austrust Ltd.* (1999) 197 C.L.R. 1 which has been criticized as based on a mechanical, even formalistic construction of the legislation: Swanton (1999) 14 J.C.L. 251, 260.

[168] Cf. *Vacwell Engineering Co. Ltd.* v. *B.D.H. Chemicals Ltd.* [1971] 1 Q.B. 88 and *Bank of Nova Scotia* v. *Hellenic Mutual War Risks Association (Bermuda) Ltd.* [1988] 1 Lloyd's Rep. 514, at p. 555; [1990] 1 Q.B. 818, rev'd on other grounds [1992] 1 A.C. 233, at p. 266. The Law Commission concluded that the Act does not apply: Law Com. No. 219 (1993) § 3.29.

[169] *Schering Agrochemicals Ltd.* v. *Reisbel N.V.S.A.* (1992, C.A.), noted by Burrows (1993) 109 L.Q.R. 175; *Barclays Bank plc* v. *Fairclough Building Ltd.* [1995] Q.B. 214.

[170] *Forsikringsaktieselskapet Vesta* v. *Butcher* [1989] A.C. 852, at p. 866, aff'd. at p. 880. Cf. *Clark Boyce* v. *Mouat* [1992] 2 N.Z.L.R. 559, at p. 564, rev'd. on other grounds [1994] 1 A.C. 428.

[171] Law Com. No. 219 (1993) Parts III and IV.

[172] [1956] A.C. 185.

awarded to G on the basis of his gross earnings before deduction of income tax and surtax (£37,720) should be reduced by the amount which he would have had to pay in tax. G was therefore left with a *net* sum of £6,695. This principle has subsequently been applied to contractual claims arising out of the wrongful dismissal of an employee[173] although it has not so far been applied to the assessment of damages in commercial cases or cases of breach of contract generally.[174] Before it can be applied, however, two conditions must be satisfied: first, the earnings or profits in respect of which the claim is made must be subject to tax; secondly, the sum awarded as damages must not be subject to tax in the claimant's hands.

The first requirement means that the principle in *Gourley*'s case does not apply to a claim in respect of the loss of a capital asset, for this would not have been subject to income tax.[175] The second excludes from its operation most claims for loss of profit, for sums awarded as damages for loss of profit are normally subject to tax in the claimant's hands as part of the profits of his or her business.[176] The case itself has been the subject of considerable criticism, since it is said that the Courts treat damages for loss of earnings arising out of personal injuries as taxable income, whereas the legislature exempts them, in part, from tax as being compensation for the loss of what may be called 'natural capital equipment'.[177] Nevertheless, the Law Reform Committee in 1958[178] recommended no change in the law, although it considered that the practical implications of the case should be kept under review.

X. INTEREST

At common law a debtor who fails to pay any sum due and owing on the date fixed for payment, is under no contractual obligation to pay interest in the absence of an express stipulation in the contract to that effect or unless such a stipulation can be implied from a previous course of dealing between the parties,[179] or from trade usage.[180]

---

[173] *Beach v. Reed Corrugated Cases Ltd.* [1956] 1 W.L.R. 807; *Re Houghton Main Colliery Co. Ltd.* [1959] 1 W.L.R. 1219; *Phipps v. Orthodox Unit Trusts Ltd.* [1958] 1 Q.B. 314. But under the Income and Corporation Taxes Act 1988, s. 148 as substituted by Finance Act 1998, s. 58, damages for wrongful dismissal are made taxable in the claimant's hands, save that tax is not chargeable on the first £30,000 of such payment and, on the excess over £30,000, relief is given by way of a regressive reduction on the taxpayer's marginal rate. It has been held that the rule in *Gourley*'s case nevertheless continues to apply to the exempted amount: *Parsons v. B.N.M. Laboratories Ltd.* [1964] 1 Q.B. 95; *Bold v. Brough, Nicholson & Hall Ltd.* [1964] 1 W.L.R. 201; *Lyndale Fashion Manufacturers v. Rich* [1973] 1 W.L.R. 73; *Shove v. Downs Surgical plc* [1984] I.C.R. 582; *Amstrad v. Seagate Technology Inc.* (1997) Build. L.R. 34.
[174] Cf. *West Suffolk C.C v. W. Rought Ltd.* [1957] A.C. 403.
[175] *Hull & Co. Ltd. v. Pearlberg* [1956] 1 W.L.R. 244. Capital gains tax is to be disregarded.
[176] *Diamond v. Campbell-Jones* [1961] Ch. 22; *Dickinson v. Jones Alexander* [1993] 2 F.L.R. 521.
[177] See Baxter (1956) 19 M.L.R. 373; Hall (1957) 73 L.Q.R. 212; Jolowicz [1959] C.L.J. 85; Tucker, *ibid.*, at p. 185; Bishop and Kay (1987) 103 L.Q.R. 211; Kerridge (1992) 108 L.Q.R. 433, 442–5.
[178] 7th Report, Cmd. 501.
[179] *Re Marquis of Angelsey* [1901] 2 Ch. 548.
[180] e.g. as in the case of bank deposits.

Since 1934, however, the Courts have been empowered to award interest on debts and damages by statute.[181] The statutory provisions enable the High Court or a county court to include in any sum for which judgment is given simple (but not compound) interest at such rate as the Court thinks fit or as rules of Court may provide, on all or part of any part of the debt or damages for which judgment is given for all or any part of the period between the date when the cause of action arose and the date of the judgment.[182] Further, if the debtor pays the debt after the institution of proceedings but before judgment, the Court has a similar power to award interest in respect of the period between the date when the cause of action arose and the date of payment.

There is, however, no general statutory power to award interest on a debt which is paid late but before proceedings to recover it were brought[183] so that the *common law* position is still of importance. The basic rule laid down reluctantly by the House of Lords in 1893 and recently, equally reluctantly, confirmed is that, at common law, interest cannot be awarded as damages for the late payment of money.[184] Given the compensatory aims of damages for breach of contract the general rule cannot be justified in principle.[185] In one respect, however, the common law rule has been relaxed. If by reason of the late payment the creditor has actually incurred interest charges in obtaining finance from an alternative source, the amount so paid may be recoverable as special damages, provided that it was in the reasonable contemplation of the parties at the time the contract was made that such charges would be incurred.[186]

The Late Payment of Commercial Debts (Interest) Act 1998 provides that it is an implied term in contracts for the supply of goods or services where both parties are acting in the course of a business[187] that any 'qualifying debt' created by the contract carries interest[188] at a rate prescribed by the Secretary of State. Where the contract provides a 'substantial remedy' for late payment of the debt, the parties are permitted to oust or vary the right to statutory interest.[189] A remedy is to be regarded as 'substantial' unless it is insufficient for the purpose of compensating for or for deterring

---

[181] Law Reform (Miscellaneous Provisions) Act 1934, s.3. See now the Supreme Court Act 1981, s. 35A and the County Courts Act 1959, s. 97A.

[182] Delay in progressing a claim may lead to lower interest: *Derby Resources A.G.* v. *Blue Corinth Marine Co. Ltd. (No. 2)* [1998] 2 Lloyd's Rep. 425.

[183] There is a statutory duty to pay interest in most European countries, see Lando & Beale, *The Principles of European Contract Law* (2000) p. 452. See also C.I.S.G. Arts. 78 and 84(1).

[184] *London, Chatham and Dover Railway Co.* v. *South Eastern Railway Co.* [1893] A.C. 429; *President of India* v. *La Pintada Co. Nav.* [1985] A.C. 104.

[185] *President of India* v. *La Pintada Co. Nav.* [1985] A.C. 104, 111, 112, 129–31; Law Com. No. 88, *Report on Interest* (1978); Mann (1985) 101 L.Q.R. 30. On the case for compound interest, see *Westdeutsche Landesbank Girozentrale* v. *Islington L.B.C.* [1996] A.C. 669, *per* Lord Goff and Lord Woolf (dissenting) at pp. 695–6, 719–21, and 735–6.

[186] *The Lips* [1988] A.C. 395; *Wadsworth* v. *Lydall* [1981] 1 W.L.R. 598.

[187] This includes a profession and the activities of government: s. 2(1). Initially only small businesses are entitled to claim interest: S.I. 1998 No. 2479, r. 2(2); S.I. 1998 No. 2481.

[188] s. 1(1)

[189] ss. 1(3) and 7–10.

late payment, and it would not be 'fair or reasonable' to allow it to be relied on to oust or vary the right to statutory interest.[190]

Where the relationship between the creditor and the debtor is not purely contractual but also gives rise to equitable duties, for example where the parties are in a fiduciary relationship, interest, including not only simple interest but also compound interest, may be recoverable in certain circumstances in the absence of any agreement or custom to that effect.[191]

XI. LOSSES SUFFERED BY THIRD PARTIES

In the case of a contract for the benefit of a third party, the third party may have a right of action under the Contracts (Rights of Third Parties) Act 1999.[192] The promisee may, alternatively or additionally, wish to sue in respect of the third party's loss.

(a) CLAIMS BY THE THIRD PARTY UNDER THE CONTRACTS (RIGHTS OF THIRD PARTIES) ACT 1999

A non-party to a contract who has a right to enforce it under the 1999 Act will be able to claim any remedy that would have been available if he had been a party to the contract. By section 1(5):

For the purpose of exercising his right to enforce a term of the contract, there shall be available to the third party any remedy that would have been available to him in an action for breach of contract if he had been a party to the contract (and the rules relating to damages, injunctions, specific performance and other relief shall apply accordingly).

In such a case it would appear that rules, such as those concerning remoteness and mitigation, would be applied by reference to the position of the third party rather than the contracting party, so that, for example, it would be the third party's loss that had to be contemplated.[193]

(b) CLAIMS BY THE PROMISEE

The promisee may be willing to enforce the contract for the benefit of the third party. In *Beswick* v. *Beswick*[194] the widow obtained her annuity because she was able to sue as

---

[190] s. 4.

[191] *Wallersteiner v. Moir (No. 2)* [1975] Q.B. 373, at p. 388; *Re Fox, Walker & Co.* (1880) 15 Ch. D. 400 (surety); *Mathew v. T.M. Sutton Ltd.* [1994] 1 W.L.R. 1453 (pawnbroker). For a wider view of the equitable jurisdiction, see *Westdeutsche Landesbank Girozentrale v. Islington L.B.C.* (*supra*, n. 185) *per* Lord Goff and Lord Woolf (dissenting) at pp. 695–6, 719–21, 735–6. Cf. the majority, *ibid.*, at pp. 717, 718–19, 737–41.

[192] See Chap. 10.

[193] An amendment to make this clear was rejected as unnecessary: H.L. Deb., 27 May 1999, col. 1052.

[194] [1968] A.C. 58. For the facts, see *ante*, p. 423.

the administratrix of her husband's estate and was treated as a party to the contract. There appears to be no procedure by which an unwilling or unco-operative promisee can be compelled to institute proceedings on behalf of the third party.[195] The existence of a right of action in the promisee does not, in consequence, necessarily ensure that the third party will obtain the performance promised in the contract.

(i) Damages for loss sustained by the promisee

The general rule is that damages are for loss suffered by the claimant. Therefore, where the breach of contract consists of failure to perform in favour of the third party, the damages will, in principle, be nominal only.[196] Thus in *Beswick* v. *Beswick*[197] the promisee's estate suffered no loss because the promisee 'died without any assets save and except the agreement which he hoped would keep him and then his widow [the third party] for their lives'.[198] In some situations, however, including many commercial transactions, the promisee will suffer loss by reason of the breach, either because an obligation it owes to the third party is not discharged, as in *Price* v. *Easton*,[199] or where the consequence is that the promisee comes under a legal obligation to the third party. In such cases substantial damages will, in principle,[200] be recoverable.

In principle, the promisee should also be able to recover substantial damages if, by reason of the breach of contract, the promisee (a) comes under a moral obligation to compensate the third party, though under no legal obligation to do so,[201] or, (b) voluntarily incurs expense in making good the default.[202] Thus if a vicar hires a coach for an outing for the choir, and the coach operator leaves the choir stranded half way, the vicar might recover substantial damages in respect of the taxi fares incurred in getting the choir home, whether the choir paid their own fares (in which case the vicar would recompense the choir from the damages recovered) or the vicar paid their fares for them.[203]

---

[195] But see the suggestion that the third party be joined as a party to the action made by Lord Denning in *Beswick* v. *Beswick* [1966] Ch. 538, at p. 554, and (in a different context) *Snelling* v. *John Snelling Ltd.* [1973] Q.B. 87 (*ante*, p. 426). Contrast *Gurtner* v. *Circuit* [1968] 2 Q.B. 587, at pp. 599, 606; *White* v. *Jones* [1995] 2 A.C. 207, at p. 267.

[196] For exceptions, see *post*, p. 622. See also Coote's argument ([1997] C.L.J. 537, at p. 549 ff.) that courts have confused loss of the enjoyments of the fruits of performance (which the promisee *has not* lost) and loss of the bargained-for contractual rights (which the promisee *has* lost).

[197] [1968] A.C. 58.

[198] *Ibid.*, at p. 102 (Lord Upjohn). See also pp. 72, 78, 101. Cf. Lord Pearce, at p. 88. Had there been other assets the loss to the estate could have been liability to provide for the widow under the statutory precursor of the Inheritance (Provision for Family and Dependants) Act 1975 or a voluntary payment made under a moral obligation, on which see *infra*, n. 201.

[199] (1833) 4 B. & Ad. 433, *ante*, p. 422.

[200] i.e., subject to the ordinary rules, including those concerning remoteness and mitigation on which see *ante*, pp. 600 and 614.

[201] *Jackson* v. *Watson* [1909] 2 K.B. 193; *Radford* v. *de Froberville* [1977] 1 W.L.R. 1262.

[202] It may be reasonable to make a voluntary payment; *Banco de Portugal* v. *Waterlow & Sons Ltd.* [1932] A.C. 452, *ante*, p. 616 (mitigation of damages). See also *Admiralty Commissioners* v. *S.S. Amerika* [1917] A.C. 38, at p. 61.

[203] *Ante*, p. 608.

There may also be certain cases of contracts for the benefit of a third party where what might at first sight appear to be the third party's loss can in fact be analysed as the promisee's. One example, discussed below, is where the promisee contracts for a family holiday.[204]

(ii) Damages for loss sustained by the third party

The principle that as a general rule substantial damages can only be given for loss suffered by the claimant, applied by the House of Lords in *Beswick* v. *Beswick*,[205] has been affirmed by the House on several occasions since then. In *Woodar Investment Development Ltd.* v. *Wimpey Construction U.K. Ltd.*:[206]

The defendants contracted to buy land from the plaintiffs for £850,000. It was agreed that on completion £150,000 was to be paid by the defendants to a third party. The plaintiffs claimed damages for breach and repudiation of the contract.

A majority of the House of Lords held that the defendants had not repudiated the contract. But their Lordships agreed that, if the contract had been repudiated, the plaintiffs could not, without showing that they had themselves suffered loss or were agents or trustees for the third party, have recovered damages for non-payment of the £150,000.

In *Jackson* v. *Horizon Holidays Ltd.*[207] Lord Denning M.R., with whom Orr L.J. agreed, had stated that whenever a contract was made for the benefit of a third party and the third party suffered loss as a result of the failure of the promisor to perform the contract, the promisee could recover damages in respect of the loss sustained by the third party, holding the damages as money had and received to the use of the third party and paying them over. In that case:

J contracted with a travel company for the provision by the company of holiday accommodation for himself, his wife and two children. The accommodation provided fell below the standard required by the contract and the whole family suffered discomfort, vexation, inconvenience and distress. The trial judge awarded J £1,100 damages including £500 for his mental distress.

The Court of Appeal upheld the award. James L.J. appeared to agree with the trial judge. Lord Denning M.R. said that, if regarded as only for the distress of the plaintiff himself, the award was excessive but held that the plaintiff could recover both for his loss and that of his family.

In *Woodar*'s case the House of Lords disapproved of this view[208] but it was said that the decision in *Jackson*'s case could be supported either on the ground that the

---

[204] An example given by Lord Denning M.R. in *Jackson* v. *Horizon Holidays Ltd.* [1975] 1 W.L.R. 1468, at pp. 1472–3.

[205] [1968] A.C. 58, at pp. 72, 78, 101, *ante*, p. 425.

[206] [1980] 1 W.L.R. 277, at pp. 283–4, 291, 293, 297, 300.

[207] *Jackson* v. *Horizon Holidays Ltd.* [1975] 1 W.L.R. 1468. Cf. in tort, where voluntary payments to victim's carer are analysed as carer's loss: *Cunningham* v. *Harrison* [1973] Q.B. 454; *Hunt* v. *Severs* [1994] A.C. 350, at p. 363, and held on trust for the carer rather than as victim's 'need'; *Donnelly* v. *Joyce* [1974] Q.B. 454; *Housecroft* v. *Burnett* [1986] 1 All E.R. 332, 343.

[208] Lord Denning had relied on a statement of Lush L.J. in *Lloyd's* v. *Harper* (1880) 16 Ch. D. 290, at p. 321

plaintiff there was recovering damages in consequence of the loss which he had himself sustained[209] or as a case which called for 'special treatment'.[210] In view of its decision on the repudiation point it was not necessary for the House to make a decision on the damages point and it did not state any rule of law regarding the recovery of damages for the benefit of third parties. Nevertheless certain members of the House of Lords were strongly critical of the result produced by the combined effect of these two aspects of the privity of contract principle; neither the third party for whom the benefit was intended nor the promisee who contracted for it could recover damages for that which the promisor had agreed, but failed, to provide. The hope was expressed that the House would soon have the opportunity of reconsidering this matter[211] but when the question again came before the House in *Linden Gardens Trust Ltd.* v. *Lenesta Sludge Disposals Ltd.* and *St Martins Property Corporation Ltd.* v. *Sir Robert McAlpine Ltd*[212] and in *Alfred McAlpine Construction Ltd.* v. *Panatown Ltd*,[213] the opportunity was not taken. There was support for a radical reformulation of the general rule so that damages for breach of a supply contract would be quantified solely by reference to the difference in value between that which was contracted for and that which is in fact supplied.[214] But in the *Linden Gardens* case the decision was that the case fell within the rationale of the exceptions to the general rule[215] and in *Alfred McAlpine Construction Ltd.* v. *Panatown Ltd* it was held that the exceptions did not apply where the third party has, as it was in that case, been given a direct contractual right against the promisor.[216]

(iii) Exceptionally third party's loss recoverable

What then are the exceptions to the general rule? A trustee-promisee may recover in respect of the beneficiary's loss,[217] an agent may recover in respect of the undisclosed principal's loss,[218] and a person with a limited interest in property who has taken out

---

which was made in the context of the 'trust of a promise' exception to the general rule; see *ante*, p. 439 and *Beswick* v. *Beswick* [1968] A.C. 58, at p. 101; *Woodar Investment Development Ltd.* v. *Wimpey Construction U.K. Ltd.* [1980] 1 W.L.R. 277, at pp. 283, 293–4, 297. The Package Travel, Package Holidays and Package Tours Regulations 1992 S.I. 1992 No. 3288, *ante* p. 447 now gives the beneficiaries of package holidays a direct right of action.

[209] [1980] 1 W.L.R. 277 at pp. 293, 297; *Jackson* v. *Horizon Holidays Ltd.* (*supra*), at p. 1474 (James L.J.).

[210] At pp. 283, 291, 293. See also *Calebar Properties Ltd.* v. *Sticher* [1984] 1 W.L.R. 287, at p. 290 (tenant's damages included sum in respect of spouse's ill-health).

[211] At pp. 291, 297–8, 300–1.

[212] [1994] A.C. 85, varying (1992) 57 B.L.R. 57 (C.A.).

[213] [2000] 3 W.L.R. 946.

[214] [1994] A.C. 85, at pp. 95, 112, *per* Lord Keith and Lord Browne-Wilkinson, with whom Lord Bridge and Lord Ackner agreed. Only Lord Griffiths (pp. 96–8) decided the case on this ground. See also *Darlington B.C.* v. *Wiltshier Northern Ltd.* [1995] 1 W.L.R. 68, at p. 80, *per* Steyn L.J. See also Cartwright (1996) 10 J.C.L. 244; Palmer & Tolhurst (1997) 12 J.C.L. 1 and 97; Coote, [1997] C.L.J. 537, at p. 549 ff.

[215] *Ibid.*, at p. 114.

[216] [2000] 3 W.L.R. 946.

[217] *Lloyd's* v. *Harper* (1880) 16 Ch. D. 290, at p. 331 on which see *ante*, p. 439. See also *St. Albans City and District Council* v. *International Computers Ltd.* [1996] 4 All E.R. 481, at p. 489 (local authority recovered in respect of chargepayer's loss).

[218] *Allen* v. *F. O'Hearn & Co.* [1937] A.C. 213, at p. 218, *post*, p. 691.

full insurance may recover the full amount of loss or damage.[219] Again, in a contract for the carriage of goods by sea, a consignor may recover substantial damages even where it has sold the goods and they are not at its risk provided it is not contemplated that the carrier would also be put into a direct contractual relationship with whomsoever might become the owner of the goods.[220] The last two exceptions concern commercial contracts about goods where the parties contemplate that the proprietary interests in the goods may be transferred after the contract has been entered into but before the breach which causes loss or damage to the goods. This principle has been held to apply to a contract for the development of land where it was contemplated that the land was going to be occupied, and possibly purchased, by third parties.[221] In such a case, where the third party owner or occupier has no direct right to sue for breach of contract, the contracting party can recover substantial damages as representing the third party's loss. It is arguable that a more general principle could be distilled from these exceptions, particularly because the ability of the promisee in these cases to recover in respect of the loss sustained by the third party was linked to the unavailability of a contractual action by the third party.[222]

XII. AGREED DAMAGES CLAUSES

(a) LIQUIDATED DAMAGES AND PENALTIES

The parties to a contract not infrequently make provision in the contract for the damages to be paid on a breach of contract. Such provision does not exclude the application of the rule that damages for breach are intended to compensate for the actual loss sustained by the claimant, and it is a question of the proper construction of the contract to decide whether a sum fixed in this way, however the parties may have described it, is a 'penalty', in which case it cannot be recovered, or a genuine attempt to 'liquidate', that is to say, to reduce to certainty, prospective damages of an uncertain amount, in which case the sum will be recoverable.

The rule against penalties originates in equity which would relieve against penalties, cutting them down to the actual damage suffered, but was taken up and applied by the common law, and reinforced by statute.[223] The Court will accept as liquidated

---

[219] *Waters v. Monarch Fire and Life Assurance Co.* (1856) 5 E. & B. 870; *Hepburn v. Tomlinson (A.) (Hauliers) Ltd.* [1966] A.C. 451. Marine Insurance Act 1906, s. 26(3). See also the right of the bailee, albeit in tort, *The Winkfield* [1902] P. 42 and the analogous fact situation in *Bovis International Inc. v. The Circle Limited Partnership* (1995) 49 Con. L.R. 12.

[220] See *ante*, p. 445. This might be by the operation of the Carriage of Goods by Sea Act 1992 or by making a separate contract. See the discussion of the exceptions in *The Albazero* [1977] A.C. 774, at pp. 846–7.

[221] *Linden Gardens Trust Ltd.* v. *Lenesta Sludge Disposals Ltd.* and *St Martins Property Corporation Ltd.* v. *Sir Robert McAlpine Ltd.* [1994] A.C. 85, at pp. 114–15 (contracting party owner of land); *Darlington B.C.* v. *Wiltshier Northern Ltd.* [1995] 1 W.L.R. 68 (contracting party had no proprietary interest).

[222] See Law Com. No. 242 (1996), § 2.46.

[223] 8 & 9 Will. III, c. 11 (an Act for the better preventing frivolous and vexatious Suits), s. 8. For history, see *Wall v. Rederiaktiebolaget Luggude* [1915] 3 K.B. 66, at pp. 72–3; Simpson (1966) 82 L.Q.R. 392.

damages the sum fixed by the parties if it is a genuine pre-estimate of the damage which seems likely to be caused if the breach provided for should occur. The question is one of construction, to be decided upon the terms and inherent circumstances of each particular contract, judged as at the time of making the contract, not as at the time of breach.[224] Or, again, if, although it is not an estimate of the probable damage, the parties had fixed that sum because they were agreed in limiting the damages recoverable to an amount less than that which a breach would probably cause, it will similarly be accepted by the Court.[225] On the other hand, if the sum was fixed *in terrorem*, the provision will be considered to be a penalty. It will be unenforceable.

In construing the terms 'penalty' and 'liquidated damages' when inserted in a contract, the Courts will not be bound by the phraseology used, but will look to the substance rather than to the form. The parties may call the sum specified 'liquidated damages' if they wish, but if the Court finds it to be a penalty, it will be treated as such. Conversely, if the parties had described the sum fixed as a 'penalty', but it turns out to be a genuine pre-estimate of the loss, it will be treated as liquidated damages.[226]

The common law rules governing such provisions must now be considered in the light of the provisions of the European Convention for the Protection of Human Rights, in particular the right to a fair trial under Article 6 and the protection of property under Article 1 of the First Protocol to the Convention.[227]

(b) RULES OF CONSTRUCTION

The leading case on penalties is that of *Dunlop Pneumatic Tyre Co. Ltd.* v. *New Garage and Motor Co. Ltd.*:[228]

The appellant sold motor tyre-covers, tyres, and tubes to the respondent which contracted not to resell them, or offer them for sale, at a price below the appellant's list prices and to pay the sum of £5 by way of liquidated damages for every breach of this agreement. The respondent sold a tyre-cover at less than the list price, and was sued by the appellant for damages for breach.

The House of Lords held that the sum fixed by the parties was a genuine pre-estimate of the damage which might ensue and not a penalty. In the course of his speech Lord Dunedin laid down the following rules:[229]

(i) 'It will be held to be a penalty if the sum stipulated for is extravagant and unconscionable in amount in comparison with the greatest loss that could conceivably be proved to have followed from the breach.'

---

[224] *Dunlop Pneumatic Tyre Co. Ltd.* v. *New Garage and Motor Co. Ltd.* [1915] A.C. 79; *Phillips Hong Kong Ltd.* v. *Att.-Gen. of Hong Kong* (1993) 61 Build. L.R. 41 (P.C.).

[225] *Cellulose Acetate Silk Co. Ltd.* v. *Widnes Foundry (1925) Ltd.* [1933] A.C. 20, for facts see *post*, p. 629.

[226] *Ibid.* See also *Union Eagle Ltd.* v. *Golden Achievement Ltd.* [1997] AC 514; *Britvic Soft Drinks Ltd.* v. *Messer U.K. Ltd.* [2002] 1 Lloyd's Rep. 20.

[227] See *Wilson* v. *First County Trust Ltd. (No. 2)* [2001] 3 W.L.R. 42.

[228] [1915] A.C. 79.

[229] At p. 87.

An illustration was provided by the Earl of Halsbury in an earlier case, where he said:[230]

For instance, if you agreed to build a house in a year, and agreed that if you did not build the house for £50, you were to pay a million of money as penalty, the extravagance of that would be at once apparent.

We shall see that there is considerable doubt as to how far this principle extends to the forfeiture of a sum already paid.[231] But in other situations the question is one of fact in each particular case. The purpose of such clauses is to promote certainty and, especially in commercial contracts, where the parties are able to protect themselves, the Court is likely to take the view that what the parties have agreed should normally be upheld and to take care not to set too stringent a standard which could defeat that purpose.[232] In the case of consumer contracts for the supply of goods or services, the common law rule has been embodied in a legislative presumption that a term requiring a consumer who fails to fulfil his obligation to pay a disproportionately high sum in compensation is unfair and not binding.[233]

> (ii) 'It will be held to be a penalty if the breach consists only in not paying a sum of money, and the sum stipulated is a sum greater than the sum which ought to have been paid.'

In *Kemble* v. *Farren*:[234]

The defendant agreed to perform at the Covent Garden Theatre for four seasons at £3 6s. 8d. a night. The contract provided that if either party refused to fulfil the agreement or any part thereof, such party should pay to the other the sum of £1,000 as 'liquidated damages'. The defendant refused to perform during the second season.

It was held that the stipulation was penal. The obligation to pay £1,000 might have arisen upon a failure to pay £3 6s. 8d. and was therefore quite obviously a penalty. The most obvious example of this presumption is where a borrower of money promises to pay the lender an additional sum if the money is not repaid by a fixed day. Such 'accelerated payment' clauses are common in sales by instalments and leasing arrangements. However, a distinction is drawn between contracts which accelerate an *existing* liability to pay on default and those which create or increase the liability to pay. The penalty rules do not apply to the former.[235] The distinction is, however, open

---

[230] *Clydebank Engineering and Shipbuilding Co. Ltd.* v. *Don Jose Ramos Yzquierdo y Castaneda* [1905] A.C. 6, at p. 10.

[231] *Post*, p. 647.

[232] *Phillips Hong Kong Ltd.* v. *Att.-Gen. of Hong Kong* (1993) 61 Build. L.R. 41 (P.C.) For the economic advantages of such clauses, including avoiding difficulties of measuring loss (on which see *ante*, p. 597) and the inability of the penalty rule accurately to identify unfairness, see Scott and Goetz (1977) 77 Col. L. Rev. 554; Rea (1984) 13 J.L.S. 147. But cf. Fenton (1975/6) 51 Ind. L.Rev. 189, at pp. 191–2.

[233] Unfair Terms in Consumer Contracts Regulations 1999 (S.I. 1999 No. 2083), reg. 5 and Sched. 2, para. 1(e). See generally, *ante*, pp. 200, 300.

[234] (1829) 6 Bing. 141.

[235] *Protector Loan Co.* v. *Grice* (1880) 5 Q.B.D. 529; *O'Dea* v. *All States Leasing System Pty Ltd.* (1983) 152 C.L.R. 359; *The Angelic Star* [1988] 1 Lloyd's Rep. 122.

to criticism on the ground that it is commercially unrealistic to hold that a debt which can only be recovered by instalments over a period is to be equated with one which can be recovered immediately and as permitting the circumvention of this rule of construction by contractual stipulation for discount if payment is made by a given date.

But even where the penalty rules apply, the presumption may be rebutted if the increase is, in the circumstances, commercially justifiable and the dominant purpose of the provision is not to deter the borrower from breach. Thus it has been held that a provision increasing by one per cent the interest chargeable on a loan from the time a borrower defaulted reflected the increased credit risk of having such a debtor, and was not therefore a penalty.[236]

> (iii) 'There is a presumption (but no more) that it is a penalty when a single lump sum is made payable by way of compensation, on the occurrence of one or more of all of several events, some of which may occasion serious and others but trifling damage.'

An illustration is offered by *Ford Motor Co.* v. *Armstrong*:[237]

A retailer of motor-cars agreed with a manufacturer *inter alia* not to sell any one of the manufacturer's cars, or any part, below the listed price. For every breach of this agreement he was to pay £250, as 'agreed damages'.

A majority of the Court of Appeal held that this was a penalty. The defendant might have become bound to pay the sum of £250 for the breach of some term which would cause only trifling damage. Similarly, in *Kemble* v. *Farren*, the same factor provided an additional reason for the Court to hold that the £1,000 was a penalty because that very large sum was to become immediately payable if 'the defendant had refused to conform to any usual regulation of the theatre, however minute or unimportant'.[238]

A single sum, as opposed to a sum proportioned to the seriousness of the breach (for example per week for delay or per item for items sold in breach of covenant), is presumed to be penal because one tests it against the least serious breach possible. The presumption does not apply where the sum is payable for breach of a single obligation which can be broken in a number of ways, for example non-completion of a building contract.[239] Where it is difficult to estimate the loss and it is therefore uncertain that losses from one breach would be greater than those from another, a Court may hold that the presumption is rebutted. It may also be rebutted where it is clear that the contractual provision has sought to average out the probable losses from all the breaches provided, however, that the disparity is not too great.[240]

On the other hand:

---

[236] *Lordsvale Finance plc* v. *Bank of Zambia* [1996] Q.B. 752.
[237] (1915) 31 T.L.R. 267.
[238] (1829) 6 Bing. 141, at p. 148.
[239] *Law* v. *Local Board of Redditch* [1892] 1 Q.B. 127.
[240] *Dunlop Pneumatic Tyre Co. Ltd.* v. *New Garage and Motor Co. Ltd.* [1915] A.C. 79, at p. 99; *English Hop Growers* v. *Dering* [1928] 2 K.B. 174.

(iv) 'It is no obstacle to the sum stipulated being a genuine pre-estimate of damage, that the consequences of the breach are such as to make precise pre-estimation almost an impossibility.'

For example, in the *Dunlop Tyre* case itself, the stipulated sum of £5 could only, at the most, be a very rough and ready estimate of the possible damage which might be suffered if a trader undercut the manufacturer's listed price. In public works contracts, such as those for the construction of roads or tunnels, the nature of the loss may in part be non-financial and therefore be particularly difficult to evaluate, but in *Phillips Hong Kong Ltd.* v. *Attorney-General of Hong Kong* it was said that a clause using a formula based on estimates of the loss of return on the capital at a daily rate, the effect of the delay on related contracts, and increased costs, was said to be sensible.[241]

But these rules are no more than presumptions as to the intention of the parties; they may be rebutted by evidence of a contrary intention, appearing from a consideration of the contract as a whole.[242]

(c) NECESSITY FOR BREACH

At common law the question whether the sum of money or other performance[243] stipulated for is a penalty or liquidated damages can only arise when the event upon which it becomes payable is a *breach of the contract between the parties*.[244] It does not arise where the obligation to pay exists on entering the contract as an advance payment or deposit,[245] or is a true alternative mode of performing the contract.[246] The distinction has given rise to litigation in the context of hire-purchase agreements. Finance companies sometimes provide that, in the event of termination of the agreement, not only shall they be entitled to take possession of the goods hired and to forfeit instalments already paid, but that the hirer shall also pay a certain sum as compensation for 'loss of profit on the transaction'. If the hiring is terminated as a result of a breach of the agreement by the hirer, the Courts may hold this payment to be a penalty *in terrorem*.[247] But if it is terminated voluntarily by the hirer, or by his death or bankruptcy, so that there is no breach of the agreement, the question of a penalty or liquidated damages cannot arise.[248] This produces the anomaly that it may

---

[241] (1993) 61 Build. L.R. 41 (P.C.).

[242] *Pye* v. *British Automobile Commercial Syndicate Ltd.* [1906] 1 K.B. 425.

[243] *Jobson* v. *Johnson* [1989] 1 W.L.R. 1026 (transfer of shares).

[244] *Export Credits Guarantee Department* v. *Universal Oil Products Co.* [1983] 1 W.L.R. 399 (H.L.) See also *Nutting* v. *Baldwin* [1995] 1 W.L.R. 201. The law on penalties does not apply to claims in debt: see *post*, p. 630.

[245] See *post*, p. 647.

[246] *Alder* v. *Moore* [1961] 2 Q.B. 57. See also *Golden Bay Realty* v. *Orchard Investment* [1991] 1 W.L.R. 981 (penalty rules not applicable to contract in statutory form).

[247] *Bridge* v. *Campbell Discount Co. Ltd.* [1962] A.C. 600; *Cooden Engineering Co. Ltd.* v. *Stanford* [1953] 1 Q.B. 86; *Financings Ltd.* v. *Baldock* [1963] 1 Q.B. 887; *Lombard North Central plc* v. *Butterworth* [1987] Q.B. 527.

[248] *Bridge* v. *Campbell Discount Co. Ltd.* (*supra*, n. 247), at pp. 613, 614, 625; cf. Lord Denning at p. 631; *Goulston Discount Co.* v. *Harman* (1962) 106 S.J. 369 (C.A.). See also *Alder* v. *Moore* [1961] 2 Q.B. 57; *Richco* v. *A.C. Toepfer* [1991] 1 Lloyd's Rep. 136.

be more expensive for a hirer to behave honourably and terminate the agreement voluntarily than to repudiate and break the contract—a situation which has now been mitigated by the Consumer Credit Act 1974 in respect of credits not exceeding £15,000 to individuals[249] and by the Unfair Terms in Consumer Contracts Regulations 1999 in respect of terms in sale and supply contracts with consumers.[250] The Courts have, however, been unwilling to extend the common law rule.[251]

(d) AMOUNTS RECOVERABLE

Where the clause is a liquidated damages clause the claimant will recover the stipulated sum without being required to prove damage and irrespective of any actual damage, even where this is demonstrably smaller than the stipulated sum.[252] However, where the actual loss is greater, the claimant is limited to the stipulated sum. In *Cellulose Acetate Silk Co. Ltd.* v. *Widnes Foundry (1925) Ltd.*:

The appellant agreed to pay 'by way of penalty the sum of £20 per week for every week we exceed 18 weeks' in the delivery of certain machinery. Calculated on this basis, the damages recoverable by the respondent on breach amounted to some £600, but its actual loss amounted to £5,850. It therefore claimed that it was entitled to disregard the penalty and to sue for the damages actually suffered.

It was, however, clear from the circumstances that the parties must have known that the damage which would be incurred might greatly exceed the stipulated sum. The House of Lords therefore held that the sum was not a penalty, but was merely the amount which the appellant had agreed to pay by way of compensation for delay, and that the damages must be limited to this agreed amount.[253]

Where a clause is held to be penal the damages incurred must be assessed in the usual way. In such circumstances the claimant might be able to recover a sum greater than the stipulated sum[254] even though it cannot be said that the clause has a penal effect in such circumstances and although this means that a claimant who has acted unfairly by inserting a penal clause would be treated more favourably than one whose clause is a genuine attempt to 'liquidate' prospective damages. However, this result can be seen as following from the principle that the validity of a clause is determined by reference to the time at which the contract is made.

---

[249] Consumer Credit Act 1974, ss. 99, 100. See also Hire-Purchase Act 1965, ss. 27, 28.

[250] S.I. 1999 No. 2083, Sched. 2, para. 1(e) (any 'failure to fulfil . . . obligation').

[251] *Else (1982) Ltd.* v. *Parkland Holdings Ltd.* [1994] 1 B.C.L.C. 130, at p. 138 *per* Evans L.J. See also *Phillips Hong Kong Ltd.* v. *Att.-Gen. of Hong Kong* (1993) 61 Build. L.R. 41.

[252] *Wallis* v. *Smith* (1882) 20 Ch.D. 243, 267.

[253] [1933] A.C. 20. See also *Diestal* v. *Stevenson* [1906] 2 K.B. 345. Cf. *AKT Reidar* v. *Arcos* [1927] 1 K.B. 352 (unliquidated damages available in respect of breaches outside ambit of clause).

[254] *Wall* v. *Rederiaktiebolaget Luggude* [1915] 3 K.B. 66; *Watts, Watts & Co.* v. *Mitsui* [1917] AC 227; *AMEV-UDC Finance Ltd.* v. *Austin* (1986) 162 C.L.R. 344 (Australia). For criticism see *Robophone Facilities* v. *Blank* [1966] 1 W.L.R. 1428, at p. 1446; Law Com. W.P. No. 61 (1975), §§ 46–8; Hudson (1974) 90 L.Q.R. 25, (1985) 101 L.Q.R. 480; Gordon (1974) 90 L.Q.R. 25.

18

SPECIFIC REMEDIES

Under certain circumstances, a contractual promise may be enforced directly. This may be by an action for the agreed sum, for instance the price it has been agreed would be paid for goods or some other performance, by an order for specific performance of the obligation, or by an injunction to restrain the breach of a negative stipulation in a contract, or to require the defendant to take positive steps to undo a breach of contract. These remedies have different historical roots, the claim for an agreed sum being a common law remedy whereas specific performance and injunctions are equitable remedies which were once exclusively administered by the Court of Chancery. At common law the breach of a contract was regarded as the breach of a purely personal obligation but equity would sometimes regard a contract as conferring a proprietary interest on the person to whom property was to be transferred, and even where this was not the case, would come to the aid of the injured party where damages would be, for that party, an inadequate redress. The specific remedies are not subject to the limits imposed on damages by, for instance, rules of remoteness and mitigation and a claimant may therefore prefer specific relief where these would limit the damages recoverable.

I. ACTIONS FOR THE AGREED SUM

Where, for example, it is agreed to sell goods for a certain price, the seller may seek payment of the agreed price.[1] The claim, a liquidated claim for the precise sum, is for the payment of a debt. The law of contract draws a clear distinction between such a claim and a claim for damages for breach of contract. The claimant need prove no loss where the claim is for the payment of a debt; 'the rules as to remoteness of damage and mitigation of loss are irrelevant; and unless the event on which payment is due is a breach of some other contractual obligation . . . the law on penalties does not apply to the agreed sum'.[2] However, a seller who suffers loss over and above the sum due may recover both the agreed sum and damages.[3] An action for an agreed sum will not be available until the contractual duty to pay has arisen, whether expressly or impliedly.[4] Subject to any provision in the contract, in sale of goods, by section 49(1)

---

[1] Burrows, *Remedies for Torts and Breach of Contract*, 2nd edn. (1994), ch. 7.
[2] *Jervis* v. *Harris* [1996] Ch. 195, at p. 202.
[3] *Overstone Ltd.* v. *Shipway* [1962] 1 W.L.R. 117.
[4] *Mount* v. *Oldham Corporation* [1973] Q.B. 309 (implied term that school fees be paid in advance).

and (2) of the Sale of Goods Act 1979 the seller is not entitled to the price unless the property in the goods has passed to the buyer or payment is due 'on a day certain irrespective of delivery'.[5] Where the goods have not been delivered, the seller's claim for the price depends on it being ready and willing to do so.[6] The contractual duty to pay and the correlative right to payment may arise on entering the contract, as in the case of the deposits required in contracts for the sale of land[7] or during the course of performance, as in the case of hire in charterparties,[8] or progress payments in building contracts.[9] By the Apportionment Act 1870, all rents, annuities (including salaries and pensions), dividends and other periodic payments in the nature of income shall be considered as accruing from day to day and are, subject to express contrary stipulation, apportionable in respect of time.[10]

Where the sum due is simply an advance payment of the price and was not required as security for due performance, the right to it is conditional upon subsequent completion of the contract. Where the contract is discharged before completion, the payment ceases to be due and the innocent party is relegated to its claim for damages.[11] Where the sum due is a deposit or other sum required as security for due performance of the contract, as a general rule it remains payable where the contract has been discharged.[12] It makes no difference whether the accrued obligation is one in favour of the innocent or the guilty party although a claim by the guilty party may be off-set by the innocent party's claim for damages. Thus, an employee who repudiates a contract of employment, can nevertheless sue for wages earned before that time.[13] There is, however, a limited jurisdiction in the Courts to provide equitable relief where it would be unconscionable for the innocent party to recover the payment.[14] Similar principles, considered *infra*, apply where the payment has been made but the payer wishes to recover it.[15]

The effect of a repudiatory breach by the party who will become liable to pay the agreed sum but before the agreed sum has fallen due has been considered in the

[5] *Stein Forbes & Co. Ltd.* v. *County Tailoring & Co. Ltd.* (1916) 86 L.J.K.B. 448 (provision for payment in cash 'against documents on arrival of steamer' means an action for the price can be brought before delivery).

[6] *Maclean* v. *Dunn & Watkins* (1828) 6 L.J. (O.S.) C.P. 184.

[7] *Howe* v. *Smith* (1884) 27 Ch. D. 87.

[8] *Leslie Shipping Co.* v. *Welstead* [1921] 3 K.B. 420.

[9] *Hyundai Heavy Industries Co. Ltd.* v. *Papadopoulos* [1980] 1 W.L.R. 1129; *Stocznia Gdanska S.A.* v. *Latvian Shipping Co.* (*infra.* n. 20) (ship-building contracts).

[10] By the Apportionment Act 1870, ss. 2, 7.

[11] *Dies* v. *British and International Mining and Finance Co. Ltd.* [1939] 1 K.B. 724, *post*, p. 646; *McDonald* v. *Dennys Lascelles* (1933) 48 C.L.R. 457, at p. 477; *Chinery* v. *Viall* (1860) 5 H. & N. 288. On the position where the payment has been made, see *post*, p. 642.

[12] *Ibid.* See also *Hinton* v. *Sparkes* (1868) L.R. 3 C.P. 161, at p. 166; *Damon Compania Naveria* v. *Hapag Lloyd* [1985] 1 W.L.R. 435, at p. 451; *Rover International Ltd.* v. *Cannon Film Sales Ltd.* (*No. 3*) [1989] 1 W.L.R. 912, at pp. 924–5. See further, *ante*, p. 580 (consequences of discharge).

[13] *Taylor* v. *Laird* (1856) 25 L.J. Ex. 329 (*ante*, p. 36); Apportionment Act 1870, s. 2. Cf. *Boston Deep Sea Fishing and Ice Co.* v. *Ansell* (1888) 39 Ch.D. 339. Note the difference of opinion in *Moriarty* v. *Regent's Garage & Engineering Co.* [1921] 1 K.B. 423. Cf. *ibid.*, *per* Lush J. at p. 434, and *per* McCardie J. at pp. 448–9.

[14] *Post*, p. 646.

[15] *Post*, p. 647.

context of discharge.[16] Although *White and Carter (Councils) Ltd. v. McGregor*[17] suggests that an injured party who can perform without the co-operation of the contract-breaker has an unfettered option to hold the contract open, to perform and to recover the sum once it becomes due, this has been criticized.[18] It is said to encourage wasteful performance and to be inconsistent with the mitigation rule (which it is said should apply to actions for an agreed sum) as well as giving what amounts to indirect specific performance of contracts which are not specifically enforceable. It has not been followed in a number of other common law jurisdictions,[19] and it does not apply where the innocent party has no legitimate interest, financial or otherwise, in completing performance,[20] although this fetter on the innocent party's right to perform and create an entitlement to the agreed sum has been stated only to apply in extreme cases.[21] Supporters of an unfettered right on the part of the innocent party point to the inconsistency of a requirement of legitimate interest with the rejection in English law, affirmed by Lord Reid,[22] of a rule that contract remedies must be exercised reasonably and to the uncertainty of the concept of legitimate interest.[23] But it is submitted that these arguments neglect a number of ways in which the law of remedies limits the possibility of abuse by the innocent party of its rights[24] and the discretionary nature of the specific remedies which have their origin in equity, to which we now turn.

II. SPECIFIC PERFORMANCE

An order for specific performance is one by which the Courts direct the defendant to perform the contract, and in accordance with its terms. By contrast to civil law systems which generally regard the innocent party's primary recourse as, in principle,

---

[16] *Ante*, p. 565.

[17] [1962] A.C. 413.

[18] Nienabar [1962] C.L.J. 213; Goodhart (1962) 78 L.Q.R. 263; Stoljar (1974) 9 Melb U.L.R. 355, at p. 368; Priestley (1990–91) 3 J.C.L. 218. But cf. (1962–66) 2 Adelaide L.R. 103; Tabachnik [1972] C.L.P. 149, at p. 164 ff.

[19] *Rockingham County v. Luten Bridge Co.* 35 F2d 301 (1929); *Restatement of Contracts* 2d, §253 (USA); *Asamera Oil Cpn. v. Sea Oil Cpn.* [1979] 1 S.C.R. 633 (Canada).

[20] *White and Carter (Councils) Ltd. v. McGregor* [1962] A.C. 413, *per* Lord Reid at p. 431. See also *Stocznia Gdanska S.A. v. Latvian Shipping Co.* [1996] 2 Lloyd's Rep. 132 but point not considered in H.L.: [1998] 1 W.L.R. 514.

[21] *Gator Shipping Cpn. v. Trans-Asiatic Oil Ltd. S.A.* [1978] 2 Lloyd's Rep. 357, at p. 374 (interest may be legitimate where the Court would have great difficulty in assessing the damages); *Clea Shipping Corp. v. Bulk Oil International Ltd. (The Alaskan Trader)* [1984] 1 All E.R. 129, at p. 137. Cf. *Attica Sea Carriers Corp. v. Ferrostaal Poseidon Bulk Reederei GmbH (The Puerto Buitrago)* [1976] 1 Lloyd's Rep. 250 (interest not legitimate where cost of repairing ship exceeds the value of the ship when repaired).

[22] *White and Carter (Councils) Ltd. v. McGregor* [1962] A.C. 413, at p. 430.

[23] Lord Hodson [1962] A.C. 413, at p. 445, stated that such a requirement would make an action in debt a discretionary remedy.

[24] Friedmann, in Beatson and Friedmann, eds., *Good Faith and Fault in Contract Law* (1995), ch. 16, lists the rules concerning penalties (*ante*, p. 624), limitation of the right to recover the cost of cure (*ante*, p. 598) and restriction of the right to recover the defendant's gain (*post*, p. 653).

to have the contract performed, the jurisdiction to order specific performance is supplementary to the common law remedy of damages. Notwithstanding this difference of principle in practice, even in civil law systems, specific performance is only granted if the innocent party has a specific interest in performance which is not satisfied by damages.[25]

(a) INADEQUACY OF DAMAGES

It has traditionally been said that specific performance will not normally be granted where damages provide adequate relief.[26] In the modern law, however, there is no absolute rule to this effect, and the scope of specific performance is wider: it may now be ordered if that remedy will 'do more perfect and complete justice than an award of damages'.[27] This may be the case where the contract provided for a series of regular payments but damages could only be sought as each payment fell due,[28] or, as discussed in Chapters 10 and 17, where the loss is suffered by a person who is not a party to the contract.[29] Nevertheless, in exercising its discretion whether or not to order specific performance, the Court will be disposed to refuse the remedy if, in the particular case before it, damages will fully compensate and will put the claimant in as beneficial a position as if the contract had been specifically performed.[30] It is submitted that although Courts are taking a more flexible and liberal approach to the availability of specific performance, two factors indicate that it should remain a secondary remedy to damages. First, specific performance, unlike damages, does not take account of the desirability of a claimant taking reasonable steps to mitigate its loss and granting it avoids the policy of the mitigation rule. Secondly, there have been many improvements in the techniques for identifying and quantifying loss recoverable by damages.[31]

(i) Sale of goods

Where personal property is concerned, damages can usually be adjusted so as to compensate for (let us say) a failure to supply goods. Section 52 of the Sale of Goods Act 1979 provides that, in any action for breach of contract to deliver specific or ascertained goods, the Court may, if it thinks fit, direct that the contract shall be performed specifically, without giving the defendant the option of retaining the goods on payment of damages. The Court of Chancery was accustomed to decree

---

[25] Lando & Beale, *The Principles of European Contract Law* (2000) p. 399.

[26] *Harnett* v. *Yielding* (1805) 2 Sch. & Lef. 549, at p. 553; *Ryan* v. *Mutual Tontine Westminster Chambers Association* [1893] 1 Ch. 116, at p. 126.

[27] *Tito* v. *Waddell (No. 2)* [1977] Ch. 106, *per* Megarry V.-C. at p. 322. See also *Beswick* v. *Beswick* [1968] A.C. 58, at pp. 77, 83, 88; *The Stena Nautica (No. 2)* [1982] 2 Lloyd's Rep. 336, at pp. 346–7.

[28] *Beswick* v. *Beswick* [1968] A.C. 58.

[29] *Beswick* v. *Beswick* [1968] A.C. 58, *ante,* p. 423. But not always, see *Co-operative Insurance Society Ltd.* v. *Argyll Stores (Holdings) Ltd.* [1998] A.C. 1 at p. 18, *post,* p. 637, wrongful closure of 'anchor' supermarket in shopping centre caused losses to other tenants.

[30] *South African Territories Ltd.* v. *Wallington* [1898] A.C. 309; *Beswick* v. *Beswick* [1968] A.C. 58, at pp. 88, 90–1, 102.

[31] Burrows, *Remedies for Torts and Breach of Contract,* 2nd edn. (1994), pp. 350–3.

specific performance only where the goods sold were of unique value to the buyer or possessed special beauty, rarity, or interest.[32] The power conferred by the Sale of Goods Act will similarly not be exercised where the chattel is 'an ordinary article of commerce' such as a piano or even a set of Hepplewhite chairs, as substitute goods can be obtained and damages are normally a sufficient remedy.[33] Even in the case of generic goods, such as petrol or steel, however, a contract falling outside section 52 of the Sale of Goods Act 1979 may be specifically enforced where scarcity of supplies means that substitutes are not available.[34]

(ii) Sale of land

On the other hand, as a general rule, either party to a contract for the sale of land is entitled to sue for specific performance of the agreement. Traditionally it is said that damages are an inadequate remedy for the breach of a contract for the sale of land; but a more convincing reason is that the purchaser acquires by the contract an equitable interest in the land sold and that the vendor is entitled to a reciprocal remedy. The power of the Court to grant specific performance is not limited to those situations in which at law damages would be recoverable. Thus specific performance may be ordered in respect of an anticipatory breach of contract in circumstances where the claimant, having elected to affirm the agreement, would have no immediate right of action for damages.[35]

(b) DISCRETIONARY REMEDY

Specific performance is a discretionary remedy. It does not follow that specific performance will necessarily be granted because damages are not an adequate compensation. The Court has a choice in the matter, and, although this does not mean that the choice will be exercised in an arbitrary or capricious manner, the Court can consider whether it would be fair to grant the remedy[36] and refuse it in circumstances which would not justify a refusal of the common law remedy of damages. 'He who comes to Equity must come with clean hands.' Thus the Court can take into account the fact that the claimant's conduct has been tricky or unfair,[37] or that the claimant has tried to take advantage of a mistake on the part of the defendant.[38] It can also take account of the conduct of the defendant,[39] and it can refuse specific performance if, to grant it,

---

[32] *Holroyd* v. *Marshall* (1862) 10 H.L. Cas. 191, at p. 209; *Falcke* v. *Gray* (1859) 4 Drew. 651, at p. 658.

[33] *Whiteley Ltd.* v. *Hilt* [1918] 2 K.B. 808, at p. 819; *Cohen* v. *Roche* [1927] 1 K.B. 169. Cf. *The Oro Chief* [1983] 2 Lloyd's Rep. 509 (ship); *Record* v. *Bell* [1991] 1 W.L.R. 853, at p. 862 (furniture in house separately sold to plaintiff).

[34] *Sky Petroleum Ltd.* v. *VIP Petroleum Ltd.* [1974] 1 W.L.R. 576 (scarcity due to oil embargo); *Howard E. Perry* v. *British Railways Board* [1980] 1 W.L.R. 1375 (steel strike).

[35] *Hasham* v. *Zenab* [1960] A.C. 316; and see *ante*, p. 573.

[36] *Shell U.K. Ltd.* v. *Lostock Garages Ltd.* [1976] 1 W.L.R. 1187.

[37] *Mortlock* v. *Buller* (1804) Ves. 292; *Walters* v. *Morgan* (1861) 3 De G.F. & J. 718; *Sang Lee Investment Co.* v. *Wing Kwai Investment Co.* (1983) 127 Sol. Jo. 410.

[38] *Webster* v. *Cecil* (1861) 30 Beav. 62; *ante*, p. 338.

[39] *Sang Lee Investment Co.* v. *Wing Kwai Investment Co.* (*supra*, n. 37).

great hardship would be caused to the defendant.[40] So, where the potential loss to the defendant was 'enormous, unquantifiable and unlimited, as well as being out of all proportion to any uncompensatable loss' suffered by the claimant, specific performance will not be granted.[41] The defendant's bad conduct may also induce the Court to grant the remedy where there has been a gross breach of personal faith or an attempt to use the threat of non-performance as blackmail.[42] But where the parties' interests are purely financial, acting 'with gross commercial cynicism' will not suffice.[43] These considerations are, of course, generally considered to be irrelevant at common law.[44]

(c) WANT OF MUTUALITY

In considering whether or not to entertain a claim for specific performance, the Court will take into account whether 'mutuality' exists between the parties. If one party were compelled to perform its obligations in accordance with the terms of the contract while the obligations of the other party under the contract, or some of them, remained unperformed, it might be unfair that the former party should be left to its remedy in damages if the latter party failed to perform any of its unperformed obligations.[45] At one time it was supposed that the Court would not grant specific performance to one party unless, at the time the contract was entered into, it could not have been enforced against that party by the other.[46] But this supposed rule was subject to a number of exceptions[47] and has since been exploded.[48] Lack of mutuality is now only relevant if, at the date of the hearing, the claimant has not performed its obligations under the contract and could not be compelled for some reason to perform its unperformed obligations specifically.[49] Even where mutuality in this sense does not exist, the Court may possibly, in the exercise of its discretion, order specific performance if damages would be an adequate remedy to the defendant for any default on the claimant's part.[50]

---

[40] *Malins* v. *Freeman* (1837) 2 Keen 25; *Denne* v. *Light* (1857) 8 De G.M. & G. 774; *Handley Page Ltd.* v. *Commissioners of Customs and Excise* [1970] 2 Lloyd's Rep. 459; *Tito* v. *Waddell (No. 2)* [1977] Ch. 106, at p. 326. But cf. *Mountford* v. *Scott* [1975] Ch. 258; *Howard E. Perry & Co.* v. *British Railways Board* [1980] 1 W.L.R. 1375.

[41] *Co-operative Insurance Society Ltd.* v. *Argyll Stores (Holdings) Ltd.* [1996] 3 W.L.R. 27, *per* Millett L.J., at p. 43. Cf. Lord Hoffmann's formulation: [1998] A.C. 1 at p. 18.

[42] *Co-operative Insurance Society Ltd.* v. *Argyll Stores (Holdings) Ltd.* [1998] A.C. 1, *per* Lord Hoffmann, at p. 18.

[43] *Ibid.*

[44] But see Friedmann, in Beatson and Friedmann, eds., *Good Faith and Fault in Contract Law* (1995), ch. 16, and *ante*, pp. 624 (the rules concerning penalties), 598 (limitation of the right to recover the cost of cure), and *post*, p. 653 (restriction of the right to recover the defendant's gain).

[45] *Price* v. *Strange* [1978] Ch. 337, at p. 361.

[46] Fry, *Specific Performance*, 6th edn., p. 219.

[47] Ames, *Lectures on Legal History* (1913), p. 370.

[48] *Price* v. *Strange* [1978] Ch. 337.

[49] *Ibid.*; *Sutton* v. *Sutton* [1984] Ch. 184.

[50] *Ibid.*, at p. 368.

(d) CONTRACTS OF PERSONAL SERVICE

The Court will not, in general, compel the performance of contracts which involve personal service.[51] In the case of contracts of employment, this principle is now embodied in legislation which provides that an employee shall not be compelled to perform a contract of employment.[52] The basis of the Courts' approach seems to be that to make one person serve or employ another against the will of the other would be improper and could 'turn contracts of service into contracts of slavery'.[53] But this is difficult to reconcile with the less personal nature of modern employment, and the fact that, by declaration, a public official[54] and a university lecturer[55] may in effect be reinstated. Certain statutes now enable a tribunal to make an order for re-engagement or reinstatement of an employee.[56] Furthermore, in exceptional circumstances, an injunction may be granted to restrain an employer from dismissing an employee and this may indirectly amount to specific enforcement of the contract of employment.[57]

(e) UNSUITABILITY

(i) Obligations ill-defined

The obligations in an agreement which it is sought to enforce may be so ill-defined, or what has to be done in order to comply with the order of the Court may not be capable of sufficient definition, that specific performance would in the circumstances be an unsuitable remedy. Thus a covenant to 'lay out £1,000 in building'[58] and a contract to construct 'a railway station' with nothing to indicate the nature, materials, style, dimensions, or anything else[59] have been held not to be specifically enforceable.

(ii) Constant supervision by the court

At one time it was said that an order for specific performance would not be granted if the Court would be required constantly to supervise the execution of the contract. Thus in *Ryan* v. *Mutual Tontine Westminster Chambers Association*[60] the Court held that it could not grant specific performance of a covenant to maintain a resident porter in constant attendance at a block of flats for the benefit of the tenants as it was

---

[51] *Rigby* v. *Connol* (1880) 14 Ch. D. 482, at p. 487; *Scott* v. *Rayment* (1868) L.R. 7 Eq. 112 (partnership).

[52] Trade Union and Labour Relations (Consolidation) Act 1992, s. 236. Cf. *Stevenson* v. *United Road Transport Union* [1977] I.C.R. 893.

[53] *De Francesco* v. *Barnum* (1890) 45 Ch. D. 430, at p. 438.

[54] *Ridge* v. *Baldwin* [1964] A.C. 40; *R.* v. *B.B.C., ex parte Lavelle* [1983] 1 W.L.R. 23. But cf. *Chief Constable of North Wales Police* v. *Evans* [1982] 1 W.L.R. 1155, at pp. 1175–6; *R.* v. *East Berkshire H.A., ex parte Walsh* [1985] Q.B. 152; *McLaren* v. *Home Office* [1990] I.C.R. 808. And cf. *Hill* v. *C. A. Parsons Ltd.* [1972] Ch. 305 (injunction).

[55] *Thomas* v. *University of Bradford* [1987] A.C. 795, at p. 824; *Pearce* v. *University of Aston (No. 2)* [1991] 2 All E.R. 469.

[56] Employment Rights Act 1996, ss. 114–15, 130. See also Race Relations Act 1976, s. 56.

[57] *Hill* v. *C. A. Parsons & Co. Ltd.* [1972] Ch. 305; *Irani* v. *Southampton and S.W. Hampshire Health Authority* [1985] I.C.R. 590; *Powell* v. *Brent L.B.C.* [1988] I.C.R. 176; *Robb* v. *Hammersmith and Fulham L.B.C.* [1991] I.R.L.R. 72. Cf. *Chappell* v. *Times Newspapers Ltd.* [1975] 1 W.L.R. 482. See also *post*, p. 640.

[58] *Moseley* v. *Virgin* (1796) 3 Ves. 184.

[59] *Wilson* v. *Northampton and Banbury Ry. Co.* (1874) 9 Ch. App. 279.

[60] [1893] 1 Ch. 116.

a contract which would require such supervision as the Court was not prepared to undertake. However, the impossibility for the Court to supervise the doing of the work has more recently been rejected as a ground for denying relief[61] and in *Posner* v. *Scott-Lewis*[62] a covenant to employ a resident porter was specifically enforced. In the case of contracts which involve continuing or complex obligations, difficulties may arise in formulating with sufficient precision (having regard to the terms of the contract) what it is that the defendant must do to comply with the order for specific performance, any breach of which is punishable as a contempt of court. If those difficulties can be overcome, there is no reason why such a contract cannot be specifically enforced if damages would be an inadequate remedy.

A narrower approach was, however, taken by the House of Lords in *Co-operative Insurance Society Ltd.* v. *Argyll Stores (Holdings) Ltd.*[63] Their Lordships refused to order the specific performance of an undertaking in a lease (which had 19 years to run) to keep a supermarket 'open for retail trade during the usual hours of business'. A distinction was drawn between cases in which the order would require the party to achieve a result, for instance building or repairing a house, and those in which it would require the party to carry on an activity, such as to run a business over an extended period of time. The more liberal approach was said to apply only to the first type of case[64] since, in the second type of case, there was a greater possibility of repeated applications to the Court to rule on whether the order would be breached. This puts the decision in *Posner* v. *Scott-Lewis*[65] into question. In the *Co-operative Insurance Society Ltd.* case it was also said to be contrary to the long-standing and settled practice of the Court to order a person specifically to perform a contract to run a business,[66] and that the contract in that case did not define the obligation sufficiently precisely to make it capable of specific performance because it said nothing about the level of trade, the areas of trade, or the kind of trade.[67]

In addition to these instances, the Court will also refuse specific performance where the interest to be transferred is merely transitory,[68] or where an entire obligation is specifically enforceable in part only.[69] Also contracts to appoint an arbitrator,[70] to convey the goodwill of a business without the business premises,[71] and to exercise a testamentary power of appointment[72] will not be specifically enforced.

---

[61] *Shiloh Spinners Ltd.* v. *Harding* [1973] A.C. 691, *per* Lord Wilberforce, at p. 724. See also the statements of Megarry V.-C. cited *post*, n. 64.

[62] [1987] Ch. 25. See also *Rainbow Estates* v. *Tokenhold Ltd.* [1998] 3 W.L.R. 980 (repairing covenant).

[63] [1998] A.C. 1.

[64] *Ibid.*, at pp. 13–15. Lord Wilberforce's rejection of the nineteenth century authorities in *Shiloh Spinners Ltd.* v. *Harding* (*supra*, n. 61) at p. 724, was made in that context and Megarry V.-C.'s statements in *C. H. Giles & Co. Ltd.* v. *Morris* [1972] 1 W.L.R. 307, at p. 318 and *Tito* v. *Waddell (No. 2)* [1977] Ch. 106, at p. 321 were said to be based on incomplete analysis.

[65] See *supra*, n. 62.

[66] *Ibid.* See also *ante*, pp. 634–5 (hardship to defendant).

[67] *Ibid.*, at p. 16–17.

[68] *Lavery* v. *Pursell* (1888) 39 Ch. D. 508, at p. 519 (tenancy for a year).

[69] *Ryan* v. *Mutual Tontine Westminster Chambers Association* [1893] 1 Ch. 116.

[70] *Re Smith & Service and Nelson & Sons* (1890) 25 Q.B.D. 545.

[71] *Baxter* v. *Connelly* (1820) 1 J. & W. 576. But see *Beswick* v. *Beswick* [1968] A.C. 58, at pp. 89, 97.

[72] *Re Parkin* [1892] 3 Ch. 510.

III. INJUNCTION

Injunctions are either prohibitory or mandatory.[73] A prohibitory injunction may be granted to restrain the breach of a negative contract or of a negative stipulation in a contract. A mandatory injunction compels the positive performance of an act and may be used to restore the situation to what it was before the breach of contract.

(a) PROHIBITORY INJUNCTIONS

Although the grant of an injunction is normally discretionary,[74] an injunction will normally be granted, without reference to 'the balance of convenience', to restrain the breach of a negative contract or stipulation.[75] A negative contract or stipulation is one whereby a promisor covenants not to do something, for example, not to carry on a certain trade,[76] or to build on land,[77] or not to ring church bells early in the morning.[78] A negative stipulation, though not express, may be implied, for example, in the case of an exclusive dealing agreement relating to a particular product,[79] or an agreement to charter a ship to a particular person,[80] the injunction being granted to restrain the promisor from buying (or selling) the product elsewhere or chartering the ship to another.

(i) Available though specific performance would not be ordered

An injunction may be granted to restrain the breach of a negative stipulation in a contract even though the Court would not order specific performance of the positive stipulations contained in the same contract.[81] Also, it may be used in a case where its effect will be to enforce performance of the contract, even though the contract is one which the Court might not normally specifically enforce. Thus in *Metropolitan Electric Supply Co. Ltd.* v. *Ginder*,[82] an express promise by the defendant to take the whole of his supply of electricity from the Company was held to import a negative promise that he would take none from elsewhere, and an injunction was accordingly granted.

---

[73] On damages in lieu of an injunction, see *post*, p. 641, and *Jaggard* v. *Sawyer* [1995] 1 W.L.R. 269.

[74] e.g. *Bankers Trust Co.* v. *P.T. Jakarta International Hotels and Development* [1999] 1 Lloyd's Rep. 910, at 911 (anti-suit injunction will only be granted where 'damages are manifestly an inadequate remedy').

[75] *Doherty* v. *Allman* (1878) 3 App. Cas. 709, at p. 720. But the grant of an *interlocutory* injunction is not obligatory: *Texaco Ltd.* v. *Mulberry Filling Station Ltd.* [1972] 1 W.L.R. 814. Cf. *Hampstead and Suburban Properties Ltd.* v. *Diomedous* [1969] 1 Ch. 248. And see generally *American Cyanamid Co.* v. *Ethicon Ltd.* [1975] A.C. 396.

[76] *Nordenfelt* v. *Maxim Nordenfelt Guns and Ammunition Co. Ltd.* [1894] A.C. 535.

[77] *Wrotham Park Estate Co.* v. *Parkside Homes Ltd.* [1974] 1 W.L.R. 798 (in relation to building that had been undertaken before the decision, see *post*, p. 614).

[78] *Martin* v. *Nutkin* (1724) 2 Peere Wms. 266.

[79] *Catt* v. *Tourle* (1869) L.R. 4 Ch. App. 654; *Evans Marshall & Co. Ltd.* v. *Bertola S.A.* [1973] 1 W.L.R. 349.

[80] *Lord Strathcona S.S. Co.* v. *Dominion Coal Co.* [1926] A.C. 108 (*ante*, p. 457); *Associated Portland Cement Manufacturers Ltd.* v. *Teigland Shipping A/S* [1975] 1 Lloyd's Rep. 581.

[81] *Lumley* v. *Wagner* (1852) De G.M. & G. 604; *Sky Petroleum Ltd.* v. *VIP Petroleum Ltd.* [1974] 1 W.L.R. 576; *Hill* v. *C.A. Parsons & Co. Ltd.* [1972] Ch. 305.

[82] [1901] 2 Ch. 799.

(ii) Contracts of personal service

Contracts of personal service cannot, of course, be specifically enforced, but it is possible by means of an injunction to encourage performance in an oblique manner. In *Lumley* v. *Wagner*,[83] for instance:

The defendant agreed to sing at the plaintiff's theatre, and during a certain period to sing nowhere else. Afterwards, she made a contract with another person to sing at another theatre, and refused to perform her contract with the plaintiff.

The Court refused to order specific performance of her positive engagement to sing at the plaintiff's theatre, but granted an injunction to restrain the breach of her promise not to sing elsewhere.

The scope of the principle in *Lumley* v. *Wagner* has, however, been confined by two restrictions:

In the first place, although in certain instances an express positive promise implies a negative undertaking not to do anything which would interfere with the performance of this promise, the Courts have normally refused in contracts of personal service to enforce by injunction anything but an express stipulation not to do some specific thing. There must have been inserted in the contract itself an express negative stipulation, and the defendant must have acted in breach of that stipulation. Thus in *Mortimer* v. *Beckett*,[84] a boxer, Joe Beckett, agreed with the plaintiff that he should have 'the sole arrangements of matching me for all my boxing contests and engagements during the period of the next seven years': afterwards he refused to be managed by the plaintiff. In terms, the contract contained no negative covenant, and so the Court held that an injunction could not be granted.

Secondly, an injunction will not be granted if its effect will be to compel the defendant to fulfil a contract for personal service or to abstain from any business whatsoever, for this would be to compel a contract-breaker to choose between specific performance and starvation. In *Ehrman* v. *Bartholomew*,[85] therefore, where a traveller promised that he would serve a firm for 10 years and would not, during that period, 'engage or employ himself in any other business', an injunction was refused, among other grounds, because to have granted it would have given him no real choice but to work for the firm. But if the employment is of a special kind, an injunction may be granted to restrain the defendant from doing similar work of that kind. So in *Warner Brothers Pictures Incorporated* v. *Nelson*:[86]

A film actress, Mrs Nelson (professionally known as Bette Davis), agreed that she would render her exclusive services as an actress to the plaintiffs for a certain period, and would not during that period render any similar services to any other person *or engage in any other occupation*. In breach of these stipulations, she entered into an agreement to appear for another film company. The plaintiffs claimed an injunction to restrain her.

---

[83] (1852) 1 De G.M. & G. 604.
[84] [1920] 1 Ch. 571. See also *Whitwood Chemical Co.* v. *Hardman* [1891] 2 Ch. 416. Cf. *Hivac Ltd.* v. *Park Royal Scientific Instruments Ltd.* [1946] Ch. 169.
[85] [1898] 1 Ch. 671.
[86] [1937] 1 K.B. 209.

Branson J. held that, although it was impossible to grant an injunction to prevent her from engaging in any other occupation as this would amount to specific performance, an injunction should be granted to restrain her from working as an actress for any other person for a period of up to three years. There were other spheres of activity which, if not so remunerative, would still be open to her, so that she would not be driven, although she might be encouraged, to perform the contract.[87] This has been criticized as implying that nothing short of idleness or starvation is compulsive and it has been said that Branson J.'s view that 'an actress of her then youth and soaring talent' might employ herself usefully and remuneratively in other spheres of activity for a period of up to three years appeared 'extraordinarily unrealistic'.[88] More recent cases have examined the practical realities of granting an injunction and have been more willing to infer compulsion where a longer term injunction was being sought and less willing to grant an injunction where the contract contained obligations of mutual trust or confidence.[89] Where there is no question of starvation, as where the employer is willing to pay wages throughout a period of notice whether or not the employee performs the contractual duties,[90] or of the employee's skills atrophying, as where the period of notice is short,[91] the Court is more willing to grant an injunction if satisfied that breach of the negative obligation, for instance to work for a third party during the contractual period of notice, will seriously prejudice the employer.

We have noted that in exceptional circumstances, however, an injunction may be granted to restrain an employer from dismissing an employee.[92]

(b) MANDATORY INJUNCTIONS

An injunction may also be granted to restore the situation which would have prevailed but for the defendant's breach of contract, e.g. to put back a tenant wrongfully evicted by a landlord.[93] Mandatory injunctions are always discretionary[94] and the Court will not intervene in this way unless it is shown that the defendant has deliberately ridden roughshod over the claimant's rights[95] or that the claimant would be gravely prejudiced if the remedy were withheld.[96]

---

[87] At p. 217.
[88] *Warren* v. *Mendy* [1989] 1 W.L.R. 853, *per* Nicholls L.J. at p. 865.
[89] *Ibid.*; *Page One Records Ltd.* v. *Britton* [1968] 1 W.L.R. 157 (injunction not granted to restrain breach of management contracts by boxer and pop group); *Young* v. *Robson Rhodes* [1998] 3 All E.R. 524, at pp. 534–5.
[90] *Evening Standard Ltd.* v. *Henderson* [1987] I.C.R. 588 (injunction granted; employer offered to permit employee to work through notice period). See also *Robb* v. *Hammersmith & Fulham LBC* [1991] I.R.L.R. 72.
[91] *Provident Financial Group plc* v. *Hayward* [1989] I.C.R. 160 (no injunction because no prejudice to employer).
[92] *Ante*, p. 640.
[93] *Luganda* v. *Service Hotels Ltd.* [1969] 2 Ch. 209.
[94] *Sharp* v. *Harrison* [1922] 1 Ch. 502, at p. 512; *Shepherd Homes Ltd.* v. *Sandham* [1971] Ch. 340.
[95] *Luganda* v. *Service Hotels Ltd.* (*supra*, n. 93).
[96] *Durell* v. *Pritchard* (1865) L.R. 1 Ch. App. 244, at p. 250; *Shepherd Homes Ltd.* v. *Sandham* (*supra*, n. 94); *Wrotham Park Estate Co.* v. *Parkside Homes Ltd.* [1974] 1 W.L.R. 798.

IV. DAMAGES AND SPECIFIC PERFORMANCE OR INJUNCTION

Since Lord Cairns' Act 1858 there has been jurisdiction to grant damages either in addition to or in substitution for specific performance or an injunction.[97] Such damages are governed by the same principles as are damages at common law.[98] They can be awarded where an order for specific performance has been made and not complied with.[99] In cases of misdescription by a vendor of land, for example where the area of the land is less than that stated in the contract, the purchaser may claim specific performance with an abatement of the purchase price to compensate for the misdescription.[100] Where the misdescription is not contained in the contract but was only a misrepresentation inducing it, the Court has power to award damages in lieu of rescission under section 2(2) of the Misrepresentation Act 1967.[101]

---

[97] See now the Supreme Court Act 1981, ss. 49, 50.
[98] *Johnson* v. *Agnew* [1980] A.C. 367, at p. 400 overruling *Wroth* v. *Tyler* [1974] Ch. 30.
[99] *Biggin* v. *Minton* [1977] 1 W.L.R. 701; *Johnson* v. *Agnew* (*supra*).
[100] Harpum [1981] C.L.J. 108.
[101] *Ante*, p. 257. Cf. *Gilchester Properties Ltd.* v. *Gomm* [1948] 1 All E.R. 493.

19

RESTITUTIONARY AWARDS

A person who pays money or supplies goods or services to the defendant pursuant to a contract which is discharged by breach may be entitled to recover the money paid or to recompense in the form of a reasonable price (*quantum valebat*) or reasonable remuneration for the goods or services (*quantum meruit*). These remedies may also be available in respect of money paid or services rendered under other ineffective agreements including those that are void, illegal, discharged for frustration, or too uncertain to amount to contracts. Such claims, which are strictly outside the scope of this part of the book, since they are not for breach of contract, have been briefly considered in the chapters on ineffective contracts.[1] Furthermore, in certain circumstances, the claimant may, by way of exception to the normal compensatory measure, be able to claim the profits the contract-breaker is alleged to have made from the breach. One of these two types of restitutionary claim may be advantageous where the innocent party has made a bad bargain,[2] where damages are limited or irrecoverable (perhaps because of the rules of remoteness or the mitigation principle), or where for some reason the innocent party finds it difficult to prove the loss suffered.[3] The first type of claim, the recovery of money paid or recompense in respect of goods or services, may also be available to a contract-breaker in certain situations.

I. THE RECOVERY OF MONEY PAID

(a) RECOVERY BY THE INNOCENT PARTY

If one party is entitled to be treated as discharged from further performance of the contract by reason of the other party's breach, and does so, any money paid by that party to the other party under the contract can be recovered provided that the consideration for the payment has failed. Although the principle is not confined to contracts,[4] many of the cases are concerned with ineffective contracts. Strictly, the rule requires that the failure be *total*, but several factors indicate that the requirement of

---

[1] *Ante*, pp. 63, 86, 207, 402, 557. See further Goff and Jones, *The Law of Restitution*, 5th edn. (1998), chs. 19–26; Beatson, *The Use and Abuse of Unjust Enrichment* (1991), pp. 1–11; ch. 3.

[2] *B.P. Exploration Co. (Libya) Ltd.* v. *Hunt (No. 2)* [1979] 1 W.L.R. 783, at p. 800, aff'd [1983] 2 A.C. 352; *Bush* v. *Canfield* 2 Conn. 485 (1818) (Connecticut). For other advantages, see *post*, pp. 664, 651.

[3] *Ante*, p. 599.

[4] *Chillingworth* v. *Esche* [1924] 1 Ch. 97 (deposit paid in transaction 'subject to contract').

totality may be 'on the turn'. We shall first consider total failure, and then the recent developments.

(i) Total failure of consideration

In *Kwei Tek Chao* v. *British Traders and Shippers Ltd.*,[5] a case concerned with a c.i.f. contract for the sale of goods, Devlin J. said:

If goods have been properly rejected, and the price has already been paid in advance, the proper way of recovering the money back is by an action for money paid on a consideration which has wholly failed, i.e. money had and received.

As well as the requirement that the failure of consideration be total, the party seeking repayment must have elected to accept the breach as discharging the contract. If the contract has been partly performed and the innocent party who is claiming repayment has either derived some benefit under it, as where goods or services have been received, or has elected to treat the contract as still continuing,[6] the money cannot be recovered unless that benefit can be and is returned to the payee. The need for a total failure of consideration is illustrated by *Hunt* v. *Silk*:[7]

The plaintiff paid £10 to the defendant in return for a promise by the defendant to give him immediate possession of certain premises, to put them into repair, and to execute a lease of them in his favour within 10 days. The plaintiff obtained possession, but left soon afterwards when the defendant failed to carry out the rest of his promise; he also sued to recover the £10.

His action failed. It was held that, the contract having been in part performed, no part of the consideration could be recovered.

The common law has required the failure of consideration to be total for two main reasons.[8] First, the common law has set its face against apportionment, partly because one cannot assume that all parts of the payee's performance are equally valuable and that the contract price is earned incrementally. For example, in a contract to build a house, the preparation of the ground and the foundations on a difficult site may involve greater expense in either time or labour than the completion of the brickwork, the roof and the interior. Secondly, in many cases the benefit the payer has received from the payee's part-performance cannot easily be valued in money. This is particularly so where it consists of services. So, where a builder who has agreed to modernize a bathroom, abandons the contract after disconnecting the old fittings and removing some of them, it is not obvious what the benefit of such part performance is to the owner of the house,[9] who will have to pay another person to clear the room as well as having the trouble of finding another builder to complete the task.

---

[5] [1954] 2 Q.B. 459, at p. 475.

[6] *Ibid.*

[7] (1804) 5 East 449.

[8] *Whincup* v. *Hughes* (1871) LR 6 CP 78, at p. 81 (Bovill C.J.). Birks, *An Introduction to the Law of Restitution* (1985) pp. 242–4. For other justifications, see Law Com. No. 121, *Pecuniary Restitution on Breach of Contract* (1983), §§ 3.8–3.10.

[9] *Sumpter* v. *Hedges* [1898] 1 Q.B. 673, *ante*, p. 514.

Failure of consideration occurs where one party has not enjoyed the benefit of any part of what it bargained for.[10] It is judged from the payer's point of view and consideration in this context refers to performance by the payee of the contractual promise.[11] This means that any performance of the actual thing promised, as determined by the contract, is fatal to recovery. The consequence of this is that the concept of total failure of consideration is somewhat arbitrary, and can ignore real benefits received by the payer and significant detrimental reliance by the payee. For instance, in the case of a contract for the sale of goods,[12] or of hire purchase,[13] a failure by the seller to convey a good title to the goods in breach of the condition implied by section 12(1) of the Sale of Goods Act 1979[14] will constitute a total failure of consideration. Thus in *Rowland* v. *Divall*:

R bought a motor-car from D for £334, repainted it and sold it on to a third party. It then turned out that the car had been stolen, although D had dealt with it in good faith. The police took possession of it on behalf of the true owner and R brought an action to recover from D the £334.

The Court of Appeal held that, since R 'had not received any part of that which he had contracted to receive—namely, the property and right to possession' of the car, there had been a total failure of consideration. He was entitled to recover the whole purchase price, notwithstanding that he and his sub-purchaser had had four months' use and enjoyment of the vehicle and that he could not restore the car to D.[15] Again, in *Butterworth* v. *Kingsway Motors*[16] the purchase price of a car (£1,275) was recovered although by the time the car, which had been used by the purchaser for nearly a year, was returned it was worth only £800. In an action for damages, account would be taken of the benefit received by purchasers in these cases.[17] Similarly, there will be a total failure of consideration even though a buyer or hirer has incurred substantial reliance expenditure for the purpose of the contract[18] or where, although there has

---

[10] *Fibrosa Spolka Akcyjna* v. *Fairbairn Lawson Combe Barbour Ltd.* [1943] A.C. 32; *Rover International* v. *Cannon Film Sales Ltd. (No. 3)* [1989] 1 W.L.R. 912; *Stocznia Gdanska S.A.* v. *Latvian S.S. Co.* [1998] 1 W.L.R. 574.

[11] *Fibrosa Spolka Akcyjna* v. *Fairbairn Lawson Combe Barbur Ltd.* [1943] A.C. 32, at p. 48.

[12] *Hudson* v. *Robinson* (1816) 4 M. & S. 475; *Rowland* v. *Divall* [1923] 2 K.B. 500.

[13] *Karflex Ltd.* v. *Poole* [1933] 2 K.B. 251; *Warman* v. *Southern Counties Car Finance Cpn. Ltd.* [1949] 2 K.B. 576.

[14] *Ante*, p. 154.

[15] [1923] 2 K.B. 500, at pp. 504, 506–7. The principle has been both criticized and defended; see Law Reform Committee, Twelfth Report, (Cmnd. 2958, 1966); Law Commission's Report on Exemption Clauses in Contracts, (Law Com. No. 24, 1969); Law Commission's Report on Sale and Supply of Goods (Law Com. No. 160, 1987), §§ 6.1–5, the last of which recommended no reform of the rule by requiring a buyer seeking to recover the price to make a money allowance in favour of the seller in respect of the use. Cf. Torts (Interference with Goods) Act 1977, s. 6(3).

[16] [1954] 1 W.L.R. 1286.

[17] *Harling* v. *Eddy* [1951] 2 K.B. 739, and *ante*, p. 616. But where a buyer has spent money on the goods while they are in its possession, damages may be the preferable remedy because this can be recovered in such an action but not in an action for the return of the price: *Mason* v. *Burningham* [1949] 2 K.B. 545.

[18] *Fibrosa Spolka Akcyjna* v. *Fairbairn Lawson Combe Barbour Ltd.* [1943] A.C. 32, *ante*, p. 557 (work done by payees in manufacturing machines); *Rover International* v. *Cannon Film Sales Ltd. (No. 3)* [1989] 1 W.L.R. 912, at pp. 932, 936, 937 (expenditure in buying back films to fulfil terms of distributorship contract).

been partial performance by the payee, the Court is able to divide the contract and hold that there has been a total failure in relation to the parts not performed,[19] or can find that the parties have impliedly acknowledged that the consideration can be 'broken up' or apportioned.[20]

(ii) Partial failure of consideration

The willingness of the Court so to divide the contract may indicate dissatisfaction with the requirement of totality. We have seen that the requirement of totality can produce fine and sometimes arbitrary distinctions. In the case of frustrated contracts, dealt with in an earlier chapter,[21] it has been removed by statute so that money paid can be recovered even though there has only been a partial failure of consideration.[22] We shall also see that where a *quantum meruit* claim is made in respect of services rendered, the difficulty of valuing the work done is not regarded as an insurmountable bar to relief.

It may, moreover, be difficult to maintain the requirement that the failure be *total* now that the principle of unjust enrichment and the defence of change of position have been recognized in English law.[23] It has been said that 'if counter-restitution is relatively simple . . . insistence on total failure of consideration can be misleading and confusing',[24] and recently, in *Goss* v. *Chilcott*,[25] the Judicial Committee of the Privy Council relaxed the requirement that the failure be total by the use of apportionment. It was held that a loan could be apportioned between the principal sum lent and the interest, so that the receipt by the lender of interest did not prevent the lender recovering the principal sum lent, and the Court indicated that it would have been willing to apportion the principal sum itself so that partial repayment of the principal sum would not have prevented a restitutionary claim, but would have merely reduced such a claim to the unpaid balance of the loan. Moreover, support has been expressed in the House of Lords for the reformulation of the total failure of consideration rule.[26] Although these cases all concerned loans or other transactions in which the part-performance received by the payer consisted of money so that the problems of valuing non-monetary performance did not arise, it is submitted that, in principle, restitution should be available in all cases in which it is relatively simple for the payer to return any benefits received.

---

[19] *D.O. Ferguson* v. *Sohl* (1992) 62 Build. L.R. 92 (building contract; total failure of consideration in respect of sum paid in excess of value of work done); *White Arrow Express Ltd.* v. *Lamey's Distribution Ltd.* (1995) 15 Tr. L.R. 69, noted Beale (1996) 112 L.Q.R. 205; *Baltic Shipping Co.* v. *Dillon* (1993) 176 C.L.R. 344, at p. 375 (High Court of Australia).

[20] *David Securities Pty. Ltd.* v. *Commonwealth Bank of Australia* (1992) 175 C.L.R. 353, at p. 383.

[21] *Ante*, p. 530.

[22] *Ante*, p. 558 (Law Reform (Frustrated Contracts) Act 1943, s. 1(2)).

[23] *Lipkin Gorman* v. *Karpnale Ltd.* [1991] 2 A.C. 548.

[24] *David Securities Pty. Ltd.* v. *Commonwealth Bank of Australia* (*supra*, n. 20) at p. 383 (High Court of Australia).

[25] [1996] A.C. 788, at p. 798.

[26] *Westdeutsche Landesbank Girozentrale* v. *Islington L.B.C.* [1996] A.C. 669, at pp. 682–3. See also Birks, *An Introduction to the Law of Restitution* (1985), pp. 259–64; Goff and Jones, (*supra*, n. 1), pp. 499–506, 525–6, but cf. Law Com. No. 121, *Pecuniary Restitution on Breach of Contract* (1983), §§ 3.8–3.9 and *Stocznia Gdanska S.A.* v. *Latvian S.S. Co.* (*supra* n. 10) at p. 590.

(b) RECOVERY BY THE PARTY IN BREACH

It is similarly possible for the party who has broken the contract to recover from the innocent party money pre-paid by it. The recoverability of such payments depends on the construction of the contract and is primarily a function of the purpose for which the payment is required. A distinction is drawn between deposits and other payments required as security for due performance on the one hand and advance payments of the price on the other.

(i) Advance payments of the contract price

Where the payment was not a deposit or otherwise required as security for due performance and where recovery was not otherwise expressly or impliedly precluded by the terms of the agreement (e.g. by express provision that it be forfeited) it may be recoverable. Thus in *Dies* v. *British and International Mining and Finance Corporation Ltd.*:[27]

The defendant contracted to sell rifles and ammunition to one Quintana at a total price of £270,000 of which £100,000 was paid before the agreed delivery date. Subsequently, in breach of contract, the purchaser failed to take delivery or to pay the balance. The defendant elected to treat the contract as discharged but refused to return the £100,000. Quintana assigned his rights to the plaintiff, who brought an action to recover the money.

Stable J. held that the plaintiff might recover it, less the amount of any damages suffered by the defendant through Quintana's breach of contract. It might seem strange, at first sight, that the party in breach should have succeeded. But as the learned Judge pointed out, the defendant was 'amply protected', since it could set off its claim for damages against the sum sought to be recovered. Again, however, in the present state of the law, the consideration for the payment must have totally failed. If the party in default has received any benefit from the subject-matter of the sale before the discharge, it cannot, subject to any equitable relief,[28] recover any part-payment made. Thus where a contract for work and materials provides for payment of the purchase price by instalments, a contractor who is bound to incur expense as the work proceeds, will be entitled to retain any instalment paid if the other party repudiates the contract before completion of the work because, subject to a *de minimis* rule, the services rendered by the innocent party are to be regarded as part of the bargained-for performance and there is thus no total failure of consideration in such a contract once performance has commenced.[29]

---

[27] [1939] 1 K.B. 724. See also *McDonald* v. *Dennys Lascelles Ltd.* (1933) 48 C.L.R. 457 (sale of land); *Rover International Ltd.* v. *Cannon Film Sales Ltd. (No. 3)* [1989] 1 W.L.R. 912; Beatson, *The Use and Abuse of Unjust Enrichment* (1991), ch. 3 (updating (1981) 97 L.Q.R. 389).

[28] See *post*, p. 647.

[29] *Hyundai Heavy Industries Co. Ltd.* v. *Papadopoulos* [1980] 1 W.L.R. 1129. The case for relaxing the rule requiring that the failure of consideration be *total* is much weaker where the person seeking recovery is a contract-breaker: see *ante*, p. 510, in the context of the rule precluding recovery for part performance of an entire obligation.

(ii) Deposits and other payments as security for due performance

It is settled law that a sum paid by way of 'deposit' for the purchase of goods or land is security for completion of the contract by the buyer and cannot as a general rule be recovered if the buyer fails to perform its side of the contract.[30] Similarly, where the contract provides that on default instalments of the price already paid shall be forfeited, there will generally be no recovery.

The general rule that deposits and other payments required as security or subject to forfeiture clauses are irrecoverable is, however, subject to statutory and equitable exceptions. By section 49(2) of the Law of Property Act 1925 the Court has an unqualified discretion to order repayment of a deposit paid under a contract for the sale of land where the justice of the case requires it.[31] Another legislative exception can be found in the Unfair Terms in Consumer Contracts Regulations 1999 which provide that a term which permits the seller or supplier 'to retain sums paid by the consumer where the latter decides not to conclude or perform the contract, without providing for the consumer to receive compensation of an equivalent amount from the seller or supplier where the latter is the party cancelling the contract' is presumptively unfair.[32] Secondly, where the provision for the forfeiture of the sum paid is penal and it is unconscionable for the payee to retain the money, equitable relief may be available.[33] It has been stated that the amount of the deposit has to be reasonable, and while long usage established the reasonableness of a 10 per cent deposit in sales of land, a larger deposit would, unless justified, be penal.[34] Thus a person who purchases goods or land by instalments, or who hires goods in return for payment of rent, may be entitled to equitable relief against forfeiture of the property or purchase money if he defaults in prompt payment of the instalments or rent when due.[35] The principle is similar to that governing penalty clauses and liquidated damages clauses[36] but the law has treated the two situations as entirely separate.[37] The 'genuine pre-estimate of damage' test does not apply to stipulations for security for due performance; 'the forfeiture rule looks at the position after the breach when the innocent party is enforcing the forfeiture'.[38]

---

[30] *Howe* v. *Smith* (1884) 27 Ch. D 89. See generally Harpum [1984] C.L.J. 134; Beatson, *The Use and Abuse of Unjust Enrichment* (1991), pp. 46–50, 76–7, 90–4.

[31] *Universal Corporation* v. *Five Ways Properties Ltd.* [1979] 1 All E.R. 552. Cf. *Macara (James) Ltd.* v. *Barclay* [1945] 1 K.B. 148 for a narrower approach to the discretion and the view that repayment could only be ordered where the vendor's conduct was open to criticism.

[32] S.I. 1999 No. 2083, Sched. 2, para. 1 (d). See generally *ante*, pp. 200, 300.

[33] See *Workers Trust & Merchant Bank Ltd.* v. *Dojap Investments Ltd.* [1993] A.C. 573. Similar principles apply where the money has not been paid and an action for the agreed sum is brought; *ante*, p. 631.

[34] *Ibid.*

[35] *Stockloser* v. *Johnson* [1954] 1 Q.B. 476; *Shiloh Spinners Ltd.* v. *Harding* [1973] A.C. 691, *per* Lord Simon at pp. 726–7. Cf. Lord Wilberforce, *ibid.*, at pp. 723–4.

[36] *Ante*, pp. 624–9. See *Public Works Commissioners* v. *Hills* [1906] A.C. 368.

[37] *Linggi Plantations Ltd.* v. *Jagatheesan* (1972) 1 M.L.J. 89, *per* Lord Hailsham L.C at p. 91; *Workers Trust & Merchant Bank Ltd.* v. *Dojap Investments Ltd.* [1993] A.C. 573. It may sometimes be hard to say whether a contract is providing for forfeiture of money paid absolutely or for a penal liability: *Else (1982) Ltd.* v. *Parkland Holdings Ltd.* [1994] 1 B.C.L.C. 130, at p. 146.

[38] *Else (1982) Ltd.* v. *Parkland Holdings Ltd.* [1994] 1 B.C.L.C. 130, *per* Hoffmann L.J., at p. 144. His Lordship also described the penalty rule as 'mechanical', *ibid.*, p. 145. See also *ibid.*, pp. 139, 143.

The scope of the jurisdiction to relieve against forfeiture is somewhat uncertain and it probably does not apply to those commercial contracts where speed and certainty are of paramount importance.[39] Although not entirely logical, it also appears that the Courts may only relieve against the forfeiture of proprietary or possessory interests as opposed to the forfeiture of 'mere contractual rights'.[40] This may, however, leave open the possibility of seeking relief where a contract is specifically enforceable and thus creates equitable rights, although in the case of breach of an essential condition as to time relief by way of specific performance is less likely to be given than relief by way of restitution, for example by repayment of retained money.[41] Apart from the uncertainty as to the scope of the equitable jurisdiction it is also possible, though unlikely, that the only form of relief available is to give the contract-breaker more time to perform the contract so that no relief will be possible if it is clear that the contract-breaker will not be able to pay after such extension of time.[42]

In the exercise of the equitable jurisdiction account has been taken of whether the sum to be forfeited is much greater than the damage caused by the breach,[43] whether the party seeking relief had received a substantial part of the consideration for the payment,[44] whether there has been any fraud or sharp practice,[45] whether it is reasonable to require the party who is *prima facie* entitled to forfeiture to accept an alternative to the property it is sought to forfeit,[46] and whether relief would permit the evasion of a contractual obligation simply because the contract has turned out to be an unwise one.[47]

[39] *The Laconia* [1977] A.C. 850; *Scandinavian Trading Tanker Co. A.B.* v. *Flota Petrolera Ecuatoriana* [1983] 2 A.C. 694; *Sport International Bussum BV* v. *Inter-Footwear Ltd.* [1984] 1 W.L.R. 776; *Union Eagle Ltd.* v. *Golden Achievement Ltd.* [1997] A.C. 514. Cf. the broader approach of the High Court of Australia: *Legione* v. *Hateley* (1983) 152 C.L.R. 406; *Stern* v. *McArthur* (1988) 165 C.L.R. 489.

[40] *BICC plc* v. *Burndy Corporation* [1985] Ch. 232, at pp. 251–2; *Nutting* v. *Baldwin* [1995] 1 W.L.R. 201. See also *Transag Haulage Ltd.* v. *Leyland DAF Finance plc* [1994] 2 B.C.L.C. 88, at p. 99; *On Demand Information plc* v. *Michael Gerson (Finance) plc* [2000] 4 All E.R. 784 (contingent interests sufficient). Cf. the broader *dictum* in *Workers Trust & Merchant Bank Ltd.* v. *Dojap Investments Ltd.* [1993] A.C. 573, at p. 578.

[41] *Union Eagle Ltd.* v. *Golden Achievement Ltd.* [1997] A.C. 514; *Steedman* v. *Drinkle* [1916] 1 A.C. 275. Cf. *Re Dagenham (Thames) Dock Co., ex parte Hulse* (1873) L.R. 8 Ch. App. 1022 and the broader Australian approach: *Legione* v. *Hateley*; *Stern* v. *McArthur* (*supra*, n. 39).

[42] *Stockloser* v. *Johnson* [1954] 1 Q.B. 476, *per* Romer L.J. (cf. Denning and Somervell L.JJ.); *Galbraith* v. *Mitchenall Estates Ltd.* [1965] 2 Q.B. 473; *Starside Properties Ltd.* v. *Mustapha* [1974] 1 W.L.R. 816; *BICC plc* v. *Burndy Corporation* [1985] Ch. 232; *Workers Trust and Merchant Bank Ltd.* v. *Dojap Investments Ltd.* [1993] A.C. 573. See also *Jobson* v. *Johnson* [1989] 1 All E.R. 621.

[43] *Stockloser* v. *Johnson* [1954] 1 Q.B. 476, at pp. 484, 490; *Transag Haulage Ltd.* v. *Leyland DAF Finance plc* [1994] 2 B.C.L.C. 88, at pp. 101–2.

[44] *Ibid.*, at pp. 484, 492.

[45] *Ibid.*, *per* Romer L.J. at pp. 495–6.

[46] *Shiloh Spinners Ltd.* v. *Harding* [1973] A.C. 691, at pp. 726–7; *Transag Haulage Ltd.* v. *Leyland DAF Finance plc* [1994] 2 B.C.L.C. 88, at pp. 101–2.

[47] *Galbraith* v. *Mitchenall Estates Ltd.* [1965] 2 Q.B. 473; *Hyundai Ship Building and Heavy Industries Co. Ltd.* v. *Pournaras* [1978] 2 Lloyd's Rep. 502, at pp. 508–9.

II. RECOMPENSE FOR GOODS AND SERVICES

A *quantum meruit* claim arises where goods are supplied or services rendered by one person to another in circumstances which entitle the former to be recompensed by the latter by receiving a reasonable price or remuneration.

Such a claim may arise in a number of different situations. Some of the situations are really contractual, the remedy being based on an implied promise or agreement.[48] In others, however, the law imposes a duty upon one party to recompense the other for a benefit received by the defendant or in respect of the claimant's reasonable reliance on the defendant's words or conduct,[49] without any promise or agreement so to do.

(a) CONTRACTUAL CLAIMS

There are two main situations where a claim for a contractual *quantum meruit* may arise. First, where one person has rendered a service to another in circumstances which indicate an understanding between them that it is to be paid for, although no particular remuneration has been specified, the law will infer a promise to pay *quantum meruit*, i.e. as much as the party doing the service has deserved, or, as it is generally described, a 'reasonable' sum.[50] The principle is precisely the same when goods are bought and sold or services rendered under a contract without an express agreement as to the price, in which case the Sale of Goods Act 1979, section 8(2) and the Supply of Goods and Services Act 1982, section 15(1) provide that the buyer and the recipient of the services must pay a reasonable price or charge.

Secondly, a *quantum meruit* claim may arise when the conduct of the parties to an express contract leads to the inference that they have agreed to substitute for it a new contract. In *Steven* v. *Bromley and Son*,[51] for example, the tender and acceptance of a completely different type of cargo from that envisaged by the original contract was held to give rise to the inference that the parties had entered into a new and substituted agreement. If no quantified remuneration can be spelled out for the new contract, then the law will imply a promise to pay a reasonable sum. It must be remembered, however, that for such a contract to arise, each party must have had the option of accepting or rejecting the substituted agreement.[52] A new and different contract cannot be forced by one party on the other against its will.

The same principle is also applied where one party has, in breach of contract, only

---

[48] Winfield, *The Province of the Law of Tort* (1931), p. 157; (1947) 63 L.Q.R. 35; Birks, *An Introduction to the Law of Restitution* (1985), p. 275.

[49] Goff and Jones (*supra*, n. 1), pp. 18–23, 530–4 and ch. 26; Beatson (*supra*, n. 27), ch. 2. Cf. Birks, (*supra*, n. 48), pp. 265–76.

[50] *Paynter* v. *Williams* (1833) 1 C. & M. 810; *The 'Batis'* [1990] 1 Lloyd's Rep. 345, at p. 352.

[51] [1919] 2 K.B. 722. See also *Sir Lindsay Parkinson & Co. Ltd.* v. *Commissioners of Works* [1949] 2 K.B. 632.

[52] *Taylor* v. *Laird* (1856) 25 L.J. Ex. 329 (for facts see *ante*, p. 36); *Foreman and Co. Pty Ltd.* v. *Ship 'Liddesdale'* [1900] A.C. 190, at p. 202.

partially performed the agreement, or performed it in a manner different from that contemplated by its terms. In such a case, if the party not in default elects to accept the partial or substituted performance, that party will have to pay *quantum meruit* the value of the benefit received. So if A plc agrees to buy from B plc certain goods, and B delivers the goods it contracted to sell mixed with goods of a different description not included in the contract, or delivers a lesser quantity of the contracted goods, if A accepts those goods,[53] it must pay a reasonable price for them.[54] By its acceptance A impliedly promises to pay a reasonable sum but again, if the party not in default has no option but to accept, then it will not be liable to a *quantum meruit* or any other action.[55]

So far we have considered claims by the innocent party. Where, however, the contractual obligation is divisible or severable so that the right to payment accrues incrementally as the services are rendered, the guilty party will also be entitled to claim in respect of performance completed, but subject to a counterclaim for damages by the innocent party in respect of loss suffered by the breach.[56]

(b) RESTITUTIONARY CLAIMS BY THE INNOCENT PARTY

Where the claim is in restitution, the obligation is imposed on the parties by the law without reference to any promise or agreement. Where a contract has been broken in such a way as to entitle the innocent party to be treated as discharged, and it has elected to be so treated, it may sue on a *quantum meruit* for the value of the work done under the contract, as an alternative to bringing an action on the contract for damages. In such a case the claim to recompense arises in restitution. Two cases provide useful illustrations of this remedy. In *Planché* v. *Colburn*:[57]

The plaintiff had contracted to write a book on custom and ancient armour for a periodical publication, called the *Juvenile Library* to be published by the defendant. For this he was to receive the sum of £100 on completion. When he had completed half, but not the whole, of his volume, the defendant abandoned the publication.

The plaintiff was held entitled to retain a verdict for £50 which the jury had awarded him. Tindal C.J. said:[58]

I agree that when a special contract is in existence and open, the plaintiff cannot sue on a *quantum meruit*: part of the question here, therefore, was whether the contract did exist or not. It distinctly appeared that the work was finally abandoned; and the jury found that no

---

[53] It is not obliged to: Sale of Goods Act 1979, s. 30(4).

[54] *Steven* v. *Bromley and Son* (*supra*, n. 51), at p. 728 (Atkin L.J.); Sale of Goods Act 1979, s. 30(1), *ante*, p. 514.

[55] *Munro* v. *Butt* (1858) 8 E. & B. 738; *Sumpter* v. *Hedges* [1898] 1 Q.B. 673 (for facts see *ante*, p. 514); *Bookmakers Afternoon Greyhound Services Ltd.* v. *Wilfred Gilbert Staffordshire Ltd.* [1994] F.S.R. 723.

[56] *Taylor* v. *Laird* (1956) 25 L.J. Ex 328 (in respect of services rendered before throwing up his command); *Button* v. *Thompson* (1869) L.R. 4 C.P. 330. On entire and divisible obligations see *ante*, p. 510; on the action for the price, see *ante*, p. 630; on acceptance of part performance of an entire obligation, see *ante*, p. 514.

[57] (1831) 8 Bing. 14.

[58] *Ibid.*, at p. 16.

new contract had been entered into. Under these circumstances, the plaintiff ought not to lose the fruit of his labour.

Again, in *De Bernardy* v. *Harding*:[59]

The defendant appointed the plaintiff his agent to advertise and sell tickets for seats to view the funeral of the Duke of Wellington, the plaintiff to receive a commission on the tickets sold. The defendant wrongfully revoked the plaintiff's authority after he had already incurred certain expenses in carrying out the contract.

It was held that the plaintiff was entitled to recover *quantum meruit* for the expenses so incurred.

(c) *QUANTUM MERUIT* COMPARED WITH DAMAGES

If the contract has not been discharged, the innocent party cannot use the *quantum meruit* remedy, but can only sue for damages. However, if the restitutionary remedy is available and the injured party chooses to sue on a *quantum meruit*, the principle of assessment differs from that which is applied in assessing damages for breach of contract and the sum which the innocent party is entitled to recover may differ from that which is recoverable as damages:[60]

Suppose that by the terms of a contract A plc is to pave one mile of road for B plc for £100,000, payable on its completion. B repudiates the contract when A has done half of the work and A accepts that repudiation as discharging it from further performance of its obligations under the contract.

It is clear that A cannot claim the stipulated sum since the work has not been completed.[61] Should it claim damages, however, it will receive £100,000 less any saving on labour and materials. If, however, a *quantum meruit* is sought, A is asking to be paid the reasonable value of the work done. Ordinarily, damages will be the more favourable remedy since the profit element in the transaction can then be recovered. But there might be special circumstances where, for instance, the contract price had been underestimated, or the costs of doing the work had risen considerably since the contract was made. In these circumstances a claimant may secure a greater measure of compensation by suing on a *quantum meruit* instead of for damages. Thus it has been held that relief by way of *quantum meruit* is not limited to a pro-ration of the contract price[62] (in our example £50,000) or the contract price itself (in our example, £100,000).[63] Although this can be criticized as inconsistent with the contract and as reallocating contractual risks, pro-ration is difficult in a complex contract and may be

---

    [59] (1853) 8 Ex. Ch. 822. See also *Prickett* v. *Badger* (1856) 1 C.B.N.S. 296.
    [60] *Heyman* v. *Darwins Ltd.* [1942] A.C. 356, at p. 398 (Lord Porter). See also *The Batis* [1990] 1 Lloyd's Rep. 345, at p. 353.
    [61] See *ante*, p. 510 (entire contracts). Cf. *ante*, p. 566 (repudiation not accepted).
    [62] *Newton Woodhouse* v. *Trevor Toys Ltd.* (20 December 1991, C.A.) Cf. *Noyes* v. *Pugin* 27 P. 548, at p. 549 (1891) (Washington).
    [63] *Lodder* v. *Slowey* (1900) 20 N.Z.L.R. 321, 358; [1904] A.C. 442; *Rover International Ltd.* v. *Cannon Film Sales Ltd. (No. 3)* [1989] 1 W.L.R. 912.

unfair because it takes no account of fixed costs which may be incurred at the early stages of a contract or of economies of scale which may have affected the determination of the contract price but be lost on part performance. Restriction to the contract price, while more attractive[64] on pragmatic grounds, would give the contract-breaker a proportion of the profits expected under the contract even though the contract has been discharged. It would also produce disequilibrium between the position of an innocent party who has only done a small proportion of the work before the contract is discharged, where the contract price limit would rarely apply, and a person who has done the bulk of the work, where the limit would be more likely to apply. So, in the example above, if the market value of half the work is in fact £200,000, the limit would not apply, and A would recover the true value of the work, £100,000, but if A has completed three-quarters of the job, it would apply and A would only recover £100,000 as the *quantum meruit*.

(d) RESTITUTIONARY CLAIMS BY THE PARTY IN BREACH

We have mentioned the contractual *quantum meruit* that is available to the party in breach who has part performed a contractual obligation which is divisible or severable. Where the contractual obligations are entire the party in breach will, however, generally obtain no recompense unless the other party freely accepted the work or otherwise waived the need for complete performance. In *Sumpter* v. *Hedges*[65] the party in breach was accordingly entitled to recover the value of materials left on the building site and used by the defendant who had a choice whether or not to use them to complete the building but not in respect of the partially completed building. This rule can work harshly where substantial benefits are conferred on an innocent party who has suffered no loss whatsoever from the breach of contract.[66] In one case it was suggested that a shipowner who deviated but delivered the goods at the port of discharge without injury or substantial delay would be entitled to reasonable remuneration.[67] Perhaps the best explanation of this is that it was not really a case of part-performance but one in which the goods' owner, in the end, got everything he had contracted for. Where, however, the innocent party has made it clear that anything other than full and precise performance is not wanted a *quantum meruit* will not be awarded.[68]

---

[64] See Goff and Jones, (*supra*, n. 1), pp. 532–4, citing *Wuchter* v. *Fitzgerald* 163 P. 819 (1917) (Oregon).

[65] [1898] 1 Q.B. 673 (for facts see *ante*, p. 514); *Bolton* v. *Mahadeva* [1972] 1 W.L.R. 1009.

[66] Law Com. No. 121, *Pecuniary Restitution on Breach of Contract* (1983) proposed reform but this was rejected by the Lord Chancellor; Law Com. No. 140, § 2.11 (19th Annual Report).

[67] *Hain S.S. Co. Ltd.* v. *Tate and Lyle Ltd.* (1936) 41 Com. Cas. 350 (H.L.).

[68] *Wilusznynski* v. *Tower Hamlets L.B.C.* [1989] I.C.R. 493. See also *British Telecommunications plc* v. *Ticehurst* [1992] I.C.R. 383. Cf. *Miles* v. *Wakefield M.B.C.* [1987] A.C. 539. See also *ante*, p. 512.

III. DAMAGES MEASURED BY BENEFIT
TO WRONGDOER

A defendant may make a gain from a breach of contract as where a financier broke his contract to invest £15,000 in the plaintiff's timber business but instead invested it in a distillery which proved much more profitable.[69] Alternatively, a defendant may gain by saving expense from its breach as where remedial work, for instance replacing soil or planting trees on the claimant's land, is not done.[70] A restitutionary award will be attractive to a claimant who suffers a smaller loss than the defendant's gain as where the diminution in the value of the claimant's land is less than the cost of the remedial work, an expense saved by the defendant.[71] It will also be attractive where the interest harmed by the breach of contract is a non-pecuniary interest such as confidentiality.[72] In general, the gain to a defendant from a breach of contract is irrelevant to the quantification of damages.[73]

The defendant's gain is, however, relevant in a number of situations in which a strict application of the principle that damages are compensatory would not do justice between the parties. In sales of land the defendant's gain is taken into account because the effect of the contract is that the purchaser has an equitable interest in the land and is accordingly entitled to the proceeds of any wrongful sale to a third party.[74] The defendant's gain will also be relevant where there has been a breach of a contractual duty of confidence[75] or a fiduciary duty,[76] or where the breach of contract involves the use of or interference with the claimant's property.[77] These are all cases of specifically enforceable contracts and it is arguable that the defendant's gains should be relevant in all such cases.

The suggestion has been made that gains should be recovered in all cases of cynical exploitation of breach for the purpose of making a gain so as to deter breaches of contract.[78] This, however, would revolutionize contract remedies since in many cases, particularly commercial cases, the breach is in fact deliberate in the sense that it is knowingly done for commercial reasons. For instance, a seller of goods may choose to

---

[69] *Teacher* v. *Calder* (1899) 1 F. 39 (H.L.).

[70] *Tito* v. *Waddell (No. 2)* [1977] Ch. 106 (for the reasons why 'cost of cure' damages were not available, see *ante*, p. 597).

[71] See generally Jones (1983) 99 L.Q.R. 442; Burrows, *Remedies for Torts and Breach of Contract*, 2nd edn. (1994), pp. 308–14; Birks [1987] L.M.C.L.Q. 421; Goodhart [1995] R.L. Rev. 3; Law Com. No. 247, *Aggravated, Exemplary and Restitutionary Damages* (1998), Part III.

[72] *Att.-Gen.* v. *Blake* [2000] 3 W.L.R. 625. See also *Snepp* v. *United States* 100 Sup. Ct. 763 (1980); *Att.-Gen.* v. *Guardian Newspapers Ltd. (No. 2)* [1990] 1 A.C. 109 and *ante*, p. 592.

[73] *Att.-Gen.* v. *Blake* [2000] 3 W.L.R. 625. See also *The Siboen* [1976] 1 Lloyd's Rep. 293, at p. 337; *Tito* v. *Waddell (No. 2)* [1977] Ch. 106, at p. 332; *Surrey CC* v. *Bredero Homes Ltd.* [1993] 1 W.L.R. 1361.

[74] *Lake* v. *Bayliss* [1974] 1 W.L.R. 1073; *Tito* v. *Waddell (No. 2)* (*supra*, n. 70), at p. 332.

[75] *Peter Pan Manufacturing Corp.* v. *Corsets Silhouette Ltd.* [1964] 1 W.L.R. 96.

[76] See *Reading* v. *Att.-Gen.* [1951] A.C. 507. See also *Hospital Products Ltd.* v. *U.S. Surgical Corp.* (1984) 156 C.L.R. 41 (Australia).

[77] *Penarth Dock Engineering Co. Ltd.* v. *Pound* [1963] 1 Lloyd's Rep. 359; *Wrotham Park Estate Co* v. *Parkside Homes Ltd.* [1974] 1 W.L.R. 798; *Jaggard* v. *Sawyer* [1995] 1 W.L.R. 269.

[78] Birks [1987] L.M.C.L.Q. 421.

breach its contract and sell to a third party who is willing to pay a premium over and above the market price. Restitutionary awards made on this basis might also permit a claimant to evade the requirements of the mitigation rule.

The liability of a contract-breaker to account for gains made from the breach was considered by the House of Lords in *Attorney-General* v. *Blake*.[79] B, a former member of the intelligence services, undertook not to divulge any official information gained as a result of his employment and broke the undertaking by publishing an auto-biography. The Crown sought to recover the royalties he was to be paid by his pub-lishers. Their Lordships confirmed that in general damages are measured by the claimant's loss, but held that in an exceptional case, where specific enforcement and injunction are inadequate compensation for a breach of contract or are not available, the Court can require the defendant to account to the claimant for benefits received from a breach of contract even where the breach of contract does not involve the use of or interference with the claimant's property.

The law recognises that a party to a contract may have an interest in performance which is not readily measurable in terms of money. On breach the innocent party suffers a loss. He fails to obtain the benefit promised by the other party to the contract. To him the loss may be as important as financially measurable loss, or more so. An award of damages, assessed by reference to financial loss, will not recompense him properly. For him a financially assessed measure of damages is inadequate.[80]

In determining whether to order an account of profits, the court will have regard to all the circumstances, including the subject matter of the contract, the purpose of the contractual provision which has been breached, the circumstances in which the breach occurred, the consequences of the breach and the circumstances in which relief is being sought. Lord Nicholls of Birkenhead (with whom Lord Goff and Lord Browne-Wilkinson agreed) stated that 'a useful general guide, although not exhaust-ive, is whether the plaintiff had a legitimate interest in preventing the defendant's profit-making activity and, hence, in depriving him of his profit'.[81] The Crown was held to have such an interest in preventing B from profiting from breaches of the undertaking in an autobiography. He was thus liable to account to the Crown for the royalties.

Their Lordships declined to give more specific guidance as to when an account of profits might be awarded for breach of contract. But they indicated that it would not in itself suffice that (a) the breach was cynical and deliberate; (b) the breach enabled the defendant to enter into a more profitable contract elsewhere; and (c) by entering into a new and more profitable contract the defendant put it out of his power to perform the contract with the claimant.[82] Their Lordships did not, moreover, consider

---

[79] *Att.-Gen.* v. *Blake* [2000] 3 W.L.R. 625.

[80] *Ibid.*, per Lord Nicholls at p. 636. Lord Hobhouse dissented on the ground (p. 652) that an account of profits, a remedy based on property rights, should not be given where the necessary property rights were absent.

[81] *Ibid.*, at p. 639. See also Lord Steyn at p. 645 (defendant's position closely analogous to that of a fiduciary). See *Esso Petroleum Co. Ltd.* v. *Niad*, 22 November 2001 (Morritt V.-C.) for a liberal approach to the availability of this remedy.

[82] [2000] 2 W.L.R. 625, 640, 645. See [1998] Ch. 439, 457, 458 (C.A.).

the two categories suggested by the Court of Appeal for 'restitutionary damages'[83] were satisfactory. The first was the case of 'skimped' performance, where defendants fail to provide the full extent of the contracted services, as where a security firm which has agreed to guard premises using a stipulated number of guards uses a much smaller number and saves a considerable sum.[84] This was said not to fall within the scope of an account of profits as ordinarily understood and in any event, an account of profits was not needed in this context. Suppliers of inferior goods have to refund the difference in price as damages for breach of contract, and a similar approach should apply in cases where the defendant provided inferior and cheaper services than those contracted for.[85] The second category suggested by the Court of Appeal, where, as in *Blake*'s case, defendants profited by doing the very thing that they contracted not to do, was considered to be too widely defined because it embraced all express negative obligations.[86]

Where a contract-breaker is liable to account for gains made from the breach it is necessary to show that the profits are occasioned directly by the breach and are attributable to the interest infringed. In some cases where the defendant makes a profit in excess of that which the claimant might have made there may be difficulties in so attributing that profit to the breach of contract as opposed to the defendant's skill and initiative so that it is difficult to say that the enrichment is 'at the expense' of the claimant.[87]

---

[83] Lord Nicholls preferred (p. 638) to avoid this term.

[84] See *City of New Orleans* v. *Firemen's Charitable Association* 9 So. 486 (1891). See also *White Arrow Express Ltd* v. *Lamey's Distribution Ltd*. (1995) 15 Tr. L.R. 69; Beale (1996) 112 L.Q.R. 205.

[85] [2000] 2 W.L.R. 625, 639, 645.

[86] *Ibid.*, at pp. 640, 645.

[87] Farnsworth (1985) 94 Yale L.J. 1339.

20

LIMITATION OF ACTIONS

At common law, lapse of time does not affect contractual rights. But it is the policy of the law to discourage stale claims, because after a long period a defendant may not have the evidence to rebut such claims and should be in a position to know that after a given time an incident which might have led to a claim is finally closed. Accordingly, in the Limitation Act 1980, the legislature has laid down certain periods of limitation after the expiry of which no action can be maintained.[1] Equity has developed a doctrine of laches, under which a claimant who has not shown reasonable diligence in prosecuting the claim may be barred from equitable relief.

I. LIMITATION ACT 1980

(a) THE GENERAL RULE

The Act provides that an action founded on a simple contract must be commenced within six years, and one created or secured by a deed, within 12 years, from the date on which the cause of action accrued.[2] In contract, the cause of action normally accrues, not, as in tort, when the damage is suffered, but when the breach of contract takes place[3] or, in the case of an anticipatory breach, when the innocent party elects to treat the contract as terminated.[4] In the case of certain loans, however, the six-year period does not start to run unless and until a demand in writing for the repayment of the debt is made by or on behalf of the creditor.[5]

A distinction is, however, drawn between a 'once and for all' breach and a

---

[1] For proposals for reform see Law Com. C.P. No. 151, *Limitation of Actions* (1998).

[2] Limitation Act 1980, ss. 5, 8. But in the case of personal injuries arising from a breach of contract, ss. 11 and 14 of the Act provide that the limitation period is to be three years from the date on which the cause of action accrued or the date of the claimant's knowledge (if later) of certain relevant facts. See also ss. 12, 13, 14 (fatal accidents).

[3] *Battley* v. *Faulkner* (1820) 3 B. & Ald. 288; *Short* v. *M'Carthy* (1820) 3 B. & Ald. 626; *Howell* v. *Young* (1826) 5 B. & C. 259. But if the claimant can establish an action in tort for negligence, the cause of action accrues when the damage is suffered: *Midland Bank Trust Co. Ltd.* v. *Hett, Stubbs & Kemp* [1979] Ch. 384; *Henderson* v. *Merrett Syndicates Ltd.* [1995] 2 A.C. 145; *First National Commercial Bank* v. *Humberts* [1995] 2 All E.R. 673. Cf. *Forster* v. *Outred & Co.* [1982] 1 W.L.R. 86; *Pirelli General Cable Works Ltd.* v. *Oscar Faber & Partners* [1983] 2 A.C. 1; *Bell* v. *Peter Browne & Co.* [1990] 2 Q.B. 495.

[4] *Reeves* v. *Butcher* [1891] 2 Q.B. 509.

[5] Limitation Act 1980, s. 6.

'continuing' breach. In the case of the former, once time has started to run it would continue to do so and a claimant cannot extend the limitation period by, for example, making repeated demands for the repayment of money owed.[6] In the case of a continuing breach, such as of an obligation to repair a building, the promisor's duty is considered as persisting and as being forever renewed until that which has been promised has been done; 'a further breach arises in every successive moment of time during which the state or condition is not as promised, during which . . . the building is out of repair'.[7] In cases of continuing breaches the claimant will be able to recover in respect of that part of the breach which occurred within the six or, in the case of an obligation created or secured by a deed, 12 years before the action was brought.

It is no answer to a plea of limitation that the claimant was unaware or could not have been aware of the existence of the cause of action for breach of contract until after the expiry of the limitation period. The 'discoverability' rule in the Latent Damage Act 1986 does not apply to a breach of contract.[8]

Where the action is in restitution, the claimant's cause of action normally accrues when the defendant is unjustly enriched whether by the receipt of money or otherwise.[9]

(b) PERSONS UNDER A DISABILITY

If on the date on which the cause of action accrued the person to whom it accrued was under a disability, i.e. was a minor or person of unsound mind,[10] the action may be brought within six years from the date when he or she ceased to be under the disability, or dies.[11] This enlargement of time does not apply when the disability supervenes after the right of action has already accrued, or where the same person is afflicted by successive disabilities (e.g. minority followed by insanity) separated by an interval in which he or she is under no disability. Again, no extension is allowed when the right of action first accrues to a person not under a disability through whom the person under a disability claims.

(c) EFFECT OF FRAUD, CONCEALMENT, AND MISTAKE

Where an action is based on the fraud of the defendant, or where any fact relevant to the right of action has been deliberately concealed from the claimant by the defendant, whether before or after the cause of action has accrued,[12] or where an action is for

---

[6] *Mahomed* v. *Bank of Baroda*, The Times, December 1998.

[7] *Larking* v. *Great Western (Nepean) Gravel Ltd.* (1940) 64 C.L.R. 221, *per* Dixon J. at 236 (High Court of Australia). See also the facts of *Midland Bank Trust Co. Ltd.* v. *Hett, Stubbs & Kemp* (*supra*, n. 3).

[8] *Iron Trades Mutual Insurance Co. Ltd.* v. *J. K. Buckenham Ltd.* [1990] 1 All E.R. 808. But it will apply if the claimant can establish an action in tort for negligence. See also Consumer Protection Act 1987, s. 5(5).

[9] *Kleinwort Benson* v. *South Tyneside M.B.C.* [1994] 4 All E.R. 972, at p. 978. See generally McLean [1989] C.L.J. 472; Virgo, *The Principles of the Law of Restitution* (1999), p. 770ff.

[10] Limitation Act 1980, s. 38(2).

[11] *Ibid.*, s. 28.

[12] *Sheldon* v. *R.H.M. Outhwaite (Underwriting Agencies) Ltd.* [1996] A.C. 102.

relief from the consequences of a mistake, the period does not begin to run until the claimant has discovered the fraud, concealment, or mistake,[13] or could with reasonable diligence have discovered it.[14] The 1980 Act further provides that a deliberate breach of duty in circumstances in which it is unlikely to be discovered for some time amounts to deliberate concealment of the facts involved in that breach of duty.[15] So, for example, if a builder fails to disclose the deliberate breach of a building contract by using defective bricks[16] or putting in inadequate foundations,[17] or if the vendors of a house knowingly fail to warn the purchaser of the risk of subsidence, when they are aware that the house has been built on a disused rubbish tip,[18] the running of the limitation period will be postponed until such time as the claimant discovers the concealment or could with reasonable diligence discover it.[19]

(d) ACKNOWLEDGEMENT AND PART PAYMENT

An acknowledgement of a debt or part payment of a debt may extend the period of limitation. The 1980 Act provides[20] that in such a case the right shall be treated as having accrued on and not before the date of the acknowledgement or payment. Thus where A owes B the sum of £500, say, as the price of goods sold and delivered, B's remedy is barred after the passing of six years from the date on which payment became due. But if A, during that period, either acknowledges the debt and its legal liability to pay it[21] or makes a part payment on account of the debt, time begins to run afresh from the date of the acknowledgement or part payment. The limitation period may thus be repeatedly extended. Once, however, it has expired, the right of action cannot subsequently be revived.[22] To be effective, an acknowledgement must be in writing and signed by the person making it or that person's agent, and either an acknowledgement or part payment must be made to the person or to the agent of the person whose claim is acknowledged or in respect of whose claim the payment is made.[23]

---

[13] Including a mistake of law, whether effected by legislation or judicially, e.g. by overruling an earlier decision: *Kleinwort Benson Ltd.* v *Lincoln City Council* [1999] 2 A.C. 349.

[14] Limitation Act 1980, s. 32. But this provision is not to affect the rights of third parties taking *bona fide* and for value. *Sed quaere* whether an action under the Misrepresentation Act 1967, s. 2(1) falls within s. 32 of the 1980 Act because of the statutory fiction of fraud: *ante*, pp. 249–50.

[15] *Ibid.*, s. 32(2).

[16] *Clark* v. *Woor* [1965] 1 W.L.R. 650.

[17] *Applegate* v. *Moss* [1971] 1 Q.B. 406.

[18] *King* v. *Victor Parsons & Co.* [1973] 1 W.L.R. 29.

[19] Note, however, these cases were decided on the wording of the Limitation Act 1939, s. 26(b), now repealed.

[20] s. 29(5).

[21] *Surrendra Overseas Ltd.* v. *Government of Sri Lanka* [1977] 1 W.L.R. 565; *Kamouh* v. *Associated Electrical Industries International Ltd.* [1980] Q.B. 199.

[22] Limitation Act 1980, s. 29(7).

[23] *Ibid.*, s. 30.

(e) STATUTE BARS REMEDY NOT RIGHT

The Act operates merely to bar the contractual remedy, but not to extinguish the right. It is procedural and not substantive. Accordingly, a debtor who pays a statute-barred debt, cannot recover the money as money not due.[24] And if the debtor owes to the creditor certain debts some of which are, and some of which are not, statute-barred, the creditor is entitled to appropriate any payment made by the debtor to those debts which are statute-barred, unless the debtor at the time expressly indicates that he is discharging a debt which is still actionable.[25]

II. BARS TO EQUITABLE RELIEF: LACHES

(a) THE STATUTE APPLIED BY ANALOGY

The statutory periods of limitation do not apply to claims for specific performance or an injunction or other equitable relief, except in so far as the Court may apply them by analogy.[26] The situations to which the statute will be applied by analogy are relatively few, and, broadly include those situations in which there is 'correspondence' between the remedies available at law and in equity, and equity is providing a remedy analogous to that which would have been available at law. For example, the statute will be applied by analogy to a claim for equitable compensation[27] and the right to a final injunction will not be barred so long as the substantive legal right which it seeks to protect has not become barred.[28]

(b) LACHES

Equitable claims or remedies to which the statute does not apply expressly or by analogy are subject to the equitable doctrine of laches. Equity has always refused its aid to stale claims. Delay which is sufficient to deprive a person of the right to claim specific performance or injunction is known technically as 'laches'. This doctrine has been described in a well-known passage in the advice of the Privy Council in *Lindsay Petroleum Co.* v. *Hurd*,[29] as follows:

The doctrine of laches in Courts of Equity is not an arbitrary or a technical doctrine. Where it would be practically unjust to give a remedy, either because the party has, by his conduct, done that which might fairly be regarded as equivalent to a waiver of it, or where by his conduct and neglect he has, though perhaps not waiving that remedy, yet put the other party in a situation in which it would not be reasonable to place him if the remedy were afterwards

[24] *Bize* v. *Dickason* (1786) 1 Term R. 286, at p. 287.
[25] *Mills* v. *Fowkes* (1830) 5 Bing. N.C. 455.
[26] Limitation Act 1980, s. 36(1).
[27] *Cie de Seguros Imperio* v. *Heath (REBX) Ltd.* [2001] 1 W.L.R. 112.
[28] *Fullwood* v. *Fullwood* (1878) 9 Ch. D. 176.
[29] (1874) L.R. 5 P.C. 221, *per* Lord Selborne at p. 239.

to be asserted, in either of these cases lapse of time and delay are most material. But in every case, if an argument against relief, which otherwise would be just, is founded upon mere delay, that delay of course not amounting to a bar by any statute of limitations, the validity of that defence must be tried upon principles substantially equitable. Two circumstances, always important in such cases, are, the length of the delay and the nature of the acts done during the interval.

Delay may therefore bar equitable remedies such as claims for rescission,[30] rectification,[31] specific performance,[32] or for an interim or interlocutory injunction.[33] The claimant must show himself to be 'ready, desirous, prompt and eager' to assert his rights, and even a short lapse of time may, in certain circumstances,[34] be fatal. But in exceptional circumstances, as where the parties have been negotiating, a lapse of time longer than the common law limitation period will not be fatal.[35]

---

[30] *Lindsay Petroleum Co.* v. *Hurd* (*supra*, n. 29).

[31] *Beale* v. *Kyte* [1907] 1 Ch. 564.

[32] *Mills* v. *Haywood* (1877) 6 Ch. D. 196. But cf. *Lazard Bros. & Co. Ltd.* v. *Fairfield Properties Co. (Mayfair) Ltd.* (1977) 121 Sol. J. 793 (two-year delay insufficient to bar specific performance of contract for sale of land); *H. P. Bulmer Ltd.* v. *J. Bollinger SA* [1977] 2 C.M.L.R. 625.

[33] *Great Western Ry.* v. *Oxford, Worcester and Wolverhampton Ry.* (1853) 3 De G.M. & G. 341; *Shepherd Homes Ltd.* v. *Sandham* [1971] Ch. 340 (four-month delay).

[34] *Lehmann* v. *McArthur* (1868) L.R. 3 Ch. App. 496 (short leasehold interest); *First National Reinsurance Co. Ltd.* v. *Greenfield* [1921] 2 K.B. 260 (shares). Cf. *Jones* v. *Jones* [1999] 1 W.L.R. 1739 (mere delay in seeking relief does not signify acquiescence).

[35] *Southcomb* v. *Bishop of Exeter* (1847) 6 Hare 213. See also *Tito* v. *Waddell* [1977] Ch. 106, at pp. 244–52 (specific performance refused 17 years after the breach of contract not because of delay; but because of futility).

PART VI

AGENCY

21

CREATION OF AGENCY

Although at common law as a general rule A cannot by contract with B confer rights or impose liabilities upon a third party, yet A may represent or act on behalf of B, with B's authority, for the purpose of bringing B into legal relations with a third party. The relationship thus constituted is called agency.[1]

I. MODES OF CREATION

Agency may be created in any one of five ways:

(1) by an actual authority to contract given by the principal to the agent;

(2) by the principal's ratification of a contract entered into by the agent on the principal's behalf but without its authority;

(3) by an ostensible authority conferred by the principal on the agent even though no actual authority has been given;

(4) by an implication of law in cases of necessity.

In the first two cases, the principal can sue and be sued by the third party and rights and duties also arise between the principal and the agent. In the last three cases, the principal can be sued but cannot always sue. We shall deal with each of these in turn, and also consider the authority which is vested in different kinds of agents.

(a) ACTUAL AUTHORITY

Actual authority to contract may be express or implied.

Normally the authority given by a principal to its agent is an express authority enabling the latter to bind the former by acts done within the scope of that authority. Such authority may, in general, be given orally. But in some cases it is necessary that the authority should be given in a special form. First, in order that an agent may make a binding contract under seal, it is necessary that authority should be received under seal. Certain transactions, for example, conveyances of land, must still be made by deed.[2]

---

[1] The leading textbooks on this subject are *Bowstead and Reynolds on Agency*, 16th edn. (1996); Powell, *The Law of Agency*, 2nd edn.

[2] On formalities for the creation of powers of attorney, see Powers of Attorney Act 1971, s. 1 (as amended by the Law of Property (Miscellaneous Provisions) Act 1989); Enduring Powers of Attorney Act 1985, s. 2.

Secondly, the Law of Property Act 1925,[3] which requires the creation or disposition of any equitable interest, or interest in land, to be in writing, signed by the grantor or the grantor's agent, lays down that in such case the agent shall be authorized in writing.

The authority of an agent may also be implied. In most cases such implied authority is said to be *incidental* to an express authority or *required* due to the circumstances of the case. The category of implied authority also includes *usual* and *customary* authority. Generally, agents have the authority *usually* possessed by agents in their position. Therefore if an agent is authorized to conduct a particular trade or business, or to perform certain duties, that agent has implied authority to do such acts as are usual in the trade or business, or ordinarily incidental to the due performance of the duties. In addition, every agent has implied authority to act in accordance with the reasonable customs and usages of the particular place, trade, or market where the agent is employed, for example, the London Stock Exchange.[4]

(b) RATIFICATION

Even if the agent enters into a contract without the authority of the principal, the principal may subsequently ratify, that is to say, adopt the benefit and liabilities of a contract made on the principal's behalf.

This may occur in one of two ways. First, when A, though contracting as P's agent, and having P in contemplation as the principal, was not at the time of the contract P's agent in fact, as no precedent authority had been received. Secondly, when A was in fact P's agent at the time of making the contract, but exceeded the authority which P had given. In either case a ratification duly made places the parties in exactly the same position in which they would have been if A had P's authority at the time the contract was made. It is said to 'relate back' to the time of contracting and to have a retrospective effect.[5] An unauthorized acceptance may therefore be ratified even though the offer has in the meantime been withdrawn. So in *Bolton Partners* v. *Lambert*:[6]

The managing director of a company, purporting to act as agent on the company's behalf, but without its authority, accepted an offer by the defendant for the purchase of some sugar works belonging to them. The defendant then withdrew his offer, but the company ratified the manager's acceptance.

It was held that the defendant was bound. The ratification related back to the time of the agent's acceptance and so prevented the defendant subsequently revoking the offer. But there can be no true ratification where an agent purports to accept an offer 'subject to ratification', or where the other contracting party has intimation of the limitation of the agent's authority. In such a case the so-called ratification would

---

[3] ss. 53(1), 54.

[4] *Pollock* v. *Stables* (1848) 12 Q.B. 765.

[5] *Wilson* v. *Tumman* (1843) 6 M. & G. 236, *per* Tindal C.J. at p. 242. The Latin maxim is *omnis ratihabitio retrotrahitur et priori mandato aequiparatur*.

[6] (1888) 41 Ch. D. 295, doubted in *Fleming* v. *Bank of New Zealand* [1900] A.C. 577, at p. 587, but followed in *Presentaciones Musicales S.A.* v. *Secunda* [1994] Ch. 271.

merely be an acceptance of the offer of the other party, which may be withdrawn at any time before the so-called ratification takes place.[7]

The following rules govern ratification:

(i) The agent must purport to act as an agent for a named or identifiable principal

An individual may not incur a personal liability and then assign it to someone else under colour of ratification. The individual must contract as agent at the time of the contract, and the principal, if not named, must at any rate be identifiable. An undisclosed principal, that is, a principal who is not disclosed by the agent to the third party at the time of contracting, may not step in and ratify acts done by the agent in excess of what had previously been authorized.[8] In *Keighley, Maxsted & Co.* v. *Durant:*[9]

A corn merchant was authorised to buy wheat at a certain price on a joint account for himself and K.M. Acting in excess of his authority, he purchased wheat at a higher price from D, but in his own name. K.M. next day ratified the transaction, but later failed to take delivery of the wheat. D brought an action against them for breach.

The action failed. The corn merchant had contracted in his own name without mentioning that K.M. were his principals. Any purported ratification by them was therefore ineffective, and they were consequently under no contractual obligation to D.

On the other hand, if this requirement is satisfied, it makes no difference that the agent's act was a fraud on the principal. So where an agent, without authority, and fraudulently, entered into a contract for the sale of wheat in the principal's name, but intending to take the benefit of it, the principal could nevertheless ratify and adopt the contract and hold the buyers to their bargain.[10] But a forged signature cannot be ratified, for one who forges the signature of another is not an agent, actually or in contemplation. The forger does not act for another; but rather personates the person whose signature has been forged.[11]

(ii) The principal must be in existence

To ratify the contract, the intended principal must have been in existence, and ascertainable, at the time that the contract was made. It is not necessary for the principal to be named as long as he or she is ascertainable.[12]

This rule is important in its bearing on the liabilities of companies for the contracts made by the promoters on their behalf before they are formed. In *Kelner* v. *Baxter:*[13]

---

[7] *Watson* v. *Davies* [1931] 1 Ch. 455; *Warehousing & Forwarding Co. of East Africa Ltd.* v. *Jafferali & Sons Ltd.* [1964] A.C. 1.

[8] Cf. *Welsh Development Agency* v. *Export Finance Co. Ltd.* [1992] B.C.L.C. 148 at pp. 159, 173, 182 (this principle is qualified by the maxim *id certum est quod certum reddi potest*, i.e. that which is capable of being made certain is to be treated as certain).

[9] [1901] A.C. 240.

[10] *Re Tiedemann and Ledermann Frères* [1899] 2 Q.B. 66.

[11] *Brook* v. *Hook* (1871) L.R. 6 Ex. 89.

[12] *National Oilwell (U.K.) Ltd.* v. *Davy Offshore Ltd.* [1993] 2 Lloyd's Rep 582, at pp. 592–7.

[13] (1866) L.R. 2 C.P. 174. See also *Natal Land and Colonization Co. Ltd.* v. *Pauline Colliery and Development Syndicate Ltd.* [1904] A.C. 120.

The promoters of an unformed company entered into a contract on its behalf, which the company when duly incorporated, ratified. It went into liquidation, and the promoters, who had contracted as agents, were sued upon the contract. They pleaded that the liability had passed, by ratification, to the company, and no longer attached to them.

The Court rejected this argument. Willes J. said:[14]

Could the company become liable by a mere ratification? Clearly not. Ratification can only be by a person ascertained at the time of the act done,—by a person in existence either actually or in contemplation of law; as in the case of assignees of bankrupts and administrators, whose title, for the protection of the estate, vests by relation.

This limitation is likely to work hardship to solicitors and others who are called in to do the preliminary work leading to the formation of a company. They will have no right of action against the company when formed, although they will normally be able to assert a right of action against the promoters in such cases, since the promoters will be considered to have incurred personal liability on the contract.[15]

(iii) Capacity of the principal to contract

'At the time the act was done the agent must have had a competent principal'.[16] Thus, if an agent enters into a contract on behalf of a principal who is, at the time, incapable of making it, no ratification is possible.[17]

   Further, the principal can only ratify the act of the agent if at the time of the purported ratification, the principal could personally do the act in question.[18] So, for example, a contract of insurance made by an agent without the principal's authority cannot be ratified after the principal has become aware that the event insured against has in fact occurred. The principal could not insure in such circumstances, and is not permitted to take advantage of the agent's unauthorized act.[19]

(iv) Manner of ratification

The principal who accepts the contract made by a person whom the principal thereby undertakes to regard as its agent, may accept by words or conduct. The principal may avow responsibility for the act of the agent, or take the benefit of the contract, or otherwise by acquiescence in what is done create a presumption of authority. In the absence of an express avowal, however, the ratification must be founded on a full knowledge of the facts,[20] and the principal must have had the option whether to accept or to refuse the contract.[21] Otherwise it will be unenforceable against the

---

[14] At p. 184.

[15] Companies Act 1985, s 36C(1). See *post*, p. 689.

[16] *Firth v. Staines* [1897] 2 Q.B. 70, at p. 75, *per* Wright J.

[17] *Ashbury Railway Carriage and Iron Co. v. Riche* (1875) L.R. 7 H.L. 653 (*ultra vires* contract); *Boston Deep Sea Fishing and Ice Co. Ltd. v. Farnham* [1957] 1 W.L.R. 1051 (alien enemy).

[18] *Presentaciones Musicales S.A. v. Secunda* [1994] Ch. 271, *per* Dillon L.J. at p. 277.

[19] An exception is created by the Marine Insurance Act 1906, s. 86, but this is an anomaly which the Courts have refused to extend, see *Grover & Grover v. Matthews* [1910] 2 K.B. 401.

[20] *La Banque Jacques-Cartier v. La Banque d'Epargne de Montreal* (1887) 13 App. Cas. 111.

[21] *Forman & Co. Pty. Ltd. v. Ship 'Liddesdale'* [1900] A.C. 190, *ante*, p. 514.

principal. It is not, however, necessary for the ratification to be communicated to the third party.[22]

(v) Time of ratification

Ratification may come too late to be effective. Thus, it has been said that 'an estate once vested cannot be divested, nor can an act lawful at the time of its performance be rendered unlawful by the doctrine of ratification'. Although the basis of this limit to the ability to ratify has been said to be wider than that property rights should not be divested retrospectively, it is not easy to discern the principle upon which ratification will be denied.[23]

(c) OSTENSIBLE AUTHORITY

The principal may, by words or conduct, create an inference that an agent has authority to act on behalf of the principal even though no authority exists in fact. In such a case, if the agent contracts within the limits of the apparent authority, although without any actual authority, the principal will be bound to third parties by the agent's acts.

(i) Representation

This doctrine of apparent authority, or ostensible authority as it is usually called, is really an application of the principle of estoppel, for estoppel means only that a person is not permitted to resist an inference which can reasonably be drawn from the principal's words or conduct. Thus where one person expressly or impliedly represents another to have authority to act as agent, so that a third party reasonably believes the person who is so held out to possess that authority and deals with that person in reliance on the representation so made, the person making the representation will be bound to the same extent as if actual authority had in fact been conferred.[24] The person making the representation is estopped from denying the ostensible authority which was thus created.

It is, however, important to note three things. First, the representation must be made by or with the authority of *the principal*.[25] Ostensible authority cannot be created simply by a representation by the agent.[26] Secondly, subject to certain

---

[22] *Shell Co. of Australia Ltd.* v. *Nat Shipping Bagging Services Ltd. (The Kilmun)* [1988] 2 Lloyd's Rep. 1 at p. 11. See also *Pagnan SpA* v. *Feed Products Ltd.* [1987] 2 Lloyd's Rep. 601.

[23] *Presentaciones Musicales S.A.* v. *Secunda* [1994] Ch. 271, at p. 280. See also *Ainsworth* v. *Crecke* (1868) L.R. 4 C.P. 476; *Bolton Partners* v. *Lambert* (1888) 41 Ch. D. 295.

[24] For examples of factual situations in which ostensible authority may exist, see *Egyptian Intl. Foreign Trade Co.* v. *Soplex Wholesale Supplies Ltd. (The Raffaella)* [1985] 2 Lloyd's Rep. 36; *Shearson Lehman Hutton Inc.* v. *MacLaine, Watson & Co. Ltd. (No. 2)* [1988] 1 W.L.R. 16; *Polish S.S. Co.* v. *A.J. Williams Fuels (Overseas Sales) Ltd. (The Suwalki)* [1989] 1 Lloyd's Rep. 511.

[25] *First Sport Ltd.* v. *Barclays Bank plc* [1993] 1 W.L.R. 1229.

[26] *Att.-Gen. for Ceylon* v. *Silva* [1953] A.C. 461, at p. 479; *Freeman & Lockyer* v. *Buckhurst Park Properties (Mangal) Ltd.* [1964] 2 Q.B. 480, at p. 505; *British Bank of the Middle East* v. *Sun Life Assurance Co. of Canada (U.K.) Ltd.* [1983] 2 Lloyd's Rep. 9 (H.L.). See also *First Energy (U.K.) Ltd.* v. *Hungarian Int'l Bank Ltd.* [1993] 2 Lloyd's Rep. 194.

exceptions discussed *infra*,[27] the third party must rely on a representation of the agent's authority to act *as agent*. The doctrine cannot apply where the third party does not know or believe that person to be an agent, for example, if the existence of the principal is unknown to the third party.[28] Thirdly, the agent's want of authority must be *unknown* to the third party.[29]

(ii) Absence of authority

These limitations mean that there will seldom be ostensible authority where a person has never at any time had authority to contract. But in *Freeman & Lockyer* v. *Buckhurst Park Properties (Mangal) Ltd.*:[30]

The articles of a company contained power to appoint a managing director. With the knowledge and approval of the board of directors, K acted as managing director, although he was never appointed to this post. K instructed the plaintiffs, a firm of architects, to do certain work for the company. The company disclaimed liability for payment for this work on the ground that K had no authority to contract on the company's behalf.

The Court of Appeal held that, although K had no actual authority to employ the plaintiffs, the company had created an ostensible authority by its conduct in permitting him to act as managing director to the knowledge of the board. Any act done within the usual ambit of that ostensible authority was therefore binding on the company.

(iii) Limited or revoked authority

The doctrine of ostensible authority is more likely to apply where an authorized agent goes beyond the limits of his actual authority, yet acts within an authority which he is made to appear to possess.[31] In particular, where a principal has publicly allowed the agent to assume an authority, that authority cannot be revoked privately. The principal will be bound by the acts of the agent if the principal has given other persons reason to suppose that they are done with authority.

Thus an employer who habitually allows employees to purchase goods on credit[32] or a husband who takes upon himself the liability in respect of his wife's past dealings with suppliers of goods or services[33] 'hold out' the employees or wife as agent. They will be liable on such contracts unless and until they actually make known to the supplier the fact that the agency has been determined.

---

[27] See *post*, pp. 669–70.

[28] *Farquharson Bros.* v. *King & Co.* [1902] A.C. 325; *Freeman & Lockyer* v. *Buckhurst Park Properties (Mangal) Ltd.* (*supra*, n. 26), at p. 503.

[29] See *Armagas Ltd.* v. *Mundogas SA* [1986] 1 A.C. 717 at pp. 777–9.

[30] [1964] 2 Q.B. 480. But see now Companies Act 1985, s. 35(1), and *ante*, p. 231 (*ultra vires* contracts).

[31] *Todd* v. *Robinson* (1825) 1 Ry. & M. 217; *Summers* v. *Solomon* (1857) 7 E. & B. 879; *Manchester Trust* v. *Furness* [1895] 2 Q.B. 539.

[32] *Summers* v. *Solomon* (*supra*, n. 31).

[33] *Drew* v. *Nunn* (1879) 4 Q.B.D. 661; *Jetley* v. *Hill* (1884) Cab. & El. 239. See also *Ryan* v. *Sams* (1848) 12 Q.B. 460 (mistress).

(iv) Partnership

Every partner is an agent of the firm and of the other partners for the business of the partnership; this is simply a case of implied authority. But any act done by a partner for carrying on in the usual way business of a kind carried on by the firm binds the firm and the other partners, even if the partner so acting has in fact no authority to act for the firm in the particular matter, unless the person with whom the partner is dealing either knows that person has no authority, or does not know or believe that person to be a partner.[34] Moreover, a partner who retires from a firm may still be liable for partnership debts contracted after retirement. A person dealing with a firm after a change in its constitution is entitled to treat all apparent members of the old firm as still being members of the firm until that person has notice of the change.[35] The retiring partner will be estopped from denying the continuation of that authority,[36] except where he was not known to be a partner by the person dealing with the firm.[37]

(d) USUAL OR INCIDENTAL AUTHORITY

There are a number of cases which establish that, in certain circumstances, a principal may be liable for the unauthorized acts of an agent, even though the third party did not rely upon any representation by the principal of the agent's authority to act *as agent*. In these cases, the existence of the principal was unknown to the third party, so that it could not be said that the principal held out the agent to have authority to act as agent and was estopped. The rule to be extracted from them is as follows: An undisclosed principal who employs an agent to conduct business is liable for any act of the agent which is incidental to or usual in that business, although such act may have been forbidden by the principal. For example, in *Watteau* v. *Fenwick*:[38]

F, a firm of brewers, bought a beer-house from one H, but kept him on as manager, and his name appeared above the door. They instructed H not to buy cigars on credit, although it was usual for such a business to deal in cigars. H bought some cigars on credit from W, who thought H was the owner of the business and gave credit to him personally. On discovering that he was employed by F, W sued F for the price of the cigars.

It was held that F was liable. Wills J. rejected the argument that a principal could only be bound where there had been a holding out of authority—which could not be said of this case where the person supplying the goods knew nothing of the existence of the principal. 'The principal', he said,[39] 'is liable for all the acts of the agent which are within the authority usually confided to an agent of that character, notwithstanding limitations as between the principal and the agent, put upon that authority'.

---

[34] Partnership Act 1890, s. 5. See also s. 8. See further, *United Bank of Kuwait Ltd.* v. *Hammoud* [1988] 1 W.L.R. 1051.

[35] Partnership Act 1890, s. 36(1). Under s. 36(2), notice in the *London Gazette* is sufficient notice as to persons who had no dealings with the firm before the change; otherwise express notice is required.

[36] *Scarfe* v. *Jardine* (1882) 7 App. Cas. 345, at p. 349.

[37] Partnership Act 1890, s. 36(3).

[38] [1893] 1 Q.B. 346.

[39] At p. 348.

This case is anomalous, and has been criticized as such.[40] An attempt has been made to explain it and similar cases on the grounds that they are cases of 'usual authority'. But as noted,[41] the usual authority of an agent is merely an example of implied authority, which could be negatived by an express limitation. If this and similar cases[42] are rightly decided, they are better regarded as examples of the operation of a quasi-tortious principle whereby an employer is rendered vicariously liable for the acts of an agent if done in the course of the agent's employment.

Another, somewhat archaic, category of agency in which there is no ostensible authority created by a holding out arises where two people are cohabiting. In such cases there is a rebuttable presumption that one has implied authority to pledge the credit of the other for necessaries in all domestic matters normally entrusted to the cohabitee who deals with the supplier.[43] The vast majority of the cases concern the liability of the husband for obligations incurred by his wife but the presumption is not confined to such cases.[44]

(e) AGENCY OF NECESSITY

In certain circumstances the law confers an authority on one person to act as agent for another without any regard to the consent of the principal. Such an agency is called an agency of necessity.[45] At common law the paradigm illustration of an agency of necessity was provided by the right of a wife, at common law, to supply the needs of herself and her children by pledging her husband's credit for necessaries. It was, however, abolished by legislation which gave the Courts power to make financial provision in the event of a husband's wilful neglect to maintain his wife or children.[46]

(i) Ship-masters and carriers

An agency of necessity can arise in the case of a carrier of goods or a master of a ship who, under certain circumstances of necessity, is empowered on behalf of the shipowner or the owner of the goods carried to dispose of the goods or to enter into such other contract as may be necessary, and will be considered to have their authority to do so.[47] In order that this agency of necessity should arise, it must be shown that the carrier or master:

---

[40] *Rhodian River Shipping S.A.* v. *Halla Maritime Corporation* [1984] 1 Lloyd's Rep. 373, *per* Bingham L.J. at pp. 378–9. See also Hornby [1961] C.L.J. 239.

[41] *Ante*, p. 664.

[42] It is not unique: see *Edmunds* v. *Bushell and Jones* (1865) L.R. 1 QB. 97. For further examples, see Powell, *The Law of Agency*, 2nd edn., pp. 72 ff., and *post*, p. 673.

[43] See generally *Bowstead and Reynolds on Agency*, 16th edn. (1996), §3–040A ff.

[44] *Debenham* v. *Mellon* (1680) 6 App. Cas. 24, at p. 336.

[45] See Birks [1971] C.L.P. 110; Rose (1989) 9 O.J.L.S. 167.

[46] Matrimonial Proceedings and Property Act 1970, s. 41 (on which see Cartwright-Sharp (1974) 37 M.L.R. 480). The repeal of this provision by the Matrimonial Causes Act 1973, s. 54 and Sched. 3 did not revive the doctrine.

[47] See, e.g. *The Choko Star* [1990] 1 Lloyd's Rep. 516. By the Merchant Shipping Act 1995, s. 224(1) the master of a ship has authority to conclude salvage agreements on behalf of the shipowner.

(1) took action which was the only practicable action in the circumstances;[48] thus a master of a ship who finds that the cargo is perishing rapidly is entitled to put into the nearest port and to sell the goods for the best price there obtainable;[49]

(2) had no opportunity in the time available of communicating with the principal;[50]

(3) acted honestly in the interests of the principal.

In the situations mentioned above, the acts of the agent bind the principal, and it has been suggested that the expression 'agency of necessity' should properly be confined to such situations.[51] But the expression is frequently used also to describe cases where one person, in an emergency, performs services or incurs expenditure to preserve the property or rights of another and seeks reimbursement,[52] or where a person claims to be protected against an action for wrongful interference with the property of another by pleading necessity.[53]

(ii) *Negotiorum gestio* not generally recognized

In principle, a person who voluntarily incurs expense by performing work or services which are 'necessary' to another cannot recover in the absence of some legal authority to incur the expense.[54] English law does not recognize the *negotiorum gestor* of Roman law—the person who voluntarily spends money upon the necessary protection of another.[55] So a person who finds a dog and spends money on its keep,[56] or a local authority which repairs a bridge which it is not bound to repair,[57] cannot recover from the owner of the property benefited.

Clear exceptions, however, exist in the case of salvage at sea (the owner of the cargo salvaged being bound to compensate the rescuer),[58] the supply of necessaries to mental patients,[59] and bills of exchange under section 65 of the Bills of Exchange Act 1882.[60] Any person, not being a party already liable on a bill of exchange, may, with the holder's consent, intervene and accept a bill *supra protest* for the honour of any party liable thereon, after it has been 'protested' for dishonour by non-acceptance. The acceptor for honour thereby makes himself liable to pay the bill, and succeeds to the rights and duties of the holder as regards the party for whose honour he pays, and all parties liable to that party. Apart from these recognized exceptions, there may yet

---

[48] *Prager* v. *Blatspiel, Stamp & Heacock Ltd.* [1924] 1 K.B. 566. Cf. *Surrey Breakdown Ltd.* v. *Knight* [1999] R.T.R. 84 (pulling stolen car out of pond did not qualify).

[49] *Couturier* v. *Hastie* (1852) 8 Exch. 40, reversed on a different point (1856) 5 H.L.C. 673.

[50] *Springer* v. *Great Western Ry.* [1921] 1 K.B. 257. See also *In re F* [1990] 2 A.C. 1, at p. 75.

[51] *China-Pacific S.A.* v. *Food Cpn. of India* [1982] A.C. 939.

[52] *Exall* v. *Partridge* (1799) 8 T.R. 308.

[53] See *Elvin & Powell Ltd.* v. *Plummer Roddis Ltd.* (1933) 50 T.L.R. 158; *Sachs* v. *Miklos* [1948] 2 K.B. 23; and now the Torts (Interference with Goods) Act 1977, s. 12.

[54] *Macclesfield Cpn.* v. *G. C. Ry.* [1911] 2 K.B. 528.

[55] *Falcke* v. *Scottish Imperial Insurance Co.* (1886) 34 Ch. D. 234, *per* Bowen L.J. at p. 248.

[56] *Binstead* v. *Buck* (1776) 2 W. Bl. 1117 (no lien on dog for expenses).

[57] *Macclesfield Cpn.* v. *Great Central Ry.* [1911] 2 K.B. 528.

[58] *The Five Steel Barges* (1890) 15 P.D. 142, at p. 146. See also Merchant Shipping Act 1995, s. 224(1).

[59] *Ante*, p. 235.

[60] See also Bills of Exchange Act 1882, s. 68 (payment for honour).

be other cases where, after some legal relationship has been created between the parties, one party reasonably incurs expenses in safeguarding the other's goods in a situation of necessity, and is entitled to reimbursement. Thus a carrier has recovered the expense of stabling an uncollected horse,[61] a salvor the expense of warehousing cargo after the salvage services had come to an end,[62] and statute enables a doctor who has given emergency treatment to the victim of a road accident to a fee.[63] These cases may be regarded either as an extension of the principle that an agent is entitled to be reimbursed expenses reasonably incurred on behalf of the principal[64] or as an example of a claim in restitution.[65]

II. DIFFERENT KINDS OF AGENTS

We note here the authority with which certain kinds of agents are invested in the ordinary course of their employment.

(a) AUCTIONEERS

An auctioneer is an agent to sell property at a public auction. Although primarily an agent for the seller, upon the property being knocked down, it has been held that the auctioneer becomes the agent of the buyer, but only for the purpose of signing a memorandum sufficient to satisfy the statutory formalities.[66] Auctioneers have authority to sell, but not to give warranties as to the property sold, unless expressly authorized by the seller.[67] Any deposit paid by the buyer is normally held by the auctioneer, not as agent of the seller, but as stakeholder.[68]

The seller will be bound if the auctioneer acts within his ostensible authority, even though disobeying instructions privately given. So, if an auctioneer through inadvertence, and contrary to instructions, puts up an article for sale without reserve, the seller will be bound by the sale.[69] But where there is a sale by auction with *notice* that it is subject to a reserve, the auctioneer cannot reasonably be supposed to have authority to accept a bid at less than the reserve fixed, and so cannot bind the seller by doing so.[70]

An auctioneer has a lien on goods sold until the whole price is paid, and, if not paid, can sue in its own name for the price.[71]

---

[61] *G.N. Ry.* v. *Swaffield* (1874) L.R. 9 Ex. 132.
[62] *China-Pacific S.A.* v. *Food Cpn. of India* [1982] A.C. 939.
[63] Road Traffic Act 1988, ss. 158–9.
[64] See *post*, p. 681.
[65] See *ante*, p. 23.
[66] See *Chaney* v. *Maclow* [1929] 1 Ch. 461, and *ante*, p. 77.
[67] *Payne* v. *Lord Leconfield* (1881) 51 L.J.Q.B. 642.
[68] *Skinner* v. *Trustee of Reed* [1967] Ch. 1194.
[69] *Rainbow* v. *Howkins* [1904] 2 K.B. 322, at p. 326.
[70] *McManus* v. *Fortescue* [1907] 2 K.B. 1, at p. 6.
[71] *Chelmsford Auctions Ltd.* v. *Poole* [1973] Q.B. 542. Cf. *Cherry* v. *Anderson* (1876) I.R. 10 C.L. 204 (land).

(b) FACTORS

A factor is an agent who has possession of the goods, authority to sell them in its own name, and a general discretion as to their sale. The factor may sell on the usual terms of credit, may receive the price, and give a good discharge to the buyer. At common law a factor has ostensible authority to do such things as are usual in the conduct of its business.[72]

This ostensible authority has been extended by a series of Factors Acts which were consolidated by the Factors Act 1889. The Act applies not only to factors, but also to any mercantile agent 'having in the customary course of his business as such agent authority either to sell goods, or to consign goods for the purpose of sale, or to buy goods, or to raise money on the security of goods'.[73]

Such a person is also deemed to have power to pledge the goods, and section 2 of the Act in effect provides that where a mercantile agent is, with the consent of the owner, in possession of goods[74] or of the documents of title to goods, any sale, pledge, or other disposition of the goods, made when acting in the ordinary course of business of a mercantile agent, is as valid as if it were expressly authorized by the owner of the goods. Accordingly, persons who, in good faith, take the goods under such a disposition, and who have not at the time notice that the agent has not the authority to dispose of them, acquire a good title to them. And so long as the agent is left in possession of the goods, revocation of authority by the principal cannot prejudice the rights of such persons to them.

(c) BROKERS

A broker is an agent primarily employed to negotiate a contract between two parties. A broker for sale has not got possession of the goods to be sold, and so has not got the authority which a factor enjoys. Nor has a broker the authority to sue in its own name on contracts made by it. A broker should be distinguished from a commission agent who is employed not to establish privity of contract between the principal and third parties, but to sell or buy goods for the principal at the most favourable price available. The commission agent receives a commission or reward, but the purchase or sale is made with the third party by the commission agent alone.[75]

(d) ESTATE AGENTS

An estate agent,[76] who is employed to find a purchaser for property, has implied authority to make representations or to give warranties relating to the property.[77] An estate agent has no authority to effect an actual contract for the sale of the property

---

[72] *Pickering* v. *Busk* (1812) 15 East. 38; see *ante*, p. 668.

[73] Factors Act 1889, s. 1(1).

[74] Provided that the possession is in the capacity of mercantile agent, and not e.g. solely as bailee: *Astley Industrial Trust Ltd.* v. *Miller* [1968] 2 All E.R. 386.

[75] See *Armstrong* v. *Stokes* (1872) L.R. 7 Q.B. 598; *post*, pp. 686–7 and Hill (1968) 31 M.L.R. 623.

[76] See Estate Agents Act 1979 and Property Misdescriptions Act 1991.

[77] *Mullens* v. *Miller* (1882) 22 Ch. D. 194.

unless expressly authorized so to do[78] and does not have implied authority to receive a deposit from an intending purchaser as agent of the vendor.[79]

(e) SOLICITORS

When undertaking litigation on behalf of a client, a solicitor has implied authority to accept process and appear for a client, but is not entitled to commence an action without express authority.[80] As against third parties, a solicitor has an ostensible authority to effect a compromise in all matters connected with an action and not merely collateral to it.[81] In certain circumstances solicitors have authority to receive payment on behalf of a client.[82]

(f) COMMERCIAL AGENTS

This and the following two chapters are primarily concerned with the basic principles of agency as developed by the common law. Brief mention is, however, also made of a new form of agency, unknown to the common law, which, as a result of the EC Directive on Commercial Agents, is now part of English law.[83] A commercial agent is a self employed intermediary with continuing authority to negotiate the sale or purchase of goods on behalf of the principal, or to negotiate and conclude the sale or purchase of goods on behalf of and in the name of the principal. A distributor buying from manufacturers and selling on at a mark-up has been held to deal as principal[84] and not to be a 'commercial agent', as has a person selling petrol under licence who did not 'negotiate' with the buyers of petrol.[85] Where the Regulations implementing the Directive apply, the freedom to terminate a commercial agency, at least without compensation, is restricted.

---

[78] *Hamer* v. *Sharp* (1874) L.R. 19 Eq. 108; *Law* v. *Robert Roberts & Co.* [1964] I.R. 292.

[79] *Sorrell* v. *Finch* [1977] A.C. 728.

[80] *Wright* v. *Castle* (1817) 3 Mer. 12.

[81] *Strauss* v. *Francis* (1866) L.R. 1 Q.B. 379; *Waugh* v. *H. B. Clifford & Sons Ltd.* [1982] Ch. 374.

[82] Law of Property Act 1925, s. 69; *Yates* v. *Freckleton* (1781) 2 Doug. K.B. 623.

[83] The Commercial Agents (Council Directive) Regulations 1993 (S.I. 1993 No. 3053) as amended by S.I. 1993 No. 3173 came into force on 1 January 1994.

[84] *AMB Imballaggii Plastici SRL* v. *Pacflex Ltd.* [1999] 2 All E.R. (Comm.) 249.

[85] *Parks* v. *Esso Petroleum Ltd.* [2000] Eu. L.R. 25.

22

EFFECT OF AGENCY

The effects of agency, when created as described above, may thus be arranged:

(1) the relations between the principal and agent;

(2) the relations between the principal and third parties;

(3) the relations between the agent and third parties.

I. THE RELATIONS BETWEEN THE PRINCIPAL AND AGENT

The rights and duties of the principal and agent depend upon the terms of the contract, whether express or implied, which exists between them. But in addition to these specific provisions, the mere existence of the relationship raises certain duties on both sides. In particular, an agent owes fiduciary duties to its principal. 'The distinguishing obligation of a fiduciary is the obligation of loyalty.'[1] Although it has been said that 'the essence of a fiduciary obligation is that it creates obligations of a different character from those deriving from the contract itself',[2] where the agency is based on a contract between the principal and the agent, the fiduciary duties may in certain cases be varied by the terms of the contract.[3]

(a) DUTIES OF THE AGENT

(i) To account

The agent is bound to account for such property of the principal as comes into its hands in the course of the employment. The agent must keep accurate accounts of the transactions which are entered into on the principal's behalf,[4] and produce them on demand to the principal.[5]

---

[1] *Bristol & West B.S.* v. *Motthew* [1998] 1 Ch. 1, at p. 17.

[2] *Re Goldcorp Exchange Ltd.* [1995] 1 A.C. 74, *per* Lord Mustill, at p. 98.

[3] *Clark Boyce* v. *Mouat* [1994] 1 A.C. 428; *Kelly* v. *Cooper* [1993] A.C. 205 (implied term of contract permitted estate agent to have conflict of interests). See also Law Com. No. 236, *Fiduciary Duties and Regulatory Rules* (1995), § 3.24 ff., but cf. *Bowstead and Reynolds on Agency*, 16th edn. (1996), p. 217; Brown (1993) 109 L.Q.R. 206.

[4] *White* v. *Lincoln* (1803) 8 Ves. Jun. 363.

[5] *Pearse* v. *Green* (1819) 1 Jac. & W. 135.

(ii) To use care and skill

The agent must also use ordinary diligence in the discharge of its duties, displaying any special skill or capacity which it may profess in relation to the work in hand.[6] Where the agency is gratuitous, the agent is only liable in tort; the standard of care is that which might reasonably be expected in the circumstances.[7]

If the agent fails in its duty, the normal remedy of the principal is to bring an action for damages or equitable compensation; but where the breach consists of a failure to pay across money received on behalf of the principal, an action for money had and received or an action for an account may also be brought by the principal.

(iii) Not to make secret profit

The fiduciary's obligation of loyalty has several facets. First, the agent must not, except with the knowledge and assent of the principal, make any profit from the transactions into which the agent enters on behalf of the principal[8] or from confidential information acquired in the capacity of agent.[9] It is immaterial that the principal has suffered no injury, or that the agent has acted throughout in good faith.[10] Any such profit made must be paid over to the principal. In *Hippisley* v. *Knee Brothers*:[11]

H employed K Brothers, auctioneers, to sell certain property for him, and undertook to pay them a commission on the sale and their out-of-pocket expenses, including those of printing and advertising. K received discounts from printers and advertisers, but charged H with the full amount in the honest belief that they were entitled to keep the discounts for themselves.

It was held that K were bound to account to H for the money. In this case, however, they did not forfeit their commission; but commission will not be payable to an agent who has acted dishonestly,[12] and, if paid in ignorance of the breach of duty, will be recoverable by the principal.

Where an agent is promised a bribe or secret commission which might induce the agent to act disloyally to the principal or which might diminish his interest in the affairs of the principal, the agent cannot recover the amount of the bribe from the person who promised it, since the transaction is a corrupt one and cannot be enforced.[13] If the agent has received the bribe, it can be claimed by the principal from both the agent[14] and the briber[15] on a restitutionary basis; the agent cannot recover or retain any remuneration from the principal in respect of the transaction.[16] Moreover,

---

  [6] *Lee* v. *Walker* (1872) L.R. 7 C.P. 121. See also *Luxmoore May* v. *Messenger May Baverstock* [1990] 1 W.L.R. 1009.

  [7] *Chaudhry* v. *Prabhakar* [1989] 1 W.L.R. 29.

  [8] *Parker* v. *M'Kenna* (1874) L.R. 10 Ch. App. 96; *Cook* v. *Deeks* [1916] A.C. 554; *English* v. *Dedham Vale Properties Ltd.* [1978] 1 W.L.R. 93; *Clark Boyce* v. *Mouat* [1994] 1 A.C. 428. See also *post*, p. 676.

  [9] *Phipps* v. *Boardman* [1967] 2 A.C. 46; *Guinness plc* v. *Saunders* [1990] 2 A.C. 663.

  [10] *Ibid.*

  [11] [1905] 1 K.B. 1.

  [12] *Andrews* v. *Ramsay & Co.* [1903] 2 K.B. 635. See also *Kelly* v. *Cooper* [1993] A.C. 205, at p. 216.

  [13] *Harrington* v. *Victoria Graving Dock Co.* (1878) 3 Q.B.D. 549.

  [14] *Boston Deep Sea Fishing and Ice Co.* v. *Ansell* (1888) 39 Ch. D. 339; *Logicrose Ltd.* v. *Southend United Football Club* [1988] 1 W.L.R. 1256.

  [15] *Arab Monetary Fund* v. *Hashim* [1993] 1 Lloyd's Rep. 543.

  [16] *Andrews* v. *Ramsay & Co.* [1903] 2 K.B. 635.

since the the agent is a fiduciary, if property or investments acquired with the bribe have increased in value, the principal has an equitable proprietary interest in the profits and is entitled to them.[17] Alternatively, it is open to a principal who discovers that its agent has been paid a bribe for bringing about a contract to recover from the agent and the person who paid the bribe, jointly and severally, damages in tort for any loss which the principal may have sustained by entering into the contract in respect of which the bribe was given. But the principal is bound to elect, at the time judgment is entered, between the claim for the amount of the bribe and the claim for damages. In *T. H. Mahesan s/o Thambiah* v. *Malaysia Government Officers' Co-operative Housing Society Ltd.*:[18]

A director and employee of a housing society in Malaysia dishonestly agreed with M that M should purchase certain land in Penang at a low price and sell it to the housing society at a profit, and that the director would not inform the housing society of the price at which the land was available nor the fact that M was selling the land to the housing society at more than double the price which he had paid for it. M made a gross profit of $488,000 on the transaction, one-quarter of which he passed on to the director as a bribe.

The Federal Court of Malaysia held that the housing society could recover from its director both the amount of the bribe and damages for the whole of the loss suffered by it as a result of the fraudulent transaction.[19] The Judicial Committee of the Privy Council, however, held that the housing society could recover either the amount of the bribe or damages for the loss suffered, but not both. In the result, since the loss suffered was (net) $443,000 and the amount of the bribe was $122,000, it was assumed that the housing society would have elected to claim the former sum, and judgment was entered for that amount.

The Prevention of Corruption Acts 1906 and 1916 also make corrupt transactions of all kinds by or with agents criminal offences punishable by fine and imprisonment.

(iv) Not to put itself in a position where interest and duty conflict

The agent must not put itself in a position where its duty and interest conflict unless full disclosure of the agent's interest (specifying its exact nature) has been made to the principal, and the principal has given its informed consent to the conflict.[20] So, an agent will in general be precluded from acting for two principals whose interests may conflict, unless the principals' assent has been obtained.[21]

Moreover, an agent may not cease to be an agent and become a principal party to the transaction even though this change of attitude does not result in injury to the

---

[17] *Att.-Gen. for Hong Kong* v. *Reid* [1994] 1 A.C. 324. Cf. *Fyffes Group Ltd.* v. *Templeman* [2000] 2 Lloyd's Rep. 643 (no entitlement if profits would have been earned anyway for services rendered by briber to P). See also *Petrotrade Inc.* v. *Smith* [2000] 1 Lloyd's Rep. 486.

[18] [1979] A.C. 374. See Beatson and Reynolds (1978) 94 L.Q.R. 344. Cf. Tettenborn (1979) 95 L.Q.R. 68.

[19] Relying on *dicta* of the Court of Appeal in *Mayor of Salford* v. *Lever* [1891] 1 Q.B. 168, which were disapproved by the Judicial Committee.

[20] *Clark Boyce* v. *Mouat* [1994] 1 A.C. 428; *Guinness plc* v. *Saunders* [1990] 2 A.C. 663. Cf. *Kelly* v. *Cooper* [1993] A.C. 205 (implied term of contract, *ante*, pp. 152–3).

[21] *Ibid.*

employer. If a person is employed to buy or sell on behalf of another, that person may not sell to or buy from the principal. Nor, if a person is employed to bring another (the principal) into contractual relations with a third party, may that person lawfully also act as agent for that third party.[22] Where an agent puts itself in a position where the agent has an interest in direct antagonism to its duty, or where, due to the conflict of duties, the agent's duty to the principal cannot be fully discharged, the principal is entitled to claim an account and payment over of any benefit which the agent has received as a result.[23]

(v) Not to delegate to another

The agent may not, as a general rule, delegate to another person the task undertaken by the contract of agency.[24] The reason for this rule, and its limitations, are outlined by Thesiger L.J. in *De Bussche* v. *Alt*:[25]

As a general rule, no doubt, the maxim '*delegatus non potest delegare*' applies so as to prevent an agent from establishing the relationship of principal and agent between his own principal and a third person; but this maxim when analyzed merely imports that an agent cannot, without authority from his principal, devolve upon another obligations to the principal which he has himself undertaken to personally fulfil; and that, inasmuch as confidence in the particular person employed is at the root of the contract of agency, such authority cannot be implied as an ordinary incident in the contract.

There are, however, a number of occasions when such authority is implied. These occasions arise from the conduct of the parties, the usage of a trade, the nature of a business, or an unforeseen emergency.[26] Also purely ministerial acts, which do not involve any special care and skill, can normally be delegated to another.[27]

Where an agent is authorized to delegate to another the employment of a sub-agent does not normally bring into being any privity of contract between the principal and the sub-agent. The sub-agent is responsible to the agent alone and cannot be sued directly in contract by the principal.[28] But where the principal expressly or impliedly authorizes the delegation, or ratifies a delegation which has already taken place, privity of contract is established.[29] The sub-agent becomes responsible to the principal for the due discharge of the duties which its employment casts upon it, and a fiduciary relationship arises between them. Where the sub-agent has been negligent, it may also be liable to the principal in tort, provided such liability is not inconsistent with the contractual structure put in place by the principal and agent.[30]

---

[22] *Anglo-African Merchants Ltd.* v. *Bayley* [1970] 1 Q.B. 311, at pp. 323–4; *North & South Trust Co.* v. *Berkeley* [1971] 1 W.L.R. 470.

[23] *De Bussche* v. *Alt* (1878) 8 Ch. D. 286.

[24] See e.g. *John McCann & Co.* v. *Pow* [1974] 1 W.L.R. 1643 (estate agent).

[25] (1878) 8 Ch. D. 286, at p. 310.

[26] *Ibid.*, at p. 310; *Re Newen* [1903] 1 Ch. 812; *Henderson* v. *Merrett Syndicates Ltd.* [1995] 2 A.C. 145, at p. 197 (although the agent remained under an obligation that the services would be carried out with reasonable skill and care).

[27] *Allam & Co. Ltd.* v. *Europa Poster Services Ltd.* [1968] 1 W.L.R. 639.

[28] *Kahler* v. *Midland Bank* [1952] A.C. 24. But see *Shamia* v. *Joory* [1958] 1 Q.B. 448.

[29] *Keay* v. *Fenwick* (1876) 1 C.P.D. 745; *De Bussche* v. *Alt* (1878) 8 Ch. D. 286.

[30] *Henderson* v. *Merrett Syndicates Ltd.* [1995] 2 A.C. 145.

(vi) *Del credere* agents

An agent is not normally responsible for ensuring that the parties with whom the principal is brought into contractual relations will pay the money which may become due under the contract into which they enter. But such a responsibility is assumed by a *del credere* agent. This is an agent employed for the purpose of sale who, in return for extra remuneration, undertakes to be liable to the principal for payment by the buyer. A *del credere* agent does not, however, become responsible to the buyer for the due performance of its contract by the principal.

(b) RIGHTS OF THE AGENT

(i) To be paid agreed remuneration

The principal must pay the agent such commission or reward as may be agreed upon between them. In the absence of any agreement, express or implied, the agent is not entitled to any reward,[31] although there is a presumption that a professional agent is to be remunerated.[32] Indeed, an agreement to pay remuneration will be implied whenever a person is employed to act as agent under circumstances which raise the presumption that the agent would, to the knowledge of the principal, expect to be paid.[33]

Before becoming entitled to remuneration, the agent must have carried out the duties, or fulfilled the conditions, stipulated for in the agreement. In particular, if the remuneration takes the form of a commission, the agent is not entitled to the commission until the event on which the commission is payable comes about. This question has frequently arisen in recent years in relation to commission payable to estate agents. The Courts have construed such provisions very strictly, and have said that a claim to commission, if no sale is actually made, must be established by the use of clear and unequivocal language.[34] Thus if the commission is payable 'on finding a purchaser', it has been held that a person found by an agent is not to be considered a 'purchaser' until that person actually purchases by entering into a contract.[35] And if the commission is payable on the introduction of a person 'ready, willing and able to purchase', that person is not 'willing' to purchase where the agreement is 'subject to contract' or where the prospective purchaser withdraws before completion;[36] and a prospective purchaser is not 'able' to purchase if any obstacles, whether legal or financial, would prevent the purchase.[37]

---

[31] *Reeve* v. *Reeve* (1858) 1 F. & F. 280.

[32] *Turner* v. *Reeve* (1901) 17 T.L.R. 592. See also Commercial Agents (Council Directive) Regulations 1993 (S.I. 1993 No 3053), reg. 6.

[33] *Way* v. *Latilla* [1937] 3 All E.R. 739 (H.L.). Cf. *Re Richmond Gate and Property Co.* [1965] 1 W.L.R. 335.

[34] *Luxor (Eastbourne) Ltd.* v. *Cooper* [1941] A.C. 108, at p. 129; *Ackroyd & Sons* v. *Hasan* [1960] 2 Q.B. 144, at p. 154; *Jaques* v. *Lloyd D. George & Partners Ltd.* [1968] 1 W.L.R. 625; *Harwood (trading as RSBS Group)* v. *Smith*, The Times, 8 December 1997. Cf. *Scheggia* v. *Gradwell* [1963] 1 W.L.R. 1049; *Christie Owen & Davies Ltd.* v. *Rapacioli* [1974] Q.B. 781. The test is similar where the Commercial Agents (Council Directive) Regulations 1993 (S.I. 1993 No. 3053) apply, see reg. 7.

[35] *Martin* v. *Perry & Daw* [1931] 2 K.B. 310.

[36] *Dennis Reed Ltd.* v. *Goody* [1950] 2 K.B. 277.

[37] *Dellafiora* v. *Lester* [1962] 1 W.L.R. 1208.

(ii) Opportunity to earn commission

Where the employment of an agent is on a commission basis, the commission being payable on results, there is no general rule which prevents the principal from taking a step which deprives the agent of the opportunity to earn commission. So, for example, a person who employs an estate agent is not necessarily bound to complete the sale,[38] and can sell the property elsewhere,[39] or simply refuse to sell at all.[40] But there may be an express term of the agreement to the contrary, and in some cases the Courts have been prepared to imply a term in order to give business efficacy to the contract.[41] It is difficult to imply such a term, however, if it means that the principal's business must be kept in existence simply for the agent's benefit. In *Rhodes* v. *Forwood*:[42]

An agreement by the defendant colliery owner with the plaintiffs, a firm of brokers, that for a term of seven years, or for so long as the plaintiffs should carry on business, the plaintiffs were to be the sole agents for the sale of any of the defendant's coal in Liverpool was not broken when, within five years, the defendants sold the colliery and ceased to carry on business.

The House of Lords held that the terms of the agreement did not bind the defendant to send any coal to Liverpool; they merely stipulated that, if coal was sent, the plaintiffs were to be the sole agents for its sale. There could therefore be no implication that the defendant should keep his colliery so that they might earn their commission.

On the other hand, in *Turner* v. *Goldsmith*:[43]

G agreed to employ T as his agent, canvasser, and traveller for five years. T was to do his utmost to obtain orders for, and sell, such various goods *manufactured or sold* by G as should from time to time be forwarded or submitted by sample to him. Within the period of five years G's factory was burnt down and he did not resume business. T brought an action for breach.

The Court of Appeal gave judgment in his favour. They implied a term that he was to be allowed to earn his commission. *Rhodes* v. *Forwood* was distinguished on the ground that, in that case, there not being any express contract to employ the agent, such a contract could not be implied.[44] The position differed where, as *Turner* v. *Goldsmith*, there is an express contract to employ the agent. Moreover, the Court held that the contract had not been frustrated by the fire, for the plaintiff's employment was not confined to articles manufactured by the defendant, but extended also to articles sold by him without reference to their origin.

---

[38] *Boots* v. *Christopher (E.) & Co.* [1952] 1 K.B. 89.

[39] *McCallum* v. *Hicks* [1950] 2 K.B. 271.

[40] *Luxor (Eastbourne) Ltd.* v. *Cooper* (*supra*, n. 34).   [41] See *ante*, p. 151.

[42] (1876) 1 App. Cas. 256. See also *French & Co. Ltd.* v. *Leeston Shipping Co. Ltd.* [1922] 1 A.C. 451. See also *Orient Overseas Management and Finance Ltd.* v. *File Shipping Co. Ltd.* (*The Energy Progress*) [1993] 1 Lloyd's Rep. 355.

[43] [1891] 1 Q.B. 544. See also *Warren & Co.* v. *Agdeshman* (1922) 38 T.L.R. 588; *Alpha Trading Ltd.* v. *Dunnshaw-Patten* [1981] Q.B. 290; *George Moundreas & Co. SA* v. *Navimpex Centrala Navala* [1985] 2 Lloyd's Rep. 515.

[44] *per* Lindley L.J. at p. 549.

(iii) Reimbursement and indemnity

Unless otherwise agreed, the agent must also be reimbursed by the principal for all expenses, and indemnified against all liabilities and claims, which the agent has reasonably incurred in the execution of its duties.[45] These rights of reimbursement and indemnity extend to cases where the agent has occasioned liability by an honest mistake,[46] but not where they have arisen from breach of duty or default by the agent.[47]

(iv) Lien

The agent is entitled to a lien on the goods of the principal in its possession in respect of any claim by the agent against the principal arising out of the agency.[48] The lien is a possessory and particular lien, i.e. the goods can only be retained by the agent in respect of the particular transaction, unless by agreement or custom a general lien is given in respect of any claim outstanding against the principal, whether connected with the agency or not.[49]

II. THE RELATIONS BETWEEN THE PRINCIPAL AND THIRD PARTIES

When a principal endows an agent with actual authority to contract, the principal is bound, as regards third parties, by all acts of the agent which are done within the limits of that authority. This rule is often expressed in the maxim, *Qui facit per alium, facit per se*, a person who acts through another acts in person.

The same rule applies where the agent is acting within its ostensible authority.[50] The principal will be liable to third parties even though the agent has acted for its own benefit and in fraud of the principal.[51] Where, however, the third party dealing with the agent is aware that the agent is acting for its own benefit, or where the circumstances of the transaction are such as to put the third party on enquiry, the principal is not bound.[52]

A principal also acquires rights against a third party under a contract entered into by an agent on its behalf where the agent has acted within the limits of its actual authority. Otherwise it appears that a principal must ratify a contract entered into without authority before it can acquire rights (as opposed to liabilities) against the third party.

---

[45] *Adamson* v. *Jarvis* (1827) 4 Bing. 66. See also *Islamic Republic of Iran Shipping Lines* v. *Zannis Cia. Naviera SA (The Tzelepi)* [1991] 2 Lloyd's Rep. 265.

[46] *Pettman* v. *Keble* (1850) 9 C.B. 701.

[47] *Lewis* v. *Samuel* (1846) 8 Q.B. 685.

[48] *Williams* v. *Millington* (1788) 1 H. Bl. 81, at p. 85.

[49] See e.g. *Snook* v. *Davidson* (1809) 2 Camp. 218 (factor); *John D. Hope & Co.* v. *Glendinning* [1911] A.C. 419 (stockbroker); *Barratt* v. *Gough-Thomas* [1951] Ch. 242 (solicitor).

[50] *Ante*, p. 667.

[51] *Hambro* v. *Burnand and others* [1904] 2 K.B. 10. See also Watts (2001) 117 L.Q.R. 300.

[52] *Reckitt* v. *Burnett, Pembroke & Slater Ltd.* [1929] A.C. 176.

(a) LIMITATIONS ON THE PRINCIPAL'S RIGHTS AND LIABILITIES

There are certain situations in which, although the agent contracts within its authority, the principal acquires no rights or liabilities under the contract. It should, however, be stated that these situations are of extremely narrow application and (with one exception) of limited importance at the present day.

(i) Agent party to deed

Technically, if an agent is a party to a deed on behalf of another, the principal cannot sue or be sued on the deed unless described in the deed as party to it, and the deed is executed in the principal's name.[53] But in practice this rule is now a dead letter,[54] and cannot in any event be applied in the case of powers of attorney,[55] and contracts into which the agent enters as trustee for the principal.[56]

(ii) Foreign principal

It was once thought to be a rule of law that a foreign principal could not sue or be sued on a contract entered into on its behalf, the agent only being liable on the contract.[57] But in modern conditions of trade this rule has no validity.[58] At the most it is but one factor to be taken into account in determining the true intent of the contract, and its weight may be minimal.[59]

(iii) Bills of exchange

A principal is not liable upon any bill of exchange or negotiable instrument unless its name is signed thereon;[60] but if it is signed there by an agent acting with authority, the principal will be liable.[61]

(iv) Undisclosed principal

The only substantial limitations upon the principal's rights and liabilities are those which are imposed in the case of an 'undisclosed principal', i.e. where the fact of the agency is not disclosed to the other party at the time that the contract is made. Normally, where an agent acts on behalf of a principal whose existence is not, at the time, disclosed, the principal can, when discovered, sue and be sued under the contract. The contractual relationship with the undisclosed principal is not separate from the subsisting contractual relationship between the agent and the other party.[62] This doctrine of the undisclosed principal is peculiar to English law, and has sometimes

---

[53] *Schack* v. *Anthony* (1813) 1 M. & S. 573.

[54] Law of Property Act 1925, ss. 56(1), 74(3); see *ante*, p. 447.

[55] Powers of Attorney Act 1971, s. 7 as amended by the Law of Property (Miscellaneous Provisions) Act 1989, Scheds. 1 and 2.

[56] *Harmer* v. *Armstrong* [1934] Ch. 65.

[57] *Elbinger Actiengesellschaft* v. *Claye* (1873) LR. 8 Q.B. 313, at p. 317.

[58] *Teheran-Europe Co. Ltd.* v. *S. T. Belton (Tractors) Ltd.* [1968] 2 Q.B. 545.

[59] *Ibid.*, at pp. 553, 558, 562. See also *Tudor Marine Ltd.* v. *Tradax Export S.A.* [1976] 2 Lloyd's Rep. 135.

[60] Bills of Exchange Act 1882, ss. 23, 89.

[61] *Ibid.*, s. 91. See also Companies Act 1985, s. 37.

[62] *Welsh Development Agency* v. *Export Finance Co.* [1992] B.C.L.C. 148 at pp. 173, 182.

been criticized as an anomaly, since it runs counter to the principles of privity of contract.[63] But it would seem to serve a useful commercial purpose, and is further subject to the qualification that the authority must have been in existence at the time the contract was made. As we have seen, it is not possible to ratify a contract unless the principal is named therein, or is at any rate identifiable. Otherwise it would be open to any stranger to intervene and sue.[64]

But the right of the undisclosed principal to intervene as a contracting party is subject to certain limitations.[65]

First, intervention is excluded if the contract is in terms which import that the agent is the real and only principal, for then the idea of agency is incompatible with the terms of the contract. Thus, in *Humble* v. *Hunter*,[66] where an agent in making a charterparty described himself therein as 'owner' of the ship, it was held that evidence was not admissible to prove that another person was the real owner and that he was merely acting as agent on his behalf. His principal could not intervene, nor could he be sued. On the other hand, where the agent was described as 'charterer',[67] 'land-lord',[68] 'tenant',[69] and even 'disponent owner',[70] evidence has been admitted to show who the real principal was. It may be that in modern law intervention of the principal will only be excluded by descriptive words where such intervention would clearly be inconsistent with the object and intent of the contract.[71]

Secondly, where the personality of the agent is of such importance that the contract must be taken to have been made with that person alone, no one else can interpose and adopt the contract.[72] For example, in the case where there is an agreement to write a book,[73] or to underwrite shares in a company,[74] or to purchase goods subject to a right of set-off,[75] if the agent contracts in its own name without disclosure of the agency, the principal cannot intervene. Of course, if the third party subsequently discovers the identity of the principal, and with an opportunity of affirming or

---

[63] Pollock (1888) 3 L.Q.R. 359; Ames, *Lectures on Legal History*, p. 453. In continental systems the absence of the doctrine of privity of contract makes such a principle commercially unnecessary. Cf. Müller-Freienfels (1953) 16 M.L.R. 299. Arguably, it can, however, be regarded as a form of assignment: see *Siu Yin Kwan* v. *Eastern Insurance Co. Ltd.* [1994] 2 A.C. 199 at p 209.

[64] *Keighley, Maxstead & Co.* v. *Durant* [1901] A.C. 240; *ante*, p. 665.

[65] See Goodhart and Hamson (1932) 4 C.L.J. 320.

[66] (1848) 12 Q.B. 310. See also *Formby* v. *Formby* (1910) 102 L.J. 116 ('proprietor'); *Asty Maritime Co. Ltd. and Panagiotis Stravelakis* v. *Rocco Guiseppe & Figli, S.N.C. (The Astyanax)* [1985] 2 Lloyd's Rep. 109 ('disponent owner').

[67] *Drughorn (Fred.) Ltd.* v. *Rederiaktiebolaget Transatlantic* [1919] A.C. 203.

[68] *Epps* v. *Rothnie* [1945] K.B. 562.

[69] *Danziger* v. *Thompson* [1944] K.B. 654.

[70] *O/Y Wasa S.S. Co.* v. *Newspaper Pulp and Wood Exports* (1949) 82 Ll. L.R. 936. Cf. *Asty Maritime Co. Ltd. and Panagiotis Stravelakis* v. *Rocco Guiseppe & Figli, S.N.C. (The Astyanax)* (*supra*, n. 66).

[71] See e.g., *J. H. Rayner (Mincing Lane) Ltd.* v. *Department of Trade and Industry* [1989] Ch 72 at pp. 190–1 and *Welsh Development Agency* v. *Export Finance Co.* [1992] B.C.L.C. 148 at pp. 159.

[72] But see *Said* v. *Butt* [1920] 3 K.B. 497, *ante*, p. 313. Cf. *Dyster* v. *Randall & Sons* [1926] Ch. 932.

[73] *Boulton* v. *Jones* (1857) 2 H. & N. 564, *per* Bramwell B. at p. 566.

[74] *Collins* v. *Associated Greyhound Racecourses Ltd.* [1930] 1 Ch. 1.

[75] *Boulton* v. *Jones* (*supra*, n. 73), *ante*, p. 326; *Greer* v. *Downs Supply Co.* [1927] 2 K.B. 28.

rejecting the contract, elects to affirm it, as, for example, by retaining goods purchased, the third party will be bound to the principal, but not otherwise.[76]

In any case, a person who contracts with an agent, honestly and reasonably believing the agent to be the principal party to the transaction, is entitled to set up against the principal, when discovered, any set-off which is available against the agent, and which accrued before the person knew that the party with whom the contract was made was in fact an agent.[77] This rule rests upon the doctrine of estoppel.[78] But a person who has not been misled cannot claim such a set-off. So in a case where a man dealt with brokers whom he knew to be in the habit of selling, sometimes as brokers for principals, and sometimes on their own account, he could not set off his indebtedness to the brokers against his debt to the principal.[79]

Upon discovering the principal, the other contracting party may elect to sue either the agent or the principal. Any act which unequivocally indicates the adoption of either principal or agent as the party liable determines the election, and the contracting party cannot afterwards sue the other.[80]

(v) Dispositions of land

A contract for the sale or other disposition of land must be in writing 'signed *by or on behalf* of each party to the contract'.[81] Although, as we have noted, the contract to which the undisclosed principal is a party is generally normally considered not to be separate from the contract between the agent and the other party,[82] the sub-section would seem to preclude an undisclosed or an unnamed principal from suing or being sued on contracts signed by their agents.[83] But the Law Commission's Working Paper stated that 'plainly agents should be permitted to sign on behalf of the parties' and that it was intended to 'let the ordinary principles of agency operate',[84] and the Commission's Report indicates that its recommendations were made on this basis.[85] So, it is arguable that, as was the case before the enactment of the 1989 Act,[86] an agent signs 'on behalf of' the principal whenever the contract is signed with authority and the agent intends to act on behalf of the principal.

---

[76] *Greer* v. *Downs Supply Co.* [1927] 2 K.B. 28, at p. 33.

[77] *Isberg* v. *Bowden* (1853) 8 Exch. 852, at p. 859; *Montagu* v. *Forwood* [1893] 2 Q.B. 350.

[78] *Cooke* v. *Eshelby* (1887) 12 App. Cas. 271, *per* Lord Watson at p. 278.

[79] *Cooke* v. *Eshelby* (*supra*, n. 78).

[80] *Scarf* v. *Jardine* (1882) 7 App. Cas. 345. Cf. *Clarkson Booker Ltd.* v. *Andjel* [1964] 2 Q.B. 775; *Pyxis Special Shipping Co. Ltd.* v. *Dritsas & Kaglis Bros. Ltd.* [1978] 2 Lloyd's Rep. 380 (institution of legal proceedings not conclusive). See Reynolds (1970) 86 L.Q.R. 318.

[81] Law of Property (Miscellaneous Provisions) Act 1989, s. 2(3), *ante*, p. 81.

[82] *Welsh Development Agency* v. *Export Finance Co.* (*ante*, n. 71).

[83] See *Bowstead and Reynolds on Agency*, 16th edn. (1996), p. 363.

[84] Law Com. W.P. No. 92 (1985), § 5.16.

[85] Law Com. No. 164 (1987), § 4.8.

[86] *Basma* v. *Weekes* [1950] A.C. 441, at p. 454, on the Law of Property Act 1925, s. 40.

(b) MISREPRESENTATION OR NON-DISCLOSURE BY THE AGENT

When a contract is made through an agent and a misrepresentation is made by the agent or, if the contract is one *uberrimae fidei*,[87] the agent fails to disclose a material fact, a number of remedies may be open to the third party.

(i) Rescission

Misrepresentation or non-disclosure renders the contract voidable by the other party just as would misrepresentation or non-disclosure on the part of the principal. The other contracting party may rescind the agreement, or set up the misrepresentation as a defence to an action for specific performance or otherwise.

(ii) Liability of principal in deceit

A principal who expressly authorizes an agent to make a statement which the principal knows to be false, or who knows that the agent has made or will make such a statement, yet deliberately does not intervene, will be liable in deceit. So, for example, a landlord who knows of facts which would deter a prospective tenant from taking a lease of a house, and deliberately employs an agent in order that it might be innocently represented that the house is sound, will be liable to an action for damages for fraud.[88] A principal is also responsible for fraudulent misrepresentations made by the agent in the course of its employment under the normal rules of vicarious liability.[89]

One of the most difficult problems, however, is to know how far the knowledge of the agent that the representation is false can be attributed to the principal. In general it is true to say that where the state of mind of a party to a contract is material, the law regards the principal and agent as one.[90] Thus in a contract *uberrimae fidei*, if there is a failure to disclose material facts which are known to the agent but not to the principal, or vice versa, the contract may be avoided.[91] But this formula is correct only 'where the employment of the agent is such that in respect of the particular matter in question, he really does represent the principal'.[92] So, if, for example, the agent of an insurance company assists the proposer by filling in the proposal form, and does so in such a way as to mislead the company, the policy is voidable by the company. No knowledge of the inaccuracies will be attributed to the company, for the agent is not employed by them to fill in proposal forms; but knowledge will be attributed to the proposer, for the company's agent became the proposer's agent for the matter in question.[93] Again, the knowledge of a person whose agency has been determined before the insurance policy sued upon had been made cannot be imputed to the principal.[94]

---

[87] *Ante*, p. 264.   [88] *Ludgater* v. *Love* (1881) 44 L.T. 694.

[89] *Lloyd* v. *Grace, Smith & Co.* [1912] A.C. 716.

[90] *Pearson (S.) & Son Ltd.* v. *Dublin Corporation* [1907] A.C. 351 (principal believes to be true, but agent knows to be false). See also Watts (2001) 117 L.Q.R. 300.

[91] *Blackburn, Low & Co.* v. *Vigors* (1887) 12 App. Case. 531, at p. 541.

[92] *Ibid.*, *per* Lord Halsbury at p. 538.

[93] *Biggar* v. *Rock Life Assurance Co. Ltd.* [1902] 1 K.B. 516; *Newsholme Bros.* v. *Road Transport etc. Insurance Co. Ltd.* [1929] 2 K.B. 365. Cf. *Stone* v. *Reliance Mutual Insurance Society* [1972] 1 Lloyd's Rep. 463.

[94] *Blackburn, Low & Co.* v. *Vigors* (1887) 12 App. Cas. 531. This case was decided before the Marine Insurance Act 1906: *ante*, p. 265.

But even where the knowledge of the principal and agent can be treated as one, in order for an action in *deceit* to lie in respect of a representation by an agent, it must be shown that one of the two was dishonest. If, upon examination, the facts resolve themselves into an 'innocent division of ingredients',[95] no deceit will be established. Although the principal knows facts which falsify the agent's representation, this does not make the principal guilty of deceit.[96] An innocent state of mind on the part of the agent cannot be added to an innocent state of mind on the part of the principal so as to produce fraud.

(iii) Negligence

It is a moot point how far these same principles would apply if a third party sought to make the principal liable in damages for negligent misstatement or under section 2(1) of the Misrepresentation Act 1967.[97] Both at common law and under the Act,[98] the principal may be liable in damages for a misrepresentation made by the agent, acting within the scope of its authority, as if the misrepresentation had been made by the principal. Although the misrepresentation may have been made by the agent without negligence and with reasonable ground to believe and belief in its truth, it may be that knowledge or means of knowledge on the part of the principal, or of a fellow agent or of an employee of the principal, of facts which would show the representation to be untrue would, in certain circumstances, be sufficient to render the principal liable in negligence or under the Act.[99]

(c) SETTLEMENT WITH THE AGENT

It often happens that either the principal or the third party incurs a debt to the other under a contract made through an agent. The principal or the third party thereupon settles with the agent, intending that the agent should pay across the money and so discharge the debt. Sometimes, however, the agent fails to do so, and makes away with the money or becomes bankrupt. Is the debtor then liable to pay over again? The answer will depend on whether it is the principal or the third party who is making the payment.

(i) Payment by principal

Where the principal pays the agent, the general rule is that the principal is not discharged.[100] But where there are indications that the third party looks to the agent alone for payment and in consequence the principal settles with the agent,[101] or where the third party's conduct leads the principal to suppose that the debt has already been

---

[95] Devlin (1937) 53 L.Q.R. 344; *Armstrong v. Strain* [1951] 1 T.L.R. 856, *per* Devlin J. at p. 871.
[96] *Armstrong v. Strain* [1952] 1 K.B. 232; *Armagas Ltd. v. Mundogas SA* [1986] A.C. 717.
[97] See *ante*, p. 248.
[98] *Gosling v. Anderson* (1972) 223 E.G. 1743.
[99] Cf. Atiyah and Treitel (1967) 30 M.L.R. 369, at p. 374.
[100] *Irvine & Co. v. Watson & Sons* (1880) 5 Q.B.D. 414.
[101] *Smith v. Ferrand* (1827) 7 B. & C. 191.

paid,[102] the third party is estopped from claiming to be paid over again. Normally, however, this is not the case. Where the third party knows that the agent is contracting on behalf of a principal, this indicates that the third party did not look exclusively to the agent for payment.[103] It is necessary to show conduct by the third party which would estop it from proceeding against the principal, or a custom of the trade to this effect.

If an undisclosed principal pays the agent for the price of goods sold to it, there is authority for saying that, once the existence of the undisclosed principal is discovered, the seller cannot sue the undisclosed principal.[104] This decision proceeded on the ground that a demand for payment could not be made from 'those who were only discovered to be principals after they had fairly paid the price to those whom the vendor believed to be the principals, and to whom alone the vendor gave credit'.[105] But this case is contrary to earlier authority,[106] and it was subsequently criticized by the Court of Appeal.[107] No estoppel could legitimately arise since the seller was unaware of the undisclosed principal's existence, and thus could not have induced it to settle with the agent. It may therefore be that it does not represent the law.

(ii) Payment by third party

If it is the third party who settles with the agent, again the general rule is that the third party is not discharged. The reason for this is that an agent who is authorized to sell is not necessarily authorized to accept the purchase money.[108] Payment, however, to an agent who has such authority, either from an express mandate of the principal or in the ordinary course of business, will constitute a good discharge.[109] It would also seem that where the principal is undisclosed, payment to the agent before disclosure would be effective, for the principal has led the third party to believe that the agent is dealing on its own account.[110]

III. THE RELATIONS BETWEEN THE AGENT AND THIRD PARTIES

An agent who is employed to establish privity of contract between the principal and a third party, in most instances will acquire no rights and incur no liabilities in respect of the contract which is entered in the capacity of agent. But 'it is not the law that, if a

---

[102] *Wyatt* v. *Hertford (Marquis of)* (1802) 3 East 147.

[103] *Irvine & Co.* v. *Watson & Sons* (1880) 5 Q.B.D. 414.

[104] *Armstrong* v. *Stokes* (1872) L.R. 7 Q.B. 598.

[105] At p. 610.

[106] *Heald* v. *Kenworthy* (1855) 10 Exch. 739, at p. 745.

[107] *Irvine & Co.* v. *Watson & Sons* (1880) 5 Q.B.D. 414, *per* Bramwell L.J. at p. 417.

[108] *Butwick* v. *Grant* [1924] 2 K.B. 483.

[109] *Howard* v. *Chapman* (1831) 4 C. & P. 508; *International Sponge Importers* v. *Watt* [1911] A.C. 279.

[110] *Curlewis* v. *Birkbeck* (1863) 3 F. & F. 894. Cf. *Drakeford* v. *Piercy* (1866) 7 B. & S. 515.

principal is liable, his agent cannot be',[111] and the agent may be found to have undertaken personal liability.[112] It is therefore our first task to discover the circumstances in
which an agent may be under a personal liability.

(a) PERSONAL LIABILITY OF THE AGENT

Where an agent contracts, as agent, for a named principal, so that the other party to
the contract looks through the agent to a principal whose name is disclosed, it may be
laid down, as a general rule, that the agent drops out of the transaction as soon as the
contract is made. The agent acquires neither rights nor liabilities.

This matter is, however, always one of the proper construction to be put upon the
conduct of the parties where the contract is oral, or upon the wording of the document and the surrounding circumstances if it is written.[113] There are, also other cases
in which the law holds an agent personally liable, even though the agent contracts on
behalf of the principal.

(i) Agent undertakes liability

There is nothing to prevent both principal and agent being severally liable on, and
entitled to enforce, a contract which the agent has made on behalf of the principal, if
that was the intention of the parties.[114] The agent may, for example, expressly or
impliedly undertake liability for payment,[115] or may be considered to have done so by
trade usage.[116] Or the document in which the contract is written may give no indication that the agent was acting as such, although both parties knew this to be the case:
'Where a person signs a contract in his own name, without qualification, he is *prima
facie* to be deemed to be a person contracting personally: and, in order to prevent this
liability from attaching, it must be apparent from the other portions of the document
that he did not intend to bind himself as principal'.[117]

(ii) Agent party to a deed

An agent who is party to a deed is bound thereby even though described as agent,[118]
except possibly where the agent is acting under a power of attorney.[119]

---

[111] *Yeung Kai Yung* v. *Hong Kong and Shanghai Banking Cpn* [1981] A.C. 787, *per* Lord Scarman at p. 795.

[112] See Reynolds (1969) 85 L.Q.R. 92.

[113] *Chapman* v. *Smith* [1907] 2 Ch. 97, at p. 103. See also *Elpis Maritime Co. Ltd.* v. *Marti Chartering Co.
Inc. (The Maria D)* [1992] 1 A.C. 21; *Punjab National Bank* v. *De Boinville* [1992] 1 W.L.R. 1138, at p. 1155.

[114] *The Swan* [1968] 1 Lloyd's Rep. 5, at pp. 13–14.

[115] *Hall* v. *Ashurst* (1833) 1 C. & M. 714; *Rusholme & Bolton, etc. Ltd.* v. *S. G. Read & Co.* [1955] 1 W.L.R.
146; *Format International Security Printers Ltd.* v. *Mosden* [1975] 1 Lloyd's Rep. 37; *Fraser* v. *Equitorial
Shipping Co. Ltd.* [1979] 1 Lloyd's Rep. 103.

[116] *Fleet* v. *Murton* (1871) L.R. 7 Q.B. 126; *Perishables Transport Co.* v. *Spyropoulos* [1964] 2 Lloyd's Rep. 379.

[117] *2 Smith's Leading Cases,* 12th edn., p. 379; *Brandt (H.O.) & Co. Ltd.* v. *Morris (H. N.) & Co. Ltd.* [1917]
2 K.B. 784; *Hichens Harrison Woolston & Co.* v. *Jackson* [1943] A.C. 266, at p. 273; *Tudor Marine Ltd.* v. *Tradax
Export S.A.* [1976] 2 Lloyd's Rep. 134. Cf. *The Santa Carina* [1977] 1 Lloyd's Rep. 478 (oral contract); *Seatrade
Gronigen B.V.* v. *Geest Industries Ltd.* [1996] 2 Lloyd's Rep. 375 (signature had to be read in conjunction with
other parts of document).

[118] *Appleton* v. *Binks* (1804) 5 East 148.

[119] Powers of Attorney Act 1971, s. 7(1), as amended by the Law of Property (Miscellaneous Provisions)

(iii) Negotiable instruments

Secondly, an agent who signs as party to a negotiable instrument, such as a bill of exchange or promissory note, either as drawer, indorser, or acceptor, will be personally liable even though words which describe the agent as such, or as filling a representative character, are added to the signature.[120] The agent must go even further and indicate clearly that the signature is only on the principal's behalf. Thus the addition of the words 'receiver',[121] 'executor',[122] or 'director'[123] will not necessarily relieve the agent of liability; but such expressions as 'for and on behalf of X as agent', or *'per pro'* will do so.[124]

(iv) Foreign principal

Although there is no rule of law to the effect that an agent who contracts on behalf of a foreign principal will be personally liable, the fact that a principal is a foreigner may be of some weight in determining whether the mutual intention of the third party and the agent was that the agent should be personally liable to be sued as well as the principal, particularly if credit has been extended by the third party.[125]

(v) Principal not in existence

An agent who contracts on behalf of a non-existent principal (for example a company before it has been incorporated) risks incurring personal liability on the contract so made.[126] At common law this was a question of construction. While the Court may assume that the agent making the contract would be personally liable,[127] there was no rule of law that an agent is automatically a party whenever there is no principal capable of being bound by the agreement.[128] The construction of the particular contract, and the signature on the contract may show that it was made with the principal alone, so that the agent acquires neither rights[129] nor liabilities[130] under the contract. Section 36C(1) of the Companies Act 1985,[131] however, provides that a contract which purports to be made by or on behalf of a company at a time when the company has not been formed has effect, subject to any agreement to the contrary, as one made with the person purporting to act for the company or as agent for it, and he

---

Act 1989, ss. 1(8) and 4. This exception probably only applies where the principal is named in the deed: *Harmer* v. *Armstrong* [1934] Ch. 65.

[120] Bills of Exchange Act 1882, s. 26. Cf. *ibid.,* s. 17. See also Companies Act 1985, s. 349(4). Cf. *Bondina* v. *Rollaway Shower Blinds Ltd.* [1986] 1 W.L.R. 517.

[121] *Kettle* v. *Dunster and Wakefield* (1927) 43 T.L.R. 770.

[122] *Liverpool Bank* v. *Walker* (1859) 4 De G. & J. 24.

[123] *Elliott* v. *Bax-Ironside* [1925] 2 K.B. 301.

[124] *Elliott* v. *Bax-Ironside* [1925] 2 K.B. 301, *per* Scrutton L.J. at p. 307; Bills of Exchange Act 1882, ss. 25, 31(5).

[125] *Teheran-Europe Co. Ltd.* v. *S. T. Belton (Tractors) Ltd.* [1968] 2 Q.B. 545, at p. 558; see *ante,* p. 682.

[126] *Kelner* v. *Baxter* (1866) L.R. 2 C.P. 174, *ante,* pp. 665–6.

[127] *Ibid.,* per Willes J. at p. 185.

[128] *Black* v. *Smallwood* (1966) 117 C.L.R. 52 (Australia).

[129] *Newborne* v. *Sensolid (Great Britain) Ltd.* [1954] 1 Q.B. 45.

[130] *Hollman* v. *Pullin* (1884) 1 Cab. & El. 254.

[131] Inserted by the Companies Act 1989, s. 130(4).

is personally liable on the contract accordingly. This provision applies whatever the form of the signature, i.e. whether the agent signs on behalf of the company or as the company itself.[132] It also seems that the person concerned can sue as well as be sued.

(vi) Misrepresentation

An agent who, while acting on behalf of the principal, is guilty of deceit, will be liable in damages in tort. Although, in certain circumstances, such an agent may also be liable for negligent misstatement,[133] where the principal owes a duty of care to the third party, it has been stated that the existence of a further duty of care is not necessary for the reasonable protection of the third party and that 'caution should be exercised before the law takes the step of concluding . . . that an agent acting within the scope of his authority on behalf of a known principal, himself owes to third parties a duty of care independent of the duty of care he owes to his principal'.[134] But it has been held that an agent cannot, *as agent*, be made liable in damages under section 2(1) of the Misrepresentation Act 1967.[135]

(vii) Unnamed principal

An agent who contracts as agent, but does *not* disclose the name of the principal, is also, as a rule, not personally liable on the contract which is made. Yet here too, as where the name of the principal is disclosed, the matter is one of construction.[136] But, although there is a *prima facie* rule that the agent drops out of the transaction, the terms of the contract or trade usage may again indicate a contrary intention.[137]

(b) 'AGENT' ACTING AS PRINCIPAL

Is it possible for a person who has purported to contract as agent for an unnamed principal, to state that he or she is in fact the real principal? The answer is that this is possible, for if the other party to the contract was willing to take the liability of an unknown person, it is hard to suppose that the agent was the one person in the world with whom the other party was unwilling to contract. At any rate, the character or the solvency of the unnamed principal could not have induced the contract. Thus in *Schmaltz* v. *Avery*:[138]

---

[132] *Phonogram Ltd.* v. *Lane* [1982] Q.B. 938.

[133] *Smith* v. *Eric S. Bush* [1990] 1 A.C. 831 (mortgagee's valuer); *Henderson* v. *Merrett Syndicates Ltd.* [1995] A.C. 145; *Resolute Maritime Inc.* v. *Nippon Kaiji Kyokai* [1983] 1 W.L.R. 857, at p. 861 (ship-brokers); *Dodds and Dodds* v. *Millman* (1964) 45 D.L.R. (2d) 472 (Canada).

[134] *Gran Gelato Ltd.* v. *Richcliff (Group) Ltd.* [1992] Ch 560, *per* Nicholls V.-C. at p. 571 (solicitor). See also *McCullagh* v. *Lane Fox & Partners Ltd.* (1996) 49 Con. L.R. 124 (estate agent); Cane (1992) 108 L.Q.R. 539.

[135] *Resolute Maritime Inc.* v. *Nippon Kaiji Kyokai* [1983] 1 W.L.R. 857 (despite the fact that s. 2(1) provides that 'the person making the misrepresentation' is to be liable).

[136] *Fleet* v. *Murton* (1871) L.R. 7 Q.B. 126, at p. 131.

[137] *Southwell* v. *Bowditch* (1876) 1 C.P.D. 374, at p. 376; *Hichens, Harrison Woolston & Co* v. *Jackson & Sons* [1943] A.C. 266; *Perishables Transport Co.* v. *N. Spyropoulos (London) Ltd.* [1964] 2 Lloyd's Rep. 379.

[138] (1851) 16 Q.B. 655. See also *Harper & Co.* v. *Vigers* [1909] 2 K.B. 549. Cf. *Sharman* v. *Brandt* (1871) L.R. 6 Q.B. 720.

S entered into a contract of charterparty with D. S described themselves as 'agents of the freighter', and it was provided in the contract that, since they were contracting 'on behalf of another party', all personal liability on their part should cease when the cargo was shipped. They then revealed themselves as principals and sought to enforce the charterparty.

It was held that they were entitled to do so. In this case, the 'agent' was allowed to sue on the contract, and by the same token ought similarly to incur liability under it.

(c) UNDISCLOSED PRINCIPAL

If the agent acts on behalf of a principal whose existence is not at the time disclosed (the 'undisclosed principal'),[139] the other contracting party, when discovering the true facts, is entitled to elect whether to treat the principal or the agent as the party with whom the contract was made.

The reason for this rule is plain. If T enters into a contract with A, T is entitled at all events to treat A, the party with whom T supposed the contract was made, as liable. If T subsequently discovers that A is in fact the representative of P, T is entitled to choose whether to accept the actual state of things, and treat P as the party to the contract, or whether to adhere to the supposed state of things upon which the contract was entered, and continue to treat A as the party to it.

The liability of the agent continues until the other contracting party has done some act which unequivocally indicates that it regards the principal as the party solely liable.[140]

(d) UNAUTHORIZED ACTS OF THE AGENT

Where a person purports to act as agent for a named principal but without any authority to do so, the party who was thus induced to enter into a contract has one of three remedies if damage has been suffered as a result.

(i) Breach of warranty of authority

First, the other party may sue on a warranty of authority. This is an implied promise on the part of the professed agent that, in consideration of the other party entering into the contract, the professed agent warrants the existence of a principal and that the contract is within the authority conferred by that principal.[141]

This rule applies not only to transactions or representations which would result in contract, but also to any representation of authority whereby one induces another to act detrimentally.[142] It is immaterial that the agent had no knowledge or means of knowledge that it was acting without authority, for 'moral innocence, so far as the person who has been induced to contract is concerned, in no way aids that person or

[139] See *ante*, p. 682.
[140] See *ante*, p. 684.
[141] *Collen* v. *Wright* (1857) 8 E. & B. 647; *Penn* v. *Bristol and West Building Society* [1997] 1 W.L.R. 1356.
[142] *Starkey* v. *Bank of England* [1903] A.C. 114.

alleviates the inconvenience and damage which he sustains'.[143] Liability is based on a promise implied by law. The warranty is, moreover, a continuing warranty, and therefore the agent is liable even though the authority, though valid at the time of the contract, has, unknown to the agent, been determined, as by the death or mental incapacity of the principal.[144]

(ii) Deceit

Secondly, if the professed agent knew that it had not the authority which it was assumed to possess, it may be sued by the third party in an action for deceit.[145]

(iii) Negligence

Finally, if the agent failed to take reasonable care in representing the existence or extent of its authority, it may be liable in damages for negligent misstatement.[146]

---

[143] *Collen* v. *Wright* (*supra*, n. 141), *per* Willes J. at p. 657. See also *Suart* v. *Haigh* (1893) 9 T.L.R. 488 (H.L.); *Yonge* v. *Toynbee* [1910] 1 K.B. 215; *post*, p. 695.

[144] See *post*, pp. 694, 695.

[145] *Polhill* v. *Walter* (1832) 3 B. & Ad. 114; *ante*, p. 245.

[146] *Hedley Byrne & Co. Ltd.* v. *Heller & Partners Ltd.* [1964] A.C. 465, at p. 532. See also *Smith* v. *Eric S. Bush* [1990] 1 A.C. 831; *Caparo Industries plc* v. *Dickman* [1990] 2 A.C. 605; *Spring* v. *Guardian Assurance plc* [1995] 2 A.C. 296; *White* v. *Jones* [1995] 2 A.C. 207; *Henderson* v. *Merrett Syndicates Ltd.* [1995] 2 A.C. 145; *Williams* v. *Natural Life Foods Ltd.* [1998] 1 W.L.R. 830.

23

TERMINATION OF AGENT'S AUTHORITY

An agent's authority may either be terminated by the act of the parties, or by operation of law. In certain circumstances, however, it will be irrevocable, and, where the Commercial Agents Regulations 1993 apply, although the agent's *authority* can be terminated, there are restrictions on the principal's ability to terminate the agency contract.[1]

I. MODES OF TERMINATION

(a) ACT OF THE PARTIES

The relation of principal and agent is generally founded on mutual consent, and may be brought to a close by the same process which originated it, by agreement.

It may also be determined, so far as the principal and the agent are concerned, by an express revocation on the part of the principal, or an express renunciation on the part of the agent, although this will not affect the rights of third parties under the doctrine of ostensible authority.[2] Agency is thus *prima facie* determinable unilaterally and at will, subject, of course, to any claim which either party may have for breach of contract.

The principal may expressly or impliedly contract not to revoke the agent's authority during a fixed period, or until the agent has carried out the act which has been authorized. In such a case the authority is sometimes loosely said to be 'irrevocable', but this is incorrect. The authority will be effectively revoked, at least from the time that the agent 'accepts' the revocation as a repudiatory breach.[3] But the principal will be compelled to pay the agent damages for breach of contract, or to provide an indemnity against any liability already incurred. The revocation is therefore effective, but unlawful.

The notice of the revocation may be given in any form, even if the original

---

[1] The Commercial Agents (Council Directive) Regulations 1993 (S.I. 1993 No. 3053) (as amended by S.I. 1993 No. 3173), regs. 14–15, 17.

[2] *Ante*, p. 667.

[3] Cf. *Atlantic Underwriting Agencies Ltd.* v. *Cia. di Assicurazione di Milano S.p.A.* [1979] 2 Lloyd's Rep. 240 (non-acceptance of repudiatory breach; see *ante*, p. 566).

authority was conferred by deed,[4] and it can take effect immediately unless the parties otherwise provide in the agreement. But where the agency is a continuing one, and analogous to a contract of service, the agent undertaking to serve the principal and the principal to pay for the services rendered, there is an implied term in the contract that the agency will not be revoked summarily, but only on reasonable notice.[5]

(b) OPERATION OF LAW

There are certain circumstances which will put an end to the relationship of principal and agent by operation of law.

(i) Insolvency

The insolvency of either the principal[6] or the agent[7] will determine an agency for most purposes. But the appointment of a receiver or the cessation of business by the agent will not.[8]

(ii) Frustration

An agency which is created to deal with certain subject-matter will normally be frustrated by the destruction of that subject-matter.[9] So, for example, if an agent is employed to effect an insurance on a particular piece of property, and the property is destroyed by fire, the agency determines. Also on the outbreak of war, whether either the principal or the agent becomes an enemy, the authority of the agent normally ceases on the ground that it is not permissible to have relations with an enemy alien, and the existence of the relationship of principal and agent necessitates such a relation.[10] But this is not invariably the case, for the agency may be of such a kind (for example, a general power of attorney)[11] that it has no tendency to assist or increase the resources of the enemy.

(iii) Death

The death[12] (or if the principal is a corporation, the dissolution)[13] of the principal determines at once the authority of the agent. The third party's remedy will be against the agent for breach of warranty of authority. It is not necessary for the agent to have notice of the death, so that there may be liability for such breach of warranty, even

---

4   *The Margaret Mitchell* (1858) Jur. N.S. 1193.

5   *Martin-Baker Aircraft Co. Ltd.* v. *Canada Flight Equipment Ltd.* [1955] 2 Q.B. 556.

6   The principal's property will be vested in the trustee in bankruptcy and an agent generally cannot dispose of it. See Insolvency Act 1986, ss. 283–4, 307, 315, 436.

7   *Beckham* v. *Drake* (1849) 2 H.L. Cas. 579. But only if the bankruptcy renders the agent unfit to perform his duties: *McCall* v. *Australian Meat Co.* (1870) 19 W.R. 188; *Bailey* v. *Thurstan & Co. Ltd.* [1903] 1 K.B. 137.

8   *Triffit Nurseries & Others* v. *Salads Etc. Ltd.* [2000] 2 Lloyd's Rep. 74.

9   *Rhodes* v. *Forwood* (1876) 1 App. Cas. 256. Cf. *Turner* v. *Goldsmith* [1891] 1 Q.B. 544; *ante*, p. 680.

10   *Sovfracht (v/o)* v. *Van Udens Scheepvaart en Agentuur Maatschappij (N.V. Gebr.)* [1943] A.C. 204, at pp. 253–5. See also *Stevenson (Hugh) & Sons Ltd.* v. *Aktiengesellschaft für Cartonnagen-Industrie* [1918] A.C. 239. Cf. *Schostall* v. *Johnson* (1919) 36 T.L.R. 75 (enemy resident in England).

11   *Hangkam Kwingtong Woo* v. *Liu Lan Fong* [1951] A.C. 707.

12   *Campanari* v. *Woodburn* (1854) 15 C.B. 400.

13   *Salton* v. *New Beeston Cycle Co.* [1900] 1 Ch. 43.

though the agent was ignorant of the fact that the authority had been determined by the death and had no means of finding out that this was so.[14] The representatives of a deceased principal may, however, ratify any contract entered into on behalf of the estate,[15] but they are in no way bound to do so.

A statutory qualification exists in the case of powers of attorney. A donee of a power of attorney who acts in pursuance of the power in ignorance of the death of the donor incurs no liability (either to the donor or to any other person) by reason of the fact that the power has been revoked by the death.[16]

The death of the agent also determines the agency[17] but where the Commercial Agents Regulations apply, compensation may be due where the agency is terminated in this way.[18]

(iv) Mental incapacity

The effect of the mental incapacity of the principal is a matter of some difficulty at common law.[19] In *Yonge* v. *Toynbee*:[20]

T, after instructing solicitors to defend on his behalf a threatened action, became insane before the action was heard. The solicitors, in ignorance of this fact, duly entered an appearance to the writ, and took all necessary steps on their client's behalf. When T's insanity became known to Y, he sought to have the appearance and all subsequent proceedings struck out, and to make the solicitors personally liable for the costs incurred, on the ground that their authority to act had been determined by T's insanity.

The Court of Appeal decided in Y's favour, holding that the solicitors had warranted an authority which they had ceased to possess. On the other hand, in *Drew* v. *Nunn*:[21]

N, being sane, held out his wife to have authority to deal with D on his behalf. He subsequently became insane, but the wife continued to deal with D who had no notice of N's insanity. N recovered, and sought to resist an action against him for the price of the goods supplied to his wife during the period of his insanity.

This defence did not succeed. The Court of Appeal did not expressly decide how far the disability affected the continuance of authority, but held that N, 'by holding out his wife as agent, entered into a contract with [D] that she had authority to act on his behalf, and that until [D] had knowledge that this authority was revoked he was entitled to act on [N's] representations'.[22]

These two cases can be reconciled on the ground that, although mental incapacity puts an end to the agency as between principal and agent, it can have no effect on

---

[14] *Blades* v. *Free* (1829) 9 B. & C. 167; *Yonge* v. *Toynbee* [1910] 1 K.B. 215. Cf. *Smout* v. *Ilbery* (1842) 10 M. & W. 1.

[15] *Re Watson* (1886) 18 Q.B.D. 116.

[16] Powers of Attorney Act 1971, s. 5(1)–(5). But see *post*, p. 697.

[17] *Friend* v. *Young* [1897] 2 Ch. 421.

[18] Commercial Agents (Council Directive) Regulations 1993 (S.I. 1993 No. 3053), reg. 17(8).

[19] See *post*, p. 698 for the effect of the Enduring Powers of Attorney Act 1985.

[20] [1910] 1 K.B. 215.

[21] (1879) 4 Q.B.D. 661.

[22] (1879) 4 Q.B.D. 661, *per* Brett L.J. at p. 669. See also *Re Parks* (1957) 8 D.L.R. (2d) 155 (Canada).

third parties who continue to contract in the belief that the agency is still in exist-ence. The principal is estopped from denying the authority of the agent unless and until the third party becomes aware of the revocation. Nevertheless the decision in *Yonge* v. *Toynbee* does produce a somewhat curious result, for, as we have seen,[23] if a person contracts with a mentally incapacitated person, the contract is good unless, at the time of contracting that person was aware of the disability. But if a contract is made by a third party with an incapacitated person through an agent, and no question of estoppel arises, the contract is void, even though the third party had no knowledge of the disability. Further, if two persons make a binding contract, and one of them, subsequently unknown to the other, becomes mentally disabled, the contract is not, in general, avoided by that event. *Yonge* v. *Toynbee*, however, obliges us to say that if the contract is one of agency, it will be an exception to this general principle. There is also the additional difficulty that, if the principal is estopped from denying the contract which the agent purported to make for the principal it is hard to see how there can have been a breach of the agent's warranty of authority at all, or if it has been technically broken, what damage the third party has suffered, since the third party's rights against the principal are exactly what the agent professed to be able to create. The decision in *Yonge* v. *Toynbee* requires reconsideration.[24]

The mental incapacity of the agent would also seem to determine the agency.

II. IRREVOCABLE AUTHORITY

The authority given to an agent may become irrevocable in three main instances: (a) when it is coupled with an interest, (b) when it is contained in a power of attorney, (c) when revocation would cause the agent personal loss.[25] Additionally, as indicated *supra*, where the Commercial Agents Regulations 1993 apply, although the agent's *authority* can be terminated, there are restrictions on the principal's ability to terminate the agency contract, at least without compensation.

(a) AUTHORITY COUPLED WITH AN INTEREST

An authority coupled with an interest is irrevocable during the subsistence of the interest. This rule has been explained by Wilde C.J. to mean that 'where an agreement is entered into on a sufficient consideration, whereby an authority is given for the purpose of securing some benefit to the donee of the authority, such an authority is irrevocable'.[26] So where a principal and agent agree for valuable consideration or under seal that the agent is to have authority, for example, to collect rents in order to

---

[23] *Ante*, pp. 234–5.
[24] See Law Commission Working Paper No. 69 (1976).
[25] Reynolds in Cranston, ed., *Making Commercial Law* (1997), p. 259.
[26] *Smart* v. *Sandars* (1848) 5 C.B. 895, at p. 917.

secure a loan,[27] or to sell certain land and discharge a debt owed to the agent by the principal out of the purchase money,[28] the principal thereby confers an interest on the agent, and the agency cannot be revoked unilaterally by the principal, or by the death, incapacity, or insolvency of the principal.[29]

But the authority must be given with the object of protecting or securing an interest of the agent, and it is not sufficient that it does so incidentally. Thus in *Smart* v. *Sandars*:[30]

The defendants, who were corn factors, were entrusted by the plaintiffs with certain wheat to sell on their behalf. They subsequently advanced the sum of £3,000 to the plaintiffs, which the plaintiffs failed to repay. The plaintiffs gave orders that the wheat was not to be sold, but the defendants nevertheless sold it to secure their advance.

In an action against them, the defendants pleaded that the agency, being coupled with an interest, was irrevocable; but the Court held that this was an improper application of the rule. The authority had not been given to secure the advance of £3,000, since it had been given prior to, and independently of, the loan.

(b) POWERS OF ATTORNEY

An instrument creating a power of attorney must be made under seal.[31] Where a power of attorney is expressed to be irrevocable and is given to secure a proprietary interest of the donee of the power, or the performance of an obligation owed to the donee, then, so long as the donee has that interest or the obligation remains undischarged, the power cannot be revoked by the donor without the consent of the donee, or by the death, incapacity, insolvency, winding-up, or dissolution of the donor.[32]

If a power of attorney is effectively revoked, the donee of the power does not incur any liability, either to the donor or to any third party, if at the time the donee of the power does not know of the revocation.[33] Similarly, where a third party, without knowledge of the revocation, deals with the donee of the power, the transaction between them is treated as valid as if the power was still then in existence.[34]

Subject to the statutory provisions outlined above, at common law a power of attorney is automatically revoked upon the donor becoming mentally incapable. Many powers of attorney are given just because of this possibility, but at a time when the assistance of the attorney became essential if the donor's affairs were to be

---

[27] *Spooner* v. *Sandilands* (1842) 1 Y. & C. Ch. 390. Cf. *Doward, Dickson & Co.* v. *Williams & Co.* (1890) 6 T.L.R. 316 (no security).

[28] *Gaussen* v. *Morton* (1830) 10 B. & C. 731.

[29] *Quaere* whether the agency persists despite the dissolution of a principal which is a company.

[30] (1848) 5 C.B. 895.

[31] Powers of Attorney Act 1971, s. 1(1) as amended by the Law of Property (Miscellaneous Provisions) Act 1989, s 1.

[32] 1971 Act, s. 4.

[33] *Ibid.*, s. 5(1).

[34] *Ibid.*, s. 5(2)–(7). See also *ibid.*, s. 6 (share transactions).

managed properly, the attorney lost its authority to act.[35] The inconvenience of this led to the enactment of the Enduring Powers of Attorney Act 1985, which allows such powers of attorney to be given if the requirements of the Act are followed. For example, the person giving the power must understand the nature of the juristic act at the time the power is given, a prescribed form (in which the powers of the donee are explained) must be followed, and following the incapacity of the donor, the donor is required to apply to the Court of Protection to register the power.[36]

(c) AGENT'S PERSONAL LIABILITY OR LOSS

Where the agent has, in pursuance of its authority, contracted a personal liability or become liable to personal loss, the agency cannot be revoked by the principal without the agent's consent, for this would be to defeat rights already established.

The liability incurred by the agent may either be a legal liability, as where the agent is bound by contract to pay to a creditor of the principal a debt which the agent has been authorized to receive;[37] or it may simply be a loss which is likely to occur in fact. Thus in *Seymour* v. *Bridge*:[38]

B employed S, who were stockbrokers, to buy shares for him according to the rules of the Stock Exchange. S purchased the shares from a jobber in the usual way, but B, before settling day, repudiated the transaction on the ground that the numbers of the shares had not been specified in accordance with Leeman's Act 1867.[39] This Act would indeed have invalidated the purchase, but the Stock Exchange forces its members to complete such bargains under pain of expulsion. B must have been taken to have known of this rule as he contracted on that basis.

It was held that S's authority could not be revoked by B so as to cause S actual loss, and that B was bound to indemnify S for the money which they had paid for the shares.

The liability or loss must have been in the contemplation of the parties at the time that the authority was conferred.[40] Thus, where an investor did not know of the custom in *Seymour* v. *Bridge*, he was held, under circumstances in other respects precisely similar to those in that case, not to be bound to pay for the shares.[41] Also the principle does not apply where the contract entered into by the agent is not merely void, but illegal.[42]

---

[35] Law Com. No. 122, *The Incapacitated Principal* (1983), § 3.2.

[36] Enduring Powers of Attorney Act 1985, s. 2; Enduring Powers of Attorney (Prescribed Form) Regulations 1990 (S.I. 1990 No. 1376); *Re K* [1988] Ch. 310. See generally Cretney, *Enduring Powers of Attorney*, 4th edn. (1996).

[37] *Hodgson* v. *Anderson* (1825) 3 B. & C. 842.

[38] (1885) 14 Q.B.D. 460.

[39] Banking Companies' (Shares) Act 1867, repealed by the Statute Law Revision Act 1966.

[40] *Read* v. *Anderson* (1884) 13 Q.B.D. 779, at p. 783.

[41] *Perry* v. *Barnett* (1885) 15 Q.B.D. 388.

[42] See *ante*, p. 407.

(d) COMMERCIAL AGENTS

Where the Commercial Agents Regulations[43] apply, the principal's freedom to terminate a commercial agency is restricted. If the contract is for an indefinite period, minimum periods of notice are specified,[44] and, save where the termination is on the ground of the agent's breach, the agent is entitled to be compensated for damage.[45] It is arguable that under the Regulations compensation is calculated by reference to the commission the agent would have earned had the contract continued to be performed in the normal manner in which the parties had intended,[46] and not, as at common law, on the basis of the principal's acting to minimize its liability to the agent.[47] This right to compensation exists even where the principal's termination of the agency contract is not a breach of contract.[48]

---

[43] The Commercial Agents (Council Directive) Regulations 1993 (S.I. 1993 No. 3053) as amended by S.I. 1993 No. 3173.

[44] The Commercial Agents (Council Directive) Regulations 1993 (S.I. 1993 No. 3053) as amended by S.I. 1993 No. 3173, reg. 15 (one month for the first year of the contract, two months for the second year, and three months for the third and subsequent years). An agreement for a fixed period which continues to be performed after that period has expired is (reg. 14) converted into one for an indefinite period.

[45] *Ibid.*, regs. 17, 18(a), as amended.

[46] *Page* v. *Combined Shipping & Trading Co. Ltd.* [1997] 3 All E.R. 656.

[47] *Ante*, p. 597.

[48] 1993 Regulations, reg. 17(1)(6).

INDEX